Fodor's 2007

W9-AAG-822

Germany

Fodor's Travel Publications • New York, Toronto, London, Sydney, Auckland
www.fodors.com

CONTENTS

MAPS

Circled letters in text correspond to letters on the photographs. For more information on the sights pictured, turn to the indicated page number Ⓐ on each photograph.

DESTINATION GERMANY

Every epoch has left its mark on Germany's landscape of fertile river valleys, rolling vineyards, and lofty peaks. Roman relics keep company with medieval castles, baroque palaces with half-timber farmhouses, and rococo urban mansions with communist-era housing. The country of oompah, cuckoo clocks, and Mercedes-Benz also gave the world Gutenberg, Luther, Bach, Beethoven, Goethe, and Marx. From the days of the Romans and Charlemagne through the Reformation to the present, it has been a tumultuous ride, and the start of the new millennium, marking the end of Germany's first decade of reunification, is a meaningful milestone. *Prost!*

Ⓐ 48

MUNICH

Ⓑ 55

Hands and beer steins down, the easygoing and fun-loving capital of Bavaria is the favorite city of both natives and visitors from abroad. Class and kitsch coexist amicably here—the former embodied in the glorious, half-mile-long Schloss Nymphenburg and the royal Ⓐ**Residenz,** home to Bavaria's art-loving Wittelsbach dynasty, and the latter the stuff of Ⓑ**Oktoberfest,** a fortnight-long tribute to beer and its consequences. Year-round, the *Gemütlichkeit* is nowhere stronger than in the city's many beer halls, of which surely the best-known is the venerable Ⓒ**Hofbräuhaus,** deafening and perennially packed. A much more tranquil refuge is Munich's 500-year-old late-Gothic Ⓓ**Frauenkirche,** whose twin domes are a city emblem. The gilded statue in nearby Marienplatz was erected in 1638 by the Catholic city in gratitude for its deliverance from the devastating Thirty Years' War. Munich is also known for its superb galleries and opera house, and the lively restaurant scene is Germany's most sophisticated. Fashionable burghers shop on broad, ele-

Ⓒ 47

gant Maximilianstrasse, designed by King Maximilian II himself, and in December artisans sell their wares at the open-air Ⓔ**Christkindlmarkt** (Christmas Market). In the huge, rolling Englischer Garten you can cross-country ski or sunbathe nude, depending on the season. And it's easy to hop on the suburban railway to the lake resorts of the Ammersee and Starnbergersee. The S-Bahn also reaches nearby Dachau, where a Holocaust memorial tells the story of those who perished at the concentration camp.

Ⓔ▷76

BAVARIAN ALPS

Ⓐ 119

Ⓑ 95

Germany is at its most photogenic in this area of majestic peaks, rocky pastures, and villages full of frescoed houses and window boxes bright with geraniums. Year-round you can find the country's finest skiing in Ⓑ**Garmisch-Partenkirchen,** and scenic hiking above mountain lakes such as fashionable Tegernsee, the quieter Schliersee, or the pristine Ⓐ **Königsee,** near Berchtesgaden. On an island in the Chiemsee is one of the palatial architectural fantasies of "Mad" King Ludwig II: Schloss Herrenchiemsee, modeled on Versailles. And once every decade in Oberammergau, noted for its wood-carvers, residents stage the Passion Play in celebration of the village's deliverance from the plague in 1633.

Ⓐ›140

Perfect for hiking, biking, and cross-country skiing, this rural, wooded area of Germany next to the Austrian and Czech borders also stands out for its reasonable prices. From one of the low-key local country resorts you can make forays to small urban centers like arts-minded Deggendorff and river-crossed Ⓑ**Passau,** a Baroque gem. Stop in the city's magnificent

BAVARIAN FOREST

Ⓐ**Dom** at noon for a performance on the world's largest church organ. Or take in the Glasmuseum, showcasing treasures produced by an important local industry. Its focal point today is Zwiesel, but master glassblowers work in studios throughout the region. Also region-wide you can visit monasteries and churches adorned with the frescoes of 18th-century Bavarian artist Cosmas Damian Asam, one of a family of artists known for their stucco work and frescoes.

Ⓑ›139

ROMANTIC ROAD

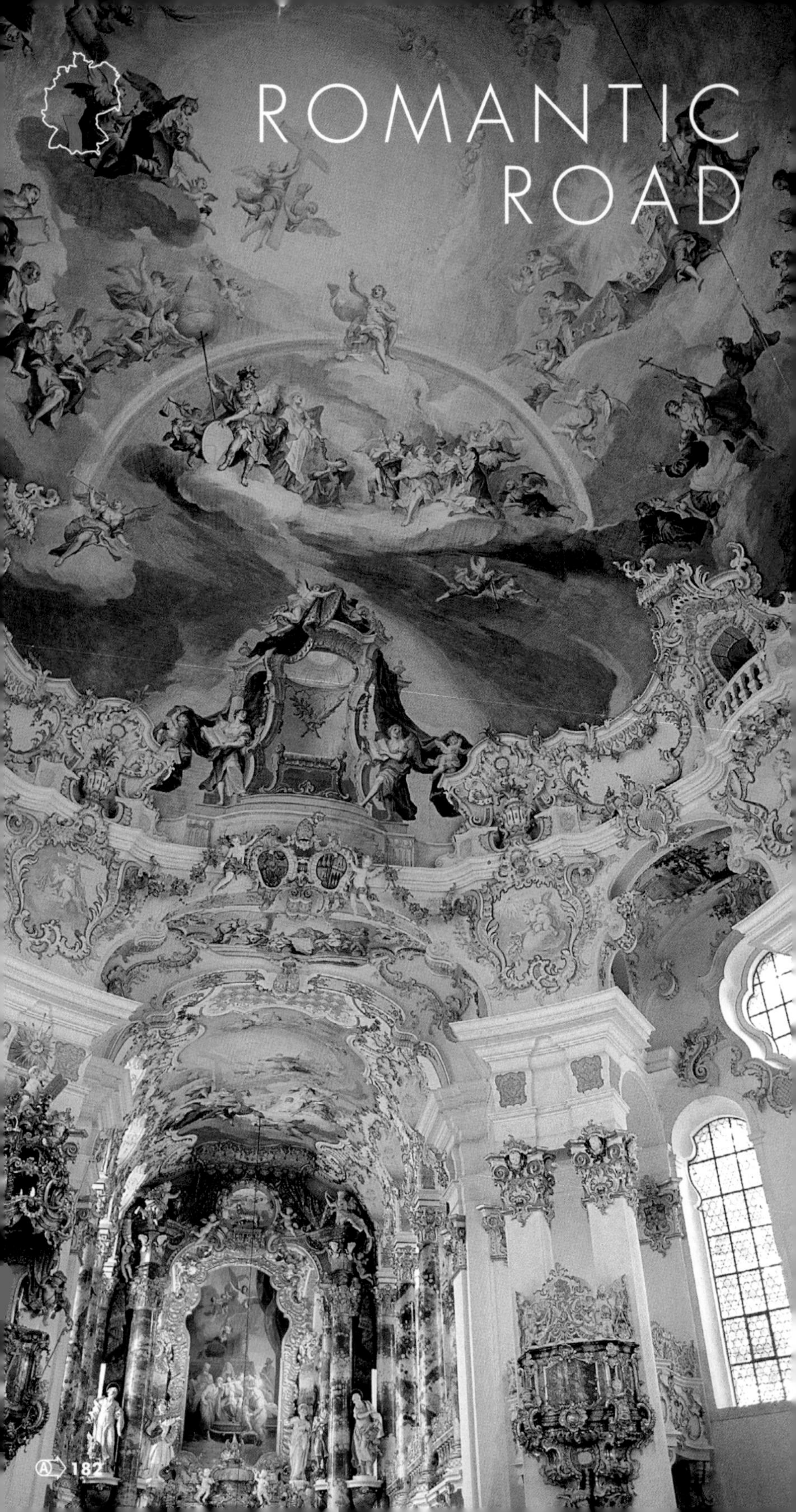

A 182

Ⓑ 183

Picturesque beyond words, the Romantic Road is 260 miles of castles and walled villages, half-timber houses and imposing churches, set in pastoral countryside. The art and architecture span centuries, and the rivers Tauber, Lech, Main, and Danube are never distant. Ⓓ**Rothenburg-ob-der-Tauber** is Europe's best-preserved medieval town, studded with turrets and towers. Ⓐ**Wieskirche,** in a meadow near Steingaden, is

Ⓒ 159

rococo. Ⓑ**Schloss Neusch-swanstein,** Ludwig II's most famous castle, is pure 19th century—as romantic as they come. Soaring and light outside, it is sepulchral and Wagnerian within. At the Ⓒ**Residenz** in Würzburg, the baroque era is at its best: the powerful prince-bishops who built it spared little expense in creating astonishing opulence. The Venetian Tiepolo painted its frescoes, including *The Four Continents,* above a remarkable split staircase by Balthasar Neumann. Augsburg was home to both the wealthy Fugger family and Marxist playwright Bertolt Brecht.

Ⓓ 164

FRANCONIA

Ⓐ▷201

Ⓒ▷214

Ⓑ▷211

The region of Franconia is rich in ancient and cultural cities. Opera fans love Bayreuth: The Wagner Festival thunders in the stark Festspielhaus each summer, and the rococo Ⓐ**Markgräfliches Opernhaus** is an intimate jewel box. The lofty Gothic Ⓑ**Schöner Brunnen** (Beautiful Fountain) anchors the market square of Nürnberg, artist Albrecht Dürer's longtime home and site of the first diets of the Holy Roman Emperors. And just outside Franconia is Ⓒ**Regensburg,** founded by Celts on the Danube 2,500 years ago and remarkably unscathed by World War II.

BODENSEE

Ⓑ⟩ 228

Ⓐ⟩ 231

Ⓒ⟩ 243

The Bodensee, or Lake Constance, is the warmest area in Germany. The island of ©**Mainau** is a colorful bouquet of tulips, hyacinths, and narcissi. The scenery is enchanting, especially when viewed from shoreline promenades or from ferries traveling between towns like terraced Meersburg and beautifully preserved Konstanz, a half hour distant. The village of Ⓐ**Wasserburg,** its castle now a hotel and its ancient streets off-limits to cars, is a perfect contemplative retreat. So is the island town of Ⓑ**Lindau,** whose maze of ancient streets contains a history reaching back to Roman Gaul. Bike routes circle the lake; pedal long enough and you'll cross into Switzerland or Austria.

Ⓐ 272

The Black Forest is synonymous with cuckoo clocks and primeval woodland: certainly thousands of acres are cloaked in pines, and at least one entire town, little Triberg, goes all atwitter every hour. But the storied Black Forest is at least as noteworthy for the beautiful people who flock to still-stately spa and casino resorts like Ⓑ**Baden-Baden** and the ultraluxurious Ⓒ**Schlosshotel Bühlerhöhe,** on a forested hilltop high above. And although pleasure is pricey here, not to worry: Elsewhere in the area, spa cures and mineral baths are far less costly—and the fresh, piney mountain air is free. There's boating and windsurfing on the Ⓓ**Titisee,** and hik-

BLACK FOREST

Ⓑ 260

Ⓒ 260

ers and cross-country skiers follow trails out of nearby Hinterzarten. Westward through the deep Hell Valley gorge is the beautifully restored university town of Freiburg, the region's largest city, with a cathedral, the Ⓐ**Münster,** that was 300 years in the making.

Ⓓ 269

HEIDELBERG AND THE NECKAR VALLEY

This is quintessential Germany—full of vineyards, castles, universities, and high-speed automobiles. In Ⓑ**Stuttgart,** swans are grace notes outside the Staatstheater, where the ballet and State Opera perform, and Porsche and Mercedes-Benz have factories and museums just outside town. Nearby is the Burgenstrasse (Castle Road), which takes in castles and villages as it makes its way through the Neckar Valley. The castle ruins in Heidelberg, a gorgeous town on Gothic foundations, inspired the German Romantics. The best views of the old town are from the Ⓐ**Alte Brücke** (Old Bridge).

Ⓑ⟩ 300

Germany goes contemporary in Frankfurt. The city is now Europe's banking capital, a focal point of power. Germany's leading stock exchange, the Ⓑ**Börse,** is here. Skyscrapers spike the skyline, and prosperity has left the art museums flush with works by Dürer, Vermeer, Rembrandt, Rubens, Monet, and Renoir, among others. Jazz is popular, and the city has Germany's oldest jazz cellar as well as fall's annual German Jazz Festival. But not everything is modern. The Römerberg square is lined with historic buildings—the gabled Gothic Römer (City Hall) and

FRANKFURT

ⒶⰤ **330**

the row of half-timber houses known as the Ostzeile. Frankfurters unwind in traditional ways, too: They head for the nearby Taunus Hills for a brisk hike and a bit of mountain air, or stop for an Apfelwein at *Ebbelwei* (cider taverns) such as Ⓐ**Zum Wagner,** which punctuate the cobbled streets of quaint Sachsenhausen, on the south bank of the Main.

ⒷⰤ**319**

PFALZ AND THE RHINE TERRACE

Wine reigns here. Bacchanalian festivals pepper the calendar between July and October, and wineries welcome drop-ins for tastings year-round. Once you've had your fill of looking at the bottom of a wineglass, head for Worms, whose streets were ancient even when Charlemagne and Luther walked them. Its Ⓐ**Judenfriedhof Heiliger Sand,** Europe's oldest Jewish cemetery, has been in use for more than a millennium. The Wormser Dom is one of the world's great Romanesque cathedrals, along with the imposing Ⓑ**Kaiserdom** in Speyer and its fortresslike, turreted sibling in Mainz, the city where Johannes Gutenberg printed the first Bible.

THE RHINELAND

Ⓐ⟩410

Ⓑ⟩389

Although it is part of western-most Germany, the Rhineland is the country's spiritual heart. Stories that originated here—telling of the Nibelungen and the Loreley—have become national legends, and tourists have been enthralled for centuries by the mighty Rhine as it flows past Koblenz, Köln, Bonn, and Düsseldorf, and the ©**Mosel,** the tributary that twists improbably past towns like Bremm. The riverbanks are graced with castles, villages, and vineyards: you can see them from your car or from one of the boats that cruise the rivers for anywhere from a few hours to as much as a week in season. Throughout the area

Ⓒ⟩402

you can stay in castle hotels such as Burghotel Auf Schönburg near Oberwesel. Ancient Trier, on the Mosel, was 1,300 years old when Caesar's legions arrived, and its 2nd-century Ⓐ**Porta Nigra** (Black Gate) testifies to its importance to the Romans. Wiesbaden, on the Rhine, was founded by Roman soldiers who discovered its hot springs, prized once again by Europe's elite in the 19th century. Restore yourself in the Ⓔ**Irish-Römisches Bad** (Irish-Roman bath). The world's best Rieslings are produced between here and half-timber Ⓑ**Rüdesheim,** a bit downstream. The region's unofficial wine capital, Rüdesheim, has plenty of cozy wine taverns. Farther north, in vibrant Ⓓ**Köln** (Cologne), a certain 18th-century eau de cologne is still for sale on Glockengasse at the address for which it is named, No. 4711.

However, the city may be most famous as the site of the country's largest and finest Gothic cathedral. Begun in the 13th century and completed in the 19th, it was intended to symbolize God's kingdom on earth, and it does so magnificently.

Ⓓ 417

Ⓔ 381

THE FAIRY-TALE ROAD

The Fairy-Tale Road, stretching 370 miles between Hanau and Bremen, is also the Road Less Traveled. (All the better for those who choose it.) This is Brothers Grimm Country, the area that the great compilers of folklore mined for their sometimes-dark tales of magic and miracles. The Grimms' imaginations were nourished during a childhood in the ©**Brüder-Grimm-Haus** in Steinau an der Strasse, a medieval beauty of a town where

Ⓑ 443

Ⓒ 443

their stories delight children today at the Ⓑ**Steinauer Marionettentheater.** In Ⓐ**Hameln** (Hamelin), sculptures, plaques, and even rat-shaped pastries recall the tale of the Pied Piper. And in Ⓓ**Bremen,** storied to have been saved by a quartet of animal musicians, drummers keep the beat during the pre-Lenten Carnival. All along the Fairy-Tale Road, misty woodlands and small towns full of half-timber houses look as if they have mysterious and compelling tales to tell. When you pass this way, it's not hard to see how the area spawned the stories that the Grimms shared with the world.

Ⓓ 463

With its international port, rusty brick warehouses, fish market, and Reeperbahn red-light district, Hamburg is undeniably gritty. But its downtown is truly elegant. The area is laced with canals spanned by small bridges. The Inner and Outer Ⓐ**Alster,** bordered with parks and shopping arcades and big enough for sailing, form the

HAMBURG

city's heart, and a 9-mile footpath lines the Elbe River banks. Despite World War II bombings, the city's architecture is diverse, encompassing the neo-Renaissance Rathaus, on a square not unlike Venice's Piazza San Marco, and turn-of-the-century Art Nouveau buildings. The dining and arts scenes thrive, as well.

SCHLESWIG-HOLSTEIN AND THE BALTIC COAST

Schleswig-Holstein and the former East Germany's Baltic coast area share a windswept landscape scattered with medieval towns, remote fishing villages, long white beaches, and summer resorts. The ©**Ahlbeck** pier dates from the 19th century, and charming Ⓐ**Stralsund** has a 13th-century redbrick Rathaus. Schwerin, the area's second-largest town after Rostock, has an amazing castle, and striking chalk cliffs edge remote, quiet Rügen island. In Schleswig-Holstein, major draws are chic Sylt island and medieval Lübeck, a stronghold of the powerful Hanseatic merchants who controlled trade on the Baltic beginning in the 13th century; the chunky gate known as the Ⓑ**Holstentor** recalls those days.

Ⓐ527

Ⓑ516

Ⓒ532

BERLIN

Ⓐ▷ 552

For Germany, restored Berlin is an emblem of national renewal. More prosaically, *urban* renewal is everywhere. Massive construction projects have replaced the vanished Wall among the sprawling city's tourist attractions, right along with grand old sights such as the Berliner Dom, looming large over the Ⓐ**Spree Canal,** and the institutions of Museum Island, which display some of the world's best-known antiquities. The Ⓒ**Brandenburger Tor** (Brandenburg Gate), which stood in a no-man's-land in divided Berlin, is a reminder of the city's history. Tree-lined Ⓑ**Kurfürstendamm,** where Berliners congregate in cafés for cakes and coffee day and night, bristles with the energy that is the city's trademark.

Ⓑ▷ 540

Ⓒ▷ 545

SAXONY, SAXONY-ANHALT, AND THURINGIA

This area's difficult transition to capitalism is much in the news, but most striking to visitors are the reminders of the area's importance in history. Weimar was home to the poets Goethe and Schiller. The Bach family home and the Thomaskirche, where Johann Sebastian served as choirmaster for 27 years, are in Leipzig, where Richard Wagner was born. Both he and Richard Strauss had premieres at the imposing Ⓐ**Semperoper** (Semper Opera House) in Dresden, whose Brühlsche Terrasse above the Elbe River was once called "Europe's balcony." It was in ©**Meissen** that an 18th-century alchemist discovered how to make fine porcelain. And Martin Luther nailed his 95 theses to the door of Wittenberg's Ⓑ**Schlosskirche** in 1517, inching closer to a break with Rome. Near Eisenach you can also see the Wartburg fortress where the excommunicated Luther sought refuge.

GREAT ITINERARIES

Highlights of Germany
12 to 18 days

Germany offers everything from opera houses to oompah bands and from seaside villages to snowcapped mountains. For a parade of early German architecture, cruise the steeply banked, vineyard-terraced Rheingau between Mainz and Koblenz, full of riverside castles. The Romantic movement, a product of this evocative setting, flourished in the university town of Heidelberg. Munich, Germany's most laid-back city and the capital of Bavaria and of beer, is the gateway to the Alps and foothill lakes. In Nürnberg, relics of the Holy Roman Empire coexist with ruins of the Third Reich. Leipzig and Dresden are the pearls of what was East Germany, and, encapsulating everything that is German, the restored capital of Berlin overwhelms with entertainment, culture, and reminders of 20th-century history.

the morning take a leisurely river cruise as far as Koblenz, breaking up your journey to overnight in a riverside Gasthof. Allow a day for exploring Koblenz, setting aside an hour to visit the scenic Deutsches Eck, the point where the Mosel flows into the Rhine, and the site of monuments to Germany's unity and division.
☞ *The Rhine Terrace in Chapter 10 and the Mittelrhein in Chapter 11*

HEIDELBERG
1 to 2 days. Generations of artists, composers, writers, and romantics have crossed the Ⓐ Alte Brücke, spanning

in a centuries-old student tavern.
☞ *Heidelberg and the Neckar-Rhine Triangle in Chapter 8*

MUNICH AND THE ALPS
3 to 4 days. Visit Munich's ©Schloss Nymphenburg and Residenz, the former Wittelsbach palaces that demonstrate Bavaria's place in German history. Follow that with an evening in a beer hall, which will confirm everything you've ever heard about beer, pork, and potato consumption in Bavaria. Relax on the morning train to Ⓑ Berchtesgaden, the Bavarian Alps a soothing cyclo-

Ⓐ▷ 284

RHINELAND-PALITINATE
● Koblenz
⑨
A61
170 km
Frankfurt
42
65 km
A60 Bingen Mainz
A61
Hessische Bergstrasse
Mannheim
103 km
Heidelberg
● Würzburg
A5
Karlsruhe
FRANCE
Stuttgart
A8
326 km
BADEN-WÜRTTEMBERG

RHINE VALLEY FROM MAINZ TO KOBLENZ
3 to 4 days. From Frankfurt take the short train ride over the Rhine to see Mainz's Dom, one of Europe's greatest Romanesque cathedrals. Continue by train through Rheingau vineyards to Bingen and stay in a castle hotel. In

the Neckar River, and climbed up the steep, winding Schlangenweg to the aptly named Philosophers' Path. At the top you'll have a view of Germany's archetypal university city and its ruined Renaissance castle. Don't leave Heidelberg without eating (and drinking)

rama beyond the window. In Berchtesgaden Hitler's Obersalzberg retreat takes priority, but find time for the most beautiful corner of Germany, the mountain-ringed Königsee.
☞ *Chapters 1 and 2*

SWITZERLAND

B 116

NÜRNBERG

1 to 2 days. In Nürnberg you'll see the full spectrum of German history. The city's massive fortress, dating from 1050, was the residence of successive Holy Roman Emperors. The former home of Renaissance artist Albrecht Dürer is now a fascinating museum. Ride the S-2 suburban rail line to the Zeppelinfeld, the enormous parade grounds where Hitler addressed the Nürnberg rallies.

☞ *Southern Franconia and Upper Palatinate in Chapter 5*

LEIPZIG AND DRESDEN

2 to 3 days. To understand the enormous political and social changes brought about by German reunification you have to visit Leipzig or Dresden—both, if possible. Deteriorated after nearly a half century of communism, they have returned to commercial and cultural prominence. A choral concert in Leipzig's Thomaskirche, where Johann Sebastian Bach was choirmaster, or a walk high above the Elbe River along Dresden's Brühlsche Terrasse is completely enchanting.

☞ *Saxony in Chapter 16*

BERLIN

2 to 3 days. Reunited and rebuilt, Berlin races forward. The German parliament is back in the Reichstag, and world-renowned architects are changing the city's face. The Mittle district holds onto its pockets of counterculture as hip restaurants and bars move in. Sights recalling World War II and the Cold War are everywhere, and antiquities steal the spotlight on Museum Island. The Zoologischer Garten, Tiergarten, and Ku'Damm cafés offer the relaxation you'll need to balance this city's energy.

☞ *Chapter 15*

C 53

By Public Transportation
Mainz is a 30-min train ride from Frankfurt, and Bingen is 40 min farther by train or bus. Cruise boats leave Bingen daily for the Rhine journey to Koblenz. Catch an InterCity train in Koblenz for the return trip south, changing at Mannheim for Heidelberg (3 hrs). Return to Mannheim by a local train (10 min) and change to an InterCity or Eurocity train to Munich (about 3 hrs). InterCity Express and Eurocity services link Munich and Nürnberg (1 hr, 45 min). InterCity and InterRegio services link Nürnberg and Leipzig (3 hrs, 40 min) and Leipzig and Dresden (1 hr). There are hourly InterCity and other express services from Dresden to Berlin (1 hr). Return from Berlin to Frankfurt by InterCity Express (3 hrs) or fly back (40 min).

BRANDENBURG
POLAND
Berlin
SPREEWALD
190 km
A13
111 km
Leipzig
A14
Dresden
SAXONY
A9
270 km
Bayreuth
A9
Nürnberg
A9
175 km
BAVARIA
A9
A8
Munich
162 km
A8
AUSTRIA
Berchtesgaden

Castles in Wine Country
6 to 9 days

Centuries of German culture unfold on a medieval castle tour through the valleys of the Rhine and its tributaries. Today castle guest rooms and restaurants provide panoramic views as well as glasses of crisp Riesling and velvety Spätburgunder (pinot noir), Germany's finest white and red wines. ⓓWine estates often post signs near their entrances that announce WEINVERKAUF (WINE FOR SALE) or WEINPROBE HEUTE (WINE TASTINGS TODAY). Come during summer or autumn, when the wine-festival season is in full swing and many a castle courtyard hosts theater and concerts.

MITTELRHEIN AND MOSEL
2 to 3 days. The Mittelrhein wine town of St. Goar is an ideal base for excursions into the Rhine and Mosel valleys. The terrace of the hotel-restaurant adjacent to Burg Rheinfels, the Rhine's largest fortress ruin, is a superb vantage point. Ferry across the river to catch a train to Rüdesheim, the liveliest town in the Rheingau wine region. Return to St. Goar on a KD Rhine steamer, and savor a glass of delicate Mosel wine or its fuller-bodied Rhine counterpart. Set aside a full day to tour the Rhine's only impregnable castle, the Marksburg, followed by a jaunt through the lower Mosel valley from Koblenz to the

fairy-tale castle Ⓔ Burg Eltz. En route you'll pass breathtakingly steep vineyards and dozens of wine estates.
☞ *The Mittelrhein and the Mosel Valley in Chapter 11*

NECKAR VALLEY
2 to 3 days. Spend one day in Heidelberg's Old Town and massive castle ruins, but beware the crowds of summer. The town straddles the Hessische Bergstrasse and northern Baden wine regions. The white varietals Riesling, Grauburgunder (Pinot Gris), and Weissburgunder (Pinot Blanc) yield the finest wines. On the Burgenstrasse (Castle Road), have lunch on the castle terrace in Hirschhorn. Neckarzimmern's Burg Hornberg, residence of a celebrated 16th-century knight, is the perfect stopover.

Atop its own terraced vineyards in the Württemberg wine region, the 12th-century castle includes guest rooms with splendid views of the Neckar Valley as well as good food and wine (try the spicy white varietals Traminer and Muskateller). There's a museum and falconry at Burg Guttenberg, and medieval Bad Wimpfen has a former imperial palace.
☞ *Heidelberg and the Neckar-Rhine Triangle, and the Burgenstrasse in Chapter 8*

TAUBER AND MAIN VALLEYS
2 to 3 days. The Baden, Württemberg, and Franken wine regions converge in the peaceful Tauber Valley. Foremost are the earthy, robust, dry white Silvaner and Rivaner (Müller-Thurgau) wines, often bottled in the flagon-shaped Bocksbeutel. Bad Mergentheim, a pretty spa and former residence of the Knights of the Teutonic

Ⓓ ▶389

E 403

Order, lies in the heart of the valley. In neighboring Weikersheim, tour the Renaissance hunting palace of the counts of Hohenlohe, after which you can sample the local wines in the shop at the gateway. Follow the course of the Tauber to its confluence with the Main River at Wertheim, also known as "little Heidelberg" because of its impressive hilltop castle ruins. In Würzburg, your next stop, you'll see many Gothic and Baroque masterpieces plus the Marienberg fortress and its successor, the Residenz. Three first-class wine estates here have wine pubs and shops.
☞ *Northern Romantic Road in Chapter 4*

By Public Transportation
Fast, frequent train service from Frankfurt to St. Goar, Koblenz, Heidelberg, or Würzburg, supplemented by local train and bus service, gets you to the above destinations within 2 hrs. The Deutsche Touring company's Europabus travels the Burgenstrasse, including Heidelberg and the Neckar Valley, as well as the Romantic Road, serving Würzburg, Bad Mergentheim, and Weikersheim. Sights are open and boats cruise the Rhine, Mosel, Neckar, and Main rivers from Easter through October.

The Great German Outdoors
7 to 10 days

Germans love the outdoors, and the autobahns are often jammed with families on their way to the countryside. News of a cold front on its way from Russia sets Germans to dusting off their skis, and the prediction of a high-pressure zone moving up from the Mediterranean fills the beds in hiking retreats. The mountains and lakes of Bavaria are Germany's playground. The Black Forest and Bodensee (Lake Constance), also in the south, are popular spa and recreation destinations. The gateway to all of them is Munich.

BAVARIAN ALPS AND LAKES
3 to 4 days. The Ammersee, ringed by cycling paths and walking trails, is a short ride from Munich. Most of the lakes in the Alps are warm enough for swimming in summer, and boatyards rent small sailboats and windsurfing boards. There are hiking trails in the mountains above Tegernsee; for more challenging walking head to Garmisch-Partenkirchen. It's one of Bavaria's three leading ski centers, with skiing virtually year-round on the glacier atop the Zugspitze, Germany's highest mountain. From here, wind your way down to the warmer clime of the Bodensee via the Deutsche Alpenstrasse.
☞ *Side Trips from Munich in Chapters 1 and 2*

BODENSEE
2 to 3 days. The Bodensee area is great for bicycling. An uninterrupted cycle path follows the shore of the lake, which you and your bike can cross via ferries. Bikes are rented at shops and some hotels. In addition, the waters of the Bodensee offer the best inland sailing in Germany, and more than 10 boatyards rent everything from sailboards to cabin cruisers. The climate here is unusually warm for

Germany. Vineyards and orchards fill the hillsides, and rare and exotic plants decorate the tiny island of Mainau.
☞ *Chapter 6*

THE BLACK FOREST
2 to 3 days. The Black Forest has wide open spaces for walking, horseback riding, cycling, and even golf. In winter, meadows become ski slopes, and forest paths are meticulously groomed as cross-country ski trails. This is also spa country, where you can rest your weary limbs in hot springs like those in opulent Ⓕ Baden-Baden.
☞ *Northern Black Forest in Chapter 7*

F 260

By Public Transportation
The lakes near Munich are easily accessible both by S-bahn suburban services and via local trains that run hourly between Munich and Garmisch-Partenkirchen. The Bodensee towns are all within 3 hrs of Munich by train, and local buses and trains travel the north shore of the lake. Baden-Baden is about 6 hrs from Munich by train via Stuttgart or Karlsruhe, and 3–4 hrs from Friedrichshafen. Local buses and trains link Baden-Baden with most Black Forest resorts.

Munich

40 km
A96
Ammersee
A8
50 km
penstrasse
A95
318
207 km
90 km
Tegernsee
Zugspitze
Garmisch-Partenkirchen

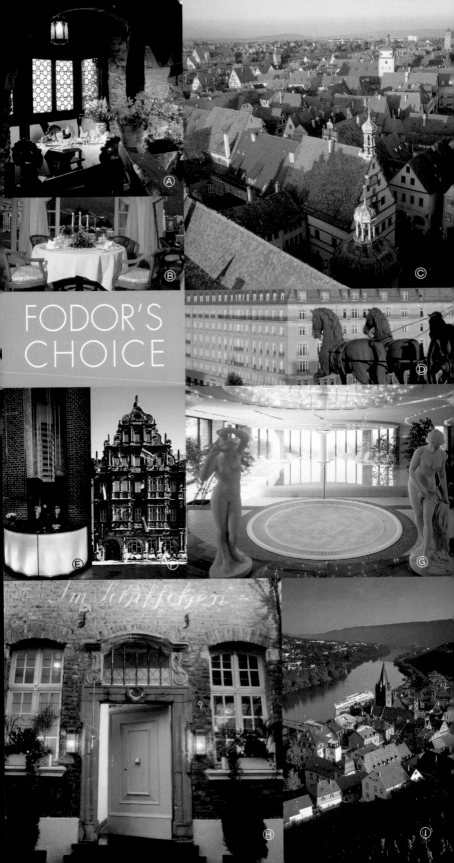

FODOR'S
CHOICE

Even with so many special places in Germany, Fodor's writers and editors have their favorites. Here are a few that stand out.

FLAVORS

Bareiss, Baiersbronn. The cuisine and champagne selection at this Black Forest mountain resort attract even the French from across the border. $$$$ ☞ p. 259

Ⓗ **Im Schiffchen, Düsseldorf.** Wear your jacket and tie for a special meal at this favorite of the Rhineland. The chef offers a lower-priced menu of local specialties at the ground-floor restaurant, Aalschokker. $$$$ ☞ p. 430

Ⓑ **Residenz Heinz Winkler, Aschau.** The reverence paid to herbs and spices here makes for sumptuous and healthy, French-leaning cuisine. Well-heeled München-ers know the trip to Heinz Winkler's Alpine inn is worth it. $$$$ ☞ p. 113

Hotel-Restaurant Luther, Freinsheim. Handsome table settings and artistic presenta-tion of imaginative meals make dining at this Baroque manor a joy for all the senses. $$$–$$$$ ☞ p. 364

Mensa, Berlin. This very trendy restaurant is the ideal place to enjoy German nouvelle cuisine and observe the capital's new business elite. $$$ ☞ p. 562

Schiffergesellschaft, Lübeck. Share a communal oak table at a historic fishermen's tavern, and order whatever is fresh from the Baltic Sea. $$–$$$ ☞ p. 517

Grossbeerenkeller, Berlin. Berliners unwind over beer and Frau Zinn-Baier's famous fried potatoes in this cellar restaurant. $ ☞ p. 562

Wein- und Speisehaus zum Stachel, Würzburg. This restaurant in the Franken wine region's capital serves its own vintages and hearty Franco-nian fare. $ ☞ p. 160

COMFORTS

Dornröschenschloss, Sababurg. This castle is said to have inspired *Sleeping Beauty*. The small, luxury hotel is still surrounded by dense woods. $$$$ ☞ p. 453

Ⓓ **Hotel Adlon, Berlin.** No other hotel in Berlin can match the Adlon's history or its prestigious location near the Brandenburger Tor. $$$$ ☞ p. 570

Ⓔ **Hotel im Wasserturm, Köln.** Neoclassic on the outside, this onetime water tower has a sleek interior. $$$$ ☞ p. 424

Ⓕ **Romantik Hotel zum Ritter St. Georg, Heidelberg.** This charming Romantik Group hotel is in Heidelberg's only Renaissance building. $$$$ ☞ p. 289

Ⓖ **Schlosshotel Bühlerhöhe, Bühl.** High on a Black Forest mountain, this resort offers everything from aromather-apy and seaweed wraps to horseback riding. $$$$ ☞ p. 260

Vier Jahreszeiten Kempinski, Munich. This Four Seasons hotel known for luxury and excellent service is perfectly placed among the premier shops of Maximilianstrasse. $$$$ ☞ p. 64

Ⓐ **Burghotel Auf Schönburg, Oberwesel.** This intimate hotel in a 900-year-old castle offers spectacular views of the Rhine from the terrace restaurant and many of the rooms. $$$–$$$$ ☞ p. 395

Hotel Robert Mayer, Frank-furt. Artists have outfitted the rooms at the "Art Hotel" with unique flair. The style of most rooms within the 1905 Art Nouveau building is coolly minimalist. $$$ ☞ p. 332

Pension Hubertus, Bad Reichenhall. This family-run pension in the eastern Bavar-ian Alps gives you a taste of Bavarian hospitality and the chance to swim in or boat on a private lake. $ ☞ p. 116

MUSEUMS

Domschatzkammer, Aachen. In one of the richest cathedral treasuries in Europe is sacred art from late antiquity and the Carolingian, Ottonian, and Hohenstaufen eras. ☞ p. 426

Kunsthalle, Hamburg. Ger-man Romantic painters

Caspar David Friedrich and Philip Otto Runge are fea-tured here, as are masters like Holbein, Rembrandt, Van Dyck, and Tiepolo. ☞ p. 478

Museum der Bildenden Künste, Leipzig. A fine collec-tion of Cranach the Elder's works is a highlight of the more than 2,700 paintings here. ☞ p. 613

Pergamonmuseum, Berlin. Within this museum are the Greek Pergamon Altar and other monuments of antiquity. ☞ p. 554

Wallraf-Richartz-Museum and Museum Ludwig, Köln. The former's pictures span the years 1300 to 1900, with Dutch and Flemish schools particularly well represented, and the latter's 20th-century works include the heavy hitters of American pop art. ☞ p. 422

TOWNS WHERE TIME STANDS STILL

Bad Wimpfen. Romans founded this ancient hill town in the 1st century AD. The remains of Barbarossa's imperial palace and a picture-postcard ensemble of Gothic and Renaissance buildings are part of the town's marked walking tour. ☞ p. 296

Ⓘ **Bernkastel-Kues.** Late-Gothic and early Renaissance facades surround the market square of this Mosel River town. ☞ p. 406

Quedlinburg. A UNESCO World Heritage site, this Harz Mountains town has more than 1,600 half-timbered houses, the oldest dating from the early 1300s. ☞ p. 623

Ⓒ **Rothenburg-ob-der-Tauber.** This walled town on the Romantic Road is a treasure of medieval towers and turrets. ☞ p. 164

St. Martin. Grapevines garland ancient houses in one of the most charming wine villages of the Pfalz region. ☞ p. 356

Wasserburg. What was born as a fortress on the site of a Roman watchtower is now a car-free island town on the Bodensee. ☞ p. 231

1 MUNICH

Chic and cosmopolitan, carefree and kitschy. As Bavaria's capital and one of Germany's biggest cities, Munich has more than its share of great museums, architectural treasures, historic sites, and world-class shops, restaurants, and hotels. The same could be said of its abundance of lederhosen and oompah bands. But it's the overall feeling of *Gemütlichkeit*—loosely translated as conviviality—that makes the city so special, with an open-air market here, a park there, and beer halls everywhere.

Updated by
Robert Tilley

MUNICH—München to the Germans—is the third-largest city in the Federal Republic and capital of the Free State of Bavaria. That Munich is the most popular vacation spot for Germans attests to the enduring appeal of the extremely likable city. Munich is kitsch and class, vulgarity and elegance. It's a city of ravishing rococo and smoky beer cellars, of soaring Gothic and sparkling shops, of sturdy Bavarian Art Nouveau (it lacks the playful grace of typical art nouveau) and pompous Prussian architecture, of ugly postwar development and late-1990s sleek steel-and-glass office buildings, of millionaires and lederhosen-clad farmers. Germany's favorite city is a place with extraordinary ambience and a vibrant lifestyle all its own, in a splendid setting within view—on a clear day—of the towering Alps.

Munich belongs to the relaxed and sunny south. Call it Germany with a southern exposure—although it may be an exaggeration to claim, as some Bavarians do, that Munich is the only Italian city north of the Alps. Still, there's no mistaking the carefree spirit that infuses the city and its easygoing approach to life, liberty, and the pursuit of happiness, Bavarian style. The Bavarians refer to this positively un-Teutonic joie de vivre as Gemütlichkeit.

What makes Munich so special? One explanation is the flair for the fanciful that is deeply rooted in Bavarian culture. And no historical figure better personifies this tradition than King Ludwig II, one of the last of the Wittelsbachs, the royal dynasty that for almost 750 years ruled over Munich and southern Germany until 1918. While Bismarck was striving from his Berlin power base to create a modern unified Germany, "Mad" Ludwig—also nicknamed the "Dream King"—was brandishing a begging bowl before Bavaria's nobility and almost bankrupting the royal treasury, all to finance a succession of fairy-tale castles and remote summer retreats (☞ Up-Close: The Dream King *in* Chapter 4).

Munich bills itself as *Die Weltstadt mit Herz* (the cosmopolitan city with heart), which it most assuredly is. A survey suggests that most Germans would prefer to live in Munich than where they currently reside, even though in many ways (housing, for instance) it's the most expensive place in Germany. But not all Germans flaunt "I Love Munich" bumper stickers. Certain buttoned-up types—in Hamburg or Düsseldorf, for example—might look down their imperious noses at Munich as being crass and tacky, and at Bavarians as only a few rungs up from the barbarians.

Munich is closely associated with the cavernous beer hall (such as the world-famous Hofbräuhaus) filled with the deafening echo of a brass oompah band and rows of swaying, burly Bavarians in lederhosen served by busty Fräuleins in flaring dirndl dresses. Every day, in different parts of the city, you'll find scenes like this. But there are also many Müncheners who never step inside a beer hall, who never go near Oktoberfest. They belong to the *other* Munich: a city of charm, refinement, and sophistication, represented by the world's finest ensemble of museums and art galleries, Europe's leading opera house and an outstanding philharmonic orchestra, high-fashion boutiques, and five-star restaurants.

Endowed with vast, green tracts of parks, gardens, and forests; grand boulevards lined with remarkable architecture; fountains and statuary; and a river spanned by graceful bridges, Munich is easily Germany's most beautiful and interesting city. If you could visit only one city in Germany, this should be it—no question.

Quietly and without fanfare, Munich has become the high-tech capital of Germany in the past decade and one of the most important cities in Europe. The concentration of electronics and computer firms—Siemens, IBM, Apple, and the like—in and around the city has turned it into the Silicon Valley of Germany.

Pleasures and Pastimes

Beer and Beer Gardens

Munich has more than 100 beer gardens, ranging from huge establishments that seat several hundred guests to small terraces tucked behind neighborhood pubs and taverns. Beer gardens are such an integral part of Munich life that a council proposal to cut down their hours provoked a storm of protest in 1995, culminating in one of the largest mass demonstrations in the city's history. They open whenever the thermometer creeps above 10°C (42°F) and when the sun filters through the chestnut trees that are a necessary part of beer-garden scenery. Most—but not all—allow you to bring along your own food, but if you do, don't defile this hallowed territory with something so foreign as pizza or a burger from McDonald's.

Dining

Old Munich Gaststätten feature *gutbürgerliche Küche,* loosely translated as good regional fare, and include brewery restaurants, beer halls, beer gardens, rustic cellars, and *Weinstuben* (wine taverns).

The city's fast-food tradition is centuries old. A tempting array of delectables is available almost anytime day or night; knowing the various Bavarian names will help. The generic term for Munich snacks is *Schmankerl,* which are served at *Brotzeit,* literally "bread time": a snack break, or what the English might call elevenses. According to a saying, *Brotzeit ist die schönste Zeit* (snack time is the best time).

In the morning in Munich, one eats *Weisswurst,* a tender minced-veal sausage—made fresh daily, steamed, and served with sweet mustard, a crisp roll or a pretzel, and *Weissbier* (wheat beer). As legend has it, this white sausage was invented in 1857 by a butcher who had a hangover and mixed the wrong ingredients. A plaque on a wall in Marienplatz marks where the "mistake" was made. It's claimed the genuine article is available only in and around Munich and served only between midnight and noon.

Another favorite Bavarian specialty is *Leberkäs*—literally "liver cheese," although neither liver nor cheese is among its ingredients. It is a spicy meat loaf baked to a crusty turn each morning and served in succulent slabs throughout the day. A *Leberkäs Semmel*—a wedge of the meat loaf between two halves of a crispy bread roll smeared with a bittersweet mustard—is the favorite Munich on-the-hoof snack. After that comes the repertoire of sausages indigenous to Bavaria, including types from Regensburg and Nürnberg.

More substantial repasts include *Tellerfleisch,* boiled beef with freshly grated horseradish and boiled potatoes on the side, served on wooden plates (there is a similar dish called *Tafelspitz).* Among roasts, sauerbraten (beef) and *Schweinebraten* (roast pork) are accompanied by dumplings and red cabbage or sauerkraut. *Haxn* (ham hocks) are roasted until they're crisp on the outside, juicy on the inside. They are served with sauerkraut and potato puree.

You'll also find soups, salads, fish and fowl, cutlets, game in season, casseroles, hearty stews, and what may well be the greatest variety and the highest quality of baked goods in Europe, including pretzels. In particular, seek out a *Käsestange*—a crispy long bread roll coated in baked cheese. No one need ever go hungry or thirsty in Munich.

Music and Opera

Munich and music complement each other marvelously. The city has two world-renowned orchestras (one, the Philharmonic, is directed by the American conductor James Levine), the Bavarian State Opera Company (managed by an ingenious British director, Peter Jonas), wonderful choral ensembles, a rococo jewel of a court theater, and a modern Philharmonic concert hall of superb proportions and acoustics—and that's just for starters.

Shopping

Munich has three of Germany's most exclusive shopping streets. At the other end of the scale, it has a variety of flea markets to rival that of any other European city. In between are department stores, where acute German-style competition assures reasonable prices and often produces outstanding bargains. The Christmas markets draw from backroom-studio artisans and artists with wares of beauty and originality. Collect their business cards—in the summer you're sure to want to order another of those little gold baubles that were on sale in December.

EXPLORING MUNICH

Munich is a wealthy city—and it shows. Everything is extremely upscale and up-to-date. At times the aura of affluence may be all but overpowering. But that's what Munich is all about these days and nights: a new city superimposed on the old; conspicuous consumption; a fresh patina of glitter along with the traditional rustic charms. Such are the dynamics and duality of this fascinating metropolis.

Numbers in the text correspond to numbers in the margin and on the Munich map.

Great Itineraries

IF YOU HAVE 2 OR 3 DAYS

Visit the tourist information office at the Hauptbahnhof (main railway station) and make for one of the cafés of the nearby pedestrian shopping zone to get your bearings. You can see the highlights of the city center and royal Munich in one day. Plan an eastward course across (or rather under) Karlsplatz and into Neuhauserstrasse and Kaufingerstrasse, plunging into the shopping crowds in this busy center of Munich commerce. You can escape the crowds whenever you want to inside one of the three churches that punctuate the route: the Bürgersaal, the Michaelskirche, or the Frauenkirche, Munich's soaring Gothic cathedral. Try to arrive in the city's central square, Marienplatz, in time for the 11 AM performance of the glockenspiel in the tower of the neo-Gothic Neues Rathaus (City Hall). Proceed to the city market, the Viktualienmarkt, for lunch, and then head a few blocks north for an afternoon visit to the Residenz, the rambling palace of the Wittelsbach rulers. End your first day with coffee at Munich's oldest café, the Tambosi, or an early evening cocktail at Käfer's, both on Odeonsplatz. Set aside days two and three for Munich's leading museums in the Maxvorstadt district. Also find time for a stroll east to the Englischer Garten, Munich's city park, for an outdoor lunch or an evening meal at one of its beer gardens or in the Seehaus, on the northern shore of the Kleinhesseloher See (lake).

IF YOU HAVE 4 OR 5 DAYS

For the first three days follow the itinerary described above. On the fourth day venture out to suburban Nymphenburg for a visit to Schloss

Nymphenburg, the Wittelsbachs' summer residence. Allow up to a whole day to view the palace's buildings and its museums and to stroll through its lovely park, breaking for lunch at the restaurant in the botanical garden. A tour of the Olympiapark is another full-day excursion. You can ride to the top of the Olympic Tower for the best view of Munich and the surrounding countryside. If you can fit it in, take a walk along the surprisingly quiet city banks of the Isar River, its rapid waters a translucent green from its mountain sources, or visit two of Munich's villa-museums, the Museum Villa Stuck and the Städtische Galerie im Lenbachhaus.

The City Center

Munich is unusual among German cities because it has no identifiable, homogeneous Old Town center. Postwar developments often separate clusters of buildings that date back to Munich's origins—and not always to harmonious effect. The outer perimeter of this tour is defined more by your stamina than by ancient city walls.

A Good Walk

Begin your walk through the city center at the **Hauptbahnhof** ①, the main train station and site of the city tourist office, which is next to the station's main entrance, on Bahnhofplatz. Pick up a detailed city map here. Cross Bahnhofplatz, the square in front of the station (or take the underpass), and walk toward Schützenstrasse, which marks the start of Munich's pedestrian shopping mall, the *Fussgängerzone,* 2 km (1 mi) of traffic-free streets. Running virtually the length of Schützenstrasse is Munich's largest department store, Hertie. At the end of the street you descend via the pedestrian underpass into another shopping empire, a vast underground complex of boutiques and cafés. Above you is the busy traffic intersection, **Karlsplatz** ②, known locally as the Stachus, with a popular fountain area.

Ahead stands one of the city's oldest gates, the Karlstor, first mentioned in local records in 1302. Beyond it lies Munich's main shopping thoroughfare, Neuhauserstrasse, and its extension, Kaufingerstrasse. On your left as you enter Neuhauserstrasse is another attractive fountain: a late-19th-century figure of Bacchus. This part of town was almost completely destroyed by bombing during World War II and has been extensively rebuilt. Great efforts were made to ensure that the designs of the new buildings harmonized with the old city, although some of the modern structures are little more than functional. Though this may not be an architectural showplace, there are redeeming features to the area. Haus Oberpollinger, on Neuhauserstrasse, is one; it's a department store hiding behind an imposing 19th-century facade. Notice the weather vanes of old merchant ships on its high-gabled roof.

Shopping, however, is not the only attraction on these streets. Worldly department stores rub shoulders with two remarkable churches: the **Bürgersaal** ③ and the **Michaelskirche** ④. The 16th-century Michaelskirche was the first Renaissance church of this size in southern Germany. Its fanciful facade contrasts wonderfully with the baroque exterior of the Bürgersaal. The massive building next to Michaelskirche was once one of Munich's oldest churches, built in the late 13th century for Benedictine monks. It was secularized in the early 19th century, served as a warehouse for some years, and today is the **Deutsches Jagd- und Fischereimuseum** ⑤.

Turn left here onto Augustinerstrasse, and you will soon arrive in Frauenplatz, a quiet square with a shallow, sunken fountain. Towering over it is the **Frauenkirche** ⑥, Munich's cathedral, whose twin

38

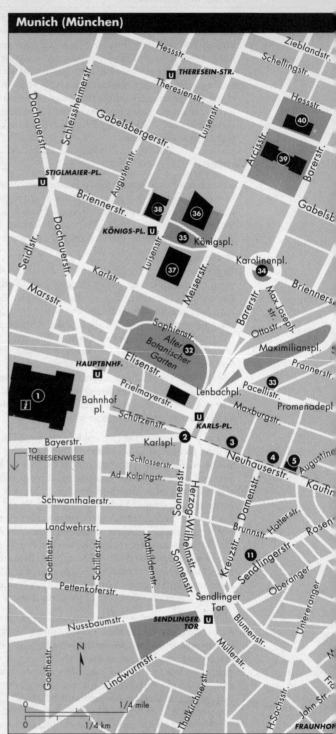

Munich (München)

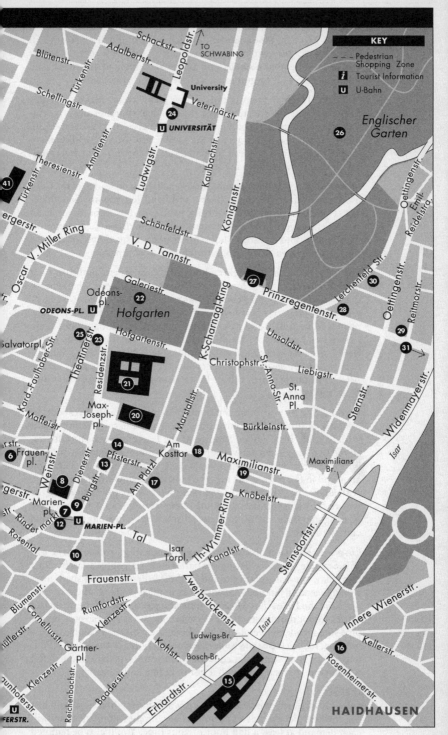

KEY

- - - Pedestrian Shopping Zone

i Tourist Information

U U-Bahn

Schackstr.

TO SCHWABING

Blütenstr.

Adalbertstr.

Leopoldstr.

University

Veterinärstr.

Türkenstr.

Schellingstr.

24

U UNIVERSITÄT

Amalienstr.

Ludwigstr.

Kaulbachstr.

Königinstr.

26

Englischer Garten

Theresienstr.

41

Türkenstr.

Schönfeldstr.

ergerstr.

Oscar V. Miller Ring

V. D. Tannstr.

K.-Scharnagl-Ring

Prinzregentenstr.

27

Lerchenfeld Str.

30

Oettingenstr.

Emil-Reidelstr.

Galeriestr.

Odeons-pl.

22

28

Oettingenstr.

ODEONS-PL. **U**

Hofgarten

29

Reimorstr.

Unsoldstr.

31

25

23

Hofgartenstr.

Theatinerstr.

Salvatorpl.

Christophstr.

St.-Anna-Str.

Liebigstr.

Kard.-Faulhaber-Str.

Residenzstr.

21

Marstallstr.

St. Anna Pl.

Sternstr.

Widenmayerstr.

Maffeistr.

Max-Joseph-pl.

20

Bürkleinstr.

Isar

6 Frauen-pl.

14

Am Kosttor

18

Maximilianstr.

Maximilians Br.

Weinstr.

Pfisterstr.

13

19

8

Dienerstr.

Burgstr.

Am platzl

17

Knöbelstr.

gerstr.

9

Marien-pl.

7

Steinsdorfstr.

12

U MARIEN-PL.

Th.-Wimmer-Ring

str.

Rindermarkt

Tal

Isar Torpl.

Kanalstr.

10

Rosental

Frauenstr.

Blumenstr.

Rumfordstr.

Zweibrückenstr.

Isar

Cornelusstr.

Klenzestr.

Innere Wienerstr.

üllerstr.

Gärtner-pl.

Ludwigs-Br.

16

Kellerstr.

Kohlstr.

Bosch-Br.

Rosenheimerstr.

Klenzestr.

Reichenbachstr.

Baaderstr.

15

aunhoferstr.

U

Erhardtstr.

HAIDHAUSEN

FERSTR.

domes are the city's main landmark and its symbol. From the cathedral follow any of the alleys heading east, and you'll reach the very heart of Munich, **Marienplatz** ⑦, which is surrounded by stores and dining spots. Marienplatz is dominated by the 19th-century **Neues Rathaus** ⑧; the **Altes Rathaus** ⑨, a medieval building of assured charm, sits modestly, as if forgotten, in a corner of the square.

Hungry? Thirsty? Help is only a few steps away. From the Altes Rathaus, cross the street, passing the Heiliggeistkirche, an early Munich church with a rococo interior added between 1724 and 1730. Heiliggeiststrasse brings you to the jumble known as the **Viktualienmarkt** ⑩, the city's open-air food market, where you can eat a stand-up lunch at any of the many stalls.

From the market follow Rosental into Sendlingerstrasse, one of the city's most interesting shopping streets, and head left toward Sendlinger Tor, a finely restored medieval brick gate. On your right as you head down Sendlingerstrasse is the remarkable **Asamkirche** ⑪. The exterior fits so snugly into the street's housefronts (the architects lived next door) that you might easily overlook the church as you pass.

From the Asamkirche, backtrack up Sendlingerstrasse and turn right onto Rindermarkt (the former cattle market), and you'll be beneath the soaring tower of the **Peterskirche** ⑫, or Alter Peter (Old St. Peter's), the city's oldest and best-loved parish church. From the Peterskirche reenter Marienplatz and pass in front of the Altes Rathaus once again to step into Burgstrasse. You'll soon find yourself in the quiet, airy **Alter Hof** ⑬, the inner courtyard of the original palace of Bavaria's Wittelsbach rulers. A short distance beyond the northern archway of the Alter Hof, on the north side of Pfisterstrasse, stands the former royal mint, the **Münze** ⑭.

If you'd like to visit some museums, extend your walk by about 10 minutes, returning down Burgstrasse to broad Tal, once an important trading route that entered Munich at the Isartor, now beautifully restored to its original medieval appearance. Continue across Isartorplatz into Zweibrückenstrasse, and you'll come to the Isar River. There, on an island in the river, is the massive bulk of the **Deutsches Museum** ⑮, with a gigantic thermometer and barometer on its tower showing the way to the main entrance. Budding scientists and young dreamers will be delighted by its many interactive displays with buttons to push and cranks to turn.

On a sunny day join the locals for ice cream and a stroll along the Isar River, where the more daring sunbathe nude on pebble islands. On a rainy day you can splash around in the Müllersches Volksbad, a restored Jugendstil (art nouveau) indoor swimming pool at Ludwigsbrücke, opposite the Deutsches Museum (one afternoon a week the Volksbad is reserved for the nudists, a very German concession). The soaring organ-pipe-like facade above on the hill above the Volksbad belongs to the modern, redbrick **Gasteig Kulturzentrum** ⑯, home of the Munich Philharmonic Orchestra and a collection of theaters, galleries, and cafés, where your tour can end with a pot of coffee and a pastry.

TIMING

Set aside at least a whole day for this walk, hitting Marienplatz when the glockenspiel plays at 11 or noon. The churches along the route will each demand at least a half hour of your time. You'll also be tempted by the department stores in the pedestrian zone. Prepare for big crowds in Marienplatz when the glockenspiel plays, and try to avoid shopping between noon and 2, when workers on lunch break make for the department stores. Aficionados of hunting or engineering could spend hours in the Deutsches Jagd- und Fischereimuseum and Deutsches Museum.

Sights to See

⑬ Alter Hof (Old Palace). This palace was the original residence of the Wittelsbachs, the ruling dynasty established in 1180. The palace now serves as local government offices. Something of a medieval flavor survives in the Alter Hof's quiet courtyard in the otherwise busy downtown area. Don't pass through without turning to admire the medieval oriel (bay window) that hides on the south wall, just around the corner as you enter the courtyard.

⑨ Altes Rathaus (Old City Hall). This was Munich's first city hall, built in 1474. Its great hall—destroyed in 1944 but now fully restored—was the work of architect Jörg von Halspach. It is used for official receptions and is not normally open to the public. The tower provides a satisfyingly atmospheric setting for a **toy museum**, accessible via a winding staircase. It includes several exhibits from the United States. ⊠ *Marienpl.,* ☎ *089/294–001.* ⌧ *Museum DM 5.* ⊙ *Daily 10–5:30.*

★ ⑪ Asamkirche (Asam Church). Munich's most unusual church has a suitably extraordinary entrance, framed by raw rock foundations. The insignificant church door, crammed between its craggy shoulders, gives little idea of the splendor within. Above the doorway St. Nepomuk, a 14th-century Bohemian monk who drowned in the Danube, is being led by angels from a rocky riverbank to heaven. The 18th-century church's official name is Church of St. Johann Nepomuk, but it is known as the Asamkirche for its architects, the brothers Cosmas Damian and Egid Quirin Asam. Inside you'll discover a prime example of true southern German, late-baroque architecture. Frescoes and rosy marble cover the walls, from which statuary and gilding explode—there's even a gilt skeleton at the sanctuary's portal. For such a small church (there are only 12 rows of pews), the opulence and lavish detailing are overwhelming. ⊠ *Sendlingerstr.* ⊙ *Daily 9–5:30.*

③ Bürgersaal (Citizens' Hall). Beneath the modest roof of this unassuming church are two contrasting levels. The Oberkirche (upper level)—the church proper—is a richly decorated baroque oratory. Its elaborate stucco foliage and paintings of Bavarian places of pilgrimage project a distinctly different ambience from that of the Unterkirche (lower level), reached by a double staircase. This gloomy, cryptlike chamber contains the tomb of Rupert Mayer, a famous Jesuit priest renowned for his energetic and outspoken opposition to the Nazis. ⊠ *Neuhauserstr. 14,* ☎ *089/223–884.* ⊙ *Oberkirche Mon.–Sat. 11–1, Sun. 9–12:30; Unterkirche Mon.–Sat. 6:30 AM–7 PM, Sun. 7–7.*

⑤ Deutsches Jagd- und Fischereimuseum (German Museum of Hunting and Fishing). Lovers of the thrill of the chase will be fascinated by this museum. It contains the world's largest collection of fishhooks, some 500 stuffed animals (including a 6½-ft-tall North American grizzly bear), a 12,000-year-old skeleton of an Irish deer, and a valuable collection of hunting weapons. ⊠ *Neuhauserstr. 2,* ☎ *089/220–522.* ⌧ *DM 5.* ⊙ *Tues., Wed., and Fri.–Sun. 9:30–5; Mon. and Thurs. 9:30–9.*

★ ⑮ Deutsches Museum (German Museum of Science and Technology). Within a monumental building next to the Isar River, this museum—filled with aircraft, vehicles, locomotives, and machinery—is an engineering student's dream. Nineteen kilometers (12 miles) of corridors, six floors of exhibits, and 30 departments make up the immense collections. Not all exhibits have explanations in English, which is why you should skip the otherwise impressive coal-mine labyrinth. The most technically advanced planetarium in Europe, it has up to six shows daily, including a

Laser Magic display. An IMAX theater—a wraparound screen six stories high—shows nature and adventure films. The Internet Café on the third floor is open daily 9–3. To arrange for a two-hour tour in English, call 089/2179–252 two weeks in advance. ✉ *Museumsinsel 1,* ☎ *089/ 21790; 089/211–25180 to reserve tickets at planetarium and IMAX.* 🎫 *Museum DM 10, Planetarium DM 12.50, IMAX DM 11.90; combined ticket for planetarium and IMAX DM 20.50 (admission for some performances is higher).* ☉ *Daily 9* AM–11 PM. ✍

OFF THE
BEATEN PATH
FRANZISKANERKLOSTERKIRCHE ST. ANNA (Franciscan Monastery Church of St. Anne) – This striking example of the two Asam brothers' work is in the Lehel district. Though less opulently decorated than the Asamkirche, this small Franciscan monastery church, consecrated in 1737, impresses with its sense of movement and its heroic scale. It was largely rebuilt after wartime bomb damage. The ceiling fresco by Cosmas Damian Asam was removed before World War II and, after restoration, now glows in all its original vivid joyfulness. The ornate altar was also designed by the Asam brothers. Towering over the delicate little church, on the opposite side of the street, is the neo-Romanesque bulk of the 19th-century church of St. Anne. You can get to Lehel on Tram 17 or U-bahn 4 or 5 from the city center. ✉ *St.-Anna-Str.,* ☎ *089/212–1820.*

★ ⑥ **Frauenkirche** (Church of Our Lady). Munich's Dom (cathedral) is a distinctive late-Gothic brick structure with two enormous towers that are Munich's chief landmark. Each is more than 300 ft high, and both are capped by very un-Gothic onion-shape domes. The towers have become the symbol of Munich's skyline—some say because they look like overflowing beer mugs.

The main body of the cathedral was completed in 20 years (1474–94)—a record time in those days. The towers were added, almost as an afterthought, in 1524–25. Jörg von Polling, the Frauenkirche's original architect, is buried here. The building suffered severe damage during the Allied bombing of Munich and was lovingly restored between 1947 and 1957. Inside, the church combines most of von Polling's original features with a stark, clean modernity and simplicity of line, emphasized by slender, white octagonal pillars that sweep up through the nave to the tracery ceiling far above. As you enter the church, look on the stone floor for the dark imprint of a large foot—the *Teufelstritt* (Devil's Footprint). According to local lore, the devil challenged von Polling to build a nave without windows. Von Polling wagered his soul and accepted the challenge, building a cathedral that is flooded with light from 66-ft-high windows that are invisible to anyone standing at the spot marked by the Teufelstritt. The cathedral houses an elaborate 15th-century black-marble memorial to Emperor Ludwig the Bavarian, guarded by four 16th-century armored knights.

A splendid view of the city is yours from an observation platform high up in one of the towers. But beware—you must climb 86 steps to reach the tower elevator! ✉ *Frauenpl.,* ☎ *089/290–0820.* 🎫 *Tower DM 4.* ☉ *Tower elevator Apr.–Oct., Mon.–Sat. 10–5.*

⑯ **Gasteig Kulturzentrum** (Gasteig Culture Center). This striking postmodern, brick cultural complex for music, theater, and film has an open-plan interior and a maze of interior courtyards and plazas, sitting high above the Isar River. The center has two theaters, where plays in English are occasionally staged. ✉ *Rosenheimerstr. 5,* ☎ *089/480–980.*

❶ **Hauptbahnhof** (Main Train Station). The city tourist office here has maps and helpful information on events around town. ✉ *Bahnhofpl.,* ☎ *089/2333–0258.*

② **Karlsplatz.** Known locally as the Stachus, this busy intersection has one of Munich's most popular fountains, a circle of water jets that acts as a magnet on hot summer days for city shoppers and office workers seeking a cool place to relax. A semicircle of yellow-front buildings with high windows and delicate cast-iron balconies back the fountain.

★ **⑦** **Marienplatz.** Bordering the ☞ Neues Rathaus, shops, and cafés, this square is named after the gilded statue of the Virgin Mary that has watched over it for more than three centuries. It was erected in 1638 at the behest of Elector Maximilian I as an act of thanksgiving for the city's survival during the Thirty Years' War, the cataclysmic religious struggle that devastated vast regions of Germany. When the statue was taken down from its marble column for cleaning in 1960, workmen found a small casket in the base containing a splinter of wood said to be from the cross of Christ. ⊠ *Bounded by Kaufingerstr., Rosenstr., Weinstr., and Dienerstr.*

④ **Michaelskirche** (St. Michael's Church). A curious story explains why this sturdy Renaissance church has no tower. Seven years after the start of construction the principal tower collapsed. Its patron, pious Duke Wilhelm V, regarded the disaster as a heavenly sign that the church wasn't big enough, so he ordered a change in the plans—this time without a tower. Completed seven years later, the Michaelskirche was the first Renaissance church of this size in southern Germany. The duke is buried in the crypt, along with 40 other Wittelsbachs, including the eccentric King Ludwig II. A severe neoclassical monument in the north transept contains the tomb of Napoléon's stepson, Eugene de Beauharnais, who married one of the daughters of King Maximilian I and died in Munich in 1824. You'll find the plain white-stucco interior of the church and its slightly barnlike atmosphere soothingly simple after the lavish decoration of the nearby Bürgersaal. ⊠ *Neuhauserstr. 6,* ☎ *089/5519–9257.* ☜ *DM 2.* ☉ *Weekdays 10–1 and 2–4:30, Sat. 10–3. Closed Sun. and public holidays.*

⑭ **Münze** (Mint). Originally the royal stables, the Münze was created by court architect Wilhelm Egkl between 1563 and 1567 and now serves as an office building. A stern neoclassical facade emblazoned with gold was added in 1809; the interior courtyard has Renaissance-style arches. ⊠ *Pfisterstr. 4.* ☜ *Free.* ☉ *Mon.–Thurs. 8–4, Fri. 8–2.*

⑧ **Neues Rathaus** (New City Hall). Munich's present city hall was built between 1867 and 1908 in the fussy, turreted, neo-Gothic style so beloved by King Ludwig II. Architectural historians are divided over its merits, though its dramatic scale and lavish detailing are impressive. Perhaps the most serious criticism is that the Dutch and Flemish style of the building seems out of place amid the baroque and rococo of so much of the rest of the city. In 1904 a glockenspiel (a chiming clock with mechanical figures) was added to the tower; it plays daily at 11 AM, noon, and 9 PM, with an additional performance at 5 PM June–October. As chimes peal out over the square, the clock's doors flip open and brightly colored dancers and jousting knights go through their paces. They act out two events from Munich's past: a tournament held in Marienplatz in 1568 and the *Schäfflertanz* (Dance of the Coopers), which commemorated the end of the plague of 1517. When Munich was in ruins after the war, an American soldier contributed some paint to restore the battered figures, and he was rewarded with a ride on one of the jousters' horses, high above the cheering crowds. You, too, can travel up there, by elevator, to an observation point near the top of one of the towers. On a clear day the view is spectacular. ⊠ *Marienpl.,* ☎ *089/2331.* ☜ *Tower DM 3.* ☉ *Mon.–Thurs. 9–4, Fri. 9–1.*

⑫ **Peterskirche** (St. Peter's Church). Munich's oldest and smallest parish church traces its origins to the 11th century and over the years has been restored in a variety of architectural styles. Today you'll find a rich baroque interior, with a magnificent late-Gothic high altar and aisle pillars decorated with exquisite 18th-century figures of the apostles. In clear weather it's well worth the climb up the 300-ft tower—the view includes glimpses of the Alps to the south. The Peterskirche has a Scottish priest who is glad to show English-speaking visitors around. ✉ *Rindermarkt*, ☎ *089/260–4828.* ▣ *Tower DM 2.50.* ☉ *Mon.–Sat. 9–7, Sun. 10–7.*

OFF THE BEATEN PATH

STREETCAR 19 – For the cheapest sightseeing tour of the city center on wheels, board this streetcar outside the ☞ **Hauptbahnhof** on Bahnhofplatz and make the 15-minute journey to Max Weber Platz. Explore the streets around the square, part of the old Bohemian residential area of Haidhausen (with some of the city's best bars and restaurants, many on the villagelike Kirchenstrasse), and then return by a different route on Streetcar 18 to Karlsplatz.

THERESIENWIESE – The site of Munich's annual beer festival—the notorious Oktoberfest—is only a 10-minute walk from the ☞ **Hauptbahnhof** or only a single stop away by subway (U-4 or U-5). It is an enormous exhibition ground, named after a young woman whose engagement party gave rise to the Oktoberfest. In 1810 the party celebrated the betrothal of Princess Therese von Sachsen-Hildburghausen to the Bavarian crown prince Ludwig, later Ludwig I. It was such a success, attended by nearly the entire population of Munich, that it became an annual affair. Beer was served then as now, but what began as a night out for the locals has become a 16-day international bonanza at the end of September and the beginning of October, attracting more than 6 million people each year (it qualifies as an *Oktober*fest by ending the first Sunday in October).

Overlooking the Theresienwiese is a 19th-century hall of fame—one of the last works of Ludwig I—and a monumental bronze statue of the maiden **Bavaria**, more than 100 ft high. The statue is hollow, and 130 steps take you up into the braided head for a view of Munich through Bavaria's eyes. ▣ *DM 4.* ☉ *Dec.–Oct., Tues.–Sun. 10–noon and 2–4.*

★ ⑩ **Viktualienmarkt.** The city's open-air food market (*Viktualien* means vittles) has a wide range of produce, German and international foodstuffs, and tables and counters for eating and drinking, which make the area a feast for the eyes as well as the stomach. It's also the realm of the garrulous, sturdy market women who run the stalls with dictatorial authority. Whether here, or at a bakery, *do not* try to select your pickings by hand; ask for help.

Royal Munich

From the relatively modest palace of the Alter Hof (☞ *above*), Munich's royal rulers expanded their quarters northward, where more space was to be found than in the jumble of narrow streets of the old quarter. The Wittelsbachs built a palace more suitable for their regal pretensions and laid out a fine garden, at first off limits to all but the nobility. Three splendid avenues radiated outward from this new center of royal rule, and fine homes arose along them. One of them—Prinzregentenstrasse—marks the southern end of Munich's huge public park, the Englischer Garten—also the creation of a Wittelsbach ruler.

A Good Walk

A good way to start this very long walk is to stoke up with a Bavarian breakfast of Weisswurst, pretzels, and beer at the **Hofbräuhaus** ⑰, perhaps Munich's best-known beer hall, on Am Platzl. Turn right from the Hofbräuhaus for the short walk along Orlandostrasse to **Maximilianstrasse** ⑱, Munich's most elegant shopping street, named after King Maximilian II, whose statue you'll see far down on the right. This wide boulevard has many grand buildings, which contain government offices and the city's ethnological museum, the **Staatliches Museum für Völkerkunde** ⑲. The Maximilianeum, on a rise beyond the Isar River, is an impressive mid-19th-century palace where the Bavarian state government now meets.

Across Maximilianstrasse as you enter from the Hofbräuhaus stands a handsome city landmark: the Hotel Vier Jahreszeiten, a historic host to traveling princes, millionaires, and the expense-account jet set.

Turn left down Maximilianstrasse, away from the Maximilianeum, and you'll enter the square called Max-Joseph-Platz, dominated by the pillared portico of the 19th-century **Nationaltheater** ⑳, home of the Bavarian State Opera Company. The statue in the square's center is of Bavaria's first king, Max Joseph. Along the north side of this untidily arranged square (marred by the entrance to an underground parking lot) is the lofty and austere south wall of the **Residenz** ㉑, the royal palace of Wittelsbach rulers for more than six centuries.

Directly north of the Residenz, on Hofgartenstrasse, lies the former royal garden, the **Hofgarten** ㉒. You can be forgiven for any confusion about your whereabouts ("Can this really be Germany?") when you step from the Hofgarten onto Odeonsplatz. To your left is the 19th-century **Feldherrnhalle** ㉓, modeled after the familiar Loggia dei Lanzi in Florence. Looking north up Ludwigstrasse, the arrow-straight avenue that begins at the Feldherrnhalle, you'll see the **Siegestor** ㉔, or victory arch, which marks the beginning of Leopoldstrasse. Completing this impressively Italianate panorama is the great yellow bulk of the former royal church of St. Kajetan, the **Theatinerkirche** ㉕, an imposing baroque structure across from the Feldherrnhalle.

Now head north up Ludwigstrasse. The first stretch of the street was designed by court architect Leo von Klenze. In much the same way that Baron Haussmann would later demolish many of the old streets and buildings in Paris, replacing them with stately boulevards, von Klenze swept aside the small dwellings and alleys that stood here to build his great avenue. His high-windowed and formal buildings have never quite been accepted by Müncheners. Most people either love it or hate it. Von Klenze's buildings end just before Ludwigstrasse becomes Leopoldstrasse, and it is easy to see where he handed construction over to another leading architect, Friedrich von Gärtner. The severe neoclassical buildings that line southern Ludwigstrasse—including the Bayerische Staatsbibliothek (Bavarian State Library), the Universität (University), and the peculiarly Byzantine Ludwigskirche—fragment into the lighter styles of Leopoldstrasse. The more delicate structures are echoed by the busy street life you'll find here in summer. Once the hub of the legendary artists' district of Schwabing, Leopoldstrasse still throbs with life from spring to fall, exuding the atmosphere of a Mediterranean boulevard, with cafés, wine terraces, and artists' stalls. In comparison, Ludwigstrasse is inhabited by ghosts of the past.

At the south end of Leopoldstrasse lies the great open quadrangle of the university. A circular area divides into two piazzas named after anti-Nazi resistance leaders: Geschwister-Scholl-Platz and Professor-Huber-Platz. The Scholls, brother and sister, and Professor Huber were members of the short-lived resistance movement known as the Weisse Rose (White Rose) and were executed after show trials. At its north end, Leopoldstrasse leads into Schwabing itself, once Munich's bohemian quarter but now distinctly upscale. Explore the streets of old Schwabing around Wedekindplatz to get the feel of the place. (Those in search of the bohemian mood that once animated Schwabing should head to Haidhausen, on the other side of the Isar.)

Bordering the east side of Schwabing is the **Englischer Garten** ㉖. Five kilometers (3 miles) long and 1½ km (about 1 mi) wide, it's Germany's largest city park, stretching from Prinzregentenstrasse, the broad avenue laid out by Prince Regent Luitpold at the end of the 19th century, to the city's northern boundary, where the lush parkland is taken over by the rough embrace of open countryside. Dominating the park's southern border is one of the few examples of Hitler-era architecture still standing in Munich: the colonnaded **Haus der Kunst** ㉗, a leading art gallery and home to Munich's most fashionable nightclub, the PI.

A few hundred yards farther along Prinzregentenstrasse are two other leading museums, the **Bayerisches Nationalmuseum** ㉘ and the **Schack-Galerie** ㉙, while around the first left-hand corner, on Lerchenfeldstrasse, is a museum of prehistory, the **Prähistorische Staatssammlung** ㉚, that brings to life the ancient past.

The column you see standing triumphant on a hill at the eastern end of Prinzregentenstrasse, just across the Isar River from the Schack-Galerie, is Munich's well-loved Friedensengel (Angel of Peace). This striking gilt angel crowns a marble column in a small park overlooking the Isar River. Just across the river, beyond the Friedensengel, is another historic home that became a major Munich art gallery—the **Museum Villa Stuck** ㉛, a jewel of Art-Nouveau fantasy.

There are innumerable walks along the banks of the Isar River and in the nearby Englischer Garten, where you can stop at one of its four beer gardens (the Chinese Tower is the largest and most popular) or visit the Seehaus, on the shore of the park's lake, the Kleinhesseloher See. Here you'll have another choice to make: a smart restaurant or a cozy *Bierstube* (beer tavern).

TIMING

You'll need a day (and good walking shoes) for this stroll, which ends in the Englischer Garten. Set aside at least two hours for a tour of the Residenz. If the weather is good, return to the southern end of the Englischer Garten at dusk, when you'll be treated to an unforgettable silhouette of the Munich skyline, black against the retreating light.

Sights to See

㉘ **Bayerisches Nationalmuseum** (Bavarian National Museum). The extensive collection here contains Bavarian and other German art and artifacts. The highlight for some will be the medieval and Renaissance wood carvings, with many works by the great Renaissance sculptor Tilman Riemenschneider. Tapestries, arms and armor, a unique collection of Christmas crèches (the Krippenschau), Bavarian arts and crafts, and folk artifacts compete for your attention. Although the museum places emphasis on Bavarian cultural history, it has artifacts of outstanding international importance and regular exhibitions that attract worldwide attention. ⊠ *Prinzregentenstr. 3,* ☎ *089/211–241.* ⊒ *DM 3, DM 8 for special exhibitions.* ☉ *Tues.–Sun. 9:30–5.*

★ ㉖ **Englischer Garten** (English Garden). This virtually endless park, which is embraced by open countryside at Munich's northern city limits, was designed for the Bavarian prince Karl Theodor by a refugee from the American War of Independence, Count Rumford. Although Rumford was of English descent, it was the open, informal nature of the park—

reminiscent of the rolling parklands with which English aristocrats of the 18th century liked to surround their country homes—that determined its name. It has a boating lake, four beer gardens, and a series of curious decorative and monumental constructions, including the Monopteros, a Greek temple designed by von Klenze for King Ludwig I and built on an artificial hill in the southern section of the park. In the center of the park's most popular beer garden is a Chinese pagoda erected in 1789. It was destroyed during the war and then reconstructed. The Chinese Tower beer garden is world famous, but the park has prettier places for nursing a beer: the Aumeister, for example, along the northern perimeter. The Aumeister's restaurant is in an early 19th-century hunting lodge.

The Englischer Garten is a paradise for joggers, cyclists, and, in winter, cross-country skiers. The Munich Cricket Club grounds are in the southern section—and spectators are welcome. The park has specially designated areas for nude sunbathing—the Germans have a positively pagan attitude toward the sun—so don't be surprised to see naked bodies bordering the flower beds and paths. ⊠ *Main entrances at Prinzregentenstr. and Koniginstr.*

㉓ Feldherrnhalle (Generals' Hall). This hall of fame that honors generals who have led Bavarian forces was modeled after the 14th-century Loggia dei Lanzi in Florence. The open-sided pavilionlike building bears two great bronze plaques honoring the generals who led the Bavarian army in three centuries of wars. Larger-than-life statues of two of these generals, Count Johann Tserclaes Tilly, who led Catholic forces in the Thirty Years' War, and Prince Karl Philipp Wrede, hero of the 19th-century Napoleonic Wars, flank two huge Bavarian lions. The imposing structure was turned into a militaristic shrine in the 1930s and '40s by the Nazis, who also found significance in the coincidence that it marked the site of Hitler's abortive coup, or putsch, which took place in 1923. All who passed it had to give the Nazi salute. A tiny alley behind the Feldherrnhalle, linking Residenzstrasse and Theatinerstrasse and now lined with exclusive boutiques, was used by those who wanted to dodge the tedious routine. ⊠ *South end of Odeonspl.*

㉗ Haus der Kunst (House of Art). This colonnaded, classical-style building is one of Munich's few remaining examples of Hitler-era architecture and was officially opened by the führer himself. In the Hitler years it showed only work deemed to reflect the Nazi aesthetic. One of its most successful postwar exhibitions was devoted to works banned by the Nazis. It stages exhibitions of art, photography, and sculpture, as well as theatrical and musical "happenings." The disco PI is in the building's west wing. ⊠ *Prinzregentenstr. 1,* ☎ *089/211–270.* ▧ *Admission depends on exhibition.* ◷ *Tues.–Sun. 9–5.*

⑰ Hofbräuhaus. Duke Wilhelm V founded Munich's most famous brewery in 1589. Hofbräu means "royal brew," which aptly describes the golden beer poured in king-size liter mugs. If the cavernous downstairs hall is too noisy for you, try the quiet restaurant upstairs. Americans, Australians, and Italians far outnumber Germans, and the brass band that performs here most days adds modern pop and American folk to the traditional German numbers. ⊠ *Am Platzl 9,* ☎ *089/221–676.*

㉒ Hofgarten (Royal Garden). The formal garden was once part of the royal palace grounds. It's bordered on two sides by arcades designed in the 19th century by the royal architect Leo von Klenze. On the east side of the garden stands the new state chancellery, built around the ruins of the 19th-century Army Museum and incorporating the remains of a Renaissance arcade. Its most prominent feature is a large copper dome. Bombed during World War II air raids, the museum stood untouched for almost 40 years as a grim reminder of the war.

In front of the chancellery stands one of Europe's most unusual—some say most effective—war memorials. Instead of looking up at a monument, you are led down to a **sunken crypt** covered by a massive granite block. In the crypt lies a German soldier from World War I. ⊠ *Hofgartenstr., north of Residenz.*

The monument is a stark contrast to the **memorial** that stands unobtrusively in front of the northern wing of the chancellery: a simple cube of black marble bearing facsimiles of handwritten wartime manifestos by anti-Nazis leaders, including members of the White Rose movement.

Ludwigskirche (Ludwig's Church). Planted halfway along the severe, neoclassical Ludwigstrasse is this curious neo-Byzantine/early Renaissance–style church. It was built at the behest of Ludwig I to provide his newly completed suburb with a parish church. It's worth a stop to see the fresco of the *Last Judgment* in the choir. At 60 ft by 37 ft, it is one of the world's largest. ⊠ *Ludwigstr. 22,* ☎ *089/288–334.* ◷ *Daily 7–7.*

⑱ **Maximilianstrasse.** Munich's sophisticated shopping street was named after King Maximilian II, who wanted to break away from the Greek-influenced classical style of city architecture favored by his father, Ludwig I. With the cabinet's approval, he created this broad boulevard, its central stretch lined with majestic buildings (now government offices and the state ethnological museum, the ☞ **Staatliches Museum für Völkerkunde**). It culminates on a rise beyond the Isar River in the stately outlines of the **Maximilianeum,** a lavish 19th-century arcaded palace built for Maximilian II and now the home of the Bavarian state parliament. Only the terrace can be visited.

③① **Museum Villa Stuck.** This museum is the former home of one of Munich's leading turn-of-the-20th-century artists, Franz von Stuck (1863–1928). His work covers the walls of the haunting rooms of the neoclassical villa, which is also used for regular art exhibits organized by the museum's Australian director. ⊠ *Prinzregentenstr. 60,* ☎ *089/ 4555–5125.* ▣ *DM 2 and up, according to exhibit.* ◷ *Tues., Wed., and Fri.–Sun. 10–5; Thurs. 10–8.*

⑳ **Nationaltheater** (National Theater). Built in the late 19th century as a royal opera house with a pillared portico, this large theater was bombed during the war but is now restored to its original splendor. Today's opera house has some of the world's most advanced stage technology. ⊠ *Max-Joseph-Pl.,* ☎ *089/2185–1920.*

③⓪ **Prähistorische Staatssammlung** (State Prehistoric Collection). This is Bavaria's principal record of its prehistoric, Roman, and Celtic past. The perfectly preserved body of a ritually sacrificed young girl, recovered from a Bavarian peat moor, is among the more spine-chilling exhibits. Head down to the basement to see the fine Roman mosaic floor. ⊠ *Lerchenfeldstr. 2,* ☎ *089/211–2402.* ▣ *DM 5; free Sun.* ◷ *Tues., Wed., and Fri.–Sun. 9–4; Thurs. 9–4 and 7–9.*

★ ㉑ **Residenz** (Royal Palace). Munich's royal palace began as a small castle in the 14th century. The Wittelsbach dukes moved here when the tenements of an expanding Munich encroached upon their Alter Hof (☞ City Center, *above*). In succeeding centuries the royal residence developed parallel to the importance, requirements, and interests of its occupants. It came to include the Königsbau (on Max-Josef-Platz) and then (clockwise) the Alte Residenz; the Festsaal (Banquet Hall); the Altes Residenztheater/Cuvilliés Theater; the now ruined Allerheiligenhofkirche (All Souls' Church); the Residenztheater; and the Nationaltheater.

Building began in 1385 with the **Neuveste** (New Fortress), which comprised the northeast section; most of it burned to the ground in 1750, but one of its finest rooms survived: the 16th-century **Antiquarium,** which was built for Duke Albrecht V's collection of antique statues (today it's used chiefly for state receptions). The throne room of King Ludwig I, the **Neuer Herkulessaal,** is now a concert hall. The accumulated Wittelsbach treasures are on view in several palace museums. The **Schatzkammer** (treasury; ⊠ DM 7; ☉ Tues.–Sun. 10–4:30) has a rich centerpiece in its small Renaissance statue of St. George, studded with 2,291 diamonds, 209 pearls, and 406 rubies; paintings, tapestries, furniture, and porcelain are housed in the **Residenzmuseum** (⊠ DM 7; ☉ Tues.–Sun. 10–4:30); antique coins glint in the **Staatliche Münzsammlung** (⊠ Residenzstr. 1; ⊠ DM 4; free Sun.; ☉ Tues., Wed., and Fri.–Sun. 10–5; Thurs. 10–6:45); and Egyptian works of art make up the **Staatliche Sammlung Ägyptischer Kunst** (⊠ Hofgarten entrance; ⊠ DM 5, free Sun.; ☉ Tues. 9–9, Wed.–Fri. 9–4, weekends 10–5).

In the summer, chamber-music concerts take place in the inner courtyard. Also in the center of the complex is the small rococo **Altes Residenztheater/Cuvilliés Theater** (⊠ Residenzstr.; ⊠ DM 3; ☉ Mon.–Sat. 2–5, Sun. 10–5). It was built by François Cuvilliés between 1751 and 1755, and it still holds performances. The French-born Cuvilliés was a dwarf who was admitted to the Bavarian court as a decorative "bauble." Prince Max Emanuel recognized his latent artistic ability and had him trained as an architect. The prince's eye for talent gave Germany some of its richest rococo treasures. ⊠ *Max-Joseph-Pl. 3, entry through archway at Residenzstr. 1,* ☎ *089/290–671.*

㉙ **Schack-Galerie.** Those with a taste for florid and romantic 19th-century German paintings will appreciate the collections of the Schack-Galerie, originally the private collection of one Count Schack. Others may find the gallery dull, filled with plodding and repetitive works by painters who now repose in well-deserved obscurity. ⊠ *Prinzregentenstr. 9,* ☎ *089/2380–5224.* ⊠ *DM 4; free Sun.* ☉ *Wed.–Mon. 10–5.*

㉔ **Siegestor** (Victory Arch). Marking the beginning of Leopoldstrasse, the Siegestor has Italian origins—it was modeled on the Arch of Constantine in Rome—and was built to honor the achievements of the Bavarian army during the Wars of Liberation (1813–15). ⊠ *Leopoldstr.*

㉓ **Staatliches Museum für Völkerkunde** (State Museum of Ethnology). Arts and crafts from around the world are displayed in this extensive museum. There are also regular ethnological exhibits. ⊠ *Maximilianstr. 42,* ☎ *089/210–1360.* ⊠ *DM 6; free Sun.* ☉ *Tues.–Sun. 9:30–4:30.*

㉕ **Theatinerkirche** (Theatine Church). This mighty baroque church owes its Italian appearance to its founder, Princess Henriette Adelaide, who commissioned it in gratitude for the birth of her son and heir, Max Emanuel, in 1663. A native of Turin, the princess distrusted Bavarian architects and builders and thus summoned a master builder from Bologna, Agostino Barelli, to construct her church. He took as his model the Roman mother church of the newly formed Theatine Order. Barelli worked on the building for 11 years but was dismissed before the project was completed. It was another 100 years before the Theatinerkirche was finished. Its lofty towers frame a restrained facade capped by a massive dome. Step inside to admire its austere, monochrome, stucco interior. ⊠ *Theatinerstr. 22,* ☎ *089/210–6960.* ☉ *Daily 7–7:30.*

Munich's oldest café, **Tambosi** (✉ Odeonspl., ☎ 089/298–322) borders the street across from the Theatinerkirche. Watch the hustle and
bustle from an outdoor table or retreat through a gate in the Hofgarten's
western wall to the café's tree-shaded beer garden. If the weather's cool
or rainy, find a corner in the cozy, eclectically furnished interior.

The Maxvorstadt and Schwabing

Here is the artistic center of Munich: Schwabing, the old artists' quarter, and the neighboring Maxvorstadt, where most of the city's leading art galleries and museums are congregated. Schwabing is no longer
the bohemian area where such diverse residents as Lenin and Kandinsky were once neighbors, but at least the solid cultural foundations of
the Maxvorstadt are immutable. Where the two areas meet (in the streets
behind the university), life hums with a creative vibrancy that is difficult to detect elsewhere in Munich.

A Good Walk

Begin with a stroll through the city's old botanical garden, the **Alter
Botanischer Garten** ㉜. The grand-looking building opposite the garden's entrance is the Palace of Justice, law courts built in 1897 in suitable awe-inspiring dimensions. On one corner of busy Lenbachplatz,
you can't fail to notice one of Munich's most impressive fountains: the
monumental late-19th-century Wittelsbacher Brunnen. Beyond the
fountain, in Pacellistrasse, is the baroque **Dreifaltigkeitskirche** ㉝.

Leave the garden at its Meiserstrasse exit and continue up the street.
On the right-hand side you'll pass two solemn neoclassic buildings closely
associated with the Third Reich. The first served as the administrative
offices of the Nazi Party in Munich. The neighboring building is the
Music Academy, where Hitler, Mussolini, Chamberlain, and Daladier
signed the prewar pact that carved up Czechoslovakia.

At the junction of Meiserstrasse and Briennerstrasse, look right to see
the obelisk dominating the circular **Karolinenplatz** ㉞. To your left will
be the expansive **Königsplatz** ㉟, bordered by two museums, the **Glyptothek** ㊱ and the **Antikensammlungen** ㊲.

After walking by the museums, turn right onto Luisenstrasse, and
you'll arrive at a Florentine-style villa, the **Städtische Galerie im
Lenbachhaus** ㊳, which has an outstanding painting collection. Continue down Luisenstrasse, turning right on Theresienstrasse to reach
Munich's three leading art galleries, the **Alte Pinakothek** ㊴, the **Neue
Pinakothek** ㊵, opposite it, and the **Pinakothek der Moderne** ㊶. They
are as complementary as their buildings are contrasting: the Alte
Pinakothek, severe and serious in style; the Neue Pinakothek, almost
frivolously Florentine; and the Pinakothek der Moderne, glass-and-concrete new.

After a few hours immersed in culture, end your walk with a leisurely
stroll through the neighboring streets of Schwabing, which are lined
with boutiques, bars, and restaurants. If it's a fine day, head for the
Elisabethmarkt, Schwabing's permanent market.

TIMING
This walk may take an entire day, depending on how long you linger
at the major museums en route. Avoid the museum crowds by visiting
as early in the day as possible. All of Munich seems to discover an interest in art on Sunday, when admission to most municipal and state-
funded museums is free; you might want to take this day off from culture
and join the late-breakfast and brunch crowd at the Elisabethmarkt,

a beer garden, or at any of the many bars and Gaststätten. Some have Sunday-morning jazz concerts. Many Schwabing bars have happy hours between 6 and 8—a relaxing way to end your day.

Sights to See

★ ❸❾ **Alte Pinakothek** (Old Picture Gallery). The towering brick Alte Pinakothek was constructed by von Klenze between 1826 and 1836 to exhibit the collection of old masters begun by Duke Wilhelm IV in the 16th century. It's now judged one of the world's great picture galleries. Among its most famous works are Dürers, Rembrandts, Rubenses (the world's largest collection), and two celebrated Murillos. ⊠ *Barerstr. 27,* ☎ *089/2380–5216.* ◩ *DM 7; free Sun.; DM 12 for a combined ticket for the Alte Pinakothek and Neue Pinakothek, valid for 2 days.* ☉ *Tues. and Thurs. 10–8; Wed. and Fri.–Sun. 10–5.*

❸❷ **Alter Botanischer Garten** (Old Botanical Garden). Munich's first botanical garden began as the site of a huge glass palace, built in 1853 for Germany's first industrial exhibition. In 1931 it shared the fate of a similarly palatial glass exhibition hall, London's Crystal Palace, when its garden burned to the ground; six years later it was redesigned as a public park. Two features from the 1930s remain: a small, square **exhibition hall,** still used for art shows, and the 1933 **Neptune Fountain,** an enormous work in the heavy, monumental style of the prewar years. At the international electricity exhibition of 1882, the world's first high-tension electricity cable was run from the park to a Bavarian village 48 km (30 mi) away. ⊠ *Entrance at Lenbachpl.*

NEED A BREAK? On the north edge of the Alter Botanischer Garten is one of the city's central beer gardens. It's part of the **Park-Café** (⊠ Sophienstr. 7, ☎ 089/598–313), which at night becomes a fashionable nightclub serving magnums of champagne for DM 1,500 apiece. Prices in the beer garden are more realistic.

❸❼ **Antikensammlungen** (Antiquities Collection). This museum at Königsplatz has a collection of small sculptures, Etruscan art, Greek vases, gold, and glass. ⊠ *Königspl. 1,* ☎ *089/598–359.* ◩ *DM 6; combined ticket to Antikensammlungen and Glyptothek DM 10.* ☉ *Tues. and Thurs.–Sun. 10–5; Wed. 10–8; tour every other Wed. at 6.*

❸❸ **Dreifaltigkeitskirche** (Church of the Holy Trinity). A local woman prophesied doom for the city unless a new church was erected: this striking baroque edifice was then promptly built between 1711 and 1718. It has heroic frescoes by Cosmas Damian Asam. ⊠ *Pacellistr. 10,* ☎ *089/290–0820.* ◩ *Daily tour DM 5.* ☉ *Daily 7–7.*

Elisabethmarkt (Elisabeth Market). Schwabing's permanent market is smaller than the popular Viktualienmarkt but hardly less colorful. It has a pocket-size beer garden, where a jazz band performs every Saturday from spring to autumn. ⊠ *Arcistr. and Elisabethstr.*

❸❻ **Glyptothek.** Greek and Roman sculptures are on permanent display here. ⊠ *Königspl. 3,* ☎ *089/286–100.* ◩ *DM 6; combined ticket to Glyptothek and Antikensammlungen DM 10; free Sun.* ☉ *Tues., Wed., and Fri.–Sun. 10–5; Thurs. 10–8; tour every other Thurs. at 6.*

❸❹ **Karolinenplatz** (Caroline Square). At the junction of Barerstrasse and Briennerstrasse, this circular area is dominated by an obelisk unveiled in 1812 as a memorial to Bavarians killed fighting Napoléon. **Amerikahaus** (America House) faces Karolinenplatz. It has an extensive library and a year-round program of cultural events. ⊠ *Karolinenpl. 3,* ☎ *089/ 552–5370.*

㉟ **Königsplatz** (King's Square). This expansive square is lined on three sides with the monumental Grecian-style buildings by Leo von Klenze that gave Munich the nickname "Athens on the Isar." The two templelike structures are now the ☞ **Antikensammlungen** and the ☞ **Glyptothek** museums. In the 1930s the great parklike square was paved with granite slabs, which resounded with the thud of jackboots as the Nazis commandeered the area for their rallies. Although a busy road passes through it, the square has regained something of the green and peaceful appearance intended by Ludwig I.

㊵ **Neue Pinakothek** (New Picture Gallery). This exhibition space opened in 1981 to house the royal collection of modern art left homeless and scattered after its former building was destroyed in the war. The exterior of the modern building mimics an older one with Italianate influences. The interior offers a magnificent environment for picture gazing, at least partly due to the superb natural light flooding in from the skylights. The highlights of the collection are probably the impressionist and other French 19th-century works—Monet, Degas, and Manet are all well represented. But there's also a substantial collection of 19th-century German and Scandinavian paintings—misty landscapes predominate—that are only now coming to be recognized as admirable products of their time. ⊠ *Barerstr. 29,* ☎ *089/2380–5195.* ☞ *DM 7; free Sun.* ☉ *Tues. and Thurs.–Sun. 10–5; Wed. 10–8.*

㊶ **Pinakothek der Moderne.** Munich's ever-delayed new museum is scheduled to open between summer and October 2001. Five outstanding art and architectural collections once distributed in separate, inadequate quarters will be joined in a striking glass-and-concrete complex: galleries of modern art, industrial and graphic design, the Bavarian State collection of graphic art, and the Technical University's architectural museum. ⊠ *Türkenstr. at Gabelsbergerstr., and Luisenstr. at Theresienstr.,* ☎ *089/ 238–05118.* ☞ *Admission fees and opening hrs unavailable at press time.*

㊳ **Städtische Galerie im Lenbachhaus** (Municipal Gallery). You'll find an internationally renowned picture collection inside a delightful late-19th-century Florentine-style villa, former home and studio of the artist Franz von Lenbach (1836–1904). It contains a rich collection of works from the Gothic period to the present, including an exciting assemblage of art from the early 20th-century *Blaue Reiter* (Blue Rider) group: Kandinsky, Klee, Jawlensky, Macke, Marc, and Münter. ⊠ *Luisenstr. 33,* ☎ *089/233–0320.* ☞ *DM 10.* ☉ *Tues.–Sun. 10–6.*

Outside the Center

BMW Museum. Munich is the home of the famous car firm, and its museum contains a dazzling collection of BMWs old and new. It adjoins the BMW factory on the eastern edge of the ☞ **Olympiapark**. You can't miss this museum, a circular tower that looks as if it served as a set for *Star Wars*. ⊠ *Petuelring 130, U-bahn 3 to Petuelring,* ☎ *089/3822–3307.* ☞ *DM 5.50.* ☉ *Daily 9–5, last entry at 4.*

Botanischer Garten (Botanical Garden). A collection of 14,000 plants, including orchids, cacti, cycads, Alpine flowers, and rhododendrons, makes up one of the most extensive botanical gardens in Europe. The garden lies on the eastern edge of ☞ **Schloss Nymphenburg** park. Take Tram 17 or Bus 41 from the city center. ⊠ *Menzingerstr. 65,* ☎ *089/1786–1350.* ☞ *DM 4.* ☉ *Oct.–Mar., daily 9–noon and 2–4:30; Apr.–Sept. daily 9–7:30; hothouses daily 9–noon and 1–4.*

☾ **Geiselgasteig Movie Studios.** Munich is Germany's leading moviemaking center, and the local Hollywood-style lot, Geiselgasteig, is on the southern outskirts of the city. The Filmexpress transports you on a 1½-hour tour of the sets of *Das Boot* (*The Boat*), *Die Unendliche Geschichte* (*The Neverending Story*), and other productions. Stunt shows are held at 11:30, 1, and 2:30 and action movies are screened in Showscan, the super-wide-screen cinema. Take U-bahn 1 or 2 from the city center to Silberhorn-strasse and then change to Tram 25 to Bavariafilmplatz. A combined ticket for a family of up to five persons, covering public transport and entry to the studios, costs DM 45. ⊠ *Bavariafilmpl. 7,* ☎ *089/6499–2304.* ⊒ *DM 17; stunt show DM 10; Showscan DM 8; combined ticket for studio tour, stunt show, and Showscan cinema DM 31.* ☉ *Nov.–Feb., daily 10–3 (tours only); Mar.–Apr., daily 9–4; May–Oct., daily 9–5.*

☽ **Hellabrun Zoo.** There are a minimum of cages and many parklike enclosures at this attractive zoo. The 170 acres include restaurants and children's areas. Take Bus 52 from Marienplatz or U-bahn 3 to Thalkirchen, at the southern edge of the city. ⊠ *Tierparkstr. 30,* ☎ *089/ 625–0834.* ⊒ *DM 10.* ☉ *Apr.–Sept., daily 8–6; Oct.–Mar., daily 9–5.*

☽ **Olympiapark** (Olympic Park). On the northern edge of Schwabing, undulating circus-tent-like roofs cover the stadiums built for the 1972 Olympic Games. The roofs are made of translucent tiles that glisten in the midday sun and act as amplifiers for the rock concerts held here. Tours of the park are conducted on a Disneyland-style train throughout the day. An elevator will speed you up the 960-ft **Olympia Tower** for a view of the city and the Alps; there's also a revolving restaurant near the top. The former Olympic cycling stadium was converted in 1999 to an **Olympic Spirit** theme park where you can compete or judge in virtual-reality Olympic sports. Take U-bahn 3 to the park. ☎ *089/3067–2414, 089/3066–8585 for restaurant.* ⊒ *Olympic Spirit DM 26; tower elevator DM 5. Tours (Apr.–Nov.): grand tour, starting 2 PM, DM 13; stadium tour, starting 11 AM, DM 8.* ☉ *Main stadium daily 9–4:30; Olympic Spirit Sun.–Thurs. 10–7, Fri. and Sat. 10–10; tower daily 9 AM–midnight.*

☽ **Schloss Blutenburg.** This medieval palace is the home of an international collection of 500,000 children's books in more than 100 languages. This library is augmented by collections of original manuscripts, illustrations, and posters. The castle chapel, built in 1488 by Duke Sigismund, has some fine 15th-century stained glass. Take any S-bahn train to Pasing station, then Bus 73 or 76 to the castle gate. The palace is beyond Nymphenburg, on the northwest edge of Munich. ⊠ *Blutenberg 35,* ☎ *089/811–3132.* ⊒ *Free.* ☉ *Weekdays 10–5.*

★ **Schloss Nymphenburg.** Five generations of Bavarian royalty spent their summers in this glorious baroque and rococo palace. Nymphenburg is the largest palace of its kind in Germany, stretching more than 1 km (½ mi) from one wing to the other. The palace grew in size and scope over a period of more than 200 years, beginning as a summer residence built on land given by Prince Ferdinand Maria to his beloved wife, Henriette Adelaide, on the occasion of the birth of their son and heir, Max Emanuel, in 1663. The princess hired the Italian architect Agostino Barelli to build both the Theatinerkirche (☞ Royal Munich, *above*)—as an expression of her gratitude for the birth—and the palace, which was completed in 1675 by his successor, Enrico Zuccalli. Within the original building, now the central axis of the palace complex, is a magnificent hall, the **Steinerner Saal**, extending over two floors and richly decorated with stucco and swirling frescoes. In the summer, chamber-music concerts are given here. The decoration of the Steinerner Saal spills over into the surrounding royal chambers, one of which houses the famous **Schönheitsgalerie** (Gallery of Beauties; ⊒ DM 4). The walls are hung from floor to ceiling with portraits of women who caught the roving eye of Ludwig I, among them a butcher's daughter and an English duchess. The most famous portrait is of Lola Montez, a sultry beauty and high-class courtesan who, after a time as the mistress of Franz Liszt and later Alexandre Dumas, captivated Ludwig I to such an extent that he lost his throne because of her.

The palace is in a park laid out in formal French style, with low hedges and gravel walks extending into woodland. Tucked away among the ancient trees are three fascinating structures. Don't miss the **Amalienburg** hunting lodge, a rococo gem built by François Cuvilliés, architect of the Altes Residenztheater ☞ Royal Munich, *above*). The silver-and-blue stucco of the little Amalienburg creates an atmosphere of courtly high life, making clear that the pleasures of the chase here did not always take place outdoors. In the lavishly appointed kennels you'll see that even the dogs lived in luxury. The **Pagodenburg** was built for royal tea parties. Its elegant French exterior disguises a suitably Asian interior in which exotic teas from India and China were served. Swimming parties were held in the **Badenburg,** Europe's first post-Roman heated pool.

Nymphenburg contains so much of interest that a day hardly provides enough time. Don't leave without visiting the former royal stables, the **Marstallmuseum,** (✉ DM 3), or Museum of Royal Carriages. It houses a fleet of vehicles, including an elaborately decorated sleigh in which King Ludwig II once glided through the Bavarian twilight, postilion torches lighting the way. On the floor above are examples of Nymphenburg porcelain, produced here between 1747 and the 1920s.

A popular museum in the north wing of the palace has nothing to do with the Wittelsbachs but is one of Nymphenburg's major attractions. The **Museum Mensch und Natur** (Museum of Man and Nature; ☎ 089/ 171–382; ✉ DM 3, free Sun.; ☉ Tues.–Sun. 9–5) concentrates on three areas of interest: the variety of life on Earth, the history of humankind, and our place in the environment. Main exhibits include a huge representation of the human brain and a chunk of Alpine crystal weighing half a ton.

Take Tram 17 or Bus 41 from the city center to the Schloss Nymphenburg stop. ☎ *089/179–080.* ✉ *Schloss Nymphenburg complex (Gesamtkarte, or combined ticket) DM 11.* ☉ *Apr.–Sept., daily 9–12:30 and 1:30–5; Oct.–Mar., daily 10–12:30 and 1:30–4. All except Amalienburg and gardens closed Mon.*

Schloss Schleissheim (Schleissheim Palace). In 1597 Duke Wilhelm V decided to look for a peaceful retreat outside Munich and found what he wanted at this palace, then far beyond the city walls but now only a short ride on a train and a bus. A later ruler, Prince Max Emanuel, added a second, smaller palace, the **Lustheim.** Separated from Schleissheim by a formal garden and a decorative canal, the Lustheim houses Germany's largest collection of Meissen porcelain. To reach the palace, take the suburban S-bahn 1 line (to Oberschleissheim station) and then Bus 292 (which doesn't run on weekends). ✉ *Maximilianshof 1, Oberschleissheim,* ☎ *089/315–5272.* ✉ *Combined ticket for palaces and porcelain collection DM 5.* ☉ *Tues.–Sun. 10–12:30 and 1:30–5.*

Südfriedhof (Southern Cemetery). At this museum-piece cemetery you'll find many famous names but few tourists. Four hundred years ago it was a graveyard beyond the city walls for plague victims and paupers. During the 19th century it was refashioned into an upscale last resting place by the city architect Friedrich von Gärtner. Royal architect Leo von Klenze designed some of the headstones, and both he and von Gärtner are among the famous names you'll find there. The last burial here took place more than 40 years ago. The Südfriedhof is a short 10-minute walk south from the U-bahn station at Sendlinger-Tor-Platz. ✉ *Thalkirchnerstr.*

EIN BIER, BITTE

HOWEVER MANY FINGERS you want to hold up, just remember the easy-to-pronounce *Bier* (beer) *Bit-te* (please) when ordering a beer. The tricky part is, Germans don't just produce *one* beverage called beer; they brew more than 5,000 varieties. Germany has about 1,300 breweries, 40% of the world's total. The hallmark of the country's dedication to beer is the purity law, *das Reinheitsgebot,* unchanged since Duke Wilhelm IV introduced it in Bavaria in 1516. The law decrees that only malted barley, hops, yeast, and water may be used to make beer, except for specialty Weiss-, or Weizenbier (wheat beers, which are a carbonated, sharp, and sour brew, often with floating yeast particles).

Most taverns have several drafts in addition to a selection of bottled beers. The type available depends upon the region you're in, and in southern Germany the choice can also depend on the time of year. The alcohol content of German beers also varies considerably. At the weaker end of the scale is the light Munich Helles (3.7% alcohol by volume); stronger brews are the bitter-flavored Pilsner (around 5%) and the dark Doppelbock (more than 7%).

Germany's biggest breweries are in the city of Dortmund, which feeds the industrial Ruhr region. Popular northern beers are Export Lagers or the paler, more pungent Pilsners. Köln and Düsseldorf breweries in the Rhine region produce "old-fashioned" beers similar to English ales. But Bavaria is where the majority of breweries—and beer traditions—are found. The Bavarians and the Saarlanders consume more beer per person than any other group in the country.

In Munich you'll find the most famous breweries, the largest beer halls and beer gardens, the biggest and most indulgent beer festival, and the widest selection of brews. Even the beer glasses are bigger: A *Mass* is a 1-liter (almost 2-pint) serving; a *Halbe* is half a *Mass,* and the standard size. The Hofbräuhaus is Munich's most well-known beer hall, but its oompah band's selections are more to Americans and Australians than to your average Münchener. You'll find the citizenry in one of the English Garden's four beer gardens. Müncheners see no conflict that their city, a most cosmopolitan place—with great art galleries and museums, an opulent opera house, and chic lifestyles—is internationally recognized as the most beer-drenched city on earth. Postcards are framed with the message "Munich, the Beer City."

Not even the widest-girthed Bavarians can be held wholly responsible for the staggering consumption of beer and food at the annual Oktoberfest, which starts at the end of September and ends in early October. Typically, 5 million liters (1,183,000 gallons) of beer, as well as 750,000 roasted chickens and 650,000 sausages, are put away by revelers of many nationalities. To partake, book lodging by April, and if you're traveling with a group, also reserve bench space with one of the 14 tents. See Munich's Web site, www.muenchentourist.de, for beer tent contacts. The best time to arrive at the grounds is lunchtime, when it's easier to find a seat—by 4 PM it's packed. The beer tents are actually huge pavilions, heaving and pulsating with thousands of beer-swilling, table-pounding "serious" drinkers, animated by brass bands pounding it out on boxing-ring-style stages. The grounds close by 11:30 PM. Take advantage of an hour or two of sobriety to tour the fairground rides, which are also an integral part of Oktoberfest. Under no circumstances attempt any of these rides—all of which claim to be the world's most dangerous—after a liter or two of the Oktoberfest beer. The opprobrium from throwing up on the figure eight is truly Germanic in scale.

— Robert Tilley

DINING

With seven Michelin-starred restaurants to its credit, Munich claims to be Germany's gourmet capital. It certainly has an inordinate number of ritzy French restaurants, some with chef-owners who honed their skills under such Gallic masters as Paul Bocuse. For connoisseurs, wining and dining at Tantris or the Königshof could well turn into the equivalent of a religious experience; culinary creations are accorded the status of works of art on a par with a Bach fugue or a Dürer painting, with tabs equal to a king's ransom. Epicureans are convinced that one can dine as well in Munich as in any other city on the Continent.

However, for many the true glory of Munich's kitchen artistry is to be experienced in those rustically decorated traditional eating places that serve down-home Bavarian specialties in ample portions. The city's renowned beer and wine restaurants offer superb atmosphere, low prices, and as much wholesome German food as you'll ever want. They're open at just about any hour of the day or night—you can order your roast pork at 11 AM or 11 PM.

What to Wear

Many Munich restaurants serve sophisticated cuisine, and they require their patrons to dress for the occasion. Other, usually less expensive, restaurants will serve you regardless of what you wear.

CATEGORY	COST*
$$$$	over DM 100
$$$	DM 75–DM 100
$$	DM 50–DM 75
$	under DM 50

per person for a three-course meal, including tax and excluding drinks

$$$$ ✕ **Am Marstall.** The latest addition to Munich's luxury restaurant scene has rapidly won acclaim—and a Michelin star. The exciting menu combines the best of French and German cuisine—lamb bred on the salt-soaked meadows of coastal Brittany, for instance, or venison from the hunting grounds of Lower Bavaria. The restaurant is on Maximilianstrasse, so if you book a window seat you can while away the time between courses by watching Bavaria's well-heeled shoppers promenading. ⊠ *Maximilianstr. 16,* ☎ *089/291–6551. Reservations essential. Jacket and tie. AE, MC, V. Closed Sun., Mon., and public holidays.*

$$$$ ✕ **Königshof.** A Michelin star was awarded the reliable old Königshof hotel restaurant in 2000, recognition at last of its place among Munich's finest and most traditional eating places. The outstanding menu is French influenced, the surroundings elegant—and if you book a window table you'll have a view of Munich's busiest squares, the Stachus, an incandescent experience at night. ⊠ *Karlspl. 25,* ☎ *089/5513–6142. Reservations essential. Jacket and tie. AE, DC, MC, V.*

$$$$ ✕ **Tantris.** Chef Hans Haas has kept this restaurant with a modernist
★   look among the top five dining establishments in Munich, and in 1994 Germany's premier food critics voted him the country's top chef. You, too, will be impressed by the exotic nouvelle cuisine on the menu, including such specialties as shellfish and creamed potato soup and roasted wood pigeon with scented rice. But you may wish to ignore the bare concrete surroundings and the garish orange-and-yellow decor. ⊠ *Johann-Fichter-Str. 7,* ☎ *089/361–9590. Reservations essential. Jacket and tie. AE, DC, MC, V. Closed Sun.*

$$$ ✕ **Bistro Terrine.** Tucked away self-effacingly in a corner of a Schwabing shopping arcade, the bistro is one of this lively area's most charming upscale restaurants. Crisp blue-and-white linen, cane-back chairs, and

art-nouveau lamps give it a French atmosphere matched by the excellent Gallic-influenced menu. A cozy aperitif bar completes the harmonious picture. ⊠ *Amalienstr. 89,* ☎ *089/281–780. AE, DC, MC, V. Closed Sun. No lunch Mon.*

$$$ ✕ **Dukatz.** Join the literary crowd at this intellectuals' scene—a smart,
★ high-vaulted bar and restaurant in the Literaturhaus, a converted city mansion where regular book readings are presented. Tables buzz with talk of publishing deals and problem authors. English-language newspapers are among the heap of reading material at your disposal in the airy café that fronts the restaurant. Food is predominantly German nouvelle cuisine, with traditional dishes such as calves' head and lamb tripe offered with a light, almost Gallic touch. ⊠ *Salvatorpl. 1,* ☎ *089/291–9600. No credit cards.*

$$–$$$ ✕ **Bistro Cezanne.** You're in for Parisian-style dining at this truly Gallic bistro-restaurant in the heart of Munich's former bohemian quarter, Schwabing. Owner-chef Patrick Geay learned his craft from some of Europe's best teachers. His regularly changing blackboard menu features the freshest market products, with vegetables prepared as only the French can. Among the fish dishes, the scallops melt in the mouth, while the coq au vin is Gallic cuisine at its most authentic. Reservations are advised. ⊠ *Konradstr. 1,* ☎ *089/391–805. AE, MC, V.*

$$–$$$ ✕ **Vinaiolo.** Less than two years after opening in the bohemian Haidhausen district, this Italian restaurant has won a Michelin star—a record even for Munich. Despite its quick rise to fame, Vinaiolo, decorated in a restful pastel green, preserves its understated charm, and even if you order just a plate of pasta, the charming Italian staff does not bat a collective Mediterranean eyelid. But why stick with spaghetti when the menu is rich with such specialties as oxtail in red-wine sauce and tender wings of the giant ray fish. Reservations are advised. ⊠ *Steinstr. 42,* ☎ *089/4895–0356. AE, MC, V.*

$$ ✕ **Austernkeller.** *Austern* (oysters) are the specialty of this cellar restaurant, although many other varieties of seafood—all flown in daily from France—help fill its imaginative menu. The lobster thermidor is expensive (DM 46) but surpasses that served elsewhere in Munich, while a rich fish soup can be had for less than DM 10. The fussy, fishnet-hung decor is a shade too maritime, especially for downtown Munich, but the starched white linen and glittering glassware and cutlery lend a note of elegance. ⊠ *Stollbergstr. 11,* ☎ *089/298–787. AE, DC, MC, V. No lunch.*

$$ ✕ **Cafe am Beethovenplatz.** The name of this charming café-restaurant is something of a misnomer because it's much more than a café. Beethoven is on the menu—along with countless other composers, whose piano and recital works are performed nightly on and around a grand piano that dominates one part of the large, art nouveau dining room. An international breakfast menu is served daily (on Sunday with live classic music), followed by suitably creative lunch and dinner menus. The pork is supplied by a farm where the free-range pigs are fed only the best natural fodder—so the Schweinebraten is recommended. Reservations are advised as a young and intellectual crowd fills the tables quickly. ⊠ *Goethestr. 51 (am Beethovenplatz),* ☎ *089/5440–4348. No credit cards.*

$$ ✕ **Glockenbach.** This small, highly popular restaurant with dark-wood paneling serves mostly fish entrées, prepared by the acclaimed chef and owner, Karl Ederer. Book ahead to enjoy specialties such as freshwater fish ragout from Starnberger Lake. Highlights of the meat menu are Bavarian Forest lamb and free-range chicken with wild mushrooms. ⊠ *Kapuzinerstr. 29,* ☎ *089/534–043. Reservations essential. AE, MC, V. Closed Sun. and Mon.*

58

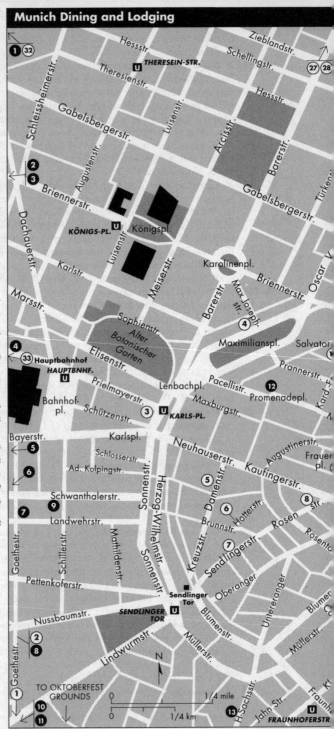

Munich Dining and Lodging

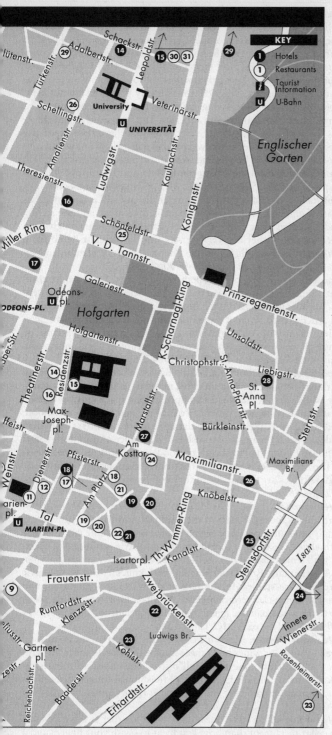

KEY

🛈 Hotels
🛈 Restaurants
ℹ️ Tourist Information
Ⓤ U-Bahn

$$ ✕ **Halali.** The Halali is an old-style Munich restaurant—polished wood paneling and antlers on the walls—that offers new-style regional specialties, such as venison in juniper-berry sauce and marinated beef on a bean salad. Save room for the homemade vanilla ice cream. ⊠ *Schönfeldstr. 22,* ☎ *089/285–909. Jacket and tie. AE, MC, V. Closed Sun.*

$$ ✕ **Hunsingers Pacific.** Werner Hunsinger, one of Germany's top restaurateurs, has brought to Munich a reasonably priced restaurant serving eclectic cuisine, borrowing from the Pacific Rim of East Asia, Australia, and North and South America. The restaurant's clam chowder is the best to be found in the city, while another praised specialty is the Chilean-style fillet steak, wrapped in a mantle of onion and eggplant-flavored maize. Lunchtime two-course meals cost less than DM 20, and evening meals cost between DM 45 and DM 55. ⊠ *Maximilianspl. 5,* ☎ *089/5502–9741. AE, MC, V. No lunch weekends.*

$$ ✕ **Ratskeller.** Munich's Ratskeller under the city hall is known for its goulash soup. Seat yourself—the space is cavernous, and the setting includes vaulted stone ceilings, alcoves, banquettes, and wrought-iron work. An atmospheric tavern serves fine Franconian wine from Würzburg's famous Juliusspital at a price that can't be matched in Munich. ⊠ *Marienpl. 8,* ☎ *089/219–9890. AE, MC, V.*

$$ ✕ **Spatenhaus.** A view of the opera house and the royal palace com-
★ plements the Bavarian mood of the wood-paneled and beamed Spatenhaus. The menu is international, however, with more or less everything from artichokes to *zuppa Romana* (alcohol-soaked, fruity Italian cake-pudding). But since you're in Bavaria, why not do as the Bavarians do? Try the Bavarian plate, an enormous mixture of local meats and sausages. ⊠ *Residenzstr. 12,* ☎ *089/290–7060. AE, MC, V.*

$$ ✕ **Spöckmeier.** This rambling, solidly Bavarian beer restaurant spread over three floors, including a snug *Keller* (cellar), is famous for its homemade Weisswurst. If you've just stopped in for a snack and don't fancy the fat breakfast sausage, order coffee and pretzels or, in the afternoon, a wedge of cheesecake. The daily changing menu also offers more than two dozen hearty main-course dishes and a choice of four draft beers. The house *Eintopf* (a rich broth of noodles and pork) is a meal in itself. The Spöckmeier is only 50 yards from Marienplatz; on sunny summer days tables are set outside in the car-free street. ⊠ *Rosenstr. 9,* ☎ *089/268–088. AE, DC, MC, V.*

$$ ✕ **Weichandhof.** If you're heading to the leafy residential suburb of Obermenzing, near the start of the Stuttgart Autobahn, a stop here is strongly recommended, but even a special trip from the city center is worthwhile. The food at this old farmhouse-style restaurant is excellent, with a menu based on traditional Bavarian and regional German and Austrian fare. Roast suckling pig, pork knuckle, and Vienna-style boiled beef are staples. In summer or on warm spring and autumn evenings the vine-clad terrace beckons. In winter tiled stoves give a warm glow to the wood-paneled dining rooms. ⊠ *Betzenweg 81,* ☎ *089/891–1600 or 089/811–1621. MC. Closed Sat.*

$$ ✕ **Weinhaus Neuner.** Munich's oldest wine tavern serves good food as well as superior wines in its three nooks: the wood-paneled restaurant, the Weinstübl, and the small bistro. The choice of food is remarkable, from nouvelle German to old-fashioned country. Specialties include home-smoked beef and salmon. ⊠ *Herzogspitalstr. 8,* ☎ *089/260–3954. AE, MC, V. Closed Sun.*

$$ ✕ **Welser Kuche.** It's less a question of what to order at this medieval-style cellar restaurant than how you'll eat it—with your fingers and a hunting knife, in the manner of 16th-century baronial banquets. You're welcomed by pretty "serving wenches" who tie a protective bib around your neck, proffer a hunting horn of mead, and show you to one of the oak trestle tables that complete the authentic-looking surroundings. It's best to go in a group, but room will always be found for couples or those dining alone. The full menu runs to 10 dishes, although you can settle for less and choose à la carte. ☒ *Residenzstr. 2,* ☎ *089/ 296–565. MC. No lunch.*

$$ ✕ **Wirtshaus im Weinstadl.** At the end of a small alley off a busy shopping street and overlooked by most passersby, the historic 16th-century Weinstadl is well worth hunting out. In summer the courtyard beer garden is a cool delight. A fountain depicting a Munich burgher quaffing a glass of wine splashes away beneath original Renaissance galleries. In winter the brass-studded oaken door opens onto a vaulted dining room where traditional Bavarian fare is served at bench-lined tables. A lunchtime menu and a glass of excellent beer leave change from DM 20. The cellar, reached via a winding staircase, features live music on Friday and Saturday evenings. ☒ *Burgstr. 5,* ☎ *089/2916– 1566. AE, DC, MC.*

$–$$ ✕ **Bamberger Haus.** The faded elegance of this historic house on the edge of Schwabing's Luitpold Park disguises an up-to-date kitchen, which conjures up inexpensive dishes of modern flair and imagination. Vegetarians are well catered to with cheap and filling vegetable gratins. The cellar beer tavern serves one of the best ales in town. In summer reserve a table on the terrace and eat under chestnut trees with a view of the park. ☒ *Brunnerstr. 2,* ☎ *089/308–8966. AE, DC, MC, V.*

$ ✕ **Augustiner Keller.** This 19th-century establishment is the flagship beer restaurant of one of Munich's oldest breweries, Augustiner. The decor emphasizes wood—from the refurbished parquet floors to the wood barrels from which the beer is drawn. The menu changes daily and offers a full range of Bavarian specialties, but try to order Tellerfleisch, served on a big wooden board. Follow that with *Dampfnudeln* (suet pudding served with custard), and you won't feel hungry again for 24 hours. The communal atmosphere of the two baronial hall-like rooms makes this a better place for meeting locals than for a quiet meal for two. ☒ *Arnulfstr. 52,* ☎ *089/594–393. AE, MC, V.*

$ ✕ **Brauhaus zum Brez'n.** This hostelry is bedecked in the blue-and-white-check colors of the Bavarian flag. The eating and drinking are spread over three floors and cater to a broad clientele—from local business lunchers to hungry night owls emerging from Schwabing's bars and looking for a bite at 2 AM. Brez'n offers a big all-day menu of traditional roasts, to be washed down with a choice of three draft beers. ☒ *Leopoldstr. 72,* ☎ *089/390–092. AE, DC, MC, V.*

$ ✕ **Dürnbräu.** A fountain plays outside this picturesque old Bavarian inn. Inside, it's crowded and noisy. Expect to share a table; your fellow diners will range from businesspeople to students. The food is resolutely traditional. Try the cream of spinach soup and the boiled beef. ☒ *Dürnbräug. 2,* ☎ *089/222–195. AE, DC, MC, V.*

$ ✕ **Erstes Münchner Kartoffelhaus.** In Munich's First Potato House tubers come in all forms, from the simplest baked potato with sour cream to gratin creations with shrimp and salmon. When potatoes were first introduced to Germany, they were dismissed as fodder fit only for animals or the very lowest strata of society. Frederick the Great was largely responsible for putting them on the dining tables of even the nobility, and now the lowly potato is an indispensable part of the German diet. This restaurant is great fun and a great value, too. ☒ *Hochbrückenstr. 3,* ☎ *089/296–331. Reservations essential. AE, MC.*

$ ✕ **Grüne Gans.** This small, chummy restaurant near the Viktualienmarkt is popular with local entertainers, whose photos clutter the walls. International fare with regional German influences dominates the menu, and there are a few Chinese dishes. Try the chervil cream soup, followed by calves' kidneys in tarragon sauce. ☒ *Am Einlass 5,* ☎ *089/266–228. Reservations essential. No credit cards. Closed Sun.*

$ ✕ **Hackerhaus.** Since the 15th century beer has been brewed or served here, the birthplace of Hacker-Pschorr, a still-active Munich brewery. Today the site is a cozy, upscale restaurant with three floors of wood-paneled rooms. In summer you can order a cheese plate and beer in the cool, flower-decorated inner courtyard; in winter you can snuggle in a corner of the Ratsstube and warm up on thick homemade potato broth, followed by schnitzel and *Bratkartoffein* (panfried potatoes), or take a table in the Bürgerstube and admire its proud centerpiece, the world's largest beer mug. ⊠ *Sendlingerstr. 14,* ☏ *089/260–5026. AE, DC, MC, V.*

$ ✕ **Haxenbauer.** This is one of Munich's more sophisticated beer restaurants. There's the usual series of interlinking rooms and sturdy yet pretty Bavarian decoration. But there is a much greater emphasis on the food here than in similar places. Try the *Schweineshaxn* (pork shanks) cooked over a charcoal fire. ⊠ *Münzstr. 2,* ☏ *089/2916–2100. AE, MC, V.*

$ ✕ **Hofbräuhaus.** The pounding oompah band draws passersby into this father of all beer halls, where singing and shouting drinkers contribute to the earsplitting din. This is no place for the fainthearted, although a trip to Munich would be incomplete without a look in. Upstairs is a quieter restaurant. In March, May, and September ask for one of the special, extra-strong seasonal beers (Starkbier, Maibock, Märzen), which complement the heavy, traditional Bavarian fare. ⊠ *Am Platzl 9,* ☏ *089/221–676 or 089/290–1360. Reservations not accepted. V.*

$ ✕ **Hundskugel.** This is Munich's oldest tavern and also one of the city's
★ smallest. You'll be asked to squeeze up and make room for latecomers looking for a place at one of the few tables that clutter the handkerchief-size dining room. The tavern dates from 1440 and in many ways doesn't appear to have changed much over the centuries. Even the menu is medievally basic and a bit hit-and-miss, although any combination of pork and potato or sauerkraut can be recommended. ⊠ *Hotterstr. 18,* ☏ *089/264–272. No credit cards.*

$ ✕ **Max-Emanuel-Brauerei.** This historic old brewery tavern is a great value, with Bavarian dishes rarely costing more than DM 20; at lunchtime that amount will easily cover the cost of an all-you-can-eat buffet including a couple of beers. The main dining room has a stage, so the bill often includes a cabaret or jazz concert. In summer take a table outside in the secluded little beer garden. ⊠ *Adalbertstr. 33,* ☏ *089/271–5158. AE, MC.*

$ ✕ **Nürnberger Bratwurst Glöckl am Dom.** Munich's most original beer tavern is dedicated to a specialty from a rival city, Nuremberg, whose delicious *Nürnberger Bratwürste* (finger-size sausages) form the staple dish of the menu. They're served by a busy team of friendly waitresses dressed in Bavarian dirndls, who flit between the crowded tables with remarkable agility. In summer tables are placed outside under a bright awning and in the shade of the nearby Frauenkirche. In winter the mellow dark-paneled dining rooms provide relief from the cold. ⊠ *Frauenpl. 9,* ☏ *089/220–385. No credit cards.*

$ ✕ **Pfälzer Weinprobierstube.** A warren of stone-vaulted rooms, wooden tables, flickering candles, dirndl-clad waitresses, and a vast range of wines add up to an experience as close to everyone's image of timeless Germany as you're likely to get. The wines are mostly from the *Pfalz* (Palatinate), as are many of the specialties on the limited menu. Here you'll find former chancellor Kohl's favorite dish, *Saumagen* (meat loaf, spiced with herbs and cooked in a pig's stomach). ⊠ *Residenzstr. 1,* ☏ *089/225–628. Reservations not accepted. No credit cards.*

$ ✕ **Weisses Bräuhaus.** If you have developed a taste for Munich's Weissbier, this is the place to enjoy it. Other beers, including a very strong Aventinus, are available, but the accent is unmistakably on the Schneider brewery's famous specialty, the Schneiderweisse, a yeast-fermented wheat beer. It's served with hearty Bavarian dishes, mostly variations of pork and dumplings or cabbage, by some of Munich's friendliest waitresses, good-humored women in crisp black dresses, who appear to match the Jugendstil features of the restaurant's beautifully restored interior. ⊠ *Tal 7,* ☎ *089/299–875. No credit cards.*

LODGING

Though Munich has a vast number of hotels in all price ranges, many are fully booked year-round; this is a major trade and convention city as well as a prime tourist destination. If you're visiting during Mode Wochen (Fashion Weeks), in March and September, or during Oktoberfest at the end of September, make reservations at least six months in advance.

Some of the large, very expensive ($$$$) hotels that cater to expense-account business travelers have very attractive weekend discount rates—sometimes as much as 50% below normal prices. Conversely, regular rates can go up during big trade fairs.

Munich's two tourist information offices—at the main railway station and in the city center (Marienplatz, in the Rathaus)—make hotel bookings. Telephone lines are usually busy, so your best bet is to visit one of the offices personally.

CATEGORY	COST*
$$$$	over DM 300
$$$	DM 200–DM 300
$$	DM 140–DM 200
$	under DM 140

*All prices are for two people in a double room, including tax and service charge.

$$$$ ⊞ **Bayerischer Hof.** Germany's most respected family-owned hotel, the Bayerischer Hof began its rich history by hosting Ludwig I's guests. Public rooms are grandly laid out with marble, antiques, and oil paintings. Laura Ashley–decorated rooms face the city's skyline of towers. Rooms facing the interior courtyard are the least expensive and begin at DM 495. Nightlife is built into the hotel, with Trader Vic's bar and dancing at the Night Club. ⊠ *Promenadepl. 2–6, D–80333,* ☎ *089/21200,* FAX *089/212–0906. 306 rooms, 45 suites. 3 restaurants, bar, pool, beauty salon, massage, sauna, nightclub, parking (fee). AE, DC, MC, V.* 🐾

$$$$ ⊞ **Park-Hotel Theresienhöhe.** Even the mansard rooms are spacious and airy in this newly constructed hotel on the edge of Munich's fairgrounds and Oktoberfest site. In fact, the hotel claims that none of its rooms is less than 400 square ft. Suites are larger than many luxury apartments, and some of them come with small kitchens. The sleek, modern rooms are mostly decorated with light woods and pastel-color fabrics and carpeting; larger rooms and suites get a lot of light, thanks to the floor-to-ceiling windows. Families are particularly welcome, and a baby-sitting service is provided. ⊠ *Parkstr. 31, D–80339,* ☎ *089/ 519–950,* FAX *089/5199–5420. 35 rooms. Restaurant, bar, baby-sitting. AE, DC, MC, V.*

$$$$ ⊞ **Platzl.** The Platzl has won awards and wide recognition for its ecologically aware management. It stands in the historic heart of Munich, near the famous Hofbräuhaus beer hall and a couple of minutes' walk from Marienplatz and many other landmarks. Its *Pfistermühle* restaurant, with 16th-century vaulting, is one of the area's oldest and most historic. ⊠ *Sparkassenstr. 10, D–80331,* ☎ *089/237–030, 800/448– 8355 in the U.S.,* FAX *089/2370–3800. 167 rooms. Restaurant, bar, sauna, steam room, exercise room, parking (fee). AE, DC, MC, V.* 🐾

$$$$ ⊞ **Rafael.** Germany's leading hotel reviewers have named the Rafael
★   the country's top grand hotel, and its restaurant, Mark's, also ranks
among the country's best. The hotel occupies a beautifully renovated
neo-Renaissance building that was a high-society ballroom in the late
19th century. Today it recaptures some of that bygone era with 24-hour
service, including such personalized amenities as in-house butlers.
Rooms are individually furnished and extravagantly decorated, in addition to offering many extras, including fax machines. ⊠ *Neuturm-
str. 1, D–80331,* ☎ *089/290–980,* ℻ *089/222–539. 67 rooms, 6
suites. Restaurant, 2 bars, pool, sauna. AE, DC, MC, V.* ✎

$$$$ ⊞ **Vier Jahreszeiten Kempinski.** The Four Seasons has been playing host
★   to the world's wealthy and titled for more than a century. It has an unbeatable location on Maximilianstrasse, Munich's premier shopping street,
only a few minutes' walk from the heart of the city. Elegance and luxury set the tone throughout; many rooms have handsome antique
pieces. The Bistro Eck is on the main floor, and the Theater bar/restau-
rant is in the cellar. ⊠ *Maximilianstr. 17, D–80539,* ☎ *089/21250, 516/
794–2670 for Kempinski Reservation Service,* ℻ *089/2125–2000. 268
rooms, 48 suites. 2 restaurants, piano bar, pool, massage, sauna, exercise room, car rental, parking (fee). AE, DC, MC, V.* ✎

$$$–$$$$ ⊞ **Bauer.** Extensive renovations in 1998 and 1999 have elevated the
family-run Bauer from country-inn status to a very comfortable hotel
indeed, although none of its Bavarian charm has been lost. Located
10 km (6 mi) from the city center, the hotel is best for those traveling
by car, although an S-bahn station with rapid access to the center of
Munich is only a short walk. ⊠ *Münchnerstr. 6, D–85622 Feldkirchen,*
☎ *089/90980,* ℻ *089/909–8414. 100 rooms. Restaurant, café, indoor
pool, sauna. AE, DC, MC, V.*

$$$–$$$$ ⊞ **Eden Hotel Wolff.** Chandeliers and dark-wood paneling in the pub-
lic rooms make for the old-fashioned elegance of this downtown fa-
vorite. It's directly across the street from the train station and near the
Theresienwiese fairgrounds. The rooms come with plush comforts, and
most are spacious. You can dine on excellent Bavarian specialties in
the intimate Zirbelstube restaurant. ⊠ *Arnulfstr. 4, D–80335,* ☎ *089/
551–150,* ℻ *089/5511–5555. 209 rooms, 7 suites. Restaurant, bar,
café, exercise room, parking (fee). AE, DC, MC, V.* ✎

$$$–$$$$ ⊞ **Torbräu.** In this snug hotel you'll sleep under the shadow of one of
Munich's ancient city gates—the 14th-century Isartor. The location is
excellent as it's midway between the Marienplatz and the Deutsches
Museum (and around the corner from the Hofbräuhaus). The hotel
has been run by the same family for more than a century. Comfort-
able rooms are decorated in a plush and ornate Italian style. Its Ital-
ian restaurant, *La Famiglia,* is one of the best in the area. ⊠ *Tal 41,
D–80331,* ☎ *089/242–340,* ℻ *089/234–235. 83 rooms, 3 suites.
Restaurant, café, in-room data ports, sauna, exercise room, bowling,
meeting rooms. AE, MC, V.* ✎

$$$ ⊞ **Admiral.** The small, privately owned Admiral enjoys a quiet side-
★   street location and its own garden, close to the Isar River and Deutsches
Museum. Many of the simply furnished and warmly decorated bedrooms have a balcony overlooking the garden. Bowls of fresh fruit are
part of the friendly welcome awaiting guests. The breakfast buffet is
a dream, complete with homemade jams, in-season strawberries, and
Italian and French delicacies. ⊠ *Kohlstr. 9, D–80469,* ☎ *089/216–350,*
℻ *089/293–674. 33 rooms. Bar, parking (fee). AE, DC, MC, V.* ✎

$$$ ⊞ **Adria.** This modern, comfortable hotel is ideally set in the upmar-
ket area of Lehel, in the middle of Munich's museum quarter. Rooms
are large and tastefully decorated, with old prints on the pale-pink walls,
Oriental rugs on the floors, and flowers beside the double beds. A spec-
tacular breakfast buffet (including a glass of sparkling wine) is included

in the room rate. There's no hotel restaurant, but the area is rich in good restaurants, bistros, and bars. ⊠ *Liebigstr. 8a, D–80538,* ☎ *089/ 293–081,* FAX *089/227–015. 46 rooms, 45 with bath. AE, MC, V.*

$$$ ⛤ **Advokat.** Owner Kevin Voigt designed much of the furniture of his exquisite new hotel and had it made by Italian craftsmen. The Italian touch is everywhere, from the sleek, minimalist lines of the bedroom furniture and fittings to the choice prints and modern Florentine mirrors on the walls. If you value modern taste over plush luxury, this is the hotel for you. ⊠ *Baaderstr. 1, D–80469,* ☎ *089/216–310,* FAX *089/ 216–3190. 50 rooms. AE, DC, MC, V.* ☙

$$$ ⛤ **ArabellaSheraton Airport.** This is not your typical airport hotel— it's a three-story, red-roof country-house-style building surrounded by greenery. The first-class lodging is only five minutes from the Franz Josef Strauss Airport, and the hotel operates a courtesy shuttle bus. Mostly businesspeople stay here, and there are plenty of leisure facilities. Rooms are furnished in light pinewood, with Laura Ashley fabrics. ⊠ *Freisingerstr. 80, D–85445 Schwaig,* ☎ *089/9272–2750,* FAX *089/9272–2800. 162 rooms, 8 suites. 2 restaurants, bar, indoor pool, sauna, steam room, exercise room, meeting rooms, airport shuttle. AE, DC, MC, V.* ☙

$$$ ⛤ **Erzgiesserei Europe.** Its location on a dull little street in an uninteresting section of the city is this hotel's only drawback, but even that is easily overcome—the nearby subway whisks you in five minutes to central Karlsplatz, convenient to the pedestrian shopping area and the main railway station. Rooms in this attractive, modern hotel are particularly bright, decorated in soft pastels with good reproductions on the walls. The cobblestone garden café is a haven of peace. ⊠ *Erzgiessereistr. 15, D–80335,* ☎ *089/126–820,* FAX *089/123–6198. 105 rooms, 1 suite. Restaurant, bar, café, parking (fee). AE, DC, MC, V.* ☙

$$$ ⛤ **Hotel Concorde.** The centrally located Concorde wants to do its bit toward relieving traffic congestion, so guests who arrive from the airport on the S-bahn can exchange their ticket at the reception desk for a welcome champagne or cocktail. The nearest S-bahn station (Isartor) is only a two-minute walk. Rooms were redecorated in 1999, in pastel tones and light woods. Fresh flowers and bright prints add a colorful touch. A large breakfast buffet is served in its stylish, mirrored Salon Margarita. ⊠ *Herrnstr. 38, D–80539,* ☎ *089/224–515,* FAX *089/ 228–3282. 67 rooms, 4 suites. Lounge. AE, DC, MC, V.*

$$$ ⛤ **Olympic** The English-style entrance lobby, with its leather easy chairs and mahogany fittings, is an attractive introduction to this friendly small hotel, a beautifully converted turn-of-the-century mansion, amid the bars and boutiques of the colorful district between Sendlinger Tor and Isartor. Most of the rooms, tucked away beneath the steep eaves of the handsome house, look out over a quiet interior courtyard. ⊠ *Hans-Sachs-Str. 4, D–80469,* ☎ *089/231–890,* FAX *089/ 231–89199. 38 rooms, 3 apartments. Parking (fee). AE, DC, MC, V.*

$$$ ⛤ **Pannonia Hotel Königin Elisabeth.** A bright, modern interior, with emphasis on the color pink, lies behind the protected neoclassical facade of this Pannonia-group hotel, a 15-minute tram ride northwest of the city center. Children under 12 stay free in their parents' room. ⊠ *Leonrodstr. 79, D–80636,* ☎ *089/126–860,* FAX *089/1268–6459. 79 rooms. Restaurant, bar, beer garden, hot tub, sauna, steam room, exercise room. AE, DC, MC, V. Closed late Dec.–early Jan.* ☙

$$$ ⛤ **Splendid.** Chandelier-hung public rooms, complete with Louis XVI– era antiques and Oriental rugs, give this small hotel something of the atmosphere of a 19th-century city residence. Bedrooms are all individually furnished. Breakfast is served in the small courtyard in summer and snacks are available at the bar. The chic shops of the Maximilianstrasse are a five-minute stroll. ⊠ *Maximilianstr. 54, D–80538,* ☎ *089/296– 606,* FAX *089/291–3176. 32 rooms, 7 suites. Bar. AE, DC, MC, V.*

$$–$$$ ▥ **Brack.** Oktoberfest revelers value the Brack's proximity to the beer festival grounds, and its location—on a busy, tree-lined thoroughfare just south of the center—is handy for city attractions. Rooms are furnished in light, friendly veneers and are soundproof (a useful feature during Oktoberfest) and have amenities such as hair dryers and cable TV. The buffet breakfast will set you up for the day. ✉ *Lindwurmstr. 153, D–80337,* ☎ *089/747–2550,* ℻ *089/7472–5599. 50 rooms. Free parking. AE, DC, MC, V.* ✎

$$–$$$ ▥ **Gästehaus am Englischen Garten.** Reserve well in advance for a room
★ at this popular converted water mill, more than 200 years old, adjoining the Englischer Garten. The hotel, complete with ivy-clad walls and shutter-framed windows, is only a five-minute walk from the bars, shops, and restaurants of Schwabing. Be sure to ask for one of the 12 nostalgically old-fashioned rooms in the main building; a modern annex down the road has 13 apartments, all with cooking facilities. In summer breakfast is served on the terrace of the main house, which has a garden on an island in the old millrace. ✉ *Liebergesellstr. 8, D–80802,* ☎ *089/383–9410,* ℻ *089/3839–4133. 12 rooms, 6 with bath or shower; 13 apartments. Free parking. AE, DC, MC, V.*

$$–$$$ ▥ **Hotel Mirabell.** This family-run hotel reports that it has "many
★ tourists from the USA," who like its friendly atmosphere, central location (between the main railway station and the Oktoberfest fairgrounds), and reasonable room rates. Three apartments are for small groups or families. All rooms have TVs and phones, and are furnished in modern, light woods and bright prints. The restaurant serves breakfast only, but snacks can be ordered at the bar. ✉ *Landwehrstr. 42 (entrance on Goethestr.), D–80336,* ☎ *089/549–1740,* ℻ *089/550–3701. 65 rooms, 3 apartments. Bar, café. AE, MC, V.*

$$–$$$ ▥ **Mayer.** If you are willing to sacrifice location for good value, head for this family-run hotel 25 minutes by suburban train from the Hauptbahnhof. The Mayer's first-class comforts and facilities cost about half of what you'd pay at similar lodgings in town. Built in the 1970s, it is furnished in Bavarian country-rustic style—lots of pine and green and red, and check fabrics. The Mayer is a 10-minute walk or a short taxi ride from Germering station on the S-5 line, eight stops west of the Hauptbahnhof. ✉ *Augsburgerstr. 45, Germering D–82110,* ☎ *089/844–071,* ℻ *089/844–094. 65 rooms. Restaurant, indoor pool. AE, DC, MC, V.* ✎

$$ ▥ **Carlton.** This is a favorite of many diplomats: a small, elegant, discreet hotel on a quiet side street in the best area of downtown Munich. The American and British consulates are a short walk away, and so are some of the liveliest Schwabing bars and restaurants. Art galleries, museums, and movie theaters are also in the immediate area. Rooms are on the small side but comfortable. A glass of champagne is included in the complimentary buffet breakfast. ✉ *Fürstenstr. 12, D–80333,* ☎ *089/282–061,* ℻ *089/284–391. 50 rooms. Sauna. AE, DC, MC, V.*

$$ ▥ **Jagdschloss.** Once a hunting lodge, the 100-year-old Jagdschloss, in Munich's leafy Obermenzing suburb, is today a delightful hotel. The rustic look has been retained, with lots of original woodwork and white stucco. Many of the comfortable pastel-tone bedrooms have wooden balconies with flower boxes bursting with color. Doubly sprung mattresses assure a good night's sleep. In the beamed restaurant or sheltered beer garden you'll be served Bavarian specialties by a staff dressed in traditional lederhosen (shorts in summer, breeches in winter). ✉ *Alte Allee 21, D–81245 München-Obermenzing,* ☎ *089/820–820,* ℻ *089/ 8208–2100. 22 rooms, 1 suite. Restaurant, beer garden, playground, free parking. MC, V.* ✎

$$ ⚐ **Kriemhild.** If you're traveling with children, you'll appreciate this welcoming, family-run pension in the western suburb of Nymphenburg, near parks and gardens. It's a 10-minute walk from Schloss Nymphenburg and around the corner from the Hirschgarten Park, site of one of the city's best beer gardens. The tram ride (No. 16 or 17) from downtown is 10 minutes. The buffet breakfast is included in the rate. ✉ *Guntherstr. 16, D–80639,* ☎ *089/171–1170,* FAX *089/1711–1755. 18 rooms. Bar, free parking. AE, MC, V.* ♿

$$ ⚐ **Kurpfalz.** Guests have praised the friendly welcome and service they receive at this centrally placed and affordable lodging. Rooms are comfortable, if furnished in a manner only slightly better than functional, and all are equipped with satellite TV. The main train station and Oktoberfest grounds are both a 10-minute walk, and the area is rich in restaurants, bars, and movie theaters. ✉ *Schwantalerstr. 121, D–80339,* ☎ *089/540–986,* FAX *089/5409–8811. 44 rooms with shower. Bar, in-room data ports. AE, MC, V.*

$ ⚐ **Fürst.** On a quiet street just off Odeonsplatz, on the edge of the uni-
★ versity quarter, this basic, clean guest house is constantly busy with families and students traveling on a budget. A cheerful touch is the collection of pictures in the pension's own art gallery. ✉ *Kardinal-Döpfner-Str. 8, D–80333,* ☎ *089/281–044,* FAX *089/280–860. 19 rooms, 12 with bath. No credit cards.*

$ ⚐ **Hotel Pension Am Siegestor.** This modest but very appealing pension
★ takes up three floors of a fin-de-siècle mansion between the Siegestor monument, on Leopoldstrasse, and the university. An ancient wood-paneled, glass-door elevator brings you to the fourth-floor reception desk. Most of the simply furnished rooms face the impressive Arts Academy across the street. Rooms on the fifth floor are particularly cozy, tucked up under the eaves. ✉ *Akademiestr. 5, D–80799,* ☎ *089/399–550 or 089/399–551,* FAX *089/343–050. 20 rooms. No credit cards.*

$ ⚐ **Hotel-Pension Beck.** American and British guests receive a particu-
★ larly warm welcome from the Anglophile owner of the rambling, friendly Beck (she and her pet canary are a regular presence). Bright new carpeting, with matching pinewood furniture, gives rooms a cheerful touch. The pension has a prime location in the heart of fashionable Lehel (convenient to museums and the Englischer Garten). ✉ *Thierschstr. 36, D–80538,* ☎ *089/220–708 or 089/225–768,* FAX *089/ 220–925. 44 rooms, 7 with shower. MC, V.* ♿

$ ⚐ **Hotel-Pension Mariandl.** The American armed forces commandeered this turn-of-the-20th-century neo-Gothic mansion in May 1945 and established Munich's first postwar nightclub, the Femina, on the ground floor (now a charming café-restaurant, ☞ Cafe am Beethovenplatz *in* Dining, *above*). Most rooms are mansion size, with high ceilings and large windows overlooking a leafy avenue. The Oktoberfest grounds and the main railway station are both a 10-minute walk. ✉ *Goethestr. 51, D–80336,* ☎ *089/534–108,* FAX *089/5440–4396. 28 rooms. Café-restaurant. No credit cards.*

NIGHTLIFE AND THE ARTS

The Arts

Bavaria's capital has an enviable reputation as an artistic hot spot. Details of concerts and theater performances are listed in "Vorschau" and "Monatsprogramm," booklets available at most hotel reception desks, newsstands, and tourist offices. Some hotels will make ticket reservations, or you can book through ticket agencies in the city center, such as **Max Hieber Konzertkasse** (✉ Liebfrauenstr. 1, ☎ 089/2900–8014), the two **Zentraler Kartenverkauf** kiosks in the underground concourse at Marienplatz (☏ 089/264–620), the **Abendzeitung Schalterhalle** (✉ Sendlingerstr. 10, ☏ 089/267–024), or **Residenz Bücherstube** (concert tickets only; ✉ Residenzstr. 1, ☏ 089/220–868). Tickets for performances at the Altes Residenztheater/Cuvilliés-Theater, Bavarian State Theater/New Residence Theater, Nationaltheater, Prinzregententheater, and Staatheater am Gartnerplatz are sold at the **central box office** (✉ Maximilianstr. 11, ☏ 089/2185–1920). It's open weekdays 10–6, Saturday 10–1, and one hour before curtain time. One ticket agency, **München Ticket** (☏ 089/5481–8181, ⬗) has a German-language Web site where tickets for most Munich theaters can be booked.

Concerts

Munich and music go together. Its world-class concert hall, the **Gasteig Culture Center** (✉ Rosenheimerstr. 5, ☏ 089/5481–8181), is a lavish brick complex standing high above the Isar River, east of downtown. Its Philharmonic Hall is the permanent home of the Munich Philharmonic Orchestra. The city has three other principal orchestras, and the leading choral ensembles are the Munich Bach Choir, the Munich Motettenchor, and Musica Viva—the latter specializing in contemporary music. The choirs perform mostly in city churches.

The Bavarian Radio Symphony Orchestra performs at the **Bayerischer Rundfunk** (✉ Rundfunkpl. 1, ☏ 089/558–080) and also at other city venues. The box office is open Monday–Thursday 9–noon and 2–4, Friday 9–noon.

The Bavarian State Orchestra is based at the **Nationaltheater** (also called the Bayerische Staatsoper; ✉ Opernpl., ☏ 089/2185–1920). The Kurt Graunke Symphony Orchestra performs at the romantic Art-Nouveau **Staatstheater am Gärtnerplatz** (✉ Gärtnerpl. 3, ☏ 089/201–6767).

Herkulessaal in der Residenz (✉ Hofgarten, ☏ 089/2906–7263) is a leading orchestral and recital venue. Concerts featuring conservatory students are given free of charge at the **Hochschule für Musik** (✉ Arcisstr. 12, ☏ 089/128–901).

Munich's major pop/rock concert venue is the **Olympiahalle** (☏ 089/3061–3577). The box office, at the ice stadium, is open weekdays 10–6 and Saturday 10–3. You can also book by calling München Ticket (☏ 089/5481–8181).

Opera, Ballet, and Musicals

Munich's Bavarian State Opera Company and its ballet ensemble perform at the **Nationaltheater** (☞ *above*). The **Staatstheater am Gärtnerplatz** (☞ *above*) presents a less ambitious but nevertheless high-quality program of opera, ballet, operetta, and musicals.

Theater

Munich has scores of theaters and variety-show venues, although most productions will be largely impenetrable if your German is shaky. Listed here are all the better-known theaters, as well as some of the smaller and more progressive spots. Note that most theaters are closed during July and August.

Altes Residenztheater/Cuvilliés-Theater (✉ Max-Joseph-Pl.; entrance on Residenzstr., ☏ 089/2185–1920). This is an intimate stage for compact opera productions such as Mozart's *Singspiele* and classic and contemporary plays (Arthur Miller met with great success here).
Amerika Haus (America House; ✉ Karolinenpl. 3, ☏ 089/343–803). A very active American company, the American Drama Group Europe, presents regular productions here.
Bayerisches Staatsschauspiel/Neues Residenztheater (Bavarian State Theater/New Residence Theater; ✉ Max-Joseph-Pl., ☏ 089/2185–

1940). This is Munich's leading stage for classic playwrights such as Goethe, Schiller, Lessing, Shakespeare, and Chekhov.

Deutsches Theater (⊠ Schwanthalerstr. 13, ☎ 089/5523–4444). Musicals, revues, and big-band shows take place here. The box office is open weekdays noon–6, Saturday 10–1:30.

Feierwerk (⊠ Hansastr. 39, ☎ 089/769–3600). English-language productions are regularly presented at this venue.

The Carl-Orff Saal and the Black Box theaters, in the **Gasteig Culture Center** (☞ *above*), occasionally present English-language plays. The box office is open weekdays 10:30–6, Saturday 10–2.

Komödie im Bayerischen Hof (⊠ Bayerischer Hof Hotel, Promenadenpl., ☎ 089/292–810) and **Kleine Komödie am Max II** ⊠ Max-II-Denkmal, Maximilianstr. 47, ☎ 089/221–859) share a program of light comedy and farce. The box office at Bayerischer Hof is open Monday–Saturday 11–8, Sunday 3–8. The box office at Max-II-Denkmal is open Monday–Saturday 11–8, Sunday 2–6.

Münchner Kammerspiele-Schauspielhaus (⊠ Maximilianstr. 26, ☎ 089/2333–7000). A city-funded rival to the nearby state-backed Staatliches Schauspiel, this theater of international renown presents the classics and new works by contemporary playwrights.

Prinzregententheater (⊠ Prinzregentenpl. 12, ☎ 089/2185–2959). Munich's Art-Nouveau theater, an audience favorite, presents not only opera but musicals and musical gala events.

Munich also has several theaters for children. With pantomime such a strong part of the repertoire, the language problem disappears. The best of these theaters are the **Münchner Theater für Kinder** (⊠ Dachauerstr. 46, ☎ 089/595–454) and the **Schauburg Theater der Jugend** (⊠ Franz-Joseph-Str. 47, ☎ 089/2333–7171). Three puppet theaters offer regular performances: the **Münchner Marionettentheater** (⊠ Blumenstr. 32, ☎ 089/265–712), the **Marionettenbühne Zaubergarten** (⊠ Nikolaistr. 17, ☎ 089/271–3373), and **Otto Bille's Marionettenbühne** (⊠ Breiterangerstr. 15, ☎ 089/150–2168). Munich is the winter quarters of the big-top **Circus Krone** (⊠ Marsstr. 43, ☎ 089/558–166), which performs from Christmas until the end of March.

Nightlife

Munich's nocturnal attractions vary with the seasons. The year starts with the abandon of Fasching, the Bavarian carnival time, which begins quietly in mid-November with the crowning of the King and Queen of Fools, expands with fancy-dress balls, and ends with a great street party on Fasching Dienstag (Shrove Tuesday) in early March. Men should forget wearing neckties on Fasching Dienstag: women posing as witches make it a point of cutting them off. From spring until late fall the beer garden dictates the style and pace of Munich's nightlife. When it rains, the indoor beer halls and taverns absorb the thirsty like blotting paper.

The beer gardens and most beer halls close at midnight, but there's no need to go home to bed: some bars and nightclubs are open until 6 AM. A word of caution about some of those bars: most are run honestly, and prices are only slightly higher than normal, but a few may intentionally overcharge. The seedier ones are near the main train station. Stick to beer or wine if you can, and pay as you go. And if you feel you're being duped, call the cops—the customer is usually, if not always, right.

Bars

Every Munich bar is singles territory. Wait until after midnight before venturing into the **Alter Simpl** (⊠ Türkenstr. 57, ☎ 089/272–3083), where a sparkling crowd enlivens the gloomy surroundings. Munich's latest "in" haunt resides within a sleek glass-and-steel interior. **Eisbach** (✉ Marstallstr. 2, ☎ 089/2280–1680) occupies a corner of the Max Planck Institute building opposite the Bavarian Parliament. The bar is among Munich's longest and is overlooked by a mezzanine restaurant area where you can choose from a limited but ambitious menu. Outdoor tables nestle in the expansive shade of huge parasols. The nearby Eisbach Brook, which gives the bar its name, tinkles away like ice in the glass. **Havana** (✉ Herrnstr. 3, ☎ 089/291–884) does its darndest to look like a rundown Cuban dive, but the chic clientele spoils those pretensions. The Bayerischer Hof's **Night Club** (✉ Promenadepl. 2–6, ☎ 089/212–0994) has live music, a small dance floor, and a very lively bar (avoid the poorly made mixed drinks). Jazz groups perform regularly there, too. On fashionable Maximilianstrasse, **O'Reilly's Irish Cellar Pub** (✉ Maximilianstr. 29, ☎ 089/293–311) offers escape from the German bar scene as it pours genuine Irish Guinness. Great Caribbean cocktails and Irish-German black and tans (Guinness and strong German beer) are made to the sounds of live jazz at the English nautical-style **Pusser's** bar (✉ Falkenturmstr. 9, ☎ 089/220–500).

Watch the barmen shake those cocktails at **Schumann's** (✉ Maximilianstr. 36, ☎ 089/229–060) anytime after the curtain comes down at the nearby opera house (the bar is closed on Saturday). Exotic cocktails are also the specialty of **Trader Vic's** (✉ Promenadepl. 2–6, ☎ 089/212–0995), a smart cellar bar in the Hotel Bayerischer Hof. The bar is particularly popular among out-of-town visitors and attracts quite a few Americans. The **Vier Jahreszeiten Kempinski** (✉ Maximilianstr. 17, ☎ 089/21250) offers piano music until 9 and then dancing to recorded music or a small combo.

Munich's gay scene stretches between Sendlingertorplatz and Isartorplatz. Its most popular bars are **Nil** (✉ Hans-Sachs-Str. 2, ☎ 089/265–545), **Sax** (✉ Hans-Sachs-Str. 3, ☎ 089/265–493), **Ochsengarten** (✉ Müllerstr. 47, ☎ 089/266–446), and **Mrs. Henderson** (✉ Müllerstr. 1, ☎ 089/263–469), which also puts on the city's best transvestite cabaret for a mixed crowd.

Dance Clubs

Schwabing is discoland, although it's getting ever greater competition from Munich's other "in" area, Haidhausen. A former Haidhausen factory hosts the city's largest rave scene: the **Kunstpark Ost** (✉ Grafingerstr. 6, S-bahn, bus, and tram stops are at Ostbahnhof, ☎ 089/490–02928). The venue has no fewer than 17 "entertainment areas," including a Latin dance club among others, bars, and a huge slot-machine and computer-game hall. Schwabing claims more than a dozen dance clubs and live music venues between its central boulevard Leopoldstrasse and the area around its central square, the Münchner-Freiheit. One, the **Skyline** (☎ 089/333–131), is at the top of the Hertie department store, which towers above the busy square. Around the corner, two streets—Feilitzstrasse and Occamstrasse—are lined with clubs, discos, and pubs. Bordering the English Garden, **Pi** (✉ Prinzregentenstr., on west side of Haus der Kunst, ☎ 089/294–252) is the trendiest club in town; good luck making it past the bouncer. **Maximilian's Nightclub** (✉ Maximilianpl. 16, ☎ 089/223–252), and the **Park-Café** (✉ Sophienstr. 7, ☎ 089/598–313) are similarly fashionable places where you'll have to talk yourself past the doorman to join the chic crowds inside.

Nachtwerk (✉ Landsbergerstr. 185, ☎ 089/570–7390), in a converted factory, blasts out a range of sounds from punk to avant-garde nightly between 8 PM and 4 AM. Live bands also perform there regularly. The real ravers ride the S-bahn to Munich's Franz-Josef-Strauss Airport, alighting at the Besucherpark station for techno and other beats until dawn at **Night Flight** (☎ 089/9759–7999). It's becoming fashionable for package-tour travelers to start their holidays here with a pre-check-in, early morning turn around the dance floor, and a bar breakfast.

Jazz

Munich likes to think it's Germany's jazz capital, and some beer gardens have taken to replacing their brass bands with funky combos. Purists don't like it, but jazz enthusiasts are happy. Some city pubs and brewery taverns set aside Sunday midday for jazz. The best of the jazz clubs are **Mr. B's** (✉ Herzog-Heinrich-Str. 38, ☎ 089/534–901), run by New Yorker Alex Best, who also mixes great cocktails; **Jazzclub Unterfahrt im Einstein** (✉ Einsteinstr. 42, ☎ 089/448–2794); **Nachtcafé** (✉ Maximilianpl. 5, ☎ 089/595–900); and **Schwabinger Podium** (✉ Wagnerstr. 1, ☎ 089/399–482). Sunday is also set aside for jazz at **Waldwirtschaft Grosshesselohe** (✉ Georg-Kalb-Str. 3, ☎ 089/795–088), in the southern suburb of Grosshesselohe. If it's a nice day, the excursion is worth it.

OUTDOOR ACTIVITIES AND SPORTS

The **Olympiapark** (☞ Outside the Center *in* Exploring Munich, *above*), built for the 1972 Olympics, is one of the largest sports and recreation centers in Europe. For general information about sports opportunities in and around Munich contact the sports emporium **Sport Scheck** (✉ Sendlingerstr. 6, ☎ 089/21660). The big store not only sells every kind of equipment but is very handy with advice.

Beaches and Water Sports

There is sailing and windsurfing on both the Ammersee and the Starnbergersee (☞ Side Trips from Munich, *below*). Windsurfers should pay attention to restricted areas at bathing beaches. Information on sailing is available from **Bayerischer Segler-Verband** (✉ Georg-Brauchle-Ring 93, ☎ 089/1570–2366). For information on windsurfing contact **Verband der Deutschen Windsurfing Schulen** (✉ Weilheim, ☎ 0881/5267).

Golf

The **Munich Golf Club** has two courses that admit visitors on weekdays. Visitors must be members of a club at home. Its 18-hole course is at Strasslach in the suburb of Grünwald, south of the city (☎ 08170/450). The greens fee is DM 120. Its nine-hole course is more centrally located, at **Thalkirchen**, on the Isar River (☎ 089/723–1304). The greens fee starts at DM 80, depending on the number of holes played.

Ice-Skating

The **Eissportstadion** in Olympiapark (✉ Spiridon-Louis-Ring 3) has an indoor rink, and outdoor rinks are available at **Prinzregenten Stadium** (✉ Prinzregentenstr. 80) and **Eisbahn-West** (✉ Agnes-Bernauer Str. 241). Depending on weather conditions, there's also outdoor skating in winter on the lake in the **Englischer Garten** and on the **Nymphenburger Canal,** where you can also go curling (*Eisstockschiessen*) by renting equipment from little wooden huts, which also sell hot drinks. Players rent sections of machine-smoothed ice on the canal. Watch out for signs reading GEFAHR (danger), warning you of thin ice. Additional information is available from **Bayerischer Eissportverband** (✉ Georg-Brauchle-Ring 93, ☎ 089/157–9920).

Jogging

The best place to jog is the **Englischer Garten** (U-bahn: Münchner-Freiheit or Universität), which is 11 km (7 mi) around and has lakes and dirt and asphalt paths. You can also jog through **Olympiapark** (U-bahn:

Olympiazentrum). The 500-acre park of **Schloss Nymphenburg** and the banks of the **Isar River** are also ideal for running. For a longer jog along the river, take the S-bahn to Unterföhring and pace yourself back to Münchner-Freiheit—a distance of 6½ km (4 mi).

Rowing

Rowboats can be rented on the south shore of the **Olympiasee** in Olympiapark and at the **Kleinhesseloher See** in the Englischer Garten.

Swimming

You can try swimming outdoors in the Isar River at Maria-Einsiedel, but because the river flows down from the Alps, the water is frigid even in summer. Warmer lakes near Munich are the **Ammersee** and the **Starnbergersee** (☞ Side Trips from Munich, *below*). There are pools at the **Cosima Bad** (✉ Englschalkingerstr. and Cosimastr., Bogenhausen), with man-made waves; the **Dantebad** (✉ Dantestr. 6), **Nordbad** (✉ Schleissheimerstr. 142, in Schwabing district), and the **Michaelibad** (✉ Heinrich-Wieland-Str. 24) have indoor and outdoor pools; the **Olympia-Schwimmhalle** (✉ Olympiapark) and the **Müllersches Volksbad** (✉ Rosenheimerstr. 1) have indoor pools.

Tennis

There are indoor and outdoor courts at **Münchnerstrasse 15,** in München-Unterföhring; at the corner of **Drygalski-Allee** and **Kistlerhofstrasse,** in München-Fürstenried; and at **Rothof Sportanlage** (✉ Denningerstr., behind the Arabella and Sheraton hotels). In addition, there are about 200 outdoor courts all over Munich. Many can be booked via the sports store **Sport Scheck** (☎ 089/21660), which has branches around town. Prices vary from DM 18 to DM 25 an hour, depending on the time of day. Full details on tennis in Munich are available from the **Bayerischer Tennis Verband** (✉ Georg-Brauchle-Ring 93, ☎ 089/157–030).

SHOPPING

Shopping Districts

Munich has an immense central shopping area, a 2-km (1-mi) *Fussgängerzone* (pedestrian zone) stretching from the train station to Marienplatz and north to Odeonsplatz. The two main streets here are Neuhauserstrasse and Kaufingerstrasse, the sites of most major department stores. For upscale shopping, Maximilianstrasse, Residenzstrasse, and Theatinerstrasse are unbeatable and contain a fine array of classy and tempting stores that are the equal of any in Europe. **Schwabing,** north of the university, has several of the city's most intriguing and offbeat shopping streets—Schellingstrasse and Hohenzollernstrasse are two to try.

Antiques

Bavarian antiques—from a chipped pottery beer mug to a massive farmhouse dresser—can be found in the many small shops around the Viktualienmarkt, including on Westenriederstrasse, just south of the market. Also try the area north of the university; Türkenstrasse, Theresienstrasse, and Barerstrasse are all filled with antiques stores.

In **Antike Uhren Eder** (✉ Prannerstr. 4, in the Hotel Bayerischer Hof building, ☎ 089/220–305), the silence is broken only by the ticking of dozens of highly valuable German antique clocks and by discreet bargaining over the high prices. The nearby **Antike Uhren H. Schley** (✉ Kardinal-Faulhaber-Str. 14a, ☎ 089/226–188) also specializes in antique clocks. **Roman Odesser** (✉ Westenriederstr. 16, ☎ 089/226–388) specializes in German antique silver and porcelain. Also on Westenriederstrasse, at Number 8, is a building that houses three antiques shops packed from floor to ceiling with curios, including a great collection of ancient dolls and toys. For Munich's largest selection of dolls and marionettes, travel to Schwabing, to **Die Puppenstube** (⊠ Luisenstr. 68, ☎ 089/272–3267). For nautical items or ancient sports equipment (golf clubs, for instance) try the **Captain's Saloon** (⊠ Westenriederstr. 31, ☎ 089/221–015).

Strictly for window-shopping—unless you're looking for something really rare and special, and money's no object—are the exclusive shops lining Prannerstrasse, at the rear of the Hotel Bayerischer Hof. Interesting and/or cheap antiques and assorted junk from all over eastern Europe are laid out at the weekend **flea markets** beneath the Donnersberger railway bridge on Arnulfstrasse (along the northern side of the Hauptbahnhof).

Department Stores

Hertie (⊠ Bahnhofpl. 7, ☎ 089/55120), occupying an entire city block between the train station and Karlsplatz, is the largest and, some claim, the best department store in the city. The basement has a high-class delicatessen with champagne bar and a stand-up bistro offering a daily changing menu that puts many high-price Munich restaurants to shame. Hertie's Schwabing branch (☎ 089/381–060)is the high-gloss steel-and-glass building on the square known as Münchner-Freiheit. **Karstadt** (⊠ Neuhauserstr. 18, ☎ 089/290–230), in the 100-year-old Haus Oberpollinger, at the start of the Kaufingerstrasse shopping mall, is another upscale department store, with a very wide range of Bavarian arts and crafts. Karstadt also has a Schwabing branch, **Karstadt am Nordbad** (⊠ Schleissheimerstr. 93, ☎ 089/13020). **Kaufhof**'s two central Munich stores (⊠ Karlspl. 21–24, ☎ 089/51250; ⊠ Corner Kaufingerstr. and Marienpl., ☎ 089/231–851) offer a range of goods in the middle price range. If you catch an end-of-season sale, you're sure to get a bargain.

Ludwig Beck (⊠ Marienpl. 11, ☎ 089/236–910) is considered a step above other departments stores by Müncheners. It's packed from top to bottom with highly original wares—from fine feather boas to roughly finished Bavarian pottery. In December a series of booths, each delicately and lovingly decorated, is occupied by craftspeople turning out traditional German toys and decorations. **Hirmer** (⊠ Kaufingerstr. 28, ☎ 089/236–830) has Munich's most comprehensive collection of German-made men's clothes, with a markedly friendly and knowledgeable staff. **K & L Ruppert** (⊠ Kaufingerstr. 15, ☎ 089/231–1470) has a fashionable range of German-made clothes in the lower price brackets.

Folk Costumes

If you want to deck yourself out in lederhosen or a dirndl or affect a green loden coat and little pointed hat with feathers, you have a wide choice in the Bavarian capital. Much of the fine loden clothing on sale at **Lodenfrey** (⊠ Maffeistr. 7–9, ☎ 089/210–390) is made at the company's own factory, on the edge of the Englischer Garten. **Wallach** (⊠ Residenzstr. 3, ☎ 089/220–871) has souvenirs downstairs and shoes and clothing upstairs (though no children's wear). The tiny **Lederhosen Wagner** (⊠ Tal 2, ☎ 089/225–697) carries lederhosen, woolen sweaters called *Walk* (not loden), and children's clothing.

Food Markets

Munich's **Viktualienmarkt** is *the* place to shop. Just south of Marienplatz, it's home to an array of colorful stands that sell everything from cheese to sausages, from flowers to wine. A visit here is more than just collecting picnic makings; it's central to an understanding of the

74

Munich Shopping

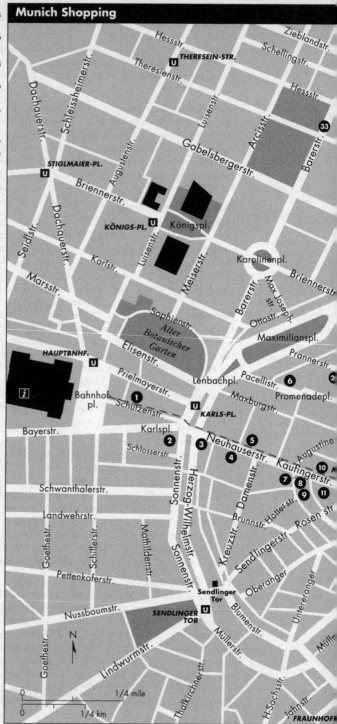

KEY

— Pedestrian Shopping Zone

🛈 Tourist Information

Ⓤ U-Bahn

Blütenstr.

Adalbertstr.

Schackstr.

Schellingstr.

Türkenstr.

Veterinärstr.

University

Ⓤ UNIVERSITÄT

Theresienstr.

Amalienstr.

Ludwigstr.

Kaulbachstr.

Königinstr.

Englischer Garten

Schönfeldstr.

Oscar v. Miller Ring

V. D. Tannstr.

Prinzregentenstr.

Lerchenfeld Str.

Oetingenstr.

Emil-Riedel str.

Galeriestr.

ODEONS-PL.

Odeons-pl.

Ⓤ

Hofgarten

K-Scharnagl-Ring

Unsoldtr.

Oetingenstr.

Reimorstr.

Hofgartenstr.

Christophstr.

St.-Anna-Pfarrstr.

Liebigstr.

St. Anna Pl.

Sternstr.

Widenmayerstr.

Salvator-pl.

Kard.-Faulhaber-Str.

Theatinerstr.

Residenzstr.

Marstallstr.

Bürkleinstr.

Isar

Max-Joseph-pl.

Maffeistrasse

Pfisterstr.

Am Kosttor

Maximilianstr.

Maximilians Br.

Frauen-pl.

Dienerstr.

Weinstr.

MARIEN-PL.

Ⓤ

Marienpl.

Am Platzl

Th.-Wimmer-Ring

Knöbelstr.

Steinsdorfstr.

Rinder markt

Tal

Isartorpl.

Kanalstr.

Rosental

Heiliggeiststr.

Westenriedstr.

Frauenstr.

Zweibrückenstr.

Blumenstr.

Cornelusstr.

Rumfordstr.

Klenzestr.

Ludwigs Br.

Innere Wienerstr.

Kohlstr.

Kellerstr.

Müllerstr.

Gärtner-pl.

Baaderstr.

Erhardtstr.

Rosenheimerstr.

Klenzestr.

Reichenbachstr.

Fraunhofer

Ⓤ

HOFERSTR.

35 36 34 32 31 29 30 28 27 26 25 24 22 21 23 20 14 15 12 13 16 17 18 19

Müncheners' easy-come-easy-go nature. If you're in the Schwabing area, the daily market at **Elisabethplatz** is worth a visit—it's much, much smaller than the Viktualienmarkt, but the range and quality of produce are comparable.

Dallmayr (⊠ Dienerstr. 14–15, ☎ 089/21350) is an elegant gourmet food store, with delights ranging from the most exotic fruits to English jams, served by efficient Munich matrons in smart blue-and-white-linen costumes. The store's famous specialty is coffee, with more than 50 varieties to blend as you wish. There's also an enormous range of breads and a temperature-controlled cigar room.

The **Zerwick Gewölbe** (⊠ Ledererstr. 3, ☎ 089/226–824) is Munich's oldest venison shop, with a mouthwatering selection of smoked meats, including wild boar.

Gift Ideas

Munich is a city of beer, and items related to its consumption are obvious choices for souvenirs and gifts. Visit **Ludwig Mory** (⊠ Marienpl. 8, ☎ 089/224–542), **Wilhelm Müller** (⊠ Sendlingerstr. 34, ☎ 089/263–969), or **Sebastian Wesely** (⊠ Rindermarkt 1 [am Peterspl.], ☎ 089/264–519).

Munich is also the home of the famous **Nymphenburg Porcelain** factory. The **Nymphenburg store** (⊠ Corner of Odeonspl. and Briennerstr., ☎ 089/282–428) resembles a drawing room of the famous Munich palace, with dove-gray soft furnishings and the delicate, expensive porcelain safely locked away in bowfront cabinets. You can also buy direct from the factory, on the grounds of **Schloss Nymphenburg** (⊠ Nördliches Schlossrondell 8, ☎ 089/1791–9710). For Dresden and Meissen ware, go to **Kunstring Meissen** (⊠ Briennerstr. 4, ☎ 089/281–532).

Bavarian craftspeople have a showplace of their own, the **Bayerischer Kunstgewerbe–Verein** (⊠ Pacellistr. 6–8, ☎ 089/290–1470); here you'll find every kind of handicraft, from glass and pottery to textiles.

Otto Kellnberger's Holzhandlung (⊠ Heiliggeiststr. 7–8, ☎ 089/226–479) specializes in wooden crafts. Looking for that pig's-bristle brush to get to the bottom of tall champagne glasses? **Geschenk Alm** (⊠ Heiliggeiststr. 7–8, ☎ 089/226–479) has nooks and crannies filled with brushes of every kind.

Obletter's (⊠ Karlspl. 11–12, ☎ 089/5508–9510) has two extensive floors of toys, many of them handmade playthings of great charm and quality. From November's end until December 24, the open-air stalls of the **Christkindlmarkt** (⊠ Marienpl.) are a great place to find gifts and warm up with mulled wine. Two other perennial Christmas market favorites are those in Schwabing (Münchner-Freiheit Square) and at the Chinesischer Turm, in the middle of the Englischer Garten.

Malls

The main pedestrian area has two malls. **Kaufinger Tor** (⊠ Kaufingerstr. 117) has several floors of boutiques and cafés packed neatly together under a high glass roof. The aptly named **Arcade** (⊠ Neuhauserstr. 5) is where the young find the best designer jeans and chunky jewelry.

SIDE TRIPS FROM MUNICH

Munich's excellent suburban railway network, the S-bahn, brings several quaint towns and attractive rural areas within easy reach for a day's excursion. The two nearest lakes, the Starnbergersee and the Ammersee, are highly recommended year-round. Dachau attracts overseas visitors, mostly because of its concentration-camp memorial site, but it's a picturesque and historic town in its own right. Landshut, north of Munich, is way off the tourist track, but if it were the same distance south of Munich, this jewel of a Bavarian market town would be over-run. Wasserburg am Inn is held in the narrow embrace of the Inn River, and it's easily incorporated into an excursion to the nearby lake, the Chiemsee (☞ Chapter 2). All these destinations have a wide selection of restaurants and hotels, and you can bring a bike on any S-bahn train.

Starnbergersee

20 km (12 mi) southwest of Munich.

The Starnbergersee was one of Europe's first pleasure grounds. Royal coaches were already trundling out from Munich to the lake's wooded shores in the 17th century; in 1663 Elector Ferdinand Maria threw a shipboard party at which 500 guests wined and dined as 100 oarsmen propelled them around the lake. Today pleasure steamers provide a taste of such luxury to the masses. The lake is still lined with the baroque palaces of Bavaria's aristocracy, but their owners now share the lake-side with public parks, beaches, and boatyards. The Starnbergersee is one of Bavaria's largest lakes—19 km (12 mi) long and 5 km (3 mi) wide—so there's plenty of room for swimmers, sailors, and wind-surfers. On its west shore is a great golf course, but it's about as dif-ficult to gain entrance there as it was for a commoner to attend one of Prince Ferdinand's boating parties.

Exploring Starnbergersee

The Starnbergersee is named after its chief resort, **Starnberg,** the largest town on the lake and the nearest to Munich. Pleasure boats set off from Starnberg's jetty for trips around the lake. The resort has a tree-lined lakeside promenade and some fine turn-of-the-century villas, some of which are now hotels. There are abundant restaurants, taverns, and chestnut-tree-shaded beer gardens. On the lake's eastern shore at the village of Berg you'll find the **King Ludwig II Memorial Chapel.** A well-marked path leads through thick woods to the chapel, built near the point in the lake where the drowned king's body was found on June 13, 1886. He had been confined in nearby Berg Castle after the Bavar-ian government took action against his withdrawal from reality and his bankrupting castle-building fantasies. Look for the cross in the lake, which marks the point where his body was recovered.

The castle of **Possenhofen,** home of Ludwig's favorite cousin, Sisi, stands on the western shore, practically opposite Berg. Local lore says they used to send affectionate messages across the lake to each other. Sisi married the Austrian emperor Franz Joseph I but spent more than 20 summers in the lakeside castle, now a luxury hotel, the **Kaiserin Elis-abeth.** ☒ *Tutzingerstr. 2–6, D–82340 Feldafing,* ☎ *08157/1013.*

Just offshore is the tiny **Roseninsel** (Rose Island), where King Maxi-milian II built a summer villa. You can swim to its tree-fringed shores or sail across in a dinghy or on a Windsurfer (Possenhofen's boatyard is one of the lake's many rental points).

Dining and Lodging

$$ ✕ **Forsthaus Ilka-Höhe.** This fine old country lodge is set amid mead-ows above the lake, an uphill stroll from the Tutzing station at the end of the S-6 suburban line. The walk is well worth the effort, for the Ilka-Höhe is one of the region's most attractive restaurants, with a view of the lake. In summer dine on its vine-clad terrace. Reservations are ad-vised, but dress is casual. ☒ *Auf der Ilkehöhe, Tutzing,* ☎ *08158/8242. MC. Closed Mon. and Tues., last 2 wks Dec., and weekends Jan.*

$$ ✕ **Seerestaurant Undosa.** This lakeside restaurant is only a short walk from the Starnberg railroad station and boat pier. Most tables command a view of the lake, which provides some of the best fish specialties on the international menu. ⊠ *Seepromenade 1,* ☎ *08151/998–930. Reservations not accepted. AE, MC, V. Closed Tues.*

$$–$$$$ ✕⌂ **Hotel Schloss Berg.** King Ludwig II spent his final days in the small castle of Berg, from which this comfortable hotel gets its name. It's on the edge of the castle park where Ludwig liked to walk and a stone's throw from the lake shallows where he drowned. The older, century-old main hotel building is on the lakeside, while a modern annex overlooks the lake from the woods. All rooms are spacious and furnished in an elegant variation of farmhouse style. The restaurant and waterside beer garden are favorite haunts of locals and weekenders. ⊠ *Seestr. 17, D–82335 Berg,* ☎ *08151/9630,* 🖷 *08151/96352. 50 rooms. Restaurant, bar, beer garden, sauna, bicycles. AE, MC, V.* ⌕

$$$ ✕⌂ **Forsthaus am See.** The handsome, geranium-covered Forsthaus faces the lake, and so do most of the rooms (they're more expensive than those at the back with woodland views but worth it). The pinewood-furnished rooms are large, many with sitting areas. The excellent restaurant has a daily-changing international menu, with lake fish a specialty. The hotel has its own lake access and boat pier, with a chestnut-shaded beer garden nearby. ⊠ *Am See 1, D–82343 Possenhofen,* ☎ *08157/93010,* 🖷 *08157/4292. 20 rooms, 1 suite. Restaurant, beer garden. AE, MC, V.*

Starnbergersee A to Z

ARRIVING AND DEPARTING

By Bus. The east bank of the lake can be reached by bus from the town of Wolfratshausen, the end of the S-bahn 7 suburban line.

By Car. Starnberg and the north end of the lake are a 40-minute drive from Munich on the A–95 Autobahn. Follow the signs to Garmisch and take the Starnberg exit. Country roads then skirt the west and east banks of the lake.

By Train. The S-bahn 6 suburban line runs from Munich's central Marienplatz to Starnberg and three other towns on the lake's west bank: Possenhofen, Feldafing, and Tutzing. The journey from Marienplatz to Starnberg takes 35 minutes.

VISITOR INFORMATION

Fremdenverkehrsverband (⊠ Wittelsbacher Str. 9 [Am Kirchpl.], D–82319 Starnberg, ☎ 08151/13008).

Ammersee

40 km (25 mi) southwest of Munich.

The Ammersee is the country cousin of the better-known, more cosmopolitan Starnbergersee, and, accordingly, many Bavarians (and tourists, too) like it all the more. Munich cosmopolites of centuries past thought it too distant for an excursion, not to mention too rustic. So the shores remained relatively free of the villas and parks that ring the Starnbergersee, and even though upscale holiday homes of Munich's moneyed class claim some stretches of the eastern shore, the Ammersee still offers more open areas for bathing and boating than the bigger lake to the west. Bicyclists can circle the 19-km-long (12-mi-long) lake (it's nearly 6 km [4 mi] across at its widest point) on a path that rarely loses sight of the water. Hikers can spread out the tour for two or three days, staying overnight in any of the comfortable inns along the way. Dinghy sailors and windsurfers can zip across in minutes with the help of the Alpine winds that swoop down from the mountains. A ferry cruises the lake at regular intervals during summer, dropping and picking up passengers at several pier stops. Board it at Herrsching.

Herrsching has a delightful promenade, part of which winds through the resort's park. The 100-year-old villa that sits so comfortably in the park, overlooking the lake and the Alps beyond, seems as if it were built by Ludwig II, such is the romantic and fanciful mixture of medieval turrets and Renaissance-style facades. It was actually built for the artist Ludwig Scheuermann in the late 19th century and became a favorite meeting place for Munich and Bavarian artists. It is now a municipal cultural center and the scene of chamber-music concerts on some summer weekends.

The Benedictine monastery of **Andechs,** one of southern Bavaria's most famous pilgrimage sites, lies 5 km (3 mi) south of Herrsching. You can reach it on Bus 951 (which also connects Ammersee and Starnbergersee). The 15th-century church is adorned with mid-18th-century rococo decoration and contains religious relics said to have been brought from the Holy Land 1,000 years ago. The church is being renovated completely in the next three years in preparation for the 550th anniversary of the monastery in 2005. Crowds of pilgrims are drawn not only by the beauty of the hilltop monastery but by the beer brewed here (600,000 liters annually). The monastery makes its own cheese as well, and it's an excellent accompaniment to the rich, almost black beer. You can enjoy both at large wooden tables in the monastery tavern or on the terrace outside. The son of the last Austro-Hungarian emperor, Archduke Otto von Habsburg, lives beside the lake. He celebrated his 80th birthday in the church in 1992, with a family party following in the tavern. ☉ *Daily 7–7.*

The little town of **Diessen,** with its magnificent baroque abbey church, is at the southwest corner of the lake. Step inside the church to admire its opulent stucco decoration and sumptuous gilt-and-marble altar. Visit in late afternoon, when the light falls sharply on its crisp gray, white, and gold facade, etching the pencil-like tower and spire against the darkening sky over the lake. Don't leave without at least peeping into neighboring St. Stephen's courtyard, its cloisters smothered in wild roses.

Dining

$$$ ✕⛬ **Landhotel Piushof.** The family-run Piushof has elegantly Bavarian guest rooms, with lots of oak and hand-carved cupboards. The beamed and pillared restaurant ($$) has an excellent menu of Bavarian specialties. ⊠ *Schönbichlstr. 18, D–82211 Herrsching,* ☎ *08152/ 968–270,* ℻ *08152/968–270. 21 rooms, 2 suites. Restaurant, indoor pool, sauna, massage, tennis court. MC, V.*

$$–$$$ ✕⛬ **Ammersee Hotel.** This very comfortable, modern resort hotel has views from an unrivaled position on the lakeside promenade. Rooms overlooking the lake are in big demand and more expensive. The Artis restaurant ($$) has an international menu. ⊠ *Summerstr. 32, D–82211 Herrsching,* ☎ *08152/96870,* ℻ *08152/5374. 40 rooms. Restaurant, Weinstube, hot tub, sauna, exercise room. AE, DC, MC, V.*

$$ ⛬ **Hotel Garni Zur Post.** Families feel particularly at home here, and children amuse themselves at the playground and small deer park. Rooms are Bavarian baroque in style, with heavy drapes and carved farmhouse furniture. ⊠ *Starnberger Str. 2, D–82346 Andechs,* ☎ *08152/3433,* ℻ *08152/2303. 32 rooms, 22 with bath. Playground. MC.*

$$ ✕⛬ **Hotel Promenade.** From the hotel terrace restaurant you can watch the pleasure boats tie up at the adjacent pier. If you're staying, ask for a room overlooking the lake; they all have geranium-hung balconies. Those under the dormer-broken roof are particularly cozy. ⊠

Summerstr. 6, D–82211 Herrsching, ☎ 08152/1088, ℻ 08152/5981. 11 rooms. Restaurant, café. DC, MC, V.

Ammersee A to Z

ARRIVING AND DEPARTING

By Bus. From the Herrsching train station Bus 952 runs north along the lake, and Bus 951 runs south and continues on to Starnberg in a 40-minute journey.

By Car. Take Autobahn 96—follow the signs to Lindau—and 20 km (12 mi) west of Munich take the exit for Herrsching, the lake's principal town.

By Train. Herrsching, on the east bank of the lake, is the end of the S-bahn 5 suburban line, a half-hour ride from Munich's Marienplatz.

VISITOR INFORMATION

Verkehrsamt (⊠ Bahnhofspl. 2, Herrsching, ☎ 08152/5227).

Dachau

20 km (12 mi) northwest of Munich.

Dachau predates Munich, with records going back to the time of Charlemagne. It's a handsome town, too, built on a hilltop with fine views of Munich and the Alps. A guided tour of the town, including the castle and church, leaves from the Rathaus on Saturday, from May through mid-October. Dachau is better known worldwide as the site of the first Nazi concentration camp, which was built just outside it. Dachau preserves the memory of the camp and the horrors perpetrated there with deep contrition while trying, with commendable discretion, to signal that it also has other points of interest.

The site of the infamous camp, now the **KZ-Gedenkstätte Dachau** (Dachau Concentration Camp Memorial), is just outside town. Photographs, contemporary documents, the few remaining cell blocks, and the grim crematorium (never used) create a somber and moving picture of the camp, where more than 30,000 of the 200,000-plus prisoners lost their lives. A documentary film in English is shown daily at 11:30 and 3:30. To reach the memorial by car, leave the center of the town along Schleissheimerstrasse and turn left into Alte Römerstrasse; the site is on the left. By public transport take Bus 724 or 726 from the Dachau S-bahn train station or the town center. Both stop within a two-minute walk from the site (ask the driver to let you out there). If you are driving from Munich, turn right on the first country road (marked B) before entering Dachau and follow the signs. ⊠ *Alte Römerstr. 75,* ☎ *08131/1741.* ⊡ *Free.* ☉ *Tues.–Sun. 9–5. Guided English tour June–Aug., Tues.–Sun. 12:30; Sept.–May., weekends 12:30.*

Schloss Dachau, the hilltop castle, dominates the town. What you'll see is the one remaining wing of a palace built by the Munich architect Josef Effner for the Wittelsbach ruler Max Emanuel in 1715. During the Napoleonic Wars the palace served as a field hospital, treating French and Russian casualties from the Battle of Austerlitz (1805). The wars made a casualty, too, of the palace, and three of the four wings were demolished by order of King Max Joseph I. What's left is a handsome cream-and-white building, with an elegant pillared and lantern-hung café on the ground floor and a former ballroom above. Concerts are held here, beneath a richly decorated and carved ceiling, with painted panels representing figures from ancient mythology. The east-facing terrace affords panoramic views of Munich and, on fine days, the distant Alps. There's also a 250-year-old *Schlossbrauerei* (castle brewery), which hosts the town's beer and music festival each year in the first two weeks of August. ⊠ *Schlosspl.,* ☎ *08131/87923.* ▣ *DM 2; tour DM 5.* ☉ *May–Sept., weekends 2–5; tour of town and Schloss May–mid-Oct., Sat. 10:30.*

St. Jacob, Dachau's parish church, was built in the early 16th century in late-Renaissance style on the foundations of a 14th-century Gothic structure. Baroque features and a characteristic onion dome were added in the late 17th century. On the south wall you can admire a very fine 17th-century sundial. A visit to the church is included in the guided tour of the town (May–mid-October, Saturday 10:30). ⊠ *Konrad-Adenauer-Str. 7,* ☉ *Daily 7–7.*

An artists' colony formed here during the 19th century, and the tradition lives on. Picturesque houses line Hermann-Stockmann-Strasse and part of Münchner Strasse, and many of them are still the homes of successful artists. The **Gemäldegalerie** displays the works of many of the town's 19th-century artists. ⊠ *Konrad-Adenauer-Str. 3,* ☎ *08131/567–516.* ▣ *DM 3.* ☉ *Wed.–Fri. 11–5, weekends 1–5.*

Dining and Lodging

$–$$ ✕ **Bräustüberl.** Near the castle, the Bräustüberl has a shady beer garden for lunches and a cozy tavern for year-round Bavarian-style eating and drinking. ⊠ *Schlossstr. 8,* ☎ *08131/725. MC. Closed Mon.*

$–$$ ✕ **Hörhammerbräu.** You can combine Bavarian farmhouse dishes such as pork knuckle and potato dumplings with the best of home-brewed Dachau beer at this inn. It's not haute cuisine, but the portions will set you up for a whole day's outing to Dachau. ⊠ *Konrad-Adenauer-Str. 12,* ☎ *08131/735–711. AE, MC, V.*

$–$$ ✕ **Zieglerbräu.** Dachau's leading beer tavern, once a 17th-century brewer's home, is a warren of cozy, wood-paneled rooms where you'll probably share a table with a party of locals on a boys' night out. The food is solidly Bavarian, basically varieties of pork, potato, and sausages in all forms. ⊠ *Konrad-Adenauer-Str. 8,* ☎ *08131/4074. No credit cards.*

Dachau A to Z

ARRIVING AND DEPARTING

By Car. Take the B–12 country road or the Stuttgart Autobahn to the Dachau exit from Munich.

By Train. Dachau is on the S-bahn 2 suburban line, a 20-minute ride from Munich's Marienplatz.

VISITOR INFORMATION

Verkehrsverein Dachau (⊠ Konrad-Adenauer-Str. 1, ☎ 08131/ 84566, ✎).

Landshut

64 km (40 mi) north of Munich.

If fortune had placed Landshut south of Munich, in the protective folds of the Alpine foothills, instead of the same distance north, in the dull flatlands of Lower Bavaria, the historic town would be teeming with tourists. Landshut's geographical misfortune is the discerning visitor's good luck, for the town is never overcrowded, with the possible exception of the three summer weeks every four years when the *Landshuter Hochzeit* (Landshut Wedding) is celebrated. The next celebration is in 2001 (June 30–July 22), and then a visit to Landshut is a must. The festival commemorates the marriage in 1475 of Prince George of Bavaria-Landshut, son of the expressively named Ludwig the Rich, to Princess Hedwig, daughter of the king of Poland. Within its ancient walls, the entire town is swept away in a colorful reconstruction of the event. The wedding procession, with the "bride" and "groom" on horseback, accompanied by pipes and drums and the hurly-burly of a medieval pageant, is held on three consecutive weekends, while a medieval-style fair fills the central streets throughout the three weeks.

Landshut has two magnificent cobblestone market streets. The one in **Altstadt** (Old Town) is one of the most beautiful city streets in Germany; the other is in **Neustadt** (New Town). The two streets run parallel to each other, tracing a course between the Isar River and the heights overlooking the town. A steep path from Altstadt takes you up to **Burg Trausnitz.** This castle was begun in 1204 and accommodated the Wittelsbach dukes of Bavaria-Landshut until 1503. ☎ 0871/22638. ⚏ DM 5, including guided tour. ☉ Apr.–Sept., daily 9–noon and 1–5; Oct.–Mar., daily 10–noon and 1–4.

The **Stadtresidenz** in Altstadt was the first Italian Renaissance building of its kind north of the Alps. The Wittelsbachs lived here during the 16th century. The Renaissance facade of the palace forms an almost modest part of the architectural splendor and integrity of the Altstadt, where even the ubiquitous McDonald's has to serve its hamburgers behind a baroque exterior. ☎ 0871/22638. ⚏ DM 4. ☉ Apr.–Sept., daily 9–noon and 1–5; Oct.–Mar., daily 10–noon and 1–4.

The **Martinskirche** (St. Martin's), with the tallest brick church tower (436 ft) in the world, soars above the other buildings with its bristling spire. The church contains some magnificent Gothic treasures and a 16th-century carved Madonna. Moreover, it is surely the only church in the world to contain an image of Hitler, albeit in a devilish pose. The führer and other Nazi leaders are portrayed as executioners in a 1946 stained-glass window showing the martyrdom of St. Kastulus. In the nave of the church is a clear and helpful description of its history and treasures in English. ☎ 0871/24277. ☉ Apr.–Sept., daily 7–6:30; Oct.–Mar., daily 7–5.

Built into a steep slope of the hill crowned by Burg Trausnitz is an unusual art museum, the **Skulpturenmuseum im Hofberg,** containing the entire collection of the Landshut sculptor Fritz Koenig. His own work forms the permanent central section of the labyrinthine gallery. ⚏ Im Hofberg, ☎ 0871/89021. ⚏ DM 6. ☉ Tues.–Sun. 10:30–1 and 2–5.

Freising (at the end of the S-bahn 1 line, a half-hour ride from central Munich) is an ancient episcopal seat and well worth including in a visit to Landshut, 35 km (22 mi) to the northeast.

Dining and Lodging

There are several attractive Bavarian-style restaurants in the Altstadt and Neustadt, most of them with beer gardens. Although Landshut brews a fine beer, look for a Gaststatte offering a Weihenstephaner, from the world's oldest brewery, in nearby Freising. Helles (light) is the most popular beer variety.

$$$ ✕▦ **Lindner Hotel Kaiserhof.** The green Isar River rolls outside the bedroom windows of Landshut's most distinctive hotel. Its steep red roof and white facade blend harmoniously with the waterside panorama. The "Herzog Ludwig" restaurant ($$–$$$) serves a sumptuous but reasonably priced lunch buffet and is an elegant place for dinner. ⚏ Papiererstr. 2, D–84034, ☎ 0871/6870, ℻ 0871/687–403. 147 rooms. Restaurant, bar, sauna, steam room, exercise room, bicycles, motorbikes. AE, DC, MC, V.

$$$ ✕▦ **Romantik Hotel Fürstenhof.** This handsome Landshut city mansion had no difficulty qualifying for inclusion in the Romantik group of hotels—it just breathes romance, from its plush little restaurant ($$–$$$) to the cozy bedrooms. A vine-covered terrace adds charm. ⚏

Stethaimerstr. 3, D–84034, ☎ *0871/92550,* FAX *0871/925–544. 24 rooms. Restaurant, sauna. AE, DC, MC, V.* 🖎

$$ ✕🖫 **Hotel Goldene Sonne.** The steeply gabled Renaissance facade of the Golden Sun fronts a hotel of great charm and sleek comfort. It stands in the center of town, near all the sights. Its dining options are a paneled, beamed restaurant, a vaulted cellar, and a courtyard beer garden, where the service is smilingly, helpfully Bavarian. ✉ *Neustadt 520, D–84028,* ☎ *0871/92530,* FAX *0871/925–3350. 55 rooms. Restaurant, beer garden, pub. AE, DC, MC, V.* 🖎

$$ ✕🖫 **Schloss Schönbrunn.** This historic country mansion is now a luxurious hotel, with many of the original features intact. Rooms in the most historic part of the building are particularly attractive, with huge double beds, and represent excellent value. The handsome house stands in the Schönbrunn district of Landshut, about 2 km (1 mi) from the center. The journey is worthwhile even for the excellent restaurant ($$–$$$), where the menu includes fish from the hotel's own pond. ✉ *Schönbrunn 1, D–84036,* ☎ *0871/95220,* FAX *0871/952–2222. 33 rooms. Restaurant, bar, beer garden, café. AE, DC, MC, V.* 🖎

Landshut A to Z

ARRIVING AND DEPARTING

By Car. Landshut is a 45-minute drive northwest from Munich on either the A–92 Autobahn—follow the signs to Deggendorf—or the B–11 highway.

By Train. Landshut is on the Plattling–Regensburg–Passau line, a 40-minute ride by express train from Munich.

VISITOR INFORMATION

Verkehrsverein (✉ Altstadt 315, ☎ 0871/922–050).

Wasserburg am Inn

51 km (30 mi) east of Munich.

Wasserburg floats like a faded ship of state in a lazy loop of the Inn River, which comes within a few yards of cutting the ancient town off from the wooded slopes of the encroaching countryside. The river caresses the southern limits of the town center, embraces its eastern boundary with rocky banks 200 ft high, returns westward as if looking for a way out of this geographical puzzle, and then heads north in search of its final destination, the Danube. Wasserburg is a perfectly preserved, beautifully set medieval town, once a vitally important trading post but later thankfully ignored by the industrialization that gripped Germany in the 19th century.

You're never more than 100 yards or so from the river in Wasserburg's **Altstadt,** which huddles within the walls of the castle that originally gave the town its name. The almost Italian look is typical of many Inn River towns. Use the north- or east-bank parking lot as the town council is expanding the traffic-free zone. It's only a few minutes' walk to the central Marienplatz. There you'll find Wasserburg's late-Gothic brick **Rathaus.** The Bavarian regional government met here until 1804, deliberating in its beautifully decorated Renaissance *Ratsstube* (council chamber). ✉ *Marienpl.* 💲 *DM 1.50.* ☉ *Guided tour Tues.–Fri. at 10, 11, 2, 3, 4; weekends at 10, 11.*

The 14th-century **Frauenkirche** (Church of Our Lady), on Marienplatz, is the town's oldest church. It incorporates an ancient watchtower. The baroque altar frames a Madonna by an unknown 15th-century artist.

Wasserburg's imposing 15th-century parish church, **St. Jakob,** has an intricately carved baroque pulpit dating from 1640.

Next to the 14th-century town gate, at the end of Wasserburg's only bridge, is the unusual **Erstes Imaginäres Museum.** The museum has a collection of more than 500 world-famous paintings, but without an original among them; every single one is a precise copy, executed by various artists. 🖾 *DM 3.* ☉ *May–Sept., Tues.–Sun. 11–5; Oct.–Apr., Tues.–Sun. 1–5.*

Wasserburg is a convenient base for walks along the banks of the Inn River and into the countryside. A pretty path west leads to the village of **Attel.** Another half hour into the Attel River valley, and you'll reach the enchanting castle-restaurant of **Schloss Hart** (☎ 08039/1774).

Dining and Lodging

$$ ✕ **Herrenhaus.** This is one of Wasserburg's oldest houses, with medieval foundations and a centuries-old wine cellar. Many pork dishes with dumplings and sauerkraut are served at the oak tables beneath vaulted ceilings. ⊠ *Herreng. 17,* ☎ *08071/2800. MC. Closed Mon. and Aug. No dinner Sun.*

$ ✕ **Gasthaus Zum Löwen.** Simple Bavarian fare is the basis of this sturdy old inn's menu. The roast pork and dumplings are legendary. You can watch the Wasserburg world go by from an outside table. ⊠ *Marienpl. 10,* ☎ *08071/7400. No credit cards.*

$$ ✕🛏 **Hotel Fletzinger Bräu.** Wasserburg's leading hotel began as a brewery, and you can sample local ales in its noisy, friendly tavern. Rooms are large and homey; many have original antiques. ⊠ *Fletzingerg. 1, D–83512,* ☎ *08071/90890,* 🖷 *08071/909–8177. 40 rooms. Restaurant, beer garden, pub. MC.*

Wasserburg A to Z

ARRIVING AND DEPARTING

By Car. Take the B–304 from Munich, which leads directly to Wasserburg. It's a 45-minute drive.

By Train. Take either the S-bahn 4 suburban line to Ebersberg and change to a local train to Wasserburg, or the Salzburg express, changing at Grafing Bahnhof to the local line. Both trips take 90 minutes.

VISITOR INFORMATION

Verkehrsamt (⊠ Rathauspl. 1, D–83512 Wasserburg am Inn, ☎ 08071/1050).

MUNICH A TO Z

Arriving and Departing

By Bus

Long-distance buses arrive at and depart from the north side of the main train station. A taxi stand is right next to it.

By Car

From the north (Nürnberg or Frankfurt), leave the autobahn at the Schwabing exit. From Stuttgart and the west, the autobahn ends at Obermenzing, Munich's most westerly suburb. The autobahns from Salzburg and the east, Garmisch and the south, and Lindau and the southwest all join the Mittlerer Ring (city beltway). When leaving any autobahn, follow the signs reading STADTMITTE for downtown Munich.

By Plane

Munich **International Airport** (☎ 089/9752–1313) is 28 km (17 mi) northeast of the city center, between the small towns of Freising and Erding.

A fast train service links the airport with Munich's main train station. The S-1 and S-8 lines operate from a terminal directly beneath the airport's arrival and departure halls. Trains leave every 10 minutes, and the journey takes around 40 minutes. Several intermediate stops are made, including the Ostbahnhof (convenient for lodgings east of the Isar River) and such city-center stations as Marienplatz. A one-way ticket costs DM 14.40, or DM 12 if you purchase a multiple-use "strip" ticket (☞ Getting Around, *below*). A family of up to five (two adults and three children under 15) can make the trip for DM 26 by buying a Tageskarte ticket. The bus service is slower and more expensive (DM 16) than the S-bahn link (☞ Getting Around, *below*) and is only recommended if you have a lot of luggage. A taxi from the airport costs between DM 90 and DM 100. During rush hours (7–10 and 4–7), allow up to an hour of traveling time. If you're driving from the airport to the city, take route A–9 and follow the signs for MÜNCHEN STADT-MITTE. If you're driving to FJS from the city center, head north through Schwabing, join the A–9 Autobahn at the Frankfurter Ring intersection, and follow the signs for the airport (FLUGHAFEN).

By Train

All long-distance rail services arrive at and depart from the Hauptbahnhof, the main train station; trains to and from some destinations in Bavaria use the adjoining Starnbergerbahnhof, which is under the same roof. The high-speed InterCity Express (ICE) trains connect Munich, Augsburg, Frankfurt, and Hamburg on one line; Munich, Nuremberg, Würzburg, and Hamburg on another. Regensburg can be reached from Munich on Regio trains. For information on train schedules, call 01805–9966333; most railroad information staff speak English. For tickets and travel information, go to the station information office or try the ABR travel agency, right by the station on Bahnhofplatz.

Getting Around

By Bicycle

Munich and its environs are easily navigated on two wheels. The city is threaded with a network of specially designated bike paths, and bikes are allowed on the S-bahn. A free map showing all bike trails is available at all city tourist offices.

You can rent bicycles from **Radl-Discount** ⊠ Benediktbeurerstr. 20–22, ☎ 089/724–2351; ⊠ Trappentreustr. 10, ☎ 089/506–285) and at **Aktiv-Rad** (⊠ Hans-Sachs-Str. 7, ☎ 089/266–506). Bikes can also be rented from April through October at the **Hauptbahnhof** (⊠ Radius Touristik, opposite platform 31, ☎ 089/596–113) and at some S-bahn and mainline stations around Munich. A list of stations that offer the service is available from the Deutsche Bahn. The cost is DM 6–DM 8 a day if you've used public transportation to reach the station; otherwise it's DM 10–DM 12, depending on the type of bike.

By Public Transportation

Munich has an efficient and well-integrated public transportation system, consisting of the **U-bahn** (subway), the **S-bahn** (suburban railway), the **Strassenbahn** (streetcars), and buses. Marienplatz forms the heart of the U-bahn and S-bahn network, which operates from around 5 AM to 1 AM. An all-night tram and bus service operates on main routes within the city. For a clear explanation in English of how the system works, pick up a copy of *Rendezvous mit München,* available free of charge at all tourist offices.

Munich Public Transit System

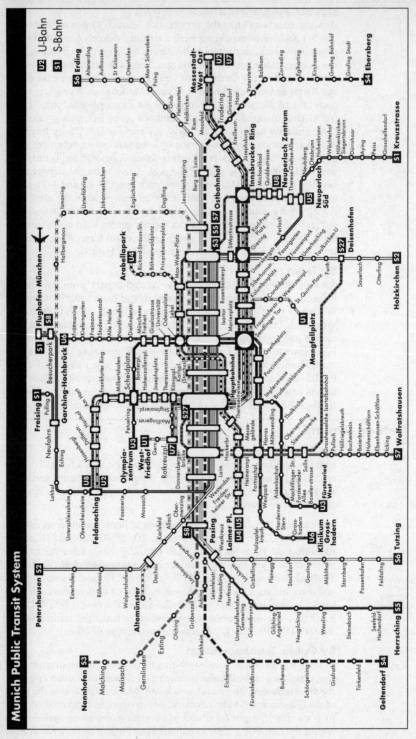

Fares are uniform for the entire system. As long as you are traveling in the same direction, you can transfer from one mode of transportation to another on the same ticket. You can also interrupt your journey as often as you like, and time-punched tickets are valid for up to four hours, depending on the number of zones you travel through. Fares are constantly creeping upward, but at press time a basic **Einzelfahrkarte** (one-way ticket) cost DM 3.60 for a ride in the inner zone and DM 1.80 for a short journey of up to four stops. If you're taking a number of trips around the city, save money by buying a **Mehrfahrtenkarte,** or multiple strip ticket. Red strip tickets are valid for children under 15 only. Blue strips cover adults. DM 15 buys a 10-strip ticket. All but the shortest inner-area journeys (up to four stops) cost two strips (one for young people between 15 and 21), which must be validated at one of the many time-punching machines at stations or on buses and trams. For a short stay the best option is the **Tageskarte** ticket, which provides unlimited travel for up to five people (maximum of two adults, plus three children under 15). It is valid weekdays from 9 AM to 6 AM the following day and at any time on weekends. The costs are DM 13 for an inner-zone ticket and DM 26 for the entire network. The **Welcome Card** covers transport within the city boundaries and includes up to 50% reductions in admission to many museums and attractions. The card, obtainable from visitor information offices, costs DM 12 for one day and DM 29 for three days. A three-day card for two people costs DM 42.

All tickets are sold at the blue dispensers at U- and S-bahn stations and at bus and streetcar stops. Bus and streetcar drivers, all tourist offices, and Mehrfahrtenkarten booths (which display a white κ on a green background) also sell tickets. Spot checks are common and carry an automatic fine of DM 60 if you're caught without a valid ticket. Holders of a EurailPass, a Youth Pass, or an Inter-Rail card can travel free on all suburban railway trains.

By Taxi
Munich's cream-color taxis are numerous. Hail them in the street or call 089/21610 (there's an extra charge of DM 2 if you call). Rates start at DM 5. Expect to pay DM 12–DM 13 for a short trip within the city. There is a DM 1 charge for each piece of luggage.

On Foot
Downtown Munich is only a mile square and is easily explored on foot. Almost all the major attractions in the city center are on the interlinking web of pedestrian streets that run from Karlsplatz, by the main train station, to Marienplatz and the Viktualienmarkt and extend north around the Frauenkirche and up to Odeonsplatz. The two tourist information offices issue a free map with suggested walking tours.

Contacts and Resources

Car Rentals
All Hauptbahnhof (train station) offices are in the mezzanine-level gallery above the Deutsche Bahn information and ticket center. Airport offices are in the central area, Zentralbereich.

Avis (✉ Airport, ☎ 089/975–97600; ✉ Hauptbahnhof, ☎ 089/550–2251; ✉ Nymphenburgerstr. 61, ☎ 089/1260–0020; ✉ Balanstr. 74, ☎ 089/403–091). **Europcar** (✉ Airport, ☎ 089/973–5020; ✉ Hauptbahnhof, ☎ 089/550–1341; ✉ Hirtenstr. 14, ☎ 089/557–145). **Hertz** (✉ Airport, ☎ 089/978–860; ✉ Hauptbahnhof, ☎ 089/550–2256; ✉ Nymphenburgerstr. 81, ☎ 089/129–5001). **Sixt** (✉ Airport, ☎ 089/526–2525; ✉ Hauptbahnhof, ☎ 089/550–2447; ✉ Seitzstr. 9, ☎ 089/223–333).

Consulates

British Consulate General (⊠ Bürkleinstr. 10, ☎ 089/211–090). **Canadian Consulate** (⊠ Tal 29, ☎ 089/219–9570). **U.S. Consulate General** (⊠ Königinstr. 5, ☎ 089/28880).

Doctors and Dentists

The American, British, and Canadian consulates (☞ *above*) have lists of recommended doctors and dentists who speak English.

Emergencies

Police (☎ 089/110). **Fire department, ambulance,** and **medical emergencies** (☎ 089/112).

English-Language Bookstores

The **Anglia English Bookshop** (⊠ Schellingstr. 3, ☎ 089/283–642) is the leading English-language bookstore in Munich, although the shop is in incredible disorder. **Hugendubel** (⊠ Marienpl. 22, 2nd floor, ☎ 089/23890; ⊠ Karlspl. 3, ☎ 089/552–2530) has a good selection. The **Internationale Presse** (☎ 089/13080) store is at the main train station. **Words'worth** (⊠ Schellingstr. 21a, ☎ 089/280–9141) is a well-kept shop with books in English.

Guided Tours

EXCURSIONS

Bus excursions to the Alps, to Austria, to the royal palaces and castles of Bavaria, or along the Romantic Road can be booked through **DER** (⊠ Hauptbahnhofpl. 2, in the main train station building, ☎ 089/5514–0100). Next to the main train station, **Panorama Tours** (⊠ Arnulfstr. 8, ☎ 089/5490–7560) operates numerous trips, including the Royal Castles Tour (Schlösserfahrt) of "Mad" King Ludwig's dream palaces; the cost is DM 78, excluding entrance fees to the palaces. Bookings for both companies can also be made through all major hotels in the city. The tours depart from in front of the Hauptbahnhof outside the Hertie department store.

The Upper Bavarian Regional Tourist Office (☞ Visitor Information, *below*) provides information and brochures for excursions and accommodations outside Munich.

ORIENTATION

A variety of city bus tours is offered by **Panorama Tours** (☞ Excursions, *above*). The blue buses operate year-round, departing from in front of the Hertie department store on Bahnhofplatz. A one-hour tour of Munich highlights leaves daily at 10, 11, 11:30, 12, 1, 2:30, 3, and 4. The cost is DM 17. A 2½-hour city tour departs daily at 10 AM and includes brief visits to the Alte Pinakothek, the Peterskirche, and Marienplatz for the glockenspiel. An afternoon tour, also 2½ hours and starting at 2:30 PM, includes a tour of Schloss Nymphenburg. The cost of each tour is DM 30. Another 2½-hour tour, departing Saturday, Sunday, and Monday at 10 AM, includes a visit to the Bavaria film studios. The cost is DM 39. A four-hour tour, starting daily at 10 AM and 2:30 PM includes a visit to the Olympic Park and the "Olympic Spirit" attraction. The cost is DM 49. The München bei Nacht tour provides 4½ hours of Munich by night and includes dinner and a show at the Hofbräuhaus, a trip up the Olympic Tower to admire the lights of the city, and a final drink in a nightclub. It departs April through November, Friday and Saturday at 7:30 PM; the cost is DM 100. Another operator, **Yellow Cab Stadtrundfahrten,** has a fleet of yellow double-decker buses, in which tours are offered simultaneously in eight languages. They leave hourly between 10 AM and 4 PM from in front of the Elisenhof shopping complex on Bahnhofplatz. A novel way of seeing the city is to hop on one of the **bike-rickshaws** which are the latest addition to the tour program. The bike-powered two-seater cabs operate between Marienplatz and the Chinesischer Turm in the Englischer Garten. Just hail one—or book ahead by calling 089/129–4808.

WALKING AND BICYCLING

Two-hour tours of the old city center are given daily in summer (March–October) and on Friday and Saturday in winter (November–February). Tours organized by the visitor center start at 10:30 and 1 in the center of Marienplatz. The cost is DM 16. **Munich Walks** (☎ 0177/227–5901) conducts tours of the old city and sites related to the Third Reich era. The cost is DM 15 (DM 12 for under-26-year-olds, free for accompanied children under 14). Tours depart daily at 11 from the Hauptbahnhof, outside the EurAide office by Track 11. **City Hopper Touren** (☎ 089/272–1131) offers daily escorted bike tours March–October. Bookings must be made in advance, and starting times are negotiable. **Radius Touristik** (✉ Arnulfstr. 3, opposite Platforms 30–36 in the Hauptbahnhof, ☎ 089/596–113) has bicycle tours from May through the beginning of October at 10:15 and 2; the cost, including bike rental, is DM 15. **Mike's Bike Tours** (☎ 089/651–4275) is run by a young American who hires German students to take visitors on a two- to three-hour spin through Munich. The tours start daily at the Old Town Hall, the Altes Rathaus, at 11:20 and 3:50. They cost DM 28, including bike rental.

Pharmacies

Internationale Ludwigs-Apotheke (✉ Neuhauserstr. 11, ☎ 089/260–3021), open weekdays 8–6 and Saturday 8–1, and **Europa-Apotheke** (✉ Schützenstr. 12, near the Hauptbahnhof, ☎ 089/595–423), open weekdays 8–6 and Saturday 8–1, stock a large variety of over-the-counter medications. Munich pharmacies stay open late on a rotating basis, and every pharmacy has a schedule in its window.

Travel Agencies

American Express, (✉ Promenadenpl. 6, ☎ 089/290–900). **DER,** the official German travel agency, has outlets all over Munich. The two most central ones are in the main railway station building (✉ Bahnhofpl. 2, ☎ 089/5514–0100) and at the Münchner-Freiheit Square, in Schwabing (✉ Münchner-Freiheit 6, ☎ 089/336–033).

Visitor Information

Munich has two tourist information offices, at the **Hauptbahnhof** (✉ Bahnhofpl. 2, next to DER travel agency, ☎ 089/2303–0300,✋), open Mon.–Sat. 9–8 and Sun. 10–6, and at the **Info-Service** (✉ Marienpl., ☎ 089/2332–8242) in the Rathaus, open weekdays 10–8, Sat. 10–4.

The monthly English-language magazine *Munich Found* is sold at most newspaper stands and in many hotels.

For information on the Bavarian mountain region south of Munich, contact the **Tourismusverband München-Oberbayern** (Upper Bavarian Regional Tourist Office; ✉ Bodenseestr. 113, D–81243, ☎ 089/829–180).

2 THE BAVARIAN ALPS

This region of fir-clad mountains stretches from Munich to the Austrian border. Quaint towns full of half-timber houses—fronted by flowers in summer, and by snowdrifts in winter—pop up among the peaks, as do the creations of "Mad" King Ludwig II. Shimmering Alpine lakes abound, and the whole area has sporting opportunities galore.

Updated by
Robert Tilley

OBERBAYERN, OR UPPER BAVARIA, is Germany's favorite year-round vacationland and comes closest to what most of us envision as "Germany." Stock images from tourist-office posters—the fairy-tale castles, those too-good-to-be-true villages with brightly frescoed facades, the window boxes abloom, or the sloping roofs heavy with snow—spring to life here. To complete the picture, onion-dome church spires rise out of the mist against the backdrop of the mighty Alps.

This part of Bavaria fans south from Munich to the Austrian border, and as you follow this direction, you'll soon find yourself on a gently rolling plain leading to lakes fed by Alpine rivers and streams and surrounded by ancient forests. In time the plain merges into foothills, which suddenly give way to jagged Alpine peaks. In places such as Königsee, near Berchtesgaden, snowcapped mountains seem to rise straight up from the gemlike lakes.

Continuing south, you'll encounter cheerful villages with richly frescoed houses, some of Germany's finest baroque churches, and several minor spas where you can stay to "take the waters" and tune up your system. Sports possibilities are legion: downhill and cross-country skiing and ice-skating in winter; tennis, swimming, sailing, golf, and, above all (sometimes literally), hiking in summer. Marked hiking trails lead from the glorious countryside, along rivers and lakes, through woods, and high into the Alps.

Pleasures and Pastimes

Castles

Popping up among the peaks are curious castles that were created at the behest of King Ludwig II. For a proper appreciation of Schloss Linderhof and Schloss Herrenchiemsee, it helps to understand this troubled man (☞ Up-Close: The Dream King *in* Chapter 4).

Dining

Designed to pack in the calories after a day's walking or skiing, the food in Bavaria's mountainous areas is understandably hearty and filling. Portions are usually huge, whether they're great wedges of roast pork, dumplings big enough to fire from a cannon, or homemade *Apfelstrudel* (apple-filled pastry), which is a meal in itself. In lakeside inns and restaurants the day's catch might be plump whitefish (*Renke*) or freshwater trout (*Forelle, Lachsforelle,* or *Bachsaibling*). Many inns have pools where the trout grow even fatter, although they lack the mountain-water tang. Most districts in the Alps distill their own brand of schnapps from mountain herbs, and you can quaff what is arguably the region's best beer on the banks of the Tegernsee.

CATEGORY	COST*
$$$$	over DM 90
$$$	DM 55–DM 90
$$	DM 35–DM 55
$	under DM 35

*per person for a three-course meal, including service, and excluding drinks

Lodging

With few exceptions, a hotel or *Gasthof* in the Bavarian Alps and lower Alpine regions has high standards and is traditionally styled, with balconies, pine woodwork, and steep roofs. Garmisch-Partenkirchen and Berchtesgaden provide plenty of accommodations in all price ranges. Check out the special seven-day packages. Private homes all through the region offer Germany's own version of bed-and-breakfasts, indicated by signs reading ZIMMER FREI (rooms available). Their rates may be less than DM 25 per person. As a general rule, the farther from the popular and sophisticated Alpine resorts you go, the lower the rates. In spas and many mountain resorts a "spa tax" is added to the hotel bill. It amounts to no more than DM 5 per person per day and allows free use of spa facilities and entry to local attractions and concerts.

CATEGORY	COST*
$$$$	over DM 200
$$$	DM 160–DM 200
$$	DM 120–DM 160
$	under DM 120

All prices are for two people in a double room, including tax and service charge.

Outdoor Activities and Sports

BIKING

With its lakeside and mountain trails, this is a mountain biker's paradise. Sports shops rent mountain bikes for around DM 20–DM 30 a day.

HIKING AND WALKING

The Bavarian Alpine range is great hiking country. If you just want an afternoon stroll in the champagne air, head for the lower slopes. If you're a serious hiker, make for the mountain trails of the Zugspitze, in Garmisch-Partenkirchen; the heights above Oberammergau, Berchtesgaden, Bad Reichenhall; or the lovely Walchensee. Well-marked trails near the Schliersee or Tegernsee (lakes) lead steadily uphill and to mountaintop inns.

SAILING

All the Bavarian Alpine lakes have sailing schools that rent sailboards as well as various types of boats. On Tegernsee you can hire motorboats at the pier in front of the Schloss Cafe, in the Tegernsee town center. Chiemsee, with its wide stretch of water whipped by Alpine winds, is a favorite for both sailing enthusiasts and windsurfers. There are boatyards all around the lake and a very good windsurfing school at Bernau.

SKIING

Garmisch-Partenkirchen was the site of the 1936 Winter Olympics and remains Germany's premier winter-sports resort. The upper slopes of the Zugspitze and surrounding mountains challenge the best ski buffs, and there are also plenty of runs for intermediate skiers and for families. The slopes above Reit im Winkl (particularly the Winklmoosalm) are less crowded, but the skiing is comparable to the Zugspitze area. All hotels in the region offer skiing packages, often including equipment rental and lift tickets.

Exploring the Bavarian Alps

Numbers in the text correspond to numbers in the margin and on the Bavarian Alps map.

Great Itineraries

The region is too extensive to cover fully in even a month's vacation, so consider basing yourself in one spot (such as Garmisch-Partenkirchen, Berchtesgaden, or a point halfway between, such as the Chiemsee or Tegernsee) and exploring the immediate area—you'll still experience just about everything the Bavarian Alps have to offer. Winter snowfalls can make traveling a nightmare, but if you want to squeeze in as

much as possible, come fair weather or foul, the German Tourist Board
has a recommended route, the Deutsche Alpenstrasse (German Alpine
Road). Allow a week to cover it.

IF YOU HAVE 3 DAYS

Choose between the western (Garmisch-Partenkirchen) area and the
eastern (Berchtesgaden) corner. If busy little ⛰ **Garmisch-Partenkirch-
en** ① is your base, devote a couple of days to exploring the magnificent countryside. Wait for good weather to take the cable car or cog
railway to the summit of Germany's highest mountain, the Zugspitze.
A comfortable day trip takes in the monastery at ⛰ **Ettal** ② and one
of King Ludwig's loveliest palaces, **Schloss Linderhof** ③. Also worth a
visit is **Oberammergau** ④, where the villagers stage the famous Passion Play every 10 years (the next performance is in 2010). Allow a
third day to visit **Mittenwald** ⑤ and its violin museum, taking in the
little village of Klais (with Germany's highest railroad station) on the
way. If you choose instead to devote your three days to ⛰ **Berchtesgaden** ⑳, allow one of them for the trip to the **Obersalzberg** ㉑, site
of Hitler's retreat, called Eagle's Nest, and a second for a boat outing
on Königsee, deep in the mountains' embrace. On the third day choose
between a trip down into Berchtesgaden's salt mine, the Salzbergwerk, or a cross-border run into the neighboring Austrian city of Salzburg.

IF YOU HAVE 5 DAYS

Spend a day or two in ⛰ **Garmisch-Partenkirchen** ①, and then head
for Bavaria's largest lake, ⛰ **Chiemsee** ⑮ (about a two-hour trip via
the autobahn). Overnight in one of the several villages on its western
shore (Prien has a main-line railway station and a boat harbor) and
take boat trips to **Schloss Herrenchiemsee** Island and to the smaller and
utterly enchanting **Fraueninsel.** Round off the journey with two days
in ⛰ **Berchtesgaden** ⑳ and the surrounding countryside.

IF YOU HAVE 7 DAYS

Begin with a day or two based in ⛰ **Garmisch-Partenkirchen** ① for excursions to **Schloss Linderhof** ③ and **Oberammergau** ④. Next strike out
east along the well-signposted Deutsche Alpenstrasse. Leave the route
after 20 km (12 mi), at Wallgau, to relax for an hour or two on the
southern shore of picturesque Walchensee, doubling back later to compare its dark waters with the fresh mountain green of dammed-up Sylvenstein Stausee, to the east. Then dodge in and out of Austria on a
highland road that snakes through the tree-lined Aachen Pass to ⛰ **Tegernsee** ⑩, where hills dip from all sides into the lake. Book two or
three nights at one of the nearby, moderately priced Gasthöfe, or spoil
yourself at one of the luxurious hotels in upscale Rottach-Egern. A day's
walk (or a 20-minute drive) takes you to Tegernsee's neighboring lake,
the shimmering **Schliersee** ⑪. From there the road becomes a switch-
back (one stretch is a privately maintained toll road), climbing from
narrow valleys to mountain ski resorts and finally plunging to the Inn
River valley. Consider leaving the Alpine route here for a stay on the
shores of the ⛰ **Chiemsee** ⑮, where King Ludwig's Schloss Herrenchiemsee stands on one of the three islands. Back on the Alpine route,
you'll inevitably head back into the mountains, dropping down again
into elegant ⛰ **Bad Reichenhall** ⑲, another recommended overnight stop.
From here it's 30 km (18 mi) to ⛰ **Berchtesgaden** ⑳, where you can
spend your final two days viewing the town, its castle museum, Hitler's
mountaintop retreat (Eagle's Nest), and the beautiful Königsee.

When to Tour the Bavarian Alps

This mountainous region is a year-round holiday destination, full of
inviting lakes and Alpine meadows, and a snowy wonderland in winter. Snow is promised by most resorts from December through March,

The Bavarian Alps

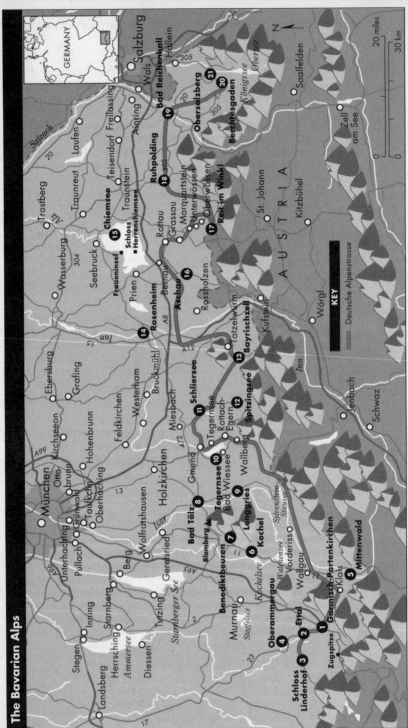

GERMANY

N

20 miles

30 km

KEY
Deutsche Alpenstrasse

Salzburg
Wals
Laufen
Teisendorf Freilassing
Ainring
Bad Reichenhall Hallein
Obersalzberg ㉑ ㉒
㉓ **Berchtesgaden**
Königssee Obersee
Saalfelden
Zell am See
Salzach
Trostberg
Traunreut
Wasserburg
Seebruck
Chiemsee ⑮ **Schloss Herrenchiemsee**
Traunstein
Traunchiemsee
Rottau
Ruhpolding ⑱
Marquartstein
Grassau
Unterwössen
Oberwössen
Reit im Winkl ⑰
St. Johann
Kitzbühel
Frauninsel
Prien
Bernau
⑯ **Aschau**
Rossholzen
⑲
A U S T R I A
Ebersburg
Grafing
Otto-
Kircheseeon
brunn
Hohenbrunn
Oberhaching
Feldkirchen
Westerham
Bruckmühl
Miesbach
Rosenheim ⑭
A8
Inn
A12
Ratzelwirm
Kufstein
Wörgl
Schwaz
Jenbach
Inn
Schliersee ⑪
Bayrischzell ⑬
Spitzingsee ⑫
München
Holzkirchen
Gmund
Tegernsee
Rottach-
Egern
Wallberg
⑩ **Tegernsee**
Wolfratshausen
Gerestried
Isar
Bad Tölz ⑧
Blomberg
Bad Wiessee
Lenggries ⑨
Spitzingsattel
Stauseee
Unterhaching
Pullach
Grünwald
Taufkirchen
Berg
Benediktbeuern
Kochelsee
Kochel ⑥
⑦
Vorderriss
Wallgau
Garmisch-Partenkirchen
Mittenwald ⑤
Inning
Starnberg
Herrsching
Tutzing
Starnberger See
Murnau
Staffelsee
Walchensee
Klais
Landsberg
Diessen
Ammersee
Oberammergau ④
② **Ettal**
Schloss Linderhof ③
Zugspitze ①

although there's year-round skiing on the glacier slopes at the top of the Zugspitze. Spring and autumn are ideal times for mountain walking. November is a between-seasons time, when many hotels and restaurants close down or attend to renovations.

Garmisch-Partenkirchen

❶ *90 km (55 mi) southwest of Munich.*

Garmisch, as it's more commonly known, is the undisputed capital of Alpine Bavaria, a bustling, year-round resort and spa. Once two separate communities, Garmisch and Partenkirchen fused in 1936 to accommodate the Winter Olympics. Today, with a population of 28,000, the area is large enough to offer every facility expected from a major Alpine resort but still not overwhelm. Garmisch is walkable but spread out, and the narrow streets and buildings of smaller Partenkirchen hold snugly to each other. In both parts of town pastel frescoes of biblical and bucolic scenes decorate facades.

Garmisch-Partenkirchen has a long history. Partenkirchen, the older half, was founded by the Romans. You can still follow the road they built between Partenkirchen and neighboring Mittenwald, which was part of a major route between Rome and Germany well into the 17th century. Partenkirchen was spared physical destruction but was devastated economically by the Thirty Years' War. By the early 18th century it was rejuvenated by the discovery of iron ore.

Winter sports rank high on the agenda here. There are more than 99 km (62 mi) of downhill ski runs, 40 ski lifts and cable cars, and 180 km (112 mi) of *Loipen* (cross-country ski trails). One of the principal stops on the international winter-sports circuit, the area hosts a week of races every January. You can usually count on good skiing from December through April (and into May on the Zugspitze).

Garmisch-Partenkirchen isn't all sporty, however. In addition to two Olympic stadiums in the Partenkirchen side of the city, there are some other attractions worth seeing. In Garmisch the pedestrian zone begins at Richard-Strauss-Platz. At its opposite end, off Marienplatz, is the 18th-century parish church of **St. Martin.** It contains some significant stuccowork by the Wessobrunn artists Schmuzer, Schmidt, and Bader. Across the Loisach River, on Pfarrerhausweg, stands another **St. Martin's,** this one dating from 1280, whose Gothic wall paintings include a larger-than-life-size figure of St. Christopher. On Frühlingstrasse are some beautiful examples of Upper Bavarian houses. At the end of Zöppritzstrasse stands the **villa of composer Richard Strauss,** who lived here until his death in 1949. It's the center of activity during the *Richard-Strauss-Tage,* an annual summer music festival devoted to the composer.

The number one attraction in Garmisch is the **Zugspitze,** the highest mountain (9,731 ft) in Germany. There are two ways up the mountain: a leisurely 75-minute ride on a cog railway from the train station in the town center, combined with a cable car ride up the last stretch; or a 10-minute hoist by cable car, which begins its giddy ascent from the Eibsee, 10 km (6 mi) outside town on the road to Austria. If it's summer or autumn (deep snow still clings to the upper slopes in spring), follow one of the well-marked paths to a point where you can pick up the railway to the bottom of the mountain again. There are two restaurants with sunny terraces at the summit and another at the top of the cog railway. A round-trip combination ticket allows you to mix your mode of travel up and down the mountain. Prices are lower in winter than in summer, even though they include use of all the ski lifts on the mountain. You can rent skis at the top. *Cog railway leaves from Olympiastr. 27,* ☎ *08821/7970.* 🎫 *Train or cable car DM 76 (DM 62 Oct.–May) round-trip, parking DM 6.* 🍽

You can take a four-seat cable car to the top of one of the lesser peaks: the **Wank** or the **Alpspitze**, some 2,000 ft lower than the Zugspitze. You can tackle both mountains on foot, provided you're properly shod and physically fit.

If you're making a day trip to the Zugspitze from Munich (or any other southern Bavarian center), take advantage of an unbeatable deal offered by Deutsche Bahn (German Railways; DM 88 for a round-trip ticket, including rail fare and a day's pass to all the Garmisch-Partenkirchen mountains).

Dining and Lodging

For information about accommodation packages with ski passes, call the **Zugspitze** (☎ 08821/7970, ℻ 08821/797–901, 🍽).

$$$ ✕ **Posthotel Partenkirchen.** A 500-year-old vaulted cellar with a hand-painted ceiling is the setting for this elegant restaurant. The menu combines traditional Bavarian dishes with French and vegetarian specialties. ✉ *Ludwigstr. 49,* ☎ *08821/93630. AE, DC, MC, V.*

$$ ✕ **Riessersee.** On the shores of a small, green, tranquil lake—a 3-km (2-mi) walk from town—this café-restaurant is an ideal spot for lunch or afternoon tea (on weekends there's live zither music 3–5). House specialties are fresh trout and local game. ✉ *Riess 6,* ☎ *08821/95440,* ℻ *08821/72589. AE, MC, V. Closed Dec. 1–15.*

$$$$ ✕🏨 **Reindl's Partenkirchner Hof.** Owner Karl Reindl ranks among the world's top hoteliers. His hotel is a real family concern, with Reindl's daughter Marianne in charge of the kitchen. She also collects awards for her international cuisine. The paneled restaurant and public rooms are furnished in a luxurious version of traditional Bavarian country style, with valuable antiques and Oriental rugs mixing harmoniously with farmhouse pieces. Each guest room has pinewood furniture and a balcony or patio. Some of the double rooms are huge. ✉ *Bahnhof-str. 15, D–82467,* ☎ *08821/58025,* ℻ *08821/73401. 65 rooms, 23 suites. Breakfast room, restaurant, bar, indoor pool, sauna, parking. AE, DC, MC, V.* 🍽

$$$–$$$$ ✕🏨 **Grand Hotel Sonnenbichl.** This elegant, established lodging on the outskirts of Garmisch offers panoramic views of the Wetterstein Mountains and the Zugspitze, but only from its front rooms—the rear rooms face a wall of rock. The large windows of its excellent main restaurant also provide a view. ✉ *Burgstr. 97, D–82467,* ☎ *08821/7020,* ℻ *08821/702–131. 90 rooms, 3 suites. 2 restaurants, bar, indoor pool, beauty salon, hot tub, sauna, exercise room. AE, DC, MC, V.*

$$$–$$$$ 🏨 **Wittelsbacher Hof.** Dramatic mountain vistas from bedroom bal-
★ conies and a spacious garden terrace make this hotel especially attractive. Public rooms are elegantly Bavarian, and the restaurant has graceful *Jugendstil* (art-nouveau) features. The bedrooms are spacious, with corner lounge areas and mahogany or cherrywood furniture. Ask for a room facing south for Zugspitze views. ✉ *Von-Brugstr. 24, D–82467,* ☎ 08821/53096, ℻ 08821/57312. *60 rooms, 2 suites. Restaurant, piano bar, indoor pool, sauna, spa. AE, DC, MC, V.*

$$–$$$$ 🏨 **Edelweiss.** Like its namesake, the "eternally white" Alpine flower of *Sound of Music* fame, this small, downtown hotel has plenty of mountain charm. Inlaid with warm pinewood, it has Bavarian furnishings and individually decorated rooms. ✉ *Martinswinkelstr. 15–17, D–82467,* ☎ *08821/2454,* ℻ *09621/4849. 21 rooms, 2 suites, 2 apart-ments. Breakfast room. V.* 🍽

$$ ☆ ⊞ **Gasthof Fraundorfer.** You can sled your way to dreamland in this beautiful old Bavarian Gasthof—some of the beds are carved like old-fashioned sleighs; others take the form of antique automobiles. By contrast, the romantic four-posters in some rooms seem almost prosaic. The colorfully painted facade, covered for most of the year with geraniums, sets the tone for the interior, where hardly a corner is left unpaneled. The tavern-restaurant presents "Bavarian evenings" of folk entertainment. Try their *Bierliquor*—a sweet concoction. ⊠ *Ludwigstr. 24, D–82467,* ☎ *08821/9270,* ℻ *08821/92799. 20 rooms, 7 suites. Restaurant, sauna, steam room. AE, MC, V.* ✍

$$ ☆ ⊞ **Hotel Bergland.** Comfort, reasonable prices, and a good location— what more could you ask of a small, traditional guest house? Great views of Zugspitze? Well, from some rooms. This hotel is in the village of Grainau, on the lower slopes of the Zugspitze, 2 km (1 mi) outside Garmisch. Rooms are furnished in traditional Bavarian style, right down to the painted cupboards and headboards. The cozy lounge, with its open fireplace, is just the place to relax after a day in the mountains. ⊠ *Alpspitzstr. 12–14, D–82491 Grainau,* ☎ *08821/98890,* ℻ *08821/988–999. 14 rooms, 3 suites. Bar, café. AE, DC, MC, V.*

$–$$ ⊞ **Hotel-Gasthof Drei Mohren.** In the historic Partenkirchen village you'll find all the simple, homey comforts you'd expect of a 150-year-old Bavarian inn. All rooms have mountain views, and most are furnished with farmhouse-style painted beds and cupboards; ask for the room with the large four-poster bed. A free bus to Garmisch and the cable car stations parks right outside the house. ⊠ *Ludwigstr. 65, D–82467,* ☎ *08821/9130,* ℻ *08821/18974. 21 rooms, 2 apartments. Restaurant, bar. No credit cards.*

Hiking and Walking

There are innumerable spectacular walks on 300 km (186 mi) of marked trails through the lower slopes' pinewoods and upland meadows. If you have the time and stout walking shoes, try one of the two trails that lead to striking gorges. The **Höllentalklamm** route starts at the Zugspitze Mountain railway terminal in town (⊠ Olympiastr. 27) and ends at the mountaintop (you'll want to turn back before reaching the summit unless you have mountaineering experience). The **Partnachklamm** route is quite challenging; to do all of it, you'll have to stay overnight in one of the huts along the way. It starts at the Olympic ice stadium in town and takes you through a spectacular, tuneled water gorge, past a pretty little mountain lake, and far up the Zugspitze. An easier way to tackle this route is to ride part of the way up in the **Eckbauer cable car** that sets out from the Olympic ice stadium at the end of Olympiastrasse. There's a handy inn at the top where you can gather strength for the hour-long walk back down to the cable car station. **Horse-drawn carriages** also cover the first section of the route in summer; in winter you can skim along it in a **sleigh** (call the local coaching society, the **Lohnkutschevereinigun,** ☎ 08821/942–920). Contact **Deutscher Alpenverein** (⊠ German Alpine Association, Von-Kahr-Str. 2–4, D–80997 Munich, ☎ 089/140–030) for details on hikes and on staying in mountain huts.

Nightlife and the Arts

Bavarian folk dancing and zither music is a regular feature of nightlife here. During the summer there's entertainment every Saturday evening at the **Bayernhalle** (⊠ Brauhausstr. 19). Wednesday through Monday the cozy tavern-restaurant of Gasthof Fraundorfer (⊠ Ludwigstr. 24, ☎ 08821/9270) hosts lots of yodeling and folk dancing. **Concerts** of classical and popular music are presented from Saturday through Thursday, mid-May through September, in the resort park bandstand in Garmisch, and on Friday in the Partenkirchen resort park.

In season there's a busy **après-ski scene.** Many hotels have dance floors, and some have basement discos that pound away until the early hours. Another option is the **casino** (☎ 08821/95990), open daily 3 PM to 3 AM, with more than 100 slot machines, roulette, blackjack, and poker tables.

Ettal

★ ❷ *16 km (10 mi) north of Garmisch-Partenkirchen, 85 km (53 mi) south of Munich.*

The village of Ettal is totally dominated by the massive bulk of **Kloster Ettal,** the great monastery founded in 1330 by Holy Roman Emperor Ludwig the Bavarian for a group of knights and a community of Benedictine monks. The abbey was replaced with new buildings in the 18th century and now serves as a school. Open to visitors, the original 10-sided church was brilliantly redecorated in 1744–53, becoming one of the foremost examples of Bavarian rococo. The church's chief treasure is its enormous dome fresco (83 ft wide), painted by Jacob Zeiller, circa 1751–52. The mass of swirling clouds and the pink-and-blue vision of heaven are typical of the rococo fondness for elaborate and glowing illusionistic ceiling painting.

Ettaler, a liqueur made from a centuries-old recipe, is still distilled at the monastery by the monks. It's made with more than 70 mountain herbs and has legendary health-giving properties. You can buy bottles of the libation from the gift shop and bookstore outside the monastery. This is the largest Benedictine monastery in Germany; approximately 55 monks live here, including one from Compton, Los Angeles. ☎ *08822/740 for guided tour of church.* ⊠ *Free.* ☉ *Daily 8–6.*

Dining and Lodging

$ ✕ **Edelweiss.** This friendly café and restaurant next to the monastery is an ideal spot for a light lunch or coffee and homemade cakes or pastries. ⊠ *Kaiser-Ludwig-Pl. 3,* ☎ *08822/4509. No credit cards.*

$$–$$$ ✕🏠 **Hotel Zur Post.** Families are warmly welcomed at this traditional Gasthof in the center of town. There's a playground in the shady garden, and the cozy Bavarian restaurant has a children's menu. ⊠ *Kaiser-Ludwig-Pl. 18, D–82488,* ☎ *08822/3596,* FAX *08822/6971. 21 rooms, 4 apartments. Restaurant, sauna, steam room, exercise room, playground. MC, V. Closed Oct. 26–Dec. 18.*

$$ ✕🏠 **Benediktenhof.** The open beams and colorfully painted walls are part of this former farmstead's 450-year history. Bedrooms are furnished in Bavarian baroque or peasant style, with brightly decorated cupboards and bedsteads. The farmhouse influence can be felt in the snug restaurant with its very Bavarian menu. The tranquil location on the edge of the Alpine forest encourages sound and undisturbed sleep. ⊠ *Zieglerstr. 1, D–82488,* ☎ *08822/4637,* FAX *08822/7288. 16 rooms, 1 apartment. Restaurant. No credit cards. Closed Nov.–Dec. 22.*

$$ ✕🏠 **Hotel Ludwig der Bayer.** Backed by mountains, this fine old Ettal hotel is run by the Benedictine order. There's nothing monastic about it, except for the exquisite religious carvings and motifs that adorn the walls. Most come from the monastery's own carpentry shop, which also made much of the sturdy furniture in the comfortable bedrooms. The hotel also has its own Bavarian-style apartments equipped with kitchens, but its eateries would tempt even the most dedicated cook. Two atmospheric restaurants and a vaulted tavern serve sturdy fare and beer brewed at the monastery. ⊠ *Werdenfelserstr. 22, D–82488,* ☎ *08822/660–102,* FAX *08822/74480. 70 rooms, 32 apartments. 2 restaurants, 2 bars, indoor pool, sauna, tennis court, bowling, exercise room, paddle tennis, bicycles. MC, V.*

Schloss Linderhof

❸ *10 km (6 mi) west of Ettal on B–23, 95 km (59 mi) south of Munich.*

Built between 1874 and 1878 on the grounds of his father's hunting lodge, Schloss Linderhof was the only one of Ludwig II's royal residences to have been completed during the monarch's short life and the one in which he spent much time. According to hearsay, while staying at Linderhof the eccentric king would dress up as the legendary knight Lohengrin to be rowed in a swan boat on the grotto pond; in winter he took off on midnight sleigh rides behind six plumed horses and a platoon of outriders holding flaring torches (in winter be prepared for an approach road as snowbound as in Ludwig's day—careful driving is called for).

Linderhof was the smallest of this ill-fated king's castles and his favorite country retreat. Set in sylvan seclusion, between a reflecting pool and the green slopes of a gentle mountain, the charming, French-style, rococo confection is said to have been inspired by the Petit Trianon at Versailles. From an architectural standpoint it could well be considered a disaster—a mishmash of conflicting styles, lavish on the outside, vulgarly overdecorated on the inside. Ludwig's bedroom is filled with brilliantly colored and gilded ornaments, the Hall of Mirrors is a shimmering dream world, and the dining room has a clever piece of 19th-century engineering—a table that rises from and descends to the kitchens below. The formal gardens contain still more whimsical touches. There's a Moorish pavilion—bought wholesale from the 1867 Paris Universal Exposition—and a grotto, said to have been modeled on Capri's Blue Grotto, and a gilded Neptune fountain that shoots a jet of water 105 ft into the air. ☎ 08822/92030. ☜ *DM 11, winter DM 8.* ☉ *Apr.–Sept., daily 9–12:15 and 12:45–5:30; Oct.–Mar., daily 10–12:15 and 12:45–4. Pavilion and grotto closed in winter.*

Oberammergau

❹ *20 km (12 mi) northwest of Garmisch-Partenkirchen, 4 km (2½ mi) northwest of Ettal, 90 km (56 mi) south of Munich.*

An amateur—and, some critics say, amateurish—theatrical production has given this small Bavarian town a fame quite out of proportion to its size. Its location alone, though, in an Alpine valley beneath a sentinel-like peak, makes it a major attraction (allow half an hour for the drive from Garmisch). Its main streets are lined with beautifully frescoed houses (such as the 1784 Pilatushaus on Ludwig-Thoma-Strasse), and in summer the village explodes with color as geraniums pour from every window box. Many of these lovely houses are occupied by families whose men are highly skilled wood-carvers, a craft that has flourished here since the depredations of the Thirty Years' War.

Oberammergau, however, is best known for its **Passion Play,** first presented in 1634 as an offering of thanks that the Black Death stopped just short of the village. In faithful accordance with a solemn vow, it will next be performed in the year 2010 as it has every 10 years since 1680. Its 16 acts, which take 5½ hours, depict the final days of Christ, from the Last Supper through the Crucifixion and Resurrection. It is presented daily on a partly open-air stage against a mountain backdrop from late May to late September.

A visit to Oberammergau when the play is on may be a mixed blessing because of the crowds (a half million or more visitors) and the difficulty of obtaining tickets (most are available only through package tours). The entire village is swept up in the production, with some 1,500 residents directly involved in its preparation and presentation. Men grow beards in the hope of capturing a key role; young women have been known to put off their weddings—the role of Mary went only to unmarried girls until the 1990 performances. In that year tradition was broken when—amid much local controversy—a 31-year-old mother of two was given the part.

You'll find many wood-carvers at work in town, and shop windows are crammed with their creations. From June through October a workshop is open free to the public at the **Pilatushaus** (✉ Ludwig-Thoma-Str. 10); working potters and traditional painters can also be seen. You can even sign up for a weeklong course in wood carving (classes are in German), at a cost of between DM 460 and DM 650, bed and breakfast included.

The immense theater in which the Passion Play is performed, the **Oberammergau Passionsspielhaus,** was totally renovated for the performances in 2000 and will again be open to the public in 2001. Hours and admission charges were not available at press time. ✉ *Passionstheater, Passionswiese,* ☎ *08822/32278.*

The **Heimatmuseum** (Natural History Museum) has historic examples of the wood craftsman's art and an outstanding collection of Christmas crèches, which date from the mid-18th century. ✉ *Dorfstr. 8,* ☎ *08822/94136.* 🖰 *DM 4.* ☉ *Mid-May–mid-Oct., Tues.–Sun. 2–6; mid-Oct.–mid-May, Sat. 2–6.*

Oberammergau's 18th-century **St. Peter and St. Paul Church** is regarded as the finest work of rococo architect Josef Schmuzer and has striking frescoes by Matthäus Günther. ✉ *Pfarrpl. 1,* ☎ *08824/553.* ☉ *Daily 9* AM*–sundown.*

Dining and Lodging

$$ ✕ **Ammergauer Stubn.** A homey beer tavern in the Wittelsbach Hotel, the Stubn offers a comprehensive menu that combines Bavarian specialties with international dishes. ✉ *Dorfstr. 21,* ☎ *08822/1011. AE, DC, MC. Closed Tues. and Nov. 7–Dec. 10.*

$ ✕ **Alte Post.** You can enjoy carefully prepared local cuisine on the original pine tables in this 350-year-old inn. There's a special children's menu, and in summer meals are also served in the beer garden. ✉ *Dorfstr. 19,* ☎ *08822/9100. AE, MC, V. Closed Nov.–Dec. 25.*

$$$ ✕🛏 **Hotel Turmwirt.** Rich wood paneling reaches from floor to ceil-
★ ing in this transformed 18th-century inn, set in the shadow of Oberammergau's mountain, the Kofel. The hotel's own band presents regular Bavarian folk evenings in the cozy restaurant. Rooms have corner lounge areas, and most come with balconies and sweeping mountain views. ✉ *Ettalerstr. 2, D–82487,* ☎ *08822/92600,* 𝖥𝖠𝖷 *08822/1437. 22 rooms. Restaurant, recreation room. AE, DC, MC, V. Closed most of Jan. and Nov.–mid-Dec.*

$$–$$$ ✕🛏 **Hotel Böld.** A boldly painted facade and geranium-hung balconies make the Böld one of the handsomest buildings in central Oberammergau. It's a rambling, friendly, family-run place. The restaurant prides itself on a menu that combines traditional fare with international cuisine. All rooms here can accommodate people in wheelchairs. ✉ *König-Ludwig-Str. 10, D–82487,* ☎ *08822/9120,* 𝖥𝖠𝖷 *08822/7102. 57 rooms, 42 with bath or shower. Restaurant, beer garden, hot tub, sauna, steam room, exercise room, paddle tennis, bicycles. AE, DC, MC, V.*

$$–$$$ ✕🛏 **Hotel Landhaus Feldmeier.** This quiet country-style hotel, idyllically set just outside the village, has mostly spacious rooms decorated with modern pinewood furniture. All have geranium-bedecked balconies,

with views of the village and mountains. The rustic restaurant is one of the region's best. ✉ *Ettalerstr. 29, D–82487,* ☎ *08822/3011,* FAX *08822/6631. 22 rooms. Hot tub, sauna, steam room, exercise room. MC, V. Closed mid-Nov.–mid–Dec.* ✇

$$–$$$ ✕☷ **Hotel Wolf.** The hotel's Hafner Stube is a popular local haunt, with a menu that will satisfy large appetites. The attractive, old hotel also draws Americans, who make up about a third of the guest list. Blue shutters punctuate its white walls, and the steeply gabled upper stories bloom with flowers. ✉ *Dorfstr. 1, D–82487,* ☎ *08822/3071,* FAX *08822/1096. 32 rooms. Restaurant, 2 bars, café, outdoor pool, sauna. AE, DC, MC, V.*

$$$ ☷ **Parkhotel Sonnenhof.** Away from the sometimes crowded town center, the modern Sonnenhof provides a balcony with every guest room, so you can sun yourself and soak up the Alpine view. There's also a children's playroom. ✉ *König-Ludwig-Str. 12, D–82487,* ☎ *08822/9130,* FAX *08822/3047. 65 rooms, 2 suites. Bar, indoor pool, sauna, bowling, billiards. AE, DC, MC, V.*

Mittenwald

❺ *20 km (12 mi) southeast of Garmisch, 90 km (56 mi) south of Munich.*

Many regard Mittenwald as the most beautiful town in the Bavarian Alps. Its medieval prosperity is reflected on its main street, with splendidly decorated houses with ornately carved gables and brilliantly painted facades. The town has a pedestrian zone to rival any city's and has restored an important historical feature by re-creating the stream that once flowed through the market square.

In the Middle Ages Mittenwald was the staging point for goods shipped from Verona by way of the Brenner Pass and Innsbruck. From there goods were transferred to rafts, which carried them down the Isar to Munich. In the mid-17th century, however, the international trade route was moved to a different pass, and the fortunes of Mittenwald declined.

In 1684 Matthias Klotz, a farmer's son–turned–master violin maker, returned from a 20-year stay in Cremona, Italy. There, along with Antonio Stradivari, he had studied under Nicolo Amati, who gave the violin its present form. Klotz taught the art of violin making to his brothers and friends; before long, half the men in the village were creating the instruments using woods from neighboring forests. Mittenwald became known as "the Village of a Thousand Violins," and stringed instruments—violins, violas, and cellos—were shipped around the world. Klotz's craft is still carried on in Mittenwald; he's memorialized as an artist at work in a vivid bronze sculpted by Ferdinand von Miller (1813–79), creator of the mighty Bavaria monument in Munich. The statue stands in front the parish church of St. Peter and St. Paul.

The **Geigenbau und Heimatmuseum** describes in fascinating detail the history of the making of the violin (in German, *Geigenbau*) in Mittenwald. Ask the museum curator to direct you to the nearest of the several violin makers who are still active—they'll be happy to demonstrate the skills handed down to them. ✉ *Ballenhausg. 3,* ☎ *08823/2511.* ☷ *DM 3.* ☉ *Weekdays 10–noon and 2–5, weekends 10–noon. Closed Nov.–mid-Dec.*

On the back of the altar in the 18th-century **St. Peter and St. Paul Church,** you'll find Matthias Klotz's name, carved there by the violin maker himself. In front of the church is a monument to him. The church, with its elaborate and joyful stuccowork coiling and curling its way around the interior, is one of the most important rococo structures in Bavaria. Note its Gothic choir loft, added in the 18th century. The bold frescoes on its exterior are characteristic of *Lüftlmalerei*, a style that reached its height in Mittenwald. Images, usually religious motifs, were painted on the wet stucco exteriors of houses and churches. On nearby streets you can see other fine examples on the facades of three famous houses: the Goethehaus, the Pilgerhaus, and the Pichlerhaus. ⊠ *Next to Geigenbau und Heimatmuseum.*

Dining and Lodging

$$–$$$ ✕ **Arnspitze.** Get a table at the large picture window and soak in the view of the towering Karwendel Mountain range as you ponder a menu that combines the best Bavarian traditional ingredients with international flair. The fish pot-au-feu is Mediterranean in flavor and appearance; the jugged hare in red wine is truly Bavarian. ⊠ *Innsbrucker Str. 68,* ☎ *08823/2425. AE. Closed Tues. and Nov.–mid-Dec. No lunch Wed.*

$$$–$$$$ ✕🏠 **Post.** Stagecoaches carrying travelers and mail across the Alps stopped here as far back as the 17th century. The hotel has changed a lot since then, but it still retains much of its historic charm. If you're having dinner, pause by the open fire in the cozy lounge-bar while you choose between the wine tavern and the low-beamed Poststüberl. The food in each is excellent, with the emphasis on hearty Bavarian fare. ⊠ *Obermarkt 9, D–82481,* ☎ *08823/1094,* 𝖥𝖠𝖷 *08823/1096. 74 rooms, 7 suites. 2 restaurants, bar, indoor pool, sauna, bowling, paddle tennis. No credit cards.*

$$ ✕🏠 **Alpenrose.** Once part of a monastery and later given a beautiful baroque facade, the Alpenrose is one of the area's handsomest hotels. Bedrooms and public rooms are decorated in typical Bavarian style, with lots of wood paneling, farmhouse cupboards, and finely woven fabrics. The restaurant devotes the entire month of October to venison dishes, for which it has become renowned. In winter the hotel organizes sleigh rides for its guests. A zither player strums away most evenings in the Josefi wine cellar. ⊠ *Obermarkt 1, D–82481,* ☎ *08823/92700,* 𝖥𝖠𝖷 *08823/3720. 16 rooms, 2 apartments. Restaurant, bar, sauna. AE, DC, MC, V.*

$$–$$$ 🏠 **Bichlerhof.** Carved oak furniture gives the rooms of this Alpine-style hotel a solid, traditionally German feel. Late-starters are catered to with a breakfast buffet, which is served until 11 AM; the solid German fare will keep the hardiest hiker going all day. Although the restaurant serves only breakfast, there's no shortage of taverns in the area. Most guest rooms have fine mountain views. ⊠ *Adolf-Baader-Str. 5, D–82481,* ☎ *08823/9190,* 𝖥𝖠𝖷 *08823/4584. 23 rooms, 2 suites. Indoor pool, sauna, steam room, exercise room. AE, DC, MC, V.*

Hiking and Walking

Mittenwald lies literally in the shadow of the mighty Karwendel Alpine range, which rises to a height of nearly 8,000 ft. A cable car and a long chairlift reach high into the mountains, giving year-round access for skiers and hikers. You can book a guide with **Bergerlebnis und Wanderschule Oberes Isartal** (☎ 08651/5835). At least a half dozen operators offer countryside sleigh rides. Try **Reisebüro Artz** (⊠ Bahnhofstr. 6, ☎ 08651/5070) or inquire at your hotel's reception desk.

Shopping

It's not the kind of gift every visitor wants to take home, but just in case you'd like a violin, cello, or even a double bass, the Alpine resort of Mittenwald can oblige. There are more than 30 craftsmen whose work is coveted by musicians throughout the world. If you're buying or even just curious, call on **Anton Maller** (⊠ Professor–Schreyögg–

Pl., ☎ 08823/5865). He's been making violins and other stringed instruments for more than 25 years. Another good place for the town's famous stringed instruments is **Geigenbau Leonhardt** (✉ Mühlenweg 53a, ☎ 08823/8010). For traditional Bavarian costumes—dirndls, embroidered shirts and blouses, and lederhosen—try **Trachten Werner** (✉ Hochstr. 1, ☎ 08823/3785). **Trachten Werner-Leichtl** (✉ Dekan-Karl-Pl. 1, ☎ 08823/8282) has a large selection of dirndls and other traditional wear for women.

En Route   One of the most beautiful stretches of the Deutsche Alpenstrasse follows the course of the fast-flowing Isar River and is lined by fir-clad slopes and rocky peaks. The first 15 km (9 mi) of this stretch from Wallgau (7 km [4½ mi] north of Mittenwald at the junction of the road north to Benediktbeuren) to Vorderiss is a toll road (DM 4 per vehicle). Vorderiss is at the western end of the Sylvenstein dam-lake, a mysterious sliver of water whose dark surface covers a submerged village. Ghosts linger in the cool air. Halfway along the lake the road divides, east to the Achen Pass and on to Tegernsee and north to the Alpine resort of Lenggries and Bad Tölz.

Walchensee

20 km (12 mi) north of Mittenwald, on the B–11 80 km (50 mi) south of Munich.

The first of the truly Alpine lakes the traveler encounters north of Mittenwald and Garmisch is the beautiful Walchensee, whose deep, blue waters are ringed by fir-clad mountains and the twin peaks of the Benediktenwand and Herzogstand. Hiking trails lead off from the town of Walchensee, and the rapidly changing winds of the Walchensee make this stretch of water a surfer's paradise. A chairlift climbs to the summit of the 5,300-ft-high **Herzogstand** (DM 22 round-trip).

Dining and Lodging

$$ ✕🏠 **Aparthotel Post.** Accommodation at this modernized country inn on the shore of the Walchensee is in spacious, comfortable, and traditionally furnished apartments—most of them with lake views. The restaurant also overlooks the lake, and on warm days you can dine outside and watch the windsurfers glide by. Specialties include whitefish right out of the lake. ✉ *Urfeld 8111, D–82431,* ☎ *08851/249,* FAX *08851/5067. 20 apartments. Restaurant. No credit cards.*

Kochel

❻ *35 km (22 mi) north of Mittenwald, on the B–11 60 km (37 mi) south of Munich.*

A serpentine mountain road leads to an almost contiguous lake, equally spectacular **Kochelsee.** The hero of the attractive little lakeside town of Kochel is the Schmied von Kochel, or Blacksmith of Kochel. His fame stems from his role—and eventual death—in the 1705 peasants' uprising at Sendling, just outside Munich. You can see his statue in the town center. The lake is a longtime favorite for summer getaways and offers good water sports and mountain walks.

The Kochelsee and the nearby, gentler, and less dramatic Staffelsee provided the inspiration for the bohemian artists who called themselves the *Blauer Reiter* (Blue Rider). Russian painters Wassily Kandinsky and Alfred Kubin and French artist Franz Marc founded the group in 1911 and were later joined by artists such as Paul Klee and August Macke. The best collection of works by the Blauer Reiter group is in Munich, at the Städtische Galerie im Lenbachhaus (☞ Exploring *in* Chapter 1).

A museum devoted to Marc's work can be found in Kochel. **Museum Franz Marc** (⊠ Herzogstandweg 43, ☎ 08851/7114; 🎟 DM 5; ⊘ Apr.–Oct., Tues.–Sun. 2–6).

🖐 The lido **Trimini,** on the shores of the Kochelsee, is one of the largest and most spectacular in Bavaria, with a collection of indoor and outdoor pools, water slides, and enough other amusements to keep a family busy the whole day. ⊠ *Trimini,* ☎ *08851/5300.* 🎟 *3-hr ticket DM 12, all-day family ticket DM 42.* ⊘ *Daily 9–8:30.*

The 5,400-ft-high **Benediktenwand,** east of Kochel, is a challenge for mountaineers.

OFF THE BEATEN PATH   **MURNAU** – On the shore of Staffelsee, Blauer Reiter group members Wassily Kandisky and his German wife, Gabriele Münter, lived for five years in Das Münter Haus–das "Russenhaus" (Russian House). The house has been restored and offers an insight into the lives of the artist couple—including furniture that they decorated to their own highly individual, colorful tastes. ⊠ *Kottmüllerallee 6, D–82418 Murnau, 16 km (10 mi) west of Kochelsee, following unmarked country road skirting northern shore of Staffelsee* ☎ *08841/628–880.* 🎟 *DM 5.* ⊘ *Tues.–Sun. 2–5.*

Dining and Lodging

$$$$ ✕🏨 **Alpenhof.** All the luxurious rooms at this handsome, Bavarian-style hotel enjoy views over meadows to the Alps beyond. They're furnished in rich dark woods and matching colors such as wine-red and forest-green. The elegant, softly lit restaurant ($$$), boasting a Michelin star, rightly claims to be one of the area's best. Window tables have sweeping Alpine views. ⊠ *Ramsachstr. 8, D–82418 Murnau,* ☎ *08841/4910,* 📠 *08841/5438. 60 rooms, 17 suites. Restaurant, Weinstube, 1 outdoor and 1 indoor pool, sauna, steam room, exercise room. AE, MC, V.* 🐾

$$–$$$ ✕🏨 **Alpenhotel Schmied von Kochel.** Under the eaves of a steep roof, flower-box-hung balconies are framed by brightly painted wall frescoes, making this the belle of Bavaria. The state's blue-and-white-check banner hangs in the tree-shaded beer garden. Farmhouse furniture and antiques complete the scene, which is given a final musical touch by the zither player who strums away regularly in the snug tavern. ⊠ *Schlehdorferstr. 6, D–82431,* ☎ *08851/9010,* 📠 *08851/7331. 33 rooms, 1 apartment. Restaurant, bar, beer garden, café, hot tub, sauna. MC, V.*

$$–$$$ ✕🏨 **Seehotel Grauer Bär.** The friendly atmosphere at this hotel, on the shore of the Kochelsee, has much to do with the family that has owned and managed it since 1905. Ask for one of the spacious rooms overlooking the lake, where the hotel also has its own stretch of private beach. Lake fish entrées often appear on the extensive menu of the airy pavilion-style restaurant, where you should try to book a table overlooking the water. ⊠ *Mittenwalderstr. 82–86, D–82431,* ☎ *08851/92500,* 📠 *08851/925–015. 26 rooms, 3 apartments. Restaurant, café, boating, bicycles. AE, DC, MC, V.*

OFF THE BEATEN PATH   **FREILICHTMUSEUM AN DER GLENTLEITEN** – This open-air museum looks and functions just as a Bavarian village did centuries ago, complete with cobbler, blacksmith, and other craftsmen who would have kept such a community self-sufficient. ⊠ *Grossweil, near Kochelsee, off Munich-Garmisch Autobahn,* ☎ *08851/1850.* 🎟 *DM 7.50.* ⊘ *Apr.–Oct., Tues.–Sun. 9–6.*

Benediktbeuren

7 *45 km (28 mi) north of Mittenwald, 52 km (32 mi) south of Munich.*

The village of Benediktbeuren has a great mid-8th-century **monastery** thought to be the oldest Benedictine institution north of the Alps. It was a flourishing cultural center in the Middle Ages; paradoxically, it also kept record of the most profane poems and songs of those times, the *carmina burana* (also known as the Goliardic songs). During the summer these songs are performed, using Bavarian composer Carl Orff's 1937 orchestration, in the monastery, where the original work was compiled in the 12th century. The frescoes of the monastery's 17th-century church were painted by the father of the Asam brothers, whose church building and artistic decoration made them famous far beyond the borders of 18th-century Bavaria. Cosmas Damian Asam, the eldest son, was born at Benediktbeuren. ☏ *08857/880 for concert information.* ▣ *DM 5.* ◷ *Monastery church daily 8–6; guided tour of monastery July–Sept., daily at 2:30; Oct.–mid-May, weekends at 2:30; mid-May–June, Sat. and Wed. at 2:30, Sun. at 10:30 and 2:30.*

Bad Tölz

8 *16 km (10 mi) northeast of Benediktbeuren, 45 km (28 mi) south of Munich.*

If you can, visit Bad Tölz on a Wednesday morning—market day—when stalls stretch along the main street to the Isar River, the dividing line between the old and new towns. The latter, dating from the mid-19th century, sprang up with the discovery of iodine-laden springs, which allowed the locals to call their town *Bad* (bath or spa) Tölz. You can take the waters, either by drinking a cupful from the local springs or going all the way with a full course of health treatments at a specially equipped hotel.

Bad Tölz clings to its ancient customs more tightly than does any other Bavarian community. Folk costumes, for example, are worn regularly. The town is also famous for its painted furniture, particularly farmhouse cupboards and chests. Several local shops specialize in this *Bauernmöbel* (farmhouse furniture) and will usually handle export formalities.

If you're in Bad Tölz on November 6, you'll witness one of the most colorful traditions of the Bavarian Alpine area: the Leonhardifahrt equestrian procession, which marks the feast day of St. Leonhard, the patron saint of horses. The procession ends north of the town at an 18th-century chapel on the Kalvarienberg, above the Isar River.

★ The **Alpamare,** Bad Tölz's very attractive lido, pumps spa water into its pools, one of which is disguised as a South Sea beach, complete with surf. Its five water slides include a 1,082-ft-long adventure run, Germany's longest. Another—the Alpa-Canyon—has 90-degree drops, and only the hardiest swimmers are advised to try it. A nightmarish dark tunnel is aptly named the Thriller. ⌧ *Ludwigstr. 13,* ☏ *08041/509–334.* ▣ *4-hr ticket DM 31 weekdays, DM 36 weekends and school holidays; between 9 AM and 11 AM and after 5 PM price drops by up to DM 11.* ◷ *Mon.–Thurs. 9–9; Fri.–Sun., and public holidays 9 AM–10 PM.* ▨

The **Heimatmuseum,** in the Altes Rathaus (Old Town Hall), has many fine examples of Bauernmöbel (Bavarian farmhouse furniture, usually hand-carved from pine), as well as a fascinating exhibition on the history of the town and its environs. ⌧ *Marktstr. 48,* ☏ *08041/504–688.* ▣ *DM 4.* ◷ *Tues., Wed., and Fri. 10–noon and 2–4; Thurs. 10–noon and 2–6; Sat. 10–4; Sun. and public holidays 10–6.*

☺ Bad Tölz's local mountain, the **Blomberg,** 3 km (2 mi) west of town,
has moderately difficult ski runs, and can also be tackled on a toboggan in winter and in summer. The winter run of 5 km (3 mi) is the longest
in Bavaria, while the artificial, concrete channel used in summer snakes
3,938 ft down the mountain. A ski-lift ride to the start of the run and
toboggan rental are included in the price. ☎ 08041/3726. ☞ DM 12
per ride. ◷ Dec.–Nov., daily 9–6; Nov.–Dec., hrs depend on weather
conditions.

Dining and Lodging

$$$$ ✕☱ **Hotel Jodquellenhof-Alpamare.** The Jodquellen are the iodine
  ★   springs that have made Bad Tölz wealthy. You can take advantage of
these revitalizing waters at this luxurious spa hotel, where the emphasis
is on fitness. Vegetarian and low-calorie entrées are served in the
restaurant. The imposing 19th-century building, with private access
to the Alpamare Lido, contains comfortable and stylish rooms, with
granite and marble bathrooms. ⊠ Ludwigstr. 13–15, D–83646, ☎
08041/5090, ℻ 08041/509–441. 81 rooms. Restaurant, pool, sauna.
AE, DC, MC, V.

$$$ ☱ **Hotel Bellaria.** This beautifully restored 19th-century villa with
baroque furnishings is just the place for lovers—or for any romantic
at heart. Its young owners will reserve the basement sauna and hot tub
for evenings à deux, with a candelabra and bottle of champagne as part
of the service. The spa park and pedestrian mall are right outside the
door. ⊠ Ludwigstr. 22, D–83646, ☎ 08041/80080, ℻ 08041/800–
844. 26 rooms, 1 apartment. Beauty salon, hot tub, sauna, exercise
room. MC, V. Closed mid-Nov.–early Dec. ✎

Nightlife and the Arts

Bad Tölz is world renowned for its outstanding **boys choir.** When it's
not on tour, the choir gives regular concerts in the Kurhaus (program
details available from the Städtische Kurverwaltung, ☎ 08041/78670)
The town has four discos; **Arena** (⊠ Demmeljochstr. 42) is considered
the best.

Shopping

Looking for a typical piece of Bavarian farmhouse furniture to ship
home? Bad Tölz and the surrounding villages provide a rich hunting
ground. Try the **Scheune** (⊠ Miesbacherstr. 33, ☎ 09041/83240), an
old barn stacked high with pine and oaken cupboards, tables, chairs,
and carved bedsteads.

Lenggries

❾ 10 km (6 mi) south of Bad Tölz, 12 km (7 mi) north of Sylvenstein
Lake, 55 km (34 mi) south of Munich.

Lenggries is a small but popular ski resort, wedged into a narrow val-
ley between the towering Benediktenwand Mountain and the peaks of
the Tegernsee Alps. There are fine walks into the Brauneck mountain
range and along the Isar, and the skiing is the best in the region.

Dining and Lodging

$$$ ✕☱ **Arabella Brauneck Hotel.** Arabella is a German chain known for
its refinements, and its leading Bavarian Alpine hotel does not disap-
point. Many rooms have views of the mountains that ring Lenggries,
and the lifts are a short walk from the hotel. The Isargrotte sauna-whirl-
pool offers great après-ski relaxation. Good international cuisine is served
in the stylish restaurant. ⊠ Münchner Str. 25, D–83661, ☎ 08042/
5020, ℻ 08042/4224. 98 rooms, 7 apartments. Restaurant, bar, hot
tub, sauna, steam room, bowling, paddle tennis, bicycles. AE, DC, MC,
V. Closed Easter and mid-July–mid-Aug.

$ ✕▣ **Altwirt.** The history of this former coaching inn stretches back to the 15th century. Its restaurant serves such regional specialties as venison with cranberry sauce and egg noodles; its rooms are neat and plain. ✉ *Marktstr. 13, D–83661,* ☎ *08042/8085,* 𝕱𝕬𝕏 *08042/5357. 20 rooms. Restaurant, sauna. MC, V.*

Tegernsee

★ ➓ *16 km (10 mi) east of Bad Tölz, 50 km (31 mi) south of Munich.*

The beautiful shores of the Tegernsee are among the most expensive properties in all Germany. So many wealthy Germans have their homes here that the locals dubbed it the Lago di Bonzo (*bonze* means "big shot," and the Italian word *lago* suggests expensive lake resorts where Mafia bosses lurk). Although many houses qualify as small palaces, most hotels have sensible rates. Tegernsee's wooded shores, rising gently to scalable mountain peaks of no more than 6,300 ft, invite hikers, walkers, and picnicking families (the tourist office in the town of Tegernsee has hiking maps). The lake itself draws swimmers and yachters. In fall the russet-clad trees provide a colorful contrast to the dark, snow-capped mountains.

On the eastern shore of the lake, the town of Tegernsee is home to a medieval **Benedictine monastery** (✉ Schlosspl.). Founded in the 8th century, this was one of the most productive cultural centers in southern Germany; the Minnesänger (musician and poet) Walther von der Vogelweide (1170–1230) was a welcome guest. Not so welcome were Hungarian invaders, who laid waste to the monastery in the 10th century. Fire caused further damage in following centuries, and secularization sealed the monastery's fate at the beginning of the 19th, when Bavarian king Maximilian I bought the surviving buildings for use as a summer retreat.

The late-Gothic **church** was refurbished in Italian baroque style in the 18th century. Opinions remain divided as to the success of the remodeling, which was the work of a little-known Italian architect named Antonio Riva. The frescoes are by Hans Georg Asam, whose work also graces the Benediktbeuren monastery. The property also houses a beer tavern, a brewery, a restaurant, and a high school. Students in what was the monastery write their exams beneath inspiring baroque frescoes.

Maximilian showed off this corner of his kingdom to Czar Alexander of Russia and Emperor Franz Josef of Austria during their journey to the Congress of Verona in October 1822, and you can follow their steps through the woods to one of the loveliest lookout points in Bavaria, the **Grosses Paraplui.** A plaque marks the spot where they admired the open expanse of the Tegernsee and the mountains beyond. The path starts opposite Schlossplatz and is well marked.

Rottach-Egern is the fashionable and upscale resort at the southern end of the lake. Its classy shops, chic restaurants, and expensive boutiques are as well stocked and interesting as many in Munich; its leading hotels are world class. Rottach-Egern's church, **St. Laurentius,** has baroque influences.

Dining and Lodging

$$–$$$ ✕ **Freihaus Brenner.** Proprietor Josef Brenner has brought a taste of nouvelle cuisine to the Tegernsee, where his attractive restaurant commands fine views from high above Bad Wiessee. Try any of his suggested dishes, ranging from wild rabbit in elderberry sauce to fresh lake fish. ✉ *Freihaushöhe 4, Bad Wiessee,* ☎ *08022/82004. DC, MC, V.*

$ ✕ **Herzogliches Bräustüberl.** Once part of Tegernsee's Benedictine monastery, then a royal retreat, the Bräustüberl is now an immensely popular beer hall and brewery. Only basic Bavarian snacks (sausages, pretzels, a deliciously marshmallowlike baked Camembert) are served in this crowded place, but hearty Bavarian meals can be ordered in the adjoining Keller. In summer quaff your beer beneath the huge chestnuts and admire the lake and mountains over the rim of your glass. ⊠ *Schlosspl. 1, Tegernsee,* ☎ *08022/4141. Reservations not accepted. No credit cards. Closed Nov.*

$ ✕ **Weinhaus Moschner.** You're pretty much expected to drink wine in this dark, old tavern on the edge of ritzy Rottach-Egern. Beer, from the monastery brewery in Tegernsee, is also served, and the waitresses probably won't protest if you order it. The menu sticks to local Bavarian fare (heavy on the sausage), but nobody comes here just to eat. Join the locals at a rough wooden table in the log-wall tavern taproom, order a plate of smoked pork and a glass of ale or Franconian wine, and leave the fine dining until tomorrow—it's the camaraderie and atmosphere here that counts. Those under 30 will love the first-floor disco, although the rough charm of the lederhosen-clad locals may distract you. ⊠ *Kisslingerstr. 2, Rottach-Egern,* ☎ *08022/5522. No credit cards. Closed Mon. and Tues.*

$$$$ ✕🏨 **Hotel Bayern.** The elegant, turreted Bayern and its two spacious annexes sit high above the Tegernsee, backed by the wooded slopes of Neureuth Mountain. Rooms overlooking the lake are in big demand despite their relatively high cost, so book early. All guests can enjoy panoramic views of the lake and mountains from the extensive terrace fronting the main building. You can dine in the hotel's stylish little restaurant or the cozy tavern. ⊠ *Neureuthstr. 23, D–83684 Tegernsee,* ☎ *08022/1820,* ℻ *08022/3775. 83 rooms, 4 suites. Restaurant, bar, indoor pool, beauty salon, spa, bowling. AE, MC, V.* ☕

$$$ ✕🏨 **Der Leeberghof.** The chamois that scramble up and down the highest Tegernsee peaks often find their way into the cooking pot of the Leeberghof's excellent kitchen. Venison of all kinds and whitefish fresh from the lake are regularly on the menu. On warm evenings take an aperitif or an after-dinner Bavarian schnapps on the bar-terrace above the lake. If you decide to stay the night, there are three very comfortable rooms and an apartment, all with balconies and lake views. ⊠ *Ellingerstr. 10, D–83684 Tegernsee,* ☎ *08022/3966,* ℻ *08022/1720. 3 rooms, 1 apartment. Restaurant, bar. AE, MC. Closed Mon. and Tues.*

$$$ ✕🏨 **Seegarten.** This lakeside hotel, with pinewood wall paneling and matching furniture, has cheerful rooms decorated in the bright primary colors typical of the Bavarian country-farmhouse style. Ask for a room with a balcony overlooking the Tegernsee. The Seegarten's kitchen is famous for its cakes, served in the restaurant or, in summer, on the lakeside terrace. In winter a log fire and hot, spiced wine welcome you in the cozy vestibule. ⊠ *Adrian-Stoop-Str. 4, D–83707 Bad Wiessee,* ☎ *08022/98490,* ℻ *08022/85087. 33 rooms. Restaurant. AE, V.*

$$–$$$ ✕🏨 **Seehotel Zur Post.** The lake views from most rooms in this hotel are somewhat compromised by the main road outside, but its central location and a fine winter garden and terrace are pluses. The restaurant serves fresh fish, but there are also special venison weeks, worthy of a long detour. ⊠ *Seestr. 3, D–83684 Tegernsee,* ☎ *08022/3951,* ℻ *08022/1699. 43 rooms, 39 with bath or shower. Restaurant. DC, MC, V. Closed Jan.–Feb. 15.*

$$$$ 🏨 **Hotel Bachmair am See.** Set in parklike grounds between the lakeside and a mountain range, this luxurious complex of five hotels and guest houses is the place for a splurge. Prices are high, but the range and quality of the amenities are unmatched in this part of Bavaria. The hotel's nightclub attracts international entertainers. Teatime in the

main building's elegant lounge, overlooking the lake, is a Savoy-style experience. ✉ *Seestr. 47, D–83700 Rottach-Egern,* ☎ *08022/2720,* FAX *08022/272–790. 100 rooms, 10 apartments. 4 restaurants, 2 bars, indoor and outdoor pools, beauty salon, sauna, 2 tennis courts, exercise room, squash, bicycles, nightclub. AE, DC, MC, V.* ☜

$$ 🏨 **Margaritenhaus.** This handsome Bavarian-style mansion has 25 individually designed and furnished apartments, all with kitchen facilities and either balconies or garden terraces, most with lake views. They're normally rented only by the week. One (Apartment Mathilde) even has a modern, glassed-in fireplace for winter evenings. The lake and mountain slopes are just a short walk. Bavarian restaurants and taverns are also nearby, as are hotels that have regular evenings of Bavarian zither music and dancing. ✉ *Adrian-Stoop-Str. 32, D–83684 Bad Wiessee,* ☎ *08022/860–340. 25 apartments. Laundry. No credit cards.*

Nightlife and the Arts

Every resort has its **spa orchestra**—in the summer they play daily in the music-box-style bandstands that dot the lakeside promenades. A strong Tegernsee tradition is the summer-long program of **festivals,** some set deep in the forest. Tegernsee's lake festival in August, when sailing clubs deck their boats with garlands and lanterns, is an unforgettable experience.

Bad Wiessee has a lakeside **casino** (☎ 08022/82028) that's open daily 3 PM–3 AM and sets the tone for a surprisingly lively after-dark scene around the Tegernsee. The **Leeberghof** (✉ Ellingerstr. 10, ☎ 08022/3966), on the edge of Tegernsee town, has a sensational terrace bar with prices to match one of Bavaria's finest views.

Shopping

Bad Tölz and nearby villages are famous for the beauty and colorful variety of their traditional dress. In Bad Tölz, follow the lovely Marktstrasse up from the river and look out for the outsize top hat at the corner of Hindenburgstrasse, at No. 61a Marktstrasse. Here you'll find all the region can offer—in the shop of Gregor and Maria Schöttl. **Trachten Brendl** (✉ Hauptstr. 8, Tegernsee, ☎ 08022/3322) has a colorful selection of Bavarian traditional costumes and other handwoven fabrics. At her workshop just outside Gmund, **Marianne Winter-Andres** (✉ Miesbacherstr. 88, Gmund, ☎ 08022/74643) creates a wide and attractive range of high-quality pottery at sensible prices.

OFF THE BEATEN PATH
WALLBERG – For the best vista in the area, climb this 5,700-ft mountain at the south end of the Tegernsee. It's a hard four-hour hike, though anyone in good shape should be able to make it since it involves no rock climbing. A cable car makes the ascent in just 15 minutes and costs DM 14 one-way, DM 23 round-trip. At the summit there are a restaurant and sun terrace and several trailheads; in winter the skiing is excellent.

Schliersee

🕚 *20 km (12 mi) east of Tegernsee, 55 km (34 mi) southeast of Munich.*

Schliersee is smaller, quieter, and less fashionable than Tegernsee, but hardly less beautiful. The difference between the two lakes is made clear in the names local people have long given them: the Tegernsee is called the Herrensee (Masters' Lake), while the Schliersee is known as the Bauernsee (Peasants' Lake). There are fine walking and ski trails on the mountain slopes that ring its placid waters. The lake is shallow and often freezes over in winter, when the tiny island in its center is a favorite hiking destination.

Like its neighbor, the Schliersee was the site of a monastery, built in the 8th century by a group of noblemen. It subsequently became a choral academy, which eventually moved to Munich. Today only the restored 17th-century **abbey church** recalls this piece of the Schliersee's history. The church has some fine frescoes and stuccowork by Johann Baptist Zimmermann.

Dining and Lodging

$$ ✕🏠 **Hotel Gasthof Terofal.** This handsome, steep-eaved, flower-filled inn is in the center of Schliersee town. In the coziest rooms, carved and painted four-poster beds are part of the traditional Bavarian furnishings. The beamed tavern-restaurant serves excellent Bavarian fare, and there's nightly zither playing. Comedy performances take place regularly at the inn's own theater. ✉ *Xaver-Terofal-Pl. 2, D–83727,* ☎ *08026/4045,* FAX *08026/2676. 23 rooms. Restaurant, beer garden. No credit cards.*

Shopping

If at the end of your Upper Bavarian tour you're still looking for *something,* stop at the busy market town of Miesbach (north of Schliersee) and climb the stairs to **Cilly's Gschirrladn** (✉ Stadtpl. 10, Miesbach, ☎ 08025/1705). A warren of rooms is stocked ceiling high with every variety of item for the home, from embroidered tablecloths to fine German porcelain.

Spitzingsee

⑫ *10 km (6 mi) south of Schliersee, 65 km (40 mi) southeast of Munich.*

Arguably the most beautiful of this group of Bavarian lakes, the Spitzingsee is cradled 3,500 ft up between the Taubenstein, Rosskopf, and Stumpfling peaks, and the ride there is spectacular. The lake is particularly beautiful in winter, usually frozen over and almost buried in snow. In summer the lake is warm enough for a refreshing swim. Walking in this area is breathtaking during every season and in every sense. The skiing is very good, too.

Dining and Lodging

$$$$ ✕🏠 **Arabella-Sheraton Alpenhotel.** For an out-of-the-way break in the mountains, head for this luxurious hotel on the shore of the small and quiet Spitzingsee, cradled among Alpine meadows. Rooms meet the high standards of comfort expected from the two hotel chains that run the establishment. If you can't stay overnight, come for a leisurely lunch of lake fish or in-season venison. ✉ *Seeweg 7, D–83727,* ☎ *08026/ 7980,* FAX *08026/798–879. 109 rooms, 13 suites. Restaurant, indoor pool, sauna, steam room, 2 tennis courts, exercise room, bowling, boating, library. AE, DC, MC, V.* 🐾

Bayrischzell

⑬ *10 km (6 mi) east of Schliersee, 65 km (40 mi) southeast of Munich.*

Bayrischzell is in an attractive family-resort area, where many a Bavarian first learned to ski. The wide-open slopes of the Sudelfeld Mountain are ideal for undemanding skiing; in summer and fall you can explore innumerable upland walking trails.

The town sits at the end of a wide valley overlooked by the 6,000-ft **Wendelstein** mountain, which attracts expert skiers. At its summit is a tiny stone-and-slate-roof chapel that's much in demand for wedding ceremonies. The cross above the entrance was carried up the mountain by Max Kleiber, who designed the 19th-century church. A **geopark** laid out beneath the summit leads visitors along paths where the 250-million-year geological history of the area is explained on 31 graphic signboards. You can reach the summit from two directions: by cable car (which sets out from Osterhofen on the Bayrischzell-Munich road and costs DM 30 round-trip) and by historic cog railway (catch it at Brannenburg, on the north side of the mountain, between Bayrischzell and the Inn Valley autobahn; a round-trip costs DM 42, and it's closed November and the first three weeks of December).

Lodging

$$ 🏨 **Hotel Feuriger Tatzelwurm.** This archetypal old Bavarian inn is named after the nearby Tatzelwurm Gorge (☞ *below*) and is ideally placed for walks in its dark depths or hikes or ski trips in the surrounding Wendelstein and Brünnstein mountain ranges. It was enlarged and received a modern wing in 2000, and it sits in isolated splendor above a forest pond, some 980 ft from the main Oberaudorf-Bayrischzell road. Traditional Bavarian dishes (also vegetarian) are served in the warren of warmly paneled dining rooms, one of which is dominated by a historic tiled stove. In summer geraniums and hanging vines cover the carved wood balconies and outside terrace. Rooms are comfortably furnished in warm pinewood. ⊠ *Am Tatzelwurm, D–82080 Oberaudorf/ Bayrischzell,* ☎ *08034/30080,* 🖷 *08034/7170. 46 rooms. Restaurant, paddle tennis, bicycles. MC.*

En Route A few miles east of Bayrischzell on the Sudelfeld Road is the **Tatzelwurm** Gorge and Waterfall, named for a winged dragon who supposedly inhabits these parts. Dragon or no, this can be an eerie place to drive through at dusk. From the gorge the road drops sharply to the valley of the Inn River, leading to the busy ski resort of Oberaudorf.

The Inn River valley, an ancient trade route, carries the most important road link between Germany and Italy. The wide, green Inn gushes here, and in the parish church of St. Bartholomew, at **Rossholzen** (16 km [10 mi] north of Oberaudorf), you can see memorials and naively painted tributes to the local people who have lost their lives in its chilly waters. The church has a baroque altar incorporating vivid Gothic elements. A simple tavern directly adjacent to the church offers an ideal opportunity for a break on the Alpine Road.

Rosenheim

🔵 *34 km (21 mi) north of Bayrischzell, 55 km (34 mi) east of Munich.*

Bustling Rosenheim is an attractive medieval market town that has kept much of its character despite the onslaught of industrial development. The arcaded streets of low-eaved houses are characteristic of Inn Valley towns. Chiemsee (☞ *below*) is nearby, and the area has a handful of pretty rural lakes of its own (Simssee, Hofstättersee, and Rinssee).

Dining and Lodging

$$-$$$ ✕🏨 **Goldener Hirsch.** Rooms maintain a high standard of comfort in this well-established hotel in the heart of Rosenheim. It's an ideal place from which to explore the Alpine region, and in the car-free streets around the hotel you'll find a wealth of restaurants and taverns. The hotel's restaurant has a large menu that combines local dishes (roast pork and dumplings, Bavarian sausage) with international ones. ⊠ *Münchnerstr. 40, D–83022,* ☎ *08031/21290,* 🖷 *08031/212–949. 31 rooms. Restaurant, bar. AE, DC, MC, V.*

Chiemsee

🔵 *20 km (12 mi) east of Rosenheim, 80 km (50 mi) east of Munich.*

Chiemsee is north of the German Alpine Road, but it demands a detour, if only to visit King Ludwig's huge palace on one of its idyllic islands. It's the largest Bavarian lake, and although it's surrounded by reedy flatlands, the nearby mountains provide a majestic backdrop. The town of **Prien** is the lake's principal resort. There are boatyards all around the lake and several windsurfing schools. The **Mistral-Windsurfing-Center,** at Gdstadt (✉ Waldstr. 20, ☎ 08054/909–906), has been in operation for 20 years. From its boatyard the average windsurfer can make it with ease to the next island.

Despite its distance from Munich, the beautiful Chiemsee drew Bavarian royalty to its shores. Its dreamlike, melancholy air caught the imagination of King Ludwig II, and it was on one of the lake's three islands that he built the sumptuous **Schloss Herrenchiemsee,** based on Louis XIV's great palace at Versailles. But this was the result of more than simple admiration of Versailles: Ludwig, whose name was the German equivalent of Louis, was keen to establish that he, too, possessed the absolute authority of his namesake, the Sun King. As with most of Ludwig's projects, the building was never completed, and the "mad" king never stayed in its state rooms. Nonetheless, what remains is impressive—and ostentatious. Regular ferries out to the island depart from the harbor shore of Stock, adjacent to Prien. If you want to make the journey in style, take the 100-year-old steam train—which glories in the name *Feuriger Elias,* or *Fiery Elias*—from Prien to Stock. A horse-drawn carriage takes you to the palace itself. Most spectacular in the palace is the Hall of Mirrors, a dazzling gallery (modeled on that at Versailles) where candlelighted concerts are held in summer. Also of interest are the ornate bedrooms Ludwig planned and the stately formal gardens. The south wing houses a **museum** containing Ludwig's christening robe and death mask, as well as other artifacts of his life. While the palace was being built, Ludwig stayed in a royal suite of apartments in a former monastery building on the island, the Altes Schloss. Germany's postwar constitution was drawn up here in 1948, and this episode of the country's history is the centerpiece of the museum housed in the ancient building, the **Museum im Alten Schloss.** ☎ 08051/68870. ☞ *Palace DM 8, King Ludwig Museum DM 4, Museum im Alten Schloss DM 3, combined ticket DM 12 (Apr.–Sept.) or DM 10 (Oct.–Mar.).* ☉ *Apr.–Sept., daily 9–5; Oct.–Mar., daily 10–4; English-language guided tours of palace, daily 11:45 and 2:25.*

The smaller **Fraueninsel** (Ladies' Island), also reached from Stock (boats call there on the way to and from Herrenchiemsee Island), is a charming retreat. The **Benedictine convent,** founded 1,200 years ago, now serves as a school. One of its earliest abbesses, Irmengard, daughter of King Ludwig der Deutsche, died here in the 9th century. Her grave in the convent chapel was discovered in 1961, the same year that early frescoes there were brought to light. The chapel is open daily from dawn to dusk. Otherwise, the island has just a few private houses, a couple of shops, and a hotel.

OFF THE
BEATEN PATH   **MUSEUM FÜR DEUTSCHE AUTOMOBILGESCHICHTE** – The world's largest small-gauge model railway competes for attention with more than 200 old automobiles at the German Automobile History Museum in Amerang, 19 km (12 mi) north of Prien. ✉ *Wasserburger Str. 38, Amerang,* ☎ *08075/8141.* ☞ *DM 12.* ☉ *Tues.–Sun. 10–6.*

Dining and Lodging

$$$ ✕🏨 **Inselhotel zur Linde.** You must catch a boat to this enchanting Bavarian inn on the traffic-free Fraueninsel, and if you miss the last connection to the mainland (at 9 PM), then you'll have to stay the night. The island is a credit-card-free zone, so be sure to bring cash. Rooms are simply furnished and decorated with brightly colored fabrics. The Linde

is one of Bavaria's oldest hotels, founded 600 years ago as a refuge for pilgrims. The lime tree after which it was named is even older. Artists have favored the inn for years, and one of the tables in the small Fischerstüberl dining room (where lake fish is the thing to order) is reserved for them. ⊠ *Fraueninsel im Chiemsee 1, D–83256,* ☎ *08054/90366,* FAX *08054/7299. 14 rooms. Restaurant, bar. No credit cards.*

$$–$$$ ✕▥ **Hotel Luitpold am See.** Boats to the Chiemsee islands tie up right outside your window at this handsome lakeside Prien hotel, which organizes shipboard disco evenings as part of its entertainment program. Rooms have traditional pinewood farm furniture, including carved cupboards and bedsteads. Fish from the lake are served at the pleasant restaurant. ⊠ *Seestr. 110, D–83209 Prien am Chiemsee,* ☎ *08051/609–100,* FAX *08051/609–175. 50 rooms. Restaurant, café. MC, V.*

$$ ✕▥ **Schlosshotel Herrenchiemsee.** This handsome mansion on the Chiemsee island of Herrenchiemsee was standing when King Ludwig was still planning his showpiece Herrenchiemsee Palace. The palace is a 15-minute walk through the woods. The rooms aren't palatial but are nonetheless comfortable. A big plus is the pavilionlike restaurant, serving fresh fish. If you're here to eat, make sure to catch the last boat to the mainland—otherwise you'll still get a good night's sleep on this traffic-free island. ⊠ *Herrenchiemsee, D–83209,* ☎ *08051/1509,* FAX *08051/1509. 12 rooms, 6 with bath or shower. Restaurant. AE, DC, MC, V.*

$$–$$$$ ▥ **Seehotel Wassermann.** The Wassermann stands in the village of Seebruck by the mouth of the River Alz, which flows into northern point of the Chiemsee. The hotel was built in the 1980s, in the traditional style of Bavarian pine. Ask for a balconied room with a four-poster bed. ⊠ *Ludwig-Thoma-Str. 1, D–83358 Seebruck,* ☎ *08667/8710,* FAX *08667/871–498. 40 rooms, 2 apartments. Indoor pool, hot tub, sauna, steam room, boating, bicycles. AE, MC, V.*

Aschau

🔟 *10 km (6 mi) south of Chiemsee, 75 km (46 mi) east of Munich.*

Aschau is an enchanting red-roof village nestling in a fold of the Chiemgauer Alps. Its **Schloss Hohenaschau** is one of the few medieval castles in southern Germany to have been restored in the 17th century in baroque style. Chamber-music concerts are presented regularly in the Rittersaal (Knights Hall) during the summer. ☎ *08052/4227.* ▧ *DM 3.* ☉ *May–Sept., Tues.–Fri. Tours at 9:30, 10:30, 11:30; Apr. and Oct., Thurs. 9:30, 10:30, and 11:30. Closed Nov.–Mar.*

Dining and Lodging

$$$$ ✕▥ **Residenz Heinz Winkler.** In 10 years star chef Heinz Winkler has
★ turned a sturdy Bavarian village inn into one of Germany's most extraordinary hotel-restaurant complexes. You step from a quiet village square, beneath the golden beech-horn insignia of the original hostelry, and through glass doors into an elegant wonderland of haute cuisine and exquisite Italian-influenced taste. Rooms in the main house are noble in proportions and furnishings, and the maisonette-style suites in the annexes are cozily romantic. All have views of the mountains. The Italianate restaurant has kept with ease the three Michelin stars that Winkler won when in charge of Munich's Tantris. A grand piano and a harp add their own notes of harmony to this deliciously sophisticated scene. It's well worth a detour. ⊠ *Kirchpl. 1,* ☎ *08052/17990,* FAX *08052/179–966. 22 rooms. Restaurant, bar, indoor pool, beauty salon, sauna, steam room. AE, DC, MC, V.* ▧

$$-$$$ ✕⊡ **Hotel Bonnschlössl.** This delightful, turreted country palace, which dates to 1477, is a dream lodging. Bavarian blue-and-white shutters, set off by a gleaming white-stucco facade, frame the windows of cozily romantic bedrooms. The Schloss is set in its own park studded with centuries-old trees. In fine weather breakfast is served on the balustraded terrace. The hotel is 6 km (4 mi) north of Aschau, and has a similarly enchanting sister property in the nearby village of Bernau, the Gasthof Alter Wirt, and apartments for rent. Both the Schloss and the Gasthof are protected by preservation orders. Emperor Maximilian I stayed overnight at the Gasthof in 1504 on his way to besiege the nearby castle of Marquartstein. ✉ *Kirchpl. 9 (for reservations for both establishments), D–83233 Bernau,* ☎ *08051/89011,* ⛶ *08051/89103. 41 rooms. Restaurant, beer garden, Weinstube, sauna, spa. MC, V.* 🐾

En Route   At Aschau you'll join the most scenic section of the Deutsche Alpenstrasse as it passes through a string of villages—Bernau, Rottau, Grassau, Marquartstein, and Oberwössen—pretty enough to make you want to linger. In summer the farmhouses of Rottau virtually disappear behind facades of flowers, which have won the village several awards. The houses of Grassau shrink beside the bulk of the 15th-century Church of the Ascension, worth visiting for its rich 17th-century stuccowork.

Reit im Winkl

⓱ *16 km (10 mi) south of Chiemsee, 100 km (62 mi) east of Munich.*

Reit im Winkl has produced at least two German ski champions, who trained on the demanding runs high above the village. **Winklmoosalm Mountain,** towering above Reit im Winkl, can be reached by bus or chairlift and is a popular ski area in winter, and a great place for bracing upland walks in summer and fall. In summer the town attracts artists because of the clarity of the light.

Dining and Lodging

$$ ✕ **Kupferkanne.** Outside, a garden surrounds the building; inside, you could be in an Alpine farmstead. The food is good country fare enhanced by some interesting Austrian specialties. Try the *Salzburger Brez'n,* a thick, creamy bread-based soup. ✉ *Weitseestr. 18,* ☎ *08640/ 1450. No credit cards. Closed Sat. and Nov.*

$$–$$$ ✕⊡ **Landgasthof Rosi Mittermaier.** Rosi Mittermaier, skiing star of the 1976 Innsbruck Olympics, owns this charming Bavarian Gasthof with her husband, Christian Neureuther, a champion skier himself. On their frequent visits to the Gasthof, they're always ready with advice about the best local ski runs or mountain walking trails. It's essential to book in advance, but even if you're not staying, the rustic Café Olympia or cozy, pine-paneled tavern-restaurant is recommended. Duck dishes are the specialty, and the *Käsekuchen* (cheesecake) is legendary. ✉ *Chiemseestr. 2a, D–83242,* ☎ *08640/1011,* ⛶ *08640/1013. 8 apartments. Restaurant, café, sauna. AE, DC, MC, V.*

Ruhpolding

⓲ *24 km (15 mi) east of Reit im Winkl, 125 km (77 mi) east of Munich.*

The Bavarian tourist boom began in this picturesque resort back in the 1930s. In those days tourists were greeted at the train station by a brass band. The welcome isn't quite so extravagant anymore, but it's still warm. In the 16th century the Bavarian rulers journeyed to Ruhpolding to hunt, and the Renaissance-style hunting lodge of Prince Wilhelm V still stands (it's now used as the offices of the local forestry service). The hillside 18th-century **Pfarrkirche St. Georg** (Parish Church of St.

George) is one of the finest baroque and rococo churches in the Bavarian Alps. In one of its side altars stands a rare 13th-century carving, the Ruhpoldinger Madonna. Note also the atmospheric crypt chapel in the quiet churchyard.

Ruhpolding has a model railway museum where youngsters are actually encouraged to play with many of the exhibits. The **Ruhpoldinger Modellbahnschau,** with a small-gauge track, claims to be one of the finest in Europe. The museum also has a display of Christmas crèches. ⊠ *Schulgasse 4, D–83324 Ruhpolding,* ☎ *08663/5613.* ☎ *DM 6.50.* ☉ *Mid-Mar.–mid-Apr., weekends 9:30–5:30; mid–Apr.–Nov., daily 9:30–5:30.*

OFF THE BEATEN PATH **HASSLBERG –** In this village near Ruhpolding you can visit a 300-year-old bell foundry, now a fascinating museum of the ancient crafts of the foundry man and blacksmith. ☎ *DM 4.50.* ☉ *Mid-May–June and mid-Sept.–mid-Oct., weekdays 10–noon and 2–4; July–mid-Sept., weekdays 10–4.*

Dining and Lodging

$$ ✕🏠 **Zur Post.** Look for the Zur Post sign in any Bavarian town or village, and you can be confident of good local fare. In business for more than 650 years, Ruhpolding's branch has been in the hands of the same family for 150 years. You can also obtain lodging here; call ahead for room reservations. ⊠ *Hauptstr. 35, D–83324,* ☎ *08663/5430,* 𝔉𝔄𝔛 *08663/1483. 56 rooms, 19 apartments. Restaurant. MC, V. Closed Wed.*

Bad Reichenhall

⑲ *30 km (19 mi) east of Ruhpolding, 20 km (12 mi) west of Salzburg.*

Bad Reichenhall shares a remote corner of Bavaria, almost surrounded by the Austrian border, with another prominent resort, Berchtesgaden. Although the latter is more famous, Bad Reichenhall is older, with saline springs that made the town rich. Salt is so much a part of the town that you can practically taste it in the air. Europe's largest saline source was first tapped in pre-Christian times; salt mining during the Middle Ages supported the economies of cities as far away as Munich and Passau. In the early 19th century King Ludwig I built an elaborate saltworks and spa house—the **Alte Saline and Quellenhaus**—in vaulted, pseudomedieval style. Their pump installations are astonishing examples of 19th-century engineering. An interesting **museum** in the same building looks at the history of the salt trade. The Alte Saline also houses a typical Upper Bavarian glass foundry and a showroom with articles for sale. *Quellenhaus and Salzmuseum:* ⊠ *Salinen Str.,* ☎ *08651/700–251.* ☎ *DM 8, foundry free.* ☉ *Apr.–Oct., daily 10–11:30 and 2–4; Nov.–Mar., Tues. and Thurs. 2–4; foundry and showroom weekdays 9–6, Sat. 9–1.*

There's even a 19th-century "saline" chapel, part of the spa's facilities and built in exotic Byzantine style at the behest of Ludwig I. Many hotels base special spa treatments on the health-giving properties of the saline springs and the black mud from the area's waterlogged moors. The waters can also be taken in the elegant, pillared **Wandelhalle** pavilion of the attractive spa gardens throughout the year. ⊠ *Salzburgerstr.* ☉ *Mon.–Sat. 8–12:30 and 3–5, Sun. 10–12:30.*

Bad Reichenhall's ancient church of **St. Zeno** is dedicated to the patron saint of those imperiled by floods and the dangers of the deep, an ironic note in a town that flourishes on the riches of its underground springs. Much of this 12th-century basilica was remodeled in the 16th and 17th centuries, but some of the original cloisters remain. ✉ *Kirchpl. 1,* ☎ *08651/4889.*

Dining and Lodging

$$$$ ✕⊡ **Parkhotel Luisenbad.** If you fancy spoiling yourself in a typical
★ German fin-de-siècle spa hotel, this is *the* place—a fine porticoed and
pillared building whose imposing pastel-pink facade holds the promise
of spacious luxury. Rooms are large, furnished in deep-cushioned,
dark-wood comfort, most with flower-filled balconies or loggias. The
elegant restaurant serves international and traditional Bavarian cuisines,
while a pine-paneled tavern, Die Holzstubn'n, pours excellent local brew.
✉ *Ludwigstr. 33, D–83435,* ☎ *08651/6040,* ℻ *08651/62928. 75
rooms, 8 suites. Restaurant, bar, beer garden, indoor pool, hot tub, sauna,
exercise room, bicycles, recreation room. DC, MC, V.*

$$$$ ✕⊡ **Steigenberger-Hotel Axelmannstein.** Ludwig would have enjoyed
the palatial air that pervades this hotel—and he would have been able
to afford the price, which rivals that of top hotels in Germany's most
expensive cities. Luxurious comfort is found in rooms ranging in style
from Bavarian rustic to Laura Ashley demure. The fine restaurant at-
tracts discerning Austrian visitors from across the nearby border. Out-
side is a manicured park and the town center. ✉ *Salzburgerstr. 2–6,
D–83435,* ☎ *08651/7770,* ℻ *08651/5932. 143 rooms, 8 suites. 2 restau-
rants, bar, indoor pool, beauty salon, sauna, spa, tennis court, bowl-
ing, exercise room, baby-sitting. AE, DC, MC, V.*

$ ⊡ **Pension Hubertus.** This delightfully traditional family-run lodging
★ stands on the shore of the tiny Thumsee, 5 km (3 mi) from the town
center. The Hubertus's private grounds lead down to the lake, where
guests can swim or boat. Rooms are Bavarian rustic in style and fur-
nished with hand-carved beds and cupboards. Ask for one with a bal-
cony overlooking the lake. You can also take breakfast with a view of the
lake in the glassed-in winter garden. ✉ *Am Thumsee 5, D–83435,* ☎
08651/2252, ℻ *08651/63845. 18 rooms. Breakfast room, exercise
room, paddle tennis, boating. AE.*

Nightlife and the Arts

Bad Reichenhall is proud of its long musical tradition and of its **or-
chestra,** founded more than a century ago. It performs six days a week
throughout the year in the chandelier-hung Kurgastzentrum Theater
or, when weather permits, in the open-air pavilion, and at a special
Mozart Week in March. Call the **Orchesterbüro** (☎ 08651/8661) for
program details. The resort has an elegant **casino** (☎ 08651/4091), open
daily 3 PM–3 AM.

Shopping

The **Josef Mack** company (✉ Ludwigstr. 36., ☎ 08651/78280) has made
medicinal herbal preparations since 1856, using flowers and herbs grown
in the Bavarian Alps. **Leuthenmayr** (✉ Ludwigstr. 27, ☎ 08651/2869)
is a youngster in the business, selling its "cure-all" dwarf-pine oil since
1908. Candle making is another local specialty, and the **Kerzenwelt
Donabauer** (✉ Reichenhaller Str. 15, Piding, ☎ 08651/8143), just out-
side Bad Reichenhall, has a selection of more than 1,000 decorative
items in wax.

Berchtesgaden

⑳ *18 km (11 mi) south of Bad Reichenhall, 20 km (12 mi) south of
Salzburg.*

Berchtesgaden's reputation is unjustly rooted in its brief association
with Adolf Hitler, who dreamed besottedly of his "1,000-year Reich"
from the mountaintop where millions of tourists before and after him

drank in only the superb beauty of the Alpine panorama. Below those giddy heights is a historic old market town and mountain resort of great charm. Although as a high-altitude ski station it may not have quite the cachet of Garmisch-Partenkirchen, in summer it serves as one of the region's most popular (and crowded) resorts, with top-rated attractions in a heavenly setting. Members of the ruling Wittelsbach dynasty started coming here in 1810. Their ornate palace is one of the town's major attractions, along with a working salt mine and the mountaintop retreat used by Hitler.

Salt—or "white gold," as it was known in medieval times—was the basis of Berchtesgaden's wealth. In the 12th century Emperor Barbarossa gave mining rights to a Benedictine abbey that had been founded here a century earlier. The abbey was secularized early in the 19th century, when it was taken over by the Wittelsbach rulers. The last royal resident of the Berchtesgaden abbey, Crown Prince Rupprecht, who died here in 1955, furnished it with rare family treasures that now form the basis of a permanent collection—the **Königliches Schloss Berchtesgaden Museum.** Fine Renaissance rooms provide the principal exhibition spaces for the prince's collection of sacred art, which is particularly rich in wood sculptures by such great late-Gothic artists as Tilman Riemenschneider and Veit Stoss. You can also visit the abbey's original, cavernous 13th-century dormitory and cool cloisters, which still convey something of the quiet and orderly life led by medieval monks. ⊠ *Schlosspl. 2,* ☎ *08652/2085.* ⊡ *DM 7.* ☉ *Easter–Sept., Sun.–Fri. 10–1 and 2–5; Oct.–Easter, weekdays 10–1 and 2–5; no admission after 4, when last tour starts.*

The **Heimatmuseum,** in the Schloss Adelsheim, displays examples of wood carving and other local crafts. Wood carving in Berchtesgaden dates to long before Oberammergau established itself as the premier wood-carving center of the Alps. ⊠ *Schroffenbergallee 6,* ☎ *08652/ 4410.* ⊡ *DM 3.* ☉ *Tues.–Sun. 10–6, guided tours at 3.*

★ Berchtesgaden has its own salt mine, the **Salzbergwerk,** one of the chief tourist attractions of the entire region. In the days when the mine was owned by Berchtesgaden's princely rulers, only select guests were allowed to see how the source of the city's wealth was extracted from the earth. Today 90-minute tours of the mines are available. Dressed in traditional miner's clothing, visitors sit astride a miniature train that transports them nearly 1 km (½ mi) into the mountain to an enormous chamber where the salt is mined. Rides down the wooden chutes used by the miners to get from one level to another and a boat ride on an underground saline lake the size of a football field are included in the 1½-hour tour. *2 km (1 mi) from center of Berchtesgaden on B–305 Salzburg Rd.,* ☎ *08652/60020.* ⊡ *DM 21.* ☉ *May–mid-Oct., daily 8:30–5; mid-Oct.–Apr., Mon.–Sat. 12:30–3:30.*

㉑ The **Obersalzberg,** site of Hitler's luxurious mountain retreat, is part of the north slope of the Hoher Goll, high above Berchtesgaden. It was a remote mountain community of farmers and foresters before Hitler's deputy, Martin Bormann, selected the site for a complex of Alpine homes for top Nazi leaders. Hitler's chalet, the Berghof, and all the others were destroyed in 1945, with the exception of a hotel that had been taken over by the Nazis, the Hotel zum Türken (☞ Dining and Lodging, *below*). Beneath the hotel is a section of the labyrinth of tunnels built as a last retreat for Hitler and his cronies, and the macabre, murky **bunkers** can be visited (⊡ DM 5; ☉ May–Oct., Tues.–Sun. 9–5; Nov.–Apr., Tues.–Sun. 10–3). Nearby, a **museum** documenting the Third Reich's history in the region opened in 1999 (⊠ Dokumentation Obersalzberg, Salzbergstr. 41, ☎ 08652/947–960, www.obersalzberg.de; ⊡

DM 5; ⊙ May–Oct., Tues.–Sun. 9–5; Nov.–Apr., Tues.–Sun. 10–3). Beyond the Obersalzberg, the hairpin bends of Germany's highest road come to the base of the 6,000-ft peak on which sat the **Kehlsteinhaus** (☎ 08652/2969), the so-called Adlerhorst (Eagle's Nest), Hitler's personal retreat and his official guest house. The road leading to it, built in 1937–39, climbs more than 2,000 ft in less than 6 km (4 mi). A tunnel in the mountain will bring you to an elevator that will whisk you up to what appears to be the top of the world, or you can walk up in about half an hour. There are refreshment rooms and a restaurant, where you can fill up before the dizzying descent to Berchtesgaden. The round-trip by bus and lift (Berchtesgaden post office to Eagle's Nest and back) costs DM 25.80 per person. By car you can travel only as far as the Obersalzberg bus station. From there the round-trip fare is DM 20. The full round-trip takes one hour. From July through September the tourist office organizes Eagle's Nest by Night tours, including a welcome cocktail and a three-course dinner accompanied by live Bavarian music. ☎ 08652/5473. ⊙ Daily 7–6; Mid-May–mid-Oct., daily 9–5. No bus service mid-Oct.–mid-May.

Dining and Lodging

One of Obersalzberg's oldest and most historic inns, the Platterhof (renamed the General Walker Hotel when it was used by U.S. service personnel after World War II) is being torn down and replaced by a luxury resort that will open in 2002.

$$ ✕ **Alpenhotel Denninglehen.** Nonsmokers will appreciate the special dining room set aside just for them in this mountain hotel's restaurant. The restaurant is 3,000 ft up in the resort area of Oberau, just outside Berchtesgaden, and its terrace offers magnificent views. ⊠ Am Priesterstein 7, Berchtesgaden-Oberau, ☎ 08652/5085. No credit cards. Closed Sat. and late Nov.–Dec. 25.

$$ ✕ **Hotel Post.** This is a centrally located and solidly reliable hostelry with a well-presented international menu. If fish from the nearby Königsee is offered, order it. In summer you can eat in the beer garden. ⊠ Maximilianstr. 2, ☎ 08652/5067. MC, V.

$ ✕ **Fischer.** You can pop into this farmhouse-style eatery for Apfelstrudel and coffee or for a meal from a frequently changing international and local menu. It's a short walk across the bridge from the railway station. ⊠ Königseerstr. 51, ☎ 08652/9550. MC. Closed Nov.–Dec. 18.

$ ✕▣ **Seehotel Gamsbock.** In the village of Ramsau, 7 km (4½ mi) west of Berchtesgaden, the Gamsbock stands directly on the shore of the Hintersee. It's ideal for anglers; the crystal-clear lake contains trout and Saibling, which often appear on the restaurant menu. Book one of the balconied rooms overlooking the lake; each is furnished in the Bavarian rustic style, with ornately hand-painted wardrobes, pinewood beds, and dried flowers. ⊠ Am See 75, D–83486 Ramsau, ☎ 08657/98800, FAX 08657/748. 15 rooms, 12 with bath or shower. Restaurant, bar, beer garden, café. No credit cards.

$$–$$$$ ▣ **Stolls Hotel Alpina.** Set above the Königsee in the delightful little village of Schönau, the Alpina offers rural solitude and easy access to Berchtesgaden. Families are catered to with special family-size apartments, a resident doctor, and a playroom. ⊠ Ulmenweg 14, D–83471 Schönau, ☎ 08652/65090, FAX 08652/61608. 44 rooms, 6 apartments. Indoor and outdoor pool, beauty salon, sauna. AE, DC, MC, V. Closed Nov. 4–Dec. 17.

$$–$$$ ▣ **Hotel Wittelsbach.** This is one of the oldest (built in 1892) and most traditional lodgings in the area. The small rooms have dark pinewood furnishings and deep-red-and-green drapes and carpets. Ask for one with a balcony. ⊠ Maximilianstr. 16, D–83471, ☎ 08652/96380, FAX 08652/66304. 26 rooms, 3 apartments. AE, DC, MC, V.

$$ ▣ **Hotel Grünberger.** The cozy rooms here have farmhouse-style furnishings and some antiques. Only a few strides from the train station, in the town center, the Grünberger overlooks the River Ache, beside which you can relax on a private terrace. A buffet breakfast is included in the rate. ✉ *Hansererweg 1, D–83471,* ☎ *08652/4560,* FAX *08652/ 62254. 65 rooms. Beer garden, indoor pool, sauna. MC, V. Closed Nov.– mid-Dec.*

$–$$ ▣ **Hotel zum Türken.** The view alone is worth the 10-minute journey from Berchtesgaden to this hotel. Confiscated during World War II by the Nazis, it's at the foot of the road to Hitler's mountaintop retreat. Beneath it are remains of Nazi wartime bunkers. There's no restaurant, although evening meals can be ordered in advance. ✉ *Hintereck 2, Obersalzberg-Berchtesgaden, D–83471,* ☎ *08652/2428,* FAX *08652/ 4710. 17 rooms, 12 with bath or shower. AE, DC, MC, V. Closed Nov.– Dec. 20.*

$ ▣ **Hotel Watzmann.** American army personnel provided the Hotel Watzmann plenty of business when there was a station in the area, and the cozy Bavarian style and good restaurant still attract American guests. Rooms are solidly furnished in oak, with such Bavarian touches as chamois hides on the walls. The hotel offers remarkable value for your money (an off-season double without bath comes for less than DM 60, and the most expensive room is DM 134). ✉ *Franziskanerpl. 2, D–83471,* ☎ *08652/2055,* FAX *08652/5174. 30 rooms, 23 with bath or shower; 2 suites. AE, MC, V. Closed early Nov.–mid-Dec.*

OFF THE
BEATEN PATH

SCHELLENBERG EISHÖHLEN – Germany's largest ice caves lie 10 km (6 mi) north of Berchtesgaden. By car take the B-305, or take the bus from the Berchtesgaden post office (fare DM 7.40) to the village of Markt-schellenberg. From there you can reach the caves on foot only by walking along the clearly marked route. The walk takes up to two hours, so you'll need to be in reasonably good physical shape. A guided tour of the caves takes one hour. 🎫 *DM 8, including guided tour.* ☉ *Mid-June– mid-Oct., daily 10–5.*

Golf

Germany's highest course, the **Berchtesgaden Golf Club** (✉ Salzbergstr. 33, ☎ 08652/2100), is on a 3,300-ft plateau of the Obersalzberg. Only fit players should attempt the demanding 9-hole course. The restored and renovated clubhouse is reputed to have been a farmhouse owned by Hitler. Seven Berchtesgaden hotels offer their guests a 30% reduction on the DM 50 greens fee—contact the tourist office or the Berchtesgaden Golf Club for details.

Berchtesgaden National Park

5 km (3 mi) south of Berchtesgaden.

The deep, mysterious, and fabled Königsee is the most photographed panorama in Germany, adorning millions of calendars. Together with its much smaller sister, the Obersee, it is nestled within the Berchtesgaden National Park, 210 square km (82 square mi) of wild mountain country where flora and fauna have been left to develop as nature intended. No roads penetrate the area, and even the mountain paths are difficult to follow. The park administration organizes guided tours of the area from June through September (contact the Nationalparkhaus, ✉ Franziskanerpl. 7, D–83471 Berchtesgaden, ☎ 08652/64343).

One less strenuous way into the Berchtesgaden National Park is by boat. A fleet of 21 excursion boats, electrically driven so that no noise disturbs the peace, operates on the **Königsee.** Only the skipper of the boat is allowed to shatter the silence with a trumpet fanfare to demonstrate the lake's remarkable echo. The notes from the trumpet bounce back and forth from the almost vertical cliffs that plunge into the dark green water. A cross on a rocky promontory marks the spot where a boatload of pilgrims hit the cliffs and sank more than 100 years ago. The voyagers, most of whom drowned, were on their way to the tiny, twin-towered baroque chapel of St. Bartholomä, built in the 17th century on a peninsula where an early Gothic church once stood. The princely rulers of Berchtesgaden built a hunting lodge at the side of the chapel; a tavern and a restaurant now occupy its rooms.

Smaller than the Königsee but equally beautiful, the **Obersee** can be reached by a 15-minute walk from the second stop on the boat tour. The lake's backdrop of jagged mountains and precipitous cliffs is broken by a waterfall, the Rothbachfall, that plunges more than 1,000 ft to the valley floor. Boat service on the Königsee runs year-round, except when the lake freezes. Round-trips can be interrupted at St. Bartholomä and at Salet, the landing stage for the Obersee. Boat trips stop only at St. Bartholomä October–April. A round-trip to the Königsee and Obersee lasts almost two hours, without stops, and costs DM 22. The shorter trip to St. Bartholomä and back costs DM 18. In summer the Berchtesgaden tourist office organizes evening cruises on the Königsee, which includes a concert in St. Bartholomä Church and a four-course dinner in the neighboring hunting lodge.

THE BAVARIAN ALPS A TO Z

Arriving and Departing

By Bus
The Alpine region is not well served by long-distance buses.

By Car
Three autobahns reach into the Bavarian Alps: A–7 coming in from the northwest (Frankfurt, Stuttgart, Ulm) and ending near Füssen in the western Bavarian Alps; A–95 from Munich to Garmisch; and A–8 from Munich to Salzburg, for the Tegernsee, Schliersee, and Chiemsee (lakes), and for Berchtesgaden. All provide speedy access to the Alpine foothills, where they connect with a comprehensive network of well-paved country roads that penetrate high into the mountains. (Germany's highest road runs above Berchtesgaden at more than 5,000 ft.)

By Plane
Munich, 95 km (59 mi) northwest of Garmisch-Partenkirchen, is the main airport for the Bavarian Alps. There is easy access from Munich to the autobahns that lead to the Alps. If you're staying in Berchtesgaden, at the east end of the Alps, the airport at Salzburg in Austria is closer but has fewer international flights.

By Train
Most Alpine resorts are connected with Munich by regular express and slower services. Trains to Garmisch-Partenkirchen depart hourly from Munich's Hauptbahnhof. Garmisch-Partenkirchen and Mittenwald are on the InterCity Express network, which has regular direct service to all regions of the country. (Klais, just outside Garmisch, is Germany's highest InterCity train station.) A train from Munich also connects to Gmund on Tegernsee. Bad Reichenhall, Berchtesgaden, Prien, and Rosenheim are linked directly to north German cities by the FD (Fern-Express) "long-distance express" service. **Deutsche Bahn** (☎ 01805/ 996–633) offers special train excursion fares from Munich and Augsburg to the top of the Zugspitze.

Getting Around

By Boat

Passenger boats operate on all the major Bavarian lakes. They're mostly excursion boats, and many run only in summer. However, there's year-round service on the Chiemsee linking the mainland with the Herrenchiemsee and Fraueninsel islands. Eight boats operate year-round on the Tegernsee, connecting the towns of Tegernsee, Rottach-Egern, Bad Wiessee, and Gmund.

By Bus

Villages not served by train are connected by postbus, but service is slow and irregular. Make inquiries either at the local tourist office or at railway stations. Larger resorts operate buses to outlying areas.

By Car

The **Deutsche Alpenstrasse** (German Alpine Road) is not a continuous highway but a series of roads that run between Lindau (on the Bodensee) and Berchtesgaden, and add up to about 485 km (300 mi). The spectacular journey skirts the northern edge of the Alps for most of the way before heading deep into the mountains on the final stretch between Inzell and Berchtesgaden. The dramatic stretch between Garmisch-Partenkirchen and Berchtesgaden runs about 300 km (186 mi) and affords wonderful views.

The **Blaue Route** (Blue Route) follows the valleys of the Inn and Salzach rivers along the German-Austrian border above Salzburg. This off-the-beaten-track territory includes three quiet lakes: the Tachingersee, the Wagingersee, and the Abstdorfersee. They are the warmest bodies of water in Upper Bavaria, ideal for family vacations. At Wasserburg, east of Munich, you can join the final section of the **Deutsche Ferienstrasse** (German Holiday Road), another combination of roads that run on to Traunstein, east of Chiemsee, and then into the Alps.

Contacts and Resources

Car Rentals

Avis (⊠ Königseerstr. 47, Berchtesgaden, ☎ 08652/69107; ⊠ St.-Martin-Str. 17, Garmisch-Partenkirchen, ☎ 08821/934–242). **Hertz** (⊠ Isarstr. 1d, Rosenheim, ☎ 08031/609–666; ⊠ Nymphenburgerstr. 81, Munich, ☎ 089/129–5001). **Sixt** (⊠ Bahnhofstr. 31, Garmisch-Partenkirchen, ☎ 08821/52055; ⊠ Seitzstr. 9–11, Munich, ☎ 089/223–333; ⊠ Hauptbahnhof [main railway station], Südtirolerplatz 1, Rosenheim, ☎ 0180/526–0250).

Emergencies

Police and **ambulance** (☎ 110). **Fire** and **emergency medical aid** (☎ 112).

Guided Tours

Bus tours to King Ludwig II's castles at Neuschwanstein and Linderhof and to the Ettal Monastery, near Oberammergau, are offered by the **DER** travel agencies (⊠ Garmisch-Partenkirchen, ☎ 08821/55125; ⊠ Oberammergau, ☎ 08822/92310). Tours to Neuschwanstein, Linderhof, Ettal, and into the neighboring Austrian Tyrol are also offered by a number of other Garmisch travel agencies: **Hans Biersack** (☎ 08821/4920), **Dominikus Kümmerle** (☎ 08821/4955), **Hilmar Röser** (☎ 08821/2926), and **Weiss-Blau-Reisen** (☎ 08821/3766). The Garmisch mountain railway company, the **Bayerische Zugspitzbahn** (☎ 08821/7970), offers special excursions to the top of the Zugspitze, Germany's highest mountain, by cog rail and/or cable car (☞ Garmisch-Partenkirchen, *above*).

In Berchtesgaden the **Schwaiger** bus company (☎ 08652/2525) offers tours of the area and across the Austrian border as far as Salzburg. An American couple runs a travel service in Berchtesgaden: **Berchtesgaden Mini-bus Tours** (☎ 08652/64971) is in the local tourist office, opposite the railroad station.

The **Aschau and Prien tourist offices** (☞ Visitor Information, *below*) have a DM 34 special offer covering a boat trip to the Herrenchiemsee and Fraueninsel, a round-trip rail ticket between the two resorts, and a round-trip ride by cable car to and from the top of Kampen Mountain, above Aschau.

Visitor Information

The Bavarian regional tourist office in Munich, **Tourismusverband München Oberbayern** (✉ Bodenseestr. 113, D–81243 Munich, ☎ 089/829–2180), provides general information about Upper Bavaria and the Bavarian Alps. There are local tourist information offices in the following towns:

Aschau (✉ Verkehrsamt, Kampenwandstr. 38, D–83229, ☎ 08052/904–937, ✍). **Bad Reichenhall** (✉ Kur-und-Verkehrsverein, im Kurgastzentrum, Wittelsbacherstr. 15, D–83424, ☎ 08651/606303, ✍). **Bad Tölz** (✉ Kurverwaltung, Ludwigstr. 11, D–83646, ☎ 08041/78670, ✍). **Bad Wiessee** (✉ Kuramt, Adrian-Stoop-Str. 20, D–837004, ☎ 08022/86030, ✍). **Bayrischzell** (✉ Kuramt, Kirchpl. 2, [mailing address: Kurverwaltung, Postfach 2, D–83735], ☎ 08023/648, ✍). **Berchtesgaden** (✉ Kurdirektion, Königseerstr. 2, D–834471, ☎ 08652/9670, ✍). **Chiemsee** (✉ Tourismusverband Chiemsee, Kurverwaltung, Alte Rathausstr. 11, D–83209 Prien, ☎ 08051/69050, ✍). **Ettal** (✉ Verkehrsamt, Kaiser-Ludwig-Pl., D–82488, ☎ 08822/3534). **Garmisch-Partenkirchen** (✉ Verkehrsamt der Kurverwaltung, Richard-Strauss-Pl. 2, D–82467, ☎ 08821/180–420, ✍). **Kochel am See** (✉ Kalmbachstr. 11, D–82431, ☎ 08851/338, ✍). **Mittenwald**(✉ Kurverwaltung, Dammkarstr. 3, D–82481, ☎ 08823/33981, ✍). **Oberammergau** (✉ Verkehrsamt, Eugen-Papst-Str. 9a, D–82487, ☎ 08822/92310, ✍). **Prien am Chiemsee** (✉ Kurverwaltung, Alter Rathausstr. 11, D–83209, ☎ 08051/69050, ✍). **Reit–im–Winkl** (✉ Verkehrsamt, Rathauspl. 1, D–83242, ☎ 08640/80020, ✍). **Rottach-Egern/Tegernsee** (✉ Kuramt, Hauptstr. 2, D–83684 Tegernsee, ☎ 08022/180–140, ✍).

3 THE BAVARIAN FOREST

Low-key, understated, and affordable, the
Bavarian Forest is a welcome alternative
to Germany's hyped-up, overcrowded
tourist regions. Farming and forestry are
mainstay industries, tourism is growing, and
glassblowing shouldn't be missed. Passau,
a 2,000-year-old town at the confluence of
three rivers, is as beautiful as it is historic.

Updated by
Robert Tilley

OR YEARS THIS PICTURESQUE, WOODED REGION of Lower Bavaria (Niederbayern) was an isolated part of western Europe, with its eastern boundary flanked by the Iron Curtain and the impenetrable, dark density of the Bohemian Forest. Together the uninterrupted expanses of the Bavarian and Bohemian forests are the largest in Europe. The flavor of Lower Bavaria is vastly different from the popular concept of Bavaria (that world supposedly populated by men in lederhosen and funny feathered green hats and buxom women in flowing dirndls, who sing along with oompah bands and knock back great steins of beer). Instead, people here are reserved; even their accent is gentler than that of their southern countrymen. Farming and forestry are the chief industries, and this combination governs the distinctly rural landscape, where the flat grainfields south of the Danube rise to wooded heights.

Villages of jumbled red roofs and onion-dome churches pepper the vast forest, which has largely buffered communities from further development. Cut off for centuries from the outside world, the small towns of the Bayerischer Wald (Bavarian Forest) developed a tough self-sufficiency, which is evident today in a kind of cultural independence not to be found in the more accessible regions of Germany. Ancient, even heathen traditions are kept alive, while each community boasts its own natural history museum or collections of local curiosities (snuffboxes, for instance). The centuries-old glassmaking industry, which was once a source of considerable wealth, is now carried on as much for the tourist trade as for the wider, international market. One of the region's official tourist routes, the Glasstrasse (the Glass Road), is constantly being extended to accommodate the small foundries whose furnaces are literally being fanned into life by the promise of tourism.

The collapse of Communism in Czechoslovakia and the formation of the Czech Republic made possible the renewal of old contacts between Germans and Bohemian Czechs. The ancient trading route between Deggendorf and Prague—the Böhmweg—has been revived for hikers. No visit to the Bavarian Forest would be complete without at least a day trip across the border; bus trips into Bohemia, as far as Prague and Plsen, are organized by every local tourist office.

The Bavarian Forest has long been a secret with Germans in search of relaxing, affordable holidays at mountainside lodges or country inns, and tourism is growing. In some parts of the forest the concentration of small hotels, pensions, and holiday apartments is the highest in Germany, but their understated presence doesn't overwhelm. In virtually all of them the accent is on sport and outdoor pleasures. All those in search of peace and quiet—hikers, nature lovers, anglers, horseback riders, skiers looking for uncrowded slopes, and golfers distressed by steep greens fees at more fashionable courses—will be satisfied here.

Pleasures and Pastimes

Dining

Food in the Bavarian Forest tends toward the wholesome and the hearty; large portions are very much the norm. The region gave Germany one of its most popular dishes, the *Pichelsteiner Eintopf,* a delicious broth of vegetables and pork. Sausages come in all varieties —the best are *Regensburger* (short, thick, spicy sausages, rather like the bratwurst of Nürnberg) and *Bauernseufzer* (literally, "farmer's sigh") sausage. Dumplings, made out of anything and everything, appear on practically every menu. Try *Deggendorfer Knödel* (bread dumplings) if you fancy something really local. The Danube provides a number of excellent types of fish, particularly *Donauwaller* (Danube catfish), from Passau, served *blau* (poached) or *gebacken* (breaded and fried). Radishes are a specialty, especially *Weichser Rettiche* (a large white radish), and are a good accompaniment to the many local beers. Passau alone has four breweries—at the Hacklberg, one of the most photogenic in all Germany, you can sample excellent beer at its tavern.

CATEGORY	COST*
$$$$	over DM 90
$$$	DM 55–DM 90
$$	DM 35–DM 55
$	under DM 35

*per person for a three-course meal, including tax and tip and excluding drinks

Lodging

Prices here are among the lowest in Germany. Many hotels offer special 14-day packages for the price of a 10-day stay, and 10 days for the price of seven. There are also numerous sports packages. All local tourist offices can supply lists of accommodations; most can help with reservations.

CATEGORY	COST*
$$$$	over DM 200
$$$	DM 160–DM 200
$$	DM 120–DM 160
$	under DM 120

*All prices are for a standard double room for two, including tax and service charge.

Outdoor Activities and Sports

GOLF

The rolling, wooded hills of the Bavarian Forest are golfing country, and in addition to attractive courses, golfers can enjoy at least two important local advantages: lower greens fees (sometimes a fraction of what's charged in Upper Bavaria) and clubs that welcome visitors. One comfortable hotel near Passau, the Golf-Hotel Anetseder, Thyrnau, is on a 21-hole golf course and has special golfing-holiday packages.

HIKING AND BIKING

The Bavarian Forest is prime hiking country, crisscrossed with trails of varied difficulty, including three officially recognized and marked hiking trails. The longest, the **Pandurensteig,** runs nearly 167 km (104 mi), from Waldmünchen, in the northwest, to Passau, in the southeast, and across the heights of the Bavarian Forest National Park. It follows an old trading route and the towns of Schönberg, Regen, and Bayerisch-Eisenstein have close access to the trail. The Pandurensteig can be covered in stages with the aid of a special tourist program that transfers hikers' luggage from one overnight stop to the next. Resorts between Deggendorf and Bayerisch-Eisenstein on the Czech border have remapped the centuries-old **Böhmweg** trading route, which connected the Danube and Moldau rivers. It can be comfortably covered in three or four days, with accommodations at village taverns en route. Cyclists can also cover this route or attempt to do others through the forest, with special deals that often include luggage transport between overnight stops. Like the Böhmweg, the **Gunterweg** strikes deep into the Czech Republic. The Gunterweg follows the thousand-year-old wanderings of the missionary St. Gunter. Passau is the starting point of several bike paths following the three rivers converging on the city. One of the bike paths leads along the Danube as far as Vienna. *See* Hiking and Biking *in* The Bavarian Forest A to Z, *below,* for information sources.

SKIING

Advanced downhill skiers make for the World Cup slopes of the Grosser Arber. The summit is reached by chairlifts from Bayerisch-Eisenstein and from just outside Bodenmais. Other ski areas in the Bavarian Forest are not as demanding, and many resorts are ideal for families. St. Englmar, Frauenau, Furth im Wald, Waldmünchen, and the villages around the Brotjackelriegel, near Deggendorf, are the best.

Cross-country skiing trails are everywhere; a map of 22 of the finest and a list of resorts offering all-inclusive ski holidays can be obtained free of charge from the Fremdenverkehrsverband Ostbayern (☞ Hiking and Biking *in* The Bavarian Forest A to Z, *below*).

Exploring the Bavarian Forest

The Bavarian Forest is a well-defined area between the Danube River and the borders of Austria and the Czech Republic. The region has only two major towns, Deggendorf and Passau, both good bases for day trips into the forest or for longer outings. Many of the larger country hotels are ideal for a family vacation, as they usually offer a very wide range of leisure and sports facilities. You could spend a week or two at such a resort and enjoy everything the Bavarian Forest has to offer without venturing beyond the village boundaries.

Numbers in the text correspond to numbers in the margin and on the Bavarian Forest and Passau maps.

Great Itineraries

IF YOU HAVE 3 DAYS

Base yourself in either Deggendorf or Passau and make day trips into the countryside. From ⛯ **Deggendorf** ⑦ it's only 7 km (4½ mi) along the Danube to the spectacular Benedictine abbey of **Metten,** founded in the 9th century by Charlemagne. It's a full day's trip north of Deggendorf to the **Grosser Arber** Mountain, the highest in both the Bavarian and the Bohemian forests, the latter on the other side of the nearby Czech frontier.

From ⛯ **Passau** ⑪–㉒ take a boat trip down the Danube into neighboring Austria and spend another day exploring the **Bavarian Forest National Park** ⑨, 50 km (31 mi) north of the city. If you're driving, take the B–85 along the valley of the pretty River Ilz.

IF YOU HAVE 5 DAYS

Make ⛯ **Deggendorf** ⑦ your starting point, and after a day or two touring the town and the nearby **Metten Abbey,** head north to the **Grosser Arber Mountain,** overnighting in ⛯ **Bodenmais** ③, ⛯ **Zwiesel** ⑤, or ⛯ **Viechtach** ②, all famous for fine glass. From Zwiesel follow the course of the Regen River as far as Frauenau and head into the **Bavarian Forest National Park** ⑨ to stay in the resort town of Grafenau. From Grafenau follow the Ilz River down to ⛯ **Passau** ⑪–㉒. Passau takes at least two days to explore, but leave time for a boat trip down the Danube and into neighboring Austria.

IF YOU HAVE 7 DAYS

Enter the Bavarian Forest through the little town of **Cham** ① at its northwest corner, stopping to admire the remains of its medieval wall. Head southeast on B–85, watching for the ruins of a medieval castle on the summit of the 2,500-ft-high **Haidstein Peak.** Farther on, between the villages of Prackenbach and Viechtach, you'll view the **Pfahl,** a ridge of glistening white quartz. Overnight in ⛯ **Viechtach** ②, and don't miss a visit to the Gläserne Scheune, a glassmaker's studio. On your second day continue on B–85, turn left at the next village, Patersdorf, and

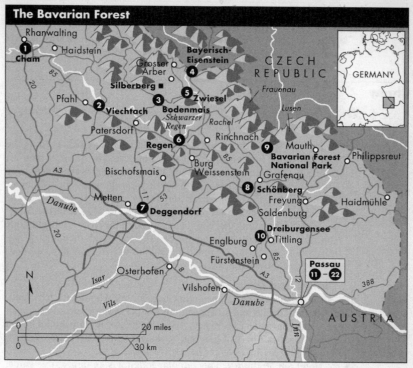

The Bavarian Forest

Rhanwalting
Cham ①
Haidstein
Grosser Arber
Silberberg ■
Bayerisch-Eisenstein ④
C Z E C H
R E P U B L I C
GERMANY
Pfahl
Viechtach ②
③ Bodenmais
⑤ **Zwiesel**
Frauenau
Patersdorf
Schwarzer Regen
Rachel
Lusen
Regen ⑥
Rinchnach
Mauth
⑨ **Bavarian Forest National Park**
Philippsreut
Bischofsmais
Burg Weissenstein
Grafenau
⑧ **Schönberg**
Metten
⑦ **Deggendorf**
Saldenburg
Freyung
Haidmühle
Danube
Dreiburgensee ⑩ Tittling
Englburg
Fürstenstein
Passau ⑪–㉒
N
Isar
Osterhofen
Vils
Vilshofen
Danube
Inn
A U S T R I A

0 ____ 20 miles
0 ____ 30 km

head through the depths of the forest for **Bodenmais** ③. The pretty resort is overlooked by the region's highest mountain, the **Grosser Arber.** The Czech border cuts through the forest on the mountain's northern slopes, and in the border town of **Bayerisch-Eisenstein** ④, the curious can peer into the country. The center of the Bavarian Forest's glass industry, **Zwiesel** ⑤, is 15 km (9 mi) south of Bayerisch-Eisenstein. The road continues south to **Regen** ⑥, a busy market town that's a good lunch stop, and then snakes through wooded uplands before dropping into Deggendorf, in the wide valley of the Danube. Allow two days for **Deggendorf** ⑦, including a side trip to the Benedictine abbey of **Metten.** Next, cross the Danube to visit the beautiful baroque church of St. Margaretha in **Osterhofen,** follow the south bank of the river to Vilshofen, and cross the bridge over the Danube there to head north again into the forest. On your fourth day base yourself at Grafenau and explore the **Bavarian Forest National Park** ⑨. On the road south to **Passau** ⑪–㉒ you'll pass through the Dreiburgenland, so named because of three famous castles that mark the route. Plan a stop at the **Dreiburgensee** ⑩, in Tittling, to see the open-air museum of reconstructed Bavarian Forest houses. From there it's an easy 20 km (12 mi) to Passau for your final two days.

When to Tour the Bavarian Forest

Summer is the time to visit the Bavarian Forest. Although local tourist offices do their best to publicize events spread throughout the calendar year, only winter-sports fans and hardy types dare venture deep into the forest in the months between late fall and early spring. November is so unpleasant—shrouding the whole region in cold, damp fog for days on end—that many hotels put up the shutters until the December vacation season begins. The cold continues through February, and snow lies deep in the ski resorts from December through March.

THE WESTERN BAVARIAN FOREST

Although the Bavarian Forest has no recognized boundaries, it can be said to end in the west where the upland, wooded slopes drop to the Franconian flatlands north of Regensburg.

Cham

❶ *58 km (36 mi) northeast of Regensburg, 58 km (36 mi) northwest of Deggendorf, 140 km (87 mi) north of Munich.*

Beautifully set on the scenic Regen River, Cham regards itself as the gateway to the forest and is further distinguished by its intact sections of original 14th-century town walls, including the massive Straubinger Turm (tower). It also has a 15th-century city hall and an even older town-wall gate, the Biertor. Every day at five minutes past noon a glockenspiel in the city-hall tower plays the French national anthem, the "Marseillaise." It's a municipal commemoration of the town's most famous son, Count Nikolaus von Luckner, who rose through the ranks of various armies to become a French marshal to whom French troops dedicated their most famous song.

Dining and Lodging

$$ ✕ **Bürgerstuben.** The Stuben is in Cham's central Stadthalle (city hall). Tasty local dishes and an appealingly simple atmosphere add up to an authentic Bavarian experience. Additional color is contributed by the nightly presence of card-playing, beer-swilling regulars. ✉ *Fürtherstr. 11,* ☎ *09971/1707. No credit cards. Closed Mon.*

$$ 🏨 **Hotel am Stadtpark.** This popular lodging is an unbeatable value, with comfortable rooms costing as little as DM 78—including a forest view and a large breakfast. The house stands on the edge of Cham's resort park. Families are especially welcome, and the hotel has three large apartments and a huge suite, which can accommodate up to eight people. There's no restaurant, but Cham has no shortage of cheap and cheerful inns. ✉ *Tilsiterstr. 3, D–93413,* ☎ *09971/2253,* FAX *09971/ 79253. 10 rooms, 1 suite, 3 apartments. MC.*

$$ 🏨 **Randsbergerhof.** Generations of German knights lived here before the house was fully restored and converted into a comfortable hotel. A suit of armor from the noble Randsberg family in the beamed restaurant recalls the hotel's romantic history. Its variety of keep-fit facilities make the hotel ideal for sports enthusiasts. ✉ *Randsbergerhofstr. 15–17, D–93413,* ☎ *09971/85770,* FAX *09971/20299. 71 rooms, 4 suites. 2 restaurants, indoor pool, sauna, bowling, squash. AE, DC, MC, V.* 🍲

Nightlife and the Arts

At Furth im Wald (20 km [12 mi] north of Cham), August brings Germany's oldest street **folk festival,** dating from medieval times. Dressed in period costume, townsfolk take part in the ritual slaying of a fire-breathing "dragon" that stalks the main street. The festival takes place between the second and third Sunday of August; call 09973/50980 or 09973/19433 for full information.

Outdoor Activities and Sports

BIKING

The **Cham Fremdenverkehrsverein** (tourist office) sends bikers off with a farewell schnapps on weeklong tours into the countryside; packages cost as little as DM 219 (including bike rental and bed-and-breakfast).

GOLF

Furth im Wald expanded its attractive and challenging course (☎ 09973/2089) from 9 holes to 18 in 2000. Visitors are warmly welcomed.

En Route As you head southeast of Cham on B–85, watch on the left for the ruins of a medieval castle perched on the 2,500-ft-high **Haidstein Peak.** Around the year 1200 it was home to the German poet Wolfram von Eschenbach, author of the metrical romance *Parzival.* On the mountain slopes is a 1,000-year-old linden tree known as Wolframslinde (Wolfram's Lime Tree). With a circumference of more than 50 ft, its hollow trunk could easily shelter 50 people. Continuing on B–85, you'll pass villages with trim streets and gardens and see two sinuous lakes created by the dammed Regen River. From here the Weisser (white) Regen soon becomes the Schwarzer (black) Regen.

Between the village of Prackenbach and the little town of Viechtach you'll see a dramatic section of the **Pfahl,** one of Europe's most extraordinary geological phenomena. The ridge of glistening white quartz juts dramatically out of the ground in an arrow-straight spur that extends more than 100 km (62 mi) through the Bavarian Forest. Here the quartz rises in folds to heights of 100 ft or more.

Viechtach

❷ *30 km (19 mi) southeast of Cham, 29 km (18 mi) north of Deggendorf.*

This little market town nestled in the folds of the Bavarian Forest won a major government prize for its environmental protection programs, and the award includes a special seal of approval (a fir tree) designating hotels and guest houses deemed "ecologically friendly." The little fir is now proudly displayed on most Viechtach houses. The town is also a center of Bavarian Forest glassmaking. The spectacularly decorated rococo church of **St. Augustin** dominates Viechtach's central market square, its severe white-and-yellow west front contrasting colorfully with the high-gable Renaissance and baroque buildings that make up the other three sides.

In the **Gläserne Scheune** (Glazed Barn), Rudolf Schmid produces his highly original sculptures of glass and wood under a roof made from a mosaic of painted glass fragments. ⊠ *Raubühl 3,* ☎ *09942/8147.* ⊡ *DM 6.* ⊙ *Apr.–Sept., daily 10–5; Oct., daily 10–4.*

Four centuries of glassmaking are documented in Viechtach's **Kristallmuseum** (Crystal Museum), which also has a vivid exhibition on the Pfahl (☞ *above*), together with samples of more than 1,000 crystals and minerals and replicas of the world's most famous diamonds. ⊠ *Linprunstr. 4,* ☎ *09942/5497.* ⊡ *DM 4.* ⊙ *Mon.–Sat. 9–6, Sun. 10–4. Closed Sun. in Feb. and Nov.*

Candle making is another ancient craft still practiced in the Bavarian Forest. Discover how beeswax is turned into candles at Viechtach's **Wachszieher & Lebzelter Museum** (Lebzelter Wax Museum). ⊠ *Ringstr. 1,* ☎ *09942/8812.* ⊡ *DM 3.* ⊙ *Sun.–Fri. 8–6.*

★ Among the most unusual museums of the Bavarian Forest is the **Ägayrischen Gewölbe** (Ägarian Vaults), a collection of 400 replicas of Egyptian antiquities spanning 4,000 years. The originals are to be seen in some of the world's leading museums. ⊠ *Spitalg. 5,* ☎ *09942/ 801–638.* ⊡ *DM 5.* ⊙ *Apr.–June and Sept.–Apr., Tues.–Sun. 10–4; July–Aug., daily 10–4.* ✎

Dining and Lodging

$$–$$$ ✕🔲 **Am Pfahl.** It's hard to imagine any wish that isn't met by this large but refreshingly personal "sports" hotel on the edge of Viechtach, right next to the famous Pfahl. Sports enthusiasts are well catered to with tennis, squash, and badminton courts; mountain bikes; and expert information about other activities in the area. The hotel's own bus operates a shuttle to ski lifts, a golf course, riding stables, and canoeing stretches in the nearby Regen River. For the less sports-minded, the hotel organizes tours to places as far away as Prague. ⊠ *Waldfrieden 1, D–94234,* ☎ *09942/95700,* 🆁🆇 *09942/957–150. 121 rooms. Restaurant, bar, indoor pool, sauna, steam room, 2 tennis courts, badminton, squash, mountain bikes. AE, MC, V.* 🥂

$$ ✕🔲 **Hotel Schmaus.** Run by the same family for 13 generations, this former stagecoach inn is for the energetic. The kitchen turns out meals on the assumption that every guest has just finished a 40-km (25-mi) hike through the forest, although the all-weather sports facilities could make you equally hungry. In summer dine in the grill garden. Ask to stay in the older section—some of the modern rooms are somewhat plain. ⊠ *Stadtpl. 5, D–94234,* ☎ *09942/94160,* 🆁🆇 *09942/941–630. 40 rooms. Restaurant, Weinstube, pool, sauna, 2 tennis courts. AE, DC, MC, V. Closed last 3 wks of Jan.*

Nightlife and the Arts

A **theater festival** with roots in the Middle Ages is held every summer in Neunussberg Castle, just outside Viechtach. Call the Viechtach tourist office (☎ 09942/1661) for details.

Shopping

For glass objects and other arts and crafts, try the **Viechtacher Kunststube,** in the Altes Rathaus (⊠ Stadtpl. 1, ☎ 09942/2441). **Glas Rötzer** (⊠ Hafnerhöhe, ☎ 09942/1340) sells forest handicrafts such as glass, pottery, and carvings. Günther Götte's **Pegasus-Studio** (⊠ Kandlbach 3, ☎ 09942/2729) has a wide range of locally made pottery.

Bodenmais

❸ *24 km (15 mi) east of Viechtach, 34 km (21 mi) north of Deggendorf.*

This health resort is in a valley below the Bavarian Forest's highest mountain, the 4,800-ft-high Grosser Arber. A nearby silver mine helped Bodenmais prosper before tourism reached this isolated part of the country.

Bodenmais's long tradition of glassmaking includes Bavaria's largest glassworks, the **Joska Waldglashütte,** which welcomes visitors at its foundry and showrooms in the Am Moosbach industrial zone. The foundry houses the **Raritäten Museum** (🔲 DM3; ☉ weekdays 9–6, weekends 9–4), a private collection of 2,000 rarities amassed over the years by a local man, Alois Lippi. The exhibits include not only glass but also rare porcelain and ceramics, clocks and watches, and religious art. The collection embraces a huge range of valuable objects spanning three centuries of craftsmanship in eastern Bavaria and Bohemia. The foundry also has a restaurant. ⊠ *Am Moosbach 1,* ☎ *09924/7790.* 🔲 *Free.* ☉ *Weekdays 9–6, Sat. 9–2.*

You can watch glassblowers at the **Austen Glashütte Foundry** (Austen Glass Foundry; ⊠ Bahnhofstr. 57, ☎ 09924/7006) and buy goods at very reasonable prices. The foundry is open weekdays 9:30–5:30 and Saturday 9:30–2:30.

OFF THE BEATEN PATH   **SILBERBERG** – The 600-year-old silver mine closed in 1962, but you can still view its workings near the summit of the 3,000-ft-high Silberberg.

The air within the mine is so pure that one of the side shafts is used to treat asthmatics and people with chronic bronchial complaints. You can walk from Bodenmais to the entrance of the mine or take the chairlift from Arber Road, about 3 km (2 mi) north of Bodenmais. ☎ *09924/ 304 for details on guided tours.* ☒ *DM 9.50.* ⊙ *Apr.–mid-June and Oct., daily 10–4; mid-June–mid-Sept., daily 9–5; Dec. 25–Jan. 8, daily 10–3; Jan. 9–Mar., Tues., Wed., Fri., and Sat. 1–3. Closed last 2 wks in Sept., Nov.–Dec. 24.*

Dining and Lodging

$$ ✕▥ **Bodenmaiser Hof.** The maisonette rooms in this expansive and meticulously run hotel are particularly large and luxurious, with galleried sleeping areas and living rooms beneath. "Ordinary" double rooms are also generously proportioned, and most have terraces or balconies with forest views. The winter-garden restaurant and a cozy tavern are warm retreats on cold days, while a glass-roof terrace beckons in summer. The hotel has its own bakery and butcher shop, which ensures the freshness and quality of the food prepared for guests. ☒ *Risslochweg 4, D–94249,* ☎ *09924/9540,* ℻ *09924/95440. 20 rooms, 10 suites. Restaurant, café, sauna, exercise room. No credit cards.* ✎

$$–$$$ ▥ **Feriengut-Hotel Böhmhof.** The Böhmhof estate, beautifully set on the edge of the forest, has been owned by the Geiger family for more than three centuries. Their long tradition can be felt throughout, from the friendly reception to the comfortable, spacious rooms, several of which were recently converted to "country-house suites" with separate living areas. One estate building provides farmhouse-style accommodations, ideal for children. The outdoor and indoor pools allow for year-round swimming; walking and cross-country ski trails start at the front door. ☒ *Böhmhof 1, D–94249,* ☎ *09924/94300,* ℻ *09924/943–013. 22 rooms, 15 suites. Restaurant, café, indoor and outdoor pool, hot tub, sauna, exercise room, recreation room. No credit cards. Closed mid-Nov.–mid-Dec.* ✎

OFF THE BEATEN PATH
GROSSER ARBER – The highest mountain of both the Bavarian Forest and the Czech Republic's Bohemian Forest (4,800 ft) is 13 km (8 mi) north of Bodenmais. Several hiking trails lead to the summit; in winter it offers challenging skiing and in 2000 was an International Skiing Federation World Cup venue. A bus service runs from Bodenmais to the base of the mountain, where a chairlift makes the 10-minute trip to the summit. There's a great view of the darkly mysterious central European stretch of woodland from here. Short walks from the bottom of the lift lead to two woodland lakes, the Grosser Arbersee and the smaller **Kleiner Arbersee**, both ideal for summer swimming and boating. Beside the Grosser Arbersee, children can wander through the Märchenwald (Fairytale Wood), which features a collection of colorful model scenes from famous stories. ☒ *Märchenwald entrance opposite Hotel Arberseehaus.* ☎ *Chairlift DM 14.* ⊙ *Easter–Oct., daily 9–5.*

Bayerisch-Eisenstein

❹ *17 km (11 mi) north of Bodenmais, 7 km (4½ mi) east of the Grosser Arber.*

Travelers who can't resist quirky sights should detour north to this little town, which sits on the Czech Republic border. The frontier actually cuts the local train station in half. More than 20 **historic old steam locomotives** are housed in one of the ancient engine sheds, and some of them regularly roll back into service for outings into the Bohemian Forest of the Czech Republic. ☒ *Bahnhofstr. 44,* ☎ *09925/1376.* ☎

Varies depending on length and duration of trip. ☉ *Apr.–Nov. and Dec. 26–Jan. 6, Tues.–Sat. 10–12:30 and 2–5; Nov.–Dec. 25 and Jan 7–Mar., weekends 10–2.*

Bayerisch-Eisenstein also has a glassblowing tradition. You can see glassblowers at work at the **Alwe Kristallglashütte** (⊠ Arberseestr., ☎ 09925/1321), in the village of Regenhütte, just outside Bayerisch-Eisenstein. The foundry is open weekdays 9–3, Saturday and holidays 9–noon. A showroom and shop are open weekdays 9–5, weekends 9–4.

Dining and Lodging

$–$$ ✕☷ **Ferienhotel Waldspitze.** Its forest location and range of facilities make this large, friendly hotel an ideal vacation base. Bohemian specialties such as *Böhmische Knödel* (bread dumplings) are included on the restaurant menu. Rooms are spacious and renovated, with new bathrooms and solid Bavarian-style furniture. A nearby apartment house is ideal for families. ⊠ *Hauptstr. 4, D–94252,* ☎ *09925/94100,* FAX *09925/941–0199. 55 rooms. Restaurant, café, indoor pool, sauna, steam room, exercise room, Ping-Pong, billiards. MC.*

Zwiesel

❺ *15 km (9 mi) south of Bayerisch-Eisenstein, 40 km (25 mi) northeast of Deggendorf, 70 km (43 mi) northwest of Passau.*

As the region's glassmaking center, Zwiesel has 18 firms and more than 2,000 townspeople involved in shaping, engraving, or painting glass. Most open their foundries to visitors. At **Kunstglasbläserei Seemann** (Seemann Artistic Glass Foundry; ⊠ Stormbergerstr. 36, ☎ 09922/1091), in the village of Rabenstein, you can try your own skill at blowing glass on Thursday from 10 to noon and take the result of your efforts home with you (for a DM 10 fee).

Just 2 km (1 mi) north of Zwiesel, in the village of Theresienthal, the **Glasmuseum zum Schlössl** (Castle Glass Museum) is one of the biggest of its kind in the Bavarian Forest. Here you'll see how glassblowing developed through the centuries. The museum is part of a glass park that includes two of Europe's oldest glass foundries, as well as showrooms, shops, and a restaurant. ⊠ *Glaspark Theresienthal,* ☎ *09922/ 1030.* ☷ *DM 1.50, including guided tour.* ☉ *Weekdays 10–2.*

The **Waldmuseum Zwiesel** (Zwiesel Forest Museum) has displays dedicated to the customs and heritage of the entire forest region during the past few centuries. ⊠ *Stadtpl. 27,* ☎ *09922/60888.* ☷ *DM 3.* ☉ *Mid-May–mid-Oct., weekdays 9–5, weekends 10–noon and 2–4; mid-Oct.–mid-May, weekdays 10–noon and 2–5, weekends 10–noon. Closed Nov.*

☾ The Bavarian Forest has a long toy-making tradition, and the **Zwiesel Spielzeugmuseum** (Zwiesel Toy Museum) has one of the region's largest collections of playthings ancient and modern. ⊠ *Stadtpl. 35,* ☎ *09922/5526.* ☷ *DM 4.* ☉ *June–Sept., daily 9–5; Oct.–May, daily 10–5. Closed Nov.–Christmas.*

Zwiesel produces a variety of beers and a notorious schnapps, Bärwurz. You can sample the house-brewed bitter Janka Pils or a malty, dark wheat brew at most of the town's taverns. The **Bayerwald Bärwurzerei** (Bayerwald Bärwurz Distillery) has added to its products a liqueur that at 40 proof rivals the schnapps for pure head-spinning effect. ⊠ *Frauenauerstr. 80–82,* ☎ *09922/84330).* ☉ *Weekdays 8–6, Sat. 9–4, Sun. and holidays 9:30–noon and 2–4.*

Lodging

$$ ⊡ **Hotel zur Waldbahn.** The great-grandfather of the current owner, assisted by 13 children, built the Hotel zur Waldbahn more than 100 years ago to accommodate train passengers traveling between Bohemia and points south. Today the emphasis is still on making the traveler feel at home within the hotel's wood-paneled walls. ⊠ *Bahnhofpl. 2, D–94227,* ☎ *09922/8570,* FAX *09922/857–222. 28 rooms. Restaurant, hot tub, sauna, exercise room. V. Closed mid-Mar.–mid-Apr.* ✉

$–$$ ⊡ **Hotel Sonnenhof.** This large, friendly pension is set in rolling countryside on the edge of Zwiesel, with panoramic views of the Bavarian Forest. It's an ideal base for exploring the area, and special rates apply for stays of a week or more. Families are warmly welcomed. ⊠ *Ahornweg 10, D–94227,* ☎ *09922/9005,* FAX *09922/60521. 46 rooms. Restaurant, indoor pool, sauna, paddle tennis, bicycles. MC. Closed Nov.* ✉

Golf

There's a beautifully landscaped 18-hole course at **Oberzwieselau** (☎ 09922/2367), near Zwiesel. The club president is an affable German baron.

Regen

❻ *10 km (6 mi) southwest of Zwiesel, 28 km (17 mi) northeast of Deggendorf, 60 km (37 mi) northwest of Passau.*

Regen, a busy market town with fine 16th-century houses around its large central square, is famous for its annual bash during the last weekend in July: a great party commemorating the 17th-century creation of *Pichelsteiner Eintopf* (pork-and-vegetable stew), a filling dish that has become a staple throughout Germany. The stylish celebrations include sports events on the Regen River, so pack a swimsuit. Regen's other claim to fame is an extraordinary display of Christmas crèches.

Frau Maria-Elisabeth Pscheidl, a Regen resident who has been crafting Nativity scene herself for more than 30 years, has amassed an inordinate number of these **Christmas crèches.** The local tourist office claims her collection is the largest and best in the world—it even has the Vatican seal of approval. Many of her creations are displayed in the **Pscheidl Bayerwald-Krippe Museum,** run by the town council in Frau Pscheidl's home. ⊠ *Ludwigsbrücke 3,* ☎ *09921/2893.* ▨ *DM 2.* ⊙ *Daily 9–11:30 and 2–4.*

OFF THE BEATEN PATH
BURG WEISSENSTEIN – The world's largest snuffbox collection is on the third floor of Weissenstein Castle, near Regen. The 1,300 snuffboxes on display were collected over a period of 46 years by Regen's former mayor, Alois Reitbauer. His reward was an entry in the *Guinness Book of Records.* In 1997 extensive excavations began on the castle grounds. You are welcome to watch the archaeologists at work and view the treasures they are bringing to light. There's a free tour of the excavations every Wednesday at 3, but you must first register with the tourist office (☎ 09921/2929). ⊠ *Weissenstein 32,* ☎ *09921/5106.* ▨ *DM 3.* ⊙ *Late May–mid-Sept., daily 10–noon and 1–5.*

Dining and Lodging

$ ✕ **Restaurant am Rathaus.** If you're anywhere in the Regen area on a Sunday, head for this atmospheric Bavarian restaurant for a great lunch or dinner deal—a quarter of a roast duck complete with red cabbage and dumplings for less than DM 10! If duck's not your favorite, there are other dishes of similarly extraordinary value on the menu, much of it cooked in traditional fashion on a hot-stone oven. ⊠ *Stadtpl. 3,* ☎ *09921/2220. Reservations not accepted. No credit cards. Closed Wed.*

$ ✕⊞ **Burggasthof Weissenstein.** The ruins of the neighboring medieval Weissenstein Castle loom above you as you breakfast on the sunny terrace overlooking the Old Town. Ask for a room with a view of either. The cellar tavern has dancing on weekends and a menu emphasizing filling local specialties, roast meats, and Bohemian-style dumplings. ⊠ *Weissenstein 32, D–94209,* ☎ *09921/2259,* ℻ *09921/8759. 15 rooms. Restaurant. No credit cards. Closed Nov.* ✥

OFF THE   **RINCHNACH** – This village, 8 km (5 mi) east of Regen, has an impressive
BEATEN PATH   monastery that began as an 11th-century monk's lonely retreat. Built in the 15th century, the church was renovated in baroque style by Johann Michael Fischer in the 1720s. Visit its expansive interior to see his masterly wrought-iron work and some typically heroic frescoes. Two early 18th-century altar paintings by Cosmas Damian Asam are also on view. ⊙ *Daily 9–dusk.*

THE EASTERN BAVARIAN FOREST

East of Deggendorf the countryside falls in hilly folds to the Danube and the beautiful border city of Passau. North of Passau the forest climbs again to the remote Dreiländereck, the spot where Germany, Austria, and the Czech Republic meet.

Deggendorf

❼ *28 km (17 mi) southwest of Regen, 140 km (87 mi) northeast of Munich.*

Between the Danube and the forested hills that rise in tiers to the Czech border, Deggendorf justifiably regards itself as the Bavarian Forest's southern gateway. The town was once on the banks of the Danube, but repeated flooding forced its inhabitants to higher ground in the 13th century. You can still see a 30-yard stretch of the protective wall built around the medieval town.

Deggendorf is unique in Lower Bavaria for its specially developed "cultural quarter," created from a section of the Old Town. Lining the leafy, traffic-free square are the city museum; a public library; a handicrafts museum, the only one of its kind in the Bavarian Forest; and the Kapuzinerstadl, a warehouse converted into a concert hall and a large foyer that is frequently used as a theater venue.

The 16th-century **Rathaus** (town hall), in the center of the wide main street, the Marktstrasse, has a central tower with a tiny apartment that traditionally housed the town watchman and lookout. From its windows you can get a fine view. The rooms haven't changed over the centuries. ⊠ *Marktstr.,* ☎ *0991/296–0169.* ⊡ *DM 5.* ⊙ *Tower can be visited as part of guided tour of the town, June–Sept. daily at 9:30.*

★ The **Heilig Grabkirche** (Church of the Holy Sepulchre) was originally built as a Gothic basilica in the 14th century. Its lofty tower—regarded as the finest baroque church tower in southern Germany—was added 400 years later by the Munich master builder Johann Michael Fischer. ⊠ *Marktstr.* ⊙ *Daily 9–sunset.*

Exhibits at the **Handwerksmuseum** (Museum of Trades and Crafts) focus on typical regional handicrafts such as glassmaking and wood carving. ⊠ *Maria-Ward-Pl. 1,* ☎ *0991/4084.* ⊡ *DM 2, also valid for admission to the Stadtmuseum.* ⊙ *Tues.–Sun. 10–4, Thurs. 10–6.*

The **Stadtmuseum** (City Museum) traces the history of the Danubian people. ⊠ *Östlicher Stadtgraben 28,* ☎ *0991/4084.* ⊡ *DM 2, also* *valid for admission to Handwerksmuseum.* ☉ *Tues.–Sun. 10–4, Thurs. 10–6.*

Dining and Lodging

$$ ✕ **Ratskeller.** In the vaulted cellar of the Rathaus, you could easily find yourself sharing a table with a town councillor, perhaps even the mayor. The menu is strictly Bavarian; the beer flows freely. ✉ *Oberer Stadtpl. 1,* ☎ *0991/6737. Reservations not accepted. No credit cards.*

$$ ✕ **Zum Grafenwirt.** In winter ask the host for a table near the fine old tile stove that sits in the dining room. Try such filling dishes as roast pork and Bavarian dumplings. In summer watch for Danube fish on the menu. ✉ *Bahnhofstr. 7,* ☎ *0991/8729. AE, MC, V. Closed 1st 2 wks in June. No dinner Tues.*

$$$$ ✕⊡ **Astron Parkhotel.** A monumental mural by Elvira Bach welcomes you in the reception area of this spacious luxury hotel, and the artistic touch is continued in the large and airy guest rooms, all with original paintings on the walls. The Tassilo restaurant and adjoining winter garden have an international menu with an Italian flair. In summer a shady beer garden beckons; in winter a log fire burns invitingly in the lounge. The Danube promenade and the Old Town center are both nearby. ✉ *Edlmairstr. 4, D–94469,* ☎ *0991/6013,* ℻ *0991/31551. 112 rooms, 13 suites. Restaurant, bar, beer garden, hot tub, sauna, exercise room, bicycles. AE, DC, MC, V.* 🐾

$$$ ✕⊡ **Schlosshotel Egg.** The "Egg" doesn't stand for something you might eat in this castle-hotel's excellent restaurant; it's derived from Ekke, the name of the 12th-century owner. Today the hotel, 13 km (8 mi) northwest of Deggendorf, is a memorable place in which to lay your head. A vaulted dining room, the Burgstall, and a paved courtyard garden maintain the medieval mood of the ivy-covered old building. There are just a few comfortable apartment-size suites, so it's essential to book ahead. ✉ *94505 Schloss Egg-Bernried, D–94505,* ☎ *09905/289,* ℻ *09905/8262. 6 suites. Restaurant, beer garden. V. Closed Jan. and Feb.*

$$–$$$ ✕⊡ **Donauhof.** This lovely 19th-century stone warehouse, painted
★ cream and white, was converted into a hotel in 1988. The spotless rooms have modern Scandinavian furniture. The Wintergarten Café is a local favorite for its homemade cakes and coffee. ✉ *Hafenstr. 1, D–94469,* ☎ *0991/38990,* ℻ *0991/389–966. 42 rooms, 3 suites. Restaurant, café, sauna. AE, DC, MC, V.* 🐾

Golf

There's a challenging course at **Schaufling** (☎ 09920/8911), high above Deggendorf, which offers views of the Bavarian Forest and the Danube Plain.

OFF THE **METTEN –** To see two outstanding examples of baroque art, you can take
BEATEN PATH the 7-km (4½-mi) trip along the Danube, heading northwest from Deggendorf, to the ancient **Benedictine abbey** of Metten, founded in the 9th century by Charlemagne. Within its white walls and quiet cloisters is an outstanding 18th-century **library**, with a collection of 160,000 books whose gilt leather spines are complemented by the heroic splendor of their surroundings—Herculean figures support the frescoed, vaulted ceiling, and allegorical paintings and fine stuccowork identify different categories of books. In the **monastery church** is Cosmas Damian Asam's altarpiece *Lucifer Destroyed by St. Michael;* created around 1720, its vivid coloring and swirling composition is typical of the time. ☎ *0991/91080.* ▧ *DM 3.* ☉ *Guided tours daily 10 and 3.*

En Route If you are driving, cross the Danube just outside Deggendorf or take the ferry at Winzer and then the Passau road (B–15) to the village of Osterhofen and the **St. Margaretha Kirche (Church of St. Margaretha).**

This structure contains important work by baroque artists, including a series of large, ornate frescoes and altar paintings by Cosmas Damian Asam, as well as elaborate sculptures of angels and cherubs, entwined on the church pillars, by Egid Quirin Asam and Johann Michael Fischer. The three worked here in a rare partnership between 1728 and 1741. Look for Cosmas Damian's self-portrait amid the extravagant decor. ⊠ *Osterhofen.* ☉ *Daily 9–7, except during Sun. services. Free guided tours Tues. and Thurs. at 3 (assemble at main church door).*

Schönberg

❽ *40 km (25 mi) northeast of Deggendorf.*

In little Schönberg's **Marktplatz** (market square), arcaded shops and houses present an almost Italian air. As you head farther south down the Inn Valley, this Italian influence—the so-called Inn Valley style—becomes more pronounced.

Lodging

$$ ⌤ **Landhaus zur Ohe.** A *Landhaus* is a country house, but this description doesn't do justice to this large holiday hotel with its huge range of amenities. The hotel backs directly onto the forest and commands a view of open, rolling countryside. Rooms are light and airy, with pale pinewood furniture. Most have balconies with panoramic views. Children are particularly well catered to, with play areas inside and out and a small zoo with domestic and farm animals. ⊠ *Maukenreuth 1, Schönberg D–94513,* ☎ *08554/96070,* FAX *08554/556. 41 rooms, 6 suites. Restaurant, bar, indoor pool, beauty salon, sauna, spa, exercise room, paddle tennis, billiards, playground. MC. Closed Nov.*

Bavarian Forest National Park

★ **❾** *15 km (9 mi) northeast of Schönberg, main entrance at Neuschönau, 50 km (31 mi) north of Passau.*

The Bavarian Forest National Park is a 32,000-acre stretch of protected dense forest. Substantial efforts have been made to reintroduce bears, wolves, lynx, and other animals to the park, though today the animals are restricted to large enclosures. Well-marked paths lead to points where wildlife can best be seen. Bracing walks also take you through the thickly wooded terrain to the two highest peaks of the park, the 4,350-ft **Rachel** and the 4,116-ft **Lusen.** Specially marked educational trails trace the geology and botany of the area, and picnic spots and playgrounds abound. In winter park wardens will lead you through the snow to where wild deer from the mountains feed. A visitor center—the **Hans-Eisenmann-Haus** (☎ 08558/96150; ☉ daily 9–5)—is at the main entrance to the park, on the edge of the village of Neuschönau. Slide shows and English-language brochures provide introductions to the area.

Tours of the national park are organized by the **Grafenau Verkehrsamt** (tourist office; ⊠ Rathausg. 1, D–94481, ☎ 08552/96230). For as little as DM 250 the Verkehrsamt offers a winter week's bed-and-breakfast package, including a visit to the national park, two tours on cross-country skis, and two on snowshoes.

There are several glass foundries in the villages bordering the national park. The **Kristallglasfabrik** (⊠ Hauptstr. 2–4, Spiegelau, ☎ 08553/2400) and the **Glasbläserhof** (⊠ Birkenweg 21, Mauth, ☎ 08557/96140) both welcome visitors, who can watch glassblowers at work and also buy the products at their source.

Neighboring **Grafenau** has two unusual and interesting museums. The **Bauernhausmuseum,** in the resort's spa-park, consists of two restored

Lower Bavarian farmhouses containing furnishings and implements from the 18th and 19th centuries. The **Schnupftabak-Museum** (Snuff Museum), in a historic almshouse (⊠ Spitalstr.), depicts (and attempts to explain) the habit of sniffing snuff. Snuffboxes from several countries disprove the theory that only Bavarians are addicted. Both museums are open mid-December–October, daily 2–5. ⊜ DM 3 for each museum.

Dining and Lodging

$$ ✕ **Adalbert Stifter.** Named after a popular 19th-century novelist, this friendly country hotel-restaurant at the foot of the Dreisessel Mountain is at its best turning out the sort of time-honored dishes Stifter knew. Try one of the Bohemian-style roasts, served with fresh dumplings. ⊠ *Frauenberg 32, Frauenberg,* ☎ *08556/355. No credit cards. Closed Nov.*

$$$ ✕🍽 **Säumerhof.** The Bavarian Forest isn't known for haute cuisine,
★ but here in Grafenau, one of its prettiest resorts, is a restaurant that bears comparison with Germany's best. It's part of a small country hotel (with 10 moderately priced and homey rooms) run by the Endl family. Gebhard Endl's territory is the kitchen, where he produces original dishes using local ingredients. Try the pheasant on champagne cabbage or the roast rabbit in herb-cream sauce. ⊠ *Steinberg 32, D– 94481 Grafenau.* ☎ *08552/408–990,* ℻ *08552/5343. 10 rooms. Restaurant, sauna. AE, DC, MC, V.*

$–$$ ✕🍽 **Gasthof-Restaurant Barnriegel.** On the edge of the Bavarian Forest National Park, this family-run restaurant caters to those made hungry by a day's walking. Sauerbraten is one of the best dishes on the menu; local lake fish is also a specialty. Fresh vegetables and herbs come from the Barnriegel's own garden. The weary will also be provided for here with a stay in one of the inexpensive but comfortable pinewood-furnished rooms. ⊠ *Halbwaldstr. 32, D–94151 Finsterau,* ☎ *08557/96020,* ℻ *08557/960–249. 24 rooms. No credit cards. Closed Mon. and Apr.–June.*

$$$$ 🍽 **Europa Congresshotel Grafenau.** If you are traveling with children, this is the hotel for you: the staff includes a *Spieltante* (playtime auntie) who keeps youngsters amused. The ultramodern hotel (formerly the Sonnenhof) is set on extensive grounds, and there's lots to do— even horse-drawn sleigh rides in winter. You can choose between two room styles: country house, with light woods and pastel tones, or rustic, with dark furnishings and brightly colored fabrics. ⊠ *Sonnenstr. 12, D–94481 Grafenau,* ☎ *08552/4480,* ℻ *08552/4680. 144 rooms, 3 suites. 2 restaurants, bar, indoor pool, beauty salon, 2 saunas, spa, miniature golf, 6 tennis courts, bowling, exercise room, nightclub. AE, DC, MC, V.* ✍

$$$–$$$$ 🍽 **Romantik Hotel Die Bierhütte.** The name means "beer hut," and it was once a royal brewery. Now a member of the select Romantik hotel group, the elegant 18th-century building has its own quiet grounds beside a lake, near the village of Hohenau. It has all the trappings of a regal residence, with ornate furnishings and tapestries in public rooms and bedrooms. ⊠ *Bierhütte 10, D–94545 Hohenau,* ☎ *08558/96120,* ℻ *08558/961–270. 37 rooms, 6 suites, 4 apartments. Restaurant, sauna, exercise room, recreation room, library. AE, DC, MC, V.* ✍

Dreiburgenland

On the Ostmarkstrasse (B–85) between Schönberg and Passau.

Fürstenstein, Englburg, and Saldenburg are the three castle-rich villages that make up Dreiburgenland, or Land of the Three Castles. The little village of Fürstenstein likes to call itself the "Pearl of the Dreiburgenland." From the walls of its castle you can get a fine view of the

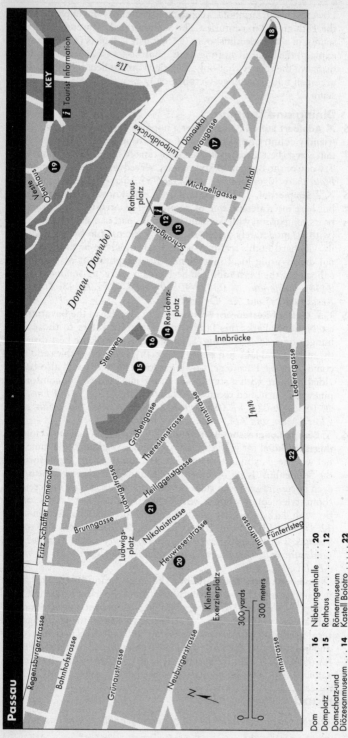

Passau

KEY

 Tourist Information

Itz

Luitpoldbrücke

Donaukai

Braugasse **17**

Michaeligasse

Innkai

Rathaus-platz

 12

13

Schrottgasse

Donau (Danube)

14 Residenz-platz

16

Steinweg

15

Innbrücke

Ledergasse

Grabengasse

Theresienstrasse

Innstrasse

Inn

22

Fritz Schäffer Promenade

Ludwigstrasse

Heiliggeistgasse

Brunngasse

21

Ludwigs-platz

Nikolaistrasse

Innrisstrasse

Fünferlsteg

Heuwieserstrasse

Regensburgerstrasse

20

Bahnhofstrasse

Kleiner Exerzierplatz

Grünaustrasse

Neuburgerstrasse

Innstrasse

Vesle Oberhaus

19

N

300 yards

300 meters

Danube plain to the south and the mountains of the Bavarian Forest to the north.

⑩ On the shore of the **Dreiburgensee** in Tittling, you'll find the **Freilicht-museum** (Open-Air Museum), which consists of 50 reconstructed Bavarian Forest houses. You can sit on the benches of a 17th-century schoolhouse, drink schnapps in an 18th-century tavern, or see how grain was ground in a 15th-century mill. ⊠ *Museumsdorf Bayerischer Wald, by Hotel Dreiburgensee, Tittling,* ☎ *08504/8482.* ⌷ *DM 5.* ⊙ *Mid-Mar.–Oct. 30, daily 8–5.*

Dining and Lodging

$–$$ ✕⌷ **Hotel Dreiburgensee.** The hotel primarily books extended vacations, but it's also convenient for an overnight stop if you're touring the Bavarian Forest or visiting the nearby open-air museum. All the hotel's rooms have balconies with views of the Dreiburgensee or the forest. Some have Bavarian-style four-poster beds with painted headboards and large, fluffy goose-down covers. Children love the sturdy bunk beds in the spacious family rooms. ⊠ *Am Dreiburgensee, Tittling/Passau, D–94100,* ☎ *08504/2092,* ℻ *08504/4926. 100 rooms. Restaurant, café, indoor pool, sauna, miniature golf, exercise room, boating, bicycles, playground. No credit cards. Closed Nov.–Jan.*

Passau

⑪ *33 km (20 mi) southeast of Schönberg, 66 km (41 mi) southeast of Deggendorf, 160 km (99 mi) northeast of Munich.*

The city perches on a narrow point of land where the Inn and the Danube meet, with wooded heights rising on the far sides of both rivers; the much smaller River Ilz also joins the Danube nearby. Most of the finest and oldest homes face the busy waterfront, where freighters and barges load and unload during journeys to and from the Black Sea and the Rhine. Narrow streets of peculiarly varying levels rise to a hill in the center of the old city. These harmonious proportions are complemented by the typical Inn Valley houses that line the streets, joined to each other by picturesque archways. Passau's Mediterranean air is due in part to the many Italian architects who worked here, and to a special quality of light that painters through the centuries have tried to capture in their work.

Passau is a remote yet important embarkation point for the traffic that has plied its way along the Danube for centuries. Settled more than 2,000 years ago by the Celts, then by the Romans, Passau later passed into the possession of prince-bishops whose domains stretched into present-day Hungary. At its height, the Passau episcopate was the largest in the entire Holy Roman Empire. The influence wielded by the prince-bishops over nearly six centuries has left its traces in the town's Residenz (bishop's palace), the Veste Oberhaus (the bishop's summer castle), and the magnificent Dom (cathedral).

For 45 postwar years Passau was a backwater in a "lost" corner of West Germany until the collapse of the Iron Curtain opened nearby frontiers, putting the historic city back on the central European map. Despite its small size, Passau has a stately, grand-dame atmosphere reminiscent of Vienna and Prague.

A Good Walk

Passau is a very snug city, sandwiched between the Danube and Inn rivers. Begin your walk at the tourist office on the west side of Rathausplatz, where you can pick up brochures and maps. Passau's 14th-century **Rathaus** ⑫ forms one side of the square and faces the Danube and its landing stages. Before leaving the square in the direction of the city center, stop by the **Glasmuseum** ⑬, in the Hotel Wilder Mann. Next, turn right at the end of the short street, Schrottgasse, and you're on Residenzplatz, dominated by the baroque bulk of the Neue Bischöfliche Residenz, where religious treasures from the city's illustrious episcopal past are housed in the **Domschatz- und Diözesanmuseum** ⑭. A flight of steps leading up from the Domschatz- und Diözesan Museum brings you to the **Domplatz** ⑮ and Passau's towering **Dom** ⑯. Leave the square by the flight of steps in the southwest corner, and you'll arrive at the Inn River. Follow the bank to the east, and you'll pass the **Kloster Niedernburg** ⑰; within 10 minutes you'll arrive at the gardens of the **Dreiflusseck** ⑱, the confluence of the Danube, Inn, and Ilz rivers. Continue along the southern bank of the Danube upstream to the Luitpoldbrücke; cross this bridge to reach the northern bank, where a steep path leads you to the **Veste Oberhaus** ⑲; you can also catch a bus to this fortress from Rathausplatz. Catch the bus back to the city center, alighting at Kleiner Exerzierplatz, bordered on one side by the immense **Nibelungenhalle** ⑳, a remainder of Nazi architecture. Now make your way back eastward to Rathausplatz, finding time to explore Passau's attractive pedestrian shopping zone (an area of eight streets); on the way, make a detour south down Obere Jägergasse to Heiliggeistgasse to visit the 15th-century **Spitalkirche Heiliger Geist** ㉑. If time permits and you're in museum mode, walk south on Heiliggeistgasse and cross the Inn River by its pedestrian bridge to the outstanding **Römermuseum Kastell Boiotro** ㉒, which holds remnants of Passau's Roman past.

TIMING

Passau can be toured leisurely in the course of one day. Try to visit the Dom at noon to hear a recital on its great organ, the world's largest. Early morning is the best time to catch the light falling from the east on the old town walls and the confluence of the three rivers. Passau shrouded in the dank river fogs of winter rivals even Venice for its brooding atmosphere.

Sights to See

⑯ **Dom** (St. Stephan's Cathedral). Passau's mighty cathedral rises majestically on the highest point of the earliest-settled part of the city, between the Danube and the Inn. A baptismal church stood here in the 6th century. Two hundred years later, when Passau became a bishop's seat, the first basilica was built. It was dedicated to St. Stephan and became the original mother church of St. Stephan's Cathedral in Vienna. A fire reduced the medieval basilica to smoking ruins in 1662; it was then rebuilt according to a design by Italian master Carlo Lurago. What you see today is an impressive building, the largest baroque basilica north of the Alps, complete with dome and flanking towers. Little in its marble- and stucco-encrusted interior reminds you of Germany, and much proclaims the exuberance of Rome. Beneath the octagonal dome is the largest church **organ** in the world. Built between 1924 and 1928 and enlarged in 1979–80, it claims no fewer than 17,774 pipes and 233 stops. ⊠ *Dompl.* ☎ *DM 2; concerts DM 4–DM 10.* ☉ *May–Oct., daily 8–11 and 12:30–6; Nov.–Apr., daily 8–dusk; tours May–Oct. and Dec. 20–25, weekdays 12:30 (assemble at cathedral's front right-hand aisle); Nov.–Dec. 19 and Dec. 26–Apr., Mon.–Sat. noon (assemble under the cathedral organ); concerts May–Oct. and Dec. 20–25, Mon.–Wed. and Fri. noon, Thurs. noon and 7:30 PM.*

⑮ **Domplatz** (Cathedral Square). In front of the ☞ **Dom**, this large square is bordered by a number of sturdy 17th- and 18th-century buildings, including the **Alte Residenz**, the former bishop's palace and now a courthouse. Domplatz is adorned by a fine statue of Bavarian king Maximilian Joseph I.

⑭ Domschatz- und Diözesanmuseum (Cathedral Treasury and Diocesan Museum). The cathedral museum houses one of Bavaria's largest collections of religious treasures, the legacy of Passau's rich episcopal history. The museum is part of the **Neue Residenz** (New Residence), which has a stately baroque entrance opening onto a magnificent staircase—a scintillating study in marble, fresco, and stucco. ⊠ *Residenzpl.* ☎ *DM 2.* ☉ *Apr.–Oct., Mon.–Sat. 10–4.*

⑱ Dreiflusseck (Junction of the Three Rivers). At this tongue of land at the eastern extremity of Passau, the Danube, Inn, and tiny Ilz rivers join together in an embrace that, thanks to a phenomenon of nature, leaves each of them with a distinct identity until they all flow out of Passau's grip and into Austria, where their waters merge into the Danube, bound for the Black Sea. For the best perspective climb to the ☞ **Veste Oberhaus** to see how the Inn's green water, typical of a mountain river, slowly gives way to the darker hues of the Danube and how the brownish Ilz adds its small contribution. It's the end of the journey for the Inn—which flows here from the mountains of Switzerland and through Austria—and the much shorter Ilz, which rises in the Bavarian Forest.

⑬ Glasmuseum (Glass Museum). The Bavarian Forest's most comprehensive exhibit of glass is in the lovely Hotel Wilder Mann (☞ Dining and Lodging, *below*). The history of central Europe's glassmaking covered through 30,000 items. ⊠ *Am Rathauspl.,* ☎ *0851/35071.* ☎ *DM 5.* ☉ *Mar.–Sept., daily 10–4; Oct.–Feb., daily 1–4.*

⑰ Kloster Niedernburg (Niedernburg Abbey). Founded in the 8th century as a convent, the abbey was destroyed by fire and rebuilt in the last century in a clumsy neo-Romanesque style. Today it's a girls' school. In its church you can see the 11th-century tomb of a queen who was once abbess here—Gisela, sister of Emperor Heinrich II and widow of Hungary's first and subsequently sainted king, Stephan, who became the patron of the Passau Cathedral. ⊠ *Bräug.* ☉ *Daily 9-dusk.*

⑳ Nibelungenhalle (Nibelungen Hall). This huge Nazi-era hall is on Passau's windswept **Kleiner Exerzierplatz** (Small Drill Square), once a Benedictine monastery garden but now an ugly parking lot. The hall's name is taken from the *Nibelungenlied,* the epic poem, written in Passau in the 12th century, that inspired Richard Wagner's immense operatic cycle *Der Ring des Nibelungen.* Later Hitler distorted the same legendary material in an attempt to legitimize the Nazi creed. His obsession with Wagner—almost surpassing that of Ludwig II—was part of his sense of himself as the preserver of a heroic Teutonic tradition. The hall is used for political rallies and trade shows and was also the reception center for the first refugees who fled East Germany in late summer 1989. ⊠ *Kleiner Exerzierpl.*

⑫ Rathaus (City Hall). Passau's 14th-century city hall sits like a Venetian merchant's house on a small square fronting the Danube. It was the home of a wealthy German merchant before being declared the seat of city government after a 1298 uprising. Two assembly rooms have wall paintings depicting scenes from local history and lore, including the (fictional) arrival in the city of Siegfried's fair Kriemhild, from the Nibelungen fable. The Rathaus tower has Bavaria's largest glockenspiel, which plays daily at 10:30, 2, and 7:25, with an additional performance at 3:30 on Saturday. ⊠ *Rathauspl.,* ☎ *0851/3960.* ☎ *DM 2.* ☉ *Apr.–Oct. and Dec. 20–25, daily 10–4.*

㉒ **Römermuseum Kastell Boiotro** (Roman Museum). A stout fortress with five defense towers and walls more than 12-ft thick came to light as archaeologists excavated the site of a 17th-century pilgrimage church on a hill known as **Mariahilfberg**, on the south bank of the Inn. The Roman citadel Boiotro was discovered along with a Roman well, its water still plentiful and fresh. Pottery, lead figures, and other artifacts from the area are housed in this museum at the edge of the site. ✉ *Ledererg. 43,* ☎ *0851/34769.* 🖙 *DM 2.* ☉ *Mar.–May and Sept.–Nov., Tues.– Sun. 10–noon and 2–4; June–Aug., Tues.–Sun. 10–noon and 1–4.*

㉑ **Spitalkirche Heiliger Geist** (Infirmary Church of the Holy Ghost). This modest city church has 16th-century stained glass and an exquisite 15th-century marble relief depicting the Way of the Cross. The church is a short walk from the ☞ **Nibelungenhalle**. Modest it may be, but the church possesses vineyards across the River Inn in neighboring Austria, and you can drink Heiliger Geist wines in several Passau taverns. ✉ *Heiliggeistg.* ☉ *Daily 9 to dusk.*

⑲ **Veste Oberhaus** (Upper House Stronghold). The powerful fortress and summer castle commissioned by Bishop Ulrich II in 1219 looks over Passau from an impregnable site on the other side of the river, opposite the Rathaus. Today the Veste Oberhaus is Passau's most important museum, containing exhibits that illustrate the city's 2,000-year history. From the terrace of its café-restaurant (open Easter–October) there's a magnificent view of Passau and the convergence of the three rivers. ✉ *Oberhausleitenstiege,* ☎ *0851/493–3512.* 🖙 *Museum DM 7. Weekdays 9–5, weekends and holidays 10–6. Closed Feb. Bus takes visitors from Rathauspl. to museum Apr.–Oct. every ½ hr 10:30–5.*

Dining and Lodging

$$–$$$ ✕ **Passauer Wolf.** The owner of this hotel, Richard Kerscher, is also master of his own kitchen, and restaurant guides crown his efforts with the highest praise. Kerscher's stylish restaurant, which commands views of the Danube from its snug window seats, is considered Passau's best. His delicacies, all based on traditional German recipes, are also served in the vaulted 16th-century wine bar. ✉ *Rindermarkt 6– 8,* ☎ *0851/931–5110. AE, DC, MC, V. Closed Sun. No lunch Sat.*

$$ ✕ **Heilig-Geist-Stiftsschänke.** For atmospheric dining this 14th-century monastery–turned–wine cellar is a must. In summer eat beneath chestnut trees; in winter seek out the warmth of the vaulted, dark-paneled dining rooms. The wines—made in Austria from grapes from the Spitalkirche Heiliger Geist vineyards—are excellent and suit all seasons. The fish comes from the Stift's own ponds. ✉ *Heiliggeistg. 4,* ☎ *0851/2607. AE, DC, MC, V. Closed Wed. and Jan. 10–Feb. 10.*

$ ✕ **Blauer Bock.** This is one of Passau's oldest houses (first mentioned in city records in 1257) and has been welcoming travelers since 1875. The Danube flows by the tavern windows, and in summer you can watch the river traffic from a beer garden. The food is as traditional as you'll find, with pork and potatoes in every variety. ✉ *Fritz-Schäffer-Promenade 20,* ☎ *0851/34637. MC, V. Closed Thurs. and Nov.–Mar.*

$ ✕ **Peschl Terrasse.** The beer you sip on the high, sunny terrace overlooking the Danube is brought fresh from the Old Town brewery below, which, along with this traditional Bavarian restaurant, has been in the same family since 1855. ✉ *Rosstränke 4,* ☎ *0851/2489. Reservations not accepted. AE, DC, MC, V. Closed Mon.*

$$$$ 🛏 **Hotel Weisser Hase.** The "White Rabbit" began accommodating travelers in the early 16th century. Rooms are decorated in sleek Ring-group style, with cherrywood and mahogany veneers and soft matching colors. The large bathrooms are finished in Italian marble. The hotel stands sturdily in the town center, at the start of the pedestrian shopping zone,

a short walk from all the major sights. All rooms have satellite TV. ✉ *Heiliggeistg. 1, D–94032,* ☎ *0851/92110,* FAX *0851/921–1100. 107 rooms, 1 suite. Restaurant, bar, in-room data ports, sauna. AE, DC, MC, V. Jan.–mid-Feb.* ✍

$$$–$$$$ ▣ **Hotel König.** Though built in 1984, the König blends successfully with the graceful Italian-style buildings alongside the elegant Danube waterfront. Rooms are large and airy; most have a fine view of the river. ✉ *Untere Donaulände 1, D–94032,* ☎ *0851/3850,* FAX *0851/385–460. 41 rooms. Bar, sauna, steam room. AE, DC, MC, V.* ✍

$$$ ▣ **Golf-Hotel Anetseder.** You don't have to be a golfer to enjoy a stay at this lodge-style hotel 7 km (4½ mi) north of Passau, although there are enticing offers that include use of the 21-hole course, which is overlooked by most of the 15 apartments. The apartments, all with kitchen facilities, are furnished in a casual, sporty style, with lots of pine wood and scatter rugs. The Bavarian Forest begins outside the hotel entrance. ✉ *Rassbach 8, Thyrnau bei Passau D–94136,* ☎ *08501/91313,* FAX *08501/91314. 14 apartments. Restaurant, kitchenettes. No credit cards. Closed Nov.–Feb.* ✍

$$–$$$ ▣ **Hotel Wilder Mann.** Passau's most historic hotel dates from the
★   11th century (renovated in the 19th and 20th centuries and kept up to contemporary standards of comfort) and shares prominence with the ancient city hall on the waterfront market square. Empress Elizabeth of Austria and American astronaut Neil Armstrong have been among its guests. On beds of carved oak you'll sleep beneath chandeliers and richly stuccoed ceilings. The swimming pool is in the 11th-century vaulted cellars. ✉ *Am Rathauspl. 1, D–94032,* ☎ *0851/ 35071,* FAX *0851/31712. 60 rooms, 5 suites. Restaurant, bar, café, indoor pool. AE, DC, MC, V.* ✍

$$ ▣ **Schloss Ort.** This 13th-century castle's latest alterations have turned its original 38 rooms into 18, giving each a spacious feel and a private bathroom. Most rooms have views of the Inn River, which flows beneath the hotel's stout walls. The restaurant is closed in winter, but the kitchen will always oblige hungry hotel guests. In summer the garden terrace is a delightful place on which to eat and to watch the river roll by. ✉ *Ort 11, D–94032.* ☎ *0851/34072,* FAX *0851/31817. 18 rooms. Restaurant, café. MC, V.* ✍

$ ▣ **Rotel Inn.** "Rotels" are usually hotels on wheels, an idea developed by a local entrepreneur to accommodate tour groups in North Africa and Asia. The first permanent Rotel Inn is on the banks of the Danube in central Passau. Its rooms are small and cabinlike, but they're clean, decorated in a pop-art style, and amazingly cheap (DM 50 for a double). The whole building breaks with traditional styles, and its design—a red, white, and blue facade and flowing roof lines—has actually been patented. It's definitely for young travelers, but also fun for families. ✉ *Am Hauptbahnhof/Donauufer, D–94032,* ☎ *0851/95160,* FAX *0851/ 951–6100. 100 rooms. No credit cards. Closed Oct.–Mar.* ✍

Golf

Europe's most extensive golf course (21 holes) is at **Thyrnau** (7 km [4½] mi northeast of Passau, ☎ 08501/91313; ☞ Golf-Hotel Anetseder *above*).

Nightlife and the Arts

Passau is the cultural center of Lower Bavaria. Its **Europäische Wochen** (European Weeks) festival—featuring everything from opera to pantomime—is a major event on the European music calendar. The festival runs from June to early August. For program details and reservations, write the Kartenzentrale der Europäischen Wochen Passau (✉ Dr.-Hans-Kapfinger-Str. 22, Passau, D–94032, ☎ 0851/560–960).

Passau's thriving theater company, the **Stadttheater,** has its home in the beautiful little baroque opera house of Passau's prince-bishops, the Fürst-bischöfliches Opernhaus. Get program details and reservations from **Stadttheater Passau** (⊠ Gottfried-Schäffer-Str. 2–4, ☎ 0851/929–1913), which hosts classical theater, opera, operetta, and occasionally ballet.

Jazz fans head to nearby Vilshofen every July for the annual international **jazz festival,** staged in a special tent on the bank of the Danube. For program details and reservations, call 08541/2080. Live jazz programs are regularly presented at Passau's **Theater im Scharfrichterhaus** (⊠ Milchg. 2, ☎ 0851/35900), home of the city's nationally famous cabaret company. The company hosts a German cabaret festival every fall from October through December.

Passau's **Christmas fair**—the Christkindlmarkt—is the biggest and most spectacular of the Bavarian Forest. It's held in and around the Nibelungenhalle from late November until just before Christmas.

OFF THE BEATEN PATH   **MT. DREISESSEL –** You can't get much more off the beaten track than in the remote corner of the country north of Passau, where the German frontier bobs and weaves along the Czech Republic and Austria. Where the border cuts across the summit of Mt. Dreisessel, west of Altre-ichenau, it's possible to walk in and out of a virtually forgotten corner of the Czech Republic—a feat that was possible even when the border was guarded everywhere else by heavily armed soldiers. *Dreisessel* means "three armchairs," an apt description of the summit and its boulders, which are shaped like the furniture of a giant's castle. If you're driving to the Dreisessel, take B–12 to Philippsreut, just before the frontier, and then follow the well-marked country road. The mountain is about 67 km (42 mi) from Passau. Several bus operators in Passau and surrounding villages offer tours. There are no visitor facilities within the forest.

THE BAVARIAN FOREST A TO Z

Arriving and Departing

By Car

The principal autobahns that link to the Bavarian Forest are the A–3 from Nürnberg and the A–92 from Munich. Traffic on both roads is always relatively light. Passau is 229 km (142 mi) from Nürnberg and 179 km (111 mi) from Munich.

By Plane

The nearest airports are in Munich and Nürnberg. Each is about 160 km (100 mi) from the western edge of the Bavarian Forest.

Getting Around

By Bus

Villages not on the railway line are well served by postbus. In winter a network of special ski buses links most of the region's resorts. Resorts on the edge of the Bavarian Forest National Park and below the Rachel and Lusen mountains are linked May–October by bus. A fleet of Igel (Hedgehog) minibuses penetrates deep into the forest on roads barred to other motor traffic. Passau has a municipal bus service that reaches into the hinterland.

By Car

The small country highways and side roads within this region are less traveled, making the entire area something of a paradise for those put off by the high-speed mayhem of most other German roads. B–85 runs the length of the Bavarian Forest from Passau to Cham, and its designation as a route of special scenic interest (the Ostmarkstrasse) extends northward to Bayreuth.

By Train

Two main rail lines cross the region: one runs west–east via Nürnberg, Regensburg, Passau, and Vienna; the other runs south–north via Munich, Landshut, and Straubing. This latter route slices right through the heart of the Bavarian Forest, making stops in Deggendorf, Plattling, and Bayerischer Eisenstein on its way to the Czech Republic (if you're going on to Prague, this is the train to take). Deutsche Bahn runs a special holiday express daily from Hamburg to Bavarian Forest resorts, with Zwiesel as its final destination. The express links up with train services from Berlin and Frankfurt International Airport. Plattling, just south of Deggendorf, and Cham are the main rail junctions for the area. Passau is the principal rail gateway on the border between southeast Germany and Austria.

Contacts and Resources

Car Rentals

Europcar (⊠ Donaustr. 2, Deggendorf, ☎ 0991/4034; ⊠ Bahnhofstr. 29, west wing of main railway station, Passau, ☎ 0851/54235). **Sixt** (⊠ Hengersbergerstr. 53, Deggendorf, ☎ 0991/340–933; ⊠ Bahnhofstr. 29, main railway station concourse, Passau, ☎ 0851/526–0250).

Cruises

Cruises on Passau's three rivers begin and end at the Danube jetties on Fritz-Schäffer Promenade. **Ludwig Wurm** (⊠ Donaustr. 71, D–94342 Irlbach, ☎ 09424/1341) has a range of small cruise-ship services upriver between Passau and Regensburg, taking in Deggendorf, Metten, Straubing, and Walhalla. **Wurm & Köck** (⊠ Höllg. 26, D–94032 Passau, ☎ 0851/929–292, ✎) runs 45-minute trips daily on the Danube, Inn, and Ilz from March through October, in the last week of December, and on weekends from mid-November to Christmas Eve. The cost is DM 11. A longer, two-hour Danube cruise aboard the newly built *Sissi* costs DM 18; cruises run daily at 11:15 and 3:15 from mid-April to mid-October. The Three Rivers trip can be combined with a cruise as far as Linz, Austria (including an overnight stay in Passau or Linz), for DM 142. Its 225-ft luxury day-cruise vessel, *Regina Danubia,* travels between Passau and Austria, usually as far as Linz.

Erste Donau-Dampfschiffahrts-Gesellschaft (DDSG; ⊠ Im Ort 14a, D–94032 Passau, ☎ 0851/33035) offers two-day cruises to Vienna, with passengers sleeping in two-bed cabins, for around DM 250 per person one-way. DDSG also offers Danube cruise connections via Budapest all the way to the Black Sea.

An Austrian shipping operator, **M. Schaurecker** (⊠ A.-Stifterstr. 34, A–4780 Schärding, ☎ 0043/771–23231), runs a daily service on the Inn River from Tuesday through Sunday, mid-March through October, between Passau and the enchanting Austrian river town of Schärding. The round-trip fare is DM 16.

Emergencies

Police and ambulance (☎ 110). **Fire and emergency medical aid** (☎ 112).

Guided Tours

Many town tourist offices (including Freyung, Furth im Wald, Grafenau, and Tittling), organize bus tours of the region and day trips to the Czech Republic (☞ Visitor Information, *below*). The **Freyung tourist office** has weekly half-day trips to the Bavarian Forest National Park and to Dreisessel Mountain for DM 8. In Tittling the **Hötl** bus company (☎ 08504/4040) has daily excursions into the Bavarian Forest in summer. From Zwiesel, **Lambürger** (✉ Stadtpl. 37, Zwiesel, ☎ 09922/84120) operates regional bus tours, as well as a tour three times a week to Prague, with a supper stop on the way home in the Plsen brewery tavern. There's a weekly tour to the Czech spas Marienbad and Karlsbad (Karlovy Vary) and another to the original home of Budweiser beer, Budweis. Guided tours of Passau are organized from April through October by the **Passau tourist office** (☎ 08551/955–980). There are two tours (at 10:30 and 2:30) on weekdays and one (at 2:30) on weekends. Tours start at the Maximilian Joseph monument in the Domplatz (cathedral square) and last one hour. The cost is DM 4.50. Day tours of the Bavarian Forest (DM 15) are offered every Monday by the **Verkehrsamt Lalling** (☎ 09904/374), the tourist office of a town near Passau. The **Wolff Ost-Reisen** bus company (☎ 09973/5080), in Furth im Wald, offers one- and two-day excursions to Prague twice a week May–October, as well as trips to the former royal spa town of Karlsbad (Karlovy Vary) in Bohemia.

Hiking and Biking

The **Fremdenverkehrsverband Ostbayern** (✉ Landshuterstr. 13, D–93047 Regensburg, ☎ 0941/57186), the **Kultur und Verkehrsamt Deggendorf** (✉ Oberer Stadtpl., ☎ 0991/296–0169, 🖂), or the **Tourismusverband Ostbayern** (☞ Visitor Information, *below*) all have details on hiking packages. Typical is a DM 225 five-day tour along the Böhmweg, which includes overnight accommodations, full breakfasts, a certificate and lapel badge, and a schnapps reception by one of the tourist offices en route. Luggage is transported from point to point along the route. **Deutsche Bahn AG** (✉ Bahnhofspl., Zwiesel D–94227, ☎ 01805/996–633), the German railway, sends hikers out on its three-day tour of the Bavarian Forest National Park with a bottle of Bärwurz schnapps. The DM 189 cost of the tour includes three nights' accommodations in a comfortable pension, breakfast, and luggage transfer. For details and maps of bike routes out of Passau, contact the tourist office in **Passau** (☞ Visitor Information, *below*).

Visitor Information

For information on the whole region, contact **Tourismusverband Ostbayern** (✉ Luitpoldstr. 20, Regensburg D–93047, ☎ 0941/585–390, 🖂).

Bayerisch-Eisenstein (✉ Verkehrsamt Bayerisch-Eisenstein, Schulbergstr., D–94252, ☎ 09925/327, 🖂). **Bodenmais** (✉ Kur-Verkehrsamt, Bahnhofstr. 56, D–94249, ☎ 09924/778–135, 🖂). **Cham** (✉ Fremdenverkehrsverein Cham, Propsteistr. 46, D–93413, ☎ 09971/857–933). **Deggendorf** (✉ Kultur–und Verkehrsamt, Oberer Stadtpl. 4, D–94469, ☎ 0991/296–0172, 🖂). **Freyung** (✉ Touristinformation/Kurverwaltung, Rathauspl. 2, D–94078, ☎ 08551/58850, 🖂). **Furth im Wald** (✉ Tourist-Information Furth im Wald, Schlosspl. 1, D–93437, ☎ 09973/50980, 🖂). **Grafenau** (✉ Verkehrsamt Grafenau, Rathausg. 1, D–94481, ☎ 08552/962–343, 🖂). **Passau** (✉ Tourist-Information Passau, Rathauspl. 3, D–94032, ☎ 0851/955–980, 🖂). **Regen** (✉ Verkehrsamt Haus des Gastes, Stadtpl., D–94209, ☎ 09921/2929, 🖂). **Schönberg** (✉ Verkehrsamt, Marktpl. 16, D–94513, ☎ 08554/960–441). **Spiegelau** (✉ Touristinformation Spiegelau, Konrad-Wilsdorf-Str. 5, D–94518, ☎ 08553/960–017, 🖂). **St. Englmar** (✉ Kurverwaltung St. Englmar, Rathausstr. 6, D–94379, ☎ 09965/840–320). **Tittling** (✉ Verkehrsamt Tittling, Marktpl. 10, D–94104, ☎ 08504/40114). **Viechtach** (✉ Tourismusverband, Rathaus, Stadtpl. 1, D–94234, ☎ 09942/1661, 🖂). **Waldkirchen** (✉ Fremdenverkehrsamt Waldkirchen, Ringmauerstr. 14, D–94065, ☎ 08581/20250, 🖂). **Zwiesel** (✉ Kurverwaltung, Stadtpl. 27, D–94227, ☎ 09922/1308, 🖂).

4 THE ROMANTIC ROAD

One of Germany's perfectly planned tour
routes, the Romantic Road is a wondrous
and fanciful journey. The southward leading
route includes Würzburg, home to a
glorious baroque palace, the medieval
town of Rothenburg-ob-der-Tauber, and
Ludwig II's fantastic Neuschwanstein
Castle. Minnesänger Walther von der
Vogelweide and medieval sculptor Tilman
Riemenschneider are among the artists
whose legacies you'll discover.

Updated by
Robert Tilley

O F ALL THE SPECIALLY DESIGNATED TOURIST ROUTES that criss-cross Germany, none rivals the aptly named Romantische Strasse, or Romantic Road. The scenery is more pastoral than spectacular, but the route is memorable for the medieval towns, villages, castles, and churches that anchor its 420-km (260-mi) length. Many of these are tucked away beyond low hills, their spires and towers poking up through the greenery.

Within the massive gates of formerly fortified settlements, half-timber houses lean against one another along narrow cobbled lanes. Ancient squares are adorned with fountains and flowers, and formidable walls are punctuated by watchtowers built to keep a lookout for marauding enemies. The sights add up to a pageant of marvels of history, art, and architecture, providing an essence of Germany at its most picturesque and romantic.

The road runs south from Würzburg, in northern Bavaria, to Füssen, on the border with Austria. You can, of course, follow it in the opposite direction, as a number of bus tours do. Either way, among the major sights you'll see are one of Europe's most scintillating rococo palaces, in Würzburg, and perhaps the best-preserved medieval town on the Continent, Rothenburg-ob-der-Tauber. Ulm, a short trip off the Romantic Road, is included here because of its magnificent cathedral. Then there's the handsome Renaissance city of Augsburg. Finally the fantastical highlight will be Ludwig II's captivating castle, Neuschwanstein.

The Romantic Road concept developed as West Germany rebuilt its tourist industry after World War II. A public-relations wizard coined the catchy title for a historic passage through Bavaria and Baden-Württemberg that could be advertised as a unit. In 1950 the Romantic Road was born. The name itself isn't meant to attract lovebirds but refers to a variation of the word *romance* that means wonderful, fabulous, and imaginative. And, of course, the Romantic Road started as a road on which the Romans traveled.

On its way the road crosses centuries-old battlefields. The most cataclysmic conflict, the Thirty Years' War, destroyed the region's economic base in the 17th century. The depletion of resources prevented improvements that would have modernized the area—thereby assuring the survival of the historic towns' now charmingly quaint infrastructures.

As you travel the Romantic Road, two names crop up repeatedly: Walther von der Vogelweide and Tilman Riemenschneider (☞ Up-Close: Tilman Riemenschneider *in* Würzburg). Walther von der Vogelweide, who died in Würzburg in 1230, was the most famous of the German *Minnesänger,* poet-musicians who wrote and sang of courtly love in the age of chivalry. Knights and other nobles would hire them to help win the favors of fair ladies. Von der Vogelweide broke with this tradition by writing love songs to maidens of less-than-noble rank. He also accepted commissions of a political nature, producing what amounted to medieval political manifestos. His work was romantic, lyrical, witty, and filled with a sighing wistfulness and philosophical questioning.

Pleasures and Pastimes

Dining

The best Franconian and Swabian food combines hearty regional specialties with nouvelle elements. Various forms of pasta are common. Try *Pfannkuchen* (pancakes) and *Spätzle* (small tagliatellelike ribbons of rolled dough), the latter often served with *Rinderbraten* (roast beef), the traditional Sunday lunchtime dish. One of the best regional dishes is *Maultaschen,* a Swabian version of ravioli, usually served floating in broth strewn with chives. Würzburg is one of the leading wine-producing areas of Germany, and the many Franconian beers range from Räucherbier (literally, "smoked beer") to the lighter ales of Ulm.

CATEGORY	COST*
$$$$	over DM 90
$$$	DM 55–DM 90
$$	DM 35–DM 55
$	under DM 35

per person for a three-course meal, including tax and excluding drinks

Golf

The countryside along the Romantic Road is ideal territory for golf; you can tee off in Aschaffenburg, Bad Mergentheim, Würzburg, at Schloss Colberg (east of Rothenburg), Augsburg, at Schloss Igling, just outside Landsberg, and virtually in the shadow of King Ludwig's fairytale castle, Neuschwanstein.

Lodging

With a few exceptions, the Romantic Road hotels are quiet and rustic, and you'll find high standards of comfort and cleanliness. Make reservations as far in advance as possible if you plan to visit in summer. Hotels in Würzburg, Rothenburg, and Füssen are often full year-round. Augsburg hotels are in great demand during trade fairs in nearby Munich. Tourist information offices can usually help with accommodations, even in high season, especially if you arrive early in the day.

CATEGORY	COST*
$$$$	over DM 230
$$$	DM 170–DM 230
$$	DM 120–DM 170
$	under DM 120

All prices are for two people in a double room.

Exploring the Romantic Road

The Romantic Road runs from the vineyard-hung slopes of the Main River valley at Würzburg to the snow-covered mountains overlooking Füssen in the Allgäuer Alps. For much of its route it follows two enchanting rivers, the Tauber and the Lech, and at one point crosses the great Danube, still a surprisingly narrow river this far from the Black Sea end of its journey. The city of Augsburg, because of its proximity to the hub of Munich, marks the natural halfway point of the Romantic Road. South of Augsburg, the road climbs gradually into the Alpine foothills and the landscape changes from the lush green of Franconian river valleys to mountain-backed meadows and forests.

Great Itineraries

Although a long-distance bus covers the Romantic Road daily during summer in less than 12 hours, each town tugs insistently at the visitor, and it's difficult to resist an overnight stay when one is sent to bed by a night watchman's bell (as in Rothenburg or Dinkelsbühl). Würzburg or Augsburg are each worth two or three days of exploration, and such attractions as the minster of Ulm are time consuming but rewarding diversions from the recognized Romantic Road.

Numbers in the text correspond to numbers in the margin and on the Romantic Road, Würzburg, Rothenburg-ob-der-Tauber, and Augsburg maps.

IF YOU HAVE 3 DAYS

Join the Romantic Road at ⛫ **Augsburg** ④⓪–⑤② and spend your first day and night immersing yourself in the Fugger family history. On the second day head north, making stops at **Donauwörth** ③⑧ (lingering for a lunchtime view of the Danube), **Nördlingen** ③⑦, **Dinkelsbühl** ③⑥, and **Feuchtwangen** ③⑤; stay overnight within the ancient walls of ⛫ **Rothenburg-ob-der-Tauber** ②⑦–③④. On the third day continue on to **Creglingen** ②⑤ to admire the Tilman Riemenschneider altar in the **Herrgottskirche** ②⑥, just outside the village, and then travel through the lovely Tauber River valley, visiting **Weikersheim** ②④, **Bad Mergentheim** ②③, and **Tauberbischofsheim** ⑤, until you reach your final destination, ⛫ **Würzburg** ⑦–②②.

IF YOU HAVE 5 DAYS

Tackle the entire length of the Romantic Road, starting with a day and night in ⛫ **Würzburg** ⑦–②②. From Würzburg follow the three-day itinerary described above in reverse order to ⛫ **Rothenburg** ②⑦–③④, where you'll spend the night. Continue to **Dinkelsbühl** ③⑥ and **Nördlingen** ③⑦ and rest after the third day in ⛫ **Augsburg** ④⓪–⑤②. Explore the rich city before joining the Lech River valley at **Landsberg am Lech** ⑤③ (where Hitler wrote *Mein Kampf* while in the town prison). Continue on to **Schongau** ⑤④, where you'll see the Alps rising up ahead; they're the signal to watch for one of the most glorious sights of the Romantic Road, the rococo **Wieskirche,** which stands in a heavenly Alpine meadow (Wiese). As it heads into the Alps, the Romantic Road has even more spectacular sights, particularly the most eccentric of "Mad" King Ludwig's castles, **Schloss Neuschwanstein** ⑤⑦. Finally, spend the day in ⛫ **Füssen** ⑤⑧ (the natural end of the Romantic Road).

IF YOU HAVE 7 DAYS

Begin at **Aschaffenburg** ①, 50 km (31 mi) east of Frankfurt, with its magnificent Renaissance castle, the Schloss Johannisburg. Next visit a smaller but no less impressive castle, **Mespelbrunn** ②, in the Spessart uplands. Continue through the Main Valley and explore the lovely old medieval towns of **Miltenberg** ③ and **Wertheim** ⑥. Devote two days to ⛫ **Würzburg** ⑦–②② before heading south. Take day four to investigate ⛫ **Rothenburg-ob-der-Tauber** ②⑦–③④ (overnighting within its medieval walls), and spend the fifth day of your tour visiting two other exquisitely preserved medieval towns, **Dinkelsbühl** ③⑥ and **Nördlingen** ③⑦. Rest your fifth night in ⛫ **Augsburg** ④⓪–⑤②. On the sixth day continue to ⛫ **Füssen** ⑤⑧, which provides a good base for day trips to **Schloss Neuschwanstein** ⑤⑦ and the lovely **Wieskirche.**

When to Tour the Romantic Road

Late summer and early autumn are the best times to travel the Romantic Road, when the grapes ripen on the vines around Würzburg and the geraniums run riot on the medieval walls of towns like Rothenburg and Dinkelsbühl. You'll also miss the high-season summer crush of tourists. Otherwise, consider visiting the region in the depths of December, when Christmas markets pack the ancient squares of the Romantic Road towns and snow gives turreted Schloss Neuschwanstein its final magic touch.

NORTHERN ROMANTIC ROAD

The northern section of the Romantic Road skirts the wild open countryside of the Spessart uplands, following the sinuous course of the Main River eastward as far as Würzburg, before heading south through the plains of Swabia and along the lovely Tauber and Lech rivers.

The Romantic Road

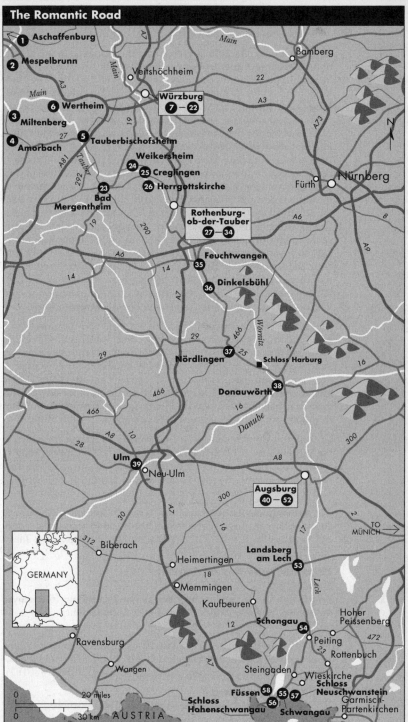

The Romantic Road

1 Aschaffenburg
2 Mespelbrunn
6 Wertheim
3 Miltenberg
4 Amorbach
5 Tauberbischofsheim
Veitshöchheim
Würzburg
7 — 22
Bamberg
Main
Main
Main
Fürth
Nürnberg
Weikersheim
24 25 Creglingen
26 Herrgottskirche
23 Bad Mergentheim
Rothenburg-ob-der-Tauber
27 — 34
35 Feuchtwangen
36 Dinkelsbühl
Schloss Harburg
37 Nördlingen
38 Donauwörth
Wörnitz
Danube
Ulm
39 Neu-Ulm
Augsburg
40 — 52
TO MÜNICH
Biberach
GERMANY
Heimertingen
Landsberg am Lech
53
Memmingen
Kaufbeuren
Hoher Peissenberg
Ravensburg
Schongau
54
Peiting
Rottenbuch
Wangen
Steingaden
Wieskirche
Schloss Neuschwanstein
Füssen
58 55 57
56
Schwangau
Garmisch-Partenkirchen
Schloss Hohenschwangau
AUSTRIA

0   20 miles
0   30 km

Aschaffenburg

❶ *50 km (31 mi) east of Frankfurt.*

Strictly speaking, Aschaffenburg isn't on the Romantic Road; it's one of the highlights of another German holiday route, the Strasse der Residenzen, which features palaces of electors and bishops. The town bears mention for its imposing Renaissance castle, **Schloss Johannisburg** (Johannisburg Palace). The prince-electors of Mainz, hereditary rulers of Aschaffenburg in the 17th and 18th centuries, lived here. The exterior of the doughty sandstone castle harks back to the Middle Ages, and four massive corner towers guard the inner courtyard. The interior contains both the **Schloss Museum** (Castle Museum), which charts the history of the town and contains a representative collection of German glass, and the **Staatsgalerie** (City Art Gallery). A small section of the latter is devoted to Lucas Cranach the Elder (1472–1553), a leading painter of the German Renaissance, known for his enigmatic nudes and haunting landscapes. The palace grounds contain a striking copy of the temple of Castor and Pollux in Pompeii, the **Pompejanum** (✉ DM 4; ☉ Mid-Mar.–mid-Oct., Tues.–Sun. 10–12:30 and 1:30–5), constructed for Ludwig I of Bavaria in 1840–50. A wine cellar–restaurant, the Schlossweinstuben, is an ideal setting for Franconian wines and food. ✉ *Schlosspl. 1,* ☎ *06021/12440.* ✉ *DM 5.* ☉ *Apr.–Oct., Tues.–Sun. 9–noon and 1–5; Nov.–Mar., Tues.–Sun. 11–4. Restaurant closed Mon.*

The **Stiftskirche** (Collegiate Church) of Sts. Peter and Alexander has a gaunt and haunting painting by Matthias Grünewald (circa 1475–1528), *The Lamentation of Christ*. It was part of a much larger and now lost altarpiece. See how, in spite of the lessons of Italian Renaissance painting, naturalism and perspective still produce an essentially Gothic image, attenuated and otherworldly. Little remains of the original Romanesque building here, save the cloisters; most of what you see dates from the 16th and 17th centuries. ✉ *Lanlingstr.* ☉ *Daily 9–dusk.*

Germany's oldest chessboard, a 14th-century treasure, can be seen in the **Stiftsmuseum** (Collegiate Church Museum), in the former chapter house of the Stiftskirche. The museum also contains ecclesiastical treasures and medieval carvings. ✉ *Stiftspl. 1a,* ☎ *06021/386–7414.* ✉ *DM 5.* ☉ *Wed.–Mon. 10–1 and 2–5.*

The **Automuseum Rosso Bianco** (Rosso Bianco Automobile Museum) claims to have the largest collection of historic sports cars in the world. ✉ *Obernauer Str. 125,* ☎ *06021/21358.* ✉ *DM 10.* ☉ *Apr.–Oct., Tues.–Sun. 10–6; Nov.–Mar., Sun. 10–6.*

Outdoor Activities and Sports

BALLOONING
British and American pilots fly a fleet of hot-air balloons for **Discover Ballooning** (☎ 06106/79641), based near Aschaffenburg.

GOLF
There are two attractive courses in the Afschaffenberg area: the 18-hole **Main-Spessart Club** at Marktheidenfeld (☎ 09391/8435) and a **nine-hole course** (✉ Am Heigenberg, Hösbach-Feldkahl, ☎ 06024/80187).

Dining and Lodging

$$ ✕🏠 **Hotel-Gasthof Zum Goldenen Ochsen.** The half-timber, lantern-hung exterior of the Golden Bull is colorful testimony to this ancient lodging, which was sheltering travelers in Renaissance times. It's been in the present family for one of its four centuries. Many of the cozy rooms have views over Schloss Johannisburg, the park, and the river valley. Wholesome Franconian fare is served in a reconstructed 200-year-old Tyrolean farm tavern. ✉ *Karlstr. 16, D–63739,* ☎ *06021/*

23132, FAX *06021/25785. 39 rooms. Restaurant, café. AE, DC, MC, V. Closed 3 wks in Aug., 1 wk in Jan.*

Mespelbrunn

❷ *14 km (9 mi) southeast of Aschaffenburg.*

The main attraction of Mespelbrunn is a **castle,** surrounded by a moat and dominated by a massive round tower dating from the mid-16th century. The **Rittersaal** (Knights' Room), on the first floor, displays suits of armor, assorted weapons, and massive dark furniture. A more delicate note is struck by the 18th-century **Chinesischer Salon** (Chinese Room), upstairs. ☎ *06092/269.* ⊡ *DM 6, including guided tour.* ☉ *Mid-Mar.–mid-Nov., Mon.–Sat. 9–noon and 1–5, Sun. 9–5.*

En Route The road south cuts through the still sparsely populated forest area of the **Spessart,** a walker's paradise that used to be the hunting grounds of the archbishops of Mainz and the haunt of Robin Hood–type outlaws. The road meets up with the River Main at the village of **Grossheubach** and then follows it on a picturesque, serpentine route to Würzburg.

Miltenberg

❸ *30 km (18 mi) south of Mespelbrunn, 70 km (43 mi) west of Würzburg.*

If you love the charm of Rothenburg-ob-der-Tauber but shrink from crowds, Miltenberg—a sleepy riverside town on the southern slopes of the forested Spessart—provides the ideal antidote. The steeply sloping **Marktplatz** is the standout attraction. A 16th-century fountain, bordered by geraniums, splashes in its center; tall half-timber houses—some six stories high, with crooked windows balancing yet more flowers—stand guard all around. One of them is the **town museum.** To see more of these appealing buildings, stroll down Hauptstrasse, site of the **Rathaus** (town hall) and the 15th-century **Haus zum Riesen** (Giant's House). The town takes its name from its **castle,** whose entrance is on the Marktplatz.

Dining and Lodging

$ ✕⊞ **Haus zum Riesen.** Built in 1590, the Giant's House is one of the oldest inns in Germany—the origins of its strange name are lost. Great roasts and fat sausages are served with excellent local beer and wines. Above the restaurant are moderately priced rooms. ⊠ *Hauptstr. 97,* ☎ *09371/3644. 14 rooms. No credit cards. Closed Jan. and Feb. No dinner Tues.*

En Route From Miltenberg you can choose one of two scenic routes to Würzburg. One road, B–426, follows the meanderings of the Main River. Taking the southern loop of B–469 to B–47 to B–27 leads you first to historic towns such as Tauberbischofsheim and Amorbach.

Amorbach

❹ *12 km (7 mi) south of Miltenberg.*

The little town of Amorbach, in the beautiful Odenwald Forest, has the impressive onetime Benedictine abbey church of **St. Maria.** You'll see works here from the 8th through the 18th centuries, one architectural style superimposed upon the next. The facade of the church seems a standard baroque structure, with twin domed towers flanking a lively and well-proportioned central section; in fact, it is a rare example of the baroque grafted directly onto a Romanesque building. Look closely and you'll notice the characteristic round arches of the Romanesque marching up the muscular towers. It's the onion-shape domes and the colored stucco applied in the 18th century that make them seem baroque. There are no such stylistic confusions in the interior, however; all is baroque power and ornamentation. The mighty baroque organ, built by the esteemed Stumm family, is recognized as one of the finest in Europe. Brief organ recitals are given during church tours May–October, Tuesday–Saturday at 11 and 3, Sunday at noon. ⊠ *Kirchpl.,* ☎ *09373/971–545.* ☑ *DM 4, including tour of church and monastery.* ☉ *Mar., Mon.–Sat. 10–noon and 1–4, Sun. 11:30–4; Apr.–Oct., Mon.–Sat. 10–noon and 1–5, Sun. 11:30–5; Nov.–Dec., Mon.–Sat. 1:30–4, Sun. 11:30–4; Jan.–Feb., weekends 1:30–4.*

Amorbach has several rustic half-timber houses; the **Templerhaus** was built in 1291 by a local nobleman. ⊠ *Bederweg.* ☑ *DM 2.* ☉ *May–Oct., Wed. 4:30–5:30, Sat. 11–noon.*

The **Sammlung Berger** (Berger Collection) has a collection of 17,000 teapots, mostly from Britain and the United States. An unusual exhibit traces the story of Pepsi-Cola, thanks to Herr Berger's personal obsession with the company. The gift shop sells a wide range of teapots made by a local firm. ⊠ *Wolkmannstr. 2,* ☎ *09373/618.* ☑ *Free.* ☉ *Apr.–Oct., Tues.–Sun. 11–6.*

OFF THE
BEATEN PATH

BURG WILDENBERG – Minnesinger Wolfram von Eschenbach (1170–1220) may have written part of his Parzival tale in this 1,000-year-old fortress. The metrical epic of the Holy Grail inspired Richard Wagner's libretto for *Parsifal.* The ruins are 5 km (3 mi) southeast of Amorbach. The castle keep is still standing, and it affords a fine view of the Odenwald Forest. ☑ *DM 2.50.* ☉ *Sun. 10–5.*

Dining

$ ✕ **Cafe Schlossmühle.** This charming café-restaurant is in the former mill of the abbey, and on warm days you can eat outside beside the mill stream. The simple menu has reasonably priced dishes, and the pastries are scrumptious. ⊠ *Schlosspl. 4,* ☎ *09373/1254. No credit cards. Closed Jan.*

Nightlife and Arts

Regular **recitals** are held on the great organ at St. Maria (☞ *above*). Call 09373/971–545 for program details.

Tauberbischofsheim

⑤   *40 km (25 mi) east of Amorbach, 36 km (22 mi) southwest of Würzburg.*

The bustling little Tauber River town of Tauberbischofsheim has a parish church, open daily 9–dusk, with a side altar richly carved by a follower of Tilman Riemenschneider. The 13th-century **Kurmainzisches Schloss** (Main Electors' Castle) has a collection of historical furnishings, tools, and costumes of commoners. ⊠ *Schlossstr. 1,* ☎ *09341/3760.* ☑ *DM 3.* ☉ *Easter–Oct., Tues.–Sat. 2:30–4:30; Sun. 10–noon and 2:30–4:30.*

Wertheim

⑥   *30 km (19 mi) east of Miltenberg*

Wertheim is the chief town on the northern Main Valley road to Würzburg and has a beautiful location at the confluence of the Main and Tauber rivers. The town was founded in 1306 and proclaims its medieval origins through a jumble of half-timber houses with jutting gables. Those in the central **Marktplatz** are the most attractive.

The romantic ruins of the **Burg Wertheim,** a 12th-century fortress built for the counts of Wertheim, have a restaurant and a memorable view of the Main Valley.

Würzburg

40 km (25 mi) east of Wertheim, 115 km (71 mi) east of Frankfurt.

The basically baroque city of Würzburg, the pearl of the Romantic Road, is a heady example of what happens when great genius teams up with great wealth. Beginning in the 10th century, Würzburg was ruled by powerful (and rich) prince-bishops, who created the city with all the remarkable attributes you see today.

This glorious city at the junction of two age-old trade routes is in a calm valley backed by vineyard-covered hills. Festung Marienberg, a fortified castle on the steep hill across the Main River, overlooks the compact town. Constructed between 1200 and 1600, the fortress was the residence of the prince-bishops for 450 years.

Present-day Würzburg is by no means completely original. On March 16, 1945, seven weeks before Germany capitulated, Würzburg was all but obliterated by Allied saturation bombing. The 20-minute raid destroyed 87% of the city and killed at least 4,000 people. Reconstruction has returned most of the city's famous sights to their former splendor. Except for a new pedestrian zone, it remains a largely authentic restoration.

A Good Walk

No two sights are more than 2 km (1 mi) from each other. Begin your tour on Marktplatz (Market Square) at the city tourist office, in the mansion **Haus zum Falken** ⑦. Collect the handy English-language tour map with a route marked out. Red signs throughout the city point the way between major sights. Next door to the Haus zum Falken is one of the city's loveliest churches, the delicate **Marienkapelle** ⑧. Leave the square at its eastern exit, and you'll find yourself on Würzburg's traffic-free shopping street, **Schönbornstrasse** ⑨, named after the city's greatest patron, the prince-bishop Johann Philipp Franz von Schönborn. Head north, passing the **Augustinerkirche** ⑩, a former Dominican church, and you'll arrive within a few minutes at the broad Juliuspromenade, dominated by the impressive baroque **Juliusspital** ⑪, an infirmary for needy citizens. Follow Juliuspromenade eastward, and you'll come to the first baroque church built in Franconia, the **Stift Haug** ⑫. Next, follow the street opposite the church, Textorstrasse, to Theaterstrasse, passing the Gothic **Bürgerspital** ⑬, another charitable institution. At the end of Theaterstrasse stands the mighty **Residenz** ⑭ of the Würzburg prince-bishops, built for Schönborn by the great baroque-era architect Balthasar Neumann.

From the Residenz walk down Domerschulstrasse and turn left onto Schönthalstrasse, where you'll find the **Alte Universität** ⑮. The southern section of the building is taken up by the Neubaukirche, a fine Renaissance church. Next, head north on Schönthalstrasse to Plattnerstrasse; where this street becomes Schönbornstrasse you'll find Würzburg's cathedral, the **Dom St. Kilian** ⑯, and the nearby **Neumünster** ⑰ church. From the cathedral take Domstrasse westward, and you'll see the high tower of the 14th-century **Rathaus** ⑱; beyond this building the **Alte Mainbrücke** ⑲ crosses the Main River. Stroll north along the riverbank to one of Würzburg's familiar city landmarks, the **Alter Kranen** ⑳, a wharf crane. To conclude your walk, cross the river on the bridge and climb the vineyard-covered hill to the great fortress that broods over Würzburg, the **Festung Marienberg** ㉑. Within its massive walls are two very interesting museums. You can ride back into central Würzburg on the bus that stops in front of the main entrance.

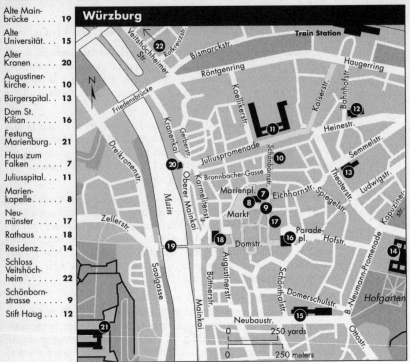

TIMING

You need two days to do full justice to Würzburg. The Residenz alone
demands several hours' attention. But if time is short, head for the Residenz as the doors open in the morning, before the first crowds assemble.
Aim to complete your tour of the Residenz by lunchtime; then continue to the nearby Juliusspital Weinstuben (☞ Dining and Lodging,
below) or one of the many traditional taverns in the area. In the afternoon explore central Würzburg and cross the Main River to visit
the Festung Marienberg and the Mainfränkisches Museum.

Sights to See

❶❾ Alte Mainbrücke (Old Main Bridge). This ancient structure crossing the
Main River began construction towards its present form in 1473.
Twin rows of infinitely graceful statues of saints line the bridge. They
were placed there in 1730, at the height of Würzburg's baroque period. Note particularly the *Patronna Franconiae* (commonly known
as the Weeping Madonna). There's also a beautiful view of the Marienberg Fortress from the bridge—statues in the foreground, Marienberg
and its vineyards as the focal point—which makes a perfect photograph
to treasure as a souvenir of this historic city.

❶❺ Alte Universität (Old University). Founded by Prince-Bishop Julius
Echter and built in 1582, this rambling institution is one of Würzburg's
most interesting Renaissance structures. ⊠ *Neubaustr. 1–9.*

❷⓪ Alter Kranen. The Old Crane, near the Main River and north of the
Old Main Bridge, was erected in 1772–73 by Balthasar Neumann's son
Franz Ignaz Michael.

❶⓪ Augustinerkirche (Church of St. Augustine). This fine baroque church,
another work by Neumann, was a 13th-century Dominican chapel; Neu-

mann retained the soaring, graceful choir and commissioned Antonio Bossi to add colorful stuccowork to the rest of the church. ⊠ *Dominikanerpl. 2,* ☎ *0961/30970.* ☉ *Daily 7–6.*

🚯 **Bürgerspital.** Wealthy burghers founded this refuge for the city's poor and needy in 1319; it now sells wine. The arcaded courtyard is baroque in style. A weekly tour (Saturday at 2) includes a glass of wine in the DM 7 price. ⊠ *Theaterstr. 19,* ☎ *0931/35030.*

🚯 **Dom St. Kilian.** St. Kilian Basilica, Würzburg's Romanesque cathedral and the fourth largest of its kind in Germany, was begun in 1045. Step inside and you'll find yourself, somewhat disconcertingly, in a shimmering rococo treasure house. This is only fitting: Prince-Bishop von Schönborn is buried here, and it's hard to imagine him slumbering amid the dour weightiness of a Romanesque edifice. His tomb is the work of his architect and builder Balthasar Neumann; Würzburg's master sculptor Tilman Riemenschneider carved the tombstones of two other bishops at the cathedral. ⊠ *Paradepl., south end of Schönbornstr.,* ☎ *0931/53691.* ▨ *Tour DM 3.* ☉ *Easter–Oct., Mon.–Sat. 10–5, Sun. 1–6; Nov.–Easter, Mon.–Sat. 10–noon and 2–5, Sun. 12:30–1:30 and 2:30–6; guided tours Easter Mon.–Oct., Mon.–Sat. noon, Sun. 12:30.*

🚯 **Festung Marienberg** (Marienberg Fortress). Beginning in the 13th century, this complex was the original home of the prince-bishops. The oldest buildings—note especially the **Marienkirche** (Church of the Virgin Mary), the core of the residence—date from around 700, although excavations have disclosed evidence that there was a already a settlement here in the Iron Age, 3,000 years ago. In addition to the rough-hewn medieval fortifications, there are a number of Renaissance and baroque apartments. To reach the hilltop Marienberg, you can make the fairly stiff climb on foot through vineyards, or take the bus from the Old Main Bridge. It runs every half hour starting at 9:45 AM.

The highlight of a visit to the Marienberg is the **Mainfränkisches Museum** (Main-Franconian Museum; ▨ DM 3.50; ☉ Apr.–Oct., Tues.–Sun. 10–5; Nov.–Mar., Tues.–Sun. 10–4). This remarkable collection of art treasures traces the rich and varied history of the city. The stand-out is the gallery devoted to Würzburg-born sculptor Tilman Riemenschneider, who lived from the late 15th to the early 16th centuries; the collection includes the originals of the great Adam and Eve statues, copies of which adorn the portal of the Marienkapelle. Two previously unknown works by Riemenschneider—a Madonna and child and a Crucifixion—were discovered in 1994–95. Both had been in private collections, where they had remained for decades without anyone suspecting they were by Riemenschneider. They were added to the Mainfränkisches Museum collection in 1996, together with two other works discovered in private possessions and thought to be by pupils of the master. Paintings by Tiepolo and Cranach the Elder and exhibits of porcelain, firearms, antique toys, and ancient Greek and Roman art are also on view. Other exhibits include enormous old winepresses and the history of Franconian wine making. ☎ *0931/43016.* ▨ *Fortress tour DM 2.* ☉ *Apr.–Oct., weekends 10, 11, 1, 2, 3, and 4.*

The Marienberg collections are so vast that they spill over into another outstanding museum that is part of the fortress, the **Fürstenbaumuseum** (Princes' Quarters Museum), which traces the 1,200 years of Würzburg's history. There are some breathtaking exhibits of local goldsmiths' art. ☎ *0931/43838.* ▨ *DM 3, combined ticket for Mainfränkisches and Fürstenbau museums DM 6.* ☉ *Apr.–Sept., Tues.–Sun. 9–5; Oct.–Mar., Tues.–Sun. 10–4.*

Close-Up

TILMAN RIEMENSCHNEIDER

TILMAN RIEMENSCHNEIDER, Germany's master of late-Gothic sculpture (1460–1531), lived an extraordinary life. His skill with wood and stone was recognized at an early age, and he soon presided over a major Würzburg workshop. Riemenschneider worked alone, however, on the life-size figures that dominate his sculptures. Details like the folds of a robe or wrinkles upon a face highlight his grace and harmony of line.

At the height of his career Riemenschneider was appointed city councillor; later he became mayor of Würzburg. In 1523, however, he made the fateful error of siding with the revolutionaries in the Peasants' Revolt. He was arrested and held for eight weeks in the dungeons of the Marienberg Fortress, above Würzburg, where he was frequently tortured. Most of his wealth was confiscated, and he returned home a broken man. He died in 1531.

For nearly three centuries he and his sculptures were all but forgotten. Only in 1822, when ditchdiggers uncovered the site of his grave, was Riemenschneider once again included among Germany's greatest artists. Today Riemenschneider is recognized as the giant of German sculpture. The richest collection of his works is in Würzburg, although other masterpieces are on view in churches and museums along the Romantic Road as well as in other parts of Germany; for example, the renowned *Windsheim Altar of the Twelve Apostles* is in the Palatine Museum in Heidelberg.

Haus zum Falken. The city's most splendid baroque mansion, formerly a humble inn, now houses the city tourist office. Its colorful rococo facade was added in 1751. ⊠ *Am Markt 1*, ☎ *0931/373–398 or 0931/372–398.* ⊗ *Weekdays 10–6, Sat. 10–2; Apr.–Oct., also Sun. 10–2.*

Juliusspital. Founded in 1576 by Prince-Bishop Julius Echter as a home for the poor, the elderly, and the sick, this enormous edifice now houses an impressive restaurant serving wine from the institution's own vineyards (☞ Dining and Lodging, *below*). It also sells wineglasses. Residents of an adjacent home for the elderly receive a free quarter liter of wine daily. A glass of wine is included in a weekly tour of the wine cellars. ⊠ *Juliuspromenade 19*, ☎ *0931/393–1400.* ▣ *DM 8.* ⊗ *Apr.–Oct., Fri. at 3.*

Marienkapelle (St. Mary's Chapel). This tranquil Gothic church (1377–1480) tucked modestly away at one end of Würzburg's market square is almost lost amid the historic old facades. Balthasar Neumann lies buried in the church. Pause beneath the finely carved portal and inspect the striking figures of Adam and Eve; you shouldn't have great difficulty recognizing the style of Tilman Riemenschneider. These are copies; the original statues are in Würzburg's Mainfränkisches Museum (☞ *above*). ⊠ *Marktpl.*, ☎ *0931/53691.* ⊗ *Daily 8–6:30.*

Neumünster (New Minster). Next to the ☞ **Dom St. Kilian**, this 11th-century Romanesque basilica was completed in 1716. The original church was built above the grave of the early Irish martyr St. Kilian, who brought Christianity to Würzburg and, with two companions, was put to death here in 689. Their missionary zeal bore fruit, however—17 years after their death a church was consecrated in their memory. By 742 Würzburg had become a diocese, and over the following centuries 39 flourishing churches were established throughout the city. The Neumünster's former cloistered churchyard contains the grave of Walther von der Vogelweide, one of the most famous German minstrels. ⊠ *Schönbornstr., ☎ 0931/53691. ⊘ Daily 7–6.*

⑱ **Rathaus.** The Gothic town hall, once headquarters of the bishop's administrator, has been the center of municipal government since 1316. A permanent exhibition in the tower documents Würzburg's destruction by Allied bombs, some examples of which are on display. ⊠ *Marktpl., ☎ 0931/370. ▤ Free. ⊘ Weekdays 9–5; tours Apr.–Oct., Sat. 10; May–Oct., Wed. 4:30, Sat. 10.*

⑭ **Residenz** (Residence). The line of Würzburg's prince-bishops lived in this glorious baroque palace after moving down from ☞ **Festung Marienberg,** their hilltop fortress. Construction of the baroque palace started in 1719 under the brilliant direction of Balthasar Neumann. Most of the interior decoration was entrusted to the Italian stuccoist Antonio Bossi and the Venetian painter Giovanni Battista Tiepolo. But the man whose spirit infuses the Residenz was the pleasure-loving prince-bishop Johann Phillip Franz von Schönborn, who financed the venture but did not live to see the completion of what is now considered one of Europe's most sumptuous buildings, known as the "Palace of Palaces." This dazzling structure is a 10-minute walk from the railway station, along pedestrians-only Kaiserstrasse and then Theaterstrasse.

From the moment you enter the building, the splendor of the Residenz is evident as the largest baroque staircase in the country, the **Treppenhaus,** stretches away from you. Halfway up, the stairway splits and peels away 180 degrees to the left and to the right.

Dominating the upper reaches of this vast space is Tiepolo's giant fresco *The Four Continents,* a gorgeous exercise in blue and pink, with allegorical figures at the corners representing the four continents known at the time. Tiepolo immortalized himself and Balthasar Neumann as two of the figures. See if you can find them; they're not too difficult to spot. Sadly, although the fresco survived the devastating wartime bombing raid on the town, it is showing signs of crumbling and urgently needs restoration.

Next, make your way to the **Weissersaal** (White Room) and then beyond to the grandest of the state rooms, the **Kaisersaal** (Throne Room). The baroque ideal of the *Gesamtkunstwerk*—fusion of all the arts— is perfectly illustrated here. Architecture melts into stucco; stucco invades the frescoes; the frescoes extend the real space of the room into their illusionary world. Nothing is quite what it seems, and no expense was spared to make it so. Tiepolo's frescoes show the 12th-century visit of Emperor Frederick Barbarossa to Würzburg to claim his bride. That the characters all wear 16th-century Venetian dress hardly seems to matter. Few interiors use such startling opulence to similar effect.

You'll find more of this expansive spirit in the **Hofkirche,** the chapel, which demonstrates the prince-bishops' love of ostentation. Among the lavish marble, rich gilding, and delicate stuccowork, note the Tiepolo altarpieces, ethereal visions of *The Fall of the Angels* and *The Assumption of the Virgin.* (⊘ Apr.–Oct., Tues.–Sun. 9–noon and 1–5; Nov.–Mar., Tues.–Sun., 9–noon and 1–4). Finally, tour the **Hofgarten;** the entrance is next to the chapel. This 18th-century formal garden, with its stately gushing fountains and trim ankle-high shrubs outlining geometric flower beds and gravel walks, is the equal of any in the country. ⊠ *Residenzpl.*, ☎ *0931/355–1712.* ☞ *DM 7, including guided tour.* ☉ *Apr.–Oct., Tues.–Sun. 9–5; Nov.–Mar., Tues.–Sun. 10–4.*

㉒ Schloss Veitshöchheim. The first summer palace of the prince-bishops is 8 km (5 mi) north of Würzburg, at Veitshöchheim. Though it has little of the glamorous appeal of the Residenz, the sturdy baroque building provides further evidence of the great wealth of the worldly rulers of Würzburg. A bus service to the palace runs from Würzburg's Kirchplatz. From mid-April to mid-October a boat service operates between Würzburg and the palace daily from 10 to 4. The 40-minute trip costs DM 8 one-way, DM 13 round-trip. ☎ *0931/91582.* ☞ *DM 3, including guided tour.* ☉ *Palace Apr.–Oct., Tues.–Sun. 9–noon and 1–5; park daily 7–dusk.*

❾ Schönbornstrasse. Würzburg's main pedestrian mall is chock-full of upscale boutiques and not-so-posh eateries. The cafés are great for people-watching.

⑫ Stift Haug. Franconia's first baroque church was designed by the Italian architect Antonio Petrini and built between 1670 and 1691. Its elegant twin spires and central cupola make an impressive exterior; unfortunately the once-exuberant interior was destroyed in the March 1945 bombing of the city. The altarpiece is a 1583 Crucifixion scene by Tintoretto. ⊠ *Bahnhofstr. at Heinestr.,* ☎ *0931/54102.* ☉ *Daily 8–6:30.*

Dining and Lodging

$$ **✕ Juliusspital Weinstuben.** The tavern serves wine from its own vineyard; the food—predominantly large portions of basic Franconian fare—takes second billing. ⊠ *Juliuspromenade 19,* ☎ *0931/393–1400. No credit cards. Closed Wed.*

$$ **✕ Ratskeller.** The vaulted cellars of Würzburg's Rathaus shelter one
★   of the city's most popular restaurants. Beer is served, but Franconian wine is what the regulars drink. The food is staunch Franconian fare. ⊠ *Beim Grafeneckart, Langg. 1,* ☎ *0931/13021. Reservations not accepted. AE, DC, MC, V.*

$ **✕ Backöfele.** More than 400 years of tradition are sustained by this old tavern. You can dine well and inexpensively on such dishes as oxtail in Burgundy sauce and homemade *Rissoles* (filled pastries) in wild-mushroom sauce. ⊠ *Ursulinerg. 2,* ☎ *0931/59059. AE, MC, V.*

$ **✕ Wein- und Speisehaus zum Stachel.** On a warm spring or summer
★   day take a bench in the ancient courtyard of the Stachel, which is shaded by a canopy of vine leaves and girded by high walls of creeper-hung stone. The entrées are satisfyingly Franconian, from lightly baked onion cake to hearty roast pork. But the real reason to come here is to sample the wine, made from the tavern's own grapes. ⊠ *Gresseng. 1,* ☎ *0931/52770. No credit cards. No dinner Sun.*

$$$$ **✕⌂ Hotel Walfisch.** You'll breakfast in a dining room on the banks of the Main with views of the vineyard-covered Marienberg. For lunch and dinner try the hotel's cozy Walfisch-Stube restaurant. Guest rooms are furnished in solid Franconian style with farmhouse cupboards, bright fabrics, and heavy drapes. ⊠ *Am Pleidenturm 5, D–97070,* ☎ *0931/ 35200,* 𝔽𝔸𝕏 *0931/352–0500. 40 rooms. Restaurant. AE, DC, MC, V.* ✿

$$$–$$$$ **✕⌂ Hotel Greifensteiner Hof.** The Greifensteiner, completely renovated in 1999, offers comfortable, individually furnished rooms in a quiet corner of the city, just off the market square. The cheaper doubles are small but lack no comforts or facilities. The hotel restaurant, the Fränkische Stuben, has very good cuisine—mostly Franconian specialties. ⊠ *Dettelbachergasse 2, D–97070,* ☎ *0931/35170,* 𝔽𝔸𝕏 *0931/ 57057. 42 rooms. Restaurant. AE, DC, MC, V.* ✿

$$$–$$$$ ✕🔁 **Ringhotel Wittelsbacher Höh.** From most of the cozy rooms under the steep eaves of this historic redbrick mansion, you'll have a view of Würzburg and the vineyards. The restaurant's wine list embraces most of the leading local vintages, and Franconian and international dishes pack the menu. In summer take a table on the terrace and soak in the view. ✉ *Hexenbruchweg 10, D–97082,* ☎ *0931/42085,* FAX *0931/ 415–458. 73 rooms, 1 suite. Restaurant, sauna. AE, DC, MC, V.* ✎

$$$ ✕🔁 **Fränkischer Hotelgasthof zur Stadt Mainz.** This traditional Franconian inn, dating from the early 15th century, is among the country's best. Its frescoed facade is a favored motif for photographers. Within, the friendly old hostelry offers comfort and a cuisine based on its own historic recipe book. Eel from the Main River, prepared in a dill sauce, and locally caught carp and pike are specialties. Homemade apple strudel is served with afternoon coffee and also finds its way onto the dinner dessert menu. The breakfast buffet is enormous. Rooms are comfortably furnished, with old-fashioned touches such as gilt mirrors and heavy drapes. ✉ *Semmelstr. 39, D–97070,* ☎ *0931/53155,* FAX *0931/58510. 15 rooms. Restaurant. AE, MC, V. Closed Dec. 20–Jan. 20.*

$$$$ 🔁 **Hotel Rebstock zu Würzburg.** This hotel's rococo facade has wel-
★ comed guests for centuries. The spacious lobby, with its open fireplace and beckoning bar, sets the tone, and an attractive winter garden was recently added. All rooms are individually decorated and furnished in English country-house style, with Laura Ashley fabrics. ✉ *Neubaustr. 7, D–97070,* ☎ *0931/30930,* FAX *0931/309–3100. 63 rooms, 9 suites. Restaurant, bar, Weinstube, no-smoking rooms. AE, DC, MC, V.*

$$ 🔁 **Strauss.** Close to the river and the pedestrians-only center, the pink-stucco Strauss has been in the same family for more than 100 years. Rooms were totally renovated in 1999 and are brightly furnished in light woods; those on the top floor are particularly cozy, some with exposed beams. The beamed Würtzburg restaurant serves Franconian cuisine, as well as international dishes, complemented by excellent Franconian wines. ✉ *Juliuspromenade 5, D–97070,* ☎ *0931/30570,* FAX *0931/305–7555. 75 rooms, 3 suites. Restaurant, bicycles. AE, DC, MC, V. Closed Dec. 20–mid-Jan.* ✎

Nightlife and the Arts

Würzburg's cultural year starts with a Classical Music Days Festival in April and May and ends with a Johann Sebastian Bach Festival in November. Its annual Mozart Festival, between May and June, attracts visitors from all over the world. Most concerts are held in the magnificent setting of the Residenz. The annual jazz festival is in November. The town hosts a series of wine festivals, climaxing in the Vintners' Festival, in September.

Outdoor Activities and Sports

Visitors are welcome to play at **Würzburg Golf Club** (✉ Giebelstädter Steige, ☎ 0931/67890). The club has a 9-hole course.

Shopping

Würzburg is the true wine center of the Romantic Road. Visit any of the vineyards that rise from the Main River and choose a *Bocksbeutel,* the distinctive green, flagon-shape wine bottle of Franconia. It's claimed that the shape came about because wine-guzzling monks found it the easiest to hide under their robes. In Würzburg itself you'll want to linger on **Schönbornstrasse** and the adjacent marketplace. Wine and Franconia's distinctive goblets are sold in many of the shops here. Homemade chocolates and other local delicacies share shelf space with the best Franconian wine and schnapps at the **Bayerisches Schokoladenhaus** (✉ Echhornstr. 2, ☎ 0961/18080).

The old **Bürgerspital** and **Juliusspital** (☞ Sights to See, *above*) both sell fine wines. The **Haus des Frankenweins** (House of Franconian Wine; ⊠ Kranenkai 1, ☎ 0931/390–110) has wine tastings for individual visitors. Some 600 Franconian wines and a wide range of wine accessories can be purchased.

En Route   From Würzburg follow the Romantic Road through Bavarian Franconia and Swabia and into the mountains of Upper Bavaria. For the first stretch, to Bad Mergentheim, take either the B–27 to Tauberbischofsheim and then the B–290, or the more direct B–19. Both routes take you through the open countryside of the Hohenloher Plain.

Bad Mergentheim

㉓ *44 km (28 mi) south of Würzburg.*

Between 1525 and 1809, Bad Mergentheim was the home of the Teutonic Knights, one of the most successful medieval orders of chivalry. Their greatest glories came in the 15th century, when they were one of the dominant powers of the Baltic, ruling large areas of present-day eastern Germany, Poland, and Lithuania. The following centuries saw a steady decline in the order's commercial success. In 1809 Napoléon expelled the Teutonic Knights from Bad Mergentheim as he marched toward his ultimately disastrous Russian campaign. The French emperor had little time for what he considered the medieval superstition of such orders. The expulsion seemed to sound the death knell of the little town. But in 1826 a shepherd discovered mineral springs on the north bank of the river. They proved to be the strongest sodium sulfate and bitter-salt waters in Europe, with health-giving properties that ensured the town's future prosperity.

The **Deutschordensschloss,** the Teutonic knights' former castle, at the eastern end of the town, has a museum that follows the history of the order. ⊠ *Schloss 16,* ☎ *07931/52212.* 🎟 *DM 6; guided tours DM 2.* ☉ *Tues.–Sun. 10–5. Tours Thurs. and Sun. at 3.*

☾ The **Wildpark Bad Mergentheim,** just outside Bad Mergentheim, is a wildlife park with Europe's largest selection of European species, including wolves and bears. ⊠ *B–290,* ☎ *07931/41344.* 🎟 *DM 12.* ☉ *Mid-Mar.–Oct., daily 9–6; Nov.–mid-Mar., weekends 10:30–5.*

OFF THE BEATEN PATH   **STUPPACH –** This village, 11 km (7 mi) southeast of Bad Mergentheim, has a chapel guarding one of the great Renaissance German paintings, the so-called *Stuppacher Madonna,* by Matthias Grünewald (circa 1475–1528). It was only in 1908 that experts finally recognized it as the work of Grünewald; repainting in the 17th century had turned it into a flat and unexceptional work. Though Grünewald was familiar with the developments in perspective and natural lighting of Italian Renaissance painting, his work remained resolutely anti-Renaissance in spirit: tortured, emotional, dark. Compare it with that of Dürer, his contemporary. While Dürer used the lessons of Italian painting to reproduce its clarity and rationalism, Grünewald used them for expressionistic purposes to heighten his essentially Gothic imagery. ☉ *Chapel Mar.–Apr., daily 10–5; May–Oct., daily 9–5:30; Nov.–Feb., daily 11–4.*

Dining and Lodging

$ ✕ **Kettler's Altfränkische Weinstube.** You'll want to come here to try the *Nürnberger Bratwürste*—finger-size spicy sausages—and to enjoy the atmosphere of a snug 180-year-old Franconian tavern. The wine list is enormous. ⊠ *Krumme Gasse 12,* ☎ *07931/7308. No credit cards.*

$$$$ ✕🏨 **Victoria.** This is one of the area's finest spa hotels, combining cosmopolitan flair with rural solitude. Rooms are large, luxurious, and furnished in the style of a country mansion, with king-size beds, well-cushioned armchairs, subdued lighting, and prints on the textile-hung walls. The lounge is scarcely less opulent, with an open fireplace and a library. The excellent Markthalle restaurant, with a magnificent tile oven taking pride of place, draws a clientele from far afield. ⊠ *Poststr. 2–4, D–97980,* ☎ *07931/5930,* 🇫🇦🇽 *07931/593–500. 75 rooms, 3 suites. Restaurant, bar, pub, beauty salon, sauna. AE, DC, MC, V.* ☕

Weikersheim

㉔ *10 km (6 mi) east of Bad Mergentheim, 40 km (25 mi) south of Würzburg.*

The Tauber River town of Weikersheim is dominated by the **castle** of the counts of Hohenlohe. The great hall of the castle is the scene each summer of an international youth music festival, and the **Rittersaal** (Knights' Hall) contains life-size stucco wall sculptures of animals, reflecting the counts' love of hunting. In the cellars you can drink a glass of cool wine drawn from the huge casks that seem to prop up the building. Outside again, stroll through the enchanting gardens and enjoy the view of the Tauber and its leafy valley. 🎫 *DM 7, gardens only DM 2.50.* ⊙ *Apr.–Oct., daily 9–6; Nov.–Mar., daily 10–noon and 1:30–4:30.*

Dining and Lodging

$$ ✕🏨 **Flair Hotel Laurentius.** This traditional old hotel on Weikersheim's market square is an ideal stopover on a tour of the Romantic Road. You can avoid the crowds and the relatively high prices of nearby Rothenburg and still be within an hour's drive of most sights on the northern route. Rooms are very comfortable and individually furnished, some with German antiques. The vaulted ground floor has a cozy wine tavern, a very good restaurant named, like the hotel, after the patron saint of cooks, and a brasserie. ⊠ *Marktpl. 5, D–97990,* ☎ *07934/91080,* 🇫🇦🇽 *07934/910–818. 13 rooms. Restaurant, brasserie, café, Weinstube, sauna. AE, DC, MC, V.* ☕

Creglingen

㉕ *20 km (12 mi) east of Weikersheim, 40 km (25 mi) south of Würzburg.*

The village of Creglingen has been an important pilgrimage site since the 14th century, when a farmer had a vision of a heavenly host plowing his field. The **Herrgottskirche** (Chapel of Our Lord) is in the Herrgottstal (Valley of the Lord), 3 km (2 mi) south of Creglingen; the way there is well signposted. The chapel was built by the counts of Hohenlohe, and in the early 16th century Tilman Riemenschneider carved an altarpiece for it. This enormous work, 33 ft high, depicts in minute detail the life and ascension of the Virgin Mary. Riemenschneider entrusted much of the background detail to the craftsmen of his Würzburg workshop, but he allowed no one but himself to attempt its life-size figures. Its intricate detail and attenuated figures are a high point of late-Gothic sculpture. 🎫 *DM 2.* ⊙ *Apr.–Oct., daily 9:15–5:30; Nov.–Mar., Tues.–Sun. 10–noon and 1–4.*

The **Fingerhutmuseum** (Thimble Museum) is opposite the Herrgottskirche. *Fingerhut* is German for "thimble," and the museum has thousands of them, some dating from Roman times. 🎫 *DM 2.* ⊙ *Apr.–Oct., daily 9–6; Nov.–Mar., daily 1–4.*

The fascinating **Feuerwehrmuseum** (Firefighting Museum), with an impressive collection of old fire engines, lies 8 km (5 mi) north of Creglingen, within the stout castle walls of Schloss Waldmannshofen. ⊠ *Waldmannshofen,* ☎ *09335/8166* ☜ *DM 4.* ◯ *Easter–Oct., daily 10–noon and 2–4.*

Lodging

$ ☏ **Heuhotel Ferienbauernhof.** For a truly off-the-beaten-track experience, book a space in the hayloft of the Stahl family's farm at Creglingen. Visitors bed down in freshly turned hay in the farmhouse granary. Bed linen and blankets are provided. The overnight rate of DM 28 includes a cold supper and breakfast. For a few marks more you can swap the granary for one of three comparatively luxurious double rooms or even an apartment. Children are particularly well catered to, with tours of the farmyard and their own playground. ⊠ *Weidenhof 1, D–97993,* ☎ *07933/378,* ℻ *07933/7515. No credit cards.* ✍

Rothenburg-ob-der-Tauber

★ *20 km (12 mi) southeast of Creglingen, 75 km (47 mi) west of Nürnberg.*

Rothenburg-ob-der-Tauber (literally, "red castle on the Tauber") is the kind of medieval town that even Walt Disney might have thought too picturesque to be true, with half-timber architecture galore and a wealth of fountains and flowers against a backdrop of towers and turrets. As late as the 17th century it was a small but thriving market town that had grown up around the ruins of two 12th-century churches destroyed by an earthquake. Then it was laid low economically by the havoc of the Thirty Years' War, and with its economic base devastated, it slumbered until modern tourism rediscovered it. It milks its best-preserved-medieval-town-in-Europe image to the fullest, undoubtedly something of a tourist trap but genuine enough for all the hype. There really is no place quite like it. Whether Rothenburg is at its most appealing in summer, when the balconies of its ancient houses are festooned with flowers, or in winter, when snow lies on its steep gables, is a matter of taste. Few people are likely to find this extraordinary little survivor from another age anything short of remarkable.

A Good Walk

Sights are dotted around town, and the streets don't lend themselves to a particular route. However, the **Rathaus** ㉗, on Rathausplatz, is a logical place to begin a tour. The **Herterlichbrunnen** ㉘ is just steps away, on Marktplatz, and a bit farther north is the **Stadtpfarrkirche St. Jakob** ㉙, where you'll find a magnificent Riemenschneider altar. From the church follow Klingengasse north to the church of **St. Wolfgang's** ㉚, built into the defenses of the town. On the outside it blends into the forbidding **Stadtmauern** ㉛. Through an underground passage you can reach the sentry walk above and follow the western stretch of the city wall to the **Reichsstadtmuseum** ㉜. Farther along the wall you'll reach the **Mittelalterliches Kriminalmuseum** ㉝. In nearby Hofbronnengasse, the **Puppen und Spielzeugmuseum** ㉞ is within a 15th-century building.

TIMING
Crowds will affect the pace at which you can tour the town. Early morning is the only time to appreciate the place in relative calm. The best times to see the mechanical figures on the Rathaus wall are in the evening, at 8, 9, or 10.

Sights to See

㉘ **Herterlichbrunnen** (Herterlich Fountain). A *Schäfertanz* (Shepherds' Dance) was performed around the ornate Renaissance fountain on the

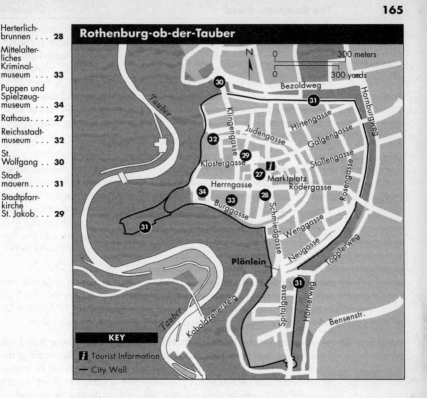

Rothenburg-ob-der-Tauber

central Marktplatz whenever Rothenburg celebrated a major event. The dance is still done, though nowadays for the benefit of tourists. It takes place in front of the Rathaus several times a year, chiefly at Easter, in late May, and regularly in June and July. ☒ *Marktpl.*

③③ **Mittelalterliches Kriminalmuseum** (Medieval Criminal Museum). The gruesome medieval implements of torture on display here are not for the fainthearted. The museum, the largest of its kind in Europe, also soberly documents the history of German legal processes in the Middle Ages. ☒ *Burgg. 3,* ☎ *09861/5359.* ☜ *DM 6.* ☉ *Apr.–Oct., daily 9:30–6; Nov., Jan., and Feb., daily 2–4; Dec. and Mar., daily 10–4.*

③④ **Puppen und Spielzeugmuseum** (Doll and Toy Museum). This complex of medieval and baroque buildings houses more than 1,000 dolls, the oldest dating from 1780, the newest from 1940, as well as a collection of dollhouses, and model shops and theaters guaranteed to charm every youngster. ☒ *Hofbronneng. 13,* ☎ *09861/7330.* ☜ *DM 5.* ☉ *Jan. and Feb., daily 11–5; Mar.–Dec., daily 9:30–6.*

②⑦ **Rathaus.** Half of the city hall is Gothic, begun in 1240; the other half is neoclassical, started in 1572. A fire in 1501 destroyed the part of the structure that is now the Renaissance section, which faces the main square. Below the building are the **Historiengewölbe** (Historical Vaults; ☜ DM 5; ☉ mid-Mar.–Apr., daily 10–5; May–Oct., daily 9–6; Oct.–mid-Dec., daily 10–5), a museum that concentrates on the Thirty Years' War. Great prominence is given to an account of the Meistertrunk (Master Drink), an event that will follow you around Rothenburg. It came about when the Protestant town was captured by Catholic forces. During the victory celebrations, the conquering general was embarrassed to find himself unable to drink a great tankard of wine in one go, as his manhood demanded. He volunteered to spare the town further destruction if any of the city councillors could drain the mighty six-pint draught. The mayor took up the challenge and succeeded, and Rothenburg was preserved. The tankard itself is on display at the Reichsstadtmuseum (☞ *below*). On the north side of the main square is a fine clock, placed there 50 years after the mayor's feat. A mechanical figure acts out the epic Master Drink daily on the hour from 11 to 3 and in the evening at 8, 9, and 10. The feat is also celebrated at two annual pageants, when townsfolk parade through the streets in 17th-century garb. ⊠ *Rathauspl.,* ☎ *09861/40492 for tower.* 🎫 *DM 1.* ☉ *Tower Apr.–Oct., daily 9:30–12:30 and 1–5; Dec., daily noon–5; Nov. and Jan.–Mar., weekends 12–3.*

㉜ Reichsstadtmuseum (Imperial City Museum). This city museum is two attractions in one. Its artifacts illustrate Rothenburg and its history. Among them is the great tankard, or *Pokal,* of the Meistertrunk (☞ Rathaus, *above*). The setting of the museum is the other attraction; it's in a former Dominican convent, the oldest parts of which date from the 13th century. Tour the building to see the cloisters, the kitchens, and the dormitory; then see the collections. ⊠ *Klosterhof 5,* ☎ *09861/939–043.* 🎫 *DM 5.* ☉ *Apr.–Oct., daily 9:30–5:30; Nov.–Mar., daily 1–4.*

㉚ St. Wolfgang (St. Wolfgang's). An historic parish church of Gothic origins with a baroque interior, St. Wolfgang's is most notable for how it blends into the forbidding city wall. ⊠ *Klingeng.,* ☎ *09861/40492.* 🎫 *DM 2.* ☉ *Apr.–Oct., daily 10–1 and 2–5; closed Nov.–Mar.*

㉛ Stadtmauern (City Walls). Rothenburg's city walls are more than 2 km (1 mi) long and provide an excellent way of circumnavigating the town from above. The walls' wooden walkway is covered by eaves. Stairs every 200 or 300 yards provide ready access. There are superb views of the tangle of pointed and tiled red roofs and of the rolling country beyond.

㉙ Stadtpfarrkirche St. Jakob (Parish Church of St. James). The church has some notable Riemenschneider sculptures, including the famous Heiliges Blut (Holy Blood) altar. Above the altar a crystal capsule is said to contain drops of Christ's blood. There are three 14th- and 15th-century stained-glass windows in the choir, and the Herlin-Altar is famous for its 15th-century painted panels. ⊠ *Klosterg. 15,* ☎ *09861/ 700–620.* 🎫 *DM 2.50.* ☉ *Easter–Oct., daily 9–5:30; Nov. and Jan.–Easter, daily 10–noon and 2–4; Dec., daily 10–5.*

Dining and Lodging

$$$ ✕ **Die Blaue Terrasse.** The view of the Tauber Valley from the windows
★ of the elegant, pillared restaurant in the Hotel Goldener Hirsch (☞ *below*) almost rivals its nouvelle cuisine, prepared with regional touches. Snails and asparagus (in season) are perennial favorites. ⊠ *Untere Schmiedg. 16–25,* ☎ *09861/7080. Jacket and tie. AE, DC, MC, V. Closed mid-Dec.–Jan.*

$$ ✕ **Baumeisterhaus.** In summer you can dine in one of Rothenburg's
★ loveliest courtyards, a half-timber oasis of peace that's part of a magnificent Renaissance house. If the weather's cooler, move inside to the paneled dining room. The menu, changed daily, features Bavarian and Franconian specialties. The Franconian sauerbraten or the Bavarian *Schweinsbraten* (a crusty hunk of roast pork in a beer-reduced sauce) are especially good. ⊠ *Obere Schmiedg. 3,* ☎ *09861/94700. AE, DC, MC, V.*

$$$$ ✕🏨 **Hotel Eisenhut.** It's fitting that the prettiest small town in Germany
★ should have one of the prettiest small hotels. It stands in the center of town and occupies what were originally four separate town houses, the oldest dating from the 12th century, the newest from the 16th. Inside there are enough oil paintings, antiques, and heavy beams to

make any Teutonic knight feel at home. Its restaurant is among the region's best. ⊠ *Herrng. 3–5, D–91541,* ☏ *09861/7050,* ⒻⒶⓍ *09861/70545. 76 rooms, 3 suites. Restaurant, café, piano bar, beer garden. AE, DC, MC, V.* 🍽

$$$–$$$$ ✕⬚ **Romantik-Hotel Markusturm.** The Markusturm began as a 13th-century customs house, an integral part of the city defense wall, and has since developed over the centuries into an inn and staging post and finally into a luxurious small hotel. Some rooms are beamed, others have four-poster beds or gaily painted bedsteads, and some have valuable antiques from as far back as medieval times. The excellent restaurant ($$) serves an international menu featuring fish from the hotel's own ponds and wines from the 700-year-old cellars. ⊠ *Röderg. 1, D– 91541,* ☏ *09861/94280,* ⒻⒶⓍ *09861/2692. 23 rooms, 2 suites. Restaurant, sauna. AE, DC, MC, V.*

$$–$$$$ ✕⬚ **Hotel-Restaurant Burg Colmberg.** This wonderfully atmospheric old castle hotel lies officially on the Burgenstrasse (Castle Road), and it's ideally placed to escape the tourist bustle of Rothenburg, just 20 km (12 mi) to the east. The 13th-century fortress was converted some 30 years ago into a hotel that combines a high standard of comfort with most of the original medieval features. Many bedrooms have historic mullioned windows, and most have valuable antiques. The beamed restaurant Zur Remise ($$) serves venison from the castle's own hunting grounds. ⊠ *Burg 1–3, D–91598 Colmberg,* ☏ *09803/91920,* ⒻⒶⓍ *09803/262. 24 rooms, 2 suites. Restaurant, Weinstube, 9-hole golf course, playground. AE, MC, V. Closed Jan.*

$$$–$$$$ ⬚ **Hotel Goldener Hirsch.** This lantern-hung, green-shuttered 15th-century patrician house is an inextricable part of Rothenburg's history. The Meistertrunk play was first performed here. Baroque antiques are everywhere, from the lobby to the uppermost, bay-windowed bedroom. ⊠ *Untere Schmiedg. 16–25, D–91541,* ☏ *09861/7080,* ⒻⒶⓍ *09861/708– 100. 72 rooms. AE, DC, MC, V. Closed mid-Dec.–Jan.* 🍽

$$–$$$$ ⬚ **Hotel-Gasthof Zum Rappen.** Close to the Würzburger Tor (a town gate) and first mentioned in town records in 1603, this tavern offers a surprisingly high standard of comfort behind its stout, yellow-stucco, geranium-smothered facade. Guest rooms have a colorful, airy touch, with light woods and floral fabrics. Those in the modern annex have balconies overlooking a quiet courtyard. Friday and Saturday are dance nights in the Rappenschmiede Weinstube. ⊠ *Würzburger Tor 6 and 10, D–91541,* ☏ *09861/95710,* ⒻⒶⓍ *09861/6076. 131 rooms. Restaurant, bar, beer garden, Weinstube. AE, DC, MC, V. Closed Jan.*

$$$ ⬚ **Burg-Hotel Relais de Silence.** This exquisite little hotel abuts the town wall and was once part of a Rothenburg monastery. Most rooms have a view of the Tauber Valley. All have plush furnishings, with antiques or fine reproductions. Breakfast is served in good weather on a terrace adjoining the wall. ⊠ *Klosterg. 1–3, D–91541,* ☏ *09861/94890,* ⒻⒶⓍ *09861/948–940. 15 rooms. AE, DC, MC, V.*

$$–$$$ ⬚ **Hotel Reichs-Küchenmeister.** Master chefs in the service of the Holy Roman Emperor were the inspiration for the name of this historic hotel-restaurant, one of the oldest trader's houses in Rothenburg. For five generations it has been run by the same family, which carries on the tradition of the old house with energy and flair. Rooms are furnished in a stylish mixture of old and new; light veneer pieces share space with heavy oak bedsteads and painted cupboards. ⊠ *Kirchpl. 8–9, D– 91541,* ☏ *09861/9700,* ⒻⒶⓍ *09861/970–409. 45 rooms, 2 suites, 3 apartments. Restaurant, pub, hot tub, sauna. AE, DC, MC, V.*

$–$$ ⬚ **Hotel Zapf An der Wörnitzquelle.** An American, Thomas Roe, runs the highly regarded restaurant in this pleasant country inn in the pretty village of Schillingfurst, 20 km (12 mi) from Rothenburg and 5 km (3 mi) from the Romantic Road. Ask for a room in the main house, a striking building with a stepped-gable Renaissance facade. Most rooms are in the less lovely modern extension; they are nevertheless comfortable and well furnished, with balconies. ⊠ *Dombühlerstr. 9, D–91583 Schillingfurst,* ☎ *09868/5029,* FAX *09868/989–390 or 09868/5464. 23 rooms, 2 apartments. Restaurant, beer garden, café, sauna, paddle tennis, bicycles. AE, DC, MC, V.* 🕸

$ 🖼 **Gasthof Klingentor.** This sturdy old staging post is outside the city walls but still within a 10-minute walk of Rothenburg's Old Town center. Rooms keep up a high standard of comfort. Its restaurant serves substantial Franconian fare. A well-marked cycle and hiking path starts outside the front door. ⊠ *Mergentheimerstr. 14, D–91541,* ☎ *09861/3468,* FAX *09861/3492. 20 rooms, 16 with bath. Restaurant, beer garden. MC, V.*

Nightlife and the Arts

Highlights of Rothenburg's annual calendar are the **Meistertrunk Festival,** over the Whitsun weekend, celebrating the famous wager that is said to have saved the town from destruction in the Thirty Years' War, and the **Reichstadt-Festtage,** on the first weekend of September, commemorating Rothenburg's attainment of Free Imperial City status in 1274. Both are spectacular festivals, when thousands of townspeople and local horsemen reenact the events in period costume.

Outdoor Activities and Sports

For scenery and a mild challenge, try the 9-hole golf course at **Burg Colmberg** (☎ 09803/615). It's 20 km (12 mi) east of Rothenburg.

Rothenburg from the air is also an enchanting sight. **Happy Ballooning** (☎ 09861/87888) conducts daily trips over the city and the countryside (DM 350).

Shopping

Die Schatztruhe (⊠ Untere Schmiedg. 13–15, ☎ 09861/1782) and the **Kunstwerke Friese** (⊠ Grüner Markt 7–8, near the Rathaus, ☎ 09861/ 7166) stock a selection of Hummel figures and beautifully crafted porcelain birds made by the Hummel manufacturer, the Goebel Porzellanfabrik; they also carry porcelain and glassware by other German manufacturers.

Käthe Wohlfahrt (⊠ Herrng. 1, ☎ 09861/4090) carries children's toys. The Weihnachtsdorf (Christmas Village), part of this store, is a wonderland of locally made toys and decorations; even in summer there are Christmas trees hung with brightly painted wood baubles.

Teddyland (⊠ Herrng. 10, ☎ 09861/8904) has Germany's largest teddy bear population. More than 5,000 of them pack this extraordinary store, all awaiting new homes. Kids adore the place, but be warned: these are pedigree teddies, and they don't come cheap.

Feuchtwangen

③⑤ *30 km (19 mi) south of Rothenburg-ob-der-Tauber.*

Feuchtwangen has a central market square with a splashing fountain and an ideal ensemble of half-timber houses. Summer is the time to visit, when, from mid-June to mid-August, open-air theater productions are staged in the low, graceful cloisters next to the **Stiftskirche** (Collegiate Church). Inside the church is a 15th-century altar carved by Albrecht Dürer's teacher, Michael Wohlgemut.

The **Fränkisches Museum** has an excellent collection of Franconian folk arts and crafts, including more than 600 ceramics. ⊠ *Museumstr. 19,* ☎ *09852/2575.* ☎ *DM 4.* ⊙ *Mar.–Dec., Tues.–Sun. 10–5.*

A state-run **casino** (☎ 09852/90060) opened in 2000. It has 12 roulette tables plus three tables for blackjack and poker. Admission is DM 5.

Dining and Lodging

$ ✕ **Ursel's Kleine Wirtschaft.** Ursel's "little tavern" is a typical Franconian establishment, cheap and cheerful, with a simple menu and a good selection of regional beers and wines. Monday evening features soups, while Friday is set aside for tripe dishes. ✉ *Herrenstr. 12, ☎ 09852/2387. No credit cards.*

$$$$ ✕▥ **Romantik Hotel Greifen Post.** The solid exterior of this historic
★ house (formerly a staging post on the medieval route between Paris and Prague) gives little hint of the luxuries within. Ask for the 17th-century room with the four-poster bed. If that's taken, settle for the romantic Louis XVI–style room, the Biedermeier-style room, or the room designed in Laura Ashley English country-house style. The indoor pool is within the original Renaissance walls of this ancient house. Frescoes of Feuchtwangen's past decorate the restaurant's walls. ✉ *Marktpl. 8, D–91555, ☎ 09852/6800, ℻ 09852/68068. 38 rooms. Restaurant, bar, indoor pool, sauna, bicycles. AE, DC, MC, V.* 🐾

Dinkelsbühl

★ ㊱ *12 km (7 mi) south of Feuchtwangen.*

Within the walls of Dinkelsbühl, a beautifully preserved medieval town, the rush of traffic seems a lifetime away. There's less to see here than in Rothenburg, and the mood is much less tourist-oriented. Like Rothenburg, Dinkelsbühl was caught up in the Thirty Years' War, and it also preserves a fanciful episode from those bloody times. Local lore says that when Dinkelsbühl was under siege by Swedish forces and in imminent danger of destruction, a young girl led the children of the town to the enemy commander and implored him in their name for mercy. The commander of the Swedish army is said to have been so moved by the plea that he spared the town. Whether or not it's true, the story is retold every year during the Kinderzech Festival, a pageant by the children of Dinkelsbühl during a 10-day festival in July.

The **Stadtpfarrkirche St. Georg** (St. George's Parish Church), on the Marktplatz, is the one standout sight. At 235 ft in length it's large enough to be a cathedral, and it is among the best examples in Bavaria of the late-Gothic style. Note especially the complex fan vaulting that spreads sinuously across the ceiling. If you can face the climb, head up the 200-ft tower for amazing views over the jumble of Dinkelsbühl's rooftops. ✉ *Marktpl.* ▦ *Church free; tower DM 3.* ☉ *Church daily 9–noon and 2–6; tower Sat. 10–6, Sun. 1–6.*

☺ The **Museum 3 Dimension** is the world's first museum of three-dimensional technology. Exhibitions describe how three-dimensional effects are achieved in photography, the cinema, and other art forms. Children enjoy the 3-D film run at various times during the day, as well as the 3-D art on display. ✉ *Nördlinger Tor, ☎ 09851/6336.* ▦ *DM 10, family ticket DM 30.* ☉ *Apr.–Oct., daily 10–6; Nov.–Mar., weekends 11–4 (exept Dec. 26–Jan. 5, daily 11–4).*

Dining and Lodging

$$–$$$ ✕▥ **Hotel Deutsches Haus.** This picture-postcard medieval inn, with a facade of half-timber gables and flower boxes, has many rooms fitted with antique furniture. One of them has a romantic four-poster bed. In the cozy restaurant you dine beneath heavy oak beams. ✉ *Weinmarkt 3, D–91550, ☎ 09851/6058 or 09851/6059, ℻ 09851/7911. 8 rooms, 2 suites. Restaurant, sauna, exercise room. AE, DC, MC, V. Closed Dec. 24–Jan. 6.* 🐾

$$–$$$ ✕🏨 **Hotel Goldene Kanne.** Within its historic walls, this central hotel, built in 1690, offers a high standard of comfort. Rooms are furnished with solid German oak; many have sitting-room corners with desks. The rooms even have fax connections—a rarity in this part of Germany. It's particularly recommended for families (seven of the rooms have children's beds), although lovers are also catered to with a special honeymoon suite. The cozy restaurant offers both local and international cuisine and has regular offbeat specialty weeks, featuring exotic pancake preparations and potato recipes. ⊠ *Segringerstr. 8, D–91550, ☎ 09851/572–910, FAX 09851/572–929. 23 rooms, 2 suites. Restaurant, café. AE, DC, MC, V.*

$$–$$$ ✕🏨 **Hotel-Restaurant Blauer Hecht.** A brewery tavern in the 18th century (beer is still brewed in the backyard), this Ring hotel is furnished with the sleek, dark-veneer and pastel-shaded contrasts favored by the group's interior designers. It's central but quiet. The restaurant serves fish from the hotel's own ponds. ⊠ *Schweinemarkt 1, D–91550, ☎ 09851/5810, FAX 09851/581–170. 43 rooms, 1 suite. Restaurant, bar, pub, Weinstube, indoor pool, sauna, steam room. AE, DC, MC, V. Closed Jan.* 🕾

Nightlife and the Arts

An annual open-air-theater festival from mid-June until mid-August has the ancient walls of Dinkelsbühl as its backdrop.

Shopping

At **Weschcke and Ries** (⊠ Segringerstr. 20, ☎ 09851/9439) Hummel porcelain figures share window space with other German porcelain and glassware.

Jürgen Pleikies (⊠ Segringerstr. 53–55, ☎ 09851/7596) is energetically trying to restore his town's former reputation for fine earthenware; he also offers courses at the potter's wheel. The **Reichstadt** Gallery (⊠ Segringerstr. 39, ☎ 09851/3123) displays a large selection of local artists' works. It has irregular opening hours, so call ahead. **Deleika** (⊠ Waldeck 33, ☎ 09857/97990) makes barrel organs to order, although it won't deliver the monkey! The firm also has a museum of barrel organs and other mechanical instruments. It's just outside Dinkelsbühl. Call ahead.

Nördlingen

③⑦ *32 km (20 mi) southeast of Dinkelsbühl, 70 km (43 mi) northwest of Augsburg.*

In Nördlingen the cry of *"So G'sell so"*—"All's well"—still rings out every night across the ancient walls and turrets. The town employs sentries to sound out the traditional message from the 300-ft-high tower of the central parish church of **St. Georg** at half-hour intervals between 10 PM and midnight. The tradition goes back to an incident during the Thirty Years' War, when an enemy attempt to slip into the town was detected by an alert townswoman. From the church tower—known locally as the Daniel—you'll get an unsurpassed view of the town and countryside, including, on clear days, 99 villages. However, the climb is only for the fit: the tower has 365 steps. ⊠ *Marktpl.* 🕾 *Tower DM 3.* ☉ *Daily 9–dusk.*

The ground plan of the town is two concentric circles. The inner circle of streets, whose central point is St. George's, marks the earliest boundary of the medieval town. A few hundred yards beyond it is the outer boundary, a wall built to accommodate expansion. Fortified with 11 towers and punctuated by five massive gates, it's one of the best-preserved town walls in Germany.

Nördlingen lies in the center of a huge, basinlike depression, the **Ries,** that until the beginning of this century was believed to be the remains of an extinct volcano. In 1960 it was proven by two Americans that the 24-km-wide (15-mi-wide) crater was caused by a meteorite at least 1 km (½ mi) in diameter that hit the ground at more than 100,000 mph. It turned the surface rock and subsoil upside down, hurling debris as far as Slovakia and wiping out virtually all plant and animal life within a radius of more than 100 mi. The compressed rock, or *Suevit,* formed by the explosive impact of the meteorite was used to construct many of the town's buildings, including St. Georg's tower. The **Rieskrater Museum** (Ries Crater Museum), housed in a converted 15th-century barn, tells the story of the Ries crater. ⊠ *Eugene-Schoemaker-Pl. 1,* ☎ *09081/273–8220.* 🖼 *DM 5.* ⊙ *Tues.–Sun. 10–noon and 1:30–4:30.*

For a spectacular view of Nördlingen and a view of the Ries crater, contact the local flying club, the **Rieser Flugsportverein** (☎ 09081/21050) for a ride in a light aircraft.

Nördlingen possesses one of Germany's largest steam railway engine museums, the **Bayerisches Eisenbahnmuseum,** adjacent to the railroad station. About a dozen times a year some of the old locomotives puff away on outings to Harburg. Call for a timetable. ⊠ *Am Hohen Weg,* ☎ *09083/340.* ⊙ *July–Aug., Tues.–Sat. noon–6, Sun. 10–6; Mar.–June, Sept.–Oct., Sun. 10–6.*

Dining and Lodging

$$$$ ✕ **Meyer's-Keller.** Choose between a table in the beer Stube or in the fancier restaurant; in summer take a place under chestnut and plane trees in the beer garden. Prices in the excellent restaurant are higher, but the menu is suitably diverse and imaginative. The Rieser Surprise Menu, for DM 45, features only fresh products from local farms, while a gourmet menu for about double the price includes a glass of carefully selected wine with each of the four courses. Fish dishes include freshly delivered Atlantic specialties. ⊠ *Marienhöhe 8,* ☎ *09081/ 4493. AE, MC, V. Closed Mon. No lunch Tues.*

$$$–$$$$ ✕🖼 **Astron Hotel Klösterle.** Where barefoot monks once went about their ascetic daily routine, you can dine amid ancient stonework. The comfortable, well-appointed guest rooms are anything but monastic. The hotel's striking white-and-yellow facade, with its Renaissance windows and steeply stepped gables, fits snugly into the Old Town center. You can admire the town's jumble of roofs from the top-floor fitness center and sauna–steam bath. ⊠ *Beim Klösterle 1, D–86720,* ☎ *09081/ 88054,* 🄵🄰🄷 *09081/22740. 92 rooms, 6 suites. Restaurant, Weinstube, sauna, steam room, exercise room, bicycles. AE, DC, MC, V.* 🍽

$–$$ ✕🖼 **Hotel Schützenhof.** This small, comfortable hotel on the outskirts of town is known for its excellent restaurant, which specializes in fresh fish from the surrounding lakes and rivers. Its special Venison Weeks, in the fall, are also very popular. ⊠ *Kaiserwiese 2, D–86720,* ☎ *09081/ 290–900,* 🄵🄰🄷 *09081/290–9038. 15 rooms. Restaurant, beer garden, bowling. AE, DC, MC, V. Closed 1st 2 wks in Aug. and 2 wks in Jan.*

$$$–$$$$ 🖼 **Kaiserhof-Hotel-Sonne.** The great German poet Goethe stayed here, only one in a long line of distinguished guests led off by Emperor Friedrich III in 1487. The vaulted-cellar wine tavern is a reminder of those days. The three honeymoon suites are furnished in 18th-century style, with hand-painted four-poster beds. ⊠ *Marktpl. 3, D–86720,* ☎ *09081/ 5068,* 🄵🄰🄷 *09081/23999. 40 rooms. Restaurant, Weinstube. AE, MC, V. Closed Dec. 26–mid-Jan.*

Nightlife and the Arts

An annual open-air **theater festival** has the ancient walls of Nördlingen's Alter Bastei (Old Bastion) as a backdrop. It's held from the end of June through July. A traditional **horse race,** the Scharlachrennen, with medieval origins, is held annually in August. It's the central focus of a show-jumping festival of international stature.

Outdoor Activities and Sports

Ever cycled around a huge meteor crater? You can do just that in the **Nördlingen Ries,** the basinlike depression left behind by the meteor that hit the area in prehistoric times. The Nördlingen tourist office (☎ 09081/ 84116) has a list of 10 recommended bike routes, including one 47-km (29-mi) trail around the northern part of the meteor crater. A two-day bike tour includes two overnight stops, half-board, and a picnic basket—all for DM 225 per person. Bikes can be rented from at least three shops in Nördlingen.

Shopping

Otto Wolf (⊠ Marktpl., ☎ 09081/4606) stocks a wide selection of Hummel figures at competitive prices. Nördlingen has a **market** in the pedestrian shopping zone on Wednesday and Saturday.

En Route   At the point where the little Wörnitz River breaks through the Franconian Jura Mountains, 20 km (12 mi) southeast of Nördlingen, you'll find one of southern Germany's best-preserved medieval castles. **Schloss Harburg** was already old when it passed into the possession of the counts of Oettingen in 1295; before that time it belonged to the Hohenstaufen emperors. The ancient and noble house of Oettingen still owns the castle, and inside you can view treasures collected by the family. Among them are works by Tilman Riemenschneider, along with illuminated manuscripts dating as far back as the 8th century and an exquisite 12th-century ivory crucifix. The castle is literally on the B–25, which runs under it through a tunnel in the rock. ⊠ *Harburg,* ☎ *09080/96990.* DM 7, *including guided tour.* ☉ *Mid-Mar.–Sept., Tues.–Sun. 9–5; Oct., Tues.–Sun. 9:30–4:30.* ✎

Donauwörth

❸❽   *11 km (7 mi) south of Harburg, 41 km (25 mi) north of Augsburg.*

At the old walled town of Donauwörth, the Wörnitz River meets the Danube. If you're driving, pull off into the clearly marked lot on B–25, just north of town. Below you sprawls a striking natural relief map of Donauwörth and its two rivers. The oldest part of town is on an island in the river. A wood bridge connects it to the north bank and the single surviving town gate, the Riederstor. North of the gate is one of the finest avenues of the Romantic Road: Reichsstrasse (Empire Street), so named because it was once a vital link in the Road of the Holy Roman Empire between Nürnberg and Augsburg. The Fuggers, a famous family of traders and bankers from Augsburg, acquired a palatial home here in the 16th century; its fine Renaissance-style facade under a steeply gabled roof stands proudly at the upper end of Reichsstrasse.

Dining and Lodging

$$–$$$ ✕🗟 **Posthotel Traube.** Mozart and Goethe are among the notable guests who have stayed at the Traube in the course of its 300-year history. It's one of the oldest coaching inns in the area. Part of the Ring group now, the hotel offers a high degree of comfort within its sturdy old walls. The restaurant is one of Donauwörth's best, with a wide-ranging menu featuring local and international cuisines. ⊠ *Kapellstr. 14–16, D–86609,* ☎ *0906/706–440,* ☎ *0906/23390. 39 rooms, 4 suites. Restaurant, Weinstube, sauna. AE, DC, MC, V.*

$$$ 🗟 **Parkhotel.** Members of the Landidyll chain of hotels have one fea-
★   ture in common: an idyllic location. This one qualifies with its fine position high above Donauwörth. Most rooms have floor-to-ceiling

windows and balconies with panoramic views. All are decorated in bright pastel tones and with wicker chairs and sofas. ✉ *Stern-schanzenstr. 1, D–86609,* ☎ *0906/706–510,* ℻ *0906/706–5180. 45 rooms. Weinstube, in-room data ports, in-room fax, indoor pool, bowling. AE, DC, MC, V.* 🐾

Shopping

Donauwörth is the home of the famous Käthe Kruse dolls, beloved for their sweet looks and frilly, floral outfits. You can buy them at several outlets in town, and they have their own museum, where more than 130 examples dating from 1912 are displayed in a specially renovated monastery building, the **Käthe-Kruse-Puppen-Museum.** ✉ *Pflegstr. 21a,* ☎ *0906/789–185.* 🎫 *DM 4.* ☼ *May–Sept. Tues.–Sun. 11–5; Apr. and Oct., Tues.–Sun. 2–5; Nov.–Mar., Wed. and weekends 2–5.*

Water Sports

There's challenging canoeing to be enjoyed on four rivers (including the Danube) in and around Donauwörth. The **Kanu-Laden in Donauwörth** (✉ Alte Augsburger Str. 12, ☎ 0906/8086) rents canoes and can provide professional advice and suggested routes.

Ulm

❸❾ *70 km (43 mi) southwest of Donauwörth, 65 km (40 mi) west of Augsburg.*

Ulm isn't strictly on the Romantic Road, but it's definitely worth visiting, if only for one reason: its mighty minster, with the world's tallest church tower (536 ft). The town's other claim to fame is that Albert Einstein was born here in 1879. To get to Ulm from Donauwörth, take the B–16 highway west, connecting with the B–28. For a prettier ride head back to Nördlingen and take the Schwäbische Albstrasse (the B–466 highway) south to Ulm. From Nördlingen it's about 60 km (37 mi).

Ulm grew as a medieval trading city thanks to its location on the Danube and, like so many other towns in the area, declined as a result of the Thirty Years' War. It was transferred between the neighboring states of Bavaria and Baden-Württemberg, becoming part of the latter in 1810. In response, Bavaria built Neu-Ulm in its territory, on the southern shore of the Danube. Today Ulm's Old Town presses against the river. In the Fisherman and Tanner quarters the cobblestone alleys and stone-and-wood bridges over the Blau (a small Danube tributary) are especially picturesque. A ticket covering entry to Ulm's two museums and other attractions costs DM 8.

Ulm's **Münster** (minster), the largest church in southern Germany, was unscathed by wartime bombing. It stands over the huddled medieval gables of Old Ulm, visible long before you hit the ugly suburbs encroaching on the Swabian countryside. Its single, filigreed tower challenges the physically fit to plod 536 ft up the 768 steps of a giddily twisting spiral stone staircase to a spectacular observation point below the spire. On clear days the highest steeple in the world will reward you with views of the Swiss and Bavarian Alps, 160 km (100 mi) to the south. The Münster was begun in the late-Gothic age (1377) and took five centuries to build, with completion in the neo-Gothic years of the late 19th century. It contains some notable treasures, including late-Gothic choir stalls and a Renaissance altar. ✉ *Münsterpl.* 🎫 *Tower DM 4.* ☼ *Daily 9–5. Organ recitals weekdays at 11.*

The central **Marktplatz** is bordered by handsome medieval houses with stepped gables. A market is held here on Wednesday and Saturday mornings.

A reproduction of local tailor Ludwig Berblinger's flying machine hangs inside the elaborately painted **Rathaus**. In 1811 Berblinger, a tailor and local eccentric, cobbled together a pair of wings and made a big splash by trying to fly across the river. He didn't make it, but he grabbed a place in German history books. ⊠ *Marktpl. 1.*

The **Ulmer Museum** (Ulm Museum), on the south side of Marktplatz, is an excellent natural history and art museum. Exhibits illustrate centuries of development in this part of the Danube Valley, and a modern art section has works by Kandinsky, Klee, Léger, and Lichtenstein. ⊠ *Marktpl. 9,* ☎ *0731/161–4330.* 🖾 *DM 5.* ☉ *Tues., Wed., and Fri.–Sun. 11–5, Thurs. 11–8; guided tour on Thurs. at 6.*

Einstein's home was a casualty of an Allied raid and was never rebuilt. The **Einstein Denkmal** (Einstein Monument), erected in 1979, marks the site opposite the main railway station. ⊠ *Friedrich-Ebert-Str.*

German bread is world renowned, so it's not surprising that a national museum is devoted to bread making. The **Deutsches Brotmuseum** (German Bread Museum) is housed in a former salt warehouse, just north of the Münster. It's by no means as crusty or dry as some might fear, with some often-amusing tableaux illustrating how bread has been baked over the centuries. ⊠ *Salzstadelg. 10,* ☎ *0731/69955.* 🖾 *DM 5.* ☉ *Tues. and Thurs.–Sun. 10–5, Wed. 10–8:30.*

Complete your visit to Ulm with a walk down to the **banks of the Danube,** where you'll find long sections of the old city wall and fortifications intact. The Ulmer Fischerstechen takes place in 2001, when teams of young men, dressed in historical costume and balancing on narrow canoelike craft, try to knock each other into the Danube with long poles—rather like jousting, but from boats. The festival is held every four years and is scheduled for July 15 and 22, 2001.

Dining and Lodging

$$ ✕ **Zunfthaus der Schiffleute.** The sturdy half-timber Zunfthaus (Guildhall) has stood here for more than 500 years, first as a fishermen's pub and now as a charming tavern-restaurant. Ulm's fishermen had their guild headquarters here, and when the nearby Danube flooded, the fish swam right up to the door. Today they land on the menu. One of the "foreign" intruders on the menu is Bavarian white sausage, *Weisswurst,* which even in Ulm should traditionally be eaten by midday. The local beer is an excellent accompaniment. ⊠ *Fischerg. 31,* ☎ *0731/64411. AE, DC, MC, V (Minimum amount: DM 50).*

$ ✕ **Barfüsser.** Ulm's leading brewery has two taverns, one just around the corner from the central Münsterplatz and the other across the river in Neu-Ulm (with a beer garden overlooking the Danube). The brewery's own Swabian pretzels are served in both taverns. ⊠ *Lautenberg 1,* ☎ *0731/602–1110;* ⊠ *Paulstr. 4,* ☎ *0731/974–480. No credit cards.*

$$$ ✕🏨 **Inter-City Hotel.** This is one of the newest and smartest of the German Inter-City hotels you'll find at many main railway stations. The hotel is in the city center, and although Ulm is a busy rail junction, you won't hear a thing from your soundproof room. Rooms have special work corners (with small desks and fax-modem data ports) for business travelers. It has a busy restaurant and a French-style bistro. ⊠ *Bahnhofpl. 1, D–89073,* ☎ *0731/96550,* 🅵🅰🆇 *0731/965–5999. 135 rooms. 2 restaurants, bar, in-room data ports. AE, DC, MC, V.*

$$–$$$ ✕🏨 **Hotel-Landgasthof Hirsch.** Five generations of the same Swabian family have run this century-old country tavern, which is now a comfortable hotel. In winter a fire burns in the large fireplace of the rustic lounge, while the excellent restaurant is a draw throughout the year. The hotel is 3 km (2 mi) from Ulm, in the Finningen district, and bus

stops are nearby. ✉ *Dorfstr. 4, D–89233 Finningen,* ☎ *0731/970–744,* FAX *0731/724–131. 22 rooms. Restaurant, lobby lounge, bowling. AE, DC, MC, V.* ✍

Nightlife and the Arts

The mighty organ of the **Münster** can be heard in special recitals every Sunday at 11:15 from Easter until November.

Ulm has a lively after-hours scene. The piano bar in the **Hotel Maritim** (✉ Basteistr. 40, ☎ 0731/9230) has nightly music. **Flash** (✉ Lessingstr. 8, Neu-Ulm, ☎ 0731/972–7274) is the best of the dance clubs. Jazz fans make for the **Jazzkeller Sauschdall** (✉ Prittwitzstr. 36, ☎ 0731/22279).

Augsburg

65 km (40 mi) east of Ulm, 41 km (25 mi) south of Donauwörth, 60 km (37 mi) west of Munich.

Augsburg is Bavaria's third-largest city, after Munich and Nürnberg. It dates to 15 years before the birth of Christ, when a son of the Roman emperor Augustus set up a military camp here on the banks of the Lech River. The settlement that grew up around it was known as Augusta, a name Italian visitors to the city still call it. It was granted city rights in 1156, and 200 years later was first mentioned in municipal records of the Fugger family, which was to Augsburg what the Medici family was to Florence.

A Good Walk

A walking tour of Augsburg is easy because signs on almost every street corner point the way to the chief sights. The signs are integrated into three color-charted tours devised by the tourist office, the Verkehrsverein. There's an office at Bahnhofstrasse 7, near the Hauptbahnhof, and on the south side of the central Rathausplatz. Pick up tour maps and begin your walk at Rathausplatz; the walk described below covers several of the sights described in the "green" tour.

On the eastern side of Rathausplatz rises the impressive bulk of the city's 17th-century town hall, the **Rathaus** ㊵. Even taller than the two onion domes of the Rathaus is the nearby **Perlachturm** ㊶. Follow the green signs north along Schlachthausgasse to the **Brecht Haus** ㊷, where the playwright was born; it's now a museum. Cross the nearby brook via the small bridge leading to Auf dem Rain and turn left into Barfüsserstrasse, leading to Jakoberstrasse. After 300 ft you'll find on the right the **Fuggerei** ㊸, a 16th-century housing project. Following the green signs, recross the brook (which follows the route of a Roman-built canal) and pass the small alley Hinterer Lech and turn left down Mittlerer Lech. This will lead you to the **Holbein Haus** ㊹, the home of painter Hans Holbein the Elder (at Vorderer Lech 20).

Continue farther south, recrossing the brook onto Oberer Graben, and head south through the Vogeltor, a Gothic city gate, to the southern extremities of the medieval defense wall. The gate here, the **Rotes Tor** ㊺, was the main entrance to Augsburg in earlier centuries. Now follow the green route north through a small park enclosed by the remains of the ancient bastion and continue northward; you'll soon see the soaring tower of the Gothic church of **Sts. Ulrich and Afra** ㊻, on Ulrichsplatz. Ulrichsplatz leads directly north into **Maximilianstrasse,** Augsburg's main thoroughfare. At No. 46 stands the **Schaezler Palais** ㊼, home of two impressive art collections. The Herkulesbrunnen, the fountain in the center of the street outside the palace, is a symbolic work by the Renaissance sculptor Adrian de Vries. You can see a second de

Brecht Haus. 42
Dom St. Maria 51
Fuggerei . . . 43
Fuggerhäuser 48
Holbein Haus. 44
Maximilian-Museum . . . 49
Mozart-Haus. 52
Perlachturm 41
Rathaus. . . . 40
Rotes Tor . . . 45
St. Annakirche . 50
Sts. Ulrich and Afra . . . 46
Schaezler Palais 47

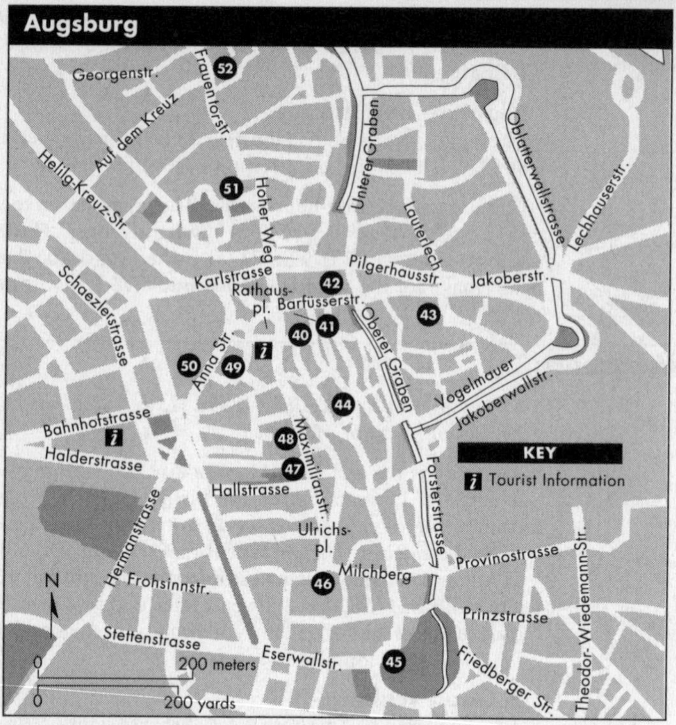

Vries fountain farther north on the same street. Just steps away on Maximilianstrasse 36 is the sturdy **Fuggerhäuser** ㊽, former home of Jakob Fugger, founder of the Fuggerei.

Wend your way across Zeugplatz, Bürgermeister-Fischer-Strasse, and Martin-Luther-Platz, to Anna-Strasse. If you have time and energy, stop at the **Maximilian-Museum** ㊾, on Phillipine-Welser-Strasse. The exquisite **St. Annakirche** ㊿ is on Anna-Strasse. Head north from here, cross busy Karlstrasse, and continue 300 ft north (through the Kesselmarkt and across Johannisgasse) to the gardens of the city cathedral, **Dom St. Maria** (51). A short walk north along Frauentorstrasse takes you to the **Mozart-Haus** (52), birthplace of Mozart's father, Leopold. By retracing your steps to the cathedral, into Hoher Weg and then Karolinenstrasse, you'll arrive within a few minutes back at Rathausplatz.

TIMING

You'll need a complete day if you linger in any of the museums. Set aside at least two hours for the Schaezler Palais, and a half hour each for the churches of Sts. Ulrich and Afra and the Dom St. Maria. There are plenty of opportunities en route for lunch or a coffee break.

Sights to See

㊷ **Brecht Haus.** This modest artisan's house was the birthplace of the renowned playwright Bertolt Brecht (1898–1956), author of *Mother Courage* and *The Three-Penny Opera.* He lived here until he moved to Munich in 1917 and then, during Hitler's reign, to Scandinavia and later the United States. After the war he settled in East Berlin to direct the Berliner Ensemble. Today the house serves as a memorial to Brecht's life and work. ✉ *Auf dem Rain 7.* *DM 2.50.* *Wed.–Sun. 10–4.*

(51) **Dom St. Maria** (Cathedral of the Virgin Mary). Augsburg's cathedral stands out within the city's panorama because of its square Gothic tow-

ers, which were built in the 9th century. A 10th-century Romanesque crypt, built in the time of Bishop Ulrich, also remains from the cathedral's early years. The heavy bronze doors on the south portal represent 11th-century craftsmanship; 11th-century windows on the south side of the nave, depicting the prophets Jonah, Daniel, Hosea, Moses, and David, form the oldest cycle of stained glass in central Europe. Five important paintings by Hans Holbein the Elder adorn the altar. The cathedral's treasures will be displayed in the ☞ **Maximilian-Museum,** pending the 2001 opening of an Episcopal Museum in the complex of ancient buildings on Domplatz. ☉ *Daily 9–dusk.*

A short walk from the cathedral will take you to the quiet courtyards and small raised garden of the former episcopal residence, a series of 18th-century buildings in baroque and rococo styles that now serve as the **Swabian regional government offices.** Although less than 64 km (40 mi) from the capital of Bavaria, you are now firmly in Swabia, once such a powerful dukedom under the Hohenstaufens that its territory covered virtually all of present-day Switzerland. Today Swabia is an administrative district of Bavaria, and Augsburg has yielded the position it once held to the younger city of Munich.

㊻ Fuggerei. This neat little settlement is the world's oldest social housing project, established by the Fugger family in 1516 to accommodate the city's deserving poor. The 104 homes still serve the same purpose; the annual rent of "one Rhenish guilder" (DM 1.72) hasn't changed, either. Residents must be Augsburg citizens, Catholic, and destitute through no fault of their own, and they must pray daily for their original benefactors, the Fugger family.

㊽ Fuggerhäuser. The 16th-century former home and business quarters of the Fugger family now houses a restaurant in its cellar and offices on the upper floors. In the ground-floor entrance are busts of two of Augsburg's most industrious Fuggers, Raymund and Anton. They are tributes from a grateful city to the wealth these merchants brought to the community. Beyond a modern glass door is a quiet courtyard with colonnades, the **Damenhof** (Ladies' Courtyard), originally reserved for the Fugger women. ✉ *Maximilianstr. 36–38.*

㊹ Holbein Haus. The rebuilt 16th-century home of painter Hans Holbein the Elder, one of Augsburg's most famous residents, is now a city art gallery, with a regularly changing program of exhibitions. ✉ *Vorderer Lech 20.* 💲 *Admission varies depending on exhibition.* ☉ *May–Oct., Tues., Wed., and Fri.–Sun. 10–5, Thurs. 10–8; Nov.–Apr., Tues., Wed., and Fri.–Sun. 10–4, Thurs. 10–8.*

㊾ Maximilian-Museum. Augsburg's main museum houses a permanent exhibition of Augsburg arts and crafts in a 16th-century merchant's mansion. ✉ *Philippine-Welser-Str. 24.* 💲 *DM 4.* ☉ *Wed.–Sun. 10–4.*

Maximilianstrasse. This main shopping street was once a medieval wine market. Today the high-gabled, pastel-color facades of the 16th-century merchant houses assert themselves against encroaching modernized shops. Most of the city's sights are on this thoroughfare or a short walk away. Two monumental and elaborate fountains punctuate the long street. At the north end the **Merkur,** designed in 1599 by the Dutch master Adrian de Vries (after a Florentine sculpture by Giovanni da Bologna), shows winged Mercury in his classic pose. Farther up Maximilianstrasse is another de Vries fountain: a bronze **Hercules** struggling to subdue the many-headed Hydra.

㊼ Mozart-Haus (Mozart House). Leopold Mozart, the father of Wolfgang Amadeus Mozart, was born in this bourgeois 17th-century residence;

he was an accomplished composer and musician in his own right. The house now serves as a Mozart memorial and museum, with some fascinating contemporary documents on the Mozart family. ✉ *Frauentorstr. 30,* ☎ *0821/5023.* ☞ *DM 2.50.* ☉ *Wed.–Sun. 10–4.*

④¹ Perlachturm (Perlach Tower). This 258-ft-high plastered brick bell tower has foundations dating to the 11th century. Although it's a long climb to the top of the tower, the view over Augsburg and the countryside is worth the effort. ✉ *Rathauspl.* ☞ *Free.* ☉ *May–mid-Oct., daily 10–6; Dec., weekends noon–7.*

④⁰ Rathaus Augsburg's city hall, on the main square, was Germany's largest when it was built in the early 17th century; it is now regarded as the finest Renaissance secular structure north of the Alps. Its **Goldenener Saal** (Golden Hall) was given its name because of its rich decoration—a gold-based harmony of wall frescoes, carved pillars, and coffered ceiling. ✉ *Rathauspl.,* ☎ *0821/5020.* ☞ *DM 3.* ☉ *10–6 on days when no official functions take place.*

④⁵ Rotes Tor (Red Gate). The city's most important medieval entrance gate once straddled the main trading road to Italy. It provides the backdrop to an open-air opera and operetta festival in June and July.

⑤⁰ St. Annakirche (St. Anna's Church). This site was formerly part of a Carmelite monastery, where Martin Luther stayed in 1518 during his meetings with Cardinal Cajetanus, the papal legate sent from Rome to persuade the reformer to renounce his heretical views. Luther refused, and the place where he publicly declared his rejection of papal pressure is marked with a plaque on ☞ **Maximilianstrasse.** Visitors can wander through the quiet cloisters of the former monastery, dating from the 14th century, and view the chapel used by the Fugger family until the Reformation. ✉ *Anna-Str., west of Rathauspl.* ☉ *Daily 9–dusk.*

④⁶ Sts. Ulrich and Afra. This imposing basilica, standing at the highest point of the city, was built on the site of a Roman cemetery where St. Afra was martyred in AD 304. The original structure was begun in the late-Gothic style in 1467; a baroque preaching hall was added in 1710 as the Protestant church of St. Ulrich. St. Afra is buried in the crypt, near the tomb of St. Ulrich, a 10th-century bishop who helped stop a Hungarian army at the gates of Augsburg in the Battle of the Lech River. The remains of a third patron of the church, St. Simpert, are preserved in one of the church's most elaborate side chapels. From the steps of the magnificent altar, look back along the high nave to the finely carved baroque wrought-iron and wood railing that borders the entrance. As you leave, pause to look into the separate but adjacent Protestant church of St. Ulrich, the former chapter house that was taken over and reconstructed by the Lutherans after the Reformation. ✉ *Ulrichspl.* ☉ *Daily 9–dusk.*

④⁷ Schaezler Palais. This elegant 18th-century city palace was built by the von Liebenhofens, a family of wealthy bankers. Schaezler was the name of a baron who married into the family. The von Liebenhofens wanted to outdo the Fuggers—but not at any price. To save money, in an age when property was taxed according to the length of its frontage on the street, they commissioned a long, narrow building running far back from Maximilianstrasse. The palace is composed of a series of interconnecting rooms leading back to a green-and-white rococo ballroom: an extravagant two-story hall heavily decorated with mirrors, chandeliers, and wall sconces. While on her way from Vienna to Paris to marry Louis XVI, in 1770, Marie Antoinette was the guest of honor at the inauguration ball.

Today the palace rooms contain the **Deutsche Barockgalerie** (German Baroque Gallery), a major art collection that features works of the 17th and 18th centuries. The palace adjoins the former church of a Dominican monastery. A steel door behind the palace's banquet hall leads into another world of high-vaulted ceilings, where the **Staatsgalerie Altdeutsche Meister,** a Bavarian state collection, highlights old-master paintings, among them a Dürer portrait of one of the Fuggers. ⊠ *Maximilianstr. 46.* ▣ *DM 4.* ◔ *Wed.–Sun. 10–4.*

Dining and Lodging

$$ ✕ **Die Ecke.** This attractive and popular restaurant is tucked away in an *Ecke* (corner) behind Augsburg's city hall. The Ecke is valued for the imaginative variety of its cuisine and the scope of its wine list. In season the venison dishes are among Bavaria's best. Fish—in particular, locally caught trout (the *truit meunière,* sautéed in butter and lightly dressed with herbs and lemon, is magnificent)—is another specialty. ⊠ *Elias-Holl-Pl. 2,* ☎ *0821/510–600. Reservations essential. AE, DC, MC, V.*

$$ ✕ **Fuggerkeller.** The vaulted cellars of the former Fugger home on Augsburg's historic Maximilianstrasse are now a bright and comfortable restaurant, owned and run by the luxurious Drei Mohren Hotel above it. The midday specials are a particularly good value; try the Swabian-style stuffed cabbage rolls in a spiced meat sauce. Prices for dinner are higher. ⊠ *Maximilianstr. 38,* ☎ *0821/516–260. AE, DC, MC, V. Closed Sun. and 1st 3 wks in Aug.*

$$ ✕ **Restaurant Oblinger.** Respected chef Albert Oblinger has moved his successful restaurant one house farther down the street, into his Oblinger Hotel. It's now smaller and more intimate, but otherwise little has changed. Some of the specialties with which he achieved national prominence are still on the menu, including Augsburg-style herb soup (rich vegetable broth spiced with rosemary and other herbs). The Swabian dumplings and regional accompaniments such as raviolilike *Maultaschen* are as good as ever. ⊠ *Pfärrle 16,* ☎ *0821/345–8392. AE, DC, MC, V. Closed Sun. and Mon. and Aug. 1–15.*

$$ ✕ **Welser Kuche.** You can practically hear the great oak tables groan
★ under the array of Swabian specialties offered here. Give a day's notice if you want the eight-course menu, however. Be sure to try the Spätzle. ⊠ *Maximilianstr. 83,* ☎ *0821/96110. No credit cards. No lunch.*

$$$$ ✕▥ **Steigenberger Drei Mohren Hotel.** Kings and princes have slept here. So did both Napoléon and the duke of Wellington, who defeated him at Waterloo. The historic hotel takes its name from three very early guests of lesser renown: Abyssinian bishops who sought shelter in this worldly German city. Dining options are the Mediterranean-style restaurant, the well-loved, traditional Maximilian's, and the busy bistro. ⊠ *Maximilianstr. 40, D–86150,* ☎ *0821/50360,* ℻ *0821/157–864. 102 rooms, 5 suites. 2 restaurants, brasserie, bar, beauty salon. AE, DC, MC, V.*

$$–$$$ ✕▥ **Romantikhotel Augsburger Hof.** A preservation order protects the beautiful Renaissance facade of this charming old Augsburg mansion, the interior of which was completely reconstructed to create a comfortable and up-to-date hotel and smart restaurant. The cathedral is around the corner; the town center is a five-minute stroll. ⊠ *Auf dem Kreuz 2, D–86152,* ☎ *0821/343–050,* ℻ *0821/343–0555. 36 rooms. Restaurant, sauna. AE, DC, MC, V.* ✦

$$$ ▥ **Dom Hotel.** Just across the street from Augsburg's cathedral, this is a snug, comfortable establishment with a personal touch. Ask for one of the attic rooms, where you'll sleep under beam ceilings and wake to a rooftop view of the city. Even if you have to settle for a room in the apartment-house extension, you'll lack no comforts. A garden terrace borders the old city walls, and there's also an indoor pool, sauna, and solarium. ⊠ *Frauentorstr. 8, D–86152,* ☎ *0821/343–390,* ℻ *0821/3439–3200. 44 rooms, 8 suites. Indoor pool, sauna. AE, DC, MC, V.*

$$$ 🍴 **Privat Hotel Riegele.** The tavern-restaurant, the *Bräustüberl,* is a local favorite. The hotel itself is a worthy successor to the Schmid family's previous house, the Hotel am Rathaus (still snugly in the shadow of the Perlachturm and recommended as an alternative lodging). All the comforts there are found in the new hotel—and, of course, the friendly service is unchanged. Public rooms and some bedrooms have plush armchairs, deep-pile rugs, and heavy drapes. ⊠ *Viktoriastr. 4, D–86150,* ☎ *0821/509–000,* ℻ *0821/517–746. 27 rooms, 1 apartment. Restaurant. AE, DC, MC, V.* 🕮

$–$$ 🍴 **Hotel-Garni Schlössle.** This family-run and very friendly little bed-and-breakfast is on the western outskirts of Augsburg, in the Stadtbergen district. A 10-minute tram ride brings you to the city center. The location offers fresh country air, walks, and sporting facilities (a golf course is within a good tee-shot's range)—and unbeatable value. Rooms under the steep eaves are particularly cozy. ⊠ *Bauernstr. 37, Stadtbergen D–86391,* ☎ *0821/243–930,* ℻ *0821/437–451. 14 rooms. AE, MC, V.*

Nightlife and the Arts

Augsburg has chamber and symphony orchestras, as well as a ballet and opera companies. The **Kongresshalle** (⊠ Gögginerstr. 10, ☎ 0821/324–2348) presents music and dance performances from September through July. For **information** about programs, call 0931/58686. The city stages a Mozart Festival of international stature in September.

Augsburg also has an annual open-air **opera and operetta** season in June and July. Productions move to the romantic inner courtyard of the **Fugger Palace** for part of July and August (☎ 0821/36604).

Children love the city's excellent **Augsburger Puppenkiste** (puppet theater; ⊠ Spitalg. 15, next to Rotes Tor, ☎ 0821/324–4976).

Outdoor Activities and Sports

Augsburg Golf Club (⊠ Engelshoferstr. 2, Augsburg-Bobingen, ☎ 08234/5621) welcomes visiting members of overseas golf clubs.

Shopping

Viktoria Passage, an arcade of diverse shops and boutiques opposite the main railway station, has some of Augsburg's best wares. **Maximilianstrasse,** the city's broad main street is also a good shopping area.

TOWARD THE ALPS

South of Augsburg, the Romantic Road climbs gradually into the foothills of the Bavarian Alps, which burst into view between Landsberg and Schongau. The route ends dramatically at the northern wall of the Alps at Füssen, on the Austrian border.

En Route   Leaving Augsburg southward on B–17—the southern stretch of the Romantic Road—you'll drive across the Lech battlefield, where Hungarian invaders were stopped in 955. Rich Bavarian pastures extend as far as the Lech River, which the Romantic Road meets at the historic town of Landsberg.

Landsberg am Lech

❺❸   *35 km (22 mi) south of Augsburg, 58 km (36 mi) west of Munich.*

Although Landsberg has a colorful history, it is most famous today because of one notorious guest—Adolf Hitler, who wrote much of *Mein Kampf* while in prison there. The town was founded by the Bavarian ruler Heinrich der Löwe (Henry the Lion) in the 12th century and grew wealthy from the salt trade. You'll see impressive evidence of Landsberg's early wealth among the solid old houses packed within its turreted walls; the early 18th-century **Altes Rathaus** (Old Town Hall) is one of the finest in the region.

The artist Sir Hubert von Herkomer (1847–1914) was born in the small village of Waal, just outside Landsberg. Within Landsberg's town walls is an unusual **monument** he built for his mother, Josefine. It's a romantic, medieval-style tower, bristling with turrets and galleries. He called it his Mutterturm, or "mother tower." The young Hubert moved with his parents to the United States and, later, to England. He died in Devon in 1914. A permanent exhibition on the artist's life and work can be seen within the tower's rough-stone walls. The admission fee includes entry to the municipal museum, the **Stadtmuseum** (⊠ Von-Kühlmann-Str., 2), interesting for its medieval religious art. ⌺ *DM 5.* ⊙ *Tues.–Sun. 2–5.*

The **Historisches Schuhmuseum** (Shoe History Museum) is devoted to the humble shoe. The exhibits—from all over the world and spanning five centuries—include slippers worn by King Ludwig II and a pair of delicate boots that once graced the feet of his beloved cousin Sisi, Empress Elisabeth of Austria. The museum is privately run, and you must call beforehand to arrange a guided tour. ⊠ *Vorderer Anger 274,* ☎ *08191/42296.* ⌺ *DM 3.* ⊙ *Weekdays 9–5.*

Outdoor Activities and Sports

You can play nine holes of golf in the beautifully landscaped grounds of a castle just outside Landsberg, at **Schloss Igling** (☎ 08248/1003).

Schongau

🖘 *28 km (17 mi) south of Landsberg, 70 km (43 mi) southwest of Munich.*

Schongau, founded in the 11th century at about the same time as Landsberg, has virtually intact wall fortifications, complete with towers and gates. In medieval and Renaissance times, the town was an important trading post on the route from Italy to Augsburg. The steeply gabled 16th-century Ballenhaus was a warehouse before it was elevated to the rank of **Rathaus.**

ⓒ A popular **Märchenwald** (fairy-tale forest) lies 1½ km (1 mi) outside Schongau, suitably set in a clearing in the woods. It comes complete with mechanical models of fairy-tale scenes, deer enclosures, and an old-time miniature railway. ⊠ *Diessenerstr. 6.* ⌺ *DM 4.* ⊙ *Easter–Oct., daily 9–7.*

Dining and Lodging

$$–$$$ ✕▥ **Alte Post.** Fancy a flight over the Bavarian Alps? You're at the right address, because Franz Lutzenburger, the host at the Alte Post, is a sparetime pilot. If he's too busy in the hotel to take guests for a joyride, he'll gladly organize flights from a nearby airfield. Costs range upward from DM 150, depending on the length of the flight. His hotel in the center of Schongau is a typically Bavarian hostelry—a sturdy, yellow-fronted inn, with comfortable accommodations and a tavern-restaurant serving hearty portions of local fare (the roast pork and dumplings are thoroughly recommended). ⊠ *Marienpl. 19, D–86956,* ☎ *08861/23200,* ⅜ *08861/232–080. 34 rooms. Restaurant, beer garden. AE, DC, MC, V.*

$$–$$$ ✕▥ **Hotel Holl.** The Alpine-style hotel on wooded slopes is a 10-minute stroll from the town center, with great views from most rooms. It's ideal for travelers seeking peace and quiet. The restaurant under

the steep eaves features imaginative fish dishes using the catch from local rivers and lakes. ⊠ *Altenstädterstr. 39, D–86956,* ☎ *08861/23310,* FAX *08861/233–112. 21 rooms, 1 suite. Restaurant, recreation room. AE, DC, MC, V.*

Outdoor Activities and Sports

The rolling meadowlands that form the foothills of the Bavarian Alps are ideal for hikers and cyclists. Tour operators focus on five main routes, providing luggage transport and arranging for accommodations. The **Schongau Verkehrsamt** (☎ 08861/7216) has details.

OFF THE
BEATEN PATH

HOHER PEISSENBERG – The Bavarian Alps rise up above lush meadowland and signal the approaching end of the Romantic Road. Some 15 km (9 mi) east of Schongau (on the B–472) is the first real peak of the Alpine chain, the 3,000-ft-high Hoher Peissenberg. A pilgrimage chapel was consecrated on the mountain in the 16th century; a century later a larger church was added, with a fine ceiling fresco and delicate carvings by local Bavarian masters.

ROTTENBUCH – The small country road B–23 (watch for the turn just before the village of Peissenberg) leads to this town, 13 km (8 mi) south of Schongau. The Augustinian order built an impressive monastery on the Ammer River here in the 11th century. The Gothic church was redecorated in rococo style in the 18th century. The lavish interior of cream, gold, and rose stuccowork and statuary is stunning.

WIESKIRCHE – This church—a glorious example of German rococo architecture—stands in an Alpine meadow just off the Romantic Road near the village of Steingaden, 9 km (5½ mi) east of Rottenbuch, on the Steingaden road. Its yellow-and-white walls and steep red roof are set off by the dark backdrop of the Trauchgauer Mountains. The architect Dominicus Zimmermann, former mayor of Landsberg and creator of much of that town's rococo architecture, built the church in 1745 on the spot where six years earlier a local woman claimed to have seen tears running down the face of a picture of Christ. Although the church was dedicated as the Pilgrimage Church of the Scourged Christ, it is now known simply as the Wieskirche (Church of the Meadow). Visit it on a bright day if you can, when light streaming through its high windows displays the full glory of the glittering interior. Together with the pilgrimage church of Vierzehnheiligen (☞ Northern Franconia *in* Chapter 5), the Wieskirche represents the culmination of German rococo ecclesiastical architecture. As at Vierzehnheiligen, the simple exterior gives little hint of the ravishing interior. A complex oval plan is animated by brilliantly colored stuccowork, statues, and gilt. A luminous ceiling fresco completes the decoration. Note the beautifully detailed choir and organ loft. Concerts are presented in the church from the end of June through the beginning of August. Contact the **Verkehrsamt** (☎ 08861/7216) in Schongau for details. Zimmermann, the church's architect, is buried in the 12th-century former abbey church of Steingaden. Although his work was the antithesis of Romanesque architecture, he was laid to rest in a dour late-Romanesque side chapel. ⊠ *Free.* ☉ *Daily 8–dusk.*

Schwangau

55 *18 km (11 mi) south of Steingaden, 105 km (65 mi) southwest of Munich.*

The lakeside resort town of Schwangau is an ideal center from which to explore the surrounding mountains. Here you'll encounter the heritage of Bavaria's famous 19th-century King Ludwig II. Ludwig spent much of his youth at Schloss Hohenschwangau; it is said that its neo-

Gothic atmosphere provided the primary influences that shaped his wildly romantic Schloss Neuschwanstein, the fairy-tale castle he built across the valley after he became king.

The two castles are 1 km (½ mi) from each other and about 2 km (1 mi) from the center of Schwangau. Road signs to the castles read KONIGSCHLÖSSER. Cars and buses are barred from the approach roads, but the mile journey to Neuschwanstein can be made in horse-drawn carriages, which stop in the village of Hohenschwangau. A bus from the village (the stop is outside the Schlosshotel Lisl, Neuschwanstein-strasse 1–3) takes a back route to an outlook called Aussichtspunkt Jugend; from there it's only a 10-minute walk to the castle. Schloss Hohenschwangau is a 15-minute walk from the village, and Neuschwanstein is a 25-minute uphill walk. There are three convenient parking areas for visitors arriving by car: at Colomannstrasse, Schwangauerstrasse, and Parkstrasse, all on the western edge of Hohenschwangau. There are four paths leading from the parking lots to Schloss Neuschwanstein and Schloss Hohenschwangau, all clearly marked.

⑤⑥ Schloss Hohenschwangau was built by the knights of Schwangau in the 12th century. Later it was remodeled by Ludwig's father, the Bavarian crown prince (and later king) Maximilian, between 1832 and 1836. Unlike Ludwig's more famous castle across the valley, Neuschwanstein, the somewhat garishly yellow Schloss Hohenschwangau has the feeling of a noble home, where comforts would be valued as much as outward splendor. It was here that the young Ludwig met the composer Richard Wagner. Their friendship shaped and deepened the future king's interest in theater, music, and German mythology—the mythology Wagner drew upon for his *Ring* cycle of operas. ☒ *DM 11, including guided tour.* ☉ *Mid-Mar.–mid-Oct., daily 8:30–5:30; mid-Oct.–mid-Mar., daily 9:30–4.*

★ ⑤⑦ Schloss Neuschwanstein was conceived by a set designer instead of an architect, thanks to Ludwig's deep love of the theater. The castle soars from its mountainside like a stage creation—it should hardly come as a surprise that Walt Disney took it as the model for his castle in the movie *Sleeping Beauty* and later for the Disneyland castle itself.

The life of the proprietor of this spectacular castle reads like one of the great Gothic mysteries of the 19th century, and the castle well symbolizes that life (☞ Up-Close: The Dream King). Yet during the 17 years from the start of Schloss Neuschwanstein's construction until his death, the king spent less than six months in the country residence, and the interior was never finished. The Byzantine-style throne room is without a throne; Ludwig died before one could be installed. The walls of the rooms leading to Ludwig's bedroom are painted with murals depicting characters from Wagner's operas—Siegfried and the Nibelungen, Lohengrin, Tristan, and others. Ludwig's bed and its canopy are made of intricately carved oak. A small corridor behind the bedroom was made as a ghostly grotto, reminiscent of Wagner's *Tannhäuser*. Chamber concerts are held in September in the gaily decorated minstrels' hall—one room, at least, that was completed as Ludwig conceived it (program details are available from the Verkehrsamt, Schwangau, ☎ 08362/81980). On the walls outside the castle's gift shop are plans and photos of the castle's construction. There are some spectacular walks around the castle. Be sure to visit the delicate **Marienbrücke** (Mary's Bridge), spun like a medieval maiden's hair across a deep, narrow gorge. From this vantage point there are giddy views of the castle and the great Upper Bavarian Plain beyond. ☒ *DM 11, including guided tour.* ☉ *Apr.–Sept., daily 8:30–5:30; Oct.–Mar., daily 10–4.*

Close-Up

THE DREAM KING

KING LUDWIG II (1845–1886), the enigmatic presence indelibly associated with Bavaria, was one of the last rulers of the Wittelsbach dynasty, which ruled Bavaria from 1180 to 1918. Though his family had created grandiose architecture in Munich, Ludwig II disliked the city and preferred isolation in the countryside. In it he constructed monumental edifices born of fanciful imagination and spent most of the royal purse on his endeavors. Although he was also a great lover of literature, theater, and opera (he was Richard Wagner's great patron), it is his fairy-tale-like castles that are his legacy.

Ludwig II reigned from 1864 to 1886, all the while avoiding political duties whenever possible. By 1878 he had completed his Schloss Linderhof retreat and immediately began Schloss Herrenchiemsee, a tribute to Versailles and Louis XIV (☞ Chapter 2). The grandest of his extravagant projects is Neuschwanstein, one of Germany's top attractions and concrete proof of the king's eccentricity. In 1886, before Neuschwanstein was finished, members of the government became convinced that Ludwig had taken leave of his senses. A medical commission declared the king insane and forced him to abdicate. Within two days of incarceration in the Berg Castle, on Starnbergersee (☞ Side Trips from Munich *in* Chapter 1), Ludwig and his doctor were found drowned in the lake's shallow waters. Their deaths are still a mystery. A poor leader, but still a visionary, Ludwig II is memorialized in a musical based in Füssen, *Ludwig II—Longing for Paradise.*

If you plan to visit Hohenschwangau or Neuschwanstein, bear in mind that more than 1 million people pass through the two castles every year. If you visit in the summer, get there early. The best time to see either castle without waiting a long time is a weekday between January and April. The prettiest time, however, is in the fall. It is hoped that a new system of timed entrance tickets will alleviate the problem of long waiting times. With a deposit or credit card number you can book your tickets in advance through **Verwaltung Hohenschwangau** (✉ Alpseestr. 12, D–87645 Hohenschwangau, ☎ 08362/930–830, ℻ 0832/930–8320). There is a DM 3 processing fee per ticket; a written confirmation will follow. You can cancel or change entrance times up to two hours before the confirmed entrance time.

Dining and Lodging

$$$$ ✕⌨ **Schlosshotel Lisl und Jägerhaus.** These jointly run 19th-century properties are across the street from one another, and both share views of the nearby castles. The intimate Jägerhaus has five suites and six double rooms, all decorated with floral wallpaper and drapery. The bathrooms have swan-motif fixtures. The Lisl's rooms were newly renovated in 2000 with bright blue carpeting and fabrics. Lisl's restaurant, Salon Wittelsbacher, provides a view of Neuschwanstein, as well as a tasty dish of Tafelspitz. ✉ *Neuschwansteinstr. 1–3, D–87643,* ☎ *08362/8870,* ℻ *08362/81107. 42 rooms, 5 suites. 2 restaurants, bar, lobby lounge. AE, MC, V.* ✎

$$$–$$$$ ✕⌨ **Hotel Müller.** Bbetween the two Schwangau castles, the Müller fits beautifully into the stunning landscape, its creamy Bavarian baroque facade complemented by the green mountain forest. Inside, the baroque influence is everywhere, from the finely furnished bedrooms to the chan-

delier-hung public rooms and restaurant ($$–$$$). The mahogany-paneled, glazed veranda (with open fireplace) provides a magnificent view of Hohenschwangau Castle. ⊠ *Alpseestr. 16, D–87643 Hohenschwangau,* ☎ *08362/81990,* ﬁﬁ *08362/819–913. 43 rooms, 2 suites. 2 restaurants, bar. AE, DC, MC, V.* ⊜

$$$–$$$$ ✕⊡ **König Ludwig.** This handsome Alpine hotel-restaurant, smothered in flowers in summer and in snow in deep winter, is named for the king who felt so at home in this area. The wood-paneled restaurant serves Bavarian fare with an international touch, and venison is a seasonal specialty. Rooms are furnished in rustic Bavarian style. Room rates include a substantial breakfast buffet. ⊠ *Kreuzweg 11–15, D–87645,* ☎ *08362/8890,* ﬁﬁ *08362/81779. 102 rooms, 36 apartments. Restaurant, pub, indoor pool, beauty salon, massage, sauna, steam room, tennis court, bowling, bicycles. No credit cards.*

Outdoor Activities and Sports

Schwangau's mountain, the Tegelberg, offers challenging upland hiking in spring, summer, and fall and good skiing in winter. There's a cable car (DM 28 round-trip) and six ski lifts. A summer sledge-run snakes for 1 km (½ mi) down the lower slopes (six rides for DM 17). At the bottom of the run is a children's playground and beer garden. Hikers can combine a stiff mountain walk with a tour of the geographic, geological, zoological, and historical landscape of this region by following the **Kulturpfad Schutzengelweg,** a trail marked by placards explaining points of interest. The trail climbs to 5,670 ft and takes about 2½ hours to complete.

At the **Golfakademie Schwangau-Alterschrofen** (☎ 08632/98300) you can play golf right below the walls of Ludwig's castle. The academy also gives golf lessons.

Füssen

❺❽ *5 km (3 mi) southwest of Schwangau, 110 km (68 mi) south of Munich.*

Füssen has a beautiful location at the foot of the mountains that separate Bavaria from the Austrian Tyrol—and a notable castle. Its **Hohes Schloss** is one of the best-preserved late-Gothic castles in Germany. It was built on the site of the Roman fortress that once guarded this Alpine section of the Via Claudia, the trade route from Rome to the Danube. Evidence of Roman occupation of the area has been uncovered at the foot of the nearby Tegelberg Mountain, and the **excavations** next to the Tegelberg cable-car station can be visited daily. The castle in Füssen was the seat of Bavarian rulers before Emperor Heinrich VII mortgaged it and the rest of the town to the bishop of Augsburg for 400 pieces of silver. The mortgage was never redeemed, and Füssen remained the property of the Augsburg episcopate until secularization in the early 19th century. The castle was put to good use by the bishops of Augsburg as their summer Alpine residence. It has a spectacular 16th-century **Rittersaal** (Knights' Hall) with a carved ceiling and a princes' chamber with a Gothic tiled stove. ⊠ *Magnuspl. 10,* ☎ *08362/903–146.* ⊡ *DM 5.* ☉ *Daily 11–4.*

The summer presence of the bishops of Augsburg ensured that Füssen received an impressive number of baroque and rococo churches. Füssen's **Rathaus** was once a Benedictine abbey, built in the 9th century at the site of the grave of St. Magnus, who spent most of his life ministering in Füssen and the surrounding area. A Romanesque crypt beneath the baroque abbey church has a partially preserved 10th-century fresco, the oldest in Bavaria. In summer chamber concerts are held in the high-ceiling baroque splendor of the abbey's **Fürstensaal** (Princes' Hall). Program details are available from the tourist office.

Füssen's main shopping street, called **Reichenstrasse,** was, like Augsburg's Maximilianstrasse, once part of the Roman Via Claudia. This cobblestone pedestrian walkway is lined with high-gabled medieval houses and backed by the bulwarks of the castle and the easternmost buttresses of the Allgäu Alps.

The Lech River, which accompanies much of the final section of the Romantic Road, rises in the Allgäu Alps and embraces the town as it rushes northward. One of several lakes in the area, the **Forggensee** is formed from a broadening of the river. The lakeside theater (☞ Nightlife & the Arts, *below,*) has restaurants. Pleasure boats cruise the lake mid-June–early October. ⌸ *DM 9–DM 14.*

Dining and Lodging

$ ✕ **Gasthaus zum Schwanen.** This modest establishment offers good regional cooking with no frills and at low prices. The excellent Swabian Maultaschen are made on the premises. ⊠ *Brotmarkt 4,* ☎ *08362/6174. MC, V. Closed Mon. and Nov. No dinner Sun.*

$$–$$$ ✕▥ **Alpen-Schlössle.** A Schlössle is a small castle, and although this comfortable, rustic hotel and restaurant doesn't quite qualify (apart from a solitary, corner tower), its mountain site, just outside Füssen, might well have appealed to King Ludwig. The elegant little restaurant, closed Tuesday, is prized for its imaginative cuisine, based on local products—the fillet of Allgäer beef is an exceptional dish. For fine-weather dining there's a very attractive, sunny terrace. The 11 small rooms are richly furnished with Russian pine, larch, and cherrywood. ⊠ *Alatseestr. 28, D–87629,* ☎ *08362/4017,* FAX *08362/39847. 11 rooms. Restaurant. MC, V.*

$$ ✕▥ **Altstadthotel Zum Hechten.** Geraniums flower for most of the year on this comfortable inn's balconies. It's one of the town's oldest lodgings, directly below the castle. The inn's own butcher shop provides the meat for its restaurant, which has sturdy, round tables and colorfully frescoed walls. Vegetarian meals are served in a separate restaurant. ⊠ *Ritterstr. 6, D–87629,* ☎ *08362/91600,* FAX *08362/916–099. 36 rooms, 30 with bath or shower. 2 restaurants, café, sauna, bowling, exercise room, paddle tennis. AE, MC.* ☙

$$ ✕▥ **Hotel Hirsch.** Mother and daughter team Christine and Eva Schwecke provide friendly service at this traditional Füssen hotel. Outside, the majestic building is its trademark stag (*Hirsch* in German); inside, the decor is pure Bavarian—large closets are brightly painted and old photographs of the hotel hang on the walls. Rooms are simply furnished with comfortable beds. In the popular Bierstuben, the pub section, guests are greeted by a painting of King Ludwig II. The brightly lighted restaurant serves good Allgäu specialties such as *Maultaschen* (a kind of huge ravioli). Luncheon special menus are very affordable (around DM 18 for a three-course meal). ⊠ *Kaiser-Maximilian-Pl. 7 D-87629,* ☎ *08362/9398-0,* FAX *08362/9398-77. 48 rooms. 2 restaurants, pub. AE, DC, MC, V. www.hotelhirschfuessen.de.*

Nightlife and the Arts

The musical *Ludwig II—Longing for Paradise* premiered in April 2000 in a specially built theater complex on the shore of the Forggensee. Subtitles in English appear above the stage. It's best to tour ☞ Neuschawanstein, *above,* and have some understanding of this lonely king's life before attending a performance. For information on tickets contact **Ludwig Musical AG & Co.** (☎ 1805/583–944; ☎ 212/972–0001 in the U.S.).

Outdoor Activities and Sports

Alpine winds ensure good sailing and windsurfing on the Forggensee, and English-speaking Andreas Hopfner is ready with advice and the right craft at his school, **Surfschule Forggensee** (☎ 08362/5517), in the tiny resort of Brunnen. The **Forgensee-Yachtschule** (✉ Seestr. 10, Dietringen, ☎ 08367/471) offers courses of up to two weeks' duration, with hotel or apartment accommodations. There are also boatyards and jetties with craft for rent at Waltenhofen.

There's good skiing in the mountains above Füssen, and cross-country enthusiasts are catered to with more than 20 km (12 mi) of prepared track. Füssen's highest peak, the Tegelberg, has a ski school, **Skischule Tegelberg A. Geiger** (☎ 08362/8455).

THE ROMANTIC ROAD A TO Z

Arriving and Departing

By Bus

☞ By Bus *in* Getting Around, *below.*

By Car

Würzburg is the northernmost city of the Romantic Road and the natural starting point for a tour. It's on the Frankfurt–Nürnberg Autobahn, the A-3, and is 115 km (71 mi) from Frankfurt. If you are using Munich as a gateway, Augsburg is 60 km (37 mi) from Munich via A-8.

By Plane

The major international airports serving the Romantic Road are Frankfurt and Munich. Regional airports include Nürnberg and Augsburg, home base of the private airline Augsburg Airways (formerly Interot ☎ 0821/96110).

By Train

Both Würzburg and Augsburg are on the InterCity and high-speed InterCity Express routes and have fast, frequent service to and from Berlin, Frankfurt, Munich, Stuttgart, and Hamburg.

Getting Around

By Bike

Wertheim is the starting point of a picturesque bike route along the Tauber River valley. The 100-km (62-mi) route follows the course of the river until Rothenburg-ob-der-Tauber. This is the most beautiful stretch of the Romantic Road, rich in ancient villages and flanked by thickly wooded heights crowned by castles and mansions. The bike route crisscrosses the river and at Tauberrettersheim passes over a bridge built by Würzburg's baroque architect Balthasar Neumann, who normally applied his talents to less mundane constructions. Bikes can be rented, and there's a luggage-transport service that will ferry your heavy baggage from hotel to hotel. For details contact the **Touristikgemeinschaft Liebliches Taubertal** (✉ Postfach 1254, D–97932 Tauberbischofsheim, ☎ 09341/820).

By Boat

Passenger service on the most romantic section of the Main, between Aschaffenburg and Wertheim, is operated by two local lines, the **Wertheimer Personenschiffahrt** (✉ Mainpl. 20, D–97877 Wertheim, ☎ 09342/1414) and the **Reederei Henneberger** (✉ Mainanlagen, D–63897 Miltenberg, ☎ 09371/3330).

By Bus

From April through October daily bus service covers the northern stretch of the Romantic Road, leaving Frankfurt at 8 AM and arriving in Munich at 8 PM; daily buses in the opposite direction leave Munich at 9 AM and arrive in Frankfurt at 8:30 PM. A second bus covers the section of the route between Dinkelsbühl and Füssen. Buses leave Dinkelsbühl daily at 4:15 PM and arrive in Füssen at 8 PM. In the other direction, buses leave Füssen daily at 8 AM, arriving in Dinkelsbühl at 12:45 PM. All buses stop at the major sights along the road. A Frankfurt–Füssen ticket costs DM 134 (DM 268 round-trip). Deutsche Touring also operates six more extensive tours along the Romantic Road and along the region's other major holiday route, the Burgenstrasse (Castle Road), which ends at Rothenburg. The tours range from two to five days and cost from DM 500 to DM 1,500. Full information can be found at the Web site touring-germany.com. Reservations are essential; contact **Deutsche Touring** (⊠ Am Römerhof 17, D–60486 Frankfurt/Main, ☎ 069/790–0350; www.deutsche-touring.com ⊠ Arnulfstr. 3, north wing of Hauptbahnhof, Munich, ☎ 089/596–133). Local buses cover much of the route but are infrequent and slow.

By Car

The Romantic Road is most easily traveled by car, starting from Würzburg as outlined above and following the B–27 country highway south to meet Roads B–290, B–19, B–292, and B–25 along the Wörnitz River.

The Romantic Road is a well-traveled two-lane route, so figure on covering no more than 70 km (40 mi) each hour, particularly in summer. The 40-km (24-mi) section of the route that's the least "romantic," the A-2 between Augsburg and Donauwörth, is also heavily used by trucks and other large vehicles traveling to northern Bavaria, so expect delays. Würzburg is the northernmost city of the Romantic Road and the natural starting point for a tour. For route maps, with roads and sights highlighted, contact the **Tourist Information Land an der Romantischen Strasse** (⊠ Kreisverkehrsamt, Crailsheimerstr. 1, D–91522 Ansbach, ☎ 0981/4680) or **Touristik-Arbeitsgemeinschaft Romantische Strasse** (⊠ Marktpl., D–91550 Dinkelsbühl, ☎ 09851/90271, ✍).

By Train

Infrequent trains link most major towns of the Romantic Road.

Contacts and Resources

Car Rentals

Avis (⊠ Klinkerberg 31, Augsburg, ☎ 0821/38241; ⊠ Nürnberger-Str. 107, Würzburg, ☎ 0931/200–3939). **Europcar** (⊠ Pilgerhausstr. 24, Augsburg, ☎ 0821/346–510; ⊠ Am Hauptbahnhof, Würzburg, ☎ 0931/12060; ⊠ Friendenstr. 15, Würzburg, ☎ 0931/881–150). **Hertz** (⊠ Werner-von-Siemens-Str. 6 [in Siemens Techno-Park], Augsburg, ☎ 0821/259–760; ⊠ Rottendorferstr. 40–42, Würzburg, ☎ 0931/784–6913). **Sixt** (⊠ Viktoriastr. 1 [in Hauptbahnhof], Augsburg, ☎ 0821/349–8502; ⊠ Bahnhofpl. 4 in Hauptbahnhof], Würzburg, ☎ 0931/465–1406).

Emergencies

Police and ambulance: ☎ 110. **Fire and emergency medical aid:** ☎ 112.

Guided Tours

BOAT TOURS

Three shipping companies offer excursions on the Main River from Würzburg. The **Fränkische Personenschiffahrt** (FPS; ⊠ Postfach 408, D–

97301 Kitzingen, ☎ 09321/91810, ✎) and the **Würzburger Personen-schiffahrt Kurth & Schiebe** (✉ St.-Norbert-Str. 9, D–97299 Zell, ☎ 0931/58573) operate excursions to the vineyards in and around Würzburg; wine tasting is included in the price. Fränkische Personenschiffahrt also offers cruises of up to two weeks on the Main, Neckar, and Danube rivers and on the Main–Danube Canal. Kurth & Schiebe and **Veitshöchheimer Personenschiffahrt** (✉ Obere Maing. 8, D–97209 Veitshöchheim, ☎ 0931/91553) offer daily service to Veitshöchheim, site of the palace that was once the summer residence of the bishops of Augsburg. Views of Aschaffenburg and its mighty palace are part of the attraction of Main cruises offered by the **Aschaffenburger Personenschiffahrt Sankt Martin** (✉ Ruhlandstr. 5, D–63741 Aschaffenburg, ☎ 06021/89099).

BUS TOURS

The **Touristik information office** (☎ 0821/502–070) in Augsburg offers morning and afternoon trips into the countryside north and south of Augsburg. *See* By Bus *in* Getting Around, *above,* for Deutsche Touring information.

CITY TOURS

All the cities and towns on the Romantic Road offer guided tours, either on foot or by bus. Details are available from the local tourist information offices. Following is a sample of the more typical tours.

In **Würzburg** two-hour bus tours of the city start at the main railway station from April through October, Monday–Saturday at 2 and Sunday and public holidays at 10:30. The fare is DM 14. Guided walking tours start at the Haus zum Falken tourist office from April through October, daily at 10:30 (tours in English are given Tuesday through Sunday at 11). The two-hour tours cost DM 13 and include a visit to the Residenz. If you'd rather guide yourself, pick up a map from the same tourist office and follow the extremely helpful directions marked throughout the city by distinctive brown signposts.

Augsburg also has self-guided walking tours, with routes posted on color-coded signs throughout the downtown area. From mid-May to mid-October a bus tour (DM 19) starts from the Rathaus at 2, Thursday through Sunday, and walking tours (DM 9) set out from the Rathaus daily at 10:30. From mid-October until May a walking tour takes place every Saturday at 2. All tours are conducted in German and English.

The costumed nightwatchman in **Rothenburg-ob-der-Tauber** conducts a nightly tour of the town, leading the way with a lantern. From April to October and in December, tours in English begin at 8 and 9:30 and cost DM 6 (a daytime tour begins at 2). The watchman in **Dinkelsbühl** does a nightly round at 9 from April through October, and though he doesn't give official tours, he's always happy to answer questions from inquisitive visitors (but don't expect a reply in fluent English). Daily guided tours of Dinkelsbühl in horse-drawn carriages (April–October) cost DM 8.

The tourist office in **Ulm** offers a 90-minute guided tour that includes a visit to the Münster, the Old Town Hall, the Fischerviertel (Fishermen's Quarter), and the Danube riverbank. From May through October there are tours at 10 and 2:30 Monday–Saturday, 11 and 2:30 Sunday; from November through April tours are at 10 on Saturday and 11 on Sunday. The departure point is the tourist information office on Münsterplatz; the cost is DM 8. From May to mid-October you can view Ulm from on board the motor cruiser *Ulmer Spatz*. There are up to five 50-minute cruises daily (DM 10). The boats tie up at the Metzgerturm, a two-minute walk from the city hall.

TRAIN TOURS

The **Deutsche Bahn** (German Rail) offers special weekend excursion rates covering travel from most German railroad stations to Würzburg and hotel accommodations for up to four nights. Details are available at any train station.

Visitor Information

A central tourist office based in Dinkelsbühl covers the entire Romantic Road: **Touristik-Arbeitsgemeinschaft Romantische Strasse** (✉ Marktpl., D–91550 Dinkelsbühl, ☎ 09851/90271, FAX 09851/90281, ✆). Their color brochure describes all the main towns and attractions along the Romantic Road.

Amorbach (✉ Verkehrsamt, Altes Rathaus, D–63916, ☎ 09373/20940, ✆). **Aschaffenburg** (✉ Dalbergstr. 6, D–63739, ☎ 06021/395–800, ✆). **Augsburg** (✉ Tourist-Information, Bahnhofstr. 7, D–86150, ☎ 0821/ 502–070, ✆). **Bad Mergentheim** (✉ Städtisches Kultur-und Verkehrsamt, Marktpl. 3, D–96980, ☎ 07931/57135, ✆). **Dinkelsbühl** (✉ Tourist-Information, Marktpl., D–91550, ☎ 09851/90240, ✆). **Donauwörth** (✉ Städtisches Verkehrs-und Kulturamt, Rathausg. 1, D–86609, ☎ 0906/ 789–151, ✆). **Feuchtwangen** (✉ Kultur-und Verkehrsamt, Marktpl. 1, D–91555, ☎ 09852/90444). **Füssen** (✉ Kurverwaltung, Kaiser-Max-imilian-Pl. 1, D–87629, ☎ 08362/93850, ✆). **Harburg** (✉ Fremden-verkehrsverein, Schlossstr. 1, D–86655, ☎ 09080/96990). **Landsberg am Lech** (✉ Kultur-und Fremdenverkehrsamt, Hauptpl. 152, D–89896, ☎ 08191/128–245, ✆). **Mespelbrunn** (✉ Fremdenverkehrsverein, Hauptstr. 158, D–63875, ☎ 06092/319). **Miltenberg** (✉ Fremden-verkehrsamt, Rathauspl., D–63897, ☎ 09371/404–119). **Nördlingen** (✉ Städtisches Verkehrsamt, Marktpl. 2, D–86720, ☎ 09081/84116). **Rothenburg-ob-der-Tauber** (✉ Tourist-Information, Rathaus, Markt-pl. 2, D–91541, ☎ 09861/40492, ✆). **Schongau** (✉ Tourist-Informa-tion, Münzstr. 5, D–86956, ☎ 08861/7216, ✆). **Schwangau** (✉ Kurverwaltung, Rathaus, Münchenerstr. 2, D–87645, ☎ 08362/81980, ✆). **Tauberbischofsheim** (✉ Marktpl. 8, D–97941, ☎ 09341/80313, ✆). **Ulm** (✉ Tourist-Information, Münsterpl. 50 [Stadthaus], D–89073, ☎ 0731/161–2830, ✆). **Weikersheim** (✉ Städtisches Kultur-und Verkehrsamt, im Rathaus, Marktpl., D–97990, ☎ 07934/10255, FAX 07934/10558). **Wertheim** (✉ Am Spitzen Turm, D–97877, ☎ 09342/ 1066). **Würzburg** (✉ Fremdenverkehrsamt, Am Congress-Centrum, D–97070, ☎ 0931/372–335, ✆).

5 FRANCONIA

A predominantly rural part of Bavaria,
Franconia was most important politically
in the days of the Holy Roman Empire.
You'll want to see its beautiful and historic
towns: Coburg, Bayreuth, Bamberg, and
Nürnberg; well-preserved Regensburg is
part of neighboring Oberpfalz. Wagner fans
especially shouldn't miss Bayreuth, where the
great composer settled and built his theater.
The annual festival that honors him brings
other town functions to a halt every summer.

ALL THAT IS LEFT OF THE HUGE ANCIENT kingdom of the Franks is the region known today as Franken (Franconia). The Franks were not only tough warriors, but also hard workers, sharp tradespeople, and burghers with a good political nose. The name *frank* means bold, wild, courageous in the old Frankish tongue. It was only in the early 19th century, following Napoléon's conquest of what is now southern Germany, that the area was incorporated into northern Bavaria. Modern Franconia stretches from the Bohemian Forest on the Czech border to the outskirts of Frankfurt. But its heart—and the focal point of this chapter—is an area known as the Fränkische Schweiz (Franconian Switzerland), bounded by Nürnberg (Nuremberg) in the south, Bamberg in the west, and the cultural center of Bayreuth in the east. Its rural appearance belies a solid economic backbone that is buttressed by the influx of businesses in what's known as the New Economy (electronics, call centers, software, etc.).

Updated by
Marton Rakai

Franconia is hardly an overrun tourist destination. But its long and rich history, its diversified landscapes and leisure activities (including skiing, golf, hiking, cycling), and its gastronomic specialties place it high on the enjoyment scale. The Oberpfalz (Upper Palatinate) district of Bavaria is south of Franconia and has earned a reputation for healthy forests, cozy villages, and picturesque castles. Regensburg, its capital, is an excellent base for excursions into the Bavarian Forest (☞ Chapter 3).

Pleasures and Pastimes

Dining

Franconia is known for its good and filling food and for its simple and atmospheric *Gasthäuser.* Many have inexpensive lunchtime menus. Pork is a staple, served either as *Schweinsbraten* (a plain roast) or sauerbraten (marinated). Nürnberg has a unique shoulder cut called *Schäfele* (little shovel), served with *Knödel* (dumplings made from either bread or potatoes). Sausages are also a specialty in Regensburg and in Nürnberg, where they are eaten either grilled or heated in a stock of onions and wine (*saurer Zipfel*).

Not to be missed are Franconia's liquid refreshments from both the grape and the grain. Franconian white wines, usually sold in distinctive flagons called *Bocksbeutel,* are renowned for their special bouquet (Silvaner is the traditional grape). The region has the largest concentration of local breweries in the world (Bamberg alone has 10, Bayreuth 7), producing a wide range of brews, the most distinctive of which is the dark, smoky *Rauchbier.*

CATEGORY	COST*
$$$$	over DM 90
$$$	DM 55–DM 90
$$	DM 35–DM 55
$	under DM 35

per person for a three-course meal, including sales tax and excluding drinks and service charge

Hiking

The wild stretches of forest and numerous nature parks in northern Franconia make this ideal hiking country. There are more than 40,000 km (25,000 mi) of hiking trails, with the greatest concentration in the Altmühltal Nature Park, a wooded gorge, and in the Frankenwald.

Lodging

Make reservations well in advance for hotels in all the larger towns and cities if you plan to visit anytime between June and September. During the Nürnberg Toy Fair at the beginning of February rooms are rare and at a premium. If you're visiting Bayreuth during the annual Wagner Festival, in July and August, consider making reservations up to a year in advance. And remember, too, that during the festival prices can be double the normal rates. Standards of comfort and cleanliness are high throughout the region, whether you stay in a simple pension or in an international chain hotel.

CATEGORY	COST*
$$$$	over DM 230
$$$	DM 170–DM 230
$$	DM 120–DM 170
$	under DM 120

All prices are for two people in a double room, including tax and service charges.

Skiing

The highest peaks of Franconia's upland region, the Fichtelgebirge and Frankenwald, rarely pass the 3,200-ft mark, but their exposed location in central Germany assures them good snow conditions most winters. Cross-country skiers also make for this region because of its lack of mass tourism. Whether Alpine style or cross-country, the skiing is cheap and ideally suited for families.

Exploring Franconia

Although many proud Franconians would dispute it, this historic homeland of the Franks, one of the oldest Germanic peoples, is unmistakably part of Bavaria. Its southern border areas end at the Danube and merge into Lower Bavaria and the Bavarian Forest, while its northern border is marked by the River Main, which is seen as the dividing line between northern and southern Germany. Despite its extensive geographic spread, however, Franconia is a homogenous region of rolling agricultural landscapes and thick forests climbing to the mountains of the Fichtelgebirge. Franconian towns like Bayreuth, Coburg, and Bamberg are practically places of cultural pilgrimage, while rebuilt Nürnberg is the epitome of German medieval beauty.

Numbers in the text correspond to numbers in the margin and on the Franconia, Nürnberg, and Regensburg maps.

Great Itineraries

IF YOU HAVE 3 DAYS

Make 🖾 **Nürnberg** ⑥–⑳ your base and take day trips on each of the three days to **Bayreuth** ④ (an imperative visit whether or not it's Wagner Festival season); **Bamberg** ⑤, once the seat of the most powerful ruling families in the country; and **Coburg** ①, home of the Saxe-Coburg duchy. Each town is only 50 minutes to an hour and 15 minutes' drive away.

IF YOU HAVE 5 DAYS

Spend the first three days following the itinerary above, making day trips from 🖾 **Nürnberg** ⑥–⑳ to **Bayreuth** ④, **Bamberg** ⑤, and **Coburg** ①. On the third and fourth days stop overnight at 🖾 **Coburg.** On the fourth day take side trips to **Banz Abbey** and **Vierzehnheiligen,** two mighty churches that stand facing each other across the valley of the River Main. On the fifth day follow the Main upstream from Coburg to **Kulmbach** ③, the beer capital of Germany. Among its several brands is reputedly the world's strongest brew.

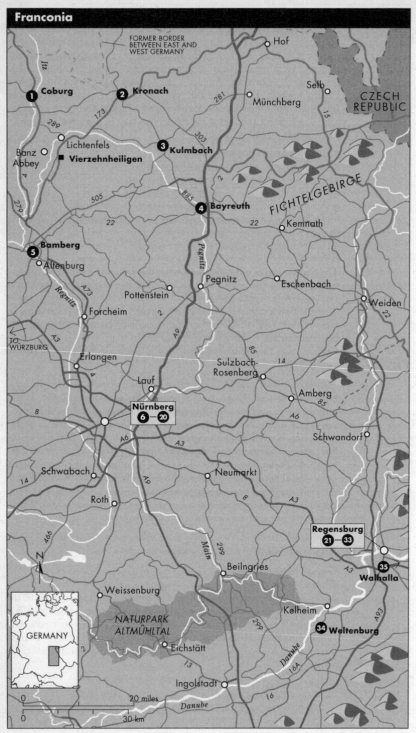

Franconia

FORMER BORDER BETWEEN EAST AND WEST GERMANY

Hof

Selb

CZECH REPUBLIC

1 Coburg

2 Kronach

Münchberg

Itz

289

173

281

303

15

Lichtenfels

Banz Abbey

■ Vierzehnheiligen

3 Kulmbach

2

FICHTELGEBIRGE

505

B85

22

4 Bayreuth

22

Kemnath

5 Bamberg

Altenburg

Pegnitz

Regnitz

A73

Pottenstein

Pegnitz

Eschenbach

Weiden

22

Forcheim

2

A9

TO WÜRZBURG

A3

Erlangen

Lauf

85

14

Sulzbach-Rosenberg

Nürnberg
6 — **20**

Amberg

85

A6

Schwandorf

8

A6

A3

Schwabach

A9

Neumarkt

14

Roth

8

A3

466

N

Main

299

Regensburg
21 — **33**

A3

35 Walhalla

Beilngries

A93

Weissenburg

NATURPARK ALTMÜHLTAL

Kelheim

34 Weltenburg

GERMANY

2

Eichstätt

299

Danube

16A

13

Ingolstadt

16

0 ———— 20 miles

0 ———— 30 km

Danube

IF YOU HAVE 7 DAYS
Begin by following the five-day itinerary above. Plan to spend your fifth night in ⊞ **Nürnberg** ⑥–⑳ before departing for medieval ⊞ **Regensburg** ㉑–㉝ on the sixth day. At Regensburg you'll meet the already broad Danube at the 12th-century **Steinerne Brücke** (Stone Bridge). From Regensburg you can embark on boat tours between towering limestone cliffs to the great abbey church of **Weltenburg** ㉞ and to Germany's 19th-century hall of fame, the Doric temple at **Walhalla** ㉟.

When to Tour

Summer is the best time to explore Franconia, though spring and fall are also fine when the weather cooperates. In spring the deciduous trees in the extensive forests take on several shades of emerald to contrast with the deep greens of the all-weather firs. In the fall the foliage takes on russet hues. Avoid the cold and wet months of November, January, and February, unless you're coming to ski. If you're in Nürnberg in December, you're in time for one of Germany's largest and loveliest Christmas markets.

NORTHERN FRANCONIA

Three major German cultural centers lie within this region of Franconia: Coburg, a town that claims blood links with royal dynasties throughout Europe; Bamberg, with its own claim to German royal history and an old town on the UNESCO World Heritage list; and Bayreuth, where composer Richard Wagner finally settled and a place of musical pilgrimage for Wagner fans from all over the world.

Coburg

❶ *105 km (65 mi) north of Nürnberg.*

Coburg is a treasure—and a surprisingly little-known one—whether it's glittering under the summer sky or frosted white with the snows of winter. The east–west border once isolated this area, but since Germany's reunification it has experienced a minor economic revolution. It was founded in the 11th century and remained in the possession of the dukes of Saxe-Coburg-Gotha until 1918; the present duke still lives there. The town is in fact most famous for the remarkable Saxe-Coburg dynasty. Though just one among dozens of German ruling families, they established themselves as something of a royal stud farm, providing a seemingly inexhaustible supply of blue-blood marriage partners to ruling houses the length and breadth of Europe. The most famous of these royal mates was Prince Albert, who married Queen Victoria, after which she gained special renown in Coburg. Legend has it that on a visit to her new husband's hometown, she had the first flush toilet in Germany installed. He reciprocated by doing his best to introduce Germany's own standards of family housing to overcrowded Victorian London. And on the subject of families, Albert and Victoria were a prolific pair. Their numerous children, married off to other of kings, queens, and emperors, helped to spread the tried-and-tested Saxe-Coburg stock even farther afield. Despite all the old history that sweats from each sandstone ashlar, Coburg is a modern and bustling town. It even is home to Europe's only Brazilian Samba Festival, a wild bacchanal held in mid-July in the august streets.

Coburg's **Marktplatz** (Market Square), has a statue of Prince Albert, the high-minded consort, proudly standing surrounded by gracious Renaissance and baroque buildings. The **Rathaus** (town hall), begun in 1500, is the most imposing structure on Marktplatz. A forest of ornate gables and spires projects from its well-proportioned facade.

Look at the statue of the **Bratwurstmännla** on the building; the staff he carries is claimed to be the official length against which the town's famous bratwursts are measured. If this sounds to you like guidebook babble, convince yourself otherwise by trying a bratwurst from one of the stands in the square; they sell them Monday–Saturday.

Schloss Ehrenburg, the ducal palace, is on Schlossplatz, Coburg's second main square. Built in the mid-16th century, it has been greatly altered over the years, principally following a fire in the early 19th century. The then-duke took the opportunity to rebuild the palace in a heavy Gothic style, although he had the sense to retain some of the original Renaissance features. It was in this dark and imposing heap that Prince Albert spent much of his childhood. The throne room; the Hall of Giants, named for the larger-than-life statues that support the stuccoed ceiling; and the baroque-style chapel can all be visited. ⊠ *Schlosspl.,* ☎ *09561/80880.* ⊠ *DM 4.* ☉ *Tour Tues.–Sun. at 10, 11, 1:30, 2:30, and 3:30 (additional tour at 4:30 Apr.–Sept.).*

Near Schloss Ehrenburg, the **Puppenmuseum** (Doll Museum) contains a fine collection of more than 900 antique dolls and art dolls, and around 150 carefully furnished dollhouses. The building itself once housed the poet and orientalist Friedrich Rückert. The museum includes a doll and toy shop. ⊠ *Rückertstr. 2–3,* ☎ *09561/74047.* ⊠ *DM 3.50.* ☉ *Apr.–Oct., Mon.–Sun. 9–5; Nov.–Mar., Tues.–Sun. 10–5)*

The **Veste Coburg** Fortress, one of the largest and most impressive in the country, is Coburg's main attraction. The brooding bulk of the castle lies on a small hill above the town. Construction began around 1055, but with progressive rebuilding and remodeling, today's predominantly late Gothic–early Renaissance edifice bears little resemblance to the original rude fortress. One part of the castle harbors the **Kunstsammlungen,** a grand set of collections including art, with works by Dürer, Cranach, and Hans Holbein, among others; sculpture from the school of the great Tilman Riemenschneider (1460–1531); furniture and textiles; magnificent weapons, armors, and tournament garb from four centuries; carriages and ornate sleighs; glass; and more. The room where Martin Luther lived for six months in 1530 while he observed the goings-on of the Augsburg Diet has an especially dignified atmosphere. The **Jagdintarsien-Zimmer** (Hunting Marquetry Room), an elaborately decorated room that dates to the early 17th century, has some of the finest woodwork in southern Germany. ☎ *09561/8790.* ⊠ *DM 6.* ☉ *Museums Apr.–Oct., Tues.–Sun. 10–5; Nov.–Mar., Tues.–Sun. 1–4; tour every ½ hr; castle Apr.–Oct., Tues.–Sun. 10–5; Nov.–Mar., Tues.–Sun. 2–5.*

The **Naturkundemuseum** (Natural History Museum) is in the castle's former palace garden, the Hofgarten. This is the country's leading museum of its kind, with more than 8,000 exhibits of flora and fauna, geology, human history, and mineralogy divided up into four major categories: Earth, Evolution, the Human Being, and Earth History. ⊠ *Veste Coburg,* ☎ *09561/808–120.* ⊠ *DM 3.* ☉ *Weekdays 9–1 and 1:30–5; weekends 9–5.*

The **Burgschänke,** Veste Coburg's own tavern, allows you to soak up centuries of history while sampling a Coburg beer and one of the traditional dishes from the basic menu. The tavern is closed Monday and January–mid-February. ⊠ *Veste Coburg,* ☎ *09561/80980.*

Perched on a hill 5 km (3 mi) to the west is **Schloss Callenberg,** until 1231 the main castle of the Knights of Callenberg. In the 16th century it was taken over by the Coburgs. From 1842 on it served as the summer residence of the hereditary Coburg prince and later Duke Ernst II. Between 1985 and 1997 the now neo-Gothic castle was renovated and opened to the public. It holds a number of important collections, including that of the Windsor gallery; art and crafts from Holland, Germany, and Italy from the Renaissance to the 19th century; precious baroque, empire, and Biedermeier furniture; table and standing clocks from three centuries; a selection of weapons; and various handicrafts. The best way to reach the castle is by car via Baiersdorf, or by taking Bus 5 from the Marktplatz. ✉ *Callenberg*, ☎ *09561/55150*. 🖅 *DM 5.* 🕓 *Tour Apr.–Oct., daily at 10, 11, noon, 2, 3, and 4; Nov.–Mar., Tues.–Sun. at 2, 3, and 4; and by appointment; closed last 3 wks of Jan.*

OFF THE BEATEN PATH

AHORN – This town 4 km (2½ mi southwest of Coburg has a wonderful museum that gives close insight into the life and times of farmers in the Coburg region. The houses of the **Grätemuseum des Coburger Landes** (Museum of Farm Appliances of the Coburg Region) date to the early 18th century. They are constructed of sandstone with harmonious half-timber superstructures. There are exhibits depicting estate life as it once was, with everything from farm implements to a smithy, while outside farm animals roam about. Snacks and drinks are available at the *Schäferstuben*, the Shepherd's Room. ✉ *On Rte. B–303 before Ahorn*, ☎ *09561/1304.* 🖅 *DM 4.* 🕓 *Apr.–Oct., Tues.–Sun. 2–5; Nov.–Mar., Sun. 2–5 and by appointment.*

SCHLOSS ROSENAU – Prince Albert was born in 1819 in this 550-year-old castle, halfway between Coburg and Neustadt. It sits in all its neo-Gothic glory in the midst of an English-style park near the village of Rödental, 9 km (5½ mi) northeast of Coburg. The castle exhibits furniture made especially for the Saxe-Coburg family by noted Viennese craftsmen, as well as other pieces from the period of Albert's youth. One room is devoted entirely to Victoria and Albert. In the garden's Orangerie is the **Museum für Modernes Glas** (Museum for Modern Glass), which displays nearly 40 years' worth of glass sculptures. *Castle:* ☎ *09563/4747.* 🖅 *DM 5.* 🕓 *Guided tour Oct.–Mar., Tues.–Sun. on the hr 10–3; Apr.–Sept., Tues.–Sun. 9–5 on the hr. Museum:* ☎ *09563/1606.* 🖅 *DM 2 (free with entrance ticket to the Veste in Coburg ☞ above).* 🕓 *Apr.–Oct., Tues.–Sun. 10–1 and 1:30–5; Nov.–Mar., Tues.–Sun. 1–4.*

Dining and Lodging

$$$$ ✕ **Coburger-Tor Restaurant Schaller.** This hotel-restaurant provides surprisingly upscale dining in softly lighted and distinctly well-upholstered quarters just south of the city center. The food is sophisticated nouvelle, with such offerings as wild-duck breasts in sherry sauce and stuffed dates with nougat sauce. Jeans are not permitted. ✉ *Ketschendorferstr. 22*, ☎ *09561/25074. Reservations essential. MC, V. Closed Sun.*

$$ ✕ **Ratskeller.** The local specialties taste better beneath the old vaults and within earshot of the Coburg marketplace. The decor is a little tacky, but the food is prepared with gusto. Try the sauerbraten, along with a glass of crisp Franconian white wine. ✉ *Markt 1*, ☎ *09561/92400. No credit cards.*

$ ★ ✕ **Goldenes Kreuz.** In business since 1477, this restaurant has all the rustic decor you'll ever want to accompany large portions of equally authentic Franconian food. Goose with dumplings provides a hearty experience. Nouvelle cuisine it is not. ✉ *Herrng. 1*, ☎ *09561/90473. No credit cards. No dinner Sun.*

$$–$$$ ★ ✕🛏 **Hotel Festungshof.** Duke Carl Eduard had this mansion built right outside the Veste in Coburg to house his guests. There could hardly be a more atmospheric location to enjoy a stay in Coburg than this turn-of-the-20th-century building with generous, comfortably (if slightly unimaginatively) furnished rooms. The restaurant has solid Franconian cooking, the café has a generous terrace for summer afternoons, and the beer garden seats 300. A bus connects to the town center, or you can take a 20-minute walk through the castle garden and the wooded landscape to reach the marketplace. ⊠ *Rosenauerstr. 30, D–96450,* ☎ *09561/80290,* FAX *09561/802–933. 14 rooms. Restaurant, beer garden, café. AE, DC, MC, V.*

$$$–$$$$ 🏩 **Romantic Hotel Goldene Traube.** Book a room overlooking the square, and on summer evenings you can fall asleep to the splash of the fountain named after Queen Victoria. The hotel feels such a strong link with Britain's former queen and empress that it even named its bar after her. The rooms are comfortable, and all have cable TV. There's also a sauna complex with solarium. ⊠ *Am Viktoriabrunnen 2, D–96450,* ☎ *09561/8760,* FAX *09561/876–222. 69 rooms, 1 suite. Restaurant, bar, sauna, steam room, miniature golf, exercise room, bicycles. AE, DC, MC, V.*

Nightlife and the Arts

Coburg's **Landestheater** has an opera season from October through mid-July. Call 09561/92742 (from 9 to 1) for tickets.

Shopping

Coburg is a culinary delight, famous for its *Schmätzen* (gingerbread) and *Elizenkuchen* (almond cake). You'll find home-baked versions in any of the many excellent **patisseries** or at a Grossman store (there are three in Coburg). Rödental, northeast of Coburg, is the home of the world-famous M. I. Hummel figurines, made by the Göbel porcelain manufacturer. There's a **Hummel Museum** (⊠ Coburgerstr. 7, Rödental, ☎ 09563/92303, 👷) devoted to them, open weekdays 9–5 and Saturday 9–noon. Besides the museum's store, there are several retail outlets in the village.

Lichtenfels

21 km (13 mi) southeast of Coburg.

Rather than speeding from Coburg to Bayreuth on the autobahn, take a detour along the small road (B–289) to Lichtenfels, just across the Main River. You might call the little town a basket case—it's known for its basket-weaving tradition. The basketwork market (☎ 09571/18283), on the third weekend in September, is one of a kind. A delightful basket museum, the **Deutsches Korb Museum Michelau,** in nearby Michelau, displays everything from furniture to decoration and household items. ⊠ *Bismarckstr. 4, Michelau,* ☎ *09571/83548.* 💳 *DM 5;* 🕐 *Apr.–Oct., Tues.–Sun. 9–noon and 1–4:30; Nov.–Mar., Mon.–Thurs. 9–noon and 1–4:30, Fri. 9–noon.*

★ Just south of Lichtenfels off the main road (B–173) to Bamberg are two religious gems, each proudly crowning the heights along the banks of the Main River. On the east side of the river is **Vierzehnheiligen,** a tall, elegant yellow-sandstone edifice, whose interior represents one of the great examples of rococo decoration. The church was built by Balthasar Neumann (architect of the Residenz at Würzburg; ☞ Chapter 4) between 1743 and 1772 to commemorate a vision of Christ and 14 saints—*vierzehn Heiligen*—that appeared to a shepherd in 1445. Thanks to clever play with light, light colors, and playful gold and blue trimmings, the interior seems to be in perpetual motion. Guided tours of the church are given on request; a donation is expected (☎ 09571/95080).

On the west bank of the Main is **Kloster Banz** (Banz Abbey), standing on what some call the "holy mountain of Bavaria." There had been a monastery here since 1069, but the present buildings—now a political-seminar center and think tank—date from the end of the 17th century.

The highlight of the complex is the **Klosterkirche** (Abbey Church), the work of architect and stuccoist Johann Dientzenhofer (1663–1726). To get to Banz from Vierzehnheiligen, drive south to Unnersdorf, where you can cross the river. From Lichtenfels take the road via Seubelsdorf and Reuendorf. ☎ 09573/7311 or 09573/5092. ☉ *Guided tour of church May–Oct., daily 9–noon and 2–5; Nov.–Apr., daily 9–noon.*

Kronach

❷ *24 km (15 mi) northeast of Lichtenfels, 120 km (74 mi) north of Nürnberg.*

Kronach is a charming little gateway to the natural splendor of the Frankenwald region. Its old section, the **Obere Stadt** (Upper Town), is a medieval gem surrounded by old walls and surmounted by a majestic fortress. Kronach is best known as the birthplace of Renaissance painter Lucas Cranach the Elder (1472–1553), but there is a running argument as to which house he was born in—Am Marktplatz 1 or in the house called Am Scharfen Eck, at Lucas-Cranach-Strasse 38, which is now an Italian restaurant.

Festung Rosenberg (Rosenberg Fortress) is a few minutes' walk from the town center. Standing below its mighty walls, it is easy to see why it was never taken by enemy forces. During World War I it served as a POW camp with no less a figure than Charles de Gaulle as a "guest." Today Rosenberg houses a youth hostel and, more importantly, the **Fränkische Galerie** (the Franconian Gallery), an extension of the Bavarian National Museum in Munich (☞ Bayerisches Nationalmuseum *in* Chapter 1) featuring paintings and sculpted works from the Middle Ages and the Renaissance. Lucas Cranach the Elder and Tilman Riemenschneider are represented, as well as artists from the Dürer School and the Bamberg School. In July and August the central courtyard serves as an atmospheric backdrop for performances of Goethe's *Faust. Fortress and Gallery:* ☎ 09261/60410. ▦ *DM 6.* ☉ *Fortress tours Apr.–Oct., Tues.–Sun. at 9:30, 11, and 2, 3:30; Nov.–Mar., Tues.–Sun. at 11 and 2; Galerie Apr.–Oct., Tues.–Sun 9–6; Nov.–Apr., Tues.–Sun. 10–4.*

Kulmbach

❸ *19 km (12 mi) southeast of Kronach, 32 km (20 mi) east of Lichtenfels.*

Kulmbach, a pretty market town on the Main, has a claim to fame that belies its size. In a country in which the brewing and beer drinking break all records, this town produces more per capita than anywhere else: 9,000 pints for each man, woman, and child. A quarter of Kulmbachers earn their living directly or indirectly from beer. A special local brew only available in winter and during the Lenten season is *Eisbock*, a dark beer that is frozen as part of the brewing process to make it stronger. The locals claim it's the sparkling clear springwater from the nearby Fichtelgebirge hills that makes their beer so special.

Kulmbach celebrates its beer every year in a nine-day festival that starts on the last Saturday in July. The main festival site, a mammoth tent, is called the Festspulhaus—literally, "festival swill house"—a none-too-subtle dig at nearby Bayreuth and its tony Festspielhaus, where Wagner's operas are performed.

The **Erste Kulmbacher Union Brewery,** (✉ Lichtenfelserstr., ☎ 09221/705–113), one of Kulmbach's six breweries, produces the strongest beer in the world—the *Doppelbock* Kulminator 28—which takes nine months to brew and has an alcohol content of more than 11%. The brewery runs the **Bayerisches Brauereimuseum Kulmbach** (the Kulmbach Brewery Museum) jointly with the nearby Mönchshof-Bräu brewery and inn. ⊠ *Hoferstr. 20,* ☎ *09221/4264.* 🎫 *Tour DM 4 (DM 2.50 if you spend DM 10 in the brewery tavern).*

Kulmbach, however, is much more than beer. The **Altstadt** (Old Town), for example, contains a warren of narrow streets that merit exploration. The **Plassenburg,** the town's castle and symbol, is the most important Renaissance castle in the country. It stands on a rise overlooking Kulmbach, a 20-minute hike from the Old Town. The first building here, begun in the mid-12th century, was torched by marauding Bavarians who were anxious to put a stop to the ambitions of Duke Albrecht Alcibiades—a man who spent several years murdering, plundering, and pillaging his way through Franconia. His successors built today's castle, starting in about 1560. Externally there's little to suggest the graceful Renaissance interior, but as you enter the main courtyard, the scene changes abruptly. The tiered space of the courtyard is covered with precisely carved figures, medallions, and other intricate ornaments, the whole comprising one of the most remarkable and delicate architectural ensembles in Europe. Inside, you may want to see the **Deutsches Zinnfigurenmuseum** (Tin Figures Museum), with more than 300,000 miniature statuettes and tin soldiers, the largest collection of its kind in the world. From April to October casting is demonstrated daily 2–5. ☎ *09221/5550.* 🎫 *DM 4.* ☉ *Daily 10–5.*

OFF THE
BEATEN PATH

NEUENMARKT – In this "railway village" near Kulmbach more than 20 beautifully preserved, gleaming locomotives huff and puff in a living railroad museum. Every now and then a nostalgic train will take you to the Brewery Museum in Kulmbach. ⊠ *Birkenstr. 5, D–95339 Neuenmarkt,* ☎ *09227/5700.* 🎫 *DM 6.* ☉ *Tues.–Sun. 10–5.*

Dining and Lodging

$$–$$$ ✕🏠 **Hotel Kronprinz.** This old hotel tucked away in the middle of Kulmbach's old town, right in the shadow of Plassenburg Castle, covers all basic needs. The furnishings are somewhat bland, but the hotel's restaurant provides a nice meal or, better yet, substantial portions of cake and coffee. ⊠ *Fischerg. 4–6, D–95326,* ☎ *09221/92180,* 🖷 *09221/921–836. 19 rooms. Restaurant, bar, café. AE, DC, MC, V.* 🐾

Bayreuth

4 *24 km (15 mi) south of Kulmbach, 80 km (50 mi) northeast of Nürnberg.*

Bayreuth is pronounced Bye-*roit,* though it might as well be called Wagner. This small Franconian town was where 19th-century composer and musical revolutionary Richard Wagner (1813–83) finally settled after a lifetime of rootless shifting through Europe, and here he built his great theater, the Festspielhaus, as a suitable setting for his grand operas on mythological Germanic themes. The annual Wagner Festival, first held in 1876, brings the town to a halt as hordes of Wagner lovers arrive, pushing prices sky high, filling hotels to bursting, and earning themselves much-sought-after social kudos in the process (to some, it's one of *the* places to be seen). The festival is held from late July until late August, so unless you plan to visit the town specifically for it, this is the time to stay away.

Built by Wagner, **Wahnfried** was the only house he ever owned. It's a simple, austere neoclassic building built in 1874, whose name, "peace from madness," was well earned. The war left only the facade; the rest was carefully rebuilt. Wagner lived here with his wife, Cosima, daughter of pianist Franz Liszt; and here they are buried. King Ludwig II of

Bavaria, the young and impressionable "fairy-tale king," who gave Wagner so much financial support, is remembered in a bust before the entrance. The exhibits, arranged along a well-marked itinerary through the house, require a great deal of German-language reading (there are no translations). The thrill is in seeing Mozart's handwriting and the original scores of such masterpieces as *Parsifal, Tristan und Isolde, Lohengrin, Der Fliegende Holländer,* and *Götterdämmerung.* You can also see designs for productions of his operas, as well as his piano and huge library. At 10, noon, and 2, excerpts from his operas are played in the living room, and a video on his life is shown at 11 and 3. The little house where Franz Liszt also lived and died is right next door and can be visited on the Wagner ticket, but be sure to express your interest in advance. It, too, is heavy on the paper, but the last rooms—with pictures, photos, and silhouettes of the master, his students, acolytes, and friends—is well worth the detour. ⊠ *Richard-Wagner-Str. 48,* ☎ *0921/757–2816.* ☞ *DM 4.* ☉ *Fri.–Mon. and Wed. 9–5; Tues. and Thurs. 9–8.*

Conspiracy theorists take note: Right around the corner from Wahnfried is the amusing little **Deutsches Freimaurer-Museum** (German Freemasons Museum), which explains the origins of the Freemasons and the ins and outs of the fraternal organization, and exhibits items from everyday life that bear the famous symbols. Though the tags are not in English, the exhibits do in most cases speak for themselves. ⊠ *Im Hofgarten 1,* ☎ *0921/69824.* ☞ *DM 2.* ☉ *Tues.–Fri. 10–noon and 2–4, Sat. 10–noon.*

The **Festspielhaus** (Festival Theater) is by no means beautiful. In fact, this high temple of the Wagner cult is surprisingly plain. The Spartan look is explained partly by Wagner's desire to achieve perfect acoustics. The wood seats have no upholstering, for example, and the walls are bare of all ornament. The stage is enormous, capable of holding the huge casts required for Wagner's largest operas. Performances take place only during the annual Wagner Festival, still masterminded by descendants of the composer. ⊠ *Auf dem Grünen Hügel,* ☎ *0921/78780.* ☞ *DM 2.50.* ☉ *Tour Tues.–Sun. at 10, 10:45, 2:15, and 3; closed Nov., during rehearsals, and afternoons during the festival.*

The **Neues Schloss** (New Palace) is a glamorous 18th-century palace built by the Margravine Wilhelmine, sister of Frederick the Great of Prussia and a woman of enormous energy and decided tastes. Though Wagner is the man most closely associated with Bayreuth, his choice of this setting is largely due to the work of a woman who lived 100 years before him. Wilhelmine devoured books, wrote plays and operas (which she directed and, of course, acted in), and had buildings constructed, transforming much of the town and bringing it near bankruptcy. Her distinctive touch is much in evidence at the palace, built when a mysterious fire conveniently destroyed parts of the original palace. Anyone with a taste for the wilder flights of rococo decoration will love it. Some rooms also have been given over to one of Europe's finest collections of faience ware. The palace is close to Wahnfried. ⊠ *Ludwigstr. 21,* ☎ *0921/759–6921.* ☞ *DM 4.* ☉ *Apr.–Sept., Tues.–Sun. 10–noon and 1:20–5; Oct.–Mar., Tues.–Sun. 10–noon and 1:30–3:30; call for English-language tour times.*

Wilhelmine's other great architectural legacy is the **Markgräfliches Opernhaus** (Margravial Opera House). Built between 1745 and 1748, it is a rococo jewel, sumptuously decorated in red, gold, and blue. Apollo and the nine Muses cavort across the frescoed ceiling. It was this delicate 500-seat theater that originally drew Wagner to Bayreuth, since he felt that it might prove a suitable setting for his own operas. In fact, although it may be a perfect place to hear Mozart, it's hard to imagine a less suitable setting for Wagner's epic works. Visitors are treated to a light and sound show. ⊠ *Opernstr.,* ☎ *0921/759–6922.* ⊠ *DM 3.* ⊘ *Apr.–Sept., Tues.–Sun. 9–noon and 1:20–5; Oct.–Mar., Tues.–Sun. 10–noon and 1:30–3:30. Light and sound shows begin at 10:15, run about every ½ hr until 4:15 in summer and 2:45 in winter. Closed Mon. and on days with performances and rehearsals.*

It is wise to remember that Bayreuth is a solid little industrious Franconian town, and that there is a lot more to it than opera and Wagner. A visit to the **Historisches Museum Bayreuth** (Bayreuth Historical Museum) is like poking around a miraculous attic with 34 rooms. It's no wonder the museum won the Bavarian Museum Award. A wonderfully eclectic collection includes items from the life of the town, be they royal remnants, faience items from the 18th-century manufacturer, clothes, or odd sports appliances. ⊠ *Kirchpl. 6,* ☎ *0921/764–0123.* ⊠ *DM 3.* ⊘ *Tues.–Sun. 10–5 (also Mon. 10–5 during the festival).*

Bayreuth's newest and proudest cultural attraction, the **Museum der modernen Bildenden Kunst** (Museum of Modern Visual Art) houses several permanent collections donated or lent by private collectors. Works by Lyonel Feininger, Max Beckmann (lithographs from his Berlin Journeys), and woodcuts by Emil Schuhmacher are highlights. An unusual collection donated by the BAT tobacco company features paintings, sculptures, and ephemera relating to tobacco, the culture of smoking, and the processing of the leaf. The museum lies within the generous rooms of the old Town Hall and shares space with a somewhat modern, upscale restaurant called Oskar. ⊠ *Maximilianstr. 33,* ☎ *0921/764–5310.* ⊠ *DM 3.* ⊘ *July–Aug., Mon.–Wed. and Fri.–Sun. 10–5, Thurs. 10–8; Sept.–June, Tues., Wed., and Fri.–Sun. 10–5, Thurs. 10–8.*

Near the center of town in the old, 1887 Maisel Brewery building, the **Brauerei und Büttnerei-Museum** (Brewery and Coopers Museum) exhibits the tradition of the brewing trade over the past two centuries. The brewery operated until 1981, when its much bigger home was completed next door. After the 90-minute tour you can quaff a cool, freshly tapped beer in the museum's own pub, which has traditional Bavarian Weissbier. ⊠ *Kulmbacherstr. 40,* ☎ *0921/401–234.* ⊠ *DM 5.* ⊘ *Tour Mon.–Thurs. at 10 AM; individual tours by prior arrangement.*

The **Altes Schloss Eremitage** (Old Palace and Hermitage), 5 km (3 mi) north of Bayreuth on B–85, makes an appealing departure from the sonorous and austere Wagnerian mood of much of the town. It's an early 18th-century palace, built as a summer palace and remodeled in 1740 by the Margravine Wilhelmine. Although her taste is not much in evidence in the drab exterior, the interior, alive with light and color, displays her guiding hand in every elegant line. The extraordinary **Japanischer Saal** (Japanese Room), filled with Asian treasures and chinoiserie furniture, is the finest room in the palace. The park and gardens, partly formal, partly natural, are enjoyable for idle strolling in summer. ☎ *0921/759–690.* ⊠ *Schloss (including guided tour every ½ hr) DM 4.* ⊘ *Apr.–Sept., Tues.–Sun. 9–4:30; Mar., Tues.–Sun. 10–11:30 and 1–2:30; Oct.–Feb., by prior arrangement only.*

The **Lohengrin Therme** (Lohengrin Spa), on the way to Seulbitz, is a modern and exciting center of wellness and the ideal place to take a break from the travel schedule. The program there includes a pool, hot tubs, Jacuzzis, a beautiful sauna area, massages, light therapy, and more. Tickets for entrance and services can range from DM 15 for the pool and Jacuzzi area to DM 40 for a full Turkish massage. ⊠ *Kurpromenade 5,* ☎ *0921/792–400.* ⊘ *Sun.–Thurs. 8–10, Fri. and Sat. 8–11; sauna and wellness Sun.–Thurs. 10–10, Fri. and Sat. 10–11.*

Dining and Lodging

$$ ✕ **Weihenstephan.** Long wooden tables, hearty regional specialties, and beer straight from the barrel (from the oldest brewery in Germany) make this hotel tavern a perennial favorite. How old is old? The famous Weihenstephan in Freising, near Munich, dates to 1040. In summer the crowded, flower-strewn terrace is the place to be. ✉ *Bahnhofstr. 5,* ☎ *0921/82288. DC, MC, V.*

$ ✕ **Brauereischänke am Markt.** They make their own bratwurst at this boisterous Old Town inn. Another local specialty is *Bierrippchen,* pork ribs braised in a dark beer sauce. The inn's yeasty Zwickel beer is the ideal accompaniment to a meal. On sunny summer days you can people-watch from the sun-drenched beer garden on the pedestrian street. ✉ *Maximilianstr. 56,* ☎ *0921/64919. AE, MC. Closed Sun.*

$ ✕ **Brauhaus-Gaststätte Hopfengwölb.** You can watch beer being brewed at this family-run tavern. But don't let being in a commercial zone bother you. Hearty Franconian-style *Frühschoppen* (midmorning meal) with lots of wurst are the tavern's specialty, and there's a daily-changing lunch menu. Thursday evening is set aside for the real blowouts, when the oak tables groan under the weight of food. ✉ *Bindlacherstr. 10,* ☎ *0921/95950. No credit cards. Closed weekends. No dinner Mon.–Wed. and Fri.–Sun.*

$$$$ ✕▣ **Jagdschloss Thiergarten.** Make reservations well in advance for this small, top-notch hotel in a 250-year-old former hunting lodge. Staying here is like being a guest of your favorite aunt if she were an elderly millionaire. Rooms are furnished either in elegant white Venetian style or heavy German baroque, and all have a plush, lived-in character. The intimate Kaminhalle, with an ornate fireplace, and the Venezianischer Salon, dominated by a glittering 300-year-old Venetian chandelier, offer regional and nouvelle cuisine. The restaurants are closed Monday, and reservations and a jacket and tie are essential. The hotel is 6½ km (4 mi) from Bayreuth in the Thiergarten suburb. ✉ *Oberthiergärtenerstr. 36, D–95448,* ☎ *09209/9840,* ℻ *09209/98429. 8 rooms. 2 restaurants, bar, indoor pool, sauna. DC, MC, V. Closed Feb. 15–Mar. 15.*

$$$ ✕▣ **Goldener Anker.** No question about it, this is *the* place to stay in
★ Bayreuth. The hotel is right next to the Markgräfliches Opernhaus and has been entertaining composers, singers, conductors, and players for more than 100 years, as the signed photographs in the lobby and the signatures in the guest book attest. The establishment has been run by the same family since 1753. Rooms are small but individually decorated; many have antique pieces. The restaurant is justly popular. Book your room well in advance. ✉ *Opernstr. 6, D–95444,* ☎ *0921/65051,* ℻ *0921/ 65500. 40 rooms. Restaurant. AE, DC, MC, V. Closed Dec. 20–Jan. 10.*

$$ ✕▣ **Goldener Löwe.** A trusty yet stylish old inn close to the town center, the Golden Lion provides a traditional Franconian welcome, especially to overseas visitors. Rooms are furnished in Franconian farmhouse style, with pinewood, floral prints, and bright red-and-white-checked linen. The kitchen is known for its selection of *Klössen* (regional-style dumplings), and you may meet some friendly folks at the tavern bar. ✉ *Kulmbacherstr. 30, D–95445,* ☎ *0921/41046,* ℻ *0921/47777. 12 rooms. Restaurant, beer garden. AE, DC, MC, V.*

Golf

At **Golfanlagen Bayreuth** (☎ *0921/970–704*), just outside Bayreuth, there's an 18-hole championship course, a pitch-and-putt nine-holer, and a driving range. Clubs can be rented, and for those too young to swing one there's a playground.

Nightlife and the Arts

Opera lovers swear that there are few more intense operatic experiences than those offered by the annual **Wagner Festival** in Bayreuth, held July–August. For tickets write to the **Bayreuther Festspiele Karten-büro** (✉ Postfach 100262, D–95402 Bayreuth, ☎ 0921/78780), but be warned: the waiting list is years long! You'll do best if you plan your visit a couple of years in advance. Rooms can be nearly impossible to find during the festival, too. If you don't get Wagner tickets, console yourself with visits to the exquisite 18th-century **Markgräfliches Opern-haus** (☎ 0921/251–416); performances are given most nights from May through September. Check with the tourist office for details.

Shopping

The **Hofgarten Passage,** off Richard-Wagner-Strasse, is one of the fan-ciest shopping arcades in the region; it's crammed with smart boutiques selling anything from high German fashion to simple local artifacts.

En Route   The B–22 highway west to Bamberg is part of the officially designated **Strasse der Residenzen** (Road of Residences), named for the many epis-copal and princely palaces along its way—including Bamberg's stun-ning Neue Residenz. The road cuts through the Fränkische Schweiz—or Franconian Switzerland—which got its name from its fir-clad upland landscape. Just north of Hollfeld, 23 km (14 mi) west of Bayreuth, the Jurassic rock of the region breaks through the surface in a bizarre, craggy formation known as the Felsgarten (Rock Garden).

Bamberg

⑤ *65 km (40 mi) west of Bayreuth, 80 km (50 mi) north of Nürnberg.*

Few towns in Germany survived the war with as little damage as Bam-berg, and it comes as no surprise that this former residence of one of Germany's most powerful imperial dynasties is on UNESCO's World Heritage site list. Bamberg rose to prominence in the 11th century thanks to the political and economic drive of its most famous offspring, Holy Roman Emperor Heinrich II. He transformed this imperial residence into a flourishing episcopal city. His cathedral, consecrated in 1237, still dominates the historic area. For a short period Heinrich II pro-claimed Bamberg the capital of the Holy Roman Empire of the Ger-man nation. Moreover, Bamberg earned fame as the second city to introduce book printing, in 1460.

The city lies on the Regnitz River, and its historic center is a small is-land in the river; to the west is the so-called Bishops Town; to the east, Burghers Town. Connecting them is a bridge on which stands the **Altes Rathaus** (Old Town Hall), a highly colorful, rickety Gothic build-ing dressed extravagantly in rococo. It was built in this unusual place so that the burghers of Bamberg could avoid paying real estate taxes to their bishops and archbishops. It's best seen from the next bridge upstream; from there it appears to be practically in danger of being swept off by the river. The preeminent pleasure of a visit is to stroll through the narrow, sinuous streets of Old Bamberg, past half-timber and gabled houses and formal 18th-century mansions. Peek into flower-filled cobblestone courtyards or take time out in a waterside café in "little Venice," watching the little steamers as they chug past the col-orful row of fishermen's houses.

The **Neue Residenz** (New Residence), Bamberg's contribution to the Road of Residences, is an immense baroque palace that was once the home of the prince-electors. Their wealth and prestige can easily be imagined as you tour the glittering interior. Most memorable is the **Kaiser-saal** (Throne Room), complete with impressive ceiling frescoes and elab-orate stuccowork. The palace also houses the **Staatsbibliothek** (State Library). Among the thousands of books and illuminated manuscripts are the original prayer books belonging to Heinrich and his wife, a 5th-century codex of the Roman historian Livy, and manuscripts by the 16th-century painters Dürer and Cranach. The rose garden behind the Neue Residenz offers an aromatic and romantic space to stroll in addition to a view of Bamberg's roof landscape. ⊠ *Dompl. 8,* ☎ *0951/ 56351; 0951/54014 for Staatsbibliothek.* ⊴ *Neue Residenz DM 4, Staatsbibliothek free.* ⊙ *Neue Residenz by tour only, Apr.–Sept., daily 9–noon and 1:30–5; Oct.–Mar., daily 9–noon and 1:30–4; Staatsbibliothek, weekdays 9–5, Sat. 9–noon. Closed Sat. in Aug.*

★ Bamberg's great **Dom** (cathedral) is one of the country's most important, a building that tells not only the town's story but that of much of Germany as well. The first building here was begun by Heinrich II in 1003, and it was in this partially completed cathedral that he was crowned Holy Roman Emperor in 1012. In 1237 it was mostly destroyed by fire, and the present late-Romanesque/early Gothic building was begun. From the outside the dominant features are the massive towers at each corner. Heading into the dark interior, you'll find one of the most striking collections of monuments and art treasures of any European church. The most famous piece is the **Bamberger Reiter** (Bamberg Rider), an equestrian statue carved—no one knows by whom—around 1230 and thought to be an allegory of chivalrous virtue or a representation of King Stephen of Hungary. The larger-than-life figure is an extraordinarily realistic work for the period, more like a poised Renaissance statue than a stylized Gothic piece. Compare it with the mass of carved figures huddled in the tympana above the church portals. In the center of the nave you'll find another great sculptural work, the massive tomb of Heinrich and his wife, Kunigunde. It's the work of Tilman Riemenschneider, Germany's greatest Renaissance sculptor. Pope Clement II is also buried in the cathedral, in an imposing tomb beneath the high altar; he is the only pope to be buried north of the Alps. ⊠ *Dompl.,* ☎ *0951/502–330.* ⊴ *DM 4.* ⊙ *Nov.–Mar., daily 9–4:45; Apr.–Oct., daily 9–6.*

The **Diözesanmuseum** (Cathedral Museum), directly next to the cathedral, contains one of many nails and splinters of wood reputed to be from the cross of Jesus, which Mark Twain pointedly took notice of while touring Europe in the 19th century. More macabre exhibits in this rich ecclesiastical collection are the elaborately mounted skulls of Heinrich and Kunigunde. The building itself was designed by Balthasar Neumann (1687–1753), the architect of Vierzehnheiligen (☞ *above*), and constructed between 1730 and 1733. ⊠ *Dompl. 5,* ☎ *0951/502– 325.* ⊴ *DM 4, tour free.* ⊙ *Tues.–Sun. 10–5; tour in English by prior arrangement.*

On the north side of the Dom is the **Alte Hofhaltung,** the former imperial and episcopal palace. It's a sturdy and weatherworn half-timber Gothic building with a large, unruly Renaissance courtyard that is used for various events. Today it contains the **Historisches Museum** (Historical Museum), with a collection of documents and maps charting Bamberg's history that will appeal most to avid history buffs and/or those who read German well. ⊠ *Dompl. 8,* ☎ *0951/871–142.* ⊴ *DM 4.* ⊙ *May–Oct., Tues.–Sun. 9–5.*

The **Hoffmann Haus** is the former home of Ernst Theodor Amadeus Hoffmann, the romantic writer, composer, and illustrator who lived and worked in Bamberg from 1808 to 1813. Hoffmann is best remembered not for his own works but because of Jacques Offenbach's opera based on them, *The Tales of Hoffmann.* The little house has been preserved much as it was when Hoffmann lived here—complete with the hole in the floor of his upstairs study through which he talked to his wife below. ⊠ *Schillerpl. 26.* ⊠ *DM 2.* ⊙ *May–Oct., Tues.–Fri. 4–6, weekends 10–noon.*

Beneath Bamberg is a maze of **catacombs,** totaling 10 km (6 mi) in length, originally excavated in the 11th century for sand but later used for storing wine, beer, and malt. During World War II the catacombs found new uses as air-raid shelters and underground munitions factories. They can only be viewed on a prearranged group tour, so call in advance. ☎ *0951/871–161.* ⊙ *Tour Mon.–Thurs.*

The **Naturkunde Museum** (Museum of Natural History) is a good complement to the city's catacombs. In an 18th-century university building, the exhibits cover a wide range of subjects, from fossils to volcanoes. The pride of the place is the collection of 800 stuffed birds in a magnificent room, which also has a whale's jawbone casually lying on the floor. ☎ *0951/863–1248.* ⊙ *Apr.–Sept., daily 9–5; Oct.–Mar. daily 10–4.*

Dining and Lodging

$ ✕ **Brauereiausschank Schlenkerla.** This old tavern was a monastery for centuries. The black furniture and wall paneling complement the beer—Rauchbier—a strong malty brew with a smoky aftertaste. The unusual flavor comes from a beechwood-smoke brewing process. There are also excellent Franconian specialties at reasonable prices. Try the *Rauchschinken* (smoked ham) or the *Bierbrauervesper*—composed of smoked meat, sour-milk cheese, and black bread and butter, all served on a wooden platter. ⊠ *Dominikanerstr. 6,* ☎ *0951/56060. No credit cards. Closed Tues. and 2 wks in Jan.*

$$ ✕⌂ **Romantik Hotel Weinhaus Messerschmitt.** Willy Messerschmitt of aviation fame grew up in this beautiful late-baroque house with its steep-eaved, green-shuttered stucco exterior. Inside, the historic house has been turned into a very comfortable hotel, with spacious and luxuriously furnished rooms, some with exposed beams and many of them lighted by chandeliers. You'll also dine under beams and a coffered ceiling in the excellent Messerschmitt restaurant, one of Bamberg's most popular culinary havens. The hotel is especially fitted for guests with disabilities. ⊠ *Langestr. 41, D–96047,* ☎ *0951/27866,* 𝐅𝐀𝐗 *0951/26141. 17 rooms. Restaurant, bar. AE, DC, MC, V.*

Nightlife and the Arts

The **Sinfonie an der Regnitz** (⊠ Muss-Str. 20, ☎ 0951/964–7200), a fine riverside concert hall, is home to Bamberg's world-class resident symphony orchestra. The **Hoffmann Theater** (⊠ Schillerpl. 5, ☎ 0951/871–433) has opera and operetta from September through July. In June and July open-air performances are also given at the **Alte Hofhaltung** (☎ 0951/25256 for tickets). The city also has the **Capella Antiqua Bambergensis,** a first-class choir concentrating on ancient music. Throughout the summer organ concerts are given in the **Dom.** For program details and tickets to all cultural events call ☎ 0951/871–161.

En Route From Bamberg you can either take the fast autobahn (A–73) south to Nürnberg or a parallel country road that follows the Main-Danube Canal (running parallel to the Regnitz River at this point) and joins the A–73 just under 25 km (15 mi) later at Forchheim-Nord. The canal, a mighty feat of engineering first envisioned by Charlemagne but only completed in the 1990s, connects the North Sea and the Black Sea by linking the Rhine and the Danube via the Main.

SOUTHERN FRANCONIA AND UPPER PALATINATE

There's no tangible division between northern and southern Franconia. You do, however, leave the thickly wooded heights of the Fichtelgebirge and the Fränkische Schweiz behind, and the countryside opens up as if to announce the imminent arrival of a more populated region, where Nürnberg and Regensburg share a historically rooted hegemony. Though also in Bavaria, Regensburg is the capital of Oberpfalz (Upper Palatinate), which includes Walhalla and Weltenburg.

Nürnberg

63 km (39 mi) south of Bamberg, 162 km (100 mi) north of Munich.

Nürnberg (Nuremberg) is the principal city of Franconia and second in size and significance in Bavaria only to Munich. With a recorded history stretching back to 1050, it's among the most historic of Germany's cities; the core of the Old Town, through which the Pegnitz River flows, is still surrounded by its original medieval walls. Nürnberg has always taken a leading role in German affairs. It was here, for example, that the Holy Roman Emperors traditionally held the first Diet, or convention of the estates, of their incumbency. And it was here, too, that Hitler staged the most grandiose Nazi rallies; later, this was the site of the Allies' war trials, where top-ranking Nazis were charged with—and almost without exception convicted of—crimes against humanity. The rebuilding of Nürnberg after the devastation wrought by the war is nothing short of a miracle.

As a major intersection on the medieval trade routs, Nürnberg became a wealthy town. With prosperity came a great flowering of the arts and sciences. Albrecht Dürer (1471–1528), the first indisputable genius of the Renaissance in Germany, was born here in 1471. He married in 1509 and bought a house in the city where he lived and worked for the rest of his life. Other leading Nürnberg artists of the Renaissance include painter Michael Wolgemut (a teacher of Dürer), stonecutter Adam Kraft, and the brass founder Peter Vischer. The tradition of the Meistersinger, poets and musicians who turned songwriting into a special craft with a wealth of rules and regulations, also flourished here in the 16th century, thanks to the high standard set by the local cobbler Hans Sachs (1494–1576), celebrated three centuries later by Wagner in his *Meistersinger von Nürnberg*. The Thirty Years' War and the shift to sea routes for transportation led to a long decline, which only ended in the early 19th century when the first railroad opened in Nürnberg. Among a great host of inventions associated with the city, the most significant are the pocket watch, gun casting, the clarinet, and the geographical globe (the first of which was made before Columbus discovered the Americas). Among Nürnberg's famous products are *Lebkuchen* (gingerbread of sorts) and Faber-Castell pencils.

Nürnberg is rich in special events and celebrations. By far the most famous is the **Christkindlesmarkt** (Christ-Child Market) an enormous pre-Christmas fair that runs from the last weekend in November to Christmas Eve. One of the highlights is the candle procession, held every second Thursday of the market season in which thousands of children march through the city streets.

A Good Walk

Start your walk at the Hauptbahnhof, the main train station, whose tourist office offers maps and brochures. Enter the Old Town through the **Königstor,** the old King's Gate. The old town walls, finished in 1452, come complete with moats, sturdy gateways, and watchtowers. Year-round floodlighting adds to their brooding romance. Take a left on Luit-poldstrasse and note on your left the **Neues Museum** ⑥, Nürnberg's new museum for contemporary art. Take a left on Vorderer Sterngasse and then a right when you reach the old wall again. Take your second right onto Strasse der Menschenrechte (Human Rights Street), with an impressive installation by the artist Dani Karavan featuring 30 columns inscribed with the articles from the Declaration of Human Rights. On the right is one of Germany's most extraordinary museums, the **Germanisches Nationalmuseum** ⑦. A few hours spent here examining the sections devoted to the city will prepare you for the step back in time you'll make during the rest of your walk through Nürnberg. Follow Kornmarkt east and turn left on Pfannenschmiedsgasse to reach the beautiful **St. Lorenz Kirche** ⑧.

Continue north on Königstrasse and cross the bridge over the Pegnitz River at its most picturesque point, where the former hospital **Heilig-Geist-Spital** ⑨ broods over the waters, and soon you'll reach the city's central market square, the **Hauptmarkt** ⑩, with the delicate late-Gothic **Frauenkirche** ⑪ standing modestly on the east side and the handsome **Schöner Brunnen** ⑫ (fountain), in the northwestern corner. Just north of the Hauptmarkt is Rathausplatz, site of another Gothic masterpiece of church architecture, **St. Sebaldus Kirche** ⑬. The restored city hall, the **Altes Rathaus** ⑭, abuts the church; behind the city hall is another pretty fountain, the **Gänsemännchenbrunnen** ⑮. To the north of the Altes Rathaus on Burgstrasse, stands the fine Renaissance Fembohaus, which contains the **Stadtmuseum** ⑯. Save some energy for the climb up Burgstrasse to the great **Kaiserburg** ⑰, which sits majestically on rocky high ground just within the northern city walls. Within the shadow of the mighty fortress and of the city walls is the **Albrecht-Dürer-Haus** ⑱, at the top of Albrecht-Dürer-Strasse, just below the castle. Follow this street southward, and you'll come to a delightful toy museum, the **Spielzeugmuseum** ⑲, on Karlstrasse. If you still have time or energy, it's about a 15-minute walk to the trains and stamps of the **DB Museum und Museum für Post und Kommunikation** ⑳, on Lessingstrasse, just south of the Germanisches Nationalmuseum. You can then return to your starting point for that much-needed refreshment. The train station has an extensive mall of restaurants and bars.

TIMING

You'll need a full day to walk around Nürnberg, two if you wish to take more time at its fascinating museums. Most of the major sights are within a few minutes' walk of each other. Begin or end your day at the Kaiserburg, whose ramparts offer a spectacular view over this medieval gem of a town.

Sights to See

★ ⑱ **Albrecht-Dürer-Haus** (Albrecht Dürer House). The great painter Albrecht Dürer lived here from 1509 until his death in 1528. This beautifully preserved late-medieval house is typical of the prosperous merchants' homes that once filled Nürnberg. Dürer, who enriched German art with Italianate elements, was more than a painter. He raised the woodcut, a notoriously difficult medium, to new heights of technical sophistication, combining great skill with a haunting, immensely detailed drawing style and complex, allegorical subject matter, while earning a good living at the same time. A number of original prints adorn the walls, and printing techniques are demonstrated in the old studio. An excellent opportunity to find out about life in the house is to take the Saturday 11 AM tour with a guide role-playing "Agnes Dürer," Dürer's

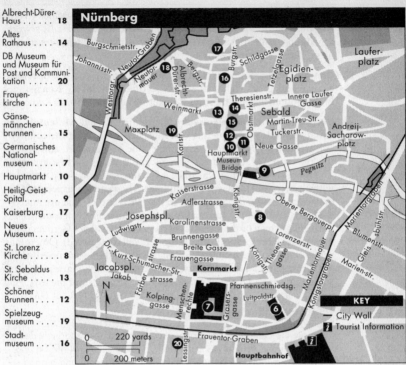

wife. ✉ *Albrecht-Dürer-Str. 39,* ☎ *0911/231–2568.* 💳 *DM 8, with tour DM 12.* ⊙ *Mar.–Oct. and during Christkindlesmarkt, Tues.–Sun. 10–5, Thurs. 10–8; Nov.–Feb., Tues.–Fri. 1–5, weekends 10–5.*

🄼 **Altes Rathaus** (Old Town Hall). This ancient building on Rathausplatz abuts the rear of ☞ **St. Sebaldus Kirche;** it was erected in 1332, destroyed in World War II, and subsequently restored. Its intact medieval dungeons, consisting of 12 small rooms and one large torture chamber called the Chapel, provide insight into the gruesome applications of medieval law. ✉ *Rathauspl.,* ☎ *0911/23360.* 💳 *DM 4.* ⊙ *Tues.–Sun. 10–5:30; mid-Oct.–Mar., Tues.–Fri. 10–5:30; Christkindlesmarkt daily 10–5:30.*

🄾 **DB Museum und Museum für Post und Kommunikation** (German Rail Museum and Museum for Post and Communication). The first train to run in Germany did so on December 7, 1835, from Nürnberg to nearby Fürth. A model of the epochal train is here, along with a series of original 19th- and early 20th-century trains and stagecoaches. Philatelists will want to check out some of the 40,000-odd stamps in the extensive exhibits on the German postal system. You can also find out about the history of sending messages, from the old coaches to optical fiber networks here. ✉ *Lessingstr. 6,* ☎ *0911/219–2428.* 💳 *DM 6.* ⊙ *Tues.–Sun. 9–5.*

🄻 **Frauenkirche** (Church of Our Lady). The fine late-Gothic Frauenkirche was built in 1350, with the approval of Holy Roman Emperor Charles IV, on the site of a synagogue that was burned down during a 1349 pogrom. The modern tabernacle beneath the main altar was designed to look like a Torah scroll as a kind of memorial to that despicable act. The church's real attraction is the **Männleinlaufen,** a clock dating from 1509, which is set in its facade. It's one of those colorful mechanical marvels at which Germans have long excelled. Every day at noon the seven electors of the Holy Roman Empire glide out of the clock to bow to Emperor Charles IV before sliding back under cover. It's worth scheduling your morning to catch the display. ⊠ *Hauptmarkt.* ⊙ *Mon.–Sat. 9–6, Sun. 12:30–6.*

⑮ Gänsemännchenbrunnen (Gooseman's Fountain). A work of rare elegance and great technical sophistication, this lovely Renaissance bronze fountain facing the Altes Rathaus was cast in 1550. ⊠ *Rathauspl.*

★ **❼ Germanisches Nationalmuseum** (German National Museum). You could spend days visiting this vast museum showcasing the country's cultural and scientific achievements, ethnic background, and history. It is the largest of its kind in Germany and perhaps the best arranged. The museum is in what was once a Carthusian monastery, complete with cloisters and monastic outbuildings. There are few aspects of German culture, from the Stone Age to the 19th century, that are not covered here, and quantity and quality are evenly matched. For some visitors the highlight may be the superb collection of Renaissance German paintings (with Dürer, Cranach, and Altdorfer well represented). Others may prefer the exquisite medieval ecclesiastical exhibits—manuscripts, altarpieces, statuary, stained glass, jewel-encrusted reliquaries—the collections of arms and armor, the scientific instruments, or the toys. Few will be disappointed. ⊠ *Kartäuserg. 1,* ☎ *0911/13310.* ▣ *DM 6.* ⊙ *Tues. and Thurs.–Sun. 10–5, Wed. 10–9.* 🐾

NEED A BREAK?   Opposite the Germanisches Nationalmuseum is a new, sparingly decorated restaurant, **Mendel** (⊠ Kartäuserg. 1, ☎ 0911/244–9774), that offers fine international cuisine, with a nod to Franconia and a good selection of wines. Entrées cost around DM 12.50.

---

❿ Hauptmarkt (Main Market). Nürnberg's central market square was at one time the city's Jewish Quarter. When the people of Nürnberg petitioned their emperor, Charles IV, for a big central market, the emperor happened to be in desperate need of money, and above all political support. The Jewish Quarter was the preferred site, but as the official protector of the Jewish people, the emperor could not just openly take away their property. Instead, he instigated a pogrom that left the Jewish Quarter in flames and more than 500 dead. The next step of razing the ruins and resettling the remaining Jews now appeared perfectly logical.

A market still operates here. Its colorful stands, piled high with produce and shaded by striped awnings, are essential to the life of the city. The market women are a formidable-looking bunch, dispensing flowers, fruit, and abuse in equal measure. It's here that the Christkindlesmarkt is held.

❾ Heilig-Geist-Spital (Holy Ghost Hospital). This ancient edifice dating from 1339 is set on graceful arches over the Pegnitz River, south of the Hauptmarkt. It has a charming courtyard, with elegant wood balconies and spacious arcades, and a restaurant. ⊠ *Spitalg. 16,* ☎ *0911/221–761.*

⑰ Kaiserburg (Imperial Castle). The city's main attraction is a grand yet playful collection of buildings standing just inside the city walls; it was once the residence of the Holy Roman Emperors. The complex comprises three separate groups. The oldest, dating from around 1050, is the **Burggrafenburg** (Castellan's Castle), with a craggy old pentagonal tower and the bailiff's house. It stands in the center of the complex. To the east is the **Kaiserstallung** (Imperial Stables), built in the 15th century as a granary and now serving as a youth hostel. The real interest of this vast complex of ancient buildings, however, centers on the westernmost part of the fortress, which begins at the **Sinwell Turm** (Sinwell Tower). The **Kaiserburg Museum** is here, a subsidiary of the Germanisches Nationalmuseum that displays ancient armors and has exhibits relating to horsemanship in the imperial era and to the history of the fortress. This section of the castle also boasts a wonderful Romanesque **Doppelkappelle** (Double Chapel). The upper part—richer, larger, and more ornate than the lower chapel—was where the emperor and his family worshiped. Also visit the **Rittersaal** (Knights' Hall) and the **Kaisersaal** (Throne Room). Their heavy oak beams, painted ceilings, and sparse interiors have changed little since they were built in the 15th century. ✉ *Burgstr.,* ☎ *0911/13310.* 🎟 *DM 9.* ☉ *Apr.–Sept., daily 9–6; Oct.–Mar., daily 10–4.*

⑥ **Neues Museum** (New Museum). Nürnberg's latest pride and joy is everything but medieval. Devoted to international design since 1945, the museum opened in mid-2000. The remarkable collection, which will be supplemented by changing exhibitions, is in a newly built edifice that has achieved the perfect synthesis between the old and the new. It is mostly built of traditional pink-sandstone ashlars, while the facade is a flowing, transparent composition of glass. ✉ *Luitpoldstr. 5,* ☎ *0911/240–2020.* 🎟 *DM 6.* ☉ *Tues.–Sun. 10–5, Wed. 10–8.*

⑧ **St. Lorenz Kirche** (St. Laurence Church). In a city with several striking churches, St. Lorenz is considered by many to be the most beautiful. It was begun around 1250 and completed in about 1477; it later became a Lutheran church. St. Lorenz is a sizable church; two towers flank the main entrance, which is covered with a forest of carvings. In the lofty interior note the works by sculptors Adam Kraft and Veit Stoss: Kraft's great stone tabernacle, to the left of the altar, and Stoss's *Annunciation,* at the east end of the nave, are their finest works. There are many other carvings throughout the building, testimony to the artistic wealth of late-medieval Nürnberg. ✉ *Lorenzer Pl.,* ☎ *0911/209–287.* ☉ *Daily 7–7.*

⑬ **St. Sebaldus Kirche** (St. Sebaldus Church). Although St. Sebaldus lacks the quantity of art treasures found in its rival ☞ St. Lorenz, its lofty nave and choir are among the purest examples of Gothic ecclesiastical architecture in Germany: elegant, tall, and airy. Veit Stoss carved the crucifixion group at the east end of the nave, while the elaborate bronze shrine, containing the remains of St. Sebaldus himself, was cast by Peter Vischer and his five sons around 1520. Not to be missed either is the **Sebaldus Chörlein,** an ornate Gothic oriel that was added to the Sebaldus parish house in 1361 (the original is in the ☞ Germanisches Nationalmuseum). ✉ *Albrecht-Dürer-Pl. 1,* ☎ *0911/225–613.* ☉ *Daily 7–7.*

⑫ **Schöner Brunnen** (Beautiful Fountain). The elegant 60-ft-high Gothic fountain carved around the year 1400 looks as though it should be on the summit of some lofty Gothic cathedral. It is adorned with 40 figures arranged in tiers—prophets, saints, local noblemen, sundry electors of the Holy Roman Empire, and one or two strays such as Julius Caesar and Alexander the Great. A gold ring is set into the railing surrounding the fountain, reportedly placed there by an apprentice carver. Stroking it is said to bring good luck. ✉ *Hauptmarkt.*

☾ **⑲** **Spielzeugmuseum** (Toy Museum). Both young and old are captivated by this playful museum, which has a few exhibits dating from the Renaissance; most, however, are from the 19th century. Simple dolls vie with mechanical toys of extraordinary complexity. There's even a little Ferris wheel. ✉ *Karlstr. 13–15,* ☎ *0911/231–3164.* 🎟 *DM 5.* ☉ *Tues. and Thurs.–Sun. 10–5, Wed. 10–9.*

⑯ **Stadtmuseum** (City Museum). This city history museum, the Fembo-haus, is a dignified patrician dwelling completed in 1598. It is one of the finest Renaissance mansions in Nürnberg. ⊠ *Burgstr. 15,* ☎ *0911/231–2595.* ☒ *DM 4.* ⊙ *Mar.–Oct., Tues.–Sun. 10–5; Nov.–Feb., Tues.–Sun. 1–5, weekends 10–5.*

OFF THE
BEATEN PATH

TIERGARTEN NÜRNBERG – The well-stocked Nuremberg Zoo has a dolphinarium that children love; it's worth the extra admission fee. The zoo is on the northwest edge of town; reach it by taking the Number 5 streetcar from the city center. ⊠ *Am Tiergarten 30,* ☎ *0911/54546.* ☒ *DM 8, Dolphinarium DM 6.* ⊙ *Zoo and dolphinarium Apr.–Sept., daily 8–7:30; Mar. and Oct., daily 8–5:30; Nov.–Feb., daily 9–5; Dolphinarium display daily at 11, 2, and 4.*

ZEPPELINFELD – The enormous parade grounds where Hitler addressed his largest Nazi rallies lie on the eastern edge of the city. Nowadays it sometimes shakes to the amplified beat of pop concerts. The central stand area contains a museum with the Fascination and Terror exhibit, which documents the political, social, and architectural history of the Nazi Party in Nürnberg. Tours of the grounds are offered by a private association called *Geschichte für Alle e.V* (History for All). ☎ *0911/869–897 for Zeppelinfeld; 0911/332–735 for tour.* ☒ *DM 2 museum, DM 9 tour. Museum:* ⊙ *Mid-May 1–Sept., Tues.–Sun. 10–6; Oct.–May, by appointment. Tours: Dec.–Mar., Sun. at 2; Apr.–Nov., weekends at 2. Meet at Luitpoldhain tram terminus (No. 9).*

Dining and Lodging

$$$$ ✕ **Entenstub'n.** "Duck Tavern" seems an inappropriate name for such a regal restaurant, which looks like an 18th-century drawing room and is in what was once a shooting lodge for Bavarian king Ludwig III. The menu, a mix of regional and nouvelle cooking styles, matches the elegant setting, with such specialties as parfait of creamed pigeon and white fish in chives galantine. It is in a remote part of town, however, so if not driving, you should take a taxi. ⊠ *Günthersbühlerstr. 145,* ☎ *0911/598–0413. AE, MC. Closed Sun. and Mon.*

$$$$ ✕ **Essigbrätlein.** Some rank this the top restaurant in the city and even
★   among the best in Germany. As the oldest restaurant in Nürnberg, built in 1550 and originally used as a meeting place for wine merchants, it is unquestionably one of the most atmospheric. Today its elegant period interior is *the* place to eat *Essigbrätlein* (roast loin of beef). Other dishes blend Franconian and nouvelle recipes. ⊠ *Weinmarkt 3,* ☎ *0911/225–131. Reservations essential. AE, DC, MC, V. Closed Sun. and Mon.*

$$ ✕ **Nassauer Keller.** The exposed-beam-and-plaster decor complements the resolutely traditional cooking. Try the duck and the apple strudel. The restaurant has a memorable setting in the cellar of a 13th-century tower beside the church of St. Lorenz. ⊠ *Karolinenstr. 2–4,* ☎ *0911/225–967. AE, DC, MC.*

$-$$ ✕ **Barfüsser Kleines Brauhaus.** The huge cellar rooms of the old grain
★   customs warehouse houses this minibrewery and restaurant. Locals meet for lunch or dinner to enjoy Franconian specialties or just plain home cooking along with the fine beer brewed on the premises. The vaulted ceiling and thick stone pillars are a simple but elegant backdrop. Try the carp, a regional specialty only available in months with the letter "r"! ⊠ *Königstr. 60,* ☎ *0911/204–242. AE, MC, V.*

$ ✕ **Historische Bratwurst-Küche Zum Gulden Stern.** A house built in 1375 holds the oldest bratwurst restaurant in the world and even survived the last war. The famous Nürnberg bratwursts are always freshly roasted on a beechwood fire; the boiled variation is prepared in a tasty stock of Franconian wine and onions. This is where the city council met in

1998 to decide upon the official size and weight of the Nürnberg bratwurst. ⊠ *Zirkelschmiedg. 26,* ☎ *0911/205–9288. No credit cards.*

$ ✕ **Heilig-Geist-Spital.** Heavy wood furnishings and a choice of more
★ than 100 wines make this 650-year-old wine tavern a popular spot.
The menu includes grilled pork chops, panfried potatoes, and German cheeses. ⊠ *Spitalg. 16,* ☎ *0911/221–761. AE, DC, MC, V.*

$$$$ ✕⌹ **Maritim.** If you value modern convenience over old-world charm, consider staying in this luxuriously modern hotel, conveniently located between the railway station and the Old Town. Clever interior designing has given the sleek decor stylized historic touches, such as coffered ceilings, checkered tiles, and lots of wood paneling. The hotel is a member of a French chain and its Gallic connection ensures fine cuisine in the Gourmet, its restaurant. Breakfast costs an extra DM 22, but the range and excellence of the buffet fully warrant the expense. ⊠ *Frauentorgraben 11, D–90443,* ☎ *0911/23630,* ⅣX *0911/236–3836, 306 rooms, 10 suites. 2 restaurants, bar, indoor pool, massage, sauna, steam room, exercise room. AE, DC, MC, V.*

$$$ ✕⌹ **Hotel-Weinhaus Steichele.** This skillfully converted former 19th-century wine merchant's warehouse is now part of the Flair hotel group but is still managed by the family that has been running it for three generations. It's handily close to the main train station yet on a quiet street of the old walled town. The rooms, decorated in Bavarian rustic decor, are cozy rather than luxurious. Two wood-paneled, traditionally furnished taverns serve Franconian fare. ⊠ *Knorrstr. 2–8, D–90402,* ☎ *0911/202–280,* ⅣX *0911/221–914. 56 rooms. Restaurant, Weinstube. AE, DC, MC, V.*

$$$ ⌹ **Agneshof.** This comfortable hotel is sandwiched north of the old town between the fortress and St. Sebaldus Church. Interiors are very modern, tastefully done, and the hotel also has a small wellness section that will be welcome after a long day exploring the Old Town. ⊠ *Agnesg. 10, D–90403,* ☎ *0911/214–440,* ⅣX *0911/2144–4144. 72 rooms. Hot tub, sauna. AE, DC, MC, V.* ✍

$$ ⌹ **Burghotel Stammhaus.** Accommodations are small but cozy, and the service is familial and friendly here. The breakfast room with its balcony overlooking the houses of the old town has a charm all its own. A pool is in the basement. ⊠ *Schildg. 14, D–90403,* ☎ *0911/203–040,* ⅣX *0911/226–503. 22 rooms. Indoor pool. AE, DC, MC, V.* ✍

Nightlife and the Arts

Nürnberg has an annual summer festival, **Sommer in Nürnberg,** from May through September, with more than 200 events. Its international organ festival in June and July is regarded as Europe's finest. From May through August classical music concerts are given in the Rittersaal of the **Kaiserburg,** while regular pop and rock shows are staged in the dry moat of the castle. In June and July open-air concerts are given in the Kaiserburg's Serenadenhof. For bookings and program details call ☎ 0911/225–726.

Shopping

Step into the **Handwerkerhof,** in the tower at the Old Town gate near the main railway station, and you'll think you're back in the Middle Ages. Craftspeople are busy at work in a "medieval mall," turning out the kind of handiwork that has been produced in Nürnberg for centuries: pewter, glassware, basketwork, wood carvings, and, of course, toys. The mall is open mid-March–December 24, weekdays 10–6:30, Saturday 10–4. December 1–24 the mall is also open on Sunday 10–6:30.

The **Scherenschnittstudio** (⊠ Albrecht-Dürer-Str. 13, ☎ 0911/244–7483) specializes in scissor-cut silhouettes. You can either come and pose yourself for owner Karin Dütz, send a picture (profile, do not smile), or just browse to pick up some items of this old and skilled craft.

Regensburg

90 km (56 mi) southeast of Nürnberg, 120 km (74 mi) northwest of Munich.

Regensburg, the capital of the Upper Palatinate, is one of the best-preserved medieval cities in Germany. Everything here is original, because the city suffered no major damage in World War II. Although it's one of Germany's most historic cities, few visitors to Bavaria venture this far off the well-trod tourist trails. Even Germans are surprised when they discover the remarkable city.

The key to Regensburg is the Danube. Until construction of the Rhine-Main-Danube Canal, completed in the 1990s, the great river was no longer navigable a few miles to the west, and this simple geographic fact allowed Regensburg to control trade along the Danube between Germany and central Europe. The Danube was a conduit of ideas as well. It was from Regensburg that Christianity spread across much of central Europe in the 7th and 8th centuries. By the Middle Ages Regensburg had become a political, economic, and intellectual center of European significance. For many centuries it was the most important city in southeastern Germany, serving as the seat of the Perpetual Imperial Diet from 1663 until 1806, when Napoléon ordered the dismemberment of the Holy Roman Empire.

Regensburg's story begins with the Celts around 500 BC. They called their little settlement Radasbona. In AD 179, as an original marble inscription in the Historisches Museum proclaims, it became a Roman military post called Castra Regina. The Porta Praetoria of the Romans remains in the Old Town, and whenever you see huge ashlars incorporated into buildings, you are looking at bits of the old Roman settlement. When Bavarian tribes migrated to the area in the 6th century, they occupied what remained of the Roman town and, apparently on the basis of its Latin name, called it Regensburg. Anglo-Saxon missionaries led by St. Boniface in 739 made the town a bishopric before heading down the Danube to convert the heathen in even more far-flung lands. Charlemagne, first of the Holy Roman Emperors, arrived at the end of the 8th century and incorporated Regensburg into his burgeoning domain.

The spirit of Regensburg is very special: On the one hand are the ancient and hallowed walls; on the other is a crowd of young and lively students from the university (founded in 1967), who are reminders that this city is not a museum. Any serious tour of Regensburg includes an unusually large number of places of worship—not for nothing is it known as "the city of churches." If your spirits wilt at the thought of inspecting them all, you should at least see the Dom (cathedral), famous for its Domspatzen (boys' choir—the literal translation is "cathedral sparrows").

A Good Walk

Begin your walk in the very center of Regensburg, on medieval Rathausplatz. At the tourist office you can book a tour of the adjacent **Altes Rathaus** ㉑ and pick up maps and brochures. Head east along Goliathstrasse, making a short detour halfway down to the bank of the Danube and the **Steinerne Brücke** ㉒, which was key to the city's rise to medieval trading power. Walk to this bridge's center for an unforgettable view of Regensburg's old town center, with the ancient tower, the **Brückturm** ㉓, acting as a gate leading to the jumble of cobblestone streets and steeply eaved houses. From the tower follow Residenzstrasse south, and within a few minutes you'll reach Domplatz, dominated by Regensburg's soaring cathedral, **Dom St. Peter** ㉔. Behind the cathedral square is the quieter Alter Kornmarkt, bordered on three sides by historic churches: the **Alte Kapelle** ㉕, the adjoining **Karmelitenkirche** ㉖, and the **Niedermünster** ㉗. At the northern exit of Alter Kornmarkt is an interesting reminder of Regensburg's Roman past, the **Porta Praetoria** ㉘, a former city gate. Other Roman remains can be viewed in Regensburg's highly interesting city museum, the **Historisches Museum** ㉙, on Dachauplatz, just south of the Alter Kornmarkt. Regensburg's oldest church, **St. Kassian** ㉚, is 200 yards west of Dachauplatz and Alter Kornmarkt, at the southern edge of another ancient city square, Neupfarrplatz, where you'll also find the city's first Protestant church, the **Neupfarrkirche** ㉛. Leave Neupfarrplatz at its southern edge and a short stroll brings you to the great bulk of Regensburg's extraordinary palace, **Schloss Emmeram** ㉜. Adjoining the palace is the church of **St. Emmeram** ㉝. To complete your walk, continue westward along Obermünsterstrasse, turning right into Obere Bachgasse. This street eventually becomes Untere Bachgasse, which will take you back within minutes to your starting point, Rathausplatz.

TIMING

Regensburg is compact; its old town center is scarcely a half-mile square. All of its attractions lie on the south side of the Danube, so you won't have to cross it more than once—and then only to admire the city from the north bank. Try to time your tour so that you arrive at lunchtime at the ancient Historische Wurstküche, a tavern nestling between the river and the bridge (☞ Dining and Lodging, *below*). You'll need about two hours or more to explore the Schloss Emmeram and the neighboring St. Emmeram Church. Schedule at least another hour to visit the cathedral.

Sights to See

㉕ **Alte Kapelle** (Old Chapel). The Carolingian structure was erected in the 9th century. Its dowdy exterior gives little hint of the joyous rococo treasures within—extravagant concoctions of sinuous gilt stucco, rich marble, and giddy frescoes, the whole illuminated by light pouring in from the upper windows. ⊠ *Alter Kornmarkt 8.* ☉ *Daily 9–dusk.*

㉑ **Altes Rathaus** (Old City Hall). The picture-book complex of medieval buildings, with half-timbering, windows large and small, and flowers in tubs, is among the best-preserved such buildings in the country, as well as one of the most historically important. It was here, in the imposing Gothic **Reichssaal** (Imperial Hall), that the Perpetual Imperial Diet met from 1663 to 1806. This parliament of sorts consisted of the emperor, the electors (seven or eight), the princes (about 50), and the burghers, who assembled to discuss and determine the affairs of the far-reaching German lands. The hall is sumptuously appointed with tapestries, flags, and heraldic designs. Note especially the wood ceiling, built in 1408, and the different elevations for the various estates. The Reichssaal is occasionally used for concerts. The neighboring **Ratsaal** (Council Room) is where the electors met for their consultations. The cellar holds the actual torture chamber of the city, the **Fragstatt** (Questioning Room), and the execution room, called the **Armesünderstübchen** (Poor Sinners' Room). Any prisoner who withstood three degrees of questioning without confessing was considered innocent and released—which tells you something about medieval notions of justice. ⊠ *Rathauspl.,* ☎ *0941/507–4411.* ☜ *DM 5.* ☉ *Daily 9–4; tour in English May–Sept., Mon.–Sat. at 3:15.*

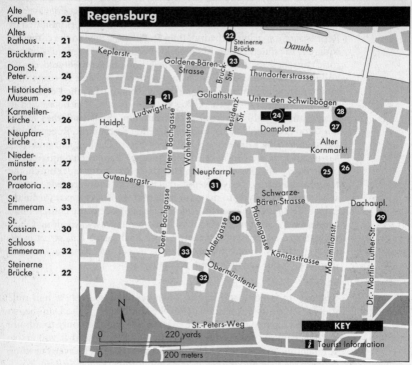

NEED A
BREAK?

Just across the square from the Altes Rathaus is the **Prinzessin Café** (⊠ Rathauspl. 2, ☎ 0941/57671), Germany's oldest coffeehouse, which first opened its doors to the general public in 1686.

㉓ Brückturm (Bridge Tower). All tiny windows, weathered tiles, and pink plaster, this picturesque 17th-century tower stands at the south end of the Steinerne Brücke. The brooding building with a massive roof to the left of the tower is an old salt warehouse that now houses the Salzstadel Wirtshaus restaurant, where you can try your first Regensburger sausages (☎ 0941/59098).

★ **㉔ Dom St. Peter** (St. Peter's Cathedral). Regensburg's transcendent cathedral, modeled on the airy, vertical lines of French Gothic architecture, is something of a rarity this far south in Germany. Begun in the 13th century, it stands on the site of a much earlier Carolingian church. Construction dragged on for almost 600 years until Ludwig I of Bavaria, then ruler of Regensburg, finally had the towers built. These had to be replaced in the mid-1950s after their original soft limestone was found to be badly eroded. Behind the Dom is a little workshop where a team of 15 stonecutters are busy full-time during the summer recutting and restoring parts of the cathedral.

Before heading into the Dom, admire the intricate and frothy carvings of its facade. A remarkable feature of the cathedral is that it can hold 7,000 people, three times the population of Regensburg when construction began. The glowing 14th-century stained glass in the choir and the exquisitely detailed statues of the archangel Gabriel and the Virgin in the crossing (the intersection of the nave and the transepts) are among the church's outstanding features. ⊠ *Dompl.,* ☎ *0941/597–1002.* ☞ *Tour DM 4.* ☉ *Cathedral tour May–Oct., weekdays at 10, 11, and 2; Sun. at noon and 2; Nov.–Apr., weekdays at 11, Sun. at noon.*

Be sure to visit the **Kreuzgang** (Cloisters), reached via the garden. There you'll find a small octagonal chapel, the **Allerheiligenkapelle** (All Saints Chapel), a typically solid Romanesque building that is all sturdy grace and massive walls. You can barely make out the faded remains of stylized 11th-century frescoes on its ancient walls. The equally ancient shell of St. Stephan's Church, the **Alter Dom** (Old Cathedral), can also be visited. The cloisters, chapel, and Alter Dom can be seen only on a guided one-hour tour. ☒ *DM 3.* ⊘ *Tour mid-May–Oct., daily at 10, 11, and 2; Nov.–Mar., weekdays at 11, Sun. at noon; Apr.–mid-May, daily at 11 and 2.*

The **Domschatzmuseum,** the cathedral museum, contains valuable treasures collected during the city's long ecclesiastical history. Some of the vestments and the monstrances are still used during special services. The entrance is in the nave. ☒ *Dompl.,* ☎ *0941/51068.* ☒ *DM 4.* ⊘ *Apr.–Oct., Tues.–Sat. 10–5, Sun. noon–5; Dec.–Mar., Fri. and Sat. 10–4, Sun. noon–4. Closed Nov.*

NEED A
BREAK?
The restaurant **Heuport,** opposite the entrance of the Dom, is in one of the old and grand private ballrooms of the city. The service is excellent, whatever you order tastes good, and the tables at the windows have a wonderful view of the Dom.

㉙ **Historisches Museum** (Historical Museum). The municipal museum vividly relates the cultural history of Regensburg. It is one of the highlights of the city, both for its unusual and beautiful setting—a former Gothic monastery—and for its wide-ranging collections, from Roman artifacts to Renaissance tapestries. The most significant exhibits are the paintings by Albrecht Altdorfer (1480–1538), a native of Regensburg and, along with Cranach, Grünewald, and Dürer, one of the leading painters of the German Renaissance. His work has the same sense of heightened reality found in that of his contemporaries, in which the lessons of Italian painting are used to produce an emotional rather than a rational effect. The real significance of Altdorfer's work is his interest in landscape, not merely as background but for its own sake. His paintings would not have seemed out of place among those of 19th-century Romantics. Far from seeing the world around him as essentially hostile, or at least alien, he saw it as something intrinsically beautiful, whether wild or domesticated. ☒ *Dachaupl. 2–4,* ☎ *0941/507–1442.* ☒ *DM 4.* ⊘ *Tues.–Sun. 10–4.*

㉖ **Karmelitenkirche** (Church of the Carmelites). This lovely church, styled in baroque from crypt to cupola, stands next to the ☞ **Alte Kapelle.** It has a finely decorated facade designed by the 17th-century Italian master Carlo Lurago.

㉛ **Neupfarrkirche** (New Parish Church). Built between 1519 and 1540, this is the first Protestant church in Regensburg, indeed one of a very few in Bavaria. It's an imposing building, substantially less ornate than any other in the city. Some may find its restraint welcome after the exuberance of so many of the other places of worship. ☒ *Neupfarrpl.* ⊘ *Daily 9–dusk.*

NEED A
BREAK?
The Dampfnudel is a kind of sweet yeast dough dumpling that is tasty and filling. The best in Bavaria can be had at **Dampfnudel Uli** (☒ Watmarkt 4), a little establishment in a former chapel. The decoration is incredibly eclectic, from Bavarian crafts to a portrait of Ronald Reagan signed: "To Uli Deutzer, with best wishes, Ronald Reagan." It's open Tuesday–Friday 10–6 and Saturday 10–3.

㉗ Niedermünster. This 12-century building with a baroque interior was originally the church of a community of nuns, all of them from noble families. For a quarter hour beginning at 12:05 PM daily, concerts are given by students of the church music school. ⊠ *Alter Kornmarkt 5,* ☎ *0941/597–1002.*

㉘ Porta Praetoria. The rough-hewn former city gate is one of the most interesting relics of Roman times in Regensburg. Look through the grille on its east side to see a section of the original Roman street, about 10 ft below today's street level.

㉝ St. Emmeram. The Thurn und Taxis family church stands across from Schloss Emmeram. The foundations of the church date to the 7th and 8th centuries. A richly decorated baroque interior was added in 1730 by the Asam brothers. St. Emmeram contains the graves of the 7th-century martyred Regensburg bishop Emmeram and the 10th-century St. Wolfgang. ⊠ *Emmeramspl. 3,* ☎ *0941/53853.* ⊙ *Mon.–Thurs. 10–4:30, Fri. 1–4:30, Sat. 10–4:30, Sun. noon–4:30.*

㉚ St. Kassian. Regensburg's oldest church was founded in the 8th century. Don't be fooled by its dour exterior; inside, it is filled with delicate rococo decoration. ⊠ *St. Kassianpl. 1.* ⊙ *Daily 9–5:30.*

㉜ Schloss Emmeram (Emmeram Palace). Formerly a Benedictine monastery, this is the ancestral home of the princely Thurn und Taxis family, which made its fame and fortune after being granted the right to carry official and private mail throughout the empire and Spain by Emperor Maximilian I (1493–1519) and by Philip I, king of Spain, who ruled during the same period. Their business extended over the centuries into the Low Countries (Holland, Belgium, and Luxembourg), Hungary, and Italy. The little horn that still symbolizes the post office in several European countries comes from the Thurn und Taxis coat of arms. For a while Schloss Emmeran was heavily featured in the gossip columns thanks to the wild parties and somewhat extravagant lifestyle of the young dowager Princess Gloria von Thurn und Taxis. In recent years, however, the princess was forced to sell much of the family treasure to pay the taxes due on the death of her husband, Prince Johannes. In 1996 the Bavarian authorities allowed her to keep what remains, on the condition it be put on public display at the palace.

The **Thurn und Taxis Palace,** with its splendid ballroom and throne room, is an eloquent witness to courtly life in the 19th century. Even more important, however, is the **Thurn und Taxis Museum,** in which every display—be it of dueling pistols, of a plain marshal's staff, of a boudoir, or even a snuffbox—has been carefully selected for its fine craftsmanship. The palace's **Marstallmuseum** (the former royal stables) displays the family's coaches and carriages and related items. ☎ *0941/50480.* ▧ *DM 8, DM 6 for Thurn und Taxis Museum alone.* ⊙ *Weekdays 11–5, weekends and holidays 10–5. Marstallmuseum is closed Nov.–Mar.*

★ **㉒ Steinerne Brücke** (Stone Bridge). This impressive old bridge resting on massive pontoons is Regensburg's most celebrated sight. It was completed in 1146 and was rightfully considered a miraculous piece of engineering at the time. As the only crossing point over the Danube for miles, it effectively cemented Regensburg's control over trade. The significance of the little statue on the bridge is a mystery, but the figure seems to be a witness to the legendary rivalry between the master builders of the bridge and those of the Dom.

Dining and Lodging

$$ ✕ **Leerer Beutel.** This restaurant lodged in a huge old warehouse serves excellent international cuisine—from antipasti to solid pork roast—in the pleasant atmosphere of a vaulted room supported by massive rough-hewn beams. The warehouse is also a venue for concerts, exhibitions, film screenings, and similar, so it's the ideal place to spend the evening. ⊠ *Bertoldstr. 9,* ☎ *0941/58997. AE, DC, MC, V.*

$$ ✕ **Salzstadel Wirtshaus.** This former salt storehouse sits squarely on the bank of the Danube next to the Steinerne Brücke, and is one of Regensburg's culinary citadels. Regensburger sausages are prominent on the menu, together with other Bavarian staples such as hocks and potato dumplings. ⊠ *An der Steinernen Brücke,* ☎ *0941/59098. MC. Closed Mon.*

$ ✕ **Historische Wurstküche.** Succulent Regensburger sausages—the best in town—are prepared right before your eyes here on an open beechwood charcoal grill in the tiny kitchen, and if you eat them inside in the tiny dining room, you'll have to squeeze past the cook. In summer they are served at trestle tables set outside on the bank of the Danube. Inside are plaques recording the levels the river reached in the various floods that have doused the restaurant's kitchen in the past 100 years. ⊠ *Thundorferstr. 3,* ☎ *0941/59098. No credit cards.*

$$$$ ✕▥ **Parkhotel Maximilian.** A handsome 18th-century building between the railway station and the Old Town is home to the most elegant and sophisticated hotel in Regensburg. Its decorative facade faces the cathedral, and the recently refurbished rooms in the front, equipped with queen- or king-size beds, offer a nice view of the church. Some rooms are equipped with fax modems and all have cable TV. The hotel has a restaurant with excellent Italian and international cuisine. ⊠ *Maximilianstr. 28, D–93047,* ☎ *0941/56850,* ℻ *0941/52942. 47 rooms, 3 suites. 2 restaurants, 2 bars, café, beauty salon, recreation room. AE, DC, MC, V.* ✍

$$$–$$$$ ✕▥ **Altstadthotel Arch.** A beautifully renovated 18th-century house with foundations laid in the 12th century, this small family hotel in the center of the old city is near all the main attractions. Rooms are decorated in great style, mostly in warm blues and shades of red, and dark wood. Try for an attic room—you'll sleep beneath the original beams. The restaurant is in a Gothic-style stone-vaulted cellar. It offers an international menu, but it's dominated by Franconian dishes such as sauerbraten; the Knödel are homemade. ⊠ *Haidpl. 4, D–93047,* ☎ *0941/ 58660,* ℻ *0941/586–6168. 62 rooms, 6 apartments. Restaurant, bar. AE, DC, MC, V.*

$$$ ✕▥ **Hotel-Restaurant Bischofshof am Dom.** This is one of Germany's most historic hostelries, a former bishop's palace where guests can sleep in an apartment that includes part of a Roman gateway. Other chambers are only slightly less historic, and some have seen emperors and princes as guests. In summer the central cobblestone courtyard is a delight. If your room overlooks it, you'll awaken to a neighboring church's carillon playing a German hymn, and you'll retire to the strains of the Bavarian national anthem. The hotel's restaurant is a gourmet mecca in these reaches of Bavaria, yet the prices are sensible. The beer comes from a brewery founded in 1649. ⊠ *Krauterermarkt 3, D–93047,* ☎ *0941/59086,* ℻ *0941/53508. 51 rooms, 3 suites. Restaurant, bar, beer garden. AE, DC, MC, V.*

$$–$$$ ✕▥ **Hotel Münchner Hof.** In this little hotel nestled in the block near the Neupfarrkirche the rooms are generous and tastefully decorated. In some the original arches of the ancient building are set against the newer plastering on the walls. The restaurant is quiet and comfortable, serving Bavarian specialties and good Munich beer. The bottom line: you get top service at a good price, and Regensburg is at your feet. ⊠ *Tändlerg. 9, D–93047,* ☎ *0941/58440,* ℻ *0941/561–709. 53 rooms. Restaurant. AE, MC, V.* ✍

$$–$$$ ✕🗓 **Kaiserhof am Dom.** Renaissance windows punctuate the green fa-
cade of this historic city mansion. The rooms, most of which were totally renovated in 1997, are 20th-century modern, with perks like
underfloor heating and cable TV. Try for one with a view of the cathedral, which stands directly across the street. Breakfast is served beneath
the high-vaulted ceiling of the former 14th-century chapel, and there's
also a smart brasserie. ✉ *Kramg. 10–12, D–93047,* ☎ *0941/585–350,*
FAX *0941/585–3595. 30 rooms. Restaurant, café. AE, DC, MC, V.*

Nightlife and the Arts

Regensburg offers a range of musical experiences, though none so
moving as a performance by the famous boys' choir at the cathedral.
The best-sung mass is held on Sunday at 9 AM. It can be a remarkable
experience, and it's worth scheduling your visit to the city to hear the
choir. A three-week program of music and theater is presented during
the **Regensburger Kultursommer**, a partly open-air festival from the
end of July to the beginning of August.

Weltenburg

★ ㉞   *25 km (15 mi) southwest of Regensburg.*

In Weltenburg you'll find the great **Stiftskirche Sts. Georg und Martin** (Abbey
Church of St. George and St. Martin), near the bank of the Danube. The
most dramatic approach to the abbey is by boat from Kelheim, 10 km
(6 mi) downstream (☞ Guided Tours *in* Franconia A to Z, *below*). On
the stunning ride the boat winds between towering limestone cliffs that
rise straight up from the tree-lined riverbanks. The abbey, constructed between 1716 and 1718, is commonly regarded as the masterpiece of the
brothers Cosmas Damian and Egid Quirin Asam, two leading baroque
architects and decorators of Bavaria. Their extraordinary composition of
painted figures whirling on the ceiling, lavish and brilliantly polished marble, highly wrought statuary, and stucco dancing in rhythmic arabesques
across the curving walls, is the epitome of Bavarian baroque. Note especially the bronze equestrian statue of St. George above the high altar, reaching down imperiously with his flamelike, twisted gilt sword to dispatch
the winged dragon at his feet. ☉ *Daily 9–dusk.*

Walhalla

★ ㉟   *11 km (7 mi) east of Regensburg.*

Walhalla is an excursion from Regensburg you won't want to miss,
especially if you have an interest in the wilder expressions of 19th-cen-
tury German nationalism. The town has an incongruous Greek-style
Doric temple that may be approached by a Danube riverboat (☞
Guided Tours *in* Franconia A to Z, *below*). To get to the temple from
the river, you'll have to climb 358 marble steps; this is not a tour to
take if you're not in good shape. There is, however, a parking lot near
the top. To drive to it, take the Danube Valley country road (unnumbered) east from Regensburg 8 km (5 mi) to Donaustauf. The Walhalla
temple is 1 km (½ mi) outside the village and well signposted. Walhalla—
a name resonant with Nordic mythology—was where the god Odin
received the souls of dead heroes. This monumental temple, on a commanding site high above the Danube, was erected in 1840 for Ludwig
I to honor German heroes through the ages. In the neoclassic style then
prevailing, it's actually a copy of the Parthenon, in Athens. Even if you
consider the building more a monument to kitsch than a tribute to the
great men of Germany, you will at least be able to muse about its
supremely well-built structure, its great smooth-fitting stones, and its
expanses of costly marble—evidence of both the financial resources and
the craftsmanship at Ludwig's command.

FRANCONIA A TO Z

Arriving and Departing

By Car

Franconia is served by five main autobahns: A–7 from Hamburg, A–3 from Köln and Frankfurt, A–81 from Stuttgart, A–6 from Heilbronn, and A–9 from Munich. Nürnberg is 167 km (104 mi) from Munich and 222 km (138 mi) from Frankfurt. Regensburg is 120 km (74 mi) from Munich and 332 km (206 mi) from Frankfurt.

By Plane

The international airports near Franconia are at Frankfurt and Munich. Nürnberg and Bayreuth have regional airports; there are frequent flights between Frankfurt and Nürnberg. If there's fog in Munich, the Nürnberg airport serves as backup.

By Train

Regular InterCity services connect Nürnberg and Regensburg with Frankfurt and other major German cities. Trains run hourly from Frankfurt to Munich, with a stop at Nürnberg. The trip takes about three hours to Munich, two hours to Nürnberg. Nürnberg is a stop on the high-speed InterCity Express north–south routes, and there are hourly trains from Munich direct to Regensburg and to Nürnberg.

Getting Around

By Bicycle

The scenic wooded terrain of the Altmühltal Valley lies halfway between Munich and Nürnberg, between Weissenburg and Ingolstadt on the Danube. It's particularly suitable for biking and is especially known for its rock formations. Otherwise the area consists of hills and landscapes dotted with pretty and sleepy villages. The **tourist board** for the Altmühltal (the Fremdenverkehrsamt Naturpark Altmühltal; ✉ Notre Dame 1, D–85072 Eichstätt, ☎ 08421/98760) issues leaflets with suggested cycling tours and lists of rental outlets. Bicycles can also be rented from most major train stations (the cost is DM 12 per day, DM 6 if you have a rail ticket).

By Boat

A total of 15 different lines operate cruises on the Altmühl and Main rivers and the Main-Donau Canal from April through October. Contact the **Fremdenverkehrsverband Franken** (✉ Fürtherstr. 21, D–90429 Nürnberg, ☎ 0911/264–202) and ask for details of the Weisse Flotte cruises.

By Bus

Bus service between major centers in Franconia is poor; it's better to drive or ride the train. The only major service is from Rothenburg-ob-der-Tauber to Nürnberg. Local buses run from most train stations to smaller towns and villages, though the service isn't frequent. Buses for the Fichtelgebirge in northern Franconia leave from Bayreuth's post office, near the train station.

By Car

Some nearby scenic driving includes the eastern section of the Burgenstrasse (Castle Road), running from Heidelberg to Nürnberg; the Bocksbeutel Strasse (Franconian Wine Road), which follows the course of the Main River from Zeil am Main along the wine-growing slopes of the valley to Aschaffenburg; and the Strasse der Kaiser und Könige (Emperors' and Kings' Road), leading from Frankfurt to Vienna through Franconia via Aschaffenburg, Würzburg, and Nürnberg.

By Train

Some InterCity trains stop in Bamberg, which is most speedily reached from Munich. Local trains from Nürnberg connect with Bayreuth and areas of southern Franconia.

Contacts and Resources

Car Rentals

The following list is of the main international rental agencies. If you shop around in one of the cities, you may find that small local agencies have specials or extra-low prices.

Avis (⊠ Markgrafenallee 6, Bayreuth, ☎ 0921/789–550; ⊠ Lossaustr. 6 [main railway station bldg.], Coburg, ☎ 09561/73075; ⊠ Allersbergerstr. 139, Nürnberg, ☎ 0911/49696; ⊠ Prüfeningerstr. 98, Regensburg, ☎ 0941/396–090). **Europcar** (⊠ Nürnberg Airport, Nürnberg, ☎ 0911/528–484; ⊠ Straubingerstr. 8, Regensburg, ☎ 0941/793–011). **Hertz** (⊠ Wasserg. 15, Coburg, ☎ 09561/24135; ⊠ Nürnberg Airport, Nürnberg, ☎ 0911/527–719).**Sixt** (⊠ Gleissbühlstr. 12–14, Nürnberg, ☎ 0911/438–710; ⊠ Im Gewerbepark C38, Regensburg, ☎ 0941/401–035).

Emergencies

Police and ambulance (☎ 110). **Fire and emergency medical aid** (☎ 112).

Guided Tours

The most popular excursions are **boat trips** on the Danube from Regensburg to Ludwig I's imposing Greek-style Doric temple of Walhalla or to the monastery at Weltenburg. There are daily sailings to Walhalla from Easter through October. The round-trip costs DM 12 and takes three hours. To reach Weltenburg from Regensburg, change boats at Kelheim—just pick up a shorter cruise beginning from Kelheim. The Regensburg–Kelheim boat ride takes 2½ hours. The journey from Kelheim to Weltenburg takes only 30 minutes (the fare is DM 9). Daylong upstream cruises from Regensburg, which take in Weltenburg via the Altmühltal, are also possible. Regensburg boats depart from the Steinerne Brücke; for information call 0941/55359. For information on **Kelheim departures**, call 09441/3402 or 09441/8290.

There are also regular trips in the summer along scenic routes following the **Main River** from Aschaffenburg to Würzburg and from Würzburg to Bamberg. These are worth considering if you plan to spend a lot of time in the region. For information contact **Fränkische Personen-Schiffahrt** (⊠ Kranenkai 1, Würzburg, ☎ 0931/55356 or 0931/51722) or the **Würzburg tourist office** (⊠ Marktpl., ☎ 0931/37398).

For boat tours around **Bamberg**, contact **Personenschiffahrt Kropf** (⊠ Kapuzinerstr. 5, ☎ 0951/26679). From March through October boats leave daily hourly beginning at 11 AM for short cruises on the Regnitz River and the Main-Danube Canal; the cost is DM 9.

In **Nürnberg** English-language bus tours of the city are conducted May–October and December, daily at 9:30, starting at the Mauthalle, Hallplatz 2. The 2½-hour tour costs DM 20. An English-language tour on foot through the Old Town is conducted daily at 2:30; it departs from the tourist information office. The tour costs DM 8. City tours are also conducted in gaily painted trolley buses April–October, daily at 45-minute intervals beginning at 10; November–March, weekends only, starting at 10 at the *Schöner Brunnen*. Tours are in German unless at least five of the participants request English. The cost is DM 7. In **Bamberg** guided walking tours set out from the tourist information office April–October, Monday–Saturday at 10:30 and 2, and Sunday at 11; November–December, Monday–Saturday at 2, and Sunday at 11; and January–March, Monday–Saturday at 2. The cost is DM 9. Guided walking tours of the historical center of **Coburg** depart at 3 every Saturday from the Albert statue in the market square. The cost is DM 3. English-language guided walking tours of **Regensburg** are conducted May–September, Wednesday and Saturday at 1:30. They cost DM 8 and begin at the tourist office.

Hiking
For maps of hiking trails in Franconia and further information, contact the **Fremdenverkehrsverband Franken** (⊠ Fürtherstr. 21, D–90429 Nürnberg, ☎ 0911/264–202).

Skiing
For information on resorts and snow conditions, call the **Tourist Information Fichtelgebirge** (☎ 09272/6255).

Travel Agencies
American Express (⊠ Adlerstr. 2, Nürnberg, ☎ 0911/232–397) makes travel arrangements.

Visitor Information
The principal regional tourist office for Franconia is **Fremdenverkehrsverband Franken e.V.** (⊠ Fürtherstr. 21, D–90429 Nürnberg, ☎ 0911/264–202). There are local tourist information offices in the following towns:

Ansbach (⊠ Johann-Sebastian-Bach-Pl. 1, D–91522, ☎ 0981/51243). **Bamberg** (⊠ Fremdenverkehrsamt, Geyerswörthstr. 3, D–96047, ☎ 0951/871–161,✎). **Bayreuth** (⊠ Fremdenverkehrsverein, Luitpoldpl. 13, D–95444, ☎ 0921/8850). **Coburg** (⊠ Fremdenverkehrs- und Kongressbetrieb, Herrng. 4, D–96450, ☎ 09561/74180,✎). **Ingolstadt** (⊠ Altes Rathaus, D–85049, ☎ 0841/305–417, FAX 0841/305–1099). **Kronach** (⊠ Marktpl., D–96317, ☎ 09261/97236). **Kulmbach** (⊠ Fremdenverkehrsbüro, Stadthalle, Sutte 2, D–95326, ☎ 09221/95880). **Lichtenfels** (⊠ Am Marktplatz 1, D–96215, ☎ 09571/7950). **Nürnberg** (⊠ Congress- und Tourismus-Zentrale Frauentorgraben 3, D–90443 Nürnberg, ☎ 0911/23360, ✎). **Regensburg** (⊠ Altes Rathaus, D–93047, ☎ 0941/507–3410,✎). **Weissenburg** (⊠ Martin-Luther-Pl. 3, D–91781, ☎ 09141/907–124).

6 THE BODENSEE

Mirrored in the Bodensee's waters is the beauty of medieval villages and towns along its shores. There are also the fertile islands and peninsulas, the vineyards and orchards that the atypically warm climate encourages. Painters, poets, and musicians retreat here to be inspired by both the lake and the landscape.

Updated by Uli
Ehrhardt

GERMANY, Switzerland, and Austria all border the Bodensee (Lake Constance), the largest lake in the German-speaking world. Though called a lake, it's actually a vast swelling of the Rhine, gouged out by a massive glacier in the Ice Age and flooded by the river as the ice receded. The Rhine flows into its southeast corner, where Switzerland and Austria meet, and flows out at its west end. On the German side, the Bodensee is bordered almost entirely by the state of Baden-Württemberg (a small portion of the eastern tip, from Lindau to Nonnenhorn, belongs to Bavaria).

The Bodensee is a natural summer playground, ringed with little towns and busy resorts. Gentle, vineyard-clad hills slope down to its shores. To the south, the Alps are a jagged and dramatic backdrop. It's one of the warmest areas of the country, too,—and not just because it's in the south, but also because of the warming influence of the water, which gathers heat in the summer and releases it in the winter like a massive radiator. The lake itself practically never freezes over—it has done so only once during the last century.

The lake's natural attractions, not least of which are its abundance of fresh fish and its fertile soil, were as compelling several thousand years ago as they are today, making this one of the oldest continually inhabited areas of Germany. Highlights include the medieval island town of Lindau; Friedrichshafen, birthplace of the zeppelin; the rococo abbey church of Birnau; and the town of Konstanz, on the Swiss-German border. A day trip to Austria and Switzerland (and to little Liechtenstein) is easy to make, and border formalities are few.

Pleasures and Pastimes

Biking
Germans pack their bikes and head for the Bodensee spring through autumn. You can rent a bike as a guest at many hotels, at some tourist offices, and from sports shops. A cycle path runs all around the lake, and bikes are allowed on the ferries.

Boating and Windsurfing
There are more than 10 boatyards and sailing schools where you can rent small sailing boats. Some also charter yachts. Motorboats and rowboats are rented without formalities in most resorts. Windsurfers can rent boards from some of the 10 windsurfing schools around the lake. For more information on boating, check with local tourist offices.

Dining
Fish specialties predominate around the Bodensee. There are 35 types of fish in the lake, with *Felchen* (a meaty white fish) the most highly prized. Felchen belongs to the salmon family and is best eaten *blau* (poached in a mixture of water and vinegar with spices called *Essigsud*) or *Müllerin* (baked in almonds). Wash it down with a top-quality Meersburg white wine. If you venture north to Upper Swabia, *Pfannkuchen* and *Spätzle,* both flour-and-egg dishes, are the most common specialties. Pfannkuchen (pancakes) are generally filled with meat, cheese, jam, or sultanas, or chopped into fine strips and scattered in a clear consommé known as *Flädlesuppe.* Spätzle are roughly chopped, golden-colored fried egg noodles that are the usual accompaniment to the Swabian Sunday roast-beef lunch of *Rinderbraten.* One of the best-known Swabian dishes is *Maultaschen,* a kind of ravioli, usually served floating in a broth strewn with chives.

Seeweine (lake wines) from area vineyards include Müller-Thurgau, Spät-burgunder, Ruländer, and Kerner.

CATEGORY	COST*
$$$$	over DM 90
$$$	DM 55–DM 90
$$	DM 35–DM 55
$	under DM 35

per person for a three-course meal, including tax and tip and excluding drinks

Lodging

The towns and resorts around the lake have a wide range of hotels, from venerable wedding-cake-style, fin-de-siècle palaces to more modest *Gasthöfe*. If you're visiting in July and August, make reservations in advance. For lower rates and a more rural atmosphere, consider staying a few miles away from the lake.

CATEGORY	COST*
$$$$	over DM 230
$$$	DM 170–DM 230
$$	DM 120–DM 170
$	under DM 120

All prices are for a standard double room for two, including tax and service charge.

Shopping

The Bodensee is artists' territory, and shopping means combing the many small galleries and artists' shops for watercolors, engravings, and prints. Local potters practice their craft and sell their pottery in many places around the lake.

Exploring the Bodensee

You can travel the entire length of the German shore of the Bodensee easily in a day—by car, train, and even by boat—but the temptation to linger in one of the enchanting towns along the way will be strong. Lindau is a pretty and unusual resort, and it's close to Austria, Liechtenstein, and the mountains of the German Allgäu. Friedrichshafen is busier and sits at the head of a road inland to Ravensburg, Weingarten, and the extraordinary churches of the baroque Road. Meersburg, built on a slope that slides down to the lakeside, is arguably the loveliest Bodensee town and is just a short ferry ride from the area's largest city, Konstanz, the local gateway to Switzerland. The small town of Bodman, on the Bodanrück Peninsula north of Konstanz, gave the lake its name. The peninsula, 20 km (12 mi) long and 3 km (2 mi) wide, is good for cycling and hiking because of its meadows, forests, and gorges.

Great Itineraries

Numbers in the text correspond to numbers in the margin and on the Bodensee (Lake Constance) map.

IF YOU HAVE 3 DAYS

Prowl around **Lindau** ①, and then make for the next "town in the lake," **Wasserburg** ②. Reserve a couple of hours for the Zeppelin Museum in **Friedrichshafen** ④, which celebrates the airships once built there. Overnight in lovely 🖬 **Meersburg** ⑤, rising early to catch the sunrise over the lake and the ferry to 🖬 **Konstanz** ⑪, on the opposite shore. From here there's a difficult choice—a day trip either to the Swiss Alps or to two Bodensee islands, **Mainau** ⑫ and **Reichenau** ⑬. After an overnight stay in Konstanz, go west to **Radolfzell** ⑭, rent a bike, and explore the **Höri** Peninsula ⑮.

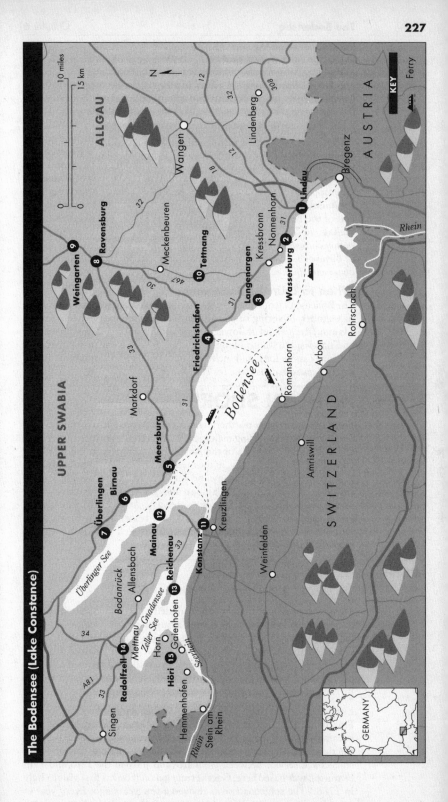

Start your itinerary at **Lindau** ①, continuing to **Wasserburg** ②, **Langenargen** ③ (for a panoramic view of the lake from Montfort Castle), and **Friedrichshafen** ④; then head inland via the B–30 to medieval ⊞ **Ravensburg** ⑧, where you can find a number of historic hostelries. Although the great baroque pilgrimage church of **Weingarten** ⑨ is only 5 km (3 mi) north of Ravensburg, allow a morning or an afternoon to do the magnificent structure justice. Return south to the lake and an overnight stay in ⊞ **Meersburg** ⑤. Catch the ferry to ⊞ **Konstanz** ⑪, on the opposite shore, and allow a full day and night to get to know this fascinating city. Devote the next day to the islands of **Mainau** ⑫ and supper in one of the ancient taverns of **Reichenau** ⑬, and then head for **Radolfzell** ⑭, at the end of the peninsula that juts into the western end of the Bodensee. From there it's a short drive around the head of the lake to ⊞ **Überlingen** ⑦, where one or two days' relaxation in its balmy clime isn't really enough. A visit to the nearby pilgrimage church of **Birnau** ⑥—a rococo masterpiece—is a marvelous finale to any Bodensee tour.

When to Tour the Bodensee

The Bodensee's temperate climate makes for pleasant weather from April to October. In spring orchard blossoms explode everywhere, and on Mainau, the "island of flowers," more than a million tulips, hyacinths, and narcissi burst into bloom. Holiday crowds come in summer, and autumn can be long and mellow. Some hotels and restaurants in the smaller resort towns close for the winter.

THE NORTHERN SHORE

From the Bodensee's northern shore you can see snowcapped mountains in Switzerland rising majestically above the opposite bank. A clear day will bring the peaks of the Austrian Vorarlberg, to the east, into view. There's a feeling here, in the midst of a peaceful Alpine landscape, that you're a part of Germany and yet separated from it—which is literally the case in towns like Lindau and Wasserburg, which sit in the lake tethered to land by narrow causeways. At the northwestern finger of the lake, Überlingen, a beauty of a resort beached on a small finger of water, attracts many vacationers as well as those seeking to restore their health.

Lindau

❶ *180 km (112 mi) southwest of Munich.*

The ancient town of Lindau is surrounded by the lake. The nicest way to arrive here is by train, as it runs along the narrow causeway linking Lindau with the mainland. Lindau's newer mainland section, the Gartenstadt (Garden Town), faces the island, and if you look from the water's edge on a hazy summer's day, the walls and roofs of Old Lindau seem to float on the shimmering water. This illusion is intensified by the miragelike backdrop of the Swiss and Austrian Alps.

Little Lindau was made a Free Imperial City within the Holy Roman Empire in 1275. Lindau had developed as a fishing settlement and then became a trading center for hundreds of years along the route between the rich lands of Swabia and Italy. (The *Lindauer Bote*, an important stagecoach service between Germany and Italy in the 18th and 19th centuries, was based here; Goethe traveled on it on his first visit to Italy in 1786.) The stagecoach was revived a few years ago: Every year in June it starts on its 10-day journey from Lindau to Italy. You can book a seat through the Lindau tourist office.

As the empire crumbled toward the end of the 18th century, battered by Napoléon's revolutionary armies, Lindau fell victim to competing political groups. It was ruled by the Austrian Empire before passing into Bavarian control in 1805.

The proud symbol of Bavaria, a **seated lion,** is one of Lindau's striking landmarks. The lion in question, 20 ft high and carved from Bavarian marble, stares out across the lake from a massive plinth at the end of one of the harbor walls.

At the edge of the inner harbor, the **Alter Leuchtturm** (Old Lighthouse) stands on the weathered remains of the original 13th-century city walls. A maze of ancient streets leading from the harbor makes up the **Altstadt** (Old Town). The main street, pedestrians-only **Maximilianstrasse**, is lined by old half-timber and gabled houses.

The **Altes Rathaus** (Old Town Hall) is the finest of Lindau's handsome historical buildings. It was constructed between 1422 and 1436 in the midst of a vineyard and given a Renaissance face-lift 150 years later, though the original stepped gables remain. Emperor Maximilian I held an imperial diet here in 1496; a fresco on the south facade depicts a scene from this high point of local history. A part of the building that served as the town prison is identified by an ancient inscription enjoining the towns folk "to turn aside from evil and learn to do good."

The **Barfüsserkirche** (Church of the Barefoot Pilgrims), built from 1241 to 1270, is now Lindau's principal theater. The Gothic choir is a memorable setting for concerts. The tourist office on Bahnhofplatz can provide details of performances.

Ludwigstrasse and Fischergasse lead to a watchtower, once part of the original city walls. Pause in the little park behind it, the **Stadtgarten** (City Park). If it's early evening, you'll see the first gamblers of the night making for the neighboring casino.

The **Peterskirche** (St. Peter's Church), on Schrannenplatz, is a solid Romanesque building, constructed in the 10th century and reputedly the oldest church in the Bodensee region. Step inside to see the frescoes by Hans Holbein the Elder (1465–1524), some of which depict scenes from the life of St. Peter, the patron saint of fishermen.

Lindau's **Marktplatz** (Market Square) is lined by a series of sturdily attractive old buildings. The Gothic **Stephanskirche** (St. Stephen's Church) is simple and sparely decorated; the **Marienkirche** (St. Mary's Church) is exuberantly baroque.

The **Haus zum Cavazzen** home dates from the 18th century and is richly decorated with stucco and frescoes. Today it's the municipal art gallery and local history museum. ⊠ *Am Marktpl.* ▣ *DM 4.* ☉ *Apr.–Oct., Tues.–Sun. 9–noon and 2–5.*

In the Gartenstadt district on the mainland, near Hotel Bad Schachen, is a wonderful English garden, **Lindenhofpark.** Its exotic old trees include gingkos and giant redwoods; an alley with tall lime trees borders the lake.

Dining and Lodging

$$$$ ✕ **Restaurant Hoyerberg Schlössle.** A commanding view across the lake
★ to Bregenz and the Alps combined with elegant nouvelle cuisine make this just about the best dining experience in Lindau. The specialties are fish and game, which change seasonally, and there are prix-fixe menus of six and eight courses; one offers lobster, noodles with white truffles and goose liver, and roast breast of squab. The decor features brick-trimmed arched windows, fresh flowers, and elegant high-back chairs.

Dine on the terrace for the terrific view. ✉ *Hoyerbergstr. 64, ☎ 08382/ 25295. Reservations essential. Jacket and tie. AE, DC, MC, V. Closed Mon. and mid-Jan.–Feb.*

$$$ ✕ **Restaurant Lanz.** Locals know the meals served in Anton Lanz's un-pretentious house are top quality. Chef Lanz has received many awards for his regional and French recipes—one of his specialties is a four-course meal with self-raised crabs from his own stream. The rooms of the restaurant are spacious and elegant. Restaurant Lanz is in the little Allgäu village of Stockenweiler, 10 km (6 mi) from Lindau on B–12. ✉ *Hergensweiler-Stockenweiler 32, ☎ 08388/99035. AE, DC, MC, V. Closed Wed. and Thurs.; 2 wks after Pentecost.*

$ ✕ **Gasthaus zum Sünfzen.** In the heart of the Old Town, the Gasthaus is an appealing old inn with small lead-glass windows and a simple wood-paneled interior. Entrées include venison from deer shot on forest hunts led by landlord Hans Grättinger, as well as fish caught locally and sausage from the restaurant's own butcher shop. Try either the spinach Spätzle or the Felchen fillet. The menu changes daily and seasonally. ✉ *Maximilianstr. 1, ☎ 08382/5865. AE, DC, MC, V. Closed Feb.*

$ ✕ **Weinstube und Galerie Zur Fischerin.** Follow the fish-shape sign to the small, pink, stepped gable house near the train station. The intimate rooms have simple wooden benches and upholstered armchairs, and art exhibits decorate the walls. Owner Fritz Scheiner not only serves wines from the Bodensee but also those from France, Italy, and Spain. The snacks include *Schmalzbrot* (a bread spread made out of pork fat), *Gulaschsuppe* (goulash), and Scheiner's special creation, the delicious *Käsesalat,* made with cheese, onions, apples, raisins, and paprika. ✉ *Ludwigstr. 50, ☎ no phone. No credit cards. Closed Tues. and Feb.*

$$$$ ✕▦ **Hotel Bayerischer Hof/Hotel Reutemann.** This is *the* address in town, a stately hotel directly on the edge of the lake, with a terrace lush with semitropical, long-flowering plants, trees, and shrubs. Most of the luxuriously appointed rooms have views of the lake and the Austrian and Swiss mountains beyond. Freshly caught pike perch is a highlight of the extensive menus in the stylish restaurants. If the hotel is full or can't provide the room you want, you will be directed to the adjacent, slightly less expensive Hotel Reutemann, which has been under the same management and ownership for three generations. ✉ *Seepromenade, D–88131, ☎ 08382/9150, FAX 08382/915–591. 98 rooms, 2 suites. Restaurant, bar, café, pool, massage, boating, bicycles, recreation room. DC, MC, V.* ✇

$$ ▦ **Gasthof Engel.** Claiming to be the oldest inn in Lindau, the Engel traces its pedigree back to 1390. Tucked into one of the Old Town's ancient, narrow streets, the family-run property creaks with history. Twisted oak beams are exposed inside and outside the terraced house. The bedrooms are simply furnished but comfortable. ✉ *Schafg. 4, D–88131, ☎ 08382/5240, FAX 08382/5644. 9 rooms, 7 with bath. Restaurant. No credit cards. Closed Nov.*

$ ▦ **Jugendherberge.** This youth hostel is open to travelers up to 26 years old and families with at least one child under 18. Rooms have anywhere from one to six beds and a shower and toilet. There are also special family rooms. ✉ *Herbergsweg 11, D–88131, ☎ 08382/96710, FAX 08382/967–150. 65 rooms. Café, cafeteria, recreation room, coin laundry. No credit cards.* ✇

Nightlife and the Arts

Lindau has a new **casino** (☎ 08382/5051) to replace its old one. It's open 3 PM–3 AM daily. The **Bregenz Casino,** in neighboring Austria, is only 8 km (5 mi) away and is more glamorous than Lindau's. The orchestral concerts and operas of the famous **Bregenzer Festspiele** (☎

0043/5574–4076, 🐝) are held from mid-July to the end of August. Great operas are performed on a stage extending into the lake. In the nearby Festspielhaus there are concert, theater, and opera performances.

Outdoor Activities and Sports

BOATING AND WINDSURFING

The best way to see Lindau is from the lake. Therefore take one of the big pleasure boats of the **Weisse Flotte** (White Fleet) that leave Lindau harbor five or six times a day for the 20-minute ride to Bregenz in Austria. Booking in advance is not needed, as these boats carry up to 800 people on three decks. Round-trip costs DM 12.

The **Bodensee Yachtschule** (✉ Christoph Eychmüller Schiffswerfte 3, ☎ 08382/944–588), in Lindau, charters yachts and has one-week camp sessions for children. You can rent windsurfing boards at **Windsurfschule Kreitmeir** (✉ Strandbad Eichwald, ☎ 08382/23346).

Shopping

Biedermann (✉ Maximilianstr. 2, ☎ 08382/944–913) carries the expensive menswear and women's wear Collections Femmes et Hommes from Italy (and accepts all credit cards). You'll also find custom-made clothing, cashmere sweaters, and Italian shoes. A find for interior decorators, **Böhm** (✉ Maximilianstr. 21 and Krummg. 6, ☎ 08382/94880) consists of three old houses holding lamps, mirrors, precious porcelain, and elegant furniture. Böhm will deliver worldwide. Michael Zeller's reputable shop, **The Colony** (✉ Binderg. 7, ☎ 08382/93020, 🐝), sells watercolors, engravings, prints, silver, and furniture. Michael Zeller also organizes the celebrated, twice-yearly Internationale Bodensee-Kunstauktion (art auction) in May and October. Smaller auctions are held during the Christmas season and in February and June.

Wasserburg

❷ *6 km (4 mi) west of Lindau.*

Wasserburg means "water castle," which describes exactly what this enchanting island town once was—a fortress, built by the St. Gallen Monastery in 924. The later owners, the counts of Montfort zu Tettnang, sold the fortress to the Fugger family of Augsburg to pay off mounting debts. They in turn became so impoverished they couldn't even afford to maintain the drawbridge that connected the castle with the shore. Instead they built a causeway. In the 18th century the castle passed into the hands of the Habsburgs, and in 1805 the Bavarian government took it over.

Wasserburg has some of the most photographed sights of the Bodensee: the yellow, stair-gabled presbytery; the fishermen's St. Georg Kirche, with its onion dome; and the little Malhaus museum, with the castle, Schloss Wasserburg, in the background.

Dining and Lodging

$$$ ✗☲ **Hotel zum Lieben Augustin am See.** On the edge of the lake and just before the peninsula is this traditional family-run hotel made up of five buildings. You can choose not only between lake or garden views, but also between rooms, suites, or apartments. There's a private beach, and you can also rent bicycles from the hotel and ride along the shore paths. ✉ *Halbinselstr. 70, D–88142,* ☎ *08382/9800,* 🆋 *08382/887–082. 40 rooms, 4 apartments, 4 suites. Restaurant, indoor pool, hot tub, beach. DC, MC, V.*

$$–$$$ ✗☲ **Hotel Lipprandt.** Most of the modern rooms in this hotel on the peninsula's edge have a lake view; those with balconies are significantly more expensive. Meals can be taken either in the restaurant or on the

terrace. ⊠ *Halbinselstr. 63–67, D–88142,* ☎ *08382/98760,* FAX *08382/ 887–245. 36 rooms. Restaurant, indoor pool, hot tub, beach. V.* 🍽

Langenargen

❸ *8 km (5 mi) west of Wasserburg.*

The small, pretty town of Langenargen is a typical Lake Constance summer resort, but as it is not as spectacular as nearby Wasserburg, there are practically no day tourists. If you walk along the shore, you'll come across the region's most unusual castle, Schloss Montfort.

Schloss Montfort (Montfort Castle)—named for the original owners, the counts of Montfort-Werdenberg—was a conventional enough medieval fortification until the 19th century, when it was rebuilt in pseudo-Moorish style by its new owner, King Wilhelm I of Württemberg. If you can, see it from a steamer on the lake; the castle is especially memorable in the early morning or late afternoon, when the softened, watery light gives additional mystery to its outline. These days the castle houses a café, restaurant, and disco. Its tower can be climbed. ⊠ *Untere Seestr. 5.* ⛫ *Tower DM 2.* ☻ *Easter–Oct., daily 9–5.*

The parish church of **St. Martin** (⊠ Marktpl. 1) was built in 1718 by Anton III of Montfort and belongs to the great churches of the Barockstrasse. The painting over the organ is presumed to be the work of the baroque painter Franz Anton Maulbertsch, born in Langenargen, who had his great successes in Vienna.

Friedrichshafen

❹ *10 km (6 mi) west of Langenargen.*

Named for its founder, King Friedrich I of Württemberg, Friedrichshafen is a young town (dating to 1811). In an area otherwise given over to resort towns and agriculture, Friedrichshafen played a central role in Germany's aeronautic tradition, which saw the development of the zeppelin airship before World War I and the Dornier seaplanes in the 1920s and '30s. The zeppelins were once launched from a floating hangar on the lake and the Dornier water planes were tested here (☞ Dornier Museum *in* Meersburg, *below*). The city was almost wiped off the map by wartime air raids on its factories. It was rebuilt after the Second World War and today is home to international firms like DASA (airplanes, rockets) and ZF (gearshifts).

Graf Zeppelin (full name, Ferdinand Graf von Zeppelin) was born across the lake in Konstanz, but Friedrichshafen was where on July 2, 1900, his first "airship"—the LZ 1—was launched. The fascinating story of

★ the Zeppelin airships is told in the **Zeppelin Museum,** which holds the world's most significant collection of things pertaining to airship history in its 43,000 square ft of exhibition space. Housed in a wing of the restored Bauhaus **Friedrichshafen Hafenbahnhof** (Harbor railway station), the main attraction is the reconstruction of an 108-ft-long section of the legendary *Hindenburg,* the LZ 129. Here you can relive how the passengers of the great Zeppelins were silently floating through air in style and luxury. Climb aboard the airship via a retractable stairway and stroll past the authentically furnished passenger rooms, the lounges, and the dining room. The illusion of traveling in a Zeppelin is followed by exhibits allowing insights into the history and technology of airship aviation. ⊠ *Seestr. 22,* ☎ *07541/38010.* ⛫ *DM 12.* ☻ *May–Oct., Tues.–Sun. 10–6; Nov.–Apr., Tues.–Sun. 10–5.* 🍽

Schloss Hofen (Hofen Castle), a short walk from town along the lakeside promenade, is a small palace that served as the summer residence of Württemberg kings until 1918. Today Duke Friedrich von Württemberg lives here with his family. The palace was formerly a priory—its foundations date from the 11th century. You can visit the adjoining priory church, a splendid example of local baroque architecture. The swirling white stucco of the interior was executed by the Schmuzer family from Wessobrunn whose master craftsman, Franz, was responsible for much of the finest work in the basilica of Weingarten. Franz Schmuzer also created the priory church's magnificent marble altar.

From Friedrichshafen you can go directly to Romanshorn in Switzerland on a car ferry that leaves every hour from the harbor. The 40-minute trip offers an impressive view from the upper passenger deck: Switzerland and its mountains ahead; Austria, also with mountains, on your left; and Germany, with rolling green hills, behind you. If you take your car, go one way by boat, and then return by driving from Romanshorn to Bregenz in Austria, then past Lindau *(☞ above)*, and back to Friedrichhafen. Round-trip per person costs DM 19.20. Car and driver one-way costs DM 32; an extra person costs DM 9.60.

Dining and Lodging

$$$–$$$$ ✕🏠 **Ringhotel Krone.** Not to be confused with the City-Krone hotel, this Bavarian-theme hotel is in the Schnetzenhausen district's semirural surroundings, ideal for an outdoor holiday. The hotel rents bikes to its guests, and the area is ideal to roam around on bicycles. All rooms have balconies. The restaurant specializes in game dishes and fish from the Bodensee. ✉ *Untere Mühlbachstr. 1, D–88045,* ☎ *07541/4080,* FAX *07541/43601. 115 rooms. Restaurant, bar, 1 indoor and 1 outdoor pool, hot tub, sauna, 4 tennis courts, bowling, exercise room, bicycles. AE, DC, MC, V.* 🐾

$$–$$$$ ✕🏠 **Ringhotel Buchhorner Hof.** This traditional hotel near the train sta-
★ tion, now part of the Ring group, has been run by the same family since it opened in 1870. Hunting trophies on the walls, leather armchairs, and Turkish rugs decorate the public areas; bedrooms are large and comfortable. The restaurant is plush and subdued, with delicately carved chairs and mahogany-paneled walls. It offers a choice of menus with dishes such as pork medallions, perch fillet, and lamb chops. ✉ *Friedrichstr. 33, D–88045,* ☎ *07541/2050,* FAX *07541/32663. 87 rooms, 4 suites, 2 apartments. Restaurant, bar, massage, sauna, miniature golf, exercise room, bicycles. AE, DC, MC, V.*

$ 🏠 **Hotel Schöllhorn.** Near the train station and Friedrichhafen's shopping mile, this simple hotel has rustic furnishings and a playroom for children. ✉ *Friedrichstr. 65, D–88045,* ☎ *07541/21816,* FAX *07541/ 33060. 46 rooms. Restaurant, bar. AE, MC, V.*

Nightlife and the Arts

Friedrichhafen's **Graf-Zeppelin-Haus** (☎ 07541/72071) is a modern convention center on the lakeside promenade, a seven-minute walk from the train station. It is also a cultural center, where musicals, light opera, and classical as well as pop-rock concerts take place several times a week. The annual **Kultur-Ufer,** an open-air festival of theater and music, is held the first week of August.

Shopping

Most of the town's shops line the pedestrian zone near the harbor. **Christina Teske** carries women's and men's clothing (✉ Seestr. 1, ☎ 07541/75356). The gift shop **Ebe** (✉ Buchhornpl., ☎ 07541/26036) sells handmade candles, dolls, and postcards.

Meersburg

⑤ *18 km (11 mi) west of Friedrichshafen.*

The most romantic way to approach Meersburg is from the lake. Seen from the water on a summer afternoon with the sun slanting low, the steeply terraced town can seem floodlighted, like an elaborate stage setting. (Meersburg is well aware of its too-good-to-be-true charm—some may find the gusto with which it has embraced tourism crass, and the town can get crowded on weekends.) If you arrive by ferry from Lindau, Konstanz, Uberlinglen, or Mainau, you'll step ashore in the Unterstadt (Lower Town). It's about a 150-ft climb to the Oberstadt (Upper Town), but the walk between the two halves is not arduous as you head up Steigstrasse, a street lined with shops and restaurants. The pretty market square is ringed by historic half-timber structures like the medieval Rathaus, and with no cars allowed, a sense of timelessness is preserved. In 1995 a hot spring was discovered on the outskirts of Meersburg, and the water now heats the municipal swimming pool.

★ Watching majestically over the town and the lake far below is the **Altes Schloss** (Old Castle), Germany's oldest inhabited castle and one of the most impressive. Meersburg is said to have been founded in 628 by Dagobert, king of the Franks, who supposedly laid the castle's first stone. The massive central tower has walls 10-ft thick and is named for King Dagobert. In 1526 the Catholic bishop of Konstanz set himself up in the castle after he was thrown out by newly converted Protestant Konstanz. Bishops remained here until the middle of the 18th century, when they built themselves what they felt to be a more suitable residence— the baroque Neues Schloss. Plans to tear down the Altes Schloss in the early 19th century were shelved when it was taken over by Baron Joseph von Lassberg, a man much intrigued by the castle's medieval romance. He turned it into a home for like-minded poets and artists, among them his sister-in-law, Annette von Droste-Hülshoff (1797–1848), one of Germany's finest poets. The Altes Schloss is still private property, but much of it can be visited, including the richly furnished rooms where Droste-Hülshoff lived and the chamber where she died, as well as the imposing knights' hall, the minstrels' gallery, and the sinister dungeons. The **Altes Schloss Museum** (Old Castle Museum) contains a fascinating collection of weapons and armor, including a rare set of medieval jousting equipment. ☎ *07532/80000.* 🎫 *DM 9.* ☉ *Mar.–Oct., daily 9–6:30; Nov.–Feb., daily 10–6.*

The spacious and elegant **Neues Schloss** (New Castle) is directly across from the older one. It was built partly by Balthasar Neumann, the leading German architect of the 18th century, and partly by an Italian, Franz Anton Bagnato. Neumann's work is most obvious in the stately sweep of the grand double staircase, with its intricate grillwork and heroic statues. The interior's other stand out is the glittering Spiegelsaal (Hall of Mirrors). In an unlikely combination of 18th-century grace and 20th-century technology, the top floor of the palace houses the **Dornier Museum,** which traces the history of the German aircraft and aerospace industries. ☎ *07532/414–071; 07532/431–110 for English tours.* 🎫 *DM 5.* ☉ *Apr.–Oct., daily 10–1 and 2–6.*

Sunbathed, south-facing Meersburg has been a center of the Bodensee wine trade for centuries. You can pay your respects to the noble profession in the **Weinbau Museum** (Vineyard Museum), one of the most comprehensive wine museums in Germany. A barrel capable of holding 50,000 liters (about the same number of quarts) and an immense wine press dating from 1607 are highlights of the collection. The museum has another claim to fame: it's in the house where the hypnotism pioneer Dr. Frank Anton Mesmer (1734–1815) lived in the early 19th century. ⊠ *Vorburg. 11,* ☎ *07532/431–110.* ⊟ *DM 3.* ☉ *Apr.–Oct., Tues., Fri., and Sun. 2–5.*

An idyllic retreat almost hidden among the vineyards, the Fürstenhäusle was built in 1640 by a local vintner and later used as a holiday home by poet Annette von Droste-Hülshoff. It's now the **Droste Museum,** containing many of her personal possessions and giving a vivid sense of Meersburg in her time. ⊠ *Stettenerstr. 9 (east of Obertor, the town's north gate),* ☎ *07532/6088.* ⊟ *DM 5.* ☉ *Easter–mid-Oct., Mon.–Sat. 10–12:30 and 2–5, Sun. 2–5.*

Dining and Lodging

$$$ ✕ **Winzerstube zum Becher.** This traditional restaurant near the new castle has been in the Benz family for three generations. If you want to try regional dishes and especially fresh fish from the lake, this is the place. Or if you like meat better, order the *canard a l'orange.* Do try the white wine from the restaurant's own vineyard. Booking ahead is advisable, as the three wood-paneled rooms have only a few tables each. ⊠ *Höllg. 4.,* ☎ *07532/9009. AE, DC, V. Closed Jan. and Mon.*

$$$ ✕▥ **Drei Stuben.** Proprietor Brigitte Drewing has seen to every imagin-
★ able detail in this restored 17th-century town house. If you have a choice, take a look at the rooms before booking as they are all decorated in different styles with great attention to details. Some have antique furniture; others are in a modern setting with paintings to match. The chef in charge of the restaurant, Stefan Marquard, is regarded as one of Germany's best. Although his avant-garde style of cooking defies categorization, Italian influences are evident in some dishes, like lamb with thyme risotto. ⊠ *Kirchstr. 7/Winzerg. 1–3, D–88709,* ☎ *07532/80020,* ℻ *07532/1367. 25 rooms. Restaurant. AE, DC, MC, V. Closed Jan.*

$$–$$$ ✕▥ **Löwen.** This centuries-old, ivy-clad tavern on Meersburg's market square is a local landmark. Its welcoming restaurant serves such regional specialties as Spätzle and Maultaschen, and, in season, venison and *Spargel* (asparagus) find their way onto the menu. Guest rooms are cozily furnished and have their own sitting corners, and some have genuine Biedermeier furniture. ⊠ *Marktpl. 2, D–88709,* ☎ *07532/43040,* ℻ *07532/430–410. 21 rooms. Restaurant, Weinstube, no-smoking rooms, bicycles. AE, DC, MC, V.* ✎

$$–$$$ ▥ **Hotel-Cafe Off.** This small and friendly hotel fronts the lake, and if your room doesn't overlook the water, it will look out over the vineyards. There's a bright, cheerful feel to the hotel, accentuated by the light woods and matching pastel tones of the furnishings. Rooms have broad beds and many homey touches. There are a playroom and sandpit for youngsters. ⊠ *Uferpromenade 51, D–88709,* ☎ *07532/44740,* ℻ *07532/447–444. 21 rooms, 2 suites. Restaurant, café, bicycles. DC, MC, V.*

$$ ▥ **Zum Bären.** Built in 1605 and incorporating 13th-century Gothic foundations, the Bären was an important staging point for Germany's first postal service. The ivy-smothered facade, with its characteristic steeple, hasn't changed much over the centuries, but interior comforts certainly have. Some rooms are furnished with Bodensee antiques and brightly painted rustic wardrobes. ⊠ *Marktpl. 11, D–88709,* ☎ *07532/ 43220,* ℻ *07532/432–244. 17 rooms. Restaurant. No credit cards. Closed Dec.–Feb.*

Nightlife and the Arts

The Spiegelsaal (Hall of Mirrors) of the Neues Schloss is the magnificent setting for an annual **international chamber music festival,** with concerts from June through September. Call 07532/431–112 for schedule information.

Birnau

❻ *10 km (6 mi) west of Meersburg.*

On a small hill overlooking the lake, the **Wallfahrtskirche** (Pilgrimage Church) of Birnau stands all by itself. If you look out from the terrace in front of the church, you will see the vineyard sloping down toward the water. The church was built by the masterful architect Peter Thumb between 1746 and 1750. Its simple exterior consists of plain gray-and-white plaster and a tapering clock-tower spire above the main entrance; the interior, by contrast, is overwhelmingly rich, full of movement, light, and color. It's hard to single out highlights from such a profusion of ornament, but seek out the *Honigschlecker* (Honey Sucker), a gold-and-white cherub beside the altar, dedicated to St. Bernard of Clairvaux, "whose words are sweet as honey" (it's the last altar on the right as you face the high altar). The cherub is sucking honey from his finger, which he's just pulled out of a beehive. The fanciful spirit of this dainty punning is continued in the small squares of glass set into the pink screen that rises high above the main altar; the gilt dripping from the walls; the swaying, swooning statues; and the swooping figures on the ceiling. ⊙ *Daily 7–7.*

En Route Just south of Birnau, near the village of Uhldingen, a settlement of **Pfahlbauten** (Pile Dwellings) sticks out of the lake—a reconstructed village of Stone Age and Bronze Age dwellings built on stilts. This is how the original lake dwellers lived, surviving off the fish that swam outside their humble huts. The nearby **Pfahlbauten Freilichtmuseum** (Open-Air Museum of German Prehistory) contains actual finds excavated in the area. ⊠ *Strandpromenade 6, Unteruhldingen,* ☎ *07556/ 8543.* ⊠ *DM 8.* ⊙ *Apr.–Oct., daily 8–7; Nov.–Mar., daily 9–6.*

Überlingen

❼ *3 km (2 mi) west of Birnau, 24 km (15 mi) west of Friedrichshafen.*

This Bodensee resort has an attractive waterfront and an almost Mediterranean flair. It's midway along the north shore of the Überlingersee, a narrow branch of the Bodensee that projects northwest out of the lake's main body. Überlingen is ancient, a Free Imperial City since the 13th century, with no fewer than seven of its original city gates and towers left, as well as substantial portions of the old city walls. What was once the moat is now a grassy place in which to walk, with the walls of the Old Town towering over you on one side and the Stadtpark stretching away on the other. The **Stadtpark** (city park) cultivates rare plants and has a famous collection of cacti. The heart of the city is the Münsterplatz.

★ The **Nikolausmünster** (Church of St. Nicholas) is a huge church for such a small town. It was built between 1512 and 1563 on the site of at least two previous churches. The interior is all Gothic solemnity and massiveness, with a lofty stone-vaulted ceiling and high, pointed arches lining the nave. The single most remarkable feature is not Gothic at all but opulently Renaissance—the massive high altar, carved from lime wood that looks almost like ivory. Statues, curlicues, and columns jostle for space on it. ⊠ *Münsterpl.*

Inside the late-Gothic **Altes Rathaus** (Old Town Hall) is a high point of Gothic decoration, the **Ratsaal**, or council chamber. Its most striking feature amid the riot of carving is the series of figures representing the states of the Holy Roman Empire. There's a naïveté to the figures—their beautifully carved heads are all just a little too large, their legs a little too spindly—that makes them easy to love. ⊠ *Münsterpl.* ⊠ *Free.* ⊙ *Apr.–mid-Oct., weekdays 9–noon and 2:30–5, Sat. 9–noon.*

The **Heimatmuseum** (Local Museum) houses exhibits tracing Bodensee history and a vast collection of dollhouses. ⊠ *Krummebergstr. 30,* ☎ *07531/991–079.* ⊡ *DM 4.* ☉ *Apr.–Oct., Tues.–Sat. 9–12:30 and 2–5, Sun. 10–3; Nov.–Mar., Tues.–Sat. 10:30–noon.*

Dining and Lodging

$$$$ ✕⊡ **Parkhotel St. Leonard.** About 2 km (1 mi) from the lake on a vine-
★ yard-covered hillside, the modern St. Leonard offers elegance and style. All rooms have balconies, but try for one with a view of the lake. Facilities include indoor and outdoor tennis courts as well as a tennis school. There are two restaurants, one sleekly contemporary and the other traditional, both in the hands of a French chef. Lake fish are a specialty, but also check to see if local lamb in spinach or the home-made Maultaschen are on the menu. In summer you'll dine on a canopied terrace. ⊠ *Obere St. Leonardstr. 71, D–88662,* ☎ *07551/ 808–100,* ℻ *07551/808–531. 140 rooms, 3 apartments. 2 restaurants, bar, indoor pool, beauty salon, sauna, 5 tennis courts, exercise room, bicycles, billiards. AE, MC, V.*

$$–$$$ ✕⊡ **Kurhotel Seehof.** This popular family hotel has direct access to a beach and boat pier, and most rooms have balconies looking out over the water. Fitness fanatics can book a cold-water cure within the hotel's health facility. The restaurant regularly serves fish caught in the lake—the pike perch is particularly tasty. ⊠ *Strandweg 6, D–88662,* ☎ *07551/63028,* ℻ *07551/68166. 35 rooms. Restaurant, sauna, beach, boating, bicycles. No credit cards. Closed Nov.–Mar.*

$–$$ ✕⊡ **Landgasthof zum Adler.** You'll appreciate the unpretentiousness of this rustic country inn with a blue-and-white half-timber facade, scrubbed wooden floors, and thick down comforters on the beds. The food is simple and delicious; trout is a specialty. ⊠ *Hauptstr. 44, D–88662 Lippertsreute,* ☎ *07553/82550,* ℻ *07553/825–570. 17 rooms. Restaurant. No credit cards. Closed 2 wks in Nov.*

Nightlife and the Arts

At the end of August organ concerts in the lakeside Kursaal make up the **Überlinger Orgelsommer.** The **Kleinkunstwoche-Kunst im Garten** runs concurrently, presenting music, theater, and pantomime. Call 07551/991–122 for details.

NORTH TO THE UPPER SWABIAN BAROQUE ROAD

From Friedrichshafen Highway B–30 leads north along the valley of the little River Schussen and links up with one of Germany's least-known but most attractive holiday routes. The *Oberschwäbische Barockstrasse* (Upper Swabian Baroque Road) follows a rich series of baroque churches and abbeys, including Germany's largest baroque church, in Weingarten.

Ravensburg

8 *20 km (12 mi) north of Friedrichshafen.*

Ravensburg once competed with Augsburg and Nürnberg for economic supremacy in southern Germany. The Thirty Years' War put an end to the city's hopes by reducing it to little more than a medieval backwater. The city's loss proved fortuitous only in that many of its original features have remained much as they were when built. Fourteen of the town gates and towers survive, for example, and the Altstadt is among the best-preserved in Germany.

That ecclesiastical and commercial life were never entirely separate in medieval towns is evident in the former **Karmeliterklosterkirche** (Carmelite Monastery Church), once part of a 14th-century monastery and now a Protestant church. The stairs on the west side of the church's chancel lead to the meeting room of the Ravensburger Gesellschaft (the Ravensburg Society), an organization of linen merchants established in 1400 to direct trade of the product that was largely responsible for the town's rapid economic growth.

Marienplatz, the central square, has many old buildings that recall Ravensburg's wealthy years: the late-Gothic **Rathaus,** with a picturesque Renaissance bay window; the 14th-century **Kornhaus** (Granary), once the corn exchange for all of Upper Swabia; the 15th-century **Waaghaus** (Weighing House), the town's weighing station and central warehouse, incorporating a tower where the watchman had his lookout; and the colorfully frescoed **Lederhaus,** once the headquarters of the city's leather workers.

One of Ravensburg's **defensive towers** is visible from Marienplatz, the **Grüner Turm** (Green Tower), so called for its green tiles; many are the 14th-century originals. Another stout defense tower is the massive **Obertor** (Upper Tower), the oldest gate in the city walls. From it you can see one of the most curious of the city's towers, the **Mehlsack,** or Flour Sack Tower (because of its bulk and the original whitewash exterior), 170 ft high and standing on the highest point of the city.

Ravensburg's true parish church, the **Liebfrauenkirche** (Church of Our Lady), is a 14th-century structure, elegantly simple on the outside but almost entirely rebuilt inside. Some of the original stained glass remains, however, as does the heavily gilt altar. In a side altar is a copy of a carved Madonna, the *Schutzmantelfrau*; the late 14th-century original is in Berlin's Dahlem Museum. ⊠ *Kirchstr. 18.* ⊙ *Daily 7–7.*

Ⓒ Ravensburg is a familiar name to all jigsaw-puzzle fans, for its eponymous Ravensburg publishing house produces the world's largest selection of puzzles, in addition to many other popular games. The history of the jigsaw puzzle plays a central role in the company's **puzzle museum.** ⊠ *Markstr. 26,* ☎ *0751/860.* ✆ *Free.* ⊙ *Thurs. 2–6.*

Ⓒ **Ravensburger Spieleland** is an amusement park designed for small children located 10 km (6 mi) from Ravensburg, in the direction of Lindau. ⊠ *Liebenau–Am Hangenwald 1, Meckenbeuren,* ☎ *07542/4000 or 07542/400–101.* ✆ *DM 26 adults; free entrance for children on their birthday.* ⊙ *Apr.–Nov. 10–6.*

Dining and Lodging

$$ ✕ **Cafe-Restaurant Central.** On the ground floor you'll find a café with good pastries, where you can also get snacks or a glass of wine. If you want more variety, climb the stairs for Italian cuisine at the restaurant on the second floor. ⊠ *Marienpl. 48,* ☎ *0751/32533. MC, V.*

$$$$ ✕▥ **Romantikhotel Waldhorn.** This historic hostelry on the market
★ square has been in the Dressel/Bouley family for more then 150 years. The menu prepared by Albert Bouley, fourth-generation proprietor and chef, draws diners from afar. Enjoy your aperitif under a big umbrella in front of the hotel before stepping into the dark wood-paneled Biedermeier dining room for the five-course Waldhorn menu. Suites and rooms in the main building overlook the square. Rooms in the annex have views into the very quiet gardens. Albert Bouley also minds the kitchen of Rebleute, the restaurant the family owns just around the corner on Schulgasse 15. The setting, an old guild hall with a beautiful *Tonnendecke* (barrel ceiling), once belonged to

the *Rebleute* (wine growers), and today serves Bouley's more regional (and less expensive) specialties. It's here that you'll meet the locals. ⊠ *Marienpl. 15, D–88212,* ☎ *0751/36120,* ℻ *0751/361–2100. 30 rooms, 3 suites, 7 apartments. Restaurant, bar, meeting rooms. AE, DC, MC, V.* 🍽

Weingarten

❾ *5 km (3 mi) north of Ravensburg.*

Weingarten is famous Germany-wide for its huge and hugely impressive pilgrimage church, which you see up on a hill from miles away, long before you get to the town.

At 220 ft high and more than 300 ft long, **Weingarten Basilica** is the largest baroque church in Germany, the basilica of one of the oldest and most venerable convents in the country, founded in 1056 by the wife of Guelph II. The Guelph dynasty ruled large areas of Upper Swabia, and generations of family members lie buried in the church. The majestic edifice was renowned because of the little vial it possesses, said to contain drops of Christ's blood. First mentioned by Charlemagne, the vial passed to the convent in 1094, entrusted to its safekeeping by the Guelph queen Juditha, sister-in-law of William the Conqueror. At a stroke Weingarten became one of Germany's foremost pilgrimage sites. On the Friday after Ascension, the anniversary of the day the relic was entrusted to the convent, a huge procession of pilgrims headed by 2,000 horsemen (many local farmers breed horses just for this procession) wends its way to the basilica. It was decorated by leading early 18th-century German and Austrian artists: stucco by Franz Schmuzer, ceiling frescoes by Cosmas Damian Asam, and a Donato Frisoni altar—one of the most breathtakingly ornate in Europe, with nearly 80-ft-high towers on either side. The organ, installed by Josef Gabler between 1737 and 1750, is among the largest in the country. ☉ *Daily 8–6.*

If you want to learn about early Germans—residents from the 6th, 7th, and 8th centuries whose graves are just outside town—visit the **Alamannenmuseum** in the Kornhaus, at one time a granary. Archaeologists discovered the hundreds of Alamanni graves in the 1950s. ⊠ *Karlstr. 28.* 🎫 *Free.* ☉ *Wed. and weekends 3–5. Closed Feb. and Nov.*

Steinhausen

33 km (19 mi) north of Weingarten on the B–30.

Follow a visit to the Weingarten pilgrimage basilica with a detour to Steinhausen. As you drive toward Bad Schussenried through forests and fields, you come around a corner to see a white, light baroque-rococo church in the fields a few miles away. Only as you come closer can you see that the church is surrounded by half a dozen houses, mostly farms, all of them less then half the size of the church. Dominikus Zimmermann built the charming late-baroque church in 1728–33. The interior forms an oval, bordered by 10 slender pillars. The walls are simply white, but the vaulted ceilings foam over with color and decoration. The frescoes glorify the life of the Virgin. If you look closely, you can see that the artist included some birds and animals of the area in his sculptures and paintings.

A local brewery in nearby Bad Schussenried runs the **Schussenried Bierkrugmuseum** (Beer-Mug Museum), with more than 1,000 exhibits of mugs spanning five centuries. On the second floor is a very nice souvenir shop with the right gift for the beer drinker back home. ⊠ *Wilhelm-Schussen-Str. 12,* ☎ *07583/40411.* 🎫 *DM 4.50.*

Tettnang

⑩ *13 km (8 mi) south of Ravensburg on the B–467.*

The old houses in the little town of Tettnang are towered over by the yellow remains of the Neues Schloss, former ancestral home of the counts of Montfort zu Tettnang. By 1780 the dynasty had fallen on such hard times that it ceded the town to the Habsburgs for hard cash, and 25 years later it passed to the Bavarian Wittelsbachs.

The **Neues Schloss** (New Castle) is an extravagant baroque palace that was built in the early 18th century, burned down in 1753, and was then partially rebuilt before the Montfort finances ran dry. Enough remains, however, to give some idea of the rulers' former wealth and ostentatious lifestyle. The palace is open only for tours. Call ahead to arrange for an English-speaking guide. ☎ *07542/953–839.* ▧ *DM 4.* ◉ *Tours in German Apr.–Oct., daily 10:30, 2:30, and 4.*

OFF THE
BEATEN PATH

HOPFENMUSEUM TETTNANG (Tettnang Hops Museum) – If you're a beer drinker, you've probably already tasted a product of the Tettnang area, because Tettnang is the second-biggest hops-growing area in Germany and exports most of its hops to the United States. This museum dedicated to brewing is in the tiny village of Siggenweiler. ⊠ *Siggenweiler,* ☎ *07542/952–206.* ◉ *May–Oct., Tues.–Sun. 2–5.*

Dining

$$ ✕ **Gasthof Krone.** This traditional German Gaststube has wood paneling, a *Stammtisch* (where the regulars sit), and good, solid German food. If it is hunting season, try the game. Owned by the Tauchser family, the Gasthof only serves beer from their own brewery, behind the restaurant. To visit the brewery and get explanations in English of how a small German brewery operates, English speakers at the tourist office may be able to oblige you. Call 07542/953–839 in advance. ⊠ *Bärenpl. 7,* ☎ *07542/7452. No credit cards.*

AROUND THE BODANRÜCK PENINSULA

Both Konstanz and Mainau, the "island of flowers," are reachable by ferry from Lindau and Meersburg. That's by far the most romantic way to cross the lake, although a main road (the B–31, then the B–34, and finally the B–33) skirts the eastern side of the Bodensee and ends its German journey at Konstanz.

Konstanz

⑪ *A ½-hr ferry ride from Meersburg.*

The university town of Konstanz is the largest on the Bodensee; it straddles the Rhine as it flows out of the lake, placing itself both on the Bodanrück Peninsula and the Swiss side of the lake. Because of its location, Konstanz suffered no wartime bombing—the Allies were unwilling to risk the inadvertent bombing of neutral Switzerland—and so Konstanz is among the best-preserved major medieval towns in Germany.

It's claimed that Konstanz was founded in the 3rd century by Emperor Constantine Chlorus, father of Constantine the Great. The story is probably untrue, though it's certain there was a Roman garrison here. By the 6th century Konstanz had become a bishopric; in 1192 it became a Free Imperial City. What really put it on the map was the Council of Constance, held between 1414 and 1418 to settle the Great Schism

(1378–1417), the rift in the church caused by two separate lines of popes, one leading from Rome, the other from Avignon. Upwards of 40,000 people are said to have descended on the city during the great assembly. The council resolved the problem in 1417 by electing Martin V as the true, and only, pope. The church had also agreed to restore the the German Holy Roman Emperor's (Sigismund's) role in electing the pope, but only if Sigismund silenced the rebel theologian Jan Hus (1372–1415) of Bohemia. Even though Sigismund had allowed Hus to come to Konstanz for the Council, he acquiesced, Hus was burned at the stake in July 1415. Konstanz became a Protestant city in the Reformation, hence the remembrances of Hus throughout the city.

For all its vivid history, most people enjoy Konstanz for its more worldly pleasures—the elegant Altstadt, trips on the lake, walks along the promenade, the classy shops, the restaurants, the views. The heart of the city is the **Marktstätte** (Market Place), near the harbor, with the simple bulk of the Konzilgebäude looming behind it. Erected in 1388 as a warehouse, the **Konzilgebäude** (Council Hall)—so called because it's claimed the council of cardinals met here to choose the new pope in 1415 (they actually met in the cathedral)—is now a concert hall. Beside the Konzilgebäude are statues of Jan Hus and native son Graf Zeppelin (1838–1917).

Hus remains a key figure in Konstanz: There's a Hussenstrasse (Hus Street); the site of his execution is marked by a stone slab (the Hussenstein) and, appropriately, the square it's in is now the Lutherplatz. The Dominican monastery where Hus was held before his execution is still here, too, doing duty as a luxurious hotel, the Steigenberger Insel-Hotel (☞ Dining and Lodging, *below*).

The **Altes Rathaus** (Old Town Hall) was built during the Renaissance and painted with vivid frescoes—swags of flowers and fruits, shields, architectural details, and sturdy knights wielding immense swords. Walk into the courtyard to admire its Renaissance restraint.

Within the medieval guild house of the city's butchers, the **Rosgartenmuseum** (Rose Garden Museum) has a rich collection of art and artifacts from the Bodensee region. Highlights include exhibits of the pile-dwelling people who inhabited the lake during the Bronze Age and sculpture and altar paintings from the Middle Ages. ⊠ *Rosgartenstr. 3–5,* ☎ *07531/900–246,* ℻ *07531/900–608.* ⊡ *DM 3.* ☉ *Tues.– Thurs. 10–5, Fri.–Sun. 10–4.*

The **St. Stephanskirche** (St. Stephen's Church), an austere, late-Gothic structure with a very un-Gothic rococo chancel, stands in a little square surrounded by fine half-timber houses. Look at the **Haus zur Katz** (House of the Cat) on the right as you walk into the square. It was a guild hall in the Middle Ages, and now it houses the city archives.

Konstanz's cathedral, the **Münster** was built on the site of the original Roman fortress. Construction on the cathedral continued from the 10th through the 19th centuries, resulting in today's odd architectural contrasts. The twin-towered facade is sturdily Romanesque, blunt, and heavy looking. However, the elegant and airy chapels along the aisles are fullblown 15th-century Gothic, the complex nave vaulting is Renaissance, and the choir is severely neoclassic. Make a point of seeing the Holy Sepulchre Tomb, a in the Mauritius Chapel behind the altar. It's a richly worked 13th-century Gothic structure, 12 ft high, with some of its original vivid coloring and gilding, and it's studded with statues of the Apostles and figures from the childhood of Jesus. ⊠ Münsterpl.).

The **Niederburg,** the oldest part of Konstanz, is a tangle of old, twisting streets leading to the Rhine. At the river take a look at the two city towers here: the **Rheintor** (Rhine Tower), the one nearer the lake, and the aptly named **Pulverturm** (Powder Tower), the former city arsenal.

OFF THE
BEATEN PATH

WOLLMATINGER RIED – Just north of Konstanz on the Bodanrück Peninsula is the 1,000-acre Wollmatinger Ried, moorland that's now a bird sanctuary. There are three-hour guided tours of the moor on Wednesday and Saturday, April through mid-October, at 4 PM, and two-hour tours from June through mid-September on Tuesday, Thursday, and Friday at 9 AM. Most of the birds you'll see are waterbirds, naturally; there are also remains of prehistoric pile houses. Bring sturdy, comfortable shoes and mosquito repellent. Binoculars can be rented. Contact DBV Naturschutzzentrum Wollmatinger Ried (✉ Fritz-Arnold-Str. 2e, Konstanz, ☎ 07531/78870).

Dining and Lodging

$$–$$$ ✕ **Barbarossa.** In the center of the Old Town, this is one of the historic buildings of Konstanz. Some of its history is depicted in the murals on the facade, and inside you can see the huge old wooden support beams. The stained-glass windows and dark wood paneling give the restaurant on the first floor a cozy, warm atmosphere. Fish and game in season are the specialties of the kitchen. ✉ *Obermarkt 8,* ☎ *07531/ 22021. AE, D, MC, V.*

$ ✕ **Zum Guten Hirten.** A traditional atmosphere is kept at this late-15th-century wine tavern, whose name means "good shepherd." In the particularly authentic Bauernstube, Swiss specialties like *Rösti*—panfried potatoes and onions mixed with chopped smoked ham—are served. Try the dish accompanied by a crisp white wine from the Bodensee Vineyards. ✉ *Zollernstr. 8,* ☎ *07531/27344. No credit cards.*

$$$$ ✕🖼 **Seehotel Siber.** The major attraction in this small hotel, in a turn-
★ of-the-century villa, is its adjoining restaurant—the most elegant dining in the region (reservations essential; jacket and tie). Prepared by Bertold Siber, one of Germany's leading chefs, the food is classical with regional touches. Try his lobster salad or bouillabaisse with local lake fish, followed by punch sorbet with ginger-flavor doughnuts. The restaurant is divided into three rooms: One resembles a library; the center room is airy and spacious, with bold modern paintings; the third has mint-color walls and a deep green carpet. In summer you can eat on a terrace overlooking the lake. Bedrooms 3 and 7 have balconies affording similar views. ✉ *Seestr. 25, D–78464,* ☎ *07531/63044,* 🖷 *07531/64813. 11 rooms, 1 suite. Restaurant, café, dance club. DC, MC, V. Hotel and restaurant closed 2 wks in Feb.*

$$$$ ✕🖼 **Steigenberger Insel-Hotel.** Equaling the Seehotel Siber (☞ *above*)
★ in reputation, this former 16th-century monastery, with its original cloisters, offers the most luxurious lodging in town. It's linked to famous historic figures as the site where Jan Hus was held before his execution and where, centuries later, Graf Zeppelin was born. Bedrooms are spacious and stylish, more like those of a private home than a hotel, and many have lake views. The Seerestaurant is very imposing, with some fine arches and superb views across the lake. The Dominikanerstube is the more intimate restaurant. Both restaurants feature regional specialties, and there's the clubby, relaxed Zeppelin Bar. Flower gardens surround the hotel, keeping the bustle of Konstanz at bay. ✉ *Auf der Insel 1, D–78462,* ☎ *07531/1250,* 🖷 *07531/26402. 100 rooms, 2 suites. 2 restaurants, bar, beach, recreation room, baby-sitting. AE, DC, MC, V.* ✆

$$–$$$$ ✕🖼 **Stadthotel.** This friendly hotel is a five-minute walk from the lake. Some rooms have a bath, others just a shower, and all have a TV. The Poseidon restaurant, on site, draws locals and guests with its Greek cuisine. ✉ *Bruderturmg. 12, D–78462,* ☎ *07531/90460,* 🖷 *07531/904–646. 24 rooms. Restaurant. AE, DC, MC, V.*

Nightlife and the Arts

The **Bodensee Symphony Orchestra,** founded in 1932, is based in Konstanz, with a season running from October through April. Konstanz's international **summer music festival** runs from mid-June to mid-July, including celebrated organ concerts in the cathedral. Performances are held in the picturesque Renaissancehof (courtyard) of the town hall. For all schedule information and tickets, contact the Konstanz tourist office (☎ 07531/133–030).

The **Stadttheater** (✉ Konzilstr., ☎ 07531/130–050 for festival office), Germany's oldest active theater, has staged plays since 1609 and has its own repertory company. The local season runs from September through June. From July through August the company moves to its summer theater in Meersburg. For **program details** contact the theater (✉ Konzilstr. 11, D–78462, ☎ 07531/20070). For the **Meersburg** program call 07532/82383.

The Bodensee nightlife scene is concentrated in Konstanz. The **casino** (✉ Seestr. 2, ☎ 07531/81570) is open 3 PM–3 AM. **Disco in Seehotel Siber** (✉ Seestr. 25, ☎ 07531/63044) is open nightly from 10 PM to 4 AM, except Tuesday. **K 9** (✉ Obere Laube 71, ☎ 07531/16713) draws all ages with its dance club, theater, and cabaret in the former Church of St. Paul. Concerts and variously themed DJ nights are held at **Kulturladen** (✉ Joseph Belli Weg 5, ☎ 07531/52954).

Shopping

Konstanz is a very good city for shopping, drawing even the Swiss from St. Gallen and Zurich across the border. It's worthwhile to roam the streets of the old part of town, where there are several gold- and silversmiths and jewelers. **Oexle–China and Glassware** (✉ Marktstätte 26, ☎ 07531/21307) carries not only famous china brands such as Meissen, Rosenthal, and Arzberg, but also beautiful china and glasses of lesser-known names like Theresienthal and Royal Copenhagen. Among their quality gift items are Hummel figures, Kristallglass, and Swiss army knives.

Outdoor Activities and Sports

BIKING

Bike rentals generally cost DM 20 per day and are cheaper when you rent for a longer period. You can rent bikes and book trips at **velotours** (✉ Fritz Arnold-Str. 2d, ☎ 07531/98280, FAX 07531/982–898, ✉).

BOATING

Small sailboats can be chartered from the **Bodensee Segelschule Konstanz/Wallhausen** (✉ Zum Wittmoosstr. 10, Wallhausen, ☎ 07533/4780).

Mainau

⑫ *7 km (4½ mi) north of Konstanz by road; by ferry, 50 min from Konstanz, 20 min from Meersburg.*

One of the most unusual sights in Europe, Mainau is a tiny island given over to the cultivation of rare plants and splashy displays of more than a million tulips, hyacinths, and narcissi in season. Rhododendrons and roses bloom from May to July, dahlias dominate the late summer. A greenhouse nurtures palms and tropical plants.

The island was originally the property of the Teutonic knights, who settled here during the 13th century. In the 19th century Mainau passed to Grand Duke Friedrich I of Baden, a man with a passion for botany. He laid out most of the gardens and introduced many of the island's more exotic specimens. His daughter Victoria, later queen of Sweden, gave the island to her son, Prince Wilhelm, and it has remained Swedish ever since. Today it's owned by Prince Wilhelm's son, Count Lennart Bernadotte, who lives in the castle. In the former main reception hall of the castle there are four or five art exhibitions during the year.

Das Schmetterlinghaus, Germany's largest butterfly conservatory, invites you into a colorful world. On a circular walk through a semitropical landscape with water cascading through rare vegetation, you will see hundreds of butterflies at close quarters flying, feeding, and mating. The exhibition in the foyer explains the butterflies' life cycle, habitats, and ecological connections. Like the park, this oasis is open year-round.

At the island's information center, called **Nature and Culture on Lake Constance,** you can view a multimedia show in which 14 projectors create a three-dimensional effect, reproducing the beauty of the countryside around Lake Constance and also addressing current environmental themes along with explaining how to observe ecologically sound behavior on vacation and at home.

Ferries to the island from Meersburg and Konstanz depart approximately every 1½ hours between 9 and 5. The entrance fee to the island is DM 18.50.

Dining

There are three restaurants on the island but no lodgings.

$$–$$$ ✕ **Schwedenschenke.** This place is geared to give fast, but good service to the lunchtime crowd. At dinnertime it becomes a stylish, candlelighted restaurant. Given that the Bernadotte family is Swedish, the specialties of the chef are Swedish dishes. Have your hotel reserve a table for you. In the evening your reservation will be checked at the gate, and then you can drive onto the island without having to pay the admission. ✉ *Insel Mainau,* ☎ *07531/3030. Reservations essential. MC, D, AE, V.*

Reichenau

⓭ *10 km (6 mi) northwest of Konstanz, 50 min by ferry from Konstanz.*

Reichenau is an island rich in vegetation, but unlike Mainau, it's less glamorous vegetables, not flowers, that prevail. In fact, Reichenau is one of the most important vegetable-growing regions in Germany, with 15% of its area covered by greenhouses and crops of one kind or another.

Though it seems unlikely, amid the cabbage, cauliflower, lettuce, and potatoes, the island has three of Europe's most beautiful Romanesque churches. Little Reichenau, 5 km (3 mi) long and 1½ km (1 mi) wide, connected to the Bodanrück Peninsula by just a narrow causeway, was a great monastic center of the early Middle Ages. Secure from marauding tribesmen on its fertile island, the monastic community blossomed from the 8th through the 12th centuries, in the process developing into a major center of learning and the arts. The churches are in each of the island's villages—**Oberzell, Mittelzell, Niederzell,** which are only separated by 1 km (mi). Along the shore are pleasant pathways for walking or biking.

The **Stiftskirche St. Georg** (Collegiate Church of St. George), in Oberzell, was built around 900; now cabbages grow in ranks up to its rough plaster walls. Small round-head windows, a simple tower, and russet-color tiles provide the only exterior decoration. Inside, look for the wall paintings along the nave; they date from around 1000 and show the miracles of Christ. Their simple colors and unsteady outlines have an innocent, almost childlike charm. The striped backgrounds are typical of Romanesque frescoes.

Begun in 816, the **Münster of St. Maria and St. Markus,** the monastery's church, is the largest and most important of the island's trio of Romanesque churches. The monastery was founded in 725 by St. Pirmin; under the abbots Waldo (786–806) and Hatto I (806–23), it became one of the most important cultural centers of the Carolingian Empire. It reached its zenith around 1000 under the rule of Abbot Hermanus Contractus, "the miracle of the century," when 700 monks lived here. It was then probably the most important center of book illumination in Germany. Though it's larger than St. George, this church has much the same simplicity. It's by no means crude, just marvelously simple, a building that's utterly at one with the fertile soil on which it stands. Visit the **Schatzkammer** (treasury) to see some of its more important treasures. They include a 5th-century ivory goblet with two carefully incised scenes of Christ's miracles and some priceless stained glass that is almost 1,000 years old. ☎ 07534/276 for guided tours. ☑ DM 1. ☉ May–Sept., daily 11–noon and 3–4. Tours possible at other times.

The **Stiftskirche St. Peter and St. Paul** (St. Peter and Paul Parish Church), at Niederzell, contains some Romanesque frescoes in the apse, uncovered in 1990 during restoration work.

A **local-history museum** in the Old Town Hall of Mittelzell offers interesting insights into life on the island over the centuries. ☑ DM 2. ☉ May–Sept., Tues.–Sun. 3–5.

Lodging

$$$–$$$$ 🏨 **Strandhotel Löchnerhaus.** The Strand (beach) Hotel stands commandingly on the water's edge, a stone's throw from the lake and about 80 yards from its own boat pier. Freshly caught lake fish figure prominently on the menu of the restaurant. Most rooms have lake views; those that don't look out over a quiet, shady garden. ⊠ An der Schiffslände 12, D–78479, ☎ 07534/8030, 📠 07534/582. 44 rooms. Restaurant, beach, boating. MC, V.

Radolfzell

⑭ 22 km (14 mi) northwest of Konstanz.

Radolfzell is a lakeside town that developed from a cell of Radolf, bishop of Verona in the 9th century. The town originally belonged to the Abbey of Reichenau, just a few miles away across the lake, until in the 15th century it became part of the Habsburg empire. The center of the town is dominated by the Gothic **Münster unserer Lieben Frau** (Minster of our Dear Lady). In the shadow of the cathedral is a farmers' market every Wednesday and Saturday morning. In the old part of town are shops in charming half-timber houses and on the lake shore a long promenade with a café, a small boat rental place, and a small harbor for sailboats and the ships of the White Fleet. In honor of the three local saints, the *Hausherrenfest* is celebrated every third Sunday in July, when a water procession of decorated boats fulfill an ancient oath.

Just east of Radolfzell is the small **Mettnau Peninsula,** which separates two fingers of the Bodensee, the Gnadensee from the Zeller See. The nature reserve, **Naturschutzgebiet Mettnau,** has free entry and guided tours of the reedy vegetation as well as bird-watching opportunities. You can spot many species of ducks, songbirds, curlews, lapwings, and cormorants. Tours depart from the **Naturfreundehaus,** which also has exhibits. ⊠ Floerickeweg 2a, ☎ 07732/12339. ☑ Free. ☉ Daily. Naturfreundehaus and tours Mar.–Oct., weekends 2–6.

Höri

⑮ *4 km (2½ mi) south of Radolfzell*

Höri is a rural peninsula, settled with small villages, between the Zeller See and Seerhein portions of Bodensee. In the village of Horn, the church **St. Johannes and Veit of Horn** is known for its beautiful location. A king of Württemberg once said: "If I weren't king, I'd like to be the priest of Horn." From here you have a view of the reedy landscape, the Zeller See and the island of Reichenau, the silhouette of Konstanz, and on a clear day, the snowcapped Alps.

In the early 1900s members of Dresden's artist group Die Brücke discovered the area. The most expressive paintings of the Bodensee landscape were created by Erich Heckel (1883–1970) and Otto Dix (1891–1969). Dix lived in the village of Hemmenhofen from 1936 until his death. You can see some of his landscapes in the **Otto Dix Haus.** ✉ *Hemmenhofen,* ☎ *07735/3151.* 🎫 *DM 5.* 🕙 *Apr.–Oct., Wed.–Sat. 2–5, Sun. 11–5.*

The Nobel laureate novelist and poet Hermann Hesse (1877–1962) lived in Gaienhofen from 1904 to 1912, before he emigrated to Switzerland. The **Hesse Haus** museum has biographical displays, books for sale, and occasional art exhibits. ✉ *Gaienhofen,* ☎ *07735/81832.* 🎫 *DM 5.* 🕙 *Apr.–Oct., Tues.–Sat. 2–5, Sun. 11–5.*

THE BODENSEE A TO Z

By Car

Construction on the A–96 autobahn that runs from Munich to Lindau is ongoing. For a more scenic route, take the B–12 via Landsberg and Kempten. If you want to take a more scenic but slower route from Frankfurt, take the B–311 at Ulm and follow the Oberschwäbische Barockstrasse (Upper Swabian Baroque Road) to Friedrichshafen. Lindau is also a terminus of the Deutsche Alpenstrasse (German Alpine Road). It runs east–west from Salzburg to Lindau.

By Plane

The closest international airport to the Bodensee is in Zurich, Switzerland, 60 km (37 mi) from Konstanz, connected by the autobahn. There are also direct trains from the Zurich airport to Konstanz. From Frankfurt there are several flights a day to the regional airport at Friedrichshafen.

By Train

From Frankfurt to Friedrichshafen and Lindau, take the ICE (InterCity Express) to Ulm and change to an IR (Inter Regio) train (3½ hours). From Frankfurt to Konstanz, board the ICE to Karlruhe, change to an IR train, and pass by the beautiful scenery of the Black Forest. From Munich to Lindau, the EC (Europe Express) train takes 2½ hours. From Zurich to Konstanz, the trip lasts 1½ hours.

Getting Around

By Boat

The **Weisse Flotte** (White Fleet) line of boats links most of the larger towns and resorts. One of the nicest trips is from Konstanz to Meersburg and then onto the island of Mainau. The round-trip cost is DM 15.20. A Bodensee-Pass is helpful only if you plan to use the boats frequently: DM 57 grants you one free day of travel plus six days of half-price travel. Passes and numerous excursions are available through **Bodensee-Schiffsbetriebe** (✉ Hafenstr. 6, D–78462 Konstanz, ☎

07531/281–389, ✆). There are also offices in **Friedrichshafen** (☎ 07541/92380) and **Lindau** (☎ 08382/944–416).

By Bus

Railway and postbuses serve most smaller communities that have no train links. Service is infrequent; use buses only if you speak a bit of German and when time is no object.

By Car

Lakeside roads in the Bodensee area are good, if crowded, in summer; all offer nice scenery during the occasional heavy traffic. Formalities at border-crossing points are few. However, in addition to your passport, you'll need insurance and registration papers for your car. For rental cars check with the rental company to verify it imposes no restrictions on crossing frontiers. Car ferries link Romanshorn, in Switzerland on the south side of the lake, with Friedrichshafen, as well as Konstanz with Meersburg. Taking either saves substantial mileage.

By Train

Local trains encircle the Bodensee, stopping at most towns and villages.

Contacts and Resources

Car Rentals

Avis (✉ Friedrichshafen Airport, ☎ 07541/930–705; ✉ Macairestr. 10, Konstanz, ☎ 07531/99000; ✉ Kemptenerstr. 25, Lindau, ☎ 08382/966–333). **Europcar** (✉ Eugenstr. 47, Friedrichshafen, ☎ 07541/23053; ✉ Von Emmerichstr. 3, Konstanz, ☎ 07531/52833). **Sixt** (✉ Zeppelinstr. 66, Friedrichshafen, ☎ 07541/33066; ✉ Karl-Benz-Str. 14, Konstanz, ☎ 07531/690–044).

Emergencies

Police and **ambulance** (☎ 110). **Fire** and **emergency medical aid** (☎ 112).

Guided Tours

BIKING TOURS

Konstanz-based **Velotours** ✉ Fritz-Arnold-Str. 2d, Konstanz, ☎ 07531/98280, ✆) arranges bicycling tours with accommodations and baggage transport around the Bodensee. Velotours also rents out bikes at DM 20 per day.

BOAT TOURS

The **Weisse Flotte** organizes excursions around the lake, lasting from one hour to a full day. Many cross to Austria and Switzerland; some head west along the Rhine to the Schaffhausen Falls, the largest waterfall in Europe. For more information contact Bodensee-Schiffsbetriebe (✉ Hafenstr. 6, D–78404 Konstanz, ☎ 07531/281–389). Information on lake excursions is also available from all local tourist offices and travel agencies.

CITY TOURS

Most of the larger tourist centers have city tours with English-speaking guides, but please call ahead to confirm availability.

SPECIAL-INTEREST TOURS

A fascinating way to view the lake is from a three-passenger Cessna operated by **Slansky/Dussmann** (☎ 07532/808–866 and 08388/1269) from Friedrichshafen's airport. They will also take you into the Alps, following your wishes.

Wine-tasting tours are available in Überlingen, in the atmospheric **Spitalweingut zum Heiligen Geist** (✉ Mühlbachstr. 115) as well as in Konstanz and Meersburg. Please call the local tourist offices for information.

Visitor Information

Information on the entire Bodensee region is available from the **Inter-nationaler Bodensee Tourismus** (⊠ Insel Mainau, D–78465 Konstanz, ☎ 07531/90940, ℻ 07531/909–494).

There are local tourist information offices in the following towns:

Bad Schussenried (⊠ Kultur-und Verkehrsamt, Georg-Kaess-Str. 10, D–88427, ☎ 07583/940–171). **Friedrichshafen** (⊠ Tourist-Information, Bahnhofpl. 2, D–88045, ☎ 07541/30010). **Konstanz** (⊠ Tourist-Information, Konstanz, Fischmarkt 2, D–78462, ☎ 07531/133–030). **Langenargen** (⊠ Langenargen Verkehrsamt, Obere Seestr. 2/2, D–88085, ☎ 07543/933–092). **Lindau** (⊠ Verkehrsverein Lindau, Ludwigstr. 68, D–88103, ☎ 08382/260–030). **Meersburg** (⊠ Verkehrsverwaltung, Kirchstr. 4, D–88709, ☎ 07532/431–110). **Radolfzell** (⊠ Städtisches Verkehrsamt, Rathaus, Marktpl. 2, D–78315, ☎ 07732/81500). **Ravensburg** (⊠ Städtisches Verkehrsamt, Kirchstr. 16, Weingartner Hof, D–88212, ☎ 0751/82324). **Reichenau** (⊠ Verkehrsbüro, Ergat 5, D–78479, ☎ 07534/92070). **Tettnang** (⊠ Verkehrsamt, Montfortpl. 1, D–88069, ☎ 07542/953–839). **Überlingen** (⊠ Kurverwaltung, Überlingen, Landungspl. 14, D–88662, ☎ 07551/991–122). **Weingarten** (⊠ Kultur-und Verkehrsamt, Münsterpl. 1, D–88250, ☎ 0751/405–125).

7 THE BLACK FOREST

Cake and smoked ham aren't the only reasons to visit the Black Forest, but they are good ones. Spa and casino resorts, outdoor activities, and cuckoo clocks are other draws. The Romans were the first to take advantage of the area's healing waters, 19 centuries ago, and royalty and the cultural elite paraded about the region in the 1800s. Here you can splurge in high-fashion, high-cost towns like Baden-Baden one day and relax in a down-home German country village the next.

Updated by
Phyllis Méras

T HE NAME BLACK FOREST—*Schwarzwald* in German—conjures up images of a wild, isolated place where time passes slowly. Dense woodland stretches away to the horizon, but this southwest corner of Baden-Württemberg (in the larger region known as Swabia) is neither inaccessible nor a backwater. The first travelers checked in here 19 centuries ago, when the Roman emperor Caracalla and his army rested and soothed their battle wounds in the natural-spring waters at what later became Baden-Baden.

In the 19th century just about everyone who mattered in Europe gravitated to Baden-Baden: kings, queens, emperors, princes, princesses, members of Napoléon's family, and the Russian nobility, along with actors, actresses, writers, and composers. Turgenev, Dostoyevsky, and Tolstoy were among the Russian contingent. Victor Hugo was a frequent visitor. Brahms composed lilting melodies in this calm setting. Queen Victoria spent her vacations here, and Mark Twain waxed poetic on the forest's beauty in his 1880 book *A Tramp Abroad,* putting the Black Forest on the map for Americans.

Today it's a favorite getaway for movie stars and millionaires, and you too can "take the waters," as the Romans first did, at thermal resorts large or small. The Black Forest sporting scene caters particularly to the German enthusiasm for hiking, with virtually limitless trails wending their way in and out of the woods. In winter the terrain is ideally suited for cross-country skiing.

The Black Forest's enviable great outdoors is blessed by dependable snow in winter and warming sun in summer. Freudenstadt, at the center of the Black Forest, claims the greatest number of annual hours of sunshine of any town in Germany. You can play tennis, swim, or bike at most resorts, and some have golf courses of international standard.

The summer's warmth also benefits the vineyards of the Badische Weinstrasse (Baden Wine Road), which often aligns with the B–3 near the French border. Gutedel and Muskateller, two of the world's oldest grape varieties, are grown here. Baden cooperatives produce mostly dry wines that go well with the region's fine traditional food.

The Black Forest also happens to be the home of the cuckoo clock, despite Orson Welles's claim in *The Third Man* that all Switzerland managed to create in 500 years of peace and prosperity was this trivial timepiece. Cuckoo clocks are still made (and sold) here, as they have been for centuries, along with hand-carved wood items and exquisite examples of glassblowing.

Despite its fame and the wealth of some of its visitors, the Black Forest doesn't have to be an expensive place to visit. It's possible to stay at a modest family-run country inn or farmhouse where the enormous breakfast will keep you going for the better part of the day—all for not much more than the price of a meal in a German city restaurant.

Pleasures and Pastimes

Biking

Bicycles can be rented in nearly all towns and many villages in the Black Forest. Several regional tourist offices sponsor tours on which the biker's luggage is transported separately from one overnight stop to the next. Six- to 10-day tours are available at reasonable rates, including bed-and-breakfast and bike rental.

Dining

Restaurants in the Black Forest range from the well-upholstered luxury of Baden-Baden's chic eating spots to simple country inns. Old *Kachelöfen* (tiled heating stoves) are still in use in many area restaurants; try to sit by one if it's cold outside. Some specialties here betray the influence of neighboring France, but if you really want to go native, try *z'Nuni,* the local farmers' second breakfast, generally eaten around 9 AM. It consists of smoked bacon, called *Schwarzwaldgeräuchertes*—the most authentic is smoked over fir cones—a hunk of bread, and a glass of chilled white wine. Swabian dishes include *Zwiebelrostbraten* (fried beefsteak with onions), *Maultaschen* (a kind of large ravioli), and *Spätzle* (small, chewy noodles). No visitor to the Black Forest will want to pass up the chance to try *Schwarzwälder Schinken* (pinecone–smoked ham) and *Schwarzwälder Kirschtorte* (kirsch-soaked layers of chocolate cake with sour cherry and whipped cream filling). *Kirschwasser,* locally called *Chriesewässerle* (from the French *cerise,* meaning "cherry"), is cherry brandy, the most famous of the region's excellent schnapps varieties.

CATEGORY	COST*
$$$$	over DM 90
$$$	DM 55–DM 90
$$	DM 35–DM 55
$	under DM 35

*per person for a three-course meal, including tax, excluding drinks

Fishing

Innumerable mountain rivers and streams make this area a fisherman's paradise. Native trout are abundant in many rivers, including the Nagold, Elz, Alb, and Wildgutach, and in mountain lakes such as the Schluchsee and Titisee. Licenses are available from most local tourist offices, which usually also provide maps and rental equipment.

Hiking and Walking

The Black Forest is ideal country for walkers. The three principal trails are well marked and cross the region from north to south, the longest stretching from Pforzheim to the Swiss city of Basel, 280 km (174 mi) away. Walks vary in length from a few hours to a week. As in many other German regions, the tourist office has gotten together with local inns to create *Wandern ohne Gepäck* (Hike Without Luggage) tours along the old clock carriers' route. Your bags are transported ahead by car to meet you each evening at that day's destination.

Horseback Riding

Farms throughout the Black Forest offer riding vacations; addresses are available from local tourist offices and the Schwarzwald Turismusverband in Freiburg (☞ Visitor Information *in* The Black Forest A to Z, *below*). Many larger towns have riding clubs and stables.

Lodging

Accommodations in the Black Forest are varied and numerous, from simple rooms in farmhouses to five-star luxury. Some properties have been passed down in the same family for generations. *Gasthöfe* offer low prices and as much local color as you'll ever want.

CATEGORY	COST*
$$$$	over DM 230
$$$	DM 170–DM 230
$$	DM 120–DM 170
$	under DM 120

*All prices are for two people in a double room, excluding service charge.

Spas and Health Resorts

There's an amazing variety of places to have a relaxing soak, from expensive spa towns to rustic places deep in the woods. Baden-Baden is stately and elegant. Bad Dürrheim has Europe's highest-brine spa. For a garden setting, head for Bad Herrenalb. Bad Liebenzell has an Olympic-size pool, and the spa towns of Feldberg and Hinterzarten also provide opportunities to hike.

Winter Sports

Despite Swiss claims to the contrary, the Black Forest is the true home of downhill skiing. In 1891 a French diplomat was sighted sliding down the slopes of the Feldberg, the Black Forest's highest mountain, on what are thought to be the world's first downhill skis. The idea caught on among the locals, and a few months later Germany's first ski club was formed. The world's first ski lift opened at Schollach in 1907. There are now more than 200 ski lifts in the Black Forest, but the slopes of the Feldberg are still the top ski area.

Exploring the Black Forest

The northern Black Forest is known for its broad ridges and thickly forested slopes; it contains the largest number of spas. The central region, Triberg in particular, is especially popular for its associations with folklore, cuckoo clocks, and the Schwarzwaldbahn (Black Forest Railway). The southern portion of the Black Forest has the most dramatic scenery and the most frequented recreation areas. Two main attractions are the Titisee and the Schluchsee, two beautiful lakes created by glaciers.

Numbers in the text correspond to numbers in the margin and on the Black Forest map.

Great Itineraries

Many first-time visitors to the Black Forest literally can't see the forest for the trees (although they have suffered in recent years from the effects of acid rain and a fierce 1999 windstorm). Take time to stray from the beaten path and inhale the cool, mysterious air of the darker recesses. Walk or ride through its shadowy corridors or across its open upland; paddle a canoe and tackle the wild water of the Nagold and Wolf rivers. Then take time out to relax in a spa, order a dry Baden wine enlivened by a dash of local mineral water, and seek out the nearest restaurant that devotes itself to local specialties. If you have money to spare at the end of your trip, return to Baden-Baden and try your luck at the gaming tables.

IF YOU HAVE 3 DAYS

Start your first day at the confluence of three rivers in **Pforzheim** ①. Envy the glittering jewelry collection at the famous Schmuckmuseum, and then visit nearby Maulbronn's beautiful 12th-century Cistercian abbey. Spend a night in the picturesque town of ▥ **Bad Liebenzell** ②, and on the second day soak in one of the Black Forest's oldest spas. After a visit to the ruined abbey in **Hirsau,** near **Calw** ③, head south to ▥ **Triberg** ⑬, site of Germany's highest waterfall and the Schwarzwaldmuseum, with regional folklore exhibits. On the last day go north to look at the farmhouses at the Open-Air Museum Vogtsbauernhof, near **Wolfach,** before driving along the Schwarzwald-Hochstrasse (Black Forest Highway) from Mummelsee (with a stop at the lake) to **Baden-Baden** ⑥, saving plenty of time for a walk around the fashionable spa.

IF YOU HAVE 5 DAYS

Begin your trip by following the first two days of the three-day itinerary described above, starting at **Pforzheim** ①, and then stopping at

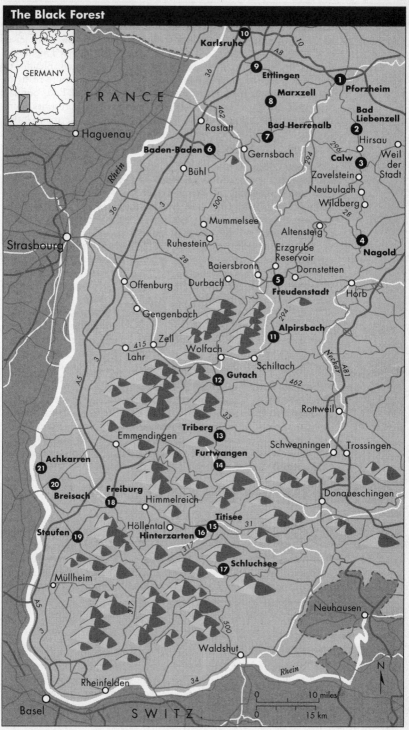

The Black Forest

Maulbronn, **Bad Liebenzell** ②, **Calw** ③, **Freudenstadt** ⑤, and ⊞
Triberg ⑬. On the third day continue directly south to **Furtwangen** ⑭
to survey Germany's largest clock museum. The ⊞ **Titisee** ⑮, the jewel
of the Black Forest lakes, is a good place to spend the third night. On
the fourth day, after taking some time to enjoy the visual splendor of
the Titisee and the mountain-enclosed **Schluchsee** ⑰, you're ready to
brave the winding road northwest through the **Höllental.** End your day
at ⊞ **Freiburg** ⑱, which lies at the foot of the Black Forest; its Münster, or cathedral, has the most perfect spire of any German Gothic
church. Drive north from Freiburg on B–3 through the Baden vineyards
to elegant ⊞ **Baden-Baden** ⑥, where you can relax on the fifth day.

IF YOU HAVE 10 DAYS

After visiting the attractions near **Pforzheim** ①, spend the first two nights
in ⊞ **Bad Liebenzell** ②. ⊞ **Freudenstadt** ⑤ is a good base for the next
two days; from here make excursions to the Schwarzwaldmuseum, at
Lossburg; the Schwarzwälder Freilichtmuseum Vogtsbauernhof, near
the **Alpirsbach** ⑪ brewery; **Gutach** ⑫; and Glasswald Lake, near Schap-
bach. On the fifth day continue on to **Triberg** ⑬ to explore its waterfall and cuckoo clock museums and then to **Furtwangen** ⑭. Spend the
fifth and sixth nights near the shores of the ⊞ **Titisee** ⑮. From the lake
visit the Feldberg, the Black Forest's highest mountain, and the
Schluchsee ⑰. Spend the following two days and nights in ⊞ **Freiburg** ⑱,
allowing time for Schauinsland Mountain; the town of **Staufen** ㉑,
where the legendary Dr. Faustus made his pact with the devil; and the
vineyards on the slopes of the Kaiserstuhl. Finally, drive north through
the Rhine Valley for two nights in ⊞ **Baden-Baden** ⑥. Indulge in the
city's attractions and take a trip to nearby Merkur Mountain.

When to Tour the Black Forest

The Black Forest is one of the most heavily visited mountain regions
in Europe, so make reservations well in advance for the better-known
spas and hotels. In summer the areas around Schluchsee and Titisee
are particularly crowded. In early fall and late spring, the Black Forest scenery is less crowded (except during the Easter holidays) but just
as beautiful. Some spa hotels close for the winter.

THE NORTHERN BLACK FOREST

This region is crossed by broad ridges that are densely wooded, with
little lakes such as the Mummelsee and the Wildsee. The Black Forest
Spa Route (270 km [167 mi]) links many of the spas in the region, from
Baden-Baden (the best known) to Wildbad. Other regional treasures
are the lovely Nagold River, ancient towns such as Bad Herrenalb and
Hirsau, and the magnificent abbey at Maulbronn, near Pforzheim.

Pforzheim

❶ *35 km (22 mi) from Karlsruhe, just off A–8 autobahn, the main Munich–Karlsruhe route.*

The Romans founded Pforzheim at the meeting place of three rivers,
the Nagold, the Enz, and the Würm. Almost totally destroyed in World
War II, it has since been rebuilt in a blocky postwar style and continues to prosper. For a sense of its past, visit the restored church of **St.
Michael** in the center of the city. The original mixture of 13th- and 15th-
century styles has been faithfully reproduced; compare the airy Gothic
choir with the church's sturdy Romanesque entrance.

Pforzheim owes its prosperity to Europe's jewelry trade, of which it is
a center. To get a sense of the "Gold City," explore the jewelry shops

on streets around Leopoldplatz and the pedestrian area. The Reuchlinhaus, the city cultural center, houses the **Schmuckmuseum** (Jewelry Museum). Its collection of 3rd-century BC to 20th-century pieces is one of the finest in the world. ⊠ *Jahnstr. 42,* ☎ *07231/392–126.* ⌷ *Free.* ⊙ *Tues.–Sun. 10–5.*

Pforzheim has long been known as a center of the German clock-making industry. In the **Technisches Museum** (Technical Museum), one of the country's leading museums devoted to the craft, you can see watch- and clock makers at work; there's also a reconstructed 18th-century clock factory. ⊠ *Bleichstr. 81,* ☎ *07231/392–869.* ⌷ *Free.* ⊙ *Wed. 9–noon and 3–6, and every 2nd and 4th Sun. of month 10–noon and 2–5.*

★ **Kloster Maulbronn** (Maulbronn Monastery), in the little town of Maulbronn, 18 km (11 mi) northeast of Pforzheim, is probably the best-preserved medieval monastery north of the Alps, with an entire complex of 30 buildings. The main buildings were constructed between the 12th and 14th centuries. The monastery's church was built in a time of architectural transition from the Romanesque to the Gothic style and had a significant influence on the spread of Gothic architecture through northern and central Europe. Next to the church is the cloister, with a fountain house and refectories for the monks and lay brothers. The monastery's fortified walls still stand and its medieval water-management system, with its elaborate network of drains, irrigation canals, and reservoirs, remains intact. ☎ *07043/175–2480.* ⌷ *DM 8.* ⊙ *Mar.–Oct., daily 9–5:30; Nov.–Feb., Tues.–Sun. 9:30–5; guided tour at 11:15 and 3.* ⊛

Dining
$$$ ✕ **Silberburg.** The Alsatian owners of this cozy restaurant outside the city center serve classic French cuisine. Try the duck in one of chef Gilbert Noesser's exquisite sauces. One of the exceptional ones emphasizes lemon. ⊠ *Dietlingerstr. 27,* ☎ *07231/441–159. AE, DC, MC, V. Closed Mon. and Aug. No lunch Tues.*

En Route The road south of Pforzheim, B–463, follows the twists and turns of the pretty little Nagold River. Gardening enthusiasts should follow the signs to the **Alpine Garden** (on the left as you leave the city limits). The garden, on the banks of the Würm River, stocks more than 100,000 varieties of plants, including the rarest Alpine flowers. ⊙ *Mid-Apr.– Oct., daily 8–7.*

Bad Liebenzell

❷ *31 km (19 mi) south of Pforzheim on Highway 463.*

The picturesque town of Bad Liebenzell has one of the Black Forest's oldest spas. Bathhouses were built here as early as 1403. Nearly six centuries later the same hot springs feed the more modern installations that have taken the place of the medieval originals. Apart from medicinal baths (highly recommended for the treatment of circulatory problems), the town has the **Paracelsusbad lido complex,** with outdoor and indoor hot-water pools. There's also mixed nude bathing at the Sauna Pinea, whose little park complex outside affords beautiful panoramic views of wooded slopes. ⊠ *Reuchlinweg 1,* ☎ *07052/408–250.* ⌷ *DM 30 for 3 hrs in bath; DM 24 for 3½ hrs in sauna.* ⊙ *Bath: Apr.–Oct., Mon.–Sat. 8 AM–9 PM, Sun. 8–8; Nov.–Mar., Mon.–Thurs. and Sat. 8:30 AM–9 PM, Sun. and Fri. 8:30–8. Sauna: year-round, weekdays 1–10, Sat. 9 AM–10 PM, Sun. 9–8.*

A principal pastime in and around Bad Liebenzell is walking along the Nagold River valley. Winding through the thick woods around the little town is a path that leads to the partially restored 13th-century castle of **Liebenzell.**

Dining and Lodging

$$$ ✕🏨 **Kronen Hotel.** Most of the rooms at this comfortable hotel are in
★   a large modern wing, with natural wood decor and large windows. The
        Black Forest landscape is nearby. One kitchen serves the hotel's three
        restaurants and prides itself on its dishes with plenty of fresh vegeta-
        bles and herbs, whole-grain products, and fruit. ⊠ *Badweg 7, D–75378,*
        ☎ *07052/4090,* 𝖥𝖠𝖷 *07052/409–420. 43 rooms. 3 restaurants, café, pool.*
        AE, DC, V. 🍽

En Route **Weil der Stadt,** a former imperial city, is in the hills behind Bad Lieben-
        zell. This small, sleepy town of turrets and gables has only its well-pre-
        served city walls and fortifications to remind you of its onetime
        importance. The astronomer Johannes Kepler, born here in 1571, was
        the first man to track and accurately explain the orbits of the planets;
        the **Kepler Museum,** in the town center, is devoted to his discoveries.
        ⊠ *Keplerg. 2,* ☎ *07033/6586.* 🖃 *DM 1.* ⊘ *Tues.–Fri. 10–noon and*
        2–4; Sat. 11–noon and 2–4; Sun. 11–noon and 2–5; Oct.–May, 1st and
        3rd Sun. of month 11–noon, 2–5.

Calw

❸ *8 km (5 mi) south of Bad Liebenzell on B–463.*

Calw, one of the Black Forest's prettiest towns, was the birthplace of
Nobel Prize–winning novelist Hermann Hesse (1877–1962). Pause on
the town's 15th-century bridge over the Nagold River; you might see
a local tanner spreading hides on the river wall to dry as his ancestors
have done for centuries. The town's market square, with its two
sparkling fountains surrounded by 18th-century half-timber houses
whose sharp gables pierce the sky, is an ideal spot for relaxing, pic-
nicking, or people-watching.

The **Hermann Hesse Museum** recounts the author of *Steppenwolf*'s life
in photographs, manuscripts, books, and documents (English transla-
tion). ⊠ *Marktpl. 30,* ☎ *07051/7522.* 🖃 *DM 5.* ⊘ *Tues.–Sun. 11–5.*

Hirsau, 3 km (2 mi) north of Calw, has ruins of a 9th-century monastery,
now the setting for the Klosterspiele Hirsau (open-air theater perfor-
mances) in July and August. Buy advance tickets at the tourist office
in Calw (⊠ Marktbrücke 1, ☎ 07051/968–844).

Dining and Lodging

$$$ ✕🏨 **Kloster Hirsau–Klosterschenke.** The hotel, a model of comfort and
★   gracious hospitality, is built just outside Calw in Calw-Hirsau, near the
        ruins of the monastery. The restaurant serves such regional specialties
        as *Schneckensuppe* (snail soup) and *Schwäbischer Rostbraten* (panfried
        beefsteak topped with sautéed onions). ⊠ *Wildbaderstr. 2, D–75365,*
        ☎ *07051/96740,* 𝖥𝖠𝖷 *07051/51795. 42 rooms. Restaurant, bowling.*
        AE, DC, MC, V.

$$ ✕🏨 **Ratsstube.** Most of the original features, including 16th-century
★   beams and brickwork, are still intact at this historic house in the cen-
        ter of Calw. Rooms aren't spacious, but they are brightly decorated
        with pastel colors and floral patterns. The restaurant offers sturdy, tra-
        ditional local fare such as *Schwäbischer Rostbraten,* and *Maultaschen.*
        ⊠ *Marktpl. 12, D–75365,* ☎ *07051/92050,* 𝖥𝖠𝖷 *07051/70826. 16*
        rooms. Restaurant. AE, D, MC, V.

OFF THE   **ZAVELSTEIN –** On the road south, watch for a sign to this tiny town 5 km
BEATEN PATH   (3 mi) out of Calw. The short detour up a side valley to this spot is well
               worth taking, particularly in spring, when surrounding meadows are car-
               peted with wild crocuses.

Bureau de change

Cambio

外国為替

In this city, you can find money on almost any street.

NO-FEE FOREIGN EXCHANGE

The Chase Manhattan Bank has over 80 convenient
locations near New York City destinations such as:

> Times Square
> Rockefeller Center
> Empire State Building
> 2 World Trade Center
> United Nations Plaza

Exchange any of 75 foreign currencies

⬠ CHASE

THE RIGHT RELATIONSHIP IS EVERYTHING.®

En Route Back on the main road going south, you'll come next to a turnoff marked TALMÜHLE/SEITZENTAL. A winding road leads to **Neubulach,** a town that was home to one of the oldest and, until it closed in 1924, most productive **silver mines** of the Black Forest. Since then doctors have discovered that the dust-free interior of the mine helps in the treatment of asthma patients. Today a therapy center is in the mine. The ancient shafts can also be visited. ☎ 07053/969–510. ✉ *Guided tour of mine DM 5.* ☉ *Apr.–Nov., daily 11–5.*

The small, fortified town of **Wildberg,** 8 km (5 mi) farther south, has a 15th-century wood town hall and the remains of a medieval castle.

Nagold

❹ *10 km (6 mi) south of Wildberg.*

The town of Nagold lies at the confluence of two gentle-flowing rivers, the Nagold and the Waldach. The town's elliptical street plan was designed some 750 years ago when Nagold was first established. Half-timber buildings, the Romanesque **Remigiuskirche** (Remigius Church), and the modest hilltop remains of a medieval castle provide further evidence of the town's long history.

Dining

$$ × **Adler.** This 17th-century half-timber inn has the kind of ambience lesser establishments can't imitate with false beams. The menu emphasizes traditional Swabian dishes, but there is also some French fare. Veal in mushroom sauce and venison (in season) are reliable favorites. ✉ *Badstr. 1,* ☎ *07452/67534,* 𝔽𝔸𝕏 *07452/67080. AE. Closed Mon.*

En Route Head west toward Freudenstadt on local Highway B–28. The road skirts another gem of the Black Forest, the ancient town of **Altensteig,** which is on a sunny terracelike slope above the Nagold River. A steep, marked route up the hill through the narrow medieval streets brings you (huffing and puffing) into an unspoiled Old Town with half-timber houses and a 13th-century castle. It's a photographer's dream and worth the effort.

In summer pause at the man-made **reservoir** by Erzgrube, 12 km (7 mi) away (follow signs to Erzgrube), for a swim, a picnic, or a hike through one of the densest parts of the Black Forest, where 200-year-old trees tower 150 ft or more.

B–28 continues, passing the oldest town of the northern Black Forest, **Dornstetten.** If you fancy another dip into the past, stop to see the 17th-century town hall, flanked by equally venerable buildings, The low eaves of their red roofs frame magnificent half-timber facades. The fountain dates from the 16th century.

Freudenstadt

❺ *40 km (25 mi) south of Nagold, 22 km (14 mi) southwest of Altensteig.*

Freudenstadt, flattened by the French in April of 1945 because the Nazis had declared it a stronghold, has been rebuilt with painstaking care. It was founded in 1599 to house both silver miners and refugees from religious persecution in what is now the Austrian province of Carinthia (*Freudenstadt* means "city of joy"). You'll find the streets still laid out in the checkerboard formation decreed by the original planners. The vast central square, more than 650 ft long, and edged with arcaded shops, is Germany's largest marketplace. It still awaits the palace that was to have been built there for the city's founder, Prince Frederick I of Württemberg, who died before work could begin. Don't miss Freudenstadt's Protestant **parish church,** just off the square. Its lofty nave is L-shaped, a rare architectural liberty in the early 17th century. It was constructed in this way so the sexes would be separated and unable to see each other during services. At 2,415 ft high, Freudenstadt claims to be the sunniest German resort. The country's largest nature preserve, the Parkwald, with miles of walking trails, abuts it.

OFF THE   **SCHAPBACH –** From this town 22 km (14 mi) southwest of Freudenstadt,
BEATEN PATH   in the enchanting Wolfach River valley, head up into the hills to
               Glaswaldsee. The tree-fringed lake will probably be all yours. Parts of
               the neighboring Poppel Valley are so wild that carnivorous flowers number among the rare plants carpeting the countryside. In July and August the bug-eating *Sonnentau* is in full bloom in the **Hohlohsee** (Hohloh Lake) nature reserve, near Enzklösterle. Farther north, just off B–500 near Hornisgrinde Mountain, a path to the remote **Wildsee** passes through a nature reserve, where rare wildflowers bloom in spring.

Biking

The **Kongresse-Touristik-Kur** office (⊠ Promenadpl. 1, ☎ 07441/8640, FAX 07441/85176) organizes bike tours of the countryside.

Dining and Lodging

$$ ✕ **Ratskeller.** If it's cold outside, ask for a place near the Kachelofen, a large, traditional tile stove. Swabian dishes usually on the menu are Zwiebelrostbraten, served with sauerkraut, and pork fillet with mushroom gravy. In season there's venison, and a specialty is the homemade trout roulade with crab sauce. ⊠ *Marktpl. 8,* ☎ *07441/2693. V. Closed Wed.*

$$ ✕ **Warteck.** Feast your senses in this Biedermeier-style restaurant.
★ Flowers spill over, even in the nooks and crannies between the leadpane windows, and the menu strikes a delicious balance between local and extraregional cuisine. Choices include succulent lamb in meadow herbs, venison with Spätzle, and veal in mushroom sauce. In season the *Spargel* (asparagus) is dressed in an aromatic hazelnut vinaigrette. ⊠ *Stuttgarterstr. 14,* ☎ *07441/91920. DC, MC, V. Closed Tues.*

$$$ ✕▦ **Schwarzwaldhotel Birkenhof.** A woodland setting and a wide
★ range of sports facilities are principal attractions of this motel-like hostelry above town. The two restaurants offer hearty Black Forest fare. ⊠ *Wildbaderstr. 95, D–72250,* ☎ *07441/8920,* FAX *07441/4763. 62 rooms. Restaurant, bar, café, indoor pool, sauna, bowling, squash. AE, DC, MC, V.*

$$ ✕▦ **Bären.** The same family has owned the sturdy old Gasthof Bären since 1878, and they strive to maintain tradition and personal service. Rooms are modern but contain such homey touches as farmhouse-style bedsteads and cupboards. The beamed restaurant (closed Monday and Friday) is a favorite with the locals. Its menu includes Swabian dishes (roasts and heavy sauces) and lighter international fare. The trout is caught locally. ⊠ *Langestr. 33, D–72250,* ☎ *07441/2729,* FAX *07441/ 2887. 33 rooms. Restaurant, parking. V.*

$$ ✕▦ **Luz Posthotel.** This old coaching inn in the heart of town has been managed by the same family since 1809. However, there's nothing 19th century about the rooms, which are both modern and cozy. The restaurant prepares Swabian delicacies. During the summer there's a coffee terrace. ⊠ *Stuttgarterstr. 5, D–72250,* ☎ *07441/8970,* FAX *07441/ 84533. 40 rooms, 4 apartments. Restaurant, Weinstube, library. AE, DC, MC, V. Closed Nov.*

Shopping

Germans prize Black Forest ham as an aromatic souvenir. You can buy one at any butcher shop in the region, but it's more fun to visit a *Schinkenräucherei* (smokehouse), where the ham is actually cured. **Hermann Wein's** Schinkenräucherei (☎ 07443/2450), in the village of Musbach, near Freudenstadt, is one of the leading smokehouses in the area. If you have a group of people, call ahead to find out if the staff can show you around.

Baiersbronn

7 km (4½ mi) northwest of Freudenstadt.

Two of Germany's leading hotel-restaurants—both famous for hospitality, cuisine, and service—grace the mountain resort of Baiersbronn. Most people come here to walk, ski, golf, and ride horseback. An interesting walk leads from restaurant to restaurant.

Dining and Lodging

$$$$ ✕🏨 **Bareiss.** This luxury modern resort resembles a cruise ship moored
★ on a hilltop above Baiersbronn. Inside, some guest rooms have dark-wood furniture and tapestry-papered walls, while others have a light and airy Laura Ashley decor. Its elegant Restaurant Bareiss (closed Monday and Tuesday) serves imaginative cuisine and carefully selected wines (30 brands of champagne alone). In its rustic Dorfstuben, homemade sausage and smoked pork loin are ever popular. By the open fire in its Kaminstube, international dishes are served. The hotel itself is among the most lavish and best equipped in the Black Forest. Some suites (DM 744 and up in season) have their own saunas, solariums, and whirlpool baths. Invigorating mountain walks and winter cross-country skiing opportunities are nearby. ⊠ *Gärtenbühlweg 14, D–07442 Mitteltal/Baiersbronn*, ☎ *07442/470,* 🞮 *07442/47320. 53 rooms, 37 apartments, 10 suites. 3 restaurants, bar, 6 indoor and 3 outdoor pools, beauty salon, sauna, 6 tennis courts, bowling, exercise room, bicycles, billiards. AE, DC, MC, V.*✑

$$$$ ✕🏨 **Traube Tonbach.** The luxurious Traube Tonbach hotel has three
★ outstanding restaurants. If the classic French cuisine of the fabulous Schwarzwaldstube (closed Monday and Tuesday) is too expensive (menus range from DM 160 to DM 205), try either the international fare of the Köhlerstube or eat at the Bauernstube, renowned for its Swabian dishes. In the latter two you dine beneath beamed ceilings at tables bright with fine silver and glassware. The hotel is a harmonious blend of old and new, and each room presents sweeping views of the Black Forest. A small army of extremely helpful and friendly staff nearly outnumbers the guests. ⊠ *Tonbachstr. 237, D–72270 Mitteltal/Baiersbronn,* ☎ *07442/4920,* 🞮 *07442/492–692. 106 rooms, 58 apartments, 8 suites. 3 restaurants, cafeteria, 3 pools, beauty salon, sauna, tennis, bowling, exercise room. AE, DC, MC, V.*✑

$$$–$$$$ ✕🏨 **Hotel Lamm.** The half-timber exterior of this 200-year-old building presents a clear picture of the traditional Black Forest hotel within. Rooms are furnished with heavy oak fittings and some fine antiques. In winter logs flicker in the lounge's fireplace, a welcome sight when returning from the slopes (the ski lift is nearby). In its beamed restaurant you can order fish fresh from the hotel's trout pools. ⊠ *Ellbacherstr. 4, D–072270 Mitteltal/Baiersbronn,* ☎ *07442/4980,* 🞮 *07442/49878. 48 rooms, 6 apartments. Restaurant, indoor pool, sauna, billiards. AE, DC, MC, V.*✑

En Route Return to the Schwarzwald-Hochstrasse now, winding through a land of myth and fable. At the little village of Ruhestein, the side road on the left leads to the **Allerheiligen** (All Saints) ruins. This 12th-century monastery was secularized in 1803, when plans were drawn up to turn it into a prison. Two days later lightning started a fire that burned the monastery to the ground. The locals claim it was divine intervention.

Five kilometers (3 miles) north of Ruhestein is the **Mummelsee,** a small, almost circular lake. Unfortunately, a plethora of souvenir shops, a hotel, and an enormous parking lot detract from what was once a tranquil spot. Because of the lake's high mineral content, there are no fish in it. According to folklore, water nymphs surface after nightfall to dance until they are called back by the king of the lake. Beware of throwing stones into it, for they say that may bring a monster out of its depths. If you can, visit during the mist-laden days of spring. The lake is a popular destination in the summer (for boating, not swimming), and if the path around the lake is too crowded, you can rent a pedal boat and head for the middle.

Bühlerhöhe

On B–500, 3 km (2 mi) after the turnoff to town of Bühl, which is 17 km (11 mi) north of Ruhestein, 16 km (10 mi) south of Baden-Baden.

Several of the finest hotels and restaurants in the Black Forest are on **Bühlerhöhe,** the thickly wooded heights above the town of Bühl. The Bühl Valley and the surrounding area have spas, ruins, quaint villages, and a legendary velvety red wine called *Affenthaler.*

Dining and Lodging

$$$$ ✗▥ **Schlosshotel Bühlerhöhe.** This premiere "castle-hotel" stands ma-
★   jestically on its own extensive grounds high above Baden-Baden, with spectacular views over the heights of the Black Forest. Walking trails start virtually at the hotel door. Its restaurant, the Imperial (closed Monday–Tuesday and January–mid-February), features French fare with regional touches, such as lamb and artichoke roulades. In its Schlossrestaurant, overlooking the Rhine Valley and open daily, the food is both more regional and international. ✉ *Schwarzwaldhochstr. 1, D–77815 Bühl/Baden-Baden,* ☎ *07226/550,* ℻ *07226/55777. 90 rooms, 16 suites. 2 restaurants, bar, indoor pool, sauna, tennis, health club. AE, DC, MC, V.* ☜

$$$–$$$$ ✗▥ **Die Grüne Bettlad.** Hand-painted furniture, bright with flowers, adds great charm to the rooms of this 300-year-old half-timber hotel down in the town of Bühl. In its cozy, old-fashioned restaurant the dishes are regional but with modern updates. Roast lamb with herbs and a ragout of prawns are among popular items. ✉ *Blumenstr. 4, D–77815 Bühl,* ☎ *07223/93130,* ℻ *07223/931–310. 6 rooms. Restaurant. MC, V. Closed Dec. 25–mid-Jan. and 2 wks in late July.*

$$ ✗▥ **Cafe-Pension Jägersteig.** Magnificent views of the wide Rhine Valley as far as the French Vosges Mountains are included in the room rate at this spectacularly situated pension, high above the town of Bühl and its vineyards. ✉ *Kappelwindeckstr. 95a, D–77815 Bühl/Baden-Baden,* ☎ *07223/98590,* ℻ *07223/985–998. 14 rooms. Restaurant. MC, V. Closed Thurs. and mid-Jan.–mid-Feb. No lunch Mon.*

Baden-Baden

★ ❻ *51 km (32 mi) north of Freudenstadt, 24 km (15 mi) north of Mummelsee.*

Baden-Baden, the famous and fashionable spa, is downhill all the way north on B–500 from the Mummelsee (☞ Baiersbronn, *above*). The town rests in a wooded valley and is atop the extensive underground hot springs that gave the city its name. Roman legions of the emperor Caracalla discovered the springs and named the area Aquae. The leisure classes of the 19th century rediscovered the bubbling waters, establishing Baden-Baden as the unofficial summer residence of many European royal families. Their palatial homes and stately villas still grace its tree-lined avenues.

This small, neat city, so harmoniously set within the forest, has a flair and style all its own. As Germany's ultimate high-fashion resort, it basks unabashedly in leisure and pleasure. Here the splendor of the belle epoque lives on to a remarkable extent. Some estimate that one out of five residents is a millionaire. In the evening Baden-Baden is a soft-music-and-champagne-in-a-silver-bucket kind of place, and in the daytime horseback riding along the bridle paths is a preferred leisure activity. Ballet performances, plays, concerts, and recitals crowd the social calendar along with exciting horse racing and high-stakes action at its renowned casino.

Baden-Baden is quite proud of its **casino** (☞ Nightlife and the Arts, *below*), Germany's first, inside the colonnaded neoclassic Kurhaus. A Parisian, Jacques Bénazet, persuaded the sleepy little Black Forest spa to build gambling rooms to enliven its evenings. In 1853 his son Edouard Bénazet commissioned Charles Séchan, a stage designer associated with the Paris opera house, to create a design along the lines of the greatest French imperial palaces. The result was a series of richly decorated gaming rooms in which even an emperor could feel at home—and did. Kaiser Wilhelm I was a regular visitor, as was his chancellor, Bismarck. The Russian novelist Dostoyevsky, the Aga Khan, and Marlene Dietrich all patronized the place. Restaurants, concert halls, and a ballroom are part of the Kurhaus complex.

Few people visit Baden-Baden to sightsee, although you could visit the **Neues Schloss** (New Castle), a 19th-century fortress that was rebuilt in the Renaissance style for the grand dukes of Baden; inside is a small handicrafts museum (✆ Apr.–Oct., Tues.–Sun. 10–12:30 and 2–5). If you've come to take the waters, be sure to have a look in the casino and perhaps take a swim in the palatial **Caracalla-Therme** (Caracalla Baths, ☞ Outdoor Activities and Sports, *below*), a vast modern complex that adjoins the casino with no fewer than seven pools. Strolling around this supremely elegant resort, you can sample the gracious atmosphere that, more than almost anywhere else in Germany, retains the feeling of a more unhurried, leisured age.

Dining and Lodging

$$$$ ✕ **Le Jardin de France.** This clean, crisp little French restaurant, whose owners are Alsatian, emphasizes elegant, imaginative dining in a simple setting. The duck might be roasted with raisins, figs, and nuts at Christmas time; the crayfish might be prepared with chanterelles. ✉ *Rotenbachtalstr. 10,* ☎ *07221/300–7860. AE, DC, MC, V. Closed Mon. and Tues.*

$$$ ✕ **Zum Alde Gott.** The mood is sophisticated and intimate at this 12-
★ table restaurant. The draw is the combination of upscale rustic appeal with distinctive nouvelle German cooking. Amid rolling vineyards in the suburb of Neuweier, you can take a table on the broad terrace and enjoy the local wine. Try the memorable figs in beer pastry dessert or the *mousse au chocolat* with pears. ✉ *Weinstr. 10, Neuweier,* ☎ *07223/5513. AE, DC, MC, V. Closed Thurs. No lunch Fri.*

$$ ✕ **Klosterschänke.** This rustic restaurant is a 10-minute drive from the center of Baden-Baden, and the food is well worth the trip, particularly on a summer evening, when you can dine outside on a tree-covered terrace. You'll probably share a rough oak table with locals; the Baden wine and locally brewed beer ensure conviviality. The menu is surprisingly imaginative, with Black Forest trout prepared in a local

meunière variation. This is the best place for venison when it's in season. ⊠ *Landstr. 84,* ☎ *07221/25854. V. Closed Mon. and 1 wk in summer. No lunch Tues.*

$ ✕ **Weinstube Zum Engel.** The Frölich family has been in charge of the Angel for four generations. Eduard Frölich is responsible for the wine, Gerti Frölich for the kitchen. It is an ideal place for traditional German food such as sauerbraten or Wiener schnitzel. The selection of wines, served by the glass, does supreme justice to the fine local vintages. ⊠ *Mauerbergstr. 62,* ☎ *07223/57243. No credit cards. Closed Mon., Tues., and 3 wks in Mar.*

$$$$ ✕🖭 **Der Kleine Prinz.** Owners Norbert Rademacher, a veteran of the
 ★   New York Hilton and Waldorf Astoria, and his interior-designer wife, Edeltraud, have skillfully combined two elegant city mansions into a unique lodging. Guest rooms are individually decorated in diverse styles. The sprawling penthouse suite has an open fireplace. Two other rooms have fireplaces, and many come with double bathtubs with whirlpool baths. In winter take an armchair in front of a blazing log fire and await your seating in the hotel's romantic little restaurant. Chef Berthold Krieg has been in charge of the kitchen for more than a decade. His nouvelle cuisine combined with unmistakable German thoroughness has won the restaurant acclaim in demanding Baden-Baden. ⊠ *Lichtentalerstr. 36, D–76530,* ☎ *07221/3464,* ℻ *07221/ 38264. 25 rooms, 13 suites. Restaurant, bar, laundry service, parking (fee). AE, DC, MC, V.* ☙

$$$$ 🖭 **Brenner's Park Hotel & Spa.** With some justification, this stately hotel
 ★   set in a private park claims to be one of the best in the world. Behind it passes leafy Lichtentaler Allee, where Queen Victoria and Czar Alexander II, among others, strolled in their day. Luxury abounds in the hotel, and all the rooms and suites (the latter costing up to DM 1,300 a day) are sumptuously furnished and appointed. ⊠ *Schillerstr. 6, D–76530,* ☎ *07221/9000,* ℻ *07221/38772. 68 rooms, 18 suites, 12 apartments. 2 restaurants, bar, indoor pool, beauty salon, sauna, spa, exercise room. AE, DC, MC, V.* ☙

$$$$ 🖭 **Quisisana.** You could hide away from the outside world for days
 ★   in this elegant hotel that had its start in the 18th century as a ladies' clinic and is set in its own spacious park. Most of the English country-house-style guest rooms have balconies, and the hotel's spa is extensive. ⊠ *Bismarck-Str. 21, D–76530,* ☎ *07221/3690,* ℻ *07221/369– 269. 60 rooms, 8 apartments. 2 restaurants, bar, indoor pool, beauty salon, massage, sauna, spa. MC, V.*

$$$ 🖭 **Belle Epoque.** This spacious two-story 1870s house, in its own garden behind wrought-iron gates, is an inviting small hotel with each of its rooms furnished in one or another 19th-century style. There are Biedermeier rooms, *Jugendstil* (art-nouveau) rooms, and rooms from earlier in the century. Colors tend to be light and gay. Comfort is a priority. ⊠ *Maria-Victoria-Str. 2b, D–76530,* ☎ *07221/300–660,* ℻ *07221/ 300–666. 16 rooms. Breakfast room. AE, D, MC, V.* ☙

$$ 🖭 **Deutscher Kaiser.** In an expensive town this central, established hotel provides homey and individually styled rooms at comfortable prices. All the double rooms have balconies on a quiet street. The hotel is a few minutes' stroll from the casino. ⊠ *Merkurstr. 9, D–76530,* ☎ *07221/ 2700,* ℻ *07221/270–270. 28 rooms, 1 apartment. AE, DC, MC, V.* ☙

$ 🖭 **Am Markt.** This 250-plus-year-old building houses a modest inn run (for more than 30 years) by the Bogner family. In the oldest part of town—a traffic-free zone—it's close to such major attractions as the Roman baths. Some rooms overlook the city. ⊠ *Marktpl. 17–18, D– 76530,* ☎ *07221/27040,* ℻ *07221/27044. 27 rooms, 12 with bath. Restaurant. AE, DC, MC, V.*

Nightlife and the Arts

Baden-Baden has one of Germany's most beautiful performance halls, the **Theater** (⊠ Am Goethepl., ☎ 07221/932–700), a late-baroque jewel built in 1860–62 in the style of the Paris Opera. It opened with the world premiere of Berlioz's opera *Beatrice et Benedict*. Today the theater presents a regular series of dramas, operas, and ballets.

In the spring of 1998 the city opened the **Festspielhaus** (⊠ Lange-Str. at Robert-Schumann-Pl., ☎ 07221/30130), a state-of-the-art concert hall. Each summer Baden-Baden holds a two-week **Philharmonischer Sommer Festival** (⊠ Schloss Solms, Solmsstr., ☎ 07221/932–791). Venues include the Kurhaus, the Kurgarten, St. Jacob's, the New Castle courtyard, and the Brenner's Park Hotel. The **Kurhaus** (⊠ Kaiserallee 1, ☎ 07221/932–700) hosts concerts year-round.

Nightlife revolves around Baden-Baden's elegant **casino** (⊠ Kaiserallee 1, ☎ 07221/21060). There's a DM 5 admission charge during gambling hours, which begin at 2 PM daily and last until 2 AM Monday–Thursday, until 3 AM Friday–Sunday; take your passport as ID. You'll have to sign a form guaranteeing that you can meet any debts you run up (minimum stake is DM 5 weekdays, DM 10 weekends; maximum DM 20,000). Half-hour guided tours (but usually in German) are offered daily from 10 to noon for DM 6. Baden-Baden tends to be a quiet place, but there is a nightclub in the Kurhaus ☞ *above*), **Equipage,** and a small one, the **Living Room,** in the Hotel Merkur (⊠ Merkurstr. 8). For a subdued evening stop by the **Oleander Bar,** in Baden-Baden's top hotel, the Brenner's Park (⊠ Schillerstr. 6). **La Cave** (⊠ Sophienstr. 15) is a good place for those 18–25 years old.

Outdoor Activities and Sports

GOLF

The 18-hole Baden-Baden course is considered one of Europe's finest. Contact the **Golf Club** (⊠ Fremersbergstr. 127, ☎ 07221/23579).

HORSEBACK RIDING

Riding facilities in Baden-Baden include an **equestrian hall** (⊠ Gunzenbachstr. 4a, ☎ 07221/949–625), a special area for riding instructions, and a sand track 1-km (½-mi) long. Annual international meets take place in late May, early June, late August, and early September.

SWIMMING

The **Caracalla-Therme** complex is the most lavish swimming pool in the Black Forest region. Built in the 1980s, it has five indoor and two outdoor pools, a sauna, a solarium, and Jacuzzis, as well as courses of thermal water-therapy treatment. ⊠ *Römerpl. 11,* ☎ *07221/275–940.* ☜ *2 hrs DM 19, 3 hrs DM 25.* ☉ *Daily 8 AM–10 PM.*

The **Friedrichsbad** is a 19th-century bathhouse. The swimming pool allows mixed nude bathing most days of the week; people who feel modest about such things should cross the Römerplatz to the Caracalla Pool. ⊠ *Römerpl. 1,* ☎ *07221/275–920.* ☜ *3 hrs DM 36; 3½ hrs, including massage, DM 48. Children under 18 not admitted.* ☉ *Mon.–Sat. 9 AM–10 PM, Sun. noon–10.*

Shopping

Like everything else in Baden-Baden, the shops lean toward elegance, with many offering high-fashion clothing for any occasion. Antiques shops, springing up in sizable numbers in recent years, also have great appeal for both collectors and browsers.

The region's wines, especially the dry Baden whites and delicate reds, are highly valued in Germany. Buy them directly from any vintner on the Baden Wine Road. At Yburg, outside Baden-Baden, the 400-year-old **Nägelsförster Hof** wine tavern and shop (✉ Nägelssörstr. 1, ☎ 07221/35550) has panoramic views of the town and wine tastings (weekdays 8–6).

En Route   The road to Gernsbach, a couple of miles east of Baden-Baden, skirts the 2,000-ft-high mountain peak **Merkur,** named after a Roman monument to the god Mercury, which still stands just below the mountain summit. You can take the cable car to the summit, but it's not a trip for the fainthearted—the incline of more than 50% is one of Europe's steepest. ✑ *Round-trip DM 7.* ☉ *Mid-Feb.–mid-Dec., daily 10–6.*

Bad Herrenalb

❼ *28 km (17 mi) northeast of Baden-Baden, 8 km (5 mi) south of Marxzell.*

The woodlands of the Alb River valley fold around the popular spa of Bad Herrenalb. Oddly enough, Baden-Baden's 19th-century train station is one of the attractions. When that city's station was modernized, preservationists saved the original from destruction by reerecting it here.

Dining and Lodging

$$–$$$ ✕▥ **Mönchs Posthotel.** Beautiful gardens surround this half-timber build-
★   ing with an ornate turret. Its Locanda restaurant, in the park (closed Monday–Tuesday and Christmas–February), offers Mediterranean fare, and the Kloster Schänke serves local dishes daily, year-round. Rooms for overnight guests are comfortable and elegantly furnished, and no two are the same. ✉ *Doblerstr. 2, D–76332,* ☎ *07083/7440,* FAX *07083/74422. 24 rooms, 1 suite, 6 apartments. 2 restaurants, pool, beauty salon, massage. AE, DC, MC, V.*

Marxzell

❽ *8 km (5 mi) north of Bad Herrenalb on road to Karlsruhe.*

In the village of Marxzell a group of ancient locomotives and other
☺   old machines at the side of the road lure you into the **Fahrzeugmuseum** (Transport Museum). Every kind of early engine is represented in this museum dedicated to the German automobile pioneer Karl Benz (1844–1929). Germans say it was he who built the first practical automobile, in 1888, a claim hotly disputed by the French. They assert a Frenchman constructed a steam-powered tricycle in 1769 that seated four and traveled for 20 minutes at 3.6 kph (2.25 mph). On display are motorcycles, Rolls Royces, Mercedes, Alfa Romeos, and Jaguars. ✉ *Albtalstr. 2,* ☎ *07248/6262.* ✑ *DM 5.* ☉ *Daily 2–5.*

Ettlingen

❾ *12 km (7 mi) north of Marxzell.*

Ettlingen is a 1,200-year-old town that's now practically a suburb of its newer and much larger neighbor, Karlsruhe, just a streetcar ride away. Bordered by the Alb River, Ettlingen's ancient center is a maze of auto-free cobblestone streets. Come in the summer for the annual Schlossberg theater and music festival in the beautiful baroque **Schloss.** The palace was built in the mid-18th century, and its striking domed chapel—today a concert hall—was designed by Cosmas Damian Asam, a leading architect of the south German baroque. Its ornate, swirling ceiling fresco is typical of the heroic, large-scale, illusionistic decoration of the period. ✉ *Schlosspl. 3,* ☎ *07243/101–273.* ✑ *Free.* ☉ *Tues.–Sun. 10–5; tour weekends at 2.*

Dining and Lodging

$$ ✕ **Ratsstuben.** Originally used to store salt, these 16th-century cellars by the fast-flowing Alb River now serve international fare and Teutonic food. ✉ *Am Markt/Kirchg. 1–3,* ☎ *07243/14754. DC, MC, V.*

$$$–$$$$ ✕🏨 **Hotel-Restaurant Erbprinz.** This is one of the most historic hotels ★ in Ettlingen, and it even has its own streetcar stop. For many, the real reason for staying here is the top-rated restaurant's magnificent nouvelle German cuisine. You might want to try pine-honey ice cream in an almond basket for dessert, for example. In summer dine in the charming garden, hidden away behind the hotel's green-and-gilt fencing. Don't let the slightly kitschy front garden with its penguin statues and Diana the Huntress put you off. ✉ *Rheinstr. 1, D–76275,* ☎ *07243/ 3220,* 🆊 *07243/16471. 41 rooms, 7 apartments. Restaurant. AE, DC, MC, V.* ✿

Rastatt

20 km (12 mi) southwest of Ettlingen. The pink-sandstone three-winged **Schloss** that is the centerpiece of Rastatt was built at the end of the 17th century by Margrave Ludwig Wilhem of Baden (known as Ludwig the Turk for his exploits in the Turkish wars). It was the first baroque palace of such enormous proportions to be built in Germany. Its highlights include its chapel, gardens, and a pagoda. Inside the palace itself are museums of German history. ✉ *Schlossstr.* 🎫 *Free.* ⊙ *Guided tours Nov.–Mar., Tues.–Sun. 10–4; Apr.–Oct., Tues.–Sun. 10–5.*

Five kilometers (3 miles) south of Rastatt, in **Förch,** Ludwig the Turk's Bohemian-born wife, Sibylle Augusta, constructed her own charming little summer palace, **Schloss Favorite** (Favorite Castle), after his death. Inside, in an exotic, imaginative baroque interior of mirrors and tiles and marble, her collection of miniatures, mosaics, and porcelain is strikingly displayed. *Off B–462.* ☎ *07222/41207.* 🎫 *DM 4.* ⊙ *Mid-Mar.– Sept. 30, Tues.–Sun. 9–11 and 1–4.*

Karlsruhe

❿ *10 km (6 mi) north of Ettlingen.*

Karlsruhe, founded at the beginning of the 18th century, is a young upstart, but what it lacks in years it makes up for in industrial and administrative importance, sitting as it does astride a vital autobahn and railroad crossroads. The town quite literally grew up around the former **Schloss** of the margrave Karl Wilhelm, which was begun in 1715. Thirty-two avenues radiate out from the palace, 23 leading into the extensive grounds, and the remaining nine forming the grid of the Old Town. It's said that the margrave fell asleep under a great oak while searching for a fan lost by his wife and dreamed that his new city should be laid out in the shape of a fan. True or false, the fact is all but one of the principal streets lead directly to the palace. The exception is the Kaiserstrasse, constructed in 1800. Today the palace houses the **Badisches Landesmuseum** (Baden State Museum), which has a large number of Greek and Roman antiquities and trophies Ludwig the Turk brought back from campaigns in Turkey in the 17th century. Most of the other exhibits are devoted to local history. ✉ *Schloss,* ☎ *0721/92665.* 🎫 *DM 5.* ⊙ *Tues. and Thurs.–Sun. 10–5; Wed. 10–7.*

Despite wartime bomb damage, much of the **Old Town** retains its elegant 18th-century appearance thanks to faithful restoration. Walk to the **Marktplatz,** the central square, to see the austere stone pyramid that marks the **margrave's tomb** and the severe neoclassic **Stephanskirche** (St. Stephen's Church), modeled on the Pantheon in Rome and built around 1810. The interior, rebuilt after the war, is incongruously modern.

★ One of the most important collections of paintings in the Black Forest region hangs in the **Staatliche Kunsthalle** (State Art Gallery). Look for masterpieces by Grünewald, Holbein, Rembrandt, and Monet, and also for work by the Black Forest painter Hans Thoma. In the **Kunsthalle Orangerie**, next door, is work by such modern artists as Braque and Beckmann. ⊠ *Hans-Thoma-Str. 2–8,* ☎ *0721/926–3355.* ✑ *DM 5 to both museums.* ☼ *Tues.–Fri. 10–5, weekends 10–6.*

★ ☙ In a former munitions factory, the vast **Zentrum für Kunst und Medientechnologie** (Center for Art and Media Technology) is an all-day adventure. You can watch movies, listen to music, try out video games, flirt with a virtual partner, or sit on a real bicycle and pedal through a virtual New York City. ⊠ *Lorenzstr. 19,* ☎ *0721/81000.* ✑ *DM 10.* ☼ *Wed.–Sun. 11–6.* ❧

Nightlife and the Arts

The best opera house in the region is Karlsruhe's **Badisches Staatstheater** (⊠ Baumeisterstr. 11, ☎ 0721/35570). Street theater is prominent in the annual **Museum Fest** centered, in summer, at the Badisches Landesmuseum. It is a popular carnival-like event.

THE CENTRAL BLACK FOREST

The Central Black Forest takes in the Simonswald, Elz, and Glotter valleys as well as Triberg and Furtwangen, with their cuckoo clock museums. The area around the Triberg Falls—the highest falls in Germany—is also renowned for pom-pom hats, thatch-roof farmhouses, and mountain railways. The Schwarzwaldbahn (Black Forest Railway; Offenburg-Villingen line), which passes through Triberg, is one of the most scenic in all of Europe.

Alpirsbach

⑪ *16 km (10 mi) south of Freudenstadt.*

The Kloster Alpirsbach monastery was built in flamboyant Gothic style and has had several restorations. The **Brauerei** (brewery) was once part of the monastery and has brewed beer since the Middle Ages. The unusually soft water gives the beer a flavor that is widely acclaimed. Call ahead before visiting. ⊠ *Marktpl. 1,* ☎ *07444/670.* ✑ *DM 6.* ☼ *Thurs. 10–noon for individual tourists; Mon.–Wed. for groups.*

The Romanesque **Stiftskirche** (Abbey Church), also on the monastery grounds, is one of the best preserved in the region. Inside, you can see some faded 12th-century frescoes in the nave. In summer concerts are held regularly in the church.

Dining and Lodging

$ ✕ **Zwickel Kaps.** Sit down at one of the massive wooden tables—next to the porcelain *Kachelofen* (tiled stove) if it's a cold day—and order a bowl of *Flädelsuppe* (broth with pancake noodles) and beef stewed in local wine. ⊠ *Marktstr. 3,* ☎ *07444/51727. No credit cards. Closed Mon., 2 wks after Carnival, and 1st wk in Nov.*

$ ▨ **Gasthof Schwanen-Post.** The rustic comforts of this small inn include clean, wood-paneled rooms and a peaceful restaurant terrace. ⊠ *Marktstr. 5, D–72275 Alpirsbach,* ☎ *07444/2205,* ℻ *07444/6003. 5 rooms. Restaurant. MC, V. Closed Tues.*

En Route South of Alpirsbach, stop at **Schiltach**, 10 km (6 mi) along B–294, to admire the outer **frescoes** on the 16th-century town hall. They tell the town's vivid history. Look for the figure of the devil, who was blamed for burning down the beautiful half-timber town on more than one occasion.

Wolfach

14 km (9 mi) south of Schiltach

This cobblestoned town is known for its 600-year-old castle, the colorful facade of its town hall, and its market square edged with turreted and half-timber houses. The Wolfach and Kinzig rivers meet here, and a loggers' rafting festival is held each July.

The **Dorotheenhütte** (Dorothea Blast Furnace) is one of the only remaining Black Forest factories where glass is blown using centuries-old techniques. ⊠ *Gashüttenweg 4*, ☎ *07834/83980.* ⊑ *DM 5.* ☉ *Mon.–Sat. 9–4:30.*

Dining and Lodging

$$ ✕⊞ **Gasthof Hecht.** There's a crisp, modern look to the rooms in this 300-year-old half-timber guest house on Wolfach's main street and a kitchen that serves such hearty fare as *Swäbischer Rostbraten* with Spätzle.* ⊠ *Hauptstr. 51, Wolfach D–77709,* ☎ *07834/538,* 🆁 *07834/47223. 17 rooms. Restaurant. AE, D, MC, V. Restaurant closed Tues., 3 wks in Jan. No dinner Mon.* 🐾

Gutach

⑫ *8 km (5 mi) south of Wolfach, 17 km (11 mi) north of Triberg.*

Gutach lies in Gutachtal, a valley famous for the traditional costume, complete with pom-pom hats, worn by the women on feast days and holidays. Married women wear black ones, unmarried women red ones. The village is one of the few places in the Black Forest where you can still see traditional thatched roofs. However, escalating costs caused by a decline in skilled thatchers, and the ever-present risk of fire, make for fewer thatched roofs than there were 20 years ago.

Near Gutach is one of the most appealing museums in the Black Forest, the **Schwarzwälder Freilichtmuseum Vogtsbauernhof** (Black Forest Open-Air Museum). Farmhouses and other rural buildings from all parts of the region have been transported here from their original locations and reassembled, complete with traditional furniture, to create a living museum of Black Forest building types through the centuries. ⊠ *B–33,* ☎ *07831/93560.* ⊑ *DM 8.* ☉ *Apr.–Oct., daily 8:30–6.*

Dining and Lodging

$$$ ✕⊞ **Romantik Hotel Stollen.** The flower-strewn balconies and low
★ roofs of this small hotel disguise a distinctive and luxurious interior. Run by the same family for 140 years, it combines understated comfort with attentive service: you are treated as if you were staying in a family home rather than a hotel. The restaurant—complete with a roaring log fire—serves regional food with nouvelle twists. ⊠ *Elzacherstr 2, D–79261 Gutach-Bleibach,* ☎ *07685/207,* 🆁 *07685/ 1550. 11 rooms, 1 suite. Restaurant. AE, MC, V. Closed 2 wks in Jan.* 🐾

OFF THE **Schwarzwalder Trachtenmuseum** (Black Forest Traditional Costume
BEATEN PATH Museum) – This museum in a former Capuchin monastery in the village

of Haslach, 10 km (6 mi) northwest of Gutach, is rich in pom-pom-topped straw hats, bejeweled headdresses, embroidered velvet vests, and *Fasnet* (Carnival) regalia of all parts of the forest. ⊠ *Altes Kapuziner Kloster,* ☎ *07832/8080.* ⌷ *DM 3.50.* ☉ *Apr.–Oct., Tues.–Fri. 9–5, Sun. 10–5; Nov.–Mar., Tues.–Fri 9–noon and 1–5; in Jan. by appointment.*

Gengenbach

20 km (12 mi) north of Gutach, 40 km (25 mi) west of Freudenstadt

Walled, half-timber Gengenbach, with its splendidly restored marketplace, is a very special place both at Carnival time and at Advent. The first day of its pre-Lenten Carnival, Schalk, the horned symbol of the festival, is awakened with much fanfare by townspeople from his resting place in the marketplace's Niggelturm, and on the last day he is escorted back. At Advent the 24 windows on the front of the town hall are opened one by one each day in the way of an Advent calendar to reveal pictures. Sometimes called the Rothenburg of Baden, because of its wall and the brightly colored medieval houses on its narrow streets, Gengenbach, in any season, is a charming sight to see.

Dining and Lodging

$$–$$$ ✕▥ **Ritter Durbach.** This 400-year-old half-timber hostelry, on the Wine Road 15 km (9 mi) north of Gengenbach, has been in the same family since 1901. Some of its rooms are spacious and airy with a view of the vineyards that climb the neighboring hillsides; others are small. Its restaurants, ever popular with the townspeople, lay emphasis on such local dishes as *Schneckensuppe* (snail soup) and *Hechtklösschen* (pike balls). Vineyards are everywhere in Durbach and the wine-card offerings are extensive. ⊠ *Talstr. 1, 77770 Durbach,* ☎ *0781/93230,* FAX *0781/932–3100. 50 rooms, 6 apartments. 2 restaurants, pool, sauna. AE, V.* ✍

Triberg

★ ⑬   *16 km (10 mi) south of Gutach.*

At the head of the Gutach Valley, the Gutach River plunges nearly 500 ft over seven huge granite steps at Triberg's **waterfall.** The pleasant 30-minute walk from the center of town to the top of the spectacular falls is well signposted. In the area there are many other fine walks, including one following the route of the cuckoo clock traders. ⊠ *Waterfall viewing DM 2.50 (may be waived in winter).*

Black Forest culture is the focus of Triberg's famous **Schwarzwaldmuseum** (Black Forest Museum). This is cuckoo clock country, and the museum's impressive collection of clocks includes one from 1640; its simple wooden mechanism is said to have been carved with a bread knife. Barrel organs and fairground organs from Berlin are newcomers to the collection. ⊠ *Wallfahrtstr. 4,* ☎ *07722/4434.* ⌷ *DM 5.* ☉ *May–Oct., daily 9–6; Nov. 1–15 and mid-Dec.–Apr., daily 10–5; Nov. 16–mid-Dec., weekends 10–5.*

To purchase a cuckoo clock, the place to look is **Haus der 1000 Uhren** (House of 1,000 Clocks). The shop lives up to its name: its in-town branches are two picturesque old houses bursting with all manner of clocks; the main branch, just out of town, is distinguished by a huge cuckoo clock on the roof and a special section devoted exclusively to *Standuhren,* or grandfather clocks. The staff is multilingual and very friendly. ⊠ *Branches on Triberg's main street below entrance to waterfall and off B–33 toward Offenburg,* ☎ *07722/96300.* ☉ *Mon.–Sat. 9–5.*

The **Schwarzwaldbahn** (Black Forest Railway) links Offenburg and Singen (Hohentwiel) in a 238-km (149-mi) stretch. The Horberg–Triberg–St. Georgen segment is one of Germany's most scenic train rides and a remarkable example of 19th-century engineering. The track winds in near circles and plunges through tunnel after tunnel to get to Triberg. For tickets and information contact the **Tourist-Information Triberg im Kurhaus** (☎ 07722/953–230).

Dining and Lodging

$$–$$$ ✕🏨 **Romantik Parkhotel Wehrle.** This imposing mansion has been in the Wehrle family's possession since 1707; its steep-eaved, wisteria-covered facade dominates the town center between the marketplace and the municipal park. The service is impeccable. The comfortable rooms are individually furnished in a variety of woods with such pleasant touches as fresh flowers. The restaurant serves trout a dozen different ways, all delicious. Try it grilled over coals with fennel. ☒ *Gartenstr. 24, D–78098 Triberg im Schwarzwald,* ☎ *07722/86020,* ℻ *07722/ 860–290. 50 rooms, 1 apartment, 1 suite. 2 restaurants, pool, indoor pool, sauna, exercise room, parking (fee). AE, DC, MC, V.* ✑

Furtwangen

⑭ *16 km (10 mi) south of Triberg.*

Furtwangen is on a tourist route dubbed "the Cuckoo Clock Road"; clock enthusiasts come to visit its **Uhren Museum** (Clock Museum), the largest such museum in Germany. It charts the development of Black Forest clocks, with the cuckoo clock taking pride of place. Its massive centerpiece is a 25-hundredweight astronomical clock built by a local master. ☒ *Gerwigstr. 11,* ☎ *07723/920–117.* ▣ *DM 5.* ⊙ *Apr.–Oct., daily 9–6; Nov.–Mar., daily 10–5.*

Across from the Clock Museum, the **Uhrenkabinett Wehrle** (Wehrle's Clock Gallery; ☒ Lindenstr. 2, ☎ 07223/53240) has an extensive selection of antique and modern clocks in all shapes and sizes.

THE SOUTHERN BLACK FOREST

In the south you'll find the most spectacular mountain scenery in the area, culminating in the Feldberg—at 4,899 ft, the highest mountain in the Black Forest. The region also has two large lakes created by glaciers: the Titisee and the Schluchsee. Freiburg is a romantic university city that incorporates vineyards, a superb Gothic cathedral, and Schauinsland Mountain.

Titisee

⑮ *37 km (23 mi) south of Furtwangen.*

The Titisee, carved by a glacier in the last ice age, is the most scenic lake in the Black Forest. The 2½-km-long (1½-mi-long) lake is invariably crowded in summer with boats and windsurfers, which can be rented at several points along the shore. The landscape is heavily wooded.

At the cuckoo clock workshop **Drubba,** clock making is demonstrated, and high-quality clocks are sold. ☒ *Seestr. 37,* ☎ *07651/981–200.*

Dining and Lodging

$$–$$$ ✕🏨 **Romantik Hotel Adler Post.** This solid old building owned and run by the Ketterer family for 140 years is in the Neustadt district of Titisee, about 5 km (3 mi) from the lake. All the rooms are comfortably and traditionally furnished. The restaurant, the Rotisserie zum Postillon, cooks up excellent local specialties. ☒ *Hauptstr. 16, D–79822 Ti-*

tisee-Neustadt, ☎ *07651/5066,* FAX *07651/3729. 24 rooms, 4 apartments. Restaurant, indoor pool, beauty salon, massage, sauna. AE, DC, MC, V. Closed mid-Mar.–early Apr.* ❧

Hinterzarten

⑯ *5 km (3 mi) west of Titisee, 32 km (20 mi) east of Freiburg.*

The lovely 800-year-old town of Hinterzarten is the most important resort in the southern Black Forest. Some buildings date from the 12th century, among them the **St. Oswaldskirche** (St. Oswald's Church), built in 1146. Hinterzarten's oldest inn, the **Weisses Rossle,** has been in business since 1347. The **Park Hotel Adler** (☞ *below*) was established in 1446, although the original building was burned down during the Thirty Years' War. A small **Schwarzwalder Ski Museum** recounts in photographs, paintings, costumes, and equipment the history of Black Forest skiing, which began in the 1890s on the nearby Feldberg. ✉ *Erlenbruchstr. 35.* ▨ *DM 5.* ⊙ *Wed. and Fri. 3–6; weekends noon–6.*

Dining and Lodging

$$$$ ✕▣ **Park Hotel Adler.** This hotel stands on nearly 2 acres of grounds
  ★   that are ringed by the Black Forest. Marie Antoinette once ate here. In its Grill Restaurant, Continental cuisine is served. In its rustic, paneled Alte Ecke there is regional fare. All rooms are sumptuously appointed. ✉ *Adlerpl. 3, D–79856,* ☎ *07652/1270,* FAX *07652/127–717. 46 rooms, 32 suites. 2 restaurants, bar, indoor pool, sauna, driving range, tennis courts, paddle tennis. AE, DC, MC, V.* ❧

$$–$$$ ▣ **Sassenhof.** Traditional Black Forest style reigns supreme here, from the steep-eaved wood exterior to the comfortable rooms furnished with rustic pieces that are brightly painted, many of them decoratively carved. A kitchen serves breakfast and small meals, but no hot dinners. ✉ *Adlerweg 17, D–79854,* ☎ *07652/1515,* FAX *07652/484. 30 rooms, 10 suites. Indoor pool, beauty salon, massage, sauna, bicycles. V. Closed mid-Nov.–mid-Dec.* ❧

Hiking and Skiing

Hinterzarten is at the highest point along the Freiburg–Donaueschingen road; from it a network of far-ranging trails fans out into the forest, making it one of Germany's most popular centers for *Langlauf* (cross-country skiing) in winter and hiking in summer. For more information contact Feldberg's tourist office.

Schluchsee

⑰ *25 km (16 mi) from Hinterzarten (take Highway B–317, then pick up B–500).*

The largest of the Black Forest lakes, mountain-enclosed Schluchsee is near Feldberg Mountain. Schluchsee is a diverse resort, where sports enthusiasts revel in swimming, windsurfing, fishing, and, in winter, skiing. For details on outfitters contact the tourist office.

Dining and Lodging

$$–$$$ ✕▣ **Kur- und Sporthotel Feldberger Hof.** This is the biggest and best-appointed hotel in the area. Amid the woods and meadows of the Feldberg, and a pleasant walk from the Schluchsee, it has everything for sports lovers—from a large pool to ski lifts, which are right outside the hotel. ✉ *Am Seebuck, D–79859,* ☎ *07676/180,* FAX *07676/1220. 140 rooms. 3 restaurants, 2 bars, café, pool, beauty salon, health club, theater. AE, DC, MC, V.* ❧

DRIVEN TO WANDERLUST

YOU'RE ON THE AUTOBAHN, not zipping through the countryside at illegal state-side speeds but crawling along at 25 mph. Far from *Fahrvergnügen* (you've seen the commercial), this is *Stau*: complete gridlock.

The facilitators of today's wanderlust, that German passion for hiking and traveling, are cars, complete with heatable upholstery and that roll of toilet paper perched on the rear window shelf, often covered by a little knitted hat. Wanderlust gains momentum when BMWs and Mercedes accelerate to a staggering 180 mph. Herein lies the true idea of wanderlust: to move freely through the countryside rather than to arrive somewhere.

Wanderlust has been a cultural leitmotiv for centuries. Living conditions were fairly harsh in Germany until the mid-1800s, and the political system and tightly organized society usually repressive. In an empire strongly defined by provincial regions, wanderlust came to represent a rebellious departure from one's homeland. In the 19th century romantic literature and art idealized the image of independent travelers. Back then, it was mostly young and confused men, such as the famous *Taugenichts* (ne'er-do-wells) of Joseph von Eichendorff's novel, who traveled the world with the navel-gazing intent of finding their inner selves. To those who did not belong to the affluent noble class, wanderlust was a means to practical training. Even today apprentices of many professions, most notably carpenters, might need to travel the country for several years, offering their services along the way, before they are considered qualified to settle down and start their own business.

The aspiring middle class in the early 19th century coined the phrase *Reisen bildet* (travel educates)—a saying many German man teenagers today, dragged through museums while on vacation, cringe to hear. Goethe, the Humboldt brothers, and their ilk set a precedent by earnestly exploring wherever they traveled. Based on the number of Germans chasing tans along beaches around the globe, it appears that wanderlust as cultural exploration may have dropped off. Still, you'll encounter organized groups of Germans at any sightseeing spot in the country. They might even be on an *Bildungsurlaub* (educational vacation), a uniquely German social institution. It's a paid "vacation" an employer is obligated to grant employees so they can travel and "improve" themselves.

But wanderlust also stands in an sharp juxtaposition to that other German passion, a longing for being settled. The best part about traveling, Germans love to say, is the return home. Wanderlust is a brief departure from that well-kept little house tucked away snugly behind that wall or fence. German companies (and the German state) encourage forays by forking out up to six weeks of vacation a year *and* a month's extra pay to be spent during wanderlust season— even if it's spent on the autobahn, for that matter.

— Jürgen Scheunemann

$ ⊡ **Hotel Waldeck.** Geraniums smother the sun-drenched balconies of the Waldeck, and in winter the decorative equivalent is the snow piling up on the slopes outside. Walking trails begin practically at the front door, and the local forest creeps up to the hotel terrace. Some rooms have traditional furnishings; others carry a generic, modern look. ⊠ *Feldberg Altglasshütten, D–79859,* ☎ *07655/364 or 07655/374,* FAX *07655/231. 23 rooms. Restaurant, bar, free parking. DC, MC, V.* 🍴

Hiking and Skiing

The best Alpine skiing in the Black Forest is on the slopes of the Feldberg. The Seebuck, Grafenmatt, and Fahl Alpin area offers 12 lifts and 25 km (15 mi) of pistes (all accessible with a single ski pass). For more information contact Feldberg's tourist office.

En Route To get to Freiburg, the largest city in the southern Black Forest, you have to brave the curves of the winding road through the **Höllental** (Hell Valley). (In 1770 Empress Maria Theresa's 15-year-old daughter—the future queen Marie Antoinette—made her way along what was then a coach road on her way from Vienna to Paris. She traveled with an entourage of 250 officials and servants in some 50 horse-drawn carriages.) The first stop at the end of the valley is a little village called, appropriately enough, **Himmelreich,** or Kingdom of Heaven. Railroad engineers are said to have given the village its name in the 19th century, grateful as they were to finally have laid a line through Hell Valley. At the entrance to Höllental is a deep gorge, the **Ravennaschlucht.** It's worth scrambling through to reach the tiny 12th-century chapel of **St. Oswald,** the oldest parish church in the Black Forest. Look for a bronze statue of a deer high on a roadside cliff, 5 km (3 mi) farther on. It commemorates the local legend of a deer that amazed hunters by leaping the deep gorge at this point. Another 16 km (10 mi) will bring you to Freiburg.

Freiburg

⑱ *Via B–31, 23 km (14 mi) from turnoff (317) to Schluchsee.*

Freiburg, or Freiburg im Breisgau (to distinguish it from the Freiberg in Saxony (☞ Chapter 16), was founded in the 12th century. After extensive wartime bomb damage, skillful restoration has helped re-create the original and compelling medieval atmosphere of one of the loveliest historic towns in Germany. The 16th-century geographer Martin Waldseemüller was born here; in 1507 he was the first to put the name *America* on a map. Freiburg has had its share of misadventures through the years. In 1632 and 1638 Protestant Swedish troops in the Thirty Years' War captured the city; in 1644 it was taken by Catholic Bavarian soldiers; and in 1677, 1713, and 1744 French troops captured it. The tourist office sponsors English walking tours April 15 through October 31, on Monday and Friday at 2:30, Wednesday–Thursday and Saturday–Sunday at 10:30. The two-hour tours cost DM 8.

Numbers in the text correspond to numbers in the margin and on the Freiburg map.

★ The **Münster** (Cathedral), Freiburg's most famous landmark, towers over the medieval streets. The pioneering 19th-century Swiss art historian Jacob Burckhardt described its delicately perforated 380-ft spire as the finest in Europe. The cathedral took three centuries to build, from around 1200 to 1515. You can easily trace the progress of generations of builders through the changing architectural styles, from the fat columns and solid, rounded arches of the Romanesque period to the lofty Gothic windows and airy interior of the choir. Of particular interest are the luminous 13th-century stained-glass windows, a 16th-

Freiburg

N — TO HAUPTBAHNHOF — *i*

Eisenbahnstr.

Rathaus
Rathauspl.

Münster
Münsterpl.

Bertholdstr.

Rathausg. Schusterstr.
Schusterstr.

Niemensstr.

Universitätsstr.

Kaiser-Joseph-Str.

Rotteckring

Herrenstr.

Universität

Löwenstr.

Grünwälderstr.

Salzstr.

Augustinermuseum
Augustinerpl.

Konvietstr.

Schloßbergring

Martinstor

Gerberau

Fischerau

Oberlinden

Schloßberg

Adelhauser Str.

Schwabentor

0 — 200 yards
0 — 200 meters

century triptych by Hans Baldung Grien, and paintings by Holbein the Younger and Lucas Cranach the Elder. If you can summon the energy, climb the tower. The reward is a magnificent view of the city and the Black Forest beyond. ⊠ *Münsterpl.,* ☎ *0761/31099; 0761/388–101 tours.* 💷 *Bell tower DM 2.50.* ۞ *Mon.–Sat. 10–6, Sun. 1–6.* 🐌

The **Münsterplatz,** the square around Freiburg's cathedral, holds a daily market, where you can buy everything from strings of garlic to scented oils in front of the 16th-century **Kaufhaus** (Market House). The square is also lined with traditional taverns serving such local specialties as Black Forest ham and Spätzle.

A visit to Freiburg's cathedral is not really complete without also exploring the **Augustinermuseum** (Augustinian Museum), at the former Augustinian cloister. Original sculpture from the cathedral is on display, as well as gold and silver reliquaries. The collection of stained-glass windows, dating from the Middle Ages to today, is one of the most important in Germany. ⊠ *Am Augustinerpl. (Salzstr. 32),* ☎ *0761/ 201–2531.* 💷 *DM 4.* ۞ *Tues.–Sun. 10–5.*

On the Rathaus Platz, Freiburg's famous **Rathaus** (town hall) is constructed from two 16th-century patrician houses joined together. Among its attractive Renaissance features is an oriel, or bay window, clinging to a corner and bearing a bas-relief of the romantic medieval legend of the Maiden and the Unicorn. ⊠ *Rathauspl. 2–4.* ۞ *Weekdays 8–12.*

For a more intimate view of Freiburg, wander through the streets around the Münster or follow the main shopping artery of **Kaiser-Joseph-Strasse.** After you pass a reconstructed city gate (this one is Martinstor; the other is called Schwabentor), follow **Fischerau** off to the left. River fishermen used to live on this little alley. You'll come to quaint shops along the bank of one of the city's larger canals, which continues past the former Augustinian cloister (☞ Augustinermuseum, *above*) to the equally picturesque area around the *Insel* (island). This canal is a larger version of the brooklets running through many streets in Freiburg's Old Town; tradition has it that anyone who steps into one of these *Bächle* (brooklets) is sure to return to Freiburg.

Dining and Lodging

$$$ ✕ **Alte Weinstube zur Traube.** The fruit of the vine is not the only item on the menu at this cozy old wine tavern, which offers a rich and varied selection of classic French and Swabian dishes. *Zander* (pike) roulade with crab sauce and braised pork with lentils are especially recommended. ⊠ *Schusterstr. 17,* ☎ *0761/32190. AE, V. Closed Sun. and 3 wks mid-Aug. No lunch Mon.*

$$$ ✕ **Markgräfler Hof.** The imaginative Mediterranean and Swabian fare
★ in this restaurant ranges from dishes like braised tomatoes and arti-
chokes with lukewarm vegetables to quail stuffed with Brussels sprouts
and walnuts in a red wine and truffle sauce. It's hard to go wrong with
the wide variety of choices. A small but fine wine list complements the
menu. ⊠ *Gerberau 22,* ☎ *0761/32540. AE, D, MC, V. Closed early
Feb., 3 wks Aug., Sun., and Mon.*

$$ ✕ **Kleiner Meyerhof.** Here you'll find an intimate Weinstube atmosphere
but with more places to sit. It's a good place to try out regional special-
ties at comfortable prices. Goose and wild game are served in the fall
and winter. ⊠ *Rathausg. 27,* ☎ *0761/26941. MC. Closed Sun. June–
Aug.*

$$ ✕ **Kühler Krug.** Wild game and goose liver terrine are among the spe-
cialties at this restaurant, which has even given its name to a distinc-
tive saddle-of-venison dish. Those who prefer fish shouldn't despair:
there's an imaginative range of freshwater varieties available. ⊠ *Torpl.
1, Günterstal,* ☎ *0761/29103. MC, V. Closed Wed.*

$ ✕ **Freiburger Salatstuben.** Come here for healthy vegetarian food pre-
pared in creative ways—try the homemade whole-wheat noodles with
cauliflower in a pepper cream sauce—and served cafeteria style. All
that nutrition and fiber costs no more than a meal at the McDonald's
around the corner. University students crowd the place at peak hours.
⊠ *Am Martinstor-Löwenstr. 1,* ☎ *0761/35155. No credit cards.
Closed Sun. No dinner Sat.*

$$$$ ✕⊡ **Colombi.** Freiburg's most luxurious hotel also has the city's finest
★ and most original restaurant in two reconstructed 18th-century Aus-
trian farmhouse rooms, now lavishly furnished and decorated with se-
lected Black Forest antiques. In the rustic part of the restaurant, which
is named after the Black Forest artist Hans Thoma, you can order such
hearty local dishes as lentil soup and venison, while in its more ele-
gant section the menu combines traditional meat and fish dishes with
innovative sauces. Restaurant reservations are essential. The hotel is
centrally located but very quiet. ⊠ *Am Colombi Park/Rotteckring 16,
D–79098,* ☎ *0761/21060,* ℻ *0761/31410. 80 rooms, 48 suites. 2 restau-
rants. AE, DC, MC, V.* ✎

$$$$ ✕⊡ **Zum Roten Bären.** A showpiece of the Ring Group, this inn,
★ which dates from 1311, retains its individual character, with very com-
fortable lodging and excellent dining in a warren of restaurants and
taverns. If it's a chilly evening, order a table next to the large Kache-
lofen (tile stove), which dominates the main, beamed restaurant. Take
a tour of the two basement floors, composed of cellars dating from the
original 12th-century foundation of Freiburg and now well stocked with
fine wines. ⊠ *Oberlinden 12, D–79098 Freiburg im Breisgau,* ☎
0761/387–870, ℻ *0761/387–8717. 25 rooms, 3 apartments. 3 restau-
rants, Weinstube, sauna, parking (fee). AE, DC, MC, V.* ✎

$$–$$$ ✕⊡ **Oberkirchs Weinstuben.** Across from the cathedral and next to
the Renaissance Kaufhaus, this wine cellar is a bastion of tradition and
local Gemütlichkeit (comfort and conviviality). The proprietor personally
bags some of the game that ends up in the kitchen. Fresh trout is an-
other specialty. In summer the dark-oak dining tables spill onto a gar-
den terrace. Approximately 20 Baden wines are served by the glass,
from white Gutedel to red Spätburgunder, many supplied from the restau-
rant's own vineyards. The Weinstuben also offers accommodation in
26 charmingly furnished rooms in the Weinstuben itself and in a neigh-
boring centuries-old house. ⊠ *Münsterpl. 22, D–79098,* ☎ *0761/
31011. 26 rooms. Restaurant. AE, MC, V. Restaurant closed Sun. and
late Dec.–Feb.*

$$–$$$ ✕⊡ **Schwär's Hotel Löwen.** Heinrich Schwär's "Lion" stands impos-
ingly on the edge of town, with its back on Freiburg's golf course. Ask

for a room with a south-facing balcony and soak up the sun in summer and the Black Forest view in winter. Most rooms are furnished in rustic Black Forest style; all are spacious. The hotel's minibus service takes guests into town. ⊠ *Kapplerstr. 120, D–79117 Freiburg-Littenweiler,* ☎ *0761/63041,* ⅢⅩ *0761/60690. 58 rooms, 3 suites. Restaurant, bar, free parking. AE, DC, MC, V.*

$$ ✕⊡ **Rappen.** In the heart of the pedestrians-only Old Town, this hotel's brightly painted farmhouse-style rooms overlook the marketplace and cathedral (and overhear the latter's bells). The rustic theme extends to the restaurant, which often has weeks of special fare, such as fish or wild game. Wine lovers will appreciate the regional vintages. There are about 40 wines (German and French) on the wine card. ⊠ *Münsterpl. 13, D–79098,* ☎ *0761/31353,* ⅢⅩ *0761/382–252. 24 rooms, 18 with bath or shower. Restaurant. AE, DC, MC, V.* ✎

$$$–$$$$ ⊡ **Park Hotel Post.** Near the train station, the renovated Post has been a hotel since the turn of the century, with good, old-fashioned service to prove it. The Jugendstil (art-nouveau) facade with stone balconies and central copper-dome tower has earned the building protected status. A large breakfast buffet is included in the room price. ⊠ *Eisenbahnstr. 35, D–79098,* ☎ *0761/385–480,* ⅢⅩ *0761/31680. 43 rooms. Breakfast room. AE, DC, MC, V.* ✎

Nightlife and the Arts

Freiburg has a multistage complex, the **Konzerthaus** (⊠ Städtische Bühne, Bertoldstr. 46, ☎ 0761/34874), near the train station. The music scene really comes alive in summer. The annual **Zeltmusik** (tent music) festival is a musical jamboree held under huge tents in June and July. The emphasis is on jazz, but most types of music, including classical, can be heard. There are summer chamber music concerts in the courtyard of the ancient Kaufhaus, opposite the Münster, and the Münster itself hosts an annual summer program of organ recitals. For program details and tickets for the above, contact **Freiburg Information** (⊠ Rotteckring 14, ☎ 0761/368–9090). Performances in Freiburg's annual **summer theater** festival are centered in the city's theater complex, spilling out into the streets and squares.

Nightlife in Freiburg takes place in the city's *Kneipen* (pubs), wine bars, and wine cellars. On Münsterplatz, **Oberkirchs Weinstuben** (⊠ Münsterpl. 22, ☎ 0761/31011) is typically atmospheric; you can also look for nightspots on any of the streets around the cathedral. For student pubs, wander around Stühlinger, the neighborhood immediately south of the train station. Leading dance clubs are **Agar** (⊠ Löwenstr. 8, ☎ 0761/380–650) and **Arena** (⊠ Schwarzwaldstr. 2, ☎ 0761/73924). Freiburg's **Jazz Haus** (⊠ Schnewlinstr. 1, ☎ 0761/34973) has live music nightly and draws big acts and serious up-and-coming artists to its brick cellar.

Staufen

⑲ *20 km (12 mi) south of Freiburg via B–31.*

Once you've braved Hell Valley to get to Freiburg, a visit to the nearby town of Staufen, where Dr. Faustus is reputed to have made his pact with the devil, should hold no horrors. The Faustus legend is remembered today chiefly because of Goethe's *Faust,* the finest drama in all of German literature. Goethe's Faust, fed up with life and the futility of academic studies, is driven to sell his soul to the devil in return for youth, knowledge, and other satanic favors. The original Faustus was a 16th-century alchemist and scientist. His pact was not with the devil but with a local baron who was convinced that Faustus could make his fortune by converting base metal into gold. While attempting to do so, Dr. Faustus caused an explosion that produced such noise and such a sulfurous stink that the townspeople were convinced the devil had carried him off. In fact, he was killed in the accident. You can visit the ancient **Gasthaus zum Löwen** (⊠ Hauptstr. 47), where Faustus lived and died, in the center of Staufen.

Dining and Lodging

$$$ ✕⊞ **Spielweg.** Half an hour's drive from Freiburg, this family-run inn
★ has everything for an indulgent holiday, with pools, tennis courts, and Karl-Josef Fuch's regional cooking. ⊠ *Hauptstr. 61, D–79244 Obermünstertal,* ☎ *07636/7090,* 𝔽𝔸𝕏 *07636/70966. 37 rooms, 2 suites. Restaurant, sauna, free parking. AE, DC, MC, V.*

$$ ✕⊞ **Die Krone.** A simple freshness is the hallmark of the rooms in this 400-year-old pink-and-gold inn in the heart of cobblestoned Staufen. In the cozy restaurant the fare is largely French and Swiss. ⊠ *Hauptstr. 30, 79219,* ☎ *7633/5840,* 𝔽𝔸𝕏 *7633/82903. 9 rooms. Restaurant. AE, MC, V. Closed first 2 wks in Feb.*

$$ ✕⊞ **Landgasthaus zur Linde.** This inn has been welcoming guests for 350 years, but the comforts inside its old walls are contemporary; the kitchen creates wholesome sustenance out of local ingredients. ⊠ *Krumlinden 13, D–79244 Obermünstertal,* ☎ *07636/7570,* 𝔽𝔸𝕏 *07636/ 1632. 16 rooms, 2 suites. Restaurant. V. Nov.*

Breisach

㉔ *20 km (12 mi) northwest of Freiburg on B–31.*

The town of Breisach stands by the Rhine River; everything you see to the west on the opposite bank is in France. Towering high above the town and the surrounding vineyards is the **Stephansmünster** (Cathedral of St. Stephen), built between 1200 and 1500 (and almost entirely rebuilt after World War II). Hotels here have terrace restaurants from which to enjoy the scenery. North of Breisach rises the **Kaiserstuhl** (Emperor's Chair), a volcanic outcrop clothed in vineyards that produce some of Baden's best wines—reds from the Spätburgunder grape and whites that have an uncanny depth.

Achkarren

㉑ *5 km (3 mi) north of Breisach.*

Sample high-quality wines—the Weissherbst, in particular—in one of the taverns of Achkarren or take a short hike along a vineyard path. The fine little **Weinmuseum** (Wine Museum) is in the village center. ☎ *Museum DM 2.* ☉ *Apr.–Oct., Tues.–Fri. 2–5, weekends 11–5.*

THE BLACK FOREST A TO Z

Arriving and Departing

By Car

The Rhine Valley Autobahn, A–5, runs the western length of the Black Forest, connecting with the autobahn system at Karlsruhe. The B–3 runs parallel to the A–5 and follows the Baden Wine Road.

Freiburg, the region's major city, is 275 km (170 mi) from Frankfurt and 410 km (254 mi) from Munich.

By Plane

The closest international airports are at Stuttgart, Strasbourg, in neighboring French Alsace, and the Swiss border city of Basel, the latter just

70 km (43 mi) from Freiburg. In Germany Frankfurt's airport is the next closest after Stuttgart's.

By Train
The main rail route through the Black Forest runs north–south, following the Rhine Valley from Karlsruhe to Basel. There are fast and frequent trains to Freiburg and Baden-Baden from most major German cities (you generally have to change at Karlsruhe).

Getting Around

By Bus
There is an extensive system of local buses in the region, particularly in the northern and central Black Forest. Details are available from the **Regionalbusverkehr Südwest** (Regional Bus Lines): **Karlsruhe** (☎ 0721/966–8620); **Offenburg** (☎ 0781/935–415); **Freudenstadt** (☎ 07441/1555).

By Car
Good two-lane highways crisscross the entire region. The main highways are the A–5 (Frankfurt–Karlsruhe–Basel), running through the Rhine Valley; the A–81 (Stuttgart–Bodensee), in the east; and the A–8 (Karlsruhe–Stuttgart), in the north. Traffic jams on weekends and holidays are not uncommon. Taking the side roads might not save time, but they are a lot more interesting. The Schwarzwald-Hochstrasse (Black Forest Highway) is one of the area's most scenic (but also most trafficked) routes, running from Freudenstadt to Baden-Baden. The region's tourist office (☞ Visitor Information *in* Contacts and Resources, *below*) has mapped out thematic driving routes: the High Road, the Low Road, the Spa Road, the Baden Wine Road, and the Clock Road. Most points along these routes can also be reached by train or bus.

By Train
Local lines connect most of the smaller towns. Two east–west routes—the Schwarzwaldbahn (Black Forest Railway) and the Höllental Railway—are among the most spectacular in the country. Details are available from **Deutsche Bahn** in Freiburg (☎ 0761/19419).

Contacts and Resources

Car Rentals
Avis (✉ Maximilianstr. 54–56, Baden-Baden, ☎ 07221/504–190; ✉ St-Georgenerstr. 7, Freiburg, ☎ 0761/19719; ✉ Westliche Karl-Friedrich-Str. 141, Pforzheim, ☎ 07231/440–828). **Europcar** (✉ Rheinstr. 29, Baden-Baden, ☎ 07221/50660 or 0180/58000; ✉ Zaehringerstr. 42, Freiburg, ☎ 0761/515–100). **Hertz** (✉ Rheinstr. 48, Baden-Baden, ☎ 07221/60002; ✉ Lörracherstr. 49, Freiburg, ☎ 0761/478–090).

Guided Tours
BIKE TOURS
Much of the Black Forest is a biker's paradise (provided the rider is stalwart since there are so many ups and downs). There are many bike rental shops throughout the region, and cycling maps are available at most tourist offices. Mountain biking is an increasingly popular sport. With advance reservations bicycles can be transported by train in most areas. For information on biking in Germany, contact the **National German Cycling Association** (✉ Postfach 107740, D–28077 Bremen, ☎ 0421/346–290).

Bus tours (some in English) of the Black Forest and parts of neighboring France and Switzerland, as well as walking tours of Freiburg, are available in Freiburg from **Freiburg Kultur** (⊠ Rotteckring 14, ☎ 0761/290–7447, FAX 0761/290–7449).

Outdoor Activities and Sports

FISHING

Licenses cost DM 8–DM 12 a day and are available from most local tourist offices, which can also usually provide maps and rental equipment. Contact the **Schwarzwald Tourismusverband** (☞ Visitor Information, *below*) for details.

HIKING AND WALKING

The regional tourist office offers *Wandern ohne Gepäck* (Hike Without Luggage) tours along the old clock-carriers' route. The participating hotels are connected by one-day hikes in a circular route, each section ranging from 16 km to 27 km (10 mi to 17 mi). Your bags are transported ahead by car to meet you each evening at that day's destination. Prices are reasonable: three nights with hotel and breakfast start at DM 331. For reservations and information contact **Wandern Ohne Gepäck** at the Uhrenträgergemeinschaft in Triberg (⊠ Hauptstr. 51, D–78094 Triberg, ☎ 07722/860–2111, FAX 07722/860–2190, ✉).

Along the Wine Road spring and summer weekend hikes will take you through vineyard country to five wineries for wine tasting. The package includes two overnights and two meals typical of the region. Information and reservations can be obtained from **Tourist-Information Durbach** (⊠ Tal 36, D–7770 Durbach, ☎ 0781/42163).

HORSEBACK RIDING

Traveling Black Forest trails on the back of a horse is an unforgettable experience. Information on renting horses and on trail rides is available in many local tourist offices or from **Schwarzwald Tourismusverband** (☞ Visitor Information, *below*).

WINTER SPORTS

Cross-country ski instruction is given in every resort. Call the **Verkehrsamt** (⊠ Hinterzarten, ☎ 07652/120–642, ✉), for details.

Visitor Information

Information for the entire Black Forest is available from **Schwarzwald Turismusverband** (⊠ Bertoldstr. 45, D–79098 Freiburg, ☎ 0761/296–2260, FAX 0761/296–2277, ✉). There are local tourist information offices in the following towns:

Baden-Baden (⊠ Baden-Baden Marketing GmbH, Augustapl. 8, D–76530, ☎ 07221/275–200, FAX 07221/275–202). **Badenweiler** (⊠ Kur- und Touristik, GmbH, Ernst-Eisenlohr-Str. 4, D–79410, ☎ 07632/72110). **Bad Herrenalb** (⊠ Kurverwaltung, D–76332, ☎ 07083/500–555). **Bad Liebenzell** (⊠ Kurverwaltung, Kurhausdamm 4, D–75378, ☎ 07052/4080). **Feldberg** (⊠ Tourist-Information [im Ortsteil Altglashütten], Kirchg. 1, D–79868, ☎ 07655/8019, FAX 07655/80143). **Freiburg** (⊠ Information, Rotteckring 14, D–79098, ☎ 0761/388–1880). **Freudenstadt** (⊠ Kongresse–Touristik–Kur, Promenadenpl. 1, D–72250, ☎ 07441/8640). **Hinterzarten** (⊠ Verkehrsamt, Freiburgerstr. 1, D–79854, ☎ 07652/120–642, ✉). **Karlsruhe** (⊠ Karlsruher Tagungs- und Touristik Service, Bahnhofpl. 6, D–76137, ☎ 0721/35530). **Pforzheim** (⊠ Stadtinformation, Rathaus, Marktpl. 1, D–75175, ☎ 07231/454–560). **Schluchsee** (⊠ Kurverwaltung, Fischbacherstr. 7, D–79859, ☎ 07656/7732). **Titisee-Neustadt** (⊠ Tourist-Information, Strandbadstr., D–79822, ☎ 07651/98040). **Triberg** (⊠ Kurverwaltung im Kurhaus, Luisenstr. 10, D–78098, ☎ 07722/953–230).

8 HEIDELBERG AND THE NECKAR VALLEY

This area bounces between industrial cities and quaint university towns—Mannheim and Stuttgart among the former, Heidelberg and Tübingen among the latter—with castles, small villages, and the Neckar River throughout. Along the scenic Burgenstrasse (Castle Road), each medieval town is guarded by a castle.

Revised by
Kerry Brady
Stewart

T HE NECKAR RIVER unites beauty and historic resonance as it flows toward the Rhine through the state of Baden-Württemberg, eventually reaching Heidelberg's graceful baroque towers and the majestic ruins of its red sandstone castle. Much of this route follows the west–east course of the Burgenstrasse (Castle Road), which stretches nearly one 1,000 km (621 mi) from Mannheim to Prague, taking in some 70 castles and palaces along the way. Every town or bend in the river seems to have its guardian castle, sometimes in ruins but often used as a museum or hotel. Off the main road, quiet side valleys and little towns slumber in leafy peace.

Pleasures and Pastimes

Dining

Fish and *Wild* (game) from the streams and woods lining the Neckar Valley, as well as seasonal favorites, such as *Spargel* (asparagus) and *Pilze* (mushrooms)—*Morcheln* (morels), *Pfifferlinge* (chanterelles), and *Steinpilze* (cèpes)—are regulars on menus in this area. Pfälzer specialties (☞ Chapter 10) are also common, but the penchant for potatoes yields to *Knödel* (dumplings) and pasta farther south. The latter includes the Swabian and Baden staples *Maultaschen* (stuffed "pockets" of pasta) and *Spätzle* (roundish egg noodles), as well as *Schupfnudeln* (finger-size noodles of potato dough), also called *Bube-* or *Buwespitzle*. Look for *Linsen* (lentils) and sauerkraut in soups or as sides. *Schwäbischer Rostbraten* (beefsteaks topped with fried onions) and *Schäufele* (pickled and slightly smoked pork) are popular meat dishes.

Considerable quantities of red wine are produced along the Neckar Valley. Crisp, light Trollinger is often served in the traditional *Viertele,* a round, quarter-liter (8-ounce) glass with a handle. Deeper-colored, more substantial reds include Spatburgunder (pinot noir) and its mutation Schwarzriesling (pinot meunier), Lemberger, and Dornfelder. Riesling, Kerner, and Müller-Thurgau (synonymous with Rivaner), as well as Grauburgunder (pinot gris) and Weissburgunder (Pinot Blanc) are the typical white wines. A birch-broom or wreath over the doorway of a vintner's home signifies a *Besenwirtschaft* (broomstick inn), a rustic pub where you can enjoy wines with snacks and simple fare.

CATEGORY	COST*
$$$$	over DM 90
$$$	DM 55–DM 90
$$	DM 35–DM 55
$	under DM 35

*per person for a three-course meal, including tax and service and excluding drinks

Festivals

Important cultural festivals for music, opera, and theater include the **Schlossfestspiele** on the castle grounds in Schwetzingen (May), Heidelberg (August), and Zwingenberg (late August). Since 1818 thousands have flocked to the Stuttgart suburb of Cannstatt in early October for the annual **Volksfest** (folk festival). Two wine festivals of particular note are the **Stuttgarter Weindorf** from late August to early September and the **Heilbronner Weindorf** in early September. Last but not least are the fabulous **fireworks** and castle illuminations in Heidelberg (with an arts-and-crafts market on the riverbank) on the first Saturday of June and September, and the second Saturday of July.

Lodging

This area is full of castle-hotels and charming country inns that range in comfort from upscale rustic to luxurious. For a riverside view ask for a *Zimmer* (room) or *Tisch* (table) *mit Neckarblick*. The Neckar Valley offers idyllic alternatives to the cost and crowds of Heidelberg. Driving time from Eberbach, for example, is half an hour; from Bad Wimpfen, about an hour.

CATEGORY	COST*
$$$$	over DM 250
$$$	DM 180–DM 250
$$	DM 120–DM 180
$	under DM 120

Prices are for two people in a double room, including tax and service.

Exploring Heidelberg and the Neckar Valley

From Heidelberg, the route follows the Neckar River upstream (east, then south), with a possible detour west to Schwetzingen. The road snakes between the river and the wooded slopes of the Odenwald (forest) before reaching the rolling, vine-covered countryside around Heilbronn. From there it's a 50-km (31-mi) drive, partly along the Neckar, to Stuttgart. About 40 km (25 mi) farther you rejoin the river at the picturesque university town of Tübingen.

Great Itineraries

Heidelberg is a destination unto itself, but it can also be seen as the major stop on the Burgenstrasse, which makes its way through the narrower parts of the Neckar Valley. Beyond that, you reach the cities of Heilbronn, Stuttgart, and Tübingen, which reflect the region's industry and history.

Numbers in the text correspond to numbers in the margin and on the Neckar Valley and Heidelberg maps.

IF YOU HAVE 3 DAYS

Spend a full day and night exploring ⌖ **Heidelberg** ①–⑯, with its university pleasures. On the second day take a trip up the Neckar to the castles of **Hirschhorn** ㉒ and ⌖ **Hornberg** ㉕ (both have hotels for an overnight stay, with excellent restaurants). On the third day visit the **Staatsgalerie** (State Gallery) in **Stuttgart** ㉙.

IF YOU HAVE 5 DAYS

Spend your first two days and nights in ⌖ **Heidelberg** ①–⑯. On the third day continue up the Neckar to **Burg Guttenberg** (with its aviary of birds of prey) and the castles of **Hirschhorn** ⑲ and ⌖ **Burg Hornberg** ㉒. Stay overnight at one of the many castle hotels in the area. Investigate the remains of the imperial palace and other sights in **Bad Wimpfen** ㉓ on the fourth day and end the trip in the medieval streets of ⌖ **Tübingen** ㉘.

IF YOU HAVE 7 DAYS

Spend your first two days and nights in ⌖ **Heidelberg** ①–⑯. On the third day head up the Neckar to **Burg Guttenberg** and the ⌖ **Hirschhorn** ⑲ Castle, staying there or in ⌖ **Eberbach** ⑳ for two nights. Continue on to explore **Mosbach** ㉑ and the castle at **Burg Hornberg** ㉒, with time out for a river cruise. Spend the fifth day and night in ⌖ **Bad Wimpfen** ㉓, with a possible side trip to the museum of bicycle and motorcycle technology at **Neckarsulm** ㉔. On the sixth day and night visit the sights and enjoy the nightlife of **Stuttgart** ㉖. On day seven stop in **Bebenhausen** ㉗ en route to ⌖ **Tübingen** ㉘, where the journey ends.

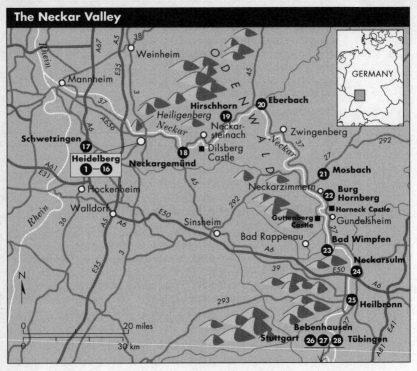

The Neckar Valley

When to Tour Heidelberg and the Neckar Valley
If you plan to visit Heidelberg in summer, make reservations well in
advance and expect to pay top rates. To get away from the crowds,
consider staying out of town and driving or taking the bus into the city.
Hotels and restaurants are much cheaper just a little upriver. A visit in
late fall, when the vines turn a faded gold, or early spring, with the
first green shoots of the year, can be captivating. In the depths of winter, river mists creep through narrow streets of Heidelberg's Old Town
and awaken the ghosts of a romantic past.

THE NECKAR-RHINE TRIANGLE

The natural beauty of Heidelberg is created by the embrace of mountains, forests, vineyards, and the Neckar River, crowned by its ruined
castle. The Neckar and the Rhine meet at nearby Mannheim, a major
industrial center and the second-largest river port in Europe. Inside its
industrial sprawl lurks an elegant Old Town that was carefully rebuilt
after wartime bomb damage. Schwetzingen, known as Germany's
Spargel (asparagus) capital, lies in the triangle's center.

Heidelberg

57 km (35 mi) northeast of Karlsruhe.

If any city in Germany encapsulates the spirit of the country, it is Heidelberg. Scores of poets and composers—virtually the entire 19th-cen-
tury German Romantic movement—have sung its praises. Goethe and
Mark Twain both fell in love here: the German writer with a beautiful
young woman, the American author with the city itself. Sigmund
Romberg set his operetta *The Student Prince* in the city; Carl Maria von
Weber wrote his lushly Romantic opera *Der Freischütz* here. Composer

Robert Schumann was a student at the university. The campaign these artists waged on behalf of the town has been astoundingly successful. Heidelberg's fame is out of all proportion to its size (population 145,000); more than 2½ million visitors crowd its streets every year.

Heidelberg was the political center of the Rhineland Palatinate. At the end of the Thirty Years' War (1618–48), the elector Carl Ludwig married his daughter to the brother of Louis XIV in the hope of bringing peace to the Rhineland. But when the elector's son died without an heir, Louis XIV used the marriage alliance as an excuse to claim Heidelberg, and in 1689 the town was sacked and laid waste. Four years later he sacked the town again. From its ashes arose what you see today: a baroque town built on Gothic foundations, with narrow, twisting streets and alleyways. The new Heidelberg changed under the influence of U.S. army barracks and industrial development stretching into the suburbs, but the old heart of the city remains intact, exuding the spirit of romantic Germany.

A Good Walk

Begin a tour of Heidelberg near Kornmarkt at the **Königstuhl Bergbahn** (funicular) ①, which will take you up to the famous **Schloss** ②, one of Germany's most memorable sights. It was already in ruins when 19th-century Romantics fell under its spell, drawn by the mystery of its Gothic turrets, Renaissance walls, and abandoned gardens. (You can also choose to hike up the winding Burgweg [castle walk] to the complex.) The fascinating **Apothekenmuseum** (Apothecary Museum) is within the castle walls. The funicular can take you higher from the Schloss to **Molkenkur** ③, the site of another castle ruin, and **Königstuhl** ④, a high hill with fine views.

From the Schloss ramparts take the Burgweg down to the city's Altstadt (Old Town), sandwiched between the Neckar River and the surrounding hills. The steep path from the castle ends abruptly near the **Kornmarkt** (Grain Market). Cross the square (north) to Hauptstrasse, an elegant pedestrian street that runs straight through the city. Bear right, and you will immediately enter Karlsplatz; on the far side are two traditional pubs, Zum Sepp'l and Zum Roten Ochsen, where fraternity students have engaged in beer-drinking contests for the last 200-some years. The pub walls are lined with swords, trophies, faded photos, and dueling and drinking paraphernalia. Going left from Kornmarkt, it is only a few steps to the **Marktplatz,** the city's main square. The **Rathaus** ⑤ is a stately baroque building dating from 1701 that fronts the market square. From the center of the square, the late-Gothic **Heiliggeistkirche** ⑥ towers over the city. Just as in medieval times, there are shopping stalls between its buttresses. **Hotel zum Ritter** ⑦, with an elaborate Renaissance facade of curlicues, columns, and gables, stands opposite Heiliggeistkirche. Walking farther down Hauptstrasse west of Marktplatz, you reach Universitätsplatz (University Square) and the **Alte Universität** ⑧, which was founded in 1386 and rebuilt in the early 18th century. It is one of four separate university complexes in the town. Go behind the Old University and down tiny Augustinerstrasse to find the **Studentenkarzer** ⑨, or student prison. Tradition once dictated that the university rather than the police should deal with unruly students. To the south, the **Neue Universität** ⑩ is on the southeast corner of Universitätsplatz. Just off Universitätsplatz, on the street called Plöck, stands the **Universitätsbibliothek** ⑪ (University Library). The Gothic **Peterskirche** ⑫, the city's oldest parish church, is opposite the library.

Next, return to Hauptstrasse and walk west a couple of blocks to visit the **Kurpfälzisches Museum** ⑬, Heidelberg's leading museum, housed in a former baroque palace. Walk back toward Marktplatz and turn

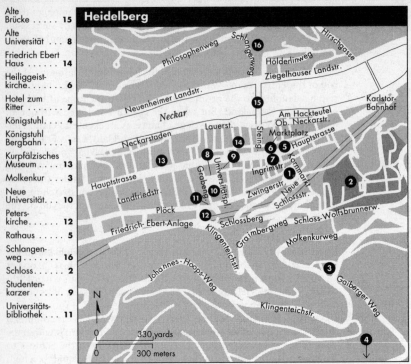

Heidelberg

left at Dreikönigstrasse; a short block brings you to Untere Strasse, where you go right, then immediately left at the first street, called Pfaffengasse. Halfway down the street on the left-hand side (No. 18) is the **Friedrich Ebert Haus** ⑭, the birthplace the president of the ill-fated Weimar Republic. Continue on to the end of the street and turn right along the river to reach the twin turrets of the **Alte Brücke** ⑮. From the bridge you'll have views of the Old Town and the castle above. For the most inspiring view of Heidelberg, climb up the steep, winding **Schlangenweg** ⑯ through the vineyards to the Philosophenweg (Philosophers' Path); then go right and continue through the woods above the river to the Hölderlin Memorial, a grove traditionally frequented by poets and scholars. Try to arrive there as the sun sets and watch the red sandstone castle turn to gold.

TIMING

Allow at least two hours to tour the Schloss—and expect long lines in summer (up to 30 minutes). For the rest of the tour, add another two hours, four if you plan on seeing the collection of the Kurpfälzisches Museum, the manuscript exhibition at the University Library, and the inside of the Student Prison.

Sights to See

⑮ **Alte Brücke** (Old Bridge). Walk onto the bridge from the Old Town under a portcullis spanned by two *Spitzhelm* towers (so called for their resemblance to old-time German helmets). The twin towers were part of medieval Heidelberg's fortifications. In the left (west) tower are three dank dungeons that once held common criminals. Between the towers, above the gate, are more salubrious lockups, with views of the river and the castle; these were reserved for debtors. Above the portcullis you'll see a memorial plaque that pays warm tribute to the Austrian forces who helped Heidelberg beat back a French attempt to capture the bridge in 1799. The bridge itself is the ninth to be built on this spot; ice floes and floods destroyed its predecessors. The elector Carl Theodor, who built it in 1786–88, must have been confident this one would last: He had a statue of himself erected on it, upon a plinth decorated with river gods and goddesses (symbolic of the Rhine, Danube, Neckar, and Mosel rivers). Just to be safe, he also put up a statue of the saint appointed to guard over it, St. John Nepomuk. From the center of the bridge you'll have some of the finest views of the Old Town and the castle above.

❽ Alte Universität (Old University). The three-story baroque structure was built in 1712–18 at the behest of the elector Johann Wilhelm on the site of an earlier university building. The present-day Universitätsplatz (University Square) was built over the remains of an Augustinian monastery that was destroyed by the French in 1693. ⊠ *Grabenstr. 3,* ☎ *06221/544–274.*

⓮ Friedrich Ebert Haus (Friedrich Ebert House). The humble rooms of a tiny back-street apartment were the birthplace of Friedrich Ebert, Germany's first democratically elected president (in 1920) and leader of the ill-fated Weimar Republic. Display cases have documents that tell the story of the tailor's son who took charge of a nation accustomed to being ruled by a kaiser. ⊠ *Pfaffeng. 18,* ☎ *06221/91070.* ⌑ *Free.* ☉ *Tues., Wed., and Fri.–Sun. 10–6, Thurs. 10–8.*

❻ Heiliggeistkirche (Church of the Holy Ghost). The foundation stone of the building was laid in 1398, but it was not actually finished until 1544. Unlike that of most other Gothic churches, the facade of the Heiliggeistkirche is uniform—you cannot discern the choir or naves from the outside. The gargoyles looking down on the south side (where Hauptstrasse crosses Marktplatz) are remarkable for their sheer ugliness. The church fell victim to the plundering General Tilly, leader of the Catholic League during the Thirty Years' War. Tilly loaded the church's greatest treasure—the *Biblioteka Palatina,* at the time the largest library in Germany—onto 500 carts and trundled it off to Rome, where he presented it to the pope. Few volumes found their way back to Heidelberg. At the end of the 17th century, French troops plundered the church again, destroying the family tombs of the Palatinate electors; only the 15th-century tomb of Elector Ruprecht III and his wife, Elisabeth von Hohenzollern, remains today. ⊠ *Marktpl.* ☉ *Daily 9–6 except during services and concerts.*

❼ Hotel zum Ritter. The hotel's name refers to the statue of a Roman knight ("Ritter") atop one of the many gables. Its French builder, Charles Bélier, had the Latin inscription *Persta Invicta Venus* added to the facade in gold letters—"Venus, Remain Unconquerable." It appears this injunction was effective, as this was the city's only Renaissance building to be spared the attentions of the invading French in 1689 and 1693. Between 1695 and 1705 it was used as Heidelberg's town hall; later it became an inn, and it is still a hotel today (☞ Dining and Lodging, *below*). ⊠ *Hauptstr. 178,* ☎ *06221/1350.*

★ ❹ Königstuhl (King's Throne). The second-highest hill in the Odenwald range—1,700 ft above Heidelberg—is only a hop, skip, and funicular ride (☞ **Königstuhl Bergbahn**) from Heidelberg. On a clear day you can see south as far as the Black Forest and west to the Vosges Mountains of France. The hill is at the center of a close-knit network of hiking trails. Signs and colored arrows from the top lead hikers through the woods of the Odenwald.

❶ Königstuhl Bergbahn (funicular). The funicular hoists visitors in 17 minutes to the summit of ☞ **Königstuhl**. On the way it stops at the ruined

Heidelberg ☞ **Schloss** and **Molkenkur.** The funicular leaves every 10 minutes in summer and every 20 or 30 minutes in winter. ✉ *Kornmarkt.* 🎫 *Round-trip to Schloss DM 5.50, round-trip to Königstuhl heights DM 8.50.*

Kornmarkt (Grain Market). One of the oldest squares in Heidelberg, it has a view of the castle ruins and a baroque statue of the Virgin Mary in its center.

⑬ **Kurpfälzisches Museum** (Palatinate Museum). The baroque palace that houses the museum was built as a residence for a university professor in 1712. It's a pleasure just to wander around, which is more or less unavoidable, since the museum's layout is so confusing. The collections chart the history of the city and its region. Among the exhibits are two standouts. One is a replica of the jaw of Heidelberg Man, a key link in the evolutionary chain thought to date from a half-million years ago; the original was unearthed near the city in 1907. The larger attraction is the **Windsheimer Zwölfbotenaltar** (Twelve Apostles Altarpiece), one of the largest and finest works of early Renaissance sculptor Tilman Riemenschneider. Its exquisite detailing and technical sophistication are evident in the simple faith that radiates from the faces of the apostles. On the top floor of the museum there's a rich range of 19th-century German paintings and drawings, many depicting Heidelberg. ✉ *Hauptstr. 97,* ☎ *06221/583–402.* 🎫 *DM 5.* ⊘ *Tues. and Thurs.–Sun. 10–5, Wed. 10–9.*

Marktplatz (Market Square). Heidelberg's main square, with the ☞ **Rathaus** on one side and the ☞ **Heiliggeistkirche** on the other, has been its focal point since the Middle Ages. Public courts of justice were held here in earlier centuries, and people accused of witchcraft and heresy were burned at the stake. The baroque fountain in the middle, the Herkulesbrunnen (Hercules Fountain), is the work of 18th-century artist H. Charrasky. Until 1740 a rotating, hanging cage stood next to it. For minor crimes, people were imprisoned in it and exposed to the laughter, insults, and abuse of their fellow citizens. The square is surrounded by narrow side streets that should be explored.

❸ **Molkenkur.** The next stop after the castle on the ☞ **Königstuhl Bergbahn,** Molkenkur was the site of Heidelberg's second castle. Lightning struck it in 1527, and it was never rebuilt. Today it is occupied by a restaurant with magnificent views of the Odenwald and the Rhine plain.

❿ **Neue Universität** (New University). The plain building on the south side of Universitätsplatz was erected between 1930 and 1932 through funds raised by the U.S. ambassador to Germany, J. G. Schurman, who had been a student at the university. The only decoration on the building's three wings is a statue of Athena, the Greek goddess of wisdom, above the entrance. The inner courtyard contains a medieval tower (1380) incorporated into the newer building—the **Hexenturm** (Witches Tower)—which is all that is left of the old city walls. Suspected witches were locked up there in the Middle Ages. It later became a memorial to former students killed in the First World War. ✉ *Grabeng.,* ☎ *06221/544–274.*

OFF THE
BEATEN PATH

NEUENHEIM – To escape the crowds of Heidelberg, walk across the Theodor Heuss Bridge to the suburb of Neuenheim. At the turn of the century this old fishing village developed into a residential area full of posh Jugendstil (Art Nouveau) villas. North of the Brückenkopf (bridgehead) you'll find antiques and designer shops, boutiques, and cafes on Brückenstrasse, Bergstrasse (one block east), and Ladenburger Strasse (parallel to the river). To savor the neighborhood spirit, visit the charming farmers' market on Wednesday or Saturday mornings at the corner of Ladenburger and Luther streets. The beer pubs Vedder's and O'Reilly's draw a young crowd; the chic bistros Le Coq, Bar d'Aix, and Pastel Rouge cater to a more mature, professional set; and Marktstübel and Dorfschänke serve good food in a casual, cozy atmosphere. All are within a five-minute walk from one another on the streets named above.

⑫ **Peterskirche** (St. Peter's Church). The city's oldest parish church has a graveyard including the final resting places, some more than 500 years old, of many famous Heidelberg citizens. ✉ *Plöck.* ☉ *Daily 9–6 except during services and concerts.*

❺ **Rathaus** (Town Hall). Work began on the town hall in 1701, a few years after the French destroyed the city. The massive coat of arms above the balcony is the work of sculptor Charrasky, who also created the statue of Hercules atop the fountain in the middle of the square. ✉ *Marktpl.*

⑯ **Schlangenweg** (Snake Path). This walkway starts just above the Alte Brücke and cuts steeply through terraced vineyards until it reaches the woods, where it crosses the **Philosophenweg** (Philosophers' Path).

★ ❷ **Schloss** (Castle). What's most striking is the architectural variety of this great complex. The oldest parts still standing date from the 15th century, though most of the castle was built in the Renaissance and baroque styles of the 16th and 17th centuries, when the castle was the seat of the Palatinate electors. There's even an "English wing," built in 1612 by the elector Friedrich V for his teenage Scottish bride, Elizabeth Stuart; its plain, square-window facade is positively foreign compared to the more opulent styles of the castle. (The enamored Friedrich also had a charming garden laid out for his young bride; its imposing arched entryway, the Elisabethentor, was put up overnight as a surprise for her 19th birthday.) The architectural highlight remains the Renaissance courtyard—harmonious, graceful, and ornate.

The castle also includes the **Apothekenmuseum** (Apothecary Museum). This museum, on the lower floor of the Ludwigsbau (Ludwig Building), is filled with ancient carboys and other flagons and receptacles (each with a carefully painted enamel label), beautifully made scales, little drawers, shelves, a marvelous reconstruction of an 18th-century apothecary shop, dried beetles and toads, and a mummy with a full head of hair. (☎ 06221/25880; ✉ DM 3; ☉ mid-Mar.–Oct., daily 10–5; Nov.–mid-Mar., weekends 10–5).

Even if you have to wait, you should make a point of seeing the **Heidelberger Fass** (Heidelberg Wine Barrel), an enormous wine barrel in the cellar, made from 130 oak trees and capable of holding 49,000 gallons. It was used to hold wines paid as taxes by wine growers in the Palatinate. During the rule of the elector Carl Philip, the barrel was guarded by the court jester, a Tyrolean dwarf called Perkeo—when offered wine, he always answered, "*Perche no?*" ("Why not?"), hence his nickname. Legend has it that he could consume frighteningly large quantities of wine and that he died when he drank a glass of water by mistake. A statue of Perkeo stands next to the two-story-high barrel.

The castle may be reached by taking the ☞ **Königstuhl Bergbahn.** Generations of earlier visitors hiked up to it on the Burgweg, a winding road. Of course, it is easier to walk down. In summer there are fireworks displays from the castle terrace (on the first Saturday in June and September and the second Saturday in July). In August the castle hosts an open-air theater festival. Performances of *The Student Prince* figure prominently. *Castle info:* ☎ 06221/538–414. ✉ *Courtyard, Great*

Cask, and Apothekenmuseum DM 4; tours of the interior, an additional DM 4. ☉ *Daily 8–5:30; tours in English weekdays 11:30, 2, 3:45, and by special arrangement.*

9 **Studentenkarzer** (Student Prison). University officials locked students up here from 1778 to 1914—mostly for minor offenses. They could be held for up to 14 days and were left to subsist on bread and water for the first three days; thereafter, they were allowed to attend lectures, receive guests, and have food brought in from the outside. A stay in the jail became as coveted as a scar inflicted in the university's fencing clubs. There's bravado, even poetic flair, to be deciphered from two centuries of graffiti that cover the walls and ceilings of the narrow cells. ✉ *Augustinerg.,* ☎ *06221/542–163.* 💳 *DM 4.* ☉ *Apr.–Oct., Mon.– Sat. 10–4; Nov.–Mar., Tues.–Fri. 10–4.*

11 **Universitätsbibliothek** (University Library). Its 2½ million volumes include the 14th-century *Manesse Codex,* a unique collection of medieval songs and poetry once performed in the courts of Germany by the *Minnesänger* (singers). Unfortunately, the original is too fragile to be exhibited. However, a copy is on display. ✉ *Plöck 107–109,* ☎ *06221/ 542–380.* 💳 *Free.* ☉ *Mon.–Sat. 10–7.*

Dining and Lodging

$$$–$$$$ ✕ **Schlossweinstube.** With its pastel tones and white stucco ceilings the Schlossweinstube's spacious baroque dining room offers refuge from the castle crowds. Apart from two beautiful tiled ovens, decor is modern and minimal. *Ente von Heidelberg* (roast duck with dumplings) is the number one favorite. The bistro Backhaus is more rustic, with wooden tables, sandstone floors, and a nearly 50-ft-high *Backkamin* (baking oven). Regional specialties as well as coffee and cake are served here. You can sample rare wines (Eiswein, Beerenauslese) by the glass in the Fasskeller, or pick up a bottle with a designer label depicting Heidelberg (a nice souvenir). Reservations are essential for terrace seating. ✉ *Schlosshof (on the castle grounds),* ☎ *06221/97970. AE, DC, MC, V. Schlossweinstube closed Jan., Wed. No lunch. Backhaus closed Oct.–Apr.*

$$$ ✕ **Simplicissimus.** Olive oil, garlic, and herbs of Provence accentuate
★ many of chef Johann Lummer's culinary delights. Saddle of lamb is a specialty; the *Dessertteller,* a sampler, is a crowning finish to any meal here. The wine list focuses on old-world estates, particularly clarets. The elegant Jugendstil interior is done in shades of red with dark wood accents. In the summer, dine alfresco in the courtyard. ✉ *Ingrimstr. 16,* ☎ *06221/183–336. AE, MC, V. Closed Tues., 10 days in Feb., and 2 wks in summer. No lunch.*

$$$ ✕ **Zur Herrenmühle.** Ursula and Günter Ueberle's gourmet cuisine is served
★ in a 17th-century grain mill that's been transformed into a romantic, cozy restaurant with an idyllic courtyard. Fish is a specialty. Try the *Variation von Edelfischen* (medley of fine fish), served with homemade noodles. The prix fixe menus (four-course, DM 85) offer good value. ✉ *Hauptstr. 239,* ☎ *06221/602–909. AE, DC, MC, V. Closed Sun. No lunch.*

$–$$ ✕ **Café Journal.** Here is an old-world paradise for coffee and cake, tasty bistro fare, and people-watching. The pedestrians strutting on the Hauptstrasse provide local theater, as do the people indoors. As in its sister cafés in Mannheim and Schwetzingen, newspapers from around the world, hung on hooks, line the walls. It closes at midnight. ✉ *Hauptstr. 162,* ☎ *06221/161–712. AE, MC, V.*

$–$$ ✕ **Schnitzelbank.** A hole-in-the-wall where tourists rarely venture, this old cooper's workshop is now a cozy, candlelit pub filled with locals seated at long wooden tables. It's hard not to fall into conversation with the people at your elbow. The menu features wines and specialties from Baden and the Pfalz, such as *Wurstsuppe* (sausage soup) or a hearty *Schlachtplatte* (a meat-and-sausage sampler). ✉ *Bauamtsg. 7,* ☎ *06221/21189. No credit cards. No lunch Mon.–Thurs.*

$–$$ ✕ **Zum Roten Ochsen.** Many of the rough-hewn oak tables here have initials carved into them, a legacy of the thousands who have visited Heidelberg's most famous old tavern. Bismarck, Mark Twain, and John Foster Dulles may have left their mark—they all ate here. You can wash down simple fare, such as goulash soup and bratwurst, or heartier dishes, like *Tellerfleisch* (boiled beef) and sauerbraten, with German wines or Heidelberg beer. The "Red Ox" has been run by the Spengel family for 160 years. ✉ *Hauptstr. 217,* ☎ *06221/20977,* ℻ *06221/164–383. Reservations essential. No credit cards. Closed Sun. and mid-Dec.–mid-Jan. No lunch Nov.–Mar.*

$ ✕ **Café Knösel.** This very traditional German coffeehouse—and Heidelberg's oldest (1863)—has always been a popular meeting place for students and professors. It's still producing café founder Fridolin Knösel's *Heidelberger Studentenkuss* (student kiss, a chocolate wrapped in paper showing two students touching lips), an acceptable way for 19th-century students to "exchange kisses" in public. ✉ *Haspelg.,* ☎ *06221/22345. No credit cards. Closed Mon.*

$$$$ ✕🏨 **Der Europäischer Hof–Hotel Europa.** This is the most luxurious of Heidelberg's hotels, centrally located, and offering a wide range of facilities. Public rooms are sumptuously furnished, and bedrooms are spacious and tasteful; all suites have whirlpools. In the elegant Kurfürsten-Stube rich shades of yellow and blue are offset by the original woodwork of 1865. In the summer meals are served on the fountain-lined terrace. There are great views of the castle from the glass-lined fitness and wellness centers. ✉ *Friedrich-Ebert-Anlage 1, D–69117,* ☎ *06221/5150,* ℻ *06221/515–506. 102 rooms, 16 suites. Restaurant, bar, coffee shop, minibars, no-smoking rooms, indoor pool, beauty salon, sauna, steam room, exercise room. AE, DC, MC, V.* ✺

$$$$ ✕🏨 **Hotel Hirschgasse.** This historical hotel (1472) is across the river
★ opposite Karlstor, yet only a 15-minute walk to the center of Old Town. The Mensur-Stube was once a tavern where university students indulged their fencing duels, and Mark Twain mentions it in *A Tramp Abroad.* Today it serves regional fare from Baden and the Pfalz. As the name implies, Le Gourmet is the more elegant, upscale of the two restaurants, serving cuisine with Mediterranean accents. Its beamed ceiling and exposed stone walls are quite cozy, as are the rooms, all decorated in Laura Ashley style. ✉ *Hirschg. 3, D–69120,* ☎ *06221/4540,* ℻ *06221/454–111. 20 suites. 2 restaurants, minibars. DC, MC, V. Le Gourmet closed Sun.–Mon. No lunch.* ✺

$$$$ ✕🏨 **Romantik Hotel zum Ritter St. Georg.** If this is your first visit to
★ Germany, try to stay here. It's the only Renaissance building in Heidelberg, and its historical ambience is unique. Some rooms are more modern and spacious than others, but all are comfortable. You can enjoy German and international favorites in the restaurant Belier or in the Ritterstube. Both are wood paneled and offer old-world charm. ✉ *Hauptstr. 178, D–69117,* ☎ *06221/1350,* ℻ *06221/135–230. 39 rooms, 36 with bath; 1 suite. 2 restaurants, minibars. AE, DC, MC, V.* ✺

$$$ ✕🏨 **Kultur-Brauerei.** Rooms with warm, sunny colors and modern decor are brilliantly incorporated into this old malt factory in the heart of Old Town. Smoking is not allowed in any guest room. The restaurant is a lively meeting place from breakfast time until well past midnight. Beer is the beverage of choice here (although there are two wines from the excellent Baden estate Dr. Heger), and both go well with the Baden and traditional German specialties. Try the *Rinderrouladen* (beef roulades) or *Spannferkel* (roast suckling pig). The cellar houses the brewery as well as a jazz club on weekends. ✉ *Grosse Leyerg. 6, D–69117,*

☎ *06221/90000,* FAX *06221/900–090.21 rooms, 1 suite. Restaurant, minibars, no-smoking rooms. AE, DC, MC, V.*

$$$ ✕⊞ **Weisser Bock.** Exposed beams and stucco ceilings are part of this hotel's charm. Rooms are individually decorated with warm wood furnishings and offer modern comfort. All rooms are no-smoking. Light and airy, the restaurant looks almost Mediterranean with its warm shades of mandarin orange and pale yellow. Art Deco fans will be charmed. Well-prepared, creative cuisine is on offer, particularly fresh fish. The homemade smoked salmon and an unusual cream of Jerusalem artichoke soup with crayfish are recommended. The proprietor is a great wine fan and the extensive wine list reflects it. ⊠ *Grosse Mantelg. 24, D–69117,* ☎ *06221/90000,* FAX *06221/900–090. 21 rooms, 21 suites. Restaurant, minibars, no-smoking rooms. AE, DC, MC, V.*

$$–$$$ ✕⊞ **Schnookeloch.** This picturesque and lively old tavern dates from 1703 and is inextricably linked with Heidelberg's history and its university. Look for men both old and young with scars on their cheeks. There are still a handful of students who duel with swords, crazy as it might sound. Every evening a piano player chimes in. Upstairs there are modern, pleasantly furnished guest rooms. ⊠ *Haspelg. 8, D–69117,* ☎ *06221/138–080,* FAX *06221/138–0813. 11 rooms. Restaurant, beer garden, minibars. AE, DC, MC, V.*

$$ ✕⊞ **Gasthaus Backmulde.** This traditional tavern in the heart of Heidelberg has a surprising range of items on its menu, from delicately marinated fresh vegetables that accompany the excellent meat dishes to imaginative soups that add modern flair to ancient recipes (a Franconian potato broth, for instance, rich with garden herbs). Guest rooms are small but comfortable. ⊠ *Schiffg. 11, D–69117,* ☎ *06221/53660,* FAX *06221/536–660. 13 rooms. Restaurant. No credit cards.*

$$$–$$$$ ⊞ **Holländer Hof.** The pink-and-white-painted facade of this ornate 19th-century building, across from the Old Bridge, stands out in the row of buildings fronting the Neckar River. Many of its rooms overlook the busy waterway and the forested hillside above the opposite shore. The rooms are modern and pleasant. ⊠ *Neckarstaden 66, D–69117,* ☎ *06221/60500,* FAX *06221/605–060. 38 rooms, 1 suite. Minibars, no-smoking floor. AE, DC, MC, V.*

$$ ⊞ **Hotel Kohler.** It's a little bit of a walk to the city's Old Town but only a couple of minutes by bus. Rooms are impeccably clean, well lighted, and equipped with solid hardwood furniture and double-glazed windows. ⊠ *Goethestr. 2, D–69115,* ☎ *06221/970–097,* FAX *06221/970–096. 43 rooms. No-smoking rooms, bicycles. MC, V. Closed late Dec.–mid.-Jan.*

$ ⊞ **Jugendherberge Tiergartenstrasse.** Here's a clean, cheap youth hostel that can provide you with a good night's sleep. If you plan to stay out past the 11:30 curfew, you'll have to get a key. A bed with breakfast costs DM 29 if you're over 27 years old. From the Hauptbahnhof, take Bus 33 to Jugendherberge (last bus 11:50 PM); reception is open 7:30 AM–9 AM and 1 PM–11:30 PM. There's wheelchair access on the first floor. ⊠ *Tiergartenstr. 5,* ☎ *06221/412–066. 200 beds. Coin laundry. No credit cards.*

Nightlife and the Arts

Information on all upcoming events is given in the monthly *Heidelberg Aktuell,* free and available from the tourist office or on the Internet (www.heidelberg-aktuell.de). Theater tickets may be purchased at the **Theaterkasse** (⊠ Theaterstr. 4, ☎ 06221/583–520).

THE ARTS

Heidelberg has a thriving theater scene. The **Kulturzentrum Karlstorbahnhof** (Cultural Center Karlstor train station; ⊠ Am Karlstor 1, ☎

06221/978–920) is a 19th-century train station reincarnated as a the-ater, cinema, and café. The **Theater der Stadt** (✉ Theaterstr. 4, ☎ 06221/583–523) is the best-known theater in town. The **Zimmer Theater** (✉ Hauptstr. 118, ☎ 06221/21069) is known for avant-garde productions. For information on **performances at the castle** during the annual Schloss-Spiele festival, call 06221/21341.

NIGHTLIFE

Heidelberg nightlife is concentrated in the area around the Heiliggeistkirche (Church of the Holy Ghost), in the Old Town. Don't miss a visit to one of the old student taverns for a drink. There are no better places to try than **Zum Roten Ochsen** and **Schnookeloch** (☞ Din-ing and Lodging, *above*), both of which have been in business for sev-eral centuries and have the atmosphere to prove it. But today's students are more likely to hang out in one of the dozen or more bars on **Un-tere Strasse,** which runs parallel to and between Hauptstrasse and the Neckar River, starting from Market Square. Begin at one end of the street and work your way down; you'll find bars that specialize in all sorts of tastes: Spanish wine, house music, motorcycles, whiskey, and "alternative" atmosphere. The fanciest bars and yuppie cafés are along **Hauptstrasse.**

Cave 54. The "54" refers to the year the Cave opened, making it one of the oldest jazz cellars in Germany. It's the only club in town for se-rious jazz fans and has a way of suddenly filling up after midnight. There's often dancing after sets. ✉ *Krämerg. 2,* ☎ *06221/27840.* 💷 *DM 10 for live performances.*

Goldener Reichsapfel. Smoky, loud, and always crowded after 10 PM, this old beer hall attracts folks with live music on some nights. It may not yet qualify as historic, but the atmosphere is cozy. ✉ *Untere Str. 35.* ☎ *06221/27950.*

Schwimmbad Musik Club. This multiculti venue is a fixture of Heidelberg nightlife, with its ambitious concert program (Nirvana used to come here), DJs, disco, videos, and movies. Theme evenings and parties round out the offerings. ✉ *Tiergartenstr. 13 (near the zoo),* ☎ *06221/470–201. Closed Mon. and Tues.*

Vetters Alt-Heidelberger Brauhaus. It's worth elbowing your way into this brewery-tavern for the brewed-on-the-premises beer. There is also a branch in Neuenheim (across the river) with a butcher shop, where the homemade sausage is produced for both pubs. ✉ *Steing. 9,* ☎ *06221/165–850.*

Outdoor Activities and Sports

SWIMMING

Heidelberg has a pool fed by thermal water at Vangerowstrasse 4 and pools at the extensive Tiergartenschwimmbad, next to the zoo.

TENNIS

Most tennis clubs along the Neckar accept visitors. In Heidelberg you can play at the **Tennis-Inn** (✉ Harbigweg 1, ☎ 06221/12106).

Shopping

Heidelberg's **Hauptstrasse,** or Main Street, is a pedestrian zone lined with shops, sights, and restaurants that stretches more than 1 km (½ mi) through the heart of town. But don't spend your money here be-fore exploring the shops on side streets like **Plöck, Ingrimstrasse,** and **Untere Strasse,** where there are candy stores, bookstores, and antiques shops on the ground floors of baroque buildings. If your budget allows, the city can be a good place to find reasonably priced German antiques, and the Neckar Valley region produces fine glass and crystal.

Heidelberg has an open-air **market** on Wednesday and Sunday mornings in Marktplatz, the central market square, between the town hall and Holy Ghost Church.

Antik Vitrine. On a side street off the Hauptstrasse, this shop is where owner Gertrud Schultz both repairs and sells antiques and small objets d'art. It's what the Germans call *klein aber fein* (small but fine). ✉ *Ziegelg. 26,* ☎ *06221/166–990.*

Aurum & Argentum. In this shop you'll find a local gold- and silversmith with impeccable craftsmanship and very reasonable prices; the finely executed pieces start at DM 150. Its hours are Tuesday–Friday 2–6:30. ✉ *Mönchhofpl. 3,* ☎ *06221/473–453.*

Edm. König. If you're looking for gifts, stop by this address for a good selection of crystal, porcelain, ceramics, and handicrafts. ✉ *Hauptstr. 124, am Uni-Pl.,* ☎ *06221/20929.*

Heidelberger Zuckerladen. The old glass display cases contain lollipops, as well as flower bouquets made out of chocolate, and wonderful apple tarts. This is the sort of place your grandparents came to for "penny" candy. ✉ *Plöck 52,* ☎ *06221/24365.*

Picobello. Even if you didn't come to Heidelberg to buy a 1950s-era ashtray or martini shaker, it's still worth crossing the street from the Gothic St. Peter's Church and looking into this shop for its collection of '50s and '60s "antiques" and household items. ✉ *Klingentorstr. 6,* ☎ *06221/164–100.*

Unholtz. Buy your cutlery and tableware here and keep it for life—it's made by Solingen, the famous German manufacturer of some of the world's best knives. ✉ *Hauptstr. 160,* ☎ *06221/20964.*

Schwetzingen

⑰ *7 mi west of Heidelberg.*

Schwetzingen is famous for its **Schloss,** a formal 18th-century palace constructed as a summer residence by the Palatinate electors. It's a noble, rose-color building, imposing and harmonious; a highlight is the charming rococo theater in one wing. The extensive park blends formal French and informal English styles, with neatly bordered gravel walks trailing off into the dark woodland. The 18th-century planners of this delightful oasis had fun adding such touches as an exotic mosque, complete with minarets and a shimmering pool (although they got a little confused and gave the building a very baroque portal), and the "classical ruin" that was de rigueur in this period. ☎ *06202/81482.* ⌂ *Palace (including tour and gardens), Apr.–Oct. DM 9; Nov.–Mar. DM 8; gardens only, Apr.–Oct. DM 4.50; Nov.–Mar. DM 3.50.* ☉ *Palace: Apr.–Oct., Tues.–Fri. 10–4, weekends 10–5; Nov.–Mar., Fri. tour at 2 PM, weekend tours at 11, 2, and 3. Gardens: Apr.–Oct., daily 8–8; Nov.–Mar., daily 9–5.*

Another rare pleasure awaits you if you're in Schwetzingen in April, May, or June: the town is Germany's asparagus center, and fresh asparagus dishes dominate the menu of every local restaurant.

Dining and Lodging

$$$ ✕▥ **Romantik Hotel Goldener Löwe.** The Lion has been a favorite staging stop for travelers for two centuries. The attractive old house, with its steep, dormer-windowed roof, was originally a butcher shop and wine tavern. Now it's a very welcoming hotel and an excellent restaurant, although the wine tavern is still in place, basically unchanged. The restaurant serves imaginatively prepared Palatinate specialties—

the marinated beef is a must. There are comfortable rooms, some with exposed beams, all individually furnished. ⊠ *Schloss Str. 4, D–68723 Schwetzingen,* ☎ *06202/28090,* ℻ *06202/10726. 15 rooms, 1 suite, 3 apartments. Restaurant, minibars. AE, DC, MC, V.*

The Arts
The leading arts event in this region is the annual **Schwetzingen Festival,** in May and June, which features operas and concerts by international artists in the lovely rococo theater of Schwetzingen Palace (☎ 06202/4933 for information from local tourist office).

THE BURGENSTRASSE (CASTLE ROAD)

Upstream from Heidelberg, the Neckar Valley narrows, presenting a landscape of orchards, vineyards, and wooded hills crowned with castles rising above the gently flowing stream. It's one of the most impressive stretches of the Burgenstrasse. The small valleys along the Neckar Valley road (B–37)—the locals call them *Klingen*—that cut north into the Odenwald are off-the-beaten-track territory. One of the most atmospheric is the **Wolfsschlucht,** which starts below the castle at Zwingenberg. The dank, shadowy little gorge inspired Carl Maria von Weber's opera *Der Freischütz* (The Marksman).

Neckargemünd

⑱ *11 km (7 mi) upstream from Heidelberg.*

The first town on the Burgenstrasse is Neckargemünd, once a bustling river town. Today it's a sleepy sort of place, although it can make a good base from which to see Heidelberg.

Dining and Lodging
$$–$$$ ✕ **Landgasthof Die Rainbach.** This long-popular country inn 2 km (1 mi) east of Neckargemünd, in the Rainbach district, offers quality cuisine and hearty traditional fare. If the weather's good, take a table on the terrace, which commands a view of the river. In winter warm up in the paneled restaurant with a dish of venison stew or any of the freshly prepared soups. ⊠ *Ortstr. 9,* ☎ *06223/2455. MC, V. Closed Mon.*

$$$ ✕🏨 **Hotel zum Schwanen.** At this family-run inn on the Neckar, op-
★ posite the village of Neckargemünd (on the northern riverbank), you can dine in a garden by the river or in the glassed-in dining room. The kitchen serves regional specialties and hearty dishes like pork medallions in a Calvados cream sauce. The owners and staff are courteous and the recently redecorated rooms have solid, rustic furnishings, river views, and thick down comforters. ⊠ *Uferstr. 16, D–69151 Neckargemünd–Kleingemünd,* ☎ *06223/92400,* ℻ *06223/2413. 20 rooms. AE, MC, V.*

$$–$$$ 🏨 **Hotel zum Ritter.** Built in the 13th century, the half-timber zum Ritter has appropriately aged exposed beams and satisfyingly creaky passages. The hotel overlooks the Neckar, as do 20 rooms. Park on the riverbank. ⊠ *Neckarstr. 40,* ☎ *06223/92350,* ℻ *06223/73339. 36 rooms. AE, MC, V.*

En Route Eight kilometers (5 miles) farther along the Neckar Valley road, perched impregnably on a hill, is **Burg Dilsberg** (🎫 DM 2; ⊙ Apr.–Oct., Tues.–Sun. 10–5:30), one of the few castles hereabouts to have withstood General Tilly's otherwise all-conquering forces in the Thirty Years' War. Until the student prison in Heidelberg was built, the castle's dungeons were used to accommodate the university's more unruly dissidents. The view from its battlements, over the valley and the green expanse of the Odenwald beyond, is worth the climb.

Opposite Dilsberg is **Neckarsteinach,** known as the *Vierburgenstadt* (Town of the Four Castles). What remains of the castles is largely ruins. The sections that are still intact make up the baronial residence of an aristocratic German family.

Hirschhorn

⑲ *8 km (5 mi) east of Neckarsteinach, 23 km (14 mi) east of Heidelberg.*

The pretty little town of Hirschhorn has a **castle,** which is one of a number of ancient structures above the Neckar that have been converted into hotel-restaurants. The view is superb. If you don't plan to stay here, a stop for lunch would certainly be worthwhile.

Dining and Lodging

$$$ ✕▥ **Schlosshotel auf der Burg Hirschhorn.** This very pleasant hotel and
★ restaurant is set in historical Hirschhorn Castle, perched high over the medieval village and the Neckar. The terrace offers splendid views (ask for table No. 30 in the corner). The rooms have pretty furnishings and offer modern comfort. Eight are in the castle and 17 in the old stables. *Wildschwein* (wild boar), *Hirsch* (venison), and fresh fish are the house specialties. The friendly proprietors, the Oberrauners, offer a delicious, warm Apfelstrudel based on a recipe from their home in Vienna. A good selection of wines is available. ✉ *D–69434 Hirschhorn/Neckar,* ☎ *06272/1373,* ⅻ *06272/3267. 25 rooms, 4 suites. Restaurant, café, minibars. AE, MC, V. Closed Dec. 15–Jan. 1.* 🐾

Eberbach

⑳ *11 km (7 mi) east of Hirschhorn.*

The landscape around romantic Eberbach is punctuated by four square towers from the medieval town fortifications and three castle ruins. Historic houses abound, and on **Alter Markt** (old market square) there is a particularly fine sgraffito facade to admire, the **Hotel Karpfen** (☞ Dining and Lodging, *below*). Stop by the **Naturpark-Informationzentrum** (Natural Park Info Center) for details about the extensive hiking trails through the Odenwald forest. The Neckar makes a wide bend here, interrupting its northerly course to flow west until its confluence with the Rhine west of Heidelberg.

Dining and Lodging

$$$ ✕▥ **Altes Badhaus.** Just walking by it, you'd never guess that this 14th-
★ century half-timber house was once the bathhouse of Eberbach's elite. Today it houses Jürgen Horn's cozy restaurant, with simpler fare in the historical vaulted cellar, and a few very pretty, modern guest rooms. Pretty shades of green, a beautiful wooden ceiling, fresh flowers, and candlelight create a wonderful ambience for Chef Ingmar Oppenberg's creative repertoire. He is fond of preparing duck, lamb, and lobster. The rustic Badstube offers regional specialties, such as Schäufele, *Kässpätzle* (a gratin version of these wonderful noodles), and boiled beef with horseradish sauce. The international wine list includes many fine local estates. ✉ *Lindenpl. 1, D–69412,* ☎ *06271/92300,* ⅻ *06271/ 923–040. 7 rooms. 2 restaurants, minibars. AE, MC, V. Restaurant Altes Badhaus closed Mon. No lunch.*

$$–$$$ ✕▥ **Hotel Karpfen.** Behind the beautiful painted facade of this traditional hotel and restaurant awaits a warm welcome from the Rohrlapper and Jung families. The wooden furnishings and floors lend the rooms warmth and a rustic charm. The restaurant has pretty wallpapered walls and antique rose accents, a nice setting for fresh *Forelle* (trout) from the streams of the Odenwald forest, game, and regional specialties, including local wines. ✉ *Am Alten Markt 1, D–69412,* ☎ *06271/71015,* FAX *06271/71010. 50 rooms. Restaurant. AE, MC, V. Closed 4 wks in Feb. and Mar. Restaurant closed Tues.*

En Route Eight kilometers (5 miles) beyond Eberbach, a castle stands above the village of **Zwingenberg,** its medieval towers thrusting through the dark woodland. Some say it's the most romantic of all the castles along the Neckar (the one at Heidelberg excepted). The annual **Schloss-Spiele** festivals take place within its ancient walls throughout the summer. For program information and tickets, contact Rathaus Zwingenberg (✉ D–69439 Zwingenberg, ☎ 06251/70030).

Mosbach

㉑ *25 km (16 mi) southeast of Eberbach.*

The little town of Mosbach is one of the most charming towns on the Neckar, and its ancient market square contains one of Germany's most exquisite half-timber buildings—the early 17th-century **Palm'sches Haus** (Palm House), its upper stories laced with intricate timbering. The **Rathaus** (town hall), built 50 years earlier, is a modest affair by comparison.

Dining and Lodging

$$–$$$ ✕ **Zum Ochsen.** Chef Achim Münch and his charming American wife,
★ Heyley, run this country inn in Nüstenbach, a suburb north of Mosbach proper. The decor is stylish—one room elegant, the other more rustic. The interesting display of antique silver is also for sale. Fresh, seasonal cuisine means there's always something new to try, but fish is always featured. Mixed *Fisch* is a good sampler, either as an entrée or as part of the very reasonably priced prix fixe menus. There is a good selection of wines available (also by the glass) at very fair prices. ✉ *Im Weiler 6,* ☎ FAX *06261/15428. No credit cards. Closed 2 wks in Feb. or Mar., 3 wks in Aug., and Tues. No lunch Mon.–Sat.*

$$ ✕▥ **Zum Lamm.** The half-timber Lamb on Mosbach's main street is one of the town's prettiest houses. Its cozy rooms are individually furnished, with flowers filling the window boxes. The restaurant, complete with requisite exposed beams, serves local and international dishes, incorporating meat from the hotel's own butcher shop. ✉ *Hauptstr. 59, D–74821,* ☎ *06261/89020,* FAX *06261/890–291. 50 rooms. Restaurant. AE, MC, V.*

Ballooning

Ebullient Irene Bering offers hot-air-balloon tours of the Neckar Valley and countryside for DM 400 per person. Flights last 1–1½ hours, but with prep time and return trip to starting point, allow 4–5 hours. Contact **Balloon Tours** (☎ 06261/18477, FAX 06261/37277) at the *Flugplatz* (airfield) in Mosbach-Lohrbach.

Neckarzimmern

5 km (3 mi) south of Mosbach.

㉒ The massive circular bulk of **Burg Hornberg** rises above the woods that drop to the riverbank and the town of Neckarzimmern. The road to the castle leads through vineyards that have been providing excellent dry white wines for centuries. Today the castle is part hotel-restaurant and part museum. In the 16th century it was home to the larger-than-life knight Götz von Berlichingen (1480–1562). When he lost his right arm fighting in a petty dynastic squabble—the War of the Landshut Succession, in 1504—he had a blacksmith fashion an iron replacement for him. The original designs for this fearsome artificial limb are on view in the castle, as is a suit of armor that belonged to him. Scenes from his life are also represented. For most Germans, the rambunctious knight is best remembered for a remark he delivered to the Palatinate elector that was faithfully reproduced by Goethe in his play (called simply, *Götz von Berlichingen*). Responding to a reprimand, von Berlichingen told the elector, more or less, to "kiss my ass" (the original German is substantially more earthy). To this day the polite version of this insult is known as a "Götz von Berlichingen." Ask the hotel receptionist where the entrance to the castle is. ⌑ *DM 3.50.*

Dining and Lodging

$$$ ✕⛫ **Burg Hornberg.** Your host is the present baron of the castle. The
★   hotel's rooms are comfortable and tastefully decorated. There are stunning views from the Panorama Restaurant and the terrace. Fresh fish and game are house specialties as are its own estate-bottled wines. They have excellent Riesling wines and the rarities Traminer and Muskateller. ✉ *D–74865 Neckarzimmern,* ☎ *06261/92460,* FAX *06261/ 924–644. 22 rooms, 2 suites. Restaurant. MC, V. Closed Jan.* ✎

Shopping

The factory **Franz Kaspar** (✉ Hauptstr. 11, ☎ 06261/923–014), known for its fine crystal, gives tours weekdays 8–3, Saturday 8–noon (call ahead for reservations) that demonstrate the manufacturing process; it has an outlet with a wide selection. Near the factory, and at the foot of the hill leading to Burg Hornberg, the **Schlosskellerei** (☎ 06261/ 5001) sells wine weekdays 10–5. Within Burg Hornberg's courtyard, the **wine shop** (☎ 06261/5001) is open from April through October, weekends 10–5.

En Route   The fine medieval **Schloss Horneck** (Horneck Castle; ⌑ DM 3; ☉ Tues.– Sun. 11–5), 5 km (3 mi) upriver, south of Burg Hornburg, was destroyed during the Peasants' War (1525) by Götz von Berlichingen and his troops. It was subsequently rebuilt and stands in all its medieval glory. Once it was owned by the Teutonic Knights; today it houses a home for the elderly and a local history museum.

A few bends of the river south of Schloss Horneck bring you to one of the best preserved of the Neckar castles, the 15th-century **Burg Guttenberg.** Within its stout stone walls is a restaurant with fine views of the river valley. The castle is also home to Europe's leading center for the study and protection of birds of prey, and some are released on demonstration flights from the castle walls from March through November, daily at 11 and 3. ☎ 06266/388. ⌑ *Castle DM 3, birds of prey demonstration DM 12. ☉ Mar.–mid-Nov., daily 9–6.*

Bad Wimpfen

★ ㉓   *8 km (5 mi) south of Neckarzimmern.*

The ancient hill town of Bad Wimpfen is one of the most stunning sights on the Neckar River. The Romans founded it in the 1st century AD, building a fortress here and a bridge across the Neckar. By the early Middle Ages, Bad Wimpfen had become an imperial center; the 12th-century emperor Barbarossa built his largest **palace** here. Much of what remains is open to the public, including the city walls, the Blue and Red towers, and imperial living quarters with their stately pillared windows, from which the royal inhabitants enjoyed fine views of the river below. ✉ *Kaiserpl.,* ☎ *07063/97200. ☉ Tours daily; reserve in advance.*

Germany's oldest sentry watchtower, the spectacular turreted **Blauer Turm** (Blue Tower) stands sentinel above Bad Wimpfen. Part of the fortress wall is intact and leads to the more austere **Roter Turm** (Red

Tower). After you've seen the towers and city walls, explore the small, winding streets of the historic center, a picture-postcard jumble of Gothic and Renaissance buildings. **Klostergasse** (Monastery Alley), a stage set of a street, is the standout. If you want to see the town in more detail, follow the walking tour marked by signs bearing the town arms—an eagle with a key in its beak; it begins at the Rathaus. Highlights of the tour are two churches. The early Gothic **Ritterstiftskirche** (Knights' Church) **of Sts. Peter and Paul** stands on a charming square shaded by gnarled chestnut trees. The rough-hewn Romanesque facade is the oldest part of the church, left standing when the town ran out of money after rebuilding the remainder of the church in Gothic style in the 13th century. The outline of the original walls is clearly visible on the floor inside. The cloisters are delightful, an example of German Gothic at its most uncluttered. The **Stiftskirche** (parish church) on the market square is among the oldest in the country. Be sure to see its 13th-century stained glass.

☞ In Germany pigs are a symbol of good luck. At the **Schweine-Museum** (Pig Museum), you'll see them in every form imaginable—depicted on posters and porcelain, modeled into household items, and as toys, including Porky Pig. In all, it's an interesting mixture of historically valuable items and kitsch. ⊠ *Kronengässchen 2,* ☎ *07063/6689.* ☞ *DM 5.* ☉ *Daily 10–5.*

Dining and Lodging

$$ ✕ **Tafelhaus Perkeo.** The interior and decor of this lovingly restored historical house is warm and inviting. Alexander Herforth and Danica Neff are the cordial young hosts, who opened this restaurant after completing a culinary apprenticeship in California. Their menu (also in English) offers upscale Swabian cooking and a generous selection of local Württemberg wines. Try the cream of garlic soup or *Schweinefilet Perkeo* (pork fillet with glazed grapes in a sherry cream sauce). ⊠ *Hauptstr. 82,* ☎ *07063/951–656. No credit cards. Closed Mon.*

$$–$$$$ ✕☒ **Hotel Schloss Heinsheim.** Since 1721 the von Racknitz family has
★ owned this baroque castle set in a beautiful park. The rooms are individually decorated—some with antiques, others are more rustic in style. You can dine on the terrace or in the restaurant, decorated in country manor style. Start with a Swabian *Hochzeitssuppe* (wedding soup), followed by breast of duck with pink peppercorns or Dover sole in champagne sauce. Most wines on the list are French or German (Baden, Württemberg). ⊠ *Gundelsheimer Str. 36, D–74906 Bad Rappenau,* ☎ *07264/95030,* ☏ *07264/4208. 40 rooms, 1 suite. Restaurant, bar, minibars, no-smoking rooms, pool, boating, bicycles. AE, DC, MC, V. Closed Jan. Restaurant closed Mon. and Tues.* ✿

$$ ✕☒ **Hotel Sonne und Weinstube Feyerabend.** This family-run hotel right in the center of town has rooms in two medieval half-timber buildings. The atmosphere is cozy throughout, with upholstered antiques, low ceilings, and thick down comforters. The tavern serves local specialties—Spätzle, fish, and game in season. ⊠ *Hauptstr. 87 and 74, D–74206,* ☎ *07063/245. 18 rooms. Restaurant, Weinstube. MC, V. Closed late Dec.–Jan. Restaurant also closed Sun. evening and Thurs.*

$$ ☒ **Hotel Neckarblick.** The Sailer family, which owns the hotel, extends the warmest of welcomes to its guests. There's a peaceful terrace, where you can sit in summer and watch the Neckar River meander by. Many rooms have a view and flower boxes in the windows. The furniture is comfortable and modern, like the hotel building. For medieval atmosphere, the heart of Bad Wimpfen is only a few blocks away. ⊠ *Erich-Sailer-Str. 48, D–74206,* ☎ *07063/961–620.* ☏ *07063/8548. 14 rooms. Lounge, minibars, bicycles. No credit cards.*

Neckarsulm

④ *10 km (6 mi) south of Bad Wimpfen.*

Motorbike fans won't want to miss the town of Neckarsulm. It's a busy little industrial center, home of the German automobile manufacturer Audi and site of the **Deutsches Zweirad Museum** (German Motorcycle Museum). It's close to the factory where motorbikes were first manufactured in Germany. Among its 350 exhibits are the world's first mass-produced motorcycles (the Hildebrand and Wolfmüller), a number of famous racing machines, and a rare Daimler machine, the first made by that legendary name. The museum also has an exhibit of early bicycles, dating from 1817, as well as early automobiles. All are arranged over five floors in a handsome 400-year-old building that belonged to the Teutonic Knights until 1806. ⊠ *Urbanstr. 11.* 🎫 *DM 7.* 🕐 *Tues.–Sun. 9–5.*

Dining and Lodging

\$\$\$–\$\$\$\$ ✕🏨 **Schloss Lehen.** Chef Friedheinz Eggensperger and his wife, Heike,
★   are the gracious hosts of this lovely castle dating from the 12th century. The former moat is now an idyllic park. All rooms are stylish, decorated with antique or modern furnishings. The restaurant Lehenstube has a rustic elegance; the restaurant Rittersaal is homey, with wood paneling and an old tiled oven. Both offer seasonal and regional specialties prepared from top-quality ingredients, and an excellent selection of wines. ⊠ *Hauptstr. 2, D–74177 Bad Friedrichshall–Kochendorf,* ☎ *07136/98970,* 𝖥𝖠𝖷 *07136/989–720. 25 rooms, 2 suites. 2 restaurants, minibars, boating, bicycles. AE, MC, V.* 🐾

SWABIAN CITIES

Heilbronn, Stuttgart, and Tübingen are all part of the ancient province of Swabia, a region strongly influenced by Protestantism and Calvinism. The inhabitants speak the Swabian dialect of German. Heilbronn lies on both sides of the Neckar. Stuttgart, the capital of the state of Baden-Würtemberg and one of Germany's leading industrial cities, is surrounded by hills on three sides, with the fourth side opening up toward its river harbor. The medieval town of Tübingen clings to steep slopes and hilltops above the Neckar.

Heilbronn

㉕ *6 km (4 mi) south of Neckarsulm, 50 km (31 mi) north of Stuttgart.*

Most of the leading sights in Heilbronn are grouped in and around the Marktplatz, which is dominated by the sturdy **Rathaus** (town hall), built in the Gothic style in 1417 and remodeled during the Renaissance. Set into the Rathaus's clean-lined facade and beneath the steep red roof
★   is a magnificently ornate 16th-century **clock.** It's divided into four distinct parts. The lowest is an astronomical clock, showing the day of the week, the month, and the year. Above it is the main clock—note how its hour hand is larger than the minute hand, a convention common in the 16th century. Above this there's a smaller dial that shows the phases of the sun and the moon. The final clock is a bell at the topmost level. Suspended from a delicate stone surround, it's struck alternately by the two angels on either side. The entire elaborate mechanism swings into action at noon. As the hour strikes, an angel at the base of the clock sounds a trumpet; another turns an hourglass and counts the hours with a scepter. Simultaneously, the twin golden rams between them charge each other and lock horns while a cockerel spreads its wings and crows. Behind the market square is the **Kilianskirche** (Church of

St. Kilian), Heilbronn's most famous church, dedicated to the Irish monk who brought Christianity to the Rhineland in the Dark Ages and who lies buried in Würzburg. Its lofty Gothic tower was capped in the early 16th century with a fussy, lanternlike structure that ranks as the first major Renaissance work north of the Alps. At its summit there's a soldier carrying a banner decorated with the city arms. Walk around the church to the south side (the side opposite the main entrance) to see the well that gave the city its name.

Dining and Lodging

$–$$$ ✕ **Ratskeller.** For sturdy and dependable regional specialties—such as pork medallions in a mushroom cream sauce—and as much Teutonic atmosphere as you'll ever want, you won't go wrong in this restaurant in the town hall cellar. ⊠ *Marktpl. 7,* ☎ *07131/84628. AE, DC, MC, V. Closed 2 wks in late Sept. and Sun.*

$–$$$ ✕ **Restaurant-Café Harmonie.** Eat on the terrace in summer to enjoy the view of the city park. Inside, the decor is traditional with a modern twist, as is the menu. For best value, try one of the prix fixe menus. Swabian specialties, such as Rostbraten and *sauere Kutteln*(tripe), are also available. ⊠ *Am Stadtgarten, Allee 28,* ☎ *07131/87954. AE, DC, MC, V. Closed Tues. and most of Aug.*

$$$–$$$$ ✕🏨 **Schlosshotel Liebenstein.** Nestled in the hills above the village of
★ Neckarwestheim, south of Heilbronn, is one of the area's most beautiful castles, Schloss Liebenstein. Behind its Renaissance facade is a modern hotel and the gourmet restaurant Lazuli. Guest rooms have views of the surrounding forests, vineyards, and golf course. Within the 3-ft-thick castle walls, the peaceful hush of centuries reigns over a setting of comfort and noble elegance. ⊠ *Schloss Liebenstein, D–74382 Neckarwestheim,* ☎ *07133/98990,* FAX *07133/6045. 22 rooms, 2 suites. 3 restaurants, beer garden, 27-hole golf course. AE, MC, V.* ❧

$$–$$$ ✕🏨 **Gutsgasthof Rappenhof.** This cheerful country inn is set on a hill in the midst of the vineyards of Weinsberg (6 km [4 mi] northeast of Heilbronn), where you can enjoy the fresh air and panoramic views from the terrace or on a scenic walk along the signposted Wine Panorama Path. The restaurant features hearty country cooking, such as sauerbraten with *Semmelknödel* (bread dumplings), and wines from the region. ⊠ *D–74189 Weinsberg,* ☎ *07134/5190,* FAX *07134/51955. 34 rooms. Restaurant, no-smoking rooms, bicycles. AE, DC, MC, V. Closed mid-Dec.–mid-Jan.*

$$$–$$$$ ✕ **Insel-Hotel.** *Insel* means "island," and that's where the luxurious Insel-Hotel is—on a river island tethered to the city by the busy Friedrich Ebert Bridge. A family-run establishment, the Insel combines a personal touch and the sleek service and facilities expected of a large chain. ⊠ *Friedrich-Ebert-Brücke, D–74072,* ☎ *07131/6300,* FAX *07131/626–060. 120 rooms, 4 suites. 2 restaurants, bar, no-smoking rooms, indoor pool, sauna, free parking. AE, DC, MC, V.*

Nightlife and the Arts

The Heilbronn tourist office distributes a monthly *Veranstaltungskalender* (calendar of events) and also sells tickets to cultural events (☎ 07131/80774). The Festhalle Harmonie and Stadttheater are the major (but not only) venues for theater, dance, opera, musicals, and concerts. The city has two resident orchestras: **Württemberg Chamber Orchestra** and **Heilbronn Symphony Orchestra.**

Shopping

The city's internationally renowned **Weindorf** wine festival, during the second week of September, showcases more than 200 wines from the Heilbronn region alone. Outside festival time, you'll find numerous shops stocking wine along Heilbronn's central pedestrian shopping zone, and you can also sample and purchase directly from private wine estates or a *Winzergenossenschaft* (vintners' cooperative winery). One of Württemberg's finest producers, the **Staatsweingut Weinsberg** (State Wine Domain in Weinsberg; ⊠ Traubenpl. 5, Weinsberg, ☎ 07134/504–167) has an architecturally striking wine shop with 70 wines and 30 other products of the grape on offer. It's open weekdays 9–5.

Stuttgart

㉖ *50 km (31 mi) south on B–27 from Heilbronn.*

Stuttgart is a place of fairly extreme contradictions. It has been called, among other things, "Germany's biggest small town" and "the city where work is a pleasure." For centuries Stuttgart, whose name derives from *Stutengarten,* or "stud farm," remained a pastoral backwater along the Neckar. Then the Industrial Revolution propelled the city into the machine age, after which it was leveled in World War II. Since then Stuttgart has regained its position as one of Germany's top industrial centers.

Here, *Schaffen*—"doing, achieving"—is all. This is Germany's can-do city, whose natives have turned out Mercedes-Benz and Porsche cars, Bosch electrical equipment, and a host of other products exported worldwide. It is only fitting that one end of the main street, Königstrasse, should be emblazoned with a neon BOSCH sigh on a high-rise and that the other end should shine with the Mercedes star.

Yet Stuttgart is also a city of culture and the arts, with world-class museums and a famous ballet company. Moreover, it's the domain of fine local wines; the vineyards actually approach the city center in a rim of green hills. Forests, vineyards, meadows, and orchards compose more than half the city, which is enclosed on three sides by woods.

An ideal introduction to the contrasts of Stuttgart is a guided city bus tour (☞ Guided Tours *in* Heidelberg and the Neckar Valley A to Z, *below*). Included is a visit to the needle-nose TV tower, high on a mountaintop above the city, affording stupendous views. Built in 1956, it was the first of its kind in the world. On your own, the best place to begin exploring Stuttgart is the Hauptbahnhof (main train station); from there walk down the pedestrian street Königstrasse to Schillerplatz, a small, charming square named after the 18th-century poet and playwright Friedrich Schiller, who was born in nearby Marbach. It is surrounded by historic buildings, many of them rebuilt after the war.

Just off Schillerplatz, the **Stiftskirche** (Collegiate Church of the Holy Cross) is Stuttgart's most familiar sight, with its two oddly matched towers. Built in the 12th century and then substantially rebuilt in a late-Gothic style (1495–1531), the church became Protestant in 1534. It was reconsecrated in 1958 after being badly damaged in a 1944 bombing raid. The choir has a famous series of Renaissance figures of the counts of Württemberg sculpted by Simon Schlör (1576–1608). ⊠ *Stiftstr. 12.*

Schlossplatz (Castle, or Royal, Square) is a huge area enclosed by reconstructed royal palaces, with elegant arcades branching off to other stately plazas. The magnificent baroque **Neues Schloss** (New Castle), now occupied by Baden-Württemberg state government offices, dominates the square.

The **Schlossgarten** (Castle Garden) borders the Schlossplatz. The garden is graced by an exhibition hall, planetarium, lakes, sculptures, and a mineral spring—the Berger Sprudler. If you continue in this park across Schillerstrasse, you'll come to the **Park Wilhelma,** home to botanical gardens and the city's renowned zoo. Here you can walk along the banks of the Neckar River.

Across the street from the Neues Schloss stands the **Altes Schloss** (Old Castle), the former residence of the counts and dukes of Württemberg. Built as a moated castle around 1320, with wings added in the mid-15th century to turn this into a Renaissance palace, the Altes Schloss was considerably rebuilt between 1948 and 1970 to repair wartime damage. The palace now houses the **Württemberggisches Landesmuseum** (Württemberg State Museum), with imaginative exhibits tracing the development of the area from the Stone Age to modern times. The displays of medieval life are especially noteworthy. ⊠ *Schillerpl. 6,* ☎ *0711/279–3400.* ⊡ *DM 5.* ☉ *Tues. 10–1, Wed.–Sun. 10–5.*

★ The **Staatsgalerie** (State Gallery) possesses one of the finest art collections in Germany. The old part of the complex, dating from 1842, has paintings from the Middle Ages through the 19th century, including works by Cranach, Holbein, Hals, Memling, Rubens, Rembrandt, Cézanne, Courbet, and Manet. Connected to the original building is the **New State Gallery**, designed by British architect James Stirling in 1984 as a melding of classical and modern, sometimes jarring, elements (such as chartreuse window mullions). Considered one of the most successful postmodern buildings, it houses works by such 20th-century artists as Braque, Chagall, de Chirico, Dali, Kandinsky, Klee, Mondrian, and Picasso. Look for Otto Dix's *Grossstadt* (*Metropolis*) triptych, which distills the essence of 1920s Germany on canvas. ⊠ *Konrad-Adenauer-Str. 30–32,* ☎ *0711/212–4050.* ⊡ *DM 9.* ☉ *Tues.–Sun. 11–7, 1st Sat. of month until midnight.*

OFF THE BEATEN PATH

GOTTLIEB DAIMLER MEMORIAL WORKSHOP – The first successful internal combustion engine was perfected here in 1883, and you can see the tools, blueprints, and models of early cars that helped pave the way for the Mercedes line. ⊠ *Taubenheimstr. 13, Stuttgart-Bad Cannstatt,* ☎ *0711/1756–9399.* ⊡ *Free.* ☉ *Tues.–Sun. 10–4.*

MERCEDES-BENZ MUSEUM – The oldest car factory in the world shows off a collection of about 100 historic racing and luxury cars here. Follow signs to the soccer stadium. ⊠ *Mercedesstr. 137, Stuttgart-Untertürkheim,* ☎ *0711/172–2578.* ⊡ *Free.* ☉ *Tues.–Sun. 9–5.*

PORSCHE MUSEUM – This Porsche factory in the northern suburb of Zuffenhausen has a small but significant collection of legendary Porsche racing cars. ⊠ *Porschepl. 1, Stuttgart-Zuffenhausen,* ☎ *0711/911–5685.* ⊡ *Free.* ☉ *Weekdays 9–4, weekends 9–5.*

WEISSENHOFSIEDLUNG – The Weissenhof Colony was a minicity created for a 1927 exhibition of the "New Home." Sixteen leading architects from five countries—among them Mies van der Rohe, Le Corbusier, and Walter Gropius—created residences that offered optimal living conditions at affordable prices. The still-functioning colony, which had a significant influence on 20th-century housing development, is on a hillside overlooking Friedrich-Ebert-Strasse. To get there from the city center, take Tram 10 toward Killesberg to the Kunstakadamie stop. The Stuttgart tourist office issues a brochure indicating which architects designed the various homes. ☎ *0711/854–641.*

Dining and Lodging

$$$$ ✗ **Wielandshöhe.** Stuttgart's culinary skyline is sprinkled with many star chefs, including Vincent Klink, whose temple is set high above the city in the suburb of Degerloch. Although he is one of Germany's top chefs, he and his wife, Elisabeth, are very down-to-earth, cordial hosts.

Flamboyant floral decorations soften the spartan black-and-white decor, but your vision—and palate—will ultimately focus on the artfully prepared and presented cuisine. Roast capon in lime-ginger stock, breast of pigeon nestled in a tangle of tagliolini, or tender duck with farmhouse red cabbage are but a few of the delicacies on the menu. The wine list is exemplary. ⊠ *Alte Weinsteige 71, Degerloch,* ☎ *0711/ 640–8848,* FAX *0711/640–9408. Reservations essential. AE, DC, MC, V. Closed Sun. and Mon.*

$$–$$$$ ✕ **Der Zauberlehrling.** The Sorcerer's Apprentice is aptly named. Indeed, there are regularly scheduled evenings of *Tischzauberei,* when magicians entertain. The enchantment on the menu features Axel Heldmann's imaginative dishes, such as quail with shiitake mushrooms and truffles, lemongrass soup with smoked monkfish, or veal fillet with nettle lasagna. You'll find excellent choices on the wine list.⊠ *Rosenstr. 38,* ☎ *0711/237–7770. AE. Closed Sun. No lunch Sat.*

$$$$ ✕🍽 **Am Schlossgarten.** Stuttgart's top accommodation is a modern struc-
★ ture set in spacious gardens in the heart of the city, a stone's throw from sights, shops, and the train station. In addition to first-class service and luxuriously appointed rooms, you can wine and dine in the restaurant Zirbelstube (French cuisine prepared by chef Andreas Goldbach, except Sunday and Monday), the Schlossgarten restaurant (classic regional favorites), or the café overlooking the garden. ⊠ *Schillerstr. 23, D–70173,* ☎ *0711/20260,* FAX *0711/202–6888. 116 rooms, 4 suites. 2 restaurants, bar, café, wine shop, minibars, bicycles. AE, DC, MC, V.* 🐾

$$$$ 🍽 **Hotel Mercure Fasanenhof.** This hotel has a light and airy design, with large windows throughout the spacious lobby, restaurant, public rooms, and comfortable bedrooms; everything is decorated in tasteful, pastel colors. It offers shuttle service to the airport (6 km [4 mi]) and downtown Stuttgart (11 km [7 mi]) can be reached by public transportation. ⊠ *Eichwiesenring 1/1, D–70567,* ☎ *0711/72660,* FAX *0711/ 726–6444. 148 rooms. Restaurant, bar, sauna, health club, free parking. AE, DC, MC, V.*

$$ 🍽 **Alter Fritz.** Katrin Fritsche describes her small country mansion as a
★ "hotel for individualists." With only 10 rooms, she is able to cater to guests' most exacting requirements with a friendly and personal touch rare in a city the size of Stuttgart. The picturesque house with its steep eaves and shuttered windows, high up on the wooded Killesberg Hill, is ideally located for visitors to the nearby trade fairground and a 15-minute bus ride from the main railway station. ⊠ *Feuerbacher Weg 101, D–70192,* ☎ *0711/135–650,* FAX *0711/135–6565. 10 rooms. Restaurant, minibars, free parking. No credit cards. Closed 2 wks in Aug. and 2 wks in Dec.*

Nightlife and the Arts

The tourist office keeps a current calendar of events.

THE ARTS

Stuttgart's internationally renowned ballet company performs in the **Staatstheater** (⊠ Oberer Schlossgarten 6, ☎ 0711/202–090). The ballet season runs from September through June and alternates with the respected State Opera. For program details contact the Stuttgart tourist office. The box office is open weekdays 10–6, Saturday 9–1.

The **STELLA Erlebnis-Center** is an entire entertainment complex (hotels, bars, restaurants, gambling casino, wellness center, cinemas, shops) built in 1994 to showcase musicals, particularly blockbuster hits from England. *Tanz der Vampire* (*Dance of the Vampire*), a musical version of Roman Polanski's parody, *The Fearless Vampire Killers,* and Walt Disney's *Die Schöne und das Biest* (*Beauty and the Beast*) were playing in 2000. ⊠ *Plieninger Str. 100, Stuttgart-Möhringen,* ☎ *0711/724– 019 Info-Hotline.* 🐾

There is no dearth of rustic beer gardens and wine pubs or sophisticated cocktail bars in and around Stuttgart. Night owls should head for the **Schwabenzentrum** on Eberhardstrasse, the **Bohnenviertel,** or "Bean Quarter" (Charlotten-, Olga-, and Pfarrstrasse), and **Calwer Strasse.**

Outdoor Activities and Sports

HIKING
Stuttgart has a 53-km (33-mi) network of marked hiking trails in the nearby hills; follow the signs with the city's emblem: a horse set in a yellow ring.

TENNIS
Stuttgart is the true tennis center of the region, and the city has several clubs that welcome visitors. The largest is **Jens Weinberger's Tennis and Sports School** (⌗ Emerholzweg 73, ☎ 0711/808–018).

Shopping
Calwer Strasse, one of the city's leading shopping streets, is home to the glitzy arcade **Calwer Passage,** full of elegant chrome and glass. Shops here carry everything from local women's fashion (Beate Mössinger) to furniture. Don't miss the beautiful Jugendstil **Markthalle** on Dorotheenstrasse. One of Germany's finest market halls, it is an archtitectural gem brimming with exotic fruits and spices, meats, and flowers.

Two of Germany's top men's fashion designers—Hugo Boss and Ulli Knecht—are based in Stuttgart. **Holy's** (⌗ Königstr. 54, ☎ 0711/221–872) is an exclusive men's boutique, which carries clothes by all the most sought-after designers.

Günter Krauss's glittering shop (⌗ Kronprinzstr. 21, ☎ 0711/297–395) specializes in designer jewelry. The design of the shop itself—walls of white Italian marble with gilt fixtures and mirrors—has won many awards.

Breuninger (⌗ Marktstr. 1–3, ☎ 0711/2110), a leading regional department-store chain, has glass elevators that rise and fall under the dome of the central arcade.

Bebenhausen

㉗ *5 km (3 mi) north of Tübingen, right at the side of the road.*

The little settlement of Bebenhausen is the first sign that you're approaching the lovely town of Tübingen. If you blink, you'll miss the turnoff, and that would be a shame because it is really worth a visit. ★ The **Zisterzienzerkloster** (Cistercian Monastery) is a rare example of an almost perfectly preserved medieval monastery dating from the late 12th century. Due to the secularization of 1806, the abbot's abode was rebuilt as a hunting **castle** for King Frederick of Württemberg. Expansion and restoration went on as the castle and monastery continued to be a royal residence into this century. Even after the monarchy was dissolved in 1918, the last Württembergs were given lifetime rights here; this came to an end in 1946 with the death of Charlotte, wife of Wilhelm II. For a few years after the war the state senate convened in the castle; today both castle and monastery are open to the public, although the castle is open for guided tours only. ⌗ *Monastery DM 5, castle DM 6, combined admission DM 9. ☉ Monastery Apr.–Oct., Mon. 9–noon and 1–6; Tues.–Sun. 9–6; Nov.–Mar., Tues.–Sun. 9–noon and 1–6. Castle tours Apr.–Oct., Tues.–Fri. hourly 9–5, weekends hourly 10–5; Nov.–Mar., Tues.–Fri. hourly 9–5 except at noon and 1, weekends hourly 10–5.*

Dining

$$$–$$$$ ✕ **Waldhorn.** Chef Ulrich Schilling and his wife, Jutta, offer extraor-
★   dinary meals and hospitality in very tasteful surroundings, whether you
opt for country elegance indoors or the streamlined garden with a cas-
tle view. "Variations of foie gras" and "essence of rose hip parfait" are
classics, as are the masterfully prepared four- or seven-course menus.
The wine list features a well-chosen selection of international wines
and top Baden and Württemberg estates. ✉ *Schönbuchstr. 49 (on B–*
27), ☎ *07071/61270. Reservations essential. No credit cards. Closed*
Mon., Tues., 1st wk in Jan., and 2 wks in summer.

Tübingen

㉘ *40 km (25 mi) south of Stuttgart on B–27 on the Neckar River.*

With its half-timber houses, winding alleyways, hilltop location, and
views overlooking the Neckar, Tübingen is popular with both German
and foreign travelers. Dating to the 11th century, the town flourished
as a trade center; Tübingen weights and measures, along with its cur-
rency, were the standard through much of the area. The town declined
in importance after the 14th century, when it was taken over by the
counts of Württemberg. Between the 14th and the 19th centuries, its
size hardly changed as it became a university and residential town, its
castle the only symbol of ruling power. Untouched by wartime bomb-
ings or even, it sometimes seems, the passage of time, the little town
still has an authentic medieval flavor, providing the quintessential Ger-
man experience.

Yet Tübingen hasn't been sheltered from the world. It resonates with
a youthful air. Even more than Heidelberg, Tübingen is virtually syn-
onymous with its university, a leading center of learning since it was
founded in 1477. Illustrious students of yesteryear include the as-
tronomer Johannes Kepler and the philosopher G. W. F. Hegel. The lat-
ter studied at the Protestant theological seminary, still a cornerstone
of the university's international reputation. One of Hegel's roommates
was Friedrich Hölderlin, a visionary poet who succumbed to madness
in his early thirties. Tübingen's population is around 85,000, of which
at least 25,000 are students. During term time it can be hard to find
a seat in pubs and cafés; during vacations the town sometimes seems
deserted. The best way to see and appreciate Tübingen is simply to stroll
around, soaking up its age-old atmosphere of quiet erudition.

A Good Walk

Tübingen's modest size makes it ideal for a walk. Begin at the Eber-
hards-Brücke with its picturesque view of the Neckar River and river-
side buildings. The bridge crosses an island with a magnificent planting
of trees—most of them at least 200 years old—known as the Platane-
nallee. If time permits, stroll up and down the island. If not, go to the
north end of the bridge, take a sharp left down a steep staircase to reach
the shore of the Neckar, and follow it to a yellow tower, the **Hölder-**
linturm. The poet Friedrich Hölderlin was housed in the tower after
he lost his mind, and it is now a small museum commemorating his
life and work. Next, walk away from the river up the steps of Hölder-
linsteg and continue left up the Bursagasse to pass by the **Bursa,** a for-
mer student dormitory that dates from the Middle Ages. Facing the
Bursa, turn left up the street called Klosterberg and then turn left again
into the courtyard of the **Evangelisches Stift.** Richer in history than in
immediate visual interest, this site was a center of European intellec-
tual thought for centuries. Proceed up Klosterberg to the narrow steps
and cobblestones of Burgsteige, one of the oldest thoroughfares in the

town and lined with houses dating from the Middle Ages. You might be a little breathless when you finally arrive at the top and enter the portal of the **Schloss Hohentübingen.** The portal is fitted as a Roman-style triumphal arch in true Renaissance spirit.

Cross the Schloss's courtyard and enter the tunnel-like passage directly in front of you; it leads to the other side of the castle. Take a moment to enjoy the view of the river from the ruined ramparts and then descend to your right through tree-shaded Kapitansweg—looking at the remains of the original city walls on your way—to Haaggasse and then left into the narrow Judengasse (Jewish Alley). Jewish citizens lived in this neighborhood until 1477, when they were driven out of the city. Next, stop at the intersection of Judengasse and Ammergasse; all around you are old half-timber buildings. The little stream that runs through Ammergasse was part of the medieval sewage system.

Across the square, Jakobsgasse leads to Jakobuskirche (Jacob's Church), in medieval times a station on the famous pilgrims' route to Santiago di Compostella in Spain. Go to the other side of the church, make a right into Madergasse, and then turn left at Schmiedtorstrasse, where you will find the Fruchtschranne on the right-hand side—a massive half-timber house little changed since it was built to store fruit and grain in the 15th century. Continue down the street to Bachgasse; turn right, then right again onto the street called Bei der Fruchtschranne and follow it a short distance to a courtyard on the left just before the intersection with Kornhausstrasse. The courtyard leads to the entrance of the 15th-century **Kornhaus,** now a city museum. Continue to Kornstrasse and go left and immediately right into Marktgasse, which takes you uphill to the **Marktplatz,** a sloping, uneven cobblestone parallelogram that dominates the heart of Tübingen's Altstadt (Old City). As is common in medieval squares, the marketplace contains a fountain—in this case the **Neptune Fountain,** graced with a statue of the sea god. The square is bounded on one side by the amazing **Rathaus.**

From the square turn into Wienergasse and then left into Münzgasse; No. 20 is the site of the former **Studentenkarzer.** The large yellow baroque building just beyond is the **Alte Aula,** for many centuries the local university's most important building. The well-preserved late-Gothic **Stiftskirche** now rises before you. Climbing the hundred-odd steps up the bell tower will allow you to take a second, faraway look at almost everything you've seen en route.

TIMING

The walk around town takes about 1½ hours. If you go inside the Hölderlinturm, Stadtsmuseum, and Stiftskirche, add half an hour for each sight.

Sights to See

Alte Aula (Old Hall). Erected in 1547, the half-timber university building was reconstructed in 1777, when it acquired an Italian roof, a symmetrical facade, and a balcony decorated with two crossed scepters symbolizing the town's center of learning. In earlier times grain was stored under the roof as part of the professors' salaries. The libraries and lecture halls were on the lower floors; for illumination, medieval students brought candles and stuck them on the tables. ☒ *Münzg.*

OFF THE
BEATEN PATH **BOTANISCHE GARTEN –** The botanical garden, north of the Neckar River above the city, is one of Tübingen's favorite modern attractions. To get there, take Bus 5 or 17 from the train station. ☒ *Hartmeyerstr. 123,* ☎ *07071/297–2609.* ☒ *Free.* ☉ *Weekdays 7:30–4:45, weekends 8–4:45.*

Bursa (Student Dormitory). The word *bursa* meant "purse" in the Middle Ages and later came to refer to student lodgings such as this former student dormitory. Despite its classical facade, which it acquired in the early 19th century, the building actually dates back to 1477. The students who lived here in medieval times had a hard life. They had to master a broad curriculum that included the *septem artes liberales* (seven liberal arts) of Grammar, Dialectic, Rhetoric, Arithmetic, Geometry, Astronomy, and Music, in addition to praying several times a day, fasting regularly, and speaking only Latin within the confines of the building. ⊠ *Bursag. 4.*

Evangelisches Stift (Protestant Seminary). From the outside you can't tell that this site has served for centuries as a center of European intellectual thought. It was founded in 1534, partly as a political move during the Reformation; the Protestant duke of Württemberg, Ulrich, wanted facilities to train Protestant clerics so that Protestantism could retain its foothold in the region (he would have been disappointed to know a major Catholic seminary arrived here in 1817). Since that time philosophical rather than political considerations have prevailed within these walls. Hegel, Hölderlin, and the philosopher Schelling all shared a room as students here—even in a university town this seems an unusually high concentration of brain power. ⊠ *Klosterg.*

Hölderlinturm (Hölderlin's Tower). "Mad" Friedrich Hölderlin (modern scholars think he suffered from schizophrenia) lived here for 36 years, until his death in 1843, in the care of the master cabinetmaker Zimmer and his daughter. If you don't speak German, you may want to arrange for an English tour to get the most out of the exhibits. You can also acquaint yourself with a couple of Hölderlin poems in translation to get a sense of the writer's imagery and notably "modern" style. ⊠ *Bursag. 6,* ☎ *07071/22040.* ☑ *DM 3.* ☉ *Tues.–Fri. 10–noon and 3–5, weekends 2–5. Tours weekends and holidays at 5 PM; English-language tours available by arrangement.*

Kornhaus (Grain House). During the Middle Ages, townspeople stored and sold grain on the first floor of this structure (built in 1453); social events were held on the second floor. Among the Kornhaus's occupants through the centuries were duelists, medieval apprentices, traveling players, 18th-century schoolchildren, an academy for young ladies, the Nazi Women's League, a driving school, and the city's restoration department. It now houses the City Museum. ⊠ *Kornhausstr.,* ☎ *07071/204–711.* ☑ *Admission varies depending on exhibition.* ☉ *Tues.–Sat. 3–6, Sun. 11–1 and 3–6.*

OFF THE
BEATEN PATH **KUNSTHALLE (Art Gallery)** – Situated north of the Neckar, the art gallery has become a leading exhibition venue and generates a special kind of "art tourism," making it difficult to find lodging if a popular show is on. ⊠ *Philosophenweg 76,* ☎ *07071/96910.* ☑ *Admission varies depending on show: DM 8–DM 12.* ☉ *Tues.–Sun. 10–6.*

★ **Marktplatz** (Market Square). Tübingen's market square is surrounded by the houses of prominent burghers of centuries gone by. At the open-air market on Monday, Wednesday, and Friday, you can buy flowers, bread, pastries, poultry, sausage, and cheese.

★ **Rathaus** (Town Hall). Begun in 1433, the Rathaus expanded over the next 150 years or so. Its ornate Renaissance facade is bright with colorful wall paintings and a marvelous astronomical clock dating from 1511. The halls and reception rooms are adorned with half-timbering and paintings from the late 19th century. ⊠ *Marktpl.*

★ **Schloss Hohentübingen** (Hohentübingen Castle). This impressive edifice was built on top of 11th-century fortifications. The Renaissance portal has the look of a Roman triumphal arch with a lot of decorative scrollwork thrown in—fruits, garlands and, at the top, the coat of arms of the Württemberg ducal family, which includes the famous Order of the Garter. A roster of deities occupies the base: Poseidon; the sea goddess Amphitrite; Nike, goddess of victory; and Athena, goddess of wisdom and war. Enter the double-doored opening and immediately notice that one-half of the courtyard is painted and the other half isn't—the result of a difference of opinion among the art historians who tried to restore the castle to its original appearance. The castle was a bone of contention during the Thirty Years' War, and the French blew up one of its towers in 1647. Now it serves an altogether more peaceable function: housing classical archaeology and several other university departments. One of the castle cellars contains an 84,000-liter wine barrel and the largest bat colony in southern Germany. The **Museum Schloss** occupies one wing and a tower with exhibits about the history of the city and the castle and a small collection of Greek and Roman artifacts. But the castle's main attraction is its magnificent view over river and town.

★ **Stiftskirche** (Collegiate Church). The late-Gothic church is in an excellent state of preservation; many of its original features have survived through the ages, including the stained-glass windows, the choir stalls, the ornate baptismal font, and the elaborate stone pulpit. The stained-glass windows are famous for their colors and were much admired by Goethe. The dukes of Württemberg from the 15th through the 17th centuries are interred beneath them in the choir. ⊠ *Holzmarkt.,* ✉ *Bell tower DM 2.* ☉ *Feb.–Oct., daily 9–5; Nov.–Jan., daily 9–4.*

Studentenkarzer (Student Prison). The oldest surviving university prison in Germany consists of just two small rooms. For more than three centuries (1515–1845) students were locked up here for offenses like swearing, failing to attend sermons, wearing clothing considered lewd, or playing dice. The figures on the walls are not graffiti but scenes from biblical history that were supposed to contribute to the moral improvement of the incarcerated students. You can enter the prison only on a guided tour (DM 1), organized by the Tübingen Tourist Board. ⊠ *Münzg. 20,* ☎ *07071/91360 for tour.*

Dining and Lodging

$–$$ ✕ **Forelle.** Beautiful ceilings painted with vine motifs, exposed beams, and an old tiled oven offer German Gemütlichkeit (coziness) at its best. This small restaurant fills up fast, not least because the Swabian cooking is excellent. All products (and the wines) are sourced locally, including the inn's namesake, Forelle. ⊠ *Kronenstr. 8,* ☎ *07071/24094. MC, V.*

$–$$ ✕ **Neckarmüller.** This shady, riverside beer garden and restaurant near the Eberhards-Brücke offers snacks, salads, and *Vesper* (sausage and cheese). For bigger appetites, the Schwabenteller, a platter of Swabian specialties (Maultaschen, Spätzle, sauerkraut, and beefsteaks in cream sauce), is more than ample. Don't wait to be served. The sign that reads SELBSTABHOLUNG means you fetch it yourself. ⊠ *Gartenstr. 4,* ☎ *07071/27848. V.*

$ ✕ **Café/Bistro Neckartor.** The café has light and airy 1960s decor and a beautiful view up and down the Neckar. Hölderlin's Tower is just a few houses upriver. The eclectic menu includes dishes like cassoulet, lasagna, and Maultaschen. The pastries are irresistible. ⊠ *Neckarg. 22,* ☎ *07071/22122. No credit cards.*

$$–$$$ ✕▦ **Hotel Am Schloss.** The climb is steep from the Altstadt to this hotel, next to the castle that towers over the town, but the reward is lovely

views from the geranium-bedecked windows of the comfortable rooms and dining terrace. Proprietor Herbert Rösch has written a number of books about regional cuisine, including one devoted to Maultaschen. He puts theory into practice at the restaurant, where an incredible 28 versions of "Swabian tortellini" are on the menu, together with other regional dishes. The wines are from Württemberg. ⊠ *Burgsteige 18, D–72070,* ☎ *07071/92940,* FAX *07071/929–410. 37 rooms. Restaurant, minibars (some rooms), bicycles. AE, MC, V.*

$$–$$$ ✕🔲 **Hotel Hospiz.** This modern, family-run hotel offers friendly service, comfort, and a convenient Altstadt location. You can enjoy hearty Swabian cuisine in the cheerful restaurant. ⊠ *Neckarhalde 2, at corner of Burgsteige, D–72070,* ☎ *07071/9240,* FAX *07071/924–200. 50 rooms, 42 with bath or shower. Restaurant, lobby lounge, minibars, meeting room. AE, MC, V.*

Nightlife and the Arts

As a student town, Tübingen has an active small **theater** scene. Check with the tourist office for a listing of what is going on—the more eclectic offerings are likely to be the better ones.

In addition to dozens of Old Town student pubs, there's a lively crowd after 9 at the **Jazzkeller** (⊠ Haaggasse 15/2, ☎ 07071/550–906) and from 5 at the cocktail bar (upstairs) at **Café Nass** (⊠ Kirchgasse 19, ☎ 07071/551–250). **Zentrum Zoo** (⊠ Schleifmühleweg 86, ☎ 07071/94480) has live music, a dance club, and a huge beer garden that is immensely popular with all ages. It's about a 20-minute walk from the town center.

Hiking

The Tübingen tourist office has maps with routes around the town, including historic and geologic *Lehrpfade,* or **educational walks.** A classic Tübingen walk goes from the castle down to the little chapel called the **Wurmlinger Kapelle,** taking about two hours. On the way it's customary to stop off at the restaurant Schwärzlocher Hof to sample the good food and great views. The tourist office can give you a map detailing the way.

OFF THE BEATEN PATH

★

Burg Hohenzollern – The Hohenzollern House of Prussia was the most powerful family in German history. It lost its throne when Kaiser William II was forced to abdicate after Germany's defeat in World War I. The Swabian branch of the family owns one-third of the castle, the Prussian branch two-thirds. Today's neo-Gothic structure is a successor of a castle dating from the 11th century. Perched high on a conical wooded hill, its majestic silhouette is visible from miles away. From its summit there are grand panoramic views. Tours are educational and interesting. In addition to seeing the Prussian royal crown, you'll see beautiful period rooms, splendid from floor to ceiling, with playful details, such as door handles carved to resemble peacocks and dogs. The royal tombs, once housed in the Christ Chapel, were returned to Potsdam in 1991 in the aftermath of German reunification. The castle restaurant, Burgschänke (closed Monday and January), is catered by the talented chefs of Hotel Brielhof at the foot of the hill, where the ascent from the B–27 begins. You can enjoy a first-class meal at the Brielhof, then enjoy a hike up to the castle in about one hour. ⊠ *D–72379 Hechingen, 25 km (15 mi) south of Tübingen on the B–27.* ☎ *07471/2428.* 🖾 *DM 9.* ☉ *Tours mid-March–mid-Oct., daily 9–5:30; mid-Oct.–mid-March, daily 9–4:30.* 🐾

HEIDELBERG AND THE NECKAR VALLEY A TO Z

Arriving and Departing

By Plane

The airports nearest to the Neckar Valley are at Frankfurt and Stuttgart. From both there's fast and easy access, by car and train, to all major centers along the Neckar.

AIRPORT TRANSFER

With advance reservations you can get to Heidelberg from the Frankfurt airport via the Heidelberg-based shuttle service **TLS** (☎ 06221/770–077, FAX 06221/770–070). The trip takes about an hour and costs DM 45 per person; with three people, DM 40 each.

Getting Around

By Bus

Europabus 189 runs the length of the Burgenstrasse daily from mid-May through September. There are stops at towns and villages all along the Neckar. For information, timetables, and reservations, contact **Deutsche Touring** (☞ Bus Travel *in* Smart Travel Tips A to Z). Local buses run from Mannheim, Heidelberg, Heilbronn, and Stuttgart to most places along the river.

By Car

Heidelberg is a 15-minute drive (6mi/10km) on A–656 from Mannheim, a major junction of the autobahn system. Heilbronn stands beside the east–west A–6 and the north–south A–81. The route followed in this chapter, the Burgenstrasse, Route B–37, follows the north bank of the Neckar from Heidelberg to Mosbach, from which it continues south to Heilbronn as B–27, the road parallel to and predating the autobahn (A–81). B–27 still leads to Stuttgart and Tübingen.

By Train

Western Germany's most important rail junction is in nearby Mannheim, with hourly InterCity trains from all major German cities. Heidelberg is equally easy to get to. Mannheim is also a major stop for the super-high-speed InterCity Express service, which reaches 250 km (155 mi) per hour on the Mannheim–Stuttgart stretch. There are express trains to Heilbronn from Heidelberg and Stuttgart and direct trains from Stuttgart to Tübingen. Local services link many of the smaller towns along the Neckar.

Contacts and Resources

Car Rentals

Avis, Europcar, Hertz and Sixt all have rental offices at the Frankfurt and Stuttgart airports and main train stations.

Avis (⊠ Karlsruherstr. 43, Heidelberg, ☎ 06221/22215; ⊠ Salzstr. 112, Heilbronn, ☎ 07131/172–077; ⊠ Katharinenstr. 18, Stuttgart, ☎ 0711/239–320).**Europcar** (⊠ Bergheimerstr. 159, Heidelberg, ☎ 06221/53990; ⊠ Neckarauerstr. 50–52, Mannheim, ☎ 0621/842–370; ⊠ Eisenbahnstr. 21, Tübingen, ☎ 07071/13370). **Hertz** (⊠ Holiday Inn, Kurfürstenanlage 1, Heidelberg, ☎ 06221/23434; ⊠ Friedrichsring 36, Mannheim, ☎ 0621/22997; ⊠ Hauptbahnhof (Arnulf-Klett-Pl. 2), Track 16, Stuttgart, ☎ 0711/226–2921).**Sixt** (⊠ Eppelheimer Str. 50C, Heidelberg, ☎ 06221/138–990).

Guided Tours

BOAT TOURS

From Easter through October there are regular **boat trips** on the Neckar from Heidelberg, Heilbronn, and Stuttgart. If time is short, take a *Rundfahrt* (round-trip excursion). The **Tübingen tourist office** organizes punting on the Neckar.

CITY TOURS

Medieval **Bad Wimpfen** offers a town walk year-round, Sunday at 2 (DM 3.50) and free guided tours in English for visitors who spend at least one night. Tell the hotel upon arrival, and it will make arrangements. There's free admission to all historic sights and museums included in the *Museumspass,* sold at the tourist office.

From April through October there are daily guided walking tours of **Heidelberg** in German (Thursday through Sunday in English) at 10 AM; in the winter, in German only, Saturday at 10; the cost is DM 10. They depart from the Löwenbrunnen, or Lion's Fountain, on Universitätsplatz. Bus tours run April–October on Thursday and Friday at 2, on Saturday at 10 and 2, on Sunday at 10. From November through March bus tours depart Saturday at 2. They cost DM 22 and depart form the central train station or Bergheimerstrasse 12, on Bismarckplatz near the Theodor Heuss Bridge. The **Heidelberg Card** costs DM 19.80 (two days) and includes free or reduced admission to most tourist attractions as well as unlimited use of all public transportation and other extras, such as free guided walking tours, bus tours for DM 17, and a city guidebook. It can be purchased at the tourist information office at the main train station, in local hotels, and cultural institutions.

Equally visitor-friendly are the (three-day) STUTTCARD (DM 25) and STUTTCARD *light* (DM 15), with or without access to free public transportation, available from the **Stuttgart** tourist office opposite the main train station. This is also the meeting point for city walking tours (year-round, Saturday at 10) for DM 10, and bus tours (January–March and November–December, Friday and Saturday at 1 PM, Sunday and Monday at 11; April–October, Monday through Saturday at 1 PM and Sunday at 11) for DM 32. These tours all last 2½ hours. A Saturday-evening tour includes a visit to a nightclub (with a show), a pub crawl, and dinner for DM 115 (year-round, 7 PM).

From March through October the **Tübingen** tourist office runs guided city tours Wednesday at 10 AM, weekends at 2:30, for DM 5, from the Rathaus on Market Square. Overnight guests receive a free Tourist-Regio-Card from their hotel (ask for it) for reduced admission fees to museums, concerts, theaters, and sports facilities.

Visitor Information

For information on the entire **Burgenstrasse,** contact the Arbeitsgemeinschaft "Die Burgenstrasse" (✉ Rathaus, D–74072 Heilbronn, ☎ 07131/562–271, FAX 07131/563–140). For information on the **Schwäbische Alb,** the hilly area south of Stuttgart and Tübingen, contact the Touristik-Gemeinschaft Schwäbische Alb (✉ Marktpl. 1, D–72574 Bad Urach, ☎ 07125/948–106, FAX 07125/948–108). There are local tourist information offices in the following towns and cities:

Bad Wimpfen (✉ Tourist-Information, Gästezentrum Alter Bahnhof, D–74206, ☎ 07063/97200). **Heidelberg** (✉ Tourist Information am Hauptbahnhof, Willy-Brandt-Pl. 1, D–69115, ☎ 06221/19433, FAX 06221/138–8111. **Heilbronn** (✉ Tourist-Information, Rathaus, Marktpl., D–74072, ☎ 07131/562–270, FAX 07131/563–349). **Mosbach** (✉

Städtisches Verkehrsamt, Rathaus, D–74821, ☎ 06261/82236, FAX 06261/82249). **Schwetzingen** (✉ Verkehrsverein, Schlosspl. 2, D–68723, ☎ 06202/4933, FAX 06202/270–827). **Stuttgart** (✉ Touristik-Information i-Punkt, Königstr. 1A, D–70173, ☎ 0711/222–8240, FAX 0711/222–8253). **Tübingen** (✉ Verkehrsverein Tübingen, An der Neckarbrücke, D–72072, ☎ 07071/91360, FAX 07071/35070).

9   FRANKFURT

Frankfurt is the gateway by air to Germany—
and to the rest of the Continent. Many
German banks are headquartered here, and
the Frankfurt Börse is Germany's leading stock
exchange. The city's New York–style skyline
would stun the 30 Holy Roman emperors
who were once elected and crowned
here. But Frankfurt is not just a commercial
metropolis; it's a cultural center as well.

U NLIKE GERMAN CITIES that reclaimed much of their prewar appearance after World War II bombings, Frankfurt looked forward and erected skyscrapers to house its many banking institutions. The city cheekily nicknamed itself Mainhattan, using the name of the Main River that flows through it to suggest that other famous city. Although modest in size (fifth among German cities, with a population of 630,000), Frankfurt is Germany's financial powerhouse. Not only is the German Central Bank (Bundesbank) here but also the newly established European Central Bank (ECB), which manages the Euro. More than 422 banks (275 of which are foreign) have offices here, including the headquarters of five of Germany's 10 largest banks. You can see how the city acquired its other nickname: "Bankfurt am Main."

Updated by
Ted Shoemaker

According to legend, a deer is said to have revealed the ford in the Main River to the Frankish emperor Charlemagne. A stone ridge, now blasted away, made the shallow river a great conduit for trade and by the early 13th century Frankfurt (*furt* means "ford") had emerged as a major trading center. Frankfurt's first international Autumn Fair was held in 1240; in 1330 it added a Spring Fair. Today these and other trade shows showcase the latest in books, cars, consumer goods, and technology. The city's stock exchange, one of the half dozen most important in the world, was established in 1595. The Rothschilds opened their first bank here in 1798. The long history of trade might help explain the Frankfurters' temperament—competitive but open-minded.

So why come to Frankfurt if not on business? Partly for its history, which spans more than 1,200 years. It was one of the joint capitals of Charlemagne's empire, the city where Holy Roman emperors were elected and crowned, the site of Gutenberg's print shop, the birthplace of Goethe (1749–1832), Germany's greatest poet, and the city where the first German parliament met.

Because of all its commercialism Frankfurt has a reputation of being crass, cold, and boring. But people who know the city think this characterization is unfair. The fun district of Sachsenhausen is as *gemütlich* as you will find anywhere. The city has world-class ballet, opera, theater, and art exhibitions; an important piece of Germany's publishing industry; a large university (40,000 students) famous for such modern thinkers as Adorno and Habermas; and two of the three most important daily newspapers in Germany, the *Frankfurter Allgemeine* and the *Frankfurter Rundschau*. In Frankfurt you find yourself in the heart of a powerful, sophisticated, and cosmopolitan nation. There may not be that much here to remind you of the Old World, but there's a great deal that explains the success story of postwar Germany.

Pleasures and Pastimes

Dining

Frankfurt's local cuisine comes from the region's farm tradition. Pork ribs and chops, stewed beef, blood sausage, potato soup, and pancakes with bacon fulfill proverbs like "better once full than twice hungry" and "you work the way you eat." The city's most famous contribution to the world's diet is the *Frankfurter Wurstchen*—a thin smoked pork sausage—better known to Americans as the hot dog. *Grüne Sosse* is a thin cream sauce of herbs served with potatoes and hard-boiled eggs. The oddly named *Handkäs mit Musik* (hand cheese with music) consists of slices of cheese covered with raw onions, oil, and vinegar, served with bread and butter (an acquired taste for many). All these things are served in Sachsenhausen *Apfelwein* (apple wine, or hard cider) taverns like Fichtekränzi and Zum Wagner (☞ Dining, *below*). Many international cuisines are represented in the financial hub of Europe. For vegetarians there's usually at least one meatless dish on a German menu, and substantial salads are popular, too (though often served with bacon).

Jazz

Frankfurt's nightlife has at least one trump card—*jazz*. Many German cities like to call themselves the jazz capital of the country, but Frankfurt probably has a better claim to the title than most. In the fall, the German Jazz Festival is held here. There are hundreds of jazz venues, from smoky backstreet cafés all the way to the Old Opera House. The Frankfurter Jazzkeller has been the most noted venue for German jazz fans for decades (☞ Nightlife and the Arts, *below*).

Museums

Frankfurt is full of museums, and 13 of them were newly built or renovated during the 1980s. Interesting for their architecture as well as for their content, the exhibition halls have increased the city's popularity. Sachsenhausen, which is largely residential, is home to seven of these museums. They line the side of the Main, on Schaumainkai, known locally as the Museumsufer (Museum Riverbank).

EXPLORING FRANKFURT

The Hauptbahnhof (main train station) area and adjoining Westend district are mostly devoted to business, and banks tower overhead. You'll find the department stores of the Hauptwache and Zeil only a few blocks east of the station, but avoid the drug-ridden red-light district, also near the station. The city's past can be found in the Old Town's restored medieval quarter and in Sachsenhausen, across the river, where pubs and museums greatly outnumber banks.

Numbers in the text correspond to numbers in the margin and on the Frankfurt map.

Great Itineraries

IF YOU HAVE 1 DAY

Begin at the Römerberg, the heart of the city, and take a look at the Römer, or city hall, and its Kaisersaal before exploring the Goethehaus und Goethemuseum, the home of Germany's greatest poet. Then go to the Museum für Moderne Kunst, one of Frankfurt's modern architectural monuments. Walk a few blocks and several centuries back in time to St. Bartholomäus and admire the magnificent Gothic carvings. After lunch cross over the Main on the Eiserner Steg to reach the Städelsches Kunstinstitut und Städtische Galerie, with its important collection of old masters and impressionists, and the Städtische Galerie Liebieghaus, which contains sculpture from the third millennium BC up to the modern age. In the evening stroll around Sachsenhausen and eat in one of the neighborhood apple-cider taverns.

IF YOU HAVE 2 DAYS

Spend your first morning in Römerberg Square, where the Römer, Nikolaikirche, Historisches Museum, and Paulskirche are all nearby. Continue on to the Goethehaus und Goethemuseum, the Museum für Moderne Kunst, and St. Bartholomäus. Take a midday break before visiting Germany's shop-'til-you-drop district on the Zeil and the Zoologischer Garten, one of Europe's best zoos. End the first evening in the Frankfurter Jazzkeller (☞ Nightlife and the Arts, *below*). The entire second day can be devoted to the museums in Sachsenhausen, starting with the Städelsches Kunstinstitut und Städtische Galerie and the Städtische Galerie Liebieghaus. Finally, explore Sachsenhausen's nightlife.

Spend your first two days following the itinerary outlined above. On the morning of the third, see the Naturkundemuseum Senckenberg; it has a famous collection of dinosaurs and giant whales. Afterward visit the nearby Palmengarten und Botanischer Garten, which have climatic zones from tropical to sub-Antarctic and a dazzling range of orchids. Take the U-bahn to the Opernplatz, and emerge before the 19th-century splendor of the Alte Oper: lunch on Fressgasse is not far away. In the afternoon, go to the visitors' gallery of the Börse to feel the pulse of Europe's banking capital. Then continue on to the less worldly Karmeliterkirche. Secularized in 1803, the church and buildings were renovated in the 1980s and now house the Museum für Vor- und Frühgeschichte. Just around the corner on the bank of the Main, in the former Rothschild Palais, the Jüdisches Museum tells the 1,000-year story of Frankfurt's Jewish quarter and its end in the Holocaust.

City Center and Westend

Frankfurt was rebuilt after World War II with little attention paid to the past. Nevertheless, important architectural monuments from its long history still stand, and the city also has its share of modern architectural masterpieces. The city is very walkable; its growth hasn't encroached on its parks, gardens, pedestrian arcades, and outdoor cafés.

A Good Walk

Römerberg ①, the historic heart of Frankfurt, has been the center of civic life for centuries. Taking up most of the west side of the square is the city hall, called the **Römer** ②. It's a modest-looking building compared with many of Germany's other city halls. In the center of the square stands the fine 16th-century Fountain of Justitia.

On the south side of the Römerberg is the red sandstone **Nikolaikirche** ③. Beside it stands the **Historisches Museum** ④, where you can see a perfect scale model of historic Frankfurt. On the east side of the square is a row of painstakingly restored half-timber houses called the Ostzeile, dating from the 15th and 16th centuries.

From the Römerberg walk up the pedestrian street called Neue Kräme. On your right you'll pass the Gothic turrets and crenellations of the **Steinernes Haus,** originally built in 1464 and rebuilt from 1957 to 1960. Today it houses an art gallery.

Next, looming up on the left is the circular bulk of the **Paulskirche** ⑤, a mostly 18th-century church building, more interesting for its political than its religious significance. It was here that the short-lived German parliament met for the first time in May 1848. From the Paulskirche keep heading along the Neue Kräme, which becomes Liebfrauenstrasse. Here, in more peaceful surroundings, you will come to the **Liebfrauenkirche** ⑥, a late-Gothic church dating from the end of the 14th century.

The **Hauptwache** ⑦ is where Liebfrauenstrasse runs into the shopping street, Zeil. The hub of the city's transportation network, the square is named after the handsome 18th-century building with a sloping roof which stands on it. The building's café can attend to your needs. A vast shopping mall lies below the square. To the south of the Hauptwache is the **Katharinenkirche** ⑧, the most important Protestant church in the city. North of the Hauptwache, Schillerstrasse leads to the Börsenplatz and Frankfurt's leading stock exchange, the **Börse** ⑨.

The **Zeil** is Frankfurt's largest pedestrian zone and main shopping street. Its department stores sell every conceivable type of consumer

316

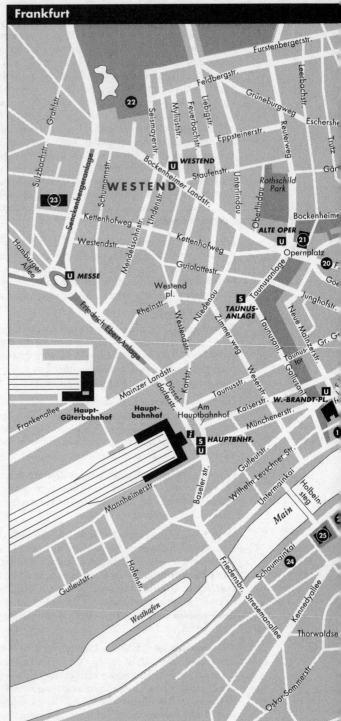

Frankfurt

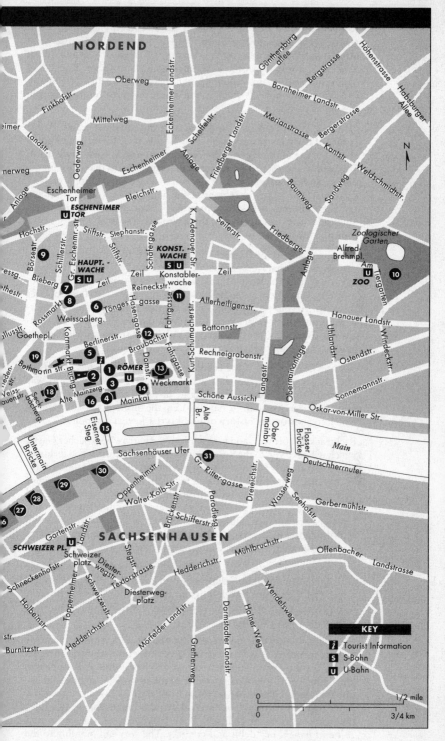

NORDEND

Oberweg

Finkhofstr.

Mittelweg

Oederweg

eimer Landstr.

nerweg

Anlage

Eschenheimer Tor

Hochstr.

Eschenheimer Bleichstr.

ESCHENEIMER U **TOR**

Stiftstr. Stephanstr.

Schäfergasse

**KONST.
WACHE**
S U

Börsenstr.

Schillerstr.

Gr. Eschenhr.-str.

Stiftstr.

**HAUPT.-
WACHE**
S U

9

Bieberg.

Zeil

Konstablerwache

Reineckstr.

Zeil

thestr.

7

Rossmarkt

8

6

Tönges-
gasse

Hasengasse

11

Fahrgasse

Allerheiligenstr.

Weissadlerg.

Goethepl.

Berlinerstr.

5

Braubachstr.

Danstr.

12

Fahrgasse

Battonnstr.

Rechneigrabenstr.

llusstr.

19

Kornmarkt Buchg.

i

1

RÖMER

13

Bethmann str.

2

3

U

Weckmarkt

Seckbächerg.

18

Alte Mainzerg.

16

4

14

Mainkai

Weiss-
fauenstr.

Schöne Aussicht

Eiserner Steg

15

Alte Br.

Ober-
mainbr.

Untermain Brücke

Sachsenhäuser Ufer

Gr. Ritter-gasse

31

Dreieichstr.

30

Oppenheimerstr.

Walter-Kolb-Str.

Brückenstr.

Paradiesg.

Wasser-

Seehofstr.

29

28

Schifferstr.

27

6

Gartenstr.

SACHSENHAUSEN

Mühlbruchstr.

SCHWEIZER PL. U

Schweizer platz

Diesterwegstr.

Stegstr.

Textorstrasse

Hedderichstr.

Schneckenhofstr.

Diesterweg-
platz

Toppenheimer str.

Schweizeistr.

Holbeinstr.

Hedderichstr.

Mörfelder Landstr.

Darmstädter Landstr.

Grethenweg

Burnitzstr.

str.

K. Adenauer Str.

Seilerstr.

Friedberger

Anlage

**Zoologischer
Garten**

Alfred-
Brehmpl.

Am
Tiergarten

U

ZOO

10

Günthersburg allee

Bornheimer Landstr.

Merianstrasse

Bergerstrasse

Kantstr.

Baumweg

Sandweg

Hanauer Landstr.

Uhlandstr.

Ostendstr.

Sonnemannstr.

Langestr.

Obermainanlage

Flosser
Brücke

Deutschherrnufer

Gerbermühlstr.

Offenbacher

Landstrasse

Wendelsweg

Hainer-Weg

Bergstrasse

Höhenstrasse

Habsburger Allee

Weidschmidtstr.

Oskar-von-Miller Str.

Main

N

KEY

i Tourist Information

S S-Bahn

U U-Bahn

0   1/2 mile

0   3/4 km

goods and can get very crowded. A 15- to 20-minute walk all the way to the end of the Zeil brings you to Alfred-Brehm-Platz and the entrance to the **Zoologischer Garten** ⑩. This is one of Frankfurt's chief attractions, ranking among the best zoos in Europe. If you don't want to go all the way down the Zeil, turn right at the square Konstabler Wache onto Fahrgasse. Follow the signs reading AN DER STAUFENMAUER to the **Staufenmauer** ⑪, which is one of the few surviving stretches of the old city wall.

Continue down Fahrgasse, and turn right onto Berlinerstrasse. At the corner of Berlinerstrasse and Domstrasse you'll see the striking wedge-shape outline of the **Museum für Moderne Kunst** ⑫. Walk south down Domstrasse a few steps and another silhouette appears, that of the grand, Gothic **St. Bartholomäus** ⑬, or the Kaiserdom as it is more popularly known. There is an archaeological site next to the church containing remains of Roman baths; from there walk through the pedestrian zone alongside the modern edifice of the **Schirn Kunsthalle** ⑭, a major venue for art exhibitions.

Continue back to the Römerberg and turn left to get to the Mainkai, the busy street that runs parallel to the tree-lined Main River. On your left you will see the Rententurm, one of the city's medieval gates, with its pinnacled towers at the base of the main spire extending out over the walls. To your right and in front is the **Eiserner Steg** ⑮, an iron footbridge connecting central Frankfurt with the old district of Sachsenhausen. River trips, boat excursions, and the old steam train leave from here (☞ Guided Tours *in* Frankfurt A to Z, *below*).

Past the Eiserner Steg is the **Leonhardskirche** ⑯, which has one of the few 15th-century stained-glass windows to have survived World War II. Return to the river and turn right. Just past the Untermainbrücke is the **Jüdisches Museum** ⑰, No. 14–15 in the former Rothschild Palais, which focuses on the history of Frankfurt's Jewish community.

Backtrack a short way, and turn left into the narrow Seckbächer Gasse, which will take you to the **Karmeliterkirche** ⑱. The church and its buildings house an early history museum and the largest religious fresco north of the Alps. Exit onto Münzgasse, turn left, and go to the junction of Bethmannstrasse and Berlinerstrasse. Use the pedestrian walkway and cross over to the north side of Berlinerstrasse; then turn left again onto Grosser Hirschgraben. Outside No. 23 there will probably be a small crowd entering and leaving the **Goethehaus und Goethemuseum** ⑲. This is where the writer Johann Wolfgang von Goethe was born in 1749.

On leaving the Goethehaus, go to Goetheplatz and continue past the Gutenberg Memorial into the pedestrian zone to Rathenau-Platz. At the end of the square turn left again, this time onto Grosse Bockenheimer Strasse, known locally as **Fressgasse** ⑳ because of its many delicatessens, bakeries, and cafés.

Fressgasse ends at Opernplatz and the **Alte Oper** ㉑, a prime venue for classical concerts as well as conferences and, every now and then, an opera. The steps of the opera house, or the Rothschild Park opposite, are a good spot from which to take in the impressive sight of Frankfurt's modern architecture. In this part of the new town you are close to the financial section. If you look down the Taunusanlage, you'll see the twin towers of the Deutsche Bank (the two towers are known as *zoll und haben,* or "debit and credit"). The very tall building to the left, topped by an antenna, is the 849-ft Commerzbank, the tallest building in Europe. Also in view is the Eurotower, headquarters of the recently established European Central Bank, which administers the Euro.

You can take the U-Bahn one stop from Alte Oper to Westend and then walk up Siesmayerstrasse to the delightful **Palmengarten und Botanischer Garten** ㉒. From here, by walking southwest, you can reach the **Naturkundemuseum Senckenberg** ㉓, with fun hands-on exhibits for both children and adults.

TIMING

Count on spending a full day on this tour. It is impossible to see all the museums on one trip. You should block out 45 minutes for the Goethehaus und Goethemuseum, an hour and 15 minutes for the Städelsches Kunstinstitut und Städtische Galerie, and an hour for the Städtische Galerie Liebieghaus. For the remaining museums it is a question of time and preference. Take your pick from the following and allow at least 45 minutes for each: the Historisches Museum, the Deutsches Filmmuseum, the Museum für Kunsthandwerk, the Deutsches Architekturmuseum, and the Jüdisches Museum. If you intend to visit the Zoologischer Garten, expect to spend 1½ hours there.

Sights to See

㉑ **Alte Oper** (Old Opera House). Built between 1873 and 1880 and gutted in World War II, Frankfurt's Old Opera House has been beautifully reconstructed. Kaiser Wilhelm I traveled from Berlin for the gala opening in 1880. After World War II the opera house remained a beautiful hollow shell for 40 years while controversy raged over its reconstruction. The new building is faithful to the classical proportions and style of the original. Even if you don't go to a performance, it's worth having a look at the ponderous and ornate lobby, an example of 19th-century neoclassicism at its most self-confident. ⊠ *Opernpl.,* ☎ *069/134–0400.*

Alter Jüdischer Friedhof (Old Jewish Cemetery). The old Jewish quarter is near Börneplatz, a short walk south of the Konstablerwache, or east of the Römer, U-bahn stations. The cemetery is east of Börneplatz and was in use between the 13th and 19th centuries. Partly vandalized in the Nazi era, it is nearly all that remains of prewar Jewish life in Frankfurt. To visit the cemetery, you must leave personal identification (like a passport) and then pick up the key. ⊠ *Kurt-Schumacher-Str. and Battonstr.,* ☎ *069/740–721.* ▣ *Free.* ☉ *Daily 8:30–4:30.*

❾ **Börse** (Stock Exchange). This is the center of Germany's stock and money market. The Börse was founded by Frankfurt merchants in 1558 to establish some order in their often chaotic dealings, but the present building dates from the 1870s. In the past, the trading on the dealers' floor was hectic. These days computerized networks and international telephone systems have removed some of the drama, but it is still an exciting scene to watch. There is a visitors' gallery. ⊠ *Börsepl.,* ☎ *069/21010.* ▣ *Free.* ☉ *Visitors' gallery weekdays 10:30–1:30.*

⓯ **Eiserner Steg** (Iron Bridge). A pedestrian walkway and the first suspension bridge in Europe, the bridge connects the city center with Sachsenhausen (☞ *below*).

Eschenheimer Turm (Eschenheim Tower). Built in the early 15th century, this tower, a block north of the Hauptwache, remains the finest example of the city's original 42 towers. ⊠ *Eschenheimer Tor.*

⓴ **Fressgasse** ("Pig-Out Alley"). Grosse Bockenheimer Strasse is the proper name of this street, one of the city's liveliest thoroughfares, but Frankfurters have given it this sobriquet because of its amazing choice of delicatessens, wine merchants, cafés, and restaurants. Food shops offer fresh or smoked fish, cheeses, and a wide range of local specialties, including Frankfurters. In the summer you can sit at tables on the sidewalk and dine alfresco.

★ ⑲ **Goethehaus und Goethemuseum** (Goethe's House and Museum). The house where Germany's most famous poet was born in 1749 is furnished with many original pieces that belonged to his family, including manuscripts in his own hand. Though Goethe is most associated with Weimar, where he lived most of his life, Frankfurters are proud to claim him as a native son. The original house was destroyed by Allied bombing and has been carefully rebuilt and restored in every detail as the young Goethe would have known it. Goethe studied law and became a member of the bar in Frankfurt but preferred the life of a writer and published his first best-seller, the drama *Götz von Berlichingen*, at the age of 20. He sealed his fame a few years later with the tragic love story *Die Leiden des jungen Werthers (The Sorrows of Young Werther)*. Goethe also wrote the first version of his masterpiece, *Faust*, in Frankfurt. The adjoining museum contains works of art that inspired Goethe (he was an amateur painter) and works associated with his literary contemporaries who were members of the Storm and Stress movement. This circle of writers and artists abandoned neoclassical ideals for the darker world of human subjectivity and helped create the romantic cult of the youthful genius in rebellion against society. ⊠ *Grosser Hirschgraben 23–25,* ☎ *069/138–800.* 🎟 *DM 7.* ☉ *Apr.–Sept., weekdays 9–6, weekends 10–4; Oct.–Mar., weekdays 9–4, weekends 10–4.*

❼ **Hauptwache.** This square is where Liebfrauenstrasse runs into the ☞ Zeil, a main shopping street; a vast underground shopping mall stretches below it. The attractive baroque building with a steeply sloping roof is the actual Hauptwache (Main Guardhouse). Built in 1729, it had been tastelessly added to over the years and was demolished to permit the excavation for the mall and subway station beneath it. The occasion was used to restore it to its original appearance. Today it houses a café.

❹ **Historisches Museum** (History Museum). This fascinating museum encompasses all aspects of the city's history over the past eight centuries. It contains a scale model of historic Frankfurt, complete with every street, house, and church. There are also an astonishing display of silver, exhibits covering all aspects of the city's life from the 16th through the 20th centuries, and a children's museum. ⊠ *Saalg. 19,* ☎ *069/2123– 5599.* 🎟 *DM 5; free Wed.* ☉ *Tues.–Sun. 10–5, Wed. 10–8.*

⑰ **Jüdisches Museum** (Jewish Museum). In the former Rothschild Palais, this museum tells the story of Frankfurt's Jewish quarter. Prior to the Holocaust it was the second largest in Germany. The museum contains extensive archives of Jewish history and culture, including a library of 5,000 books, a large photographic collection, and a documentation center. ⊠ *Untermainkai 14–15,* ☎ *069/2123–4856.* 🎟 *DM 5.* ☉ *Tues. and Thurs.–Sun. 10–5, Wed. 10–8.*

⑱ **Karmeliterkirche** (Carmelite Church and Monastery). Secularized in 1803, the church and adjacent buildings were renovated in the 1980s and now contain the **Museum für Vor- und Frühgeschichte** (Museum of Prehistory and Early History; ⊠ Karmeliterg. 1, ☎ 069/2123– 5896; 🎟 DM 5, free Wed.; ☉ Tues. and Thurs.–Sun. 10–5, Wed. 10– 8). The main cloister of this former monastery houses the **Galerie im Karmeliterkloster** (⊠ Münzg. 9; 🎟 free; ☉ weekdays 8:30–5, weekends 10–5), which displays rotating exhibitions of modern art and the largest religious fresco north of the Alps, a 16th-century representation of Christ's birth and death by Jörg Ratgeb.

❽ **Katharinenkirche** (St. Catherine's Church). This church was originally built between 1678 and 1681, the first independent Protestant church in Gothic style. It was in the original church that the first Protestant sermon was preached in Frankfurt, in 1522. Goethe was confirmed here. Step inside to see the simple, postwar stained glass. ⊠ *An der Hauptwache and Katherinenpfad.* ⊙ *Daily 10–5.*

⑯ Leonhardskirche (St. Leonard's Church). Begun in the Romanesque style and continued in the late-Gothic style, this beautifully preserved church contains five naves, two 13th-century Romanesque arches, and 15th-century stained glass. The "pendant," or hanging vaulting, was already a major Frankfurt tourist attraction in the 17th century. ⊠ *Leonhardstr. and Untermainkai.* ⊙ *Wed., Fri., and Sat. 10–noon and 3–6; Tues. and Thurs. 10–noon and 3–6:30; Sun. 9–1 and 3–6.*

❻ Liebfrauenkirche (Church of Our Lady). Dating from the 14th century, this late-Gothic church still has a fine tympanum relief over the south door and ornate rococo wood carvings inside. Outside is a delightful rococo fountain. ⊠ *Liebfrauenberg 3,* ☎ *069/284–612.* ⊙ *Daily 7– 7, except during services.*

Messe (Exhibition Halls). This huge complex is Europe's busiest trade fair center and is full of congresses, conferences, and seminars. Important international trade fairs showcase the latest books, cars, fashion, medical and high technology, and consumer goods. In addition to the two major fairs in spring and fall, there is an automobile show in September of odd-numbered years, the Fur Fair at Easter, and the International Book Fair in the fall. ⊠ *Ludwig-Erhard-Anlage 1,* ☎ *069/75750.*

⑫ Museum für Moderne Kunst (Museum of Modern Art). Austrian architect Hans Hollein designed this distinctive triangular building, shaped like a slice of wedding cake. The collection features American pop art and works by such German artists as Gerhard Richter and Joseph Beuys. ⊠ *Domstr. 10,* ☎ *069/2123–0447.* ▣ *DM 7.* ⊙ *Tues. and Thurs.–Sun. 10–5, Wed. 10–8.*

☙ ㉓ Naturkundemuseum Senckenberg (Natural History Museum). An important collection of fossils, animals, plants, and geological exhibits is upstaged by the famous diplodocus dinosaur, imported from New York—the only complete specimen of its kind in Europe. Many of the exhibits on prehistoric animals have been designed with children in mind, and there is a whole series of dioramas in which stuffed animals are presented. ⊠ *Senckenberganlage 25,* ☎ *069/75420.* ▣ *DM 7.* ⊙ *Mon., Tues., Thurs., and Fri. 9–5, Wed. 9–8, weekends 9–6.*

❸ Nikolaikirche (St. Nicholas Church). This small red sandstone church was built in the late 13th century as the court chapel for emperors of the Holy Roman Empire. Try to time your visit to coincide with the chimes of the carillon, which rings out three times a day, at 9, noon, and 5. ⊠ *South side of Römerberg.* ⊙ *Mon.–Sat. 10–5.*

☙ ㉒ Palmengarten und Botanischer Garten (Tropical Garden and Botanical Gardens). A splendid cluster of tropical and semitropical greenhouses contains a wide variety of flora, including cacti, orchids, and palms. The surrounding park has many recreational facilities. There is a little lake where you can rent rowboats, a play area for children, and a wading pool. Between the Palmengarten and the adjoining Grüneburgpark, the botanical gardens have a wide assortment of wild, ornamental, and rare plants from around the world. Special collections include a 2½-acre rock garden as well as rose and rhododendron gardens. During most of the year there are flower shows and exhibitions; in summer concerts are held in an outdoor music pavilion. ⊠ *Siesmayerstr. 63,* ☎ *069/2123–3939.* ▣ *DM 7.* ⊙ *Mar.–Sept., daily 9–6; Oct. and Feb., daily 9–5; Nov.–Jan., daily 9–4.*

⑤ Paulskirche (St. Paul's Church). This church was the site of the first all-German parliament in 1848. The parliament lasted only a year, having achieved little more than offering the Prussian king the crown of Germany. Today the church, which has been secularized and not very tastefully restored, remains a symbol of German democracy and is used mainly for ceremonies. The German Book Dealers' annual Peace Prize is awarded in the hall, as is the Goethe Prize. ⊠ *Paulspl.* ⊘ *Daily 11–3.*

② Römer (City Hall). Its gabled Gothic facade with an ornate balcony is widely known as the city's official emblem. Three individual patrician buildings make up the Römer. From left to right, they are the Alt-Limpurg, the Zum Römer (from which the entire structure takes its name), and the Löwenstein. The mercantile-minded Frankfurt burghers used the complex not only for political and ceremonial purposes but also for trade fairs and other commercial ventures.

The most important events to take place in the Römer were the festivities celebrating the coronations of the Holy Roman emperors. These were mounted starting in 1562 in the glittering **Kaisersaal** (Imperial Hall), last used in 1792 to celebrate the election of the emperor Francis II, who would later be forced to abdicate by Napoléon. It is said that 16-year-old Goethe posed as a waiter to get a firsthand impression of the banquet celebrating the coronation of Emperor Joseph II. The most vivid description of the ceremony is told in his book *Dichtung und Wahrheit* (*Poetry and Truth*). When no official business is being conducted, you can see the impressive, full-length 19th-century portraits of the 52 emperors of the Holy Roman Empire, which line the walls of the reconstructed banquet hall. ⊠ *West side of Römerberg,* ☎ *069/2123–4814.* ⊠ *DM 3.* ⊘ *Daily 10–1 and 2–5. Closed during official functions.*

① Römerberg. This square north of the Main River, lovingly restored after wartime bomb damage, is the historical focal point of the city. The ☞ **Römer**, the ☞ **Nikolaikirche**, the ☞ **Historiches Museum**, and the half-timber Ostzeile houses are all found here. The 16th-century Fountain of Justitia (Justice) stands in the center of the Römerberg. At the coronation of Emperor Matthias in 1612, wine flowed from the fountain instead of water. This practice has been revived by the city fathers on special occasions.

⑬ St. Bartholomäus (Church of St. Bartholomew). Because the Holy Roman emperors were chosen and crowned here from the 16th to the 18th centuries, the church is also known as the Kaiserdom (Imperial Cathedral). But it isn't really a cathedral. It was built largely between the 13th and 15th centuries and survived World War II with most of its treasures intact. It replaced a church established by Charlemagne's son, Ludwig the Pious, on the present site of the Römerberg. The many magnificent, original Gothic carvings include a life-size crucifixion group and the fine 15th-century *Maria-Schlaf* (Altar of Mary Sleeping). The most impressive exterior feature is the tall, red sandstone tower (almost 300 ft high), which was added between 1415 and 1514. It was the tallest structure in Frankfurt before the skyscrapers, and the view from the top remains an exciting panorama. In 1953 excavations in front of the main entrance revealed the remains of a Roman settlement and the foundations of a Carolingian imperial palace.

The **Dommuseum** (Cathedral Museum) occupies the former Gothic cloister. ⊠ *Dompl. 1.* ⊠ *Dommuseum DM 2.* ⊘ *Church daily (9–6 in summer, shorter hrs in winter) except during services; Dommuseum Tues.–Fri. 10–5, weekends 11–5.*

⑭ **Schirn Kunsthalle** (Schirn Art Gallery). One of Frankfurt's most modern museums is devoted exclusively to changing exhibits of modern art and photography. Past shows include the German symbolist movement between 1870 and 1920; the works of a contemporary news photographer, and Polish landscapes of the 19th and 20th centuries. It's opposite St. Bartholomäus Church. ⊠ *Am Römerberg 6a,* ☎ *069/299–8820.* 🎟 *DM 6–DM 9, depending on exhibition.* ☉ *Tues. and Fri.–Sun. 10–7, Wed. and Thurs. 10–10.*

⑪ **Staufenmauer** (Staufen Wall). The Staufenmauer is one of the few remaining sections of the old city's fortifications and dates from the 12th century.

Steinernes Haus (Stone House). Originally built in 1464, destroyed in World War II, and rebuilt between 1957 and 1960 with an altered interior, this Gothic-style patrician house has also served as a trading post. The Frankfurt Kunstverein (Art Association) regularly mounts special exhibits here. ⊠ *Markt 44,* ☎ *069/285–339.* 🎟 *Varies with exhibition.* ☉ *Tues.–Sat. noon–7.*

🄲 **Struwwelpeter-Museum** (Slovenly Peter Museum). This museum contains a collection of letters, sketches, and manuscripts by Dr. Heinrich Hoffmann, physician and creator of the children's book hero Struwwelpeter, or "Slovenly Peter," the character you see as a puppet or doll in Frankfurt's shops. ⊠ *Schirm am Römerberg,* ☎ *069/281–333.* 🎟 *Free.* ☉ *Tues. and Thurs.–Sun. 11–5, Wed. 11–8.*

Zeil. The heart of Frankfurt's shopping district is this ritzy pedestrian street, running east from Hauptwache Square. City officials claim it's the country's busiest shopping street. The Zeil is also known as "the Golden Mile" (☞ Shopping, *below*).

★ 🄲 ⑩ **Zoologischer Garten** (Zoo). Founded in 1858, this is one of the most important and attractive zoos in Europe, with many of the animals and birds living in a natural environment. Its remarkable collection includes some 5,000 animals of 600 different species, a bears' castle, an exotarium (aquarium plus reptiles), and an aviary, reputedly the largest in Europe. Nocturnal creatures move about in a special section. The zoo has a restaurant and a café, along with afternoon concerts in summer. ⊠ *Alfred-Brehm Pl. 16,* ☎ *069/2123–3727.* 🎟 *DM 11.* ☉ *Nov. 1–Mar. 31, daily 8–5; Apr. 1–Oct. 31, daily 8–8.*

Sachsenhausen

★ The old quarter of Sachsenhausen, on the south bank of the Main River, has been sensitively preserved and its cobblestone streets, half-timber houses, and beer gardens make it a very popular area to stroll. Sachsenhausen's two big attractions are the Museumufer (Museum Riverbank), which has seven museums almost next door to one another, and the famous *Ebbelwoi* (apple-wine or cider) taverns around the Rittergasse pedestrian area. A green pine wreath above a tavern's entrance tells passersby that a freshly pressed—and alcoholic—apple cider is on tap. You can eat well in these small inns, too. Formerly a separate village, Sachsenhausen is said to have been established by Charlemagne, who settled the Main's banks with a group of Saxon families in the 8th century. It was an important bridgehead for the crusader Knights of the Teutonic Order and in 1318 officially became part of Frankfurt.

A Good Walk

The best place to begin is at the charming 17th-century villa housing the **Städtische Galerie Liebieghaus** ㉔, the westernmost of the museums. It has an internationally famous collection of classical, medieval, and

Renaissance sculpture. From it you need only turn to your right and follow the riverside road, Schaumainkai, for about 2 km (1 mi), passing all of the museums and winding up around the Rittergasse.

The other museums are strung out before you. The **Städelsches Kunstinstitut und Städtische Galerie** ㉕ houses one of the most significant art collections in Germany, and the **Museum für Post und Kommunication** ㉖ displays postal coaches, ancient telephones that work, and a huge stamp collection. The **Deutsches Architekturmuseum** ㉗ traces man's structures from Stone Age huts to high-rises. Film artifacts and classic film videos are featured at the **Deutsches Filmmuseum** ㉘. After this museum, you could take a break at an Apfelwein tavern on Schweizer Strasse (☞ Need a Break, *below*). The next museum after the bridge is the **Museum für Volkerkunde** ㉙, which holds ethnological artifacts from the Pacific, Indonesia, Africa, and America. A stunning collection of European and Asian applied art in the **Museum für Kunsthandwerk** ㉚ comes next. Continue down the river road (the name changes from Schaumainkai to Sachsenhäser Ufer) to the **Kuhhirtenturm** ㉛, the only remaining part of Sachsenhausen's original fortifications.

Just beyond the first bridge carrying car traffic, follow Grosse Rittergasse to the right. You will immediately be in the heart of the Apfelwein district, which is especially lively on summer evenings when it becomes one big outdoor festival. Some of the apple-wine taverns and other watering places are also open weekday afternoons. The area has a distinctly medieval air, with narrow back alleys, quaint little inns, and quiet squares that escaped the modern developer, yet it's also full of new shops, cafés, and bars thronging with people.

Timing

Allow an hour and 15 minutes for the Städelsches Kunstinstitut and Städtische Galerie, and an hour for the Städtische Galerie Liebieghaus. You could spend at least 45 minutes in each of the other museums along the walk. At the end of the day relax in an apple-wine tavern.

Sights to See

㉗   **Deutsches Architekturmuseum** (German Architecture Museum). Created by German architect Oswald Mathias Ungers, this 19th-century villa contains an entirely modern interior. There are five floors of drawings, models, and audiovisual displays that chart the progress of architecture through the ages, as well as many special exhibits. ⊠ *Schaumainkai 43,* ☏ *069/2123–8844.* ⌑ *DM 8.* ☉ *Tues.–Sun. 10–5, Wed. until 8.*

㉘   **Deutsches Filmmuseum** (German Film Museum). Germany's first museum of cinematography houses an exciting collection of film artifacts. Visitors can view its collection of classic film videos, and a theater in the basement has regular evening screenings of every sort of film from avant-garde to Hungarian to silent-era flicks. ⊠ *Schaumainkai 41,* ☏ *069/2123–8830.* ⌑ *DM 5.* ☉ *Tues., Thurs., Fri., and Sun. 10–5, Wed. 10–8, Sat. 2–8.*

NEED A
BREAK?   Two of Sachsenhausen's swingingest Apfelwein taverns are well removed from the Rittergasse and handy to the Museumufer. Once beyond the Deutsches Filmmuseum, turn right on Schweizer Strasse and walk five minutes to the neighboring **Zum Gemalten Haus** (⊠ Schweizer Str. 67, ☏ 069/614–559) and **Zum Wagner** (⊠ Schweizer Str. 71, ☏ 069/612–565) for all the hard cider or Gemütlichkeit you could want.

㉛   **Kuhhirtenturm** (Shepherd's Tower). This is the last of nine towers, built in the 15th century, that formed part of Sachsenhausen's fortifications. The composer Paul Hindemith lived in the tower from 1923 to 1927, while working at the Frankfurt Opera.

㉚ Museum für Kunsthandwerk (Museum of Decorative Arts). The American architect Richard Meier designed this museum, which opened in 1985. More than 30,000 objects representing European and Asian handicrafts are exhibited, including furniture, glassware, and porcelain. ⊠ *Schaumainkai 17,* ☎ *069/2123–4037.* ⛬ *DM 6; free Wed.* ☉ *Tues. and Thurs.–Sun. 10–5, Wed. 10–8.*

㉖ Museum für Post und Kommunication (Museum for Post and Communication). On display are the various means of transporting mail through the ages—from the mail coach to the airplane. There's also an exhibition of stamps and stamp-printing machines, as well as a reconstructed 19th-century post office. ⊠ *Schaumainkai 53,* ☎ *069/60600.* ⛬ *Free.* ☉ *Tues.–Sun. 10–5.*

㉙ Museum für Völkerkunde (Ethnological Museum). The exhibits depict the lifestyles and customs of aboriginal societies from around the world. The collection includes masks, ritual objects, and jewelry. ⊠ *Schaumainkai 29,* ☎ *069/2123–1510.* ⛬ *DM 6; free Wed.* ☉ *Tues. and Thurs.–Sun. 10–1 and 1:30–5, Wed. 10–8.*

★ ㉕ Städelsches Kunstinstitut and Städtische Galerie (Städel Art Institute and Municipal Gallery). Here you will find one of Germany's most important art collections, with paintings by Dürer, Vermeer, Rembrandt, Rubens, Monet, Renoir, and other masters. The section on German expressionism is particularly strong, with representative works by Frankfurt artist Max Beckmann. ⊠ *Schaumainkai 63,* ☎ *069/605–0980.* ⛬ *DM 8; free Wed.* ☉ *Tues. and Thurs.–Sun. 10–5, Wed. 10–8.*

★ ㉔ Städtische Galerie Liebieghaus (Liebieg Municipal Museum of Sculpture). The sculpture collection here from 5,000 years of civilizations and epochs is considered one of the most important in Europe. From antiquity the collection includes a statue of a Sumarian functionary and a relief from the temple of Egyptian king Sahure (2455–2443 BC). From the Middle Ages there is an 11th-century throned Madonna with child from Trier, and from the Renaissance an altar relief by the noted Florentine sculptor Lucca della Robbia (1399–1482). Works such as the *Immaculata,* by Matthias Steinl (1688), represent the baroque era. Some pieces are exhibited in the lovely gardens surrounding the house. ⊠ *Schaumainkai 71,* ☎ *069/2123–8617.* ⛬ *DM 5.* ☉ *Tues. and Thurs.–Sun. 10–5, Wed. 10–8.*

DINING

Make reservations in advance for any of the fancier restaurants in Frankfurt. Many serve bargain lunch menus. For example, **Erno's Bistro** and **Gargantua** have midday menus for DM 49. At the apple-wine taverns there's always room for a couple more at the long tables, and patrons are very accommodating when it comes to squeezing together.

CATEGORY	COST*
$$$$	over DM 100
$$$	DM 75–DM 100
$$	DM 50–DM 75
$	under DM 50

*per person for a three-course meal, including tax and service, excluding drinks

City Center

$$$$ ✕ **Restaurant Français.** Frankfurt's oldest hotel-restaurant, in the Steigenberger Frankfurter Hof (☞ Lodging, *below*), offers sophisticated international fare with a French accent. The ornate green-and-gold dining room with Louis XVI furnishings and well-spaced tables is a perfect place for a business meal or to enjoy the seven-course tasting menu, including breast of quail in lentil soup, followed by duck supreme or baked turbot fillets in a mango-and-ginger sauce. ⊠ *Bethmannstr. 33,* ☎ *069/215–138. Reservations essential. Jacket and tie. AE, DC, MC, V. Closed Sun., Mon., and 4 wks in July or Aug. (depending on summer vacation). No lunch Sat.*

$$$$ ✕ **Sand.** The restaurant proudly boasts that Lebanon is the "mother of Arabic cuisine." As is usual with Middle Eastern restaurants, the emphasis is on lamb, and there is a big selection of hors d'oeuvres, with spiced vegetables, lamb sausages, sheep cheese, and yogurt. Many make a meal of two or three of them. It also, unaccountably, has a bar where you can get skillfully made American cocktails, a rarity even in Frankfurt. Most of the tables are in a pleasant courtyard to the rear, which is covered in inclement weather with a sliding translucent roof. A pianist helps with the mood. ⊠ *Kaiserstr. 25,* ☎ *069/2424–9440. AE, DC, MC, V. Closed Sun.*

$$$ ✕ **Mikuni.** A few paper lanterns and wall posters don't do much to offset the German furnishings, but the many Japanese patrons here vouch for the authentic Japanese fare. The menu is in Japanese as well as German, each arriving guest gets a hot towel, soup is drunk from the bowl, and even Germans seldom ask for a knife and fork to replace their chopsticks. Prices are more reasonable here than at other sushi bars. ⊠ *Fahrg. 91–95,* ☎ *069/283–627. AE, MC.*

$$ ✕ **Kangaroo's.** The man-size ceramic kangaroo that greets you at the door sets the tone for this Australia-themed restaurant. The adventurous will try the meat of such Down Under critters as emu or barramundi (but Aussies, too, eat beef, chicken, and salads.) Most people patronize this incredibly popular downtown establishment for the food, but it's also a friendly place to gather for a Foster's beer, play pool, or watch events on the large-screen TV. ⊠ *Grosse Eschersheimer Str.,* ☎ *069/ 131–0339. AE, DC, MC, V.*

$ ✕ **Café Karin.** An understated café that attracts an interesting cross section of patrons, this is a great place to breakfast (only a few marks), to recover from a shopping spree, or to eat something healthy in preparation for a night out. Sample the goat cheese salad or whole-grain ratatouille crepes. Cakes and baked goods come from the whole-grain bakery next door. There is a no-smoking section. ⊠ *Grosser Hirschgraben 28,* ☎ *069/295–217. No credit cards.*

$ ✕ **Historix.** It goes without saying that Apfelwein is an important part of Frankfurt, so what could be more logical than the Historisches Museum to have a permanent exhibition on apple wine? Inside the museum, the Historix serves the beverage in *Bembel* pitchers and with all the typical food items and other accoutrements of the hard-cider business. The wall facing the street is one big plate-glass window, something you're not likely to find in a real tavern, but the decor more than makes up for this. What Sachsenhausen locale would have a display of historic bembels and every inch of wall space covered with schmaltzy old pictures of the apple-wine scene? The place is overshadowed by a fake apple tree with huge fruit. ⊠ *Saalg. 19,* ☎ *069/294400. No credit cards. Closed Mon. No dinner weekends.*

$ ✕ **Steinernes Haus.** Diners share long wooden tables beneath prints of old Frankfurt and traditional clothing mounted on the walls. The house specialty is a rump steak brought to the table uncooked with a heated rock tablet on which it is prepared. The beef broth is the perfect antidote to cold weather. The menu has other old German standards along with daily specials. If you don't specify a *Kleines*, or small glass of beer, you'll automatically get a liter mug. Traditional fare popular with locals includes *Frankfurter Rippchen* (smoked pork) and *Zigeunerhackbraten* (spicy meat loaf). ⊠ *Braubachstr. 35*, ☎ *069/283–491. Reservations essential. MC, V.*

Westend

$$$$ ✕ **Erno's Bistro.** Erno's is something of a Frankfurt institution. It's small and chic—*very* popular with visiting power brokers—and offers classic French cuisine. Fish dishes predominate—all the fish is flown in daily, most of it from France—and specials vary according to what's available in the markets that day. This is one of those rare restaurants where you can sit back and let the staff choose your meal for you. All the waiters speak English. ⊠ *Liebigstr. 15*, ☎ *069/721–997. Reservations essential. Jacket and tie. AE, DC, MC, V. Closed weekends, 1 wk at Easter, and July–Aug.*

$$$ ✕ **Gargantua.** One of Frankfurt's most creative chefs, Klaus Trebes serves up new versions of German classics and French-accented dishes in a Westend dining room decorated with contemporary art. His menu features dishes like artichoke risotto with goose liver, lentil salad with stewed beef, and grilled dorado served on puréed white beans and pesto. One corner of the restaurant is reserved for those who only want to sample the outstanding wine list. ⊠ *Liebigstr. 47*, ☎ *069/720–718. AE, DC, MC, V. Closed Sun. No lunch Sat.*

$$ ✕ **Jewel of India.** The elegant decor, gracious service, and delicious Indian-Pakistani food make the Jewel a good choice for lunch (it's just a couple of blocks from the trade-fair grounds). It's a lot calmer and quieter than the neighborhood's popular Italian restaurants. The chicken tandoori in saffron-yogurt marinade and lamb dishes such as *rogan josh* harmoniously blend spices and flavors without being overpowering. ⊠ *Wilhelm-Hauff-Str. 5*, ☎ *069/752–375. AE, MC, V. No lunch Sat.*

$$ ✕ **Omonia.** This cozy cellar locale offers the best Greek cuisine in town. Those with a good appetite should try the Omonia Platter, with lamb in several forms, plus Greek-style pasta and vegetables. The place is popular and the tables few, so make a reservation. ⊠ *Vogtstr. 43*, ☎ *069/593314. AE, DC MC, V.*

$$ ✕ **Pizzeria Romanella.** Don't let the name and unpretentious exterior fool you. This is a true *ristorante* with a very extensive menu of Italian fare. All the tables are full at supper time, when diners enjoy pastas and veal dishes. The pizza pies are good, but no better than elsewhere. ⊠ *Wolfsgangstr. 84*, ☎ *069/596–1117. No credit cards. Closed Sat.*

$ ✕ **Café Laumer.** The ambience of an old-time Viennese café, with a subdued decor, ballustraded terrace, and rear garden, is well preserved here. Come for the variety of coffees and mouthwatering cake buffet. In a compromise with the café tradition, meals are also served until closing time, but there's no lingering over dinner. It's open for breakfast, lunch, and afternoon coffee but closes at 7 PM. ⊠ *Bockenheimer Landstr. 67*, ☎ *069/727–912. No credit cards.*

Sachsenhausen

$$$$ ✕ **Maingau Stuben.** Chef Werner Döpfner himself greets you and ★ lights your candle at this very "in" restaurant. Well-heeled patrons are drawn by the linen tablecloths, subdued lighting, and such nearly forgotten practices as carving the meat at the table and pouring a bit of

Frankfurt Dining and Lodging

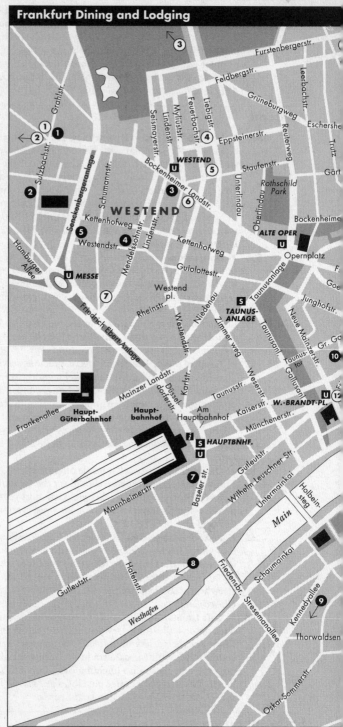

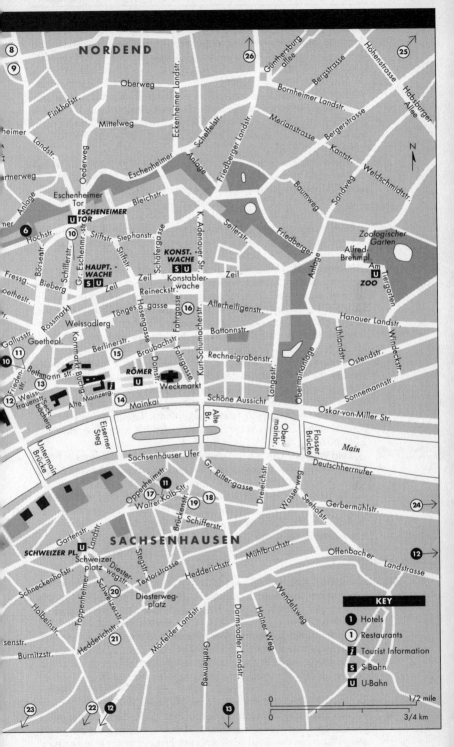

NORDEND

Oberweg

Finkhofstr.

Mittelweg

Oederweg

Eschenheimer Landstr.

Eckenheimer Landstr.

Scheffeleldr.

Friedberger Landstr.

Günthersburg allee

Bornheimer Landstr.

Bergstrasse

Höhenstrasse

Habsburger Allee

Merianstrasse

Bergerstrasse

Sandweg

Weldschmidtstr.

Kantstr.

Baumweg

Anlage

Eschenheimer

Bleichstr.

Seilerstr.

Friedberger

Eschenheimer Tor

ESCHENEIMER TOR 🅄

Hochstr.

Börsenstr.

Schillerstr.

Stiftstr.

Stephanstr.

Schäfergasse

K. Adenauer Str.

KONST. WACHE 🆂🅄

Anlage

Zoologischer Garten

Alfred-Brehmpl.

Am Tiergarten

ZOO

HAUPT.-WACHE 🆂🅄

Gr. Eschenmr.str.

Zeil

Reineckstr.

Konstabler-wache

Zeil

Allerheiligenstr.

Hanauer Landstr.

Bieber

Rossmarkt

Weissadlerg.

Tönges-gasse

Hasengasse

Fahrgasse

🅃🅄

Battonnstr.

Uhlandstr.

Ostendstr.

Windeckstr.

Fressg.

Goethestr.

Goethepl.

Berlinerstr.

Braubachstr.

Kurt-Schumacherstr.

Rechneigrabenstr.

Langestr.

Obermainanlage

Sonnemannstr.

Gallusstr.

Bethmann str.

Buchg.

RÖMER 🅄

Domstr.

Weckmarkt

Schöne Aussicht

Oskar-von-Miller Str.

Friedensstr.

Weissfrauenstr.

Seckbächerg.

Alte Mainzerg.

Mainkai

Alte Br.

Obermainbr.

Flosser Brücke

Main

Deutschherrnufer

Eiserner Steg

Sachsenhäuser Ufer

Gr. Ritter-gasse

Dreieichstr.

Wasserweg

Seehofstr.

Gerbermühlstr.

Untermain Brücke

Oppenheimstr.

Walter-Kolb-Str.

Brückenstr.

Schifferstr.

SACHSENHAUSEN

SCHWEIZER PL. 🅄

Gartenstr.

Landstr.

Schweizer platz

Diester-wegstr.

Stegstr.

Textorstrasse

Hedderichstr.

Mühlbruchstr.

Offenbacher

Landstrasse

Schneckenhofstr.

Toppenheimer Landstr.

Schweizerstr.

Diesterweg-platz

Mörfelder Landstr.

Wendelsweg

Hainer Weg

Holbeinstr.

Hedderichstr.

Burnitzstr.

senstr.

Greifhenweg

Darmstädter Landstr.

KEY

❶	Hotels
①	Restaurants
🄸	Tourist Information
🆂	S-Bahn
🅄	U-Bahn

0 ____ 1/2 mile

0 ____ 3/4 km

the newly arrived wine for your approval. Chef Döpfner is one of Frankfurt's best, serving contemporary dishes like seafood salad with scallops and lobster mousse, and rack of venison in a walnut crust. He also has a cellar full rare German wines. ⊠ *Schifferstr. 38–40,* ☎ *069/610–752. AE, MC. Closed Mon. No lunch Sat.*

$$$ ✕ **Bistrot 77.** Proprietor-chef Dominique, who learned his trade in the French Alsace region, serves a three-course regional meal daily in this spare bistro with plain walls and a tile floor. The emphasis is on fresh vegetables and fine cuts of meat, such as rosettes of lamb with young runner beans. ⊠ *Ziegelhüttenweg 1–3,* ☎ *069/614–040. AE, MC, V. Closed Sun. No lunch Sat.*

$$ ✕ **Edelweiss.** This place, "where the Alps melt in your mouth," is full of homesick Austrians enjoying their native cuisine, including the genuine Wiener schnitzel, and Kaiser Franz Josef's favorite, *Tafelspitze,* made of boiled beef with a chive sauce. Then there is the roast chicken with a salad made of "earth apples" (potatoes) and the beloved *Kaiserschmarrn*: egg pancakes with raisins, apples, cinnamon, and jam. The decor is rustically wooden within, and there is a pleasant terrace. ⊠ *Schweizer Str. 96,* ☎ *069/619–696. AE, DC, MC, V.*

$ ✕ **Fichtekränzi.** This is the real thing—a traditional apple-cider tavern in the heart of Sachsenhausen. In summer the courtyard is the place to be; in winter you sit in the noisy tavern proper at long tables with benches. It's often crowded, so if there isn't room when you arrive, order a glass of apple cider and hang around until someone leaves. Traditional cider-tavern dishes include *Rippchen* (smoked pork). ⊠ *Wallstr. 5,* ☎ *069/612–778. No credit cards.*

$ ✕ **Tandure.** The aroma of the clay oven—called a *tandure*—wafts through the dining room in this small Turkish restaurant decorated with Turkish carpeting and Anatolian handicrafts. As an appetizer you might want to try the *sigara böregi* (phyllo pastry stuffed with sheep's cheese) or *imam bayildi* (stewed eggplant). Lamb, marinated and cooked in the tandoori, is the house specialty. It's open until midnight. ⊠ *Wallstr. 10,* ☎ *069/612–543. AE, V.*

$ ✕ **Zum Wagner.** This is a Sachsenhausen classic that succeeds in being
★ touristy and traditional all at once. The kitchen produces the same hearty German dishes as those of other apple-wine taverns—only better. Try the *Tafelspitz mit Frankfurter Grüner Sosse* (stewed beef with a sauce of green herbs) or come on Friday for fresh fish. Beer and wine are served as well as cider. ⊠ *Schweizer Str. 71,* ☎ *069/612–565. Reservations not accepted. No credit cards.*

Outer Frankfurt

$$$$ ✕ **Papillon.** Although it's part of the Sheraton Hotel at the airport, the
★ Papillon has won over the country's most respected food critics. No whisper of a jet engine can be heard, and there's no rush or bustle in the velvety, luxurious dining room. It concentrates on a small but imaginative changing contemporary menu, on which you'll find such delicacies as rolled pike-perch coated in wild rice or lamb fillet served with eggplant baked in a sour-cream dough. Even though this is an airport restaurant, there is a strict jacket-and-tie rule. ⊠ *Hugo-Eckener-Ring 15/Terminal 1, Frankfurt Airport,* ☎ *069/6977–1238. Jacket and tie. AE, DC, MC, V. Closed Sun. No lunch Sat.*

$$$ ✕ **Altes Zollhaus.** Within this beautiful 200-year-old half-timber house you can enjoy very good traditional German specialties. Try one of the game dishes, or the sliced pork with mushrooms in apple-wine sauce. In summer you can eat outside while chefs grill in the huge garden. ⊠ *Friedberger Landstr. 531,* ☎ *069/472–707. AE, DC, MC, V. Closed Mon. No lunch.*

$$$ ✕ **Gerbermühle.** Many think this is the finest garden restaurant in the city. It's right on the banks of the Main and can be reached with a pleasant riverside hike from downtown. The city's favorite son, Goethe, liked to patronize it, which ought to be recommendation enough. The menu is typically Frankfurt and German. ⊠ *Deutschherrnufer 105,* ☎ *069/ 965–2290. AE.*

$$ ✕ **Arche Nova.** This sunny establishment is a feature of Frankfurt's Ökohaus, which was built according to environmental principles (solar panels, catching rainwater, etc.) In keeping with the character of the place, it's more or less vegetarian with such dishes as a vegetable platter with feta cheese or a curry soup with grated coconut and banana. Much of what's served, even some of the beers, is organic. ⊠ *Kasselerstr. 1a,* ☎ *069/707–5859. No credit cards.*

$$ ✕ **Zum Rad.** Named for the huge *Rad* (wagon wheel) that decorates it, this Apfelwein tavern is one of the few not in Sachsenhausen. It's in a little district called Seckbach, off the northeastern edge of the city, that retains its village character. Outside tables are under the spreading chestnut trees of an extensive courtyard. The typically Hessian cuisine includes dishes like *Ochsenbrust* (brisket of beef) and Handkäs. ⊠ *Leonhardsg. 2, Seckbach,* ☎ *069/479–128. No credit cards. Closed Mon. and Tues.*

$ ✕ **Dr. Flotte.** This smoky place is right out of another era, with high ceilings, arched windows, and a collection of ancient appliances, including radios and sewing machines. It's in the middle of the university district, and the students join the 80-year-old ladies in quaffing beer. The varied, largely German cuisine is quite affordable. ⊠ *Gräfstr. 87,* ☎ *069/704–595. No credit cards.*

$ ✕ **Wäldches.** This is Frankfurt's busiest brew-pub, in a countrified lo★ cation nevertheless handy to a rapid transit station, and a favorite stop for bikers and hikers. By noon on a pleasant summer Sunday, the big beer garden can be standing room only. The home-brewed light and dark beer goes nicely with the largely German cuisine, which is substantial but not stodgy. If you like the beer, you can take some of it with you in an old-fashioned bottle with a wired porcelain stopper. ⊠ *Am Ginnheimer Wäldchen 8,* ☎ *069/520–522. No credit cards.*

LODGING

Businesspeople descend on Frankfurt year-round, so most hotels in the city are expensive (though many also offer significant reductions on weekends) and are frequently booked up well in advance. Many hotels add as much as a 50% surcharge during trade fairs (*Messen*), of which there are about 30 a year. The majority of the larger hotels are close to the main train station, fairgrounds, and business district and are a 20-minute walk from the Old Town. Lower prices and—for some, anyway—more atmosphere are found at smaller hotels and pensions in the suburbs; the efficient public transportation network makes them easy to reach.

Information about trade fairs is available from the **German-American Chamber of Commerce** (☎ 212/974–8830; 0171/734–0543 in London) or the Tourismus und Congress Büro GmbH Frankfurt/Main (☞ Visitor Information *in* Frankfurt A to Z, *below*).

CATEGORY	COST*
$$$$	over DM 300
$$$	DM 200–DM 300
$$	DM 140–DM 200
$	under DM 140

*All prices are for two people in a double room, including tax and service.

City Center

$$$$ 🏨 **Hilton Frankfurt.** Frankfurt's newest chain hotel opened in 1999 with all the latest things the business traveler wants, from fax and modem lines to voice mail and video on command. Its Pacific Colors Restaurant has a large terrace overlooking a park. The Vista Bar & Lounge is just below the hotel's airy and transparent atrium. ✉ *Hochstr. 4,* ☎ *069/133–8000,* 𝙵𝙰𝚇 *069/1338–1338. 342 rooms. Restaurant, 2 bars, air-conditioning, in-room data ports, in-room safes, minibars, room service, indoor pool, beauty salon, hot tub, massage, sauna, steam room, health club, meeting rooms, parking (fee). AE, DC, MC, V.* 😊

$$$$ 🏨 **Steigenberger Frankfurter Hof.** This 19th-century Renaissance-style
★   building has one of the most imposing facades you'll ever see. Although it fronts a courtyard, you must enter it through a modest side entrance. Its full-bodied luxury makes this the first choice for many visitors. The atmosphere throughout is one of old-fashioned, formal elegance, with burnished woods, fresh flowers, and a thick-carpeted hush. The Restaurant Français (☞ Dining, *above*) is among the gourmet high spots of Germany; the bar is a classy late-night rendezvous. ✉ *Am Kaiserpl., D–60311 Frankfurt am Main,* ☎ *069/21502,* 𝙵𝙰𝚇 *069/215–900. 332 rooms, 10 suites. 2 restaurants, 2 bars. AE, DC, MC, V.* 😊

$ 🏨 **Pension Aller.** Quiet, solid comforts for a modest price and a friendly welcome are right near the train station. The third floor of a sociologist's private home offers cozy, well-lighted rooms in the back of the building. Reserve in advance because it gets a lot of return guests. ✉ *Gutleutstr. 94, D–60329 Frankfurt am Main,* ☎ *069/252–596,* 𝙵𝙰𝚇 *069/232–330. 10 rooms with shower. No credit cards.*

Westend

$$$ 🏨 **An der Messe.** This little place, whose name means "At the Fairgrounds," is a pleasing change from the giant hotels of the city. It's stylish, with a pink marble lobby and chicly appointed bedrooms. The staff is courteously efficient. The only drawback is the lack of a restaurant. ✉ *Westendstr. 104, D–60325 Frankfurt am Main,* ☎ *069/747–979,* 𝙵𝙰𝚇 *069/748–349. 46 rooms, 2 suites. AE, DC, MC, V.*

$$$ 🏨 **Hotel Robert Mayer.** For creative types who shun the sterile decor
★   of international hotel chains, Frankfurt's "Art Hotel" offers an alternative: 11 rooms, each decorated by a different Frankfurt artist, with furniture designs by the likes of Rietveld and Frank Lloyd Wright. The room designed by Therese Traube contrasts abstract newspaper collage with a replica Louis XIV armchair. It has no restaurant, but a large breakfast buffet is included in the price of the room. ✉ *Robert-Mayer-Str. 44, D–60486 Frankfurt am Main,* ☎ *069/970–9100,* 𝙵𝙰𝚇 *069/9709–1010. 11 rooms. AE, DC, MC, V.* 😊

$$$ 🏨 **Palmenhof.** Named for its proximity to the botanical garden, this
★   luxuriously modern hotel occupies a renovated Jugendstil (art nouveau) building in Frankfurt's Westend. The high-ceiling rooms have up-to-date comfort but retain the elegance of the old building. In the basement is a cozy restaurant, the Bastei, with an expensive nouvelle cuisine menu. ✉ *Bockenheimer Landstr. 89–91, D–60325 Frankfurt am Main,* ☎ *069/753–0060,* 𝙵𝙰𝚇 *069/7530–0666. 43 rooms, 37 apartments, 2 suites. Restaurant, parking (fee). AE, DC, MC, V.*

$$ 🏨 **Hotel-Pension West.** For home comforts, a handy location (near the university and U-bahn), and good value, try this family-run pension. It's in an older building and scores high for old-fashioned appeal. The rooms are more than adequate for a night or two. ✉ *Gräfstr. 81, D–60486 Frankfurt am Main,* ☎ *069/247–9020,* 𝙵𝙰𝚇 *069/707–5309. 20 rooms. AE, DC, MC, V.*

$ 🏨 **Hotel Westend.** "*Klein aber fein*" ("small but nice") is what the Germans say about a place like this. Everywhere you turn in the stylish, family-run establishment, you'll trip over French antiques. The hotel itself has no restaurant, but the classy neighborhood has plenty. ✉ *Westendstr. 15, D–60325 Frankfurt am Main,* ☎ *069/74670,* 🖷 *069/ 745–396. 20 rooms, 15 with bath or shower. AE, MC, V.*

Sachsenhausen

$$ 🏨 **Maingau.** In the middle of the lively Sachsenhausen quarter, the hotel is still within easy reach of the downtown area by public transit. Rooms are modest but spotless, comfortable, and equipped with TVs; the room rate includes a substantial breakfast buffet. The Maingau Stuben is one of the city's best restaurants (☞ Dining, *above*). ✉ *Schifferstr. 38–40, D–60594 Frankfurt am Main,* ☎ *069/609–140,* 🖷 *069/620–790. 100 rooms. Restaurant, parking (fee). AE, MC.*

Outer Frankfurt

$$$$ 🏨 **Sheraton Frankfurt.** This huge hotel is immediately accessible to one of Frankfurt Airport's terminals. It, like the airport, is also adjacent to the Frankfurter Kreuz, the major autobahn intersection, with superhighway connections to all of Europe. Not to worry about noise, the rooms are all soundproofed. In addition to the usual comforts, each room is equipped with an answering machine and a modem. Fortyfour of the rooms have ISDN connections that permit a fax machine, printer, and copier. Despite the hustle and bustle, the Papillon (☞ Dining, *above*) is one of the city's most renowned restaurants and provides a relaxing environment. ✉ *Hugo-Eckener-Ring 15, Flughafen Terminal 1,* ☎ *069/69770,* 🖷 *069/6977–2209. 1,020 rooms, 30 suites. 3 restaurants, 2 bars, air-conditioning, in-room data ports, minibars, indoor pool, massage, sauna, steam room, exercise room, concierge, meeting rooms, parking. AE, DC, MC, V.*

$$$ 🏨 **Dorint Hotel.** The Frankfurt member of the Dorint chain is a modern, well-appointed hotel with all the comforts and facilities expected from this well-run group, including a palm-fringed indoor pool. The hotel is south of the river in the Niederrad district, but there are good bus and subway connections with the city center and Sachsenhausen. ✉ *Hahnstr. 9, D–60492 Frankfurt-Niederrad,* ☎ *069/663–060,* 🖷 *069/ 6630–6600. 183 rooms, 8 suites. 2 restaurants, bar, no-smoking rooms, indoor pool, sauna, parking (fee). AE, DC, MC, V.* ⊛

$ 🏨 **Waldhotel Hensels Felsenkeller.** Helmut Braun's hotel is one of Frankfurt's least expensive, but the setting is one of the most pleasant: it backs onto the woods that ring Frankfurt. And the city center is just a 15-minute train ride (the nearest stop is a three-minute walk). Rooms are basic; the less expensive ones have shared showers in the hallway. ✉ *Buchrainstr. 95, D–60599 Frankfurt am Main,* ☎ *069/652–086,* 🖷 *069/658–379. 15 rooms, 7 with bath. Restaurant. No credit cards.*

NIGHTLIFE AND THE ARTS

The Arts

Frankfurt has the largest budget for cultural affairs of any city in the country. The **Städtische Bühnen**—municipal theaters, including the city's opera company—are the leading venues. Frankfurt has what is probably the most lavish theater in the country, the **Alte Oper** (Old Opera House), a magnificently ornate 19th-century edifice. However, the building is no longer used for opera, but as a multipurpose hall for pop and classical concerts, dances, and the like.

Theater tickets can be purchased from the **tourist office** at Römerberg 27 and from theater box offices. **Frankfurt Ticket GmbH** (⊠ Hauptwache Passage, ☎ 069/134–0400) is one of the best ticket agencies. You can also get tickets at **Ticket Direct** (⊠ Ottostr. 3a, ☎ 069/201–156), **Kartenvorverkauf GmbH** (⊠ Liebfrauenberg 52–54, ☎ 069/920–300), and at the ticket office in the **Hertie department store** (⊠ Zeil 90, ☎ 069/294–848).

Ballet, Concerts, and Opera

The most glamorous venue for classical music concerts is the **Alte Oper** (⊠ Opernpl., ☎ 069/134–0400). Tickets to performances can range from DM 20 to nearly DM 300. The **Frankfurt Opera** (⊠ Städtische Bühnen, Untermainanlage 11, ☎ 069/2123–7999) has made a new name for itself as a company for dramatic artistry. Sharing the same venue as the Frankfurt Opera, the world-renowned **Frankfurt Ballet** is under the modern-thinking direction of American William Forsythe.

The **Festhalle** (⊠ Ludwig-Erhard-Anlage 1, ☎ 069/7575–6404), on the fairgrounds, is the scene of many rock concerts, horse shows, ice shows, sporting events, and other large-scale spectaculars. It is sometimes used for fair exhibits, especially ones with large pieces of equipment, but more modern halls handle most of this nowadays.

Film

Frankfurt's new **IMAX** theater (⊠ Zeil 112–114, ☎ 069/1338–4830) entirely surrounds the spectator with a 979-ft screen. An old building at the Eschenheimer Tor is being converted into a multiplex theater, and the city is also a center of broadcasting.

Orfeo's Erben Kino & Kantine is a movie theater that has added on a restaurant and shows everything from children's matinees to silent-era horror films. You can dine by candlelight in the restaurant, then retire with wine and finger food to a plush theater seat. ⊠ *Hamburger Allee 45,* ☎ *069/7076–9100,* ☉ *Sun.–Thurs. 11:30 AM–3 PM and 5:30 PM– 2 AM, Fri. and Sat. 5:30 PM–2 AM. AE, DC, V.*

Theater

The **Künstlerhaus Mouson Turm** (⊠ Waldschmidtstr. 4, ☎ 069/4058–9520) is a cultural center that hosts a regular series of concerts of all kinds, as well as plays and exhibits. The municipally owned **Schauspielhaus** (⊠ Willy-Brandt-Pl., ☎ 069/2123–7999) has a repertoire including works by Sophocles, Goethe, Shakespeare, Brecht, and Beckett. For a zany theatrical experience, try **Die Schmiere** (⊠ Seckbächerg. 2, ☎ 069/281–066), which offers trenchant satire and also disarmingly calls itself "the worst theater in the world." Renowned for international experimental productions, including dance theater and other forms of nonverbal drama, is **Theater am Turm** (TAT; ⊠ Bockenheimer Warte, ☎ 069/2123–7999), in the Bockenheimer Depot, a former trolley barn.

If you're looking for English-language productions, try the **English Theater** (⊠ Kaiserstr. 52, ☎ 069/2423–1620), which creates its own productions with artists from England and the United States.

Nightlife

Frankfurt at night is a city of stark contrasts. Old hippies and baby-faced counterculturalists, Turkish and Greek guest workers, people on pensions, chess players, exhibitionists, and loners all have their piece of the action. People from the banking world tend to seek different amusements than the city's 40,000-plus students. But their paths cross in places like the cider taverns in Sachsenhausen and the gay bars of the Nordend. Sachsenhausen (Frankfurt's "Left Bank") is a good place to start for bars, discos, clubs, and **Apfelwein taverns,** which traditionally have a green wreath above their door to indicate they pour hard cider. The ever-more-fashionable district of **Bornheim,** northeast of downtown, has an almost equal number of bars and clubs but fewer tourists. Frankfurt is one of Europe's leading cities for Techno, the computer-generated music of ultrafast beats that's a theme song of German youth culture. Most bars close between 2 AM and 4 AM.

Bars and Nightclubs

Wagons and pushcarts decorate the cellar Irish pub **An Sibin** (✉ Wallstr. 9, ☎ 069/603–2159), presumably to remind you of the Emerald Isle's folksy character. Serious elbow lifting and heartfelt conversations take place in English, Gaelic, Hessian dialect, and German. There is live music most nights along with Guinness right out of the keg and some good pub grub. It's closed Sunday.

The tiny, cozy **Balalaika** (✉ Dreiköigstr. 30, ☎ 069/612–226), in Sachsenhausen, provides intimacy and live music without charging the fancy prices you'd expect at such a place. The secret is proprietress Anita Honis, a professional American singer from Harlem, who usually gets out her acoustic guitar several times during an evening.

If you're seeking something soothing, sit down at **Casablanca Bar** (✉ Parkhotel, Wiesenhüttenpl. 28, ☎ 069/26970) and listen to the piano music. For something a little stronger, ask the bartender to shake up a "Tropica Girl" or "Humphrey's Special." **Cooky's** (✉ Am Salzhaus 4, ☎ 069/287–662) is open into the wee hours and is one of the most popular local haunts for rock music; live bands perform on Monday night. You can also dance and have a meal.

Frankfurt teems with Irish pubs, but **Fox and Hound** (✉ Niedenau 2, ☎ 069/9720–2009) is the only *English* pub in town. The patrons, mainly British, come to watch constant satellite transmissions of the latest soccer, rugby, and cricket matches, to enjoy the authentic pub grub (try the basket of chips), and to participate in the Sunday-night quiz for free drinks and cash prizes. It's a noisy bunch.

Jimmy's Bar (✉ Friedrich-Ebert-Anlage 40, ☎ 069/7540–2961) is classy and expensive—like the Hessischer Hof Hotel in which it's located. It's a favorite with high-flying executives and other big spenders but attracts local color as well. There's live music every night after 10, and you can also get something to eat. You must ring the doorbell to get in. Regulars have a key.

Newcomer **Living** (✉ Kaiserstr. 29, ☎ 069/242–9370) is one of the biggest bar-restaurants in Germany and is as "in" as the Eurotower in which it's located, the headquarters of the newly established European Central Bank. On Friday and Saturday it offers a "subdued" disco, geared to the easy-listening preferences of the banking community, but it's not so prudish as to exclude regular gay entertainment. Its spacious, terraced interior has drawn architectural praise.

The best place in Frankfurt to see variety shows, as well as circus performances, and to dance, dine elegantly and much more is **Tigerpalast** (✉ Heiligkreuzg. 16–20, ☎ 069/9200–2250). Shows often sell out, so book tickets as far in advance as possible. It's closed Monday. Popular with crowds before and after performances at the nearby Old Opera, **Vinum** (✉ 9 Kleine Hochstr. ☎ 069/293–037) is in an arched cellar lined with wine kegs. The food, unlike the wine, is overpriced.

Dance Clubs

Bizarre as it may seem, **Dorian Gray** (✉ Terminal 1, Section C, Level O, ☎ 069/6902–2121) is at the airport and is one of Frankfurt's best clubs for techno music. It's easily reached by the S-bahn. It's closed Monday and Tuesday.

The very trendy **Fantasy Garden** (⊠ Seilerstr. 34, ☎ 069/285–055) is a bistro, bar, and dance club in one with an Asian-Egyptian-Californian atmosphere. Drinks have names like "Orgasmus," and mescal is served with a worm. California-style food leans toward salads and vegetables (served until midnight). There is a terrace for cooling off.

New on the scene is **King Kamahameha** (⊠ Hanauer Landstr. 192, ☎ 069/4059–1194). Beneath the heating pipes of a former brewery are a dance floor and stage. When there isn't a live concert or a DJ on the stage, there may be comedy, cabaret, or a fashion show. If the noise is too much, there's a quiet bar downstairs. It's closed Monday.

Jazz
Der Frankfurter Jazzkeller (⊠ Kleine Bockenheimer Str. 18a, ☎ 069/288–537). The oldest jazz cellar in Germany was founded by legendary trumpeter Carlo Bohländer. It offers hot, modern jazz, often free (but the cover charge for some performances is around DM 25). It's closed Monday.

Dreikönigskeller (⊠ Faerberstr. 71, ☎ 069/629–273). The cellar fills up with jazz and jazz enthusiasts, as well as smoke. Anything can happen, and you might hear 1940s or '50s jazz, blues, funk, rock-wave, or indie-punk. It's patronized mostly by students, as well as a sprinkling of older, hip people.

Sinkkasten (⊠ Brönnerstr. 5–9, ☎ 069/280–385). The club is a class act—a great place for jazz, rock, pop, and African music. It's sometimes hard to get in but worth the effort. There's live music Tuesday–Wednesday and weekends.

OUTDOOR ACTIVITIES AND SPORTS

South of the city, the 4,000-acre **Stadtwald** is the Frankfurters' biggest outdoor playground. With its innumerable paths and trails, bird sanctuaries, and impressive sports stadiums, the Stadtwald is great for recreation and relaxation. The park also has a number of good restaurants. The Stadtwald was the first place in Europe where trees were planted from seed (they were oaks, sown in 1398), and there are still many extremely old trees here. The Waldlehrpfad is a trail leading past a series of rare trees, each identified by a small sign. The Oberschweinstiege stop on streetcar Line 14 is right in the middle of the park. Alternately, you can take Bus 36 from Konstablerwache to Hainerweg.

The **Taunus Hills** are also a great getaway for Frankfurters, and the public transportation gets you there without hassle. Take U-bahn 3 to Hohemark. In the Seckbach district, northeast of the city, Frankfurters hike the 590-ft **Lohrberg Hill,** as the climb yields a fabulous view of the town and the Taunus, Spessart, and Odenwald hills. Along the way you'll also see the last remaining vineyard within the Frankfurt city limits, the Seckbach Vineyard. Take the U-4 subway to Seckbacher Landstrasse, then Bus 43 or 38.

For information on sports clubs and organizations within Frankfurt, as well as public pools, call the **city sports office** (☎ 069/2123–3565).

Biking
Frankfurt's outer parks and forests are terrific for recreational biking. In summer you can rent bikes at the **Goetheturm** (Goethe Tower; ☎ 069/49111), on the northern edge of the Stadtwald.

Fitness Centers

Near the central Hauptwache, the **Fitness Company** (⊠ Zeil 109, ☎ 069/9637–3100) has everything anyone needs to work out. There are more than 60 aerobics and other classes and 150 different fitness machines, from Nautilus to StairMaster. English is spoken. A day's training costs DM 35. The **Fitness Center für Frauen** (Fitness Center for Women; ⊠ Studio 1, Gallusstr. 1, ☎ 069/9637–3500) is DM 45 per day.

Jogging

The banks of the Main River are a good place to jog, and to avoid retracing your steps, you can always cross a bridge and return down the opposite side. In the city center, **Grüneberg Park** is 2 km (1 mi) around, with a *Trimm Dich* (get fit) exercise facility in the northeast corner. The **Anlagenring,** a park following the line of the old city walls around the city, is also a popular route. For a vigorous forest run, go to the **Stadtwald** or the **Taunus** (☞ *above*).

Skating

The **Eissporthalle** (⊠ Am Bornheimer Hang, ☎ 069/2123–0810), near the Ostpark, provides indoor ice-skating in the winter and roller skating in the summer.

Swimming

Incredible as it may seem, the banks of the Main also used to be a place to swim. Pictures from as recently as the 1930s show happy crowds splashing in a roped-off area. That day is long gone (you'd probably dissolve), but there are a number of indoor and outdoor pools. The often-crowded **Brentanobad** (⊠ Rödelheimer Parkweg, ☎ 069/2123–9020) is an outdoor pool surrounded by lawns and old trees. The **Rebstockbad** (⊠ August-Euler-Str. 7, ☎ 069/708–078) leisure center has an indoor pool, a pool with a wave machine and palm-fringed beach, and an outdoor pool with giant water chutes. The **Stadionbad** (⊠ Morfelder Landstr. 362, ☎ 069/678–040) has an outdoor pool, a giant water chute, a solarium, and exercise lawns. For everything from "adventure pools" to squash courts, head to the **Titus Therme** (⊠ Walter-Möller-Pl. 2, ☎ 069/958–050) pool complex.

Tennis

Europa Tennis & Squash Park (⊠ 49 Ginnheimer Landstr., ☎ 069/532–040) has 20 courts. **Waldstadion** (⊠ 362 Moerfelder Landstr., ☎ 069/678–7346) has three indoor and five outdoor courts. Book in advance.

SHOPPING

Shopping Districts

The tree-shaded pedestrian zone of the **Zeil** is claimed to be the richest shop-'til-you drop mile in Germany. Other cities ask where Frankfurt gets the figures to prove this claim, but there is no doubt that the Zeil, between **Hauptwache** and **Konstablerwache**, is incredible for its variety of department and specialty stores.

The two department stores that have competed in the Zeil for many years, **Kaufhof** (⊠ Zeil 116–126, ☎ 060/21910) and **Hertie** (⊠ Zeil 90, ☎ 069/929–050), now have a strong competitor in the newly built branch of Britain's **Marks and Spencer** (⊠ Zeil 121, ☎ 069/138–7250). The new store is somewhat less of a one-stop center than the other two, since it lays its heaviest emphasis on clothing and food. But it is making a real challenge to Hertie's long-standing reputation as the best place in town to fulfill gourmet fantasies.

The Zeil is only the centerpiece of the downtown shopping area. On the opposite side of the Hauptwache are two parallel streets highly regarded by shoppers. One is the luxurious **Goethestrasse,** lined with boutiques, art galleries, jewelry stores, and antique shops. The other is **Grosse Bockenheimer Strasse,** better known as the Fressgasse ("Pig Out Alley"). Cafés, restaurants, and, especially, pricey food stores line the street, offering everything from crumbly cheeses and smoked fish to vintage wines and chocolate creams.

The Zeil area abounds in arcades. The moderately priced **Zeilgallerie** (⊠ Zeil 112–114, ☎ 069/9207–3414) has 56 shops and a brand new IMAX theater. The nearby **Schillerpassage** (⊠ Rahmhofstr. 2) is strong on men's and women's fashion boutiques, and there is still another arcade on the Fressgasse. The subway station below the **Hauptwache** also doubles as a vast underground mall.

Heading southward toward the cathedral and the river there is an area of art and antiques shops on **Braubachstrasse, Fahrgasse,** and **Weckmarkt.**

Clothing Stores

Men shop at **Bailly & Diehl** (⊠ Börsenstr. 2–4, ☎ 069/20845) for well-known labels. **Pfüller Modehaus** (⊠ Goethestr. 15–17, ☎ 069/1337–8070) offers a wide range of choices for women, from classic to trendy. **Prenatal** (⊠ An der Hauptwache 7, ☎ 069/288–001) sells a comprehensive collection of baby and maternity clothes.

Flea Markets

Frankfurt has a weekend flea market on Saturday from 8 to 2 in Sachsenhausen between **Dürerstrasse** and the **Eiserner Steg.** There's a wide range of goods (and a lot of junk). Get there early for the bargains because better-quality items sometimes reward the diligent browser. Shopping success or no, the market is fun to explore.

Gift Ideas

Souvenirs are not the first things that spring to mind when thinking about the financial capital of Germany. It does produce fine porcelain, though, and it can be bought at the **Höchster Porzellan Manufaktur,** in the suburb of Höchst (☞ Side Trips, *below*).

One thing typical of Frankfurt is the **Äpfelwein** (hard cider). You can get a bottle of it at any grocery store, but more enduring souvenirs would be *Bembel* (pitchers) and glasses that are equally a part of the Apfelwein tradition. The blue-stoneware Bembel have a fat belly, and the glasses are ribbed to give them "traction" (in the old days this was good for preventing the glass from slipping from greasy hands). **Lorey** (⊠ Schillerstr. 16, ☎ 069/299–950) sells apple-wine pitchers and glasses along with a big assortment of tableware and other household items.

A famous children's book in Germany, *Struwwelpeter* (Slovenly Peter), was the work of a Frankfurt doctor, Heinrich Hoffmann. He wrote the poems and drew the rather amateurish pictures in 1844 just to warn his own children of the dire consequences of being naughty. He did not originally intend to publish the book, but the reaction of his kids and his friends convinced him he had a gem on his hand. You can get a copy of the book, probably even in English, at most bookstores. Dolls of the fuzzy-headed main character are also available. Try the **Struwwelpeter Museum** (⊠ Schirm am Römerberg, ☎ 069/281–333).

Another potable you can take home is the Frankfurter sausage, which gave America one of its favorite sandwiches. The hot dog, on a long roll, made its first appearance at Chicago's World's Columbian Exhibition in 1893, and this sausage, sent over in cans from Frankfurt, was the basic ingredient. It's still available in cans. Try **Plöger** on the Fress-gasse (⊠ Grosse Bockenheimer Str. 30, ☏ 069/138–7110). One taste of this high-quality smoked sausage will convince you that today's American imitation resembles the true Frankfurter only in size and shape.

Pastry Shops

The pastry shop **Konditorei Lochner** (⊠ Kalbächerg. 10, ☏ 069/920–7320) has local delicacies such as *Bethmännchen und Brenten* (marzipan cookies) or *Frankfurter Kranz* (a kind of creamy cake). All types of sweets and pastries are found at the café **Laumer** (⊠ Bockenheimer Landstr. 67, ☏ 069/727–912).

SIDE TRIPS FROM FRANKFURT

Frankfurt is so centrally located in Germany that the list of possible excursions—day trips and longer treks—is nearly endless. It's the ideal starting point for journeys to the Rhineland, in the west; the Neckar Valley, in the south; and Franconia, in the southeast. The following destinations are reachable by the local transportation system.

The Taunus Hills

Just to the northwest and west of Frankfurt lie the Taunus Hills, an area of mixed pine and hardwood forest, medieval castles, and photogenic towns that many Frankfurters regard as their own territory. It's home to Frankfurt's wealthy bankers and businesspeople, and on weekends you can see them enjoying their playground: hiking through the hills, climbing the **Grosse Feldberg,** taking the waters at Bad Homburg's health-enhancing mineral springs, or just lazing in such elegant stretches of lawn and garden as the Kurpark or Schlosspark.

The area has many royal associations. Emperor Wilhelm II, the infamous "kaiser" of World War I, spent a month each year at **Bad Homburg,** the area's principal city. And it was the kaiser's mother, the daughter of Britain's Queen Victoria, who built the magnificent palace, now a luxurious hotel, in the Taunus town of Kronberg. Another frequent visitor to Bad Homburg was Britain's Prince of Wales, later King Edward VII, who made the name *Homburg* world famous by attaching it to a hat. Until recent decades the Homburg hat was the headgear of preference of diplomats, state dignitaries, and other distinguished gentlemen worldwide. It remains in occasional use and still is manufactured.

Bad Homburg's greatest attraction has been the **Kurpark** (spa), in the heart of the Old Town, with more than 31 fountains. Romans first used the springs, which were rediscovered and made famous in the 19th century. In the park you'll find not only the popular, highly saline Elisabethenbrunnen Spring but also a Siamese temple and a Russian chapel, mementos left by more royal guests—King Chulalongkorn of Siam and Czar Nicholas II. The Kurpark is a good place to begin a walking tour of the town; Bad Homburg's tourist office is here (☞ Visitor Information, *below*). ⊠ *Between Paul-Ehrlich-Weg and Kaiser-Friedrich-Promenade.*

Bad Homburg's **casino,** adjacent to the Kurpark, boasts with some justice that it is the "Mother of Monte Carlo." The first casino in Bad Homburg, one of the first in the world, was established in 1841, but closed down in 1866 because Prussian law forbade gambling. The proprietors moved their operation to the French Riviera and the Bad Homburg casino wasn't reopened until 1949. ⊠ *Im Kurpark,* ☏ *06172/17010.* ⊠ *DM 5 for the full gaming area, DM 2 for the slot machines only.* ☉ *Slot machines, 2 PM–1 AM, remainder 3 PM–3 AM.*

The most historically noteworthy sight in Bad Homburg is the 17th-century **Schloss,** where the kaiser stayed when he was in residence. The 172-ft **Weisser Turm** (White Tower) is all that remains of the medieval castle that once stood here. The Schloss was built between 1680 and 1685 by Friedrich II of Hesse-Homburg, and a few alterations were made in the 19th century. The state apartments are exquisitely furnished, and the Spiegelkabinett (Hall of Mirrors) is especially worthy of a visit. In the surrounding park look for two venerable trees from Lebanon, both now almost 150 years old. ⊠ *Schlosspl., Bad Homburg,* ☎ *06172/6750.* 🖾 *DM 4.* ◔ *Mar.–Oct., Tues.–Sun. 10–5; Nov.–Feb., Tues.–Sun. 10–4.*

The **Hutmuseum** (Hat Museum), a part of the Museum im Gotisches Haus, is a shrine to headgear. Its collection includes everything from 18th-century three-cornered hats to silk toppers, from simple bonnets to the massive, feathered creation of 19th-century milliners. But mainly it's a shrine to the distinguished hat that was developed in Bad Homburg and bears its name. The Homburg hat was made around the turn of the century for Britain's Prince of Wales, later King Edward VII, a frequent visitor. He liked the shape of the Tyrolean hunting hat, but found its green color and decorative feather a bit undignified. So, for him, the Homburg hatters removed the feather, turned the felt gray, and established an enduring fashion item. ⊠ *Tannenwaldweg 102, Bad Homburg,* ☎ *06172/ 37618.* ◔ *Tues. and Thurs.–Fri. 2–5, Wed. 2–7, Sun. 10–6.*

Just a short, convenient bus ride from Bad Homburg is the highest mountain in the Taunus, the 2,850-ft, eminently hikeable **Feldberg.**

Another Taunus town, **Kronberg,** 15 km (9 mi) northwest of Frankfurt, boasts not only the **Schlosshotel,** with magnificent grounds and a restaurant (☞ Dining and Lodging *below*), but also the **Opel Zoo** (☞ *below*). Kronberg's half-timber houses and crooked, winding streets, all on a steep hillside, were so picturesque that a whole 19th-century art movement was built around them.

Only 6½ km (4 mi) from Bad Homburg, and accessible by direct bus service, is the **Römerkastell-Saalburg** (Saalburg Roman Fort). Built in AD 120, the fort could accommodate a cohort (500 men) and was part of the fortifications along the Limes Wall, which ran from the Danube to the Rhine and was meant to protect the Roman Empire from barbarian invasion. On the initiative of Kaiser Wilhelm II the fort was rebuilt as the Romans originally left it—with wells, armories, parade grounds, and catapults, as well as shops, houses, baths, and temples. All of these are for viewing only. You can't take a bath or buy a souvenir in the shops, though there is a contemporary restaurant on the grounds. There is also a **museum** with Roman exhibits. ☎ *06175/93740.* 🖾 *DM 3.* ◔ *Fort and museum daily 8–5.*

About a 30-minute walk from the Römerkastell-Saalburg is an open-air museum at **Hessenpark,** near Neu Anspach. The museum presents a clear, concrete picture of the world in which 18th- and 19th-century Hessians lived, using 135 acres of rebuilt villages with houses, schools, and farms typical of the time. The park, 15 km (9 mi) outside Bad Homburg in the direction of Usingen, is also reachable from the Frankfurt main station on the Taunusbahn, whose trains run about every half hour until about 9 PM. ☎ *06081/58854.* 🖾 *DM 7.* ◔ *Mar.–Oct., Tues.– Sun. 9–6.*

★ ✺ ➓ **Opel Zoo.** Established by a very wealthy heir of the man who created the automobile that bears that name, this large open-air zoo has more than 1,000 native and exotic animals, plus a petting zoo and a playground with more than 100 rides and pieces of equipment. There are also a nature path and a picnic area with grills that can be reserved. Camel rides are offered in the summer. ⊠ *Königsteiner Str. 35,* ☎ *06173/ 79749.* 🎟 *DM 10.* ☉ *Apr.–Sept., daily 8:30–6; Oct.–Mar., daily 9–5.*

Dining and Lodging

Although most of the well-known spas in Bad Homburg have expensive restaurants, there are still enough affordable places to eat.

$$$ ✕ **Sänger's Restaurant.** You get a quintessential spa experience here: fine dining at high prices. But service is friendly, and the truffle risotto may make you forget the bill. ⊠ *Kaiser-Friedrich-Promenade 85, Bad Homburg,* ☎ *06172/928–839. AE, MC. Closed Sun. No lunch Mon. and Sat.*

$$ ✕ **Zum Wasserweibchen.** Chef Inge Kuper is a local culinary legend.
★ Although prices are high for some items on the menu, the portions are large. The clientele sometimes includes celebrities, and the service is friendly and unpretentious. You can't go wrong with the potato cakes with salmon mousse, the brisket of beef, or any of the desserts. ⊠ *Am Mühlberg 57, Bad Homburg,* ☎ *06172/29878. AE, MC, V. Closed Sat.*

$ ✕ **Kartoffelküche.** This simple restaurant serves traditional dishes accompanied by potatoes cooked every way imaginable. The potato and broccoli gratin and the potato pizza are excellent, and for dessert try potato strudel with vanilla sauce. ⊠ *Audenstr. 4, Bad Homburg,* ☎ *06172/21500. No credit cards.*

$$$ ✕🏠 **Maritim Kurhaus Hotel.** Standing on the edge of a spa park, the hotel offers large, richly furnished rooms with king-size beds and deep armchairs. You can dine in style in the hotel's elegant Park restaurant (pink table linen, fine silverware, and candlelight) with nouvelle cuisine, or more cheaply (but evenings only) in the cozy Bürgerstube, with local meat dishes; the latter is worth a visit just to see its collection of dolls. Despite the difference in prices, both restaurants draw on the same excellently managed kitchen. ⊠ *Ludwigstr. am Kurpark, D–61348 Bad Homburg,* ☎ *06172/6600,* 🆇 *06172/660–100. 138 rooms, 10 suites. Restaurant, 2 bars, 2 cafés. AE, DC, MC, V.*

$$$$ 🏠 **Schlosshotel Kronberg.** It looks like it was built for an empress, and indeed it was. Kaiserin Victoria, daughter of the British queen of the same name and mother of Wilhelm II, was empress for only a few months, in 1888. This magnificent palace was built for her after she was widowed. It's richly endowed with her furnishings and works of art and is surrounded by a park with old trees, a grotto, a rose garden, and an 18-hole golf course. It's one of the few hotels left where you can leave your shoes outside your door for cleaning and where fresh fruit is left in your room daily. Jimmy's Bar, with pianist, is a local rendezvous. There is free transfer to a nearby fitness center. ⊠ *Hainstr. 25, D–61476 Kronberg im Taunus,* ☎ *06173/70101,* 🆇 *06173/ 701–267. 51 rooms, 7 suites. Restaurant, bar, in-room data ports, minibars, room service, beauty salon, massage, sauna, 18-hole golf course, horseback riding, laundry service. AE, DC, MC, V.*

$$$$ 🏠 **Steigenberger Bad Homburg.** This prestigious hotel chain is well
★ represented in Bad Homburg. Across from the Kurpark, the hotel has luxurious rooms furnished in art deco style. One of its restaurants, Charly's Le Bistro, serves traditional bistro-style cuisine while the other, Charly's Parkside Restaurant, is devoted to American cooking. ⊠ *Kaiser-Friedrich-Promenade 69–75, D–61348 Bad Homburg,* ☎ *06172/1810,* 🆇 *06172/181–630. 152 rooms, 17 suites. 2 restaurants, bar, air-conditioning, in-room data ports, in-room safes, in-room VCRs, minibars, room service, sauna, steam room, jogging, laundry service, concierge, meeting rooms. AE, DC, MC, V.*

Bad Homburg A to Z

ARRIVING AND DEPARTING

By Bus and Train. Bad Homburg and Kronberg are easily reached by the S-bahn from Hauptwache, the main station, and other points in downtown Frankfurt. The S–5 goes to Bad Homburg, the S–4 to Kronberg. There is also a Taunusbahn (from the main station only) that stops in Bad Homburg and then continues into the far Taunus, including the Saalburg and Hessenpark.

By Car. About 30–45 minutes of driving on the A–5 (Frankfurt–Dortmund) will take you to Bad Homburg. You can get to Kronberg in about the same time by taking the A–66 (Frankfurt–Wiesbaden) to the Nordwestkreuz interchange and following the signs to Eschborn and Kronberg.

Höchst

Höchst, a town with a castle and an **Altstadt** (Old Town) right out of a picture book, has been politically a part of Frankfurt since 1928. However, it still looks and feels like a separate town and should be explored separately.

The name *Höchst* is synonymous with chemicals because of the huge firm that has its headquarters and manufacturing facilities here. Unlike Frankfurt, Höchst was not devastated by wartime bombing, so the castle and the market square, with its half-timber houses, are well preserved. These are also well removed from the industrial area; concern about chemicals has been a major contributor to the Altstadt's fine state of repair.

The **Höchster Schloss,** first built in 1360, houses two **museums,** one about company history and one about Höchst history, the latter with an excellent collection of porcelain. (The castle and a nearby villa were used for decades following the war by the American military broadcaster AFN.) ⊠ *Museum: Bolongaro at Königsteinerstr.,* ☏ *069/305–7366.* ▨ *Free.* ☉ *Daily 10–4.*

For a week in summer the whole Höchst Old Town is hung with lanterns for the Schlossfest, one of Frankfurt's more popular outdoor festivals.

Of special interest in town is the **Höchster Porzellan Manufaktur.** Höchst was once a porcelain-manufacturing town to rival Dresden and Vienna. Production ceased in the late 18th century but was revived by an enterprising businessman in 1965. Its **outlet** (⊠ Berlinerstr. 60, at Kornmarkt, ☏ 069/295–299) sells everything from figurines to dinner services, as well as a selection of glassware and silver. ⊠ *Bolongaro Str. 186,* ☏ *069/300–9020; 069/2123–8953 to arrange guided tour of the works.*

On Bolongaro Strasse, not far from the Höchster Schloss, you can also see a fine exhibit of porcelain at the **Bolongaropalast** (Bolongaro Palace), a magnificent residence facing the river. It was built in the late 18th century by an Italian snuff manufacturer. Its facade—almost the length of a football field—is nothing to sneeze at. ⊠ *Museum: Bolongaro at Königsteinerstr.,* ☏ *069/305–7366.* ▨ *Free.* ☉ *Daily 10–4.*

Höchst's most interesting attraction is the **Justiniuskirche** (Justinius Church), Frankfurt's oldest building. Dating from the 7th century, the church is part early Romanesque and part 15th-century Gothic. The view from the top of the hill is well worth the walk. ⊠ *Justiniuspl. at Bolongaro Str.*

Lodging

$ 🏨 **Hotelschiff** *Peter Schlott*. This is Frankfurt's most unusual hotel—
a riverboat moored in the Main at Höchst. Few comforts are lacking,
although unsurprisingly the rooms are on the small side. Still, they offer
fine views of the Main River, which laps outside the portholes. Caution is advised when returning home after a night out in Frankfurt. ✉
Mainberg, D–65929 Frankfurt am Main, 🕾 *069/300–4643,* 📠 *069/
307–671. 19 rooms, 10 with shower. Restaurant. AE, MC, V.* 🍽

Arriving and Departing

Höchst can be reached via the S-1 and S-2 suburban trains from Frankfurt's main train station (Konstablerwache).

Neu-Isenburg

Though an extensive forested area to the south of Frankfurt was leveled to make room for the airport, a considerable stretch remains, and
Neu-Isenburg is the center of it. At the time of the airport's construction in the mid-1930s, Germans believed that the future of the air age
lay in the lighter-than-air Zeppelin (the 1937 *Hindenburg* disaster lay
such notions to rest). **Zeppelinheim,** a once-independent town, now a
part of Neu Isenburg, was constructed to provide hangar space and
housing for Zeppelin flight and maintenance crews.

In the shadow of the airport, the **Zeppelin Museum** is dedicated to the
history of airships in Germany. Exhibits include big, 1:100 models of
some of the Zeppelins and a reconstruction of the Hindenburg's promenade deck, with a "view" of Rio de Janeiro. The domed construction
gives you impression you're actually aboard one of the airships. ✉
Kapitän-Lehmann-Str. 2, Neu-Isenburg, 🕾 *069/694–390.* 🎫 *Free.* 🕘
Fri.–Sun. 9–5.

$$$$ 🏨 **Hotel Gravenbruch Kempinski.** The atmosphere of the 16th-century
★ manor house that forms the core of this elegant, sophisticated hotel
still remains at this parkland site, a 15-minute drive south of the downtown area. It's a combination of substantial modern luxury with old-
world charm that works. All rooms are spacious and classy and have
views of the lake or the park, and there is a splendid golf course
nearby. ✉ *An der Bundesstr. 459, D–63263 Neu-Isenberg,* 🕾 *06102/
5050,* 📠 *06102/505–900. 255 rooms, 28 suites. 2 restaurants, bar, 1
indoor and 1 outdoor pool, beauty salon, massage, sauna, tennis
courts, convention center. AE, DC, MC, V.* 🍽

Arriving and Departing

Neu-Isenburg can be reached with Streetcar 14 from Frankfurt's Sud-
bahnhof or with Bus 68 from the airport.

FRANKFURT A TO Z

Arriving and Departing

By Bus

More than 200 European cities—including most major German cities—
have bus links with Frankfurt. Buses arrive and depart from the south
side of the Hauptbahnhof. For information and tickets, contact **Deutsche
Touring** (✉ Am Römerhof 17, 🕾 069/79030).

By Car

Frankfurt is the meeting point of a number of major autobahns. The
most important are A–3, running south from Köln and then west on
to Würzburg, and A–5, running south from Giessen and then on
toward Mannheim and Heidelberg. A complex series of beltways sur-

rounds the city. If you're driving to Frankfurt on A–5 from either north or south, exit at Nordwestkreuz and follow A–66 to the Nordend district, just north of downtown. Driving south on A–3, exit onto A–66 and follow the signs to Frankfurt-Höchst and then the Nordend district. Driving west on A–3, exit at Offenbach onto A–661 and follow the signs for Frankfurt-Stadtmitte.

By Plane

Frankfurt Airport is the biggest on the Continent, second in Europe only to London's Heathrow. There are direct flights to Frankfurt from many U.S. cities and from all major European cities. It's 10 km (6 mi) southwest of the downtown area by the Köln–Munich A–3 Autobahn, and it now has its own railway station for the high-speed InterCity (IC) and InterCity Express (ICE) trains.

BETWEEN THE AIRPORT AND DOWNTOWN

Getting into Frankfurt from the airport is easy. The S-bahn 8 (suburban train) runs from the airport to downtown. Most travelers get off at the Hauptbahnhof (main train station) or at Hauptwache, in the heart of Frankfurt. Trains run at least every 15 minutes, and the trip takes about 15 minutes. The one-way fare is DM 5.90. A taxi from the airport into the city center normally takes around 20 minutes; allow double that during rush hours. The fare is around DM 40. If driving a rental car from the airport, take the main road out of the airport and follow the signs reading STADTMITTE (downtown).

By Train

EuroCity, InterCity, and InterCity Express trains connect Frankfurt with all German cities and many major European ones. The InterCity Express line links Frankfurt with Berlin, Hamburg, Munich, and a number of other major hubs. All long-distance trains arrive at and depart from the Hauptbahnhof, and many also stop at the new long-distance train station at the airport. Be aware that the red-light district is just northeast of the train station. For information call **Deutsche Bahn** (German Railways; ☎ 069/19419) or go to its office in the station.

Getting Around

By Bike

Theo Intra's shop (✉ Westerbachstr. 273, ☎ 069/342–780) has a large selection of bikes, from tandems to racing models. Be sure to reserve bikes in advance for weekends and holidays. Bicycles can be rented at the Hauptbahnhof for DM 15 a day. Contact the **Deutsche Bahn** (German Railway) at 069/2653–4834.

By Public Transportation

Frankfurt's smooth-running, well-integrated public transportation system (called **RMV**) consists of the U-bahn (subway), S-bahn (suburban railway), Strassenbahn (streetcars), and buses. Fares for the entire system are uniform, though they are based on a complex zone system. Streetcar, bus, and subway tickets are interchangeable; within the time that your ticket is valid (one hour for most inner-city destinations), you can transfer from one part of the system to another. Tickets may be purchased from automatic vending machines, which are at all U-bahn and S-bahn stations. Machines accept coins and notes and make change. Bus drivers also sell tickets, but only if you boarded at a stop that does not have a vending machine. Weekly and monthly tickets are sold at central ticket offices and newsstands. If you are caught on the subway without a ticket, there's a fine of DM 60.

A basic one-way ticket for a ride in the inner zone costs DM 3.50 (DM 3 in off-peak hours: 9 AM–4 PM, 6:30 PM–1 AM). There is also a reduced, "short stretch," fare of DM 3 (DM 2.10 off-peak). Each station has a list of short-stretch destinations that can be reached from it, and if you're going to one of them, press the *Kurzstrecke* button on the vending machine. A day ticket for unlimited travel in the inner zones costs DM 12 and includes transport to the airport.

The Frankfurt tourist office offers a one- or two-day ticket—the **Frankfurt Card**—allowing unlimited travel in the inner zone (and to the airport) and a 50% reduction on admission to 15 museums (DM 12 for one day, DM 19 for two days). If you are attending a conference in Frankfurt, go to the tourist office and ask for a Congress Ticket (DM 5), a one-day ticket valid for unlimited travel in the city and to the airport.

By Taxi

Fares range from DM 2.30 to DM 2.60 per kilometer, depending on the time of day, plus a basic charge of DM 3.80. Count on paying from DM 12 to DM 14 for a short city ride. You can hail taxis in the street or call them (☎ 069/250–001, 069/230–033, or 069/545–011); there's an extra charge if you phone ahead to be picked up.

Contacts and Resources

Car Rentals

Avis (✉ Schmidtstr. 39, ☎ 069/730–111). **Europcar** (✉ Kennedyallee 280, ☎ 069/6772–0291). **Hertz** (✉ Hanauer Landstr. 117, ☎ 069/449–090).

Consulates

Australian Consulate (✉ Grüneburgweg 58–62, D–60322, ☎ 069/905–580). **British Consulate General** (✉ Bockenheimer Landstr. 42, D–60323, ☎ 069/170–0020). **U.S. Consulate General** (✉ Siesmayerstr. 21, D–60323, ☎ 069/75350).

Emergencies

Police (☎ 110). **Fire and Emergency Vehicle Direction Center** (☎ 112). **On-Call Emergency Doctors** (☎ 069/7950–2200 or 069/19292). **Pharmacies** (☎ 069/11500). **Dental Emergencies** (☎ 069/660–7271). For a listing of **pharmacies** and **pet doctors** available after hours call 011500.

English-Language Bookstore

British Bookshop (✉ Börsenstr. 17, ☎ 069/280–492).

Guided Tours

CRUISES

Day trips on the River Main run from March through October and leave from the Frankfurt Mainkai am Eiserner Steg, just south of the Römer complex. The **Frankfurt Personenschiffahrt GmbH** company (✉ Mainkai 36, ☎ 069/133–8370) has boat trips along the Main and excursions to the Rhine, which, unlike the Köln-Düsseldorfer ships (☞ The Pfalz and the Rhine Terrace A to Z *in* Chapter 10), depart from Frankfurt.

EXCURSIONS

Deutsche Touring (✉ Am Römerhof 17, ☎ 069/79030) and **Gray Line** (✉ Wiesenhüttenpl. 39, ☎ 069/230–492) offer tours in the areas immediately around Frankfurt as well as farther afield. Destinations include the Rhine Valley, with steamship cruises and wine tasting, as well as day trips to Heidelberg and Rothenburg-ob-der-Tauber.

A casino bus runs daily to the casino at Bad Homburg in the Taunus. It leaves every hour between 2 PM and 10 PM from the Frankfurt Hauptbahnhof (south side). The last bus back to Frankfurt leaves Bad Homburg after the casino closes. The DM 12 fare will be refunded after the DM 5 entry fee has been deducted.

Two-and-a-half-hour city bus tours with English-speaking guides are offered throughout the year. From April through October tours leave from outside the main tourist information office at Römerberg 27 daily at 10 AM and 2 PM; all these buses leave from the south side of the train station 15 minutes later. The tour includes the price of visits to the Goethe Haus and the Historical Museum. November through March, tours leave daily at 2 from the Römer office, stopping at 2:15 at the south side of the train station. The cost is DM 44. **Gray Line** (☎ 069/230–492) offers two-hour city tours by bus four times a day; the price (DM 50) includes a typical Frankfurt snack. The tours leave from the line's office at Wiesenhüttenplatz 39.

The **City Transit Authority** (☎ 069/2132–2425) runs a brightly painted old-time streetcar—the *Ebbelwoi Express* (Cider Express)—on weekend and holiday afternoons. Departures are from the Bornheim-Mitte U- and S-bahn station, and the fare, DM 6, includes a glass of Apfelwein.

The **Historische Eisenbahn Frankfurt** (☎ 069/436–093) runs a vintage steam train along the banks of the Main River on weekends. The train runs from the Eiserner Steg west to Frankfurt-Griesham and east to Frankfurt-Mainkur. The fare is DM 6.

There are special tours offered by the tourist office by prior arrangement for clubs and other groups up to a maximum of 30 persons: the first covers Frankfurt's architecture (from its historic remains to its skyscrapers), the second traces the city's Jewish history, and the third follows Goethe's footsteps. For an English-speaking guide, the cost is DM 200 plus tax for up to two hours, and DM 100 per hour after that. For further information call the **tourist office** (☎ 069/2123–8953).

Walking tours are available on request at the **tourist office** (☎ 069/2123–8849). Tours can be tailored to suit individual requirements, and costs vary accordingly.

Travel Agencies

American Express International (✉ Theodor Heuss Allee 112, ☎ 069/97970). **Thomas Cook** (✉ Kaiserstr. 11, ☎ 069/134–733). **Hapag-Lloyd Reisebüro** (✉ Kaiserstr. 14, ☎ 069/216–216).

Visitor Information

For advance information write to the **Tourismus und Congress Büro GmbH Frankfurt/Main** (✉ Kaiserstr. 56, D-60329 Frankfurt am Main, ☎ 069/2123–8800, ✍). The **main tourist office** is at Römerberg 27 (☎ 069/2123–8708), in the heart of the Old Town. It's open daily 9–6. A secondary **information office** (☎ 069/2123–8849) is in the main hall of the train station (Hauptbahnhof). This branch is open weekdays 8 AM–9 PM, weekends 9–6. Both offices can help you find accommodations.

Two airport information offices can also help with accommodations. The **FAG Flughafen-Information,** on the first floor of Arrivals Hall B, is open daily 6:45 AM–10:15 PM. The **DER Deutsches Reisebüro,** in Arrivals Hall B-6, is open daily 8 AM–9 PM.

10 THE PFALZ AND THE RHINE TERRACE

The Romans planted the first Rhineland vineyards 2,000 years ago. By the Middle Ages viticulture was flourishing at the hands of the Church and the state, and a bustling wine trade had developed in Speyer, Worms, and Mainz. The vineyard area that once supplied these imperial residences is now Germany's two largest wine regions, Rheinhessen and the Pfalz.

THE STATE OF RHEINLAND-PFALZ (Rhineland Palatinate) is home to six of Germany's 13 wine-growing regions, including the two largest, Rheinhessen and the Pfalz. Bordered on the east by the Rhine and stretching from the French border north to Mainz, these two regions were the "wine cellar of the Holy Roman Empire." Thriving viticulture and splendid Romanesque cathedrals are the legacies of the bishops and emperors of Speyer, Worms, and Mainz. Two routes parallel to the Rhine link dozens of wine villages. In the Pfalz follow the Deutsche Weinstrasse (German Wine Road); in eastern Rheinhessen (the Rhine Terrace), the home of the mild wine Liebfraumilch, the Liebfrauenstrasse guides you from Worms to Mainz.

The Pfalz has a mild, sunny climate and an ambience to match. Vines carpet the foothills of the thickly forested Haardt Mountains, an extension of the Alsatian Vosges. The Pfälzerwald (Palatinate Forest) is the region's other natural attraction. Well-marked hiking and cycling trails lead through the vineyards, the woods, and up to castles on the heights. As the Deutsche Weinstrasse winds its way north from the French border, idyllic wine villages beckon with flower-draped facades and courtyards full of palms, oleanders, and fig trees. WEINVERKAUF (wine for sale) or WEINPROBE (wine tasting) signs are posted everywhere, each one an invitation to stop in to sample the wines.

The border between the Pfalz and Rheinhessen is invisible. Yet a few miles into the hinterland, a profile takes shape. Rheinhessen is a region of gentle, rolling hills and expansive farmland, where vines are but one of many crops and vineyards are often scattered miles apart. The slopes overlooking the Rhine between Worms and Mainz—the so-called Rhine Terrace—are a notable exception. This is a nearly uninterrupted ribbon of vines culminating with the famous vineyards of Oppenheim, Nierstein, and Nackenheim on the outskirts of Mainz.

Pleasures and Pastimes

Biking
Country roads and traffic-free vineyard paths are a cyclist's paradise. There are also well-marked cycling trails, such as the Radwanderweg Deutsche Weinstrasse, which runs parallel to its namesake from the French border to Bockenheim, and the *Radweg* (cycling trail) along the Rhine between Worms and Mainz. The Palatinate Forest, Germany's largest single tract of woods, has more than 10,000 km (6,200 mi) of paths.

Dining
The best introduction to regional country cooking is the *Pfälzer Teller*, a platter of bratwurst (grilled sausage), *Leberknödel* (liver dumplings), and slices of *Saumagen* (a spicy meat-and-potato mixture encased in a "sow's stomach"), with *Weinkraut* (sauerkraut braised in wine) and *Kartoffelpüree* (mashed potatoes) on the side. Rheinhessen is known for the hearty casseroles *Dippe-Has* (hare and pork baked in red wine) and *Backes Grumbeere* (scalloped potatoes cooked with bacon, sour cream, white wine, and a layer of pork). *Spargel* (asparagus), *Wild* (game), chestnuts, and mushrooms, particularly *Pfifferlinge* (chanterelles), are seasonal favorites. During the grape harvest, from September through November, try *Federweisser* (fermenting grape juice) and *Zwiebelkuchen* (onion quiche)—specialties unique to wine country.

Above all, savor the local wines. Many are sold as *offene Weine* (wines by the glass) and are *trocken* (dry) or *halbtrocken* (semidry). The classic white varieties are Riesling, Silvaner, Müller-Thurgau (also called Rivaner), Grauburgunder (pinot gris), and Weissburgunder (pinot blanc), while Spätburgunder (pinot noir), Dornfelder, and Portugieser are the most popular red wines. The word *Weissherbst* after the grape variety signals a rosé wine.

CATEGORY	COST*
$$$$	over DM 90
$$$	DM 55–DM 90
$$	DM 35–DM 55
$	under DM 35

per person for a three-course meal, including tax and service and excluding drinks,

Festivals

Wine and *Sekt* (sparkling wine) flow freely from March through October at festivals small and large. The latter include parades, fireworks, and rides. The Pfalz is home to the world's largest wine festival in mid-September, the Dürkheimer Wurstmarkt (sausage market, so named because of the 400,000 pounds of sausage consumed during eight days of merrymaking). In Neustad, the German Wine Queen is crowned during the 10-day Deutsches Weinlesefest (German wine harvest festival) in October. The Mainzer Johannisnacht (in honor of Johannes Gutenberg) in late June, the Wormser Backfischfest (fried-fish festival) in late August, and the Brezelfest (pretzel festival) in Speyer on the second weekend in July are the major wine and folk festivals along this part of the Rhine.

Hiking

The Wanderweg Deutche Weinstrasse, a walking route that traverses vineyards, woods, and wine villages, covers the length of the Pfalz. It connects with many trails in the Palatinate Forest that lead to Celtic and Roman landmarks and dozens of castles dating primarily from the Salian and Hohenstaufen periods (11th to 13th centuries). South of Annweiler, between the Deutsche Weinstrasse and Daun, are the fascinating geological formations and sandstone cliffs of the Wasgau. In Rheinhessen you can hike along two marked trails parallel to the Rhine: the Rheinterrassenwanderweg and the Rheinhöhenweg along the heights. Both regions have many *Lehrpfade* (educational paths) signposted at intervals with information about the flora and fauna.

Lodging

Accommodations in all price categories are plentiful, but book in advance if your visit coincides with a large festival. Bed-and-breakfasts abound. Look for signs reading FREMDENZIMMER or AIMMER FREI (rooms available). A *Ferienwohnung* (holiday apartment), abbreviated FeWo in tourist brochures, is an economical alternative if you plan to stay in one location for several nights.

CATEGORY	COST*
$$$$	over DM 250
$$$	DM 180–DM 250
$$	DM 120–DM 180
$	under DM 120

All prices are for two people in a double room, including tax and service.

Shopping

There is no dearth of places to sample and purchase wine and Sekt. Rarities, such as the dessert wines Beerenauslese, Eiswein, and Trockenbeerenauslese, are good souvenirs. *Trester* (German grappa), often sold in stunning designer bottles, *Weinessig* (wine vinegar), *Weingelee* (wine jelly), or wine-related accessories such as table linens and coasters with grape motifs, or unusual corkscrews and bottle-stoppers, make lovely gifts. Some local tourist offices as well as many wine estates and *Winzergenossenschaften* (wine growers' cooperatives) have good shops.

Throughout the region there are many *offene Ateliers* (artist workshops open to the public) selling everything from sculptures to paintings; for pottery look for a *Töpferei*.

Exploring the Pfalz and Rhine Terrace

The Pfalz and Rheinhessen wine regions lie west of the Rhine in the central and southern part of the state of Rheinland-Pfalz. The trip begins on the French border in Schweigen-Rechtenbach and continues north for some 80 km (50 mi) to Bockenheim. The area between Schweigen and Neustadt is known as the Südliche Weinstrasse (Southern Wine Road, abbreviated sÜw) and is the most romantic and serpentine part of the Wine Road. The scene farther north is more spacious and the vineyards fan out onto the vast Rhine Plain. The 45-km (28-mi) stretch between Worms and Mainz along the Rhine takes in Rheinhessen's most prestigious vineyards. From here you are poised to explore the northern portion of the Rhineland (☞ Chapter 11).

Great Itineraries

If time is short, it is best to explore the Pfalz and Rheinhessen by car. There are, however, many scenic paths for hikers and cyclists, and public transportation is excellent.

Numbers in the text correspond to numbers in the margin and on the Pfalz and the Rhine Terrace and Worms maps.

IF YOU HAVE 3 DAYS

Start at the French border in **Schweigen-Rechtenbach** ①, then visit two sites west of the Wine Road: enchanting Dörrenbach and the legendary **Burg Trifels,** near **Annweiler** ④. For a contrast, tour the Pompeian-style palace **Schloss Villa Ludwigshöhe,** overlooking Edenkoben on the Wine Road, then continue uphill via chairlift to the vantage point at the **Rietburg castle.** Stay overnight in ⊞ **St. Martin** ⑥. The next day travel via **Neustadt** ⑦ to **Speyer** ⑧ to see the Romanesque imperial cathedral, the **Kaiserdom,** and the world's oldest bottle of wine in the **Historisches Museum der Pfalz.** Backtrack to the Wine Road to overnight in either ⊞ **Deidesheim** ⑨ or ⊞ **Bad Dürkheim** ⑩. Begin your third day with a visit to the magnificent **Limburg Monastery** ruins above Bad Dürkheim. Continue north on the Wine Road, with detours to the romantic medieval towns of **Freinsheim** ⑪ and Neuleiningen. Your journey and the Wine Road end in **Bockenheim.**

IF YOU HAVE 5 DAYS

From **Schweigen-Rechtenbach** ① visit **Dörrenbach** before exploring the cliffs and castles of the **Wasgau** area west of **Bad Bergzabern** ②. Overnight in ⊞ **Gleiszellen** or ⊞ **Herxheim-Hayna.** Devote the second day to the sights between **Klingenmünster** and **Edenkoben,** with an excursion to **Burg Trifels.** After staying in ⊞ **St. Martin** ⑥, see the **Kalmit,** the region's highest peak, before heading for **Speyer** ⑧. Back on the Wine Road, visit **Deidesheim** ⑨ en route to ⊞ **Bad Dürkheim** ⑩, home base for two nights. In the morning visit **Limburg Monastery** or **Hardenburg Fortress;** then relax at the spa, hike or bike through the Palatinate Forest, or tour a wine estate. The final day take in the northern end of the Wine Road via **Freinsheim** ⑪ and Neuleiningen, before turning east to **Worms** ⑫–⑲ for a look at the amazing **Wormser Dom** and the **Judenfriedhof,** Europe's oldest and largest Jewish cemetery.

Pfalz and the Rhine Terrace

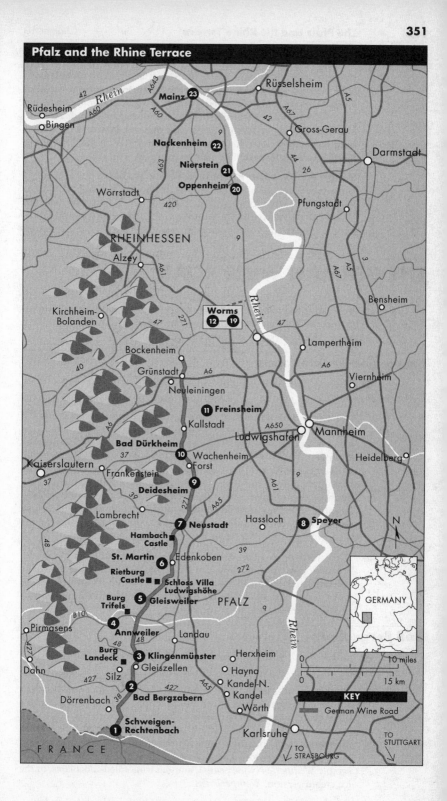

Follow the five-day itinerary above, overnighting in ⊞ **Worms** ⑫–⑲ the fifth night. Proceed north (B–9) to see Rheinhessen's most famous wine villages. In **Oppenheim** ⑳ visit the **Katharinenkirche,** a beautiful Gothic church, and in **Nierstein** ㉑ enjoy a Rhine panorama. Spend a peaceful night in ⊞ **Nackenheim** ㉒ or end the day in ⊞ **Mainz** ㉓ with a pub crawl. On the seventh day see the **Mainzer Dom** and the **Gutenberg Museum,** devoted to the history of printing. Visit the **Kupferberg Sekt Cellars** for a sparkling finale to your trip.

When to Tour the Pfalz and Rhinehessen

The wine festival season begins in March with the *Mandelblüten* (blossoming of the almond trees) along the Deutsche Weinstrasse and continues through October. By May the vines' tender shoots and leaves appear. At the start of the wine harvest in autumn, foliage takes on reddish-golden hues.

THE GERMAN WINE ROAD

The Deutsche Weinstrasse spans the length of the Pfalz wine region. You can travel from north to south or vice versa. Given its central location, the Pfalz is convenient to visit before or after a trip to the Black Forest, Heidelberg, or the northern Rhineland.

Schweigen-Rechtenbach

❶ *21 km (13 mi) southwest of Landau on B–38.*

The southernmost wine village of the Pfalz lies on the French border. During the economically depressed 1930s, local vintners established a route through the vineyards to promote tourism. The German Wine Road was inaugurated in 1935; a year later the massive stone **Deutsches Weintor** (German Wine Gate) was erected to add visual impact to the marketing concept. There's an open gallery halfway up the gateway that offers a fine view of the vineyards—to the south, French; to the north, German. Schweigen is also the birthplace of Germany's first **Weinlehrpfad** (educational wine path), created in 1969. This 1-km (½-mi) path through the vineyards, marked with signs and exhibits, explains the history of viticulture from Roman times to the present.

En Route   Drive north on B–38 toward Bad Bergzabern. Two kilometers (1 mile) before you reach the town, turn left to see the enchanting village of **Dörrenbach.** It has an uncommon Gothic *Wehrkirche* (fortified church) that overlooks the Renaissance town hall, considered the most beautiful half-timber building in the Pfalz.

Bad Bergzabern

❷ *10 km (6 mi) north of Schweigen-Rechtenbach on B–38.*

The landmark of this little spa is the baroque **Schloss** (palace) of the dukes of Zweibrücken. Walk into the *Schlosshof* (palace courtyard) to see the elaborate portals of earlier residences on the site. The town's other gem is nearby: an impressive stone building with scrolled gables and decorative oriels. Built about 1600, it houses the wine restaurant **Zum Engel** (☞ Dining and Lodging, *below*). There are many historic facades to admire along Marktstrasse Stop at No. 48, **Café Herzog,** to sample *Weinperlen* (wine pearls), unusual wine-filled chocolates, or the ice cream version, *Weinperleneis.*

Continue north on the Wine Road—now B–48 (B–38 leads to Landau)—toward Klingenmünster. Four kilometers (2½ miles) north of Bad Bergzabern turn left and drive to **Gleiszellen** to see the Winzergasse (Vintners' Lane). This little vine-canopied street is lined with a beautiful ensemble of half-timber houses. Try a glass of the town's specialty: spicy, aromatic Muskateller wine, a rarity seldom found elsewhere in Germany.

Dining and Lodging

$–$$ ✕ **Zum Engel.** Enjoy fish, game, or Palatinate specialties in the prettiest Renaissance house of the Pfalz. The wines are from local producers and very reasonably priced. ✉ *Königstr. 45, Bad Bergzabern,* ☎ *06343/4933. No credit cards. Closed Tues. and 2 wks in Feb. No dinner Mon.*

$$$–$$$$ ✕▦ **Hotel Zur Krone.** The simple facade belies the upscale inn that offers modern facilities, tasteful decor, and above all, a very warm welcome from the Kuntz family. Reservations are essential at the main restaurant ($$$$; closed Monday and Tuesday). Chef Karl-Emil Kuntz masterfully transforms fresh local products into gourmet delights. To start, order the *Gruss aus der Küche* (greetings from the kitchen), a creative medley of appetizers. Terrines and parfaits are specialties as is the homemade goat cheese. The same kitchen team prepares Pfälzer dishes at the Pfälzer Stube. The wine list is excellent. Hayna, an idyllic suburb of Herxheim, lies between the Rhine and the Wine Road, 20 km (12 mi) east of Bad Bergzabern via the B–427. ✉ *Hauptstr. 62–64, D–76863 Herxheim-Hayna,* ☎ *07276/5080,* ⅄ *07276/50814. 50 rooms, 3 suites. 2 restaurants, bar, Bierstube, minibars, no-smoking rooms, indoor pool, sauna, steam room, 2 tennis courts, bicycles. AE, MC, V. Closed 1st 2 wks in Jan. and 2 wks in July–Aug.* ✎

$$ ✕▦ **Gasthof Zum Lam.** Flowers cascade from the windowsills of this half-timber inn in the heart of Gleiszellen (to the north of Bad Bergzabern). Exposed beams add rustic charm to the airy rooms; the bathrooms are bright and very modern. The restaurant is no less inviting with its dome-shape tile stove, natural stone walls, and wooden beams everywhere. In summer you can dine on the vine-shaded terrace. ✉ *Winzerg. 37, D–76889 Gleiszellen,* ☎ *06343/939–212,* ⅄ *06343/939–213. 11 rooms, 1 suite. Restaurant, beer garden. MC, V. Closed Jan. Restaurant closed Wed. No lunch Nov.–Mar., except Sun.*

Klingenmünster

❸ *8 km (5 mi) north of Bad Bergzabern on B–48.*

The village grew out of the **Benedictine monastery** founded here by the Merovingian king Dagobart in the 7th century. The monastery church is still in use. Despite its baroque appearance, parts of it date from the 12th century, as do the remains of the cloister. On the hillside above are the ruins of **Burg Landeck,** built in circa 1200 to protect the monastery. The keep and inner walls are accessible via a drawbridge that spans a 33-ft-deep moat. You can walk through the chestnut forest from the monastery to the castle in about half an hour. Your reward will be a magnificent view over the Rhine Valley and south as far as the Black Forest.

Annweiler

❹ *11 km (7 mi) northwest of Klingenmünster at the junction of B–48 and B–10.*

In 1219 Annweiler was declared a Free Imperial City by Emperor Friedrich II. Stroll along Wassergasse, Gerbergasse (Tanners' Lane), and Quodgasse to see the half-timber houses and the waterwheels on the Queich River (more like a creek). Annweiler is a gateway to the **Was-**

gau, the romantic southern portion of the Palatinate Forest, marked by sandstone cliffs and ancient castles.

★ **Burg Trifels,** one of Germany's most imposing castles, is perched on the highest of three sandstone bluffs overlooking Annweiler. Celts, Romans, and Salians all had settlements on this site, but it was under the Hohenstaufen emperors (12th and 13th centuries) that Trifels was built on a grand scale. It housed the crown jewels from 1125 to 1274 (replicas are on display today). It was also an imperial prison, perhaps where Richard the Lion-Hearted was held captive in 1193–94.

Although it was never conquered, the fortress was severely damaged by lightning in 1602. Reconstruction began in 1938, shaped by visions of grandeur to create a national shrine of the imperial past. Accordingly, the monumental proportions of some parts of today's castle bear no resemblance to those of the original Romanesque structure. The imperial hall is a grand setting for the *Serenaden* (concerts) held in summer. ☎ 06346/8470. ☜ DM 6. ☉ Apr.–Sept., daily 9–5:30; Oct.–Mar., daily 9–4:30. Closed Dec.

OFF THE BEATEN PATH

MUSEUM "DIE" SCHUHFABRIK" (Shoe Factory Museum) – In this former shoe factory in Hauenstein, 12 km (7½ mi) west of Annweiler on B–10, ♨ you can learn about the history of shoe making, once an important industry in this part of Germany. Demonstrations on historical machinery and seven factory outlet stores nearby make this a worthwhile excursion. ✉ Turnstr. 5, ☎ 06392/915–165. ☜ DM 6. ☉ Daily 10–4.

♨ **Wild- und Wanderpark Südliche Weinstrasse** (Game and Hiking Park of the Southern Wine Road) – Deer, Scottish Highland cattle, rare wild sheep, mountain goats, and eagles and snowy owls roam freely through this forested game and hiking park near Silz, 10 km (6 mi) south of Annweiler or 6 km (4 mi) west of Klingenmünster. Allow one hour for the *kleiner Rundgang* (short circuit) and half an hour more for the longer trail. A petting zoo, playground, and restaurant are on the grounds. ✉ Silz, ☎ 06346/5588. ☜ DM 7. ☉ Mid-Mar.–mid-Nov., daily 9–dusk; mid-Nov.–mid-Mar., daily 10–dusk.

Dining and Lodging

$–$$ ✕ **Burg-Restaurant Trifels.** In summer terrace tables have a terrific view of the Burg Trifels. The menu features seasonal specialties, such as asparagus in spring or game in autumn, and Pfälzer fare year-round. ✉ Auf den Schlossäckern, next to parking lot ☎ 06346/8479. MC, V. Closed Mon. and Tues. in Nov.–Feb.

$–$$ ✕ **Zur alten Gerberei.** An open fireplace, exposed beams, and sandstone walls give this old *Gerberei* (tannery) a cozy feel, while the outdoor seats overlook the Queich. In addition to Pfälzer specialties and vegetarian dishes, you can try Alsatian *Flammkuchen,* similar to pizza, but baked on a wafer-thin crust. There are 15 Pfälzer wines by the glass. ✉ Am Prangertshof 11, at Gerberg., ☎ 06346/3566. No credit cards. Closed Mon. and 4 wks in winter. No lunch Tues.–Sat.

$$$ ✕▥ **Landhaus Herrenberg.** A flower-filled courtyard welcomes guests to this country inn. The rooms are modern and spacious, with blond-wood furnishings. The suite comes with a whirlpool. The Lergenmüllers are vintners known for award-winning red wines. In the restaurant (dinner only) they showcase their wines with fine regional cuisine using many homegrown ingredients. Try a *Degustationsmenü,* a three- or four-course menu with wines preselected to accompany each course. You can pick up some good souvenirs here, such as pickled pumpkin, *grüne Nüsse* (marinated nuts), and excellent still and sparkling wines. ✉ Lindenbergstr. 72, D–76829 Landau-Nussdorf, ☎ 06341/60205, ℻ 06341/60709. 8 rooms, 1 suite. Restaurant, minibars. AE, MC, V.

Outdoor Activities and Sports

BIKING, CLIMBING, AND HIKING

Dozens of marked trails guide you to the Wasgau's striking geological formations, sandstone cliffs, and castles carved into the cliffs. For an overview make a circular tour from Annweiler by proceeding west on B–10 to Hinterweidenthal, then south on B–427 to Dahn, and continuing southeast to Erlenbach. Return to Annweiler via Vorderweidenthal and Silz. Each town is a good starting point for a scenic ride, climb, or hike.

GOLF

The **Golfanlagen Landgut Dreihof Südliche Weinstrasse** (☎ 06348/4282), between Essingen and Offenbach, circa 5 km (3 mi) east of Landau, has an 18-hole championship course, a 9-hole course, pitch-and-putt greens, and a driving range.

HORSEBACK RIDING

Gallop through the Wasgau with Jutta Weiland, equestrian expert and owner of **Schönbacherhof** (✉ Hauptstr. 88, ☎ 06346/5875). Castle-to-castle tours are her specialty. The stables are near Silz, less than 10 km (6 mi) south of Annweiler or 6 km (4 mi) west of Klingenmünster. The **Ferien- und Reiterhof Munz** (✉ Auf dem Berg 2, Gossersweiler-Stein, ☎ 06346/5272), a complex of stables and holiday cottages, is less than 3 km (2 mi) north of Silz. Near Essingen go riding in the vine-filled Hainbach Valley from Bützler's riding stables, **Gut Dreihof** (☎ 06348/7971).

SWIMMING

Erlebnis means "adventure" or "experience," and this is what Landau's **Erlebnisbad LaOla** promises with its 330-ft-long slide (partly in a tunnel with special lighting effects), six pools, outdoor thermal baths, simulated ocean waves, whirlpools, and saunas. ✉ *Horstring 2, Landau,* ☎ *06341/55115.* ▨ *DM 7 (1½ hrs), DM 14 (all day); DM 2 supplement weekends and holidays; DM 11 supplement for sauna.* ☺ *Sun. 10–9, Mon. 2–11, Tues.–Thurs. and Sat. 10–11, Fri. 10–midnight.*

SHOPPING

The **süw Shop** (▨ An der Kreuzmühle 2, ☎ 06341/940–407), in Landau's Südliche Weinstrasse regional tourist office (☞ Contacts and Resources *in* The Pfalz and Rheinhessen A to Z, *below*), offers gifts, products of the grape, wine-related accessories, and detailed maps of cycling and hiking trails. The shop is closed weekends.

Gleisweiler

❺ *16 km (10 mi) north of Klingenmünster on the Wine Road; 11km (7 mi) northeast of Annweiler.*

The little town of Gleisweiler is reputedly the warmest spot in Germany. The flourishing **subtropical park** on the grounds of the sanatorium Klinik Bad Gleisweiler supports the claim with its camellias in spring, bananas and lemons in summer, and exotic trees (cedars, ginkgos, and a 130-ft-high sequoia) year-round. Cool off in the *Walddusche* (forest shower), an unusual waterfall and wading pond. These were set up circa 1850 as cold-water therapeutic baths by the founder of the sanatorium. It's a 20-minute walk from town via Hainbachtal Strasse.

En Route   Venerable old chestnut trees line **Theresienstrasse** in **Rhodt.** It rivals Gleiszellen's Winzergasse as one of the most picturesque lanes of the Pfalz. Fragrant, spicy Traminer (or Gewürztraminer) is a specialty here, and on the eastern outskirts of town, opposite the cooperative winery on Edesheimer Strasse, you can see a plot of 350-year-old Traminer grapes, Germany's oldest producing vines.

Bavaria's King Ludwig I built a summer residence on the slopes over-looking Edenkoben, in what he called "the most beautiful square mile of my realm." You can reach the neoclassical **Schloss Villa Ludwigshöhe** by car or bus or take a scenic 45-minute walk through the vineyards along the Weinlehrpfad. Historical wine presses and vintners' tools are displayed at intervals along the path. It starts at the corner of Landauer Strasse and Villa Strasse.

The layout and decor—Pompeian-style murals, splendid parquet floors, and Biedermeier and Empire furnishings—of the palace offer quite a contrast to the medieval castles elsewhere in the Pfalz. It also houses an extensive collection of paintings and prints by the leading German impressionist Max Slevogt (1868–1932). ⊠ ▩ *DM 5. ☉ Apr.–Sept., Tues.–Sun. 10–6; Oct.–Mar., Tues.–Sun. 10–5. Closed Dec.*

From the palace you can hike (30 minutes) or ride the Rietburgbahn chairlift (10 minutes) up to the **Rietburg** castle ruins for a sweeping view of the Pfalz. A restaurant, game park, and playground are on the grounds. ▩ *DM 8 round-trip, DM 5.50 one-way. ☉ Mar., Sun. 9–5; Good Friday–Oct., daily 9–5.*

St. Martin

6   *7 km (4½ mi) north of Gleisweiler, slightly west of the Wine Road. Turn left at the northern edge of Edenkoben.*

This is one of the most charming wine villages of the Pfalz. The entire **Altstadt** (Old Town) is under historical preservation protection. For 350 years the Knights of Dalberg lived in the castle **Kropsburg,** the romantic ruins of which overlook the town. Their Renaissance tombstones are among the many artworks in the late-Gothic Church of **St. Martin.** The town's namesake is honored with a parade and wine festival on November 11.

Dining and Lodging

$$$ **St. Martiner Castell.** The Mücke family transformed a simple vint-ner's house into a fine hotel and restaurant, retaining many of the orig-inal features, such as exposed beams and an old wine press. Although in the heart of town, the hotel is an oasis of peace, particularly the rooms with balconies overlooking the pretty garden. A native of the Loire Val-ley, Frau Mücke adds French flair to the menu, including a six-course *Schlemmer-Menü* (gourmet menu). The wine list offers a good selec-tion of bottles from a neighboring wine estate. ⊠ *Maikammerer Str. 2, D–67487,* ☎ *06323/9510,* ℻ *06323/951–200. 26 rooms. Restau-rant, Weinstube, no-smoking rooms, sauna. MC, V. Closed Feb. Restau-rant closed Tues.* ✎

$$ **Landhaus Christmann.** This bright, modern house in the midst of the vineyards offers stylish rooms decorated with 17th- and 18th-cen-tury antiques. Some rooms have balconies with a view of the Ham-bacher Schloss (☞ *below*). Vintners and distillers, the Christmanns offer 20 wines by the glass in their restaurant Gutsausschank Kabinett, as well as culinary wine tastings. ⊠ *Riedweg 1, D–67487,* ☎ *06323/94270,* ℻ *06323/942–727. 6 rooms, 1 apartment. Restaurant. No credit cards. Restaurant closed Mon.–Wed. No lunch.*

Nightlife and the Arts

Schloss Villa Ludwigshöhe, Kloster Heilsbruck (a former Cistercian convent near Edenkoben), and **Schloss Edesheim** are backdrops for con-certs and theater in summer. For a calendar of events contact the Südliche Weinstrasse regional tourist office in Landau (☞ Contacts and Resources *in* The Pfalz and Rheinhessen A to Z, *below*).

Shopping

Artist Georg Wiedemann is responsible for both content and design of the exquisite products of Germany's premier **wine vinegar estate** (⊠ Raiffeisenstr. 5, ☏ 06323/5505) in Venningen, 2 km (1 mi) east of Edenkoben. Make an appointment for a unique vinegar tasting and tour of the cellars or pick up a gift at his shop. He's open Monday–Saturday 8–2 and Wednesday until 6.

En Route Depart St. Martin via the Totenkopf-Höhenstrasse, a very scenic road through the forest. Turn right at the intersection with Kalmitstrasse and proceed to the vantage point atop the **Kalmit**, the region's highest peak (2,200 ft). The view is second to none. Return to the Kalmitstrasse, drive toward Maikammer, and stop at the chapel **Mariä-Schmerzen-Kapelle** (Our Lady of Sorrows Chapel) in Alsterweiler. It houses the work of an unknown master, a remarkable Gothic triptych depicting the crucifixion. Maikammer has half-timber houses, patrician manors, and a baroque church, and is the last (or first) wine village in the Südliche Weinstrasse district.

Back on the Wine Road it's a brief drive to the Neustadt suburb of Hambach. Majestically perched on the hillside above is the **Hambacher Schloss,** considered the "cradle of German democracy." It was here, on May 27, 1832, that 30,000 patriots demonstrated for freedom and German unity, raising the German colors for the first time. Inside, there are exhibits about the uprising and the history of the castle. The French destroyed the 11th-century imperial fortress in 1688. It has been largely rebuilt during the past 50 years in neo-Gothic style. It is an impressive setting for theater and concerts. You can enjoy a view from the terrace restaurant. On a clear day you can see the spire of Strasbourg Cathedral and the northern fringe of the Black Forest. ⊠ *Hambach,* ☏ *06321/30881.* 🎫 *DM 9.* ☉ *Mar.–Nov., daily 10–6.*

Neustadt

❼ *8 km (5 mi) north of St. Martin; 5 km (3 mi) north of Hambach on the Wine Road.*

Neustadt and its nine wine suburbs are at the midpoint of the Wine Road and the edge of the district known as Deutsche Weinstrasse–Mittelhaardt. With around 5,000 acres of vines, they jointly comprise Germany's largest wine-growing community. The German Wine Harvest Festival culminates every October with the coronation of the German Wine Queen and a parade with more than 100 floats. You can sample some 100 Neustadt wines year-round at the **Haus des Weines** (House of Wine), which is opposite the town hall in a Gothic house from 1276 bordered by a splendid Renaissance courtyard. ⊠ *Rathausstr. 6,* ☏ *06321/355–871. Closed Sun. and Mon.*

The **Marktplatz** (market square) is the focal point of the Old Town and a beehive of activity on Tuesday, Thursday, and Saturday, when the farmers come to sell their wares. The square itself is ringed by baroque and Renaissance buildings (Nos. 1, 4, 8, and 11) and the Gothic **Stiftskirche** (Collegiate Church), built as a burial church for the counts Palatine. In summer there are concerts in the church (Saturday 11:30–noon), after which you can ascend the southern tower (187 ft) for a bird's-eye view of the town. The world's largest cast-iron bell—weighing more than 17 tons—hangs in the northern tower. Indoors, see the elaborate tombstones near the choir and the fanciful grotesque figures carved into the baldachins and corbels.

The Pfalz is home to the legendary, elusive **Elwetritschen,** part bird and part human, said to roam the forest and vineyards at night. "Hunting

Elwetritschen" is both a sport and an alibi. Local sculptor Gernot Rumpf has immortalized them in a fountain on Marstallplatz. No two are alike. On the market square, hunt for the one that "escaped" from its misty home. End a walking tour of the Old Town on the medieval lanes Metzgergasse, Mittelgasse, and Hintergasse to see beautifully restored half-timber houses, many of which are now pubs, cafés, and boutiques.

Thirty historical train engines and railway cars are on display at the **Eisenbahn Museum,** behind the *Hauptbahnhof* (main train station). Take a ride through the Palatinate Forest on one of the museum's historical steam trains, the *Kuckucksbähnel* (DM 20), which rides every other Sunday between Easter and mid-October. It takes an hour and a half to cover the 13-km (8-mi) stretch from Neustadt to Elmstein. ⊠ *Neustadt train station, Schillerstr. entrance,* ☎ *06325/8626.* ☒ *DM 6.* ☉ *Weekends and holidays 10–4.*

Dining and Lodging

$–$$$ ✕ **Altstadtkeller.** Tucked behind a wooden portal, this vaulted sandstone "cellar" (it's actually on the ground floor) is a cozy setting for very tasty food. The regular menu offers a number of salads and a good selection of fish and steaks, while the daily specials are geared to what's in season. Owner Jürgen Reiss is a wine enthusiast and his well-chosen list shows it. ⊠ *Kunigundenstr. 2,* ☎ *06321/32320. AE, DC, MC, V. Closed Mon.*

$–$$$ ✕ **Weinstube Eselsburg.** Always packed with regulars, this popular wine
★ pub is decorated with original artwork by the owner, Peter Wiedemann, and his late father, Fritz, the pub's founder. Enjoy top Pfälzer wines in the flower-filled courtyard in summer or in the warmth of an open hearth in winter. The *Esel* (donkey) lends its name to Mussbach's best-known vineyard, *Eselshaut* (donkey's hide); this pub; and one of its specialties, *Eselsuppe,* a hearty soup of pork, beef, and vegetables. ⊠ *Kurpfalzstr. 62, Neustadt-Mussbach,* ☎ *06321/66984. No credit cards. Closed Sun.–Tues. and mid-Dec.–mid-Jan. No lunch.*

$–$$ ✕ **Weinstube Kommerzienrat.** You could come here for eight months
★ running and sample a different Pfälzer wine every evening. In addition, there are 160 wines from around the world. Try a *Rumpsteak* (beef steak), served with braised onions, mustard sauce, or herbed butter. The usual side dishes are *Bratkartoffeln* (home-fried potatoes) or *Rösti* (fried potato pancakes) and a salad. ⊠ *Loblocherstr. 34, Neustadt-Gimmeldingen,* ☎ *06321/68200. AE, DC, MC, V. Closed Thurs. No lunch.*

$–$$$ ✕☑ **Burgschänke Rittersberg.** From the terrace of the Rusche family's restaurant, you have a view of the Hambacher Schloss towering above and the vineyards below. The menu has something for every taste, such as homemade *Wildschinken* (ham made from game) or fresh trout or salmon in a sorrel sauce. The rooms are modern and the surroundings peaceful. ⊠ *Hambacher Schloss 19, D–67434 Neustadt-Hambach,* ☎ *06321/39900,* ☎ *06321/32799. 5 rooms. Restaurant, Weinstube. MC, V. Closed 2 wks in Jan. and 2 wks in summer. Restaurant closed Thurs.*

$ ☑ **Gästehaus Reber.** This little 18th-century stone vintner's house has been renovated to offer modern comfort but not at the expense of its charm. Every room has a balcony or terrace, and there's breakfast in the cozy vaulted cellar. Close to the Palatinate Forest and on the Wanderweg Deutsche Weinstrasse, it is ideal for hikers. ⊠ *Heidenburgstr. 12, D–67435 Neustadt-Gimmeldingen,* ☎ *06321/96360,* ☎ *06321/ 60560. 4 rooms. Lounge. No credit cards.*

Nightlife and the Arts

The **Saalbau,** opposite the train station, is Neustadt's convention center and main venue for concerts, theater, and special events. In summer there is open-air theater at **Villa Böhm,** which also houses the city's history museum. Concerts, art exhibits, and wine festivals are held at the **Herrenhof,** in the suburb of Mussbach. Owned by the Johanniter-Orden (Order of the Knights of St. John) from the 13th to 18th centuries, it is the oldest wine estate of the Pfalz. Contact the Neutstadt tourist office (☞ Contacts and Resources *in* The Pfalz and Rheinhessen A to Z, *below*) for program details and tickets.

Outdoor Activities and Sports

BIKING AND HIKING

The Neustadt tourist office (☞ Contacts and Resources *in* The Pfalz and Rheinhessen A to Z, *below*) has brochures and maps that outline circular tours, including the educational wine paths in Gimmeldingen and Haardt.

En Route   The **Holiday Park,** in Hassloch, 10 km (6 mi) east of Neustadt, is one of Europe's largest amusement parks. The admission fee (free on your birthday) covers all attractions, from shows to giant-screen cinema, and special activities for children. The free-fall tower, hell barrels, and Thunder River rafting are just a few of many fun rides. ☒ ☏ 06324/599–3900. ☜ DM 35.50. ☼ *Summer, daily 9–6; spring and autumn, daily 10–6.*

Speyer

8 *25 km (15 mi) east of Neustadt via B–39, 22 km (14) mi south of Mannheim via B–9 and B–44.*

Speyer was one of the great cities of the Holy Roman Empire, founded in pre-Celtic times, taken over by the Romans, and expanded in the 11th century by the Salian emperors. Between 1294, when it was declared a Free Imperial City, and 1570, no fewer than 50 imperial diets ★ were convened here. Ascend the **Altpörtel,** the impressive town gate, for a grand view of Maximilianstrasse, the street that led kings and emperors straight to the cathedral.

★ The **Kaiserdom** (Imperial Cathedral), one of the finest Romanesque cathedrals in the world, conveys the pomp and majesty of the early Holy Roman emperors. It was built in some 30 years, between 1030 and 1061, by the emperors Konrad II, Henry III, and Henry IV. The latter replaced the flat ceiling with groined vaults in the late 11th century, an innovative feat in its day. A restoration program in the 1950s returned the building to almost exactly its original condition.

See the exterior before venturing inside. You can walk most of the way around it, and there's a fine view of the east end from the park by the Rhine. Much of the architectural detail, including the dwarf galleries and ornamental capitals, was inspired and executed by stone masons from Lombardy, which belonged to the German Empire at the time. The four towers symbolize the four seasons and that the power of the empire extends in all four directions. Look up as you enter the nearly 100-ft-high portal. It is richly carved with mythical creatures. In contrast to Gothic cathedrals, whose walls are supported externally by flying buttresses, allowing for a minimum of masonry and a maximum of light, at Speyer the columns supporting the roof are massive. The **Krypta** (crypt) lies beneath the chancel. The largest in Germany and strikingly beautiful in its simplicity, it is the burial site of four emperors, four kings, and three empresses. ☒ *Dompl.* ☜ *Donation requested.* ☼ *Apr.–Oct., daily 9–7; Nov.–Mar., daily 9–5. Closed during services.*

★ Opposite the cathedral, the **Historisches Museum der Pfalz** (Palatinate Historical Museum) houses the **Domschatz** (Cathedral Treasury).

Other collections chronicle the art and cultural history of Speyer and the Pfalz from the Stone Age to modern times. Try to see the precious "Golden Hat of Schifferstadt," a golden, cone-shape object used for religious purposes during the Bronze Age. The **Wine Museum** exhibits artifacts from Roman times to the present, including the world's oldest bottle of wine, from circa AD 300. ⊠ *Dompl.,* ☎ *06232/13250.* ⊠ *DM 8; free Tues. 4–6.* ☉ *Tues.–Sun. 10–6, Wed. 10–8.* ❧

Speyer was an important medieval Jewish cultural center. In the **Jewish quarter,** behind the Palatinate Historical Museum, you can see synagogue remains from 1104 and Germany's oldest (pre-1128) ritual baths, the 33-ft-deep *Mikwe.* ⊠ *Judenbadg.,* ☎ *06232/291–971.* ⊠ *DM 1.50.* ☉ *Apr.–Oct., weekdays 10–1 and 2–4, weekends 10–5.*

☺ A turn-of-the-century factory hall houses the **Technik-Museum** (Technology Museum), a large collection of locomotives, aircraft, old automobiles, fire engines, and automatic musical instruments. Highlights here are the 420-ton U-boat (you can go inside) and the monumental 3-D IMAX cinemas. ⊠ *Geibstr. 2,* ☎ *06232/67080.* ⊠ *Museum or IMAX DM 13, combination ticket DM 24.* ☉ *Daily 10–6.*

Dining and Lodging

$$$–$$$$ ✕ **Backmulde.** Bread is still baked daily in this historic bakery, now a
  ★   tastefully designed wine restaurant. Homemade bread, homegrown fruits and vegetables, and local products are all part of chef and proprietor Gunter Schmidt's requirements of freshness. The aromas and flavors of his fare often have a Mediterranean accent. The wine list features more than 600 wines—including half from the Pfalz and a well-chosen selection from abroad. Schmidt's own wines are from the Heiligenstein vineyard on the outskirts of Speyer. ⊠ *Karmeliterstr. 11–13,* ☎ *06232/ 71577. AE, DC, MC, V. Closed Sun., Mon., and mid-Aug.–early Sept.*

$–$$$ ✕ **Wirtschaft Zum Alten Engel.** This 200-year-old vaulted brick cellar, with its rustic wood furnishings and cozy niches, is an intimate setting for a hearty meal. Seasonal dishes supplement the large selection of Pfälzer and Alsatian specialties, such as *Ochsenfetzen* (slices of beef), coq au vin (chicken baked in wine), or *Choucroute* (similar to a Pfälzer Teller). The wine list is manageable (Pfalz and international), with 17 wines available by the glass. ⊠ *Mühlturmstr. 1a,* ☎ *06232/70914. No credit cards. Closed Sun. and 2 wks in Aug. No lunch.*

$$–$$$ ✕⊡ **Kutscherhaus.** Charming rustic decor and a profusion of flow-
  ★   ers have replaced the *Kutschen* (coaches) in this turn-of-the-century coachman's house. The menu offers regional cuisine as well as creative vegetarian and pasta dishes. In summer you can sit beneath the old plane trees in the beer garden and select from a sumptuous buffet. Three modern, comfortable suites can sleep up to four persons each. ⊠ *Am Fischmarkt 5a, D–67346,* ☎ *06232/70592,* FAX *06232/620–922. 3 suites. Restaurant, beer garden. AE, DC, MC, V. Restaurant closed Wed. and 4 wks in July and Aug.* ❧

$$–$$$ ⊡ **Hotel Goldener Engel.** Near the Gothic town gate at Maximilianstrasse, the Golden Angel is a traditional house with some antique touches such as baroque garderobes. The rooms, however, have sleek modern furniture. The **Wirtschaft Zum Alten Engel** (☞ *above*) adjoins the hotel. ⊠ *Mühlturmstr. 1a, D–67346,* ☎ *06232/13260,* FAX *06232/132–695. 44 rooms, 2 suites. Bicycles. AE, DC, MC, V. Closed last 2 wks in Dec.*

Nightlife and the Arts

The **Stadthalle** is the main theater. Highlights for music lovers are **Orgelfrühling,** the organ concerts in the Gedächtniskirche (Memorial Church) in spring, and the concerts in the cathedral during September's **Internationale Musiktage.** Call the Speyer **tourist office** (☎ 06232/142–392) for program details and tickets.

Deidesheim

⑨ *8 km (5 mi) north of Neustadt via the Wine Road, now B–271.*

Deidesheim is the first of a trio of villages on the Wine Road renowned for their vineyards and the wine estates known as the "three Bs of the Pfalz"—Bassermann, Buhl, and Bürklin.

The half-timber houses and historical facades framing Deidesheim's **Marktplatz** form a picturesque group, including the Church of St. Ulrich, a Gothic gem inside and out, and the old **Rathaus**, whose doorway is crowned by a baldachin and baroque dome. The attractive open staircase leading up to the entrance is the site of the festive *Geissbock-Versteigerung* (billy-goat auction) every Pentecost Tuesday, followed by a parade and folk dancing. The goat is the tribute neighboring Lambrecht has paid Deidesheim since 1404 for grazing rights. Inside see the richly appointed **Ratssaal** (council chamber) and the museum of wine culture. ⊠ *Marktpl.,* ⊙ *Mar.–Dec., Wed.–Sun. 4–6.*

Vines, flowers, and *Feigen* (fig trees) cloak the houses behind St. Ulrich on Heumarktstrasse and its extension, Deichelgasse (nicknamed Feigengasse). Cross the Wine Road to reach the grounds of **Schloss Deidesheim**, now a wine estate and pub (closed Wednesday and Thursday). The bishops of Speyer built a moated castle on the site in the 13th century. Twice destroyed and rebuilt, the present castle dates from 1810 and the moats have been converted into gardens.

Dining and Lodging

$$$–$$$$ ✕ **Weinstube St. Urban.** St. Urban is the vintners' patron saint and considered responsible for the outcome of the harvest between his name day on May 25 until the harvest in autumn. This is not a "typical" Weinstube, but rather an upscale wine restaurant offering very good regional cuisine and wines in several beautifully decorated rooms. It's in the Hotel Deidesheimer Hof (☞ *below*). ⊠ *Am Marktpl. 1,* ☎ *06326/ 96870. AE, DC, MC, V.*

$$–$$$ ✕ **Weinschmecker.** Herbert Nikola, an expert on Pfälzer wines and fes-
★ tivals, opened his restaurant and Vinothek on the eastern edge of town a couple of years ago. Italian tiles and whitewashed walls give it a light, airy Mediterranean look—the menu reflects the same. The focus, however, is on top-quality Pfälzer wines, 200 of which (from about 40 estates) are featured; 120 are available by the glass. ⊠ *Steing. 2,* ☎ *06326/ 980–460. No credit cards. Closed Sun. and Mon. No lunch.*

$$$$ ✕▥ **Hatterer's Hotel-Restaurant Le Jardin d'Hiver.** Clément Hatterer,
★ the hospitable Alsatian owner and chef, offers all the modern comforts you could ask for in this stylish hotel. Whether you dine in the winter garden, decorated in soothing shades of lilac, or in the sunny courtyard garden filled with exotic plants, the food and wine are exceptional. Like the menu, the wine list features Pfälzer and Alsatian specialties. ⊠ *Weinstr. 12, D–67146,* ☎ *06326/6011,* 🖷 *06326/7539. 57 rooms. Restaurant, bar, bicycles. AE, DC, MC, V.*

$$$$ ✕▥ **Hotel Deidesheimer Hof.** If your timing's right, you could rub el-
★ bows with the heads of state, entertainers, or sports stars who frequent this house, first built in 1781 for a wine merchant. Despite the glitter of the guest book, the hotel retains its country charm and friendly service. Rooms are luxurious, and several have baths with round tubs or whirlpools. The restaurant Schwarzer Hahn ($$$$) is for serious wining and dining. The set menus, from three to seven courses, are an excellent choice. À la carte you can sample Pfälzer specialties, including sophisticated renditions of the region's famous dish, Saumagen. More than 600 wines grace the wine list. ⊠ *Am Marktpl. 1, D–67146,* ☎ *06326/96870,* 🖷 *06326/7685. 19 rooms, 3 suites. Restaurant, bar, We-*

instube, minibars. AE, DC, MC, V. Closed 1st wk in Jan. Restaurant closed Sun. and Mon.

$-$$ 🖭 **Gästehaus Johanna.** Expect a warm welcome from the Doll family. Their guest rooms are no less cheerful and completely modern. Ask for a room with a balcony facing the Haardt Mountains. ⊠ *Kathrinenstr. 1, D–67146,* ☎ *06326/96700,* FAX *06326/7668. 9 rooms. Minibars. No credit cards.*

Shopping

The Biffar family not only runs a first-class **wine estate** (⊠ Niederkircher Str. 13–15, ☎ 06326/5028) but also manufactures very exclusive candied fruits and ginger (delicious souvenirs).

En Route **Forst** and **Wachenheim,** both a few minutes' drive north of Deidesheim, complete the trio of famous wine villages. As you approach Forst, depart briefly from B–271 (take the left fork in the road) to see the Old Town with its vine- and ivy-clad sandstone and half-timber vintners' mansions. Peek through the large portals to see the lush courtyards. Many estates on this lane have pubs, as does the town's *Winzerverein* (cooperative winery). Wachenheim is another 2 km (1 mi) down the road. Its cooperative, Wachtenburg Winzer, is on the left at the entrance to town. Head for the Wachtenburg (castle) ruins up on the hill for a glass of wine. The Burgschänke (castle pub) is open if the flag is flying.

★ A couple of miles east of the Wine Road, between Wachenheim and Friedelsheim, is the **Villa Rustica,** a fascinating open-air museum showing the foundations of a Roman farm dating from circa AD 20.

Bad Dürkheim

🔟 *6 km (4 mi) north of Deidesheim on B–271.*

This pretty spa is nestled into the hills at the edge of the Palatinate Forest and ringed by vineyards on the other three sides. The saline springs discovered here in 1338 are the source of today's drinking and bathing cures, and at harvest time there's also a detoxifying *Traubenkur* (grape juice cure). A trip to the neoclassical **Kurhaus** and its beautiful gardens might be just the ticket if you've overindulged at the Dürkheimer Wurstmarkt, the world's largest wine festival. Legendary quantities of *Weck, Worscht un Woi* (dialect for rolls, sausage, and wine) are consumed at the fair, including half a million *Schoppen,* the region's traditional pint-size glasses of wine. The festival grounds are also the site of the world's largest wine cask, the **Dürkheimer Riesenfass,** with a capacity of 1.7 million liters. Built in 1934 by an ambitious cooper, the cask is a restaurant that can seat well over 450 people (☞ Dining and Lodging, *below*).

The **Palatinate Forest,** with its beautiful pine and chestnut trees, is popular for hiking and biking and will interest history buffs, too. Northwest of town is the **Heidenmauer** (heathen wall), the remains of an ancient Celtic ring wall more than 2 km (1 mi) in circumference and up to 20 ft thick in parts, and nearby are the rock drawings at **Krimhildenstuhl,** an old Roman quarry where the legionnaires of Mainz excavated sandstone.

Overlooking the suburb of Grethen are the ruins of **Kloster Limburg** (Limburg Monastery). Emperor Konrad II laid the cornerstone in 1030, supposedly on the same day as he laid the cornerstone of the Kaiserdom in Speyer. The monastery was never completely rebuilt after a fire in 1504, but it is a majestic backdrop for open-air performances in summer. Its secular counterpart, the massive ruins of 13th-century **Hardenburg** Fortress, lies 3 km (2 mi) farther west (via B–37). In its heyday it was inhabited by more than 200 people. It succumbed to fire in 1794. ⊠ *B–37.* ▦ *DM 4.* ⊙ *Tues.–Sun. 9–1 and 2–5. Closed Dec.*

Dining and Lodging

$$–$$$ ✕ **Dürkheimer Riesenfass.** The two-story "giant cask" is divided into various rooms and niches with rustic wood furnishings. Ask to see the impressive *Festsaal mit Empore* (banquet hall with gallery) upstairs. Regional wines, Pfälzer specialties, and international dishes are served year-round and specialties in season. The terrace seats 300. ⊠ *St. Michael Allee 1,* ☎ *06322/2143. AE, MC, V.*

$$ ✕ **Weinstube Bach-Mayer.** From the warmth of the tile stove to the pol-
★ ished wooden tables and benches, this small wine pub appeals with its down-home atmosphere, tasty country cooking, and hearty Pfälzer wines. It's a local favorite. ⊠ *Gerberstr. 13,* ☎ *06322/92120. MC, V. Closed Sun. No lunch.*

$$$$ ✕▦ **Kurparkhotel.** Part of the Kurhaus complex, the Kurparkhotel is
★ the place to be pampered from head to toe. Haus A has the most elegant rooms, several with balconies. Haus B, also modern and comfortable, is less exclusive. This is a typical, elegant spa hotel, with extensive health and beauty facilities, thermal baths, a casino, and concerts in the garden (except Monday). ⊠ *Schlosspl. 1–4, D–67098,* ☎ *06322/7970,* ℻ *06322/797–158. 113 rooms. Restaurant, bar, mini-bars, no-smoking rooms, indoor pool, sauna, spa, steam room, Turkish bath, bowling, casino, laundry service. AE, DC, MC, V.* ✎

$–$$ ✕▦ **Weingut und Gästehaus Ernst Karst und Sohn.** This cheerful guest house is adjacent to the Karst family's wine estate, in the midst of the vineyards. Rooms are light and airy, furnished mostly in pine; all of them have splendid views of the countryside—which you are invited to explore on the bikes the Karsts loan. Tastings and cellar tours are possible, or sample the wines with regional dishes at the nearby restaurant, Weinrefugium, at Schlachthausstrasse 1a. ⊠ *In den Almen 15, D–67098,* ☎ *06322/2862,* ℻ *06322/65965. 3 rooms, 5 apartments. Restaurant, minibars, bicycles. No credit cards. Closed Nov.–Jan.* ✎

$$$ ▦ **Weingut Fitz-Ritter.** Konrad Fitz and his American wife, Alice, have
★ a lovely vacation cottage (no smoking) that sleeps two to four people on the parklike grounds of their 216-year-old wine estate. The minium stay is one week. In addition to the wine business, they run Germany's second-oldest sparkling wine operation and a gift shop. There are concerts and festivals in the garden, courtyard, and vaulted cellars. Tastings and tours of the cellars, vineyards, and garden are possible. ⊠ *Weinstr. Nord 51, D–67098,* ☎ *06322/5389,* ℻ *06322/66005. 1 cottage. Kitchen, pool. MC, V.* ✎

Nightlife and the Arts

The **Spielbank** (casino) in the Kurparkhotel is a daily diversion after 2 PM (▦ DM 5); jacket and tie are required. The **Limburg Monastery** (☞ *above*) offers concerts and theater. Contact the local **tourist office** (☎ 06322/935–156) for program details.

Outdoor Activities and Sports

GOLF

Tee up amid the vineyards at an 18-hole course with a driving range and pitch-and-putt greens. The **Golfanlage Deutsche Weinstrasse** is in Dackenheim, 8 km (5 mi) north of Bad Dürkheim. ⊠ *Im Bitzgrund,* ☎ *06353/989–210.*

SWIMMING

The **Staatsbad** (⊠ Kurbrunnenstr. 14, ☎ 06322/9640) houses all kinds of bathing facilities for leisure and wellness, including thermal baths, herbal steam baths, a sauna, and the Turkish bath Hamam. It's open weekdays 9–9 and weekends 9–5.

En Route   When the vineyards of Ungstein, a suburb north of Bad Dürkheim, were modernized in 1981, a **Roman wine estate** was discovered. Among the finds was an ancient *Kelterhaus* (pressing house). Watch for signs to Villa Weilberg, to the left of the Wine Road (B–271).

Around Freinsheim

⓫ *7 km (4½ mi) northeast of Bad Dürkheim, via Kallstadt (the right turn to Freinsheim is signposted midway through Kallstadt).*

The next village on the Wine Road north of Bad Dürkheim is **Kallstadt,** where you can enjoy Saumagen in your glass and on your plate—for this is the home of the excellent **Saumagen Vineyard.** Both its wine and the specialty dish are served with pride everywhere in town, not just at the *Saumagenkerwe* (wine festival) the first weekend in September.

Off the Wine Road to the west, **Freinsheim's** Stadtmauer (town wall), probably built between 1400 and 1540, is one of the best-preserved fortifications in the Pfalz. Walk along it to see the massive town gates (Eisentor and Haintor) and the numerous towers, two of which can be rented as holiday apartments (☞ Dining and Lodging, *below*). Many of the town's historical houses are baroque, including the **Rathaus** (1737), with its covered stairway and sandstone balustrade. Next to it is a **Protestant church,** a Gothic structure to which Renaissance and baroque elements were added over the years. No fewer than five large festivals are celebrated here between April and September—quite a showing for a town this small.

Drive 5 km (3 mi) west to Weisenheim am Berg (you'll cross over the Wine Road at Herxheim) and watch for signs toward Bobenheim and Kleinkarlbach. This road, which runs parallel to the Wine Road and along the **vineyard heights,** affords a wonderful panorama of the expansive vineyards stretching onto the Rhine Plain. Follow the signs to **Neuleiningen,** then wind your way uphill to reach the romantic Old Town, ringed by a medieval wall. The ruins of the 13th-century castle are a good start for a town walk.

Dining and Lodging

$–$$$ ✕ **Weinhaus Henninger.** Walter Henninger numbers among the elite
★   of Pfälzer vintners, but there's nothing pretentious about the atmosphere or cooking at his cozy, wood-paneled wine pub. It's a jovial place, frequented by locals who come for the delicious, hearty fare and excellent wines. The soups and *Eintopf* dishes (stews), Rumpsteak with sautéed onions, and daily specials are recommended. ⌧ *Weinstr. 93, Kallstadt,* ☎ *06322/2277. No credit cards. Closed Mon. No lunch Tues.– Fri. in Feb.*

$$$–$$$$ ✕🏠 **Hotel-Restaurant Alte Pfarrey.** The Old Rectory is perched on the
★   hilltop above the Old Town of Neuleiningen. The comfortable inn with modern facilities is made up of several Gothic houses. Rooms are distinctive for their antique furnishings. Susanne and Utz Überschaer tend to the personal service and first-rate culinary delights. The focus is on light international favorites prepared with fresh, local ingredients. The wine list is very good, with offerings from the New and Old World. ⌧ *Unterg. 54, D–67271 Neuleiningen,* ☎ *06359/86066,* 🅵🅰🆇 *06359/86060. 9 rooms. Restaurant. DC, MC, V. Closed Mon. and 3 wks in Aug. No lunch Tues.*

$$$–$$$$ ✕🏠 **Hotel-Restaurant Luther.** This elegant country inn and restaurant
★   is set in a baroque manor right inside Freinsheim's town wall. The rooms provide modern comfort amid refined decor, with fresh flowers throughout the house. Gisela Luther's handsome table settings and Dieter Luther's artistic meal presentations make dining here a joy for all the

senses. One of Germany's leading chefs, he is known for his imaginative combinations, such as shrimp with artichokes in vanilla sauce or squab liver ravioli with warm shallot preserves. The fish and shellfish have Mediterranean hints. Save room for the chocolate hazelnut cake filled with Valrhona chocolate. ⊠ *Hauptstr. 29, D–67251 Freinsheim,* ☎ *06353/93480,* 🅵🅰🆇 *06353/934–845. 23 rooms. Restaurant, sauna. AE, MC, V. Closed Sun. and Feb. No lunch.*

$$$–$$$$
★ ✕🏠 **Hotel-Restaurant Weincastell zum Weissen Ross.** Behind the cheerful facade of this half-timber house, with its wrought-iron sign depicting a *weisser Ross* (white stallion), you can experience Pfälzer hospitality at its best. Jutta and Norbert Kohnke offer service and cuisine that are top-notch. The superb wines come from her brother's wine estate next door, Weingut Koehler-Rupprecht, and there's a well-chosen selection of international red wines. This is the best place in the Pfalz to sample "Saumagen twice." ⊠ *Weinstr. 80–82, D–67169 Kallstadt,* ☎ *06322/5033,* 🅵🅰🆇 *06322/66091. 14 rooms, 1 apartment. Restaurant. AE, DC, MC. Closed Mon., Tues., Jan., and 1 wk in late July or early Aug.*

$$
🏠 **Town Wall Tower.** For a room with a view in a highly original setting, overnight in a medieval *Turm* (tower). The Hahnenturm sleeps two; the Herzogturm can accommodate a family. Contact the Freinsheim tourist office for reservations. ⊠ *Hauptstr. 2, D–67251 Freinsheim,* ☎ *06353/989–294,* 🅵🅰🆇 *06353/989–904. 2 rooms. Kitchenettes. No credit cards.*

En Route Neuleiningen is 4 km (2½ mi) west of the Wine Road town Kirchheim. **Bockenheim,** 10 km (6 mi) north, is dominated by an imposing gateway. Like its counterpart in Schweigen-Rechtenbach, the **Haus der Deutschen Weinstrasse** marks the end (or start) of its namesake, the German Wine Road.

THE RHINE TERRACE

Like Speyer, the cities of Worms and Mainz were Free Imperial Cities and major centers of Christian and Jewish culture. Germany's first synagogue and Europe's oldest surviving Jewish cemetery, both from the 11th century, are in Worms. The imperial diets of Worms and Speyer in 1521 and 1529 stormed around Martin Luther (1483–1546) and the rise of Protestantism. In 1455 Johannes Gutenberg (1400–68), the inventor of movable type, printed the Gutenberg Bible in Mainz.

Worms

15 km (9 mi) east of Bockenheim via B–47 from Monsheim, 45 km (28 mi) south of Mainz on B–9.

Worms (pronounced *vawrms*), although devastated in World War II, is among the most ancient cities of Germany. It was founded at least 6,000 years ago and settled by the Romans and later became one of the imperial cities of the Holy Roman Empire. More than 100 imperial diets were held here, including the 1521 meeting where Martin Luther pleaded his cause. In addition to having a great Romanesque cathedral, Worms is a center of the wine trade. The Rheinhessen wines are often sleeker and less voluminous than their Pfälzer counterparts.

Worms developed into an important garrison town under the Romans, but it is better known for its greatest legend, the *Nibelungenlied,* derived from the short-lived kingdom established by Gunther and his Burgundian tribe in the early 5th century. The complex and sprawling story was given its final shape in the 12th century and tells of love, betrayal, greed, war, and death. It ends when Attila the Hun defeats the Nibelungen (Burgundians), who find their court destroyed, their treasure lost, and their heroes dead. One of the most famous incidents tells how Hagen, treacherous and scheming, hurls the court riches into the Rhine. Near the Nibelungen Bridge there's a bronze statue of him caught in the act. The *Nibelungenlied* may be legend, but the story is based on fact. A Queen Brunhilda, for example, is said to have lived here. It's also known that a Burgundian tribe was defeated in 436 by Attila the Hun in what is present-day Hungary.

Not until Charlemagne resettled Worms almost 400 years later, making it one of the major cities of his empire, did the city prosper again. Worms was more than an administrative and commercial center, it was a great ecclesiastical city as well. The first expression of this religious importance was the original cathedral, consecrated in 1018. Between 1130 and and 1181 it was rebuilt in three phases into the church you see today.

★ ⑫ If you've seen Speyer Cathedral, you'll quickly realize that the **Wormser Dom St. Peter** (Cathedral of St. Peter), by contrast, contains many Gothic elements. In part this is simply a matter of chronology. Speyer Cathedral was completed nearly 70 years before the one in Worms was even begun, long before the lighter, more vertical lines of the Gothic style evolved. Furthermore, once built, Speyer Cathedral was left largely untouched in later periods; the Worms Cathedral was remodeled frequently as new architectural styles and new values developed. The Gothic influence can be seen both inside and out, from the elaborate tympanum with biblical scenes over the southern portal (today's entrance), to the great rose window in the west choir, to the five sculptures recounting the life of Christ in the north aisle. The cathedral was completely gutted by fire in 1689 in the War of the Palatinate Succession. For this reason many of the furnishings are baroque, including the magnificent gilt high altar from 1742, designed by the master architect Balthasar Neumann (1687–1753). The choir stalls are no less decorative. They were built between 1755 and 1759 in rococo style. Walk around the building to see the artistic detail of the exterior. ⊠ *Dompl.,* ☎ *06241/6115.* ⊡ *Donation requested.* ⊙ *Apr.–Oct., daily 8–6; Nov.–Mar., daily 9–5. Closed during services.*

An imperial palace once stood in what is now the **Heylshofgarten,** a park just north of the cathedral. This was the site of the fateful meeting between Luther and Emperor Charles V in April 1521 that ultimately led to the Reformation. Luther refused to recant his theses demanding Church reforms and went into exile in Thuringia (☞ Chapter 16), where he translated the the New Testament in 1521 and 1522.

★ ⑬ The **Kunsthaus Heylshof** (Heylshof Art Gallery) is also in the park. One of the leading art museums of the region, it has an exquisite collection of German, Dutch, and French paintings as well as stained glass, glassware, porcelain, and ceramics from the 15th to 19th centuries. ⊠ *Stephansg. 9,* ☎ *06241/22000.* ⊡ *DM 3.* ⊙ *May–Oct., Tues.–Sun. 10–5; Nov.–Apr., Tues.–Sat. 2–4, Sun. 10–noon and 2–4.*

⑭ The Lutheran **Dreifaltigkeitskirche** (Church of the Holy Trinity) is just across the square from the Heylshofgarten. Remodeling during the 19th and 20th centuries produced today's austere interior, although the facade and tower are still joyfully baroque. ⊠ *Marktpl.* ⊙ *Apr.–Sept., daily 9–5; Oct.–Mar., daily 9–4.*

⑮ The **Lutherdenkmal** (Luther Monument) commemorates Luther's appearance at the Diet of Worms. He ended his speech with the words: "Here I stand. I have no choice. God help me. Amen." The 19th-century monument includes a large statue of Luther ringed by other figures from the Reformation. It is set in a small park on the street named Lutherring.

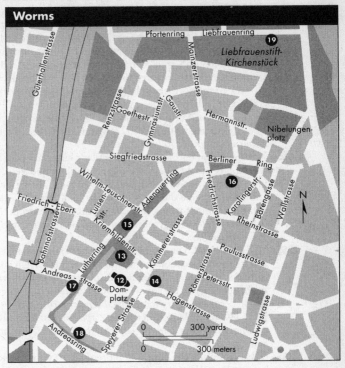

The Jewish quarter is along the town wall between Martinspforte and
Friesenspitze and between Judengasse and Hintere Judengasse. The first
★ ⑯ **Synagoge** (synagogue) was built in 1034, rebuilt in 1175, and expanded
in 1212 with a building for women. Destroyed in 1938, it was rebuilt
in 1961 using as much of the original masonry as had survived. ⊠ *Hintere Judeng.* ⊙ *Apr.–Oct., daily 10–12:30 and 1:30–5; Nov.–Mar., daily
10–noon and 2–4.*

The **Raschi-Haus,** the former study hall, dance hall, and Jewish hospital, is next door to the synagogue. It houses the city archives and the
Jewish Museum. ⊠ *Hintere Judeng. 6,* ☎ *06241/853–4700.* ⊡ *DM
3.* ⊙ *Apr.–Oct., Tues.–Sun. 10–12:30 and 1:30–5; Nov.–Mar., 10–12:30
and 1:30–4:30.*

⑰ The **Judenfriedhof Heiliger Sand** (Holy Sand Jewish Cemetery) is the
oldest Jewish cemetery in Europe. The oldest of some 2,000 tombstones
date from 1076. ⊠ *Andreasstr. and Willy-Brandt-Ring.* ⊙ *Daily.*

⑱ To bone up on the history of Worms, visit the **Städtisches Museum** (Municipal Museum), housed in the cloisters of a Romanesque church in
the Andreasstift. ⊠ *Weckerlingpl. 7,* ☎ *06241/946–390.* ⊡ *DM 4.* ⊙
Tues.–Sun. 10–5.

On the northern outskirts of Worms, the twin-towered Gothic
⑲ **Liebfrauenkirche** (Church of Our Lady) is set amid vineyards. The church
is the namesake of the mild white wine named Liebfraumilch, literally,
the "Milk of Our Lady." Today this popular wine is made from grapes
grown throughout Rheinhessen, the Pfalz, the Nahe, and the Rheingau wine regions. This one small vineyard surrounding the church was
the first to grow the grape.

Dining and Lodging

$$$–$$$$ ✕ **Rôtisserie Dubs.** A pioneer of the Rheinhessen restaurant scene, Wolfgang Dubs focused on creative regional cuisine and seasonal specialties long before it was in vogue. Old favorites, such as fillet of pork cooked in hay and *arme Ritter* (French toast with a frothy white-wine sauce), or expertly prepared fish, lamb, and game make the 9-km (5½-mi) trek to the northern suburb of Rheindürkheim worthwhile. Wine enthusiast Dubs offers his own wines, top German and French estates, and a few New World wines, such as Opus One. ✉ *Kirchstr. 6, Worms-Rheindürkheim,* ☎ *06242/2023. MC. Closed Tues., 2 wks in Jan., and 2 wks in summer. No lunch Sat.*

$–$$$ ✕ **Bistro Léger.** Barbara and Jorg Seider's bistro caters to baby boomers
★ who appreciate the casual, friendly atmosphere and fresh, well-prepared food. The salads are outstanding. Very popular are the menus with variations on a theme during "fish weeks" and "fowl weeks." There's a good selection of wines, including local vintages from the P. J. Valckenberg estate (☞ *Shopping, below*). ✉ *Siegfriedstr. 2,* ☎ *06241/46277. MC. Closed Sun.*

$$$ ✕🏨 **Dom-Hotel.** The appeal of this modern hotel lies in its friendly staff and its terrific location in the heart of the pedestrian zone (a parking garage is available). At the hotel's upscale restaurant you can watch the happenings on the square below. The focus is on international and regional cuisine and wines. ✉ *Obermarkt 10, D–67547,* ☎ *06241/ 9070,* FAX *06241/23515. 53 rooms, 2 apartments. Restaurant, minibars, no-smoking rooms, laundry service. AE, DC, MC, V. Restaurant closed Sun. and 2 wks in Aug. No lunch Sat.*

$$ 🏨 **Haus Kalisch am Dom.** For more than 30 years the Kalisch family have welcomed guests to its little inn opposite the cathedral. There are no frills, but the rooms are comfortable and have private baths and TVs. ✉ *Neumarkt 9, D–67547,* ☎ *06241/27666,* FAX *06241/25073. 13 rooms. No credit cards. Closed 3 wks in Dec. and Jan.*

$ 🏨 **Land- und Winzerhotel Bechtel.** The Bechtel family, winegrowers and proud parents of a former German Wine Queen, offer very pleasant accommodations on the grounds of their wine estate in the suburb of Heppenheim, about 10 km (6 mi) west of Worms proper. The rooms are modern, and all have balconies. There is no restaurant per se, but meals can be organized, as can wine tastings in the vaulted cellars. ✉ *Pfälzer Waldstr. 100, D–67551 Worms-Heppenheim,* ☎ *06241/3142,* FAX *06241/34745. 12 rooms. Sauna, bicycles. AE, MC, V.*

Nightlife and the Arts

The **Städtisches Spiel- und Festhaus** on Rathenaustrasse is the cultural hub of Worms, presenting theater, concerts, ballet, and special events. Concerts are also held in the **Municipal Museum,** in the Andreasstift, and at the 19th-century palace **Schloss Herrnsheim,** in the northern suburb of Herrnsheim. The annual **jazz festival** (first weekend in July) is staged primarily around Weckerlingplatz and the cathedral. Contact the **tourist office** (☎ 06241/853–8800 or 06241/25045) for program details.

Worms's nine-day wine and folk festival, the **Backfischfest** (Fried-Fish Festival), begins the last weekend of August. It evolved from the thanksgiving celebrations held by the once-powerful fishers' guild. There are rides, entertainment, a parade, fireworks, and *Fischerstechen* (jousting in the harbor).

Shopping

For tasteful wine accessories and excellent wines drop by P. J. Valckenberg's wine shop, **Der Weinladen** (✉ Weckerlingpl. 1, ☎ 06241/911–180). The winery owns nearly all of the Liebfrauenstift-Kirchenstuck vineyard surrounding the Liebfrauenkirche (☞ *above*). The store is closed Sunday and Monday and does not accept credit cards.

Oppenheim

⑳ *26 km (16 mi) north of Worms and 23 km (16 mi) south of Mainz on B–9.*

★ En route to Oppenheim, the vine-covered hills parallel to the Rhine gradually steepen. Then, unexpectedly, the spires of the Gothic **St. Katharine's Church** come into view. The contrast of its pink sandstone facade against a bright blue sky is striking. Built between 1220 and 1439, it is the most important Gothic church between Strasbourg and Köln. The interior affords a rare opportunity to admire original 14th-century stained-glass windows and two magnificent rose windows, the Lily Window and the Rose of Oppenheim. The church houses masterfully carved tombstones, while the chapel behind it has a *Beinhaus* (charnel house) that contains the bones of 20,000 citizens and soldiers from the 15th to 18th centuries. The church is open daily 9–5 in winter, 8–6 in summer.

Concerts are held in St. Katharine's, and open-air theater is in the **Burgruine Landskrone,** the 12th-century imperial fortress ruins a few minutes' walk northwest of the church. From here there is a wonderful view of the town and the vineyards, extending all the way to Worms on a clear day. For more jovial entertainment, accompanied by *Blasmusik* (brass-band oompah music), attend the **wine festival** in mid-August on the market square, which is ringed by pretty half-timber houses and the 16th-century Rathaus.

Oppenheim and its neighbors to the north, Nierstein and Nackenheim, are home to Rheinhessen's finest vineyards. The **Deutsches Weinbaumuseum** (German Viticultural Museum) has wine-related artifacts that chronicle the region's 2,000-year-old wine-making tradition and the world's largest collection of mousetraps. ⊠ *Wormser Str. 49,* ☎ *06133/ 2544.* ⊙ *Apr.–Oct., Tues.–Fri. 2–5, weekends 10–noon and 2–5.*

Nierstein

㉑ *3 km (2 mi) north of Oppenheim on B–9.*

Surrounded by 2,700 acres of vines, Nierstein is the largest winegrowing community on the Rhine and boasts Germany's oldest documented **vineyard** (AD 742), the "Glöck," surrounding St. Kilian's Church. The **Winzergenossenschaft** (cooperative winery; ⊠ Karolingerstr. 6) is an excellent place to sample the wines and the starting point of an easy hike or drive to the vineyard heights and the vantage point at the *Wartturm* (watch tower). Tasting stands are set up along the same route, providing delightful wine presentations in the vineyards *am roten Hang* (referring to the steep sites of red soils of slate, clay, and sand) in mid-June. Early August brings the **wine festival,** with stands throughout the town and a festive parade in medieval costumes.

Nackenheim

㉒ *5 km (3 mi) north of Nierstein on B–9.*

This wine village lies slightly to the west of B–9; turn left and cross the railroad tracks (opposite the tip of the island in the Rhine) to reach the town center, 2 km (1 mi) down the country road. The writer Carl Zuckmayer (1896–1977) was born here and immortalized the town in his farce *Der fröhliche Weinberg* (*The Merry Vineyard*) in 1925. He described Rheinhessen wine as "the wine of laughter . . . charming and appealing." You can put his words to the test the last weekend of July, when **wine festival** booths are set up between the half-timber town hall on Carl-Zuckmayer-Platz and the baroque **Church of St. Gereon.** Its scrolled gables, belfry, and elaborate altars are worth seeing.

Dining and Lodging

$$ ✕ **Zum alten Zollhaus.** Walk through the arched gateway to reach the beautiful garden and the entrance to this historical house. Cozy niches, fresh flowers, and handsome antiques provide a very pleasant setting for very good food and wine. Ilse Hees, the friendly proprietor, offers daily specials as well as standards such as *Spanferkelkottelete* (cutlet of roast suckling pig). The *Trilogie vom Lachs* (cold salmon) and elegant *pochiertes Lachsmedaillon* (poached salmon steak), both served with a mustard sauce, are excellent. The wine list focuses on Rheinhessen wines, and a good number are available by the glass. ✉ *Wormser Str. 7, next to Carl-Gunderloch-Pl.,* ☎ *06135/8726. No credit cards. Closed Sun. and Mon. No lunch.*

$$ ✕▣ **Landhotel und Weinstube St. Gereon.** The Jordan family's charm-
★   ing country inn is in a half-timber house they lovingly restored a few years ago. The modern rooms feature pale shades of yellow, blond-wood floors, and light-color furnishings. Stone walls and light pine furniture on terra-cotta tiles give the restaurant a warm, rustic look, too. Try a *Winzerauflauf* (vintner's soufflé) of pasta, potatoes, onions, wine, and cheese or ask if the hearty regional specialties Dippe-Has or Backes Grumbeere are available. All 20 wines served come from Rheinhessen. ✉ *Carl-Zuckmayer-Pl. 3, D–55299,* ☎ *06135/92990,* ℻ *06135/929–992. 15 rooms. Restaurant, no-smoking rooms, laundry service. MC, V. Restaurant closed Tues. and Wed. and 2 wks in Sept.–Oct.*

Outdoor Activities and Sports

BIKING

The old towpath along the riverbank is an ideal *Radweg* (cycling trail) to Mainz or Worms, and the vineyard paths are well suited for exploring the countryside.

GOLF

Seven kilometers (4½ miles) southwest of Nackenheim, the **Golfanlage Domtal Mommenheim** (✉ Am Golfpl., Mommenheim, ☎ 06138/ 92020) is in the midst of and named after the Nierstein vineyard site Domtal. It's a beautiful setting to play 18 holes or to just unwind at the driving range.

HIKING

Enjoy the views from the vineyard heights on the **Rheinhöhenweg** trail. Allow three hours to hike the 10-km (6-mi) stretch between Nackenheim, Nierstein, and Oppenheim. Start at the corner of Weinbergstrasse and Johann-Winkler-Strasse. The educational wine path through the St. Alban vineyard is a pleasant walk in Bodenheim (4 km [2½] mi northwest of Nackenheim).

Mainz

㉓   *14 km (9 mi) north of Nackenheim, 45 km (28 mi) north of Worms on B–9, and 42 km (26 mi) west of Frankfurt on A–3.*

Mainz is the capital of the state of Rheinland-Pfalz. Today's city was built on the site of a Roman citadel from 38 BC, though some of the local artifacts in the Landesmuseum (☞ *below*) date from 300,000 BC. Given its central location at the confluence of the Main and Rhine rivers, it's not surprising that Mainz has always been an important trading center, rebuilt time and time again in the wake of wars. The city's fine museums and historical buildings bear witness to a splendid past.

To see the sights, head for the Touristik Centrale (tourist office) to pick up a **Mainz Card,** a terrific one-day pass for DM 10 that includes a basic walking tour, unlimited use of public transportation, and free entry to museums and the casino, as well as a reduction in price on some hotel rooms, KD cruises, and theater tickets.

The **market square** and *Höfchen* (little courtyard) around the cathedral, the focal points of the town, are especially colorful on Tuesday, Friday, and Saturday, when farmers set up their stands to sell produce and flowers. This is also the site of the *Sektfest* (sparkling wine festival) in early June and the *Johannismarkt,* a huge wine festival with fireworks, a few weeks later.

★ The entrance to the **Dom** (Cathedral of St. Martin and St. Stephan) is on the south side of the market square, midway between the eastern and western chancels that symbolize the worldly empire and the sacerdotal realm, respectively. Emperor Otto II began building the oldest of the Rhineland's trio of grand Romanesque cathedrals in 975, the year in which he named Willigis archbishop and chancellor of the empire. Henry II, the last Saxon emperor of the Holy Roman Empire, was crowned here in 1002, as was his successor, Konrad II, the first Salian emperor, in 1024. In 1009, on the very day of its consecration, the cathedral burned to the ground. It was the first of seven fires the Dom has endured in the course of its millennium. Today's cathedral dates mostly from the 11th to 13th centuries. During the Gothic period, remodeling diluted the Romanesque identity of the original; an imposing baroque spire was added in the 18th century. Nevertheless, the building remains essentially Romanesque and its floor plan demonstrates a clear link to the cathedrals in Speyer and Worms. The interior is a virtual sculpture gallery of elaborate monuments and tombstones of archbishops, bishops, and canons, many of which are significant artworks from the 13th to 19th centuries. ⊠ *Markt.* ✇ *Donations requested.* ☉ *Nov.–Feb., weekdays 9–5; Mar.–Oct., weekdays 9–6:30. Year-round, Sat. 9–4, Sun. 1–2:45 and 3:45–5 or 6:30. Aug. and Sept., Sun. 1–6:30. Closed during services.*

From the Middle Ages until secularization in the early 19th century, the archbishops of Mainz, who numbered among the imperial electors, were extremely influential politicians and property owners. The wealth of religious art treasures they left behind can be viewed in the **Dom und Diözesanmuseum,** in the cathedral cloisters. ⊠ *Domstr. 3,* ☎ *06131/ 253–344.* ✇ *DM 5.* ☉ *Tues.–Sun. 10–5.*

★ Opposite the east end of the cathedral (closest to the Rhine) is the **Gutenberg Museum,** devoted to the history of writing and printing from Babylonian and Egyptian times to the present. Exhibits include historical printing presses, incunabula, and medieval manuscripts with illuminated letters, as well as a precious 42-line Gutenberg Bible printed in circa 1455. A replica workshop demonstrates how Gutenberg implemented his invention of movable type. After extensive renovations the museum reopened in 2000, the Gutenberg Memorial Year. ⊠ *Liebfrauenpl. 5,* ☎ *06131/1226–4044.* ✇ *DM 8.* ☉ *Tues.–Sat. 9–5, Sun. 10–5.*

★ The Kurfürstliches Schloss (Electoral Palace) houses the **Römisch-Germanisches Zentralmuseum,** a wonderful collection of original artifacts and copies of items that chronicle cultural developments in the area up to the early Middle Ages. ⊠ *Ernst-Ludwig-Pl. on Grosse Bleiche,* ☎ *06131/91240.* ✇ *Free.* ☉ *Tues.–Sun. 10–6.*

The remains of five 4th-century wooden Roman warships and two full-size replicas are on display at the **Museum für Antike Schiffahrt**

(Museum of Ancient Navigation). These were unearthed in 1981 when the foundation for the Hilton's new wing was dug. For more than a decade the wood was injected with a water-and-paraffin mixture to restore hardness. ⊠ *Neutorstr. 2b,* ☎ *06131/286–630.* ⊠ *Free.* ⊙ *Tues.–Sun. 10–6.*

★ The various collections of the **Landesmuseum** (Museum of the State of Rheinland-Pfalz) are in the former electors' stables, easily recognized by the statue of a golden stallion over the entrance. Exhibits range from the Stone Age to the 20th century. Among the highlights are a tiny Celtic glass dog from the 1st or 2nd century BC, Roman masonry, paintings by Dutch masters, artworks from the baroque to Jugendstil periods, and collections of porcelain and faience. ⊠ *Grosse Bleiche 49–51,* ☎ *06131/28570.* ⊠ *DM 5.* ⊙ *Tues. 10–8, Wed.–Sun. 10–5.*

Ⓒ The animals in Mainz's **Naturhistorisches Museum** (Natural History Museum) may all be stuffed and mounted, but these lifelike groups can demonstrate the relationships among various families of fauna better than any zoo. Fossils and geological exhibits show the evolution of the region's plants, animals, and soils. ⊠ *Reichklarastr. 1,* ☎ *06131/122–646.* ⊠ *DM 3.* ⊙ *Wed. and Fri.–Sun. 10–5, Tues. and Thurs. 10–8.*

Schillerplatz, ringed by beautiful baroque palaces, is the site of the ebullient **Fastnachtbrunnen** (Carnival Fountain), with 200 figures related to Mainz's "fifth season" of the year. From here it is but a short walk
★ up the Gaustrasse to **St. Stephanskirche** (St. Steven's Church), which affords a hilltop view of the city. In 990 Willigis built a basilica on the site; today's Gothic hall church dates from the late 13th and early 14th centuries. Postwar restoration included the installation of six stained-glass windows depicting scenes from the Bible, designed in the 1970s by the Russian-born painter Marc Chagall. The windows' vivid blue beautifully complements the Gothic decor of the church. ⊠ *Kleine Weissg. 12,* ☎ *06131/231–640.* ⊙ *Dec. and Jan., weekdays 10–noon and 2–4:30; Feb.–Nov., weekdays 10–noon and 2–5.*

On an adjacent hillside is the **Kupferberg Sektkellerei** (sparkling wine cellars), built in 1850 on a site where the Romans cultivated vines and built cellars. The Kupferberg family expanded them into 60 seven-story deep vaulted cellars—the deepest in the world. The winery has a splendid collection of glassware, posters from the Belle Epoque period (1898–1914), richly carved casks from the 18th and 19th centuries, and the **Traubensaal** (Grape Hall), a tremendous example of the Jugendstil style. Tours last 2½ hours and include a tasting of five sparkling wines. Reservations are required. ⊠ *Kupferbergterrasse 17–19,* ☎ *06131/923–205.* ⊠ *DM 17.* ⊙ *Shop weekdays 10–1 and 3–6, Sat. 10–1.*

Dining and Lodging

$$–$$$ ✕ **Heiliggeist.** This once very traditional restaurant reopened in 2000 as an upbeat café-bistro-bar that keeps late hours. Modern, minimal decor provides an interesting contrast to the historical vaulted ceilings. The compact menu offers elaborate salad platters as well as creatively spiced and sauced fish and meat dishes. One house specialty worth trying is the *Croustarte,* an upscale version of pizza. There is an extensive drinks list of teas and coffees, fresh-pressed juices, and the usual wines and spirits you'd expect at a bar. Wines by the glass are pricey, but bottles are very reasonably calculated. ⊠ *Mailandsg. 11,* ☎ *06131/225–757. No credit cards.*

$–$$$ ✕ **Fischrestaurant Jackob.** Fresh fish (the fish shop next door belongs to the restaurant) is served at reasonable prices in a setting of old foghorns and ship photographs. *Muscheln* (mussels) are available in season. ⊠

Fischtor 7, ☎ 06131/229–299. No credit cards. Closed Sun. No dinner Mon.–Thurs. and weekends.

$–$$$ ✕ **Gebert's Weinstuben.** Gebert's traditional wine restaurant offers re-
★ fined versions of regional favorites. Try the *Handkäs-Suppe* (cheese soup)
or Saumagen made not of pork, but rather *Wildschwein* (wild boar).
Gans mit Schmoräpfel und Klöse (goose with braised apples and
dumplings) or duck in orange sauce are always delicious. German wines
dominate the excellent wine list. ⊠ *Frauenlobstr. 94, ☎ 06131/611–
619. AE, DC, MC, V. Closed Sat. and 3 wks in summer. No lunch Sun.*

$–$$$ ✕ **Haus des Weines.** In addition to the pleasant ambience, tasty food,
★ and a great selection of wines, the late hours are consumer-friendly (11
AM–1 AM). The daily specials and huge salads offer very good value
and the menu covers a broad range, from snacks to full-course meals.
Enjoy a glass of wine with the Mainz specialties *Spundekäs* (cheese
whipped with cream and onions) or *Handkäse mit Musik* (pungent,
semihard cheese served with diced onions in vinaigrette). ⊠ *Gutenbergpl. 3, ☎ 06131/221–300. AE, MC, V.*

$–$$ ✕ **Eisgrub-Bräu.** It's loud, it's lively, and the beer is brewed in the vaulted
cellars on site. An Eisgrub brew is just the ticket to wash down a hearty
plate of *Haxen* (pork hocks), *Bratkartoffeln* (home fries), and sauerkraut.
Breakfast and a buffet lunch are also served. Brewery tours are free,
but make a reservation in advance. It's open daily 9 AM–1 AM. ⊠
Weisslilieng. 1a, ☎ 06131/221–104. MC, V.

$$$$ ✕🏨 **Hilton International.** The riverside location adjacent to the Old Town
★ can't be beat nor can the high standard of comfort and service you would
expect of this chain. Both restaurants have Rhine views (ask for a window table): the buffets in the Römische Weinstube are excellent, while
the Brasserie, on the first floor, is more posh and serves creative cuisine. ⊠ *Rheinstr. 68, D–55116, ☎ 06131/2450, FAX 06131/245–589.
433 rooms, 9 suites. 2 restaurants, café, piano bar, minibars, no-smoking rooms, beauty salon, massage, sauna, exercise room, casino (jacket
and tie required), laundry service. AE, DC, MC, V.*

$$ 🏨 **Hotel Ibis.** Modern, functional rooms and a great location on the
edge of the Old Town are what the Ibis offers. Except during trade fairs
and major events, there's a weekend discount rate of about 15%, but
for this rate rooms cannot be booked in advance; it's show up and take
your chances. ⊠ *Holzhofstr. 2, at Rheinstr., D–55116, ☎ 06131/
2470, FAX 06131/234–126. 144 rooms. Restaurant, bar, no-smoking
rooms, laundry service. AE, DC, MC, V.*

$–$$ 🏨 **Hotel Weinhaus Rebstock.** This 15th-century house is tucked away
in the Old Town's pedestrian zone. A family-run operation, it offers
friendly service and comfortable rooms, seven with a view of the cathedral. Park at the garage of the Hertie department store (entrance on
Weissliliengasse), a minute's walk. ⊠ *Heiliggrabg. 6, near Bischofspl.
D–55116, ☎ 06131/230–317, FAX 06131/230–318. 11 rooms, 5 with
bath. No credit cards.*

Nightlife and the Arts

Mainz offers a broad spectrum of cultural events, music from classical
to avant-garde, as well as dance, opera, and theater performances, at many
venues throughout the city. The home stage of the Staatstheater Mainz,
the **Grosses Haus** (⊠ Gutenbergpl.) is being renovated and is due to re-
open in 2001. In the interim, performances are held at the high-tech
Phönixhalle (⊠ Hauptstr. 17–19, ☎ 06131/962–830), in the suburb of
Mombach. Its other stages include the **Kleines Haus** (⊠ Gutenbergpl.,
☎ 06131/28510) and **TiC** (⊠ Spritzeng. 2, ☎ 06131/28510). **Mainzer
Kammerspiele** (⊠ Rheinstr. 4, Fort Malakoff Park, ☎ 06131/225–002)
is also a multiarts venue. The Mainzer Forum-Theater (cabaret) performs
in the **Unterhaus** (⊠ Münsterstr. 7, ☎ 06131/28510).

Music lovers can also attend **concerts** in venues ranging from the cathedral, the Kurfürstliches Schloss, the **Frankfurter Hof** (✉ Augustinerstr. 55), the **Villa Musica** (✉ Auf der Bastei 3), and the Kupferberg sparkling wine cellars to the Rathaus and several historic churches in the city. There are open-air concerts on the market square in summer. Contact the **tourist office** (☎ 06131/286–210) for program details and tickets.

Nightlife is centered in the numerous **wine pubs.** Rustic, charming, and cozy, they're packed with locals who come to enjoy a meal or snack with a glass (or more) of local wine. Most are on the Old Town's main street, Augustinerstrasse, and its side streets (Grebenstrasse, Kirschgarten, Kartäuserstrasse, Jakobsbergstrasse) and around the Gutenberg Museum, on Liebfrauenplatz. The traditional wine pubs **Wilhelmi** (✉ Rheinstr. 51) and **Schreiner** (✉ Rheinstr. 38) are also recommended.

Carnival season runs from November 11 at 11:11 AM to Ash Wednesday.

Shopping

The **Old Town** is full of boutiques, and the major department stores (Hertie and Kaufhof-Galeria) offer everything imaginable, including food halls in their lower levels. The shopping district lies basically between the Grosse Bleiche and the Old Town and includes the **Am Brand** Zentrum, an ancient marketplace that is now a pedestrian zone brimming with shops.

The excellent **Weincabinet** (✉ Leichhofstr. 10, behind the cathedral, ☎ 06131/228–858) sells an array of the region's best wines and accessories. The bustling flea market, the **Krempelmarkt,** is on the bank of the Rhine between the Hilton Hotel and Kaiserstrasse. It takes place from 7 to 1 the first and third Saturday of the month from April to October and the first Saturday from November to March.

PFALZ AND THE RHINE TERRACE A TO Z

Arriving and Departing

By Car

Autobahn access to Mainz, the northernmost point of the itinerary, is fast and easy. A–63, A–61, and A–65 run through the area roughly north–south, and A–8 approaches the southern part of the German Wine Road via Karlsruhe.

By Plane

Frankfurt is the closest major international airport for the entire Rhineland. International airports in Stuttgart and France's Strasbourg are closer to the southern end of the German Wine Road.

By Train

Mainz and Mannheim are hubs for IC (InterCity) and ICE (InterCity Express) trains.

Getting Around

By Bike

There is no charge for transporting bicycles on local trains throughout Rheinland-Pfalz weekdays after 9 and anytime weekends and holidays. The train stations in the towns of this chapter, however, do not rent bicycles. For maps, suggested routes, bike rental locations, and details on *Pauschal-Angebote* (package deals) or *Gepäcktransport* (luggage-forwarding service), contact Pfalz-Touristik or Rheinhessen-Information (☞ Contacts and Resources, *below*).

By Car

It's 162 km (100 mi) between Schweigen-Rechtenbach and Mainz, the southernmost and northernmost points of this itinerary. The main route is the Deutsche Weinstrasse, which is a *Bundesstrasse* (two-lane highway), abbreviated "B," as in B–38, B–48, and B–271. The route from Worms to Mainz is B–9. The autobahn, abbreviated "A," parallel to the Wine Road in the Pfalz is A–65 from Kandel to Kreuz Mutterstadt (the junction with A–61, south of Ludwigshafen), and in Rheinhessen, A–61 to Alzey, and, finally, A–63 to Mainz. The A–6 runs west to east through the Pfalz from Kaiserslautern to Kreuz Frankenthal (the junction with A–61, north of Ludwigshafen).

By Public Transportation

An excellent network of public transportation called *Rheinland-Pfalz-Takt* operates throughout the region with well-coordinated *RegioLinie* (buses) and *Nahverkehrszüge* (local trains). The travel service of the **Deutsche Bahn** (German Railway; ☎ 01805/996–633) provides information on schedules, connections, prices, and so on, 24 hours daily from anywhere in Germany.

Contacts and Resources

Boat Tours

The Köln-Düsseldorfer Deutsche Rheinschiffahrt (KD Rhine steamers; ☞ Cruise Travel *in* Smart Travel Tips A to Z) offers excursions from Mainz to Köln (☞ Chapter 11).

Car Rentals

Each company below also has a rental office at Frankfurt's airport and main train station.

Avis (⊠ Rheinallee 183, Mainz, ☎ 06131/625–523; ⊠ Wormser Landstr. 22, Speyer, ☎ 06232/32068; ⊠ Alzeyerstr. 44, Worms, ☎ 06241/591–081). **Europcar** (⊠ Rheinallee 195, Mainz, ☎ 06131/913–500; ⊠ Wormser Landstr. 46, Speyer, ☎ 06232/35075). **Hertz** (⊠ Alte Mainzer Str. 127, Mainz, ☎ 06131/985–644; ⊠ Klosterstr. 45, Worms, ☎ 06241/411–462). **Sixt** (⊠ Bingerstr. 19, Mainz, ☎ 06131/270–710).

Guided Walking Tours

Except where noted, tours begin at the tourist information office. **Bad Dürkheim** has free tours March to mid-November, departing Monday at 10:30 from the fountain in front of the train station. **Deidesheim** offers tours on Saturday at 10 (DM 6), from the *Geissbockbrunnen* (Billy-Goat Fountain) in front of the Stadthalle. **Mainz** has year-round tours departing Saturday at 10 (DM 6) from the Touristik Centrale. The office is one story above street level on the footbridge over Rheinstrasse. Another tour during July and August takes place daily at 2 (DM 10) and departs from the cathedral information desk. **Neustadt** tours cost DM 5 and take place April through mid-November, Wednesday at 10:30 and Saturday at 2. **Speyer** tours are at 11 on Sunday between May and October; the cost is DM 5. **Worms** begins its tours at the southern portal (main entrance) of the cathedral on Saturday at 10:30 and Sunday at 2, between mid-April and October. The cost is DM 5.

Visitor Information

The regional and local wine and tourist information offices in the southern Pfalz, the northern Pfalz, and Rheinhessen can help you make the most of your visit.

The **German Wine Information Bureau** promotes the wines of all 13 German wine regions. To receive general background information and invaluable free brochures like the German wine festivals schedule and *Vintners to Visit* (a roster of visitor-friendly wineries), contact GWIB (✉ 245 5th Ave., Suite 2204, New York, NY 10016, ☎ 212/896–3336, FAX 212/896–3342, ✆).

There are local tourist-information offices in the following towns:

Bad Dürkheim (✉ Tourist-Information, Mannheimer Str. 24, D–67098, ☎ 06322/935–156, FAX 06322/935–159). **Deidesheim** (✉ Tourist-Information, Bahnhofstr. 5, D–67146, ☎ 06326/96770, FAX 06326/967–718). **Landau** (✉ Büro für Tourismus, Marktstr. 50, D–76829, ☎ 06341/13181, FAX 06341/13195). **Mainz** (✉ Touristik Centrale, ✉ Brückenturm am Rathaus, D–55116, ☎ 06131/286–210, FAX 06131/286–2155). **Neustadt-an-der-Weinstrasse** (✉ Tourist-Information, Hetzelpl. 1, D–67433, ☎ 06321/926–892, FAX 06321/926–891). **Speyer** (✉ Verkehrsamt, Maximilianstr. 11, D–67346, ☎ 06232/142–392, FAX 06232/142–332). **Wachenheim** (✉ Verkehrsamt, Weinstr. 16, D–67157, ☎ 06322/958–032, FAX 06322/958–059). **Worms** (✉ Tourist-Information, Neumarkt 14, D–67547, ☎ 06241/853–8800 or 06241/25045, FAX 06241/26328).

PFALZ REGION

Contact **Pfalzwein** (✉ Chemnitzer Str. 3, D–67433 Neustadt a.d. Weinstrasse, ☎ 06321/912–328, FAX 06321/12881) for wine information. **Pfalz-Touristik** (✉ Landauer Str. 66, D–67434 Neustadt a.d. Weinstrasse, ☎ 06321/39160, FAX 06321/391–619) has general tourist information.

For information on the southern Pfalz: **Südliche Weinstrasse** (✉ An der Kreuzmühle 2, D–76829 Landau, ☎ 06341/940–407, FAX 06341/940–502). For information on the northern Pfalz: **Deutsche Weinstrasse** (✉ Chemnitzer Str. 3, D–67433 Neustadt a.d. Weinstrasse, ☎ 06321/912–333, FAX 06321/912–330).

RHEINHESSEN AREA

Rheinhessenwein (✉ An der Brunnenstube 33–35, D–55120 Mainz-Mombach, ☎ 06131/99680, FAX 06131/682–701) has information on the area's wine. For tourist information contact **Rheinhessen-Information** (✉ Wilhelm-von-Erlanger-Str. 100, D–55218 Ingelheim, ☎ 06132/787–566, FAX 06132/787–560).

11 THE RHINELAND

Vater Rhein, or "Father Rhine," is Germany's historic lifeline, and the region from Mainz to Koblenz is its heart. Its banks are crowned by magnificent castle after castle and by breathtaking, vine-terraced hills that provide the livelihood for many of the villages hugging the shores. In the words of French poet Victor Hugo, "The Rhine combines everything. The Rhine is swift as the Rhône, wide as the Loire, winding as the Seine . . . royal as the Danube and covered with fables and phantoms like a river in Asia . . ."

Updated by
Kerry Brady
Stewart

THE IMPORTANCE of the Rhine can hardly be overestimated. Although not the longest river in Europe (the Danube is more than twice its length), the Rhine has been the main river-trade artery between the heart of the Continent and the North Sea (and Atlantic Ocean) throughout recorded history. The Rhine runs 1,320 km (820 mi) from the Bodensee (Lake Constance) west to Basel, then north through Germany, and finally, west through the Netherlands to Rotterdam.

Wine and tourism have significantly contributed to the Rhineland's economic success for centuries. Vineyards, a legacy of the Romans, are an inherent part of the Rhine landscape from Wiesbaden to Bonn. The Rhine tempers the climate sufficiently for grapes to ripen this far north. Indeed, the wine regions along the Rhine, such as the Rheingau, and its most important tributary, the Mosel, are synonymous with the world's finest Riesling wines. Thanks to the river, these wines were shipped far beyond the borders of Germany, which in turn gave rise to the wine trade that shaped the fortune of many a riverside town. Rüdesheim, Bingen, Koblenz, and Köln (Cologne) remain important commercial wine centers to this day.

The Rhine became Germany's top tourist site 200 years ago. Around 1790 a spearhead of adventurous travelers from throughout Europe arrived by horse-drawn carriages to explore the stretch of the river between Bingen and Koblenz, now known as the Rhine gorge or Mittelrhein (Middle Rhine). The Prussian-Rhine Steamship Co. (forerunner of the Köln-Düsseldorfer) started passenger service between Mainz and Köln in 1827. Shortly thereafter, the railroad opened the region to an early form of mass tourism.

The river is steeped in legend and myth. The Loreley, a steep jutting slate cliff, was once believed to be the home of a beautiful and bewitching maiden who lured boatmen to a watery end in the swift currents. Heinrich Heine's poem *Song of Loreley* (1827), inspired by Clemens Brentano's *Legend of Loreley* (1812) and set to music in 1837 by Friedrich Silcher, has been the theme song of the landmark ever since. The Nibelungen, a Burgundian race said to have lived on its banks, serve as subjects for Wagner's epic opera cycle *Der Ring des Nibelungen* (1852–72).

William Turner captured misty Rhine sunsets on canvas. Famous literary counterparts, such as Goethe's *The Feast of St. Roch* (1814), Lord Byron's *Childe Harold's Pilgrimage* (1816), or Mark Twain's *A Tramp Abroad* (1880), captured the spirit of Rhine Romanticism on paper, encouraging others to follow in their footsteps.

No less romantic is the dreamy landscape of the Mosel Valley. Vines and forests still carpet the steep, slate slopes lining the river from Trier, the former capital of the western Roman Empire, to its confluence with the Rhine at Koblenz. En route there is a wealth of Roman artifacts, medieval churches, and castle ruins to admire.

Pleasures and Pastimes

Dining

Regional cuisine features fresh fish and *Wild* (game), as well as sauces and soups based on the local Riesling and Spätburgunder (pinot noir) wines. *Tafelspitz* (boiled beef) and *Rheinischer Sauerbraten* (Rhenish marinated pot roast in a sweet-and-sour raisin gravy) are traditional favorites. The *Kartoffel* (potato) is prominent in soups, in *Reibekucken* and *Rösti* (potato pancakes), and in *Dibbe-* or *Dippekuchen* (dialect: *Döppekoche*), a casserole baked in a *Dibbe* (cast-iron pot) and served with apple compote. *Himmel und Erde,* literally, "Heaven and Earth," is a mixture of mashed potatoes and chunky applesauce, topped with panfried slices of blood sausage and onions.

Although Düsseldorf, Köln, and Wiesbaden are home to many talented chefs, some of Germany's most creative classic and contemporary cooking is also found in smaller towns or country inns.

CATEGORY	COST*
$$$$	over DM 90
$$$	DM 55–DM 90
$$	DM 35–DM 55
$	under DM 35

*per person for a three-course meal, including tax and service and excluding drinks

Festivals

The Rhineland is a stronghold of Germany's **Fastnacht** (Carnival festivities), which takes place from 11:11 AM on November 11 to Ash Wednesday, culminating with huge parades in Düsseldorf, Köln, and Mainz (☞ Chapter 10) on the Monday before Lent.

Festivals lasting well over a week at venues throughout the Rheingau are the **Gourmet Festival** (mid-March) and **Glorreiche Tage** (mid-November); the **Rheingau Musik Festival** (mid-June through August), with more than 100 concerts, often held at Kloster Eberbach, Schloss Johannisberg, or Wiesbaden's Kurhaus; and theater and concerts during the **Burghof Spiele** in and near Eltville (late June to late August). Wiesbaden hosts the region's largest wine festival, the **Rheingauer Weinwoche** (mid-August), and the **Internationale Maifestspiele** (throughout May), featuring performances by world-renowned artists.

The spectacular fireworks display **"Rhine in Flames"** takes place the first Saturday evening in May (Linz–Bonn), July (Bingen–Rüdesheim), August (Andernach); the second Saturday evening in August (Koblenz), September (Oberwesel); and the third Saturday evening in September (St. Goar).

Lodging

The most romantic places to lay your head are the old riverside inns and castle hotels. Ask for a *Rheinblick* (Rhine view) room. Hotels are often booked well in advance, especially for festivals and when there are trade fairs in Köln, Düsseldorf, or Frankfurt, making rooms in Wiesbaden and the Rheingau scarce and expensive. Many hotels close for the winter.

CATEGORY	COST*
$$$$	over DM 250
$$$	DM 180–DM 250
$$	DM 120–DM 180
$	under DM 120

All prices are for two people in a double room, including tax and service.

Music

Few regions in Europe rival the quality of classical music performances and venues on the Rhine. Beethoven was born in Bonn, and the city hosts a Beethoven festival every two years (the next one is in 2001). Düsseldorf, once home to Mendelssohn, Schumann, and Brahms, has the finest concert hall in Germany after Berlin's Philharmonie: the Tonhalle, in a former planetarium. Köln also has one of Germany's best concert halls, and its opera company is known for exciting classical and contemporary productions. The cathedrals of Aachen, Köln, and Trier are magnificent settings for concerts and organ recitals.

Wine

Riesling is the predominant white grape and Spätburgunder (pinot noir) the most important red variety in the Rheingau, Mittelrhein, and Mosel wine regions covered in this chapter. Three abutting wine regions, Rheinhessen and the Nahe, near Bingen, and the Ahr, southwest of Bonn, add to the variety of wines available along this route.

Exploring the Rhineland

Travel begins in the Rheingau, where the village of Hochheim, east of Wiesbaden, lends its name to the generic term for all Rhine wines, *hock*. At Rüdesheim and Bingen the slopes steepen to dramatic heights and the valley narrows. The thickly wooded hills—now on both sides of the river—are interspersed by vineyards perched on steep, terraced slopes. Around every bend ancient castles tower above the tiny wine villages on the shores. Past Boppard, where the Rhine makes its largest loop, and the Mosel conflux at Koblenz, the valley widens and the scenery is tamer. One last set of peaks, the basalt cliffs known as the Siebengebirge (Seven Hills) rise up south of Bonn, concluding the most romantic portion of the Rhine Valley. The landscape flattens out in the Cologne Lowlands, the German part of the Lower Rhine. Köln and Düsseldorf are the principal cities. Not far from the Rhine, on the Belgian and Dutch borders, is the city of Aachen, site of the most important Carolingian (pre-Romanesque) cathedral in Europe.

Great Itineraries

Driving is the ideal way to travel—up one side of the Rhine and down the other—with time out for a cruise. But even the train route between Wiesbaden and Koblenz offers thrilling views.

IF YOU HAVE 3 DAYS

Travel down the Rhine toward Rüdesheim, stopping near **Eltville** ② to visit the historical monastery **Kloster Eberbach,** the cultural wine center of the Rheingau. Take in the beauty of the Rhine gorge, with its steep vineyards, legendary castles, and the **Loreley** rock, on a Rhine steamer cruise from ⛴ **Rüdesheim** ④ to **St. Goarshausen** ⑩. Return by train and overnight in a Rheingau wine village between Eltville and Rüdesheim. The second day, ferry from Rüdesheim to **Bingen** ⑤ for a closer look at the romantic Mittelrhein. The period rooms in Rheinstein, Reichenstein, and Sooneck castles evoke the region's medieval past, as do the town walls, towers, and historic buildings in the wine villages of **Bacharach** ⑥, **Oberwesel** ⑧, **St. Goar** ⑨, and **Boppard** ⑪. The latter also has significant relics from Roman times. From there drive about 20 km (12 mi) to the Mosel Valley (toward Brodenbach) to overnight in a wine village (Dieblich, ⛴ **Alken** ㉓, or ⛴ **Treis-Karden** ㉔). Start the third day with a visit to the fairy-tale castle **Burg Eltz.** Follow the Mosel downstream to its confluence with the Rhine at ⛴ **Koblenz** ⑫–㉑, spending the rest of the day exploring the sights of the city or the nearby castles **Stolzenfels, Marksburg,** and **Ehrenbreitstein.**

IF YOU HAVE 5 DAYS

Spend an afternoon and night in ⛴ **Wiesbaden** ① to enjoy the thermal springs, elegant shops, and nightlife. The next morning visit **Kloster Eberbach** and a wine estate, or proceed to ⛴ **Rüdesheim** ④ for a Rhine steamer cruise to **St. Goarshausen** ⑩. Return by train and take the cable car to the Niederwald-Denkmal (monument) overlooking Rüdesheim for an outstanding panoramic view of the Rhine Valley. The third morning continue downstream to **Kaub** ⑦ to visit the **Pfalz,** a medieval fortress. Ferry across the Rhine to **Bacharach** ⑥. See the medieval towns of **Oberwesel, St. Goar** ⑨, and **Boppard** ⑪. Overnight in ⛟ **Koblenz** ⑫–㉑. The fourth day travel along the Mosel River to **Burg Eltz,** followed by stops in ⛟ **Cochem** ㉕ and a few of the charming wine villages upstream. Overnight in or near ⛟ **Bernkastel-Kues** ㉘ with its picturesque market square, wine museum, and wine-tasting centers. On day five enjoy the natural beauty of the Mosel during an hour-long boat excursion from Bernkastel before following the river upstream to ⛟ **Trier** ㉙–㊷, the former capital of the western Roman Empire.

IF YOU HAVE 7 DAYS

Follow the five-day itinerary above. Travel from ⛟ **Trier** ㉙–㊷ to ⛟ **Köln** ㊿–㉒ via the autobahn. Spend the sixth day and night in Köln, visiting the **Dom** ㊿, a masterpiece of Gothic architecture, and one or more of the Romanesque churches and excellent museums. Devote the last day to **Aachen,** an elegant spa and the single greatest storehouse of Carolingian architecture in Europe.

When to Tour the Rhineland

The peak season for cultural, food, and wine festivals is March–mid-November, followed by colorful Christmas markets in December. The season for many hotels, restaurants, riverboats, cable cars, and sights is from Easter through October, particularly in smaller towns. Opening hours at castles, churches, and small museums are shorter during winter. Orchards blossom in March and the vineyards are verdant from May until mid-September, when the vines turn a shimmering gold.

THE RHEINGAU

The heart of the region begins in Wiesbaden, where the Rhine makes a sharp bend and flows east to west for some 30 km (19 mi) before resuming its south–north course at Rüdesheim. Wiesbaden is a good starting point to follow any of the well-marked cycling, hiking, and driving routes through the Rheingau's villages and vineyards. These are known as the Rheingauer Riesling–Radwanderweg, –Pfad, and –Route, respectively. The cycling and hiking trails extend to Kaub in the Mittelrhein. Nearly every Rheingau village has an outdoor *Weinprobierstand* (wine-tasting stand), usually near the riverbank. They are staffed and stocked by a different wine estate every weekend in the summer.

Wiesbaden

❶ *40 km (25 mi) west of Frankfurt via A–66.*

Wiesbaden, the capital of the state of Hesse, is a small city of tree-lined avenues with elegant shops and handsome facades. Its hot mineral springs have been a drawing card since the days when it was known as Aquis Mattiacis (the waters of the Mattiaci)—the words boldly inscribed on the portal of the Kurhaus—and Wisibada (the bath in the meadow). In the first century AD the Romans built thermal baths here, a site then inhabited by a Germanic tribe, the Mattiaci. Today visitors can "take the waters" in an ambience reminiscent of Roman times in the **Irisch-Römisches Bad** (Irish-Roman bath) at the Kaiser-Friedrich-Therme, a superb Jugendstil (Art Nouveau) bathhouse from 1913 (☞ Outdoor Activities and Sports, *below*). On nearby Kranzplatz, 15 of Wiesbaden's 26 springs converge at the steaming **Kochbrunnen** Fountain, where you can taste the healthful waters.

Modern Wiesbaden dates from the 19th century, when the dukes of Nassau and, later, the Prussian aristocracy, commissioned the grand

The Rhineland

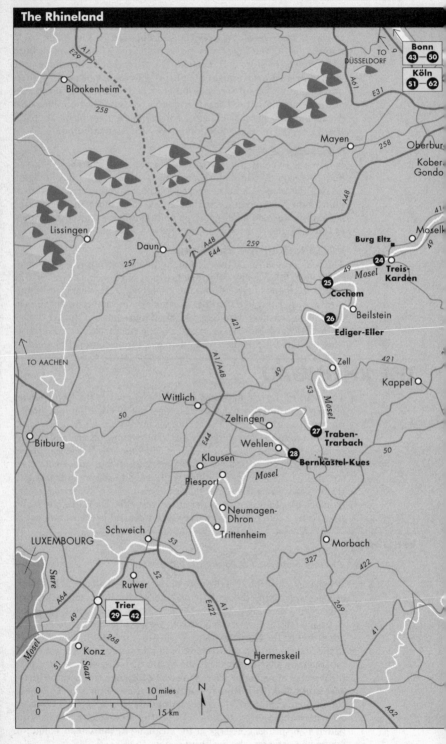

Bonn
43—50
Köln
51—62

TO
DÜSSELDORF

TO AACHEN

Blankenheim

258

E29
A1

Mayen

258

Oberbur

Kober-
Gondo

Mosel

A61

E31

A48

Lissingen

Daun

257

A48
E44

259

421

Burg Eltz

24
Treis-
Karden

25
Cochem

Mosel

49

A1/
A48

A1/A48

Beilstein

26
Ediger-Eller

Zell

421

Kappel

Wittlich

50

Zeltingen

Wehlen

53

Mosel

27
Traben-
Trarbach

50

Bitburg

E44

Klausen

28
Bernkastel-Kues

Mosel

Piesport

Neumagen-
Dhron

Schweich

53

Trittenheim

Morbach

327

422

LUXEMBOURG

Sure

A64

52

Ruwer

A1

E422

269

41

49

Trier
29—42

Konz

268

A62

Mosel

51

Saar

Hermeskeil

0
0

10 miles

15 km

N

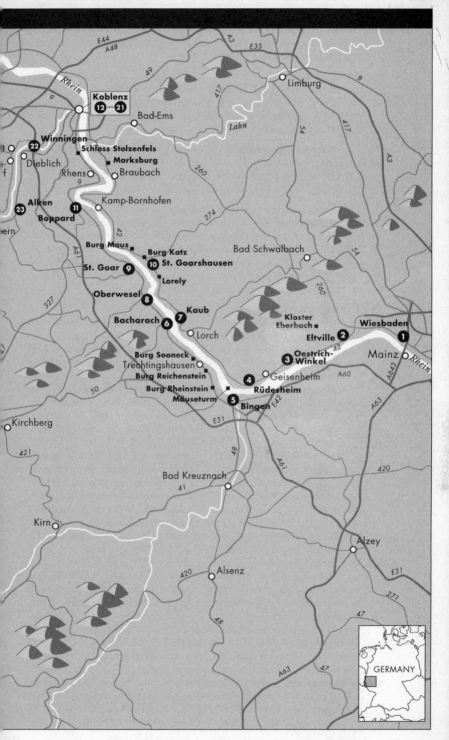

public buildings and parks that shape the city's profile today. Wiesbaden developed into a fashionable spa that attracted the rich and the famous. Their ornate villas on the Neroberg and turn-of-the-century town houses are part of the city's flair.

The Kurhaus complex is the social-cultural center of town. The neoclassical **Kurhaus** (1907) houses the casino and the Thiersch-Saal, a splendid setting for concerts. It is flanked by the Staatstheater (1894), opulently appointed in baroque and rococo revival style, and two beautifully landscaped parks.

The **Museum Wiesbaden** is known for its collection of expressionist paintings, particularly the works of the Russian artist Alexej Jawlensky. ⊠ *Friedrich-Ebert-Allee 2,* ☎ *0611/335–2250.* ☑ *DM 5.* ⊙ *Tues. 12–8, Wed.–Fri. 10–4, weekends 10–5.*

Historical buildings ring the **Schlossplatz** (Palace Square) and the adjoining **Marktplatz** (Market Square), site of the farmers' market (Wednesday and Saturday). Behind the neo-Gothic brick Marktkirche (Market Church) food and wine vendors also ply their wares in the vaulted cellars of the Marktkeller. The **Altstadt** (Old Town) is just behind the Schloss (now the seat of parliament, the Hessischer Landtag) on Grabenstrasse, Wagemannstrasse, and Goldgasse.

Dining and Lodging

$–$$$ ✕ **Käfer's.** An upscale clientele frequents this popular Kurhaus bistro with striking Jugendstil decor, a grand piano (live music nightly), and a good-size bar. Book a table for two in one of the window alcoves (Nos. 7, 12, 25, and 29) for some privacy among the otherwise close-set tables. *Neue deutsche Bescheidenheit* (sevruga caviar on a potato pancake, garnished with arugula) is a house tradition and the Wiener schnitzel is excellent. There is a good international selection of wines, and a bottle of Veuve Clicquot Brut Champage at DM 75 is an excellent value. The huge beer garden behind the Kurhaus is catered by Käfer's. ⊠ *Kurhauspl. 1,* ☎ *0611/536–200. AE, MC, V.*

$ ✕ **Sherry & Port.** Gerd Royko's neighborhood bistro-pub is a friendly place with live music Friday and Saturday from September to March. During warm months dining is at outdoor tables that ring a huge fountain on tree-lined Adolfsallee. In addition to the fantastic number of sherries (35), ports (19), and malt whiskeys (20) by the glass, there's a good selection of beers (Guinness on tap) and wines to accompany everything from tapas, salads, and pasta to steaks. ⊠ *Adolfsallee 11,* ☎ *0611/373–632. No credit cards. Closed Sun. No lunch.*

$$$$ ✕🖾 **Nassauer Hof.** Wiesbaden's premiere address for well over a century, this elegant hotel opposite the Kurhaus lies on the site of a Roman fortress that was converted into a spa and ultimately, a guest house. It is internationally renowned for its luxuriously appointed rooms, topflight service, and restaurants, die Ente (closed two weeks in January) and l'Orangerie—both open daily for lunch and dinner. ⊠ *Kaiser-Friedrich-Pl. 3, D–65183,* ☎ *0611/1330,* 🅵🅰🆇 *0611/133–632. 178 rooms, 20 suites. 2 restaurants, piano bar, lobby lounge, minibars, no-smoking rooms, indoor pool, massage, sauna. AE, DC, MC, V.* 🕸

$$$ 🖾 **Hansa Hotel.** This is a very comfortable, modern hotel in a Jugendstil house centrally located between the main train station and the Old Town. ⊠ *Bahnhofstr. 23, D–65185,* ☎ *0611/3995,* 🅵🅰🆇 *0611/300–319. 80 rooms, 1 suite. AE, DC, MC, V. Closed between Christmas and New Year's.*

$$ 🖾 **Ibis.** These two modern hotels offer excellent value and locations within walking distance of all sights: the first is on the edge of the Old Town, opposite the Kochbrunnen; the second is in the heart of the shop-filled pedestrian zone. ⊠ *Kranzpl. 10, D–65183,* ☎ *0611/36140,* 🅵🅰🆇

0611/361–4499. 132 rooms. Bar. AE, DC, MC, V; ⊠ *Mauritiusstr. 5-7, D–65183,* ☎ *0611/16710,* Ⅸ *0611/167–1750. 149 rooms. Bar. AE, DC, MC, V.*

Nightlife and the Arts

The tourist office provides schedules and sells tickets for most venues listed below.

The **Hessisches Staatstheater** (⊠ Chr.-Zais-Str. 3, ☎ 0611/132–325) presents classical and contemporary opera, theater, ballet, and musicals on three stages: Grosses Haus, Kleines Haus, and Studio. Great classics and avant-garde films, as well as dance and small theatrical productions, are specialties of the **Caligari Filmbühne** (⊠ Marktpl. 9, behind Marktkirche, ☎ 0611/313–779). Smaller dramatic productions and cabaret are performed at the intimate **Pariser Hoftheater** (⊠ Spiegelg. 9, ☎ 0611/300–607). **Thalhaus** is a lively, multiarts venue (⊠ Nerotal 18, ☎ 06111/851–267).

The Hessian State Orchestra performs in the **Kurhaus** (⊠ Kurhauspl. 1, ☎ 0611/17290). Concerts and musicals are staged at the **Rhein-Main-Hallen** (⊠ Rheinstr. 20, ☎ 0611/1440). Other venues for concerts are **Villa Clementine** (⊠ Frankfurter Str. 1, ☎ 0611/313–642), the **Henkell & Söhnlein** sparkling wine cellars (⊠ Biebricher Allee 142, ☎ 0611/630), and many churches. There are free organ concerts Saturdays at 11:30 in the **Marktkirche.**

The **Spielbank** (casino) with the Grosses Spiel (roulette, blackjack) in the Kurhaus and the Kleines Spiel (slots) in the neighboring Kolannade are lively from 3 PM to 3 AM and 2 PM–2 AM, respectively. The former is one of Europe's grand casinos, where jacket and tie are required. Minimum age is 21 (bring your passport). ⊠ *Kurhauspl. 1,* ☎ *0611/536–100.* ▣ *Grosses Spiel DM 5, Kleines Spiel DM 2. Closed holidays.*

In addition to the casino, restaurants, bars, and beer garden at the **Kurhaus,** nightlife is centered in the many bistros and pubs on **Taunusstrasse** and in the Old Town.

Outdoor Activities and Sports

SWIMMING

Renovated in 1999, the **Kaiser-Friedrich-Therme** offers thermal spring and cold-water pools, various steam baths and saunas, two solaria, massage, and a score of health and wellness treatments in elegant Jugendstil surroundings. Towels and robes can be rented on site, but come prepared for "textile-free" bathing. Children under 16 are not admitted. ⊠ *Langg. 38-40 (the entrance faces Webergasse),* ☎ *0611/172–9660.* ▣ *2 hrs DM 19.50, 4 hrs DM 31.50, for pools, steam baths and saunas.* ☉ *Sat.–Thurs. 10–10, Fri. 10–midnight (Tues. women only; Wed. men only).*

The **Opelbad,** a large outdoor swimming pool on the Neroberg, is idyllically situated on the edge of the city forest, overlooking Wiesbaden and the Rheingau. ⊠ *Neroberg,* ☎ *0611/172–9885.* ▣ *DM 10.* ☉ *May–Sept., daily 7 AM–8 PM.*

The **Thermalbad Wiesbaden** has large indoor and outdoor thermal spring pools, five saunas, an outdoor Finnish garden sauna, and a steam bath. ⊠ *Leibnizstr. 7 (near the Aukamm clinics),* ☎ *0611/172–9880.* ▣ *DM 10 swimming only, DM 20 swimming and saunas. Children under 3 not admitted.* ☉ *Mon. 12:30–10, Tues.–Thurs. 7:30 AM–10 PM, Fri. 7:30 AM–11 PM, weekends 7:30–7.*

Shopping

Broad, tree-lined **Wilhelmstrasse,** with designer boutiques housed in its fin-de-siècle buildings, is one of Germany's most elegant shopping streets. Wiesbaden is also known as one of the best places in the country to find antiques; **Taunusstrasse** has excellent antiques shops. The **Altstadt** is full of upscale boutiques; **Kirchgasse** and its extension, **Langgasse,** are the heart of the shop-filled pedestrian zone.

Eltville

❷ *14 km (9 mi) west of Wiesbaden via A–66 and B–42.*

Eltville, Alta Villa in Roman times, was first in the Rheingau to receive town rights (1332). It flourished as a favorite residence of the archbishops of Mainz in the 14th and 15th centuries, and it was during this time that the **Kurfürstliche Burg** (electors' castle) was built. The castle has an exhibition commemorating Johannes Gutenberg (1400–68), the inventor of movable type. He lived in Eltville on and off and it was here that he was named a courtier by elector Adolf II of Nassau in 1465. ✉ *Burgstr. 1,* ☎ *no phone.* 🎫 *DM 2.50.* ⊙ *Open only 1st Sun. every month, tours at 3 PM.*

The parish church of **Sts. Peter and Paul** has late-Gothic frescoes, Renaissance tombstones, and a carved baptismal by the Rhenish sculptor Hans Backoffen (or his studio). Also worth seeing are Burg Crass on the riverbank (☞ Dining and Lodging, *below*) and the half-timber houses and aristocratic **manors** on the lanes between the river and Rheingauer Strasse (B–42), notably the Bechtermünzer Hof (Kirchgasse 6), Stockheimer Hof (Ellenbogengasse 6), and Eltzer Hof (at the Martinstor gateway).

The tree-lined Rhine promenade hosts the annual *Sekt* (sparkling wine) festival during the first weekend of July. Sekt production in the Rheingau is concentrated here, in Wiesbaden, and in Rüdesheim.

The administrative headquarters and main cellars of the **Hessian State Wine Domains** are in Eltville. It owns nearly 400 acres of vineyards throughout the Rheingau and in the Hessische Bergstrasse wine region south of Frankfurt. As a result, its shops in the Jugendstil press house built in 1900 and at nearby Kloster Eberbach (☞ *below*) offer a comprehensive regional selection. ✉ *Schwalbacher Str. 56-62,* ☎ *06123/92300.* ⊙ *Weekdays 9–noon and 1–6, Sat. 10–4. MC, V.*

For a good look at the central Rheingau, make a brief circular tour. Drive 3 km (2 mi) north via the Kiedricher Strasse to the Gothic village of **Kiedrich.** In the distance you'll see the tower of Scharfenstein castle (1215) and the spires of **St. Valentine's Church** and St. Michael's Chapel, both from the 15th century. Try to visit the church on a Sunday for the 10:15 mass to admire the splendid Gothic furnishings and star vaulting amid the sounds of one of Germany's oldest organs and Gregorian chants. The chapel next door, once a charnel house, has a unique chandelier sculpted around a nearly life-size, two-sided Madonna.

These Gothic gems have survived intact thanks to 19th-century restorations patronized by the English baronet John Sutton. Today Sutton's beautiful villa south of the church is home to one of Germany's leading wine estates, **Weingut Robert Weil.** Its famed Kiedricher Gräfenberg Riesling wines can be sampled in the ultramodern *Vinothek* (tasting room and wineshop). ✉ *Mühlberg 5,* ☎ *06123/2308.* ⊙ *Weekdays 8–5, weekends by appointment.*

★ The former Cistercian monastery **Kloster Eberbach** is idyllically set in a secluded forest clearing 3 km (2 mi) west of Kiedrich. Its Romanesque and Gothic buildings (12th–14th centuries) look untouched by time—one reason why Umberto Eco's medieval murder mystery *The Name of the Rose,* starring Sean Connery, was partially filmed here. The monastery's impressive collection of old wine presses and the historical Cabinet Cellar, once reserved for the best barrels, bear witness to a viticultural tradition that spans nearly nine centuries. The wines can be sampled in the **Cabinet Cellar** on weekends, from April through October, and year-round in the **wineshop** or restaurants on the grounds (☞ Dining and Lodging, *below*). The church, with its excellent acoustics, and the large medieval dormitories are the settings for concerts, wine auctions, and festive wine events. ⊠ *Stiftung Kloster Eberbach, Eltville,* ☎ *06723/91780.* 🎫 *DM 5.* ☉ *Apr.–Oct., daily 10–6; Nov.–Mar., weekdays 10–4, weekends 11–4.* 🐾

From Eberbach take the road toward Hattenheim, stopping at the first right-hand turnoff to admire the monastery's premier vineyard, **Steinberg**. It is encircled by a 2½-km-long (1½-mi-long) stone wall (13th–18th centuries). The vineyard has an outdoor pub, Brot und Wein (bread and wine). ☉ *May–Sept., weekends 11–7.*

The *Brunnen* (springs) beneath the vineyards of **Hattenheim** and **Erbach,** both on the Rhine, lend their name to three excellent vineyards: Nussbrunnen, Wisselbrunnen, and Marcobrunnen—on the boundary between the two towns. As you return to Eltville (2 km [1 mi] east of Erbach on B–42) you will pass the elegant 19th-century palace **Schloss Reinhartshausen** (☞ Dining and Lodging, *below*).

Dining and Lodging

$$$$ ✕🏨 **Kronenschlösschen.** The atmosphere of this stylish Jugendstil house (1894) is intimate, and the individually designed rooms have antique furnishings and marble baths. Chef Patrik Kimpel oversees both the gourmet restaurant Kronenschlösschen and the more casual Bistro. Try the smoked saddle of venison or the *loup de mer* (sea bass) on macaroni au gratin with salami. Fish and lamb are the specialties at the bistro. You can also dine in the parklike garden. The wine list focuses on the finest Rheingau estates for whites and Old and New World estates for reds. ⊠ *Rheinallee, D–65347 Eltville-Hattenheim,* ☎ *06723/640,* 📠 *06723/7663. 8 rooms, 10 suites. 2 restaurants, minibars. AE, DC, MC, V. No lunch weekdays at Kronenschlösschen.* 🐾

$$$$ ✕🏨 **Schloss Reinhartshausen.** A palace in every sense of the word, this hotel and wine estate majestically overlooks the Rhine and beautifully landscaped gardens. Antiques and artworks fill the house and some rooms have fireplaces and whirlpools. The restaurant Marcobrunn (named after the famed vineyard site) is known for superb classical cuisine. Sautéed foie gras on a compote of peaches, beans, and ginger is but one of the specialties. Lighter fare is served in the airy Wintergarten, and regional dishes are served in the Schlosskeller. Approximately 1,000 wines are on the menu. The estate's wines are also available in the Vinothek. ⊠ *Hauptstr. 43, D–65337 Eltville-Erbach,* ☎ *06123/6760,* 📠 *06123/676–400. 40 rooms, 14 suites. 3 restaurants, bar, lobby lounge, wineshop, minibars, no-smoking rooms, indoor pool, sauna, exercise room, bicycles. AE, DC, MC, V. Marcobrunn closed Mon. and 2 wks in Jan. No lunch Tues. Schlosskeller closed Mon.* 🐾

$$$–$$$$ ✕🏨 **Burg Crass.** The riverfront side of this ancient castle (1076) has been fitted with floor-to-ceiling windows that open onto a magnificent terrace in the summer. High ceilings, tall plants, chic dark wood furnishings, and many works of art are a stunning setting for contemporary cuisine and excellent wines and sparkling wines, many of which are available by the glass and for sale at the Vinothek. The set food-and-wine menus offer good value, and Sunday every item on the menu, from appetizers through desserts, costs DM 9. Rooms are modern, with the charming decor you would expect in a country inn. ⊠ *Freygässchen 1 (from B–42, on the eastern edge of town), D–65343 Eltville,*

☎ 06123/69060, FAX 06123/690–669. 6 rooms. Restaurant, wineshop. No credit cards. Restaurant closed Mon. Nov.–Easter.

$$–$$$ ✕⌖ **Klosterschänke und Gästehaus Kloster Eberbach.** The monks never had it this good: the Marschollek family's light, modern, and comfortable rooms are a far cry from the unheated, stone dormitories of the past. Beneath the vaulted ceiling of the Klosterschänke you can sample the wines of the Hessian State Wine Domains with regional cuisine. Try the *Weinfleisch* (pork goulash in Riesling sauce) or *Zisterzienser Brot,* "Cistercian bread," minced meat in a plum-and-bacon dressing with boiled potatoes. ⊠ *Kloster Eberbach, D–65346 Eltville, via Kiedrich or Hattenheim,* ☎ 06723/9930, FAX 06723/993–100. 30 rooms. Restaurant, snack bar. AE, MC, V.

$$–$$$ ✕⌖ **Zum Krug.** Winegrower Joself Laufer more than lives up to the hospitality promised by the wreath and *Krug* (earthenware pitcher) hanging above the front door. The rooms have modern baths and dark wood furnishings. Equally cozy is the wood-paneled restaurant, with its old tiled oven. The German fare includes wild duck, goose, game, or Sauerbraten served in rich, flavorful gravies. The wine list is legendary for its scope (600 Rheingau wines) and large selection of older vintages. ⊠ *Hauptstr. 34, D–65347 Eltville,* ☎ 06123/99680, FAX 06123/996– 825. 10 rooms. Restaurant, no-smoking rooms. Closed 1st half of Jan. and 2nd half of July. Restaurant also closed Mon.; no dinner Sun.

Oestrich-Winkel

❸ *21 km (13 mi) west of Wiesbaden, 7 km (4½ mi) west of Eltville on B–42.*

Oestrich's vineyard area is the largest in the Rheingau. Lenchen and Doosberg are the most important vineyards. You can sample the wines opposite the 18th-century crane at the outdoor wine tasting stand.

The village of Winkel (pronounced *vin*-kle) lies west of Oestrich. A Winkeler Hasensprung wine from the fabulous 1811 vintage was Goethe's wine of choice during his stay here in 1814 with the Brentano family, who still welcome visitors to their home (☞ Dining and Lodging, *below*). The oldest (1211) of Germany's great private wine estates, **Schloss Vollrads,** lies 3 km (2 mi) north of town (depart on Schillerstrasse; turn right on Greiffenclaustrasse). The picturesque moated tower (1330) was the Greiffenclau residence for 350 years until the present palace was built in the 17th century. The period rooms are open during concerts, festivals, and wine tastings. ⊠ ☎ 06723/660. ⊙ Office: weekdays 8–5. Tasting stand: Apr.–Oct., weekends 11–6.

From Vollrads retrace your route via Greiffenclaustrasse to Schillerstrasse. Turn right and proceed all the way uphill (there is a fine view at the top). After the road curves to the left, watch for the left turn to

★ **Schloss Johannisberg.** The origins of this grand wine estate date from 1100, when Benedictine monks built monastery and planted vines on the slopes below. The palace and remarkable cellars (visits by appointment only) were built in the early 18th century by the prince-abbots of Fulda. Every autumn a courier was sent from Johannisberg to Fulda to obtain permission to harvest the grapes. In 1775 he returned after considerable delay. Although the harvest was later and the grapes far riper than usual, the wines were exceptionally rich and fruity. *Spätlese* (literally, "late harvest," pronounced *shpate*-lay-zeh) wines have been highly esteemed ever since. A statue in the courtyard commemorates the "late rider." There are tastings at the Vinothek and the *Gutsauschank* (estate's restaurant, ☞ *below*). ⊠ *Weinbaudomäne Schloss Johannisberg, D–65366 Geisenheim-Johannisberg,* ☎ 06722/70090. ⊙ Vinothek: weekdays 10–1 and 2–6, weekends 11–6. ☙

Dining and Lodging

$$–$$$ ✕ **Gutsausschank Brentano Haus.** Part of the Brentano family's home and lovely garden, once a favorite meeting place of the Rhine Romanticists, has been converted into a cozy wine pub that serves regional cuisine with Baron von Brentano's estate-bottled wines. Tischbein's famous portrait of Goethe adorns the house wine label. The Goethe Zimmer (Goethe Room), with mementos and furnishings from Goethe's time, may be visited by appointment only. ✉ *Am Lindenpl. 2 (in Winkel),* ☎ *06723/7426 pub, 06723/2068 estate. No credit cards. Closed Thurs. No lunch weekdays. Closed weekdays Jan. and Feb.*

$$–$$$ ✕ **Gutsausschank Schloss Johannisberg.** The glassed-in terrace affords a spectacular view of the Rhine and the vineyards from which the wine in your glass originated. Rheingau Riesling soup and *Bauernnente* (farmer's duck) are house specialties. ✉ *Schloss Johannisberg,* ☎ *06722/96090. MC, V.*

$$–$$$ ✕ **Gutsrestaurant Schloss Vollrads.** Chef Matthias Böhler's "farmers' specialties" and creative seasonal menus are served with the estate's wines in the cavalier house (1650) or on the flower-lined terrace facing the garden. ✉ *Schloss Vollrads, north of Winkel,* ☎ *06723/5270. MC, V. Closed Wed., Apr.–Oct.; Tues.–Thurs., Nov.–Mar.; 2 wks in Jan. and 2 wks in Nov.*

$$$–$$$$ 🏨 **Hotel Schwan.** This green-and-white half-timber inn has been in the Wenckstern family since it was built in 1628. All rooms offer modern comfort; the decor in the guest house is simpler than in the historical main building. Many rooms afford a Rhine view, as does the beautiful terrace. The staff is friendly and helpful. ✉ *Rheinallee 5, D–65375 Oestrich-Winkel,* ☎ *06723/8090,* 📠 *06723/7820. 53 rooms, 1 suite. Restaurant, bar, minibars. AE, DC, MC, V. Closed mid-Dec.–mid-Jan.*

Rüdesheim

④ *30 km (19 mi) west of Wiesbaden, 9 km (5½ mi) west of Oestrich-Winkel on B–42.*

Tourism and wine are the heart and soul of Rüdesheim and best epitomized by the **Drosselgasse** (Thrush Alley). Less than 500 ft long, this narrow, pub-lined lane is abuzz with music and merrymaking from noon until well past midnight every day from Easter through October.

The **Asbach Weinbrennerei** (wine distillery) has produced Asbach, one of Germany's most popular brands of *Weinbrand* (wine brandy, the equivalent of Cognac) here since 1892. It is a key ingredient in its brandy-filled *Pralinen* (chocolates) and in the local version of Irish coffee, Rüdesheimer Kaffee. A tour of the distillery operations concludes with a tasting. ✉ *Asbach Besucher Center Ingelheimer Str. 4, on the eastern edge of town,* ☎ *06722/497–345.* 🎫 *DM 5.* ☉ *Mon.–Thurs. 9–5, Fri. 9–noon; weekends Apr.–Oct. 9–5, Dec. 9–4.*

The **Weinmuseum Brömserburg,** housed in one of the oldest castles on the Rhine (circa 1000 AD), displays wine-related artifacts and drinking vessels dating from Roman times. You can enjoy a glass of Rüdesheimer wine and a good view on the terrace. ✉ *Rheinstr. 2,* ☎ *06722/2348.* 🎫 *Museum DM 5; DM 9 with glass of wine, souvenir tasting glass, tour; DM 13 (as above, with 4 wines).* ☉ *Mid-Mar.–mid-Nov., daily 9–6.*

☖ The 15th-century **Brömserhof** (Brömser Manor) holds Germany's largest collection of mechanical music instruments. Tours are educational and entertaining. ✉ *Siegfried's Mechanisches Musikkabinett, Oberstr. 29,* ☎ *06722/49217.* 🎫 *DM 9.* ☉ *Mar.–Dec., daily 10–6.*

High above Rüdesheim and visible for miles stands "Germania," a colossal female crowning the **Niederwald-Denkmal** (Niederwald Monument). It was built from 1877 to 1883 to commemorate the rebirth of the German Empire after the Franco-Prussian War (1870–71). There are splendid panoramic views from the monument and from other vantage points on the edge of the forested plateau. You can reach the monument on foot, by car (via Grabenstrasse), or by sweeping over the vineyards in the *Seilbahn* (cable car). There is also a *Sessellift* (chairlift) to and from Assmannshausen, a red wine enclave, on the west side of the hill. ⊠ *Oberstr. 37,* ☎ *06722/2402.* ⊠ *One-way DM 6.50, round-trip or combi-ticket for cable car and chairlift DM 10.* ⊙ *Mid-Mar.–Oct., daily 9:30–4 (June–Sept. until 7).*

With the wings of a glider you can silently soar over the Rhine Valley. At the **Luftsport-Club Rheingau** you can catch a 30–60-minute *Segelflug* (glider flight) on a glider plane between Rüdesheim and the Loreley; allow 1½ hours for pre- and postflight preparations. ⊠ *3 mi (1 km) north of the Niederwald-Denkmal and Landgut Ebenthal,* ☎ *06722/2979.* ⊠ *DM 20 (10 mins) and DM 1 (each additional min).* ⊙ *Apr.–Oct., weekends 10–7.*

Dining and Lodging

$–$$$ ✕ **Rüdesheimer Schloss.** In a tithe house built in 1729, this wine tavern specializes in Hessian cuisine and Rheingauer Riesling and Spätburgunder wines from the Breuer family's own estate and its illustrious neighbors throughout the region. The selection of older vintages is remarkable. Start with the delectable *Sauerkrautsuppe* (sauerkraut soup). Benedictine-style *"Schloss Ente"* (duck with dates and figs), *Ochsenbrust* (boiled breast of beef), and *Woihinkel* (chicken in Riesling sauce) are all excellent. Typical Drosselgasse music and dancing are an entertaining backdrop indoors and in the tree-shaded courtyard. ⊠ *Drosselg.,* ☎ *06722/90500. AE, DC, MC, V. Closed Jan.–Mar.*

$–$$ ✕ **Breuer's Restaurant und Gutsausschank.** In an airy, uncluttered setting you can enjoy tasty bistro fare (pasta, salads, dishes with Asian accents) and excellent wines, not least those of the renowned Rheingau estate Weingut Georg Breuer. The Vinothek next door sells the estate's wines and tasteful wine accessories. ⊠ *Grabenstr. 8,* ☎ FAX *06722/1026. AE, DC, MC, V. Closed Mon. and Tues. No lunch.*

$$$$ ✕▥ **Hotel Krone Assmannshausen.** This elegant, antique-filled hotel and restaurant offers first-class service and fine wining and dining. Classic cuisine prepared by chef Willi Mittler and wines from the family's own vineyards as well as an overall superb collection of wines make for very memorable meals indoors or on the terrace overlooking the Rhine. ⊠ *Rheinuferstr. 10, D–65385 Rüdesheim-Assmannshausen,* ☎ *06722/4030,* FAX *06722/3049. 46 rooms, 19 suites. Restaurant, bar, minibars, pool, sauna. AE, DC, MC, V.* ❧

$$$–$$$$ ▥ **Breuer's Rüdesheimer Schloss.** Gracious hosts Susanne and Heinrich Breuer have beautifully integrated modern designer decor into the historic walls of this stylish hotel. The Constantinescu Suite (No. 20) and the Rhine Suite (No. 14), with its large terrace, are especially popular; most rooms offer a vineyard view. Cellar or vineyard tours and wine tastings can be arranged. ⊠ *Steing. 10, D–65385 Rüdesheim,* ☎ *06722/90500,* FAX *06722/47960. 18 rooms, 3 suites. Restaurant, bar, minibars, bicycles. AE, DC, MC, V. Closed late Dec.–early Jan.* ❧

THE MITTELRHEIN

Bingen, like Rüdesheim, is a gateway to the Mittelrhein. From here to Koblenz is the greatest concentration of Rhine castles. Most date from the 12th and 13th centuries but were destroyed in 1689 when French troops systematically blew them up and burned them down during the war of Palatinate succession. It is primarily thanks to the Prussian royal family and its penchant for historical preservation that numerous Rhine castles were rebuilt or restored in the 19th and early 20th centuries.

Two roads run parallel to the Rhine: B–42 (east side) and B–9 (west side). The spectacular views from the heights can best be enjoyed via the routes known as the Loreley-Burgenstrasse (east side), from Kaub to the Loreley to Kamp-Bornhofen, or the Rheingoldstrasse (west side), from Rheindiebach to Rhens. The Rheinhöhenweg (Rhine Heights Path) affords hikers the same splendid views, including descents into the villages en route. These marked trails run between Oppenheim on the Rhine Terrace (☞ Chapter 10) and Bonn for 240 km (149 mi) and between Wiesbaden and Bonn-Beuel for 272 km (169 mi). The traffic-free paths through the vineyards and along the riverbanks are wonderful routes for hikers and cyclists alike.

Bingen

⑤ *35 km (22 mi) west of Wiesbaden via Mainz and A–60; ferry from the wharf opposite Rüdesheim's train station.*

Bingen overlooks the Nahe-Rhine conflux near a treacherous stretch of shallows and rapids known as the Binger Loch (Bingen Hole). Early on, Bingen developed into an important commercial center, for it was here —as in Rüdesheim on the opposite shore—that goods were moved from ship to shore to circumvent the unnavigable waters. Bingen was also the crossroad of Roman trade routes between Mainz, Koblenz, and Trier. Thanks to this central location, it grew into a major center of the wine trade and remains so today. Wine is celebrated during 11 days of merrymaking in early September at the annual **Winzerfest.**

Bingen was destroyed repeatedly by wars and fires, thus there are many ancient foundations but few visible architectural remains of the past. Since Celtic times the Kloppberg (Klopp Hill), in the center of town, has been the site of a succession of citadels, all named **Burg Klopp** since 1282. The terrace affords good views of the Rhine, the Nahe, and the surrounding hills.

Not far from the millennium-old Drususbrücke, a stone bridge over the Nahe, is the late Gothic **Basilica of St. Martin.** It was originally built in 793 on the site of a Roman temple. The 11th-century crypt and Gothic and baroque furnishings merit a visit.

★ The **Historisches Museum am Strom** (History Museum), is housed in a former power station (1898) on the riverbank. Here you can see an intact set of Roman surgical tools (2nd century), period rooms from the Rhine Romantic era, and displays about the Abbess St. Hildegard von Bingen (1098–1179), one of the most remarkable women of the Middle Ages. An outspoken critic of papal and imperial machinations, she was a highly respected scholar, naturopath, and artist whose mystic writings and music are much in vogue today. ⊠ *Museumsstr. 3,* ☎ *06721/990–654.* ≊ *DM 8.* ☉ *Tues.–Sun. 10–5.* ☜

The forested plateau of the *Rochusberg* (St. Roch Hill) is the pretty setting of the **Rochuskapelle** (St. Roch Chapel). Originally built in 1666 to celebrate the end of the plague, it has been rebuilt twice. Goethe attended the consecration festivities on August 16, 1814, the forerunner of today's Rochusfest, a weeklong folk festival in mid-August. The chapel (open during Sunday services at 8 and 10) contains an altar dedicated to St. Hildegard and relics and furnishings from the convents she founded on the Ruppertsberg (in the suburb of Bingerbrück) and in Eibingen (east of Rüdesheim). The **Hildegard Forum,** near the chapel, has exhibits related to St. Hildegard, a medieval herb garden, and a restaurant serving tasty, wholesome foods (*Dinkel,* or spelt, is a main ingredient) based on Hildegard's nutritional teachings. ☎ *06721/181–000.* ✆ *Tues.–Fri. 2–6, weekends 11–6.*

Dining and Lodging

$–$$$ ✕ **Schlösschen am Mäuseturm.** Dining on the terrace of this Schlösschen (little castle) with its view of the Mäuseturm (☞ *below*) and the Rhine makes for a very pleasant evening. The Steiningers serve traditional favorites as well as Pfälzer specialties (☞ Chapter 10). The wine list offers 24 wines by the glass, including Trockenbeerenauslese, a rare, liqueurlike wine. ✉ *Stromberger Str. 28 (in suburb of Bingerbrück),* ☎ FAX *06721/36699. MC. Closed Sun. and 2 wks in summer. No lunch.*

$–$$$ ✕ **Weinstube Kruger-Rumpf.** It is well worth the 10-minute drive from Bingen (just across the Nahe River) to enjoy Cornelia Rumpf's refined country cooking with Stefan Rumpf's exquisite Nahe wines (Riesling, Weissburgunder [pinot blanc], and Silvaner are especially fine). House specialties are a rich potato soup with slices of fried blood sausage, boiled beef with green herb sauce, and *Winzerschmaus* (casserole of potatoes, sauerkraut, bacon, cheese, and herbs). The house dates from 1790; the wisteria-draped garden beckons in the summer. ✉ *Rheinstr. 47, Münster-Sarmsheim, 4 km (2½ mi) southwest of Bingen,* ☎ *06721/ 43859. Reservations essential. MC. Closed Mon.; 2 wks in late Dec.– early Jan.; 2 wks in Feb. and Mon. No lunch.*

$$$$ ✕🏨 **Hotel Stromburg.** It's a pretty 15-minute drive through the *Binger Wald* (Bingen Forest) to this luxurious castle hotel and restaurant overlooking Stromberg. Johann Lafer is a multistarred chef who pioneered cooking shows in Germany. In the elegant Le Val d'Or (reservations essential), specialties include *gebratene Gänsestopfleber* (sautéed foie gras) in Port wine jus and a medley of Asian seafood with Singapore noodles. The less formal Turmstube offers tasty regional dishes. Try the *Dessertimpression* for a sample of Lafer's renowned desserts. The wine list features 200 top Nahe wines and several hundred Old and New World wines, with a particularly fine collection from Bordeaux and Burgundy. ✉ *Am Schlossberg 1, D–55442 Stromberg, 12 km (7½ mi) west of Bingerbrück via Weiler and Waldalgesheim,* ☎ *06724/93100,* FAX *06724/931–090. 13 rooms, 1 suite. 2 restaurants, bar, lobby lounge, minibars. AE, DC, MC, V.* ✆

Outdoor Activities and Sports

HIKING AND WALKING

There are excellent signposted wine and nature trails in the park on the heights of the **Höhenpark Rochusberg.** In the **Binger Wald** (near Bingerbrück), information panels along the **Erlebnispfad** ("experience path") detail the forest's flora and inhabitants. The tourist office has brochures outlining circular walks.

En Route On the 5-km (3-mi) drive on B–9 to Trechtingshausen, you will pass by Bingen's landmark, the **"Mäuseturm"** (mice tower), perched on a rocky island near the Binger Loch. The name derives from a gruesome legend. One version tells that during a famine in 969, the miserly Archbishop Hatto hoarded grain and sought refuge in the tower to escape the peasants' pleas for food. The stockpile attracted scads of mice to the tower, where they devoured everything in sight, including Hatto. In fact, the tower was built by the archbishops of Mainz in the 13th–14th centuries as a *Mautturm* (watch tower and toll station) for their fortress Ehrenfels on the opposite shore (now a ruin). It was restored in neo-Gothic style by the king of Prussia in 1855, who also rebuilt Sooneck Castle (☞ *below*).

The three **castles** open for visits near Trechtingshausen will fascinate lovers of history and art. As you enter each castle's gateway, you can't help but marvel at what a feat of engineering it was to have built such a massive

Burg (fortress or castle) on the stony cliffs overlooking the Rhine. They have all lain in ruin once or more during their turbulent histories. Their outer walls and period rooms still evoke memories of Germany's medieval past as well as the more recent era of Rhine Romanticism. You can enjoy superb Rhine vistas from the castles' terraces, where coffee and cake and local wines are served, except Monday. Reichenstein also serves meals.

★ ♨ **Burg Rheinstein** was the home of Rudolf von Habsburg from 1282 to 1286. To establish law and order on the Rhine, he destroyed the neighboring castles of Burg Reichenstein and Burg Sooneck and hanged their notorious robber barons from the oak trees around the Clemens Church, a late-Romanesque basilica near Trechtingshausen. The Gobelin tapestries, 15th-century stained glass, wall and ceiling frescoes, and antique furniture—including a rare "giraffe spinet" upon which Kaiser Wilhelm I is said to have tinkled the ivories—are well worth seeing. Rheinstein was the first of many a Rhine ruin to be rebuilt by a royal Prussian family in the 19th century. ⊠ *55413 Trechtingshausen,* ☎ *06721/6348.* ▦ *DM 6.50.* ⊙ *Mid-Mar.–Apr. and Oct.–mid-Nov., daily 10–5; May–Sept., daily 9:30–5:30.* ⊛

Burg Reichenstein has collections of decorative cast-iron slabs (from ovens and historical room-heating devices), hunting weapons and armor, period rooms, and paintings. ⊠ *55413 Trechtingshausen,* ☎ *06721/6117.* ▦ *DM 6.* ⊙ *Mid-Mar.–mid-Nov., Tues.–Sun. 10–6.*

Burg Sooneck, on the edge of the Soon (pronounced zone) Forest, houses a valuable collection of Empire, Biedermeier, and neo-Gothic furnishings, medieval weapons, and paintings from the Rhine Romantic era. ⊠ *55413 Niederheimbach,* ☎ *06743/6064.* ▦ *DM 5.* ⊙ *Apr.–Sept., Tues.–Sun. 10–6; Oct. and Nov., and Jan.–Mar., Tues.–Sun. 10–5. Closed Dec. and Mon.*

Bacharach

❻ *16 km (10 mi) north of Bingen; ferry 3 km (2 mi) north of town, to Kaub.*

Bacharach, a derivative of the Latin *Bacchi ara* (altar of Bacchus), has long been associated with wine. Like Rüdesheim, Bingen, and Kaub, it was a shipping station where barrels would interrupt their Rhine journey for land transport. Wine from the town's most famous vineyard, the Bacharacher Hahn, is served on the KD Rhine steamers. You can sample wines at the *Weinblütenfest* (vine blossom festival) in the side valley suburb of **Steeg** (late June) or the *Winzerfest* (wine festival) in Bacharach proper (early October).

Park on the riverbank and enter the town through one of its medieval gateways. You can ascend the 14th-century **town wall** for a walk along the ramparts facing the Rhine, then stroll along the main street (one street, but three names: Koblenzer Strasse, Oberstrasse, and Mainzer Strasse) for a look at **patrician manors,** typically built around a *Hof* (courtyard), and **half-timber houses.** Haus Sickingen, Posthof, Zollhof, Rathaus (town hall), and Altes Haus (☞ Dining and Lodging, *below*) are fine examples. The massive tower in the center of town belongs to the parish church of **St. Peter.** A good example of the transition from Romanesque to Gothic styles, it has an impressive four-story nave. From here a set of stone steps (signposted) leads to Bacharach's landmark, the sandstone ruins of the Gothic **Werner Kapelle,** highly admired for its filigree tracery. The chapel's roof succumbed to falling rocks in 1689, when the French blew up Burg Stahleck. Originally a Staufen fortress (11th century), the castle lay dormant until 1925, when a youth hostel was built on the foundations. The sweeping views it affords are worth the 10-minute walk.

Dining and Lodging

$–$$$ ✕ **Weinhaus Altes Haus.** Charming inside and out, this medieval half-timber house is a favorite setting for films and photos. The cheerful proprietor, Irina Weber, uses the freshest ingredients possible and buys her meat and game from local butchers and hunters. *Rieslingrahmsuppe* (Riesling cream soup), *Reibekuchen* (potato pancakes), and the hearty *Hunsrücker Teller* (boiled beef with horseradish sauce) are favorites, in addition to the seasonal specialties. She offers a good selection of wines from the family's own vineyards. ⊠ *Oberstr. 61,* ☎ *06743/1209. AE, MC, V. Closed Wed. and mid-Dec.–Easter.*

$ ✕ **Gutsausschank Zum Grünen Baum.** Winegrower Fritz Bastian runs this cozy tavern in a half-timber house from 1579. He is the sole owner of the vineyard Insel Heyles'en Werth, on the island opposite Bacharach. The "wine carousel" is a great way to sample a full range of flavors and styles (15 wines), at its best under the tutelage of the congenial host. Snacks are served, including delicious homemade, air-dried *Schinken* (ham), as well as sausages and cheese. ⊠ *Oberstr. 63,* ☎ *06743/ 1208. No credit cards. Closed Thurs. and Feb.*

$$ ✕🖾 **Rhein-Hotel Andreas Stüber.** This friendly family operation offers modern rooms (each named after a vineyard) with Rhine or castle views. The restaurant has an excellent selection of Bacharacher wines to help wash down hearty regional specialties, such as *Hinkelsdreck* (chicken liver pâté), *Stichpfeffer* (peppery pork ragout), or *Rieslingbraten* (beef marinated in wine). ⊠ *Langstr. 50 (on the Stadtmauer, the town wall), D–55422 Bacharach,* ☎ *06743/1243,* 𝖥𝖠𝖷 *06743/1413. 14 rooms. Restaurant, wine pub, minibars, bicycles. MC, V. Closed Nov.–mid-Mar. Restaurant closed Tues.*

$$–$$$ 🖾 **Altkölnischer Hof.** Flowers line the windows of the Scherlicht family's pretty, half-timber hotel near market square. The rooms are simply but attractively furnished in country style and some have balconies. ⊠ *D–55422 Bacharach,* ☎ *06743/1339,* 𝖥𝖠𝖷 *06743/2793. 20 rooms. Restaurant, minibars (some rooms). AE, MC, V. Closed Nov.–Mar.*

Kaub

❼ *19 km (12 mi) north of Rüdesheim; ferry from Bacharach.*

The village of Kaub (pronounced cowp), once a major customs post, has profited from its slate quarries and wine for centuries. On New Year's Eve 1813–14, General Blücher led his troops from here across the Rhine on a pontoon bridge of barges to expel Napoléon's troops from the Rhineland. The small **Blüchermuseum** with furnishings and militaria from that time is housed in his former headquarters. ⊠ *Metzgerg. 6,* ☎ *06774/400.* 🖾 *DM 4.* ☉ *Apr.–Oct., Tues.–Sun. 10–noon and 2–4; Nov.–Mar. weekdays 10–noon.*

☉ **Pfalzgrafenstein** Castle—known locally as the "Pfalz"—is built on a rock in the middle of the Rhine. Originally a five-sided tower, it was later enclosed by a six-sided defense wall that makes it look like a stone ship anchored in the Rhine. It was never destroyed. Unlike the elaborate period rooms of many Rhine castles, the Pfalz provides a good look at sparse medieval living quarters and has an interesting collection of ordinary household goods. ☎ *06774/222 Kaub tourist office.* 🖾 *DM 7, including boat ride to and from Kaub.* ☉ *Apr.–Sept., daily 9–1 and 2–6; Oct.–Mar., Tues.–Sun. 9–1 and 2–5. Closed Dec.*

Dining and Lodging

$$–$$$ ✕🖾 **Zum Turm.** Set next to a medieval *Turm* (tower) near the Rhine, this little inn offers spacious guest rooms on the floors above its cozy restaurant and terrace. Fish, game, and produce chef Harald Kutsche can't source from local farms are imported from the market halls of Paris. For a starter try the home-smoked salmon, venison carpaccio, or goose liver terrine, followed by beech-wood-smoked breast of duck or cassoulet of lobster. The daily set menus (three–six courses) are excellent options. The Mittelrhein and Rheingau are the focus of the wine list. ⊠ *Zollstr. 50, D–56349,* ☎ *06774/92200,* FAX *06774/922–011. 6 rooms. Restaurant, minibars, bicycles. DC, MC, V. Closed 2 wks in Feb., 2 wks in Nov. Restaurant closed Tues.; lunch on request only Nov.–Mar.* ✎

Oberwesel

8 *8 km (5 mi) north of Bacharach*

Oberwesel retains its medieval silhouette. Sixteen of the original 21 towers and much of the town wall still stand in the shadow of **Schönburg** Castle. Both Gothic churches are worth visiting. The **Liebfrauenkirche** (Church of Our Lady), popularly known as the "red church" because of its brightly colored exterior, has a superb rood screen, masterful sculptures, tombstones and paintings, and one of Germany's oldest altars (1331). Set on a hill at the opposite end of the town is **St. Martin**—the so-called white church—with a fortresslike tower, beautifully painted vaulting, and a magnificent baroque altar. The "town of towers," is also renowned for its Riesling wines, celebrated at two lively wine festivals, the *Weinmarkt,* in early and mid-September.

Dining and Lodging

$–$$ ✕ **Historische Weinwirtschaft.** Tables in the flower-laden garden in front of this lovingly restored stone house are at a premium in the summer, yet seats in the nooks and crannies indoors are just as inviting. Dark beams, exposed stone walls, and antique furniture set the mood on the ground and first floors, while the vaulted cellar houses contemporary art exhibitions. Ask Iris Marx, the ebullient proprietor, to translate the menu (it's in local dialect) of regional dishes. She offers country cooking at its best. The wine list is excellent and features 32 wines by the glass. ⊠ *Liebfrauenstr. 17,* ☎ *06744/8186. AE, MC, V. Closed Tues. and Jan. No lunch except Sun. May–Sept.*

$$$–$$$$ ✕🖬 **Burghotel Auf Schönburg.** Part of the Schönburg Castle complex
★   (12th century) has been restored as a romantic hotel and restaurant (closed Monday), with terraces in the courtyard and overlooking the Rhine. Antique furnishings and historical rooms (library, chapel, prison tower) add to the ambience. Your hosts, the Hüttls, will transfer your luggage from the parking lot—simply ask upon arrival. ⊠ *D–55430,* ☎ *06744/93930,* FAX *06744/1613. 20 rooms, 2 suites. Restaurant, minibars. AE, DC, MC, V. Closed Jan.–Mar. and mid-Dec.* ✎

$$–$$$ ✕🖬 **Römerkrug.** Rooms with exposed beams, pretty floral prints, and historic furnishings are tucked within the half-timber facades (1458) of Elke Matzner's small inn on the market square. Fish and game are house specialties, but there's light cuisine with Asian accents as well as Rhine specialties, such as Himmel und Erde. There is a well-chosen selection of Mittelrhein wines. ⊠ *Marktpl. 1, D–55430,* ☎ *06744/7091,* FAX *06744/1677. 7 rooms. AE, MC, V. Hotel closed Jan. Restaurant closed Wed. and Jan.*

St. Goar

9 *7 km (4½ mi) north of Oberwesel; ferry to St. Goarshausen.*

St. Goar and its counterpoint on the opposite shore, St. Goarshausen, are named after a Celtic missionary who settled here in the 6th century. He became the patron saint of innkeepers—an auspicious sign for both towns that now live from tourism and wine. St. Goar's tomb once rested in the 15th-century collegiate church, the **Stiftskirche,** built over a Romanesque crypt reminiscent of those of churches in Speyer and Köln.

The extensive castle ruins of **Burg Rheinfels** overlooking the town bear witness to the fact that St. Goar was once the best-fortified town in the Mittelrhein. From its beginnings in 1245, it was repeatedly enlarged by the counts of Katzenelnbogen, a powerful local dynasty, and their successors, the landgraves of Hesse. Although it repelled Louis IV's troops in 1689, Rheinfels was blasted by the French in 1797. Take time for a walk through the impressive ruins and the museum, which has an exquisite model of how the fortress looked in its heyday. ☎ 06741/383. ▣ DM 6. ◷ *Apr.–Oct., daily 9–6; Nov.–Mar., weekends (weather permitting) 10–5.*

September is especially busy, with *Weinforum Mittelrhein* (a major wine-and-food presentation in Burg Rheinfels) on the first weekend, and on both sides of the Rhine, wine festivals and the splendid fireworks display "Rhine in Flames" on the third weekend.

Dining and Lodging

$$$–$$$$ ✕▥ **Schloss-Hotel & Villa Rheinfels.** Directly opposite Burg Rheinfels, this hotel offers modern comfort in very pleasant surroundings. The expansive views from the restaurant's terrace make a meal or glass of wine especially memorable. Regional and seasonal specialties are served in the main restaurant, Auf Scharfeneck, and evenings, the Burgschänke offers rustic fare in the cellar. Highly recommended is the *Wispertal Forelle* (trout from the Wisper Valley). ▨ *Schlossberg 47, D–56329,* ☎ *06741/8020,* ⅏ *06741/802–802. 55 rooms, 2 suites. 2 restaurants, bar, minibars, indoor pool, sauna, bicycles. AE, DC, MC, V.* ◔

$$–$$$ ✕▥ **Hotel Landsknecht.** The Nickenig family makes everyone feel at home in their riverside restaurant and hotel north of St. Goar. Daughter Martina, a former wine queen, and Joachim Lorenz, a wine maker, operate the Vinothek, where you can sample his prize-winning Bopparder Hamm wines. These go well with the restaurant's hearty local dishes. Friday evenings in the summer there is a barbecue on the splendid Rhine terrace. Rooms are individually furnished and quite comfortable; some offer a Rhine view (Nos. 4, 5, and 8 are especially nice). ▨ *Rheinuferstr. (B–9), D–56329 St. Goar-Fellen,* ☎ *06741/2011,* ⅏ *06741/7499. 14 rooms. Restaurant, minibars, shop. AE, DC, MC, V. Closed mid-Dec.–Feb.* ◔

St. Goarshausen

⑩   *29 km (18 mi) north of Rüdesheim; ferry from St. Goar.*

St. Goarshausen lies at the foot of two 14th-century castles whose names, Katz (cat) and Maus (mouse), reflect but one of the many the power plays on the Rhine in the Middle Ages. Territorial supremacy and the concomitant privilege of collecting tolls fueled the fires of rivalry. In response to the construction of Burg Rheinfels, the archbishop of Trier erected a small castle north of St. Goarshausen to protect his interests. In turn, the masters of Rheinfels, the counts of Katzenelnbogen, built a bigger castle directly above the town. Its name was shortened to "Katz," and its smaller neighbor was scornfully referred to as "Maus." Katz is not open to the public. **Maus** has a terrace café (great views) and demonstrations featuring eagles and falcons in flight. ☎ 06771/7669. ▣ DM 12. ◷ *Apr.–Sept., daily at 11 and 2:30. Sun. also at 4:30.*

Some 10 km (6 mi) north, near Kamp-Bornhofen, is a similar castle duo, separated by a "quarrel wall": **Liebenstein** and **Sterrenberg,** known as the *Feindliche Brüder* (rival brothers). Both impressive ruins have terrace cafés that afford good views.

One of the Rhineland's main attractions lies 4 km (2½ mi) south of St. Goarshausen: the steep (430 ft-high) slate cliff named after the beautiful blond nymph **Loreley.** Here she sat, singing songs so lovely that sailors and fishermen were lured to the treacherous rapids—and their demise. The legend stems from a tale by Clemens Brentano, retold as a ballad by Heinrich Heine and set to music by Friedrich Silcher at the height of Rhine Romanticism in the 19th century. The summit is a great vantage point.

Boppard

⑪ *17 km (11 mi) north of St. Goar; ferry to Filsen.*

Boppard is a pleasant little resort that evolved from a Celtic settlement into a Roman fortress, Frankish royal court, and Free Imperial City. The Roman garrison Bodobrica, established here in the 4th century, was enclosed by a 26-ft-high rectangular wall (1,010 by 505 ft) with 28 defense towers. You can see portions of the wall and towers that were excavated in 1990 in the fascinating open-air **archaeological park** (⊠ Angertstr., near the B–9 and railroad tracks). The **Stadtmuseum** (town museum), housed in the 14th-century Kurfürstliche Burg (elector's castle) built by the archbishop of Trier, has additional exhibits on Boppard's Roman and medieval past, as well as an extensive collection of bentwood furniture designed by the town's favorite son, Michael Thonet (1796–1871). The cane-bottomed *Stuhl Nr. 14* (chair No. 14) is the famous classic found in coffeehouses around the world since 1859. ⊠ *Burgstr.,* ☎ *06742/10369.* ⊡ *Free.* ☉ *Apr.–Oct., Tues.–Sun. 10–noon and 2–5.*

Excavations in the 1960s revealed ancient Romans baths beneath the twin-towered, Romanesque **Church of St. Severus** (1236) on the market square. The large triumphal crucifix over the main altar and a lovely statue of a smiling Madonna date from the 13th century. Two baroque altars dominate the interior of the Gothic **Carmelite Church** on Karmeliterstrasse, near the Rhine. It houses intricately carved choir stalls and tombstones, and several beautiful Madonnas. Winegrowers still observe the old custom of laying the first-picked *Trauben* (grapes) at the foot of the Traubenmadonna (1330) to ensure a good harvest. The annual wine festival takes place in late September, just before the Riesling harvest.

On the northern edge of Boppard the Rhine makes its largest loop, skirting the majestic, vine-covered hill known as the **Bopparder Hamm.** From the Mühltal station let the *Sessellbahn* (chairlift) whisk you 1,300 ft uphill to the **Vierseenblick** (four-lake vista), a vantage point from which the Rhine looks like a chain of lakes. ⊡ *DM 11 round-trip, DM 7.50 one-way.* ☉ *Apr.–Oct., daily 10–5 (summer 9:30–6:30).*

Dining and Lodging

$$–$$$ ✕⌂ **Best Western Hotel Bellevue.** You can enjoy a Rhine view from many of the rooms in this traditional hotel or from the terrace next to the pretty Rhine promenade. Afternoon tea, dinner, and Sunday lunch are accompanied by piano music (except Wednesday) in the main restaurant. Try the hearty *Reblaus-Teller* of pork medallions in a grape sauce. The other restaurant offers sumptuous buffets. ⊠ *Rheinallee 41, D–56154,* ☎ *06742/1020,* FAX *06742/102–602. 94 rooms, 1 suite. 2 restaurants, bar, minibars, pool, sauna, steam bath, exercise room. AE, DC, MC, V.*

$ ✕⌂ **Weinhaus Heilig Grab.** This wine estate's tavern, Boppard's oldest, is full of smiling faces: the wines are excellent, the fare is simple but hearty, and the welcome is warm. Old chestnut trees shade tables in the courtyard. Rooms are furnished with rustic pine furniture. If you'd like to visit the cellars or vineyards, ask your friendly hosts, Rudolf and Susanne Schoeneberger. They also arrange wine tastings. ⌧ *Zelkesg. 12, D–56154,* ☎ *06742/2371,* ⅋⅋ *06742/81220. 5 rooms. Weinstube, bicycles. No credit cards. Hotel closed Nov.–Easter. Weinstube closed Tues.* ✎

Outdoor Activities and Sports

GOLF

The **Jakobsberg** (⌧ Im Tal der Loreley, Boppard/Rhens, ☎ 06742/8080), 10 km (6 mi) north of Boppard via Spay and Siebenborn, is one of the most magnificent settings in Germany to play a challenging round of 18 holes. The views are superb.

HIKING

The 10-km (6-mi) **Weinwanderweg** (wine hiking trail) through the Bopparder Hamm, from Boppard to Spay, begins north of town on Peternacher Weg. Many other marked trails in the vicinity are outlined in maps and brochures available from the tourist office.

En Route On the outskirts of Koblenz the neo-Gothic towers of **Schloss Stolzenfels** come into view. The castle's origins date from the mid-13th century, when the archbishop of Trier sought to counter the influence (and toll rights) of the archbishop of Mainz, who had just built Burg Lahneck, a castle at the confluence of the Lahn and Rhine rivers. Its superbly furnished period rooms and beautiful gardens are well worth a visit. It is a wonderful setting for concerts. ☎ *0261/51656.* ⌧ *DM 5.* ☉ *Easter–Sept., Tues.–Sun. 10–6; Oct., Nov., and Jan.–Easter, Tues.–Sun. 10–5. Closed Dec.*

☾ On the eastern shore, overlooking the town of Braubach, is the **Marksburg.** Built in the 12th century to protect the silver and lead mines in the area, it is the only land-based castle on the Rhine to have survived the centuries intact. Within its massive walls are a collection of weapons and manuscripts, a medieval botanical garden, and a restaurant. ☎ *02627/206.* ⌧ *DM 8.* ☉ *Easter–Oct., daily 10–5; winter, daily 11–4. Closed last half Dec. Restaurant closed mid-Dec.–mid-Feb.*

Koblenz

20 km (12 mi) north of Boppard.

The ancient city of Koblenz is at a geographic nexus known as the **Deutsches Eck** (German Corner) in the heart of the Mittelrhein region. Rivers and mountains converge here: the Mosel flows into the Rhine on one side; the Lahn flows in on the other; and three mountain ridges intersect. Koblenz is one of the Rhineland-Palatinate's cultural, administrative, and business centers.

Founded by the Romans in AD 9, the city's first name was Castrum ad Confluentes (Fort at the Confluence). It became a powerful city in the Middle Ages, when it controlled trade on both the Rhine and the Mosel. Air raids during World War II destroyed 85% of the city, but extensive restoration has done much to re-create its former atmosphere. English-speaking walking tours of the Old Town can be arranged by the tourist office on request.

Koblenz is centered on the west bank of the Rhine. On the east bank
⑫ stands Europe's largest fortress, **Festung Ehrenbreitstein,** offering a commanding view from 400 ft above the river. Take the **Sesselbahn** (cable car; ☉ Apr., May, Sept., and Oct., daily 10–4:50; June–Aug., daily 9–5:50) if the walk is too daunting; the round-trip fare is DM 12.50 (including admission to the fortress). The earliest buildings date from about 1100, but the bulk of the fortress was constructed in the 16th century. In 1801 it was partially destroyed by Napoléon and the French occu-

pied Koblenz for the next 18 years. As for the fortress's 16th-century **Vogel Greif cannon,** the French absconded with it in 1794, the German took it back in 1940, and the French commandeered it again in 1945. The 15-ton cannon was peaceably returned by French president François Mitterrand in 1984 and is now part of the exhibit on the history of local technologies, from wine growing to industry, in the fortress's **Landesmuseum** (State Museum; ☎ 0261/97030; 💰 DM 4; ☉ Mid-Mar.–mid-Nov., daily 9–12:30 and 1–5). The fortress can be reached by ferry (DM 2) from Pegelhaus on the Koblenz side of the Rhine. ☎ 0261/974–2444. 💰 DM 2. ☉ Daily 9:30–5.

⑬ The **Pfaffendorfer Brücke** (Pfaffendorf Bridge) marks the beginning of the Old Town. At its west end, between the modern blocks of the Rhein-
⑭ Mosel-Halle and the Hotel Mercure, is the **Weindorf,** a wine "village" constructed for a mammoth exhibition of German wines in 1925 (☞ Dining and Lodging, below).

⑮ The **Rheinanlagen** (Rhine Gardens), a 10-km (6-mi) promenade, runs along the riverbank past the Weindorf. Strolling along the promenade
⑯ toward town, you'll pass the gracious **Kurfürstliches Schloss,** the prince-elector's palace. It was built in 1786 by Prince-Elector Clemens Wenzeslaus as an elegant escape from the grim Ehrenbreitstein fortress. He lived here for only three years, however; in 1791 he was forced to flee to Augsburg when the French stormed the city. The palace is used for city offices and is closed to visitors.

⑰ The squat form of the **Rheinkran** (Rhine Crane), built in 1611, is one of Koblenz's landmarks. Marks on the side of the building indicate the heights reached by floodwaters of bygone years. In the mid-19th century a pontoon bridge consisting of a row of barges spanned the Rhine here; when ships approached, two or three barges were simply towed out of the way to let them through.

⑱ The **Deutsches Eck** (German Corner) is at the sharp intersection of the Rhine and Mosel, a pointed bit of land jutting into the river like the prow of some early ironclad warship. One of the more effusive manifestations of German nationalism—an 1897 statue of Kaiser Wilhelm I, first emperor of the newly united Germany—was erected here. It was destroyed at the end of World War II and replaced in 1953 with a ponderous, altarlike monument to Germany unity. After German reunification a new statue of Wilhelm was placed atop this monument in 1993. Pieces of the Berlin Wall stand on the Mosel side—a memorial to those who died as a result of the partitioning of the country.

⑲ The **Ludwig Museum** stands just behind the Deutsches Eck, housed in the spic-and-span *Deutschherrenhaus,* a restored 13th-century building. Industrialist Peter Ludwig, one of Germany's leading contemporary art collectors, has founded museums in many Rhineland cities; he's filled this one with part of his huge collection. ⊠ Danziger Freiheit 1, ☎ 0261/304–040. 💰 DM 5. ☉ Tues.–Sat. 10:30–5, Sun. 11–6.

⑳ The **St. Kastor Kirche** (St. Castor Church) is a sturdy Romanesque basilica consecrated in 836. It was here in 842 that plans were drawn for the contract signed as the Treaty of Verdun, formalizing the division of Charlemagne's great empire and leading to the creation of Germany and France as separate states. Inside, compare the squat Romanesque columns in the nave with the intricate fan vaulting of the Gothic sections. **The St. Kastor Fountain** outside the church is an intriguing piece of historical one-upmanship. It was built by the occupying French to mark the beginning of Napoléon's ultimately disastrous Russian campaign of 1812. When the Russians reached Koblenz after having roundly defeated the French, they added an ironic SEEN AND APPROVED

400

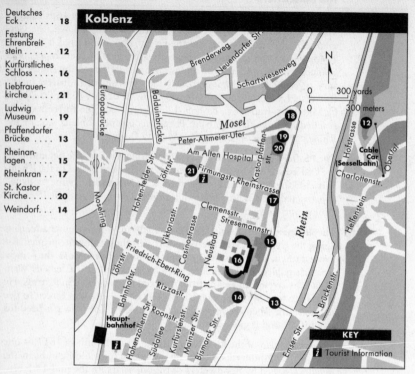

to the fountain's inscription. ⊠ *Kastorhof.* ⊗ *Daily 9–6 except during services.*

The **Altstadt** (Old Town) can be reached from the Deutsches Eck via the Moselanlagen (Mosel Promenade). This walkway leads to Koblenz's oldest restaurant, the Deutscher Kaiser, which marks the start of the Old Town. War damage is evidenced by the blend of old buildings and modern store blocks on and around the central square of **Am Plan.** Near Am Plan, the **Mittelrhein Museum** houses the city's art collection in a lovely 16th-century building. ⊠ *Florinsmarkt 15,* ☏ *0261/129–2520.* ☜ *DM 5.* ⊗ *Tues.–Sat. 10:30–5, Sun. 11–6.*

㉑ The **Liebfrauenkirche** (Church of Our Lady) stands on Roman foundations at the Old Town's highest point. The bulk of the church is of Romanesque design, but its choir is one of the Rhineland's finest examples of 15th-century Gothic architecture, and the west front is graced with two 17th-century baroque towers. ⊠ *Am Plan.* ⊗ *Mon.–Sat. 8–6, Sun. 9–8 except during services.*

Dining and Lodging

$$–$$$$ ╳ **Loup de Mer.** Chef Hermann Christiaans has a passion for fish, cooked to perfection, and for good German wines. Start with one of the excellent fish soups. You can dine amid modern art on display from the gallery next door or in the flower-lined courtyard. ⊠ *Neustadt 12/ Schlossrondell,* ☏ *0261/16138. AE, DC, MC, V. Closed Sun. May– Sept. and 3 wks in summer. No lunch.*

$$–$$$ ╳ **Café Balthazar.** The multistory atrium of a historic house (once a furniture store) has been turned into a very classy, yet comfortable, meeting point. Three meals a day are served amid fabulous Jugend-stil decor, complete with huge palm trees. You can also come for coffee and cake, or snacks and drinks late into the night. Weekends, the

lower level is a disco. Outdoor fans will love the huge terrace on Gör-res Square. ⊠ *Firmungstr. 2, Am Görrespl.,* ☎ *0261/105–834. AE, DC, MC, V.*

$–$$$ ✕ **Weindorf.** This reconstructed "wine village" of half-timber houses grouped around a tree-shaded courtyard is popular with locals and vis-itors alike. There's country cooking (from Bratwurst to Sauerbraten), a very reasonably priced selection of German wines (15 are available by the glass), and live music nightly, from Easter through October, and year-round on Sunday 11–1. ⊠ *Julius-Wegeler-Str. 2,* ☎ *0261/31680. AE, MC, V. Closed Mon. in winter.*

$ ✕ **Pomm & Toffel.** The abbreviated Franco-German names for potato (*pomme de terre, Kartoffel*) sum it up: everything on the menu revolves around the Teutonic tuber of choice. Here you can try a great version of the Rhineland potato casserole Döppekoche or a delicious *Kartof-felpizza,* with a crust made of potato dough, in a casual, cozy atmo-sphere. ⊠ *Clemensstr. 17,* ☎ *0261/100–2323. No credit cards.*

$$–$$$ ✕🏠 **Zum weissen Schwanen.** Guests have found a warm welcome in this half-timber inn and mill since 1693, a tradition carried on by the Kunz family today. Situated next to a 13th-century town gateway, it is a thoroughly charming place to overnight or enjoy well-prepared re-gional specialties, contemporary German cuisine, and an excellent se-lection of local wines. Rooms are individually decorated with period furniture ranging from Biedermeier to Belle Epoque. ⊠ *Brunnenstr. 4, D–56338 Braubach, 12 km (7½ mi) south of Koblenz via B–42,* ☎ *02627/559 or 02627/9820,* 🖷 *02627/8802. 16 rooms, 2 suites. Restau-rant. AE, DC, MC, V. Restaurant closed Wed. and 3 wks in summer. No lunch Mon.–Sat.* 🕭

$$$ 🏠 **Hotel Mercure.** This modern high-rise on the Rhine is next to the city's conference and events center, the Rhein-Mosel-Halle, and but a short walk to all major sights. Rooms are modern and well appointed; some have fabulous views. ⊠ *Julius-Wegeler-Str. 6, D–56068,* ☎ *0261/ 1360,* 🖷 *0261/136–1199. 167 room, 1 suite. 2 restaurants, bar, mini-bars, hot tub, sauna, bicycles. AE, DC, MC, V.*

$$ 🏠 **Hotel An der Mosel.** The Hundertwasser-inspired look of this hotel is unique. Behind the colorful facade there are pleasant, mod-ern rooms (some with waterbeds). You can dine on a terrace sur-rounded by artificial pools and eclectic "works of art." ⊠ *Pastor-Klein-Str. 11, D–56073 Koblenz-Rauental, 2 km (1 mi) from the Deutsches Eck,* ☎ *0261/40650,* 🖷 *0261/406–5188. 185 rooms, 7 apartments. Restaurant, bar, minibars (in some rooms), massage, sauna. AE, DC, MC, V.*

Nightlife and the Arts

The **Staatsorchester Rheinische Philharmonie** (Rhenish Philharmonic Orchestra; ⊠ Julius-Wegeler-Str., ☎ 0261/129–1651) plays regularly in the Rhein-Mosel-Halle. The gracious neoclassic **Theater der Stadt Koblenz** (☎ 0261/129–2840), built in 1787, is still in regular use.

Night owls frequent **Café Balthazar** (☞ Dining and Lodging, *above*) and the many pubs on **Florinsmarkt.** The **Blaue Biwel** (⊠ Entenpfuhl 9, ☎ 0261/35577) and its sister club in the suburb of Güls, **Café Hahn** (⊠ Neustr. 15, ☎ 0261/42302), feature everything from cabaret and stand-up comedians to popular musicians and bands.

Shopping

Koblenz's most pleasant shopping is in the Old City streets around the market square Am Plan. **Löhr Center,** a modern, American-style, win-dowless mall, has some 130 shops and restaurants and will give you an authentic German shopping experience.

En Route At the **Garten der lebenden Schmetterlinge** (Garden of Living Butterflies) you can walk among butterflies from South America, Asia, and
Africa as they flit back and forth over your head between the branches
of banana trees and palms. It is far more inspiring than seeing them
pinned to the bottom of a dusty museum case. You'll find it 15 km (9
mi) north of Koblenz (Bendorf exit off the B–42). ✉ *Im Fürstlichen
Schlosspark, D–56170 Bendorf-Sayn,* ☎ *02622/15478.* 🎫 *DM 7.* ☉
Easter–Sept., daily 9–6; Oct., daily 9–5.

THE MOSEL VALLEY

The Mosel is one of the most hauntingly beautiful river valleys on earth.
Here, as in the Rhine Valley, forests and vines carpet steep hillsides;
castles and church spires dot the landscape; and picturesque, medieval
wine villages line the riverbanks. The Mosel landscape is no less majestic, but it is less narrow and more peaceful than that of the Rhine
gorge; the river's countless bends and loops slow its pace and lend the
region a special charm.

From Koblenz to Tries-Karden, two roads run parallel to the Mosel:
B–416 (west side) and B–49 (east side). Thereafter, only one road con-
tinues upstream, occasionally traversing the river as it winds toward
Trier: until Alf, it is B–49; afterwards, B–53.

The signposted routes between Koblenz and Trier include the Mosel
Weinstrasse (Mosel Wine Road) along the riverbank and, on the
heights, the hiking trails on both sides of the river known as the Mosel-
höhenweg. The latter extends 224 km (140 mi) on the Hunsrück (eastern) side and 164 km (102 mi) on the Eifel (western) side of the river.
Driving time for the river route is at least three hours. On the autobahn (A–1) the distance between Koblenz and Trier can be covered in
about an hour. Cyclists can follow the marked route of the Radroute
Nahe-Hunsrück-Mosel from Trier to Bingen, which partially overlaps
with the Moselradwanderweg from Koblenz to Trier.

Winningen

㉒ *11 km (7 mi) southwest of Koblenz on B–416.*

Winningen is a gateway to the *Terrassenmosel* (terraced Mosel), the
portion of the river characterized by steep, terraced vineyards. Mono-
rails and winches help winegrowers, and their tools make the ascent,
but tending and harvesting the vines is all done by hand. For a bird's-
eye view of the valley drive up Fährstrasse to Am Rosenhang, the start
of a pleasant walk along the *Weinlehrpfad* (educational wine path).

The renowned vineyard site **Uhlen** lies upstream between Winningen
and Kobern-Gondorf. Kobern's Oberburg (upper castle) and the St.
Matthias Kapelle, a 12th-century chapel, are good vantage points. Near
the picturesque market square in the village below, you can see an old
half-timber house (1321), now quarters for Kobern's tourist office.

Dining and Lodging

$$–$$$ ✕ **Alte Mühle.** Tucked away in a valley beneath Kobern's castle ruins
is Thomas and Gudrun Höreth's lovingly restored "old mill" (1026)—
a labyrinth of little rooms and cellars grouped around romantic, ole-
ander- and flower-lined courtyards. Wine presses are on display, along
with many wine-related artifacts. The menu offers something for every
taste but the absolute hits are the homemade cheeses, terrines, and pâtés,
and *Entensülze* (goose in aspic), served with home-fried potatoes. Mature Bordeaux wines supplement the Höreths' own estate-bottled
wines, including Riesling, chardonnay, and pinots (Spätburgunder/pinot

noir, Grauburgunder/pinot gris, Weissburgunder/pinot blanc). ⊠ *Mühlental 17 (via B–416), Kobern,* ☎ *02607/6474. No credit cards. Closed Feb. No lunch weekdays.*

$$–$$$ ✕⚏ **Halferschenke.** This *Schenke* (inn) was once an overnight stop for "Halfer" who, with their horses, towed cargo-laden boats upstream. Today the stone house inn (1832) is run by a friendly young couple, Thomas and Eva Balmes. Light walls, dark wood, and lots of candles and flowers are a lovely setting for his artfully prepared food. An excellent selection of Terrassenmosel wines is available. The rooms, each named after an artist, are modern, airy, and bright. ⊠ *Hauptstr. 36, D–56332 Dieblich, via B–49, opposite Kobern,* ☎ *02607/1008,* ⴼ *02607/960–294. 4 rooms. Restaurant. AE, MC, V. Closed Mon. and 2 wks in autumn. No lunch Tues.–Sat.*

Alken

㉓ *22 km (13½ mi) southwest of Koblenz.*

The 12th-century castle **Burg Thurant** towers over the village and the Burgberg (castle hill) vineyard. Wine and snacks are served in the courtyard; castle tours take in the chapel, cellar, tower, and a weapons display. Allow a good half hour for the climb from the riverbank. ☎ *02605/2004.* ⴲ *DM 5.* ⏱ *Daily 10–5.*

Dining and Lodging

$–$$$ ✕⚏ **Burg Thurant.** The Kopowski's stylish restaurant and guest house lie at the foot of the castle, next to a venerable stone tower on the riverbank (B–49). They serve tasty renditions of *Mosel Aal* (Mosel eel), *Bachforelle* (fresh stream trout) in almond butter, and *Entenbrust mit Brombeerjus* (breast of duck in blackberry sauce), accompanied by wines from the region's finest producers. The modern guest rooms are outfitted with a mixture of antiques and country-style furnishings. ⊠ *Moselstr. 16, D–56332,* ☎ *02605/3581,* ⴼ *02605/2152. 5 rooms, 1 suite. Restaurant, no-smoking rooms, bicycles. No credit cards. Closed Mon., Tues., and Feb.*

En Route **Burg Eltz** (Eltz Castle) is one of Germany's most picturesque, gen-
★ ⏳ uinely medieval castles (12th–16th centuries) and merits as much (if not more) attention as King Ludwig's trio of castles in Bavaria. Nestled deep within the forested Eltz River Valley, the approach to the castle is a downhill walk. The 40-minute tour, with excellent commentary on the castle's history and furnishings, guides you through the period rooms and massive kitchen, but does not include the treasure chamber, a collection of fascinating artworks displayed in five historical rooms. In the summer the lines are long, so bring some water, particularly if you are traveling with kids. To get here, exit B–416 at Hatzenport (opposite and southwest of Alken), proceed to Münstermaifeld, and follow signs to the parking lot near the Antoniuskapelle. From here it is a 15-minute walk or take the shuttle bus (DM 2). Hikers can reach the castle from Moselkern in 40 minutes. ⊠ *Burg Eltz/Münstermaifeld,* ☎ *02672/950–500.* ⴲ *Castle tour DM 9, treasure chamber DM 4.* ⏱ *Apr.–Oct., daily 9:30–5:30.* ✎

Treis-Karden

㉔ *39 km (24 mi) southwest of Koblenz; Karden is on B–416; Treis is on B–49.*

Treis-Karden are two towns joined for administrative purposes. The richly furnished Romanesque and Gothic **Church of St. Castor,** named after the saint who introduced Christianity to the area in the middle of the 4th century, is well worth a visit, as is its museum in the historical tithe house (1238) behind the church. The two stars on the weather vane symbolize the star of Bethlehem and allude to church's precious "altar of the three kings," Europe's only remaining terra-cotta altar (1420). Attend Sunday service to hear the magnificent baroque organ (1728) built by Johann Michael Stumm, founder of one of the world's greatest organ-building dynasties. ⊠ *St.-Castor-Str. 1, Karden.*

Dining and Lodging

$$–$$$ ✕⊡ **Schloss-Hotel Petry.** From a simple guest house a century ago, this family-run hotel has developed into a complex of buildings with very attractive, comfortably furnished rooms and modern facilities. House specialties are *Aal Grün* (green eel), cooked eel served cold with a green herb sauce, and rib roast of lamb. The wine list has a good selection of Mosel wines. ⊠ *St.-Castor-Str. 80 (B–416), D–56253 Treis-Karden,* ☎ *02672/9340,* ℻ *02672/934–440. 55 rooms, 19 suites. Restaurant, bar, Weinstube, minibars, no-smoking rooms, hot tub, sauna, bowling, exercise room, Ping-Pong, billiards, bicycles. No credit cards. Restaurant closed Tues. and Wed.*

Cochem

㉕ *51 km (31½ mi) southwest of Koblenz on B–49, approximately 93 km (58 mi) from Trier.*

Cochem is one of the most attractive towns of the Mosel Valley, with a riverside promenade to rival any along the Rhine. It is especially lively during the wine festivals in June and late August. If time permits, savor the landscape from the deck of a **boat**—many excursions are available, lasting from one hour to an entire day. The tourist office on Endertplatz has an excellent English-language outline for a walking tour of the town. The 15-minute walk to the **Reichsburg** (Imperial Fortress), the 1,000-year-old castle overlooking the town, will reward you with great views. ☎ *02671/255.* ⊟ *DM 7, including 40-min tour.* ☺ *Mid-Mar.–mid-Nov., daily 9–5.*

A ride on the **cable car** to the Pinner Kreuz also provides great vistas. ⊠ *Endertstr.,* ☎ *02671/989–063.* ⊟ *DM 9.50 round-trip.* ☺ *Mar.–mid-Nov., daily 10–6.*

From the **Enderttor** (Endert Town Gate) you can see the entrance to Germany's longest railway tunnel, the Kaiser-Wilhelm, an astonishing example of 19th-century engineering. The 4-km-long (2½-mi-long) tunnel saves travelers a 21-km (13-mi) detour along one of the Mosel's great loops.

Dining and Lodging

$$$ ✕⊡ **Weissmühle.** This century-old mill is set amid the forested hills of the Enderttal (Endert Valley). It's an oasis from traffic and crowds yet only 2½ km (1½ mi) from Cochem. The rooms are individually decorated—some in an elegant country manor style; others have rustic, farmhouse furnishings. Beneath the exposed beams and painted ceiling of the restaurant you can enjoy fresh baked goods, meat, or trout from the hotel's own bakery, butcher shop, and fishponds. German (particularly Mosel) and French wines are served. ⊠ *Im Enderttal, D–56812, via Endertstr., toward Greimersburg; from A–48 exit Kaisersesch,* ☎ *02671/8955,* ℻ *02671/8207. 36 rooms. Restaurant, bar, lounge, minibars, sauna, steam room, bowling, helipad. DC, MC, V.* ✆

$$–$$$ ✕⊡ **Alte Thorschenke.** Next to the Enderttor near the river, this inn dates from 1332. Winding staircases, ancient wooden beams, and historical decor set the mood. Many of the rooms have period furniture (some with elaborate, four-poster beds). Hunting trophies and portraits of prince elec-

tors adorn the wood-paneled walls of the restaurant. There is also a cozy Weinstube and a patio for alfresco dining. Highly recommended are the fresh trout or the *Wildplatte* (game platter) of wild boar, venison, and hare. The parent firm, Weingut Freiherr von Landenberg, supplies the excellent Mosel wines. If you'd like to visit the wine estate, ask your delightful hosts, the Kretz family, to make arrangements. ⊠ *Brückenstr. 3, D–56812,* ☎ *02671/7059,* FAX *02671/4202. 33 rooms, 1 suite. Restaurant, Weinstube, minibars (in most rooms), bicycles, shop. AE, DC, MC, V. Closed Jan.–mid-Mar. Restaurant closed Wed. Nov.–mid-Dec.* 🍴

$$–$$$ ✕🏠 **Lohspeicher–l'Auberge du Vin.** In times past, oak bark for leather tanners was dried and stored in this house (1834) near the market square. Today it is a charming inn with a pretty terrace, run by a vivacious young couple, Ingo and Birgit Beth. His delicacies, such as quail stuffed with foie gras on red onion marmalade, are a pleasure for the palate and the eye. At least one saltwater and one freshwater fish are featured daily. Some 20 French and Italian wines supplement the family's own estate-bottled wines. The rooms are pleasant and modern. ⊠ *Oberg. 1, Am Marktpl., D–56812,* ☎ *02671/3976,* FAX *02671/1772. 9 rooms. Restaurant, bicycles. AE, MC, V. Closed Wed. and Feb.*

En Route   Ten kilometers (6 miles) south of Cochem, on the opposite shore, the ruins of Metternich Castle crown the Schlossberg (Castle Hill) vineyard next to the romantic village of **Beilstein.** Take in the stunning Mosel loop panorama from the castle's terrace café before heading for the market square below. Then ascend the *Klostertreppe* (monastery steps) leading to the baroque monastery church for views of the winding streets lined with half-timber houses.

Ediger-Eller

㉖ *61 km (38 mi) southwest of Koblenz on B–49.*

Ediger is another picturesque wine village with well-preserved houses and remnants of the medieval town wall. The **Martinskirche** (St. Martin's Church; ⊠ Kirchstr.) is a remarkable amalgamation of art and architectural styles, inside and out. Take a moment to admire the 117 carved bosses in the star-vaulted ceiling of the nave. Among the many fine sculptures throughout the church and the chapel is the town's treasure: a Renaissance stone relief of "Christ in the Wine Press."

Dining and Lodging

$$–$$$ ✕🏠 **Zum Löwen.** The drawing cards of this hotel and wine estate run by Saffenreuther family are the friendly service and the excellent cuisine. The house specialties are game (from their own preserve) and fine, fruity Rieslings (a mature Riesling with a balance of acidity and naturally ripe sweetness is superb with venison and boar). The rooms have simple decor. In addition to wine tastings, fishing or hunting trips can be arranged. ⊠ *Moselweinstr. 23, D–56814 Ediger-Eller,* ☎ *02675/ 208,* FAX *02675/214. 21 rooms. Restaurant, bicycles. AE, MC, V. Closed Christmas and Jan. Restaurant closed Wed. Feb.–Apr.*

En Route   As you continue along the winding course of the Mosel, you'll pass Europe's steepest vineyard site, **Calmont,** opposite the romantic ruins of a 12th-century Augustinian convent before the loop at Bremm. **Zell** is a popular village full of pubs and wineshops plying the crowds with Zeller Schwarze Katz, "black cat" wine, a commercially successful product and the focal point of a large wine festival in late June. Some 6 million vines hug the slopes around Zell, making it one of Germany's largest wine-growing communities. The area between Zell and Schweich (near Trier), known as the middle Mosel, is the home of some of the world's finest Riesling wines.

Traben-Trarbach

㉗ *30 km (19 mi) south of Cochem.*

Traben-Trarbach straddles the Mosel, offering pleasant promenades on both sides of the river. Its wine festivals are held the second and last weekends in July. Traben's **Jugendstil buildings** are worth seeing (Hotel Bellevue, gateway on the Mosel bridge, post office, train station, and town hall). For a look at fine period rooms and exhibits on the historical development of the area, visit the **Mittelmosel Museum** in Haus Böcking (1750). ⊠ *Casino Str. 2,* ☎ *06541/9480.* ☒ *DM 4.* ☉ *Mid-Apr.–Oct., Tues.–Fri. 9:30–noon and 1:30–5, weekends 10–1.*

En Route During the next 24 km (15 mi) you'll pass by world-famous vineyards, such as Erdener Treppchen, Ürziger Würzgarten, the *Sonnenuhr* (sundial) sites of Zeltingen and Wehlen, and Graacher Himmelreich, before reaching Bernkastel-Kues.

Bernkastel-Kues

㉘ *22 km (14 mi) southwest of Traben-Trarbach, 100 km (62 mi) southwest of Koblenz on B–53.*

Bernkastel and Kues straddle the Mosel, on the east and west banks, respectively. Elaborately carved half-timber houses (16th–17th centuries) and a Renaissance town hall (1608) frame St. Michael's Fountain (1606), on Bernkastel's photogenic **market square.** In early September the square and riverbank are lined with wine stands for one of the region's largest wine festivals, the Weinfest der Mittelmosel. From the hilltop ruins of the 13th-century castle **Burg Landshut** there are splendid views. It was here that Trier's Archbishop Boemund II is said to have recovered from an illness after drinking the local wine, henceforth known as the "Doctor." This legendary vineyard soars up from Hinterm Graben street near the town gate Graacher Tor. You can purchase these exquisite wines from Weingut J. Lauerburg (one of the three original owners of the tiny site) at the estate's tasteful wineshop. ⊠ *Am Markt 27.* ☎ *06531/2481.* ☉ *Apr.–Oct., weekdays 10–5, Sat. 11–5.*

The philosopher and theologian Nikolaus Cusanus (1401–64) was born in Kues, where special events and concerts will be held in his honor during the Cusanus Memorial Year 2001. The **St.-Nikolaus-Hospital** is a charitable *Stiftung* (foundation) he established in 1458, and it still operates a home for the elderly and a wine estate. Within it is the **Mosel-Wein-museum** (wine museum; ☒ DM 3; ☉ mid-Apr.–Oct., daily 10–5; Nov.–mid-Apr., daily 2–5), as well as a bistro and a wineshop. You can sample more than 100 wines from the entire Mosel-Saar-Ruwer region in the **Vinothek** (☒ DM 17; ☉ mid-Apr.–Oct., daily 10–5; Nov.–mid-Apr., daily 2–5) in the vaulted cellar. The hospital's famous library, with precious manuscripts, cloister, and Gothic chapel, may be visited only on tours. ⊠ *Cusanus-Str. 2,* ☎ *06531/4141 or 06531/2101.* ☒ *Historical rooms (tours): DM 5.* ☉ *Mid-Apr.–Oct., Tues. 10:30, Fri. 3, or by appointment.*

Some 3,500 winegrowers throughout the region deliver their grapes to the **Moselland Winzergenossenschaft** (cooperative winery), where the wines are produced, bottled, and marketed. It is an impressive operation, and the large wine shop is excellent. ⊠ *Bornwiese 6, in the industrial park,* ☎ *06531/570.* ☉ *Tours Tues. and Thurs. 3, or by appointment. Wineshop weekdays 9–noon and 1–6, Sat. 9–noon.*

Dining and Lodging

$$$$ ✕☒ **Waldhotel Sonnora.** Helmut and Ulrike Thieltges offer guests one
★   of Germany's absolute finest dining and wining experiences in their elegant country inn set within the forested Eifel Hills. Mr. Thieltges is a

multistarred chef, renowned for transforming exclusive ingredients (foie gras, truffles, Persian caviar) into culinary masterpieces, such as roulades of *poussin* larded with Périgord truffles, served with a macaroni timbale stuffed with foie gras, or a tart of Persian caviar and beef tartar served on a potato pancake. The wine list is equally superb. The dining room, with gilded and white-wood furnishings and plush red carpets, has a Parisian look. The guest rooms are attractive. ⊠ *Auf dem Eichelfeld, D–54518 Dreis, 8 km (5 mi) southwest of Wittlich, which is 18 km (11 mi) west of Kues via B–50; from A–1, exit Salmtal,* ☎ *06578/98220,* 𝔽𝔸𝕏 *06578/1402. Reservations essential. 20 rooms. Restaurant, minibars (most rooms). AE, MC, V. Closed Mon., Tues., and Jan.*

\$\$–\$\$\$ ✕🗊 **Gutshotel Reichsgraf von Kesselstatt.** This is a lovely country inn, stylishly decorated with light wood furnishings. The rooms, restaurant, and terrace are peaceful and very pleasant. Chef Dieter Braun has a fondness for fresh Mosel fish, such as *Hecht* (pike), *Zander* (pike-perch), and *Aal* (eel), and lamb dishes. His potato soup is delicious, as is his homemade *Sülze* (aspic; ingredients vary). The inn is affiliated with the prestigious wine estate Reichsgraf von Kesselstatt, whose prize-winning Rieslings are on the wine list. ⊠ *Balduinstr. 1, D–54347 Neumagen-Dhron, 20 km (12½ mi) southwest of Bernkastel via B–53,* ☎ *06507/2035,* 𝔽𝔸𝕏 *06507/5644. 15 rooms, 5 suites. Restaurant, minibars, indoor pool, sauna, bicycles. AE, MC, V. Closed mid-Jan.–mid.-Feb. Restaurant closed Mon. No lunch Tues.–Fri.*

\$\$–\$\$\$ ✕🗊 **Zur Post.** The Rössling family will make you feel welcome in their house (1827) with its comfortable guest rooms and cozy restaurant and Weinstube. It's near the riverbank, and the picturesque market square is just around the corner. Try the Mosel trout *nach Müllerin Art* (dredged in flour and fried). The wine list is devoted exclusively to Mosel Rieslings. ⊠ *Gestade 17, D–54470 Bernkastel-Kues,* ☎ *06531/96700,* 𝔽𝔸𝕏 *06531/976–050. 42 rooms, 1 suite. Restaurant, Weinstube, minibars, sauna. DC, MC, V. Closed Jan. Restaurant closed Wed.*

\$\$ 🗊 **Gästehaus E. Prüm.** The traditional wine estate S.A. Prüm has state-of-the-art cellars, a tastefully designed Vinothek, and a beautiful guest house with an idyllic patio facing the Mosel. The spacious rooms and baths are individually decorated in a winning mixture of contemporary and antique furnishings. In all, the ambience is warm and Mediterranean-like. Erika Prüm is a charming hostess; husband Raimund (the redhead) an excellent wine maker, who is happy to organize wine tastings and cellar tours. ⊠ *Uferallee 25, D–54470 Bernkastel-Wehlen, north of Kues,* ☎ *06531/ 3110,* 𝔽𝔸𝕏 *06531/8555. 8 rooms. MC, V. Closed mid-Dec.–Jan.* ✎

En Route The 55-km (34-mi) drive from Bernkastel to Trier takes in another series of outstanding hillside vineyards, including those 6 km (4 mi) upstream at **Brauneberg,** where Thomas Jefferson was enchanted by a 1783 Brauneberger Kammer Auslese during his visit here in 1788. Today, the vineyard is solely owned by Weingut Paulinshof (⊠ Paulinsstr. 14, Kesten, ☎ 06535/544; ◷ weekdays 8–6, Sat. 9–5). On a magnificent loop 12 km (7½ mi) farther southwest is the famous village of **Piesport.** Wines from its 35 vineyards are collectively known as Piesporter Michelsberg; however, the finest individual site and one of Germany's very best, is the Goldtröpfchen (little droplets of gold). On the western edge of the town, the largest Roman press house (4th century) north of the Alps is on display.

Trier

55 km (34 mi) southwest of Bernkastel-Kues via B–53, 150 km (93 mi) southwest of Koblenz; 30 mins by car to Luxemburg airport.

By 400 BC a Celtic tribe, the Treveri, had settled the Trier Valley. Eventually Julius Caesar's legions arrived at this strategic point on the river and Augusta Treverorum (the town of Emperor Augustus in the land of the Treveri) was founded in 16 BC. It was described as a most opulent city, as beautiful as any outside Rome.

Around AD 275 an Alemannic tribe stormed Augusta Treverorum and reduced it to rubble. But it was rebuilt in even grander style and renamed Treveris. Eventually it evolved into one of the leading cities of the empire and was promoted to "Roma secunda" (a second Rome) north of the Alps. As a powerful administrative capital it was adorned with all the noble civic buildings of a major Roman settlement, as well as public baths, palaces, barracks, an amphitheater, and temples. The Roman emperors Diocletian (who made it one of the four joint capitals of the empire) and Constantine both lived in Trier for years at a time.

Trier survived the collapse of Rome and became an important center of Christianity and, ultimately, one of the most powerful archbishoprics in the Holy Roman Empire. The city thrived throughout the Renaissance and baroque periods, taking full advantage of its location at the meeting point of major east–west and north–south trade routes and growing fat on the commerce that passed through. It also became one of Germany's most important wine-exporting centers. A later claim to fame is the city's status as the birthplace of Karl Marx. Trier is a city of wine as well as history, and beneath its streets are cellars capable of storing nearly 8 million gallons. To do justice to Trier, consider staying for at least two full days. The **Trier Card** entitles the holder to free public transportation and admission to museums, as well as discounts on tours, admission to Roman sights, and sports and cultural venues. It costs DM 21 and is valid for three days. There is also a ticket good for all the Roman sights for DM 9 (for details on tours, *see* Contacts and Resources, *below*).

A Good Walk

Nearly all of Trier's main sights are close together. Begin your walk where Simeonstrasse passes around the city gate of the Roman city— the **Porta Nigra** ㉙—one of the grandest Roman buildings still standing. Climb up inside for a good view of Trier from the tower gallery. The **Städtisches Museum Simeonstift** ㉚, in a courtyard just off the Porta Nigra, contains the remains of the Romanesque church honoring the early medieval hermit Simeon. From here follow Simeonstrasse just past the tourist information office and make a right on Margaretengässchen to visit the **Vinothek WELCOME** ㉛, the city's new wine-tasting and information center. Return to Simeonstrasse and walk toward the **Hauptmarkt** ㉜, the center of the Old Town. You'll find yourself surrounded by old gabled houses, with facades from several ages—medieval, baroque, and 19th century. Turn left into Domstrasse and come almost immediately face to face with Trier's **Dom** ㉝, the oldest Christian church north of the Alps. The 13-century Gothic **Liebfrauenkirche** ㉞ stands right next door. Just behind the Dom, the **Bischöfliches Museum** ㉟ houses many antiquities unearthed in excavations around the cathedral.

Next, walk south of the cathedral on Liebfrauenstrasse, curving left through a short street (An-der-Meer-Katz) to Konstantinplatz for a look at the **Römische Palastaula** ㊱, the largest surviving single-hall structure of the ancient world. The **Rheinisches Landesmuseum** ㊲, with an extensive collection of Roman antiquities, stands south of the Palastaula, facing the grounds of the prince-elector's palace. The ruins of the **Kaiserthermen** ㊳, or Imperial Baths, are just 200 yards from museum. The smaller **Barbarathermen** ㊴ lie west of the Kaiserthermen on Südallee, while the remains of the **Amphitheater** ㊵ are just east of the Kaiserthermen. Continue from the Barbara-Thermen toward the town center along Lorenz-Kellner-Strasse to Brückenstrasse to visit the **Karl-Marx-Haus** ㊶. Then proceed to Viehmarkt, east of St. Antonius Church, to visit the **Thermen-Museum** ㊷, and an excavated Roman bath. From here Brotstrasse will lead you back to the main market square.

TIMING

Although the walk itself will take a good two hours, investigating specific sights will add another two or three to your day. It takes extra time to climb the tower of the Porta Nigra, walk through the vast interior of the Dom and its treasury, visit the underground passageways of the Kaiserthermen, and examine the cellars of the Amphitheater. Allow another half hour each for the Städtisches Museum Simeonstift, the Bischöfliches Museum, and Thermen-Museum, as well as an additional hour for the Rheinisches Landesmuseum.

Sights to See

㊵ **Amphitheater.** The sheer size of Trier's oldest Roman structure (circa AD 100) is impressive. In its heyday it seated 20,000 spectators; today it is a stage for the Antiquity Festival. You can climb down to the cellars beneath the arena—animals were kept in cells here before being unleashed to do battle with gladiators. ✉ *Olewiger Str. 25.* 🎫 *DM 4.* 🕙 *Jan.–Easter, Oct., and Nov., daily 9–5; Easter–Sept., daily 9–6; Dec., daily 10–4.*

㊴ **Barbarathermen** (Barbara Baths). These Roman baths are much smaller and two centuries older than the ☞ **Kaiserthermen.** ✉ *Südallee 48, near Friedrich-Wilhelm-Str. and the river.* 🎫 *DM 4.* 🕙 *Jan.–Easter, Oct., and Nov., Tues.–Sun. 9–1 and 2–5; Easter–Sept., Tues.–Sun. 9–1 and 2–6.*

㉟ **Bischöfliches Museum** (Bishop's Museum). The collection here focuses on medieval sacred art, but there are also fascinating models of the cathedral as it existed in Roman times and 15 Roman frescoes (AD 326), discovered in 1946, that may have adorned the emperor Constantine's palace. ✉ *Windstr. 6,* ☎ *0651/710–5255.* 🎫 *DM 4.* 🕙 *Apr.–Oct., Mon.–Sat. 9–5, Sun. 1–5; Nov.–Mar., Tues.–Sat. 9–1 and 2–5, Sun. 1–5.*

㉝ **Dom** (Cathedral). Practically every period of Trier's past is represented here. The Dom stands on the site of the Palace of Helen, named for the mother of the emperor Constantine, who tore the palace down in AD 330 and put up a large church in its place. The church burned down in 336 and a second, even larger one was built. Parts of the foundations of this third building can be seen in the east end of the present structure (begun in about 1035). The cathedral you see today is a weighty and sturdy edifice with small, round-head windows, rough stonework, and asymmetrical towers, as much a fortress as a church. Inside, Gothic styles predominate—the result of remodeling in the 13th century—although there are also many baroque tombs, altars, and confessionals.

The **Domschatzkammer** (Cathedral Treasure Chamber; 🎫 DM 2; 🕙 Apr.–Oct., Mon.–Sat. 10–5, Sun. 1:30–5; Nov.–Mar., Mon.–Sat. 11–4, Sun. 1:30–4) houses many extraordinary objects. The highlight is the 10th-century Andreas Tragaltar (St. Andrew's Portable Altar), constructed of oak and covered with gold leaf, enamel, and ivory by local craftsmen. It is a reliquary for the soles of St. Andrew's sandals, symbolized by the gilded, life-size foot on the top of the altar. 🕙 *Dom: Apr.–Oct., daily 6:30–6; Nov.–Mar., daily 6:30–5:30.*

㉜ **Hauptmarkt.** The main market square of Old Trier is easily reached via Simeonstrasse. The market cross (958) and richly ornate St. Peter's Fountain (1595), dedicated to the town's patron saint, stand in the square. The farmers' market is weekdays 7–6:30 and Saturday 7–1.

㊳ **Kaiserthermen** (Imperial Baths). This enormous 4th-century bathing palace once housed cold- and hot-water baths and a sports field. Al-

though only the masonry of the **Calderium** (hot baths) and the vast basements remain, they are enough to give a fair idea of the original splendor and size of the complex—it covered an area 270 yards long and 164 yards wide. Originally 98 ft high, the walls you see today are 62 ft high. ✉ *Corner of Weimarer-Allee and Kaiserstr.* 🎟 *DM 4.* ☉ *Jan.–Easter and Oct.–Nov., Tues.–Sun. 9–5; Easter–Sept., Tues.–Sun. 9–6; Dec. Tues.–Sun. 10–4.*

㊶ Karl-Marx-Haus. Marx was born in this solid bourgeois house in 1818. Visitors with a serious interest in social history will be fascinated by its small museum. A signed first edition of *Das Kapital,* the study in which Marx sought to prove the inevitable decline of capitalism, has a place of honor. ✉ *Brückenstr. 10,* ☏ *0651/970–680.* 🎟 *DM 3.* ☉ *Apr.–Oct., Mon. 1–6, Tues.–Sun. 10–6; Nov.–Mar., Mon. 2–5, Tues.–Sun. 10–1 and 2–5.*

㉞ Liebfrauenkirche (Church of Our Lady). This is the first Gothic church in Germany, built in the 13th century on the site of a Roman basilica. The original statues from the portal (those that have survived) are in the ☞ Bischöfliches Museum. Inside, the decoration is austere except for the Canon Karl von Metternich's 17th-century tomb. ✉ *Liebfrauenstr.* ☉ *Daily 8–noon and 2–6.*

㉙ Porta Nigra (Black Gate). The best preserved Roman structure in Trier was originally a city gate, built in the 2nd century (look for holes left by the iron clamps that held the structure together). Its name is misleading, however; the sandstone gate is not black but dark gray. The gate also served as part of Trier's defenses and was proof of the sophistication of Roman military might and its ruthlessness. Attackers were often lured into the two innocent-looking arches of the Porta Nigra, only to find themselves enclosed in a courtyard. In the 11th century the upper stories were converted into a twin church, in use until the

18th century. The tourist office is next door. ✉ *Porta-Nigra-Pl.* 🖼 *DM 4.* ☉ *Jan.–Easter, Oct., and Nov., daily 9–5; Easter–Sept., daily 9–6; Dec., daily 10–4.*

㊲ Rheinisches Landesmuseum (Rhenish State Museum). The largest collection of Roman antiquities in Germany is housed here. Pride of place goes to the 4th-century stone relief of a Roman ship transporting barrels of wine up the river. This tombstone of a Roman wine merchant was discovered in 1874 when Constantine's citadel in Neumagen was excavated. Have a look at the 108-square-ft model of the city as it looked in the 4th century—it provides a sense of perspective to many of the sights you can still visit today. ✉ *Weimarer-Allee 1,* 🕿 *0651/97740.* 🖼 *DM 7.* ☉ *Tues.–Fri. 9:30–5, weekends, 10:30–5.*

㊱ Römische Palastaula (Roman Basilica). An impressive reminder of Trier's Roman past, this edifice is now Trier's major Protestant church. When first built by the emperor Constantine around AD 310, it was the imperial throne room of the palace. At 239 ft long, 93 ft wide, and 108 ft high, it demonstrates the astounding ambition of its Roman builders and the sophistication of their building techniques. The basilica is one of the two largest Roman interiors in existence (the other is the Pantheon in Rome). Look up at the deeply coffered ceiling; more than any other part of the building, it conveys the opulence of the original structure. ✉ *Konstantinpl.,* 🕿 *0651/72468 or 42570.* ☉ *Apr.–Oct., Mon.–Sat. 9–6, Sun. noon–6; Nov.–Mar., Tues.–Sat. 11–noon and 3–4, Sun. noon–1.*

㉚ Städtisches Museum Simeonstift (Simeon Foundation City Museum). Built around the remains of the Romanesque Simeonskirche, this church is now a museum. It was constructed in the 11th century by Archbishop Poppo in honor of the early medieval hermit Simeon, who for seven years shut himself up in the east tower of the Porta Nigra. Collections include art and artifacts produced in Trier from the Middle Ages to the 19th century. ✉ *An der Porta Nigra,* 🕿 *0651/718–1454.* 🖼 *DM 3.* ☉ *Apr.–Oct., daily 9–5; Nov.–Mar., Tues.–Fri. 9–5, weekends 9–3.*

㊷ Thermen-Museum. Trier's third Roman bath (early 4th century) was discovered beneath Viehmarktplatz when ground was broken for a parking garage. Finds of the excavations from 1987–94 are now beneath a protective glass structure. You can visit the baths and see the cellar of a baroque Capuchin monastery. ✉ *Viehmarktpl.,* 🕿 *0651/994–1057.* 🖼 *DM 4.* ☉ *Tues.–Sun. 9–5.*

㉛ Vinothek WELCOME. At the city's wine-tasting and information center you can sample and purchase from a large selection of Mosel, Saar, and Ruwer wines and sparkling wines. Other products of the grape, wine accessories, gifts, and souvenirs are also sold here. Trier Card (☞ *above*) holders receive a free glass of wine or Sekt. ✉ *Margaretengässchen 2a,* 🕿 *0651/994–0540.* ☉ *Mon.–Sat. 10–7, Sun. 10–5.*

Dining and Lodging

$$$–$$$$ ✕ **Pfeffermühle.** For nearly three decades chef Siegbert Walde has offered guests classic cuisine in elegant surroundings. The 18th-century house on the northern edge of town offers two stories of cozy niches, with beautiful table settings in shades of pink; the terrace directly overlooks the Mosel. Foie gras is a favorite ingredient, served in a terrine or sautéed and served in *Ahorn-jus* (maple-flavor juices). White wines from the Mosel's finest producers and top red Bordeaux wines predominate the excellent wine list. ✉ *Zurlaubener Ufer 76,* 🕿 *0651/ 26133. Reservations essential. MC, V. Closed Sun. No lunch Mon.*

$$–$$$ ✕ **Palais Kesselstatt.** This baroque palace opposite the Liebfrauenkirche is a wonderful setting for fine dining—elegant but not pretentious. There is also seating in the beautiful courtyard in the summer. Katja Weiler is responsible for the efficient, friendly service; Burkhard Weiler reigns in the kitchen. Specialties are rack of lamb or lamb medallions as well as fish dishes. Wines from the Reichsgraf von Kesselstatt estate predominate the wine list, supplemented by Old and New World reds. ⊠ *Liebfrauenstr. 10,* ☎ *0651/40204. AE, MC, V. Closed Mon. and Jan.*

$$–$$$ ✕ **Schlemmereule.** The name literally means "gourmet owl," and, indeed, chef Peter Schmalen caters to gourmets within the 19th-century Palais Walderdorff opposite the cathedral. Lots of windows lend a light, airy look, and there is courtyard seating in the summer. Try the pike-perch in a potato crust and the fabulous crème brûlée. The wine list features 10 wines by the glass and 180 by the bottle, with an emphasis on Mosel wines. ⊠ *Palais Walderdorff, Domfreihof 1,* ☎ *0651/ 73616. Reservations essential. AE, DC, MC, V. Closed Tues.*

$$–$$$ ✕ **Schloss Monaise.** Hubert and Birgit Scheid have infused a breath of fresh air into this 18th-century palace in the suburb of Zewen (southwest of Trier, via B-49 toward Igel and Luxembourg). The decor is modern classic, with Thonet chairs, contemporary art, and pastel colors. The three-course menu for DM 49.50 offers excellent value, and there's an extensive wine list. Part of the terrace is reserved for fine dining; the other part is a beer garden, a laid-back venue for spareribs, salads and pasta. ⊠ *Schloss Monaise 7, Zewen,* ☎ *0651/828-670. MC, V. Closed 2 wks in Feb.*

$$–$$$ ✕ **Zum Domstein.** Whether you opt for cozy dining indoors or outdoor
★ seating in front of or behind this historic house on market square, don't miss the collection of Roman artifacts on display in the cellar. Here you can order menus based on recipes of the Roman gourmet Apicius. Proprietor Rose-Marie Gracher is an expert on the subject. It is a unique experience and highly recommended. ⊠ *Am Hauptmarkt 5,* ☎ *0651/74490. MC, V.*

$–$$ ✕ **Walderdorff's Vinothek-Café-Club.** This lively trio moved into the 19th-century palace when renovations were completed in the spring of 2000. The café-bistro offers breakfast, sandwiches, salads, pasta, and light fare—prepared by the Schlemmereule team (☞ *above*); some 250 local and Old and New World are sold in the Vinothek; and the club offers music and dancing in the baroque cellars. ⊠ *Palais Walderdorff, Domfreihof 1,* ☎ *0651/9946–9210. DC, MC, V.*

$–$$ ✕ **Weinstube Palais Kesselstatt.** The Hilgers family runs this casual offshoot of Palais Kesselstatt (☞ *above*). The interior has exposed beams and polished wood tables; the shady terrace is popular in summer. Two soups daily, light fare, and fresh, regional cuisine are served with wines from the Reichsgraf von Kesselstatt estate. ⊠ *Liebfrauenstr. 10,* ☎ *0651/ 41178. MC, V. Closed Jan.*

$$–$$$ ✕🏨 **Weinhaus Becker.** This family-run hotel, restaurant, and wine estate is in the peaceful suburb of Olewig, near the amphitheater. The rooms are individually decorated with light wood furnishings; some have balconies. The restaurant has romantic, candlelighted niches. You can also dine on the terrace. Try the sole stuffed with scallops and Persian caviar sauce. *Geeister Rieslingschaum,* a light parfait, is a delicious finale. Bordeaux and Burgundy wines are offered in addition to the estate's own wines. The Beckers are happy to organize wine tastings, cellar visits, and guided tours on the wine path. ⊠ *Olewiger Str. 206, D–54295 Trier-Olewig,* ☎ *0651/938–080,* 🖷 *0651/938–0888. 19 rooms. Restaurant, bicycles. MC, V. Restaurant closed Mon., 3 wks Jan. and Feb., 1 wk late July. No lunch except Sun.*

$$$ 🏨 **Römischer Kaiser.** Centrally located near the Porta Nigra, this handsome patrician manor from 1895 (restored in 1994) offers well-appointed, attractive, modern rooms. ⊠ *Am Porta-Nigra-Pl. 6, D–54292,* ☎ *0651/97700,* 🖷 *0651/977–099. 43 rooms. Restaurant, minibars. AE, DC, MC, V.*

$$ 🏨 **Hotel Petrisberg.** The Pantenburg's family-run hotel is high on Petrisberg hill overlooking Trier, not far from the amphitheater. You can walk to the Old Town in 20 minutes. The individually decorated rooms have solid pine furnishings; some have balconies with a fabulous view. The wine pub serves light fare and very good wines. ☒ *Sickingenstr. 11-13, D–54296,* ☎ *0651/4640,* ℻ *0651/46450. 26 rooms, 4 apartments. Weinstube, no-smoking rooms, bicycles. MC, V*

Festivals

The **Europa-Volksfest** (European Folk Festival), in early June, features specialties from several European countries, in addition to rides and entertainment. In late June the entire Old Town is the scene of the **Altstadtfest.** The Kaiserthermen and Amphitheater are impressive stages for the theatrical performances of the **Antikenfestspiele** (Antiquity Festival) from late June to mid-July. The **Moselfest,** with wine, sparkling wine, beer, and fireworks, takes place in early July along the riverbank in Zurlauben, followed by a large **Weinfest** (wine festival) in Oelwig in early August, the **Elblingfest** (festival with still and sparkling wines from the grape variety Elbling), in mid-August, and the **Sektgala** (sparkling wine gala), in front of the Porta Nigra in late August.

Nightlife and the Arts

Theater Trier (☒ Am Augustinerhof, ☎ 0651/718–1818 box office) offers opera, theater, ballet, and concerts.

In addition to **Walderdorff's** in Palais Walderdorff (☞ *above*), there is music and dancing at **Riverside** (☒ Zurmaiener Str. 173, near traffic circle on northern edge of town, ☎ 0651/21006), a large entertainment center.

BONN AND THE COLOGNE LOWLANDS

Updated by
Matthew
Schneider

Bonn, the former capital of Germany, is the next major stop on the Rhine, northwest of Koblenz, where the Mosel joins the Rhine. It's close to the legendary Siebengebirge (Seven Hills), a national park and site of Germany's northernmost vineyards. According to German mythology, Siegfried (hero of the Nibelungen saga) killed a dragon here and bathed in its blood to make himself invincible. The lowland, a region of gently rolling hills north of Bonn, lacks the drama of the Rhine gorge upstream but offers Köln (Cologne), an ancient cathedral town, and Düsseldorf, an elegant city of art and fashion. Although not geographically in the Rhineland proper, Aachen is an important side trip for anyone visiting the region. Its stunning cathedral and treasury are the greatest storehouses of Carolingian art and architecture in Europe.

Bonn

44 km (27 mi) north of Koblenz, 28 km (17 mi) south of Köln.

Bonn was the postwar seat of the federal government and parliament until the capital returned to Berlin in 1999. Aptly described in the title of John Le Carré's spy novel *A Small Town in Germany,* the quiet university town was chosen as a stopgap measure to prevent such weightier contenders as Frankfurt from becoming the capital, a move that would have lessened Berlin's chances of regaining its former status. No one knows what final effect the exodus of the government from Bonn will have on this city. In reality many of the government ministries and civil servants remain in Bonn, while the entire move is expected to take a number of years. To help fill the remaining void, plans for moving a number or other organizations and industries to Bonn are in the works, and Bonn's status as a UN city is also expected to be strengthened dur-

ing this time, with additional UN offices taking residence in some of
the old government buildings.

Although Bonn seems to have sprung into existence only after the war,
the Romans settled this part of the Rhineland 2,000 years ago, calling
it Castra Bonnensia. Life in Bonn's streets, old markets, pedestrian malls,
and handsome Südstadt residential area is unhurried. The town center is a car-free zone; an inner ring road circles it with parking garages
on the perimeter. A convenient parking lot is just across from the railway station and within 50 yards of the tourist office.

A Good Walk

After picking up what you need at the tourist office at Windeckstrasse
2, continue to the cathedral **Münster** ㊸, the site where two Roman soldiers were executed in AD 253 for holding Christian beliefs. Across from
the cathedral are the **Kurfürstliches Schloss** ㊹ and its gardens. Walk away
from the river and down chestnut-tree-lined Poppelsdorfer Allee to the
Poppelsdorfer Schloss ㊺. To get to the leafy cemetery, **Alter Friedhof** ㊻
(final resting place of famous soldiers and of scholars and composers
Robert and Clara Schumann), retrace your steps along the Poppelsdorfer Allee to Quantiusstrasse. Follow it north until it becomes Her-
warthstrasse; before the street curves, turning into Endenlicherstrasse,
take the underpass below the railroad line. You'll then be on Thomas-
trasse, which borders the cemetery. Berlinerplatz is on the northeast
corner. Cross it and enter the Sternstrasse; a left on Bonngasse leads
to the modest **Beethovenhaus** ㊼, the residence of the great composer
until he was 22. Farther down Sternstrasse is the Markt and its lavish
rococo **Rathaus** ㊽. From the square take Stockenstrasse past the
Friedrich-Wilhelm University and its Hofgarten. Crossing Adenauerallee, you will reach the Rhine river. The **Haus der Geschichte** ㊾ is about
1½ km (1 mi) southeast along the Rhine down Adenauerallee. The **Kunst-
und Austellungshalle der Bundesrepublik Deutschland** ㊿ is around the
corner on Friedrich-Ebert-Allee.

TIMING

Allow about three hours for the walk, not including time spent in museums or window shopping.

Sights to See

㊻ The **Alter Friedhof** (Old Cemetery). This ornate graveyard is the resting place of many of the country's most celebrated sons and daughters. Look for the tomb of composer Robert Schumann and his wife,
Clara. ✉ *Am Alten Friedhof.* ☉ *Mar.–Aug., daily 7:15 AM–8 PM; Sept.
and Feb., daily 8–8; Oct., daily 8–7; Nov.–Jan., daily 8–5.*

★ ㊼ **Beethovenhaus** (Beethoven House). Beethoven was born in Bonn in 1770
and, except for a short stay in Vienna, lived there until the age of 22.
The house where he grew up is a museum celebrating his career. You'll
find scores, paintings, a grand piano (his last, in fact), and an ear trumpet or two. Perhaps most impressive is the room in which Beethoven
was born—empty save for a bust of the composer. ✉ *Bonng. 20,* ☎
0228/981–7525. 🎫 *DM 8.* ☉ *Apr.–Oct., Mon.–Sat. 10–6, Sun. 11–
4; Nov.–Mar., Mon.–Sat. 10–5, Sun. 11–4.*

㊾ **Haus der Geschichte** (House of History). German history since World
War II is the subject of this museum, which begins with "hour zero,"
as the Germans call the unconditional surrender of 1945. The museum
displays an overwhelming amount of documentary material organized
on five levels and effectively utilizes various types of media. ✉ *Adenauerallee 250,* ☎ *0228/91650.* 🎫 *Free.* ☉ *Tues.–Sun. 9–7.*

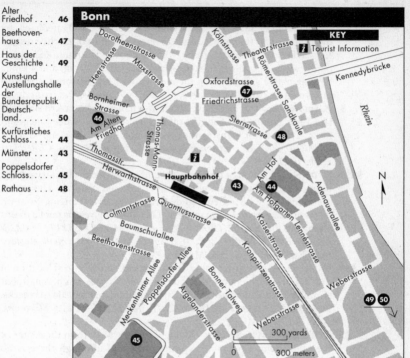

Bonn

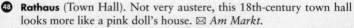

㊿ Kunst- und Austellungshalle der Bundesrepublik Deutschland (Art and Exhibition Hall of the German Federal Republic). This exhibition hall is one of the Rhineland's most important venues for major exhibitions about culture and science. Its modern design, by Viennese architect Gustave Peichl, employs three rooftop cones (there is also a garden) and 16 columns. ⊠ *Friedrich-Ebert-Allee 4,* ☎ *0228/917–1200.* ⊡ *DM 10.* ⊙ *Tues. and Wed. 10–9, Thurs., Fri., and Sun. 10–7; Sat. 9–9.*

The large **Kunstmuseum** (Art Museum), next door to the exhibition hall, is devoted to contemporary art. ⊠ *Friedrich-Ebert-Allee 2,* ☎ *0228/ 776–260.* ⊡ *DM 15.* ⊙ *Tues.–Sun. 10–6 (Wed. until 9).*

㊹ Kurfürstliches Schloss (Prince-Electors' Palace). Built in the 18th century by the prince-electors of Köln, this grand palace now houses a university. If it's a fine day, stroll through the Hofgarten (Palace Gardens).

㊸ Münster (Cathedral). The 900-year-old cathedral is vintage late-Romanesque, with a massive octagonal main tower and a soaring spire. It saw the coronations of two Holy Roman Emperors (in 1314 and 1346) and was one of the Rhineland's most important ecclesiastical centers in the Middle Ages. The 17th-century bronze figure of St. Helen and the ornate rococo pulpit are highlights of the interior. ⊠ *Münsterpl.,* ☎ *0228/633–344.* ⊙ *Daily 7–7.*

㊺ Poppelsdorfer Schloss (Poppelsdorf Palace). This former electors' palace was built in the baroque style between 1715 and 1753. The building houses the university's botanical garden, with an impressive display of tropical plants. ⊠ *Meckenheimer Allee 171,* ☎ *0228/732–259.* ⊡ *Free.* ⊙ *Apr.–Sept., weekdays 9–6, weekends 9–1; Oct.–Mar., weekdays 9–4.*

㊽ Rathaus (Town Hall). Not very austere, this 18th-century town hall looks more like a pink doll's house. ⊠ *Am Markt.*

Dining and Lodging

$$ ✕ **Haus Daufenbach.** The stark white exterior of the Daufenbach, by the church of St. Remigius, disguises one of the most distinctive restaurants in Bonn. The mood is rustic, with simple wood furniture and antlers on the walls. Specialties include *Spanferkel* (suckling pig) and a range of imaginative salads. Wash them down with wines from the restaurant's own vineyards. ✉ *Brüderg. 6,* ☎ *0228/969–4600. No credit cards.*

$ ✕ **Em Höttche.** Travelers have taken sustenance at this tavern since the late 14th century, and today it offers one of the best-value lunches in town. The interior is rustic; the food stout and hearty. ✉ *Markt 4,* ☎ *0228/690–009. Reservations not accepted. No credit cards. Closed last 2 wks in Dec.*

$$$$ 🏨 **Domicil.** A group of buildings around a quiet, central courtyard has been converted into a hotel of great charm and comfort. The rooms are individually furnished and decorated—in styles ranging from fin de siècle romantic to Italian modern. Lots of glass gives the public rooms a spacious airiness. ✉ *Thomas-Mann-Str. 24–26, D–53111,* ☎ *0228/ 729–090,* FAX *0228/691–207. 36 rooms, 3 suites, 1 apartment. Restaurant, bar, sauna. AE, DC, MC, V.*

$$$ 🏨 **Sternhotel.** For good value, solid comfort, and a central location in the Old Town, the family-run Stern is tops. Rooms can be small, but all are pleasantly furnished. There's no restaurant, but the café has snacks. ✉ *Markt 8, D–53111,* ☎ *0228/72670,* FAX *0228/726–7125. 80 rooms. Café. AE, DC, MC, V.*

$$ 🏨 **Rheinland.** This modest lodging is a short walk from the center of the Old Town. Rooms are comfortable, and although there is no restaurant, a good buffet breakfast greets the day. ✉ *Berliner Freiheit 11, D–53111,* ☎ *0228/658–096,* FAX *0228/472–844. 31 rooms. V.*

Nightlife and the Arts

MUSIC

The Bonn Symphony Orchestra opens its season in grand style every September with a concert on the market square, in front of city hall. Otherwise, concerts are held in the **Beethovenhalle** (✉ Wachsbleiche 17, ☎ 0228/72220); they're free on Sunday morning. Chamber-music concerts are given regularly at the **Schumannhaus** (☎ 0228/773–666). The **Pantheon** theater (✉ Bundeskanzlerpl., ☎ 0228/212–521) has become a leading venue for all manner of pop concerts and cabaret. Bonn also hosts a **Beethoven Festival** every September with indoor and outdoor concerts held at numerous venues around the city; call the tourist office for a schedule of events.

Opera productions are staged regularly at the **Oper der Stadt Bonn** (✉ Am Böselagerhof 1, ☎ 0228/778–000), popularly known as "La Scala of the Rhineland."

THEATER AND DANCE

Musicals and ballet are performed at the **Oper der Stadt Bonn** (☞ *above*). From May through October the **Bonner Sommer** festival offers folklore, music, and street theater, much of it outdoors and most of it free.

Shopping

The international comings and goings have established a prolific market for antiques in this little town. **Paul Schweitzer** (✉ Löbestr. 1, ☎ 0228/362–659), closed Monday, is a respected dealer. The family-run **Ehlers Antiquitäten** (✉ Berliner Freiheit 28, ☎ 0228/676–853) is another reliable antiques outlet.

Despite its name, Bonn's **Wochenmarkt** (Weekly Market) is open daily, filling Marktplatz with vendors of produce and various edibles. Bargain hunters flock to the city's renowned—and huge—**flea market**

(*Flohmarkt*), held on the third Saturday of each month from April through October at Rheinaue (Ludwig-Erhard-Strasse), where you can find secondhand goods and knickknacks of all descriptions. **Pützchens Markt,** a huge country fair, is held in the Bonn area the second weekend of September.

Königswinter

12 km (7 mi) northeast of Bonn.

The town of Königswinter has one of the most visited castles on the Rhine, the **Drachenfels.** Its ruins crown one of the highest hills in the Siebengebirge, Germany's oldest nature reserve, with a spectacular view of the Rhine. The reserve has more than 100 km (62 mi) of hiking trails. The castle was built in the 12th century by the archbishop of Köln. Its name commemorates a dragon said to have lived in a nearby cave. As legend has it, the dragon was slain by Siegfried, hero of the epic *Nibelungenlied.*

Dining

$$–$$$ ✕ **Gasthaus Sutorius.** Across from the church of St. Margaretha, this wine tavern serves refined variations on German cuisine with an intelligent selection of local wines. In summer food is served outdoors beneath the linden trees. ⊠ *Oelinghovener Str. 7,* ☎ *02244/912–240. No credit cards. Closed Mon. No lunch except Sun.*

Brühl

20 km (12 mi) southwest of Bonn.

★ In the heart of Brühl you'll discover the Rhineland's most important baroque palace. **Schloss Augustusburg** and the magnificent pleasure park that surrounds it were created in the time of Prince Clemens August, between 1725 and 1768. The palace contains one of the most famous achievements of rococo architecture, a staircase by Balthasar Neumann. **Concerts** are held here in summer (☎ 02232/941–884 for tickets and information). ⊠ *Schloss Str. 6,* ☎ *02232/44000.* ☑ *DM 6.* ☉ *Feb.–Nov., Tues.–Sun. 9–noon and 1:30–4.*

The smaller **Jagdschloss Falkenlust,** at the end of an avenue leading straight through the Augustusburg's grounds, was built as a getaway where the prince could indulge his passion for falconry. ⊠ *Schloss Str. 6,* ☎ *02232/12111.* ☑ *DM 4.50.* ☉ *Feb.–Nov., Tues.–Sun. 9–noon and 2–4:30.*

Köln

28 km (17 mi) north of Bonn, 47 km (29 mi) south of Düsseldorf, 70 km (43 mi) southeast of Aachen.

Köln is the largest city on the Rhine (the fourth largest in Germany) and one of the most interesting. Although not as old as Trier, it has been a dominant power in the Rhineland since Roman times. Known throughout the world for its scented toilet water, eau de cologne (first produced here in 1705 from an Italian formula), Köln is today a major commercial, intellectual, and ecclesiastical center. The city is vibrant and bustling, with something of the same sparkle that makes Munich so memorable. At its heart is tradition, manifested in the abundance of bars and brew houses serving the local Kölsch beer and old Rhine cuisine—these are the meeting places of Köln, and the starting place for many a person's night on the town. Köln also puts on a wild carnival every February, with three days of orgiastic revelry, bands, parades, and parties that last all night. Tradition, however, is mixed with the contemporary, found in a host of elegant shops, sophisticated restaurants, and modern bars and dance clubs. The numerous trade fairs held in the two massive convention centers on the east side of the Rhine (in the Deutz district) are also a draw for many.

Köln was first settled by the Romans in 38 BC. For nearly a century it grew slowly, in the shadow of imperial Trier, until a locally born noblewoman, Julia Agrippina, daughter of the Roman general Germanicus, married the Roman emperor Claudius. Her hometown was elevated to the rank of a Roman city and given the name Colonia Claudia Ara Agrippinensium. For the next 300 years Colonia (hence Cologne, or Köln) flourished. Today there's evidence of the Roman city's wealth in the Römisch-Germanisches Museum (☞ *below*). When the Romans left, Köln was ruled first by the Franks, then by the Merovingians. In the 9th century Charlemagne, the towering figure who united the sprawling German lands (and ruled much of present-day France) as the first Holy Roman Emperor, restored Köln's fortunes and elevated it to its preeminent role in the Rhineland. Charlemagne also appointed the first archbishop of Köln. The city's ecclesiastical heritage is one of its most striking features; it has a full dozen Romanesque churches and the largest and finest Gothic cathedral in Germany.

Köln eventually became the largest city north of the Alps, and in time evolved into a place of pilgrimage second only to Rome. In the Middle Ages it was a member of the powerful Hanseatic League, occupying a position of greater importance in European commerce than either London or Paris.

Köln entered modern times as the number-one city of the Rhineland. Then, in World War II, bombings destroyed 90% of it. Only the cathedral remained relatively unscathed. Almost everything else had to be rebuilt, including all of the glorious Romanesque churches. Early reconstruction was accomplished in a big rush—and it shows. Like many German cities that sprang up, mushroomlike, in the "Economic Miracle" of the 1950s, Köln is a mishmash of old and new, sometimes awkwardly juxtaposed. A good part of the former Old Town along the Hohe Strasse (old Roman High Road) was turned into one of Germany's first, yet remarkably charmless, pedestrian shopping malls. The ensemble is framed by six-lane expressways winding along the rim of the city center—barely yards from the cathedral—perfectly illustrating the problems, as well as the blessings, of postwar reconstruction.

Among the blessings is the fact that much of the Altstadt (Old Town), ringed by streets that follow the line of the medieval city walls, is closed to traffic; most major sights are within this area and are easily reached on foot. Here, too, you'll find the best shops.

The **tourist office,** across from the cathedral, can make hotel bookings for you at a cost of DM 6.

A Good Walk

Any tour of the city should start beneath the towers of the extraordinary Gothic cathedral, the **Dom** ㊿, comparable to the great French cathedrals and a highlight of a trip to Germany. Spend some time admiring the outside of the building (you can walk almost all the way around it). Notice how there are practically no major horizontal lines—all the accents of the building are vertical. Climb to the top of the bell tower to get the complete vertical experience. The cathedral's treasures are kept in the **Dom Schatzkammer,** the cathedral treasury. Just a few steps across Roncalli Platz is a superb museum complex, the **Wallraf-Richartz-Museum/Museum Ludwig** ㊾, which houses the largest art collection in the Rhineland. The **Römisch-Germanisches Museum** ㊿, right next door, has a large mosaic dating from Roman times. From the museum walk away from the cathedral across the square and turn left on Am Hof Strasse. Walk one block, turn right, and continue down Burg Strasse. A few more steps (crossing Kleine Budengasse) brings you to the **Altes Rathaus** ㉝. Next, enter the small alley beneath the Rathaus tower (to the left as you face it) and walk a few steps to the **Alter Markt** ㉟. Cross the square and enter Lintgasse; after taking a few steps, you will be in the shadow of the outstanding **Gross St. Martin** ㊱, one of Köln's 12 Romanesque churches. You are also near the bank of the Rhine. Walk left through the Rhein Garten park for a view of the river. Soon you'll reach Heinrich-Böll-Platz, named after the native son who was Germany's greatest postwar novelist. Just three blocks north, along the Rhine, stands **St. Kunibert's** ㊲, the last of Köln's famous Romanesque churches to be built. Continuing from Heinrich-Böll-Platz, go up the steps and walk past the cathedral again, continuing beyond the Dom Hotel and across Hohe Strasse, an ugly pedestrian shopping street, into Burgmauer Strasse. Follow the waist-high, block-long remnant of the old city walls to Mohrenstrasse. Go right two blocks, then left to a square. On the other side of the square stands **St. Gereon's** ㊳, the jewel of the city's Romanesque churches.

Sights to the south that can easily be reached on foot by heading back down the Mohrenstrasse and following the street all the way to Cäcilienstrasse are the **Schnütgen Museum** ㊴, a fine collection of medieval art (on Cäcilienstrasse, east of the Neumarkt); the 15th-century hall of **Gürzenich** ㊵ (Martinstrasse, north of the Heumarkt); and the somber 11th-century **St. Maria im Kapitol** ㊶ (west of the Heumarkt). On the Rhine, beneath the Deutzer Bridge, is the **Imhoff-Stollwerck-Museum for the History of Chocolate** ㊷.

TIMING
Allow two hours just for the walk. To see the interior of the cathedral and the cathedral treasury, and to climb the cathedral tower will add almost an hour. The museum collections could take several hours depending on your interests. Visits to the Wallraf-Richartz-Museum/Museum Ludwig and the Römisch-Germanisches Museum require at least 45 minutes each.

Sights to See

㉟ **Alter Markt** (Old Market). The square has an eclectic assembly of buildings, most of them postwar; two 16th-century houses survived the war intact—Numbers 20 and 22. The oldest structure dates from 1135.

㉝ **Altes Rathaus** (Old Town Hall). This is the oldest town hall in Germany, if you don't count the fact that the building was entirely rebuilt after the war; it was originally erected in the 14th century. There was a seat of local government here in Roman times, and directly below the current Rathaus are the remains of the Roman city governor's headquarters, the Praetorium. The 14th-century **Hansa Saal,** a meeting hall, has tall Gothic windows and a barrel-vaulted wood ceiling, both potent expressions of medieval civic pride. The figures of the prophets that decorate the town hall, standing on pedestals at one end, are all from the early 15th century. Ranging along the south wall are nine additional statues, the so-called *Nine Good Heroes,* carved in 1360. Charlemagne and King Arthur are among them. Beneath a small glass pyramid by the south corner of the Rathaus is the **Mikwe,** a 12th-century ritual bath from the medieval Jewish quarter. ✉ *Rathauspl.,* ☎ 0221/2212–6484. ⊙ *Mon.–Thurs. 7:30–4:45, Fri. 7:30–2.*

★ ㊾ **Dom** (Cathedral). This Köln landmark is one of the purest expressions of the Gothic spirit in Europe. The desire to pay homage to God took

Köln (Cologne)

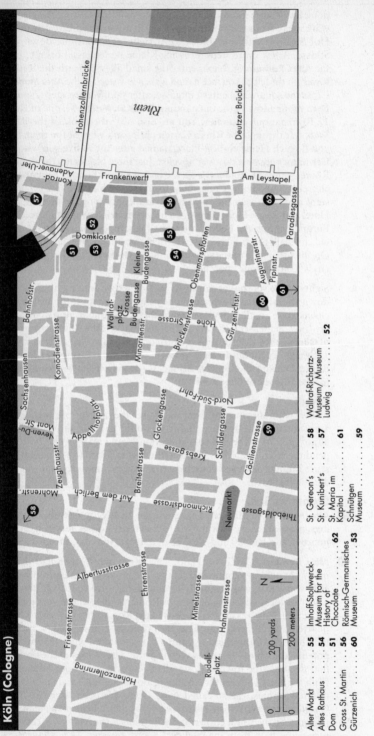

the form of building the largest and most lavish church possible, a tangible expression of God's kingdom on earth. Its spires soar heavenward, and its immense interior is illuminated by light filtering through acres of stained glass. It may come as a disappointment to learn that the cathedral, begun in 1248, was not completed until 1880. Console yourself with the knowledge that it was still built to original plans. At 515 ft high, the two west towers of the cathedral were by far the tallest structures in the world when they were finished. The cathedral was built to house what were believed to be the relics of the Magi, the three kings who paid homage to the infant Jesus (the trade in holy mementos was big business in the Middle Ages—and not always scrupulous). Since Köln was by then a major commercial and political center, it was felt that a special place had to be constructed. Anxious to surpass the great cathedrals then being built in France, the masons set to work. The size of the building was not simply an example of self-aggrandizement on the part of the people of Köln, however; it was a response to the vast numbers of pilgrims who arrived to see the relics. The ambulatory, the passage that curves around the back of the altar, is unusually large, allowing cathedral authorities to funnel large numbers of visitors up to the crossing (where the nave and transepts meet, and where the relics were originally displayed), around the back of the altar, and out again. Today the relics are kept just behind the altar, in the original enormous gold-and-silver **reliquary.** The other great treasure of the cathedral, in the last chapel on the left as you face the altar, is the **Gero Cross,** a monumental oak crucifix dating from 971. Other highlights are the stained-glass windows, some dating from the 13th century; the 15th-century altarpiece; and the early 14th-century high altar with its glistening white figures and intricate choir screens. ⊠ *Dompl.,* ☎ *0221/9258–4730.* ☉ *Daily 6 AM–7 PM; Dom stairwell daily 9–7.* ✍

The **Dom Schatzkammer,** the cathedral treasury, includes the silver shrine of Archbishop Engelbert, who was stabbed to death in 1225. ⊠ *Dompl.,* ☎ *0221/9258–4730.* ◪ *DM 3.* ☉ *Apr.–Oct., Mon.–Sat. 9–7, Sun. 12:30–7; Nov.–Mar., Mon.–Sat. 9–4, Sun. 1–4.*

⑤⑥ **Gross St. Martin** (Big St. Martin). This remarkable Romanesque parish church was rebuilt after being flattened in World War II. Its massive 13th-century tower, with distinctive corner turrets and an imposing central spire, is another landmark of Köln. The church was built on the site of a Roman granary. ⊠ *Lintg.,* ☎ *0221/1642–5650.* ☉ *Weekdays 10:15–6, Sat. 10–12:30 and 1:30–6, Sun. 2–4.*

⑥⓪ **Gürzenich.** At the south end of Martinsviertel, this Gothic structure was all but demolished in World War II but carefully reconstructed afterward. It is named after a medieval knight (von Gürzenich) from whom the city acquired a quantity of valuable real estate in 1437. The official reception and festival hall built on the site has played a central role in the city's civic life through the centuries. At one end of the complex are the remains of the 10th-century Gothic church of **St. Alban,** which were left ruined after the war as a memorial. On what's left of the church floor, you can see a sculpture of a couple kneeling in prayer, *Mourning Parents,* by Käthe Kollwitz, a fitting memorial to the ravages of war. ⊠ *Gürzenichstr.*

⑥② **Imhoff-Stollwerck-Museum for the History of Chocolate.** This riverside museum explores 3,000 years of civilization's production and delectation of chocolate, from the Maya to the colonizing and industrializing Europeans. It is also a real factory with lava flows of chocolate, milk-chocolate bars stacked to the ceiling, and a conveyer belt jostling thousands of truffles. ⊠ *Rheinauhafen 1a* ☎ *0221/9318–8811.* ◪ *DM 10.* ☉ *Tues.–Fri. 10–6, weekends 11–7.*

Martinsviertel (St. Martin's Quarter). The colorful old city neighborhood, with ☞ **Gross St. Martin** at the north end and the ☞ **Gürzenich** at the south, is an attractive combination of reconstructed, high-gabled medieval buildings, winding alleys, and tastefully designed modern apartments and business quarters. Head here after sunset, when the restaurants, brew houses, and *Kneipen* (pubs) begin to overflow with people.

★ ⑤ **Römisch-Germanisches Museum** (Roman-Germanic Museum). This cultural landmark was built in the early 1970s around the famous Dionysius mosaic discovered there during the construction of an air-raid shelter in 1941. The huge mosaic, more than 100 yards square, once formed the dining-room floor of a wealthy Roman trader's villa. Its millions of tiny earthenware and glass tiles depict some of the adventures of Dionysius, the Greek god of wine and, to the Romans, the object of a widespread and sinister religious cult. The pillared 1st-century tomb of Lucius Publicius, a prominent Roman officer, some stone Roman coffins, and a series of memorial tablets are among the museum's other exhibits. Bordering the museum on the south is a restored 90-yard stretch of the old Roman harbor road. ✉ *Roncallipl. 4,* ☎ *0221/2212–4438.* 💳 *DM 5.* ⊙ *Tues.–Sun. 10–5.*

⑤⑧ **St. Gereon's.** Experts regard St. Gereon's as one of the most noteworthy medieval structures in existence. This exquisite Romanesque church stands on the site of an old Roman burial ground six blocks west of the train station. An enormous dome rests on walls that were once clad in gold mosaics. Roman masonry forms part of the structure, which is believed to have been built over the grave of its namesake, the 4th-century martyr and patron saint of Köln. ✉ *Gereonsdriesch 2–4,* ☎ *0221/134–922.* ⊙ *Mon.–Sat. 9–12:30 and 1:30–6, Sun. 1:30–6.*

⑤⑦ **St. Kunibert's.** The most lavish of the churches from the late-Romanesque period is by the Rhine, three blocks north of the train station. Its precious stained-glass windows have filtered the light of day for over 700 years. Consecrated in 1247, the church contains an unusual room, concealed under the altar, which gives access to a pre-Christian well once believed to promote fertility in women. ✉ *Kunibertklosterg. 6,* ☎ *0221/121–214.* ⊙ *Daily 9–noon and 2–6.*

⑥① **St. Maria im Kapitol.** Built in the 11th and 12th centuries on the site of a Roman temple, St. Maria's is best known for its two beautifully carved 16-ft-high doors and its enormous crypt, the second largest in Germany after the one in Speyer's cathedral (☞ Chapter 10). ✉ *Kasinostr. 6,* ☎ *0221/214–615.* ⊙ *Daily 10–6.*

⑤⑨ **Schnütgen Museum.** A treasure house of medieval art from the Rhine region, the museum has an ideal setting in a 12th-century basilica. Don't miss the crucifix from the St. Georg Church or the original stained-glass windows and carved figures from the ☞ **Dom.** Many of the exhibits—intricately carved ivory book covers, rock crystal reliquaries, illuminated manuscripts—require intense concentration to be fully appreciated. ✉ *Cäcilienstr. 29,* ☎ *0221/2212–3620.* 💳 *DM 5.* ⊙ *Tues.–Fri. 10–5 (every 1st Wed. until 8), weekends 11–5.*

★ ⑤② **Wallraf-Richartz-Museum/Museum Ludwig.** The Wallraf-Richartz-Museum contains paintings spanning the years 1300 to 1900. Dutch and Flemish schools are particularly well represented, as is the 15th- to 16th-century Cologne school of German painting. Its two most famous artists are the Master of the Saint Veronica (whose actual name is unknown) and Stefan Lochner, represented by two luminous works, *The Last Judgment* and *The Madonna in the Rose Bower.* Large canvases by Rubens, who spent his youth in Köln, hang prominently on the second floor. There are also outstanding works by Rembrandt, Van Dyck, and Frans Hals. Among the other old masters are Tiepolo, Canaletto, and Boucher. Some of the great impressionists bring the collection into this century.

The Museum Ludwig is devoted exclusively to 20th-century art. Its American pop art collection (including Andy Warhol, Jasper Johns, Robert Rauschenberg, Claes Oldenburg, and Roy Lichtenstein) rivals that of New York's Guggenheim Museum.

The **Agfa Foto-Historama** (Agfa Photography Museum) is in the same complex as the Museum Ludwig. It has one of the world's largest collections of historic photographs and cameras, but not everything is on display at the same time. ✉ *Bischofsgartenstr. 1,* ☎ *0221/2212–2379, 0221/2212–2382, or 0221/2212–2411.* ✉ *All 3 museums DM 10.* ☉ *Tues. 10–8, Wed.–Fri. 10–6, weekends 11–6.*

Dining and Lodging

$$$–$$$$ ✕ **Le Moissonnier.** Part of the charm of this restaurant—arguably the
★ best in the city—is its lack of pretension. In contrast to the gray neighborhood, the turn-of-the-century bistro decor radiates warmth from its mirrors, Tiffany lamps, and painted flowers. Owners Vincent and Liliane Moissonnier greet their guests in person, seating them at one of 20 tables and overseeing every detail of their evening. Chef Eric Menchon crafts cuisine that is French at its base but intertwines an array of global influences, serving dishes such as scampi with caraway seeds wrapped in potatoes with a white bean sauce and oyster hash, or a bouillabaisse with thick turbot and calamari and ginger balls. ✉ *Krefelder Str. 25,* ☎ *0221/729–479. Reservations essential. No credit cards. Closed Sun. and Mon.*

$$$ ✕ **Bizim.** The extraordinary chef Enis Akisik has made his Bizim a can-
★ didate for best Turkish restaurant in Germany. Forget shish kebab and prepare yourself for a leisurely, gourmet experience that might include scampi with tarragon sauce, eggplant-coated lamb fillets with a garlic yogurt sauce, or quail grilled on a rosemary spit and served in its own juices. The four-course lunch menu (DM 55) is highly recommended. ✉ *Weideng. 47–49,* ☎ *0221/131–581. Reservations essential. AE, D, MC, V. Closed Sun. and Mon.*

$$$ ✕ **Fischer's.** This modestly decorated modern restaurant provides a relaxed and friendly dining experience with elegant food and wine at a reasonable price. The kitchen experiments with regional cuisine with influences from France and the Mediterranean to as far off as Southeast Asia, and the menu is complemented by a selection of more than 400 wines, 40 of which can be bought by the glass. The expert staff will help you pick the perfect wine for each dish, and if you like it, you can even buy a bottle to take home with you. ✉ *Hohenstaufenring 53,* ☎ *0221/310–8470. Reservations essential. No credit cards. No lunch Sat. Closed Sun.*

$$ ✕ **Die Tomate.** If you don't like tomatoes, stay away from this popular little restaurant. The red fruit may be seen growing at the door, and the menu may feature tomato carpaccio with tomato paste and escallop of pork, as well as dishes without tomatoes, such as steak in a red-wine sauce. For dessert try the delicious pancakes filled with apples. ✉ *Aachenerstr. 11,* ☎ *0221/257–4307. AE. Closed Sun.*

$$ ✕ **Früh am Dom.** For real down-home German food, there are few places that compare with this time-honored former brewery. Bold frescoes on the vaulted ceilings establish the mood; the authentically Teutonic experience is complete with such dishes as *Hämmchen* (pork knuckle). The beer garden is delightful for summer dining. ✉ *Am Hof 12–14,* ☎ *0221/258–0396. No credit cards.*

$ ✗ **Haus Töller.** There is no better tavern in Köln in which to imbibe Kölsch, the city's home brew. You won't sit long in front of an empty glass before another glass is placed before you. The Teutonic specialties include bean soup, schnitzel, Hämmchen, and potato pancakes. ✉ *Weyerstr. 96,* ☎ *0221/240–9187. No credit cards. No lunch. Closed Sun.*

$ ✗ **Moderne Zeiten.** At this friendly Internet café, near the Breite Strasse in the Future Point media center, you can check your e-mail over eggs and toast for breakfast or while lunching on soups, salads, pasta, and milk shakes. ✉ *Richmodstr. 13,* ☎ *0221/206–7206. No credit cards.*

$$$$ ✗⊡ **Dom-Hotel.** Old-fashioned, formal, and gracious, with a stunning location right by the cathedral, the Dom offers old-world elegance and discreetly efficient service. The antiques-filled bedrooms, generally in Louis XV or Louis XVI style, are subdued in color, high-ceilinged, and spacious. Each room is individually furnished. Service is, for the most part, exemplary, unhurried, and personal. The view of the cathedral is something to treasure. Enjoy it from the glass-enclosed Atelier am Dom, where you can dine informally on such specialties as marinated lamb carpaccio with grated Parmesan or sautéed mullet on a bed of spicy tomato ragout and basil pasta. ✉ *Domkloster 2A, D–50667,* ☎ *0221/20240,* FAX *0221/202–4444. 125 rooms. Restaurant, bar. AE, DC, MC, V.*

$$$$ ✗⊡ **Excelsior Hotel Ernst.** The Empire-style lobby is striking in sump-
★   tuous royal blue, bright yellow, and gold, and a similarly bold grandeur extends to the other public rooms in this 1863 hotel. Old-master paintings (including a Van Dyck) are everywhere; you'll be served breakfast in a room named after the Gobelin tapestries that hang there. Ultimately, it's the genuine warmth and helpfulness of the staff that make dining here a memorable experience. The Hansestube restaurant, which attracts a local business crowd with its lunch specials, has a more hushed ambience in the evening, when it serves French haute cuisine with an occasional nod to the health conscious. Mushroom lovers will want to try the veal medallions in a rich cream sauce with a huge mound of morels. The wine cellar is famous for its French burgundies and Bordeaux. ✉ *Trankg. 1, D–50667,* ☎ *0221/2701,* FAX *0221/135–150. 140 rooms, 20 suites. Restaurant, bar, beauty salon, massage. AE, DC, MC, V.*

$$ ✗⊡ **Chelsea.** This designer hotel has a very strong following among artists and art dealers. The decor is a cross between Rietveld, Philippe Starck, and a half dozen others. Bathrooms and bathtubs are luxuriously roomy, and there is no end to the mirrors decorating the walls. Breakfast is served until noon. The restaurant-café downstairs is great for encounters of an informal kind and for people-watching. It's 20 minutes to the city center on foot, 10 by subway or tram. ✉ *Jülicherstr. 1, D–50674,* ☎ *0221/207–150,* FAX *0221/239–137. 30 rooms. Restaurant. AE, DC, V.*

$$$$ ⊡ **Hotel im Wasserturm.** What used to be Europe's tallest water tower
★   is now an 11-story luxury hotel-in-the-round, opened at the end of 1989 after a $70 million conversion. The neoclassic look of the brick exterior was retained by order of Köln conservationists. The ultramodern interior was the work of the French designer Andrée Putman, known for her minimalist work on the hotel Morgans, in New York. The 11th-floor restaurant has a view of the city. ✉ *Kayg. 2, D–50676,* ☎ *0221/20080,* FAX *0221/200–8888. 54 rooms, 34 suites and maisonettes. Restaurant, bar, room service, exercise room, sauna. AE, DC, MC, V.* ✎

$$$–$$$$ ⊡ **Carat Hotel.** Besides bright, well-sized rooms, the true strength of this modern hotel is it's location at the southern edge of the Altstadt. After starting your day with a generous buffet breakfast, you can also quickly reach either the Rhine or the Kö with a three-block walk. ✉ *Benratherstr. 7a, D–40213,* ☎ *0211/13050,* FAX *0211/322–214. 73 rooms, 1 suite. Bar, air-conditioning (some), sauna. AE, DC, MC, V. CP.*

$$–$$$ ⊞ **Das Kleine Stapelhäuschen.** One of the few houses along the river-bank to have survived World War II bombings, this is one of the old-est buildings in Köln. You can't beat the location, overlooking the river and right by Gross St. Martin; yet the rooms are reasonably priced, making up in age and quaintness for what they lack in luxury. The restaurant is in a slightly higher price bracket and does a respectable enough job with spruced-up versions of German specialties. ⊠ *Fischmarkt 1–3, D–50667,* ☎ *0221/257–7862,* ℻ *0221/257–4232. 31 rooms. Restaurant. AE, MC, V.*

Nightlife and the Arts

THE ARTS

Köln's Westdeutsche Rundfunk Orchestra performs regularly in the city's excellent concert hall, the **Philharmonie** (⊠ Bischofsgartenstr. 1, ☎ 0221/280–280). The Gürzenich Orchestra gives regular concerts in the Philharmonie, but the natural setting for its music is the restored **Gürzenich,** medieval Köln's official reception mansion. Köln's opera company, the **Oper der Stadt Köln,** is known for exciting classical and contemporary productions. Year-round organ recitals in Köln's cathedral are supplemented from June through August with a summer season of organ music. Organ recitals and chamber concerts are also presented in many of the Romanesque churches and in **Antoniterkirche** (⊠ Schilderg.). Call for details on all **church concerts** (☎ 0221/9258–4745).

Köln's principal theater is the **Schauspielhaus** (⊠ Offenbachpl. 1, ☎ 0221/2212–8252). The Schauspielhaus is also home to the 20 or so private theater companies in the city. The city's small ballet company, the **Kölner Tanzforum** (☎ 0221/9514–6914), hosts an international festival every July.

NIGHTLIFE

Köln's nightlife is centered in three distinct areas: between the Alter Markt and Neumarkt in the Old Town; on Zulpicherstrasse; and around the Friesenplatz S-bahn station.

In summer head straight for the **Stadtgarten** (⊠ Venloerstr. 40, ☎ 0221/9529–9420) and sit in the Bier Garten for some good outdoor Gemütlichkeit. Any other time of year it is still worth a visit for its excellent jazz club that regularly brings class acts to the city. **Papa Joe's Biersalon** (⊠ Alter Markt 50–52, ☎ 0221/258–2132) is kind of kitschy but often has classic jazz and draws locals as well as tourists.

Many streets off the Hohenzollernring and Hohenstaufenring, particularly Roonstrasse, also provide a broad range of nightlife. **Das Ding** (⊠ Hohenstaufenring 30–34, ☎ 0221/246–348), literally, "the Thing," is a student club that is never empty, even on weeknights. The **Savoy Club** (⊠ Hohenstaufenring 25, ☎ 0221/969–2559) is devoted to house and techno. For the last word in disco experience, make for the **Alter Wartesaal** (⊠ Am Hauptbahnhof, Johannisstr. 11, ☎ 0221/912–8850) in the Hauptbahnhof on Friday or Saturday night. The old train-station waiting room has been turned into a concert hall and disco, where dancers swivel on ancient polished parquet and check their style in original mahogany-framed mirrors.

Shopping

A good shopping loop begins at **Wallrafplatz,** and continues clockwise down Hohe Strasse, Schildergasse, Neumarkt, Mittelstrasse, Hohenzollernring, Ehrenstrasse, Breite Strasse, Tunisstrasse, Minoritenstrasse, and then back to Wallrafplatz.

Hohe Strasse, south of the cathedral, is the main artery of Köln's huge pedestrian shopping zone. The area's stores, including many of the main

German department store chains—Kaufhof, Hertie, and Karstadt—are rich in quantity if not always in quality, and certainly a center of city life. Mittelstrasse and Hohe Strasse are best for German fashions and luxury goods. **Offermann's** (✉ Breite Str. 48-50, ☎ 0221/252–018) has a large selection of fine leather items and beautifully finished travel accessories.

Köln's most celebrated product is, of course, **eau de cologne**. In **Glock-engasse** (✉ No. 4711, ☎ 0221/925–0450) you can visit the house where the 18th-century Italian chemist Giovanni-Maria Farina first concocted it. The shop has extended its selection to include other scents in addition to 4711, but the original product remains the centerpiece, available in all sizes from a purse-size bottle to a container that holds a quart or so.

Aachen

70 km (43 mi) west of Köln.

At the center of Aachen, the characteristic *drei-Fenster* facades, three windows wide, give way to buildings dating from the days when Charlemagne made Aix-la-Chapelle (as it was then called) one of the great centers of the Holy Roman Empire. Roman legions had been drawn here for the healing properties of the sulfur springs emanating from the nearby Eifel Mountains. Charlemagne's father, Pepin the Short, also settled here to enjoy the waters that gave Bad Aachen—as the town is also known—its name; the waters continue to attract visitors today. But it was certainly Charlemagne who was responsible for the town's architectural wealth. After his coronation in Rome in 800, he spent more and more time in Aachen, building his spectacular palace and ruling his vast empire from within its walls. Aachen is now home to almost 30,000 students, keeping this beautiful old town a bustling center of activity. One-hour walking tours depart from the tourist information office weekends at 11, year-round, and weekdays at 2, from April through October. **English tours** can be set up by prior arrangement (☎ 0241/180–2960).

★ The stunning **Dom** (Cathedral) in Aachen, the "Chapelle" of the town's earlier name, remains the single greatest storehouse of Carolingian architecture in Europe. Though it was built over the course of 1,000 years and reflects architectural styles from the Middle Ages to the 19th century, its commanding image is the magnificent octagonal royal chapel, rising up two arched stories to end in the cap of the dome. It was this section, the heart of the church, that Charlemagne saw completed in AD 800. His bones now lie in the Gothic choir, in a golden shrine surrounded by wonderful carvings of saints. Another treasure is his marble throne. Charlemagne had to journey all the way to Rome for his coronation, but the next 32 Holy Roman emperors were crowned here in Aachen, and each marked the occasion by presenting a lavish gift to the cathedral. In the 12th century Barbarossa donated the great chandelier now hanging in the center of the imperial chapel; his grandson, Friedrich II, donated Charlemagne's shrine. Emperor Karl IV journeyed from Prague in the late 14th century for the sole purpose of commissioning a bust of Charlemagne for the cathedral; now on view in the treasury, the bust incorporates a piece of Charlemagne's skull. ✉ *Münsterpl.,* ☎ *0241/4770–9127.* ⊙ *Daily 7–7.* 🐾

★ The **Domschatzkammer** (Cathedral Treasury) houses sacred art from late antiquity and the Carolingian, Ottonian, and Hohenstaufen eras; highlights include the Cross of Lothair, the Bust of Charlemagne, and the Persephone Sarcophagus. ✉ *Am Domhof, entrance via Klosterg.,* ☎ *0241/ 4770–9127.* 🎫 *DM 5.* ⊙ *Mon. 10–1, Tues.–Sun. 10–6, Thurs. 10–9.*

The back of the **Rathaus** (Town Hall) is opposite the cathedral, across Katschhof Square. It was built beginning in the early 14th century on the site of the *Aula*, or "great hall," of Charlemagne's palace. Its first major official function was the coronation banquet of Emperor Karl IV in 1349, held in the great Gothic hall you can still see today (though this was largely rebuilt after the war). On the north wall of the building are statues of 50 emperors of the Holy Roman Empire. The greatest of them all, Charlemagne, stands in bronze atop the Kaiserbrunnen (Imperial Fountain) in the center of the market square. ⊠ *Marktpl.,* ☎ *0241/180–2960.* ⊠ *DM 3.* ⊙ *Daily 10–1 and 2–5.*

An old Aachen tradition that continues today is "taking the waters." The arcaded, neoclassical **Elisenbrunnen** (Elisa Fountain), built in 1822, is south of the cathedral. It contains two fountains with thermal drinking water. Experts agree that the spa waters here—the hottest north of the Alps—are effective in helping to cure a wide range of ailments. Drinking the sulfurous water in the approved manner can be unpleasant; but as you hold your nose and gulp away, you're emulating the likes of Dürer, Frederick the Great, and Charlemagne. In Dürer's time there were regular crackdowns on the orgiastic goings-on at the baths—a far cry from today's rather clinical atmosphere. You can try sitting in the spa waters at the **Kurbad Quellenhof** (⊠ Monheimsallee 52, ☎ 0241/180–2920; ⊠ DM 17) or at Aachen's newest spa, opened in the fall of 2000, the **Carolus-Thermen** (⊠ Stadtgarten/Passtr., ☎ 0241/180–2911).

Like many famous German spa towns, Aachen has its **Spielbank** (casino). It's housed in the porticoed former Kurhaus, on the parklike grounds fronting Monheimsallee and facing the Kurbad Quellenhof. Jacket and tie are required. Bring your passport for identification. ⊠ *Monheimsallee 44,* ☎ *0241/18080.* ⊠ *DM 5.* ⊙ *Mon.–Thurs. and Sun. 3 PM–2 AM, Fri. and Sat. 3 PM–3 AM.*

Aachen has its modern side as well—one of the world's most important art collectors, Peter Ludwig, has endowed two museums in his hometown. The **Ludwig Forum für Internationale Kunst** holds a portion of Ludwig's truly enormous collection of contemporary art and hosts traveling exhibits. ⊠ *Jülicher Str. 97–109,* ☎ *0241/18070.* ⊠ *DM 6.* ⊙ *Tues. and Thurs. 10–5, Wed. and Fri. 10–8, weekends 11–5.*

The **Suermont-Ludwig Museum** is devoted to classical painting up to the beginning of the 20th century. ⊠ *Wilhelmstr. 18,* ☎ *0241/479–800.* ⊠ *DM 6.* ⊙ *Tues., Thurs., and Fri. 11–7; Wed. 11–9; weekends 11–5.*

Dining and Lodging

$$$$ ✕ **Gala.** For the most elegant dining in Aachen, reserve a table at the
★ Gala restaurant adjoining the casino. Dark-paneled walls and original oil paintings make the mood discreetly classy; chef Roger Achterrath's cooking is regional, with nouvelle and creative touches. There is no ordering à la carte. The set menu (DM 175) includes wine. ⊠ *Monheimsallee 44,* ☎ *0241/153–013. Reservations essential. Jacket and tie. AE, DC, MC, V. Closed Sun. and Mon. No lunch.*

$$$ ✕ **La Becasse.** Sophisticated French nouvelle cuisine is offered in this upscale modern restaurant just outside the Old Town by the Westpark. Try the distinctively light calves' liver. ⊠ *Hanbrucherstr. 1,* ☎ *0241/74444. Reservations essential. Jacket and tie. AE, DC, MC, V. Closed Sun. No lunch Sat. and Mon.*

$$ ✕ **Der Postwagen.** This annex of the more upscale Ratskeller is worth a stop for the building alone, a half-timber medieval edifice at one corner of the old Rathaus. Sitting at one of the low wooden tables, surveying the marketplace through the wavy old glass, you can dine very respectably on solid German fare. If you really want to go local, try

Unser Puttes, a kind of blood sausage. ⊠ *Am Markt,* ☎ *0241/35001. AE, DC, MC, V.*

$ ✕ **Am Knipp.** At this historic old Aachen Bierstube, guests sit at low wooden tables next to the tile stove. Pewter pots and beer mugs hang from the rafters. ⊠ *Bergdriesch 3,* ☎ *0241/33168. No credit cards. Closed Tues.*

$$$$ ✕🏨 **Hotel Quellenhof.** Built during World War I as a country home
★   for the kaiser, this is one of Europe's grande dames: spacious, elegant, and formal. Reopened in 1999 after two years of remodeling, the rooms have high ceilings, a mix of conservative-style furniture, a walk-in baggage room, and huge, modern bathrooms. It has a flower-filled bistro called La Brasserie, and Orchidee (Orchid) is an oasis of Asian cuisine in northern Germany. The hotel is near the Kurpark and the casino, and guests have direct access by elevator to the thermal baths. ⊠ *Monheimsallee 52, D–52062,* ☎ *0241/91320,* 🖷 *0241/91100. 175 rooms, 2 suites. 2 restaurants, spa. AE, DC, MC, V.*

$$–$$$ 🏨 **Hotel Brülls am Dom.** In the historic heart of the city, this family-run hotel offers not only tradition and convenience but also considerable comfort. It's a short walk to nearly all the major attractions. ⊠ *Hühnermarkt, D–52062,* ☎ *0241/31704,* 🖷 *0241/404–326. 10 rooms. Restaurant. No credit cards.*

Nightlife and the Arts

Aachen has a municipal orchestra that gives regular concerts in the **Kongresszentrum Eurogress** (⊠ Monheimsallee 48, ☎ 0241/91310). The most activity in this town is concentrated around the market square and the Pontstrasse, a pedestrian street that radiates off of the square. Start out at Aachen's most popular bar, the **Dom Keller** (⊠ Hof 1, ☎ 0241/34265), to mingle in low light over old wooden tables with locals of all ages. Then head over to the Irish pub **Wild Rover** (⊠ Hirschgraben 13, ☎ 0241/35453) which serves Guinness on tap to live music every night starting at 9:30.

Shopping

Don't leave Aachen without stocking up on the traditional local gingerbread, *Aachener Printen.* Most bakeries in town offer assortments. Some of the best are at the **Alte Aachener Kaffeestuben,** also known as the *Konditorei van den Daele* (⊠ Büchel 18, ☎ 0241/35724). The store-café is worth a visit for its atmosphere and tempting aromas, whether or not you intend to buy anything. It also ships goods.

Düsseldorf

47 km (29 mi) north of Köln.

At first glance, Düsseldorf may suffer by comparison to Köln's remarkable skyline, but the elegant city has more than enough charm to justify including it on a Rhineland itinerary. It has gained a reputation for being the richest city in Germany, with an extravagant lifestyle that epitomizes the economic success of postwar Germany. Although 80% of prewar Düsseldorf was destroyed in World War II, the city has since been more or less rebuilt from the ground up—in part re-creating landmarks of long ago and restoring a medieval riverside quarter.

Hard as it may be to believe, this dynamic city at the confluence of the Rivers Rhine and Düssel started as a small fishing town. The name means "village on the Düssel," but obviously this Dorf is a village no more. Raised expressways speed traffic past towering glass-and-steel structures; within them, glass-enclosed shopping malls showcase the fanciest outfits, furs, jewelry, and leather goods that famous designers can create and those with plenty of money can buy.

★ The **Königsallee,** the main shopping avenue, is the epitome of Düssel-dorf affluence; it's lined with the crème de la crème of designer bou-tiques and stores. Known as the Kö, this wide, double boulevard is divided by an ornamental waterway that is actually a part of the River Düssel. Rows of chestnut trees line the Kö, shading a string of side-walk cafés. Beyond the Triton Fountain, at the street's north end, be-gins a series of parks and gardens. In these patches of green you can sense a joie de vivre hardly expected in a city devoted to big business.

The lovely **Hofgarten Park,** once the garden of the elector's palace, is reached by heading north to Corneliusplatz. Laid out in 1770 and com-pleted 30 years later, the Hofgarten is an oasis of greenery at the heart of downtown and a focal point for Düsseldorf culture.

The baroque **Schloss Jägerhof,** at the far-east edge of the Hofgarten, is more a combination town house and country lodge than a castle. It houses the **Goethe Museum,** featuring original manuscripts, first edi-tions, personal correspondence, and other memorabilia of Germany's greatest writer. ⊠ *Jacobistr. 2,* ☎ *0211/899–6262.* ⊑ *DM 4.* ۞ *Tues.–Fri. and Sun. 11–5, Sat. 1–5.*

The **Kunstmuseum Düsseldorf im Ehrenhof** (Museum of Fine Arts) lies at the northern extremity of the Hofgarten, close to the Rhine. It fea-tures a collection of paintings that run the gamut from Rubens, Goya, Tintoretto, and Cranach the Elder to the romantic Düsseldorf School and such modern German expressionists as Beckmann, Kirchner, Nolde, Macke, and Kandinsky. ⊠ *Ehrenhof 5,* ☎ *0211/899–2460.* ⊑ *DM 5.* ۞ *Tues.–Sun. 11–6.*

The **Kunstsammlung Nordrhein-Westfalen** (North Rhineland–Westphalia Art Collection) displays a dazzling array of 20th-century classic mod-ern paintings, including works by Bonnard, Braque, Matisse, Léger, Johns, and Pollock; there are also many by Paul Klee because the Swiss painter lived in Düsseldorf for a time and taught at the National Academy of Art. The collection is across the street from the city opera house. ⊠ *Grabbepl. 5,* ☎ *0211/83810.* ⊑ *DM 12.* ۞ *Tues.–Sun. 10–6, Fri. 10–8.*

The restored **Altstadt** (Old Town) faces the Rhine. Narrow alleys thread their way to some 200 restaurants and taverns offering a wide range of foreign and local cuisines, all crowded into the 1-square-km (½-square-mi) area between the Rhine and Heine Allee. Occasionally you can still see the *Radschläger,* young boys who demonstrate their cartwheeling abilities, a Düsseldorf tradition, for the admiration (and tips) of visitors.

A plaque at **Bolkerstrasse 53** indicates where poet Heinrich Heine was born in 1797. The **Heinrich Heine Institute** has a museum and an archive of significant manuscripts. Part of the complex was once the residence of the composer Robert Schumann. ⊠ *Bilkerstr. 12–14,* ☎ *0211/899–2902.* ⊑ *DM 4.* ۞ *Tues.–Fri. 11–5, Sat. 1–5.*

The traffic-free cobblestone streets of the Old Town lead to **Burgplatz** (Castle Square). The 13th-century **Schlossturm** (Castle Tower) there is all that remains of the castle built by the de Berg family, which founded Düsseldorf. The tower also houses the **Schiffahrt Museum,** which charts 2,000 years of Rhine boatbuilding and navigation. ⊠ *Burgpl. 30,* ☎ *0211/899–4195.* ⊑ *DM 3.* ۞ *Wed. and Sat. 2–6, Sun. 11–6.*

The Gothic **St. Lambertus** (St. Lambertus Church) is near Burgplatz, on Stiftsplatz. Its spire became distorted because unseasoned wood was used in its construction. The Vatican elevated the 14th-century brick church to a basilica minor (small cathedral) in 1974 in recognition of its role in church history. Built in the 13th century, with additions from 1394, St. Lambertus contains the tomb of William the Rich and a graceful late-Gothic tabernacle.

Dining and Lodging

$$$$ ✕ **Im Schiffchen.** Although it's a bit out of the way, dining in one of
★   Germany's best restaurants makes it worth a trip. This is grande luxe, with cooking that's a fine art. The restaurant Aalschokker, on the ground floor, features local specialties created by the same chef but at lower prices. ⊠ *Kaiserwerther Markt 9,* ☎ *0211/401–050 or 0211/401–948. Reservations essential. Jacket and tie. AE, DC, MC, V. Closed Sun. and Mon. No lunch.*

$$$$ ✕ **Weinhaus Tante Anna.** This charming restaurant is furnished with antiques; the cuisine presents another facet of German tradition, showing that there's a lot more to the country's cooking than the standard platters of wurst and sauerkraut. The wine selection is particularly fine. ⊠ *Andreasstr. 2,* ☎ *0211/131–163. AE, DC, MC, V. Closed Sun. No lunch.*

$ ✕ **Zum Uerige.** Among beer buffs, Düsseldorf is famous for its *Altbier,* so called because of the old-fashioned brewing method still used. The mellow and malty copper-color brew is produced by eight breweries in town. This tavern provides the perfect atmosphere for drinking it. The beer is poured straight out of polished oak barrels and served by bustling waiters in long blue aprons. ⊠ *Bergerstr. 1,* ☎ *0211/866–990. No credit cards.*

$$$$ 🏨 **Steigenberger Parkhotel.** Miraculously quiet despite its central lo-
★   cation on the edge of the Hofgarten and at the beginning of the Königsallee, this old hotel is anything but stodgy. The soaring ceilings add to the spaciousness of the guest rooms, each individually decorated in a restrained, elegant style. The pampering continues at the breakfast buffet, served in the Menuette restaurant, where champagne and smoked salmon are appropriate starters for a shopping expedition on the Kö. ⊠ *Corneliuspl. 1, D–40213,* ☎ *0211/13810,* FAX *0211/138–1592. 123 rooms, 12 suites. Restaurant, 2 bars. AE, DC, MC, V.* ✆

$$$ 🏨 **Günnewig Hotel Esplanade.** This small, modern hotel has an exceptionally quiet, leafy location still close to the action. From the inviting lobby to the attractive decor in the rooms, the ambience here is one of intimacy. ⊠ *Fürstenpl. 17, D–40215,* ☎ *0211/386–850,* FAX *0211/374–032. 80 rooms, 2 suites. Pool, sauna. AE, DC, MC, V.* ✆

$$ 🏨 **Hotel Cristallo.** Clearly someone took great pains with the slightly tacky but nonetheless striking decor of this well-located, midprice hotel. If you like gilt angels in the breakfast room, this is the place for you. The hotel is centrally located near the Kö and has pleasant, eclectically furnished rooms, with comfortable sofas and color TVs even in singles. ⊠ *Schadowpl. 7,* ☎ *0211/84525,* FAX *0211/322–632. 35 rooms. AE, DC, MC, V.*

Nightlife and the Arts

Düsseldorf, once home to Mendelssohn, Schumann, and Brahms, has the finest concert hall in Germany after Berlin's Philharmonie: the **Tonhalle** (⊠ Ehrenhof 41, ☎ 0211/899–6123), a former planetarium on the edge of the Hofgarten. It's the home of the Düsseldorfer Symphoniker, which play from September to mid-June. **Deutsche Oper am Rhein** (⊠ Heinrich Heine Allee 16a, ☎ 0211/890–8378) showcases the city's highly regarded opera company and ballet troupe.

Düsseldorf nightlife is mostly concentrated in the **Altstadt,** a landscape of pubs, discotheques, ancient restored brewery houses, and jazz clubs in the vicinity of the Marktplatz and along cobblestone streets named Bolker, Kurze, Flinger, and Mühlen. These places may be crowded, but some are very atmospheric. A more sophisticated mood is set in the modern part of the city. **Bei Tino** (⊠ Königsallee 21) is a fashionable upscale bar. **Front Page** (⊠ Mannesman Ufer) is a slick watering hole. **Sam's West,** on the Kö, is the most popular dance club.

Shopping

The east side of the **Königsallee** is lined with some of Germany's trendiest boutiques, grandest jewelers, and most extravagant furriers. **Kö Center** (⊠ Königsallee 30), an upscale shopping arcade, features the most famous names in fashion, from Chanel to Louis Vuitton. **Kö Galerie** (⊠ Königsallee 60) has trendy fashion boutiques, where you can find the creations of local designers such as Ute Raasch. Kö Galerie also includes the Mövenpick restaurant on its luxurious two-story premises. **Schadow Arcade** (⊠ Off Schadowpl., at the end of the Kö Galerie) caters to normal budgets, with such stores as Hennes and Mauritz and Habitat. The area around Hohe Strasse has antiques. Try **Arts Decoratifs** (⊠ Hohe Str. 28, ☎ 0211/324–553) for Art Deco furniture, tableware, and knickknacks.

THE RHINELAND A TO Z

Arriving and Departing

By Plane

The Rhineland is served by three international airports: Frankfurt, Düsseldorf, and Köln-Bonn. Bus and rail lines connect each airport with its respective downtown area and provide rapid access to the rest of the region. The **Luxembourg Findel International Airport** (a 30-minute drive from Trier) provides the best access to the upper Mosel River Valley.

Getting Around

By Bike

The Mosel Valley, with its small hamlets lining the riverbanks, is an excellent area for biking. The train stations in Trier and Cochem rent bikes.

By Boat

No visit to the Rhineland is complete without at least one river cruise, and there are many options from which to choose here (☞ Guided Tours *in* Contacts and Resources, *below*). Rowboats and canoes can be rented at most Rhine and Mosel river resorts. Contact local tourist offices (☞ Visitor Information, *below*) for more information.

By Car

The autobahns and other highways of the Rhineland are busy, so allow plenty of time for driving. Frankfurt is 126 km (78 mi) from Koblenz, 175 km (109 mi) from Bonn, 190 km (118 mi) from Köln, and 230 km (143 mi) from Düsseldorf (the A–3 links Frankfurt with Köln and Düsseldorf and passes near Koblenz and Bonn). The most spectacular stretch of the Rhineland is along the Middle Rhine, between Mainz and Koblenz. Highways hug the river on each bank (B–42 on the north/eastern side, and B–9 on the south/western side), and car ferries crisscross the Rhine at many points.

By Train

InterCity and EuroCity expresses connect all the cities and towns of the area. Hourly InterCity routes run between Düsseldorf, Köln, Bonn, and Mainz, with most services extending as far south as Munich and as far north as Hamburg. The Mainz–Bonn route runs beside the Rhine, between the river and the vine-covered heights, offering spectacular views all the way. The city transportation networks of Bonn,

Köln, and Düsseldorf are linked by S-bahn (for information contact the **Kölner Verkehrs-Betriebe (KVB)** (☎ 0221/547–3333).

Contacts and Resources

Car Rentals

Each of the companies below has a rental office at the Frankfurt Airport. Avis, Europcar, and Hertz have offices at the Luxembourg Airport as well. Europcar and Sixt have offices at Wiesbaden's main train station. **Avis** (✉ Römerstr. 4, Bonn, ☎ 0228/631–433; ✉ Berliner Allee 32, Düsseldorf, ☎ 0211/865–6220; ✉ Schmidtstr. 39, Frankfurt/Main, ☎ 069/730–111; ✉ Andernacher Str. 190–192, Koblenz, ☎ 0261/800–366; ✉ Herzogenbuscher Str. 31, Trier, ☎ 0651/270–770; ✉ Dotzheimer Str., Wiesbaden, ☎ 0611/449–030).

Europcar (✉ Potsdammer Pl. 7, Bonn, ☎ 0228/652–961; ✉ Burgunderstr. 40, Düsseldorf, ☎ 0211/950–980; ✉ Frankfurt Airport Hall A, arrival level, Frankfurt/Main, ☎ 069/697–970; ✉ Andernacher Str. 199, Koblenz, ☎ 0261/889–180; ✉ Köln-Bonn Airport, Köln, ☎ 02203/402–555; ✉ Wasserweg 16, Trier, ☎ 0651/146–540).

Hertz (✉ Juelicherstr. 250, Aachen, ☎ 0241/162–686; ✉ Adenauerallee 216, Bonn, ☎ 0228/223–047; ✉ Immermannstr. 65, Düsseldorf, ☎ 0211/357–025; ✉ Otto-Shönhagen-Str. 3, Koblenz, ☎ 0261/8450; ✉ Bismarckstr. 19–21, Köln, ☎ 0221/515–084; ✉ Gutleutstr. 87, Frankfurt/Main, ☎ 069/2425–2627; ✉ Loeb Str. 4, Trier, ☎ 0651/23137).

Sixt (✉ Tilde-Klose-Weg 6, Düsseldorf, ☎ 0211/471–310; ✉ Friedrich-Mohr-Str. 10A, Koblenz, ☎ 0261/86095; ✉ Eurener Str. 5, Trier, ☎ 0651/827–950).

Consulates

British General Consulate (✉ Yorckstr. 19, D–40476 Düsseldorf, ☎ 0228/94480).

Canadian Consulate (✉ Benratherstr. 8, D–40213 Düsseldorf, ☎ 0211/172–170).

Guided Tours

BOAT TRIPS

Trips along the Rhine and Mosel range in length from a few hours to days or even a week or more. One of the major lines is **Köln-Düsseldorfer Rheinschiffahrt** (☞ Cruise Travel *in* Smart Travel Tips A to Z). Ships travel the Rhine between Köln and Mainz, and the Mosel from Koblenz to Cochem, daily from Easter to late October. A day ticket is good for up to four trips in one day, or you can buy tickets for single destinations. The KD also offers various cruises on ships with cabins, which travel to destinations along the entire length of the Rhine and up the Mosel and range in length from 2 to 14 days. Cruises on the Mosel run from Köln, Frankfurt, and Würzburg to Trier, and from Trier to Würzburg. One special package is a weeklong "floating wine seminar" aboard the pride of its fleet, the motor ship *Heinrich Heine*, which makes stops at vineyards on both the Mosel and Rhine rivers and ends in Breisach, Germany.

From March through November the **Hebel-Line** (☎ 06742/2420) in Boppard cruises the Lorelei Valley; night cruises have music and dancing. Trips along the Mosel are also available through **Mosel-Personenschiffahrt Bernkastel-Kues** (✉ Goldbachstr. 52, Bernkastel-Kues, ☎ 06531/8222).

Several shipping companies in Koblenz organize short "castle cruises" from Easter through September. Two boats, the *Undine* and the *Marksburg*, ply the Rhine between Koblenz and Boppard, passing 10 castles during the 75-minute, one-way voyage. Details and reservations are available from **Personenschiffahrt Merkelbach** (✉ Emserstr. 87, Koblenz-Pfaffendorf, ☎ 0261/76810). **Personenschiffahrt Josef Vomfell** (✉ Koblenzer Str. 64, Spay am Rhein, ☎ 02628/2431) organizes cruises on the Middle Rhine. The Koblenz operator **Rhein und Moselschiffahrt Gerhard Collee-Holzenbein** (✉ Rheinzollstr. 4, ☎ 0261/37744) runs day cruises as far as Rüdesheim on the Rhine and Cochem on the Mosel.

From Köln three shipping companies operate boat tours on the Rhine (all tours leave from the landing stages near the Hohenzollern Brücke, a short walk from the cathedral). The **Köln-Düsseldorfer** line (☞ *above*) has hourly trips starting at 10:30 daily, April through October. The **KölnTourist Personenschiffahrt am Dom** (✉ Konrad Adenauer-Ufer, ☎ 0221/121–714) has daily departures every 45 minutes starting at 10, April through September. The **Dampfschiffahrt Colonia** (✉ Lintg. 18, ☎ 0221/257–4225) has daily departures every 45 minutes beginning at 10, April through October.

BUS TOURS

Limousine Travel Service (✉ Wiesenhüttenpl. 39, Frankfurt/Main, ☎ 069/230–492) has a daily bus trip from Frankfurt to Rhine wine country. From Rüdesheim travel continues by boat to St. Goarhausen; return to Frankfurt is by bus. The DM 120 fee includes lunch and a wine tasting.

Bus trips into the Köln countryside (to the Eifel Hills, the Ahr Valley, and the Westerwald) are organized by several city travel agencies. Leading tour operators are: **Globus Reisen** (✉ Hohenzollernring 86, ☎ 0221/912–8270), **Univers-Reisen** (✉ Am Rinkenpfuhl 57, ☎ 0221/209–020), and **Siebert's Bustouristik** (✉ Venloerstr. 411, ☎ 0221/541–204).

CITY TOURS

City tours of **Bonn** start from the tourist office. Two-hour and three-hour tours for DM 22 are conducted April–October, Tuesday–Sunday, and November–March, Saturday only. Call ahead to check times for tours in English.

The **Koblenz** tourist office has guided tours on Saturday at 2:30, May through October, departing from the "i-Punkt" opposite the KD Rhine steamer landing stage.

Bus tours of **Köln** leave from outside the tourist office, opposite the main entrance to the cathedral, hourly 10–3, April–October, and at 11 and 2, November–April. The tour lasts two hours and costs DM 26; it is conducted in English and German. A two-hour Köln walking tour is available by prior arrangement with the tourist office. Most central hotels offer a special tourist package, the KölnTourismus Card, which entitles you to a sightseeing tour, admission to all the city's museums, free city bus and tram travel, and other reductions. The package costs DM 30.

The **Trier** tourist office offers two-hour daily walking tours from April through October at 11 and 2 in German, and from May through October at 1:30 in English (DM 10).

Bilingual tours of **Wiesbaden** depart from the bus stop in front of the Staatstheater on Kurhausplatz. The bus tour (DM 20) is offered year-round, Wednesday at 2:30 and Saturday at 2. The walking tour (DM 10) is conducted April through October, Saturday at 10 (November through March, the first and third Saturday).

Travel Agencies

American Express (✉ Königs-Allee 98a, D–40215 Düsseldorf, ☎ 0211/386–910; ✉ Burgmauer 14, D–50667 Köln, ☎ 0221/925–9010).

Visitor Information

The Rhineland regional tourist office, **Rheinland-Pfalz-Information** (⊠ Löhrstr. 103–105, D–56068 Koblenz, ☎ 0261/915–200, FAX 0261/915–2040), provides general information on the entire region.

Aachen (⊠ Aachen Tourist Service, Friedrich-Wilhelm-Pl., Postfach 2007, D–52022, ☎ 0241/180–2960, ✇). **Bernkastel-Kues** (⊠ Tourist-Information, Gestade 5, D–54470, ☎ 06531/402–324, FAX 06531/7953). **Bingen** (⊠ Tourist-Information, Rheinkai 21, D–55411, ☎ 06721/16275). **Bonn** (⊠ Bonn Information, Windeckstr. 2 am Münsterpl., D–53111, ☎ 0228/775–000, ✇). **Boppard** (⊠ Tourist-Information, Marktpl., D–56154, ☎ 06742/3888, FAX 06742/81402). **Cochem** (⊠ Tourist-Information, Endertpl. 1, D–56812, ☎ 02671/60040, FAX 02671/600–444). **Düsseldorf** (⊠ Verkehrsverein, Konrad Adenauer Pl. 12, D–40210, ☎ 0211/172–020, ✇). **Koblenz** (⊠ Tourist-Information, Löhrstr. 141, D–56068, ☎ 0261/31304, FAX 0261/100–4388). **Köln** (⊠ KölnTourismus Office, Unter Fettenhenen 19, D–50667, ☎ 0221/2212–3345, ✇). **Rüdesheim** (⊠ Städtisches Verkehrsamt, Rheinstr. 16, D–65385, ☎ 06722/19433, FAX 06722/3485). **Trier** (⊠ Tourist-Information, An der Porta Nigra, D–54290, ☎ 0651/978–080, FAX 0651/44759). **Wiesbaden** (⊠ Tourist Information, Marktstr. 6, D–65183, ☎ 0611/172–9780, FAX 0611/172–9798).

12 THE FAIRY-TALE ROAD

If you're in search of Sleeping Beauty, the Pied Piper, and Rumpelstiltskin, the Fairy-Tale Road is the place to look. One of Germany's special tour routes, it leads through the landscapes that inspired the Brothers Grimm. From its start in Hanau, just east of Frankfurt, to its end in Bremen, 600 km (370 mi) north, it passes dozens of picturesque towns full of half-timber houses and guarded by castles.

Updated by
Ted Shoemaker

T HE FAIRY-TALE ROAD, or Märchenstrasse, leads deep into the heart of the country, as well as the German character. It begins just 20 minutes east of Frankfurt in the town of Hanau, and from there wends its way northward some 600 km (about 370 mi), mainly through the states of Hesse and Lower Saxony, following the Fulda and Weser rivers and traversing a countryside as beguiling as any in Europe.

One of the most recent of Germany's designated tour routes, the Fairy-Tale Road doesn't have the glamour of the Romantic Road, but it also doesn't have the crowds and commercialism. It's perhaps even a route more in tune with romantics. Fairy tales come to life in forgotten villages where black cats snooze in the windows of half-timber houses, in castles surrounded by ancient forests where wild boar snort at timid deer, and in misty valleys where the silence of centuries is broken only by the splash of a ferryman's oar. The meandering, progressive path seems to travel backward in time, into the reaches of childhood, imagination, and the German folk consciousness, to visit old-world settings steeped in legend and fantasy.

This part of Germany shaped the lives and imaginations of the two most famous chroniclers of German folk history and tradition, the Brothers Grimm. From their childhood, the Grimms were enthralled by tales of enchantment, of kings and queens, of golden-haired princesses saved from disaster by stalwart princes—folk tales, myths, epics, and legends that dealt with magic and wicked witches, predatory stepmothers, and a supporting cast of goblins and wizards.

The Grimms did not invent these tales; they were in the public domain long before the brothers began collecting them. The Grimms' devotion to fairy tales could be considered merely a sideline to their main careers. Jacob (1785–1863) was a linguist who formulated Grimm's Law, an explanation of how German, along with Greek and Latin, evolved from an ancestral Indo-European language. Wilhelm (1786–1859) was a literary scholar and critic. Together they spent most of their energies compiling a massive dictionary of the German language. But it is as the authors of the *Kinder und Hausmärchen* (Children's and Household Tales), a work that has been called the best-known book after the Bible, that they are remembered. In 1812 the Grimms introduced the world to some 200 of their favorite stories, with a cast of characters that included Cinderella, Hansel and Gretel, Little Red Riding Hood, Rapunzel, Rumpelstiltskin, Sleeping Beauty, Snow White, and other unforgettable stars of the world of make-believe.

The degree to which the brothers have influenced the world's concept of fairy tales is remarkable, matched only by *The Arabian Nights*. But it would be a mistake to imagine them as kindly, bewhiskered old gents telling stories in their rose-clad cottage for the pleasure of village children. They were serious and successful academics, with interests ranging far beyond what we may think of as amusements for children. Their stories probe deep into the German psyche and deal with far more complex emotions than is suggested by the occasional happily-ever-after endings.

The zigzag course detailed in this chapter follows the spine of Fairy-Tale country and includes a number of side trips and detours. Although the route is best explored by car, most of the attractions along its meandering path can also be reached by train.

Pleasures and Pastimes

Dining

A specialty of Northern Hesse is sausages with *Beulches,* made from potato balls, leeks, and black pudding. *Lauterbacher Strolch* is a special Camembert named after the little fellow who lost his sock in that town. *Weck,* which is local dialect for heavily spiced pork, appears either as *Musterweck,* served on a roll, or as *Weckewerk,* a frying-pan concoction with white bread. Heading north into Lower Saxony you'll encounter the ever-popular *Speckkuchen,* a heavy and filling onion tart. Another favorite main course is *Pfefferpothast,* a sort of heavily browned goulash with lots of pepper. The "hast" at the end of the name is from the old German word *Harst,* meaning "roasting pan." Trout and eels are common in the rivers and streams around Hameln, and by the time you reach Bremen, North German cuisine has taken over the menu. *Aalsuppe grün,* eel soup seasoned with dozens of herbs, is a must in summer, as the hearty *Grünkohl mit Pinkel,* a cabbage dish with sausage, bacon, and cured pork is in winter. And be sure to try the coffee. Fifty percent of the coffee served in Germany comes from beans roasted in Bremen. The city has been producing the stuff since 1673 and knows just how to serve it in *gemütlich* surroundings.

CATEGORY	COST*
$$$$	over DM 90
$$$	DM 55–DM 90
$$	DM 35–DM 55
$	under DM 35

per person for a three-course meal, including tax and excluding drinks and service charge

Golf

There are golf courses at Bad Orb, Bad Pyrmont, Bremen, Fulda, Göttingen, Hanau, Kassel, and Polle-Holzminden; guests are welcome at all locations (provided they can produce a handicap from their local clubs). The courses at Hanau (on the former hunting grounds at Wilhelmsbad) and Kassel (high above the city on the edge of Wilhelmshöhe Park) are particularly attractive. At Schloss Schwöbber, near Hameln, golfers tee off on the extensive castle grounds.

Hiking

The hills and forests between Hanau and Hameln are a hiker's paradise. The valleys of the Fulda, Werra, and Weser rivers make enchanting walking country, with ancient waterside inns positioned along the way. Another hiking route runs from Hannoversch-Münden, in the south, to Porta-Westfalica, where the Weser River breaks through the last range of North German hills and into the plain of Lower Saxony.

Horseback Riding

This part of Germany is horse country, and most resorts have riding stables. There are large and well-equipped equestrian centers at Löwensen, near Bad Pyrmont, and Hameln.

Lodging

Make reservations well in advance if you plan to visit during the summer. Though it's one of the less-traveled tourist routes in Germany, the main points of the Fairy-Tale Road are popular. Hannover is particularly busy during trade fair times.

CATEGORY	COST*
$$$$	over DM 250
$$$	DM 175–DM 250
$$	DM 125–DM 175
$	under DM 125

All prices are for two people in a double room, excluding service charge.

Water Sports

Great canoeing and motorboating can be enjoyed on the Fulda, Weser, and Werra rivers.

Exploring the Fairy-Tale Road

This isn't a route for travelers in a hurry. The road extends about half the length of Germany, from the banks of the Main River, which marks the border between northern and southern Germany, to the North Sea ports of Bremen and Bremerhaven. The diverse regions have been linked together for the benefit of tourism—to highlight the region's connection with the Grimm brothers and their stories. Some towns on the journey—Bremerhaven and Hanau, for example—are modern, while others, such as Steinau an der Strasse, Hannoversch-Münden, and Hameln, might have stepped right out of a Grimm story.

Numbers in the text correspond to numbers in the margin and on the Fairy-Tale Road map.

Great Itineraries

The itineraries below assume you'll be starting off from Frankfurt, Germany's transportation hub. You could also approach the Fairy-Tale Road from Hamburg in the north.

IF YOU HAVE 3 DAYS

You won't get much farther than the first stretch of the route, but that's enough for an introduction to the influence of the region on the Grimm brothers. Skip **Hanau** ① altogether and begin with **Schloss Philippsruhe,** the oldest French-style baroque palace east of the Rhine, and the spa town of **Wilhelmsbad** ②, where European royalty and aristocrats once took the waters. Make 🔀 **Gelnhausen** ③ your next stop, for a visit to the remains of Barbarossa's greatest castle. Plan an overnight stay at the **Romantisches Hotel Burg Mühle** or at least dine in its restaurant. Devote your second day to exploring **Steinau an der Strasse** ④, where the Grimm brothers spent much of their childhood, and then continue on to 🔀 **Fulda** ⑤, which has an impressive bishop's palace and cathedral.

IF YOU HAVE 5 DAYS

Follow the itinerary described above but include a short stop in **Hanau** ①. On your third day proceed north of Fulda, calling at the medieval towns of **Lauterbach** and **Alsfeld,** both of which are perfect settings for Grimm tales. Spend the night in 🔀 **Kassel** ⑦ and try to catch the sunset from the heights of the Wilhelmshöhe. On the fourth day, traverse the valley of the Fulda River to where it meets the Weser, at **Hannoversch-Münden** ⑧, which claimed a place on geographer Alexander von Humboldt's list of the world's most beautiful towns. Follow the lazily winding Weser northward now, making a short detour to **Göttingen** ⑨ for lunch in one of the student taverns in this busy university city. Try to fit in an overnight stay at one of Germany's most romantic hotels, Sleeping Beauty's Castle, the 🔀 **Sababurg** ⑩, half hidden in the depths of the densely wooded Reinhardswald. On the fifth day return to the Weser River valley road and find time for stops at **Bad Karlshafen** ⑪, **Höxter** ⑫, and **Bodenwerder** ⑬ to explore their streets of half-timber houses, examples of the Weser Renaissance style of building. End your trip at 🔀 **Hameln** ⑭, the Pied Piper's town.

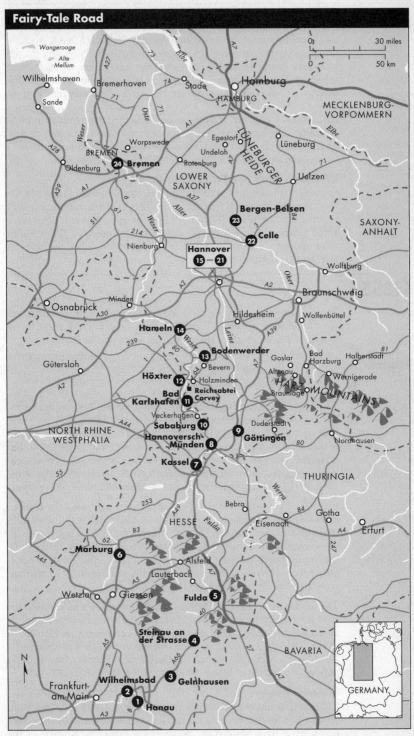

After the five-day itinerary described above, leave the Fairy-Tale Road at Hameln for a detour to 🔤 **Hannover** ⑮–㉑, which has a magnificent royal park. An overnight stay in Hannover will give you the opportunity to enjoy some nightlife after the tranquillity of much of the Weser Valley route. Or you can postpone that amusement until 🔤 **Bremen** ㉔, 110 km (68 mi) northwest. Bremen is the northernmost frontier of the Grimm brothers' influence, represented by several statues of the donkey, dog, cat, and rooster of the Bremen town musicians fable. It would be a shame to travel all this way without venturing the final 66 km (40 mi) to the seaport of **Bremerhaven** ㉕, which has Germany's largest maritime museum, the Deutsches Schiffahrtsmuseum.

When to Tour the Fairy-Tale Road

Summer is the ideal time to travel through this varied landscape, although in spring you'll find the river valleys carpeted in the season's first flowers, while in fall the sleepy current of the Weser is often blanketed in mist; both sights linger in the mind. Travel the Weser Valley road early in the morning or late in the afternoon, when the light has a softening touch on the river.

HESSE

The first portion of the Fairy-Tale Road, from Hanau to Kassel, lies within the state of Hesse. Frankfurt, the gateway to the state, is less than a half hour south of the road's starting point in Hanau.

Hanau

❶ *16 km (10 mi) east of Frankfurt.*

The Fairy-Tale Road begins in "once upon a time" fashion at Hanau, the town where the brothers were born: Jacob in 1785, Wilhelm a year later. Although Grimm fans will want to start their pilgrimage here, Hanau is now a traffic-congested suburb of Frankfurt, with post–World War II buildings that are not particularly attractive. Hanau was almost completely obliterated by wartime bombing raids, and there's little of the Altstadt (Old Town) that the Grimm brothers would recognize now.

Hanau's main attraction can be reached only on foot—the **Nationaldenkmal Brüder Grimm** (Brothers Grimm Memorial) in the Neustädter Marktplatz. The bronze memorial, erected in 1898, is a larger-than-life-size statue of the brothers, one seated, the other leaning on his chair, the two of them pondering an open book—a fitting pose for these scholars who unearthed so many medieval myths and legends, earning their reputation as the fathers of the fairy tale.

The solid bulk of Hanau's 18th-century **Rathaus** (town hall) stands behind the Grimm brothers statue. Every day at noon its bells play tribute to another of the city's famous sons, the composer Paul Hindemith (1895–1963), by chiming out one of his canons. On Wednesday and Saturday mornings the Rathaus is the backdrop for the largest street market in the state of Hesse. ⊠ *Marktpl. 14,* ☎ *06181/277–515.*

The **Altes Rathaus** (Old Town Hall), behind the Rathaus, dominates a corner that has been faithfully reconstructed. This handsome 16th-century Renaissance building has two half-timber upper stories weighted down by a steep slate roof. Today it's a museum. Known as the **Deutsches Goldschmiedehaus** (German Goldsmiths' House), it has both permanent and temporary exhibitions of the craft, contemporary and historical, of the goldsmith and silversmith. ⊠ *Altstädter Markt 6,* ☎ *06181/295–430.* 🎟 *Free.* ⊙ *Tues.–Sun. 10–noon and 2–5.*

OFF THE
BEATEN PATH

SCHLOSS PHILIPPSRUHE (Philippsruhe Palace) – This baroque palace on the bank of the Main River in the suburb of Kesselstadt (Bus 1 or 10 will take you there in 10 minutes) has much more than Grimm exhibits to offer. Philippsruhe might remind you of Versailles, although its French-trained architect, Julius Ludwig Rothweil, planned it along the lines of another palace in the Paris area, the much smaller Clagny Palace. Philippsruhe—as its name, Philipp's Rest," suggests—was built for Count Philipp Reinhard von Hanau, who laid the cornerstone in 1701. He didn't enjoy its riverside peace for long, however; he died less than three months after moving in. During the first weekend of September the people of Hanau crowd the palace grounds at a magnificent party commemorating the rebuilding of their war-ravaged town. Historical Hanau treasures, including a priceless collection of faience, are on display in the palace museum, as are exhibits of 17th- to 19th-century paintings, 19th- and early 20th-century industry, and cardboard toy theaters popular in the 19th century. A café with a terrace overlooks the Main.

In the early 19th century, following the withdrawal of the French from Hanau, the original formal gardens were replanned as an informal, English-style park. The contrast between the formal palace and informal wooded grounds is striking. Pause to study the entrance gate; its gilding was the work of Parisian masters. ⊠ *Schloss Philippsruhe, Kesselstadt,* ☎ *06181/295–516.* ⊇ *DM 3.* ☉ *Tues.–Sun. 11–6.*

Wilhelmsbad

② *3 km (2 mi) west of Hanau, 14 km (9 mi) east of Frankfurt.*

Just north of Schloss Philippsruhe and a short bus ride from the center of Hanau is the spa city of Wilhelmsbad. It was built at the end of the 18th century by Crown Prince Wilhelm von Hessen-Kassel at the site where two peasant women, out gathering herbs, discovered mineral springs. For a few decades Wilhelmsbad rivaled Baden-Baden as Germany's premier spa and fashionable playground. Then, about 100 years ago, the springs dried up, the casino closed, and Europe's wealthy and titled looked for other amusements. But this is still Grimm fairy-tale land, and Wilhelmsbad, the Sleeping Beauty–like spa, awoke from its slumber in the 1960s to become a rejuvenated resort. Today you'll find baroque buildings and bathhouses; informal, English-style parkland; riding stables; five taverns and restaurants; and one of Germany's loveliest golf courses laid out where the leisure classes once hunted pheasants.

The spa's Arkadenbau (arcade) contains the **Hessisches Puppenmuseum** (Hesse Doll Museum), one of Germany's largest doll museums, with examples dating back 2,000 years. ⊠ *Parkpromenade 4,* ☎ *06181/ 86212.* ⊇ *DM 5.* ☉ *Tues.–Sun. 10–noon and 2–5.*

Dining and Lodging

$$$ ╳☱ **Golfhotel.** An occasional "fore" heard from the neighboring golf course or bird songs coming from the backyard woods are the only sounds likely to disturb you at this rural retreat on the edge of the Wilhelmsbad park. Golfers love the hotel, but nonsporting types also feel at home, relaxing at the friendly bar or, in warm weather, on the outside terrace (overlooking the golf links, of course). The hotel's da Enzo restaurant serves excellent Italian cuisine. There are only seven rooms, so it's essential to book in advance. ⊠ *Wilhelmsbader Allee 32, D– 63454,* ☎ *06181/83219,* ℻ *06181/87722. 7 rooms. Restaurant, bar, café. AE, DC, MC, V.*

Gelnhausen

❸ *20 km (12 mi) northeast of Hanau, 35 km (21 mi) northeast of Frankfurt.*

At Gelnhausen you'll find an island in the sleepy little Kinzig River with the remains of **Burg Barbarossa,** a castle that may well have stimulated the imagination of the Grimm brothers. Emperor Friedrich I—known as Barbarossa, or Red Beard—built the castle in this idyllic spot in the 12th century; in 1180 it was the scene of the first all-German Imperial Diet, a gathering of princes and ecclesiastical leaders. Although on an island, the castle was hardly designed as a defensive bastion and was accordingly sacked in the Thirty Years' War. Today only parts of the russet walls and colonnaded entrance remain. Still, stroll beneath the castle's ruined ramparts on its water site, and you'll get a tangible impression of the medieval importance of the court of Barbarossa. ⊠ *Follow signs to Burg Barbarossa,* ☎ *06051/8305.* ⊟ *DM 3.* ⊙ *Mar.– Oct., Tues.–Sun. 9–5; Nov.–Dec. and Feb., Tues.–Sun. 9–4. Closed Jan.*

The **Hexenturm** (Witches Tower), a grim prison, remains from the time when Gelnhausen was the center of a paranoiac witch-hunt in the late 16th century; dozens of women were burned at the stake or thrown— bound hand and foot—into the Kinzig River. Suspects were held in the Hexenturm of the town battlements. Today it houses a bloodcurdling collection of medieval torture instruments. A visit to the tower is included in a weekly summer season tour of the town, beginning at the Rathaus. ⊠ *Barbarossastr.* ⊟ *DM 5.* ⊙ *May–Oct., tour Sun. at 2:30.*

Dining and Lodging

$$–$$$ ✕⊞ **Romantisches Hotel Burg Mühle.** *Mühle* means "mill," and this hotel was once the tithe mill of the neighboring castle, delivering flour to the community until 1948. In the restaurant the mill wheel churns away as you eat. Ask for one of the cozy rooms in the oldest part of the hotel. ⊠ *Burgstr. 2, D–63571,* ☎ *06051/82050,* FAX *06051/820– 554. 41 rooms. Restaurant, bar, massage, sauna, exercise room. DC, MC, V.* ⊗

Steinau an der Strasse

❹ *30 km (18 mi) northeast of Gelnhausen, 65 km (40 mi) northeast of Frankfurt.*

For clear evidence of its formative influence on the Brothers Grimm, you need only travel to the little town of Steinau—full name Steinau an der Strasse (Steinau "on the road," referring to an old trade route between Frankfurt and Leipzig). Here Father Grimm served as local magistrate and the Grimm brothers spent much of their childhood. They were preschoolers on arrival and under 12 when they left after their father's untimely death.

Steinau dates from the 13th century and is typical of villages in the region. Marvelously preserved half-timber houses are set along cobblestone streets; imposing castles bristle with towers and turrets. In its woodsy surroundings you can well imagine encountering Little Red Riding Hood, Snow White, or Hansel and Gretel. A major street is named after the brothers; the building where their father was employed is now known as the "Brothers Grimm House."

★ A **castle** straight out of a Grimm fairy tale stands at the top of the town. Originally an early medieval fortress, it was rebuilt in Renaissance style between 1525 and 1558 and first used by the counts of Hanau as their summer residence, later to guard the increasingly important trade route between Frankfurt and Leipzig. It's not difficult to imagine the young Grimm boys playing in the shadow of its great gray walls or venturing into the encircling dry moat.

The castle houses a **Grimm Museum**, one of two in Steinau. This one exhibits the family's personal effects, including portraits of the Grimm relatives, the family Bible, an original copy of the Grimms' dictionary (the first in the German language), and all sorts of mundane things like spoons and drinking glasses. Climb the tower for a breathtaking view of Steinau and the countryside. ⊠ *Schloss Steinau,* ☎ *06663/6843.* ⌨ *DM 3.50, tour of castle and museum DM 5.50, tower DM 2.* ⊙ *Tues.– Sun. 9–5. Closed Christmas–mid-Jan.*

☼ The **Steinauer Marionettentheater** (Steinau Marionette Theater) is in the castle's former stables and portrays Grimm fairy tales and other children's classics. Performances are held most weekends at 3. ⊠ *Marstall am Schloss,* ☎ *06663/245.* ⌨ *DM 10.*

★ The carefully restored **Brüder-Grimm-Haus** is a few hundred yards from the castle and contains a museum devoted to the Grimms. Among the exhibits are books and pictures, some dating from their time, plus reminders of the Grimms' work as lexicographers. ⊠ *Brüder-Grimm-Str. 80,* ☎ *06663/7605.* ⌨ *DM 3.* ⊙ *Mar.–Dec., daily 2–5.*

The Gothic church of **St. Catherine** (⊠ Am Kumpen), where the Grimm brothers' grandfather Friedrich was parson, stands in front of the castle in Steinau's ancient market square. In the square's center, the **Märchenbrunnen** (Fairy-Tale Fountain) dates only from 1985, but its timeless design blends well with the rest of the town.

The 16th-century **Rathaus** has six bronze figures on its white stucco facade; they represent a cross section of 16th-century Steinau's population—from the builder who helped construct the town to the mother and child who continue its traditions. ⊠ *Brüder-Grimm-Str. 70,* ☎ *06663/96310.*

☼ A 3-km (2-mi) detour north of Steinau brings you to the **Teufelshöhlen** (Devil's Caves). The caves are 2½ million years old and have two immense chambers, the *Dom* (cathedral) and *Kapelle* (chapel). Weird stalactite formations have accumulated over the millennia, including one in the shape of a giant beehive. ⊠ *Landstr. 3179,* ☎ *06663/96310.* ⌨ *DM 3.* ⊙ *Easter–June, Sat. 1–7, Sun. 10–7; July–Oct., weekdays 1– 5, Sat. 1–7, Sun. 10–7.*

Dining and Lodging

$ ✕⌨ **Brathänchenfarm.** All meat here is charcoal-grilled, something your nose will tell you the minute you step into the cheery hotel-restaurant. The name "Roast Chicken Farm" tells you right away what the specialty is, but lamb or pork kebabs, spareribs, and other grilled delicacies can also be had. Many of the rooms face the surrounding forest. ⊠ *Im Ohl, D–36396,* ☎ *06663/961–236,* 𝔽𝔸𝕏 *06663/579. 15 rooms. Restaurant, bowling. AE, V.*

$ ⌨ **Burgmannenhaus.** This sturdy, steep-eaved Steinau house has small, cozy, and traditionally furnished rooms, and those under the eaves have exposed beams and woodwork. ⊠ *Brüder-Grimm-Str. 49, D–36396,* ☎ *06663/5084,* 𝔽𝔸𝕏 *06663/5087. 5 rooms. Restaurant. MC, V.*

$ ⌨ **Weisses Ross.** If the nearby Burgmannenhaus is full, this is a good second choice. It may be a simple inn, but you can sleep within its gnarled walls in the knowledge that the Grimm brothers dined and imbibed in its tavern almost 200 years ago. Rooms facing the street have views of ancient buildings but suffer from traffic noise. ⊠ *Brüder-Grimm-Str. 48, D–36396,* ☎ *06663/5804. 7 rooms, 5 with shower. No credit cards.*

Shopping

The Steinau area was renowned for centuries as a pottery center, and in the 1880s the town had 40 potteries. Official records from 1391 mention the tradition in the neighboring village of Marjoss, 12 km (7 mi) south of Steinau, where two potteries are still functioning. Bernhard Breitenberger's **Bauerntöpferei** (⊠ Distelbachstr. 24, ☎ 06660/1224) prides itself on traditional Hessian pottery modeled on old pieces. It's especially known for its *Bauerntopf* (farmer's pot) with two handles and a screw top, formerly used to carry soup and coffee to the fields. The other Marjoss pottery is run by the **Georg Ruppert family** (⊠ Brückenauer Str. 21, ☎ 06660/304). All the traditional Steinau potteries have gone out of business, but **Hans Krüger** (Hans Krüger Kunsttöpferei; ⊠ Ringstr. 52, ☎ 06663/6413) set up shop several years ago and makes modern pieces.

En Route   Gelnhausen and Steinau an der Strasse both lie on the German Half-Timber Road (Deutsche Fachwerkstrasse). Towns with historic half-timber buildings make up the route, which stretches from near Frankfurt to north of Bremen and meets the Fairy-Tale Road at several points. A map and brochure can be obtained from the Deutsche Fachwerkstrasse (⊠ Propstei Johannesberg, D–36041 Fulda, ☎ 0661/43680, FAX 0661/495–3105, ✆).

Fulda

⑤ *32 km (20 mi) northeast of Steinau an der Strasse, 100 km (62 mi) northeast of Frankfurt.*

The episcopal city of Fulda is a treasure trove of baroque architecture and worth a detour off the Fairy-Tale Road. It also has a half-timber Old Town where the streets are so narrow and twisty that it can be served only by a tiny bus, the Transity, which can be stopped at the wave of a hand. The city's grandest example of baroque design is the immense **Stadtschloss** (City Palace). This great collection of buildings began as a Renaissance palace in the early 17th century and was transformed into its present baroque splendor a century later by Johann Dientzenhofer. Much of the palace is now used as municipal offices, but you can visit the apartments of the prince-abbots. The **Fürstensaal** (Princes' Hall), on the second floor, provides a breathtaking display of baroque decorative artistry, with ceiling paintings by the 18th-century Bavarian artist Melchior Steidl and fabric-clad walls. Concerts are regularly held here (contact the city tourist office in the palace for program details, ☎ 0661/102–346). The palace also has permanent displays of the faience for which Fulda was once famous, as well as some fine Fulda porcelain.

Pause at the windows of the Grünes Zimmer (Green Chamber) to take in the view across the palace park to the **Orangerie**, a large garden with summer-flowering shrubs and plants. If you have time after your palace tour, stroll over for a visit. There's a pleasant café on the first floor. ⊠ Schlossstr. ☒ DM 4. ☉ Mon.–Thurs. 10–6, Fri. 2–6.

The **Dom** (cathedral), Fulda's 18th-century cathedral with tall twin spires, stands across the broad boulevard that borders the palace park. The cathedral was built by Dientzenhofer on the site of an 8th-century basilica, which at the time was the largest church north of the Alps. The basilica had to be big enough to accommodate the ever-growing number of pilgrims from all parts of Europe who converged on Fulda to pray at the grave of the martyred St. Boniface, the "Apostle of the Germans." A black alabaster bas-relief depicting his death marks the martyr's grave in the crypt. The **Cathedral Museum** contains a document bearing his writing, along with several other treasures, including Lucas Cranach the Elder's fine 16th-century painting of Christ and the Adulteress (who looks very comely in her velvet Renaissance costume). ⊠ *Dompl.* ⌨ *Museum DM 4.* ☉ *Apr.–Oct., Tues.–Sat. 10–5:30, Sun. 12:30–5:30; Nov.–Dec. and Feb.–Mar., Tues.–Sat. 10–12:30 and 1:30–4, Sun. 12:30–4.*

The **Vonderau Museum** is housed in the former Jesuit seminary. Its exhibits chart the cultural and natural history of Fulda and eastern Hesse. A popular section of the museum is its **planetarium,** with a variety of shows, including one for children. Since it has only 35 seats an early reservation is advisable. You get a unique impression of wandering alone through the stars to the sound of music. Performances take place Friday at 5 and 8, Saturday at 3 and 8, and Sunday at 10:30 and 3. ⊠ *Jesuitenpl. 2,* ☎ *0661/928–3510.* ⌨ *Museum DM 4, planetarium DM 5.* ☉ *Tues.–Sun. 10–6, tour Fri.–Sun. at 3:30.*

The **Michaelskirche** (Church of St. Michael) is one of Germany's oldest churches, built in the 9th century along the lines of the Church of the Holy Sepulchre in Jerusalem. It has a harmony and dignity that equal the majesty of the baroque facade of the neighboring Dom. ⊠ *Michaelsberg 1.*

The **Rathaus** (city hall) is quite possibly the finest town hall in this part of the country. The particularly delicate half-timbering separates the arcaded first floor from the steep roof and its incongruous but charming battery of small steeples. ⊠ *Schlossstr. 1,* ☎ *0661/102–345.*

If you need a break from cultural pursuits, head to the **Gokart Bahn** (Go-Cart Track) on the southern outskirts of Fulda. Hop into one of the 5.5 HP Honda machines and navigate the 11 curves of an 820-ft long indoor track. A special "top grip" surface keeps you safely on the piste. It's expensive fun, but where else can you play at being Schumacher for that price? ⊠ *Frankfurter Str. 142,* ☎ *0661/402–053.* ⌨ *DM 18 per ride.* ☉ *Mon.–Thurs. 3–11, Fri. 3 PM–1 AM, Sat. 1 PM–1 AM, Sun. 10 AM–11 PM.*

Dining and Lodging

$–$$ ✕ **Zum Stiftskämmerer.** This former episcopal treasurer's home is now a charming tavern-restaurant, its menu packed with local fare prepared with imagination and flair. A four-course menu priced around DM 60 is an excellent value, although à la carte dishes can be ordered for as little as DM 10. Try the *Schlemmertöpfchen,* a delicious (and very filling) combination of pork, chicken breast, and venison steak. ⊠ *Kämmerzeller Str. 10,* ☎ *0661/52369. DC, MC, V. Closed Tues.*

$$$$ 🏨 **Maritim Hotel am Schlossgarten.** This is the luxurious showpiece of the Maritim chain, housed in an 18th-century baroque building overlooking Fulda Palace Park. Chandeliers and oil paintings maintain the historic style, which contrasts with the hotel's modern atrium. The historic atmosphere of the grand old building, however, extends to the basement foundations, where you can dine beneath centuries-old vaulted arches in the Dianakeller restaurant. Many of the rooms have balconies or terraces with views over the park. ⊠ *Pauluspromenade 2, D–36037,* ☎ *0661/2820,* ℻ *0661/282–499. 113 rooms, 2 suites. 2 restaurants, bar, café, indoor pool, sauna. AE, DC, MC, V.* ⌘

$$$$ 🏨 **Romantik Hotel Goldener Karpfen.** Fulda is famous for its baroque
★ buildings, and this hotel is a short walk from the finest of them. The hotel, too, dates from the baroque era but has a later facade. Inside it's been renovated to a high standard of comfort. Afternoon coffee in the tapestry-upholstered chairs of the hotel's lounge is one of Fulda's delights, while dining in the elegant restaurant, with linen tablecloths,

Persian rugs, and subdued lighting, is another. ✉ *Simpliciusbrunnen 1, D–36037,* ☎ *0661/86800,* ⅎ𝖠𝖷 *0661/868–0100. 55 rooms. Restaurant, Weinstube, sauna, exercise room. AE, DC, MC, V.* ✆

$$$–$$$$ ☒ **Hotel Kurfürst.** Behind a baroque facade, this first-class hotel maintains the charm of the original historic house. It's in the heart of the Old Town, within easy walking distance of all attractions. ✉ *Schlossstr. 2, D–36037,* ☎ *0661/83390,* ⅎ𝖠𝖷 *0661/833–9339. 22 rooms. Restaurant, bar. AE, DC, MC, V.* ✆

Nightlife and the Arts

Chamber-music concerts are held regularly from September through May in the chandelier-hung splendor of the bishop's palace. One wing of the palace is now the city's main theater. Organ recitals are given regularly in Fulda's Dom. Call 0661/102–345 for details on all of Fulda's **cultural events.**

En Route   Kassel is the next major stop on the road north. If you're in a hurry, you can reach Kassel from Fulda in less than an hour via A–7. But the Fairy-Tale Road gives autobahns a wide berth, so if you have time, take B–254 into the Vogelsberg Mountains via Grossenluder to Lauterbach, some 25 km (15 mi) northeast of Fulda.

Lauterbach, a resort town of many medieval half-timber houses, has two castles—the **Riedesel** and the **Eisenbach.** The town is the setting of a well-known folk song in which a little fellow complains of having lost his sock. (The lyrics never crossed the Atlantic, but the tune did, as "Oh Where, Oh Where Has My Little Dog Gone?") Lauterbach's other unique claim to fame is its garden gnomes, which are right up there with beer steins and cuckoo clocks as a beloved, folklorish, German export. These gnomes, made in all shapes and sizes by the firm of Heissner Keramik, stand out on lawns at night with lighted lanterns, direct choruses of birds with batons, or fish in goldfish ponds. A selection featuring Grimm fairy-tale characters is sold at the **Heissner Shop** (✉ Schlitzerstr. 24, ☎ 06641/860).

The Fairy-Tale Road continues north to **Alsfeld** (34 km [21 mi] northwest of Fulda), notable for its beautifully preserved half-timber houses on narrow, winding cobbled streets. The jewel of Alsfeld—and one of Germany's showpieces—is the **Altes Rathaus** (Old Town Hall), built in 1512. Its facade, combining a ground floor of stone arcades, half-timber upper reaches, and a dizzyingly steep, top-heavy slate roof punctured by two pointed towers shaped like witches' hats—would look right at home in Walt Disney World. To get an unobstructed snapshot of this remarkable building (which is closed to the public), avoid the Marktplatz on Tuesday and Friday, when market stalls clutter the square.

The route next follows the little Schwalm River through a picturesque region so inextricably linked with the Grimm fairy tales that it's known as Rotkäppchenland (Little Red Riding Hood Country). **Schwalmstadt** is the capital of the area, and during the town's many festival days, local people deck themselves out in traditional folk costumes. You'll notice that the women's costume includes a little red cap *(Rotkäppchen)* covering a topknot. This is what gave Little Red Riding Hood her name.

Marburg

➏ *60 km (35 mi) northwest of Fulda.*

"I think there are more steps in the streets than in the houses." That is how Jacob Grimm described the half-timber hillside town of Marburg. He and his brother Wilhelm studied at the town's famous university from 1802 to 1805.

Marburg rises steeply from the Lahn River to the spectacular castle that crowns the hill, 335 ft up. Many of the winding, crooked "streets" are indeed stone staircases, and nowadays there is an elevator that gets you from level of the river to the marketplace. Several of the hillside houses have a back door five stories above the front door.

And the architecture is stunning. A great deal of money was spent in recent decades restoring the buildings to their original appearance. Half-timbering was out of fashion for most of the centuries since the 1600s, and the building facades had been stuccoed over. Marburg's most important building is the **Elisabethkirche** (St. Elizabeth Church; ⊠ Elisabethstr. 3), which marks the burial site of St. Elizabeth (1207–31), the town's favorite daughter. She was a Hungarian princess, betrothed at 4 and married at 12 to the landgrave Ludwig IV of Thuringia. She was widowed in 1228 when her husband fell in one of the Crusades and thereafter gave up all worldly pursuits. She moved to Marburg, founded a hospital, gave her wealth to the poor, and spent the rest of her very short life in poverty, caring for the sick and the aged. She is largely responsible for what Marburg became. Because of her selflessness she was made a saint only four years after her death. The Teutonic Knights built the Elisabethkirche, which quickly became the goal of pilgrimages, enabling the city to prosper. You can visit the shrine in the sacristy that once contained her bones, a masterpiece of the goldsmith's art. The church is a veritable museum of religious art, full of statues and frescoes.

The hilltop **castle,** residence of the counts of Hesse, was started by Elizabeth's daughter, Sophie, but it dates mainly from the 14th and 15th centuries. It contains a **museum** of the history of the state of Hesse, and its **Rittersaal** is the largest secular Gothic hall in Germany.

Much of the old city is closed to automobile traffic, which is just as well because the streets are paved with cobblestones that are slippery when wet, especially on a steep hillside. One of the main streets of the old city is named Barfussstrasse (Barefoot Street) because it led to a Franciscan monastery, the residents of which were sworn to humility and poverty.

The university and its students are the main influence on the town's social life, which pulsates through the many street cafés, restaurants, and student hangouts around the marketplace. Because so many of the streets are traffic-free, the whole area is filled with outdoor tables when the weather cooperates.

For those who prefer nature to history the Lahn Valley is idyllic. There are paths for biking and hiking, and the river itself can be explored by paddleboat.

Dining and Lodging

$ ✕ **Cafe Vetter.** This has unquestionably the most spectacular view in a town that's famed for its panoramas. The outdoor terrace is pleasant in good weather, but there's also a glassed-in terrace and two floors of dining rooms with windows facing the valley. It bakes its own cakes and is known for its literary Sundays. ⊠ *Reitg. 4,* ☎ *06421/25888. No credit cards. No dinner.*

$$$$ ✕⊞ **Sorat Hotel Marburg.** This rather unconventional luxury hotel opened in 1997 at the river level, just across the street from the elevator to the marketplace. The color scheme is orange, apricot, and yellow, contrasted with fiery red tables and upholstered furniture. Its Tartagua Restaurant, with bar, terrace, and beer cellar, has become a hip meeting place for those who can afford it. In addition to the usual rolls, eggs, and sausages, the breakfast buffet includes smoked salmon

and champagne. ⊠ *Pilgrimstein 29, D–35037,* ☎ *06421/9180,* FAX *06421/918–444. 143 rooms, 3 suites. 2 restaurants, bar, beer garden, air-conditioning, in-room data ports, minibars, sauna, fitness center, shops, meeting rooms, parking (fee). AE, DC, MC, V.*

Kassel

❼ *100 km (62 mi) northeast of Marburg.*

The Brothers Grimm spent time in Kassel as librarians at the court of the king of Westphalia, Jerome Bonaparte (Napoléon's youngest brother), and for the elector of Kassel. In researching stories and legends, their best source was not books but storyteller Dorothea Viehmann, who was born in the Knallhütte tavern, which still is in business in nearby Baunatal (☞ Dining and Lodging, *below*).

The **Brüder Grimm Museum,** in the center of Kassel, occupies five rooms of the Palais Bellevue, where the brothers once lived and worked. Exhibits include furniture, memorabilia, letters, manuscripts, and editions of their books, as well as paintings, watercolors, etchings, and drawings by Ludwig Emil Grimm, a third brother and a graphic artist of note. ⊠ *Palais Bellevue, Schöne Aussicht 2,* ☎ *0561/787–2033.* ☜ *DM 3.* ⊙ *Daily 10–5.*

The 18th-century **Schloss Wilhelmshöhe** served as a royal residence from 1807 to 1813, when Jerome was king of Westphalia. Later it became the summer residence of the German emperor Wilhelm II. The great palace, with a collection of antique furniture, stands at the end of the 5-km-long (3-mi-long) Wilhelmshöher Allee, an avenue that runs straight as an arrow from one side of the city to the other.

The giant 18th-century **statue of Hercules** that crowns the Wilhelmshöhe heights is an astonishing sight, standing on a massive red-stone octagon. At 2:30 PM on Sunday and Wednesday from mid-May through September, water gushes from a fountain beneath the statue, rushes down a series of cascades to the foot of the hill, and ends its precipitous journey in a 175-ft-high jet of water. It's a natural phenomenon, with no pumps. It takes so long to accumulate enough water that the sight can be experienced only on those two days, on holidays, and on the first Saturday evenings of June, July, August and September. On those occasions the cascade is also floodlighted and the whole palace is illuminated by candlelight. You can climb the statue from within for a rewarding look over the entire city, spread out over the plain and bisected by the straight line of the Wilhelmshöher Allee. Tramline 1 runs from the city to the Wilhelmshöhe. A café lies a short walk from the statue, and there are several restaurants in the area. ⊠ *Schloss Wilhelmshöhe,* ☎ *0561/93570.* ☜ *DM 6.* ⊙ *Tues.–Sun. 10–5.*

The Wilhelmshöhe was laid out as a baroque park—Europe's largest palace grounds—its elegant lawns separating the city from the thick woods of the Habichtswald (Hawk Forest). It comes as something of a surprise to see the turrets of a romantic medieval castle, the **Löwenburg** (Lion Fortress), breaking the harmony. There are more surprises, for this is no true medieval castle but a fanciful, stylized copy of a Scottish castle, built 70 years after the Hercules statue that towers above it. The architect was a Kassel ruler who displayed an early touch of the mania later seen in the castle-building excesses of Bavaria's eccentric Ludwig II. The Löwenburg contains a collection of medieval armor and weapons, tapestries, and furniture. ⊠ *Schloss Wilhelmshöhe,* ☎ *0561/ 935–7200.* ☜ *DM 6, including tour.* ⊙ *Mar.–Oct., Tues.–Sun. 10–noon and 1–5; Nov.–Feb., Tues.–Sun. 10–noon and 1–4.*

When it Comes to Getting Local Currency at an ATM,

Same Thing.

Whether you're in Yosemite or Yemen, using your Visa® card or ATM card with the PLUS symbol is the easiest and most convenient way to get local currency. For example, let's say you're in France. When you make a withdrawal, using your secured PIN, it's dispensed in francs, but is debited from your account in U.S. dollars. This makes it easy to take advantage of favorable exchange rates. And if you need help finding one of Visa's 627,000 ATMs in 127 countries worldwide, visit **visa.com/pd/atm**. We'll make finding an ATM as easy as finding the Eiffel Tower, the Pyramids or even the Grand Canyon.

It's Everywhere You Want To Be.

Savings all over the map.

Enjoy even greater savings with Hertz Affordable Europe.

Whatever direction you're headed, Hertz is there to greet you with even greater savings throughout Europe. Like 15% off Affordable Europe Non-Prepaid Weekly Rates on Intermediate cars and above. Just call **1-800-654-3001** and mention **CDP# 1209761**. Or for an even better deal, receive 20% off when you book on hertz.com and enter **CDP# 1209762**.

But, just because you're vacationing in Europe, it doesn't mean you can't feel at home. English is spoken at all Hertz European locations. Plus, you'll also receive the peace of mind that comes with our toll-free Affordable Europe Helpline and 24-Hour Emergency Roadside Assistance. For complete details call **1-800-654-3001**, or visit us on the web at hertz.com and you'll soon be on the road to savings. Another reason nobody does it exactly like Hertz.

Hertz ®

Kassel's leading art gallery and the state art collection lie within the Wilhelmshöhe Palace as part of the newly renovated **Staatliche Museen.** Its esteemed collection includes 11 Rembrandts as well as outstanding works by Rubens, Hals, Jordaens, Van Dyck, Dürer, Altdorfer, Cranach, and Baldung Grien. ⊠ *Schloss Wilhelmshöhe,* ☎ *0561/ 93777,* ᴰᴬˣ *0561/937–7666.* ⊒ *DM 5; free Fri.* ☉ *Tues.–Sun. 10–5.*

The **Deutsches Tapeten Museum,** (German Wallpaper Museum), the world's most comprehensive museum of wallpaper, has more than 600 exhibits tracing the art through the centuries. ⊠ *Brüder-Grimm-Pl. 5,* ☎ *0561/78460.* ⊒ *DM 5; free Fri.* ☉ *Tues.–Sun. 10–5.*

To the southeast, outside Hessisch-Lichtenau, is the **Hohe Meissner,** a high hill from which the Grimms' Mother Holle is said to have shaken out her featherbed, causing it to snow. Mother Holle, a good fairy, supposedly lives at the bottom of a pond on the Hohe Meissner.

Dining and Lodging

$$ ✕ **Autobahnrastätte Knallhütte.** This brewery–cum–coaching inn, established in 1752, was the home of village storyteller Dorothea Viehmann. The Grimms got the best of their stories from her, including Little Red Riding Hood, Hansel and Gretel, and Rumpelstiltskin. The coach road is now the autobahn, and there are numerous reminders of the tavern's history, starting with its name: The crack of a whip (*knall*) sounded the arrival of horse-drawn carriages struggling up the hill. In the Dorothea Viehmann Room, weary travelers once slept on straw on the floor; the tables can be hinged upward and affixed to the wall to make more room (the straw has been replaced with real beds should you want to spend the night). You can sample the brewery's unique beers while enjoying the Knallhütte's menu, which includes a grill night with salad buffet on Thursday and Friday. ⊠ *Baunatal,* ☎ *0561/492–076. MC, V.*

$ ✕ **Ratskeller.** Rustic German cuisine is served here within the embracing cellar vaults. The kitchen's North Hessian duck, fresh daily from the oven, is much beloved, as is its *Riesenbratwurst,* a 1½-ft-long and circular roast sausage, served with sauerkraut. ⊠ *Obere Konigstr. 8,* ☎ *0561/15928. AE, DC, MC, V.*

$$$–$$$$ ✕▥ **Hotel Gude.** This modern hotel is 10 minutes by public transportation to the city center. Rooms are spacious and come with marble bathrooms. The Pfeffermühlene is one of the region's finest restaurants, with an inventive international menu including German fare. The hotel is ideal for conferences, with its central location, variable meeting rooms for up to 200 persons, and its own underground garage. ⊠ *Frankfurter Str. 299, D–34134,* ☎ *0561/48050,* ᴰᴬˣ *0561/ 480–5101. 84 rooms. Restaurant, bar, air-conditioning (some), in-room safes, in-room data ports, minibars, refrigerators, indoor pool, massage, sauna, exercise room, meeting rooms, parking. AE, DC, MC, V.* ✎

$$$$ ▥ **Schlosshotel Wilhelmshöhe.** Set in the beautiful baroque Wilhelmshöhe Park, 5 km (3 mi) from town, this is no ancient palace but a contemporary hotel with a sleek gambling casino. Secure a window table in the elegant restaurant for a view of the park grounds. Sports facilities in the immediate vicinity include an 18-hole golf course, tennis courts, and horse stables. The park's palace is a two-minute walk. ⊠ *Schlosspark 8, D–34131,* ☎ *0561/30880,* ᴰᴬˣ *0561/308–8428. 106 rooms, 7 suites. Restaurant, bar, café, no smoking rooms, indoor pool, sauna, casino. AE, DC, MC, V.* ✎

$$$ ▥ **City-Hotel.** Just a few minutes from the Rathaus, this city-center hotel is designed to integrate with its ancient surroundings. Rooms are stylishly decorated and furnished. ⊠ *Wilhelmshöher Allee 38–42, D–*

34119, ☎ 0561/72810, ℻ 0561/728–1199. *43 rooms. Restaurant, bar, café, sauna. AE, DC, MC, V. Closed Christmas wk.*

Nightlife and the Arts

THE ARTS

Outdoor concerts are held in Wilhelmshöhe Park on Wednesday, Saturday, and Sunday afternoons from May through September. Classical concerts are given by the municipal orchestra in the Stadttheater. The Kasseler Musiktage, at the end of October and beginning of November, are devoted to music of the 20th century; call 0561/10940 for program details of all concerts and tickets at the **Stadttheater.**

Kassel has no fewer than 35 **theater companies.** The principal venues are the Schauspielhaus, the Tif-Theater, the Stadthalle, and the Komödie. Call 0561/109–4222 for program details and tickets for all.

NIGHTLIFE

Kassel's pulsating nightlife is concentrated in the bars and discos of **Friedrich-Ebert-Strasse.** The **casino** (✉ Schlosspark 8, ☎ 0561/930–850) in the Schlosshotel Wilhelmshöhe provides a note of elegance with its gray-blue-silver decor and windows that afford a spectacular view of the city below. It's open daily 3 PM–3 AM. Pick up the Kassel hotel guide from the local tourist office for a free admission pass. Otherwise admission is DM 5 for the main area's roulette and card games, and DM 2 for the slot machines.

Shopping

Kassel's chic **Königsgalerie,** a glass-roofed atrium, is packed with boutiques, restaurants, and bars.

In the village of Immenhausen, just north of Kassel, a local glass museum, **Glasmuseum Immenhausen** (✉ Am Bahnhof 3, ☎ 05673/2060; 🎫 DM 4; ⊙ weekdays 9–5, Sat. 10–1, Sun. 10–5) has regular exhibitions of work by German glassblowers; many of the pieces are for sale. The centerpiece of the museum is a permanent exhibition of work by the celebrated but now closed Immenhausen glass foundry, the Glashütte Süssmuth.

LOWER SAXONY

Lower Saxony (Niedersachsen), Germany's second-largest state after Bavaria, was formed from an amalgamation of smaller states in 1946. The state's landscape is quite diverse, but the focus here is on the Weser River's course from Hannoversch-Münden, in the south, to its end in the North Sea at Bremenhaven. Between Hannoversch-Münden and Hameln is one of Germany's most haunting river roads (B–80 to Bad Karlshafen, B–83 the rest of the way), where the fast-flowing Weser snakes between green banks that hardly show where land ends and water begins. Standing sentinel along the banks are superb little towns, whose half-timber architecture has given rise to the expression "Weser Renaissance."

The states of Lower Saxony and Saxony share the Harz Mountains; *see* Chapter 16 for complete coverage of the region.

Hannoversch-Münden

★ ⑧ *24 km (15 mi) north of Kassel, 150 km (93 mi) south of Hannover.*

This delightful town, seemingly untouched by recent history, shouldn't be missed. In the 18th century the German scientist and explorer Alexander von Humboldt (1769–1859) included it on his short list of the world's most beautiful towns (Passau, in eastern Bavaria, was another choice; ☞ The Eastern Bavarian Forest *in* Chapter 3). You'll have to travel a long way through Germany to find a grouping of half-timber houses (700 of them) as harmonious as these. A 650-year-old bridge over the Weser River leads into the old, walled settlement. The town is surrounded by forests and the Fulda and Werra rivers, which join and flow as the Weser River to Bremen and the North Sea.

Much is made of the fact that the quack doctor to end all quacks died here. Dr. Johann Andreas Eisenbart (1663–1727) would be forgotten today if a ribald 19th-century drinking song *(Ich bin der Doktor Eisenbart, Widda widda wit, boom! boom!)* hadn't had him shooting out aching teeth with a pistol, anesthetizing with a sledgehammer, and removing boulders from the kidneys. He was, as the song has it, a man who could make "the blind walk and the lame see." But this was libelous: Dr. Eisenbart was as good a doctor as any in his day, which admittedly isn't saying much. The town stages Eisenbart plays each summer and a Glockenspiel on the city hall depicts his feats. There's a statue of the doctor in front of his home at Langestrasse 79, and his grave is outside the St. Ägidien Church. For information on the plays, contact the **Touristik Naturpark Münden** (✉ *Lotzestr. 2,* ☎ *05541/75313,* FAX *05541/75404,* ✆).

Göttingen

❾ *30 km (19 mi) northeast of Hannoversch-Münden, 110 km (68 mi) south of Hannover.*

Although Göttingen is not strictly on the Fairy-Tale Road, it is closely associated with the Brothers Grimm, for they served as professors and librarians at the city's university from 1830 to 1837.

The university dominates life in Göttingen, and most houses more than a century old bear plaques that link them to a famous university student or professor. In one of the towers of the city's old defense wall, Otto von Bismarck, the Iron Chancellor and founder of the 19th-century German Empire, pored over his books as a 17-year-old law student. It looks like a romantic student's den now (the tower is open to visitors), but Bismarck was a reluctant tenant—he was banned from living within the city center because of his "riotous behavior" and fondness for wine. The taverns where Bismarck and his cronies drank are still there, all of them associated with Göttingen luminaries.

The statue of **Gänseliesel,** the little Goose Girl of German folklore, stands in the central market square, symbolizing the strong link between the students and their university city. The girl, according to the story, was a princess who was forced to trade places with a peasant, and the statue shows her carrying her geese and smiling shyly into the waters of a fountain. Above her pretty head is a charming wrought-iron art nouveau bower of entwined vines. The students of Göttingen contributed money toward the bronze statue and fountain in 1901 and gave it a ceremonial role: traditionally, graduates who earn a doctorate bestow a kiss of thanks upon Gänseliesel. Göttingen's citizens say she's the most-kissed girl in the world. There was a time, however, when the city fathers were none too pleased with this licentious practice, and in 1926 they banned the tradition. A student challenged the ban before a Berlin court but lost the case. Officially the ban still stands, although neither the city council nor the university takes any notice of it.

Behind the Gänseliesel statue is the **Altes Rathaus** (Old City Hall), begun in the 13th century but basically a part-medieval, part-Renaissance building. The bronze lion's-head knocker on the main door dates from early in the 13th century. Inside, the lobby's striking murals tell the city's story. Beneath the heavily beamed ceiling of the medieval council chamber, the council met, courts sat in judgment, visiting dignitaries were officially received, receptions and festivities were held, and traveling theater groups performed. ⊠ *Markt 9,* ☎ *0551/54000,* ℻ *0551/ 400–2998.* ☞ *Free.* ⊙ *Weekdays 8:30–6, Sat. 10–1.*

In the streets around the Rathaus you'll find magnificent examples of Renaissance architecture. Many of these half-timber, low-gabled buildings house businesses that have been there for centuries.

The **Ratsapotheke** (pharmacy) across from the Rathaus is one of the town's oldest buildings; medicines have been doled out there since 1322. ⊠ *Weenderstr. 30,* ☎ *0551/57128.*

The 16th-century **Schrödersches Haus** (Schröder House), a short stroll from the town hall up Weenderstrasse, is the most appealing storefront— with an ornate, half-timber front—you're likely to find in all Germany. A clothing store called the Camel Shop is inside. ⊠ *Weenderstr. 62.*

On the way to the Schrödersches Haus, you'll pass the ancient student tavern Zum Szültenbürger. Another, Zum Altdeutschen, is around the corner on Prinzenstrasse (named after three English princes, sons of King George III, who lived on this street while studying in Göttingen from 1786 to 1791). Don't be shy about stepping into either of these taverns or any of the others that catch your eye; the food and drink are inexpensive, and the welcome is invariably warm and friendly.

The **Städtisches Museum** (City Museum) is in Göttingen's only noble home, a 16th-century palace. It charts the history of Göttingen and its university with exhibits of church art, glass objects, and crafts, and has a valuable collection of antique toys and a reconstructed apothecary's shop. ⊠ *Ritterplan 7–8,* ☎ *0551/400–2843.* ☞ *DM 3.* ⊙ *Tues.–Fri. 10–5, weekends 11–5.*

Just to the east of Göttingen is Ebergötzen, with a rustic mill containing a museum honoring a man who could justifiably be called "the godfather of the comic strip." More than a century ago, Wilhelm Busch (1832–1908) wrote and illustrated a very popular children's book, still in print, called *Max und Moritz.* These were very bad boys who mixed gunpowder in the village tailor's pipe tobacco, and with fishing lines down the chimney, filched roasting chickens off the fire. The first American comic strip, *The Katzenjammer Kids* (1897), not only drew on Busch's naughty boys (they even spoke with a German accent) but also on his loose cartoon style. The mill, with a wheel that still turns, belonged to a friend of Busch's. There is a more extensive Busch Museum in Hannover.

Dining and Lodging

$$ ✕ **Historischer Rathskeller.** Dine in the vaulted underground chambers of Göttingen's Rathaus and choose from a traditional menu with the friendly assistance of chef Peter Ollhof. ⊠ *Altes Rathaus, Markt 9,* ☎ *0551/56433. AE, DC, MC, V.*

$ ✕ **Zum Schwarzen Bären.** The Black Bear is one of Göttingen's old-
★ est tavern-restaurants, a 16th-century half-timber house that breathes history and hospitality. The specialty of the house is *Bärenpfanne,* a generous mixture of beef, pork, and lamb. ⊠ *Kurzestr. 12,* ☎ *0551/ 58284. AE, DC, MC, V. Closed Mon. No dinner Sun.*

$$$$ ⌂ **Gebhards Hotel.** Though just across a busy road from the train station, this family-run hotel stands aloof and unflurried on its own grounds, a sensitively modernized 18th-century building that's something of a local landmark. Rooms are furnished in dark woods and floral prints highlighted by bowls of fresh flowers. The suites are par-

ticularly spacious, with completely separate bedrooms. ⊠ *Goethe-Allee 22–23, D–37073,* ☎ *0551/49680,* Ⅸ *0551/496–8110. 53 rooms, 7 suites. Restaurant, hot tub, sauna. AE, DC, MC, V.*

$$ ⊡ **Hotel Beckmann.** The Beckmann family runs this pleasant and homey hotel with friendly efficiency. Rooms are furnished in modern style, with light woods and pastel shades. The hotel is 5 km (3 mi) out of town, with good bus links to downtown. ⊠ *Ulrideshuser-Str. 44, D–37077 Göttingen-Nikolausberg,* ☎ *0551/209–080,* Ⅸ *0551/209–0810. 27 rooms, 21 with bath or shower. Sauna. DC, V.* ⊜

Nightlife and the Arts

Göttingen's symphony orchestra presents about 20 concerts a year. In addition, the city has a nationally known boys choir and an annual Handel music festival in June. Call 0551/54000 for program details and tickets for all three.

Göttingen's two theater companies—the 100-year-old **Deutsches Theater** and the **Junge Theater** (Young Theater)—are known throughout Germany; call 0551/496–911 for program details and tickets. Outdoor performances of Grimm fairy tales are presented on a woodland stage at Bremke (10 km [6 mi] southeast of Göttingen, near Gleichen) on certain summer weekends. Check with the local tourist office for dates.

The ancient student taverns that crowd the downtown area are the focus of local nightlife, but for something more sophisticated try the **Blue Note** jazz club and dance club (⊠ Wilhelmspl. 3, ☎ 0551/46907) or the **Outpost** dance club (⊠ Königsallee 243, ☎ 0551/66251).

En Route To pick up the Fairy-Tale Road where it joins the scenic Weser Valley Road, return to Hannoversch-Münden and head north on B–80. This is a beautiful route served by neither buses nor trains. In the village of Veckerhagen take a left turn to the signposted Sababurg.

Sababurg

★ ⑩ *10 km (6 mi) north of Göttingen, 100 km (62 mi) south of Hannover.*

Sababurg is home to the **Dornröschenschloss** (Sleeping Beauty's Castle). It stands just as the Grimm fairy tale tells us it did, in the depths of the densely wooded Reinhardswald, still inhabited by deer and wild boar. Sababurg was built in the 14th century by the archbishop of Mainz to protect a nearby pilgrimage chapel. Later it was destroyed and ultimately rebuilt as a turreted hunting lodge for the counts of Hesse. Today it is a fairly fancy hotel (☞ Dining and Lodging, *below*). Even if you don't stay the night, a drive to the castle is a highlight of the Fairy-Tale Road. There's a nominal fee to tour the grounds, which include a rose garden and ruins.

Ⓒ Adjacent to the castle is the **Tierpark Sababurg,** one of Europe's oldest wildlife refuges. Bison, red deer, wild horses, and all sorts of waterfowl populate the park. There's also a children's zoo. ⊠ *Kasinoweg 22,* ☎ *05671/800–1251.* ⅨⅠ *DM 7.* ☉ *Apr.–Sept., daily 8–7; Oct. and Mar., daily 9–5; Nov.–Feb., daily 10–4.*

Dining and Lodging

$$$–$$$$ ✕⊡ **Dornröschenschloss Sababurg.** The medieval fortress thought to have
★ been the inspiration for the Grimm brothers' tale of *The Sleeping Beauty* is now a small luxury hotel snugly set in the castle walls and surrounded by the oaks of the Reinhardswald. Concerts and plays are held on the grounds in summer, and it is a popular place for weddings. The castle was built in 1334, but many of the palatial improvements came during the 17th and 18th centuries. Since 1960 the Koseck family has been enthusiastically welcoming guests to the hotel and showing them the magic

of the area. The restaurant serves a fine haunch of venison in the autumn, and the fresh trout with a Riesling-based sauce in the spring is equally satisfying. ⊠ *Sababurg, D–34369 Hofgeismar,* ☎ *05671/8080,* FAX *05671/808–200. 18 rooms. Restaurant. AE, DC, MC, V.*☟

En Route A short distance over back roads is another hilltop castle hotel, **Trendelburg.** Legend has it that its tower is the one in which a wicked witch imprisoned Rapunzel. Since it had neither a door nor stairs, the witch, and eventually a handsome prince, could get to Rapunzel only by climbing her long, golden tresses. From Trendelburg follow more back roads to the Weser Valley riverside village of Oberweser. Turn left and take B–80 north.

Bad Karlshafen

⑪ *42 km (26 mi) north of Hannoversch-Münden, 55 km (34 mi) northwest of Göttingen, 125 km (77 mi) south of Hannover.*

From the inland harbor of the pretty little spa of Bad Karlshafen, German troops of the state of Waldeck embarked to join the English forces in the American War of Independence. Flat barges took the troops down the Weser to Bremen, where they were shipped across the North Sea for the long voyage west. Many American families can trace their heritage to this small spa and the surrounding countryside.

Viewed from one of the benches overlooking the harbor, there's scarcely a building that's not in the imposing baroque style. The grand **Rathaus** (⊠ Hafenpl. 8) behind you is the best example. Bad Karlshafen stands out in solitary splendor amid the simple Weser Renaissance style of other riverside towns.

Dining and Lodging

$$–$$$$ ✕🏨 **Romantik Hotel Menzhausen.** The half-timber exterior of this 16th-century establishment in the small town of Uslar, 12 km (7 mi) east of the Weser River, is matched by the cozy interior of its comfortable, well-appointed restaurant. Ask for a guest room in the Mauerschlösschen, if you're looking for the romance in Romantik; this is a luxurious hotel extension, which incorporates traditional Weser Renaissance design, such as half-timbering and carved beams. ⊠ *Langestr. 12, D–37170 Uslar,* ☎ *05571/92230,* FAX *05571/922–330. 41 rooms. Restaurant, Weinstube, indoor pool, sauna, meeting room. AE, DC, MC, V.*

$ ✕🏨 **Gaststätte-Hotel Weserdampfschiff.** You can step right from the deck of a Weser pleasure boat into the welcoming garden of this popular hotel-tavern. Fish from the river land straight into the tavern's frying pan. The rooms are snug; ask for one with a river view. The restaurant is closed Monday. ⊠ *Weserstr. 25, D–34385,* ☎ *05672/2425,* FAX *05672/8119. 14 rooms. Restaurant. No credit cards.*

$ ✕🏨 **Hessicher Hof.** In the heart of town, this inn started as a tavern for the locals and now includes several comfortably furnished bedrooms. The restaurant serves good, hearty fare. Breakfast is included in the room price, or you may request half-pension. ⊠ *Carlstr. 13–15, D–34385,* ☎ *05672/1059,* FAX *05672/2515. 17 rooms. Restaurant, bar. AE, MC, V.*

Shopping

There are some excellent small, privately run potteries and glassworks in the area. At **Die Glashütte** (⊠ Weserstr. 43, ☎ 05672/1414) glassblowers will fashion and engrave to order.

Höxter

⑫ *24 km (14 mi) north of Bad Karlshafen, 100 km (62 mi) south of Hannover.*

Stop at Höxter to admire its **Rathaus,** a perfect example of the Weser Renaissance style, combining three half-timber stories with a romantically crooked tower. Though it has no better claim than any other town to the story of Hansel and Gretel, Höxter presents a free performance of the Hansel and Gretel story on the first Saturday of each month, May to September.

Einbeck, another storybook town 20 km (12 mi) east of Höxter, is where bock beer originated. Starting in 1341 the good burghers brewed it in their houses, and the name *Bockbier* is a corruption of the original Einbecker Bier. The **Einbecker Brauhaus** (brewery) still makes the strong brew, and groups can visit it with an advance written request (⊠ Papenstr. 4–7, D–37574 Einbeck, ☎ 05561/7970). There is also an exhibit on bock in the **city museum** (⊠ Steinweg 11, ☎ 05561/971710).

OFF THE
BEATEN PATH

REICHSABTEI CORVEY – Across the river and 3 km (2 mi) east of Höxter lies the Imperial Abbey of Corvey, idyllically set between the wooded heights of the Solling region and the Weser River. The 1,100-year history of the abbey is closely tied with the early development of the German nation. Optimistically described by some as the "Rome of the North," it hosted several sessions of the imperial council in the 12th century and provided lodging for several Holy Roman emperors. In the 16th century the first six volumes of the Roman historian Tacitus's annals were discovered in its vast library. Heinrich Hoffmann von Fallersleben (1798–1874), author of the poem "Deutschland, Deutschland über Alles," worked as librarian here in the 1820s. The poem, set to music by Joseph Haydn, became the German national anthem in 1922. A music festival is held in the church and great hall, the Kaisersaal, in May and June. ☎ 05271/68116. ☑ DM 6.50, abbey church DM 1. ☉ Apr.–Oct., daily 9–6.

Dining and Lodging

$$$ ✕ **Schloss Bevern.** You'll dine like a baron here, within the honey-color
★ walls of a Renaissance castle in the little town of Bevern, just north of Höxter on the other side of the river. In the enchanting inner courtyard, a solitary dome-topped, half-timber tower stands sentinel over a 17th-century fountain. The romance carries into the stylish restaurant, which serves such traditional country dishes as roast pheasant, lamb, or fish at tables with finely cut glassware. ⊠ *Am Schloss, Bevern,* ☎ *05531/8783. Reservations essential. AE, DC, MC, V. Closed Mon. No lunch Tues.*

$$ ✕ **Schlossrestaurant Corvey.** In summer you can dine under centuries-
★ old trees at the Reichsabtei Corvey's excellent restaurant. It is closed in the winter, except by special arrangement. With advance notice, a *Fürsten-Bankett,* or "princely banquet," can be arranged for groups in the vaulted cellars. ⊠ *Reichsabtei Corvey,* ☎ *05271/8323. V.*

$$–$$$ ✕🏠 **Niedersachsen Ringhotel.** Behind the three-story, half-timber facade of this fine old Höxter house is a hotel with modern comfort and amenities, a member of the respected Ring group. The restaurant has a shady garden terrace and features fresh river fish. ⊠ *Grubestr. 3–7, D–37671,* ☎ *05271/6880,* ℻ *05721/688–444. 80 rooms. Restaurant, bar, indoor pool, sauna. AE, DC, MC, V.* ✎

Shopping

Germany's oldest **porcelain factory** is at Fürstenberg, 8 km (5 mi) south of Höxter, in a baroque castle high above the Weser River. The crowned Gothic letter *F,* which serves as its trademark, is world famous. You'll find Fürstenberg porcelain in Bad Karlshafen and Höxter, but it's more fun to journey to the 18th-century castle, where production first began in 1747, and buy directly from the manufacturer. Fürstenberg and most dealers will take care of shipping arrangements and any tax refunds. The factory has a sales outlet, a museum, and a café. ⊠ *Schloss Fürstenberg,* ☎ *05271/401–161.* 🗺 *Museum DM 5.* ⊗ *Museum: Apr.–Oct., Tues.–Sun. 10–6; Nov.–Mar., weekends 10–5. Shop: Apr.–Oct., Tues.–Sun. 10–6; Nov.–Mar., Tues.–Sat. 10–5.*

Bodenwerder

🔞 *34 km (21 mi) north of Höxter, 70 km (43 mi) south of Hannover.*

The charming Weser town of Bodenwerder plays a central role in German popular literature. It is the home of the Lügenbaron (Lying Baron) von Münchhausen (1720–97), who was known as a teller of whoppers. His reputation was not without foundation, but it was mainly created by a book based in part on the baron's stories and published anonymously by an acquaintance. According to one tale, the baron rode a cannonball toward an enemy fortress but then, having second thoughts, returned to where he started by leaping onto a cannonball heading the other way.

The **Münchhausen-Erinnerungszimmer** (Münchhausen Memorial Room), in the imposing family home in which Baron von Münchhausen grew up (now the Rathaus), is crammed with mementos of his adventurous life, including his cannonball. A fountain in front of the house represents another story. The baron, it seems, was puzzled when his horse kept drinking insatiably at a trough. Investigating, he discovered that the horse had been cut in two by a closing castle gate and that the water ran out as fast as the horse drank. The water in the fountain, of course, flows from the rear of a half-horse. On the afternoon of the first Sunday of the month from May through October, townspeople retell von Münchhausen's life story with performances in front of the Rathaus. ⊠ *Münchhausenpl. 1,* ☎ *05533/40541.* 🗺 *Museum DM 2.* ⊗ *Apr.–Oct., daily 10–noon and 2–5.*

Dining and Lodging

$$ ✗🖭 **Hotel Deutsches Haus.** The fine half-timber facade of this comfortable country hotel vies for attention with the nearby home of Baron von Münchhausen, now Bodenwerder's town hall. Original wood beams and oak paneling add to the rural feel inside. The hotel's own extensive grounds adjoin the town park, and the Weser River is a short walk away. The restaurant's terrace adjoins the Münchhausen house. A specialty is *Münchhausen Kugeln* (Cannonballs), a dish with turkey, pork, vegetables, and croquettes. ⊠ *Münchhausenpl. 4, D–37619,* ☎ *05533/3925,* 🅵🅰🆇 *05533/4113. 42 rooms. Restaurant, bowling, bicycles. AE, MC, V. Closed Jan.* 🕭

$ ✗🖭 **Hotel Goldener Anker.** The Weser boats tie up right outside this simple half-timber tavern and hotel, and the sleepy river flows right past your bedroom window. The restaurant prepares hearty German fare and sometimes fresh Weser fish; in summer a shady terrace beckons. ⊠ *Weserstr. 13, D–37619,* ☎ *05533/2135,* 🅵🅰🆇 *05533/3057. 13 rooms. Restaurant, bicycles. MC.*

Hameln

★ 🔞 *24 km (15 mi) north of Bodenwerder, 47 km (29 mi) southwest of Hannover.*

Hameln (or Hamelin, in English) is home to the story of the gaudily attired Pied Piper, who rid the town of rats by playing seductive melodies on his flute. The rodents followed him willingly, waltzing their way right into the Weser. When the town defaulted on its contract and refused to pay the piper, he settled the score by playing his merry tune to lead Hameln's children on the same route. As the children reached the river, the Grimms wrote, "they disappeared forever." The tale is included in the Grimms' book *German Legends*. The origin of the story is lost in the mists of time, but the best guess is that it is associated with the forced resettlement of young people to the sparsely populated eastern territories. Also, during the 13th century, an inordinate number of Hameln's young men were conscripted to fight in an unpopular war in Bohemia and Moravia.

The Pied Piper tale is immortalized in an ultramodern sculpture set above a reflecting pool in the town's pedestrian zone. There are even rat-shape pastries in the windows of Hameln's bakeries. On central Osterstrasse you'll see several beautiful half-timber houses, including the **Rattenfängerhaus** (Rat-Catcher's House) and the **Hochzeitshaus** (Wedding House), a 17th-century, Weser Renaissance building now containing city offices. Every Sunday from mid-May to mid-September, the story of the Pied Piper is played out at noon by local actors and children on the Hochzeitshaus terrace. The half-hour performance is free; get there early to ensure a good place. The carillon of the Hochzeitshaus plays a Pied Piper song every day at 9:35 and 11:35, and mechanical figures enact the story on the west gable of the building at 1:05, 3:35, and 5:35.

Dining and Lodging

$–$$ ✕ **Rattenfängerhaus.** This brilliant example of Weser Renaissance
★ architecture is Hameln's most famous building, reputedly where the Pied Piper stayed during his rat-extermination assignment (actually, it wasn't built until centuries after his supposed exploits). A plaque in front of it fixes the date of the incident at June 26, 1284. Rats are all over the menu, from the "rat-remover cocktail" to a "rat-tail flambé." But don't be put off: the traditional dishes are excellent, and the restaurant is guaranteed rodent free. ⊠ *Osterstr. 28,* ☎ *05151/3888. AE, DC, MC, V.*

$$$$ ⛨ **Hotel zur Börse.** Thoroughly renovated as a luxury establishment, this hotel, with terrace, offers comfortable accommodations and friendly service. The bar serves snacks. ⊠ *Osterstr. 41, entrance on Kopmanshof, D–31785,* ☎ *05151/7080,* 🖷 *05151/25485. 31 rooms. Bar, bistro. AE, DC, MC, V.*

$$$–$$$$ ⛨ **Hotel zur Krone.** If you fancy a splurge, ask for the split-level suite.
★ With prices starting at DM 380 a night, it's an expensive but delightful comfort. The building dates from 1645 and is a half-timber marvel. Avoid the modern annex, however; it lacks all charm. ⊠ *Osterstr. 30, D–31785,* ☎ *05151/9070,* 🖷 *05151/907–217. 32 rooms, 5 apartments. Restaurant. AE, DC, MC, V.*

Nightlife and the Arts

The **Theater Hameln** (⊠ Sedanstr. 4, ☎ 0515/916–222) has a top-class, year-round program of dance, drama, opera, and orchestral concerts.

Hannover

47 km (29 mi) northeast of Hameln.

Hannover is somewhat off the Fairy-Tale Road, yet its culture and commerce influence the quieter surrounding towns. As a trade-fair center, Hannover competes with such cities as Munich and Leipzig—it wrapped up hosting the world's fair, EXPO 2000, in October. It's also an exemplary arts center, with leading museums, an opera house of international repute, and the finest baroque park in the country. Its patronage of the arts is evident in unexpected places: in an international competition, architects and designers created nine unique bus stops for the city.

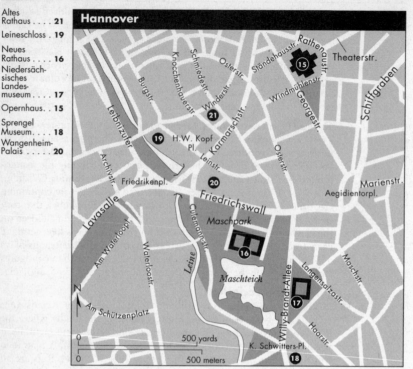

Hannover

A Good Walk

You can start your tour at the big Kröpke U-bahn station, which is also the place to catch Tramline 5 to the gardens of **Herrenhausen** and the **Wilhelm Busch Museum.** Just a short distance south of the station on Georgstrasse is Hannover's beautiful classical theater, the **Opernhaus** ⑮. From here continue south on Georgstrasse, the city's main shopping street, to Georgesplatz, then veer right on Georgeswall to Breite Strasse and turn right to Theodor Lessing Platz. A left under the elevated Friedrichswall gets you into Maschpark, containing the vast bulk of the **Neues Rathaus** ⑯. Behind the Rathaus you can stroll through the park, skirting the east edge of the pond to Willy-Brandt-Allee, on which you will find the **Niedersachsisches Landesmuseum** ⑰ with its celebrated art collection. At the end of the street is the appropriately named Kurt-Schwitters-Platz, with the **Sprengel Museum** ⑱ and its modern art collection. Retrace your steps to the Rathaus, once again cross under Friedrichswall, and just to the west you will come to two royal palaces important in Hannoverian history. The larger one, standing above the River Leine, is the **Leineschloss** ⑲, the seat of the Lower Saxony State Parliament. Facing Leinstrasse is **Wangenheim-Palais** ⑳, a smaller palace where one of the Hannoverian kings resided. Up Karmarschstrasse and two blocks on the left is Hannover's first city hall, the 14th-century **Altes Rathaus** ㉑, a notable example of Hannoverian brick architecture. The central market square behind it is dominated by the Marktkirche, with a splendid Gothic carved altar and fine stained glass inside.

Sights to See

㉑ **Altes Rathaus.** It took nearly 100 years, starting in 1410, to build this gabled brick edifice, which once contained a merchants hall and an apothecary. In 1844 it was restored to the style of about 1500. The facade's fired clay frieze depicts coats of arms and representation of princes, and a medieval game somewhat comparable to arm wrestling. Inside is a modern interior with boutiques and a restaurant. ⊠ *Köbelingerstr.*

<table>
<tr><td>OFF THE
BEATEN PATH</td><td>**HERRENHAUSEN** – The gardens of the former Hannovarian royal summer residence is the city's showpiece (the 17th-century palace was never rebuilt after wartime bombing). The grounds recently underwent a DM 50 million renovation. There are 4 km (2½ mi) of new hedges and chestnut trees, 36 new flower beds, and a "fig garden" with a collapsible shelter to protect it in the winter. A new gastronomy pavilion lies behind the grotto (also restored). The baroque park is unmatched in Germany for its formal precision, with patterned walks, gardens, and copses framed by a placid moat. From Easter until October fountains play for a few hours daily (weekdays 11–noon and 3–4, weekends 10–noon and 3–5). Herrenhausen is outside the city, a short ride on Tramline 4 or 5. ⊠ *Herrenhauser Str.* 🚋 *DM 3.* ☉ *May–Oct., daily 8–8; Nov.–Apr., daily 8–4:30.*</td></tr>
</table>

An 18th-century residence at the edge of the park is now a museum, the **Fürstenhaus Herrenhausen-Museum,** affording fascinating insight into Hannoverian court life and its links with England. ⊠ *Alte Herrenhauser Str. 14,* ☎ *0511/750–947.* 🚋 *DM 5.* ☉ *Tues.–Sun. 10–5.*

⑲ **Leineschloss.** The former Hannoverian royal palace stands above the River Leine and is now the seat of the Lower Saxony State Parliament. From 1714 until 1837 rulers of the house of Hannover also sat on the British throne as Kings George I–IV. The first of them, George I, spoke no English. George III presided over the loss of the American colonies in the Revolutionary War but sent no Hannoverian troops to help fight, even though he hired troops from other German states for this purpose. The period of joint rule came to an end when Queen Victoria ascended the throne (Hannover didn't allow female monarchs). Call the tourist office (☎ 0511/301–422) if you'd like to visit. ⊠ *Leinstr.*

⑯ **Neues Rathaus.** The new city hall was built at the start of the century in Wilhelmine style (for Kaiser Wilhelm), at a time when pomp and circumstance were important ingredients of heavy German bureaucracy. An elevator rises to the dome for a splendid view. ⊠ *Friedrichswall.* 🚋 *Dome DM 3.* ☉ *Daily 9:30–7.*

⑰ **Niedersächsisches Landesmuseum** (Lower Saxony State Museum). This prestigious museum was thoroughly renovated in time for EXPO 2000. Its priceless early art collection includes works by Tilman Riemenschneider, Veit Stoss, Hans Holbein the Younger, and Lucas Cranach. ⊠ *Willy-Brandt-Allee 5,* ☎ *0511/98075.* 🚋 *DM 6.* ☉ *Tues., Wed., and Fri.–Sun. 10–5, Thurs. 10–7.*

⑮ **Opernhaus.** Hannover's late classical opera house, completed in 1852, has two large wings and a covered, colonnaded portico adorned with statues of great composers and poets. This enabled the finely attired operagoers to disembark from their coaches with dry feet, a function now taken over by an underground garage. The building originally served as the court theater but now is used almost exclusively for opera. It was gutted by fire in a 1943 air raid and restored in 1948. The acoustics were completely renewed in 1985. Unless you have tickets, the only part of the interior you can visit is the foyer with ticket windows. ⊠ *Opernpl. 1,* ☎ *0511/999–900.*

⑱ **Sprengel Museum.** An important museum of modern art, the Sprengel holds major works by Max Beckmann, Max Ernst, Paul Klee, Emil Nolde, and Pablo Picasso. The works of Schwitters, a native son and prominent dadaist, is also here. ⊠ *Kurt-Schwitters-Pl.,* ☎ *0511/1684–*

3875. ☜ *DM 7; free with tourist office's Hannover Card.* ☉ *Tues. 10–8, Wed.–Mon. 10–6.*

⑳ Wangenheim-Palais. This is one of the more delightful works of the noted architect Georg Friedrich Laves, who also designed the opera and several buildings at Herrenhausen and thoroughly renovated the Leineschloss. After the death of the Count Wangenheim, for whom it was built in 1833, it briefly became the royal palace. Hannoverian king Georg V lived there from 1851 to 1862 before moving to Herrenhausen. It was then the city hall for 50 years and now serves as the offices of the Lower Saxony Economics Ministry. ☒ *Friedrichswall.*

OFF THE
BEATEN PATH

WILHELM BUSCH MUSEUM – Many effects and original drawings of the "godfather of the comic strip" (☞ Göttingen, *above*) are on display in this section of the Georgspalais, which is near the Herrenhausen Gardens. ☒ *Georgengarten 1,* ☎ *0511/714–076.* ☜ *DM 2.* ☉ *Tues.–Sat. 10–4, Sun. 10–6.*

Dining and Lodging

$$$ ✕ **Basil.** Constructed in 1867 as a riding hall for the Royal Prussian military, this hip restaurant's home is as striking as the menu. Cast-iron pillars support the vaulted brick ceiling, and two-story drapes hang in the huge windows. The menu changes every three weeks, and includes eclectic dishes from the Mediterranean to Asia. Game and white *Spargel* (asparagus) are served in season. ☒ *Dragonerstr. 30A,* ☎ *0511/622–636. AE. Closed Sun.*

$–$$ ✕ **Brauhaus Ernst August.** This brewery has so much artificial greenery that you could imagine yourself in a beer garden. Hannoverian pilsner is brewed on the premises, and regional specialties are the menu's focus. There's a souvenir shop where besides beer paraphernalia such as mugs and coasters, you can purchase, empty or full, a huge old-fashioned beer bottle with a porcelain stopper. In the early postwar years American soldiers christened the bottles "snap daddies." Many patrons precede their beer and food with a shot of *Brauerschluck* (Brewer's Gulp), the pub's own potent schnapps. It, too, is sold in a miniature snap daddy. There is live music most evenings (no cover charge) and a merry mood prevails with dancing. ☒ *Schmiedstr. 13,* ☎ *0511/365–950. V.*

$–$$ ✕ **Grapenkieker.** An ancient pot steams in the aromatic, farmhouse-style kitchen of the half-timber Grapenkieker, and simple, hearty fare prevails. Proprietors Gabriele and Karl-Heinz Wolf are locally famous for their prowess in the kitchen and the warm welcome they give their guests. The restaurant is 5 km (3 mi) from the city center, in the Isernhagen District, but it's well worth seeking out. ☒ *Hauptstr. 56, Isernhagen,* ☎ *05139/88068. AE, DC, MC, V. Closed Sun. and Mon.*

$$$$ ✕🏠 **Kastens Hotel Luisenhof.** This very traditional hotel, both in appearance and service, is a few steps from the main train station. Antiques are everywhere: tapestries on the lobby walls, an elegant wardrobe on every floor, oil paintings in the foyer, and copper engravings in the bar. The hotel takes pride in having been in the family since 1856. Although the building was bombed during World War II, it has a charming facade and a thoroughly renovated interior. The restaurant is international with French touches. ☒ *Luisenstr. 1–3, D–30159,* ☎ *0511/30440,* 🖷 *0511/304–4807. 150 rooms, 5 suites. Restaurant, bar, meeting rooms. AE, DC, MC, V.*

$$$–$$$$ ✕🏠 **Hotel Benther Berg.** This large country-house hotel with a modern extension sits amid parkland and woods in Ronneberg-Benthe, a southwest suburb. Rooms are large and furnished mostly in modern dark woods and pastel shades. The restaurant attracts Hannover regulars, who value its international cuisine. ☒ *Vogelsangstr. 18, D–*

30952 Ronneberg-Benthe, ☎ *05108/64060,* 𝔽𝔸𝕏 *05108/640–650. 70 rooms. Restaurant, café, indoor pool, sauna. AE, DC, MC, V.* ✎

$$–$$$ ✕🏠 **Hotel Körner.** The modern Körner has an almost old-fashioned feel about it, probably created by the friendly and personal service. Rooms are comfortably furnished in light veneers and pastel shades. The small courtyard terrace has a fountain; breakfast is served here in the summer. The Lüzower Jäger restaurant is decorated with memorabilia from the Hannoverian wars of liberation, and the menu consists of Lower Saxony specialties. ✉ *Körnerstr. 24–25, D–30159,* ☎ *0511/16360,* 𝔽𝔸𝕏 *0511/18048. 75 rooms. Restaurant, indoor pool, exercise room. AE, DC, MC, V.*

Nightlife and the Arts

The **opera company** of Hannover is internationally known, with productions staged in one of Germany's finest 19th-century classical opera houses. Call 0511/368–1711 for program details and tickets. Hannover's elegant **casino** (✉ Am Maschsee, ☎ 0511/980660) is open from 3 PM.

Outdoor Activities

Hannover's inland lake, the **Maschsee,** is a favorite local recreation area. In summer you can swim there or hire a sailboat.

Shopping

Hannover has what it claims is Germany's oldest **Flohmarkt** (flea market)—certainly one of the largest and most interesting. It's held every Saturday on the bank of the River Leine (Am Hohen Ufer) from 7 to 4. The colorful sculptures by Niki de St. Phalle you'll see on the opposite bank (Am Leibnitzufer) were commissioned by the city, which then had to prevent them from being added to the flea-market junk. Art advocates prevailed, and the sculptures (huge, maternal "nanas") are now an indispensable part of the city landscape.

Hannover is one of northern Germany's most fashionable cities, and its central pedestrian zone has international shops and boutiques, as well as the very best of German-made articles, from stylish clothes to handmade jewelry. In the glassed-over **Galerie Luise** (✉ Luisenstr. 5) you can spend a couple of hours browsing, with a leisurely lunch or afternoon tea at one of the several restaurants and cafés.

En Route The Fairy-Tale Road continues north of Hannover as far as Bremen, even though any connection to the Grimm brothers is faint here. You can reach Bremen in less than an hour on the A–27. An alternative is to return to Hameln and follow the Weser as it breaks free of the Wesergebirge uplands at Porta Westfalica. The idle, meandering route runs through the northern German plains to the sea and Bremen.

Celle

㉒ *60 km (35 mi) northeast of Hannover.*

The main street of Celle's Old Town is quite different from the narrow, twisting streets you'd expect to find in a half-timber town. The **Stechbahn** is very broad, and was once used for jousting tournaments. A horseshoe sunk in the pavement in front of the Löwenapotheke supposedly marks where the man who established Celle's present location, Duke Otto the Severe, died in such a tournament.

This charming city, with more than 500 half-timber buildings, is also the southern gateway to the Lüneburg Heath, one of Germany's most pleasant pastoral areas. It's a landscape of bizarrely shaped juniper bushes, of heather that flowers in pinkish purple in the late summer, and of grazing flocks of the heath's own breed of sheep, the cuddly Heidschnucken.

Thanks to a bend in the Aller River and a small tributary, Celle was protected on three sides by streams. To guard the fourth side from invasion by robber barons, Duke Otto built a fortified castle. This became the city's present **palace,** set in a lush park with the oldest baroque theater in Germany still used for performances. The castle chapel is the only complete Renaissance place of worship north of the Alps. The city hall (Rathaus) also traces its origins back to Duke Otto's time. It was extended and elaborately decorated in the 14th and 16th centuries.

The **Bomann Museum** is a must for anyone charmed by old furnishings. Its aim is to depict the folk culture of the area along with the history of Celle and of the Kingdom of Hannover. You can see a completely furnished reconstruction of a farmhouse and numerous reconstructed interiors, including a cartwright shop and a smithy. ⊠ *Schlosspl. 7,* ☎ *05141/12544.* ⊡ *DM 4.* ☉ *Apr.–Oct., Tues.–Sun. 10–5; Nov–Mar., Tues.–Sat. 10–5, Sun. 10–1.*

The very specialized **Deutsche Stickmuster-Museum** (German Needlework Museum) dedicates itself to needlework and embroidery. The display includes native costumes, shirts, pillows, bedspreads and the like all adorned with needlework flowers, birds, animals, human figures, and abstract designs. If you want to make your own sampler, you can buy a kit to do just that. ⊠ *Palais im Prinzengarten,* ☎ *05141/382–626.* ⊡ *DM 5.* ☉ *Tues.–Thurs., weekends 10–5.*

Dining and Lodging

$$ ✕ **Ratskeller Celle.** This subterranean establishment with a vaulted stone ceiling lays claim to being the oldest restaurant in Lower Saxony. If you can stand slow service, it's a good place to try the regional specialties, notably lamb dishes from the Heidschnucken. Boar is also a heath specialty, as is tender white asparagus, served in May and June, with an endless variety of accompaniments. ⊠ *Markt 14,* ☎ *05141/29099. AE, V. Closed Tues.*

$$$$ ✕⊞ **Hotel Fürstenhof.** This baroque hunting chateau is surrounded by huge trees in the center of town. Chef Hans Sobotka's specialty in the Endtenfang restaurant is *le canard du duc,* in which the breast is served with a pepper sauce and potatoes au gratin, and the legs, after a sorbet to clear the palate, with a port wine sauce and mushrooms. The grand salon, with its groupings of leather chairs, has a mirrored ceiling supported by Grecian columns. Try to get one of the four rooms with antique furnishings in the original lodge. The other rooms are in a modern wing without much character. ⊠ *Hannoverische Str. 55, D–29221,* ☎ *05141/201–140,* FAX *05141/201–120. 76 rooms. 2 restaurants, bar, indoor pool, sauna. AE, DC, MC, V.* ⊛

$$ ⊞ **Hotel Celler Hof.** This moderately priced hotel is right in the heart of the half-timber old city, just steps from the Rathaus, palace, and Bomann Museum. Since it is owned by the same group as the nearby **Hotel Fürstenhof** (☞ *above*), guests are welcome to use the indoor pool and solarium there. ⊠ *Stechbahn 11, D–29221,* ☎ *05141/911–960,* FAX *05141/911–9644. 49 rooms. Bar, lobby, sauna, exercise room. AE, DC, MC, V.* ⊛

Bergen-Belsen

㉓ *25 km (15 mi) north of Celle.*

Just outside Celle is a sobering contrast to the charm of half-timbering and heather. At the site of the infamous concentration camp on the Lüneburg Heath, the **Gedenkstätte Bergen-Belsen** (Bergen-Belsen Memorial) is a memorial to the victims of the Holocaust. Diarist Anne Frank was among the more than 80,000 persons who died here.

Only the gruesome photographs on display will tell what the camp looked like. There is nothing left of it. The British liberators found thousands and thousands of unburied corpses all over the camp, so as a precaution against disease, they burned everything down.

Those who venture onto the site of the camp may be surprised at its pleasant, parklike appearance. Reminders of the horrors that once were include numerous burial mounds, mostly overgrown with heather and with stones with such inscriptions as HERE LIE 1,000 DEAD. Anne Frank probably lies in one of them. The SS officers had hoped to have the dead buried and out of sight before the British forces arrived, but the starving prisoners were too weak for the job. Under the direction of the British, the graves you see were dug and filled by the SS officers themselves. The British also tried and executed the camp's SS commandant, Josef Kramer, better known as the "Beast of Belsen."

The foundations of the barracks were unearthed in recent years by volunteer youth groups. Monuments and shrines include a Jewish memorial dating to 1946, with a commemorative stone dedicated by the Israeli president in 1987; an obelisk and memorial wall erected by the British; a wooden cross dating to only weeks after the liberation, and a commemorative stone from the German government.

The main feature of the memorial is a permanent exhibition on the history of the camp and the Nazi persecution system. Though all signs are in German, there are supplementary guides (DM 5) in English and eight other languages, including Hebrew. There are also regular showings of a video on the camp in English, German, and French. Children under 12 are not admitted to the showings, and it is said that one of the British photographers who made the footage couldn't bear to look at his work in later years. ⊠ *Just off the unnumbered hwy. connecting Bergen and Winsen,* ☎ *05051/6011.* 🎟 *Free.* ☉ *Daily 9–6.*

Dining and Lodging

$ 🏠 **Hof Averbeck.** People who think the Lüneburg Heath looks like an ideal place for a farm vacation will find confirmation here. The typical heath farm doubles as a bed-and-breakfast. Well off the main highway, it's great for children, with ponies to ride, animals to feed, and a playground. The farm, which is handy to the Bergen-Belsen Memorial and central for day trips to Hamburg and Hannover, also has cattle, with boar and deer in the surrounding forest and meadows. ⊠ *Hassel 3, D–29303 Bergen,* ☎ *05054/249,* 🖷 *05054/269. 14 rooms, 2 apartments. No credit cards.*

BREMEN

㉔ Germany's smallest city-state, **Bremen** is also Germany's oldest port, second in size to Hamburg. Together with Hamburg and Lübeck, Bremen was an early member of the merchant-run Hanseatic League, and its rivalry with the larger port on the Elbe River is still tangible. Though Hamburg may still claim its title as Germany's "door to the world," Bremen likes to boast: "But we have the key."

Bremen is also central to the fable of the Bremer Stadtmusikanten, or Bremen Town Musicians—a rooster, cat, dog, and donkey quartet that came to Bremen to seek its fortune. (Their music and singing was so awful that it caused a band of robbers to flee in terror, thus saving the town.) Their feats are reenacted in a free, open-air play in the market square at noon and 1:30 each Sunday, from May to October. You'll find statues of this group in various parts of the city.

Exploring Bremen

Bremen's **Marktplatz** is one of Europe's most impressive market squares. It's bordered by an imposing, 900-year-old Gothic cathedral, an ancient Rathaus, a 16th-century guildhall, and a modern glass-and-steel state parliament building, with gabled town houses finishing the panorama. Alongside the northwest corner of the Rathaus is the famous bronze statue of the four **Bremen Town Musicians,** one atop the other in a sort of pyramid. Another well-known figure on the square is the stone statue of the knight in service to Charlemagne, **Roland,** erected in 1404. Three times larger than life, the statue serves as Bremen's good-luck piece and a symbol of freedom and independence.

Construction of the **St. Petri Dom** (St. Peter's Cathedral) began in the mid-11th century. Its two prominent towers are Gothic, but in the late 1800s the cathedral was restored in the Romanesque style. It served as the seat of an archbishop until the Reformation turned the cathedral Protestant. ✉ *Marktpl.,* ☎ *no phone.* 🎫 *Free.* ☉ *Weekdays 10–5, Sat. 10–2, Sun. 2–5.*

Charlemagne had established a diocese here in the 9th century, and a 15th-century statue of him, together with seven princes, adorns the Gothic **Rathaus,** which acquired a Weser Renaissance facade during the early 17th century. Tours are given in German. ✉ *Marktpl.* 🎫 *Tour DM 5.* ☉ *Tours Mon.–Sat. 11, noon, 3, and 4; Sun. 11 and noon.*

The **Übersee Museum** (Overseas Museum) has unusual displays on the histories and cultures of the many peoples with whom Bremen traders came into contact. One section is devoted to North America. ✉ *Bahnhofspl. 13,* ☎ *0421/361–9201.* 🎫 *DM 6.* ☉ *Tues.–Sun. 10–6.*

Don't leave Bremen without strolling down **Böttcherstrasse** (Barrel-Maker's Street), at one time inhabited by coopers. Between 1924 and 1931 their houses were torn down and reconstructed in a style at once historically sensitive and modern by Bremen coffee millionaire Ludwig Roselius. (He was the inventor of decaffeinated coffee and held the patent for many years; Sanka was its brand name in the United States.) Many of the restored houses are used as galleries for local artists. At one end of Böttcherstrasse is the **Roselius-Haus,** a 14th-century building that is now a museum showcasing German and Dutch paintings, as well as wood carvings, furniture, textiles, and decorative arts from the 12th through the 18th centuries. Notice also the arch of Meissen bells at the rooftop. These chime daily at noon, 3, and 6. ✉ *Böttcherstr. 6–10,* ☎ *0421/336–5077.* 🎫 *DM 8.* ☉ *Tues.–Sun. 11–6.*

★　Also take a walk through the idyllic **Schnoorviertel** (Schnoor District), a jumble of houses, taverns, and shops once occupied or frequented by fishermen and tradespeople. This is Bremen's oldest district, dating back to the 15th and 16th centuries. Over the last decade the area has become fashionable among artists and craftspeople, who have restored the tiny cottages to serve as galleries and workshops. Other buildings have been converted into popular small cafés and pubs.

....

OFF THE
BEATEN PATH

BREMERHAVEN – This busy port city belongs to Bremen and is 66 km (41 mi) upriver, where the Weser empties into the North Sea. You can take in the enormity of the port from a promenade or from a platform in the North Harbor. The country's largest and most fascinating maritime museum, the **Deutsches Schiffahrtsmuseum** (German Maritime Museum) is a fun place to explore. Part of the museum consists of a harbor with seven old trading ships. A train to Bremerhaven from Bremen takes about one hour. ✉ *Hans-Scharoun-Pl. 1, from Bremen take A–27 to exit* *for Bremerhaven-Mitte,* ☎ *0471/482–070.* 🎫 *DM 6.* ☺ *Tues.–Sun. 10–6. Harbor closed Oct.–Mar.*

Dining and Lodging

$$$$ ✕ **Park Restaurant.** Thanks to Chef Henry Precht, the Park is one of the
★ finest dining establishments in Germany. Within the Park Hotel Bremen
(☞ *below*), it is somewhat small, but the floor-to-ceiling windows and
lacquered ceiling open up the room. The stunning dining room is decorated in yellow, black, and cream, with shimmering crystal chandeliers,
classical moldings, marble urns, and Louis XVI chairs. Chef Precht in-
troduces a dash of fantasy to his classic French and Italian dishes, which
may include air-dried ham and pickled salmon. Reservations are advised.
✉ *Im Bürgerpark,* ☎ *0421/340–8633. Jacket and tie. AE, DC, MC, V.*

$$ ✕ **Comturei.** The vaults of Bremen's ancient Heiliggeistkirche (Church
of the Holy Spirit) were secularized some time ago, becoming a beer
cellar and restaurant, where the traditional German cuisine is devil-
ishly good if not exactly heavenly. Special medieval banquet menus are
served to groups of more than 10, but there's often a place for a lone
diner—and it's a great way to meet the locals. ✉ *Ostertorstr. 30–32,*
☎ *0421/325–050. AE, MC, V.*

$$ ✕ **Grashoff's Bistro.** Locals fill the closely packed tables at this popu-
★ lar lunchtime bistro. The menu has a French touch, with an accent on
fresh fish from the Bremerhaven market. Old prints and photographs
cover the walls. ✉ *Contrescarpe 80,* ☎ *0421/14740. DC, V. Closed
Sun. No dinner.*

$$ ✕ **Ratskeller.** Said to be Germany's oldest and most renowned town-
★ hall restaurant, this one specializes in solid, typical northern German
fare, including creatively prepared poultry and fresh seafood. Shortly
after the restaurant opened beneath the Rathaus in 1408, the city fa-
thers decreed that only wine could be served there, and the ban on beer
still exists. The cellar is lined with wine casks, including an 18th-cen-
tury barrel that could house a small family. Connoisseurs have more
than 600 wine labels from which to choose—and they're all German.
✉ *Am Markt,* ☎ *0421/321–676. AE, DC, MC, V.*

$$$$ ✕🏨 **Park Hotel Bremen.** This palatial lakeside hotel has the atmosphere
★ of an exclusive country mansion. A quiet dignity pervades, from the
corridors bathed with natural ceiling light to the beautiful bedrooms,
each decorated in an individual style, from opulently Moorish to min-
imalist Japanese. If you manage to secure a room in the magnificent
cupola, you'll awaken to sun streaming through mansard windows.
There are views of the surrounding park from all rooms, including many
from the exquisite marble bathrooms. The Park Restaurant (☞ *above*)
is the best fine dining around. ✉ *Im Bürgerpark, D–28209,* ☎ *0421/
34080, 800/223–6800 for reservations in the U.S.,* 📠 *0421/340–8602.
194 rooms, 13 suites. 2 restaurants, bar, café, beauty salon, massage,
bicycles. AE, DC, MC, V.* ♿

$$$–$$$$ ✕🏨 **Mercure Columbus.** Under the French management of the Accor
group, this elegant hotel is adjacent to the train station and only a short
stroll from the Old Town. Rooms are spacious; the double-bed rooms
actually have two queen-size beds. Breakfast is not included in the room
rate, but the enormous buffet is worth the price. ✉ *Bahnhofpl. 5–7,
D–28195,* ☎ *0421/30120,* 📠 *0421/15369. 143 rooms, 5 suites. Bar,
sauna, solarium. AE, DC, MC, V.*

$$–$$$ 🏨 **Hotel Landhaus Louisenthal.** This half-timber country-house hotel
★ on the outskirts of Bremen is 150 years old. Its old-world charm also
comes from the caring, family-run management. ✉ *Leher Heerstr.
105, D–28359,* ☎ *0421/232–076,* 📠 *0421/236–716. 61 rooms.
Restaurant, sauna. AE, DC, MC, V.* ♿

Nightlife and the Arts

Bremen may be Germany's oldest seaport, but it can't match Hamburg for racy nightlife. Nevertheless, the streets around the central Marktplatz and in the historic Schnoor District are filled with all sorts of taverns and bars.

The Bremen and Bremerhaven casinos attract gamblers from as far as Hamburg. The **Bremen casino** (⊠ Böttcherstr. 3–5, ☎ 0421/329–000) is open daily 3 PM to 1 AM, and the **Bremerhaven casino** (⊠ Theodor-Heuss-Pl. 3, ☎ 0471/413–641) is open daily until midnight.

Bremen has a **philharmonic orchestra** of national stature, which plays regularly at the city's concert hall. It also has three theaters, which regularly stage classical and modern dramas, comedies, and musical comedies: the **Schauspielhaus** (⊠ Goethepl. 1), the **Concordia,** (⊠ Schwachhäuser Heerstr. 1), and the **Musiktheater** (⊠ Goethepl. 1-3). Call 0421/365–3333 for program details and tickets. The **Bremen Shakespeare Company** (⊠ Leibnitzpl. 1, ☎ 0421/500–333) has achieved national fame for its excellent productions.

Shopping

In Bremen bargain hunters should head to the **Schnoorviertel** (☞ *above*). Bremerhaven has one of Germany's oldest established shoemakers, **Leder-Koopmann** (⊠ Georgstr. 56, ☎ 0471/302–829), where you can buy first-class footwear and all kinds of leather goods, made with the kind of care that has kept the firm in business since 1898.

THE FAIRY-TALE ROAD A TO Z

Arriving and Departing

By Bus
Bremen, Kassel, Göttingen, Fulda, and Hanau all are reachable via Europabus. For information, timetables, and reservations, contact **Deutsche Touring** (⊠ Am Römerhof 17, D–60486 Frankfurt am Main, ☎ 069/790–350, ℻ 069/790–3219, 🖭).

By Car
Major north–south and east–west autobahns crisscrossthe region, affording easy and speedy access to major cities.

By Plane
Frankfurt, Hannover, and Hamburg have the closest international airports to the area. Frankfurt is less than half an hour from Hanau, and Hamburg is less than an hour from Bremen.

By Train
Hanau, Fulda, Kassel, and Göttingen all are on both the InterCity Express Frankfurt–Hamburg line and the Frankfurt–Berlin line (not all of these trains stop at Hanau). The Frankfurt-Hamburg line also stops in Hannover, and there is additional ICE service to Hannover and to Bremen from Frankfurt and other major cities.

Getting Around

By Boat
From May through September the **Oberweser-Dampfschiffahrt** (⊠ Inselstr. 3, D–31787 Hameln, ☎ 05151/22016) runs its six ships daily on the Weser River between Hameln, Bodenwerder, and Bad Karlshafen.

A Kassel company, the **Rehbein-Linie Kassel** (✉ Weserstr. 5, D–34125 Kassel, ☎ 0561/18505) operates a boat service between Kassel, Hannoversch-Münden, and Bad Karlshafen.

By Bus

Frankfurt, Kassel, Göttingen, and Bremen all have city bus services that extend into the countryside along the Fairy-Tale Road.

By Car

The Fairy-Tale Road incorporates one of Germany's loveliest scenic drives, the **Wesertalstrasse,** or Weser Valley Road, between Hannoversch-Münden and Hameln. The autobahn network penetrates deep into the area, serving Hanau, Fulda, Kassel, Göttingen, and Bremen directly. Bremen is 60 km (35 mi) northeast of Hannover.

By Train

Four cities, though too small for ICE service, are big enough for rail service. They are Hannoversch-Münden, Marburg (change for both at Kassel), Hameln, and Celle (change for both at Hannover).

Contacts and Resources

Car Rentals

Avis (✉ Kirchbachstr. 200, Bremen, ☎ 0421/201–060; ✉ Am Klagesmarkt 22, Hannover, ☎ 0511/121–740). **Hertz** (✉ Flughafenallee 22, Bremen, ☎ 0421/555–350; ✉ Langenhagen Airport, Hannover, ☎ 0551/779–041). **Sixt** (✉ Duckwitzstr. 60, Bremen, ☎ 0421/510–055; ✉ Schulenburger Landstr. 66, Hannover, ☎ 0511/352–1213; ✉ Weserstr. 6, Kassel, ☎ 0561/500–880).

Emergencies

Police and ambulance (☎ 110). **Fire and emergency medical aid** (☎ 112).

Guided Tours

Bremen's tours depart daily at 10:30 from the central bus station. **Fulda** has a tour of the Old Town, starting at the Stadtschloss, April–October daily; November–March, weekends and holidays at 11:30. **Göttingen** shows visitors around April–October, weekends at 2:30 (starting from the Old Town Hall). To sit back and see the sights in comfort, you can hire one of the several city taxi drivers who double as guides (☎ 0551/69300). A city-tour taxi isn't cheap: DM 55 for one hour. But when were you last shown around by a taxi driver who *really* knew what he or she is talking about? **Hameln** offers tours April–October, Monday–Saturday at 3 and Sunday at 10 and 3, leaving from the tourist office (✉ Diesterallee 3). The major sights of **Hannover** are strung together on a tourist trail marked by red signs. The "Red Thread" is also clearly marked on a map obtainable from the tourist office. Guided bus tours of Hannover start from outside the tourist office May–September, daily at 1:30; October–April, Saturday at 1:30. With advance notice, **Hannoversch-Münden's** tourist office can set up tours for groups (☎ 05541/75313). Guided bus tours of **Kassel** set off from Königsplatz May–October, every Saturday at 2. Tours are free if you buy a ServiceCard, which costs DM 12 for 24 hours and DM 29 for three days (the card also entitles you to free travel on all city trams and buses, reduced admission to museums, and free admission to the casino). The tourist office of **Steinau an der Strasse** (☎ 06663/963–133) can set up group tours by prearrangement.

BOAT TOURS

The **Oberweser-Dampfschiffahrt** operates summer services on the Weser River between Hameln and Bad Karlshafen and will give you advice on how to combine a boat trip with a tour by bike, bus, or train. It has a five-day round-trip cruise from Bodenwerder to Bad Karlshafen. Included in the price of DM 585 per person in a double room is a daily breakfast buffet, four other meals, and tours to Bodenwerder, the Reichsabtei Corvey, and the Fürstenberg porcelain factory. It also has daily excursions from Hameln, Hannoversch-Münden, Bad Karlshafen, and Bodenwerder, and in the summer months a day trip (Tuesday–Sunday) between Holzminden and Bad Karlshafen, with lunch, tea, and a guided tour of the Corvey Abbey included in the DM 69 fare. Call for details and reservations (☎ 05151/22016). The **Rehbein-Linie Kassel** operates a service from Kassel to Bad Karlshafen. One of its two boats, the *Deutschland,* even has a bowling alley aboard. For schedule information and bookings, contact the company at its Kassel headquarters (✉ Weserstr. 5, D–34125, ☎ 0561/18505, ⨳ 0561/102–839). Another Kassel company, **Personenschiffahrt K. & K. Söllner** (✉ Die Schlagd Rondell, D–34125, ☎ 0561/774–670), has two excursion boats plying between Kassel and Hannoversch-Münden.

There are two enjoyable boat excursions from Bremerhaven: a one-hour trip around the harbor for DM 13 and an all-day round-trip to the fortress North Sea island of **Helgoland** for DM 58. Call 0471/946–4610 for information. If you're in a hurry to see Helgoland, there's a quicker daily round-trip flight for DM 264 per person from the **Bremerhaven Airport** (☎ 0471/77188 for flight details).

BUS TOURS

Year-round tours of the region are offered by a Hameln company, **Rattenfänger-Reisen** (✉ Bahnhofstr. 18/20, ☎ 05151/811–414), and by **Radke–Reisen** (✉ Sonnental Str. 89, Hessisch Oldendorf, ☎ 05152/94480). The Radke-Reisen tours can be joined at several points in Hameln, including the train station. Some local authorities—those in Bad Karlshafen, for example—also organize bus tours. Contact individual tourist offices for details.

Outdoor Activities and Sports

BIKING

The Fulda and Werra rivers have 190 km (118 mi) of cycle paths, and you can cycle the whole length of the Weser River from Hannoversch-Münden to the outskirts of Bremen without making too many detours from the river valley. The tourist authority, **Touristik Naturpark Münden** (✉ Rathaus, Am Markt, D–34346 Hannoversch-Münden, ☎ 05541/75313), organizes five- and seven-day cycle tours of the Fulda and Werra River valleys, including bike rentals, overnight accommodations, and luggage transport between stops.

GOLF

Schloss Schwöbber (☎ 05154/9870), near Hameln, has two 18-hole golf courses.

HIKING

Fremdenverkehrsverband Weserbergland-Mittelweser (✉ D–31785 Hameln, ☎ 05151/93000) can supply information for numerous pleasant walks in the hilly, densely forested region that characterizes the area.

HORSEBACK RIDING

There is an **equestrian center** at Löwensen, near Bad Pyrmont (☎ 05281/10606). **Hameln** also has stables (☎ 05151/3513). Katrin Graf's **Circle K Ranch** (☎ 06663/5321), at Steinau-Marborn, rents horses trained to be ridden western style.

WATER SPORTS
Canoes can be rented from **Busch Freizeitservice** (⊠ Postweg Nord 7, 37671 Höxter, ☎ 05271/921363), which also organizes boat trips on the Fulda, Weser, and Werra rivers.

Visitor Information

Information on the Fairy-Tale Road can be obtained from the **Deutsche Märchenstrasse** (⊠ Königspl. 53, D–34117 Kassel, ☎ 0561/707–7120).

There are local tourist information offices in the following towns:

Alsfeld (⊠ Verkehrsbüro Touristcenter, Ritterg. 5, D–36304, ☎ 06631/182–165, ✆). **Bad Pyrmont** (⊠ Touristik Information, Europapl. 1, D–31812, ☎ 05281/940–511, www.badpyrmont.de). **Bodenwerder** (⊠ Städtische Verkehrsamt, Weserstr. 3, D–37619, ☎ 05533/40521,✆). **Bremen** (⊠ Verkehrsverein, Findorffstr. 105, D–28215, ☎ 0421/19433,✆). **Bremerhaven** (⊠ Verkehrsamt der Seestadt Bremerhaven, Van-Ronzelen-Str. 2, D–27568, ☎ 0471/946–4610, ✆). **Fulda** (⊠ Städtische Verkehrsbüro, Schlossstr. 1, D–36037, ☎ 0661/102–346, ✆). **Gelnhausen** (⊠ Verkehrsverein, Am Obermarkt, D–63571, ☎ 06051/480–721, ✆). **Göttingen** (⊠ Fremdenverkehrsverein, Altes Rathaus, D–37073, ☎ 0551/54000,✆). **Hameln** (⊠ Hameln Marketing und Tourismus, Deisterallee 3 (am Bürgergarten), D–31785, ☎ 05151/202–617,✆). **Hanau** (⊠ Verkehrsbüro, Altstädter Markt 1, D–63450, ☎ 06181/277–515, ✆). **Hannover** (⊠ Hannover Information, Ernst-August-Pl., D–30159, ☎ 0511/301–421 or 0511/301–422, ✆). **Hannoversch-Münden** (⊠ Verkehrsbüro, Rathaus am Markt, D–34346, ☎ 05541/75313, ✆). **Höxter** (⊠ Fremdenverkehrsverein, Historisches Rathaus, Weserstr. 11, D–37671, ☎ 05271/963–431,✆). **Kassel** (⊠ Tourist-Information, Königspl. 53, D–34117, ☎ 0561/707–707,✆). **Marburg** (⊠ Pilgrimstein 26, D–35037 ☎ 06421/99120). **Steinau an der Strasse** (⊠ Verkehrsamt, Bruder-Grimm-Str. 70, D–36396, ☎ 06663/963–133).

13 HAMBURG

Water—in the form of the Alster Lakes and the River Elbe—is Hamburg's defining feature and the key to the city's success. The city-state's official title, the Free and Hanseatic City of Hamburg, reflects its kingpin status in the medieval Hanseatic League, a union that dominated trade on the North and the Baltic seas. The seafaring life has given the city some of its most distinctive attractions, from the fish market to the red-light district (the Reeperbahn).

H AMBURG IS FOREMOST a harbor city with an international past, and is still probably the most tolerant and open-minded of German cities. The media have made Hamburg their capital by planting some of the leading newspapers, magazines, and television stations here. Add to that the slick world of advertising, show business, and model agencies, and you have a populace of worldly and fashionable professionals. Not surprisingly, the city of movers and shakers is also the city with most of Germany's millionaires.

The *Hanseaten*—members of the distinguished city business and political elite—act with an understatement, modesty, and sincerity that have gained them a formidable reputation throughout Germany. Downtown and in fashionable restaurants, Hanseaten are easily recognizable by their conservative dress code of navy blue and gray. Those accustomed to the warm Gemütlichkeit (conviviality) and jolly camaraderie of Munich should be advised that Hamburg initially presents a more somber face, as do most northern German cities. People here are reputed to be notoriously frugal and cool, yet within their own *Kiez* (street and neighborhood) they are generous and hospitable hosts with a penchant for indulging in the most refined delicacies.

For Europeans, the port city invariably triggers thoughts of the gaudy Reeperbahn underworld, that sleazy strip of clip joints, sex shows, and wholesale prostitution that helped earn Hamburg its reputation as "Sin City." Today the infamous red-light district is just as much a hip meeting place for young Hamburgers and tourist crowds, who flirt with the bright lights and chic haunts of the not-so-sinful Reeperbahn, especially on warm summer nights.

Hamburg, or "Hammaburg," was founded in 810 by Charlemagne. For centuries it was a walled city, its gigantic outer fortifications providing a tight little world relatively impervious to outside influences. The city is at the mouth of the Elbe, one of Europe's great rivers and the 97-km (60-mi) umbilical cord that ties the harbor to the North Sea. Its role as a port gained it world renown. It was one of the kingpins of the Hanseatic League, the medieval union of northern German merchant cities that dominated shipping in the Baltic and North seas, with satellites in Bergen, Visby, Danzig, Riga, Novgorod, and elsewhere.

The Thirty Years' War left Hamburg unscathed, and Napoléon's domination of much of the continent in the early 19th century also failed to affect it. Indeed, it was in the 19th century that Hamburg reached the crest of its power, when the largest shipping fleets on the seas with some of the fastest ships afloat were based here. Its merchants traded with the far corners of the globe. Ties to New York, Buenos Aires, and Rio de Janeiro were stronger than those to Berlin or Frankfurt. During the four decades leading up to World War I, Hamburg became one of the world's richest cities. Its aura of wealth and power continued right up to the outbreak of World War II. Nowadays about 15,000 ships sail up the lower Elbe each year, carrying more than 50 million tons of cargo—from petroleum and locomotives to grain and bananas.

What you see today is the "new" Hamburg. The Great Fire of 1842 all but obliterated the original city; a century later World War II bombing raids destroyed port facilities and leveled more than half of the city proper. The miracle is that in spite of the 1940–44 raids, Hamburg now stands as a remarkably faithful replica of that glittering prewar city— a place of enormous style, verve, and elegance, with considerable architectural diversity, including turn-of-the-century *Jugendstil* (Art Nouveau) buildings. Of particular interest are the 14th-century houses of Deichstrasse—the oldest residential area in Hamburg—and the Kontorhausviertel (Merchant Quarter). The latter contains some unique clinker-brick buildings from the 1920s.

The comparison that Germans like to draw between Hamburg and Venice is somewhat exaggerated. But the city *is* threaded with countless canals and waterways spanned by about 1,000 bridges, even more than you'll find in Venice. Swans glide on the canals. Arcaded passageways run along the waterways. In front of the Renaissance-style Rathaus (city hall) is a square that resembles the Piazza San Marco.

The distinguishing feature of downtown Hamburg is the Alster (Alster Lakes). Once an insignificant waterway, it was dammed in the 18th century to form an artificial lake. Divided at its south end, it is known as the Binnenalster (Inner Alster) and the Aussenalster (Outer Alster)—the two separated by a pair of graceful bridges, the Lombard Brücke and the John F. Kennedy Brücke. The Inner Alster is lined with stately hotels, department stores, fine shops, and cafés; the Outer Alster, is framed by the spacious greenery of parks and gardens against a backdrop of private mansions. From late spring into fall, sailboats and surfboards skim across the surface of the Outer Alster and white excursion steamers ferry back and forth. The view from these vessels (or from the shore of the Outer Alster) is of the stunning skyline of six spiny spires (five churches and the Rathaus) that is Hamburg's identifying feature. It all creates one of the most distinctive downtown areas of any European city.

Pleasures and Pastimes

Dining
Hamburg is undoubtedly one of the best places in the country to enjoy fresh seafood. The flotilla of fishing boats brings a wide variety of fish to the city—to sophisticated upscale restaurants as well as simple harborside taverns. One of the most celebrated dishes among the robust local specialties is *Aalsuppe* (eel soup), a tangy concoction not entirely unlike Marseilles's famous bouillabaisse. A must in summer is *Aalsuppe grün* (eel soup seasoned with dozens of herbs). *Räucheraal* (smoked eel) is equally good. In the fall try *Bunte oder Gepflückte Finten,* a dish of green and white beans, carrots, and apples. Available anytime of year is *Küken* ragout, a concoction of sweet breads, spring chicken, tiny veal meatballs, asparagus, clams, and fresh peas cooked in a white sauce. Other northern German specialties include *Stubenküken* (young, male, oven-fried chicken), *Vierländer Mastente* (duck stuffed with apples, onions, and raisins), *Birnen, Bohnen, und Speck* (pears, beans, and bacon), and the sailors' favorite, *Labskaus*—a stew made from pickled meat, potatoes, and (sometimes) herring, garnished with a fried egg, sour pickles, and lots of beets.

The Harbor
A cruise of Germany's gateway to the world is a must. The energy from the continuous ebb and flow of huge cargo vessels and container ships, and the harbor's prosperity and international flavor best symbolize the city's spirit. The narrow cobblestone streets and late-medieval warehouses in the older parts of town testify to Hamburg's powerful Hanseatic past. Bars and nightclubs have transformed some of the harbor area into a hot spot for eyebrow-raising entertainment.

Shopping
Although not as rich or sumptuous on first sight as Düsseldorf or Munich, Hamburg is nevertheless expensive and ranks first among Germany's shopping experiences. Chichi boutiques sell primarily

distinguished and somewhat conservative fashion; understatement is the style here. Some of the country's premier designers, such as Karl Lagerfeld, Jil Sander, and Wolfgang Joop, are either native Hamburgers or have worked here for quite some time. Hamburg has the greatest number of shopping malls in the country, mostly small but elegant downtown arcades offering entertainment, fashion, and fine food.

EXPLORING HAMBURG

Hamburg's most important attractions stretch between the Alster Lakes, to the north, and the harbor and the Elbe River, to the south. This area consists of three unique quarters. The first is the business district around the Hauptbahnhof (central train station) and the Rathaus (town hall); the second, the historic neighborhood clustered near the harbor; and the third, the shabby but thrilling district of St. Pauli, including the Reeperbahn, the strip of sex clubs and bars.

Numbers in the text correspond to numbers in the margin and on the Hamburg map.

Great Itineraries

Though Hamburg, with more than 1.7 million citizens, is Germany's second-largest city, it's nevertheless manageable. Easily traversed on foot, the business district retains its relatively small medieval scale, yet it's dominated by broad shopping boulevards and modern buildings. You can reach the historic quarters near the harbor and St. Pauli in minutes by subway and then explore them on foot.

IF YOU HAVE 2 DAYS

With two days you can see all the major sights in town. Start at the Alster Lakes and head toward the main shopping boulevards of Jungfernstieg and Mönckebergstrasse. A short walk south of Mönckebergstrasse takes you to the majestic Rathaus Square, while a brief walk north on the same street leads to the equally impressive Hauptbahnhof, the largest steel-and-glass construction of its kind in Europe. To the southeast, the Kontorhausviertel is one of the nicest parts of town, a collection of old brick warehouses dating back to the 1920s.

Take a quick tour of the Freihafen Hamburg, Hamburg's port, on your second day. Compare the port's modern warehouses with their antique counterparts on photogenic Deichstrasse in the Altstadt (Old City). You may want to inspect at least one of the city's great churches; a good choice is the city's premier baroque landmark, St. Michaeliskirche. Finally, head over to the Landungsbrücken, the starting point for boat rides in the harbor and along the Elbe River. And don't leave Hamburg without a jaunt down St. Pauli's Reeperbahn.

IF YOU HAVE 3 DAYS

Begin a day watching wild animals roam free at Hagenbecks Tierpark. Equally green are the two parks, Planten und Blomen and the Alter Botanischer Garten, in the business district. After exploring the downtown's other attractions, from the Alster to the Hauptbahnhof, detour to the Kunsthalle and the Museum für Kunst und Gewerbe, both showcasing some of the best paintings and artwork in Germany.

Devote another day to historic Hamburg and the harbor. Take in the docks and don't miss the Speicherstadt's 19th-century warehouses. After a walk among the charming houses on Deichstrasse, continue on to the meticulously restored Krameramtswohnungen, the late-medieval shopkeepers' guild houses. Next, visit the Museum für Hamburgische Geschichte for an excellent overview of the city's dramatic past.

Save a day for St. Pauli, too. Early one morning, mingle with locals at the Fischmarkt, a boisterous market. Board one of the boats at the Landungsbrücken for a sightseeing tour through the harbor. One evening should be spent along the Reeperbahn, perhaps including the Erotic Art Museum, one of the few tasteful displays of eroticism on the strip.

IF YOU HAVE 4 DAYS

You'll be able to make some trips off the beaten path with this many days. To get a glimpse of Hamburg's playful turn-of-the-century Jugendstil architecture, start the first day west of the lakes at the Dammtorbahnhof and make quick trips to Hagenbecks Tierpark and the Planten und Blomen and Alter Botanischer Garten parks. The inner-city district has many highlights, from the Alster to the Kontorhausviertel, including the Chilehaus and St. Jacobikirche, a medieval church with Gothic altars.

On the second day explore Hamburg's past at the harbor and in other old parts of town. Begin with the St. Katharinenkirche, the city's perfectly restored baroque church. Then spend the afternoon at Hamburg's harbor and its historic attractions, from the Freihafen Hamburg to Krameramtswohnungen, including the Alte St. Nikolaikirche, a church ruin now preserved as a memorial. End the day by viewing the city from the giant Bismarck-Denkmal. Spend a third day in St. Pauli. On the fourth day return to the Landungsbrücken and embark on a boat ride to the terraced, waterside village of Blankenese. This is old Hamburg at its best.

Downtown Hamburg

The city's heart is centered on two extensive shopping boulevards, the Jungfernstieg and the Mönckebergstrasse. The area was heavily bombarded during World War II, so most of the buildings here were constructed after it; they now house banks, insurance companies, and other big businesses. Downtown may not be the most beautiful part of town, but its atmosphere is invigorating.

A Good Walk

Begin at **Dammtorbahnhof** ①, a fine example of Hamburg's Jugendstil architecture. Departing from the south exit, you can easily take a detour to Hamburg's zoo, **Hagenbecks Tierpark** ②, one of Germany's oldest and most popular urban animal habitats. It has its own subway stop on the U–2 line. After visiting the zoo, return to the south exit of the Dammtor station; on your right you'll see the SAS Plaza Hotel and the Congress Centrum Hamburg (CCH), a vast, modern conference-and-entertainment complex. Continue past the Congress Centrum and bear left in a sweeping arc through the ornamental park **Planten und Blomen** ③. When you leave the park, make your way to the northeast entrance of the **Alter Botanische Garten** ④ at Stephansplatz and head south to cross over the Esplanade. Both the park and the gardens are in the larger Wallringpark, which encompasses four parks in all. Walk down Colonnaden to reach the **Alster Lakes** ⑤ and the **Jungfernstieg** ⑥, the most elegant boulevard in downtown Hamburg.

Turn right off the **Jungfernstieg** ⑥ onto Reesendamm and make your way to the **Rathaus** ⑦ and its square. Leave by its east side, perhaps pausing to join those relaxing on the steps of the memorial to the poet Heinrich Heine, a great fan of the city.

Beyond the memorial lies **Mönckebergstrasse** ⑧, Hamburg's not-so-elegant but always-bustling shopping boulevard. At its end you'll meet the busy main road of Steintorwall, which was the easternmost link of the defense wall encircling the Old Town in the 17th century. Take the pedestrian underpass to the **Hauptbahnhof** ⑨, Hamburg's impressive central train station. Leave the Hauptbahnhof the way you entered and turn right on Steintorwall, which continues as Glockengiesserwall, until you come to the major art museum, **Kunsthalle** ⑩, on the corner of Ernst-Merck-Strasse.

A quite different but equally fascinating perspective on art is offered by the nearby **Museum für Kunst und Gewerbe** ⑪. To reach it, head in the direction from which you came and turn left on Steintordamm, crossing over the railroad tracks. The large, yellow museum is across the street, its entrance on Brockestrasse.

Turn right when leaving the museum, then right again onto Kurt-Schumacher-Allee. Cross over Steintorwall near the subway and continue west along Steinstrasse to the **St. Jacobikirche** ⑫—you'll recognize it by its needle spire. Cross over Steinstrasse when leaving the church and head down Burchardstrasse, which will bring you to Burchardplatz. This area between Steinstrasse and Messberg is known as the Kontorhausviertel, a restored quarter with redbrick commercial buildings dating to the 1920s. The most famous building is at the south end of Burchardplatz: the **Chilehaus** ⑬ resembles a huge ship.

TIMING

You need half a day for just walking the proposed tour, depending on how much time you devote to the parks, the zoo (both are crowded but most enjoyable on summer weekends), and to shopping (which isn't advisable on Saturday morning because of the crowds). If you add two hours for visits to the museums and the Rathaus and two more hours for the delightful boat tour on the Alster Lakes, you'll end up spending more than a full day downtown.

Sights to See

❺ **Alster** (Alster Lakes). These twin lakes provide downtown Hamburg one of its most memorable vistas. In summer the boat landing at the Jungfernstieg, below the Alsterpavillion, is the starting point for the *Alsterdampfer,* the flat-bottom passenger boats that traverse the lakes (☞ Guided Tours *in* Hamburg A to Z, *below*). Small sailboats and rowboats, hired from yards on the shores of the Alster, are very much a part of the summer scene.

Every Hamburger dreams of living within sight of the Alster, but only the wealthiest can afford it. Some lucky millionaires own the magnificent garden properties around the Alster's perimeter, known as the Millionaire's Coast. But you don't have to be a guest on one of these estates to enjoy the waterfront—the Alster shoreline has 6 km (4 mi) of tree-lined public pathways. Popular among joggers, these trails are a lovely place for a stroll. ⊠ *U-bahn: Jungfernstieg.*

❹ **Alter Botanische Garten** (Old Botanical Gardens). This green and open park within Wallringpark cultivates rare and exotic plants. Tropical and subtropical species grow under glass in hothouses, and specialty gardens, including herbal and medicinal plantings, are clustered around the moat. ⊠ *Stephanspl.,* ☏ *no phone.* ☞ *Free.* ☉ *Daily 8–6. U-bahn: Stefansplatz.*

❸ **Chilehaus** (Chile House). This building is the most representative example of the northern German clinker-brick architecture of the 1920s. The fantastical 10-story structure, which at first looks like a vast landlocked ship, was commissioned by businessman Henry Sloman, who traded in saltpeter from Chile. The building is the most famous one in the **Kontorhausviertel**, a series of imaginative clinker-brick buildings designed in the New Objectivity style of 1920s civic architect Fritz Schumacher. ⊠ *Burchardspl. U-bahn: Messberg.*

Hamburg

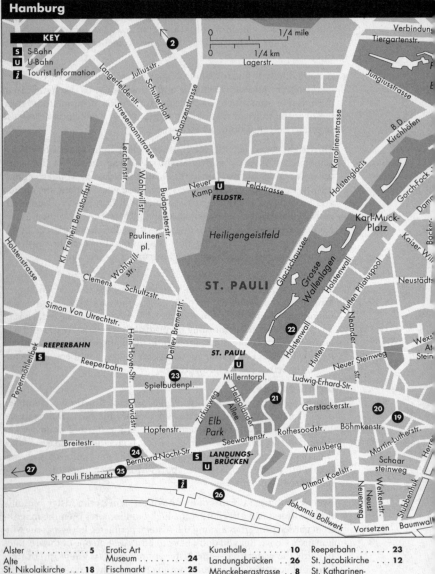

KEY
- **S** S-Bahn
- **U** U-Bahn
- **i** Tourist Information

0 — 1/4 mile
0 — 1/4 km

Verbindung
Tiergartenstr.

Lagerstr.

Langerfelderstr.
Juliusstr.
Schulterblatt
Schanzenstrasse
Stresemannstrasse
Lerchenstr.
Wohlwillstr.
Budapesterstr.
Jungiusstrasse
Karolinenstrasse
Holstenglacis
B.D.
Kirchhöfen
Gorch-Fock-Wall
Neuer
Kamp
U Feldstrasse
FELDSTR.
Kl. Freiheit Bernstorffstr.
Paulinen-
pl.
Heiligengeistfeld
Karl-Muck-
Platz
Kaiser Will
Holstenstrasse
Clemens
Wohlwill
str.
Schultzstr.
Simon Von Utrechtstr.
Glacischaussee
Grosse
Wallanlagen
Holstenwall
Huften Pilatuspool
Neustädts
Neuander
ST. PAULI
REEPERBAHN
Pepermöhlenbek
S
Reeperbahn
Hein-Hoyer-Str.
Detlev Brenerstr.
ST. PAULI
U
Millerntorpl.
Holstenwall
Holstenwall
Huften
Neuer Steinweg
Ludwig-Erhard-Str.
Wexst
At
Stein
23
Spielbudenpl.
Davidstr.
Zirkusweg
Helgoländer
Allee
21
Gerstackerstr.
Böhmkenstr.
20
19
Hopfenstr.
Elb
Park
Seewartenstr.
Rothesoodstr.
Venusberg
Martin-Luther-str.
Breitestr.
24
Bernhard-Nocht-Str.
S
LANDUNGS-
BRÜCKEN
Schaar
steinweg
Herre
27
St. Pauli Fishmarkt
25
U
Ditmar Koelstr.
Werkenstr.
Neust
Neuerweg
Slubbenhuk
Baumwal
i
26
Johannis Bollwerk
Vorsetzen
22

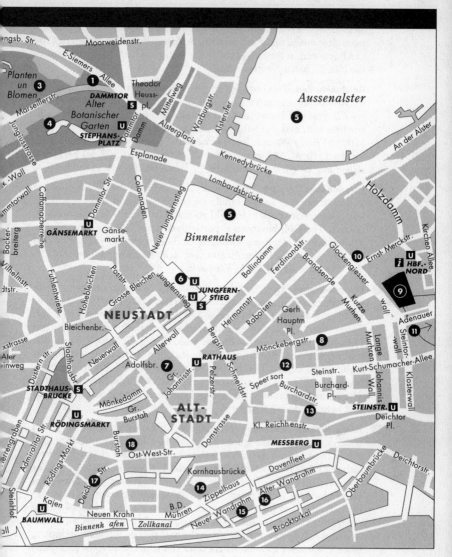

❶ Dammtorbahnhof (Dammtor Train Station). Built in 1903, this elevated steel-and-glass Jugendstil structure is one of Hamburg's finest train stations. It is one of many art nouveau buildings you'll see in the city. You can buy a map at the newsstand in the station to find your way through the city. ⊠ *Ernst-Siemers-Allee.*

Deichtorhallen. This complex of warehouses built in 1911–12 is near the Kontorhausviertel (☞ **Chilehaus,** *above*) and is now one of the country's largest exhibition halls for modern art. Its interior resembles an oversize loft, and its changing exhibits, presenting the works of such artists as Andy Warhol, Roy Lichtenstein, and Miró, have dazzled the local art crowd. ⊠ *Deichtorstr. 1–2,* ☎ *040/321–0307.* ☞ *Fees vary, depending on current exhibition.* ☉ *Tues.–Fri. 11–6, weekends 10–6.*

❷ Hagenbecks Tierpark (Hagenbecks Zoo). One of the country's oldest and most popular zoos is family-owned. Founded in 1848, it was the world's first city park to let wild animals roam freely in vast, open-air corrals. The **Dolphinarium** is particularly popular with kids. ⊠ *Hagenbeckallee at Hamburg-Stellingen,* ☎ *040/5400–014748.* ☞ *Zoo DM 21, Dolphinarium DM 6.* ☉ *Summer, daily 9–sunset; winter, daily 9–4:30. U-bahn: Hagenbecks Tierpark.*

❾ Hauptbahnhof. This central train station's cast-iron-and-glass architecture evokes the grandiose self-confidence of imperial Germany. The building was completed in 1906 and completely renovated in 1991. Today it sees a heavy volume of international, national, and suburban rail traffic. Despite being badly damaged during the Second World War and being modernized many times, it continues to have tremendous architectural impact. The chief feature of the enormous 394-ft-long structure is its 460-ft-wide glazed roof supported only by pillars at each end. The largest structure of its kind in Europe, it is remarkably spacious and light inside. ⊠ *Steintorpl.*

❻ Jungfernstieg. This wide promenade looking out over the Alster Lakes is the city's premier shopping boulevard. Its attractive promenade, laid out in 1665, used to be part of a muddy millrace that channeled water into the Elbe. The two lakes meet at the 17th-century defense wall at Lombard Brücke, the first bridge visible across the water. Hidden from view behind the sedate facade of Jungfernstieg is a network of nine covered arcades that together account for almost a mile of shops selling everything from souvenirs to haute couture. Many of these air-conditioned passages have sprung up in the past two decades (☞ Shopping, *below*), but some have been here since the 19th century; the first glass-covered arcade, called Sillem's Bazaar, was built in 1845.

NEED A BREAK?   Hamburg's best-known and oldest café, the **Alsterpavillon** (⊠ Jungfernstieg 54, ☎ 040/355–0920) is an ideal vantage point from which to observe the constant activity on the Binnenalster (Inner Alster).

★ ❿ Kunsthalle (Art Gallery). One of the most important art museums in Germany, the Kunsthalle has 3,000 paintings, 400 sculptures, and a coin and medal collection that dates from the 14th century. In the postmodern, cube-shape building designed by Berlin architect O. M. Ungers, the **Galerie der Gegenwart** houses a collection of international modern art created since 1960, including works by Andy Warhol, Joseph Beuys, Georg Baselitz, and David Hockney. Graphic art is also well represented, with a special collection of works by Picasso and the late Hamburg artist Horst Janssen, famous for his satirical world view. In the old wing, you can view works by local artists dating from the 16th century. The outstanding collection of German Romantic paintings includes works by Runge, Friedrich, and Spitzweg. Paintings by Holbein,

Rembrandt, Van Dyck, Tiepolo, and Canaletto are also on view, while late-19th-century impressionism is represented by works by Leibl, Liebermann, Manet, Monet, and Renoir. ✉ *Glockengiesserwall 1,* ☎ *040/4285–42612.* 🖅 *DM 12.* 🕙 *Tues., Wed., and Fri.–Sun. 10–6, Thurs. 10–9. U-bahn: Hauptbahnhof.* 🕮

8 **Mönckebergstrasse.** This broad, bustling street of shops—Hamburg's major thoroughfare—cuts through both the historic and new downtown areas. It was laid out in 1908 when this part of the Old Town was redeveloped. The shops here are not as exclusive as those of ☞ **Jungfernstieg;** the stores and shopping precincts on both sides of the street provide a wide selection of goods at more affordable prices.

11 **Museum für Kunst und Gewerbe** (Arts and Crafts Museum). The museum houses a wide range of exhibits, from 15th- to 18th-century scientific instruments to an art nouveau interior complete with ornaments and furnishings. It was built in 1876 as a combination museum and school. Its founder, Justus Brinckmann, intended it to be a bastion of the applied arts that would counter what he saw as a decline in taste due to industrial mass production. A keen collector, Brinckmann amassed a wealth of unusual objects, including a collection of ceramics from all over the world. ✉ *Steintorpl. 1,* ☎ *040/4285–42630.* 🖅 *DM 10.* 🕙 *Tues., Wed., and Fri.–Sun. 10–6, Thurs. 10–9. U-bahn: Hauptbahnhof.*

3 **Planten und Blomen** (Plants and Flowers Park). Opened in 1935, this park is known all over Germany for its well-kept gardens. There are many places to rest and admire the flora. The park lies within the remains of the 17th-century fortified wall that guarded the city during the Thirty Years' War. The walls and moats have been cleverly integrated into a huge, tranquil park. If you visit on a summer evening, you'll see the Wasserballet, the play of an illuminated fountain set to organ music. Make sure you get to the lake in good time for the show—it begins at 10 PM each evening during the summer (at 9 PM in September). Also during the summer, traditional tea ceremonies are presented in the Japanese Garden, the largest of its kind in Europe.

The Plants and Flowers Park is part of the larger **Wallringpark,** which also includes the ☞ **Alter Botanischer Garten** and the Kleine and Grosse Wallanlagen parks to the south, whose special appeal is their well-equipped leisure facilities, including a children's playground and theater, a model-boat pond, roller- and ice-skating rinks, and outdoor chess. ✉ *Planten un Blomen: Stephanspl.* 🖅 *Free.* 🕙 *Mar.–Oct., daily 9–4:45; Nov.–Feb., daily 9–3:45.*

★ **7** **Rathaus** (Town Hall). To most Hamburgers this large building is the symbolic heart of the city. As a city-state—an independent city and simultaneously one of the 16 federal states of Germany—Hamburg has a city council and a state government, both of which have their administrative headquarters in the Rathaus. A pompous neo-Renaissance affair, the building dictates political decorum in the city. To this day, the mayor of Hamburg never welcomes VIPs at the foot of its staircase but always awaits them at the very top—whether it's a president or the queen of England.

Both the Rathaus and the **Rathausmarkt** (Town Hall Market) lie on marshy land, a fact vividly brought to mind in 1962, when the entire area was severely flooded. The large square, with its surrounding arcades, was laid out after Hamburg's Great Fire of 1842. The architects set out to create a square with the grandeur of Venice's Piazza San Marco. Building on the Rathaus was begun in 1866, when 4,000 piles were sunk into the moist soil to support the structure. It was completed in 1892, the year a cholera epidemic claimed the lives of 8,605 people in 71 days. A fountain and monument to that unhappy chapter in Hamburg's history is in a rear courtyard of the Rathaus.

This immense building, with its 647 rooms (six more than Buckingham Palace) and imposing central clock tower, is not the most graceful structure in the city, but the sheer opulence of its interior is astonishing. Although you only get to see the state rooms, their tapestries, huge staircases, glittering chandeliers, coffered ceilings, and grand portraits give you a sense of the city's great wealth in the 19th century and its understandable civic pride. The starting point for the 45-minute tours of the Rathaus interior is the ground-floor Rathausdiele, a vast pillared hall. ⊠ *Rathausmarkt,* ☎ *040/428–310.* ☜ *English-language tour DM 2.* ☉ *Tours Mon.–Thurs. hourly 10:15–3:15, Fri.–Sun. hourly 10:15–1:15. U-bahn: Mönckebergstr.* ☜

⓬ **St. Jacobikirche** (St. James's Church). This 13th-century church was almost completely destroyed during World War II. Only the furnishings survived. Reconstruction was completed in 1962. The interior is not to be missed—it houses such treasures as the vast baroque organ on which Bach played in 1720 and three Gothic altars from the 15th and 16th centuries. ⊠ *Jacobikirchhof 22/Steinstr.,* ☎ *040/327–744.* ☉ *Mon.–Sat. 10–5, Sun. 10–noon. U-bahn: Mönckebergstr.*

The Harbor and Historic Hamburg

Hamburg's historic sections are a fascinating mixture of the new and old; the modern harbor contrasts sharply with the surviving late-medieval and 19th-century warehouses. Narrow cobblestone streets with richly decorated mansions lead to churches of various faiths reflecting the diverse origins of the sailors and merchants drawn to the city.

A Good Walk

This tour takes you south to the picturesque quarters around the harbor area (bring your passport as there's a customs point on the walk). Start with a visit to the restored **St. Katharinenkirche** ⑭. To get there from the Messberg U-bahn station, cross the busy Ost-West-Strasse and continue down Dovenfleet, which runs alongside the Zoll Kanal (Customs Canal). Continue until Dovenfleet turns into Bei den Mühren, and you'll see the church's distinctive green-copper spire.

Head back a short way to the bridge you previously passed, the Kornhausbrücke. Notice the sign on the bridge announcing your entrance to the **Freihafen Hamburg** ⑮ and the **Speicherstadt** ⑯, the complex of 19th-century warehouses lining the waterfront. As you leave the Free Port over the Brooksbrücke (two bridges down from the Kornhausbrücke), you'll pass through a customs control point, at which you may be required to make a customs declaration. Turn left after the bridge, where Bei den Mühren becomes Bei dem Neuen Krahn. Take your second right onto **Deichstrasse** ⑰, the city's 18th-century business district, which runs alongside Nikolaifleet, a former channel of the Alster and one of Hamburg's oldest canals. After exploring this lovely area, take the Cremon Bridge, at the north end of Deichstrasse. This angled pedestrian bridge spans Ost-West-Strasse. You may wish to make a small detour down one of the narrow alleys (Fleetgänge) between the houses to see the fronts of the houses facing the Nikolaifleet.

The Cremon Bridge will take you to Hopfenmarkt Square, just a stone's throw from the ruins of the **Alte St. Nikolaikirche** ⑱. From here head west on Ost-West-Strasse and cross to the other side at the Rödingsmarkt U-bahn station. Continue along Ost-West-Strasse, which turns into Ludwig-Erhard-Strasse, until you reach Krayenkamp, a side street to your left that will take you to the historic **Krameramtswohnungen** ⑲, or shopkeepers' guild houses. The distance from the Nikolaikirche to Krayenkamp is about 1 km (½ mi). Hamburg's best-loved and most famous landmark, the **St. Michaeliskirche** ⑳, is on the other side of the alley Krayenkamp.

From St. Michaeliskirche, walk west on Bömkenstrasse until you reach a park and the enormous **Bismarck-Denkmal** ㉑, rising high above the greenery. From the monument's northeast exit cross Ludwig-Erhard-Strasse and continue on Holstenwall to the **Museum für Hamburgische Geschichte** ㉒, with exhibits depicting the city's past.

TIMING

This can be a rather short walk, manageable in a half day if you only stroll through the historic harbor quarters. You may wish to spend another 1½ hours at the Museum of Hamburg History and still another hour taking a closer look inside the churches.

Sights to See

⑱ **Alte St. Nikolaikirche** (Old St. Nicholas's Church). The tower and outside walls of this 19th-century neo-Gothic church, which survived World War II, serve as a monument to those killed and persecuted during the war. Next to the tower is a center documenting the church. It is run by a citizens organization that is also spearheading private efforts to partially rebuild the church and redesign the surrounding area. Beneath the former church a cellar wine store is open for browsing and wine tasting. ⊠ *Ost-West-Str. by Hopfenmarkt,* ☎ *040/220–3200.* ☉ *Weekdays 10–5, weekends 11–4. U-bahn: Rathaus or Rödingsmarkt.*

㉑ **Bismarck-Denkmal** (Bismarck Memorial). The colossal 111-ft granite monument, erected between 1903 and 1906, is an equestrian statue of Otto von Bismarck, Prussia's Iron Chancellor, who was the force behind the unification of Germany. The plinth features bas-reliefs of various German tribes. Created by sculptor Hugo Lederer, the statue calls to mind Roland, the famous warrior from the Middle Ages, and symbolizes the German Reich's protection of Hamburg's international trade. *U-bahn: St. Pauli.*

⑰ **Deichstrasse.** The oldest residential area in the Old Town of Hamburg, which dates from the 14th century, now consists of lavishly restored houses from the 17th through the 19th centuries. Many of the original houses on Deichstrasse were destroyed in the Great Fire of 1842, which broke out in No. 42 and left approximately 20,000 people homeless; only a few of the early dwellings escaped its ravages. Today Deichstrasse and neighboring **Peterstrasse** (just beneath Ost-West-Strasse) are of great historical interest. At No. 39 Peterstrasse, for example, is the baroque facade of the Beylingstift complex, built in 1700. Farther along, No. 27, constructed as a warehouse in 1780, is the oldest of its kind in Hamburg. All the buildings in the area have been painstakingly restored, thanks largely to the efforts of individuals. *U-bahn: Rödingsmarkt.*

NEED A
BREAK?

There are three good basement restaurants in this area. The **Alt–Hamburger Aalspeicher** (⊠ Deichstr. 43, ☎ 040/362–990) serves fresh fish dishes; the **Alt Hamburger Bürgerhaus** (⊠ Deichstr. 37, ☎ 040/373–633) specializes in traditional Hamburg fare; and the **Nikolaikeller** (⊠ Cremon 36, ☎ 040/366–113), an upscale old Hamburg tavern, offers the most extensive herring menu in Germany.

⑮ **Freihafen Hamburg.** Hamburg's Free Port, the city's major attraction, dates to the 12th century, when the city was granted special privileges by Holy Roman Emperor Frederick I (Barbarossa). One of these was the freedom from exacting duties on goods transported on the Elbe River. The original Free Port was where the Alster meets the Elbe, near Deichstrasse, but it was moved farther south as Hamburg's trade expanded. When Hamburg joined the German Empire's Customs Union in the late 1800s, the Free Port underwent major restructuring to make way for additional storage facilities. An entire residential area was torn down (including many Renaissance and baroque buildings), and the ☞ **Speicherstadt** warehouses, the world's largest block of contiguous storage space, came into being between 1885 and 1927. *U-bahn: St. Pauli Landungsbrücken.*

⑲ Krameramtswohnungen (Shopkeepers' Guild Houses). The shopkeepers' guild built this tightly packed group of courtyard houses between 1620 and 1626 for members' widows. The houses became homes for the elderly after 1866. The half-timber, two-story dwellings, with unusual twisted chimneys and decorative brick facades, were restored in the 1970s and are now protected. The house marked "C" is open to the public. A visit inside gives you a sense of what life was like in those 17th-century dwellings. Tour buses stop here, and some of the houses have been converted to shops. ⊠ *Historic House "C," Krayenkamp 10,* ☎ *040/3110–2624.* ⊠ *DM 2.* ☉ *Tues.–Sun. 10–5. U-bahn: Rödingsmarkt.*

NEED A
BREAK? **Krameramtsstuben** (⊠ Krayenkamp 10, ☎ 040/365–800) is a rustic bar-cum-restaurant where you can sample hearty traditional local dishes, mostly made with fish. It's open daily from 10 AM to midnight.

✋ ㉒ Museum für Hamburgische Geschichte (Museum of Hamburg History). The museum's vast and comprehensive collection of artifacts gives you an excellent overview of Hamburg's development, from its origins in the 9th century to the present. Among the museum's many attractions are an exhibit that describes, through pictures and models, the history of the port and shipping between 1650 and 1860, and a 16th-century architectural model of Solomon's Temple, measuring 11 square ft. ⊠ *Holstenwall 24,* ☎ *040/4284–12380.* ⊠ *DM 10.* ☉ *Tues.–Sat. 10–5, Sun. 10–6. U-bahn: St. Pauli.*

⑭ St. Katharinenkirche (St. Catherine's Church). Completed in 1660, this house of worship was severely damaged during World War II but has since been carefully reconstructed. Almost none of the original interior furnishings escaped destruction. Only two 17th-century epitaphs (to Moller and to von der Feehte) remain. ⊠ *Katharinenkirchhof 1,* ☎ *040/336–275.* ☉ *Apr.–Sept., daily 9–5; Oct.–Mar., daily 9–4. U-bahn: Messberg.*

★ ⑳ St. Michaeliskirche (St. Michael's Church). The Michel, as it is called locally, is Hamburg's principal church and northern Germany's finest baroque ecclesiastical building. Constructed between 1649 and 1661 (the tower followed in 1669), it was razed after lightning struck almost a century later. It was rebuilt between 1750 and 1786 in the decorative Nordic baroque style but was gutted by a terrible fire in 1906. The replica completed in 1912 was demolished during the Second World War. The present church is a reconstruction.

The Michel has a distinctive 433-ft brick-and-iron tower bearing the largest tower clock in Germany, 26 ft in diameter. Just above the clock is a viewing platform (accessible by elevator or stairs) that affords a magnificent panorama of the city, the Elbe River, and the Alster Lakes. Twice a day, at 10 AM and 9 PM (Sunday at noon), a watchman plays a trumpet solo from the tower platform, and during festivals an entire wind ensemble crowds onto the platform to perform. The **Multivisionsshow** (slide and audio show) recounts Hamburg's history. ⊠ *St. Michaeliskirche,* ☎ *040/3767–8100.* ⊡ *St. Michael's Church and Tower: elevator or staircase DM 4.50. Combined ticket for tower, crypt, the exhibition Michaelica, and the show: DM 11.* ☉ *Apr.–Sept., Mon.–Sat. 9–6, Sun. 11:30–5:30; Oct.–Mar., Mon.–Sat. 10–5, Sun. 11–5:30; shows Thurs. and weekends at 12:30, 1:30, 2:30, and 3:30. U-bahn: Landungsbrücken or Rödingsmarkt.*

NEED A
BREAK?

> Just opposite the Michel is one of Hamburg's most traditional restaurants, the **Old Commercial Room** (⊠ Englische Planke 10, ☎ 040/366–319). Try one of the local specialties, such as Labskaus or Aalsuppe. If you don't make it to the restaurant, you can buy its dishes (precooked and canned) in department stores in both Hamburg and Berlin.

⑯ Speicherstadt (Warehouse District). These imposing warehouses in the ☞ Freihafen Hamburg reveal yet another aspect of Hamburg's extraordinary architectural diversity. A Gothic influence is apparent here, with a rich overlay of gables, turrets, and decorative outlines. These massive rust-brown buildings are still used to store and process every conceivable commodity, from coffee and spices to raw silks and handwoven Oriental carpets. Although you won't be able to enter the buildings, the nonstop comings and goings you'll see as you stroll around this area will give you a good sense of a port at work. If you want to learn about the history and architecture of the old warehouses, detour to the Speicherstadtmuseum. ⊠ *St. Annenufer 2, Block R,* ☎ *040/321–191.* ⊡ *DM 5.* ☉ *Tues.–Sun. 10–5. U-bahn: Messberg.*

St. Pauli and the Reeperbahn

The run-down maritime district of St. Pauli is sometimes described as a "Babel of sin," but that's not entirely fair. The Reeperbahn, its major thoroughfare as well as a neighborhood moniker, offers a broad menu of entertainment in addition to the striptease and sex shows. Beyond this strip of pleasure, St. Pauli and Altona are dominated by their Elbe waterfront.

A Good Walk

Starting from the St. Pauli U-bahn station, you are at the very beginning of a long, neon-lighted street stretching nearly 1 km (½ mi). This is the red-light **Reeperbahn** ㉓, full of nightlife entertainment and sex clubs. The best areas to check out are the Grosse Freiheit, Hans-Albers-Platz, and Davidstrasse. Walk down Davidstrasse to reach the not-to-be-missed **Erotic Art Museum** ㉔, exhibiting all the hidden sides of human sexuality. But as the bright lights begin to fade sometime around daybreak, those who are made of stern stuff continue their entertainment at the **Fischmarkt** ㉕, a shopper's paradise stocked with fresh fish, meat, and produce (only open Sunday). From the museum walk west on Hafenstrasse until you see the first market booths.

From the market you can head back on Hafenstrasse to the nearby piers at **Landungsbrücken** ㉖, where ferries depart for short round-trips. To find the booking hall and departure point from the Fischmarkt, turn left up the hill to the U-bahn station and bear right toward the long limestone building with two towers.

One trip you should try to make is to the riverside village of **Blankenese** ㉗, 14½ km (9 mi) west of Hamburg. From there you can make the return journey by ferry, by S-bahn, or on foot. The celebrated Elbe River walk is long, but it's one of Hamburg's prettiest.

TIMING

This tour can last a full day and a long night, including a very enjoyable boat trip through the harbor, and a few hours in the theaters and bars along the Reeperbahn. However, you might just want to walk down the red-light strip and check out the Erotic Art Museum and the Landungsbrücken, all in less than three hours. You have to be an early riser to catch the Fischmarkt on Sunday.

Sights to See

㉗ Blankenese. Blankenese is another of Hamburg's surprises—a suburb west of the city with the character of a quaint fishing village. Some Germans like to compare it to the French and Italian rivieras; many consider it the most beautiful part of Hamburg. In the 14th century Blankenese was an important ferry terminal, but it wasn't until the late 18th and 19th centuries that it became a popular residential area. The most picturesque part of town is the steeply graded hillside, where paths and stairs squeeze between closely placed homes. The town has a lively fruit and vegetable market, open Tuesday 8–2, Friday 8–6, and Saturday 8–1. ◷ *HADAG ferries depart from Pier 3 for Blankenese late Apr.–Sept., weekdays at 10 and 2, and late Mar.–early Oct., weekends at 10 and 2; from Blankenese late Apr.–Sept., weekdays at 12:30 and 5:30, and late Mar.–early Oct., weekends at 12:30 and 5:30.*

NEED A
BREAK?   A fine view and well-prepared fish await you at **Sagebiel's Fährhaus** (⊠ Blankeneser Hauptstr. 107, ☎ 040/861–514), a former farmhouse where Kaiser Wilhelm once celebrated his birthday.

㉔ Erotic Art Museum. Sexually provocative art from 1520 to the present— 1,800 original works (mostly photographs) in all—is showcased here. The collection is presented with such great taste and decorum that it has won the respect of many who would not normally view such an exhibit. Special exhibits of modern erotic photography or comic art are in a building on Bernhard-Nocht-Strasse. ⊠ *Main bldg.: Nobistor 10a, at Reeperbahn; photo exhibits at Bernhard-Nocht-Str. 69, ☎ 040/317– 8410. Minimum age 16. ▣ DM 15 for Erotic Art Museum, DM 10 for photo exhibit; combined ticket for both exhibitions DM 15. ◷ Sun.– Thurs. 10 AM–midnight, Fri.–Sat. 10 AM–1 AM. U-bahn: St. Pauli.*

㉕ Fischmarkt (Fish Market). The open-air Altona Fischmarkt is by far the most celebrated of Hamburg's many markets, and for which it is worth getting out of bed early. The pitch of fervent deal making is unmatched in Germany. Offering real bargains, the market's barkers are famous for their sometimes rude but usually successful bids to shoppers.

Sunday fish markets became a tradition in the 18th century, when fishermen sold their catch before church services. Today freshly caught fish are only a part of the scene. You can find almost anything here—from live parrots and palm trees to armloads of flowers and bananas, from valuable antiques to fourth-hand junk. ⊠ *Between Grosse Elbestr. and St. Pauli Landungsbrücken. ◷ Apr.–Sept., Sun. 5 AM–10 AM; Oct.–Mar., Sun. 7 AM–10 AM. U-bahn: Landungsbrücken.*

㉖ Landungsbrücken (Piers). A visit to the port is not complete without a tour of one of the most modern and efficient harbors in the world. Hamburg is Germany's largest seaport, with 33 individual docks and 500 berths lying within its 78 square km (30 square mi). Tours of the harbor begin at the main passenger terminal, where a whole range of ferry and barge rides depart. There's usually a fresh breeze, so do dress warmly enough for your trip. Don't expect rolling surf and salty air, however, as Hamburg's port is 56 nautical mi from the North Sea (☞ Guided Tours *in* Hamburg A to Z, *below*). *Rickmer Rickmers*, an old sailing ship that once traveled as far as the West Indies, is now open to visitors and is docked at Pier 1. ⊠ *St. Pauli Landungsbrücken 1,* ☎ *040/319–5959.* 🎫 *Rickmer Rickmers DM 6.* ☼ *Daily 10–6. U-bahn: Landungsbrücken.*

㉓ Reeperbahn. The hottest spots in town are concentrated in the St. Pauli Harbor area, on the Reeperbahn thoroughfare, and on a little side street known as the Grosse Freiheit (Great Liberty—and that's putting it mildly!). The striptease shows are expensive and explicit, but a walk through this area is an experience in itself and costs nothing. Saturday night finds St. Pauli pulsating with people determined to have as much fun as possible. It's *not* advisable, however, to travel through this part of the city alone in the wee hours of the morning.

It's no understatement to say that although some of the sex clubs may be relatively tame, a good many others are pornographic in the extreme. None of them gets going until about 10 PM; all will accommodate you until the early hours. Order your own drinks rather than letting the hostess do it and pay for them as soon as they arrive, double-checking the price list again before handing over the money.

Among the attractions in the St. Pauli area are theaters, clubs, music pubs, discos, and a bowling alley. The Schmidt Theater, on Reeperbahn, has a repertoire of live music, vaudeville, chansons, and cabaret, while the St. Pauli Theater, on Speilbudenplatz, presents popular lowbrow productions in Hamburger dialect (☞ Nightlife, *below*). *U-bahn: St. Pauli.*

DINING

Hamburg has plenty of chic restaurants to satisfy the fashion-conscious local professionals, as well as the authentic salty taverns typical of a harbor town.

CATEGORY	COST*
$$$$	over DM 100
$$$	DM 75–DM 100
$$	DM 50–DM 75
$	under DM 50

per person for a three-course meal, excluding drinks

$$$$ ✕ **Landhaus Dill.** A fin de siècle building with views of the Elbe provides a home for this stylish restaurant. The dining room has an air of cool elegance, with crisp linen, glistening tile floors, and a high standard of incredibly light cuisine. The lobster salad is prepared at your table, and the rack of lamb comes hot from the kitchen with an aromatic thyme sauce. For dessert try *Weissweinparfait mit Portwein-Feigensauce,* a light white-wine cream with a sauce made of port wine and figs. Reservations are advised. ⊠ *Elbchaussee 94,* ☎ *040/390–5077. Jacket and tie. AE, DC, MC, V. Closed Mon.*

$$$$ ✕ **Landhaus Scherrer.** Though this establishment is only minutes from the downtown area, in Altona, its parklike setting seems worlds away from the high-rise bustle of the city. The mood is elegantly low-key— the building was originally a brewery—with wood-paneled walls and soft lighting. The food fuses sophisticated nouvelle specialties with more down-to-earth local dishes. The wine list is exceptional. ⊠ *Elbchaussee 130,* ☎ *040/880–1325. Jacket and tie. AE, DC, MC, V. Closed Sun.*

$$$$ ✕ **Le Canard.** One of Hamburg's top and restaurants, Le Canard en-
★ joys a much-coveted location overlooking the harbor and historic vessels at Övelgönne, with enviably elegant decor and nouvelle cuisine to match. Chef Viehhauser's skills and creativity keep the restaurant's standards high. Fish dishes predominate, but the roasted duck with red cab-

Hamburg Dining and Lodging

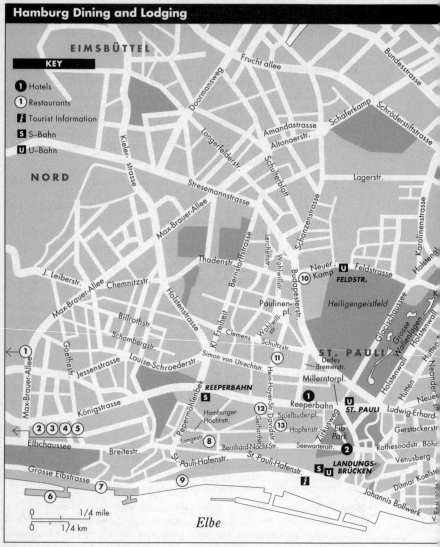

EIMSBÜTTEL

KEY

- ① Hotels
- ① Restaurants
- ⓘ Tourist Information
- Ⓢ S–Bahn
- Ⓤ U–Bahn

NORD

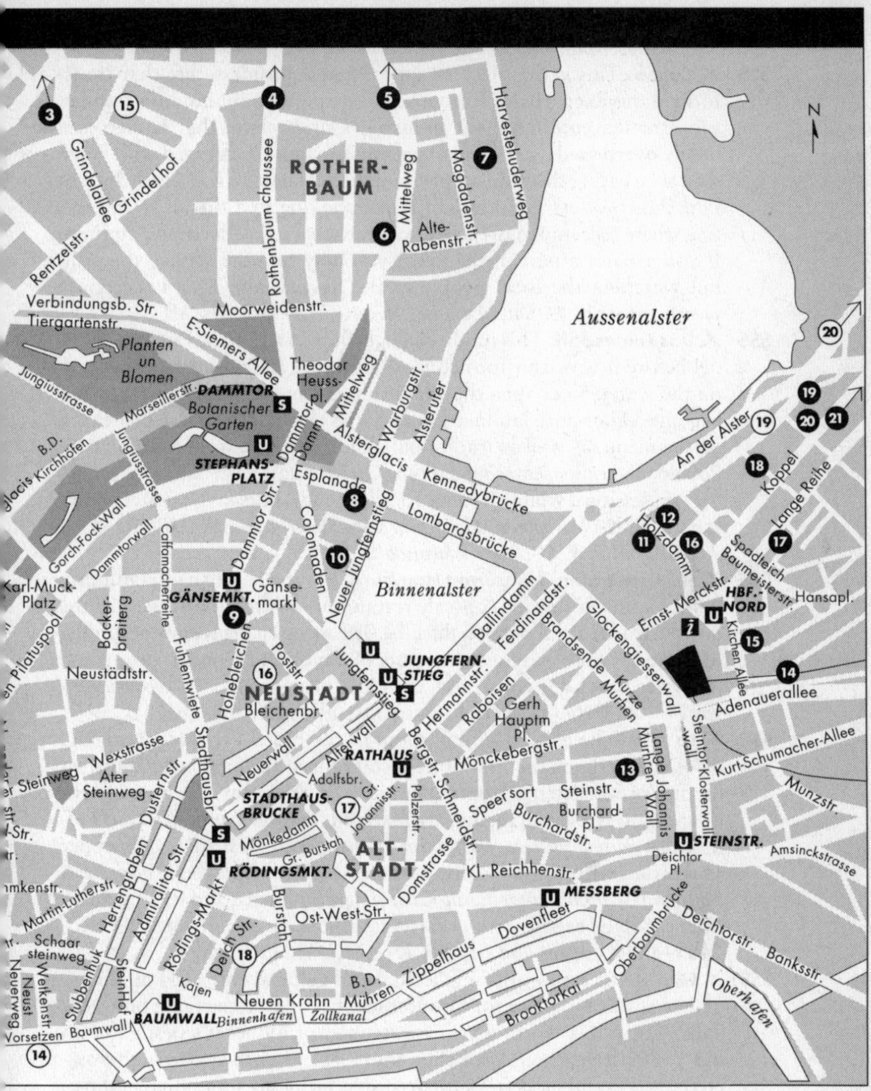

Aussenalster

ROTHER-
BAUM

N

Binnenalster

Planten
un
Blomen

DAMMTOR
Botanischer
Garten

STEPHANS-
PLATZ

Gänse-
markt

GÄNSEMKT.

NEUSTADT

JUNGFERN-
STIEG

Karl-Muck-
Platz

RATHAUS

STADTHAUS-
BRÜCKE

ALT-
STADT

RÖDINGSMKT.

HBF.
NORD

STEINSTR.

MESSBERG

BAUMWALL

Mellingburger
Schleuse **4**
Nippon Hotel **21**
Park Hyatt
Hamburg **13**
Steen's Hotel **16**
Vier Jahreszeiten . . . **10**
Wedina **18**

bage is worth sampling. ⊠ *Elbchaussee 139,* ☎ *040/880–5057. Reservations essential. Jacket and tie. AE, DC, MC, V. Closed Sun.*

$$$ ✕ **Cuneo.** This is the place to spot the new business elite that transformed the Reeperbahn from a seedy strip into a multimillion-dollar, fun-oriented entertainment industry. Critics claim that Cuneo is a highly overpriced eatery where patrons are more concerned with being seen then eating the unimaginative Italian dishes. This is a little bit unfair. Cuneo offers good Italian home cooking in a tiny crowded setting where red, smoke-drenched walls are covered with cheap paintings. If you are not a part of the gang, you may find the service sluggish, but watching the local people of the Reeperbahn Kiez is certainly worth the wait. ⊠ *Davidstr. 11,* ☎ *040/312–580. AE, MC, V.*

$$$ ✕ **Das Feuerschiff.** This bright-red lightship served in the English Channel before it was transformed in 1989 into a restaurant and tiny pub on the water. Since then the small ship docked in the city harbor has become a Hamburg landmark. Fresh and tasty German fish dishes are on the menu, as well as traditional seafood entrées from Scandinavia, Poland, and other seafaring nations. On Monday, local bands meet here for jam sessions, while on some Tuesdays and Thursdays cabaret shows are staged. ⊠ *Vorsetzen, Hamburg City Sporthafen,* ☎ *040/362–553. AE, DC, MC, V. U-bahn: Baumwall.*

$$$ ✕ **Fischereihafen-Restaurant Hamburg.** For the best fish in Hamburg, book a table at this big, upscale restaurant in Altona, just west of the downtown area and right on the Elbe. The menu changes daily according to what's available in the fish market that morning. The restaurant and its oyster bar is a favorite with the city's beau monde. ⊠ *Grosse Elbstr. 143,* ☎ *040/381–816. Reservations essential. AE, DC, MC, V.*

$$$ ✕ **La Mer.** The elegant dining room of the Hotel Prem (☞ Lodging, *below*) is perhaps the best hotel restaurant in the city, beautifully set on the Aussenalster, a 10-minute ride from downtown. A host of subtle specialties, ever changing, are featured. Try the *Zanderfilet auf Pefferkraut mit gefüllten Waffelkartoffeln* (pike-perch fillet on pepper sauerkraut with stuffed waffle potatoes) or *Brust und Keule vom Perlhuhn auf Schwarzwurzeln mit Kartoffelgratin* (breast and leg of guineafowl on black salsify with potato gratin). ⊠ *An der Alster 9,* ☎ *040/ 2483–4040. Jacket and tie. AE, DC, MC, V. No lunch.*

$$$ ✕ **Nil.** Media types—the intellectual and cultural elite of Hamburg—
★ gather at this hip place for business lunches and prepartying on weekends. The Nil is worth a visit for its interior alone: it's nestled in an old 1950s-style, three-floor shoe shop. The kitchen serves high-powered seafood and modern German cuisine, including four different three- to six-course menus, offering delicious fare such as *Rinderfilet mit Walnuss-Rosmarinkruste, Schwarzwurzeln und Madeirasauce* (beef fillet in a walnut-rosemary crust with black salsify and Madeira sauce). ⊠ *Neuer Pferdemarkt 5,* ☎ *040/439–7823. Reservations essential for dinner. No credit cards. Closed Mon. and Tues.*

$$$ ✕ **Rive.** This restaurant dubs itself an "oyster bar," and rightfully so.
★ Its fresh oysters, clams, and other seafood are served right at the harbor in a building that looks like a ship. It is mostly patronized by media people enjoying the spectacular view of the harbor. The Rive would not be a Hamburg establishment without serving at least some local dishes, so make your choice between hearty *Matjes mit drei Saucen* (herring with three sauces), *Gegrillte Scampi mit Glasnudelsalat und Chilisaucee* (barbecue shrimp with glass-noodle salad and chili sauce), or fancy lobster with aioli. ⊠ *Van der Smissen Str. 1, Kreuzfahrt-Center,* ☎ *040/380–5919. Reservations essential. AE.*

$$ ✕ **Abendmahl.** The small Abendmahl, off the Reeperbahn, is always jammed with a crowd getting ready for the bars and clubs. No wonder that the good but not impressive cuisine plays second fiddle to the inexpensive and inventive drinks and the flirtatious atmosphere. The fresh dishes on the small menu focus on French and Italian cuisine. ⊠ *Hein-Köllisch-Pl. 6,* ☎ *040/312–758. No credit cards.*

$$ ✕ **Ahrberg.** Next to the river in Blankenese, the Ahrberg has a cozy, wood-paneled dining room and a terrace for summer dining. The menu features traditional German dishes and seafood specialties. Try the shrimp-and-potato soup or, in season, the fresh carp. ⊠ *Strandweg 33, Blankenese,* ☎ *040/860–438. AE, MC.*

$$ ✕ **Deichgraf.** This small and elegant fish restaurant in the heart of the old harbor warehouse district has been a Hamburg classic for years. It's one of the best places to get traditional Hamburg dishes such as *Hamburger Panfisch* (fried pieces of the day's catch prepared in a wine and mustard sauce) at a very reasonable price of DM 34.50. The restaurant is in an old merchant house, and the dining room is decorated with historic oil paintings depicting the hardships of the fisherman of the late 19th century. Reservations are essential on weekends. ⊠ *Deichstr. 23,* ☎ *040/319–1214. AE, DC, MC, V. Closed Sun.*

$$ ✕ **Eisenstein.** The food is fantastic, considering the low prices, and the
★ crowd bubbly and mostly stylish. A sure bet are the daily menus or the Italian-Mediterranean dishes, including pastas and some of Germany's presumably best pizzas. The Pizza Helsinki (made with tomatoes, sour cream, onions, and fresh gravlox) is truly delicious. The setting, a 19th-century industrial complex with high ceilings and dark redbrick walls, is very rustic. ⊠ *Friedensallee 9,* ☎ *040/390–4606. Reservations essential for dinner. No credit cards.*

$$ ✕ **Ratsweinkeller.** For atmosphere and robust local specialties, there are few more compelling restaurants than this cavernous, late-19th-century haunt under the city hall. The simple tables are wooden, and ship models hang from the high stone-and-brick arches. You can order surprisingly fancy or no-nonsense meals. Fish specialties predominate, but there's a wide choice of other dishes, too. ⊠ *Grosse Johannisstr. 2,* ☎ *040/364–153. AE, DC, MC, V. No dinner Sun.*

$$ ✕ **Restaurant Esprit.** The elegant restaurant at the Ramada Renaissance Hotel, in the Hanseviertel, has won awards for its cuisine and service and has become a choice city-center dining haunt. The extensive menu focuses on northern German fare such as *Scholle mit Büsumer Krabben und Bratkartoffeln* (plaice with shrimp and fried potatoes). Reservations are advised; ask for a table close to the open kitchen, where you can watch your order being prepared. ⊠ *Grosse Bleichen,* ☎ *040/3491–8935. AE, DC, MC, V.*

$$ ✕ **Weite Welt.** The restaurant's name recalls the longing of Hamburg's
★ seafaring folk to see the "great wide world." In an old fish smokehouse on the Reeperbahn's notorious Grosse Freiheit (the live sex shows are just a few steps away), the Weite Welt attracts regulars who feel right at home thanks to owner Niko Bornhofen's hospitality. Don't be surprised if he himself tends to your needs and addresses you with the casual *"Du"* rather than the more formal and appropriate *"Sie."* The menu is inventive and changes daily. The fish dishes cross the continents of Europe and Asia, and the theme dishes (like the "Last Supper of the Titanic") are a good value. Weite Welt is an absolute must if you are visiting St. Pauli. Reservations are essential on weekends. ⊠ *Grosse Freiheit 70,* ☎ *040/319–1214. V.*

$ ✕ **At Nali.** This is one of Hamburg's oldest and most popular Turkish restaurants, and it's open until 1 AM, handy for those seeking a late-night kebab. Prices are low, service is reliable and friendly, and the menu is extensive. Reservations are essential on weekends. ⊠ *Rutschbahn 11,* ☎ *040/410–3810. AE, DC, MC, V.*

$ ✕ **Avocado.** The imaginative vegetarian menu at this popular restaurant is an excellent value. In the pleasant Uhlenhorst District, close to the Aussenalster, it is one of Hamburg's few no-smoking restaurants. If you're really hungry, try one of the four- or six-course "surprise" dinners (DM 44–DM 66 per person). ⊠ *Kanalstr. 9,* ☎ *040/220–4599. Reservations essential. No credit cards. Closed Mon.*

$ ★ ✕ **Fischerhaus.** The family-owned fish restaurant may look mediocre, but the food, prepared from family recipes, is truly delicious. Most dishes focus on North Sea fish and Hamburg specialties such as *Orly-Rotbarschfilet in Bierteig* (rose-fish fillet wrapped in beer dough) or the several dishes with plaice: A favorite is the *Scholle Finkenwerder Art,* panfried plaice with smoked ham and potato salad. When making a reservation, ask for a table upstairs to get a harbor view. ⊠ *Fischmarkt 14,* ☎ *040/314–053. AE, MC, V.*

$ ★ ✕ **Phuket.** This tiny Thai restaurant, just around the corner from the Reeperbahn's infamous Davidwache, Germany's toughest police station, is one of the best-kept dining secrets in Hamburg. The seedy-looking basement restaurant will remind you of a shabby sailor's tavern, but the food is simply delicious, the service attentive and smooth. The best dish is not listed on the long menu of spicy Thai specialties: *Huhn in Erdnusssosse* (chicken in a hot peanut sauce)—ask the waiter for it. ⊠ *Davidstr. 31,* ☎ *040/315–854. No credit cards.*

LODGING

Hamburg has a full range of hotels, from five-star, grande-dame luxury enterprises to simple pensions. Nearly year-round conference and convention business keeps most rooms booked well in advance, and the tariffs are high. But many of the more expensive hotels lower their rates on weekends, when businesspeople have gone home. The tourist office can help with reservations if you arrive with nowhere to stay (☞ Contacts and Resources *in* Hamburg A to Z, *below*); ask about the many Happy Hamburg special-accommodation packages.

CATEGORY	COST*
$$$$	over DM 300
$$$	DM 200–DM 300
$$	DM 150–DM 200
$	under DM 150

All prices are for two people in a double room, including tax and service charge.

$$$$ ★ 🏨 **Hotel Abtei.** On a quiet, tree-lined street about 2 km (1 mi) north of the downtown area, in Harvestehude, this elegant period hotel offers understated luxury and very friendly, personal service. If you want a room with a four-poster bed, ask when making a reservation. One of the nicest rooms is Number 7, which was completely renovated in 1999. All guest rooms have English antique cherrywood and mahogany furniture. Three suites even have their own private conservatories. You can have your breakfast in the beautiful garden and afternoon tea in the antique-furnished sitting room. In the evening acclaimed chef Ulrich Heimann prepares international dishes in the intimate restaurant; he may even cook a personalized meal following your suggestions. ⊠ *Abteistr. 14, D–20149,* ☎ *040/442–905,* FAX *040/449–820. 8 rooms, 3 suites. Restaurant, in-room safes, minibars, room service, dry cleaning, laundry service, free parking. AE, DC, MC, V.*

$$$$ ★ 🏨 **Kempinski Atlantic Hotel Hamburg.** There are few hotels in Germany more sumptuous than this gracious Edwardian palace facing the Aussenalster. The stylish mood is achieved with thick-carpeted, marble-inlaid panache, along with sophisticated lighting, and the lobby is positively baronial. Whether the rooms are traditionally furnished or more modern, they are all typical of Hamburg in their understated lux-

ury. All have spacious sitting areas with a writing desk and easy chairs, as well as large bathrooms, most with two washbasins, a bathtub, and a separate shower stall. Service at the Atlantic is hushed and swift. In fine weather guests can lounge in the formal outdoor courtyard, where only the gurgling fountain disturbs the peace. ⊠ *An der Alster 72–79, D–20099,* ☎ *040/28880,* FAX *040/24729. 254 rooms, 13 suites. 3 restaurants, bar, café, in-room data ports, in-room safes, minibars, no-smoking floor, room service, indoor pool, barbershop, beauty salon, sauna, health club, jogging, boating, shops, baby-sitting, dry cleaning, laundry service, concierge, business services, meeting rooms, parking (fee). AE, DC, MC, V.* ✍

$$$$ 🏨 **Marriott.** This was the first Marriott in Germany, and it remains the showpiece—from the extraordinary barrel-roof ceiling of the reception area to the expansive comfort of its guest rooms. The rooms' modern green furniture isn't particularly inspired, but you do get amenities such as pay-per-view TV and modem and fax lines. The hotel has a central location—an unbeatable spot on Hamburg's Gänsemarkt, in one of the best shopping areas. The hotel's aptly named American Place is one of the better city-center restaurants. The health club is one of the most modern in northern Germany. ⊠ *ABC-Str. 52, D–20354,* ☎ *040/ 35050,* FAX *040/3505–1777. 277 rooms, 5 suites. Restaurant, bar, piano bar, in-room data ports, minibars, no-smoking rooms, room service, indoor pool, barbershop, beauty salon, massage, sauna, exercise room, baby-sitting, dry cleaning, laundry service, concierge, business services, meeting rooms, parking (fee). AE, DC, MC, V.* ✍

$$$$ 🏨 **Park Hyatt Hamburg.** This ultramodern hotel is hidden behind the
★ historic walls of the Levantehaus, an old warehouse, not far from the train station. Guest rooms have bright and modern furnishings, somewhat minimalist and Asian in style. Original artworks by local painters adorn the suites. The Club Olympus pool and fitness area is breathtaking, both for its streamlined design and the variety of activities. The Regency Club floor offers such special treats as a free Continental breakfast and a light evening snack. Bagels are smeared in the New York Deli hotel restaurant. ⊠ *Bugenhagenstr. 8–10, D-20095,* ☎ *040/ 3332–1234,* FAX *040/3332–1235. 221 rooms, 31 apartments. 2 restaurants, bar, in-room data ports, minibars, no-smoking rooms, room service, indoor pool, barbershop, beauty salon, massage, sauna, exercise room, baby-sitting, dry cleaning, laundry service, concierge, business services, meeting rooms, parking (fee). AE, DC, MC, V.* ✍

$$$$ 🏨 **Vier Jahreszeiten.** Some claim that this handsome 19th-century
★ town house on the edge of the Binnenalster is the best hotel in Germany. Friedrich Haerlin founded the hotel in 1897, and the Japanese company that acquired it in 1989 runs it as perfectly as the Haerlin family did. Antiques—the hotel has a set of near-priceless Gobelin tapestries—fill the public rooms and accentuate the stylish bedrooms; there are fresh flowers in massive vases; rare oil paintings hang on the walls; and all rooms are individually decorated with superb taste. One of the three restaurants, the Jahreszeiten-Grill, has been restored to its 1920s Art Deco look with dark woods and is worth a visit. If you want a lake-view room, especially one with a balcony, reserve well in advance. ⊠ *Neuer Jungfernstieg 9–14, D–20354,* ☎ *040/34940,* FAX *040/ 3494–2600. 158 rooms, 23 suites. 3 restaurants, bar, wine shop, in-room data ports, minibars, no-smoking rooms, room service, barbershop, beauty salon, baby-sitting, dry cleaning, laundry service, concierge, business services, meeting rooms, parking (fee). AE, DC, MC, V.* ✍

$$$ 🏨 **Aussen Alster.** Crisp and contemporary in design, this boutique hotel prides itself on giving personal attention to its guests. Rooms are compact; most have a full bathroom, but a few have a shower only. Stark white walls, white bedspreads, and light-hued carpets create a bright, fresh ambience. A small bar is open in the evening, and a tiny garden is available for summer cocktails. The restaurant serves Italian fare for lunch and dinner. The Aussenalster, where the hotel keeps a sailboat for the use of guests, is at the end of the street. ⊠ *Schmilinskystr. 11, D–20099,* ☎ *040/241–557,* FAX *040/280–3231. 27 rooms. Restaurant, bar, room service, sauna, boating, bicycles, baby-sitting, dry cleaning, laundry service, business services, meeting rooms, parking (fee). AE, DC, MC, V.* ❧

$$$ ⛫ **Garden Hotels Hamburg.** The location in chic Pöseldorf, 2 km (1 mi) from the downtown area, may discourage those who want to be in the thick of things, but otherwise this is one of the most appealing hotels in Hamburg, offering outstanding personal service and classy, chic accommodations in three attractive mansions. It's very much the insider's choice. There's no restaurant, but breakfast and light, cold meals are served in the bar and the airy winter garden. ⊠ *Magdalenenstr. 60, D–20148,* ☎ *040/414–040,* FAX *040/414–0420. 57 rooms, 3 suites. Bar, in-room data ports, minibars, no-smoking rooms, room service, barbershop, beauty salon, massage, baby-sitting, dry cleaning, laundry service, concierge, business services, meeting rooms, parking (fee). AE, DC, MC, V.*

$$$ ⛫ **Hotel Prem.** Facing the Aussenalster, this extremely personable, quiet, small hotel is Hamburg's gem. Most guests are regulars who have their favorite rooms; no two rooms are the same. The Adenauer Suite (named after the chancellor, who stayed here) is traditionally furnished, including an antique chaise longue and a period writing desk in an alcove with a lake view. Room 102, across the hall, has contemporary furnishings and a platform bed. Suite 2 has two rooms with modern furnishings and a terrace overlooking the lake. The bar is intimate, and the dining at La Mer (☞ Dining, *above*) is superb. ⊠ *An der Alster 9, D–20099,* ☎ *040/2483–4040,* FAX *040/280–3851. 51 rooms, 3 suites. Restaurant, bar, in-room data ports, minibars, room service, massage, sauna, baby-sitting, dry cleaning, laundry service, concierge, business services, meeting rooms, free parking. AE, DC, MC, V.* ❧

$$$ ⛫ **Hotel Senator.** At this modern hotel near the main train station, every room has a fresh look and modern conveniences, from hair dryers to cable TV. The largest and quietest rooms are on the fifth floor at the back of the building. Most rooms have a full bath; a few have only a shower. On the first floor the reception area has a pleasant glass-enclosed terrace for breakfast, as well as a bar and a lounge. ⊠ *Lange Reihe 18–20, D–20099,* ☎ *040/241–203,* FAX *040/280–3717. 56 rooms. Bar, snack bar, in-room data ports, in-room safes, minibars, no-smoking rooms, room service, baby-sitting, dry cleaning, laundry service, meeting rooms, parking (fee). AE, DC, MC, V.* ❧

$$–$$$ ⛫ **Hotel Hafen Hamburg and Hotel Residenz Hafen Hamburg.** In one building complex just across the famous St. Pauli Landungrbücken, both hotels are good value considering their three- and four-star status, respectively. The older Hotel Hafen Hamburg, with its smaller but nicely renovated rooms, offers a great view of the harbor, while the larger, ultramodern and upscale Hotel Residenz Hafen annex has less flair but more comfort. A very good deal are the Residenz's double rooms, which come at the price of a single room. The location makes this hotel a perfect starting point for exploring St. Pauli and the Reeperbahn. ⊠ *Seewartenstr. 7–9, D–20459,* ☎ *040/3111–3600,* FAX *040/3111–3755. Hotel Hafen 115 rooms, 10 suites; Hotel Residenz 230 rooms. Restaurant, 3 bars, sauna, in-room safes, minibars, no-smoking rooms, sauna, baby-sitting, dry cleaning, laundry service, meeting rooms, parking (fee). AE, DC, MC, V.* ❧

$$ ⛫ **Baseler Hof.** It's hard to find a fault in this central hotel near the Binnenalster and the opera house. Service is friendly and efficient, most rooms have been renovated and are neatly furnished, and prices are quite reasonable for this expensive city. The hotel caters to both individuals and convention groups, so at times the lounge area can become crowded. ✉ *Esplanade 11, D–20354,* ☎ *040/359–060,* ℻ *040/ 3590–6918. 151 rooms, 2 suites. Restaurant, bar, in-room data ports, no-smoking rooms, room service, baby-sitting, dry cleaning, laundry service, concierge, meeting rooms, parking (fee). AE, DC, MC, V.*

$$ ⊞ **Hotel-Garni Mittelweg.** With chintz curtains, flowered wallpaper, old-fashioned dressing tables, and a country-house-style breakfast room, this hotel offers small-town charm in big-business Hamburg. The converted mansion is in upmarket Pöseldorf, a short walk from the Aussenalster and a quick bus ride from the city center. ✉ *Mittelweg 59, D– 20149,* ☎ *040/414–1010,* ℻ *040/4141–0120. 38 rooms, 1 apartment. In-room safes, minibars, room service, baby-sitting, dry cleaning, laundry service, meeting rooms, parking (fee). No credit cards.*

$$ ⊞ **Hotel-Pension am Nonnenstieg.** The owner, Frau Hodermann, is friendly and helpful and makes this unassuming little hotel homey. Extra beds for younger children can be put in rooms at no extra charge. Ask for a room with a kitchen alcove if you want to cook for yourself. There is no restaurant; only breakfast is offered. ✉ *Nonnenstieg 11, D–20149,* ☎ *040/480–6490,* ℻ *040/4806–4949. 30 rooms. MC, V.*

$$ ⊞ **Ibis Hamburg Alster.** This French chain hotel may have few frills, but in this costly city it offers smart, uniformly decorated rooms at reasonable rates. Each room has a bathroom with a shower and a closet with just enough space to hang your clothes. On the ground floor the helpful English-speaking staff is welcoming, and the lobby bar creates camaraderie among the guests. The location, across the street from the Atlantic Kempinski, is just a five-minute walk from the train station and two minutes from the Alster Lakes. ✉ *Holzdamm 4–12/16, D–20099,* ☎ *040/248–290,* ℻ *040/2482–9999. 165 rooms. Restaurant, bar, no-smoking rooms, business services, meeting rooms, parking (fee). AE, DC, MC, V.*

$$ ⊞ **Kronprinz.** For its humble position (on a busy street opposite the railway station) and its moderate price, the Kronprinz is a surprisingly attractive hotel, with a whiff of five-star flair. Rooms are individually styled, modern but homey. ✉ *Kirchenallee 46, D–20099,* ☎ *040/243– 258,* ℻ *040/280–1097. 73 rooms. Restaurant, minibars, no-smoking rooms, parking (fee). AE, DC, MC, V.*

$$ ⊞ **Mellingburger Schleuse.** If you prefer off-the-beaten-track lodgings, this member of the Ringhotels association is a 20-minute drive from the downtown area, idyllically set in a forest. The Alsterwanderweg hiking trail passes right by the doorstep. The hotel is more than 200 years old, with a thatch roof, peasant-style furnishings, and a restaurant that serves traditional northern German dishes. ✉ *Mellingburgredder 1, D–22395,* ☎ *040/6024–00103,* ℻ *040/602–7912. 40 rooms. 2 restaurants, bar, indoor pool, billiards, bowling, concierge, meeting rooms, free parking. AE, DC, MC, V.*

$$ ⊞ **Nippon Hotel.** You'll be asked to remove your shoes before entering your room at the Nippon, western Germany's second exclusively Japanese hotel (the first is in Düsseldorf). There are tatami on the floor, futon mattresses on the beds, and an attentive Japanese staff. The authenticity might make things a bit *too* spartan and efficient for some, but by cutting some Western-style comforts, the hotel offers a good value in the attractive Uhlenhorst District. The Nippon has a Japanese restaurant and sushi bar. ✉ *Hofweg 75, D–22085,* ☎ *040/227–1140,* ℻ *040/2271–1490. 41 rooms, 1 suite. Restaurant, in-room safes, minibars, no-smoking rooms, dry cleaning, laundry service, concierge, meeting rooms, parking (fee). AE, DC, MC, V.*

$$ ⊞ **Wedina.** Rooms at this small hotel are neat, compact, and completely
★ renovated. When you make a reservation, ask for a room in the Italian-style "Yellow House," with its elegant parquet floor. In the main building the bar and breakfast area face the veranda and a small gar-

den with an outdoor pool that bring Tuscany to mind. All lodgings are a half block from the Aussenalster and a brisk 10-minute walk from the train station. ✉ *Gurlittstr. 23, D–20099,* ☎ *040/243–011,* FAX *040/280–3894. 27 rooms. Bar, in-room safes, no-smoking rooms, baby-sitting, concierge, parking (fee). AE, DC, MC, V.*

$ 🖭 **Hotel Monopol.** There is no other hotel in the Reeperbahn neigh-
★ borhood where budget travelers can enjoy a safe and clean stay in the heart of Europe's most bizarre red-light district. The small rooms are not up-to-date, and some look like an odd mixture of 1950s and '80s designs, but the service is warm and has an original touch of Hamburger Kiez. You might run into an artist performing in a Hamburg musical—or in the live sex shows on Reeperbahn, for that matter. ✉ *Reeperbahn 48, D–20359,* ☎ *040/311–770,* FAX *040/3117–7151. 82 rooms. Restaurant, bar, no-smoking rooms, room service, dry cleaning, laundry service, meeting rooms, parking (fee). AE, DC, MC, V.*

$ 🖭 **Hotel Village.** Until 1991 the small and charming Hotel Village was
★ a typical brothel near the central train station. The interior of the 14 rooms—decorated with glossy red-and-black carpets and wallpaper— is a nod to the hotel's past. Some rooms even have their old large beds, replete with baldachin and a revolving mirror on the ceiling. The service (including a 24-hour coffee bar) is extremely friendly and casual. The hotel has gained a reputation as an "in" place where celebrities hide out whenever they want to keep a low profile. ✉ *Steindamm 4, D–20099,* ☎ *040/246–137,* FAX *040/4503–0030. 14 rooms. Minibars, dry cleaning, laundry service, parking (fee). AE, DC, MC, V.*

$ 🖭 **Steen's Hotel.** This small, family-run hotel in a narrow, four-story
★ white city town house near the central train station provides modest but very congenial service for budget travelers. The rooms are spacious and clean but lack atmosphere. Bathrooms are tiny. A great plus are the comfortable beds with reclining head and foot rests. The breakfasts amply make up for the uninspired rooms, and the hotel's garage is a big added feature since there's never a parking space in this neighborhood. ✉ *Holzdamm 43, D–20099,* ☎ *040/244–642,* FAX *040/280–3593. 11 rooms. Minibars, free parking. No credit cards.*

NIGHTLIFE AND THE ARTS

The Arts

The arts flourish in this elegant metropolis. The city's ballet company is one of the finest in Europe, and the Ballet Festival in July is a cultural high point. Information on events is available in the magazines *Hamburger Vorschau*—pick it up in tourist offices and most hotels for DM 2.30—and *Szene Hamburg,* sold at newsstands for DM 5.

The best way to order tickets for all major Hamburg theaters, musicals, and most cultural events is the central phone **HAM-Hotline:** ☎ 040/3005–1300. In addition, a number of travel agencies sell tickets for plays, concerts, and the ballet. There's also a ticket office in the tourist office at the St. Pauli **Landungsbrücken** (✉ Landungsbrücken, between Piers 4 and 5, ☎ 040/3005–1200 or 040/3005–1203). Or try these downtown ticket agencies: **Theaterkasse im Alsterhaus** (✉ Jungfernstieg 16, ☎ 040/352–664) and **Theaterkasse Central** (✉ Gerhart-Hauptmann-Pl. 48, ☎ 040/337–124), at the Landesbank-Galerie.

Ballet and Opera

One of the most beautiful theaters in the country, **Hamburgische Staatsoper** (✉ Grosse Theaterstr. 35, ☎ 040/351–721) is the leading northern German venue for opera and ballet. The Hamburg Ballet is directed by American John Neumeier.

The **Operettenhaus** (⊠ Spielbudenpl. 1, ☎ 0180/54444 or 040/311–170) puts on light opera and musicals and, at press time, was still offering Andrew Lloyd Webber's *Cats*.

Concerts
Both the Hamburg Philharmonic and the Hamburg Symphony Orchestra appear regularly at the **Musikhalle** (⊠ Johannes-Brahms-Pl., ☎ 040/346–920). Visiting orchestras from overseas are also presented.

Film
The British Council Film Club (⊠ Rothenbaumchaussee 34, ☎ 040/446–057) screens films in English.

Theater
Deutsches Schauspielhaus (⊠ Kirchenallee 39, ☎ 040/248–713). One of Germany's leading drama stages is a beautiful theater, lavishly restored to its full 19th-century opulence and now the most important Hamburg venue for classical and modern theater.

English Theater (⊠ Lerchenfeld 14, ☎ 040/227–7089). This is the city's only stage presenting English-language drama.

Hansa Theater (⊠ Steindamm 17, ☎ 040/241–414). This variety-show dinner theater is a real German rarity, both for its nostalgia and the excellent artists and singers dishing out premier evening entertainment.

Neue Flora Theater (⊠ Stresemannstr. 159a, at Alsenstr., ☎ 0180/54444 or 040/3005–1350). Hamburg is by far Germany's capital for musicals and the Neue Flora offers the best deal. At press time the theater was continuing its long run of *The Phantom of the Opera*.

Metropol Musicaltheater (⊠ Norderelbstr. 6, at Hamburger Hafen, follow signs to Schuppen 70, ☎ 040/3005–1150). The latest addition to Hamburg's musical scene presents *Buddy*, a musical devoted to the life and songs of one America's great rock-and-roll stars, Buddy Holly.

Thalia-Theater (⊠ Alstertor, ☎ 01805–1997 or 040/3281–4444). This used to be one of the country's most controversial theaters, where the sets and staging of classical drama, from Shakespeare to Schiller, were perceived as scandalous by many Germans.

Nightlife

The Reeperbahn
Whether you think it sordid or sexy, the Reeperbahn, in the St. Pauli District, is as central to the Hamburg scene as are the classy shops along Jungfernstieg. A walk down **Herbertstrasse** (men only, no women or children permitted), just two blocks south of the Reeperbahn, can be quite an eye-opener. Here prostitutes sit displayed in windows as they await customers. On nearby **Grosse Freiheit** are a number of the better-known sex-show clubs: **Colibri**, at No. 30; **Safari**, at No. 24; and **Salambo**, at No. 11. They cater to the package-tour trade as much as to those on the prowl by themselves. Prices are high. If you order a drink, ask for the price list, which must be displayed by law, and pay as soon as you're served. Not much happens here before 10 PM.

Schmidt Theater (⊠ Spielbudenpl. 24, ☎ 040/3177–8899 or 040/3005–1400) and **Schmidts Tivoli** (⊠ Spielbudenpl. 27–28, ☎ 040/3177–8899 or 040/3005–1400) have become Germany's leading variety theaters. Their shows are nationally televised, and the classy repertoire of live music, vaudeville, chansons, and cabaret is quite hilarious and worth the entrance fee. If you don't get a ticket (which is likely to happen), relax in one of their cafés.

A veteran of the age of velvet and plush, **St. Pauli-Theater** (✉ Spiel-budenpl. 29, ☎ 040/314–344) usually serves up a popular brand of low-brow theater in Hamburger dialect, which is even incomprehensible to other northern Germans.

Dance Clubs

One of the biggest clubs in Hamburg, **After Shave** (✉ Spielbudenpl. 7, ☎ 040/319–3215) is packed with young, trendy, and very flirtatious Hamburgers and tourists. Sometimes a name says it all: the **Funky Pussy Club** (✉ Grosse Freiheit 26, ☎ 040/314–236) is a small but always-packed disco in a former brothel. The mixed crowed dances to European house and American funk music. **La Cage** (✉ Reeperbahn 136, ☎ 040/3179–0481) is a huge dance club and the best place for house music. The scene is fairly young, and on Sunday a special gay disco, the *La Cage aux Folles,* is staged. A favorite of the more mature business crowd meets at **Top of the Town** (✉ Marseiller Str. 2, ☎ 040/3502–3432), on the 26th floor of the SAS Plaza Hotel. It's both elegant and expensive, as most Hamburg clubs are.

Jazz and Live Music Clubs

Birdland (✉ Gärtnerstr. 122, ☎ 040/405–277) is one of the leading clubs among Hamburg's more than 100 venues. The jazz scene in Hamburg is pulsing as never before, and the Birdland has everything from traditional New Orleans sounds to avant-garde electronic noise. The **Cotton Club** (✉ Alter Steinweg 10, ☎ 040/343–878), Hamburg's oldest jazz club, offers classic New Orleans jazz as well as Swing. **Docks** (✉ Spielbudenplatz 19, ☎ 040/31788) has a stylish bar and is Hamburg's largest venue for live music. It also puts on disco nights.

OUTDOOR ACTIVITIES AND SPORTS

Biking

There are bike paths throughout downtown and many outlying areas. You can rent bikes at many of the bigger hotels or at the **Fahrrad-Centrum** (✉ Ludolfstr. 39–41, ☎ 040/461–015).

Golf

There are two leading clubs that members of foreign clubs can visit: **Hamburger Golf-Club Falkenstein** (✉ In de Bargen 59, ☎ 040/812–177) and **Golf-Club auf der Wendlohe** (✉ Oldesloerstr. 251, ☎ 040/550–5014).

Horseback Riding

With many of Germany's premier derbies staged in Hamburg, the city has a traditional affection for horseback riding. Stables include the **Gut Wendlohe** (✉ Oldesloerstr. 236, ☎ 040/550–4945) and the **Reitschule in der Alten Wache** (✉ Bredenbekstr. 63, ☎ 040/605–0586).

Jogging

The best places for jogging are the Planten un Blomen and Alter Botanischer Garten parks and along the leafy promenade around the Alster. The latter is about 6 km (4 mi) long.

Sailing

You can rent rowboats and sailboats on the Alster in the summer between 10 AM and 9 PM. Rowboats cost around DM 12 an hour, sailboats around DM 25 an hour, plus DM 3 per additional person.

Squash and Tennis

One of the nicest tennis facilities in town is the **Eichenhof-Tennisanlage** (✉ Duvenstedt, Puckaffer Weg 18, ☎ 040/4480–2593). It offers seven outdoor and five indoor courts. In downtown Hamburg try the smaller **Fit-Fire** (✉ Wandsbeker Zollstr. 29, ☎ 040/689–0848. For squash, the

Sportwerk Hagenbeckstrasse (⊠ Hagenbeckstr. 124a, ☎ 040/546–074) has 11 courts, a swimming pool, a sauna, and a solarium.

Swimming

You can't swim in the Elbe or the Alster—they're health hazards. There are, however, pools—indoor and outdoor—throughout the city. Two of the nicest indoor pools are the 19th-century spa **Bartholomäus-therme** (⊠ Bartholomäusstr. 95, ☎ 040/221–283) and the **Alster Schwimmhalle** (⊠ Ifflandstr. 21, ☎ 040/223–012).

SHOPPING

Shopping Districts

Hamburg's shopping districts are among the most elegant on the Continent, and the city has Europe's largest expanse of covered shopping arcades, most of them packed with small, exclusive boutiques. The streets **Grosse Bleichen** and **Neuer Wall,** which lead off Jungfernstieg, are a high-price-tag zone. The Grosse Bleichen leads to six of the city's most important covered (or indoor) malls, many of which connect. The marble-clad **Galleria** is modeled after London's Burlington Arcade. Daylight streams through the immense glass ceilings of the **Hanse-Viertel,** an otherwise ordinary reddish-brown brick building. The **Kaufmannshaus,** also known as the Commercie, and the upscale (and former first-class hotel) **Hamburger Hof** are two of the oldest and most fashionable indoor malls. There are also the **Alte Post** and the **Bleichenhof.**

Jungfernstieg. Hamburg's premier shopping street is just about the most upscale and expensive in the country. It's lined with jewelers' shops— Wempe, Brahmfeld & Guttruf, and Hintze are the top names—and chic clothing boutiques such as Linette, Ursula Aust, Selbach, Windmöller, and Jäger & Koch.

Pöseldorf. In this fashionable district north of downtown, take a look at Milchstrasse and Mittelweg. Both are filled with small boutiques, restaurants, and cafés.

Spitalerstrasse. This boulevard, running from the main train station to Gerhard-Hauptmann-Platz, is a pedestrians-only street lined with stores. Prices here are noticeably lower than those on Jungfernstieg.

Antiques

Antik-Center (⊠ Klosterwall 9–21, ☎ 040/326–285). This assortment of 39 shops in the old market hall, close to the main train station, features a wide variety of antiques from all periods.

St. Georg. Take a look at the shops in this city district behind the train station, especially those between Lange Reihe and Koppel. You'll find a mixture of genuine antiques (*Antiquitäten*) and junk (*Trödel*). You won't find many bargains, however. ABC-Strasse is another happy hunting ground for antiques lovers.

Department Stores

Alsterhaus (⊠ Jungfernstieg 16–20, ☎ 040/359–010). Hamburg's most famous department store is both large and elegant; it's a favorite with locals and a must for visitors. Don't miss its food department. Reward yourself for having braved the crowds by ordering a glass of *Sekt* (German champagne) and fresh seafood.

Karstadt (⊠ Mönckebergstr. 16, ☎ 040/30940). Germany's leading department-store chain offers the same goods as the Alsterhaus at similar prices. Hamburg's downtown Karstadt is the city's best place to shop for sports clothing.

Kaufhof (⊠ Mönckebergstr. 3, ☏ 040/333–070). Kaufhof offers far more bargains than most other department stores here.

Stilwerk (⊠ Grosse Elbstr. 68, ☏ 040/306–210). Hamburg's new shopping mall resembles a department store and primarily houses furniture and home accessory stores.

Flea and Food Markets

Blankenese. A lively fruit and vegetable market in the heart of this suburb manages to preserve the charm of a small village. ⊠ *Bahnhofstr.* ◷ *Tues. 8–2, Fri. 8–6, Sat. 8–1. S-bahn: Blankenese.*

Fischmarkt (☞ St. Pauli and the Reeperbahn *in* Exploring Hamburg, *above*).

Gift Ideas

Binikowski (⊠ Lokstedter Weg 68, ☏ 040/462–852). This shop sells the most famous must-buy *Buddelschiffe* (ships in bottles). There are few better places to shop for one, or for a blue-and-white-striped sailor's shirt, a sea captain's hat, ship models, even ship's charts.

Brücke 4 (⊠ St. Pauli Landungsbrücken, ☏ 040/316–373). This Hamburg institution is an experience not to be missed, the best place for all of the city's specialty maritime goods.

Harry's Hafenbasar (⊠ Bernhard-Nocht-Str. 89–91, ☏ 040/312–482). You can finger the dusty goods traders and seamen have brought back from all of the world in this eerie, bazaarlike store. It's jam-packed and a bargain hunter's paradise for anything maritime.

Seifarth and Company (⊠ Robert-Koch-Str. 19, ☏ 040/524–0027). Hamburg is one of the best places in Europe to buy tea. Smoked salmon and caviar are terrific buys here as well. Seifarth and Company also offers lobsters, salmon, and other expensive fish.

Jewelry

Wempe (⊠ Jungfernstieg 8, ☏ 040/3344–8824). This is the flagship store (of three Hamburg locations) of Germany's largest and most exclusive jeweler, which also sells watches.

Men's Clothing

Doubleeight. Another Level (⊠ Jungfernstieg 52, ☏ 040/3571–5510). The stylish store offers both designer and less expensive fashions you wear can everyday. A Hamburg classic and a must for the fashion-conscious traveler, **Thomas I-Punkt** (⊠ Mönckebergstr. 21, ☏ 040/327–172 sells both conservative suits and casual wear of its own label.

Women's Clothing

High-priced fashion, designed by one of Hamburg's newcomers, Petra Rodeck, is found at **bitch** (⊠ Fehlandstr. 41, ☏ 040/343–606). The clothes here is daring, cool, and definitely not mainstream. The upscale shopping complex **Kaufrausch** (⊠ Isestr. 74, ☏ 040/477–154) has mostly clothing and accessories stores for women. The name literally translates as "shopping spree." Visit on a Saturday, and you'll witness how the wives of Hamburg's millionaires spend money. A small but elegant and very personal store, **Linette** (⊠ Eppendorfer Baum 19, ☏ 040/4604–963) features only top designer labels.

SIDE TRIPS FROM HAMBURG

Hamburg is surrounded by the fertile green marshlands of the neighboring states of Schleswig-Holstein and Lower Saxony (Niedersachsen). Two of the most beautiful and popular side trips are described here; for others, *see* Schleswig-Holstein (☞ Chapter 14).

Altes Land

23 km (14 mi) west of downtown Hamburg (on Finkenwerder Str. and Cranzer Hauptdeich).

The marshy Altes Land extends 30 km (19 mi) west from Hamburg along the south bank of the Elbe River to the town of Stade (☞ *below*). This traditional fruit-growing region is dotted with huge half-timber farmhouses and crisscrossed by canals. The fertile land is popular for hikes, especially in spring, when the apple and cherry trees are in blossom. Some of the prettiest walks take you along the dikes running next to the Rivers Este and Lühe. Much of the territory is best covered on foot, so wear walking shoes. You may want to bring a picnic lunch as well and spend a long (summer) day here.

From the dock at Cranz, walk south into the suburb of **Neunfelde.** Here you can visit the **St. Pancras Kirche** (Church of St. Pancras), a baroque church with an unusual painted barrel roof, worth a visit for its altar inside. It was built in 1688, and the organ, dating from the same period, was designed by Arp Schnitger, an organ builder and local farmer. ⊠ *Am Organistenweg,* ☎ *040/745–9296.* ◷ *Daily 9–4.*

The village of **Jork** lies some 9 km (5½ mi) on foot to the west of Neunfelde, just beyond the confluence of the Este and Elbe rivers. Take in it's early 18th-century church and decorative farmhouses. The windmill in nearby **Borstel** is worth a short detour.

Stade

60 km (37 mi) west of Hamburg on B–73

The town of Stade is on the western edge of the Altes Land. Thanks to one of Germany's largest reconstruction programs in the 1960s and '70s, the city of 46,000 has regained its late-medieval and baroque appearance. Founded some time before AD 994 and once a thriving member of the Hanseatic League, Stade then began losing business to Hamburg, which had the better harbor. Stubborn Stade decided to leave the Hanseatic League in 1601 and was subsequently conquered by the Swedes, who controlled the city for 70 years—and their heritage is still visible. Marshland, rivers, and small lakes surround the small city.

A walk through the **Altstadt** (Old City), on an island, gives you a vivid impression of what a northern German city looked like some 300 years ago. Many of the buildings are built in the half-timber or redbrick styles typical of the region. The heart of the Old City is the **Altes Rathaus** (Old Town Hall), built in 1667, a redbrick blend of Dutch Renaissance and early baroque recalling the city's proud mercantile days. Exhibitions are sometimes held in the historic main hall. ⊠ *Hökerstr. 22,* ☎ *04141/4010. Weekdays 8:30–5.*

Not far away, off Johannisstrasse, is the city's most impressive church, the baroque **St. Cosmae** (⊠ Cosmaekirchhof, ☎ 04141/43042), whose tower offers a wonderful view of Stade and the countryside.Close to the **Alter Hafen,** the old harbor, which looks rather like a narrow canal, is Stade's most beautiful (and lively) square, the tiny **Fischmarkt**. Nearby streets, particularly **Wasser West,** have not only many cafés and restaurants but also some of the best-preserved Renaissance and baroque merchants' mansions. Here you can visit the **Schwedenspeicher-Museum** (Swedish Warehouse Museum). It once stored food for the Swedish garrison and now traces the city's history from the Stone Age to the present. ⊠ *Wasser West 39,* ☎ *04141/3222.* ⊠ *DM 2.* ◷ *Tues.–Fri. 10–5, weekends 10–6.*

Altes Land and Stade A to Z

ARRIVING AND DEPARTING

By Boat. Ferries depart from the Landungsbrücken (☞ St. Pauli and the Reeperbahn, *above*) twice daily during the week and four times daily on the weekends from mid-April through August and on weekends only in September. Take the ferry to Lühe. To reach Neunfelde, take the ferry from Blankenese (☞ St. Pauli and the Reeperbahn, *above*). For ferry information contact the **HADAG** (☎ 040/311–7070).

A 45-minute ride on a high-speed boat on the Elbe River may be the most exciting way of reaching Stade or Altes Land. Elbe-city-jets departs five times a day for Stade from the St. Pauli Landungsbrücken between 6:40 AM and 6:15 PM and cost DM 32 (round-trip). You can also reach the Cranz dock in Altes Land by Elbe-city-jet. For information contact **SAL Schiffahrtskontor** (☎ 04142/81810 or 040/317–7170).

By Car. Take B–73 west from Hamburg.

By Train. Trains to Stade depart from Hamburg's main central station.

VISITOR INFORMATION
Stade Tourismus GmbH (✉ Schiffertorstr. 6, D–21682 Stade, ☎ 04141/4091–7074, FAX 04141/409–110, ✎).

HAMBURG A TO Z

Arriving and Departing

By Bus

Hamburg's bus station, the **Zentral-Omnibus-Bahnhof** (✉ ZOB, Adenauerallee 78, ☎ 040/247–575) is right behind the main train station. You can also contact **Deutsche Touring** (✉ Am Römerhof 17, D–60486 Frankfurt/Main, ☎ 069/79030) for bus information.

By Car

Several autobahns (A–1, A–7, A–23, A–24, and A–250) connect with Hamburg's three beltways, which then easily take you to the downtown area. Follow the STADTZENTRUM signs.

By Ferry

The **MS Hamburg** (☎ 040/389–0371) carries passengers and cars three times a week for the 24-hour run between Hamburg and Harwich, England.

By Plane

Hamburg's international airport, **Fuhlsbüttel** (☎ 040/50750), is 11 km (7 mi) northwest of the city.

BETWEEN THE AIRPORT AND DOWNTOWN
The **Airport-City-Bus** runs nonstop between the airport and Hamburg's main train station daily at 20-minute intervals between 5:40 AM and 10:30 PM. Tickets are DM 8. The **Airport-Express** (Bus 110) runs every 10 minutes between the airport and the Ohlsdorf U- and S-bahn stations, a 17-minute ride from the main train station. The fare is DM 4.10. A **taxi** from the airport to the downtown area will cost about DM 30. If you're driving a **rental car** from the airport, follow the signs to STADTZENTRUM (downtown).

By Train

EuroCity and InterCity trains connect Hamburg with all German cities and many major European ones. Two InterCity Express "supertrain" lines link Hamburg with Berlin, Frankfurt, and Munich, and with Würzburg and Munich. There are two principal stations: the centrally located Hauptbahnhof (main train station) and Hamburg-Altona, west of the downtown area. For information call 040/19419.

Getting Around

By Bicycle

Most major streets in Hamburg have bicycle lanes. Some of the major hotels will accommodate their guests with free rental bikes.

By Car

Hamburg is easier to handle by car than many other German cities, and traffic is relatively uncongested. During rush hours, however, there can be as much gridlock as in any other big German city.

By Public Transportation

The **HVV,** Hamburg's public transportation system, includes the U-bahn (subway), the S-bahn (suburban train), and buses. A one-way fare starts at DM 2.60, which covers approximately four stops; DM 4.10 covers one unlimited ride in the Hamburg city area. Tickets are available on all buses and at automatic machines in all stations and at most bus stops. A **Tageskarte** (all-day ticket), valid from 9 AM to 1 AM, costs DM 8 for unlimited rides on the HVV system. If you're traveling with family or friends, a **Gruppen-** or **Familienkarte** (group or family ticket) is a good value—a group of up to four adults and three children can travel for the entire day for only DM 13.80. Available from all Hamburg tourist offices, the **Hamburg CARD** allows unlimited travel on all public transportation within the city, admission to state museums, and approximately 30% discounts on most bus, train, and boat tours. The Hamburg CARD is valid for 24 hours (beginning at 6 PM through 6 PM the following day) and costs DM 12.80 for one adult and up to three children under the age of 12; the family card costs DM 24 for four adults and up to three children under the age of 12. The Hamburg CARD for three days (valid starting at noon the first day) costs DM 26.50, DM 43 for the family card. A new Hamburg CARD light ("light" meaning inexpensive) costs DM 10 (DM 21 for a group of five) and is valid for three days but does not include public transportation.

You must validate your ticket at a machine at the start of your journey. If you are found without a validated ticket, the fine is DM 80.

In the north of Hamburg the HVV system connects with the **A-bahn** (Alsternordbahn), a suburban train system that extends into Schleswig-Holstein. **Night buses** (Nos. 600–640) serve the downtown area all night, leaving the Rathausmarkt and Hauptbahnhof every hour.

Hamburg Passenger Transport Board (Hamburger Verkehrsverbund; ⊠ Steinstr. 7, D–20015, ☎ 040/19449) provides information on the HVV system. It's open daily 7 AM–8 PM.

By Taxi

Taxi meters start at DM 4, and the fare is DM 2.30 per km (DM 2.50 at night and on weekends), plus 50 pfennigs for each piece of luggage. You can hail taxis on the street or at stands, or call 040/441–011, 040/686–868, or 040/611–061.

Contacts and Resources

Car Rentals

Avis (⊠ Airport, ☎ 040/5075–2314; ⊠ Drehbahn 15–25, ☎ 040/341–651; ⊠ Herderstr. 52, ☎ 040/220–1188). **Hertz** (⊠ Airport, ☎ 040/5935–1367; ⊠ Kirchenallee 34–36, opposite the Hauptbahnhof, ☎ 040/2801–2013). **Sixt** (⊠ Airport, ☎ 040/593–9480; ⊠ Spaldingstr. 110, ☎ 040/232–393).

Consulates

Ireland (✉ Feldbrunnenstr. 43, ☎ 040/4418–6213). **New Zealand** (✉ Heimhuder Str. 56, ☎ 040/442–5550). **U.S.** (✉ Alsterufer 28, ☎ 040/411–710). **U.K.** (✉ Harvestehuder Weg 8a, ☎ 040/448–0320).

Emergencies

Regarding medical emergencies, welcome to German bureaucracy: 112 is a direct line to the ambulance service operated by the fire department; 110 is the general ambulance service; 040/228–022 is a special city ambulance service providing doctors in an ambulance. The kind of service provided does not differ, only the institution behind it.

Police and ambulance (☎ 110). **Fire and emergency medical aid** (☎ 112). **Medical emergencies** (☎ 040/228–022). **Poison Information Center** (☎ 040/6385–3345). **Dentist** (☎ 040/468–3260 or 040/11500).

English-Language Bookstore

Frensche International (✉ Spitalerstr. 26c, ☎ 040/327–585) stocks American and British books.

Guided Tours

BOAT TOURS

Water dominates Hamburg, and there are few better ways to get to know the city than by taking a trip around the massive harbor. During the summer excursion boats and barges leave every half hour from the Landungsbrücken—Piers 1, 2, 3, and 7. In winter departures are every hour. The **HADAG line** and other companies organize round-trips in the port, lasting about one hour (DM 15) and taking in several docks. ☎ *HADAG: 040/311–7070 or 040/313–130, 040/314–280 for schedules and other information, 040/3178–2231 for English-language tour.* ☉ *Tours Apr.–late Sept., daily every ½ hr 8–6; early Oct.–Mar., every hr; English-language tour leaves from Pier 1 Mar.–Nov., daily at 11:15.*

You can combine an evening trip around the harbor with a cold buffet dinner, including as much beer as you can drink. Other watery options include renting rowboats on the Stadtpark Lake and surrounding canals and dancing on "party ships." To make a reservation call the **Bordparty-Service** cruise line or check for available tickets at its visitor information booth at Landungsbrücken, Pier 9. ☎ *040/313–687.* 🎫 *DM 69.* ☉ *Departures late Apr.–Dec., Sat. 8 PM between Piers 7 and 9. Inquire at visitor information booth about other special cruises.*

For additional information on harbor tours, call the general numbers (☎ 040/311–7070, 040/313–130, 040/313–959, or 040/314–611).

Boat trips around the **Alster Lakes** and through the canals leave from the Jungfernstieg promenade in the city center. From April through November they leave every half hour, less regularly in winter. ✉ *Alster Touristik, Jungfernstieg,* ☎ *040/3574–2419.* 🎫 *Aussenalster 50-min lake tour DM 16, combination lake and canal tour DM 25.* ☉ *Boats for lake tour leave every ½ hr Apr.–Oct. 3, daily 10–6; less often rest of yr. Combination lake and canal tours leave Apr.–Oct. 3, daily at 9:45, 12:15, 2:45, 5:15.*

From May through September there's a romantic twilight tour, called Dämmertour, of the Alster Lakes leaving the Jungfernstieg every evening at 8 (DM 21). For information on these and other Alster tours, call **Alster Touristik** (☎ 040/357–4240).

ORIENTATION TOURS

Sightseeing **bus tours** (☎ 040/227–1061) of the city, all with guides who quickly narrate in both English and German, leave from Kirchenallee by the main train station. A bus tour lasting 1¾ hours sets off every

15 minutes daily between 9:30 and 4:45 between April and September and daily at 11 and 3 between October and March, and costs DM 22. A longer tour, lasting 2½ hours, starts at 10 and 2, costing DM 32. For an additional DM 11, both tours can be combined with a one-hour boat trip. Departure times for tours vary, according to season. City tours aboard the nostalgic *Hummelbahn* (converted railroad wagons pulled by a tractor) are offered, starting from the Kirchenallee stop. They run April–October, daily 10:30, 12:30, 2:30, and 4:30; and November–March, weekends at 10:30, 12:30, and 2:30. The fare is DM 25 for 1¾ hours. From May to September, Friday and Saturday at 8 PM, the *Hummelbahn* (☎ 040/792–8979) also offers a three-hour evening tour of the city at a cost of DM 58 (including a drink).

WALKING TOURS

Tours of downtown, the harbor district, and St. Pauli are offered from April to October at 2:30 by the **Tourismus-Zentrale Hamburg** (✉ Steinstr. 7, D–20015, ☎ 040/3005–1144). All guided walking tours (DM 10) are conducted in German, and they start at different locations.

Downtown tours by **StattreisenHamburg** (☎ 040/430–3481) are held on Saturday (February to November) and are conducted in German only. English-language bus tours are offered by **AG Hamburg Rundfahrt.** To check for hours and themes, call 040/641–3731.

Late-Night Pharmacies

Pharmacies offer late-night service on a rotating basis. Every pharmacy displays a notice indicating the schedule. For **emergency pharmaceutical assistance,** inquire at the nearest police station or call 112.

Travel Agencies

Reiseland American Express (✉ Ballindamm 39, ☎ 040/309–080; ✉ Airport Fuhlsbüttel at Terminal 4, Level 2, ☎ 040/500–5980). **Hapag-Lloyd** (✉ Verkehrspavillon Jungfernstieg, ☎ 040/325–8560).

Visitor Information

Hamburg has tourist offices around the city. The main branch of the tourist office is in the **Hauptbahnhof** (main train station; ☎ 040/3005–1200). It's open daily 7 AM–11 PM. At the harbor there's an office at the St. Pauli **Landungsbrücken** (✉ Between Piers 4 and 5, ☎ 040/3005–1200 or 040/3005–1203), open November–February, daily 10–7, and March–October, daily 10–5:30.

In addition to its comprehensive hotel guide, the tourist office also co-publishes *Hamburger Vorschau*, a monthly program of events in the city. It costs DM 2.30. The illustrated magazine *Hamburg Tips* is issued quarterly and details major seasonal events; it's free.

All tourist offices can help with accommodations, and there's a central call-in booking office for hotel and ticket reservations and general information, the **HAM-Hotline** (☎ 040/3005–1300, 🖉). A DM 5 fee is charged for every room reserved.

14 SCHLESWIG-HOLSTEIN AND THE BALTIC COAST

The far north of Germany is a lush, green landscape of marshlands, endless beaches, fishing villages, and lakes—all under a wide open sky. Beachgoers head to the islands of Schleswig-Holstein, which juts out between the often stormy North Sea and the quiet waters of the Baltic. The stretches of limestone cliffs and recondite coves that make up the neighboring Baltic Coast, along eastern Germany's shoreline, beckon those in search of solitude.

Gᴇʀᴍᴀɴʏ'ꜱ ᴛʀᴜᴇ ɴᴏʀᴛʜ is a quiet and peaceful region that
belies its past status as one of the most powerful trading centers in Europe. The salty air and great outdoors is the main
pleasure here, not sightseeing. On foggy November evenings or during the hard winter storms that sometimes strand islanders from the
mainland, you can well imagine the fairy tales spun by the Vikings who
lived here.

By Jürgen
Scheunemann

Schleswig-Holstein, Germany's northernmost state, is the smallest and
poorest of the western states. The Danish-German heritage here is the
result of centuries of land disputes between the two nations—you
could call this area southern Scandinavia. Since World War II its shores
and islands have become popular weekend and summer retreats for
the well-to-do from Hamburg and Berlin. The island of Sylt, in particular, is known throughout Germany for its rich and beautiful sunbathers.

The rest of Schleswig-Holstein, though equally appealing in its green
and mostly serene landscape, is far from rich and worldly. Most people farm or fish and often speak Plattdütsch, or low German, which
is difficult for outsiders to understand. Cities such as Flensburg,
Schleswig, the state capital of Kiel, and even Lübeck all exude a laid-
back, small-town charm.

The neighboring state of Mecklenburg-Vorpommern, once part of the
former German Democratic Republic (commonly referred to by its German acronym, DDR), includes the Baltic Coast and is even quieter and
perhaps closer to nature. Germany's almost forgotten eastern shoreline is as unfamiliar to most western Germans as it is to foreigners. On
the islands of Hiddensee and Rügen, the clock appears to have stopped
before World War II; the architecture, the pace of life, even the old-
fashioned trains seem like products of a magical time warp.

This area was not always a restful retreat. Between the 12th and 16th
centuries the sea was crucial to the rise of Hanseatic League, a con-
sortium of merchants who monopolized trade across the Baltic. You'll
see their wealth invested in buildings; some of the finest examples of
North German Gothic and Renaissance redbrick architecture, with tall,
stepped gables, are found here. The shipbuilding industry in Schleswig-
Holstein closed down more than 20 years ago, and the mid-1990s
bankruptcy of the industry in Rostock and Stralsund further depressed
the economy. Unemployment rates in both Schleswig-Holstein and
Mecklenburg-Vorpommern are among the highest in Germany.

Pleasures and Pastimes

Beaches

Beaches stretch all along the coast of the North Sea and the Baltic. Virtually all these sandy beaches are clean and safe, sloping gently into
the water, which is equally gentle and calm. Vacationers pack the seaside resorts during the high season (July–August). Be aware that water
temperatures even in August rarely exceed 20°C (65°F). The busiest
beaches are at Westerland (Sylt Island), Bansin (Usedom Island), Binz
(Rügen Island), Ostseebad Kühlungsborn, and Warnemünde. The most
beautiful beaches are at Timmendorf on Poel Island (you can drive there
from Wismar or take a White Fleet boat); Kap Arkona (reachable
only on foot); and Hiddensee Island, off Rügen. The more remote coves
can be found at Kampen on Sylt, at the Ahrenshoop Weststrand, on
the Darss Peninsula; at Nienhagen (near Warnemünde); and the Grosser
Jasmunder Bodden, on Rügen Island to the west of Lietzow.

There's an *Kurtaxe* (entrance fee) of DM 3–DM 10 for most beaches; the fees on Sylt are the most expensive, with an average of DM 6 per entry. Some beaches allow nude bathing. In German it's known as *Freikörperkultur* (literally, "free body culture"), or FKK for short. The most popular of these bare-all beaches are on Sylt island, at Nienhagen and Prerow (on Darss).

Churches

Throughout the region medieval churches with red and white facades are prime examples of the German redbrick Gothic style. In Mecklenburg-Vorpommern even the smallest village proudly boasts a redbrick church, and the cathedrals in cities like Wismar or Stralsund testify to the region's prosperous past as Hanseatic seaports.

Dining

The restaurants in both coastal states serve mostly seafood such as *Scholle* (flounder) or *Krabben* (shrimp), often with fried potatoes, eggs, and bacon. Mecklenburg specialties to look for are *Mecklenburger Griebenroller,* a custardy casserole of grated potatoes, eggs, herbs, and chopped bacon; *Mecklenburger Fischsuppe,* a hearty fish soup with vegetables, tomatoes, and sour cream; *Gefüllte Ente* (duck with bread stuffing); and *Pannfisch* (fish patty). A favorite local nightcap since the 17th century is grog, a strong blend of rum, hot water, and local fruits.

CATEGORY	COST*
$$$$	over DM 50
$$$	DM 40–DM 50
$$	DM 25–DM 40
$	under DM 25

per person for a three-course meal, excluding drinks

Lodging

In northern Germany you'll find both small *Hotelpensionen* and fully equipped large hotels; along the eastern Baltic Coast, many hotels are renovated high-rises dating from DDR times. Much of the entrepreneurial spirit of the east has been directed toward the tourism industry, and privately owned small hotels and pensions have opened throughout Mecklenburg-Vorpommern. In high season all accommodations, especially on the islands, are in great demand. If you can't book well in advance, inquire at the local tourist office.

CATEGORY	COST*
$$$$	over DM 250
$$$	DM 175–DM 250
$$	DM 125–DM 175
$	under DM 125

All prices are for two people in a double room, including tax and service charge.

Exploring Schleswig-Holstein and the Baltic Coast

Except for such cities as Kiel, Lübeck, Schwerin, and Rostock, both states are essentially rural and enjoy a countryside of lakes, lush green meadows, fertile fields, and tree-lined roads. The three major areas of interest are the western coastline of Schleswig-Holstein—primarily Sylt Island—eastern Mecklenburg, and Vorpommern's secluded, tundralike landscape of sandy heath and dunes. In Mecklenburg-Vorpommern any interesting roads that head off to the north are likely to lead to the coast. Vorpommern ends at the Polish border.

Numbers in the text correspond to numbers in the margin and on the Schleswig-Holstein and Baltic Coast maps.

Great Itineraries

This chapter follows a route through five main ports of the medieval Hanseatic League—Lübeck, Rostock, Stralsund, Flensburg, and Wismar. A standard itinerary will take you from the pleasure island of Sylt, then east along the Baltic coast but slightly inland, and finally to the island of Usedom. You could easily drive through the whole region from west to east in less than two days, but that would be the surest way to miss all the hidden treasures—churches and little sightseeing gems—in the quaint villages and medieval cities along the way. Instead, try to do it like the natives—at a slow pace. Should you indulge in a week-long sojourn, you'll certainly perceive the rest of the world as villagers do—as just a faint memory far, far away.

IF YOU HAVE 3 DAYS

Start your trip in **Flensburg** ①, less than two hours from Hamburg, and make **Schleswig** ④ a stop as you head toward ☷ **Lübeck** ⑦, western Germany's only Hanseatic town. On the following day visit **Wismar's** ⑧ delightful market square and grand churches and make a side trip south to **Schwerin** ⑨, which is known for its lakes and its magnificent castle, the **Schweriner Schloss.** Next head to ☷ **Rostock** ⑪, once the center of eastern Germany's shipbuilding industry. On the last day pay a visit to **Stralsund** ⑮, a much smaller but more charming medieval town. It serves as a gateway to the most remote and solitary part of the Baltic Coast: the island of **Rügen** ⑯. The **Stubbenkammer** ⑲ and the **Königstuhl** there are outstanding chalk cliffs.

IF YOU HAVE 5 DAYS

Devote a morning to the palace at **Ahrensburg** ⑥, just outside Hamburg, and continue on to the cities of **Schleswig** ④ and ☷ **Flensburg** ①. Both still have an abundance of old northern German fishing and farming traditions. When you finish exploring Flensburg, head to medieval ☷ **Lübeck** ⑦ to overnight. After seeing Lübeck, visit **Wismar** ⑧ before spending the night in ☷ **Schwerin** ⑨. On the fourth day, after a tour of the Schweriner lakes and the Schweriner Schloss, continue your eastward journey via **Bad Doberan** ⑩ and Kühlungsborn, a top beach resort. The little Molli train pulled by a steam locomotive connects the resort and Bad Doberan. Spend the late afternoon and night in ☷ **Rostock** ⑪ and the beach resort at **Warnemünde** ⑫. On the fifth day explore the medieval port of **Stralsund** ⑮ and the island of **Rügen** ⑯.

IF YOU HAVE 8 DAYS

Spend your first day and night in ☷ **Flensburg** ① and the next in the romantic fishing town of ☷ **Husum** ②. On the third morning take the train onto the island of ☷ **Sylt** ③. You may find it more economical to leave your car at the Niebüll train embarkment and use bikes or buses on the island. On your fourth day visit **Schleswig** ④ and **Kiel** ⑤ on your way to ☷ **Lübeck** ⑦. From Lübeck head east to **Wismar** ⑧ and ☷ **Schwerin** ⑨. The sixth day you can sightsee around **Rostock** ⑪ and shop in **Ribnitz-Damgarten** ⑬, the center of Germany's amber industry. If you don't find a souvenir here, you might be luckier in **Ahrenshoop** ⑭, a small coastal village that was once an artists' colony. Spend your sixth night in ☷ **Stralsund** ⑮ and your seventh day and night on the island of ☷ **Rügen** ⑯. A visit to Vorpommern wouldn't be complete without a trip to **Greifswald** ㉒, the last of the medieval Hanseatic towns on eastern Germany's coastline. If you still have time on this eighth day, drive to **Wolgast** and over the causeway to **Usedom Island** ㉔.

When to Tour Schleswig-Holstein and the Baltic Coast

Unfortunately, the region's climate is at its best when the two states are also most crowded—in July and August, the high season for vacationers from Hamburg or Berlin. Winter is extremely harsh in this

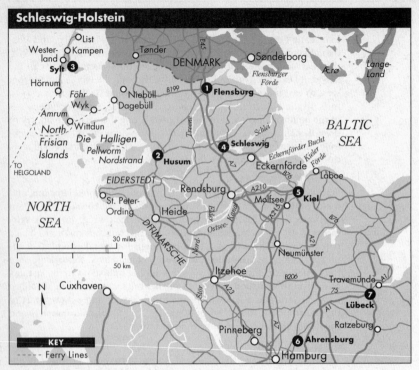

Schleswig-Holstein

List
Wester-land Kampen Tønder DENMARK Sønderborg Ærø Lange-Land
Sylt **3** Flensburger Förde
Hörnum **1** Flensburg
Föhr Niebüll B199
Wyk Dagebüll
Amrum Wittdun Schlei BALTIC
North Die Halligen **4** Schleswig SEA
Frisian Pellworm Eckernförder Bucht
Islands Nordstrand **2** Husum Eckernförde Laboe
TO HELGOLAND EIDERSTEDT Rendsburg A210 **5** Kiel
NORTH St. Peter- Molfsee
SEA Ording Heide Ostsee-Kanal
30 miles DITHMARSCHE Neumünster
50 km Itzehoe B206
Cuxhaven Travemünde
N **7**
Lübeck
Pinneberg Ratzeburg
KEY **6** Ahrensburg
---- Ferry Lines Hamburg

area, and even spring and fall are rather windy, chilly, and rainy. If you want to avoid the crowds, schedule your trip for June or September. But don't expect reasonable water temperatures or hot days on the beach.

SCHLESWIG-HOLSTEIN

This region once thrived, thanks to the Hanseatic League and the Salzstrasse (Salt Route), a merchant route connecting northern Germany's cities. The kings of Denmark warred with the dukes of Schleswig, and, later, the German Empire over the prized northern territory of Schleswig-Holstein. The northernmost strip of land surrounding Flensburg became German in 1864. The state is relatively poor now but is also known for the artists it produced: writers such as Thomas Mann and Theodor Fontane, and painters and sculptors such as Emil Nolde and Ernst Barlach. The quiet, contemplative spirit of the region's people, the marshland's special light, and the ever-changing face of the sea is inspiring. Today the world-famous Schleswig-Holstein-Musikfestival ushers in classical concerts to old farmhouses, palaces, and churches.

Flensburg

1 *182 km (114 mi) north of Hamburg.*

Germany's northernmost city is known for its superb beer, Flensburger Pils, and the lovely, quiet marshland surrounding it. For centuries people in this border region between Denmark and Germany have lived more or less peacefully, except when distant empires clashed over their land. Locals have a laid-back, dry-humor attitude, and the mixed Danish-German heritage is reflected in the culture and food. The 87,000 residents of the area are nicknamed *Nordlichter* (northern lighters), not for their presumed brightness but rather for the lack of light in a region plagued—in fall and winter—by fog and rain.

Most of Flensburg has retained its special small-town charm, with red-brick warehouses, Gothic churches, half-timber houses, and cobble-stone squares. Many of the city's landmarks are off the streets **Holm, Grosse Strasse,** and **Norderstrasse,** which wind their way through the city center to the waterfront. Around the picturesque **Südermarkt,** the Old City's South Market, are several typical commercial warehouses.

The **St. Nikolai-Kirche** (St. Nicholas Church) is named for the patron saint of sailors and was built in 1390. The church's real attraction is hidden inside, one of the most stunning Renaissance organ facades in Germany. ⊠ *Nikolaikirchhof,* ☎ *0461/26137.* ☞ *Free.* ⊙ *Daily 9–5.*

The **Museumsberg Flensburg** (Flensburg Museum Mountain), a unique complex of three museums, reveals the rich diversity of crafts and art in an otherwise rural area. In addition to a collection of local *Jugendstil* (art-nouveau) furniture and tapestries, the **Heinrich-Sauermann-Haus** also exhibits art from the Middles Ages to the present. The museum even houses several original living rooms from North German island farms of the 17th and 18th centuries. Paintings by local artists of the 19th and 20th centuries are hung in the **Hans-Christiansen-Haus.** Some of the more interesting pieces are by Emil Nolde, Ernst Barlach, and Erich Heckel, all of whom were fascinated by the special and at times mysterious light and atmosphere of North Germany's marshlands. ⊠ *Museumsberg,* ☎ *0461/852–956.* ☞ *DM 5.* ⊙ *Apr.–Oct., Tues.–Sun. 10–5; Nov.–Mar., Tues.–Sun. 10–4.*

The **Nordermarkt** (North Market) is surrounded by old alleyways such as the **Rote Strasse,** which is lined by redbrick warehouses now converted into galleries, restaurants, and pubs. The marketplace also preserves a reminder of medieval justice: at a small arcade you can see the metal for a neck ring used to publicly humiliate people convicted of certain crimes.

The **Schifffahrtsmuseum** (Maritime Museum) is in the old customs ware-house and can be spotted from far away thanks to the wooden masts of the old sailing vessels lying at anchor in the museum's harbor. The museum itself tells the story of the sea trade that made Flensburg pros-perous in the Middle Ages and sent the city's sons as far away as Green-land and the West Indies. A special **Rum-Museum** explains how the city traded and manufactured some of Germany's finest rum. ⊠ *Schiffbrücke 39,* ☎ *0461/852–970.* ☞ *DM 5.* ⊙ *Apr.–Oct., Tues.–Sun. 10–5; Nov.–Mar., Tues.–Sun. 10–4.*

Only 14 km (9 mi) northeast of Flensburg is the bright white **Schloss Glücksburg,** the chief residence of the dukes of Schleswig-Holstein. Built in 1582–87, Glücksburg, like many other palaces of the period, was a combination of a castle and palace completely surrounded by water. It is also known as the cradle of European high nobility, as the six chil-dren of Christian IX, king of Denmark and duke of Schleswig, were married to different European royal families. The palace museum showcases paintings, sculptures, furniture, and porcelain, mostly from the 17th century. ⊠ *Glücksburg, off B–199,* ☎ *04631/2213 or 04631/ 2243.* ☞ *DM 8.50.* ⊙ *Apr.–Oct., daily 10–6; Nov.–Mar., weekends 10–5; closed Mon. in Oct.*

Dining and Lodging

$$ ✕ **Schwarzer Walfisch.** The Black Whale has been serving local fish
★ since 1751, and its house and dining hall are protected monuments. Especially recommendable is the *Walfischteller* (with salmon, fried cod, shrimp from the North Sea, an egg sunny-side up, and fried pota-toes). Such dishes must be washed down with the dark local beer on

tap. ✉ *Angelburgerstr. 44,* ☎ *0461/13525. Reservations essential. No credit cards. Closed Sun.*

$$$ ✕🍴 **Alter Meierhof Vitalhotel.** The Meierhof is a former dairy farm, out-
★   side Flensburg on an inlet of the Baltic Sea. The hotel is luxurious but sur-
prisingly inexpensive and caters primarily to those who want to pamper
themselves with massages, mud packs, beauty treatments, and special baths.
The fitness and wellness areas—under an artificial star-spangled sky—
are all state-of-the-art. Rooms are fairly spacious and have reproductions
of 19th-century furnishings. When making a reservation, ask for the spe-
cial Wellness or Health weekend packages, which include massages, skin
treatments, and special meals. ✉ *Uferstr. 1, D–24960 Glücksburg,* ☎
04631/61990, ℻ *04631/619–999. 69 rooms, 6 suites. 2 restaurants, bar,
in-room data ports, in-room safes, minibars, no-smoking rooms, room
service, indoor pool, beauty salon, hot tub, massage, sauna, steam room,
Turkish bath, health club, beach, bicycles, baby-sitting, dry cleaning,
laundry service, meeting rooms, free parking. AE, DC, MC, V.*❧

$$ 🏨 **Mercure Hotel Flensburg.** The newly built hotel, a part of the upscale German Mercure hotel chain, is a rather somber-looking build-
ing whose appeal is its proximity to the harbor. Reserve a room on one
of the upper floors, and you'll enjoy a wonderful view. All rooms are
fairly spacious, with modern furnishings and cable television. ✉
Norderhofenden 6–9, D–24937, ☎ *0461/84110,* ℻ *0461/841–1299.
87 rooms, 4 suites. Bar, minibars, no-smoking rooms, sauna, meeting
rooms, parking (fee). AE, DC, MC, V.*

Shopping

Holm-Passage (✉ Holm 39, ☎ 04621/21955), the only shopping mall
in the city's historic downtown area, has many upscale fashion and specialty stores. A rather exclusive antiques shop, **Kunst und Antiquitäten
Rote Strasse** (✉ Rotestr. 10, ☎ 0461/29161) primarily sells 19th-cen-
tury furniture and White Gold, fine porcelain from Copenhagen.

Husum

❷ *45 km (28 mi) southeast of Flensburg, 158 km (98 mi) northeast of
Hamburg.*

The town of Husum is the epitome of northern German lifestyle and
culture. Immortalized in a poem as the "gray city upon the sea" by its
famous son, Theodor Storm, Husum is in fact a popular vacation spot
in summer. Its wonderful, deserted beaches and proximity to Sylt and
the Danish border make it a perfect place to fully relax.

The central **Marktplatz** (market square) is bordered by 17th- and 18th-
century buildings, including the historic Rathaus (town hall), which
houses the tourist information office. The best impression of Husum's
beginnings in the mid-13th century is found south of the Marktplatz,
along **Krämerstrasse,** the **Wasserreihe,** a narrow and tortuous alley,
and **Hafenstrasse,** right next to the narrow **Binnenhafen** (city harbor).

The most famous house on Wasserreihe is the **Theodor-Storm-Haus,**
where writer Theodor Storm (1817–88) lived between 1866 and 1880.
It is a must if you're interested in German literature as well as if you
want to gain insight into the life of the few well-to-do people in this
region during the 19th century. The small museum features the poet's
living room and a small *Poetenstübchen* (poets' parlor) where he wrote
many of his novels, including the famous *Schimmelreiter* (*The Rider
on the Gray Horse*). All rooms, the furniture, and many of the writer's
belongings showcased are original. ✉ *Wasserreihe 31,* ☎ *04841/666–
270.* 🎫 *DM 4.* ☉ *Apr.–Oct., Tues.–Fri. 10–noon and 2–5; Mon. and
weekends 2–5; Nov.–Mar., Tues., Thurs., and Sat. 2–5.*

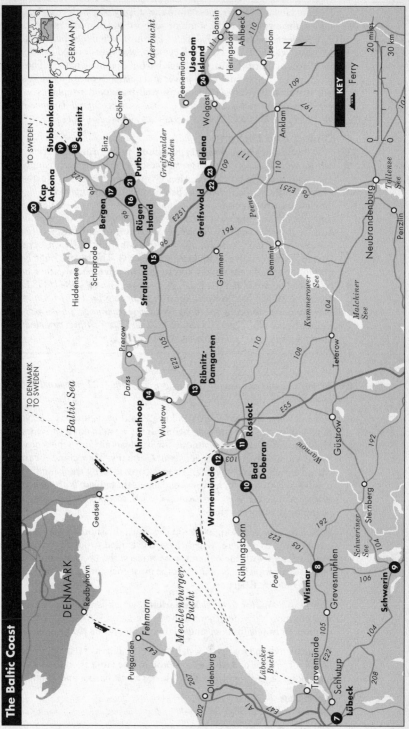

The Baltic Coast

GERMANY

Oderbucht

Baltic Sea

TO SWEDEN

TO DENMARK
TO SWEDEN

Hiddensee

Schaprode

20 Kap Arkona

19 Stubbenkammer
18 Sassnitz

Binz

Göhren

17 Bergen

21 Putbus

16 Rügen Island

15 Stralsund

Prerow

Darss

14 Ahrenshoop

Wustrow

13 Ribnitz-Damgarten

105

E22

Greifswalder
Bodden

96

E251

Grimmen

22 **23** Greifswald

Eldena

Wolgast

Peenemünde

24 Usedom Island

Heringsdorf

Ahlbeck

Bansin

111

Usedom

110

109

Anklam

197

E251

96

E55

Neubrandenburg

Tollense

Penzlin

Demmin

194

Peene

110

108

Malchiner
See

Teterow

104

Kummerower
See

Güstrow

192

Sternberg

11 Rostock

12 Warnemünde

103

10 Bad Doberan

Gedser

DENMARK

Rødbyhavn

Fehmarn

Putgarden

Oldenburg

202

207

Mecklenburger
Bucht

Kühlungsborn

Poel

8 Wismar

Grevesmühlen

9 Schwerin

Schweriner
See

Warnow

105
E22

192

106

104

Lübecker
Bucht

Travemünde

105
E22

Schlutup

7 Lübeck

208

104

A1

E47

Mecklenburger
Bucht

KEY
Ferry

N

20 miles
30 km

111

Despite Husum's remoteness amid the stormy sea, wide marshes, and dunes, the city used to be a major seaport and administrative center. The **Schloss vor Husum** (Palace of Husum), originally built as a Renaissance castle in the late 16th century, was transformed in 1752 by the dukes of Gottorf into a redbrick baroque country palace. The odd-looking blend of a church-bell tower and bastion is one of its most striking features, as well as the many well-preserved fireplaces whose mantelpieces are richly decorated. ⊠ *Professor-Ferdinand-Tönnies-Allee,* ☎ *04841/2545.* 🎫 *DM 4.* ☉ *Apr.–Oct., Tues.–Sun. 11–5.*

Dining and Lodging

$$$ ✕🏨 **Romantik-Hotel Altes Gymnasium.** In a former redbrick high
★   school behind an orchard of pear trees, you'll find a surprisingly elegant country-style hotel. The Altes Gymnasium combines North German friendly service with English and Italian country-style design. The rooms are spacious with wood-panel floors and modern office amenities. The restaurant Eucken serves game (from its own hunter) and local dishes such as *Gegrilltes Steinbuttfilet auf karamelisiertem Chicorée mit Krustentierkroketten* (fried halibut fillet on caramel-coated Belgian endives with crustacean fries). The hotel's huge health and indoor pool area makes you forget the often bad weather in this region. ⊠ *Süderstr. 6, D–25813,* ☎ *04841/8330,* 📠 *04841/83312. 66 rooms, 6 suites. Restaurant, bar, in-room data ports, in-room safes, minibars, no-smoking rooms, room service, indoor pool, massage, sauna, health club, exercise room, bicycles, baby-sitting, dry cleaning, laundry service, free parking. AE, DC, MC, V.* 🐾

Sylt

❸ *44 km (27 mi) northwest of Husum, 196 km (122 mi) northwest of Hamburg.*

Sylt is a long, narrow island (38 km [24 mi] by as little as 222 yards) of unspoiled beaches and marshland off the western coast of Schleswig-Holstein and Denmark. Famous for its clean air and white beaches, Sylt is the hideaway for the jet set of Germany. They come for the secluded beaches, and the exclusiveness provided by the island's inaccessibility. Nature itself, however, endangers the habitat: with each winter storm, wind and wave erosion chew off pieces of land, constantly changing the island's shape.

Wattwanderungen (long walks in the Watt, the shoreline tidelands) is a popular activity here, whether on self-guided or guided tours. The small villages with their thatch-roof houses, the beaches, and the nature conservation areas make Sylt the most enchanting German island, rivaled only by Rügen.

The island's major town is **Westerland,** which is not quite as expensive but more crowded than Kampen (☞ *below*). An ugly assortment of modern hotels lines an undeniably clean and broad beach.

If you are looking for privacy, detour to the villages of **List,** on the northern tip of Sylt, or to **Archsum** or **Hörnum.** The latter is on the southernmost point on the island and, like List, has a little harbor and a lighthouse.

Kampen

9 km (6 mi) from Westerland.

The island's unofficial capital is charming Kampen, which is the main destination for the wealthier crowd. Their redbrick or shining white thatch-roof houses spread along the coastline. The real draw—apart from the fancy restaurants and chic nightclubs—are the beaches. One
★   of the island's best-known features is the **Rotes Kliff** (Red Cliff), a dune

cliff on the northern end of the Kampen beaches, which turns an eerie yet beautiful dark red when the sun sets.

The **Naturschutzgebiet Kampener Vogelkoje** (Birds' Nest Nature Conservation Area) once served as a mass trap for wild geese and was built in the mid-17th century. Nowadays it serves as a nature preserve for wild birds. ⊠ *Lister Str., Kampen,* ☎ *04651/871–077.* ☞ *DM 3.* ◷ *Apr.–Oct., daily 10–4.*

For a glimpse of the rugged lives of 19th-century fishermen, visit the small village of **Keitum** to the south and drop in on the **Altfriesisches Haus** (Old Frisian House), which preserves an old-world peacefulness in its lush garden setting. The house also documents a time when most seamen thrived on extensive whale hunting. ⊠ *Am Kliff 13, Keitum,* ☎ *04651/31101.* ☞ *DM 3.* ◷ *Apr.–Oct., daily 10–5.*

The tower of the 800-year-old church **St. Severin,** built on the highest elevation in the region, once served the island's fishermen as a beacon. Strangely enough, the tower also served as a prison until 1806. Today the church is a popular site for weddings. ⊠ *Keitum,* ☎ *04651/33733.* ☞ *Free.* ◷ *Apr.–Oct., tours Mon. and Thurs. at 5; in winter at 11.*

The small **Sylter Heimatmuseum** (Sylt Island Museum) tells the centuries-long history of the island's seafaring people. It features traditional costumes tools and other gear from fishing boats and tells the stories of prominent islanders such as Uwe Jens Lornsen, who fought for Sylt's independence. ⊠ *Am Kliff 19, Keitum,* ☎ *04651/31669.* ☞ *DM 4.* ◷ *Apr.–Oct., daily 10–5.*

Dining and Lodging

$$$ ✕ **Dorfkrug Rotes Kliff.** The Dorfkrug has fed the island's seafaring inhabitants since 1876. Today you can enjoy meals such as *Steinbuttfilet* (halibut fillet) or *Gebratener Zander* (fried perch fillet) in a homey setting, where the walls are covered in traditional blue-white Frisian tiles. ⊠ *Braruper Weg 3, Kampen,* ☎ *04651/43500. AE, MC.*

$$$ ✕ **Sansibar.** Sansibar is one of the island's most popular restaurants.
★ The cuisine includes seafood and fondue with fish or scampi, served with any one of more than 800 wines. To get a table even in the afternoon, you must reserve well in advance. ⊠ *Strand, Rantum-Süd, Rantum,* ☎ *04651/964–646. Reservations essential. No credit cards.*

$$$$ ✕🏠 **Hotelrestaurant Jörg Müller.** The old thatched farmhouse hotel has
★ only a handful of lovely rooms combining Frisian-style designs with classical elegance. The restaurant serves a rather unusual (but high-quality) blend of cuisine from the Baden region and local seafood dishes. All room prices include a breakfast. ⊠ *Süderstr. 8, D–25980 Westerland,* ☎ *04651/27788,* 🖷 *04651/201–471. 7 rooms, 4 suites. Restaurant, bar, in-room safes, minibars, room service, sauna, dry cleaning, laundry service, free parking. AE, DC, MC, V.*

$$$ ✕🏠 **Landhaus Nösse.** Perched on a small elevation in the midst of the Nösse nature conservation area, this excellent hotel and restaurant not only serves Michelin-starred food but also offers secluded accommodations. Most rooms have white painted wooden walls and ceiling beams, old-style German windows tucked away under the thatch roof, and a beautiful view of the sea and marshes. When making reservations, inquire about the hotel's special weekend and other packages. ⊠ *Nösistieg 13, D–25980 Sylt-Ost Morsum,* ☎ *04651/97220,* 🖷 *04651/ 891–658. 10 rooms. Restaurant, café, pub. AE, MC, V.* 🕭

Water Sports

The island is a mecca for windsurfers, who rely on constant strong winds. Each September they meet for the Surf Cup competition off the **Brandenburger Strand,** which is also the best surfing spot.

Nightlife and the Arts

The nightspots in Kampen are generally more upscale and quite expensive compared to the pubs and clubs of Westerland. Two of the classic clubs are **Club Rotes Kliff** (⊠ Alte Dorfstr., Kampen, ☎ 04651/43400) and the **Compass** (⊠ Friedrichstr. 42, Westerland, ☎ 04651/23513).

Schleswig

❹ *37 km (23 mi) south of Flensburg, 114 km (71 mi) north of Hamburg.*

Schleswig-Holstein's oldest city is also one of its best-preserved examples of a typical North German town. Once the seat of the dukes of Schleswig-Holstein, it has not only their palace but also remains of the area's first rulers, the Vikings. Those legendary and fierce warriors from Scandinavia brought terror (but also commerce) to northern Germany between 800 and 1100. Under a wide sky, Schleswig lies on the Schlei River in a landscape of freshwater marshland and lakes, making it a good departure point for bike or canoe tours.

The fishing village comes alive along the **Holm,** an old settlement with tiny and colorful houses. The windblown buildings give a good impression of what villages in northern Germany looked like some 150 years ago. Relax in one of the cafés or further inspect the city's history at the **Städtisches Museum** (Municipal Museum). In a typical noble country palace of the late 17th century, you can explore Schleswig's history from the Stone Age forward. ⊠ *Günderothscher Hof, Friedrichstr. 9–11,* ☎ *04621/936–820.* ⊡ *DM 4.* ⊘ *Tues.–Sun. 10–5.*

The more impressive baroque **Schloss Gottorf,** dating from 1703, is the state's largest secular building and once housed the ruling family. It has been transformed into the **Schleswig-Holsteinisches Landesmuseum** (State Museum of Schleswig-Holstein) and holds a collection of art and handicrafts of northern Germany from the Middle Ages to the present, including paintings by Lucas Cranach the Elder. Among the museum's archaeological exhibits are ancient mummified corpses retrieved from nearby swamps. ⊠ *Schloss Gottorf,* ☎ *04621/8130.* ⊡ *DM 9.* ⊘ *Mar.–Oct., daily 9–5; Nov.–Feb., Tues.–Sun. 9:30–4.*

The most thrilling museum in Schleswig, the **Wikinger-Museum Haithabu** (Haithabu Viking Museum), is at the site of a Viking settlement. This was the Vikings' most important German port. They left boats, gold jewelry, and graves, all of which are displayed in the museum. ⊠ *Haddeby,* ☎ *04621/8130.* ⊡ *DM 4.* ⊘ *Apr.–Oct., daily 9–5; Nov.–Mar., Tues.–Sun. 10–4.*

Dining and Lodging

$$ ✕ **Stadt Flensburg.** This small restaurant in a city mansion that dates to 1699 serves mostly fresh fish from the Schlei River. Fishermen living on the Holm will have caught your dinner. The food is rather solid regional fare such as *Zanderfilet* (perch fillets) or *Butt* (flounder). The familial, warm atmosphere and the local dark tap beers more than make up for the simplicity of the setting. Reservations are advised. ⊠ *Lollfuss 102,* ☎ *04621/23984. AE, DC, MC, V. Closed Wed.*

$$ ✕▥ **Ringhotel Strandhalle Schleswig.** A modern hotel overlooking the small yacht harbor and the Schlei, this establishment has surprisingly low rates and a good value for its many services. The rooms are furnished in timeless dark furniture, and all have cable television. If you plan to stay a couple of days, ask about the special weekend packages that include nightly four-course meals and other extras. ⊠ *Strandweg 2, D–24837,* ☎ *04621/9090,* 𝖥𝖠𝖷 *04651/891–658. 25 rooms. Restaurant, in-room safes, no-smoking rooms, minibars, pool, bicycles, boating, meeting rooms, free parking. AE, DC, MC, V.*

Shopping

The tiny **Keramik-Stube** (✉ Rathausmarkt, ☎ 04621/24757) offers craft work and beautiful local, handmade pottery. It's the ideal place to buy a gift. The best place to buy tea is **Teekontor Hansen** (✉ Kornmarkt 3, ☎ 04621/23385). Try their *Schliekieker,* a special and very strong blend of different teas.

Kiel

⑤ *53 km (33 mi) southeast of Schleswig, 130 km (81 mi) north of Hamburg.*

The sleepy state capital Kiel is known throughout Europe for its annual *Kieler Woche,* a festival and regatta that attracts hundreds of sailing boats from around the world. Despite the many wharves and industries concentrated in Kiel, the **Kieler Föhrde** (Bay of Kiel) has remained mostly unspoiled. Unfortunately, this cannot be said about the city itself. Because of Kiel's strategic significance during World War II—it served as the German submarine base—the historic city, founded more than 750 years ago, was completely destroyed. Kiel's buildings are mostly modern, and its attraction lies in its outlying beaches, parks, and small towns.

At the **Kieler Hafen** (Kiel Harbor), Germany's largest passenger shipping harbor, you can always catch a glimpse of one of the many ferries leaving for Scandinavia from the **Oslokai** (Oslo Quay). In the background you can spot some of the shipbuilding wharves and—in the Kiel Bay—sometimes even a German submarine charting its way home. In the past, however, it was primarily the fishing industry that built the city.

The **Schifffahrtsmuseum** (Maritime Museum), housed in a hall of the old fish market, includes two antique fishing boats. ✉ *Wall 65,* ☎ *0431/901–3428.* 🎟 *DM 2.* ☉ *Apr. 15–Oct. 14, daily 10–6; Oct. 15–Apr. 14, Tues.–Sun. 10–5.*

A grim reminder of a different marine past is exhibited at the **U-Boot-Museum** (Submarine Museum) in Kiel-Laboe. The vessels of the much-feared German submarine fleet in World War I were mostly built and stationed in Kiel, before leaving for the Atlantic where they attacked American and British supply convoys. Today the submarine U995 serves as a public viewing model of a typical German submarine. The 280-ft-high **Marineehrenmal** (Marine Honor Memorial), in Laboe, was built in 1927–36. All German submarine personnel are required to salute when passing the memorial. You can reach Laboe via ferry from the Kiel harbor or take B–502 north. ✉ *Strandstr. 92, Kiel-Laboe,* ☎ *04343/42700.* 🎟 *Memorial DM 5, museum DM 3.50.* ☉ *Apr. 16–Oct. 15, daily 9:30–6; Oct. 16–Apr. 15, daily 9:30–4.*

One of northern Germany's best (though small) collections of modern art can be found at the **Kunsthalle zu Kiel** (Kiel Art Gallery), which specializes in Russian art of the 19th and early 20th centuries, German expressionism, and contemporary international art. The collections include paintings, prints, and sculptures. ✉ *Düsternbrooker Weg 1,* ☎ *0431/597–3751.* 🎟 *DM 8.* ☉ *Tues.–Sun. 10:30–6, Wed. 10:30–8.*

Two attractive beach towns close to Kiel, **Laboe** and **Strande,** are crowded with sun-loving Kielers on summer weekends. Both retain their fishing-village appeal, and you can buy fresh fish directly from the boats in the harbor. Most fishermen here still smoke the fish on board, preparing, for example, the famous *Kieler Sprotten,* a small salty fish somewhat like sardines. Though you can get to Laboe and Strande by car, it's more fun to catch a ferry leaving from Kiel.

Dining and Lodging

$$ ✕ **Kieler Ansichten.** Sitting high above the Nord-Ostsee-Kanal (North
★ Sea–Baltic Canal) and the Kieler Föhrde, you can watch the marine traf-
fic from your seat on the restaurant's terrace. The Kieler Ansichten is
a 15-minute drive from downtown Kiel, but it is worth the trip to enjoy
the delightful view while tasting *Lachs im Kartoffelmantel mit Gemüse*
(salmon in a baked coat of potatoes, served with vegetables and saf-
fron sauce). ✉ *Zum Kesselort 40,* ☎ *0431/239–730. Reservations es-
sential. No credit cards.*

$$$ ✕🖬 **Hotel Kieler Yachtclub.** This traditional hotel offers standard yet
elegant rooms in the main building and completely new, bright ac-
commodations in the *Villentrakt.* The restaurant serves mostly local
fish dishes; in summer try to get a table on the terrace. The club overlooks the Kieler Föhrde. ✉ *Hindenburgufer 70, D–24105,* ☎ *0431/
88130,* 🖷 *0431/881–3444. 55 rooms, 3 suites. Restaurant, bar, minibars, no-smoking rooms, room service, dry cleaning, laundry service,
concierge, meeting rooms, parking (fee). AE, DC, MC, V.*

Nightlife and the Arts

Despite its medium size (250,000 inhabitants), the city has a thriving
nightlife. One of the many chic and hip bars is the **Hemingway** (✉ Alter
Markt, ☎ 0431/96812). Another popular bar, the **Nachtcafé,** has a basement disco, **Velvet** (✉ Eggerstedtstr. 14, ☎ 0431/95550).

Ahrensburg

❻ *25 km (16 mi) northeast of Hamburg.*

One of Schleswig-Holstein's major attractions is within a Hamburg suburb. The romantic, 16th-century **Schloss Ahrensburg** (Ahrensburg
Castle) is surrounded by lush parkland on the bank of the Hunnau.
The whitewashed, brick, moated Renaissance castle stands much as it
did when first constructed by Count Peter Rantzau. Its interior has had
several remodelings, the first after financier Carl Schimmelmann purchased the estate in 1759.

Furniture and paintings, most dating from the early 19th century, fine
porcelain, and exquisite crystal are exhibited on the two museum floors.
On the grounds stands a simple 16th-century church; the west tower was
a later addition, and baroque alterations were made in the 18th century.
The church is nestled between two rows of 12 almshouses, or *Gottes-
buden* (God's cottages). ✉ *On bank of the Hunnau,* ☎ *04102/42510.*
🖾 *DM 6.* ☉ *Apr.–Sept., Tues.–Sun. 10–12:30 and 1:30–5; Oct., Feb.–
Mar., Tues.–Sun. 10–12:30 and 1:30–4; Nov.–Jan., Tues.–Sun. 10–3.*

Lübeck

★ **❼** *38 km (24 mi) northeast of Ahrensburg, 60 km (37 mi) southeast of
Kiel, 56 km (35 mi) northeast of Hamburg.*

The ancient core of Lübeck, one of Europe's largest Old Towns dating from the 12th century, was a chief stronghold of the Hanseatic merchant princes who controlled trade on the Baltic. But it was the roving
Heinrich der Löwe (King Henry the Lion) who established the town
and, in 1173, laid the foundation stone of the redbrick Gothic cathedral. The town's famous landmark gate, the **Holstentor,** built between
1464 and 1478, is flanked by two round, squat towers and serves as
a solid symbol of Lübeck's prosperity as a trading center.

In the **Altstadt** (Old Town), proof of Lübeck's former position as the
golden queen of the Hanseatic League is found at every step. More 13th-
to 15th-century buildings stand in Lübeck than in all other large north-

ern German cities combined, which has earned the Altstadt a place on UNESCO's register of the world's greatest cultural and natural treasures. The **Rathaus,** dating from 1240, is among the buildings lining the arcaded Marktplatz, one of Europe's most striking medieval market squares. It has been subjected to several architectural face-lifts that have added Romanesque arches, Gothic windows, and a Renaissance roof. ✉ *Breitestr. 64,* ☎ *0451/122–1005.* ▦ *Guided tour in German DM 4.* ☉ *Tour weekdays at 11, noon, and 3.*

The impressive redbrick Gothic **Marienkirche** (St. Mary's Church), which has the highest brick nave in the world, looms behind the Rathaus. ✉ *Marienkirchhof,* ☎ *0451/74901.* ☉ *Mar. and Oct., daily 10–5; Apr.–Sept., daily 10–6; Nov., weekdays 10–6, weekends 10–5; Dec.–Feb., daily 10–4.*

The **Buddenbrookhaus,** a highly respectable-looking mansion, takes its name from German novelist Thomas Mann's saga *Buddenbrooks.* Mann's family once lived in the house, which is now the **Heinrich and Thomas Mann Zentrum** (Heinrich and Thomas Mann Center). This museum documents the lives and works of two of the most important German writers of this century. A tour and video in English are offered. ✉ *Mengstr. 4,* ☎ *0451/122–4192.* ▦ *DM 5.* ☉ *Daily 10–5. Closed Mon. in Jan. and Feb.*

Take a look inside the entrance hall of the Gothic **Heiligen-Geist-Hospital** (Hospital of the Holy Ghost). It was built in the 14th century by the town's rich merchants and is still caring for the infirm. ✉ *Am Koberg,* ☎ *0451/122–2040.* ☉ *Apr.–Sept., Tues.–Sun. 10–5; Oct.–Mar., Tues.–Sun. 10–4.*

Building of the **Lübecker Dom** (Lübeck Cathedral), the city's oldest building, began in 1173. Both the Dom and the Marienkirche (☞ *above*) present frequent organ concerts, a real treat in these magnificent redbrick Gothic churches. ✉ *Domkirchhof,* ☎ *0451/74704.* ☉ *Mar.–Oct., daily 10–6; Nov.–Feb., daily 10–3.*

Dining and Lodging

$$$–$$$$ ✕ **Wullenwever.** Culinary experts say this restaurant set a new standard of dining sophistication for Lübeck. It is certainly one of the most attractive establishments in town, with dark furniture, chandeliers, and oil paintings on pale pastel walls. In summer tables fill a quiet flower-strewn courtyard. ✉ *Beckergrube 71,* ☎ *0451/704–333. Reservations essential. Jacket and tie. AE, DC, V. Closed Sun. and Mon. No lunch.*

$$–$$$ ✕ **Schiffergesellschaft.** Not even the scent of a woman was allowed in
★ the Schiffergesellschaft from its opening in 1535 until 1870. Today men and women alike sit in church-style pews at long 400-year-old oak tables. At each end of the pew is a sculpted coat of arms of a particular city. Ship owners had their set trading routes, and they each had their own pew and table. A good meal here is the *Ostseescholle* (plaice), fried with bacon and served with potatoes and cucumber salad. ✉ *Breitestr. 2,* ☎ *0451/76776. No credit cards.*

$$$$ ✕▧ **SAS Radisson Hotel Lübeck.** Close to the famous Holstentor, the new
★ Radisson is an ultramodern hotel whose daring architecture still reveals a North German heritage: The redbrick building, with its oversize windows and generous, open lobby, mimics an old Lübeck warehouse. Rooms in this ascetic yet elegant hotel are fairly large, decorated in soft, warm brown and yellow tones. A big plus are the very comfortable beds, which are large by German standards. The Nautilo restaurant serves light Mediterranean cuisine (with an emphasis on fish). At the lively bar the local Hanseaten and tourists mingle over beer and aquavit, the strong North German schnapps. ✉ *Willy-Brandt-Allee 6, D–23554,* ☎ *0451/*

1420, ℻ 0451/142–2222. 217 rooms, 7 suites. 2 restaurants, bar, in-room data ports, minibars, no-smoking rooms, room service, indoor pool, beauty salon, massage, sauna, spa, health club, baby-sitting, dry cleaning, laundry service, concierge, meeting rooms, parking (fee). AE, DC, MC, V. ✸

$$$ ✕🍴 **Jensen.** Only a stone's throw from the Holsten Gate, this hotel is close to all the main attractions and faces the moat that surrounds the Old Town. It's family run and very comfortable, with modern rooms, mostly decorated with bright cherrywood furniture. Though not large, the guest rooms are big enough for two twin beds and a coffee table and come with either a shower or a bath. The popular Yachtzimmer restaurant offers a mix of regional and international dishes. ⊠ *An der Obertrave 4–5, D–23552,* ☎ *0451/71646,* ℻ *0451/73386. 41 rooms, 1 suite. Restaurant. AE, DC, MC, V.*

$$$ 🍴 **Kaiserhof.** The most comfortable hotel in Lübeck consists of two early 19th-century merchants' houses linked together, retaining many of the original architectural features. It's just a five-minute walk from the cathedral. Although the hotel lacks a full restaurant, a marvelous breakfast (included in the room cost) is served. The spacious bedrooms all have a restful, homey ambience, and the quietest of them overlook the garden at the back. ⊠ *Kronsforder Allee 11–13, D–23560,* ☎ *0451/703–301,* ℻ *0451/795– 083. 60 rooms, 6 suites. Bar, minibars, in-room safes, room service, indoor pool, sauna, exercise room, free parking. AE, DC, MC, V.* ✸

$ 🍴 **Klassik Altstadt-Hotel.** Behind the landmark old facade stands a modern hotel that opened in 1984. The studios, fitted with small kitchens, are a particularly good value if you plan to stay a few days. There is no restaurant, but breakfast (included in the price) is served in the hotel. ⊠ *Fischergrube 52, D–23552,* ☎ *0451/72083,* ℻ *0451/73778. 25 rooms, 2 suites. Breakfast room. AE, DC, MC, V.* ✸

Nightlife and the Arts

Contact the **Musik und Kongresshallen Lübeck** (⊠ Willy-Brandt-Allee 10, D–23554, ☎ 0451/790–400) for schedules of the myriad concerts, operas, and theater performances in Lübeck.

In summer try to catch a few performances of the **Schleswig-Holstein Music Festival** (mid-July–late August), which features orchestras composed of young musicians from more than 25 countries. Some concerts are held in the Dom or the Marienkirche; some are staged in barns in small towns and villages. The sight of the late Leonard Bernstein conducting a complete classical orchestra where cows and chickens are normally fed is still remembered. The La Scala Orchestra and the music of Goethe were featured in 1999. For exact dates and tickets, contact **Schleswig-Holstein Konzertorganisation** (⊠ Kartenzentrale Kiel, Postfach 3840, D–24037 Kiel, ☎ 0431/570–470, ℻ 0431/570–4747).

Shopping

The city's largest downtown mall, **Holstentor-Passage** (⊠ An der Untertrave 111, ☎ 0451/704–425), is next to the Holstentor and is home to stores most of which sell clothing or home accessories. **Konditorei-Café Niederegger** (⊠ Breitestr. 89, ☎ 0451/530–1126) sells the famous Lübeck marzipan molded into a multitude of imaginative forms. It's hard to believe that the almond-paste treat was first introduced during the great medieval Lübeck famine.

WESTERN MECKLENBURG

This long-forgotten Baltic Coast region, pinned between two sprawling urban areas—the state capital of Schwerin, in the west, and Rostock, in the east—is thriving again. Despite its perennial economic woes, this part of Germany, and Schwerin in particular, has attracted many new businesses, which suggests a light at the end of the tunnel. Though the region is close to the sea, it is made up largely of seemingly endless fields of wheat and yellow rape and a dozen or so wonderful lakes. "When the Lord made the Earth, He started with Mecklenburg," wrote native novelist Fritz Reuter.

Wismar

★ ❽ *60 km (37 mi) east of Lübeck on Rte. 105.*

The old city of Wismar was one of the original three sea-trading towns, along with Lübeck and Rostock, that banded together in 1259 to combat Baltic pirates. From this mutual defense pact grew the great and powerful private trading bloc, the Hanseatic League, which dominated the Baltic for centuries. The Thirty Years' War halved the prewar population—and the power of the Hanseatics was broken. Wismar became the victim of regular military tussles and finally fell to Sweden. In 1803 the town was leased for 100 years to a German Mecklenburg duke, and only when the lease expired did Wismar legally rejoin Germany. The wealth generated by the Hanseatic merchants can still be seen in Wismar's ornate architecture.

★ The **Marktplatz** (Market Square), one of the largest and best preserved in Germany, is framed by patrician gabled houses. Their style ranges from redbrick late Gothic through Dutch Renaissance to 19th-century neoclassical. In 1922 filmmaker Friedrich Wilhelm Murnau used the tortuous streets of Wismar's Old Town in his expressionist horror film classic, *Nosferatu.* The square's **Wasserkunst,** the ornate pumping station done in Dutch Renaissance style, was built between 1580 and 1602 by the Dutch master Philipp Brandin. Not only was it a work of art, it supplied the town with water until the mid-19th century.

The **Alter Schwede,** a seamen's tavern since 1878, has entertained guests ranging from sailors to the Swedish royal family. Dating from 1380, it's the oldest building on the Marktplatz and is easily identified by its stepped gables and redbrick facade. ⊠ *Am Markt 19–22,* ☎ *03841/283–552.*

The ruins of the **Marienkirche** (St. Mary's Church) with its 250-ft tower, bombed in World War II, lie just behind the Marktplatz; the church is still undergoing restoration. At noon, 3, and 5, listen for one of 14 hymns played on its carillon. The **Fürstenhof** (Princes' Court), home of the former dukes of Mecklenburg, stands next to Marienkirche. It is an early 16th-century Italian Renaissance structure with touches of late Gothic. The facade is a series of fussy friezes depicting scenes from the Trojan War. The **Georgenkirche** (St. George's Church), another victim of the war, is next to the Fürstenhof. Today it's the biggest Gothic religious ruin in Europe.

The late-Gothic **St. Nikolaikirche** (St. Nicholas's Church), with a 120-ft-high nave, was built between 1381 and 1487. A remnant of the town's long domination by Sweden is the additional altar built for Swedish sailors. ⊠ *Marktpl.,* ☎ *03841/215–739.* ☉ *Apr.–May, Mon.–Sat. 10–noon and 1–4; Sun. 1–4; June–Sept., Mon.–Sat. 10–12:30, Sun. 1–5:30; Oct.–March, Mon.–Sat. 11–noon and 1–3, Sun. 1–3.*

If you have an hour to spare, wander among the jetties and quays of the port, a mix of the medieval and the modern. **To'n Zägenkrog,** a seamen's haven decorated with sharks' teeth, stuffed seagulls, and maritime gear, is a picturesque pit stop along the harbor. ⊠ *Ziegenmarkt 10,* ☎ *03841/282–716.*

Dining and Lodging

$$ ✕ **Alter Schwede.** Regarded as one of the most attractive, authentic taverns on the Baltic—and correspondingly busy—this eatery focuses

on Mecklenburg's traditional game and fish dishes, such as *Mecklen-burger Rippenbraten mit Backpflaumen, Rotkraut und Kartoffeln* (pork spareribs with baked plums, red cabbage, and potatoes.) ⊠ *Am Markt 19–22,* ☎ *03841/283–552. AE, MC, V.*

$$ ✕ **Reuterhaus.** The rustic, historic restaurant at the Old Market square
★ is one of the most traditional places to visit in Wismar. Chef Kirsten Tautel serves many hearty Mecklenburg fish and sausage dishes, such as *Mecklenburger Grünkohl* (with green cabbage) or *Rote Grütze* (a sweet red pudding with vanilla sauce). Be careful with their furniture— some of it is more than 300 years old. ⊠ *Am Markt 19,* ☎ *03841/ 211–790. No credit cards.*

$$ ✕🏨 **Privathotel Alter Speicher.** This small and very personal family-
★ owned hotel is behind a restored facade of an old merchant house in the historic downtown area. Some of the rooms may be tiny, but they add to the cozy and warm atmosphere the hotel exudes. The lobby and restaurants are decorated with wooden beams and panels. The main restaurant primarily serves game, but it also offers regional dishes such as *Rauchwarme Räucherfischhappen auf Kräuterrührei und Brot* (smoke-warm smoked fish pieces on scrambled eggs with herbs and bread). ⊠ *Bohrstr. 12–12a, D–23966,* ☎ *03841/211–746,* FAX *03841/ 211–747. 70 rooms, 3 suites, 2 apartments. Restaurant, bar, café, in-room safes, minibars, no-smoking rooms, massage, sauna, exercise room, meeting rooms, parking (fee). DC, MC, V.* 🐾

$$$ 🏨 **Arkona-Hotel Stadt Hamburg.** This completely remodeled first-class hotel hides behind a rigid gray facade dating to the early 19th century. Behind it is an open, airy interior, with skylights and a posh lobby. The rooms have elegant cherrywood art-deco-style furnishings. Downstairs, the hotel's Bierkeller, a cavernous 17th-century room with vaulted ceilings, is a trendy nightspot. When making a reservation, ask for special package deals such as the *Genuss total,* which includes a three-course dinner, a sightseeing tour, and complimentary cocktails. ⊠ *Am Markt 24, D–23966,* ☎ *03841/2390,* FAX *03841/239–239. 103 rooms. Restaurant, café, minibars, no-smoking floor, massage, sauna, exercise room, meeting rooms. AE, DC, MC, V.* 🐾

Nightlife and the Arts

At the **Niederdeutsche Bühne** (⊠ Philipp-Müllerstr. 5, ☎ 03841/705–501), plays in German and operas are performed regularly, and con-certs are occasionally presented.

Schwerin

★ ❾   *32 km (20 mi) south of Wismar on Rte. 106.*

Schwerin, the second-largest town in the region after Rostock and the capital of the state of Mecklenburg-Vorpommern, is worth a trip just to visit its giant island palace. On the edge of Lake Schwerin, the **Schweriner Schloss** housed the Mecklenburg royal family. When Henry the Lion founded Schwerin in 1160, he enlarged the original palace, which dated from 1018. Surmounted by 15 turrets, large and small, the palace is reminiscent of a French château, and, indeed, portions of it were later modeled on Chambord, in the Loire Valley. The part of it that's neo-Renaissance style along with its many ducal staterooms date from between 1845 and 1857.

North of the main tower is the **Neue Lange Haus** (New Long House), built between 1553 and 1555 and now used as the **Schlossmuseum.** The Communist government restored and maintained the fantastic op-ulence of this rambling, 80-room reminder of an absolutist monarchy— and then used it to board kindergarten teachers in training. A fifth of the rooms are now used for government offices. Antique furniture, objets d'art, silk tapestries, and paintings are sprinkled throughout the salons (the throne room is particularly extravagant), but of special interest are the ornately patterned and highly burnished inlaid wooden floors and wall panels. The parkland contains many beautiful and rare species of trees. Sandstone replicas of Permoser sculptures adorn the boulevards. ⊠ *Lennéstr. 1,* ☎ *0385/565–738.* ▣ *DM 8.* ⊙ *Mid-Apr.–mid-Oct., Tues.–Sun. 10–6; mid-Oct.–mid-Apr., Tues.–Sun. 10–5.*

The **Alte Garten** (Old Garden), the town's showpiece square, was the setting of military parades during the years of Communist rule. It is dominated by two buildings: the ornate neo-Renaissance state theater, constructed in 1883–86; and the **Staatliches Museum** (State Museum), which houses an interesting collection of paintings by Max Liebermann and Lovis Corinth, plus an exhibition of Meissen porcelain. ⊠ *Alter Garten 3,* ☎ *0385/59580.* ▣ *DM 7.* ⊙ *Mid-Apr.–mid.-Oct., Wed.–Sun. 10–6, Tues. 10–8; mid-Oct.–mid-Apr., Wed.–Sun. 10–5, Tues. 10–8.*

The **Dom,** a Gothic cathedral, is the oldest building (built 1222–48) in the city. The bronze baptismal font is from the 14th century; the altar was built in 1440. Religious scenes painted on its walls date from the Middle Ages. Sweeping views of the Old Town and lake await those with the energy to climb the 219 steps to the top of the 320-ft-high cathedral tower. ⊠ *Am Dom 4,* ☎ *0385/565–014.* ⊙ *Tower and nave May–mid-Oct., Mon.–Sat. 10–4, Sun. noon–4; mid-Oct.–Apr., weekdays 11–2, Sat. 11–4, Sun. noon–3.*

⊙ The **Mecklenburgisches Volkskundemuseum** (Ethnology Museum) is a living-history museum representing traditional work and farm life in Germany. Children and history buffs in particular will enjoy wandering through the 17 preserved buildings, which include a blacksmith's shop dating from 1736, a village school from the 19th century, and a traditional fire station. You can watch demonstrations of the tools. ⊠ *Alte Crivitzer Landstr. 13, 6 km (4 mi) south of Schwerin,* ☎ *0385/208–410.* ▣ *DM 5.* ⊙ *May–Oct., Tues.–Sun. 10–6.*

A visit to Schwerin wouldn't be complete without a boat tour of the lakes (☞ Contacts and Resources *in* Schleswig-Holstein and the Baltic Coast A to Z, *below.*)

Dining and Lodging

$$$ ✕ **Weinhaus Uhle.** One of the most traditional and popular eateries ★ in Schwerin, this restaurant is named after the wine merchant who opened the restaurant back in 1740. The new *Weinbistro* (wine bistro) offers primarily German wine tasting and a small menu (mostly cheese plates or soups such as lobster cream soup). In the restaurant, regional specialties and international mixed grills are served in a rustic setting, accompanied by a piano player on Friday and Saturday nights. ⊠ *Schusterstr. 13–15,* ☎ *0385/562–956.* AE, MC, V.

$$–$$$ ✕ **Zum Goldenen Reiter.** The classic elegance here provides a sharp contrast to the current crop of glossy restaurant chains and mossy old taverns. The dark-wood, candlelighted rooms generate a sophisticated yet comfortable atmosphere. Head chef Jörg Reimer serves *Mecklenburger Entenbrust,* a tender breast of duck stuffed with apples and red cabbage, a recipe lifted from an 1896 cookbook of regional specialties. ⊠ *Puschkinstr. 44,* ☎ *0385/565–036.* AE, MC.

$–$$ ✕▥ **Alt-Schweriner Schankstuben.** A small family-owned restaurant ★ and hotel, the Schankstuben offers standard but very personal service with emphasis on Mecklenburg tradition. The hotel is within three old houses in the historic downtown district. Its restaurant serves local dishes such as *Rinderfilet unter der Zwiebel-Senfkruste* (beef fillet under an onion-mustard crust). The fish on the menu is equally delicious; ask for the catch of the day. The guest rooms are small but bright and furnished with simple pine furniture. ⊠ *Schlachtermarkt 9–13, D–19055,* ☎ *0385/592–530,* FAX *0385/557–4109. 16 rooms. Restaurant, café, no-smoking rooms, meeting rooms, free parking. AE, V.*

$$$$ ⊞ **Crowne Plaza Schwerin.** This new hotel looks a little somber from
★ the outside, but once you've entered the elegant dark-marble and mahogany lobby, you'll be surprised. The rooms are sumptuously decorated with thick dark blue or red carpets and reproduction antiques of the late 19th century. Instead of booking a double room, spend some DM 50 extra for a large apartment with a kitchenette. The hotel's location is ideal for exploring Schwerin on foot because it sits right on the banks of Ostorfer Lake. The restaurant and health club offer views of the lake. ⊠ *Bleicher Ufer 23, D–19053,* ☎ *0385/57550,* FAX *0385/575–5777. 84 rooms, 8 suites, 8 apartments. Restaurant, bar, in-room data ports, in-room safes, minibars, no-smoking floors, room service, massage, sauna, health club, bicycles, baby-sitting service, dry cleaning, laundry service, concierge, meeting rooms, parking (fee). AE, DC, MC, V.* ✎

$$–$$$ ⊞ **Hotel Arte Schwerin.** This new hotel is small and distinguished. The redbrick building is a fully restored farmhouse whose humble exterior contrasts with its modern and luxurious interior. The hotel is on peaceful Ostorfer Lake, close to the Schweriner Schloss. ⊠ *Dorfstr. 6, D–19061,* ☎ *0385/63450,* FAX *0385/634–5100. 40 rooms. Restaurant, bar, in-room safes, minibars, no-smoking rooms, room service, hot tub, sauna, dry cleaning, laundry service, meeting rooms, free parking. AE, DC, MC, V.*

Nightlife and the Arts

The **Mecklenburgisches Staatstheater** (⊠ Am Alten Garten, ☎ 0385/53000) stages German drama and opera. In June the **Schlossfestspiele** offer open-air drama or comedy performances.

The **Achteck** (⊠ Wittenburgerstr. 120, ☎ 0385/760–860) is one of the city's largest dance clubs and attracts a stylish young crowd.

Shopping

Antiques and bric-a-brac that have languished in cellars and attics since World War II are still surfacing throughout eastern Germany, and the occasional bargain can be found. The best places to look in Schwerin are on and around **Schmiedestrasse, Schlossstrasse,** and **Mecklenburgstrasse.**

Bad Doberan

⑩ *60 km (37 mi) east of Wismar on Rte. 105, 90 km (56 mi) northeast of Schwerin.*

★ Bad Doberan has a meticulously restored redbrick **Klosterkirche** (monastery church), one of the finest of its kind in the region. It was built by Cistercian monks between 1294 and 1368 in the northern German Gothic style, with a central nave and transept. The main altar dates from the early 14th century and features a 45-ft-tall cross. ⊠ *Klosterstr. 2,* ☎ *038203/62716.* 🎫 *DM 2, tours DM 3.* ⊙ *May–Sept., Mon.–Sat. 9–6, Sun. noon–6; Mar., Apr., and Oct., Mon.–Sat. 9–4, Sun. noon–4; Nov.–Feb., Tues.–Fri. 9–noon and 2–4, Sat. 9–4, Sun. noon–4; Apr.–Sept., tours at 9, 10, and 2; Oct.–Mar., tours at 2 and 3.*

No visit to this part of the world would be complete without a ride on
★ *Molli,* a quaint steam train that has been chugging up and down a 16-km (10-mi) narrow-gauge track between Bad Doberan and the nearby beach resorts of **Heiligendamm** and **Kühlungsborn** since 1886. The train was nicknamed after a little local dog that barked its approval every time the smoking iron horse passed by. At the start of the 45-minute

journey the engine and its old wooden carriages make their way through the center of Bad Doberan's cobbled streets. In summer *Molli* runs 13 times daily between Bad Doberan and Kühlungsborn. ⊠ *Mecklenburgische Bäderbahn Molli, Küstenbus GmbH,* ☎ *038203/ 4150.* ⊑ *DM 16.50 for round-trip on same day.* ⊙ *May–Sept., daily 6:44–6:36; Oct.–Apr., daily 6:44–4:40.*

Dining and Lodging

$$ ✕ **Weisser Pavillon.** Here's a mixed setting for you: a 19th-century Chinese pagoda–type structure in an English-style park. Come for lunch or high tea; regional specialties are featured. In summer the café closes at 10 PM. ⊠ *Auf dem Kamp,* ☎ *038203/62326. No credit cards.*

$$$–$$$$ ✕▥ **Romantik-Hotel Bad Doberan.** Built in 1793 for a Mecklenburg
★ duke, this historic whitewashed member of the Romantik Hotel group has accommodated guests for more than 200 years. Completely restored and renovated, each room exudes old-world elegance with modern comforts. ⊠ *August-Bebel-Str. 2, D–18209,* ☎ *038203/63036,* ⅀ *038203/ 62126. 40 rooms, 2 suites, 3 apartments. Restaurant, café, minibars, no-smoking rooms, room service, sauna, bicycles, free parking. AE, DC, MC, V.* ✆

$$–$$$ ✕▥ **Hotel und Apartments Röntgen.** This white mansion has spacious one- to three-bedroom apartments with kitchenettes, as well as a nice little restaurant specializing in fish dishes. In the heart of seaside Kühlungsborn, it is run by the Röntgen family, who are not only proud of their tradition as bakers but also of their highly personalized service. ⊠ *Strandstr. 30a, D–18225 Kühlungsborn,* ☎ *038293/7810,* ⅀ *038293/78199. 17 apartments. Restaurant, café. AE, MC, V.*

Rostock

⓫ *14 km (9 mi) east of Bad Doberan on Rte. 105.*

Rostock, the biggest port and shipbuilding center of the former East Germany, was founded around 1200. Of all the Hanse cities, the once-thriving Rostock suffered the most from the dissolution of the League in 1669. Although Hamburg, Kiel (to the west), and Stettin (to the east; now part of Poland) became leading port cities, Rostock languished until the late 1950s. The newly formed DDR reestablished Rostock as a major port, but since reunification, port work has been cut in half and though ferries come from Gedser (Denmark) and Trelleborg (Sweden), there is little traffic. Today the biggest local attraction is Hanse Sail, a week of yacht racing held in August.

Because it was home to wartime armament factories, the city suffered severe bombings, but much of the Old Town's core has been rebuilt. The main street, the pedestrians-only **Kröpelinerstrasse,** begins at the old western gate, the Kröpeliner Tor. Here you'll find the finest examples of the late-Gothic and Renaissance houses of rich Hanse merchants. The triangular **Universitätsplatz** (University Square), commemorating the founding of northern Europe's first university here in 1419, is home to Rostock University's Italian Renaissance–style main building, finished in 1867.

At the **Neuer Markt** (Town Square) you'll immediately notice the architectural potpourri of the **Rathaus.** Basically 13th-century Gothic with a baroque facade, the building spouts seven slender, decorative towers, looking like candles on a peculiar birthday cake. The square is surrounded by historic gabled houses.

Four-centuries-old **St. Marienkirche** (St. Mary's Church), the Gothic architectural prize of Rostock, boasts a bronze baptismal font from 1290 and some interesting baroque features, notably the oak altar (1720) and organ (1770). Unique is the huge astronomical clock dating from 1472; it has a calendar extending to the year 2017. ⊠ *Am Ziegenmarkt,* ☎ *0381/492–3396.* ☉ *Mon.–Sat. 10–5, Sun. 11–noon.*

☺ The **Schifffahrtsmuseum** (Maritime Museum) traces the history of shipping on the Baltic and displays models of ships, which especially intrigue children. It is just beyond the city wall, at the old city gateway, Steintor. ⊠ *August-Bebel-Str. 1,* ☎ *0381/252–060.* ☑ *DM 4.* ☉ *Tues.–Sun. 10–6.*

☺ The **Schiffbaumuseum** (Shipbuilding Museum) is housed in the hold of the *Dresden,* a 10,000-ton old freighter. Built in 1952, the ship also contains a youth hostel. The *Dresden* is moored to the riverbank on the right-hand side of the road, in the Warnow River about 5 km (3 mi) north of the center of Rostock. ⊠ *Traditionsschiff Rostock Schmarl,* ☎ *0381/121–9726.* ☑ *DM 4.* ☉ *Tues.–Sun. 9–5.*

The **Port Centre** is a ship that was commandeered and moored alongside the riverbank to become a complex of stores, boutiques, bars, and restaurants. After the collapse of state communism, there weren't enough buildings to house shops, so the ship offered additional space. ⊠ *Kapuzenhof.*

☺ The **Zoologischer Garten** (Zoological Garden) has one of the largest collections of exotic animals and birds in northern Germany. This zoo is particularly noted for its polar bears, some of which were bred in Rostock. If you're traveling with kids, a visit is a must. ⊠ *Rennbahnallee 21,* ☎ *0381/20820.* ☑ *DM 9.* ☉ *Oct.–Apr., daily 9–4; May–Sept., daily 9–5.*

Dining and Lodging

$ ★ ✕ **Zur Kogge.** Looking like the cabin of some ancient sailing vessel, the oldest sailors' beer tavern in town serves mostly fish. Order the *Mecklenburger Fischsuppe* (Baltic Coast fish soup) if it's on the menu; *Grosser Fischteller,* consisting of three kinds of fish—depending on the day's catch—served with vegetables, lobster and shrimp sauce, and potatoes is also a popular choice. ⊠ *Wokrenterstr. 27,* ☎ *0381/493–4493. Reservations essential. AE, DC, MC, V.*

$$ ☒ **Courtyard by Marriott.** This hotel in a 19th-century mansion is a genuine part of Rostock's historic Old Town. It provides smooth service, and the modern rooms are tastefully decorated. Despite its downtown location, it is a quiet place to stay. ⊠ *Schwaansche/Kröpeliner Str., D–18055,* ☎ *0381/49700,* ☒ *0381/497–0700. 148 rooms, 2 suites. Restaurant, bar, minibars, no-smoking floor, room service, sauna, exercise room, dry cleaning, laundry service, meeting rooms, parking (fee). AE, DC, MC, V.* ☜

Nightlife and the Arts

The summer season brings with it a plethora of special concerts, sailing regattas, and parties on the beach. The **Volkstheater** (⊠ Doberanerstr. 134/35, ☎ 0381/2440) presents plays and concerts.

The bar/café **Kajahn** (⊠ Patriotischer Weg 126, ☎ 0381/201–8893) is a stylish nightspot. **Speicher–Discothek** (⊠ Am Strande 3a, ☎ 0381/492–3031), a split-level disco, appeals to all ages.

Shopping

Echter Rostocker Doppel-Kümmel und -Korn, a kind of schnapps made from various grains, is a traditional liquor of the region around Rostock. Fishermen have numbed themselves to the cold for centuries with this 80-proof beverage; a 7-liter bottle costs DM 15–DM 20.

Warnemünde

⑫ *14 km (9 mi) north of Rostock on Rte. 103.*

Warnemünde is a quaint seaside resort with the best hotels and restaurants in the area, as well as 20 km (12 mi) of beautiful white beach. For years it has been a popular summer getaway for families in eastern Germany. Children enjoy climbing to the top of the town landmark, a 115-ft-high **Leuchtturm** (lighthouse), dating from 1898; on clear days it offers views of the coast and Rostock Harbor. Inland from the lighthouse is the yacht marina known as **Alter Strom** (Old Stream). Once the entry into the port of Warnemünde, it now has bars, cozy restaurants, and specialty shops.

Dining and Lodging

$$ ✕ **Fischerklause.** Sailors have stopped in at this restaurant's bar since the turn of the century, but it's not *that* kind of place. The smoked fish sampler served on a lazy Susan is delicious, and the house specialty of fish soup is best washed down with some Rostocker Doppel-Kümmel schnapps. An accordionist entertains the crowd on Friday and Saturday evenings. ⊠ *Am Strom 123,* ☎ *0381/52516. Reservations essential. AE, DC, MC, V.*

$–$$ ✕▥ **Landhotel Ostseetraum.** This family-owned hotel is an outstand-
★ ing example of blending modern style with rural architecture. The farmhouse with a thatch roof is fairly secluded, in an area outside Warnemünde, just 500 yards from the beach. ⊠ *Stolteraaweg 34b, D–18119 Warnemünde-Diedrichshagen,* ☎ 🖷 *0381/51719. 18 rooms. Restaurant, free parking. AE, MC, V.*

$$$$ ▥ **Hotel Neptun.** The 19-story concrete-and-glass Neptun is an eyesore on the outside, but inside it has the redeeming qualities of a luxury hotel. Every one of the neat and lovingly decorated rooms has a sea view. To get first-class atmosphere for less money, ask for the hotel's special "Happy Weekend" and "Vacation on the Sea" rates. The hotel's Spa Arkona is one of eastern Germany's finest fitness and sauna clubs. ⊠ *Seestr. 19, D–18119,* ☎ *0381/7770,* 🖷 *0381/777–800. 340 rooms, 5 suites. 4 restaurants, 2 bars, café, in-room safes, minibars, no-smoking rooms, room service, indoor saltwater pool, beauty salon, sauna, spa, exercise room, boating, bicycles, dance club, baby-sitting, dry cleaning, laundry service, meeting rooms, parking (fee). AE, DC, MC, V.* ✆

$$–$$$ ▥ **Hotel Germania.** At the harbor entrance and only one block from the beach and the Alter Strom promenade, this small hotel's location alone makes it a good choice. All rooms are tastefully decorated in pale blue tones and mahogany furnishings and equipped with a TV. With so many good eateries nearby you probably won't miss having a hotel restaurant. ⊠ *Am Strom 110–111, D–18119,* ☎ *0381/519–850,* 🖷 *0381/519–8510. 18 rooms. Minibars, parking (fee). AE, DC, MC, V.*

Fishing

Fishing is a rapidly expanding leisure industry in the area. Every port along the coast now has small boats for rent, and some boatmen will lead you to the shoals. For information on equipment availability, contact the **Rostock tourist office** (☎ 0381/51142) for **Warnemünder Hafen** (Warnemünde Harbor).

Nightlife

In Warnemünde nearly all the seaside hotels and resorts, down to the smallest, have almost nightly dances during the summer months. Head to the large hotels to search for fun. The pubs in **Alter Strom** are gathering places for locals and visitors alike.

The **Skybar,** on the 19th floor of the Neptun Hotel (⊠ Seestr. 19, ☎ 0381/7770), is open until 4 AM. Roof access gives you the chance to sit under the stars and watch ship lights twinkle on the sea.

Ribnitz-Damgarten

⓭ *30 km (19 mi) northeast of Warnemünde, 26 km (16 mi) east of Rostock on Rte. 105.*

Ribnitz-Damgarten is the center of the **amber** (in German, *Bernstein*) business, unique to the Baltic Coast. Amber is a yellow-brown fossil formed from the sap of ancient conifers and is millions of years old. Head for a beach and join the locals in the perennial quest for amber stones washed up among the seaweed. Pebbles with a hole worn through the middle are prevalent on this coast; locals call them *Hühnergötter* (chicken gods) and believe they bring good luck. In the **Bernsteinmuseum** (Amber Museum), which adjoins the main factory, you can see a fascinating exhibit of how this precious "Baltic gold" is collected from the sea and refined to make jewelry. The museum has examples of amber that are between 35 and 50 million years old. The biggest lump of raw amber ever harvested from the sea weighed more than 23 pounds. ⊠ *Im Kloster 1–2,* ☎ *03821/2931.* ☜ *DM 5.* ☉ *Apr.–Oct, daily 9:30–5:45; Nov.–Mar., Wed.–Sun. 9:30–5.*

Shopping

You can buy amber jewelry, chess figures, and ornate jewelry boxes in the Bernsteinmuseum. The jewelry, often designed with gold and silver as well as amber, costs from DM 100 to DM 1,000. Fossils are often embedded in the stone—a precious find. (Hint: only true amber floats in a glass of water stirred with 2 teaspoons of salt.)

VORPOMMERN

The best description of this region is found in its name, which simply means "before." This area, indeed, seems trapped between Mecklenburg and the authentic, old Pommerania farther east, now part of Poland. Although Vorpommern is not the dull, monotonous backwater it is made out to be, its tundralike appearance, pine barrens, heaths, and dunes are not typical tourist draws, either. Its very remoteness and poverty ensure an unforgettable view of unspoiled nature, primarily attracting families and a young crowd.

Ahrenshoop

⓮ *75 km (47 mi) north of Ribnitz-Damgarten.*

Ahrenshoop is typical of the seaside villages on the half-island of **Darss.** This curved finger of land was once three islands that became one from centuries of shifting sand. In the late 19th century painters from across Germany and beyond formed an art colony here. After World War II Ahrenshoop again became a mecca of sorts for artists, musicians, and writers of the DDR, but that scene has long dispersed. Continue toward Prerow to get back to the mainland, but be sure to stop at the 17th-century seamen's church on the edge of town.

Since 1966 much of Darss has been a nature reserve, partly to protect the ancient forest of beech, holly, and juniper. The island's best beach is the **Weststrand** (West Beach), a broad stretch of fine white sand that is free of auto traffic and most development.

Stralsund

⑮ *59 km (37 mi) east of Ahrenshoop, 42 km (26 mi) east of Ribnitz-Damgarten on Rte. 105.*

Although it was rapidly industrialized, this jewel of the Baltic features a historic city center. Following an attack by the Lübeck fleet in 1249, a defensive wall was built around Stralsund, parts of which you'll see on your left as you come into the Old Town. In 1815 the Congress of Vienna awarded the city, which had been under Swedish control, to the Prussians.

The old market square, the **Alter Markt,** has the best local architecture, ranging from Gothic through Renaissance to baroque. Most buildings were rich merchants' homes, notably the late-Gothic **Wulflamhaus,** with 17 ornate, steeply stepped gables. Stralsund's architectural masterpiece, however, is the 13th-century **Rathaus,** considered by many to be the finest secular example of redbrick Gothic.

The 13th-century Gothic **St. Nikolaikirche** (St. Nicholas's Church)—note how many churches are named after the sailors' patron saint—faces the market square. Its treasures include a 15-ft-high crucifix from the 14th century, an astronomical clock from 1394, and a baroque altar. ⊠ *Alter Markt,* ☎ *03831/297–199.* ⊙ *Apr.–Sept., Mon.–Sat. 10–5, Sun. 11–12 and 2–4; Oct.–Mar., Mon.–Sat. 10–noon and 2–4, Sun. 11–noon and 2–4.*

The **Katherinenkloster** (St. Catherine's Monastery) is a former cloister; 40 of its rooms now house two museums: the famed **Deutsches Meeresmuseum** (Sea Museum), with its aquarium (☞ *below*), and the **Kulturhistorisches Museum** (Cultural History Museum), exhibiting diverse artifacts from more than 10,000 years of this coastal region's history. Highlights include a toy collection and 10th-century Viking gold jewelry found on Hiddensee. You'll reach the museums by walking along Ossenreyerstrasse through the Apollonienmarkt on Mönchstrasse. ⊠ *Kulturhistorisches Museum, Mönchstr. 25–27,* ☎ *03831/ 28790.* 🎫 *DM 6.* ⊙ *Tues.–Sun. 10–5.*

The Stralsund aquarium of Baltic Sea life is part of the marine museum
🆑 **Deutsches Meeresmuseum,** which also displays the skeletons of a giant whale and a hammerhead shark, and a 25-ft-high chunk of coral. ⊠ *Katharinenberg 14–20, entrance on Mönchstr.,* ☎ *03831/26500.* 🎫 *DM 7.* ⊙ *Daily 10–5.*

The monstrous **St. Marienkirche** (St. Mary's Church) is the largest of Stralsund's three redbrick Gothic churches. With 4,000 pipes and intricate decorative figures, the magnificent 17th-century Stellwagen organ is a delight to see and hear. The view from the church tower of Stralsund's old city center is well worth the 349 steps you must climb to reach the top. ⊠ *Neuer Markt, entrance at Bleistr.,* ☎ *03831/293–529.* 🎫 *Tour of church tower DM 2.* ⊙ *Mon.–Sat. 10–4, Sun. 11:30–4; church tower tour daily.*

Dining and Lodging

$$ ✕ **Wulflamstuben.** This restaurant is on the ground floor of
★ *Wulflamhaus,* a 14th-century gabled house on the old market square. Steaks and fish are the specialty of the house; if you plan to visit in late spring or early summer, get the light and tasty *Ostseeflunder* (grilled plaice), fresh from the North Sea. ⊠ *Alter Markt 5,* ☎ *03831/ 291–533. Reservations essential. AE, DC, MC, V.*

$–$$ ✕ **Zum Alten Fritz.** It's worth the trip here just to see the rustic interior and copper brewing equipment. Good, old German beer and ale of all shades are the main focus. In summer the atmosphere becomes rambunctious in the beer garden. ⊠ *Greifswalder Chaussee 84–85, at B–96a,* ☏ *03831/255–500. MC, V.*

$$ ▣ **Hotel zur Post.** This redbrick hotel is a great deal for travelers who
★   want to enjoy a homey yet first-class atmosphere. It's on the market square near the Old Town. The hotel's interior is a thoughtful blend of traditional North German furnishings and modern design. ⊠ *Am Neuen Markt, Tribseerstr. 22, D–18439,* ☏ *03831/200–500,* ℻ *03831/ 200–510. 104 rooms, 2 suites, 8 apartments. Restaurant, bar, in-room safes, minibars, no-smoking rooms, room service, sauna, dry cleaning, laundry service, meeting rooms, parking (fee). AE, MC, V.* ✆

$$ ▣ **Norddeutscher Hof.** Don't let the weathered facade fool you; the hotel was completely renovated a few years ago. Unfortunately, the lobby and restaurant were not as tastefully redecorated as the guest rooms. Still, you get the basics at a fair price. ⊠ *Neuer Markt 22, D–18439,* ☏ *03831/293–161,* ℻ *03831/287–939. 13 rooms. AE, MC, V.*

Nightlife

The new **Bar Hemingway** (⊠ Tribseerstr. 22, ☏ 03831/200–500) has the best cocktails in town and attracts a thirtysomething clientele. A young crowd dances at **Fun und Lollipop** (⊠ Grünhofer Bogen 11–14, ☏ 03831/399–039). A genuine old harbor *Kneipe* (tavern) is the **Kuttel Daddeldu** (⊠ Hafenstr./Hafeninsel, ☏ 03831/299–526).

Shopping

Buddelschiffe (ships in a bottle) are a symbol of the once-magnificent sailing history of this region. They look easy to build, but they aren't, and they're quite delicate. Expect to pay more than DM 120 for a 1-liter bottle. Also look out for **Fischerteppiche** (fisherman's carpets). Eleven square feet of these traditional carpets take 150 hours to create, which explains why they're only meant to be hung on the wall—and why they cost from DM 500 to DM 2,000. They're decorated with traditional symbols of the region, such as the mythical griffin.

Rügen Island

⑯   *4 km (2½ mi) northeast of Stralsund on Rte. 96.*

What Rügen lacks in architectural allure it makes up for in natural beauty. Its diverse and breathtaking landscapes have inspired poets and painters for more than a century. Railways in the mid-19th century brought the first vacationers, and many of the grand mansions and villas on the island date from this period. The island's main route runs between the **Grosser Jasmunder Bodden** (Big Jasmund Inlet), a giant sea inlet, and a smaller expanse of water—the **Kleiner Jasmunder Bodden** (Little Jasmund Inlet Lake)—to the port of Sassnitz. You're best off staying at any of the island's four main vacation centers—Sassnitz, Binz, Sellin, and Göhren.

Bergen

⑰   *34 km (21 mi) northeast of Stralsund on Rte. 96.*

Bergen, the island's administrative capital, was founded as a Slavic settlement some 900 years ago. It's worth a visit for the **Rugard,** a small hill, 298 ft above sea level, which offers a fantastic panoramic view of the whole island. A few remnants of the old fortification wall can be found on the hill.

Sassnitz

⑱   *25 km (16 mi) northeast of Bergen on Rte. 96.*

From Sassnitz, where ferries run to Sweden, walk into **Jasmund Nationalpark** to stare in awe at the Königstuhl cliffs. For information about the park, contact the Sassnitz tourist office. Off the northwest corner of Rügen is a smaller island called Hiddensee. The undisturbed solitude of this sticklike island attracted such visitors as Albert Einstein, Thomas Mann, Rainer Maria Rilke, and Sigmund Freud. As Hiddensee is an auto-free zone, leave your car in Schaprode, 46 km (29 mi) west of Sassnitz, and take a ferry.

Ten kilometers (6 miles) north of Sassnitz are the twin chalk cliffs of **⑲** Rügen's main attraction, the **Stubbenkammer** headland, on the east coast of the island. From here you can best see the much-photographed chalk cliff called the **Königstuhl,** rising 351 ft from the sea. A steep trail leads down to a beach.

Kap Arkona

⑳ *21 km (13 mi) northwest of Stubbenkammer.*

Kap Arkona has a lighthouse marking the northernmost point in eastern Germany, and you can see the Danish island of Moen from a restored watchtower next door. The blustery sand dunes of Kap Arkona are a nature lover's paradise.

Putbus

㉑ *59 km (37 mi) southeast of Kap Arkona, 8 km (5 mi) south of Bergen.*

From Putbus you can take a ride on the 90-year-old miniature steam train, the *Rasender Roland* (Racing Roland), which runs 24 km (16 mi) to Göhren, at the southeast corner of the Rügen. Trains leave hourly; the ride takes 70 minutes one-way and costs DM 15. For a splendid view in all directions, climb the cast-iron spiral staircase of the lookout tower of **Jagdschloss Granitz,** a hunting lodge near Binz built in 1836 by Karl Friedrich Schinkel. It stands on the highest point of East Rügen and has an excellent hunting exhibit. ⊠ *Binz,* ☎ *038393/2263.* ☞ *DM 5.* ☉ *May–Sept., daily 9–6; Oct.–Apr., Tues.–Sun. 10–4.*

Dining and Lodging

$$$ ✕▥ **Nordperd.** Built in 1990, with an addition in 1994, this four-story hotel is one of the better-equipped accommodations on the island. The decor is white and bright, with cheerful patterned upholstery and curtains, although space is at a premium. Some rooms have coastal views, thanks to the hotel's hilltop setting at the southeast tip of the island, in the seaside resort village of Göhren. In the restaurant, look for *Rügenwild,* a pot roast made with game, available in winter months. In summer you'll find the *Trilogie vom Fischfilet,* an assortment of three Baltic Sea fish. ⊠ *Nordperdstr. 11, D–18586 Göhren-Rügen,* ☎ *038308/70,* ℻ *038308/7160. 95 rooms. Restaurant, bar, beer garden, minibars, no-smoking rooms, room service, sauna, dry cleaning, laundry service, free parking. AE, DC, MC, V.*

$ ✕▥ **Hotel Godewind.** Two hundred yards from the beaches of Hiddensee that have so inspired writers, this small hotel offers solid food and lodging at very reasonable prices. In addition, the hotel rents small cottages and apartments around the island, which are a good value if you intend to stay for more than a few days. Godewind's restaurant is known on the island for its traditional regional dishes. ⊠ *Süderende 53, D–18565 Vitte-Hiddensee,* ☎ *038300/6600,* ℻ *038300/660–222. 23 rooms, 15 cottages. Restaurant. No credit cards.* ✍

$$–$$$$ ▥ **Hotel Vineta.** This great white building at the promenade in Binz is ★ one of the most beautiful on Rügen Island. Its name derives from a local fairy tale that tells of the destruction of the prosperous but sinful city of Vineta in a winter storm. According to the legend, you can still hear the golden bells of the sunken city's towers ringing through the fog. ⊠ *Hauptstr. 20, D–18609 Binz-Rügen,* ☎ *038393/390,* ℻ *038393/39444. 25 rooms, 12 apartments. 2 restaurants, in-room safes, minibars, sauna, exercise room, parking (fee). AE, MC, V.*

$$ ★   🏨 **Hotel Villa Granitz.** The little town of Baabe claims to have the most beautiful beach on Rügen Island. This mansion, built in the romantic art-nouveau style popular at the turn of the century, is a small and quiet retreat for those who want to avoid the masses in the island's other resorts. ⊠ *Birkenallee 17, D–18586 Baabe,* ☎ *038303/1410,* FAX *038303/14144. 44 rooms, 9 apartments. Refrigerators, no-smoking rooms, dry cleaning, laundry service, free parking. No credit cards.*

$–$$ ★   🏨 **Villa Daheim and Villa Elisabeth.** Two of the most beautiful old city mansions on the island of Rügen, these small hotels both offer a familylike, warm atmosphere in a late-19th century setting. The houses, just 100 yards apart, have been renovated à la the old glamour of German *Bäderarchitektur,* the style of seaside cottages along the Baltic Coast. The mansions are in the historic heart of Sassnitz yet offer a panoramic view of the sea. ⊠ *Rosenstr. 8 and Bergstr. 20, D–18546 Sassnitz,* ☎ *038392/22278,* FAX *038392/35001. 19 apartments. Bicycles, car rental, free parking. No credit cards.*

Shopping

At the end of the 19th century 16 pieces of 10th-century Viking jewelry were discovered on the Baltic coastline (presently housed in the Kulturhistorisches Museum in Stralsund). Gold and silver replicas of the **Hiddensee Golden Jewelry** are a great souvenir, and their distinctive patterns are found in shops on Rügen Island and on Hiddensee Island.

Water Sports

As private enterprise revives, a wide range of water-based activities is becoming available: windsurfing, sailing, surfing (although the waves here are modest), and pedal-boat riding. Equipment is available for hire at the beach resorts. If you have difficulty locating what you want, contact the local tourist offices. The best-protected area along the coast for sailing is **Grosser Jasmunder Bodden,** a huge bay on Rügen Island. Boats for the bay can be hired at Lietzow and Ralswiek.

Greifswald

  ㉒   *64 km (40 mi) southeast of Putbus, 32 km (20 mi) southeast of Stralsund on Rte. 96.*

Greifswald is the last in the string of Hanseatic ports on the Baltic Coast. The town became a backwater during the 19th century, when larger ships couldn't negotiate the shallow Ryck River leading to the sea. In 1945 a colonel's surrender of the town to Soviet forces spared its destruction; yet time has taken its toll on some historic buildings.

Splendid redbrick Gothic houses border the **Marktplatz.** The medieval Rathaus, rebuilt in 1738–50 following a fire, was modified during the 19th century and again in 1936.

Three churches shape the silhouette of the city. The 13th-century **Dom St. Nikolai** (St. Nicholas's Cathedral), at the start of Martin-Luther-Strasse, is a Gothic church with an impressive view from its 300-ft-high tower. ⊠ *Domstr.,* ☎ *03834/2627.* ☉ *May–Oct., Mon.–Sat. 10–4, Sun. 10–1; Nov.–Apr., Mon.–Sat. 11–1, Sun. 10–1.*

The 14th-century **Marienkirche** (St. Mary's Church), the oldest surviving church in Greifswald, has remarkable 60-ft-high arches and a striking four-corner tower. ⊠ *Friedrich-Loeffler-Str. 68 at Brüggstr.,* ☎ *03834/2263.* ☉ *June–Nov., weekdays 10–noon and 2–4.*

Greifswald is the birthplace of two great German artists—Caspar David Friedrich (1774–1840), the painter of German romanticism, and Wolfgang Koeppen, one of the country's most important postwar novelists. The new **Pommersche Landesgalerie** (Pommeranian State Gallery) showcases the development of European romantic painters and focuses on works by Caspar David Friedrich. His house in Greifswald has been destroyed, but his legacy lives on in famous paintings such as *Ruine Eldena im Riesengebirge* (Eldene Ruins in the Riesengebirge) or *Greifswalder Marktplatz* (Greifswald Market Square). Other works of art in the gallery include Dutch painters of Friedrich's time. ⊠ *Mühlenstr. 15,* ☎ *03834/894–357.* ☜ *DM 5.* ⊙ *Tues.–Sun. 10–6.*

㉓ In the suburb of **Eldena** stand the ruins of a 12th-century **Zisterzenserkloster** (Cistercian monastery). The Gothic monastery was made famous in a painting by Caspar David Friedrich (now at Schloss Charlottenburg's Gallery of Romanticism in Berlin). The monastery, which led to the founding of Greifswald, was plundered by rampaging Swedish soldiers early in the Thirty Years' War. Today it is a protected national monument.

Dining and Lodging

$–$$ ✕⌂ **Alter Speicher.** Its broad selection of delectable grilled items and its wine list have brought this comfortable steak house regional renown. It also offers small but modern guest rooms; all have private baths. The Alter Speicher is on the edge of the old city center. ⊠ *Rossmühlenstr. 25, D–17489,* ☎ *03834/77700,* 🖷 *03834/777–077. 14 rooms. Restaurant, free parking. AE, DC, MC, V.*☙

$$ ⌂ **Best Western Hotel Greifswald.** The hotel's decor—curtains, bedcovers, and lamp shades covered in bold stripes and flowers—stands out from the American Southwestern–style palette and patterns common in chain hotels of this region. To make up for the garishly bright rooms, the hotel provides modern amenities, a convenient location, and a helpful staff. ⊠ *Hans-Beimler-Str. 1–3, D–17491,* ☎ *03834/8010,* 🖷 *03834/801–100. 51 rooms, 4 apartments. Restaurant, bar, minibars, no-smoking rooms, room service, barbershop, sauna, exercise room, meeting rooms, free parking. AE, DC, MC, V.* ☙

$ ⌂ **Hotel Maria.** The facilities at this small hotel are clean and modern—and the friendly service is what you'd hope for from a family-owned place. The hotel is right on the harbor; the terrace is the perfect place to linger over a drink while watching the panorama of sailboats. ⊠ *Dorfstr. 45, D–17493,* ☎ *03834/841–426,* 🖷 *03834/840–136. 13 rooms. Restaurant, free parking. MC.*

Usedom Island

㉔ On its seaboard side, 40-km-long (25-mi-long) **Usedom Island** has almost 32 km (20 mi) of sandy shoreline and a string of resorts. Much of the island's untouched landscape is a nature preserve that provides refuge for a number of rare birds, including the giant sea eagle, which has a wingspan of up to 8 ft. Even in the summer this island is more or less deserted and is ready to be explored by bicycle.

Wolgast

32 km (20 mi) southeast of Greifswald on Rte. 109, then Rte. 111.

Wolgast is near the causeway crossing to the island of Usedom. Its **Rathausplatz** (Town Hall Square) holds a baroque Rathaus and the pretty mid-17th-century half-timber house known as the Kaffeemühle (Coffee Mill). The Kaffeemühle, far from serving coffee, contains the local history museum, or **Stadtgeschichtliches Museum.** ⊠ *Rathauspl. 6,* ☎ *03836/203–041.* ☜ *DM 5.* ⊙ *June–Aug., Tues.–Fri. 10–6, weekends 10–2; Sept.–May, Tues.–Fri. 10–5, Sat. 10–2.*

The massive redbrick Gothic **St. Petri Kirche** (St. Peter's Church) sits on the highest point of the Old Town. The church has 24 paintings of

Holbein's *Totentanz (Dance of Death)*. ⊠ *Kirchpl. 7.* 🏰 *Tower DM 3.* ☉ *Weekdays 10–11:30 and 1:30–5.*

Peenemünde
16 km (10 mi) north of Wolgast.

At the northern end of Usedom Island is Peenemünde, the launch site of the world's first jet rockets, the V1 and V2, developed by Germany toward the end of World War II and fired at London. You can view these rockets as well as models of early airplanes and ships at the popular **Historisch-Technisches Informationszentrum** (Historical-Technical Information Center). One exhibit covers the secret underground plants where most of the rocket parts were assembled. Thousands of slave laborers died there. ⊠ *Im Kraftwerk,* ☎ *038371/5050.* 🏰 *DM 6.* ☉ *Apr.–Oct., Tues.–Sun. 9–6; Nov.–Mar., Tues.–Sun. 10–4.*

Ahlbeck
46 km (29 mi) southeast of Peenemünde on Rte. 111.

Ahlbeck, one of the best resorts on Usedom and the island's main town, features an unusual 19th-century wooden pier with four towers. Ahlbeck's promenade is lined with turn-of-the-century villas, some of which are now small hotels. If you stroll along the beach to the right of Ahlbeck's pier, you'll arrive at the Polish border—the easternmost corner of the island belongs to Poland.

Dining and Lodging

$$–$$$ ✕ **Seebrücke.** Perched on pilings over the Baltic, the Sea Bridge is in the historic center of Ahlbeck. The emphasis is on seafood, but the menu has other choices, from *Königsberger Klopse* (spicy meatballs in a thick, creamy sauce) to a tender fillet of lamb. You can also enjoy the view over coffee and a delectable piece of cake. ⊠ *Dünenstr., Ahlbeck,* ☎ *038378/2660. AE, MC, V. Closed Oct.–Apr.*

$$ ✕ **Café Asgard.** A visit here is a step back into the 1920s, which is when this restaurant first opened its doors. You'll dine amid silk wallpaper, potted plants, crisp white napery, and fresh flowers. The Asgard is open all day, so if you stop by between meal times, settle for a homemade pastry. ⊠ *Strandpromenade 15, Bansin,* ☎ *038378/29488. No credit cards.*

$$$ ✕🏨 **Romantik Seehotel Ahlbecker Hof.** This first-class resort lacks
★ the coziness of Usedom's other (and smaller hotels) but undoubtedly is one of the regions best and has been meticulously restored to imperial glamour. The baths in the guest rooms are luxurious, and there's a fantastic wellness and swimming pool area. A real draw is the hotel's *Kleopatrabad,* a Turkish steam bath. The restaurant serves some of the finest seafood along the Baltic coastline. ⊠ *Dünenstr. 47, D–17419 Ahlbeck,* ☎ *038378/620,* 📠 *03378/62100. 39 rooms, 9 suites. Restaurant, bar, brasserie, in-room safes, minibars, room service, pool, beauty salon, massage, sauna, 18 hole- golf, exercise room, bicycles, dry cleaning, laundry service, meeting rooms, parking (fee). AE, MC, V.* 🐾

$$$ ✕🏨 **Romantik Strandhotel Atlantic.** The small but elegant hotel once served as the intimate summer retreat for Berlin's rich and beautiful. These days, the upscale restaurant and the lavishly decorated guest rooms—all with venerable 19th-century glamour—make this hotel one of the island's best (and most coveted). ⊠ *Strandpromenade 18, D–17429 Bansin,* ☎ *038378/605,* 📠 *03378/60600. 24 rooms, 2 suites. Restaurant, bar, pub, in-room safes, minibars, room service, bicycles, dry cleaning, laundry service, meeting room, parking (fee). AE, MC, V.* 🐾

$$ ✕🏨 **Ringhotel Ahlbeck Ostseehotel.** Generations of families have stayed at this snug, if slightly dated, hotel in a 19th-century villa on Ahlbeck's promenade. Rooms are airy but modestly furnished, and most have a view of the sea. The restaurant serves mainly hearty, though standard, local dishes. ✉ *Dünenstr. 41, D–17419 Ahlbeck,* ☎ *038378/600,* 𝔉𝔞𝔵 *03378/60100. 58 rooms, 12 apartments. Restaurant, bar, no-smoking rooms, room service, indoor pool, bicycles, parking (fee). AE, MC, V. Closed Oct.–Mar.*

Outdoor Activities and Sports

BIKING

The coastal region and the islands in particular are ideal for cycling (read: flat). Most large hotels provide bicycles for guests, and many shops rent bikes at modest rates. Some train stations also rent bicycles. Escorted tours are organized by the tourist offices; contact the regional tourist office (☞ Contacts and Resources *in* Schleswig-Holstein and the Baltic Coast A to Z, *below*) for more information.

CAMPING

There are 150 campsites along the coast and on the islands. Contact the local tourist offices for a list of locations and facilities offered.

SCHLESWIG-HOLSTEIN AND THE BALTIC COAST A TO Z

Arriving and Departing

By Car

Sylt island is 196 km (122 mi) from Hamburg via Autobahn A–7 and Bundesstrasse 199 and is ultimately reached via train; *see* By Train *in* Getting Around, *below*. Lübeck, the gateway to Mecklenburg-Vorpommern, is 56 km (35 mi) from Hamburg via the A–1 autobahn (E–22). From Berlin take A–11 and head toward Prenzlau for B–109 all the way to Usedom Island, a distance of 162 km (100 mi).

By Plane

The international airport closest to Schleswig-Holstein is in **Hamburg.** For an eastern approach to the Baltic Coast tour, use **Berlin**'s Tegel Airport.

By Train

Train travel is much more convenient than bus travel in this area. Sylt, Kiel, Lübeck, Schwerin, and Rostock have InterCity train connections to either Hamburg, Berlin, or both.

Getting Around

By Boat

The **Weisse Flotte** (White Fleet) line operates ferries linking the Baltic ports, as well as short harbor and coastal cruises. Boats depart from Warnemünde, Wismar, Sassnitz, and Stralsund. For information call 0381/519–860 for boats departing Warnemünde; 0381/268–116 in summer for all other ports; or call the city's tourist office (☞ *below*). Harbor and coastal cruises also operate from Lübeck; contact the **Lübeck tourist office** for details (☎ 0451/122–8109). In addition, ferries run between Rostock, Warnemünde, Stralsund, and Sassnitz and Sweden, Denmark, and Finland.

By Bus

Local buses link the main train stations with outlying towns and villages, especially the coastal resorts. Buses operate throughout Sylt, Rügen, and Usedom islands.

By Car

With the exception of July and August, roads along the coast aren't overcrowded. B–199 and the A–7 autobahn cover much of the journey through Schleswig-Holstein. Using the Bundesstrassen takes more time, but these often tree-lined roads are by far more scenic than the autobahn. B–199 cuts through some nice countryside, and instead of the A–7 or B–76 between Flensburg, Schleswig, and Kiel, you could take the slow route through the coastal hinterland (B–199, 203, 503).

B–105 leads to all sightseeing spots in Mecklenburg-Vorpommern. The main road over the causeway from Stralsund (Route 96) cuts straight across Rügen Island southwest to northeast, a distance of 51 km (32 mi). If you are returning to Berlin from Usedom Island, you can leave the island by a causeway at the southwest corner, reached from the town of Usedom and emerging on the mainland at Anklam. From Anklam you can reach Berlin by taking Route 109 to A–11.

By Train
A north–south train line links Schwerin and Rostock. An east–west route connects Kiel, Hamburg, Lübeck, and Rostock, and some trains continue through to Stralsund and Sassnitz, on Rügen Island. Train service between the smaller cities of former East Germany is generally much slower than in the west.

Trains are the *only* way to access **Sylt,** which is connected to the mainland via the train causeway **Hindenburgdamm.** Deutsche Bahn will transport you and your car from central trains stations at Dortmund, Düsseldorf, Hamburg, Stuttgart, and Frankfurt directly onto the island. In addition, a daily shuttle car train leaves **Niebüll** every 30 minutes from 6 AM to 9 PM (☎ 04651/22561). There are no reservations on this train.

Contacts and Resources

Car Rentals
Avis (✉ Willy-Brandt-Allee 6, Lübeck, ☎ 0451/72008; ✉ Am Warnowufer 6, Rostock, ☎ 0381/202–1170; ✉ Wittenburgerstr. 120, Schwerin, ☎ 0385/761–000; ✉ Am Flughafen, Westerland, Sylt, ☎ 04651/23734). **InterrentEuropcar** (✉ Esso-Station am Bahnhof Westerland, Sylt, ☎ 04651/7178). **Hertz** (✉ Willy-Brandt-Allee 1, Lübeck, ☎ 0451/702–250; ✉ Röverzhagener Chaussee 5, Rostock, ☎ 0381/683–065; ✉ Schwerinerstr. 31, Wismar, ☎ 03841/703–259; ✉ Bremsweg 1, Schwerin, ☎ 0385/487–5555).

Emergencies
Police and ambulance (☎ 110).

Guided Tours
Although tourist offices and museums have worked to improve the quality and amount of English-language literature about this area, English-speaking tours are infrequent and must be requested ahead of time through the local tourist office. Because most tours are designed for groups, there is usually a flat fee of DM 40–DM 60. Towns currently offering tours are: Lübeck, Stralsund, and Rostock.

Tours of **Old Lübeck** depart daily from the tourist offices on the Alter Markt (☎ 0451/122–8106) between mid-April and mid-October and on weekends only from mid-October to mid-April.

In Schwerin, **Weisse Flotte** has two-hour tours of the region's seven pristine lakes. A trip to the island of Kaninchenwerder, a small sanctuary for more than 100 species of water birds, is an unforgettable experience. Boats depart daily 10:30–4:30 May–September and 12:30–3:30 October–April from the pier adjacent to the Schweriner Schloss. ✉ *Anlegestelle Schlosspier,* ☎ *0385/581–1596.* ▣ *DM 20.*

Many of the former fishermen in these towns give sunset tours of the harbors or shuttle visitors between neighboring towns. This is a unique opportunity to ride on an authentic fishing boat. In **Flensburg, Kiel, Rostock,** and on **Sylt,** cruise lines make short trips through the respective bays and/or islands off the coast, sailing even as far as Denmark and Sweden. Inquire at the local tourist office about companies and times, as well as about fishing boat tours.

Visitor Information

The regional tourist associations for Schleswig-Holstein and the Baltic Coast are **Schleswig-Holstein Tourismus** (✉ Niemannsweg 31, D–24105 Kiel, ☎ 0431/560–0210, FAX 0431/560–0200, ✎); Tᴏᴜʀʙᴜ-**Zentrale, Landesfremdenverkehrsverband Mecklenburg-Vorpommern** (✉ Platz der Freundschaft 1, D–18059 Rostock, ☎ 0381/403–0500, FAX 0381/403–0555, ✎).

The following towns and cities have tourist offices. When writing to any of these offices, address your letter to "Touristeninformation" and then add the city's name.

Bad Doberan (✉ Goethestr. 1, D–18209, ☎ FAX 038203/62154, ✎). **Flensburg** (✉ Amalie-Lamp-Speicher, Speicherlinie 40, D–24937, ☎ 0461/23090, FAX 0461/17352, ✎). **Greifswald** (✉ Schuhhagen 22, D–17489, ☎ 03834/3460, ✎). **Husum** (✉ Grossstr. 27, D–25813, ☎ 04841/89870, ✎). **Kampen** (✉ Kurverwaltung, Hauptstr. 12, D–25999, ☎ 04651/46980, FAX 04651/469–840, ✎). **Kiel** (✉ Kiel, Sophienblatt 30, D–24103, ☎ 0431/679–100, FAX 0431/679–1099, ✎). **Lübeck** (✉ Breite Str. 62, [Mailing address: ✉ Beckergrube 95, D–23552], ☎ 0451/122–1909, FAX 0451/122–1202, ✎). **Rostock** (✉ Schnickmannstr. 13–14, D–18055, ☎ 0381/497–990, FAX 0381/497–9923, ✎). **Rügen Island** (✉ Tourismusverband Rügen, Am Markt 4, D–18528 Bergen, ☎ 03838/80770, FAX 03838/254–440, ✎). **Sassnitz** (✉ Seestr. 1, D–18546, ☎ 038392/5160, FAX 038392/51616, ✎). **Schleswig** (✉ Plessenstr. 7, D–24837, ☎ 04621/24878, FAX 04621/981–619, ✎). **Schwerin** (✉ Am Markt 10, D–19055, ☎ 0385/592–5212, FAX 0385/555–094, ✎). **Stralsund** (✉ Ossenreyerstr. 1–2, D–18439, ☎ 03831/24690, FAX 03831/246–949, ✎). **Usedom Island** (✉ Tourismusverband Insel Usedom e.V., Bäderstr. 4, D–17459 Seebad Ückeritz, ☎ 038375/23410, FAX 038375/23429, ✎). **Warnemünde** (✉ Heinrich-Heine-Str. 17, D–18119, ☎ 0381/51142, FAX 0381/497–9923, ✎). **Westerland** (✉ Strandstr. 33, [mailing address: ✉ Stephanstr. 6, Postfach 1260 D–25969], ☎ 04651/9980, FAX 04651/998–234, ✎). **Wismar** (✉ Stadthaus, Am Markt 11, D–23966, ☎ 03841/19433, FAX 03841/251–813, ✎).

15 BERLIN

Germany's capital is resuming its role as a
true international metropolis. The historic
eastern parts of the city continue to be
shaped by commercial and government
developments and by both high and
alternative culture. As ever, life in Berlin
is on the cutting edge.

Updated by
Jürgen
Scheunemann

BERLIN'S ROLE AS THE FOCAL POINT and touchstone of the new and reunited Germany began on November 9, 1989, when East Germans finally breached the infamous Berlin Wall. The federal parliament's return to Berlin culminated 10 years later, making the city once again the German capital. For nearly 30 years Berlin suffered under one of the greatest geographic and political anomalies of all time, a city split in two by a concrete wall—its larger western half an island of capitalist democracy surrounded by an East Germany run by hard-line Communists. The wall's demolition signaled the change sweeping over Iron Curtain countries.

Compared to other German cities, Berlin is quite young and, ironically, began as two cities more than 760 years ago. Museum Island, on the Spree River, was once called Cölln, while the mainland city was always known as Berlin. As early as the 1300s, Berlin prospered from its location at the intersection of important trade routes. After the ravages of the Thirty Years' War, Berlin rose to power as the seat of the Hohenzollern dynasty, as the Great Elector Friedrich Wilhelm, in the almost 50 years of his reign (1640–88), touched off a renaissance in the city, especially by the construction of such institutions as the Academy of Arts and the Academy of Sciences. Later, Frederick the Great made Berlin and Potsdam his glorious centers of the enlightened yet autocratic Prussian monarchy.

In the late 19th century, Prussia, ruled by the "Iron Chancellor" Count Otto von Bismarck, proved to be the dominant force in unifying the many independent German states. Berlin maintained its status as Germany's capital for the duration of the German Empire (1871–1918), through the post–World War I Weimar Republic (1919–33), and also through Hitler's so-called Third Reich (1933–45). But the city's golden years were the Roaring '20s, when Berlin, the energetic, modern, and sinful counterpart to Paris, became a center for the cultural avant-garde. World-famous writers, painters, and artists met here while the impoverished bulk of its 4 million inhabitants lived in heavily overpopulated quarters. This "dance on the volcano," as those years of political and economic upheaval have been called, came to a grisly and bloody end after January 1933, when Adolf Hitler assumed power. The Nazis made Berlin their capital but ultimately failed to remodel the city into a silent monument to their power. During World War II Berlin was bombed to smithereens. By the war's end there was more rubble in Berlin than in all other German cities combined.

Along with the division of Germany after World War II, Berlin was partitioned into American, British, and French zones in the west, and a Soviet zone to the east. By 1947 Berlin had become one of the cold war's first testing grounds. The three western-occupied zones gradually merged, becoming West Berlin, while the Soviet-controlled eastern zone defiantly remained separate. Peace conferences repeatedly failed to resolve the question of Germany's division, and in 1949 the Soviet Union established East Berlin as the capital of its new puppet state, the German Democratic Republic (DDR). The division of the city was cruelly finalized in concrete in August 1961, when the East German government constructed the Berlin Wall, dividing families and friends.

With the wall relegated to the souvenir pile of history, visitors can now appreciate the qualities that mark the city as a whole. Its particular charm has always lain in its spaciousness, its trees and greenery, and its racy atmosphere. Moreover, the really stunning parts of the prewar capital are in the historic eastern part of town, which has grand avenues, monumental architecture, and world treasures in its museums.

What really makes Berlin tick, however, are the intangibles—the fascinating juxtaposition of *Macht und Geist* (power and intellect) and the spirit and bounce of the city and its citizens. Berliners come off as brash, witty, no-nonsense types who speak German with their own piquant dialect and are considered by their fellow countrymen as a most rude species. The bracing air, the renowned *Berliner Luft,* gets part of the credit for their high-voltage energy. That energy is also attributable to the many residents who have faced adversity all their lives, and have managed to do so with a mordant wit and cynical acceptance of life.

Pleasures and Pastimes

Dining

Dining in Berlin can either mean sophisticated nouvelle specialties in chic restaurants or hearty local specialties in inexpensive pubs; the range is as vast as the city itself. Specialties include *Eisbein mit Sauerkraut* (knuckle of pork with pickled cabbage), *Rouladen* (rolled stuffed beef), *Spanferkel* (suckling pig), *Berliner Schüsselsülze* (potted meat in aspic), *Hackepeter* (ground beef), and *Kartoffelpuffer* (fried potato cakes). Spicy *Currywurst* is a chubby frankfurter that's served with thick tomato sauce, curry, and pepper. It's sold at *Bockwurst* stands all over the city. Turkish specialties are also an integral part of the Berlin diet. On almost every street you'll find snack stands selling *Döner kepab* (grilled lamb with salad in a flat-bread pocket).

Museums

Berlin is home to some of the world's finest museums, art galleries, and exhibition halls. Its more than 100 state and private museums showcase the arts from ancient times through the medieval and Renaissance periods and up to the modern avant-garde. Among the jewels of Berlin's museum holdings are superb monuments of Greek, Byzantine, and Roman architecture on the renowned Museum Island, and the collections of the two Egyptian museums, which include the famous bust of Queen Nefertiti. Some state museums and exhibitions may be closed for periods of time through 2000 as they continue to be reorganized.

Nightlife

Berlin is the only European city without official closing hours, so you can enjoy your drinks until the wee hours of the morning without fear of a last call. A peculiar leftover from the days of Allied occupation, liberal drinking hours has transformed Berlin into a nightlife El Dorado, with more than 6,000 pubs, music and dancing clubs, cabarets, and theaters. The city presents Germany's leading dramatic and musical productions, as well as lively variety shows in some of Europe's largest theaters, including the Friedrichstadtpalast. Berlin is also a mecca for fans of acid jazz, house, and techno music.

EXPLORING BERLIN

Unlike most other large German cities, Berlin is a young and partly planned capital, with streets and boulevards organized in an unusually clear manner. Yet Berlin is also laid out on an epic scale—western Berlin alone is four times the size of the city of Paris. When the city-state of Berlin was incorporated, it swallowed towns and villages far beyond the downtown area. Of its 23 boroughs, the five of most interest to visitors are Charlottenburg in the west, Tiergarten and Kreuzberg in the downtown western area, the historic eastern part of town in Mitte, and Prenzlauer Berg in the northeast. Southwest Berlin has lovely parks, and secluded forests and lakes in the Grunewald area.

Numbers in the text correspond to numbers in the margin and on the Berlin map.

Great Itineraries

Although public transportation makes most sights convenient and inexpensive to reach, the sheer magnitude of the city and its wealth of attractions make it hard for newcomers to see all the important sights.

In two days you can just about fit in the highlights of both the western downtown and the eastern historic districts. Three days allow you a more leisurely pace that will give you time to absorb Berlin's dramatic history and dynamic present. Even a stay of four days is not enough time to experience the real, electrifying atmosphere of this city, or to visit sights off the beaten track.

IF YOU HAVE 2 DAYS

Start in western, downtown Berlin by strolling past the shops and cafés of Kurfürstendamm to the stark shell of the Kaiser-Wilhelm-Gedächtniskirche. Pick up a snack from the elegant Kaufhaus des Westens and catch the double-decker Bus 100 (on Budapester Strasse), which takes you past the Reichstag and the Government district to the Brandenburger Tor. Exit here to explore historic eastern Berlin, the pre–World War II pride of the city. Shops on Unter den Linden and Friedrichstrasse are recapturing prewar glamour, and there's a wealth of architectural monuments to explore, including those on the Gendarmenmarkt, Berlin's finest square. The real cultural highlights to save time for are the antiquities on Museuminsel on the Spree Canal.

The next day visit Potsdamer Platz, a study in urban renewal and a playground for architects in recent years. From here take the U-bahn west to Charlottenburg to explore the palace and nearby museums.

IF YOU HAVE 3 DAYS

In Charlottenburg tour Schloss Charlottenburg and either of the nearby museums. By taking the U-bahn next to Adenauerplatz, you can browse the most elegant of the Kurfürstendamm boutiques before reaching the grittier scene of Breitscheidplatz, where locals and street performers gather. Stop inside the Kaiser-Wilhelm-Gedächtniskirche, a war memorial, before heading for the always entertaining Zoologischer Garten. If you need a meal, the famous Kaufhaus des Westens department store is just a bit farther down Tauentzienstrasse. You will have had a full day, but you can still visit the unusual Erotik-Museum in the evening, as it's open until midnight.

Start the next day in the Tiergarten, an enormous landscaped park with monuments, gardens, fields, and playgrounds. Visit the Kulturforum museums and Potsdamer Platz, just outside the park, before taking in such symbols of German history as the Reichstag, the country's revived parliamentary building, and Brandenburger Tor, at the park's eastern end. Continue east along Unter den Linden, which leads to historic eastern Berlin's shops and imperial architecture. Spend the evening around the Hackesche Höfe in the Mitte district.

Eastern Berlin holds still more attractions for your third day. Visit the historic sights near the vast Alexanderplatz, including the museums on the Spree canal's Museuminsel, before exploring the capital's backyard around Oranienburger Strasse. Not far away, at the Gedenkstätte Berliner Mauer, you can inspect the last remains of the Berlin Wall.

IF YOU HAVE 5 DAYS

Follow the three-day itinerary above, but continue east to the old working-class district of Prenzlauer Berg after viewing the Gedenkstätte

Berliner Mauer. Finish your day at a café near Kollwitzplatz, or with evening entertainment at the old Kulturbrauerei.

Begin your fourth day in the district of Kreuzberg. Start with the former Preussischer Landtag (Prussian State Legislature), now housing the city-state's legislature, and the Prinz-Albrecht-Gelände, where former Nazi prison cellars were excavated. Proceed to one of Berlin's cold-war hot spots—Checkpoint Charlie, the former border station at the Berlin Wall. Before hitting the heart of Kreuzberg via Oranienstrasse, detour to see what's developed at the new Jüdisches Museum.

Spend your last day in southern Berlin at the Dahlem Museums, the Gedenk- und Bildungsstätte Haus der Wannsee-Konferenz, and the Grunewald (forest) and the Pfaueninsel. If you have time left, you may want to visit the East Side Gallery, where a preserved section of the wall has been transformed into an open-air art gallery; or the Sachsenhausen Memorial concentration camp, north of the city.

The Kurfürstendamm and Western Downtown Berlin

The Ku'damm, as Berliners affectionately call the tree-lined Kurfürstendamm, Berlin's busiest shopping avenue, stretches for 3 km (2 mi) through the heart of the city's western downtown section. The popular thoroughfare is full of shops, department stores, art galleries, theaters, movie houses, and hotels, as well as some 100 restaurants, bars, clubs, and sidewalk cafés. It bustles with shoppers and strollers most of the day and far into the night.

A Good Walk

Start your tour on the far western end of the **Kurfürstendamm** ①, either at Olivaer Platz or at Adenauerplatz, farther west. As you make your way east along the boulevard, stopping at boutiques or one of the cafés along the way, you will pass the new multimedia exhibit, **The Story of Berlin** ②, which is worth a visit. Farther down, almost at the end of the boulevard, is the **Kaiser-Wilhelm-Gedächtniskirche** ③, the very heart of western Berlin. The ruin serves as a memorial to the horrors of war and the surrounding square is a vibrant meeting point for Berliners, outcasts, performers, and tourists alike.

Just steps away from the ruin is the **Europa Center** ④, a shopping mall; the Berlin tourist information office is at its back on Budapester Strasse. Across from the tourist office, you'll find the Elefantentor (Elephant Gate), the main entrance to the **Zoologischer Garten** ⑤, western Berlin's zoo and aquarium. Allow yourself two hours here before strolling down Tauentzienstrasse, the boulevard that runs southeast away from the corner of Europa Center. Tauentzienstrasse, or the Tauentzien, as Berliners call this not-very-fashionable shopping strip, leads straight to Europe's largest and Germany's most elegant department store, the **Kaufhaus des Westens** ⑥, nicknamed KaDeWe.

You could easily spend hours at this consumer's paradise. To reach the tour's final stop, catch the U-bahn at the Wittenbergplatz station, first completed in 1913 and now painstakingly restored. Get out after one stop (Zoologishcher Garten), and head south on Joachimstaler Strasse to the **Erotik-Museum** ⑦, a peculiar exhibition on the art and culture of sexuality.

TIMING

A leisurely walk from the western end of the Kurfürstendamm down to its beginning at Breitscheidplatz takes at least four hours, including a quick breakfast or lunch. Amidst the urban buzz, you could easily spend at least three hours around the Kaiser-Wilhelm-Gedächtniskirche, the Europa Center, and in the shops along the Tauentzien and the KaDeWe. A trip to the admirable zoo and aquarium will take at least two hours, and watching feeding times and monkey-play is worth skipping some shopping opportunities. The Ku'damm is extremely crowded on Saturday mornings.

Sights to See

❼ Erotik-Museum. The culture and art of human sexuality in all its sometimes peculiar manifestations is exhibited here, though primarily in paintings and other works of art from Europe and Asia. Outstanding exhibits document the history of German scientist Magnus Hirschfeld, whose institute for sexuality was destroyed by the Nazis, and recount Berlin painter Heinrich Zille's often humorous tales of sexual behavior in the city's working-class tenements. The museum is extremely tasteful, but it is owned and run by the Beate Uhse company, Germany's largest retailer of X-rated videos and other bedroom paraphernalia. Only adults over 18 years of age are admitted. ⊠ *Kantstr. (corner Joachimstaler Str.),* ☎ *030/886–0666.* 🎟 *DM 10.* ⊙ *Daily 9 AM–midnight.*

❹ Europa Center. This vast shopping and business complex was erected on the site of the renowned Romanisches Café, the hot spot for writers and actors during the Roaring '20s. The plaza in front of the Europa Center is where Berliners, hippies, homeless people, and tourists mingle in summer. The 22-story tower built in the 1960s—nicknamed "Pepper's Manhattan" after its owner—is a remarkable though somewhat depressing leftover from the good old days of West Berlin, when the city was pampered with federal money and business boomed around Kurfürstendamm. Today the Europa Center's past glamour has faded into shabbiness, especially when compared to its new counterparts in eastern Berlin. The center houses more than 100 shops, restaurants, and cafés, two cinemas, a comedy club, and the Verkehrsamt (tourist information center). Two pieces of the Berlin Wall stand by the Tauentzienstrasse entrance. ⊠ *Breitscheidpl.*

★ **❸ Kaiser-Wilhelm-Gedächtniskirche** (Kaiser Wilhelm Memorial Church). This ruin stands as a dramatic reminder of World War II's destruction. The bell tower, which Berliners call "hollow tooth," is all that remains of the once-imposing church, which was built between 1891 and 1895 and originally dedicated to the emperor, Kaiser Wilhelm I. On the hour the tower chimes out a melody composed by the last emperor's great-grandson, the late Prince Louis Ferdinand von Hohenzollern.

In stark contrast to the old bell tower are the adjoining Memorial Church and Tower, designed by the noted German architect Egon Eiermann in 1959–61. These ultramodern octagonal structures, with their myriad honeycomb windows, are perhaps best described by their nicknames: the lipstick and the powder box. The interior is dominated by the brilliant blue of its stained-glass windows, imported from Chartres. Church music and organ concerts are presented in the church regularly.

An exhibition inside the old tower focuses on the devastation of World War II, with a cross constructed of nails recovered from the ashes of Coventry Cathedral in England, destroyed in a German bombing raid in November 1940. ⊠ *Breitscheidpl.,* ☎ *030/218–5023.* 🎟 *Free.* ⊙ *Old Tower, Mon.–Sat. 10–4; Memorial Church, daily 9–7.* 🏛

★ **❻ Kaufhaus des Westens** (Department Store of the West). The KaDeWe isn't just Berlin's classiest department store; it's also Europe's largest, a grand-scale emporium in modern guise. Its seven floors hold an enormous selection, but it is best known for its two top floors' food and delicatessen counters, restaurants, champagne bars, and beer bars,

Berlin

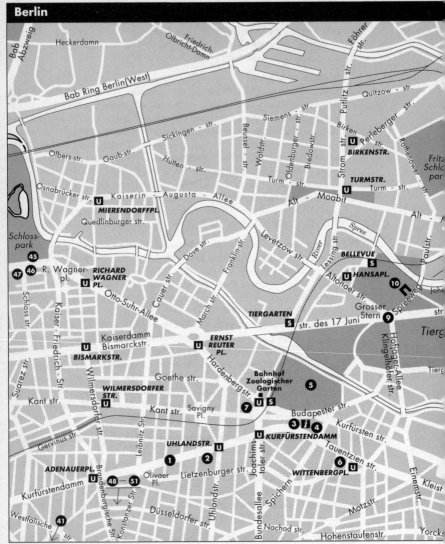

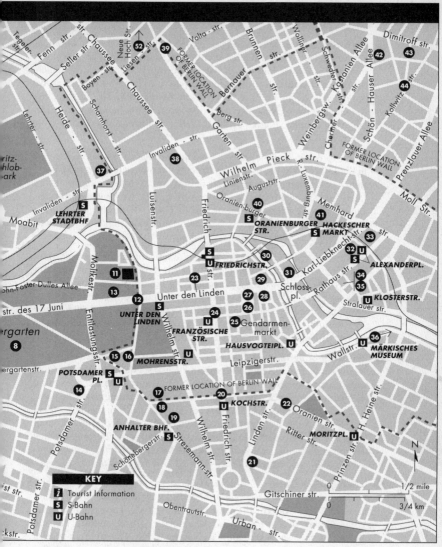

KEY

- **i** Tourist Information
- **S** S-Bahn
- **U** U-Bahn

and for its crowning rooftop winter garden. ⊠ *Tauentzienstr. 21,* ☎ *030/21210.*

❶ Kurfürstendamm. This grand boulevard, nicknamed the Ku'damm, is certainly the liveliest and most exciting stretch in Berlin. The busy thoroughfare was first laid out in the 16th century as the path by which the elector Joachim II of Brandenburg traveled from his palace on the Spree River to his hunting lodge in the Grunewald. The Kurfürstendamm (Elector's Causeway) was developed into a major route in the late 19th century, thanks to the initiative of Bismarck, Prussia's Iron Chancellor.

Don't look for house Number 1—when the Ku'damm was relocated in the early 1920s, the first 10 address numbers were just dropped. Back then, the Ku'damm was relatively new and by no means elegant; it was fairly far removed from the old heart of the city, which was Unter den Linden in the eastern section of Berlin. The Ku'damm's prewar fame was due mainly to the rowdy bars and dance halls that studded much of its length and its side streets.

Along with the rest of Berlin, the Ku'damm suffered severe wartime bombing. Almost half of its 245 late-19th-century buildings were destroyed in the 1940s, and the remaining buildings were damaged in varying degrees. What you see today (as in most of western Berlin) is either restored or was constructed in recent decades. Some of the 1950s buildings have been replaced by skyscrapers, in particular at the corner of Kurfürstendamm and Joachimstaler Strasse.

❷ The Story of Berlin. In a city with such a turbulent history, this multimedia show and museum built over a nuclear shelter (which is the most eerie part of the exhibition) off Kurfürstendamm is almost as exciting as the historic events. The odd mixture of history museum, theme park, and movie theater covers 800 years of city history, from the first settlers to the fall of the Wall, and is displayed on four floors. Many original items are woven together in an interactive design in the 26 rooms, which is both entertaining and informative. ⊠ *Ku'damm Karree, Kurfürstendamm 207–208,* ☎ *01805/992–010.* ⊡ *DM 18.* ☺ *Daily 10–6.*

★ ☪ ❺ Zoologischer Garten (Zoological Gardens). Germany's oldest zoo opened in 1844, and today it's the world's largest. After the destruction of World War II the zoo was carefully redesigned to create surroundings as close as possible to the animals' natural habitats. The zoo houses more than 14,000 animals belonging to 1,400 different species and has been successful at breeding rare and endangered species. The Asian-style **Elefantentor** (Elephant Gate) is the main entrance to the zoo and is also next to the aquarium. ⊠ *Hardenbergpl. 8 and Budapester Str. 34,* ☎ *030/254–010.* ⊡ *Zoo DM 14, aquarium DM 14, combined ticket to zoo and aquarium DM 22.50.* ☺ *Zoo Nov.–Feb., daily 9–5; early Mar., daily 9–5:30; late Mar.–late Sept., daily 9–6:30; Oct., daily 9–6; aquarium daily 9–6.*

NEED A
BREAK?

The **Einstein Café** (⊠ Kurfürstenstr. 58, ☎ 030/261–5096) offers a variety of exotic coffees. The Viennese-style coffeehouse is in the beautiful 19th-century mansion of German silent-movie star Henny Porten.

Tiergarten and the Government District

The Tiergarten, a beautifully laid-out, 630-acre park with lakes and paths, is the "green lung" of Berlin. In the 17th century it served as the hunting grounds of the Great Elector. Now it's swamped in summer with sunbathers and family barbecues. Its eastern end, between the grandiose landmarks of the Reichstag and the Brandenburger Tor, is being developed into the new seat of the federal government.

A Good Walk

From the Hardenbergplatz entrance to the Zoologischer Garten (☞ *above*), you can set off diagonally through the greenery of the idyllic **Tiergarten** ⑧. At the center of the park is the traffic intersection known as the Grosser Stern (Big Star), so called because five roads meet here. The **Siegessäule** ⑨ column provides a lookout from the center of the rotary. Follow the Spreeweg Road from the Grosser Stern to **Schloss Bellevue** ⑩, the residence of Germany's president. Next head east along John-Foster-Dulles Allee, keeping the Spree River in sight on your left. You'll soon pass the former Kongresshalle (Congress Hall), which houses cultural exhibitions.

Continuing east, you'll reach the monumental **Reichstag** ⑪, the German Empire's old parliament building that has been refitted to house the federal parliament. Just south of the Reichstag, where Strasse des 17. Juni meets Unter den Linden, is the mighty **Brandenburger Tor** ⑫, probably the most significant icon of German triumph and defeat.

Back in the park, along Strasse des 17. Juni—a name that commemorates the 1953 uprising of East Berlin workers that was quashed by Soviet tanks—you will see the **Sowjetisches Ehrenmal** ⑬. Turn south from the memorial onto Entlastungsstrasse and cross the tip of the Tiergarten to nearby Kemperplatz, with its **Kulturforum** ⑭, a large square with a series of fascinating museums and galleries.

TIMING

You can do the whole tour in a day, provided you take Berlin's least expensive public transportation, Bus 100. It starts at the U-bahn station Zoologischer Garten and makes several stops in the western downtown and Tiergarten area. You can leave and reboard the bus whenever you like. All buildings in the Tiergarten, with the exception of the former Kongresshalle, are closed to the public, so you can explore the park in less than two hours, even if you walk. Reserve at least three hours for the Kulturforum museums around Kemperplatz.

Sights to See

★ ⑫ **Brandenburger Tor** (Brandenburg Gate). This massive gate, once the pride of imperial Berlin and the city's premiere landmark, was left in an eerie no-man's-land when the Wall was built. Since the Wall's dismantling, the gate has become the focal point of much celebrating and is the nation's central party venue for New Year's Eve. This is the sole remaining gate of 14 built by Carl Langhans in 1788–91, designed as a triumphal arch for King Frederick Wilhelm II. It's virile classical style pays tribute to Athens's Acropolis. The quadriga, a chariot drawn by four horses and driven by the Goddess of Peace, was added in 1794. Troops paraded through the gate after successful campaigns—the last time in 1945, when victorious Red Army troops took Berlin. The upper part of the gate, together with its chariot and Goddess of Peace, was destroyed in the war. In 1957 the original molds were discovered in West Berlin, and a new quadriga was cast in copper and presented as a gift to the people of East Berlin. The square behind the gate, **Pariser Platz,** has regained its traditional, prewar design: Looking east, the left side of the square is dominated by a bank and the French and American embassies. To the right stands the ultramodern glass box of yet another bank and the new **Akademie der Künste**, the city's famous Academy of Arts. At the prestigious address of "Unter den Linden No. 1," the **Hotel Adlon Berlin,** the meeting point of Europe's jet set in the 1920s, has been rebuilt. The hotel has quickly gained a reputation as the unofficial guest house for state visitors and royalty. Toward Potsdamer Platz, south of the Brandenburg Gate, the new **Holocaust Mahnmal**, Germany's national Holocaust memorial, is being built. Designed by American architect Peter Eisenman, it will consist of 2,600 concrete pillars.

⑭ Kulturforum (Cultural Forum). With its unique ensemble of museums, galleries, libraries, and the Philharmonic Hall, the complex is considered one of Germany's cultural jewels. The **Gemäldegalerie,** which opened in 1997, reunites formerly separated collections from east and west Berlin. It is one of Germany's finest art galleries and houses an extensive selection of European paintings from the 13th to the 18th centuries. Several rooms are reserved for paintings by German masters, among them Dürer, Cranach the Elder, and Holbein. A special collection has works of the Italian masters—Botticelli, Titian, Giotto, Lippi, and Raphael—as well as paintings by Dutch and Flemish masters of the 15th and 16th centuries: Van Eyck, Bosch, Brueghel the Elder, and van der Weyden. The museum also holds the world's second-largest Rembrandt collection. ⊠ *Matthäikirchpl. 8,* ☎ *030/2660, 030/2090–5555 for all state museums in Berlin.* ☜ *DM 4; a Tageskarte (day card) is available for DM 8 and covers 1-day admission to all museums at Kulturforum. It is available at all museums.* ☉ *Tues.–Sun. 10–6.*

Steps away from the Gemäldegalerie are two examples of ultramodern architecture. The **Kunstbibliothek** (Art Library; ☎ 030/2090–5555; ☉ Mon. 2–8, Tues.–Fri. 9–8) contains art posters, a costume library, ornamental engravings, and a commercial art collection. The exhibitions at the **Kupferstichkabinett** (Drawings and Prints Collection) include European woodcuts, engravings, and illustrated books from the 15th century to the present. Also on display are several pen-and-ink drawings by Dürer, 150 drawings by Rembrandt, and a photographic archive. Another building displays paintings dating from the late Middle Ages to 1800. ⊠ *Matthäikirchpl. 6,* ☎ *030/266–2002.* ☜ *Free.* ☉ *Tues.–Fri. 10–6, weekends 11–6.*

The roof that resembles a great tent belongs to the **Philharmonie** (Philharmonic Hall), home to the renowned Berlin Philharmonic Orchestra since 1963 (☞ Nightlife and the Arts, *below*). The smaller Chamber Music Hall adjoining it was built in 1987. Both these buildings and the **Staatsbibliothek** (National Library), one of the largest libraries in Europe, were designed by Hans Scharoun.

The Philharmonie's **Musikinstrumenten-Museum** (Musical Instruments Museum) has a fascinating collection of keyboard, string, wind, and percussion instruments. ⊠ *Tiergartenstr. 1,* ☎ *030/254–810.* ☜ *DM 4; free 1st Sun. of every month; tour DM 3.* ☉ *Tues.–Fri. 9–5, weekends 10–5; guided tour Sat. at 11; presentation of Wurlitzer organ 1st Sat. of month at noon.*

Inside the **Kunstgewerbemuseum** (Museum of Decorative Arts), which is opposite the Philharmonie, you'll find a display of European arts and crafts from the Middle Ages to the present. Among its notable exhibits are the Welfenschatz (Welfen Treasure), a collection of 16th-century gold and silver plates from Nürnberg, as well as ceramics and porcelains. ⊠ *Matthäikirchpl. 8,* ☎ *030/266–2902.* ☜ *DM 4; free 1st Sun. of every month.* ☉ *Tues.–Fri. 9–6, weekends 11–6.*

The glass-and-steel **Neue Nationalgalerie** (New National Gallery) was designed by Mies van der Rohe and built in the mid-1960s. The collection comprises paintings, sculptures, and drawings from the 19th and 20th centuries, with an accent on works by such impressionists as Manet, Monet, Renoir, and Pissarro. Other schools represented are German Romantics, realists, expressionists, and surrealists. The gallery frequently showcases outstanding international art exhibitions. ⊠ *Potsdamer Str. 50,* ☎ *030/266–2662.* 🎫 *DM 12.* ⊙ *Tues.–Thurs., Sun. 9–6; Fri. and Sat. 10–8.*

⓫ Reichstag (Parliament Building). The Bundestag, Germany's federal parliament, returned to its traditional seat in the spring of 1999. British architect Sir Norman Foster did extensive remodeling to the gray monolithic structure, adding its glass dome, which has quickly become one of the city's main attractions: you can walk up a snail-like, gently rising staircase reminiscent of Frank Lloyd Wright's New York Guggenheim Museum while taking in a spectacular view of Berlin. Short tours include a view of the chambers before you ascend the dome. Visit either in the early morning or evening to avoid the longest lines. The last time people flocked to the Reichstag was to see it comically wrapped in 1995 by American artists Christo and Jeanne-Claude.

The Reichstag was erected between 1884 and 1894 to house the imperial German parliament and later served a similar function during the ill-fated Weimar Republic. On the night of February 28, 1933, the Reichstag burned down under mysterious circumstances, an event that provided the Nazis with a convenient pretext for outlawing all opposition parties. It was rebuilt but again badly damaged in 1945. The graffiti of the victorious Russian soldiers can still be seen on some of walls in the hallways. The finished building is surrounded by construction sites, mostly for new government offices. The largest is for the **Kanzleramt,** the new chancellery, almost adjacent to the Reichstag. The huge, boxlike construction for the German chancellor will not be finished until the year 2002. ⊠ *Platz der Republik 1,* ☎ *030/2270.* 🎫 *Free.* ⊙ *Daily 8 AM–10 PM.* 🕸

⓾ Schloss Bellevue (Bellevue Palace). This small palace has served as the official residence of Germany's federal president since 1959. It was built on the Spree River in 1785 for Frederick the Great's youngest brother, Prince August Ferdinand. In 1994 then-president Richard von Weizsäcker made it his main residence. Since then it has been closed to the public. To the left of the palace is the new egg-shape executive building—all marble, glass, and steel. Erected in 1998, it was the first new building built by the federal government in Berlin. It's powered by solar-energy panels on the roof. ⊠ *Schloss Bellevue Park.*

❾ Siegessäule (Victory Column). The 227-ft-high granite, sandstone, and bronze column has a splendid view across much of Berlin. It was erected in front of the Reichstag in 1873 to commemorate Prussia's military successes and then moved to the Tiergarten in 1938–39. The climb of 285 steps up through the column to the observation platform can be tiring, but the view is rewarding. ⊠ *Am Grossen Stern,* ☎ *030/391–2961.* 🎫 *DM 2.* ⊙ *Apr.–Sept., daily 9:30–6:30; Oct.–Mar., daily 9:30–5:30 (last admission 1 hr before closing).*

⓭ Sowjetisches Ehrenmal (Soviet Memorial). Built directly after World War II, this semicircular monument stands as a reminder of the bloody Soviet victory over the shattered German army in Berlin in May 1945. It features a bronze statue of a soldier atop a marble plinth taken from Hitler's former Reichkanzlei (headquarters). The memorial is flanked by what are said to be the first two T-34 tanks to have fought their way into the city in the last days of the war. ⊠ *Str. des 17. Juni.*

❽ Tiergarten (Animal Garden). For Berliners the quiet greenery of the 630-acre Tiergarten is a beloved green oasis in the heart of urban turmoil. In the summer the park, with some 23 km (14 mi) of footpaths, playgrounds, and white marble sculptures, becomes the embodiment of multicultural Berlin: Turkish families gather in the green meadows for spicy barbecues, children play soccer, and gay couples sunbathe. The inner park's 6½ acres of lakes and ponds were landscaped by garden architect Joseph Peter Lenné in the mid-1800s. On the shores of the lake in the southwestern part of the park, you can relax at the **Café am Neuen See**, a café and beer garden. In the center of the Tiergarten is the former **Kongresshalle** (✉ John-Foster-Dulles Allee 10, ☎ 030/397–870; ◷ Tues.–Sun. 9–6), nicknamed the "pregnant oyster" for its design; it's now home to the World Culture House.

In the past few years the tranquillity of the Tiergarten has been disturbed by the construction of a huge autobahn, railway, and metro tunnel, the multibillion-dollar **Nord-Süd-Tunnel**. It will redirect downtown traffic when all branches of the federal government have finally moved into the new government quarter and the new central train station at **Lehrter Stadtbahnhof** is finished.

Potsdamer Platz to Kreuzberg

World War II and the division of Berlin reduced bustling Potsdamer Platz to a sprawling, empty lot at the southeastern end of the Tiergarten. In the mid-1990s it became Europe's largest construction site, with corporate giants such as debis, the software subsidiary of DaimlerChrysler, and Sony erecting headquarters next to malls devoted to shopping and entertainment. Today the square and its surrounding, narrow streets are a modern version of prewar Potsdamer Platz, then the epitome of the urbane Berlin of the Roaring '20s. Neighboring Kreuzberg is still one of the most lively of Berlin's districts. A largely Turkish population lives cheek-by-jowl with a variegated assortment of political radicals, New Agers, down-at-the-heel artists real and fake, and bohemians of all nationalities.

A Good Walk

Begin at **Potsdamer Platz** ⑮, scene of corporate construction in recent years. At the center of the new buildings is the **Potsdamer Platz Arkaden** ⑯, a shopping and entertainment complex with plenty of eateries. From here head southeast along Stresemannstrasse and turn left on Niederkirchnerstrasse, where the Berlin Wall once ran; the fragment of the wall here is one of only four sections still standing.

This is yet another strip of German history, with the old **Preussischer Landtag** ⑰, the seat of Berlin's parliament, and the **Martin-Gropius-Bau** ⑱, one of the city's premier exhibition halls. Right next door is the **Prinz-Albrecht-Gelände** ⑲, which contains the underground ruins of Nazi SS headquarters. Continuing east on Niederkirchnerstrasse, cross Wilhelmstrasse to its intersection with Kochstrasse. Head east on Kochstrasse until you reach the corner of Friedrichstrasse. Gripping stories of the Wall, refugees, and spies are told in the museum at the former **Checkpoint Charlie** ⑳. From here continue east on Kochstrasse and detour right onto Lindenstrasse for the **Jüdisches Museum** ㉑, Germany's largest museum of Jewish culture. To find a place to relax next, backtrack and turn right on **Oranienstrasse** ㉒. This is the heart of the Kreuzberg district, with Turkish shops, alternative cafés, and nearby street markets.

TIMING

You can cover this walk in less than four hours. In addition, reserve at least an hour for any of the museums you visit and take in some of the scenery in Kreuzberg. Oranienstrasse and the neighboring side streets are filled with cafés that are perfect for unwinding.

Sights to See

★ ⑳ **Checkpoint Charlie.** This famous crossing point between the two Berlins is where American and Soviet tanks faced off in the tense months of the Berlin blockade (1948–49). All evidence of the crossing point disappeared along with the Wall, but the **Haus am Checkpoint Charlie** (House at Checkpoint Charlie—The Wall Museum) is still here to tell the Wall's fascinating stories. The museum reviews the events leading up to its construction and displays actual tools and equipment, records, and photographs documenting methods used by East Germans to cross over to the West (one of the most ingenious instruments of escape was a miniature submarine). The new building behind the museum, the **American Business Center,** was erected on the eastern side of the former Iron Curtain. ⊠ *Friedrichstr. 43–45,* ☎ *030/253–7250.* ⊡ *DM 8.* ☉ *Daily 9 AM–10 PM.*

NEED A BREAK? Try your best to conjure up an image of the Wall from a window seat at **Café Adler** (⊠ Friedrichstr. 206, ☎ 030/251–8965), which once bumped right up against it. The soups and salads are all tasty and cheap.

OFF THE BEATEN PATH **EAST SIDE GALLERY –** This stretch of concrete amounts to nothing less than the largest open-air gallery in the world. Between February and June of 1990, 118 artists from around the globe created unique works of art on the longest remaining section—1.3 km (.8 mi)—of the Berlin Wall; it has been declared an historic monument. One of the best-known works, by Russian artist Dmitri Vrubel, depicts Brezhnev and Honnecker (the former East German leader) kissing, with the caption "My God. Help me survive this deadly love." ⊠ *Mühlenstr./Oberbaumbrücke.*

㉑ **Jüdisches Museum** (Jewish Museum). Berlin's newest museum has yet to reveal its exhibits, yet its very creation and striking architecture makes it the most talked-about museum in the city. The lightning bolt–like building designed by architect Daniel Libeskind draws frequent comparisons to a broken star of David. Meant to showcase the long history and culture of the country's Jewish community—one of the world's largest prior to the Holocaust—the museum plans to open in September 2001. The long delay is the result of protracted debates among historians, politicians, and curators over how to present the Holocaust. ⊠ *Lindenstr. 9–14,* ☎ *030/2599–3300.*

Mariannenplatz. Restored 19th-century tenement houses surround this square, the highlight of which is the **Künstlerhaus Bethanien**, a former deaconesses' hospital, where artists from around the world are given studio space. A gallery presents works of artists in residence. Turn north on Mariannenstrasse from Oranienstrasse to reach the square. ⊠ *Mariannenpl. 2,* ☎ *030/616–9030.* ☉ *Wed.–Sun. 2–7 (hrs vary depending on exhibition).*

⑱ **Martin-Gropius-Bau.** This renowned exhibition hall is home to a city museum with galleries of local art and Jewish culture in Berlin. It stands opposite the Preussischer Landtag (☞ *below*). ⊠ *Niederkirchnerstr. 7,* ☎ *030/2548–67877.* ☉ *Weekdays 10–8 (hrs vary depending on exhibit).*

㉒ **Oranienstrasse.** The core of life in the Kreuzberg district, Oranienstrasse and its hard-core appeal has tempered into funkiness since reunification. When Kreuzberg literally had its back against the Wall, West German social outcasts, punks, and the radical left made this old working-class street their own private hideout. Since the 1970s the population has been largely Turkish, and many of yesterday's outsiders have turned into successful owners of trendy shops and restaurants. Oranienstrasse is a good case study of West Berlin's past and the slow changes that have taken place since the Wall fell. You'll find a lively and curious mixture of Muslim culture, alternative lifestyles, offbeat fashion shops, and hip restaurants—the contrasts in the streets of this neighborhood couldn't be starker.

To the south of Oranienstrasse is the depressing and seedy Kottbusser Platz. Its social housing projects date to the 1970s, and there's drug dealing in the area (stay away from both the dealers and drug addicts and do not give them any money).

⑮ Potsdamer Platz (Potsdam Square). The once-divided capital is rejoined on this square, which was Europe's busiest plaza before World War II and Berlin's inner-city center. Looking at today's new buildings of steel, glass, and concrete, it's hard to imagine the square was once a no-man's-land with the infamous Wall cutting across it. Only a painted red line on the streets to the east traces the line of the old border. Where the British, American, and Russian sectors once met, Sony, debis, Asea Brown Boveri, and other companies have built their new headquarters.

The two high-rise towers dominating the square are part of the headquarters of debis, the software subsidiary of DaimlerChrysler. The debis center was designed by star architect Renzo Piano.

The light glass-and-steel construction of the **Sony Center**, wrapped around a spectacular 4,800-square-yard forum, is an architectural jewel designed by German-American architect Helmut Jahn. Sony's European headquarters are here, as well as the unusual attraction of the old **Kaisersaal** (Emperor's Hall), a café, and meeting rooms from the prewar Grand Hotel Esplanade that once stood on this spot. The hall is all that survived World War II bombings. It originally stood some 50 yards away, but was moved lock, stock, and barrel to its present location. Its restored interior has been meticulously integrated into the modern Sony Center. Also in the center is the **Marlene Dietrich Collection**, a small museum exhibiting such personal belongings of the German-born movie star as dresses, movie memorabilia, and letters.

⑯ Potsdamer Platz Arkaden. This shopping and entertainment mecca covers 40,000 square yards and houses 140 shops and restaurants on three levels. Right next to it are Berlin's newest first-class hotel, the Grand Hyatt Berlin, the movie complex Cinemaxx, and a 3D-IMAX cinema, as well as the new Berlin casino and Germany's largest musical theater. ⊠ *IMAX, Marlene-Dietrich-Pl. 4,* ☎ *030/4431–6131.* 🎫 *DM 11.50.* ⊙ *Daily 10–midnight; shows start every hr.*

⑰ Preussischer Landtag (Prussian State Legislature). The monumental parliament building on the north side of Niederkirchnerstrasse now houses Berlin's House of Deputies and is one of Germany's most impressive 19th-century administration buildings. Even if the house isn't in session, you should take a look inside and admire the huge entrance hall. ⊠ *Niederkirchnerstr. 3–5,* ☎ *030/23250.* ⊙ *Weekdays 9–6.*

⑲ Prinz-Albrecht-Gelände (Prince Albrecht Grounds). The headquarters of the SS, the Main Reich Security Office, and other Nazi security organizations were housed on this site from 1933 until 1945. After the war the buildings were leveled. The grounds remained untouched until 1987, when the basements of the buildings, once used as "house prisons" by the SS, were excavated, and an open-air exhibit on their history and Nazi atrocities was opened—the Topography of Terror. Tours are available by appointment. ⊠ *Niederkirchnerstr. 8,* ☎ *030/254–5090.* 🎫 *Free.* ⊙ *Oct.–Apr., daily 10–6; May–Sept., daily 10–8.*

COPING WITH THE PAST

IN THE NEW MILLENNIUM, will Germany shed decades of self-loathing about the Holocaust and World War II? Critical self-examination began as late as the 1960s, when an angry young generation pointedly questioned what their parents did during the 12 years of fascism. This generation has now grown up and seems comfortable declaring its slate clean.

Baby boomers now hold key positions in the media, politics, science, and culture. They've opened the door for Germans wishing for a normalcy they feel has long eluded the country. Gerhard Schröder (born 1944) won the chancellorship in 1998 largely because of his domestic economic platform, but his election also signaled a historic shift in leadership: Schröder is the first postwar chancellor not to have experienced World War II. He and his generation are well aware of Germany's past but do not seem burdened by its weight. The new government is straightforward, outspoken, and less apt to worry that the world will hold Germany's past over its head. This open, unpretentious approach is a political style that has gone over well with Germany's neighbors, most significantly Poland and France.

But the past is never far from German consciousness. During the late 1990s American historian Daniel J. Goldhagen's book *Hitler's Willing Executioners* triggered the most profound shock wave of *Vergangenheitsbewältigung* (coping with the past) the nation has felt in recent years. Goldhagen reminded people that the Holocaust was carried out by ordinary Germans, not just by a minority of fanatical Nazis.

Also, in 1999, the very year the federal government returned to Berlin—representing an end to the country's post–World War II division—a heated debate flared over the Holocaust. As historians and politicians argued over how to express German responsibility, shame, and guilt, plans for a national Holocaust memorial derailed, and controversy surrounded Berlin's new Jewish Museum. Some of the country's most respected elder writers and politicians stressed the importance of examining the German traits that allowed the genocide to occur. This renewed reflection on the idea of a national character flaw once again aroused the country's insecurities. After years of debating, the construction of the disputed memorial will be begin in summer 2001, next to the Brandenburg Gate, and the Jewish Museum will open in September 2001.

Germany continues to address issues of its past. The much-feared political successes of right-wing parties that had appeared so imminent in the mid-1990s did not materialize. Right-wing attacks on foreign workers have decreased, and a new citizenship law established in 2000 has begun to (at least legally) integrate Germany's alien residents. German corporations have established reparation funds for World War II slave-laborers. These days, accepting and exploring Germany's past has taken a somewhat quieter and more balanced approach. And that is probably the best sign that the nation has truly accepted its history.

— Jürgen Scheunemann

TÜRKENMARKT (Turkish Market) – On Tuesday and Friday from noon to 6:30 you can find the country's best selection of Arab and Turkish foods along the Landwehrkanal. Vendors line the bank roads of Maybachufer and the Paul-Lincke-Ufer. You can walk here from Kreuzberg's Kottbusser Tor U-bahn station via Kottbusser Damm. The cafés and restaurants on Paul-Lincke-Ufer are great places for a cup of coffee.

Unter den Linden to Alexanderplatz

Unter den Linden and Friedrichstrasse, the main streets of eastern Berlin, proudly roll out restored landmarks, museums, and new shopping malls. The old boulevards were once almost forgotten in the shadow of the Wall. Some rather unattractive office buildings along Unter den Linden, hastily erected in the 1970s, are reminders that the boulevard was remodeled by Communist East Germany. At the very end of Unter den Linden, around the vast Alexanderplatz, eastern Berlin's handful of skyscrapers cluster around one of the city's premier landmarks, the Berlin TV tower. Northeast of it, the old working-class district of Prenzlauer Berg is home to wonderfully restored 19th-century tenement houses.

A Good Walk

Begin your walk at Pariser Platz, right behind the Brandenburger Tor (☞ Tiergarten, *above*), and take a long walk east down **Unter den Linden** ㉓. This eastern and older counterpart to Kurfürstendamm is both more historic and more elegant, with landmarks like the famous Hotel Adlon next to the Brandenburger Tor. On your way, you'll pass several parliamentary offices and consulates, among them the huge Russian embassy, and souvenir shops. From the turn of the century until the beginning of World War II, the intersection of Unter den Linden and **Friedrichstrasse** ㉔ was the busiest in all Berlin. Turn right here, passing both quaint and fancy shops, then left at Französische Strasse to reach **Gendarmenmarkt** ㉕, one of Europe's finest early 19th-century plazas.

Head farther down Französische Strasse to **St. Hedwigskathedrale** ㉖, Berlin's leading Catholic church, and the **Staatsoper Unter den Linden** ㉗, the city's premier opera house. These buildings, along with the **Kronprinzenpalais** ㉘—which adjoins the opera house—and Humboldt University, form the Forum Fridericianum, the model of Prussian glory, designed by Frederick the Great himself. Back on Unter den Linden, opposite the Kronprinzenpalais and next to the university, is the **Deutsches Historisches Museum** ㉙. Turn left to follow the Spree Canal to **Museumsinsel** ㉚, the site of Berlin's two original medieval settlements. From the museum complex follow the Spree Canal back to Unter den Linden and turn left to reach the enormous cathedral **Berliner Dom** ㉛ and the adjacent **Palast der Republik,** the former parliament building of Socialist East Germany.

Next, follow Karl-Liebknecht-Strasse to take a look at the 13th-century **St. Marienkirche** ㉜ and the bordering **Alexanderplatz** ㉝, a wide-open square. Walk across the lower end of the square past the **Berliner Rathaus** ㉞, the city's town hall, and the **Nikolaiviertel** ㉟, Berlin's historic quarter with the medieval St. Nikolaikirche (St. Nicolas Church). To reach the redbrick **Märkisches Museum** ㊱, which displays the history of Berlin, wander down Spreeufer to the Mühlendamm, turn left onto this boulevard and cross the Spree River. Turn left again into onto Fischerinsel, and then make another left onto Wallstrasse.

TIMING

Exploring the historic heart of Berlin might seem just as exhausting as the city's past has been dramatic. The walk down Unter den Linden past Alexanderplatz to the St. Nikolaiviertel takes about two hours if you don't look closely at any museums or highlights. Allow at least the same amount of time for the Museumsinsel. You won't regret one minute. Most of the other sights can be seen in less than one hour each. The Museumsinsel, Friedrichstrasse, and the Galeries Lafayette are crowded on weekends, so try to visit there early or during the week.

Sights to See

㉝ Alexanderplatz. This square once formed the hub of East Berlin. German writer Alfred Döblin dubbed it the "heart of a world metropolis." It's a bleak sort of place today, open and windswept and surrounded by grimly ugly modern buildings, with no hint of its prewar activity—a reminder not just of the Allied bombing of Berlin but of the ruthlessness practiced by the East Germans when they demolished the remains of the old buildings.

Finding Alexanderplatz is no problem; just head toward the **Berliner Fernsehturm,** the soaring TV tower, completed in 1969 and 1,198 ft high (not accidentally 710 ft higher than western Berlin's broadcasting tower and 98 ft higher than the Eiffel Tower in Paris). The tower's observation platform offers the best view of Berlin; on a clear day you can see for 40 km (25 mi). You can also enjoy a coffee break up there in the city's highest café, which rotates for your panoramic pleasure. ⊠ *Panoramastr. 1a,* ☎ *030/242–3333.* ⊡ *DM 8.* ☉ *Nov.–Apr., daily 10 AM–midnight; May–Oct., daily 9 AM–1 AM (last admission at 11:30 PM).*

★ **㉛ Berliner Dom** (Berlin Cathedral). The impressive 19th-century cathedral, with its enormous green copper dome, is one of the great ecclesiastical buildings in Germany. Its main nave was reopened in June 1993 after a 20-year renovation. There's an observation balcony that allows a view of the cathedral's ceiling and interior. More than 80 sarcophagi of Prussian royals are on display in the cathedral's catacombs. ⊠ *Am Lustgarten,* ☎ *030/2026–9136.* ⊡ *DM 5, with balcony DM 8.* ☉ *Church: Mon.–Sat. 9–7, Sun. noon–8; balcony: Mon.–Sat. 9–7, Sun. noon–5; imperial staircase and crypt: Mon.–Sat. 9–8, Sun. noon–7.*☜

㉜ Berliner Rathaus (Red Town Hall). The former Rotes Rathaus is known for its redbrick design and friezes depicting the city's history. After the city's reunification, this pompous symbol of Berlin's 19th-century urban pride again became the seat of the city government. ⊠ *Jüdenstr. at Rathausstr.,* ☎ *030/90290.* ⊡ *Free.* ☉ *Weekdays 9–6.*

㉙ Deutsches Historisches Museum (German History Museum). This magnificent baroque building, constructed between 1695 and 1730, was once the Prussian arsenal (Zeughaus) and normally houses Germany's National History Museum. Due to major reconstruction, including a new wing designed by Japanese architect I. M. Pei, the building is closed until late 2001. Exhibitions are temporarily in the ☞ **Kronprinzenpalais,** across the street. ⊠ *Unter den Linden 2,* ☎ *030/203–040.*

★ **㉔ Friedrichstrasse.** There's probably no other street in the whole of eastern Germany that has changed as dramatically as Friedrichstrasse. The once-bustling 5th Avenue of Berlin's prewar days has risen from the rubble of war and Communist negligence to recover its glamour of old, though it doesn't offer the sheer number of establishments as the competing Ku'damm.

Heading south on Friedrichstrasse, you'll pass various new business buildings, including the **Lindencorso** and the **Rosmarin-Karree,** which are worth a look both for their architecture and fancy shops. The jewel of this street is the **Friedrichstadtpassagen,** a gigantic shopping and business complex of three buildings praised for their completely different designs. The buildings are connected by an underground mall of elegant shops and eateries. At the corner of Französische Strasse a daring building, designed by French architect Jean Nouvel, houses the French department store **Galeries Lafayette.** Its interior is dominated by a huge steel-and-glass funnel surrounded by six floors of merchandise. ⊠ *Französische Str. 23,* ☎ *030/209–480.* ☉ *Weekdays 9:30–8, Sat. 9–4.*

★ ㉕ **Gendarmenmarkt.** This large square is the site of the beautifully reconstructed 1818 **Schauspielhaus,** one of Berlin's main concert halls, and the **Deutscher Dom and Französischer Dom** (German and French cathedrals). The French cathedral contains the **Hugenottenmuseum,** with exhibits charting the history and art of the Protestant refugees from France—the Huguenots—expelled at the end of the 17th century by King Louis XIV. Their energy and commercial expertise did much to help boost Berlin during the 18th century. ⊠ *Gendarmenmarkt 5,* ☎ *030/229–1760.* 💳 *DM 3.* ☉ *Tues.–Sat. noon–5, Sun. 11–5.*

The **Deutscher Dom** (German Cathedral) has an extensive historical exhibition sponsored by the Bundestag, the German parliament. It's worth a visit if you're interested in an official view of German history with a particular accent on the cold war and the division of Germany. A café and bookstore with attractive books on Berlin are on the top floor. ⊠ *Gendarmenmarkt 1,* ☎ *030/2273–0431.* 💳 *Free.* ☉ *Tues.–Sun. 10–5.*

㉘ **Kronprinzenpalais** (Crown Prince's Palace). Now used as a temporary exhibition hall for the ☞ **Deutsches Historisches Museum,** this magnificent baroque-style building was originally constructed in 1732 by Philippe Gerlach for Crown Prince Friedrich (later Frederick the Great). ⊠ *Unter den Linden 3,* ☎ *030/203–040.* 💳 *Free, English-speaking guide DM 60.* ☉ *Thurs.–Tues. 10–6.*

㊱ **Märkisches Museum** (Brandenburg Museum). This showcase for Berlin's history includes exhibits on the city's theatrical past and a fascinating collection of mechanical musical instruments. They are demonstrated on Sunday at 11 and Wednesday at 3. ⊠ *Am Köllnischen Park 5,* ☎ *030/308–660.* 💳 *DM 8, instrument demonstration DM 4.* ☉ *Tues.–Sun. 10–6.*

★ ㉚ **Museumsinsel** (Museum Island). On the site of one of Berlin's two original settlements, this unique complex of four world-class museums is an absolute must—and not just for museum buffs. The **Nationalgalerie** (Old National Gallery, entrance on Bodestrasse) reopens in early 2001. It houses an outstanding collection of 18th-, 19th-, and early 20th-century paintings and sculptures. Works by Cézanne, Rodin, Degas, and one of Germany's most famous portrait artists, Max Liebermann, are part of the permanent exhibition, which is temporarily on display at the **Altes Museum** (Old Museum). The austere neoclassical building just north of the old Lustgarten (entrance at Am Lustgarten) also features antique sculptures, clay figurines, and bronze art, which are part of the collection of antiquities from the Pergamonmuseum.

★ Even if you think you aren't interested in the ancient world, make an exception for the **Pergamonmuseum** (entrance on Am Kupfergraben). It is not only the standout in this complex, but one of the world's greatest museums. The museum's name is derived from its principal and best-loved display, the Pergamon Altar, a monumental Greek temple discovered in what is now Turkey and dating from 180 BC. The altar was shipped to Berlin in the late 19th century. Equally impressive is the Babylonian processional way in the Asia Minor department.

The **Antikensammlung** (Antiquities Collection) is home to a collection of ceramics and bronzes as well as everyday utensils from ancient

Greece and Rome and a number of Greek vases from the 6th to 4th centuries BC.

Please note: Due to the continuing reconstruction of the Museumsinsel, the Altes Museum and parts of the Pergamonmuseum will be closed in 2001. ✉ *Entrance to Museumsinsel: Am Kupfergraben. Museumsinsel:* ☎ *030/209–050.* ☞ *Each museum on Museumsinsel DM 8; free 1st Sun. of every month; Tageskarte (day card, DM 8), available at each museum, covers 1-day admission to all museums.* ☉ *All museums Tues.–Sun. 10–6.* ✍

❸❺ **Nikolaiviertel** (Nicholas Quarter). The complex of buildings centering around the medieval twin-spire **St. Nikolaikirche** (St. Nicholas Church), dating from 1230, gives you an idea of what old Berlin looked like. The quarter with its tiny cobblestone streets that grew up around Berlin's oldest parish church is filled with stores, cafés, and restaurants. The adjacent Fischerinsel (Fisherman's Island) area was the heart of Berlin 750 years ago, and today retains some of its medieval character. At Breite Strasse you'll find two of Berlin's oldest buildings: No. 35 is the **Ribbeckhaus**, the city's only surviving Renaissance structure, dating from 1624, and No. 36 is the early baroque **Marstall**, built by Michael Matthais between 1666 and 1669. ✉ *Church: Nikolaikirchpl.,* ☎ *030/240–020.* ☞ *DM 5.* ☉ *Tues.–Sun. 10–6.*

Palast der Republik (Palace of the Republic). This colossal building housed East Germany's so-called People's Chamber (parliament). The palace was closed in 1991, and the future use of this unappealing socialist leftover is still undecided. Nothing about the structure and the vast square in front of it suggests that this was the very spot where the Hohenzollern city palace once stood. It was heavily damaged by bombings during the war and was then dynamited by the Communist regime. The smaller building at the southern end of Schlossplatz used to house East Germany's **Staatsrat** (State Senate). Ironically, it now serves as the chancellor's provisional Berlin office until the new Chancellery next to the Reichstag is completed. The palace stands opposite the Berliner Dom (☞ *above*). ✉ *Schlosspl.*

❷❻ **St. Hedwigskathedrale** (St. Hedwig's Cathedral). Similar to the Pantheon in Rome, this substantial circular building is Berlin's premier Catholic church. When the cathedral was erected in 1747, it was the first Catholic church built in resolutely Protestant Berlin since the Reformation. It was Frederick the Great's effort to appease Prussia's Catholic population after his invasion of Catholic Silesia. ✉ *Bebelpl.,* ☎ *030/203–4810.* ☉ *Weekdays 10–5, Sun. 1–5.*

❸❷ **St. Marienkirche** (St. Mary's Church). This medieval church, one of the finest in Berlin, is worth a visit for its late-Gothic, macabre fresco *Der Totentanz* (*Dance of Death*). The cross on top of the church tower was an everlasting annoyance to Communist rulers, as its golden metal was always mirrored in the windows of the Fernsehturm TV tower, the pride of socialist construction genius. ✉ *Karl-Liebknecht-Str. 8,* ☎ *030/242–4467.* ☞ *Tour free.* ☉ *Mon.–Thurs. 10–4, weekends noon–4; tour Mon.–Tues. at 1, Sun. at 11:45.*

❷❼ **Staatsoper Unter den Linden** (State Opera). The lavishly restored opera house, Berlin's prime opera stage, lies at the heart of the Forum Fridericianum. This ensemble of buildings was designed by Frederick the Great himself to showcase the splendor of his enlightened rule. Daniel Barenboim is maestro of the opera house. ✉ *Unter den Linden 7,* ☎ *030/2035–4555.* ☉ *Box office weekdays 10–6, weekends 2–6; reservations by phone weekdays 10–8, weekends 2–8.*

The **Opernpalais** (✉ Unter den Linden 5, ☎ 030/202–683), right next
to the opera house, is home to four restaurants and cafés, all famous for
their rich German cakes, pastries, and original Berlin dishes.

㉓ **Unter den Linden.** The name of this major Berlin thoroughfare means
"under the linden trees"—and as Marlene Dietrich once sang: "As long
as the old linden trees still bloom, Berlin is still Berlin." Once the most
elegant and famous Berlin address, the grand boulevard is slowly re-
gaining its old glamour. Lined by grand hotels, an opera house, some
cafés and shops, parliamentary buildings, embassies, and consulates,
the avenue reminds visitors that Berlin once was the proud capital of
the German Empire. The ☞ **Kronprinzenpalais,** ☞ **Deutsches Historisches Museum,** and **Humboldt-Universität** (Humboldt University;
✉ Unter den Linden 6, ☎ 030/20930) border the avenue. The university was built in 1766 as a palace for the brother of Friedrich II of
Prussia. It became a university in 1810, and both Karl Marx and
Friedrich Engels once studied here. The main hall of the university is
open Monday–Saturday 6 AM–10 PM.

Next to the university is the **Neue Wache** (New Guardhouse). Constructed in 1818, it served as the Royal Prussian War Memorial until
the declaration of the Weimar Republic in 1918. Badly damaged in World
War II, it was restored by the East German state and rededicated as a
memorial for the victims of militarism and fascism in 1960. After unification it was restored to its Weimar Republic appearance and, in
November 1993, inaugurated as Germany's central war memorial.

Mitte and Prenzlauer Berg

The district of Mitte (Middle) is close to the center of Berlin and served
as the government district during the era of the Prussian kings, the German emperors, and, later, the German Democratic Republic governments. In 1999 Mitte resumed its role of yore when the German
government finally relocated here. The district includes the historic heart
of old Berlin and abounds with landmarks on the grand boulevards
(☞ Unter den Linden to Alexanderplatz, *above*). But the atmosphere
of this smallest of all Berlin districts is best experienced in its alleyways.
The old working-class district of Prenzlauer Berg used to be one of the
poorest sections of Berlin. In socialist East Germany, the old (and
mostly run-down) tenement houses attracted the artistic avant-garde,
which transformed the district into an oasis for alternative lifestyles.
Today both Mitte and Prenzlauer Berg charm their visitors with a
blend of rugged, turn-of-the-century architecture and the city's liveliest nightlife.

A Good Walk

From the S-bahn station of Lehrter Stadtbahnhof, walk east on Invalidenstrasse, passing the **Hamburger Bahnhof** ㊲, Berlin's museum for
contemporary art. At the intersection of Invalidenstrasse and
Chausseestrasse, turn right and walk south to find the **Brecht-Weigel-
Gedenkstätte** ㊳, a museum in the living quarters of the famous German playwright Bertolt Brecht, and the bordering graveyard, where
many famous figures are buried. A short walk back toward Invalidenstrasse, and farther to the northeast, on Bernauer Strasse, is the
Gedenkstätte Berliner Mauer ㊴, the only section of the Berlin Wall still
in its original form and location. From here you can continue south
on Gartenstrasse, Kleine Hamburger Strasse, and Auguststrasse to
reach the heart of the Mitte district, Oranienburger Strasse. This is also
the center of the old Jewish quarter, spread around the massive **Neue
Synagoge** ㊵. From here continue east on Oranienburger Strasse to the

Hackesche Höfe ㊶, an Art Deco warehouse complex. Jump on the nearby S-bahn to Alexanderplatz and transfer to the subway (U–2), getting off two stops later at Senefelderplatz station in Prenzlauer Berg. It's an easy walk north on Schönhauser Allee to the fringe art and culture center **Kulturbrauerei** ㊷, an old brewery and a typical example of late-19th-century industrial architecture. Finally, to take in some of the district's scenery, follow the small Sredzkistrasse to the east until you reach the center of Berlin's old working-class district, the completely restored 19th-century **Husemannstrasse** ㊸ and **Kollwitzplatz** ㊹.

TIMING

If you want to indulge in the art exhibitions at Hamburger Bahnhof or relax at any of the many cafés along the way, reserve a full day for Mitte and Prenzlauer Berg. It's also possible to take in all spots along the tour within four hours.

Sights to See

㊳ Brecht-Weigel-Gedenkstätte (Brecht-Weigel Memorial Site). You can visit the former working and living quarters of playwright Bertolt Brecht and his wife, Helene Weigel, and there's a library for Brecht scholars. The downstairs restaurant serves Viennese cuisine using Weigel's recipes. Brecht is buried next door, along with his wife and more than 100 other celebrated Germans, in the **Dorotheenstädtischer Friedhof** (Dorotheenstadt Cemetery). ✉ *Chausseestr. 125,* ☎ *030/28305–7044, 030/461–7279 cemetery.* 🎟 *Apartment DM 6, library free.* 🕙 *Apartment: Tues.–Wed., Fri. 10–noon; Thurs. 10–noon and 5–7; Sat. 9:30–noon and 12:30–2; Sun. 11–6; tours every ½ hr, every hr on Sun.; library Tues.–Fri. 9–3; cemetery: daily 8–7.*

★ **㊳ Gedenkstätte Berliner Mauer** (Berlin Wall Memorial Site). This is the only nearly original piece of the Berlin Wall border system left in the city. The museum took almost seven years to realize, as most East Berliners living nearby didn't want a reminder of the gruesome symbol of German separation right in front of their homes. The museum shows a 230-ft-long piece of the whole Wall system, which consisted of two walls, and a control path between them used by border guards and their German shepherds or army jeeps. Standing behind one wall, you can look through small observation windows to the other. ✉ *Bernauer Str. 111.* ☎ *030/464–1030.* 🎟 *Free.* 🕙 *Wed.–Sun. 10–5.*

★ **㊶ Hackesche Höfe** (Hacke Warehouses). Built in 1905–07, the completely restored Hackesche Höfe are the finest example of *Jugendstil* (Art Nouveau) industrial architecture in Berlin. The huge complex is comprised of nine courtyards connected by narrow passageways. Most of the buildings are covered with white tiles and decorated in blue and gray mosaics. Today the Hackesche Höfe are the center of the bustling nightlife in Mitte, with several style-conscious bars and pubs, the restaurant Hackescher Hof (☞ Dining, *below*), the variety theater Chamäleon Vareté (☞ Nightlife, *below*), a drama stage, and a movie theater. On warm weekend nights in summer, the courtyards are full. ✉ *Rosenthaler Str. 40–41.* 🐾

㊲ Hamburger Bahnhof, Museum für Gegenwart–Berlin (Museum of Contemporary Art). This museum is perhaps the best place in Berlin to get a survey of Western art after 1960. The early 19th-century structure was originally a train station. When it was remodeled, a huge and spectacular new wing was added, designed by Berlin architect J. P. Kleihues. The addition is worth a visit itself for its stunning interplay of glass, steel, colorful decor, and sunlight coming through skylights. You can see installations by German artists Joseph Beuys and Anselm Kiefer as well as paintings by Andy Warhol, Cy Twombly, Robert Rauschenberg, and Robert Morris. ⊠ *Invalidenstr. 50–51,* ☎ *030/397–8340.* 🖾 *DM 12.* ☉ *Tues.–Fri. 10–6, weekends 11–6.*

❹❸ Husemannstrasse. This completely restored cobblestone street in the old part of Prenzlauer Berg gives a vivid impression of life in the late-19th century. With their squat advertising pillars, wrought-iron parapets on the balconies, and stucco decorations, the houses bring to life a time when handicrafts and small shops flourished amid the large tenements built for the working class. The socialist East German government began renovating the street in 1987, and though it may be a bit too nostalgic in its depiction of the past, the street nevertheless gives a good insight into daily life in a big city.

NEED A
BREAK?

For coffee and cake or a good German beer, stop by at the **Restauration 1900** (⊠ Husemannstr. 1, ☎ 030/442–2494), one of the few popular cafés and restaurants from socialist times still in business today.

❹❹ Kollwitzplatz (Kollwitz Square). Named for painter, sculptor, and political activist Käthe Kollwitz, who lived nearby, the square is the center of the old working-class district of Prenzlauer Berg. It is dominated by a sculpture by Kollwitz, whose many art works portray the life and hard times of ordinary people living in the district. An enlarged copy of one of her sculpture, *Trauernde Mutter mit totem Sohn* (Grieving Mother with Dead Son), stands at the Neue Wache on Unter den Linden (☞ Unter den Linden to Alexanderplatz, *above*).

OFF THE
BEATEN PATH

JÜDISCHER FRIEDHOF (Jewish Cemetery) – More than 150,000 graves make this peaceful retreat in Berlin's Weissensee district Europe's largest Jewish cemetery. The cemetery and tombstones are in excellent condition—a seeming impossibility, given its location in the heart of the Third Reich. To reach the cemetery, take Tram 2, 3, 4, or 13 from Hackescher Markt to Berliner Allee and head south on Herbert-Baum-Strasse. ☎ *030/925–3330.* ☉ *Sun.–Thurs. 8–4, Fri. 8–3.*

❹❷ Kulturbrauerei (Culture Brewery). The redbrick buildings of the old Schultheiss brewery now house a fringe arts and entertainment center, containing a movie center, art galleries, pubs, and a concert hall. Parts of the brewery were built in 1842. Around the turn of the century the complex was expanded to house the main brewery of Berlin's famous Schultheiss beer. It was then the largest brewery in the world. The buildings were completely restored in 1997–99, though no beer is brewed here now. ⊠ *Schönhauser Allee 36–39,* ☎ *030/441–9269.*

❹⓿ Neue Synagoge (New Synagogue). This meticulously restored landmark, built between 1859 and 1866, is an exotic amalgam of styles, the whole faintly Middle Eastern. When its doors opened, it was the largest synagogue in Europe, with 3,200 seats. The synagogue was largely ruined on the night of November 9, 1938, the infamous *Kristallnacht* (Night of the Broken Glass), when Nazi looters rampaged across Germany, burning synagogues and smashing the few Jewish shops and homes left in the country. Further destroyed by Allied bombing in 1943, it remained untouched until restoration began under the East German regime in the mid-1980s. The building is connected to the modern **Centrum Judaicum,** a center for Jewish culture and learning that frequently has exhibitions and other cultural events. ⊠ *Oranienburger Str. 28–30,* ☎ *030/2840–1316.* ☉ *Sun.–Thurs. 10–6, Fri. 10–2.*

Scheunenviertel (Barn Quarter), or Jüdisches Viertel (Jewish Quarter). The area to the northeast of the Neue Synagoge (☞ *above*) is known as the stable quarters, or Jewish quarter. During the second half of the

17th century, the Great Elector brought artisans, small businessmen, and Jews into the country to improve his financial situation. As industrialization intensified, the quarter became poorer, and in the 1880s many East European Jews escaping pogroms settled here. By the 20th century the quarter had a number of bars, stores, and small businesses frequented by gamblers, prostitutes, and the poor. The Nazis deliberately used the presence of these undesirables to stigmatize the middle-class Jewish families living there.

Palaces, Parks, and Museums in Outer Berlin

The city's outlying areas abound with palaces, lakes, and museums set in lush greenery. To the west, the Charlottenburg district, once an independent and wealthy city that only became a part of Berlin in 1920, boasts the baroque Charlottenburg Palace. The vast Grunewald (forest) covers most of southwestern Berlin; it's an ideal spot for hiking or for relaxing on one of the lake's islands. Some of the city's most intriguing museums are found in the well-to-do neighborhood of Dahlem. To the north, however, in the town of Oranienburg, stands a grim reminder of German history: the former Sachsenhausen concentration camp, now a museum and memorial complex.

A Good Tour

Begin at the museums of **Schloss Charlottenburg** ㊺, the adjacent **Ägyptisches Museum** ㊻, and the **Sammlung Berggruen** ㊼. To reach Schloss Charlottenburg, take the U–2 subway in the direction of Ruhleben. Get off at the Bismarckstrasse stop and then take the U–7 in the direction of Rathaus Spandau to Richard-Wagner-Platz. From here walk northwest on Otto-Suher-Allee toward the dome of the palace. (From Zoologischer Garten the total U-bahn ride takes about 20 minutes.)

Your next stop should be the two **Dahlem Museums** ㊽, which lie south of the Charlottenburg district in the neighborhood of Dahlem. The best way to get there is by the U–1 in the direction of Krumme Lanke to Dahlem-Dorf station. To reach the Dahlem Museums from Schloss Charlottenburg, walk to Richard-Wagner-Platz station and ride the U–7 in the direction of Rudow until you reach the stop Fehrbelliner Platz. Change trains here and take U–1 to Dahlem-Dorf. The trip from the palace to the museums takes about 45 minutes.

After either the Charlottenburg or Dahlem Museums, it's time for the great outdoors. From the Dahlem Museums it's a short ride on the U–1 to the Krumme Lanke station. Change trains at the suburban railway station at nearby Mexikoplatz and take a ride on the S-bahn No. 1 (in the direction of Wannsee) to the Nikolassee or Wannsee stations. If you want to continue to the Grunewald station, change trains and take S-bahn 7 (in the direction of Friedrichstrasse). Each of these stations serves as a starting point for hour-long hikes through the greenbelt of the **Grunewald** ㊾ and Wannsee lakes with the **Pfaueninsel** ㊿ and its romantic small palace. A grim reminder of the area's past is the **Bildungs- und Gedenkstätte Haus der Wannsee-Konferenz** (51), an old villa where the Holocaust was planned. You can reach the Pfaueninsel by taking Bus A16 or 316; the Wannsee Conference House can be reached on Bus 114. All buses depart from the Wannsee S-bahn station.

Finally, you can make a trip to Sachsenhausen, 35 km (22 mi) north of Berlin, where you'll find the **Sachsenhausen Gedenkstätte** (52), the only Nazi concentration camp near Berlin. To reach Sachsenhausen, take the S-bahn 1 from Friedrichstrasse to Oranienburg, the last stop. The ride will take 45 to 50 minutes. From the station it's a 25-minute walk, or you can take a taxi.

TIMING

To take in all the attractions above, you will need at least one full day, with the morning devoted to Schloss Charlottenburg and the Dahlem Museums and the rest of the day for the Grunewald area. It takes about three hours to detour and visit Oranienburg. If you skip the museums at Schloss Charlottenburg and Dahlem, you will still need a full day to visit the other places.

Sights to See

★ ㊻ **Ägyptisches Museum** (Egyptian Museum). The former east guardhouse and residence of the Prussian king Friedrich I's bodyguard is now home to the exquisite portrait bust of **Queen Nefertiti.** The 3,300-year-old sculpture of the Egyptian queen is the centerpiece of a collection of works that traces Egypt's history from 4000 BC and includes some of the best-preserved mummies outside Cairo. The museum is across from ☞ Schloss Charlottenburg. ✉ *Schlossstr. 70,* ☎ *030/320–911.* 🎫 *DM 8.* ⏲ *Tues.–Fri. 10–6, weekends 11–6.*

(51) **Bildungs- und Gedenkstätte Haus der Wannsee-Konferenz** (Wannsee Conference Memorial Site). The lovely setting of this typical Berlin villa belies the unimaginable Holocaust atrocities planned here. This elegant edifice hosted the fateful conference held on January, 20, 1942, at which Nazi leaders and German bureaucrats under SS leader Reinhard Heydrich planned the systematic deportation and mass extinction of Europe's Jewish population. Today this so-called *Endlösung der Judenfrage* ("final solution of the Jewish question") is illustrated in the villa in a small exhibition that documents the conference, its results, and the history of the house itself. ✉ *Am Grossen Wannsee 56–58,* ☎ *030/805–0010.* 🎫 *Free.* ⏲ *Weekdays 10–6, weekends 2–6; library weekdays 10–6.*

㊽ **Dahlem Museums.** This complex of four museums includes the **Ethnologisches Museum** (Ethnographic Museum) as well as museums for Indian, East Asian, and early European art. It is internationally known for its art and artifacts from Africa, Asia, the South Seas, and the Americas. The large collection of Maya, Aztec, and Incan ceramics and stone sculptures should not be missed. ✉ *Lansstr. 8,* ☎ *030/83011.* 🎫 *DM 4; free 1st Sun. of every month.* ⏲ *Tues.–Fri. 9–6, weekends 11–6.*

㊾ **Grunewald.** Together with its Wannsee lakes, this splendid forest is the most popular green retreat for Berliners. In good weather Berliners come out in force, swimming, sailing their boats, tramping through the woods, and riding horseback. In winter a downhill ski run and even a ski jump operate on the modest slopes of Teufelsberg Hill. Excursion steamers ply the water wonderland of the Wannsee and the Havel River (☞ Guided Tours *in* Berlin A to Z, *below*).

★ ㊿ **Pfaueninsel** (Peacock Island). The Pfaueninsel is a small oasis which served as a romantic hideaway for Prussian king Friedrich Wilhelm II and his mistresses. **Schloss Pfaueninsel,** the ruinlike small palace on the island in the Great Wannsee, was erected in 1794 according to the ruler's plans and—in accordance the taste of his era—was built as a fake ruin. In the early 19th century garden architect Joseph Peter Lenné designed an English garden on the island, which ultimately became western Berlin's favorite summer retreat. ✉ *Pfaueninselchaussee,* ☎ *030/805–3042.* 🎫 *DM 2.* ⏲ *Daily 10–4.*

(52) **Sachsenhausen Gedenkstätte** (Sachsenhausen Memorial). The only Nazi concentration camp near the Third Reich capital was established in 1936, later becoming a Soviet internment and prison camp for German soldiers. In 1961 the camp was made into a memorial to its more than 100,000 victims. The area has a few preserved facilities and bar-

racks, as well as a memorial and museum. ✉ *Str. der Nationen 22, Oranienburg,* ☎ *03301/803–719.* ✆ *Free.* ☉ *Apr.–Sept., daily 8:30– 6; Oct.–Mar., daily 9–4:30 (last admission 30 mins before closing).*

★ ㊼ **Sammlung Berggruen** (Berggruen Collection). This small museum in the historic Stüler-Bau (once a museum of ancient art) focuses on the history of modern art, with representative work from such artists as Van Gogh and Cézanne, Picasso, Giacometti, Klee, and more contemporary artists. Heinz Berggruen, a businessman who emigrated to the United States in the 1930s, collected the excellent paintings on display. Opened in 1996, this intimate museum has become one of Berlin's most beloved art venues. ✉ *Schlosstr. 1,* ☎ *030/326–9580.* ✆ *DM 8.* ☉ *Tues.–Fri. 9–6, weekends 11–6.* ✎

㊺ **Schloss Charlottenburg** (Charlottenburg Palace). This showplace of western Berlin, the most monumental reminder of imperial days, served as a city residence for the Prussian rulers. You can easily spend a full day here. The gorgeous palace started as a modest royal summer residence in 1695, built on the orders of King Friedrich I for his wife, Sophie-Charlotte. In the 18th century Frederick the Great made a number of additions, such as the dome and several wings designed in the rococo style. By 1790 the complex had evolved into the massive royal domain you see today. Behind heavy iron gates the Court of Honor—the front courtyard—is dominated by a fine baroque statue of the Great Elector on horseback.

The **Altes Schloss** is the main building with the suites of Friedrich I and his wife. Paintings include royal portraits by Antoine Pesne, a noted court painter of the 18th century. On the first floor you can visit the Oak Gallery, the early 18th-century palace chapel, and the suites of Friedrich Wilhelm II and Friedrich Wilhelm III, furnished in the Biedermeier style.

The **Neuer Flügel** (New Wing; ✆ DM 5; ☉ Tues.–Fri. 10–6, weekends 11–6), where Frederick the Great once lived, is also called the Knobbeldorff-Flügel. It showcases the 138-ft-long **Goldene Galerie** (Golden Gallery), the palace's ballroom. West of the staircase are the rooms of Frederick, in which the king's extravagant collection of works by Watteau, Chardin, and Pesne are displayed. Visits to the royal apartments are by guided tour only; tours leave every hour on the hour from 9 to 4.

Also in the Neuer Flügel is the **Galerie der Romantik** (Gallery of Romanticism), the National Gallery's collection of masterpieces from such 19th-century German painters as Karl Friedrich Schinkel and Caspar David Friedrich, the leading members of the German Romantic school.

The park behind the palace was laid out in the French baroque style beginning in 1697 and was transformed into an English garden in the early 19th century. In it stand the **Belvedere teahouse** (☎ 030/320–911; ✆ DM 4; ☉ Tues.–Fri. 9–6, weekends 11–6), overlooking the lake and the Spree River and housing a collection of Berlin porcelain, and the Schinkel Pavilion.

The **Museum für Vor- und Frühgeschichte** (Museum of Pre- and Early History; ☎ 030/3267–4840; ✆ DM 4; free 1st Sun. of month; ☉ weekdays 10–6, weekends 11–6) traces the evolution of mankind from 1 million BC to the Bronze Age. It's in the western extension of the palace opposite Klausener Platz. ✉ *Luisenpl.,* ☎ *030/3209–1275.* ✆ *Altes Schloss DM 10. A Tageskarte (day card) for DM 15 covers the admission for all bldgs. and exhibits.* ☉ *Altes Schloss: Tues.–Thurs. 9–5, Fri. 9– 5, weekends 11–6.*

DINING

CATEGORY	COST*
$$$$	over DM 100
$$$	DM 75–DM 100
$$	DM 50–DM 75
$	under DM 50

*per person for a three-course meal, including tax and service, excluding drinks

Charlottenburg

$$$$ ✕ **Alt-Luxemburg.** This popular restaurant is tastefully furnished, and
★   attentive service enhances the intimate setting. Chef Karl Wannemacher uses only the freshest ingredients for his nouvelle German dishes, including his divine lobster lasagna. ⊠ *Windscheidstr. 31,* ☎ *030/323–8730. AE, DC, V. Closed Sun.*

$$$ ✕ **Ana e Bruno.** A Berlin classic with consistently high-quality offerings,
★   this Italian restaurant is expensive but rewards the patron with a warm and homey atmosphere thanks to the heartfelt hospitality of the owners Bruno and his wife, Ana. Don't expect hearty Italian home cooking, though: the chef values a low-calorie reinterpretation of Mediterranean cuisine and prefers fresh vegetables and salads over pasta. The four-course meals and daily specials are good value. ⊠ *Sophie-Charlotten-Str. 101,* ☎ *030/3257–110. Reservations essential. AE. Closed Sun. and Mon.*

$$$ ✕ **Mensa.** Contrary to all trends, this is one of the few new restaurants
★   to be opened in the west part of town, and it's packed on weekends. The name ("Mensa," meaning the student refectories) is something of a joke since the cuisine here has nothing in common with cafeterias. Instead, it serves inventive nouvelle cuisine with an emphasis on light fish, beef, or veal dishes. The wine and dessert list is extraordinary, with vintages and recipes from all over the world. Chef Markus Semmler, former head chef of the Berlin Ritz-Carlton, has also opened a second restaurant, the Stil in Charlottenburg. In both restaurants, the service is outstanding and yet casual—something unheard of in Berlin's somewhat stiff and unfriendly service landscape. ⊠ *Lützowpl. 5,* ☎ *030/2579–9333. Reservations essential. AE, MC, V;* ⊠ *Stil, Kantstr. 17,* ☎ *030/315–1860. AE, MC, V.*

$$ ✕ **XII Apostel.** One of the nicest and liveliest Italian restaurants in Berlin, the XII Apostel should be avoided by the pious. The restaurant made its debut with 12 pizzas, one for each apostle of Jesus Christ—the biggest (and tastiest) is called the Judas. These and other pizzas are outstanding for their thin and crunchy crust; most people flock to this place, however, simply because it is hip. The colorful walls are reminiscent of Renaissance decorations in Italian churches. ⊠ *Bleibtreustr. 49,* ☎ *030/312–1433. No credit cards.*

Kreuzberg

$ ✕ **Grossbeerenkeller.** This cellar restaurant, with its massive, dark-oak
★   furniture and decorative antlers, is undoubtedly one of the most original dining spots in town. Its old-fashioned, warm Berlin hospitality is hard to find elsewhere. Owner and bartender Ingeborg Zinn-Baier presents such dishes as *Sülze vom Schweinekopf mit Bratkartoffeln und Remoulade* (diced pork with home fries and herb sauce), *Kasseler Nacken mit Grünkohl* (boiled salt pork meat with green cabbage), and other traditional Berlin meals. Her fried potatoes are said to be the best in town. ⊠ *Grossbeerenstr. 90,* ☎ *030/251–3064. No credit cards. Closed Sun. and holidays.*

Mitte

Dressler Unter den Linden (☞ Dressler, *in* Western Downtown, *below*).

$$$$ ✕ **VAU.** Trendsetter VAU ushered in the movement of expensive and
★ hip restaurants to the Mitte district a couple of years ago. The excellent German fish and game dishes prepared by Chef Kolja Kleeberg
might earn him a second Michelin star. Daring combinations include
Geschmorter Ochsenschwanz mit Trüffelkruste (braised oxtail wrapped
in truffles dough) and *Steinbutt mit Kalbbries auf Rotweinschalotten*
(turbot with veal sweet bread on shallots in red wine). The VAU's cool
interior is all style and modern art: it was designed by one of Germany's
leading industrial designers. ✉ *Jägerstr. 54/55,* ☎ *030/202–9730.*
Reservations essential. AE, DC, MC, V. Closed Sun.

$$$ ✕ **Borchardt.** This is one of the most fashionable of the celebrity meet-
★ ing places that have sprung up in the historic Mitte district. The high
ceiling, columns, red plush benches, and Art Nouveau mosaic (discov-
ered during renovations) create the impression of a 1920s café. The cui-
sine is high-quality French-Mediterranean, including several dishes with
fresh fish and veal, such as *Praline vom Steinbutt und Hummer im grü-
nen Reismantel* (fillet of stone flounder and lobster with green rice). ✉
Französische Str. 47, ☎ *030/2038–7110. Reservations essential. AE, V.*

$$$ ✕ **Ermelerhaus.** The Ermelerhaus offers two restaurants under one roof.
The more traditional Raabediele and its Tabaklounge offers good old
German cooking. The Ermelerhaus à la carte restaurant relies on an
exceptional mixture of Californian and Italian cuisine (with an accent
on seafood) to attract old and new patrons. Its lavishly decorated rococo Rosenzimmer is one of the nicest historic dinner settings in Berlin.
✉ *Märkisches Ufer 10,* ☎ *030/2406–2904. AE, DC, MC, V.*

$$$ ✕ **Kaiserstuben.** Next to the Pergamonmuseum, soft candlelight spills
★ onto the cobblestone street, inviting gourmets to make their way down
into the Kaisersuben's half-basement. The restaurant (German for
"Emperor's Parlor") serves ingeniously prepared cuisine that carefully
balances regional heritage with influences from all over the world. The
young chef Tim Raue, a rising star in Berlin's gourmet firmament, sur-
prises guests with constantly changing combinations such as *Gebratene
Gänseleber mit Rhabarber und grünem Pfeffer* (fried goose livers with
rhubarb and green pepper kernels). The wine list is one of the most
extensive in Berlin. This is the perfect place in Mitte to enjoy a meal
in a sophisticated yet cozy environment. ✉ *Am Kupfergraben 6a,* ☎
030/2045–2980. AE, MC, V. No dinner Sun.

$$ ✕ **Barist.** This elegant restaurant is typical of the hip nightlife scene in
the Mitte district. The Barist is a mixture of jazz bar, restaurant, and
pub, tucked away under the railroad viaducts. The food is not the biggest
attraction here, even though most dishes—an assortment of some Italian and French, but mostly Austrian recipes—are delicious: The Barist
is probably the best place in Berlin to enjoy a spicy and huge Wiener
schnitzel with the best potato salad you have ever tasted outside Vienna. On weekend nights a jazz singer and pianist entertain the artsy
crowd. If it's too noisy and giddy in the main room, a second, more
quiet room is reserved exclusively for dining. ✉ *Am Zwirngraben, S-
Bahnbögen 13–14,* ☎ *030/2472–2613. AE, MC, V.*

$$ ✕ **Die Möwe.** The Seagull name refers to East Berlin's famous artists'
club that is housed in the same building. The restaurant emphasizes
its affection for the arts: there's a piano player—rather unusual even
for the best German restaurants—and a special *Kunstgenuss* (art en-
joyment) dinner on Monday night, a two-course dinner created along
an artistic theme. The light German nouvelle cooking is very tasty, with
a tendency toward fish such as *Dialog von Meeresfrüchten auf Wild-
dreis,* a combination of perch, salmon, loup de mer on wild rice. ✉

Berlin Dining and Lodging

Dining

Alt-Luxemburg 3
Alt-Cöllner
Schankstuben 28
Ana e Bruno 2
Bamberger Reiter . . . 10
Barist 23
Blockhaus
Nikolskoe 4
Borchardt 19
Café Oren 21
Die Möwe 17

Diekmann im
Weihaus Huth 13
Dressler
Kurfürstendamm . . . 8
Dressler Unter
den Linden 15
Ermelerhaus 29
First Floor 11
Florian 7
Ganymed 16
Grossbeerenkeller . . 14
Hackescher Hof . . . 22
Kaiserstuben 18

Mensa 12
Paris Bar 9
Reinhard's
Nikolaiviertel 26
Reinhard's
Kurfürstendamm . . . 5
Rockendorf's 1
Schwarzenraben . . . 24
XII Apostel 6
VAU 20
Zur Letzten
Instanz 25
Zur Rippe 27

Lodging

Bristol Hotel
Kempinski 6
Charlottenberger
Hof 4
Dorint Hotel Berlin
Müggelsee 25
Econtel 1
Estrel Residence
Congress Hotel . . . 24
Forum Hotel
Berlin 19
Four Seasons Hotel
Berlin 21

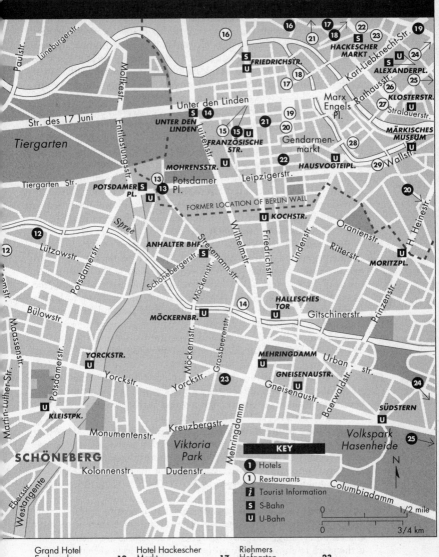

KEY

- **1** Hotels
- **1** Restaurants
- **i** Tourist Information
- **S** S-Bahn
- **U** U-Bahn

0 ——— 1/2 mile

0 ——— 3/4 km

Grand Hotel Esplanade **12**	Hotel Hackescher Markt **17**	Riehmers Hofgarten **23**
Grand Hyatt Berlin **13**	Hotel Palace **10**	Ritz-Carlton Schlosshotel **3**
Heinrich-Heine City-Suites **20**	Hotel-Pension Dittberner **5**	Steigenberger Berlin **9**
Hilton Berlin **22**	Hotel-Pension Kastanienhof **18**	Westin Grand Hotel **15**
Hotel Adlon Berlin **14**	Hotel-Pension Korfu II **8**	
Hotel am Scheunenviertel **16**	Inter-Continental Berlin **11**	
Hotel Astoria **7**	Landhaus Schlachtensee **2**	

Am Festungsgraben 1, at the Palais am Festungsgraben, ☎ *030/201–2029. AE, DC, MC, V. Closed Sun.*

$$ ✕ **Ganymed.** Ganymed has reappeared at its original location right next to the Brecht Ensemble theater, once again becoming a typical, though upscale, Berlin *Theaterkneipe,* a place to meet after the theater. The food served on elegantly decorated tables is by and large French, with a smattering of regional fare such as spicy *Berliner Kartoffelsuppe* (potato soup). Still, the food—tasty as it is—does not play the main role here: most people join actors and other theater lovers for a good glass of wine from an extensive list. ✉ *Schiffbauerdamm 5,* ☎ *030/2859–9046. AE, MC, V.*

$$ ✕ **Hackescher Hof.** The restaurant's setting in the hopping Hackesche Höfe makes it without question one of the most *in* restaurants in the Mitte district and a great place to experience the upswing in the old East. With oversize industrial lamps, the large, high-ceilinged rooms have an urban and breathless atmosphere. The food is a mixture of international nouvelle cuisine and beefy German cooking—there is also a special dinner menu with more refined dishes. Reservations are advised. ✉ *Rosenthaler Str. 40/41,* ☎ *030/283–5293. AE, MC, V.*

$$ ✕ **Reinhard's.** In the Nikolai Quarter, friends meet here to enjoy the carefully prepared entrées and to sample spirits from the amply stocked bar, all served by friendly, colorful tie–wearing waiters. The honey-glazed breast of duck, *Adlon,* is one its specialties. If you just want to hug the bar but find no room, don't despair; head two doors down to Italian Otello (under the same management). Reinhard's second restaurant on Ku'damm is much smaller but more elegant, and one of the trendiest places in town. Both the menu and prices are the same. ✉ *Poststr. 28,* ☎ *030/242–5295;* ✉ *Kurfürstendamm 190,* ☎ *030/881–1621. Reservations essential. AE, DC, MC, V.*

$$ ✕ **Zur Rippe.** This popular place in the Nikolai Quarter serves wholesome food in an intimate setting with oak paneling and ceramic tiles. Specialties include the cheese platter and a herring casserole. ✉ *Poststr. 17,* ☎ *030/242–4248. AE, DC, MC, V.*

$ ✕ **Alt-Cöllner Schankstuben.** A tiny restaurant and pub reside within this charming, historic Berlin house. The section to the side of the canal on the Kleine Gertraudenstrasse, where there are tables set outside, serves as a café. The menu is relatively limited, but the quality—like the service—is good. ✉ *Friederichsgracht 50,* ☎ *030/201–1299. Reservations not accepted. AE, DC, MC, V.*

$ ✕ **Café Oren.** This popular vegetarian eatery is next to the Neue Synagoge on Oranienburger Strasse. The restaurant buzzes with loud chatter all evening, and the atmosphere and service are friendly. This is the place to enjoy traditional Jewish cooking, long absent from the old Jewish quarter of Berlin. Try the gefilte fish, a tasty (and very salty) German-Jewish dish, or *Baichsaibling in schämender Butter* (red-meat trout in hot butter). The small backyard is a wonderful spot to enjoy a cool summer evening or a warm autumn afternoon. ✉ *Oranienburger Str. 28,* ☎ *030/282–8228. AE, MC, V.*

$ ✕ **Zur Letzten Instanz.** Established in 1621, Berlin's oldest restaurant
★ combines the charming atmosphere of old Berlin with a limited (but very tasty) menu. Napoléon is said to have sat alongside the tile stove in the front room, and Mikhail Gorbachev enjoyed a beer here during a visit in 1989. The emphasis is on beer, both in the recipes and in the mugs. Service can be erratic, though always engagingly friendly. ✉ *Waisenstr. 14–16,* ☎ *030/242–5528. AE, DC, MC, V.*

Prenzlauer Berg

$$ ✕ **Schwarzenraben.** No other restaurant in Berlin exemplifies the ar-
★ rival of the New East better than the Schwarzenraben. At its white-

clothed tables, uncomfortably squeezed together in a long, narrow room, the rich and beautiful of the new metropolis gather to enjoy their success. The atmosphere is noisy and not very elegant. The cooking lets you discover new Italian recipes such as Milanese veal hocks. ⊠ *Neue Schönhauser Str. 13,* ☎ *030/2839–1698. Reservations essential. AE, DC, MC, V.*

Reinickendorf

$$$$ ✕ **Rockendorf's.** Berlin's premier restaurant only has prix-fixe menus, some with up to nine courses. Exquisitely presented on fine porcelain, the mainly nouvelle specialties are sometimes fused with classic German cuisine. The wine list—with 800 choices, one of the world's best—has the appropriate accompaniment to any menu. The closest S-bahn station is Waidmannslust. Rockendorf's will probably move to the Kurfürstendamm neighborhood in 2001, so call ahead. ⊠ *Düsterhauptstr. 1,* ☎ *030/402–3099. Reservations essential. AE, DC, MC, V. Closed Sun. and Mon., Dec. 25–Jan. 6, and 3–4 wks in summer.*

Schöneberg

$$$$ ✕ **Bamberger Reiter.** One of the city's leading restaurants, the Bamberger Reiter is now presided over by chef Christoph Fischer from Freiburg. Like his famous predecessor, Franz Raneburger, he relies on fresh market produce for his *Neue Deutsche Küche* (new German cuisine), but adds a more international touch. The menu changes daily. ⊠ *Regensburgerstr. 7,* ☎ *030/218–4282. Reservations essential. AE, MC, V. Closed Sun., Mon., and Jan. 1–15. No lunch.*

$$$$ ✕ **First Floor.** This newcomer to Europe's firmament of Michelin stars
★ is a German exception, as only a few hotel-restaurants are so outstanding that they become a sensation. It is even more unusual that Chef Matthias Buchholz succeeds with traditional German fare, and not with the typical menu of light nouvelle cuisine. The menu changes according to the season and the chef's moods, but most of the dishes are new interpretations of heavy German dishes such as *Geschnetzelte Ochsenbacke in Rotweinsauce an Mark-Nockerln* (sliced ox cheeks in red wine sauce, served with Bavarian noodles). ⊠ *Hotel Palace, Budapester Str. 42,* ☎ *030/2502–1020. Reservations essential. AE, DC, MC, V. No lunch Sat.*

Tiergarten

$$ ✕ **Diekmann im Weinhaus Huth.** The new Dieckmann is a fascinating place to eat, not so much for the ordinary French cooking, but for its location. The old Weinhaus Huth once was the last building standing in the no-man's-land of Potsdamer Platz. Now it's surrounded by the shiny new company headquarters of Sony and debis. The service is smooth and friendly, the interior tries to imitate a Paris bistro but lacks some warmth. It's a more inexpensive, more casual alternative to Borchardt (☞ *above*). One outstanding exception on the reliable menu are the fresh oysters, which are less expensive than elsewhere in Berlin. ⊠ *Alte Potsdamer Str. 5,* ☎ *030/2529–7524. MC, V.*

Western Downtown

$$$ ✕ **Dressler.** Both in its cuisine and in its service, the Dressler is a mixture of French brasserie culture and German down-to-earth reliability. Accordingly, the dishes are conceived for a wide range of palates: duck with red cabbage or cod with Pommery mustard sauce, for example. The menu changes according to season. Compared to other French restaurants in Germany, the Dressler's *plateaux de fruits de mer* with oysters, lobster, and clams is a good value and beautiful to behold as well. Of the two (very similar) Dressler establishments, the one on Kurfürstendamm is livelier, with a genuinely French atmosphere. Reservations are advised. ⊠ *Kurfürstendamm 207/208,* ☎ *030/883– 3530;* ⊠ *Unter den Linden 39,* ☎ *030/204–4422. AE, DC, MC, V.*

$$$ ✗ **Paris Bar.** Just off the Ku'damm, this trendy restaurant attracts a polyglot clientele of film stars, artists, entrepreneurs, and executives who care more for glamour than gourmet food. The cuisine, including such delights as Jacques oysters and lamb chops with Provençal herbs, is reliable French cooking. ⊠ *Kantstr. 152,* ☎ *030/313–8052. AE.*

$$ ✗ **Florian.** In a big city like Berlin, the idea of creating a series of dishes
★ based on down-home Swabian cuisine might have seemed a joke were there not so many successful Swabians in Berlin. Florian turned out to be one of the most popular restaurants in town. The food, a high-gear combination of Swabian cuisine with a slight French accent, is only one of this intimate little place's draws: most people come for the warm, relaxed atmosphere and to watch the writers, artists, and film people that congregate here. ⊠ *Grolmanstr. 52,* ☎ *030/313–9184. Reservations essential. No credit cards.*
Reinhard's (☞ Mitte, *above.*)

Zehlendorf

$$ ✗ **Blockhaus Nikolskoe.** Prussian king Frederick Wilhelm III built this Russian-style wooden lodge for his daughter Charlotte, wife of Russian czar Nicholas I. South of the city, in Glienecker Park, it offers open-air, riverside dining in summer. Game dishes are prominently featured. Wannsee is the closest S-bahn station. ⊠ *Nikolskoer Weg 15,* ☎ *030/ 805–2914. DC, MC, V. Closed Thurs.*

LODGING

As a European metropolis, Berlin attracts all major international first-class hotel chains. These modern luxury resorts are but a faint reminiscence of the prewar past, when Berlin was considered Europe's finest lodging capital. Elegance and style were bombed to rubble during World War II, and only a few native havens were rebuilt. Moderately priced pensions and small hotels offering good value are common in western districts like Charlottenburg, Schöneberg, or Wilmersdorf; many of them date from the turn of the century, preserving some traditional character.

Year-round business conventions and the influx of summer tourists mean you should make reservations well in advance. If you arrive without reservations, consult hotel boards at airports and train stations, which show hotels with vacancies; or go to the tourist offices at Tegel Airport, at the Hauptbahnhof or Zoologischer Garten train stations, or in the Europa Center for help with reservations (☞ Contacts and Resources *in* Berlin A to Z, *below*).

CATEGORY	COST*
$$$$	over DM 350
$$$	DM 200–DM 350
$$	DM 150–DM 200
$	under DM 150

All prices are for two people in a double room, including tax and service.

Charlottenburg

$$ 🏨 **Econtel.** This family-oriented hotel is within walking distance of Charlottenburg Palace. The spotless rooms have a homey feel and provide

closet safes and cable TV; some have a minibar. Family rooms have four beds and are especially decorated for kids. A crib, bottle warmer, and kiddie toilet are available on request free of charge. The breakfast buffet provides a dazzling array of choices to fill you up for a day of sightseeing. ✉ *Sömmeringstr. 24–26, D–10589,* ☏ *030/346–810,* FAX *030/3468–1163. 205 rooms. Restaurant, bar, in-room safes, no-smoking rooms, baby-sitting, dry cleaning, laundry service. AE, MC, V.*

$–$$
★ 🏨 **Charlottenburger Hof.** A convenient location across from the Charlottenburg S-bahn station and low rates make this low-key hotel a great value for no-fuss travelers. Kandinsky, Miró, and Mondrian are the muses here; their prints and primary color schemes inspire the rooms and common spaces. Rooms are individually designed and crafted by the staff, and their variety can suit travelers from friends to couples to families. Whether facing the street or the courtyard, all rooms receive good light; room amenities include TVs and hair dryers. The 24-hour café serves healthy dishes and is patronized by locals. The Ku'damm is a 10-minute walk, taxis are easy to catch at the S-bahn station, and the bus to and from Tegel Airport stops a block away. ✉ *Stuttgarter Pl. 14, D–10627,* ☏ *030/329–070,* FAX *030/323–3723. 46 rooms. Restaurant, lounge, in-room safes, no-smoking rooms, coin laundry, laundry service, parking (fee). MC, V.*

Köpenick

$$
🏨 **Dorint Hotel Berlin Müggelsee.** Berlin's largest and some say most beautiful lake in the southeastern outskirts is just beyond your balcony at this reliable and more efficient than friendly hotel. The rooms are renovated, comfortable, and fairly spacious. Each of the hotel's three floors features a different style; rooms on the ground floor are furnished with heavy, dark German woods; the second floor has an Italian accent (with elegant cherrywood furniture); and the third floor is reminiscent of a Japanese house. ✉ *Am Grossen Müggelsee, D–12559,* ☏ *030/658–820,* FAX *030/6588–2263. 172 rooms, 4 suites. Restaurant, bar, in-room data ports, no-smoking rooms, room service, beauty salon, massage, sauna, tennis court, health club, dry cleaning, laundry service, convention center, meeting rooms, free parking. AE, DC, MC, V.*

Mitte

$$$$
★ 🏨 **Four Seasons Hotel Berlin.** One of the best hotels in town, the Four Seasons combines turn-of-the-century luxury (reminiscent of the *Grand Hotel* of Vicki Baum's novel) with smooth, up-to-date services like portable phones and fax machines for the weary business traveler. The large guest rooms have first-class amenities, including free newspapers, overnight dry cleaning, and valet parking. Behind the modern facade, thick red carpets, heavy crystal chandeliers, and a romantic restaurant, complete with an open fireplace, create a sophisticated and serene atmosphere. ✉ *Charlottenstr. 49, D–10117,* ☏ *030/20338,* FAX *030/2033–6166. 162 rooms, 42 suites. Restaurant, bar, minibars, in-room data ports, no-smoking rooms, room service, massage, sauna, exercise room, baby-sitting, dry cleaning, laundry service, concierge, business services, meeting rooms, parking (fee). AE, DC, MC, V.*

$$$$
★ 🏨 **Grand Hyatt Berlin.** Europe's first Grand Hyatt is probably also the most modern first-class hotel on the continent. The hotel's minimalist-style yet elegant architecture is a mix of Japanese and Bauhaus design elements. Situated in the new center of Berlin, the establishment offers large guest rooms (they start at 406 square ft) featuring dark cherrywood furniture and marble bathrooms (accessed through Asian-style sliding doors). The gym and swimming pool on the top floor have a wonderful view of Berlin's skyline. The Regency Club floor provides

special services geared toward businesspeople. The hotel's Vox restaurant serves international and Asian cuisine; it whets the appetite with a "show kitchen," where you can watch the chef preparing your dinner. ☒ *Marlene-Dietrich-Pl. 2, D–10785,* ☎ *030/2553–1234,* FAX *030/2553–1235. 327 rooms, 15 suites. Restaurant, café, bar, in-room data ports, in-room safes, minibars, no-smoking floors, room service, indoor pool, massage, sauna, exercise room, baby-sitting, dry cleaning, laundry service, concierge, business services, meeting rooms, parking (fee). AE, DC, MC, V.* ☺

$$$$ 🖫 **Hilton Berlin.** All the right touches are here, from heated bathtubs to special rooms for businesswomen and travelers with disabilities. An executive floor offers a private lounge, free breakfast, late check-in, and larger rooms. It is also one of the few German first-class hotels offering discounts for parents traveling with children and teenagers. The Hilton overlooks the Gendarmenmarkt and the German and French cathedrals, as well as the classic Schauspielhaus. ☒ *Mohrenstr. 30, D–10117,* ☎ *030/20230,* FAX *030/2023–4269. 454 rooms, 46 suites. 3 restaurants, 2 bars, cafeteria, 2 pubs, in-room data ports, minibars, no-smoking rooms, room service, indoor pool, massage, sauna, exercise room, dance club, baby-sitting, dry cleaning, laundry service, concierge, business services, meeting rooms, parking (fee). AE, DC, MC, V.* ☺

$$$$ 🖫 **Hotel Adlon Berlin.** Berlin's premiere hotel lives up to its almost myth-
★   ical predecessor, the old Hotel Adlon, which, until its destruction during the war, was considered to be Europe's ultimate luxury resort, hosting the likes of Kaiser Wilhelm II and Greta Garbo. These days, the Adlon has become the unofficial guest house of the German government. The lobby is large and light, thanks to its creamy marble and limestone and a stained-glass cupola. The dark blue, garnet, and ocher color scheme continues in the guest rooms. All are identically furnished in 1920s style with cherrywood trim, myrtle-wood furnishings, and elegant bathrooms in black marble. The more expensive rooms overlook the Brandenburger Tor. ☒ *Unter den Linden 77, D–10117,* ☎ *030/22610,* FAX *030/2261–2222. 337 rooms, 82 suites. 2 restaurants, 2 bars, café, in-room data ports, in-room safes, minibars, no-smoking floors, room service, indoor pool, beauty salon, massage, sauna, health club, shops, baby-sitting, dry cleaning, laundry service, concierge, business services, meeting rooms, parking (fee). AE, DC, MC, V.* ☺

$$$ 🖫 **Forum Hotel Berlin.** With its 40 stories, this hotel (owned by Inter-Continental) at the top of Alexanderplatz competes with the nearby TV tower for the title of tallest downtown landmark. As one of the city's largest hotels, it is understandably less personal, at times even unfriendly. When booking, ask for a newly decorated room. Its casino is the highest in Europe and is open until 3 AM. ☒ *Alexanderpl. 8, D–10178,* ☎ *030/23890,* FAX *030/2389–4311. 945 rooms, 12 suites. 3 restaurants, 2 bars, in-room data ports, minibars, no-smoking floors, room service, massage, sauna, exercise room, casino, baby-sitting, dry cleaning, laundry service, concierge, business services, parking (fee). AE, DC, MC, V.* ☺

$$$ 🖫 **Westin Grand Hotel.** Since the takeover of former East Berlin's top hotel by the Westin Hotel Group in 1997, the Grand Hotel on historic Friedrichstrasse has undergone several major modernizations. The neoclassical pink-marble lobby, with its soaring six-story atrium, has polished brass accents, stuccowork, and richly decorated wallpaper. Standard rooms are tastefully decorated in muted tones; bathrooms have large tubs. The service sometimes lacks a genuine first-class approach, but the setting and architecture of this grand hotel make it a preferred choice among American travelers. ☒ *Friedrichstr. 158–164, D–10117,* ☎ *030/20270,* FAX *030/2027–3419. 358 rooms, 35 suites. 2 restaurants, bar, lobby lounge, in-room data ports, minibars, no-smok-*

ing floors, room service, indoor pool, barbershop, beauty salon, hot tub, sauna, steam room, shops, baby-sitting, children's programs, dry cleaning and laundry service, concierge, business services, convention center, meeting rooms, parking (fee). AE, DC, MC, V. ✈

$$ ⊞ **Heinrich-Heine City-Suites.** Named after rebellious German poet Heinrich Heine, this new apartment hotel close to the historic Nikolai Quarter primarily caters to business travelers on an extended stay. Even if you only want to spend a couple of days, the Heinrich Heine's junior suites are one of the best deals in town. All rooms are tastefully decorated with timeless furniture and have a full kitchen as well a mini-office. The hotel offers a wide variety of extra services, including a newspaper and fresh German rolls every morning. ⊠ *Heinrich-Heine-Pl. 11, D–10179,* ☎ *030/278–040,* 𝔽𝔸𝕏 *030/2780–4780. 38 apartments. Breakfast room, kitchenettes, no-smoking rooms, room service, concierge, parking (fee). AE, DC, MC, V.*

$$ ⊞ **Hotel Hackescher Markt.** Not far from the nightlife around the Hackescher Markt and Rosenthaler Platz, this newly built hotel provides discreet and inexpensive service. Unlike those of many older hotels in eastern Berlin, guest rooms here are spacious and light and nicely furnished with bright pine furniture in rustic style. You can enjoy a coffee in the small courtyard in summer. The staff is quite friendly and attentive. The price is right, and it's a great location for travelers primarily interested in the historic sights in eastern Berlin. ⊠ *Grosse Präsidentenstr. 8, D–10178,* ☎ *030/280–030,* 𝔽𝔸𝕏 *030/2800–3111. 28 rooms, 3 suites. Bar, in-room data ports, in-room safes, minibars, no-smoking rooms, room service, baby-sitting, dry cleaning, laundry service, parking (fee). AE, DC, MC, V.*

$$ ⊞ **Hotel-Pension Kastanienhof.** This small hotel in a 19th-century ten-
★ ement house represents the working-class counterpart to the more luxurious pensions in the western part of Berlin. The rooms are spacious but simply furnished: functionality is the point rather than antique authenticity. All rooms are equipped with amenities usually found only in first-class hotels. The Kastanienhof is an excellent deal for those bent on exploring the new eastern Berlin and nightlife in Prenzlauer Berg and Mitte. ⊠ *Kastanienallee 65, D–10119,* ☎ *030/443–050,* 𝔽𝔸𝕏 *030/4430–5111. 34 rooms, 2 apartments. Bar, in-room safes, no-smoking rooms, dry cleaning, laundry service, meeting room, parking (fee). AE, DC, MC, V.*

$ ⊞ **Hotel am Scheunenviertel.** This simply furnished but well-kept small hotel is a good alternative to equally inexpensive pensions in western Berlin. It offers personal service, a wonderful breakfast buffet, and three restaurants (Mexican, Russian, and German) under one roof. The biggest advantage is its location in the old, eastern *Scheunenviertel* (Barn Quarter), the old Jewish neighborhood around the New Synagogue, which is only a few steps away. If you want to indulge in Berlin's hip nightlife, you'll be near the major cultural and entertainment hot spots. ⊠ *Oranienburger Str. 38, D–10117,* ☎ *030/282–2125,* 𝔽𝔸𝕏 *030/282–1115. 18 rooms with shower. 3 restaurants, dry cleaning, laundry service. AE, DC, MC, V.*

Neukölln

$$–$$$ ⊞ **Estrel Residence Congress Hotel.** Europe's biggest hotel may seem huge and anonymous, but it's the best deal in town for upscale rooms and service. The hotel is in the unappealing working-class district of Neukölln, some 20 minutes away from the downtown areas. But the modern hotel offers all amenities you can think of and guarantees quiet efficiency and smooth comfort at incredibly low prices. Rooms are decorated with Russian art. The lobby hall is a breathtakingly bright

atrium with water basins, plants, and huge trees. The festival center adjoining the hotel features musicals. ✉ *Sonnenallee 225, D–12057,* ☎ *030/68310,* 🖷 *030/6831–2346. 1,045 rooms, 80 suites. 5 restaurants, bar, lobby lounge, in-room data ports, minibars, no-smoking floors, beauty salon, sauna, exercise room, theater, baby-sitting, children's programs, dry cleaning, laundry service, concierge, business services, convention center, parking (fee). AE, DC, MC, V.* ♺

Schöneberg

$$$$ 🖥 **Grand Hotel Esplanade.** The Grand Hotel Esplanade exudes luxury in its uncompromisingly modern design, its stylish rooms, and its artworks by some of Berlin's most acclaimed artists. Many rooms on the upper floors have panoramic views of the city, though the furnishings, an homage to the cool Bauhaus style, may not be to everyone's taste. You'll appreciate superb facilities and impeccable service. The enormous grand suite comes complete with sauna, whirlpool, and a grand piano—for DM 2,600 per night. ✉ *Lützowufer 15, D–10785,* ☎ *030/254–780,* 🖷 *030/265–1171. 369 rooms, 33 suites. 3 restaurants, bar, lobby lounge, in-room data ports, minibars, no-smoking rooms, room service, indoor pool, hot tub, sauna, steam room, exercise room, shops, piano, baby-sitting, dry cleaning, laundry service, concierge, business services, convention center, meeting rooms, parking (fee). AE, DC, MC, V.* ♺

$$$ 🖥 **Riehmers Hofgarten.** The small Riehmers Hofgarten attracts an
★   atypical clientele. The hotel's rooms may be too spartan for many travelers, but they are modern, quiet, and functional. The Riehmers's true appeal comes from its location in an impressive, late-19th-century tenement house in the Kreuzberg district and in its special courtyard. The architecture, with its richly decorated facade, reminds you that 100 years ago the aristocratic officers of Germany's imperial army lived here. ✉ *Yorckstr. 83, D–10965,* ☎ *030/7809–8800,* 🖷 *030/7809–8808. 20 rooms. Restaurant, bar, no-smoking rooms, room service, dry cleaning and laundry service, parking (fee). AE, MC, V.* ♺

Western Downtown

$$$$ 🖥 **Bristol Hotel Kempinski.** Destroyed in the war and rebuilt in 1952, the "Kempi" is a renowned Berlin classic. On the Ku'damm, it has the best shopping at its doorstep and some fine boutiques of its own within. All rooms and suites are luxuriously decorated and have marble bathrooms and cable TV. Reserve a room in the "superior" category, which will give you all the elegance you'll need at a fair rate. Children under 12 stay for free if they share their parents' room. ✉ *Kurfürstendamm 27, D–10719,* ☎ *030/884–340,* 🖷 *030/883–6075. 301 rooms, 52 suites. 2 restaurants, bar, lobby lounge, in-room data ports, minibars, no-smoking rooms, room service, indoor pool, beauty salon, massage, sauna, exercise room, shops, baby-sitting, dry cleaning, laundry service, concierge, business services, meeting rooms, parking (fee). AE, DC, MC, V.* ♺

$$$$ 🖥 **Hotel Palace.** This is probably the most individualized luxury hotel
★   in town and the only first-class hotel directly in the heart of the western downtown area. Each room has its own design, color, and style. The interior is mostly done in dark blue or red colors and dark-color woods. The spacious business and corner suites are a good deal; you might also want to ask for the special Panda-Suite or the Zackebarsch-Suite, both personally designed by the hotel's directors. Due to its low-profile status in the city, it is also a favorite among international film stars who stay at the Palace during the Berlin Film Festival in February. ✉ *Europa-Center, Budapester Str. 26, D–10789,* ☎ *030/25020,*

FAX *030/2502–1197. 234 rooms, 48 suites. 3 restaurants, 2 bars, in-room data ports, in-room safes, minibars, no-smoking floors, room service, indoor-outdoor pool, barbershop, hot tub, massage, sauna, steam room, health club, shops, baby-sitting, dry cleaning, laundry service, concierge, business services, convention center, meeting rooms, parking (fee). AE, DC, MC, V.* ✍

$$$$ 🖫 **Inter-Continental Berlin.** Popular with American business travelers, the rooms and suites here are all of the highest standard, and their decor shows exquisite taste, with such refinements as luxuriously thick carpets and elegant bathrooms. The recently renovated east wing offers rooms with views of the vast Tiergarten Park. Service is efficient and smooth, but compared to hotels of similar quality, the atmosphere here is bland. ⊠ *Budapester Str. 2, D–10787,* ☎ *030/26020,* FAX *030/2602–1182. 510 rooms, 67 suites. 3 restaurants, bar, in-room data ports, minibars, no-smoking floors, room service, indoor pool, hot tub, sauna, exercise room, baby-sitting, dry cleaning, laundry service, concierge, business services, convention center, meeting rooms, parking (fee). AE, DC, MC, V.* ✍

$$$ 🖫 **Steigenberger Berlin.** The Steigenberger group's exemplary Berlin hotel is very central, only steps from the Ku'damm, but remarkably quiet. All rooms have stylish maple-wood furniture. The classy rooms of the Executive Club feature late check-in, complimentary ironing and shoe-shine service, a lounge, and a small breakfast. ⊠ *Los-Angeles-Pl. 1, D–10789,* ☎ *030/21270,* FAX *030/212–7799. 397 rooms, 11 suites. 2 restaurants, café, piano bar, in-room data ports, in-room safes, minibars, no-smoking floor, room service, indoor pool, massage, sauna, baby-sitting, dry cleaning, laundry service, concierge, meeting rooms, parking (fee). AE, DC, MC, V.* ✍

$$ 🖫 **Hotel Astoria.** This is one of the most traditional hotels in Berlin, and it shows. Privately owned and run, it provides every service with a personal touch. Rooms are spacious, though the 1980s furniture may seem outdated. The location is good for exploring the Ku'damm area, yet it's a quiet side street. The hotel offers weekend specials with discounts of DM 20 (single) or DM 70 (double) per night for a two-night stay. It also has several package deals for stays of up to six nights. ⊠ *Fasanenstr. 2, D–10623,* ☎ *030/312–4067,* FAX *030/312–5027. 31 rooms, 1 suite. Bar, minibars, in-room safes, no-smoking rooms, room service, dry cleaning, laundry service, parking (fee). AE, DC, MC, V.*

$$ 🖫 **Hotel-Pension Dittberner.** If you ever wanted to stay in a real Berlin
★ pension, this is the place to go. The Dittberner, close to Olivaer Platz and next to the Ku'damm, is a typical, family-run small hotel in an old turn-of-the-century house. Staying in a large room, walking through the endless floors, you might feel the glamour of Berlin's high society that once met here. The service sometimes may be a bit disorganized, and some of the furniture in the (now mostly renovated) rooms a little worn, but the warm atmosphere, breakfast buffet, and good rates more than make up for it. ⊠ *Wielandstr. 26, D–10707,* ☎ *030/884–6950,* FAX *030/885–4046. 22 rooms. Dry cleaning, laundry service, concierge, meeting room. No credit cards.*

$ **Hotel-Pension Korfu II.** This small pension on one of the quiet side streets off the Ku'damm is a modern, inexpensive, and comfortable alternative to small hotels. The Korfu II lacks the atmosphere that so many other smaller Berlin hotels still have, but the rooms, with their high ceilings and simple but functional furniture, are clean and well kept. Some of the double rooms are more modern and definitely more appealing, decorated with elegant black-and-white furniture. All rooms have a phone and color television. The breakfast buffet is included in the price—altogether a good deal. ⊠ *Rankestr. 35, D–10789,* ☎ *030/212–4790,* FAX *030/211–8432. 19 rooms. Parking (fee). AE, MC, V.*

Zehlendorf

$$$$ ⬚ **Ritz-Carlton Schlosshotel.** The small but extremely luxurious Schlosshotel, the city's most expensive hotel, has regained its reputation for first-class comfort after being taken over by the Ritz-Carlton hotel group. In the beautiful, verdant setting of the Grunewald, the palace-like hotel is full of classic style and is lavishly decorated. You might be reminded of a late 19th-century chateau. It was designed by Chanel's Karl Lagerfeld, who also completed a special suite for himself, which is made available to guests if the master himself is not staying in Berlin. The service is amazingly personal but never intruding. ⊠ *Brahmsstr. 10, D–14193,* ☎ *030/895–840,* 𝖥𝖠𝖷 *030/8958–4800. 54 rooms. Restaurant, bar, lobby lounge, in-room data ports, minibars, no-smoking rooms, room service, indoor pool, beauty salon, massage, sauna, exercise room, baby-sitting, dry cleaning, laundry service, concierge, business services, meeting rooms, parking (fee). AE, DC, MC, V.* ⬙

$$ ⬚ **Landhaus Schlachtensee.** This former villa is a cozy bed-and-breakfast offering personal and efficient service, well-equipped rooms, and a quiet location in the Zehlendorf district. The nearby Schlachtensee and Krumme Lanke lakes beckon you to swim, boat, or walk along their shores. ⊠ *Bogotastr. 9, D–14163,* ☎ *030/809–9470,* 𝖥𝖠𝖷 *030/8099– 4747. 20 rooms. Breakfast room, free parking. AE, MC, V.*

NIGHTLIFE AND THE ARTS

The Arts

Today's Berlin has a tough task living up to the reputation it gained from the film *Cabaret*. In the 1920s it was said that in Berlin, if you wanted to make a scandal in the theater, you had to have a mother committing incest with *two* sons; one wasn't enough. Even if nightlife has toned down since the 1920s and '30s, the arts and the avant-garde still flourish.

The **Berlin Festival Weeks,** held annually from August through September, include concerts, operas, ballet, theater, and art exhibitions. For information and reservations, write **Festspiele GmbH** (Kartenbüro, ⊠ Budapester Str. 50, D–10787 Berlin, ☎ 030/254–890, 𝖥𝖠𝖷 030/2548– 9111).

In addition to the many hotels that book seats, there are several ticket agencies, including **Showtime Konzert- und Theaterkassen** at KaDeWe (⊠ Tauentzienstr. 21, ☎ 030/217–7754) and Wertheim (⊠ Kurfürstendamm 181, ☎ 030/882–2500); and **Theater- und Konzertkasse City Center** (⊠ Kurfürstendamm 16, ☎ 030/882–6563). The **Hekticket office** (⊠ Karl-Liebknecht-Str. 12 and Zoo-Palast movie theater, ☎ 030/2431–2431 or 030/2309–930), at Alexanderplatz, offers discounted and last-minute tickets. Most of the big stores (Hertie, Wertheim, and Karstadt, for example) also have ticket agencies. Detailed information about what's going on in Berlin is covered in the *Berlin Programm,* a monthly tourist guide to Berlin arts, museums, and theaters; and the magazines *Prinz, tip,* and *zitty,* which appear every two weeks and provide full arts listings. For the latest information on Berlin's bustling house, techno, and hip-hop club scene, pick up a copy of *(030),* a free weekly flyer magazine. The only English-language magazine available is *Berlin–the magazine,* published four times a year by the city's tourist information center.

Concerts

Among the major symphony orchestras and orchestral ensembles in Berlin is one of the world's best, the Berliner Philharmonisches Orchester, which resides at the **Philharmonie mit Kammermusiksaal** (⊠ Matthäikircherstr. 1, ☏ 030/254–880 or 030/2548–8132). The Kammermusiksaal is dedicated to chamber music.

Grosser Sendesaal des SFB (⊠ Haus des Rundfunks, Masurenallee 8–14, ☏ 030/30310) is part of the Sender Freies Berlin, one of Berlin's broadcasting stations, and the home of the Radio Symphonic Orchestra. **Konzerthaus Berlin**'s (⊠ Schauspielhaus, Gendarmenmarkt, ☏ 030/2030–92101) beautifully restored hall is a prime venue for classical music concerts in historic Berlin. The concert hall of the **Hochschule der Künste** (University of Arts) (⊠ Hardenbergstr. 33, ☏ 030/3185–2374) is Berlin's second largest.

Waldbühne (⊠ Am Glockenturm, close to Olympic Stadium, ☏ 030/305–5079) is modeled after an ancient open-air Roman theater and accommodates nearly 20,000 people at opera, classical, or rock concerts.

Dance, Musicals, and Opera

Berlin's three opera houses each have their own ballet companies: the **Deutsche Oper Berlin** (⊠ Bismarckstr. 34–37, ☏ 030/3410–249 or 030/343–8401); the **Komische Oper** (⊠ Behrenstr. 55–57, ☏ 030/4799–7400 or 01805/304–168); and the **Staatsoper Unter den Linden** (⊠ Unter den Linden 7, ☏ 030/2035–4555), Germany's leading opera house. The **Neuköllner Oper** (⊠ Karl-Marx-Str. 131–133, ☏ 030/6889–0777) has showy, fun performances of long-forgotten operas as well as humorous musical productions.

For musicals such as *West Side Story, Shakespeare & Rock 'n' Roll, A Chorus Line,* and *Cabaret* (all translated into German), head for the **Estrel Festival Center** (⊠ Sonnenallee 225/Ziegrastr. 21–29, ☏ 030/6831–6831); the **Theater des Westens** (⊠ Kantstr. 12, ☏ 030/882–2888), Germany's leading musical theater; or the **Stella Musical Theater** (⊠ Marlene-Dietrich-Pl. 1, ☏ 01805–4444), which stages the *Hunchback of Notre-Dame.* The **Freie Volksbühne** (⊠ Schaperstr. 24, ☏ 030/882–2888) also shows musical guest productions both from Germany and the United States. Experimental and modern-dance performances are presented at **Podewil** (⊠ Klosterstr. 68–70, ☏ 030/2474–9777), **Tanzfabrik** (⊠ Möckernstr. 68, ☏ 030/786–5861), and the **Theater am Halleschen Ufer** (☞ Theater, *below*).

Film

Berlin has more than 100 movie theaters. International and German movies are shown in the big theaters around the Ku'damm; the off-Ku'damm theaters show less-commercial movies. For (undubbed) movies in English, go to the **Babylon** (⊠ Dresdnerstr. 126, ☏ 030/614–6316), the **Odeon** (⊠ Hauptstr. 116, ☏ 030/781–5667), or the **UFA Arthouse die Kurbel** (⊠ Giesebrechtstr. 4, ☏ 030/883–5325).

In February Berlin hosts the **Internationale Filmfestspiele,** an international festival at which the Golden Bear award is bestowed on the best films, directors, and actors. Call 030/254–890 for information.

Theater

Theater in Berlin is outstanding, but performances are usually in German. The exceptions are operettas and the (nonliterary) cabarets. Of the city's impressive number of theaters, the most renowned for both their modern and classical productions are the **Schaubühne am Lehniner Platz** (⊠ Kurfürstendamm 153, ☏ 030/890–023) and the **Deutsches Theater** (⊠ Schumannstr. 13, ☏ 030/2844–1222 or 030/2844–1225), which has an excellent studio theater next door, the **Kammerspiele** (☏ 030/2844–1226).

The **Berliner Ensemble** (⊠ Bertolt Brecht-Pl. 1, ☎ 030/282–3160) is dedicated to Brecht and works of other international playwrights. The **Hebbel Theater** (⊠ Stresemannstr. 29, ☎ 030/259–00427) showcases international theater and dance troupes. The **Maxim Gorki Theater** (⊠ Am Festungsgraben 2, ☎ 030/2022–1115) also has a superb studio theater. The **Renaissance-Theater** (⊠ Hardenbergstr. 6, ☎ 030/312–4202) shows German productions of international hit drama plays. The **Volksbühne am Rosa-Luxemburg-Platz** (⊠ Rosa-Luxemburg-Pl., ☎ 030/247–6772 or 030/2406–5661) is known for its radical interpretations of dramas. For **boulevard plays** (fashionable social comedies), try the **Hansa Theater** (⊠ Alt-Moabit 48, ☎ 030/391–4460), the **Komödie** (⊠ Kurfürstendamm 206, ☎ 030/4702–1010), and, at the same address, the **Theater am Kurfürstendamm** (☎ 030/4799–7440).

For smaller, more alternative theaters, which generally showcase guest productions, try **Theater am Halleschen Ufer** (⊠ Hallesches Ufer 32, ☎ 030/251–0941) or **Theater Zerbrochene Fenster** (⊠ Fidicinstr. 3, ☎ 030/6912–932).

Social and political satire has a long tradition in cabaret theaters here. The **BKA–Berliner Kabarett Anstalt** (⊠ Mehringdamm 34, ☎ 030/251–0112), **Die Wühlmäuse** (⊠ Nürnbergerstr. 33, ☎ 030/213–7047), and the **Stachelschweine** (⊠ Europa Center, Breitscheidpl., ☎ 030/261–4795) carry on that tradition with biting wit and style. Eastern Berlin's equivalent is the **Distel** (⊠ Friedrichstr. 101, ☎ 030/204–4704).

For children's theater head for the world-famous **Grips Theater** (⊠ Altonaer Str. 22, ☎ 030/391–4004) or **Hans Wurst Nachfahren** (⊠ Gleditschstr. 5, ☎ 030/216–7925). Both are nominally for children but can be good entertainment for adults as well.

For English-language theater try the **Friends of Italian Opera** (⊠ Fidicinstr. 40, ☎ 030/691–1211), presenting both classical British and American drama as well as modern productions.

Variety Shows

Berlin's variety shows can include magicians, circus performers, musicians, and classic cabaret stand-ups. Intimate and intellectually entertaining is the **Bar jeder Vernunft** (⊠ Spiegelzelt, Schaperstr. 24, ☎ 030/883–1582), whose name is a pun, literally meaning "devoid of any reason." The **Chamäleon Varieté** (⊠ Rosenthaler Str. 40/41, ☎ 030/282–7118) has risen to near stardom in the city's offbeat scene thanks to its extremely funny shows, and is fairly accessible to non-German speakers. The world's largest variety show takes place at the **Friedrichstadtpalast** (⊠ Friedrichstr. 107, ☎ 030/2326–2326), a glossy showcase for revues, famous for its female dancers. The new **Grüner Salon** (⊠ Freie Volksbühne, Rosa-Luxemburg-Pl., ☎ 030/2859–8936) is one of Berlin's hip venues for enjoying live music, cabaret, dancing, and drinks. The programs change almost daily. The **Wintergarten** (⊠ Potsdamer Str. 96, ☎ 030/2308–8230 or 030/2500–8863) pays romantic homage to the old days of Berlin's original variety theater in the 1920s.

Nightlife

In Berlin, as in most German big cities, the term "bar" connotes a somewhat upscale setting, where tall drinks and cocktails are served but not food or snacks. Most people frequent bars later in the evening, past 10 PM. Contrary to other German cities, Berlin pubs usually don't know a last call. Many of the places listed are open until the wee hours of the morning. Kneipen, by contrast, are more down-to-earth places and comparable to English pubs. Bartenders and servers expect a 2%–5% tip.

Bars

Bar am Lützowplatz (⊠ Am Lützowpl. 7, ☎ 030/262–6807). A Berlin classic, this fancy bar with the longest counter in town is a must for nighthawks. The bar attracts beautiful women, who sip American cocktails while flirting with the handsome bartenders.

Harry's New York Bar (⊠ Am Lützowufer 15, ☎ 030/2547–8821). The Grand Hotel Esplanade has probably the best lobby bar in town. It's also one of the few in the city that features live piano music. Businessmen try to relax under the portraits of American presidents and modern paintings on the walls.

Kumpelnest 3000 (⊠ Lützowstr. 23, ☎ 030/261–6918). Whether you think the red velvet walls make the place look like a brothel or not, it's still for kinky nightclubbers only, where a crowd of both gays and heteros mingle. Nobody really cares about the quality of the drinks, although the beer is good.

Newton (⊠ Charlottenstr. 57, ☎ 030/2061–2999). Via larger-than-life photos, nude women photographed by American Helmut Newton gaze out from the walls. This elegant bar is one of the stylish *in* places in the new Berlin.

Casinos

Spielbank Berlin (⊠ Marlene-Dietrich-Pl. 1, ☎ 030/255–990). Berlin's newest and leading casino on Potsdamer Platz, with roulette tables, three blackjack tables, and slot machines, stays open from 2 PM to 3 AM. The **Casino Berlin** is less fashionable and international but is worth a visit for its breathtaking location on top of the Forum Hotel at Alexanderplatz (⊠ Alexanderpl., ☎ 030/2389–4113).

Clubs

Blu (⊠ Marlene-Dietrich-Pl. 4, ☎ 030/8261–882). This new high-tech disco high above the Potsdamer Platz offers soul and funk music on three floors. The crowd is mixed—teenagers from East Berlin dance next to young managers. The view of the Berlin skyline is magnificent.

Golgatha (⊠ Dudenstr. 48–64, in Viktoriapark, ☎ 030/785–2453). Offering a beer garden, a pub, and a small dance floor, the Golgatha attracts a large student crowd every weekend. The atmosphere is easy-going and extremely flirtatious.

Metropol Tanztempel (⊠ Nollendorfpl. 5, ☎ 030/217–3680). Berlin's largest disco, which also stages concerts, is a hot spot for younger tourists. The black dance floor upstairs is the scene of a magnificent laser light show. Its occasional gay dances are hugely popular. The disco is open Friday and Saturday only.

90 Grad (⊠ Dennewitzstr. 37, ☎ 030/262–8984). This jam-packed disco plays hip-hop, soul, and some techno and really gets going around 2 AM. Women come fashionably dressed and go right in, but men usually have to wait outside until they get picked by the doorman.

Gay and Lesbian Bars

Berlin is unmistakably Germany's gay capital, and many Europeans come to partake of the city's gay scene. Concentrated in Schöneberg (around Nollendorfplatz) and Kreuzberg, and growing in Mitte and Prenzlauer Berg in eastern Berlin, the scene offers great diversity.

The following places are a good starting point for information. Also check out the magazines *Siegessäule, (030),* and *Sergej* (free and available at the places listed below as well as many others around town).

Anderes Ufer (✉ Hauptstr. 157, ☎ 030/784–1578). A young gay and lesbian crowd frequents this hip Kneipe. It has a mellow atmosphere and 1950s and '60s music.

Connection (✉ Welserstr. 24, ☎ 030/218–1432). Close to Wittenbergplatz, this dance club offers heavy house music and lots of dark corners. It's open Friday and Saturday, midnight until 6 AM.

Hafenbar (✉ Motzstr. 18, ☎ 030/211–4118). The decor and the energetic crowd make this bar endlessly popular and a favorite singles place. At 4 AM people move next door to Tom's Bar, open until 6 AM.

Mann-O-Meter (✉ Motzstr. 5, ☎ 030/216–8008). You can get extensive information here about gay life, groups, and events. Talks are held in the café, which has a variety of books and magazines. It's open weekdays 3–11, Saturday 3–10.

Schwuz (✉ Mehringdamm 61, ☎ 030/694–1077). This gay gathering spot sponsors various events. Every Saturday starting at 11 PM there's an "open evening" for talk and dance.

Kneipen

The city's roughly 6,000 bars and pubs all come under the heading of *Kneipen*—the place around the corner where you stop in for a beer, a snack, and conversation—and sometimes to dance. Other than along Ku'damm and its side streets, the happening places in western Berlin are around Savignyplatz in Charlottenburg, Nollendorfplatz and Winterfeldplatz in Schöneberg, Ludwigkirchplatz in Wilmersdorf, and along Oranienstrasse and Wienerstrasse in Kreuzberg. In eastern Berlin (Mitte) most of the action is north of and along Oranienburger Strasse, and around Rosenthaler Platz and the Hackesche Höfe. Kollwitzplatz is the hub in Prenzlauer Berg.

Green Door (✉ Winterfeldstr. 50, ☎ 030/215–2515). At this Schöneberg classic, at the former location of Berlin's legendary Havanna Bar, the city's hip and wildly dressed crowd gets together for outstanding cocktails.

Hackbarths (✉ Augustr. 49a, ☎ 030/282–7706). This is only one of many similar alternative bars and clubs, mostly frequented by students in the Oranienburger Strasse neighborhood.

Keyser Soze (✉ Tucholskystr. 31, ☎ 030/2859–9489). One of Berlin's trendiest pubs in an understated and cool setting. The service may be sluggish, but the drinks and the atmosphere are just great.

Leydicke (✉ Mansteinstr. 4, ☎ 030/216–2973). This historic spot is a must for out-of-towners. The proprietors operate their own distillery and have a superb selection of sweet wines and liqueurs.

Jazz Clubs

Berlin's lively music scene is dominated by jazz and rock. For jazz enthusiasts *the* events of the year are the summer **Jazz in the Garden** festival and the autumn international **Jazz Fest Berlin.** For information call the **tourist information center** (☎ 030/262–6031).

A-Trane Jazzclub (✉ Pestalozzistr. 105, ☎ 030/313–2550). A stylish newcomer, the A-Trane has found its fans among Berlin's jazz community. The club is often used for radio recordings.

B-Flat (✉ Rosenthaler Str. 13, ☎ 030/280–6349). This new jazz club presents mostly young German artists almost every night. The jam sessions focus on free and experimental jazz. Once a week, dancers come for swing night; call for details.

Eierschale (I) (✉ Podbielskiallee 50, ☎ 030/832–7097). A variety of jazz groups appears here at the Egg Shell, one of Berlin's oldest jazz clubs, open daily from 8:30 PM. Admission is free.

Flöz (✉ Nassauische Str. 37, ☎ 030/861–1000). The sizzling jazz at this club sometimes accompanies theater presentations.

Quasimodo (✉ Kantstr. 12a, ☎ 030/312–8086). The most established and popular jazz venue in the city has a great basement atmosphere and a good seating arrangement.

OUTDOOR ACTIVITIES AND SPORTS

Biking
There are bike paths throughout the downtown area and the rest of the city. *See* Getting Around *in* Berlin A to Z, *below,* for details on renting bikes.

Golf
Berlin's leading club is the **Golf- und Land Club Berlin-Wannsee e.V.** (✉ Am Golfweg 2, ☎ 030/806–7060).

Horseback Riding
Horses can be rented at the **Reitsportschule Onkel Toms Hütte** (✉ Onkel-Tom-Str. 172, ☎ 030/813–2081), **Reitschule Stall-Schmitz** (✉ Hennigsdorfer Str. 162, Berlin-Heiligensee, ☎ 030/431–9393), and **Reitsportschule Haflinger Hof** (✉ Feldweg 21, Fredersdorf, ☎ 03343/96371).

Jogging
The **Tiergarten** is the best place for jogging in the downtown area. Run its length and back, and you'll have covered 8 km (5 mi). Joggers can also take advantage of the grounds of **Charlottenburg Palace,** 3 km (2 mi) around. For longer runs, anything up to 32 km (20 mi), make for the **Grunewald.** In general, all of these woods are safe. You should, however, avoid Grunewald and Tiergarten on dark winter evenings.

Sailing
If you can provide a sailing certificate, sailboats can be rented at the sailing clubs and stands around Wannsee.

Squash and Tennis
Ask your hotel to direct you to the nearest tennis court and squash center. **Tennis & Squash City** (✉ Brandenburgische Str. 53, Wilmersdorf, ☎ 030/873–9097) has six tennis courts and 11 squash courts. At **Tennisplätze am Ku'damm** (✉ Cicerostr. 55A, ☎ 030/891–6630), you can step right off the Ku'damm and onto a tennis court.

Swimming
The **Wannsee,** the **Halensee,** and the **Plötzensee** all have beaches that get crowded during summer weekends. There are public pools throughout the city, so there's bound to be at least one near where you're staying. For full listings ask at the tourist office. Berlin's most impressive pool is the **Olympia-Schwimmstadion** at Olympischer Platz (U-bahn: Olympiastadion). The **Blub Badeparadies** lido (✉ Buschkrugallee 64, ☎ 030/606–6060) has indoor and outdoor pools, a sauna garden, hot whirlpools, and a solarium (U-bahn: Grenzallee).

SHOPPING

Berlin is a city of alluring stores and boutiques. Despite its cosmopolitan gloss, shop prices are generally lower than in cities like Munich and Hamburg.

Shopping Districts

Charlottenburg

For trendier clothes try the boutiques along the side streets off the Ku'-damm, such as Fasanenstrasse, Knesebeckstrasse, Mommsenstrasse, Bleibtreustrasse, Schlüterstrasse, and Uhlandstrasse. **Kantstrasse** west of the corner of Uhlandstrasse has reemerged as a stylish shopping area. Most shops here offer home furniture and accessories or designer stationary. For less trendy and much less expensive shopping try the pedestrian zone at **Wilmersdorfer Strasse** (U–7 station of same name), where price-conscious Berliners do their shopping.

Mitte

This rebuilt boulevard offers the most elegant shops in historic Berlin, including the Galeries Lafayette department store. Nearby Unter den Linden has a mix of expensive boutiques, including a Meissen ceramic showroom and tourist souvenir shops. Around **Alexanderplatz,** more affordable stores offer everything from clothes to electronic goods to designer perfumes. Many smaller clothing and specialty stores have sprung up in and around the **Nikolai Quarter.**

Kurfürstendamm

The city's liveliest and most famous shopping area is still found around Kurfürstendamm and its side streets, especially between Breitscheid-platz and Olivaer Platz. Running east from Breitscheidplatz is **Tauentzien-strasse,** another shopping street. At the end of it is Berlin's most celebrated department store, the **Kaufhaus des Westens** or KaDeWe. The elegant **Uhland-Passage** (⊠ Uhlandstr. 170) has leading name stores as well as cafés and restaurants. The **Kempinski Plaza** (⊠ Uhlandstr. 181–183) features exclusive boutiques and a pleasant atrium café.

Potsdamer Platz

The city's newest shopping mall, **Potsdamer Platz Arkaden** (⊠ Potsdamer Pl., ☎ 030/2559–270) has 140 shops, cafés, and restaurants under high glass ceilings.

Department Stores

Department Store Quartier 206 (⊠ Friedrichstr. 71, ☎ 030/2094–6276). The smallest and most luxurious department store in town offers primarily French women's and men's designer clothes, perfumes, and home accessories.

Galeries Lafayette (⊠ Französische Str. 23, ☎ 030/209–480). This intimate and elegant counterpart to the KaDeWe has evolved as the city's most popular department store. Only a sixth of the size of KaDeWe, it carries almost exclusively French products, including designer clothes, perfume, and all the French produce you might need for preparing yourown haute cuisine at home.

Galleria Kaufhof (⊠ Alexanderpl., ☎ 030/247–430). At the north end of Alexanderplatz, the Kaufhof is worth a visit for its stunning gourmet food department.

Kaufhaus des Westens (KaDeWe) (⊠ Tauentzienstr. 21, ☎ 030/21210). The largest department store in Europe, even surpassing London's Harrods, is the undeniably classy KaDeWe. It has a grand selection of goods on seven floors, as well as food and deli counters, champagne bars, restaurants, and beer bars on its two upper floors.

Stilwerk (⊠ Kantstr. 17, ☎ 030/315–150). The new and unique Stilwerk is not a real department store but an upscale mall with 48 shops and restaurants all catering to design and style. Most shops sell home accessories.

Wertheim (✉ Kurfürstendamm 181, ☎ 030/8800–3206). This downtown store is neither as big nor as attractive as KaDeWe, but Wertheim offers a large selection of fine wares.

Gift Ideas

Gipsformerei der Staatlichen Museen Preussischer Kulturbesitz (✉ Sophie-Charlotten-Str. 17, ☎ 030/326–7690). If you long to have the Egyptian Museum's Queen Nefertiti bust on your mantelpiece at home, check out the state museum's shop, open weekdays 9–4, which sells plaster casts of treasures from the city's museums.

Königliche Porzellan Manufaktur. Fine porcelain is still produced by this former Royal Prussian Porcelain Factory, also called KPM. You can buy this delicate handmade, hand-painted china at KPM's two stores (✉ Kurfürstendamm 27, ☎ 030/886–7210; ✉ Unter den Linden 35, ☎ 030/206–4150), but it may be more fun to visit the **factory salesroom** (✉ Wegelystr. 1, ☎ 030/390–090), which also sells seconds at reduced prices.

Puppenstube im Nikolaiviertel (✉ Propststr. 4, ☎ 030/242–3967). This is the ultimate shop for any kind of (mostly handmade) dolls, including designer models as well as old-fashioned German dolls.

Scenario (✉ Savignypassage, Bogen 602, ☎ 030/312–9199). Tucked under the elevated tram tracks, Scenario sells stationery articles, gifts of any kind, and a lot of leather wares and jewelry. The designs here are always at the cutting edge of what's state-of-the-art in Europe.

Spielen Berlin (✉ Neue Schönhauser Str. 8, ☎ 030/281–7183). This small shop in the Mitte district has a unique blend of traditional German wooden toys of yore and modern, educational toys and games for kids.

Wohnart Berlin (✉ Uhlandstr. 179–180, ☎ 030/882–5252). For stylish European furnishings, lamps, glass, porcelain or stationery items, this is the place to "shop till you drop."

Specialty Stores

Antiques

Not far from Wittenbergplatz lies Keithstrasse, a street full of antiques stores. Eisenacher Strasse, Fuggerstrasse, Kalckreuthstrasse, Motzstrasse, and Nollendorfstrasse—all close to Nollendorfplatz—have many antiques stores of varying quality. Another good street for antiques is Suarezstrasse, between Kantstrasse and Bismarckstrasse.

Berliner Antik- und Flohmarkt. This is one of the largest, more established, and expensive areas dealing in antique art. The series of stores offer everything from costly lamps to bargain books. Other antiques stores are found under the tracks at the Friedrichstrasse station (☎ 030/208–2645), open Monday and Wednesday–Sunday 11–6.

Berliner Kunstmarkt (Berlin Art Market). On weekends from 10 to 5, the colorful and lively antiques and handicrafts fair on Strasse des 17. Juni swings into action. Don't expect to pick up many bargains.

Villa Grisebach (✉ Fasanenstr. 25, ☎ 030/885–9150). One of the city's most classic arts and antiques auction houses also hosts exhibitions and special events at which you can buy paintings.

Jewelry

Bucherer (✉ Kurfürstendamm 26a, ☎ 030/880–4030). One of Berlin's new and upscale jewelers, Bucherer carries fine handcrafted jewelry, watches, and other stylish designer accessories.

Bulgari (✉ Fasanenstr. 70, ☎ 030/885–7920). The intimate but ultimate Berlin jeweler exclusively offers Italian-made jewelry.

Men's Clothing

Budapester Schuhe (✉ Kurfürstendamm 199, ☎ 030/881–1707). This old-style shop for men's shoes offers the largest selection of business shoes in all designs and colors.

Mientus (✉ Wilmersdorfer Str. 73, ☎ 030/323–9077; ✉ Kurfürstendamm 52, ☎ 030/323–9077). This large, exclusive men's store offers conventional and business wear, as well as sporty and modern looks.

Selbach (✉ Kurfürstendamm 195/196, ☎ 030/262–7038). A wealthy young crowd shops here for elegant evening wear and designer labels.

Women's Clothing

Jil Sander (✉ Kurfürstendamm 185, ☎ 030/886–7020). The new flagship store of German designer legend Jil Sander carries her complete line of clothes.

Kramberg (✉ Kurfürstendamm 56, ☎ 030/327–9010). If you're looking for international labels, including Gucci, Armani, and Chanel, drop by here and enjoy the first-class atmosphere.

Modehaus Horn (✉ Kurfürstendamm 213, ☎ 030/881–4055). For German designer wear, try this boutique. It's not cheap, and the styling is more conservative than chic.

Peek und Cloppenburg (✉ Tauentzienstr. 19, ☎ 030/212–900). "P and C" offers women's, men's, and children's clothes on five floors. The special Joop! designer store on the top floor and the international designer department in the basement should not be missed.

SIDE TRIPS FROM BERLIN

A trip to Berlin wouldn't be complete without paying a visit to Potsdam and the Palace of Sanssouci, both in Brandenburg, the poor rural state that surrounds the city. In contrast to Berlin, Brandenburg's lovely countryside is a pleasant surprise, with green meadows to the north and pine barrens to the east and south. The two rivers of the region, the Havel and the Spree, offer miles of unspoiled shores for walking.

Potsdam

Potsdam still retains the imperial character lent it by the many years during which it served as a royal residence and garrison quarters. The central **Alter Markt** (Old Market Square) sums it all up: the stately, domed **Nikolaikirche** (St. Nicolas Church; built in 1724), a square baroque church with classical columns; an **Ägyptischer Obelisk** (Egyptian obelisk) erected by Schloss Sanssouci architect von Knobelsdorff; and the officious facade of the old **Rathaus** (city hall; built in 1755) with a gilded figure of Atlas atop the tower. Wander around some of the adjacent streets, particularly Wilhelm-Külz-Strasse, to admire the handsome restored burghers' houses.

The **Holländisches Viertel** (Dutch Quarter) lies three blocks north of the Alter Markt. This settlement was built by Friedrich Wilhelm I in 1732 to entice Dutch artisans to a city in need of labor to support its

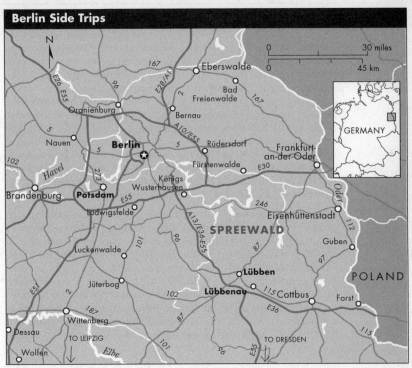

rapid growth. Few Dutch came, and the gabled, hip-roofed brick houses were largely used to house staff.

From the historic downtown district, you can walk down Gutenbergstrasse or Brandenburger Strasse to the west to reach Potsdam's famous Sanssouci Palace. Prussia's most famous king, Friedrich II—Frederick the Great—spent more time at his summer residence, **Sanssouci** in Potsdam, than in the capital Berlin. Its name means "without a care" in French, the language Frederick tried to cultivate in his own private circle and within the court. Some experts believe Frederick actually named the palace "Sans, Souci," which they translate as "with and without a care," a more apt name; its construction caused him a lot of trouble and expense and sparked furious rows with his master builder, Georg Wenzeslaus von Knobelsdorff. His creation nevertheless became one of Germany's greatest tourist attractions.

Executed according to Frederick's impeccable French-influenced taste, the palace, built between 1745 and 1747, is extravagantly rococo, with scarcely a patch of wall left unadorned. To the west of the palace are the **New Chambers** (☎ 0331/969–4206; ☜ guided tour DM 5; ⏱ Apr.–mid-May, weekends 10–5; mid-May–mid-Oct., Tues.–Sun. 10–5), which housed guests of the king's family; originally it functioned as a greenhouse until it was remodeled in 1771–74. Just east of Sanssouci Palace is the **Bildergalerie** (Picture Gallery; ☎ 0331/969–4181; ☜ DM 4; ⏱ mid-May–mid-Oct., Tues.–Sun. 10–5), with expensive marble from Siena in the main cupola. The gallery displays Frederick's collection of 17th-century Italian and Dutch paintings, including works by Caravaggio, Rubens, and Van Dyck. ✉ *Sanssouci Central Visitor Information, Besucherzentrum an der Historischen Mühle,* ☎ *0331/969–4190, 0331/969–4202, and 0331/969–4203; 0331/969–4204 for recorded information.* ☜ *DM 20 for a special ticket pass, valid for 1*

*day and all bldgs. and museums in Sanssouci and Potsdam; guided tour
DM 10.* ☼ *Apr.–Oct., daily 9–5; Nov.–Mar., Tues.–Sun. 9–4.* ☜

The **Neues Palais** (New Palace), a much larger and grander palace than
Sanssouci, stands at the end of the long, straight avenue that runs
through Sanssouci Park. It was built after the Seven Years' War (1756–
63), when Frederick loosened the purse strings. It's said he wanted to
demonstrate that the state coffers hadn't been depleted too severely by
the long conflict. The Neues Palais has much of interest, including an
indoor grotto hall with walls and columns set with shells, coral, and
other aquatic decor. The upper gallery contains paintings by 17th-cen-
tury Italian masters and a bijou court theater in which drama and
opera performances are still given. ⊠ *Strasse am Neuen Palais,* ☎
0331/969–4255. ⊡ *DM 8, including guided tour.* ☼ *Apr.–Oct., daily
9–5; Nov.–Mar., Sun.–Sat. 9–4.* ☜

Schloss Charlottenhof stands on its own grounds in the southern part
of Sanssouci Park. After Frederick died in 1786, the ambitious Sanssouci
building program ground to a halt, and the park fell into neglect. It
was 50 years before another Prussian king, Frederick William III, restored Sanssouci's earlier glory. He engaged the great Berlin architect
Karl Friedrich Schinkel to build this small palace for the crown prince.
Schinkel gave it a classical, almost Roman appearance, and he let his
imagination loose in the interior, too—decorating one of the rooms as
a Roman tent, with its walls and ceiling draped in striped canvas. ☎
0331/969–4228. ⊡ *Guided tour DM 6.* ☼ *Mid-May–mid-Oct., Tues.–
Sat. 10–5.*

Just north of Schloss Charlottenhof on the path back to Sanssouci are
later additions to the park. In 1836 Friedrich Wilhelm II built the **Römische Bäder** (Roman Baths; ☎ 0331/969–4224; ⊡ DM 3, additional
charge for special exhibitions; ☼ mid-May–mid-Oct., Tues.–Sun. 10–
5). The **Orangerie** (☎ 0331/969–4280; ⊡ guided tour DM 5; ☼ mid-
May–mid-Oct., Tues.–Sun. 10–5) was completed in 1860; its two massive towers linked by a colonnade evoke an Italian Renaissance palace.
Today it houses 47 copies of paintings by Raphael. The **Chinesisches
Teehaus** (Chinese Teahouse; ☎ 0331/969–4222; ⊡ DM 2; ☼ mid-May–
mid-Oct., Tues.–Sun. 10–5) was erected in 1757 in the Chinese style,
which was then the rage. The **Italianate Peace Church** (1845–48)
houses a 12th-century Byzantine mosaic taken from an island near
Venice.

NEED A
BREAK?   Halfway up the park's Drachenberg Hill, above the Orangerie, stands
           the curious **Drachenhaus** (Dragon House), modeled in 1770 after the
           Pagoda at London's Kew Gardens and named for the gargoyles orna-
           menting the roof corners. It now houses a popular café.

Resembling a rambling, half-timber country manor house, **Schloss Cecilienhof** (Cecilienhof Palace), the final addition to Sanssouci Park, was
built for Crown Prince Wilhelm in 1913 in a newly laid-out stretch of
the park bordering the Heiliger See, called the New Garden, on the
northeastern side of the city. It was here that the Allied leaders Truman, Attlee, and Stalin hammered out the fate of postwar Germany
at the 1945 Potsdam Conference. From Sanssouci you can reach the
New Garden with any tram or bus going toward the Neuer Garten station. ☎ *0331/969–4244.* ⊡ *DM 8, including guided tour.* ☼ *Apr.–Oct.,
Tues.–Sun. 9–5; Nov.–Mar., Tues.–Sun. 9–4.* ☜

Not far away, on a small hill called **Pfingstberg** in the park's western
section, are the dark ruins of the palacelike building the **Belvedere**. Built
in 1849–52 as an observation platform for the royals, the building is

currently being restored. The spectacular view from the hill, however, can be enjoyed from the rooftop of the small **Pomonatempel** below the Belvedere.

Dining and Lodging

$ ✕ **Preussischer Hof.** If you are up to genuine Berlin and Brandenburg cooking, try this restaurant in the historic heart of downtown Potsdam. The old building looks just like the city at the time when Frederick the Great ruled the country, and the dishes are just as hearty. Among the favorites is *Gepökeltes Eisbein auf Weinsauerkraut mit Erbspüree und Salzkartoffeln* (pickled hocks on wine sauerkraut with mashed peas and boiled potatoes). If the relatively small menu doesn't appeal to you, ask for their specials of the week. Reservations are advised. ⊠ *Charlottenstr. 11,* ☎ *0331/270–0762. No credit cards.*

$$ 🏨 **Hotel am Luisenplatz.** This intimate hotel hides a warm, upscale el-
★ egance and friendly, personal service behind a somber-looking facade. The large rooms are decorated in typically Prussian colors—dark blue and yellow—and all have a bathtub. The biggest draw, however, is the hotel's location, offering a spectacular view of historic Luisenplatz and its restored Prussian city mansions. ⊠ *Luisenpl. 5, D–14471,* ☎ *0331/ 971–900,* 𝖥𝖠𝖷 *0331/971–9019. 25 rooms, 3 suites. In-room safes, minibars, dry cleaning, laundry service, meeting room, parking (fee). AE, DC, MC, V.* ✺

$$ 🏨 **Schlosshotel Cecilienhof.** This English country–style mansion is where Truman, Attlee, and Stalin drew up the 1945 Potsdam Agreement and where Truman received news of the first successful atom bomb test. The hotel rooms are somewhat plain, although comfortable and adequately equipped. The Schloss is set in its own parkland bordering a lake and is a pleasant 15-minute stroll from Sanssouci and the city center. ⊠ *Neuer Garten, D–14469,* ☎ *0331/37050,* 𝖥𝖠𝖷 *0331/292–498. 36 rooms, 6 suites. Restaurant, minibars, room service, sauna, dry cleaning, laundry service, concierge, meeting rooms, free parking. AE, D, MC, V.* ✺

Potsdam A to Z

ARRIVING AND DEPARTING

Potsdam is virtually a suburb of Berlin, some 20 km (12 mi) southwest of the city center and a half-hour journey by car, bus, or S-bahn. City traffic is heavy, however, and a train journey is recommended. The most effortless way to visit Potsdam and its attractions is to book a tour with one of the big Berlin operators (☞ Guided Tours *in* Berlin A to Z, *below*).

By Boat. Boats leave Wannsee, landing hourly, between 10 and 6; until 8 in summer.

By Bus. There is regular service from the bus station at the Funkturm on Messedamm 8 (U–1 U-bahn: Kaiserdamm).

By Car. From Berlin center (Strasse des 17. Juni), take the Potsdamer Strasse south until it becomes Route 1 and then follow the signs to Potsdam. A faster way is taking the highway from Funkturm through Zehlendorf to Potsdam.

By Train. Take the S-bahn 7 line to Potsdam-Stadt (for the city and Schloss Sanssouci). Change there for the short rail trip to the Potsdam-Charlottenhof (for Schloss Charlottenhof) and Wildpark (for Neues Palais) stations. You can also take Bus 116 from Wannsee to the Glienecker Brücke, and then take a ride on the streetcar to Potsdam's Bassanplatz station. From there you can walk down Brandenburger Strasse to Platz der Nationen and on to the Green Gate, the main entrance to Sanssouci Park.

GUIDED TOURS

All major sightseeing companies (☞ Guided Tours *in* Berlin A to Z, *below*) offer three- to four-hour-long tours of Potsdam and Sanssouci for DM 54. The **Potsdam Tourist Office** also runs two tours from April through October. Its three-hour tour, including Sanssouci, costs DM 35; the 1½-hour tour of the city alone is DM 27 (☞ Visitor Information, *below*).

VISITOR INFORMATION

The **Potsdam tourist office** has information on tours, attractions, and events, and also reserves hotel rooms for tourists. Their branch office at Brandenburger Strasse 18 also sells tickets for the Neues Palais theater. ⊠ *Touristenzentrum am Alten Markt, Friedrich-Ebert-Str. 5, Postfach 601220, D–14467 Potsdam,* ☎ *0331/275–580.* ☉ *Apr.–Oct., weekdays 9–8, Sat. 10–6, Sun. 9–4; Nov.–Mar., weekdays 10–6, weekends 10–2;* ⊠ *Brandenburger Str. 18,* ☎ *0331/275–5888.* ☉ *Weekdays 10–6, Sat. 10–2. www.potsdam.de.*

Spreewald

The Spreewald is a unique natural conservation area southeast of Berlin. This almost pristine landscape of wetlands, dark forests, canals, and uncharted waterways, rivers, and lakes covers nearly 500 square mi and is one of the most popular getaways for Berliners. Summer weekends are very crowded, but it's better in the late spring or fall. The Spreewald is also known for its people, a blend of Germans and the Slavic Sorben, and for specialties such as freshwater fish and *Spreewald-Gurken* (pickles), and the many fairy tales which have come from this rugged and mysterious area.

From one of the region's major towns, **Lübben,** or **Lübbenau,** explore the small rivers by boarding one of the flat-bottom wooden boats called *Kähne,* which are punted along with long poles just like the gondolas in Venice. You can have lunch or dinner when your boat docks at one of the hidden forest islands that have a restaurant. Smaller villages with ports such as **Straupitz** or **Raddusch** offer more personal tours with paddleboats or gondolas.

Lübben, the region's old residence of the Saxon prince electors, is also home to **Schloss Lübben,** a castle whose main defense tower is the only accessible building. ⊠ *Ernst-von-Houwald-Damm,* ☎ *no phone.* ☉ *Tues.–Sun. 10–5.*

The city of Lübbenau has the largest harbor in the Spreewald region. Before boarding a boat here, follow the nature trail to the **Freiland-museum Lehde** (Lehde Open-Air Museum), which features three old farmhouses typical of the Spreewald, historic handicrafts, traditional costumes, and one of the area's oldest barge-building shops. ⊠ *Lehde, An der Gliglitza,* ☎ *03542/2472.* ☑ *DM 3.* ☉ *Apr.–Oct., daily 10–6; Nov.–Mar., daily 10–5.*

The small but fascinating **Spreewald-Museum** features an art exhibit and many historic items of local craft work. ⊠ *Torhaus, Am Topfmarkt 12,* ☎ *03542/2472.* ☑ *DM 3.* ☉ *Apr.–Oct., daily 10–6; Nov.–Mar., daily 10–5.*

The sleepy village of **Straupitz** has three mills under one roof: The Holländermühle has a grandiose waterwheel that once powered a sawmill, an oil mill, and a corn mill. A closer inspection of the inside is possible, but you must register in advance for a tour. ⊠ *Lassower Str. 11a,* ☎ *035475/16997.*

Dining and Lodging

$ ✕⊞ **Hotel-Pension Dubkow-Mühle.** The family-owned pension in the small village of Leipe, north of Raddusch, is one of the oldest pubs (established 1737) in the Spreewald. The building is an old mill in a lovely garden surrounded by water and wetlands. Guest rooms are quiet and spacious, and the hotel's restaurant serves solid local fare. The hotel also offers individual boat trips. ✉ *Leipe/Spreewald, D–03226,* ☎ *03542/2297,* 𝔽𝔸𝕏 *03542/41722. 19 rooms, with bath, 2 with shower. Restaurant, boating, bicycles. No credit cards.*

Spreewald A to Z

ARRIVING AND DEPARTING

By Car. The Spreewald is 60 km (37 mi) southeast of Berlin and easily accessible with a 45-minute ride on the A–13 toward Cottbus. To reach Lübben, take B–87 to the north; smaller villages like Straupitz and Raddusch can be reached via B–320 and B–115, respectively.

By Train. Trains to Lübbenau depart from Berlin's Alexanderplatz station and the Hauptbahnhof (train Lines RB 41 and RE 2).

GETTING AROUND

By Boat. The easiest way to explore the Spreewald region is by boat. There are several organized boat tours departing from the Grosser Hafen in Lübbenau. Tours usually cost DM 5 for one hour and can last as long as eight hours. For DM 9 for one hour (or DM 31 for a whole day), you can rent your own paddleboat from **Bootsverleih Petrick** (✉ Schlossbezirk 22, Lübbenau, ☎ 03542/3620; ☉ Apr.–Oct., daily 8–7) and **Bootsverleih Ingrid Hannemann** (✉ Am Wasser 1, Lübbenau, ☎ 03542/3647; ☉ Apr.–Oct., daily 8–7).

Larger boat tour operators are to be found at the **Kahnabfahrtsstelle Am Holzgraben,** in Lübbenau (✉ Dammstr. 72, ☎ 03542/2221). In Straupitz boats depart from the barge dock at the village church.

VISITOR INFORMATION

Fremdenverkehrsverein Lübben (✉ Ernst-von-Houwald-Damm 15, D–15907 Lübben, ☎ 03546/3090, 𝔽𝔸𝕏 033546/2543); **Fremdenverkehrsverein Lübbenau** (✉ Ehm-Welk-Str. 15, D–03222 Lübbenau, ☎ 03542/3668, 𝔽𝔸𝕏 03542/46770, ✍); **Heimat- und Fremdenverkehrsverein Straupitz** (✉ Lübbener Str. 28, D–15913 Straupitz, ☎ 035475/16771); **Tourismusverband Spreewald e.V.** (✉ Lindenstr. 1, D–03226 Raddusch, ☎ 035433/72299, 𝔽𝔸𝕏 035433/7228, ✍).

BERLIN A TO Z

Even a decade after the official unification of the two Germanys, the nuts-and-bolts work of joining up the halves is not complete, and uncertainties abound. We have given addresses, telephone numbers, and other logistical details based on the best available information, but please understand that telephone numbers in particular are still changing.

Arriving and Departing

By Bus

Buses are slightly cheaper than trains. Berlin is linked by bus to 170 European cities. The Omnibusbahnhof, the central bus terminal, is at the corner of Masurenallee 4–6 and Messedamm. Reserve through DER (a state agency), commercial travel agencies, or the station itself. For information call 030/301–8028 between 9 and 5:30.

By Car

The German autobahn system links Berlin with the eastern German cities of Magdeburg, Leipzig, Rostock, Dresden, and Frankfurt an der Oder. At press time, speed restrictions of 130 kph (80 mph) still applied.

By Plane

Most international airlines serve western Berlin's **Tegel Airport** after a first stop at a major European hub (such as Frankfurt). Because of increased air traffic following unification, the former military airfield at **Tempelhof** is used as an alternate airport for commuter flights to western Germany. Eastern Berlin's **Schönefeld Airport** is about 24 km (15 mi) outside the downtown area. It is used principally by charter airlines. You can reach all three airports by calling the central service phone number (☎ 0180/500–0186).

BETWEEN THE AIRPORT AND DOWNTOWN

Tegel Airport is only 6 km (4 mi) from the downtown area. The No. 109 and X09 airport buses run at 10-minute intervals between Tegel and downtown via Kurfürstendamm, Bahnhof Zoologischer Garten, and Budapester Strasse. The trip takes 30 minutes; the fare is DM 3.90. Expect to pay about DM 25 for the same trip by taxi. If you rent a car at the airport, follow the signs for the Stadtautobahn into Berlin. The Halensee exit leads to Kurfürstendamm. Tempelhof is linked directly to the city center by the U–6 subway line. From Schönefeld a shuttle bus leaves every 10–15 minutes for the nearby S-bahn station; S-bahn trains leave every 20 minutes for the Friedrichstrasse station, in downtown eastern Berlin, and for the Zoologischer Garten station, in downtown western Berlin. Bus 171 also leaves every 10 or 15 minutes for the western Berlin Rudow subway station. A taxi ride from the airport takes about 40 minutes and will cost around DM 55. By car, follow the signs for Stadtzentrum Berlin.

By Train

There are six major rail routes to Berlin from the western part of the country (from Hamburg, Hannover, Köln, Frankfurt, Munich, and Nürnberg). Ask about reduced fares within Germany. Some trains now stop at and depart from more than one of Berlin's four main train stations, but generally trains from the west and north arrive at Friedrichstrasse and Zoologischer Garten, and trains from the east and south at Hauptbahnhof or Lichtenberg. For details on rates and information, call **Deutsche Bahn Information** (☎ 030/19419).

Getting Around

By Bike

Bicycling is popular in Berlin. Although it's not recommended in the downtown area, it's ideal in outlying areas. Bike paths are generally marked by red bricks on the walkways; many stores that rent or sell bikes carry the Berlin biker's atlas to help you find the paths. Call the **Allgemeiner Deutscher Fahrrad-Club, ADFC** (✉ Brunnenstr. 28, ☎ 030/448–4724) for information and rental locations, or rent your bikes at some of the major hotels for approximately DM 30 for 24 hours.

Fahrradstation (✉ Bergmannstr. 9 in Kreuzberg, ☎ 030/215–1566; ✉ Rosenthaler Str. 40–41, ☎ 030/2859–9895) rents green bikes. You must leave your passport as a security deposit. Call for their other locations. **Fahrrad Vermietung Berlin** (☎ 030/261–2094) rents black bikes with baskets, which they keep in front of the Marmorhaus movie theater on Kurfürstendamm, opposite the Gedächtniskirche. Bikes are rented by the day (not 24 hours), and you must leave either a DM 200 deposit or your passport as security. If no one is there, just wait, or see if there's a sky-blue bus parked nearby. The attendant is probably signing up a bus tour there and will return shortly.

By Car

Berliners are famous for their reckless driving, so exploring the city by car can be extremely frustrating for out-of-towners. Due to the many construction sites, traffic on many streets is often detoured, and rush hour is stop-and-go for every driver. It's best to leave your car at the hotel and take the public transit system.

By Subway

Berlin is too large to be explored on foot. To compensate, the city has one of the most efficient public-transportation systems in Europe, a smoothly integrated network of subway (U-bahn) and suburban (S-bahn) train lines, buses, trams (in eastern Berlin only), and even a ferry across the Wannsee, making every part of the city easily accessible. Get a map from any information booth. Extensive all-night bus and tram service operates seven nights a week (indicated by the letter N next to route numbers).

A DM 3.90 ticket covers not only the downtown areas (fare Zones A and B) but the outlying areas (fare Zone C) as well, and allows you to make an unlimited number of changes between trains, buses, and trams within two hours.

If you are just making a short trip, buy a **Kurzstreckentarif.** It allows you to ride six bus stops or three U-bahn or S-bahn stops for DM 2.50. The best deal for visitors who plan to travel around the city extensively is the **day card,** for DM 8.30, good for 24 hours after validation on all trains and buses. The **group day card,** DM 22.50, offers the same benefits as the day card but for two adults and up to three children. A seven-day **tourist pass** costs DM 40 and allows unlimited travel on all city buses and trains for fare Zones A and B; DM 48 buys all three fare zones. The **Berlin WelcomeCard** entitles one person (DM 16) or one adult and up to three children (DM 29) to three days of unlimited travel as well as free admission or reductions of up to 50% for sightseeing trips, museums, theaters, and other events and attractions.

All tickets are available from vending machines at U-bahn and S-bahn stations. Punch your ticket into the red machine on the platform. For information about public transportation, call the **Berliner Verkehrsbetriebe** (☎ 030/19449 or 030/752–7020) or go to the BVG-information office on Hardenbergplatz, directly in front of the Bahnhof Zoo train station. If you're caught without a ticket, the fine is DM 60.

By Taxi

The base rate is DM 4, after which prices vary according to a complex tariff system. Figure on paying around DM 15 for a ride the length of the Ku'damm. Ask for a special fare called *Kurzstreckentarif,* which allows for a short ride of less than 2 km (1 mi) or five minutes in a cab hailed in the street only. You can also hail one at a taxi stand or order a cab by calling 030/9644, 030/210–202, 030/691–001, or 030/261–026. U-bahn employees will call a taxi for passengers after 8 PM.

Students operate *Velotaxis,* a rickshaw service system, along Kurfürstendamm and Unter den Linden. Just hail one of the orange or red bicycle cabs on the street or look for the VELOTAXI-STAND signs along the boulevards mentioned. The fare is DM 2 for up to 1 km (½ mi), DM 5 for a tour between sightseeing landmarks (for example, Europa Center to the Brandenburger Tor), and DM 15 for 30 minutes of travel. Velotaxis operate April–October, daily 1–8.

Hints for Travelers with Disabilities

All major S- and U-bahn stations have elevators, and most buses have hydraulic lifts. Check the public transportation maps or call the **Berliner Verkehrsbetriebe** (☎ 030/19449). **Service-Ring-Berlin e.V.** (☎ 030/859–4010) and **Verband Geburts- und anderer Behinderter e.V.** (☎ 030/341–1797) provide information and van and wheelchair rentals.

Contacts and Resources

Car Rentals

Avis (⊠ Schönefeld Airport, ☎ 030/6091–5710; ⊠ Tegel Airport, ☎ 030/4101–3148; ⊠ Budapester Str. 43, at Europa Center, ☎ 030/230–9370; ⊠ Holzmarktstr. 15–18, ☎ 030/240–7940). **Europcar** (⊠ Schönefeld Airport, ☎ 030/634–9160; ⊠ Tegel Airport, ☎ 030/417–8520; ⊠ Kurfürstenstr. 101-104, ☎ 030/235–0640). **Hertz** (⊠ Schöne-feld Airport, ☎ 030/6091–5730; ⊠ Tegel Airport, ☎ 030/4101–3315; ⊠ Tempelhof Airport, ☎ 030/6951–3818; ⊠ Budapester Str. 39, ☎ 030/261–1053). **Sixt** (⊠ Schönefeld Airport, ☎ 030/6091–5690; ⊠ Tegel Airport, ☎ 030/4101–2886; ⊠ Tempelhof Airport, ☎ 030/6951–3816; ⊠ Nürnberger Str. 65, ☎ 030/212–9880; ⊠ Spandauer Str., at SAS Radisson Hotel, ☎ 030/243–9050).

Consulates

Australia (⊠ Friedrichstr. 200, ☎ 030/880–0880). **Canada** (⊠ Inter-national Trade Center, Friedrichstr. 95, ☎ 030/261–1161). **Ireland** (⊠ Friedrichstr. 200, ☎ 030/220–720). **New Zealand** (⊠ Friedrich-str. 60, ☎ 030/206–210). **United Kingdom** (⊠ Unter den Linden 32–34, ☎ 030/201–840). **United States** (⊠ Neustädtische Kirchstr. 4–5, ☎ 030/238–5174).

Emergencies

Police (☎ 030/110). **Ambulance** (☎ 030/112). **Dentist** (☎ 030/8900–4333).

English-Language Bookstores

Books in Berlin (⊠ Goethestr. 69, Charlottenburg, ☎ 030/313–1233). **British Bookshop** (⊠ Mauerstr. 83–84, ☎ 030/238–4680). **Buch-handlung Kiepert** (⊠ Hardenbergstr. 4–5, ☎ 030/311–0090). **Duss-mann Kulturkaufhaus** (⊠ Friedrichstr. 90, ☎ 030/20250). **Hugendubel** (⊠ Tauentzienstr. 13, ☎ 030/214–060). **Marga Schoeller Bücherstube** (⊠ Knesebeckstr. 33, ☎ 030/881–1112).

Guided Tours

BOAT TRIPS

Tours of downtown Berlin's **canals** take in sights such as the Charlot-tenburg Palace and the Congress Hall. Tours depart from Kottbusser Bridge in Kreuzberg and cost around DM 10.

A tour of the **Havel Lakes** is the thing to do in summer. Trips begin at Wannsee (S-bahn: Wannsee) and at the Greenwich Promenade in Tegel (U-bahn: Tegel). You'll sail on either the whale-shape vessel *Moby Dick* or the *Havel Queen,* a Mississippi-style boat, and cruise 28 km (17 mi) through the lakes and past forests. Tours last 4½ hours and cost between DM 20 and DM 25. There are 20 operators. The following are the leading ones:

Reederei Bruno Winkler (⊠ Mierendorffstr. 16, ☎ 030/349–9595). **Reed-erei Heinz Riedel** (⊠ Planufer 78, ☎ 030/693–4646). **Stern- und Kreiss-chiffahrt** (⊠ Helmstedter Str. 4–17, ☎ 030/211–7451).

BUS TOURS

Four companies offer more or less identical tours (in English) cover-ing all major sights in Berlin, as well as all-day tours to Potsdam, Dresden, and Meissen. The Berlin tours cost DM 15–DM 45; those to Potsdam, DM 50–DM 70; and to Dresden and Meissen, approximately DM 100.

Berliner Bären Stadtrundfahrten (BBS; ✉ Seeburgerstr. 19b, ☎ 030/3519–5270) tours depart from the corner of Rankestrasse and Kurfürstendamm and, in eastern Berlin, from Alexanderplatz, opposite the Forum Hotel. **Berolina Berlin-Service** (✉ Kurfürstendamm 220, corner Meinekestr., ☎ 030/8856–8030) tours depart from the corner of Kurfürstendamm and Meinekestrasse and, in eastern Berlin, from Alexanderplatz, opposite the Forum Hotel. **Bus Verkehr Berlin** (BVB, ✉ Kurfürstendamm 225, ☎ 030/885–9880) tours leave from Kurfürstendamm 225. **Severin & Kühn** (✉ Kurfürstendamm 216, ☎ 030/880–4190) tours leave from clearly marked stops along the Kurfürstendamm.

SPECIAL-INTEREST TOURS

Sightseeing tours with a cultural/historical focus are offered weekends at a cost of approximately DM 15 by **StattReisen** (✉ Malplaquetstr. 5, ☎ 030/455–3028). Tours include "Jewish History" and "Prenzlauer Berg Neighborhoods" and are in German; English tours are offered upon request. All tours given by **Berlin Walks** (✉ Harbigstr. 26, ☎ 030/301–9194) are in English. The introductory "Discover Berlin" tour takes in the major downtown sites in 2½–3 hours. Other theme tours (Third Reich sites and Jewish life) are shorter and run March–November. Tours depart at the taxi stand in front of the main entrance to the Zoologischer Garten train station and cost DM 15, plus S-bahn transportation.

Late-Night Pharmacies

Pharmacies in Berlin offer late-night service on a rotating basis. Every pharmacy displays a notice indicating the location of the nearest shop with evening hours. For **emergency pharmaceutical assistance,** call 030/01189.

Travel Agencies

Reiseland American Express Reisebüro (✉ Wittenbergerpl., Bayreuther Str. 37, ☎ 030/2149–8363; ✉ Friedrichstr. 172, ☎ 030/238–4102).

Visitor Information

The **Berlin Tourismus Marketing** (main tourist office) is in the heart of the city in the Europa Center. If you want materials on the city before your trip, write **Berlin Tourismus Marketing GmbH** (✉ Am Karlsbad 11, D–10785 Berlin). For information on the spot, the office in the Europa Center is open Monday–Saturday 8 AM–10 PM, Sunday 9–9. Other offices are found at the **Brandenburger Tor,** open Monday–Saturday 9:30–6, and at **Tegel Airport,** open daily 5 AM–10:30 PM.

The **Berlin-Hotline** provides the latest tourist information via phone (☎ 030/250–025) or fax (FAX 030/2500–2424, ✎).

For information in English on all aspects of the city, pick up a copy of *Berlin—the magazine* (DM 3.50) from any tourist office. The Berlin daily newspaper *Die Welt* publishes a special editorial page written in English everyday.

16 SAXONY, SAXONY-ANHALT, AND THURINGIA

These three states in eastern Germany have a great many secrets in store and some gems of German culture. Cities such as Dresden and Leipzig have treasures of art and music, and milestones of history are found in Weimar and Wittenberg, the city of Martin Luther. An old-world state of mind is found here, the likes of which you will never find in western Germany.

THE SMALL TOWNS in the eastern states of Saxony, Saxony-Anhalt, and Thuringia will reveal much more about an older Germany than the pace of Frankfurt, Hamburg, Stuttgart, or Köln can afford. Communism never penetrated the culture here as deeply as did the American influence in West Germany. The German Democratic Republic (commonly referred to by its German acronym—DDR) clung to its German heritage, proudly preserving connections with such national heroes as Luther, Goethe, Schiller, Bach, Handel, Wagner, and the Hungarian-born Liszt. Towns in the regions of the Thüringer Wald (Thuringian Forest) or the Harz Mountains—long considered the haunt of witches—are drenched in history and medieval legend.

East Germans rebuilt extensively after World War II bombings devastated most of their cities; though you will see eyesores of industrialization and stupendously bland housing projects, many historic centers were returned to their old glamour. Some of Europe's most famous palaces and cultural wonders—-the Zwinger and Semperoper in Dresden, the Wartburg at Eisenach, the Schiller and Goethe houses in Weimar, Luther's Wittenberg—await the long-delayed traveler.

Traditional tourist sights aside, eastern Germany is also worth visiting precisely because it still *is* in transition. In 1989 the resolute people of Leipzig, with their now legendary *Montagsdemonstrationen* (Monday demonstrations) through the streets of their proud city, startled the East German regime and triggered the peaceful revolution. A year later the initiative for unification came as much from the West as it did from the East, though many former East Germans have not been altogether happy with the results. The closing of factories and a shrunken welfare system have left many jobless (unemployment has run as high as 30%).

But apart from all the economic woes that still haunt the region, a new class of young East German entrepreneurs has transformed cities like Leipzig and Dresden. It's all part of a new wave of start-up businesses, an upswing that echoes that region's tradition of hard work. Consider this in light of the past. When the DDR was communism's "Western Front," it was largely isolated from Western ideas. Saxony's Dresden area, in particular, was nicknamed *Tal der Ahnungslosen* (Valley of the Know-Nothings), as residents there couldn't receive Western television or radio signals.

The three states described here survived under a harsh political regime and have now embarked on a new and promising future. Eastern Germany used to move very slowly, but nowadays the pace of many cities has overtaken that of their West German counterparts.

Pleasures and Pastimes

Dining

CATEGORY	COST*
$$$$	over DM 60
$$$	DM 40–DM 60
$$	DM 25–DM 40
$	under DM 25

per person for a three-course meal, including tax and tip, excluding drinks

Enterprising young managers and chefs are beginning to establish themselves in the east, so look out for new and mostly small restaurants along the way. Some of the restaurants recommended here are successfully blending nouvelle German cuisine with such regional specialties as *Thüringer Sauerbraten mit Klössen* (roast corned beef with dumplings), spicy *Thüringer Wurst* (sausage), *Bärenschinken* (cured ham), *Harzer Köhlerteller mit Röstkartoffeln* (charcoal-grilled meat with fried potatoes), *Harze Käse* (a strong-smelling cheese), and *Moskgauer Bauerngulasch mit Klump* (goulash with dumplings).

Fine Wines

Saxony has cultivated vineyards for more than 800 years and is known for its dry red and white wines, among them Müller-Thurgau, Weissburgunder, Ruländer, and the spicy Traminer. The Sächsische Weinstrasse (Saxon Wine Route) follows the course of the Elbe River from Diesbar-Seusslitz (north of Meissen) to Pirna (southeast of Dresden). Meissen, Radebeul, and Dresden have upscale wine restaurants, and wherever you see a green seal with the letter *S* and some grapes, good local wine is being served. Most of the hotels and restaurants listed in this chapter also have their own wine cellars.

Lodging

A crash building program has filled the accommodation gaps in Thuringia and Saxony, but not in Saxony-Anhalt. All major hotel chains are present in the larger cities, most of them within beautifully restored mansions. Smaller and family-run hotels often combine a good restaurant with fairly good accommodations. In an effort to further improve tourism, most big hotels offer special (weekend) or activity-oriented packages that aren't found in the western part of the country.

During the trade fairs and shows of the **Leipziger Messe**, particularly in March and April, most Leipzig hotels increase their prices.

CATEGORY	COST*
$$$$	over DM 250
$$$	DM 200–DM 250
$$	DM 160–DM 200
$	under DM 160

All prices are for two people in a double room, including tax and service charge.

Old Railway Engines and Boats

Eastern Germany is a treasure house of old steam-driven tractors, factory engines, train engines, and riverboats, many lovingly restored by enthusiasts. Deutsche Bahn (German Railways) regularly runs trains from the years 1899–1930 on a small-gauge line that penetrates deep into the Saxon countryside and the Fichtelberg Mountains. In Saxony-Anhalt you can ride the steam-powered narrow-gauge Brockenbahn to the Harz Mountains' highest point. The world's largest and oldest fleet of paddle steamers (Weisse Flotte) plies the Elbe. Eight old steamers (all of them under official technical-preservation orders) and two reconstructed ships ply up and down the Elbe, following the Saxon Wine Route as far as the Czech Republic.

Outdoor Activities and Sports

You can canoe on the Elbe, Gera, and Saale rivers and seldom see another paddle. Contact the tourist offices in Dresden, Gera, or Halle for rental information.

Hiking is good in the Harz Mountains, particularly around Thale and Wittenberg. Maps and guides to bicycle and walking trails are available in most hotels and bookstores. The Thale and Wernigerode tourist offices and the Wittenberg District Rural Information Office have great resources (☞ Contacts and Resources *in* Saxony, Saxony-Anhalt, and Thuringia A to Z, *below*).

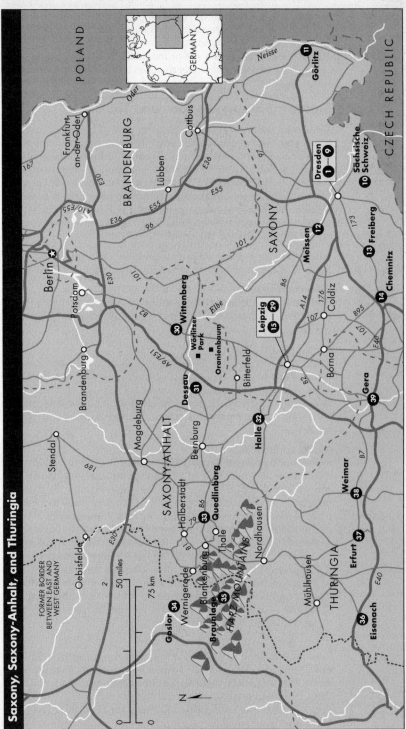

Saxony, Saxony-Anhalt, and Thuringia

Braunlage, in the Harz, offers good family skiing. The elevated, dense Thuringian Forest is a popular holiday destination in summer and in winter. Its center is Suhl, administrative heart of an area where every 10th town and village is a spa or mountain resort. The region south of Erfurt, centering around Oberhof, has comfortable hotels and full sports facilities.

Exploring Saxony, Saxony-Anhalt, and Thuringia

These three states cover the southeastern part of the former East Germany, and some of the old and now run-down industrial towns will remind you of its communist past. Some of Germany's most historically important cities are here, and reconstruction programs are slowly restoring them. Dresden is promoting its reputation as the "Florence of the Elbe," and, just downstream, Meissen has undergone an impressive face-lift. Weimar, one of the continent's old cultural centers, and Leipzig, in particular, have washed off their grime and have almost completely restored historic city centers.

Numbers in the text correspond to numbers in the margin and on the Saxony, Saxony-Anhalt, and Thuringia, Leipzig, and Dresden maps.

Great Itineraries

Rail transportation in the east has improved rapidly, so the region can be comfortably toured by train. East–west and north–south autobahns crisscross the three states.

IF YOU HAVE 3 DAYS

Spend your first day in ⊞ **Dresden** ①–⑨, with its impressive Zwinger complex and fine museums. On your second day stop in **Meissen** ⑫ to see how its famous porcelain is produced. Then head northwest to ⊞ **Leipzig** ⑮–㉙, where Bach once resided. If there's still time, continue southwest to visit **Weimar** ㉘, where the poets Goethe and Schiller once lived.

IF YOU HAVE 5 DAYS

Spend your first day and night in ⊞ **Dresden** ①–⑨. Finish taking in its splendors in the morning and continue to **Meissen** ⑫, stopping long enough for a visit to the porcelain factory, before closing the day in ⊞ **Leipzig** ⑮–㉙. When you've explored your fill, head north to the birthplace of Martin Luther and the Reformation, **Wittenberg** ㉚. An indirect route takes you on the third day to the old Harz Mountain towns of **Quedlinburg** ㉝, **Wernigerode,** and **Goslar** ㉞, the unofficial capital of the Harz region. Skirt through the Harz Mountains and drive south to ⊞ **Eisenach** ㉗, where you can prowl through the Wartburg Castle, where Luther translated the Bible in hiding. The final stops are **Erfurt** ㉘, a city of towers that mostly managed to escape wartime bombing, and ⊞ **Weimar** ㉙, where you might want to peek into its most famous hotel, the charming and luxurious Elephant.

IF YOU HAVE 7 DAYS

Your first day should be fully devoted to the various sights in ⊞ **Dresden** ①–⑨, before exploring the **Sächsische Schweiz** ⑩, a mountainous region south of the city, the next day. Depending on how long you hiked through the mountains, you will still have enough time to drive to the Polish-border town of ⊞ **Görlitz** ⑪. Spend the night there and travel to **Meissen** ⑫, and then follow a northern route on the A–14 autobahn to ⊞ **Leipzig** ⑮–㉙ and spend the rest of the day there. Leave enough time in Leipzig for visits to its outstanding museums, including the Grassimuseum complex and the Museum der Bildenden Künste. On your fourth and fifth days, from Leipzig, drive back to the sights at **Halle** ㉜ before touring the old towns of **Wittenberg** ㉚ and **Quedlinburg** ㉝. You can spend the nights in any of the Harz towns and venture into the mountains for some fresh air. The sixth day is best spent at the Wartburg in **Eisenach** ㊱, which can be reached either by following the country roads or the autobahn from the Harz Mountains toward the south, and then on to **Erfurt** ㊲ and ⛯ **Weimar** ㊳. Spend your last day either in both cities or concentrate fully on the culture and museums in Weimar. If time permits, also detour to **Gera** ㊴.

When to Tour Saxony, Saxony-Anhalt, and Thuringia

Winters in this part of Germany can be cold, wet, and dismal, so unless you plan to ski in the Harz Mountains or the Thüringer Wald, visit in late spring, summer, or early autumn. Avoid Leipzig at trade fair times, particularly in March and April.

SAXONY

Updated by
Jürgen
Scheunemann

As you travel east into Saxony, close to the Czech and Polish borders, the villages and landscape show signs of having languished for decades in this almost-forgotten corner of Germany. The people of this state are known for their laid-back attitude toward the rest of Germany. Their point of view is echoed by the Saxon dialect, which is the target of endless jokes and puns about the somewhat indecipherable accent of its speakers, though the dialect often sounds like gentle singing. Three cities are rebuilding themselves magnificently: Dresden and Leipzig—the showcase cities of eastern Germany—and the smaller town of Görlitz, on the Neisse River. If you make your way toward Dresden from Freiberg, you can follow the Freital road or first cut north to the Elbe River and the enchanting little city of Meissen.

Dresden

205 km (127 mi) south of Berlin.

Saxony's capital city sits in baroque splendor on a wide sweep of the Elbe River, and its proponents are working with German thoroughness to recapture the city's old reputation as the "Florence of the North." Its yellow and pale green facades are enormously appealing, and their mere presence is even more overwhelming when you compare what you see today with photographs of Dresden from February 1945, after an Allied bombing raid destroyed the city overnight. Though some parts of the city center still look halfway between demolition and construction, the present city is an enormous tribute to Dresdeners' skills and dedication. Despite lack of funds, the people of Dresden succeeded in rebuilding what was once one of Europe's architectural and cultural treasures. The resemblance of today's riverside to Dresden cityscapes painted by Canaletto in the mid-1700s is remarkable.

Dresden was the capital of Saxony as early as the 15th century, although most of its architectural masterpieces date from the 18th century and the reigns of Augustus the Strong and his son, Frederick Augustus II. Both were widely traveled and sought out architects and designers capable of creating monuments like those they admired in Italy.

Life is Dresden is slowly returning to the level of its prewar busy economic and cultural past. Dresdeners are known for their industriousness and very efficient way of doing business, but they also know how to spend a night out. Contrary to Leipzig, the city still struggles to regain its architectural beauty: The war-inflicted gaps in the urban landscape are too big to be closed.

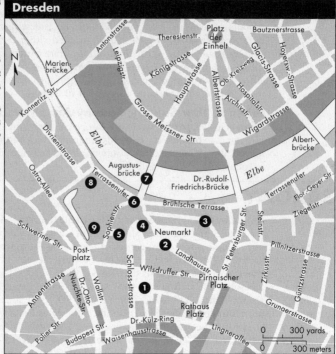

A Good Walk

From the main railway station (which has adequate parking), you'll first have to cross a featureless expanse surrounded by postwar high-rises to reach the old part of the city and its treasures. Pick up any materials you like at the tourist information office on pedestrians-only Pragerstrasse (No. 8).

The downtown area of Dresden is easily covered on foot. Buildings representing several centuries of architecture border the **Altmarkt** ①. At the square's northwest side, the narrow Schlosstrasse connects to Dresden's historic heart, the Neumarkt (New Market). On your right is the baroque **Frauenkirche** ②, rising up from its rubble. Just behind the church, off Brühlsche Gasse, stands the impressive **Albertinum** ③, which has one of the world's leading art galleries. If you leave the Albertinum by the Brühlsche Terrasse exit, you'll find yourself on what was once known as the "Balcony of Europe," a terrace high above the Elbe, carved from a 16th-century stretch of the city fortifications; from the terrace, a breathtaking vista of the Elbe and the Dresden skyline opens up. Back at the Neumarkt's northwestern corner, you'll see the **Johanneum** ④, part of the former palace that now houses a transportation museum. The outside wall of the Johanneum has a unique porcelain-tile painting of a royal procession; walk along the wall, and at the end of the street you'll reach the **Dresdner Schloss** ⑤, which is still under reconstruction.

Next walk a short distance north on any of the small paths from the Neumarkt, crossing Augustusstrasse in the direction of Terrassenufer; cross Schlossplatz and then turn left, where you'll encounter Sophienstrasse. If you turn left, you can't miss Saxony's largest church, the **Katholische Hofkirche** ⑥. North of the church off the Terrassenufer lies the **Augustusbrücke** ⑦, an intriguing, reconstruction of the old baroque bridge that once spanned the Elbe River. Just opposite the church on the Theaterplatz is the architecturally wondrous **Semperoper** ⑧, one of Europe's finest opera houses. Theaterplatz has as its centerpiece a proud equestrian statue of King Johann, who ruled Saxony when Gottfried Semper was at work. Don't be misled by Johann's confident pose in the saddle—he was terrified of horses and never learned to ride. Five minutes south of the Semperoper is the world-famous **Zwinger** ⑨, a richly decorated baroque palace with an entrance off Ostra-Allee.

TIMING

In winter and early spring, it can get quite windy on the wide, open squares. Small wonder, then, that most of the main attractions are hidden inside the impressive historic buildings. A full day is sufficient for a quick tour of historic Dresden, but if you plan to explore any of the museums, such as the Zwinger, or take a guided tour of the Semperoper, you'll need more than a day. Allow at least two hours each for the Zwinger, the Johanneum, and the Albertinum. In summer, schedule some time to relax in one of the cafés along the Elbe River.

Sights to See

❸ **Albertinum.** The massive, imperial-style building houses Dresden's leading art museum, one of the world's great galleries. The Albertinum is named after Saxony's King Albert, who between 1884 and 1887 converted a royal arsenal into a suitable setting for the treasures he and his forebears had collected. The upper story of the Albertinum, accessible from the Brühlsche Terrasse, houses the **Gemäldegalerie Neue Meister** (Gallery of Modern Masters), with displays of 19th- and 20th-century paintings and sculpture. Permanent exhibits include outstanding work by German masters of the 19th and 20th centuries (Caspar David Friedrich's haunting *Das Kreuz im Gebirge* is here) and French Impressionists and Postimpressionists.

The **Grünes Gewölbe** (Green Vault) draws the most attention. Named after a green room in the palace of Augustus the Strong, this part of the Albertinum (entered from Georg-Treu-Platz) contains an exquisite collection of unique objets d'art fashioned from gold, silver, ivory, amber, and other precious and semiprecious materials. Among the crown jewels are the world's largest "green" diamond, 41 carats in weight, and a dazzling group of tiny gem-studded figures called *Hofstaat zu Delhi am Geburtstag des Grossmoguls Aureng-Zeb* (The Court at Delhi during the Birthday of the Great Mogul Aureng-Zeb). The unwieldy name gives a false idea of the size of the work, dating from 1708; some parts of the tableau are so small they can be admired only through a magnifying glass. Somewhat larger and less delicate is the drinking bowl of Ivan the Terrible, perhaps the most sensational of the treasures in this extraordinary museum. Next door is the **Skulpturensammlung** (Sculpture Collection), which includes ancient Egyptian and classical works and examples by Giovanni da Bologna and Adriaen de Vries. ⊠ *Am Neumarkt, Brühlsche Terrasse,* ☎ *0351/491–4619.* ⚲ *DM 7, including admission to Gemäldegalerie Neue Meister, Grünes Gewölbe, Münzkabinett (coin collection), and Skulpturensammlung.* ⊙ *Fri.–Wed. 10–6.*

❶ **Altmarkt** (Old Market Square). Although dominated by the nearby unappealing Kulturpalast (Palace of Culture), a concrete leftover from the 1970s, the broad square and its surrounding streets are the true center of Dresden. Its colonnaded beauty (from the Stalinist-era architecture of the early 1950s) survived the disfiguring efforts of city planners to turn it into a huge outdoor parking lot. The Altmarkt's church, the **Kreuzkirche,** is an interesting combination of baroque and Jugendstil (art nouveau) architecture and decoration. There was already a church on this spot in the 13th century, but the present structure dates from the late 1700s. Other interesting buildings bordering the Altmarkt include the rebuilt **Rathaus** and the yellow-stucco, 18th-century Landhaus, which contains the **Stadtmuseum Dresden** (Municipal Museum; ✉ Wilsdruffer Str. 2, ☎ 0351/498–660; ⊡ DM 4; ☉ Sat.–Thurs. 10–6).

❽ Augustusbrücke (Augustus Bridge). This bridge, which spans the river in front of the ☞ **Katholische Hofkirche**, is a reconstruction of a 17th-century bridge blown up by the SS shortly before the end of World War II. The bridge was restored and renamed for Georgi Dimitroff, the Bulgarian Communist accused by the Nazis of instigating the Reichstag fire; after the fall of communism the original name, honoring August the Strong, was reinstated.

OFF THE
BEATEN PATH

DEUTSCHES HYGIENE-MUSEUM DRESDEN – A unique museum (even in a country with a national tendency for excessive cleanliness), the museum relates the history of public health and often features special art exhibits. ✉ Lingnerpl. 1, ☎ 0351/48460. ⊡ DM 5. ☉ Tues., Thurs., and Fri. 9.–5; Wed. 9–8:30; weekends 10–5.

❺ Dresdner Schloss (Dresden Palace). Restoration work is still under way behind the Renaissance facade of this former royal palace, much of which was built between 1709 and 1722. Some of the finished rooms in the reopened **Georgenbau** host historical exhibitions, among them an excellent exhibit on the reconstruction of the palace itself. The palace's main gate, the Georgentor, has regained its original appearance, complete with an enormous statue of the fully armed Saxon count George. In summer (April–October), the palace's old **Hausmannsturm** (Hausmann Tower) offers a wonderful view of the city and the Elbe River. The palace housed August the Strong's ☞ Grünes Gewölbe before it was moved in its entirety to the **Albertinum**. ✉ *Schlosspl.*, ☎ *0351/491–4619.* ⊡ *DM 5.* ☉ *Tues.–Sun. 10–6.*

❷ Frauenkirche (Church of Our Lady). The ruins here are all that remain of Germany's greatest Protestant church after the February 1945 bombing raid. These jagged, precariously tilting walls were once a mighty baroque church, so sturdily built that it withstood a three-day bombardment during the Seven Years' War, only to fall victim to the flames that followed the World War II raid. A painstaking reconstruction of the Frauenkirche is under way; it is hoped that it can be reconsecrated in the year 2006, the 800th anniversary of the founding of Dresden. ✉ *An der Frauenkirche.*

❹ Johanneum. At one time the royal stables, this 16th-century building now houses the **Verkehrsmuseum** (Transportation Museum), a collection of historical conveyances, including vintage automobiles and engines. The former **stable exercise yard,** behind the Johanneum and enclosed by elegant Renaissance arcades, was used in the 16th century as an open-air festival ground. A ramp leading up from the courtyard made it possible for royalty to reach the upper story to view the jousting below without having to dismount. You'll find the scene today much as it was centuries ago, complete with jousting markings in the ground. More popular even than jousting in those days was *Ringelstechen,* a risky pursuit in which riders at full gallop had to catch small rings on their lances. Horses and riders often came to grief in the narrow confines of the stable yard.

On the outside wall of the Johanneum is a remarkable example of **Meissen porcelain art:** a Meissen tile mural of a royal procession, 336 ft long. More than 100 members of the royal Saxon house of Wettin, half of them on horseback, are represented on the giant mosaic of 25,000 porcelain tiles, painted in 1904–07 after a design by Wilhelm Walther.

The Johanneum is reached by steps leading down from the Brühlsche Terrasse. ⊠ *Am Neumarkt at Augustusstr. 1,* ☎ *0351/86440.* ☑ *DM 4.* ☉ *Tues.–Sun. 10–5.*

⑥ Katholische Hofkirche (Catholic Court Church). The largest church in Saxony is also known as the Cathedral of St. Trinitatis. Frederick Augustus II (reigned 1733–63) brought architects and builders from Italy to construct a Catholic church in a city that had been the first large center of Lutheran Protestantism (like his father, Frederick Augustus II had to convert to Catholicism to be eligible to wear the Polish crown). They worked in secret, so the story goes, and Dresden's Protestant citizens were presented with a fait accompli when the church was finally consecrated in 1754. Seventy-eight statues of historical and biblical figures decorate the baroque facade; inside, the treasures include a beautiful stone pulpit by the royal sculptor Balthasar Permoser and a 250-year-old organ said to be one of the finest ever to come from the mountain workshops of the famous Silbermann family. In the cathedral's crypt are the tombs of 49 Saxon rulers and a precious vessel containing the heart of August the Strong. Due to restoration work, the cathedral's opening hours may change daily. ⊠ *Schlosspl.,* ☎ *0351/4844–712.* ☑ *Free.* ☉ *Weekdays 9–5, Sat. 10–5, Sun. noon–5.*

OFF THE BEATEN PATH

Radebeul – Follow the road along the north bank of the Elbe to Meissen. The small town of Radebeul, on the way, is a mecca for fans of westerns. Radebeul is the birthplace of Germany's well-loved novelist Karl May, who wrote highly popular, convincing Westerns without once visiting America. A museum explains just how he did it. ⊠ Karl-May-Str. 5, ☎ 0351/837–300. ☑ DM 9.50. ☉ Mar.–Oct., daily 9–6; Nov.–Feb., daily 10–4.

⑧ Semperoper (Semper Opera House). One of Germany's best-known and most popular theaters, this magnificent opera house saw the premieres of Richard Wagner's *Rienzi, Der fliegende Holländer* and *Tannhäuser,* and Richard Strauss's *Salome, Elektra* and *Der Rosenkavalier.* The Dresden architect Gottfried Semper built the house in 1838–41 in Italian Renaissance style, then saw his work destroyed in a fire caused by a careless lamplighter. Semper had to flee Dresden after participating in a democratic uprising, so his son Manfred rebuilt the theater in the neo-Renaissance style you see today. Even Manfred Semper's version had to be rebuilt after the devastating bombing raid of February 1945. On the 40th anniversary of that raid—February 13, 1985—the Semperoper reopened with a performance of *Der Freischütz,* by Carl Maria von Weber, another artist who did much to make Dresden a leading center of German music and culture. Even if you're no opera buff, the Semper's lavish interior can't fail to impress. Velvet, brocade, and marble (much of it imitation) create an atmosphere of intimate luxury (it seats 1,323). Guided tours of the building are offered throughout the day, depending on the opera's rehearsal schedule. Tours begin at the entrance to your right as you face the Elbe. ⊠ *Theaterpl. 2,* ☎ *0351/491–1496.* ☑ *Tour DM 8.* ☉ *Tours usually start at 1:30, 2, and 3 weekdays, 10 weekends.*

⑨ Zwinger. Dresden's magnificent baroque showpiece and perhaps one of the greatest examples of baroque architecture in Europe is entered by way of the mighty Kronentor (Crown Gate), off Ostra-Allee. Augustus the Strong hired a small army of artists and artisans to create a "pleasure ground" worthy of the Saxon court on the site of the former bailey (German: *Zwinger*), part of the city fortifications. They were placed under the general direction of the architect Matthäus Daniel Pöppelmann, who was called reluctantly out of retirement to design what came to be his greatest work, begun in 1707 and completed in 1728. Completely enclosing a central courtyard filled with lawns and pools, the complex is made up of six linked pavilions, one of which boasts a carillon of Meissen bells, hence its name: Glockenspielpavillon.

The Zwinger is quite a scene—a riot of garlands, nymphs, and other baroque ornamentation and sculpture on the edge of an urban landscape etched in somber gray. The contrast would have been much greater had Semper not closed in one side of the Zwinger, which was originally open to the riverbank. Stand in the center of this quiet oasis, where the city's roar is kept at bay by the outer wings of the structure, and imagine the court festivities held here. One notable occasion celebrated here was the marriage of Frederick Augustus, son of Augustus the Great, to Maria Josepha, daughter of Emperor Joseph I, in 1719. The ornate carriage-style lamps shone; the fountains splashed in the shallow pools; and wide staircases beckoned to galleried walks and to the romantic Nymphenbad, a coyly hidden courtyard where statues of nude women perch in alcoves to protect them from a fountain that spits unexpectedly.

The **Sempergalerie** (Semper Gallery), in the northwestern corner of the Zwinger complex, was built by the great architect to house portions of the royal art collections. It contains the world-renowned **Gemäldegalerie Alte Meister** (Old Masters Gallery). The Zwinger Palace complex also contains a porcelain collection, a zoological museum, and the Mathematisch-Physikalischer Salon, which displays old scientific instruments.

Among the priceless paintings in the Sempergalerie collection are works by Dürer, Holbein, Jan van Eyck, Rembrandt, Rubens, van Dyck, Hals, Vermeer, Raphael (*The Sistine Madonna*), Titian, Giorgione, Veronese, Velázquez, Murillo, Canaletto, and Watteau. On the wall of the entrance archway you'll see an inscription in Russian, one of the few amusing reminders of World War II in Dresden. It reads, in rhyme: "Museum checked. No mines. Chanutin did the checking." Chanutin, presumably, was the Russian soldier responsible for checking one of Germany's greatest art galleries for anything more explosive than a Rubens nude. ☎ *0351/491–4619.* 🎫 *DM 7.* 🕐 *Tues.–Sun. 10–6.*

The Zwinger's **Porzellansammlung** (Porcelain Collection; ☎ 0351/491–4619; 🎫 DM 3; 🕐 Fri.–Wed. 10–6), stretching from the curved gallery that adjoins the Glockenspielpavillon to the long gallery on the east side, is considered one of the best of its kind in the world. The focus, naturally, is on Dresden and Meissen china, but there are also outstanding examples of Japanese, Chinese, and Korean porcelain. The **Rüstkammer** (armory; ☎ 0351/491–4619; 🎫 DM 3; 🕐 Tues.–Sun. 10–6) showcases medieval and Renaissance suits of armor and weapons. The **Zoologisches Museum** (Zoological Museum; ☎ 0351/495–2503; 🎫 DM 2; 🕐 Tues.–Sun. 9–4) has a small but very interesting collection of natural history exhibits, including skeletons of wild animals that once roamed the Elbe Valley. The **Staatlicher Mathematisch-Physikalischer Salon** (State Mathematics and Physics Salon) (☎ 0351/495–1364; 🎫 DM 3; 🕐 Fri.–Wed. 9:30–5) is packed with rare and historic scientific instruments. ✉ *Zwinger entrance, Ostra–Allee.*

Dining and Lodging

$$ ✕ **Sophienkeller.** The most exciting (and probably the friendliest)
★ restaurant in town is in the basement of the Taschenbergpalais and re-
creates an 18th-century beer-cellar atmosphere. Waitresses wear period
costumes, and the furniture and porcelain are as rustic as the food is
original. Most of the dishes are standard regional fare, including
Schweinekrustenbraten mit Rotkraut und Knödeln (crunchy pork roast
with red cabbage and dumplings) or the typically Saxon *Gesindeessen*
(rye bread, panfried with mustard, slices of pork, and mushrooms and
baked with cheese). ✉ *Taschenbergpalais, Taschenberg 3,* ☎ *0351/497–
260. AE, DC, MC, V.*

$–$$ ✕ **Haus Altmarkt.** The choice of eateries in this busy corner of the colonnaded Altmarkt is enormous—from the McDonald's that has wormed
its way into the city landscape to the upscale Amadeus restaurant on
the ground floor. Between these extremes are a jolly, bistrolike café and,
downstairs, a vaulted restaurant, the *Altmarkt-Keller,* with a secluded
bar. The Zum Humpen restaurant is the best value, with midday menu
offerings of less than DM 20. In warm weather you can eat outside on
a terrace and watch the marketplace bustle. ✉ *Wilfdruffer Str. 19–21,*
☎ *0351/495–1212. AE, MC, V.*

$–$$ ✕ **Italienisches Dörfchen.** The name, which means "Italian village," is
a reference to the fact that this historic building on the bank of the Elbe
once housed Italian craftsmen. They had been brought to Dresden to
work on the Hofkirche. Today the lavishly restored, colorful rooms
offer a warm welcome. There are a beer tavern, a café, and a shady
garden for alfresco eating. The menu is mostly Saxon; the Bellotto restaurant upstairs serves upscale, but not Italian, cuisine such as *Schnitzel
mit Parmaschinken und Salbei* (schnitzel with Parma bacon, fresh vegetables, and roasted potatoes). ✉ *Theaterpl. 3,* ☎ *0351/498–160.
AE, DC, MC, V.*

$$$–$$$$ ✕🏨 **Bülow-Residenz.** One of the most intimate first-class hotels in east-
★ ern Germany, the Bülow-Residenz is also one its most luxurious, with
a focus on old-world elegance. The baroque palace was built in 1730
by a wealthy Dresden city official. Each spacious room is tastefully dec-
orated with thick carpets and mostly dark, warm cherrywood furni-
ture, and has individual accents and modern amenities. In summer the
verdant courtyard is a romantic setting for dinner. The Carousel
restaurant, holds Saxony's sole Michelin star, and offers a surprisingly
large variety of sophisticated fish and game dishes. The bar is under-
neath the building's old vaulted ceilings. ✉ *Rähnitzg. 19, D–01097,*
☎ *0351/80030,* 📠 *0351/800–3100. 25 rooms, 5 suites. Restaurant,
bar, in-room safes, minibars, no-smoking floor, room service, baby-sit-
ting, dry cleaning, laundry service, meeting rooms, concierge, parking
(fee). AE, DC, MC, V.* ≋

$–$$ ✕🏨 **Hotelschiff Florentina.** Dresden's celebrated river panorama is
right outside your cabin window on this cruise-liner hotel, moored just
below the historic Augustus Bridge and an easy stroll from all the major
sights. The boat has spacious public lounges and a restaurant with the
finest view in town. In summer you can eat on deck; if the weather
cools, you can move inside to a plant-hung winter garden. Cabins—
furnished "maritime-style"—all have showers and toilets and come
equipped with TV, radio, and telephone. ✉ *Terrassenufer, D–01069,*
☎ *0351/459–0169,* 📠 *0351/459–5036. 64 cabins. Restaurant. AE,
DC, MC, V.*

$$$$ 🏨 **Kempinski Hotel Taschenbergpalais Dresden.** Destroyed in wartime
★ bombing but now rebuilt, the historic Taschenberg Palace—the work
of the Zwinger architect Matthäus Daniel Pöppelmann—reopened as
a magnificent hotel in early 1995. It's Dresden's premier address, a show-

piece of the Kempinski group and the last word in luxury, as befits the former residence of the Saxon crown princes. Rooms are as big as city apartments, while suites earn the adjective palatial; they are all furnished with bright elm-wood furniture and have several phone lines, as well as fax machines and data ports. ✉ *Taschenberg 3, D–01067,* ☎ *0351/ 49120,* FAX *0351/491–2812. 188 rooms, 25 suites. 2 restaurants, 2 bars, in-room data ports, in-room safes, minibars, no-smoking rooms, room service, indoor pool, barbershop, beauty salon, massage, sauna, shops, baby-sitting, dry cleaning, laundry service, concierge, business services, meeting rooms, parking (fee). AE, DC, MC, V.* 🕮

$$$$ 🏨 **Westin Bellevue Dresden.** Across the river from the city core, this modern hotel cleverly incorporates an old restored mansion, which also has the best rooms. From the outside the hotel may look unappealing, but most rooms on the upper floors have spectacular views of the city skyline and Elbe River. If you don't get a room with a view, you can enjoy vistas from the fitness club's panoramic windows. Guest rooms and suites in the old mansion are furnished with restored or reproduced pieces in the 18th-century style. ✉ *Grosse Meissner Str. 15, D–01097,* ☎ *0351/8050,* FAX *0351/805–609. 323 rooms, 16 suites. 3 restaurants, bar, café, in-room data ports, in-room safes, minibars, no-smoking rooms, room service, indoor pool, barbershop, massage, sauna, exercise room, shops, children's programs, concierge, meeting rooms, free parking. AE, DC, MC, V.* 🕮

$$$ 🏨 **artotel Dresden.** The artotel keeps the promise of its rather unusual name. It's all modern, designed by Italian interior architect Denis Santachiara and decorated with more than 600 works of art by Dresden-born painter and sculptor A. R. Penck. It's definitely a place for the artsy crowd; you might find the heavily styled rooms a bit much. The Kunsthalle Dresden and its exhibits of modern art is right next door. Apart from offering art, the hotel's rooms and service have genuine first-class appeal at considerably lower prices. ✉ *Ostra-Allee 33, D–01067,* ☎ *0351/49220,* FAX *0351/492–2777. 158 rooms, 16 suites. 2 restaurants, bar, in-room data ports, in-room safes, minibars, no-smoking rooms, room service, indoor pool, massage, sauna, steam room, exercise room, shops, baby-sitting, dry cleaning, laundry service, concierge, business services, meeting rooms, parking (fee). AE, DC, MC, V.* 🕮

$ 🏨 **Hotel Schloss Röhrsdorf.** Surrounded by rolling parkland, this beautifully restored country palace is just a short drive from Dresden. Rooms have been renovated to a high standard of comfort, with mostly modern furnishings but some original antique touches. The vaulted restaurant is of equally high standard. The hotel has its own stables, and the terrain is ideal for riding. ✉ *Hauptstr. 3, D–01809 Röhrsdorf,* ☎ *0351/ 285–770,* FAX *0351/2857–7263. 21 rooms, 1 suite. Restaurant, bar, minibars, no-smoking rooms, meeting rooms, free parking. AE, MC, V.*

Nightlife and the Arts

The opera in Dresden regained its international reputation when the **Semper Opera House** (Sächsische Staatsoper Dresden; ✉ Theaterpl.) reopened in 1985 following an eight-year reconstruction. Tickets are reasonably priced but also hard to get; they're often included in package tours. Try your luck at the evening box office (Abendkasse, left of the main entrance; ☎ 0351/491–1705) about a half hour before the performance; there are usually a few tickets available. If you're unlucky, take one of the opera house tours (☞ Sights to See, *above*).

Dresden's fine **Philharmonic Orchestra** takes center stage in the city's annual music festival, from mid-May to early June. In addition to the annual **film** festival in April, open-air "Riverside Film Nights" take place on the bank of the Elbe from mid-July to mid-August.

May brings an annual international Dixieland **jazz** festival, and the Jazz Autumn festival follows in October. Jazz musicians perform most nights of the week at the friendly, laid-back **Tonne Jazz Club** (⊠ Waldschlösschen, Am Brauhaus 3, ☎ 0351/802–6017). Folk and rock music are regularly featured at **Bärenzwinger** (⊠ Brühlscher Garten, ☎ 0351/4965–153). Two of the best bars and pubs in town are the American-style bar **Pinta** (⊠ Louisenstr. 49, ☎ 0351/8026–612), and **Planwirtschaft** (⊠ Louisenstr. 20, ☎ 0351/8013–187). Both are in the **Äussere Neustadt,** the city's liveliest nightspot. Two hip dancing clubs are **Dance Factory,** in an old Stasi garrison (⊠ Bautzner Str. 118, ☎ 0351/8020–066), and the **Motown Club** (⊠ St. Petersburger Str. 9, ☎ 0351/4874–150). Both clubs attract a younger crowd.

Shopping

Dresden is almost as famous as Meissen for its porcelain. It's manufactured outside the city in **Freital,** where there's a showroom and shop (⊠ Bachstr. 16, Freital, ☎ 0351/647130), open weekdays 9–6. Within Dresden you'll find exquisite Meissen and Freital porcelain at the **Karstadt** department store (⊠ Prager Str. 12, ☎ 0351/490–6833). The **Kunststube am Zwinger** (⊠ Hertha-Lindner-Str. 10–12, ☎ 0351/490–4082) sells wooden toys and all the famous Saxon *Rächermännchen* (Smoking Men) and *Weihnachtspyramiden* (Christmas Lights Pyramids) manufactured by hand in the Erzbirge Mountains.

Sächsische Schweiz

❿ *42 km (26 mi) southeast of Dresden.*

True mountain climbers may smile at the name of the **Sächsische Schweiz** (Saxon Switzerland), the mountainous region southeast of Dresden. The highest summit in Saxon Switzerland is a mere 182 ft, but the scenery in this region, a mixture of cliffs, gorges, and small canyons, is almost as dramatic as the Alps. The stone formations are at least 100 million years old and are a geological leftover of the Elbe River's sandstone deposits. In time, the soft stone was sculpted by wind and water into often grim but fantastic-looking tall columns of stone.

The **Nationalpark** (national park), which covers 97 square km (37 square mi) of the region, was only established 11 years ago. Thanks to its inaccessibility, Saxon Switzerland is home to game and many other wild animals (such as the lynx), which are otherwise extinct in Germany. The national park is divided into two different parts, which can be explored by foot, either following marked routes or by registering with the park rangers for guided tours. To reach the national park from Dresden, drive southeast on the B–172 toward Pirna, or take the S-bahn from the central train station and get off at **Königstein** or **Bad Schandau;** both towns are served by buses and minitrains that take you to the most towns of the region. The train ride itself takes close to an hour. ⊠ *Nationalparkverwaltung Sächsische Schweiz, An der Elbe 4, D–01814 Bad Schandau,* ☎ *035022/90060.* 🎫 *Free.*

Görlitz

⓫ *60 km (38 mi) northeast of Dresden, 265 km (165 mi) southeast of Berlin.*

Quiet, narrow cobblestone alleys and late-medieval and 19th-century mansions make Görlitz one of the most charming finds in eastern Germany. Once a major commercial hub between Dresden and Wroclaw, Görlitz, Germany's easternmost city, fell into small-town oblivion after World War II. The Germans blew up all of the city's bridges over the Neisse

River in the last days of the war (the eastern bank of the city now belongs to Poland), but the city was barely touched by Allied bombings.

A vivid reminder of the city's wealthy past is the richly decorated Renaissance homes and warehouses on the **Obermarkt** (Upper Market). During the late Middle Ages, the most common merchandise here was cloth, which was bought and sold from covered wagons jamming the market and the first floors of many buildings. On **Verrätergasse** (Traitors' Alley), off the Obermarkt, is the **Peter-Liebig-Haus;** note the letters DVRT above the doorway. In 1527 the city's cloth makers secretly met here to prepare a rebellion against the city council. Their plans were uncovered, and the plotters were hanged. The initials of the first four words of their meeting place, *Der verräterischen Rotte Tor* (The treacherous gang's gate) were inscribed above the door.

Görlitz's rich past is displayed at two locations of the **Städtische Kunstsammlung** (Municipal Art Collection). The massive **Kaisertrutz** (Emperor's Fortress; ⊠ *Am Obermarkt*) once protected the western city gates and now houses late-Gothic and Renaissance art from and around Görlitz. The **Barockhaus Neissestrasse** (Baroque House on Neisse Street; ⊠ Neissestr. 30) mostly displays furniture and art from the 17th to the 19th centuries. ☎ *03581/671–351.* ⊠ *DM 3.* ☉ *Tues.–Sun. 10–5. Kaisertrutz closed Apr.–Nov.*

The city's oldest section surrounds the **Untermarkt** (Lower Market), whose most prominent building is the **Rathaus.** Its winding staircase is as peculiar as the statue of the goddess of justice, whose eyes—contrary to European tradition—are not covered. The corner house on the square, the **Alte Ratsapotheke** (Old Council Pharmacy) has a sundial on the facade (painted in 1550) based on the 12 signs of the zodiac.

Not far away from the Untermarkt is the **Biblisches Haus** (Biblical House), whose sandstone facade is carved with scenes from the Old and New testaments. The upper series shows the life of Christ; the lower series of ornaments depicts scenes from the book of Genesis. ⊠ *Neissestr. 29, near corner of Weberstr.*

The **Karstadt** department store off busy Marienplatz dates to 1912–13 and is Germany's only original Art Nouveau department store. The main hall has a colorful glass cupola and several stunning freestanding staircases.

Perched high above the river is the **Kirche St. Peter und Paul** (Sts. Peter and Paul Church), one of Saxony's largest late-Gothic churches, dating to 1423. The real draw of the church is its famous organ, built in 1703 by Eugenio Casparini. Its full and deep sound can be heard during guided tours (which must be prearranged by phone). ⊠ *Bei der Peterkirche 5,* ☎ *03581/409–590.* ⊠ *Free.* ☉ *Mon.–Sat. 10:30–4, Sun. 11:30–4; guided tours Thurs. and Sun. at noon.*

Dining and Lodging

$$ ✕ **Le Trou Normand.** Behind the thick walls of a historic baroque building on the Untermarkt, this charming little restaurant features the cuisine of northern France. The wine list is impressive, the atmosphere friendly and familial. ⊠ *Untermarkt 13,* ☎ *03581/417–037.* MC, V.

$$ ✕▥ **Hotel Tuchmacher.** The city's best hotel is also its most modern
★   accommodation in antique disguise. In a mansion dating to 1528, the guest rooms are sparsely furnished with modern dark-cherrywood furniture, wooden floors, and ceilings with thick beams. The colorful ceilings may remind you of Jackson Pollock paintings, but they are original ornaments from the Renaissance. The hotel's atmosphere is

warm and laid-back. The Schneider-Stube serves traditional Saxon dishes such as *Rinderroulade in Rotweinsud* (beef roulade in red-wine gravy). All room prices include a luxurious breakfast buffet. ⊠ *Peterstr. 8, D–02826,* ☎ *03581/47310,* FAX *03581/473–179. 47 rooms, 5 suites. Restaurant, bar, minibars, no-smoking rooms, room service, sauna, exercise room, dry cleaning, laundry service, meeting rooms, free parking. AE, DC, MC, V.*

Meissen

⑫ *25 km (16 mi) northwest of Dresden.*

This romantic city on the Elbe River is known the world over for its porcelain, bearing the trademark crossed blue swords. The first European porcelain was made in this area in 1708, and in 1710 the Royal Porcelain Workshop was established in Meissen, close to the local raw materials.

The story of how porcelain came to be produced in Meissen reads like a German fairy tale: the Saxon elector Augustus the Strong, who ruled from 1694 to 1733, urged alchemists at his court to search for the secret of making gold, something he badly needed to refill a state treasury depleted by his extravagant lifestyle. The alchemists failed to produce gold, but one of them, Johann Friedrich Böttger, discovered a method for making something almost as precious: fine hard-paste porcelain. Already a rapacious collector of Oriental porcelains, Prince August put Böttger and a team of craftsmen up in a hilltop castle—Albrechtsburg—and set them to work. Augustus hoped to keep their formula a state secret, but within a few years fine porcelain was being produced in many parts of Europe. Meissen porcelain is found in one form or another all over town.

The **Albrechtsburg,** where the story of Meissen porcelain began, sits high above Old Meissen, towering over the Elbe River far below. The 15th-century castle is Germany's first truly residential one, a complete break with the earlier style of fortified bastions. It fell into neglect as nearby Dresden rose to prominence, but it's still an imposing collection of late-Gothic and Renaissance buildings. In the central *Schutzhof,* a typical Gothic courtyard protected on three sides by high rough-stone walls, is an exterior spiral staircase, the **Wendelstein,** a masterpiece of early masonry hewn in 1525 from a single massive stone block. The ceilings of the castle halls are richly decorated, although many date only from a restoration in 1870. Adjacent to the castle is a towered early Gothic cathedral. It's a bit of a climb up Burgstrasse and Amtsstrasse to the castle, but a bus runs regularly up the hill from the Marktplatz. ☎ *03521/47070.* ✑ *DM 6, tour DM 3.* ✆ *Mar.–Oct., daily 10–6; Nov.–Feb., daily 10–5. Closed Jan. 10–31.*

A set of porcelain bells at the late-Gothic **Frauenkirche** (Church of Our Lady) on the central Marktplatz was the first of its kind anywhere when installed in 1929. Also of interest in the town center are the 1569 **Alte Brauerei** (Old Brewery; ⊠ An der Frauenkirche 3), graced by a Renaissance gable and now housing city offices, and **Franziskanerkirche** (St. Francis Church), a former monastery, where a museum showcases the city's medieval past. ⊠ *Heinrichspl. 3,* ☎ *03521/458–857.* ✑ *DM 3.* ✆ *Daily 10–5.*

The **Staatliche Porzellan–Manufaktur Meissen** (Meissen Porcelain Works) outgrew its castle workshop in the mid-19th century, and today you'll find it on the southern outskirts of town. One of its buildings has a demonstration workshop and a museum whose Meissen collection rivals that of the Porcelain Museum in Dresden (☞ *Zwinger in* Dresden, *above*). ⊠ *Talstr. 9,* ☎ *03521/468–700.* 🖾 *Museum DM 9; workshop DM 5, including guided tour.* ☼ *May–Oct., daily 9–6; Nov.–Apr., daily 10–5.*

Near the porcelain works is the **Nikolaikirche** (St. Nicholas Church; ⊠ Neumarkt 29), which holds the largest set of porcelain figures ever crafted (8.2 ft) and also has remains of early Gothic frescoes.

Dining and Lodging

$–$$ ✕ **Domkeller.** Part of the centuries-old complex of buildings ringing the town castle, this ancient and popular hostelry is definitely one of the best places to enjoy fine wines and hearty German dishes in Meissen. It's also worth a visit for the sensational view of the Elbe River valley from its large dining room and tree-shaded terrace. ⊠ *Dompl. 9,* ☎ *03521/457–676. AE, DC, MC, V.*

$$$–$$$$ ✕🖾 **Meissen Pannonia Parkhotel.** This Jugendstil (art nouveau) villa on the bank of the Elbe, across from the hilltop castle, serves meals prepared with an international flair in a dining room with original stained glass and elegantly framed doors. Although most of the luxuriously furnished and appointed rooms are in the newly built annexes, try for one in the villa—and for an unforgettable experience book the *Hochzeitssuite* (wedding suite), on the top floor (around DM 307 a night). The view of the river and the castle from its two rooms and from the large private terrace is sensational. ⊠ *Hafenstr. 27–31, D-01662,* ☎ *03521/72250,* ꜰᴀx *03521/722–904. 76 rooms, 17 apartments, 4 suites. Restaurant, bar, in-room data ports, minibars, no-smoking rooms, room service, hot tub, massage, sauna, exercise room, babysitting, dry cleaning, laundry service, meeting rooms, free parking. AE, DC, MC, V.*

Nightlife and the Arts

Meissen's cathedral, the **Dom,** has a yearlong music program, with organ and choral concerts every Saturday during the summer. Call (☎ 03521/452–490) for details. Regular **concerts** are held at the Albrechtsburg, and in early September the *Burgfestspiele*—open-air evening performances—are staged in the castle's romantic courtyard (☎ 03521/47070 for details).

Shopping

Meissen porcelain can be bought directly from the **Staatliche Porzellan–Manufaktur Meissen** (⊠ Talstr. 9, ☎ 03521/468–700) and in every china and gift shop in town. To wine connoisseurs, the name *Meissen* is associated with vineyards producing top-quality wines much in demand throughout Germany—try a bottle of Müller-Thurgau, Weissburgunder, or Goldriesling.

Freiberg

🔞 *40 km (25 mi) south of Meissen.*

Once a prosperous silver-mining community, Freiberg's highlights are two picturesque Gothic town squares, the Upper and Lower markets. The late-Gothic cathedral, with its Golden Gate, constructed in 1230, has a richly decorated interior and a Silbermann organ dating from 1711.

The **Stadtmuseum** (City Museum), on central Domplatz, vividly describes the history of silver mining in and around Freiberg. ⊠ *Stadt- und Bergbaumuseum, Am Dom 1,* ☎ *03731/23197.* 🖾 *DM 4.* ☼ *Tues.– Sun. 10–5.*

En Route Take the winding Freital Valley road west to Chemnitz. You'll pass through a village called **Frankenstein** on the way. It has no relation to Mary Shelley's fictional scientist-baron, but there are some ancient castle ruins in the vicinity.

Chemnitz

⓮ *35 km (22 mi) west of Freiberg, 80 km (50 mi) southeast of Leipzig.*

On older maps Chemnitz may appear as Karl-Marx-Stadt, an appellation imposed on the city in 1953 to remind the East German working community of the man who really started it all. In 1990 the inhabitants, free to express a choice, overwhelmingly voted to restore the original name. Still, in front of the district council building in the new city center is one of the few remaining Karl Marx memorials in eastern Germany (thanks to the hard-fighting pro-Marx lobby), a massive stylized head sculpted by the Soviet artist Lew Kerbel. Behind it is the motto WORKING MEN OF ALL COUNTRIES, UNITE!—in German, Russian, French, and English. Badly damaged during World War II, Chemnitz has revived as a center of heavy industry, but it never had the architectural attractions of other cities in the area.

Chemnitz's main visual attraction is its 12th-century **Rote Turm** (Red Tower), in the center of the city. The **Altes Rathaus** (Old City Hall), dating from 1496–98, incorporates a variety of styles from many reconstructions. Outside the city museum (which is not particularly exciting) on Theaterplatz is a group of 250-million-year-old **petrified tree trunks,** unique in Europe and looking for all the world like a modern work of sculpture.

Dining and Lodging

$$ ✕▥ **Adelsberger Parkhotel Hoyer.** The first hotel built in Chemnitz after reunification has a modern, graceful exterior and elegant, comfortable guest rooms. The apartments under the steeply sloping eaves are particularly attractive, especially where sunlight streams through large dormer windows. The restaurant's royal-blue-and-white furnishings are flooded with light from floor-to-ceiling bay windows. The imaginative menu includes international cuisine and some hearty Saxon specialties. ⊠ *Wilhelm-Busch-Str. 61, D–09127,* ☎ *0371/773–303,* ᐧᐧ *0371/773–377. 23 rooms, 3 suites. Restaurant, minibars, room service, sauna, solarium, exercise room, baby-sitting, dry cleaning, laundry service, meeting rooms, free parking. AE, MC, V.* ✺

$$$ ▥ **Günnewig Hotel Chemnitzer Hof.** This city-center hotel was built in 1930 in early Bauhaus style, in which ornamentation was discarded in favor of abstract design (it is now on the National Historic Register). The spacious rooms are furnished with fine veneers and attractive shades of blue. ⊠ *Theaterpl. 4, D–09111,* ☎ *0371/6840,* ᐧᐧ *0371/676–2587. 100 rooms, 1 suite, 3 apartments. Restaurant, bar, in-room safes, minibars, no-smoking rooms, room service, barbershop, dry cleaning, laundry service, meeting rooms, parking (fee). AE, DC, MC, V.* ✺

En Route Bundestrasse 95 leads to Leipzig, but for a scene out of World War II, detour at Borna for 176 to **Colditz.** A pretty river valley holds the town whose name still sends a chill through Allied veterans. During the war the Germans converted the town's massive, somber castle into what they believed would be an escape-proof prison for prisoners regarded as security risks. But many managed to flee, employing a catalog of ruses that have since been the stuff of films and books. The castle is now a home for the elderly, but the courtyards and some of the installations used during the war can be visited. You can continue to Leipzig via 107 to the autobahn.

Leipzig

80 km (50 mi) northwest of Chemnitz, 32 km (20 mi) southeast of Halle.

With a population of about 560,000, Leipzig is the second-largest city in eastern Germany (after Berlin) and has long been a center of printing and bookselling. Astride major trade routes, it was an important market town in the Middle Ages, and it continues to be a trading center, thanks to the *Leipziger Messe* (trade and fair shows throughout the year) that bring together buyers from east and west.

Those familiar with music and German literature will associate Leipzig with the great composer Johann Sebastian Bach (1685–1750), who was organist and choir director at the Thomaskirche. The city celebrated Bach throughout 2000 with special concerts and events. The 19th-century composer Richard Wagner was born here in 1813; and German poets Goethe and Schiller both lived and worked in the area.

On the city's outskirts, Prussian, Austrian, Russian, and Swedish forces stood ground against Napoléon's troops. In 1813 the Völkerschlacht (Battle of the Nations) was fought here, a prelude to the French general's defeat two years later at Waterloo.

World War II left little of old Leipzig intact. Restoration conveys touches of the city's Renaissance character and Jugendstil (Art Nouveau) flair, although some of the newer buildings (notably the university's skyscraper tower) distort the perspective and proportions of the old city.

A Good Walk

Start your tour of downtown Leipzig at the gigantic **Hauptbahnhof** ⑮, the city's main train station and premier shopping mall. Cross the broad expanse of Willy-Brandt-Platz to walk south on Goethestrasse. On your left you'll see the modern **Opernhaus** ⑯, whose socialist facade is a sad contrast to the magnificent old architecture of the Hauptbahnhof. Turn right onto Grimmaischestrasse and after a short walk turn right onto Nikolaistrasse, where you can visit the **Nikolaikirche** ⑰. Returning south, Nikolaistrasse turns into Universitätstrasse, where the rather unappealing **Leipzig Universitätsturm** ⑱ looms above every other building in the city center. On its east side, the tower faces the vast Augustusplatz; across this square stands the **Neues Gewandhaus** ⑲, home of the city's renowned orchestra. Return north to Grimmaischestrasse and walk west; on your left you'll pass by the **Mädlerpassage** ⑳, one of the city's finest shopping arcades, which dates to the turn of the 20th century. Continue a bit farther west, and just off the street on your right is the market square, the **Markt** ㉑, with the old city hall and its museum devoted to Leipzig's past. Not far away, off the narrow Barfussgässchen, is the new **Museum zum Arabischen Kaffeebaum** ㉒, a coffeehouse and museum devoted to the bitter bean. From here it's just a five-minute walk northwest to the **Museum in der Runden Ecke** ㉓, a special exhibition about East Germany's secret police, the Stasi. Take the Dittrichring to **Thomaskirche** ㉔, where Johann Sebastian Bach once worked as choirmaster. Opposite the church is the **Johann-Sebastian-Bach-Museum** ㉕. Follow Dittrichring and Harkortstrasse south to the **Museum der Bildenden Künste** ㉖, the city's leading art gallery. Right next to the museum stands a 19th-century neo-Gothic monstrosity that serves as Leipzig's city hall.

Leipzig's other main sights are on the walk's periphery. If you turn east from Goethestrasse onto Grimmaischestrasse, you'll reach the **Gras-**

Leipzig

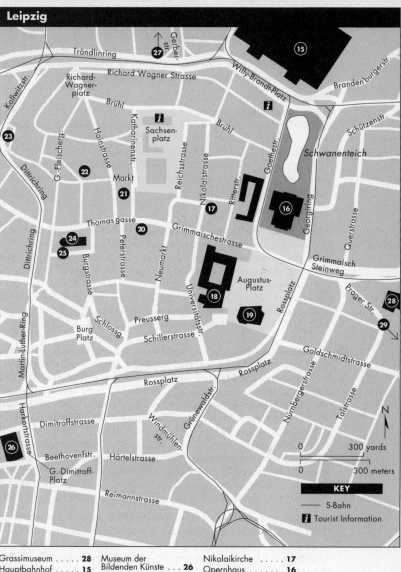

Trändlinring
Gerberstr.
27
15
Richard Wagner Strasse
Willy-Brandt-Platz
Brandenburgerstr.
Richard-Wagner-platz
Brühl
Schützenstr.
Kollwitzstr.
23
G.-Fleischerg.
Hainstrasse
Katharinenstr.
Sachsen-platz
Reichsstrasse
Nikolaistrasse
Brühl
Goethestr.
Schwanenteich
Dittrichring
22
Markt
21
Ritterstr.
16
Georgring
Querstrasse
Thomas gasse
20
Grimmaischestrasse
17
24
Peterstrasse
Neumarkt
18
Grimmaisch Steinweg
25
Burgstrasse
Universitätsstr.
Augustus-Platz
19
Rossplatz
Prager Str.
28
Schlossg.
Preusserg.
Schillerstrasse
29
Burg Platz
Martin-Luther-Ring
Rossplatz
Goldschmidtstrasse
Nürnbergerstrasse
Talstrasse
Harkortstrasse
Dimitroffstrasse
Windmühlen-str.
Grünewaldstr.
Rossplatz
N
26
Beethovenfstr.
Härtelstrasse
0   300 yards
G.-Dimitroff-Platz
0   300 meters
Reimannstrasse
KEY
— S-Bahn
i Tourist Information

simuseum ㉘ in about 10 minutes. After a stop here, you can take a streetcar (No. 15 to Meusdorf) from Johannisplatz (in front of the museum) to the **Völkerschlachtdenkmal** ㉙, a huge memorial to the battle that marked the beginning of Napoléon's final defeat in 1815. For another side trip, take streetcar No. 6 to the **Schillerhaus** ㉗, once the home of German poet and playwright Friedrich Schiller.

TIMING

It's possible to walk around the historic downtown area of Leipzig in just about three hours and still stop at some of the sights mentioned above. The churches can be inspected in less than 20 minutes each. But if you're interested in German history and art, you'll need perhaps two full days because you can spend a whole day just visiting the museums, particularly the Grassimuseum. The Völkerschlachtdenkmal is perfect for a half-day side trip.

Sights to See

OFF THE
BEATEN PATH

BOTANISCHER GARTEN (Botanical Garden) – This set of splendid open-air gardens and greenhouses incorporates Germany's oldest university botanical garden, which dates from 1542. The journey to the Botanischer Garten stop takes about 15 minutes on Tram 2 or 21 (get off at the Johannisallee stop). ✉ Linnestr. 1, ☎ 0341/973–6850. ☞ Free. ☺ Gardens Nov.–Mar., daily 9–4; Apr. and Oct., daily 9–6; May–Sept., daily 9–8. Greenhouses Nov.–Feb., daily 9–4; Mar.–Apr. and Oct., daily 9–6; May–Sept., daily 9–8. Butterfly house Apr.–Oct., Tues.–Sun. 10–6.

㉘ **Grassimuseum.** This major cultural venue is a fine example of German Art Deco. It was built between 1925 and 1929 to house three important museums. The **Museum für Kunsthandwerk** (Museum of Arts and Crafts; ☞ DM 5–6, depending on exhibit; ☺ Tues. and Thurs.–Sun. 10–6, Wed. noon–8) showcases European works from the Middle Ages to the early 20th century. The **Museum für Völkerkunde** (Ethnological Museum; ☞ DM 5; ☺ Tues.–Fri. 10–5:30, weekends 10–5) has exhibits on prehistoric cultures from all five continents. The **Musikinstrumentenmuseum** (Musical Instruments Museum; ✉ Enter from Täubchenweg 2e; ☞ DM 5; ☺ Tues.–Sat. 10–5, Sun. 10–1) contains some 5,000 instruments. ✉ *Johannespl. 5–11,* ☎ *0341/21420.* ☞ *DM 9 for a combined ticket for all 3 museums, valid for 2 full days.*

⑮ **Hauptbahnhof.** Leipzig's main train station is a major attraction. In 1991 it expanded to accommodate the anticipated postreunification increase in traffic, and with its 26 platforms the station is the largest in Europe. The station next transformed into a huge shopping center, with more than 150 upscale shops and eateries. But its fin de siècle grandeur remains, particularly in the staircases that lead majestically up to the platforms. As you climb them, take a look at the great arched ceilings high above you. There's also a tourist information office opposite Platform 3, open weekdays 9–5. ✉ *Willy-Brandt-Pl.*

㉕ **Johann-Sebastian-Bach-Museum.** The Bach family home, the old Bosehaus, still stands opposite the Thomaskirche and is now a museum devoted to the composer's life and work. Musical instruments on display date to Bach's time. The exhibits are in German only; an English-language guide can be purchased in the shop. In 2000 the museum celebrated the 75th annual Bachfestival with concerts and other events. ✉ *Thomaskirchhof 16,* ☎ *0341/964–4135.* ☞ *DM 4, DM 8 with guided tour.* ☺ *Daily 10–5.*

⑱ **Leipziger Universitätsturm** (Leipzig University Tower). Towering over Leipzig's city center is this 470-ft-high structure, which houses administrative offices and lecture rooms. Some of the University of Leipzig students have dubbed it the "Jagged Tooth"; students were also largely responsible for changing the university's name, replacing the postwar title of Karl Marx University with its original moniker. The **Augustusplatz** spreads out below the university tower like a space-age campus.

㉑ Mädlerpassage (Mädler Mall). This shopper's paradise is Leipzig's finest arcade, where the ghost of Goethe's Faust lurks in every marble corner. Goethe set one of the scenes of his *Faust* in the famous Auerbachs Keller restaurant (☞ Dining and Lodging, *below*), at No. 2. A bronze group of characters from the play, sculpted in 1913, beckons you down the stone staircase to the restaurant. A few yards away down the arcade is a delightful Jugendstil bar called Mephisto, done in devilish reds and blacks.

㉑ Markt. Leipzig's showpiece is its huge, old market square. One side is occupied completely by the recently restored Renaissance city hall, the **Altes Rathaus,** which now houses the **Stadtgeschichtliches Museum,** where Leipzig's past is well documented. ✉ *Markt 1,* ☎ *0341/965–130.* 🎫 *DM 5.* ☉ *Tues. 2–8, Wed.–Sun. 10–6.*

★ **㉖ Museum der Bildenden Künste** (Museum of Fine Arts). The city's leading art gallery occupies the ground floor of the former Reichsgericht, the court where the Nazis held a show trial against the Bulgarian Communist Georgi Dimitroff, accused of masterminding the burning of the Reichstag in 1933. The museum has more than 2,700 paintings representing the German Middle Ages to contemporary American art; one of its finest collections focuses on Cranach the Elder ☞ Wittenberg, *below*). ✉ *Grimmaische Str. 1–7,* ☎ *0341/216–990.* 🎫 *DM 5; free 2nd Sun. of month.* ☉ *Tues. and Thurs.–Sun. 10–6, Wed. 1–9:30.*

★ **㉓ Museum in der Runden Ecke** (Museum in the Round Corner). The museum's name may sound funny, but behind its thick walls lies one of the darkest chapters of recent Leipzig history: the building once served as the headquarters of the city's secret police, the dreaded *Staatssicherheitsdient.* The exhibition, *Stasi—Macht und Banalität*(Stasi—Power and Banality), not only presents the offices and surveillance work of the Stasi, but also shows hundreds of documents revealing the magnitude of its interests in citizens' private lives. The material is written in German, but the items and the atmosphere still give an impression of how life under such a regime might feel. ✉ *Dittrichring 24,* ☎ *0341/961–2443.* 🎫 *Free.* ☉ *Wed.–Sun. 2–6.*

㉒ Museum zum Arabischen Kaffeebaum (Arabic Coffee Tree Museum). This museum and café tells the fascinating history of coffee culture in Europe, particularly in Saxony. The café, on the first floor, is one of the oldest on the Continent and once proudly served a cup of good coffee to such luminaries as Lessing, Schumann, Goethe, and Liszt. The museum features many paintings, Arabian coffee vessels, and coffeehouse games. It also explains the basic principles of roasting coffee. ✉ *Kleine Fleischerg. 4,* ☎ *0341/965–1321.* 🎫 *Free.* ☉ *Daily 11–7.*

⑲ Neues Gewandhaus (New Orchestra Hall). In the shadow of the ☞ **Leipzig University Tower** is the glass-and-concrete home of the city orchestra, one of Germany's greatest. Kurt Masur, its former director, now leads the New York Philharmonic Orchestra and Herbert Blomstedt is currently at the helm. The statue of Beethoven that stands in the foyer, by sculptor Max Klinger, won first prize at the 1912 World Art Exhibition in Vienna. On the foyer's ceiling, a staggering allegorical painting by Sighard Gilles is devoted to the muse of music. Owing to the world-renowned acoustics of the concert hall, a tone resonates here for a full two seconds. ✉ *Augustuspl. 8,* ☎ *0341/127–0280.*

★ ⑰ **Nikolaikirche** (St. Nicholas Church). This church with its undistinguished facade has taken a central place in the city's contemporary life as well as in its past; demonstrations here are credited with helping to bring down the Communist regime. Every Monday for months before the government collapsed, thousands of citizens gathered in front of the church chanting, "*Wir sind das Volk*" ("We are the people"). Inside is a soaring Gothic choir and nave. Note the unusual patterned ceiling supported by classical pillars that end in palm tree–like flourishes. Luther is said to have preached from the ornate 16th-century pulpit. ✉ *Nikolaikirchhof*, ☎ *0341/960–5270.* 🎫 *Free.* ◷ *Mon.–Sat. 10–6, Sun. services 9:30, 11:15, and 5.*

⑯ **Opernhaus** (Opera House). Leipzig's stage for operas was the first postwar theater to be built in Communist East Germany. Its solid, boxy style is the subject of ongoing local controversy. ✉ *Opposite Gewandhaus, on north side of Augustuspl.*

㉗ **Schillerhaus** (Schiller House). This small residence was for a time the home of the German poet and dramatist Friedrich Schiller. After more than two years of extensive renovation, mostly funded by private donors, the house has reopened. To reach the Schillerhaus, take streetcar Line 6, 20, or 24 to Menckestrasse or Fritz-Seger-Strasse. ✉ *Menckestr. 42,* ☎ *0341/566–2170.* 🎫 *DM 3.* ◷ *Tues.–Sun. 11–6.*

★ ㉔ **Thomaskirche** (St. Thomas's Church). Bach was choirmaster at this Gothic church for 27 years, and Martin Luther preached here on Whitsunday 1539, signaling the arrival of Protestantism in Leipzig. Originally the center of a 13th-century monastery rebuilt during the 15th century, the tall church now stands by itself, but the names of adjacent streets recall the cloisters. Bach wrote most of his cantatas for the church's famous boys' choir, the Thomasknabenchor, which was founded in the 13th century; the church continues as the choir's home as well as a center of Bach tradition.

Bach's 12 children and the infant Richard Wagner were baptized in the early 17th-century font; Karl Marx and Friedrich Engels also stood before this same font, godfathers to Karl Liebknecht, who grew up to be a revolutionary as well.

The great music Bach wrote during his Leipzig years commanded little attention in his lifetime, and when he died, he was given a simple grave, without a headstone, in the city's Johannisfriedhof (St. John Cemetery). It wasn't until 1894 that an effort was made to find where the great composer lay buried, and after a thorough, macabre search his coffin was removed to the Johanniskirche. That church was destroyed by Allied bombs in December 1943, and Bach subsequently found his final resting place in the church he would have selected: the Thomaskirche. His gravestone below the high altar is never without a floral tribute. Fresh flowers also constantly decorate the statue of Bach that stands before the church, erected on the initiative of the composer Mendelssohn, who performed his own music in the church and revered its great master. ✉ *Thomaskirchhof, off Grimmaischestr.,* ☎ *0341/960–2855.* 🎫 *Free.* ◷ *Daily 9–6.* 🍃

㉙ **Völkerschlachtdenkmal** (Memorial to the Battle of the Nations). The battle that put Leipzig on the military map of Europe, the 1813 Battle of the Nations, is commemorated by this enormous 1913 monument on the city's outskirts. The somber, gray pile of granite and concrete is more than 300 ft high. Despite its ugliness, the site is well worth a visit, if only to wonder at the lengths—and heights—to which the Prussians went to celebrate their military victories and to take in the view from a windy platform (provided you can climb the 500 steps to get there). The Prussians did make one concession to Napoléon in designing the monument: a stone marks the spot where he stood during the three-day battle. An exhibition hall explains the history of the memorial. The memorial can be reached via Streetcar 15 or 21 (leave the tram at the Probstheida station). ⊠ *Prager Str.,* ☎ *0341/878–0471.* ☎ *DM 6.* ☉ *Nov.–Apr., daily 9–4; May–Oct., daily 10–5; tour daily at 10:30, 11:30, 1:30, and 2:30.*

Dining and Lodging

$$$
★ ✕ **Auerbachs Keller.** Amazingly, this most famous of Leipzig's restaurants went bankrupt in 1995, an indication of the economic turmoil in eastern Germany. Under new ownership the restaurant and food have bounced back. It's been around since 1530, after all, and Goethe immortalized it in his *Faust.* The menu features regional dishes from Saxony, often with Faustian names. There is also a good wine list. ⊠ *Mädlerpassage, Grimmaische Str. 2–4,* ☎ *0341/216–1040. Reservations essential. Jacket and tie. AE, MC, V.*

$$ ✕ **Apels Garten.** This elegant little restaurant in the city center pays homage to nature with landscape paintings on the wall, floral arrangements on the tables, and fresh produce on the imaginative menu. In winter the wild-duck soup with homemade noodles is an obligatory starter; in summer try the *Räucherfischsuppe* (smoked fish soup)—you won't find another soup like it in Leipzig. ⊠ *Kolonnadenstr. 2,* ☎ *0341/960–7777. AE, MC, V. No dinner Sun.*

$$ ✕ **Barthels Hof.** This beamed and paneled Gasthaus is a local favorite. The hearty Saxon food has an international touch; some dishes try to be nouvelle German cuisine but lack inspiration and spices. Still, the Barthels Hof is a place to have dinner and a cold beer (or heavy Saxon red wine). The breakfast buffet is impressive, too. If you don't understand the menu, which employs German puns, ask one of the waitresses for an explanation. ⊠ *Hainstr. 1,* ☎ *0341/141–310. AE, DC, MC, V.*

$$ ✕ **Paulaner Restaurant Hutter Culinaria.** Munich's Paulaner Brewery returned to its Leipzig subsidiary of prewar times and transformed the building into a vast complex, with restaurants, a banquet hall, a café, and a beer garden. There's something here for everyone, from intimate dining to noisy, Bavarian-style tavern-table conviviality. The food, such as *Schweinshaxen mit* (salty pork with sauerkraut), is a mix of Bavarian and Saxon. The Paulaner beer is a perfect accompaniment. ⊠ *Klosterg. 3–5,* ☎ *0341/211–3115. AE, DC, MC, V.*

$$ ✕ **Zill's Tunnel.** The "tunnel" refers to the barrel-ceiling ground-floor
★ restaurant, where foaming glasses of excellent local beer are served with a smile. The friendly staff will also help you decipher the Old Saxon descriptions of the menu's traditional dishes. Upstairs there's a larger wine restaurant with an open fireplace; wine buffs will single out the rare Saxon wine from a Saale Valley vineyard. In December goose prepared in a variety of ways (including marinated in heavy brown sauce with wild berries, then oven-baked) is a staple. ⊠ *Barfussgässchen 9,* ☎ *0341/960–2078. AE, MC, V.*

$$$ ✕🖬 **Renaissance Leipzig Hotel.** One of the largest hotels in this city of fairs, the Renaissance Leipzig attracts business travelers with its quiet atmosphere. It has large, elegant rooms—with fashionable bathrooms in dark marble—all equipped with fax, ISDN-phone system, and cable television. When making a reservation, ask for a room on the Club Floor: for about DM 40 a day, you get a free Continental breakfast and access to the Club Lounge. The hotel's restaurant, Four Seasons, serves light nouvelle German cuisine. The Renaissance is in the heart of old Leipzig, a perfect spot from which to explore the city on foot. ⊠

Querstr. 12, D–04103, ☎ 0341/12920, FAX 0341/129–2800. 295 rooms, 61 suites. Restaurant, bar, in-room data ports, minibars, no-smoking floor, room service, indoor pool, massage, sauna, exercise room, dry cleaning, laundry service, concierge, business services, meeting rooms, parking (fee). AE, DC, MC, V. ✆

$$$$ 🖭 **InterContinental.** The "Interconti" is still one of the city's most luxurious hotels, but it has competition. Although the hotel's service is outstanding, the high-rise edifice and its accommodations lack true atmosphere. The Japanese owners have included a Japanese restaurant and garden. Rooms offer every luxury, including bathrooms with marble floors and walls and full air-conditioning—and you'll be close to the main train station. ☒ *Gerberstr. 15, D–04105, ☎ 0341/9880, FAX 0341/988–1229. 426 rooms, 24 suites. 3 restaurants, bar, in-room data ports, in-room safes, minibars, no-smoking rooms, room service, indoor pool, barbershop, beauty salon, massage, sauna, spa, bowling, exercise room, shops, casino, baby-sitting, dry cleaning, laundry service, concierge, business services, meeting rooms, parking (fee). AE, DC, MC, V.* ✆

$$$$ 🖭 **Kempinski Hotel Fürstenhof Leipzig.** The city's grandest hotel, and
★ one of the country's best, is inside the renowned Löhr-Haus, a revered old mansion that the Kempinski group restored to its former elegance. The stunning banquet section is the epitome of 19th-century grandeur, with red wallpaper and dark mahogany wood; the bar is a lofty meeting area under a bright glass cupola. Rooms are spacious and decorated with dark cherrywood designer furniture. The incredible fitness facilities include a dreamy swimming pool, a Finnish sauna, and a Roman steam-bath. Service throughout the hotel is attentive and impeccable. The hotel has a sleek cocktail bar in the front and a more elegant piano bar in the lobby area. ☒ *Tröndlinring 8, D–04105, ☎ 0341/1400, FAX 0341/140–3700. 84 rooms, 8 suites. Restaurant, bar, in-room data ports, in-room safes, minibars, no-smoking rooms, room service, indoor pool, massage, sauna, spa, exercise room, baby-sitting, dry cleaning, laundry service, concierge, business services, meeting rooms, parking (fee). AE, DC, MC, V.* ✆

$$$ 🖭 **Park Hotel-Seaside Hotel Leipzig.** A few steps from the central train station, the Park Hotel is primarily geared toward the business traveler. It opened in 1913 as the city's premiere first-class hotel, and today the interior has been completely remodeled. The modern rooms may lack some individuality and are definitely not designed for romantic weekends, but the warm service and exceptional bathrooms and swimming pool area more than make up for it. Add to that the Orient Express restaurant, a reconstruction of the famous 19th-century train, and you'll enjoy a pleasant and smooth stay. ☒ *Richard-Wagner-Str. 7, D–04109, ☎ 0341/98520, FAX 0341/985–2750. 281 rooms, 9 suites. Restaurant, bar, in-room safes, minibars, no-smoking floor, room service, hot tub, baby-sitting, dry cleaning, laundry service, concierge, meeting rooms, parking (fee). AE, DC, MC, V.* ✆

$$ 🖭 **Ringhotel Adagio Leipzig.** The quiet Adagio, tucked away behind the facade of a 19th-century city mansion, is centrally located between the Grassimuseum and the Neues Gewandhaus. All rooms are individually furnished; when making a reservation, ask for a "1920s room," which features the style of the Roaring '20s and bathtubs almost as large as a whirlpool. The Champagner-Offerte package includes a dinner in the hotel's restaurant and a city tour. ☒ *Seeburgstr. 96, D–04103, ☎ 0341/216–699, FAX 0341/960–3078. 30 rooms, 1 suite, 1 apartment. Restaurant, bar, no-smoking rooms, dry cleaning, laundry service, meeting rooms, parking (fee). AE, DC, MC, V.* ✆

Nightlife and the Arts

The **Neues Gewandhaus,** a controversial piece of architecture, is home to an undeniably splendid orchestra. Tickets to concerts are very difficult to obtain unless you reserve well in advance and in writing only (Gewandhaus zu Leipzig, ✉ Augustuspl. 8, D–04109). Sometimes spare tickets are available at the box office a half hour before the evening performance. Leipzig's annual music festival, **Music Days,** is in June.

One of Germany's most famous cabarets, the **Leipziger Pfeffermühle** (✉ Thomaskirchhof 16, ☎ 0341/960–3196) has a lively bar off a courtyard opposite the Thomaskirche. On pleasant evenings the courtyard fills with benches and tables, and the scene rivals the indoor performance for entertainment. Equally entertaining is the variety theater **Krystallpalast** (✉ Magazinstr. 4, ☎ 0341/140–660), which features a blend of circus, vaudeville, and comedy.

The **Gohliser Schlösschen** (Gohlis Mansion ✉ Menckestr. 23, ☎ 0341/589–690), a small rococo palace outside Leipzig's center, frequently holds concerts. It's easily reached by public transportation: Take streetcar No. 20 or No. 24, then walk left up Poetenweg; or take streetcar No. 6 to Menckestrasse. Daytime tours can be arranged for groups.

Two of the top **dance clubs** are the hip **Spizz Keller** (✉ Markt 9, ☎ 0341/9608–043) and the **Tanzpalast,** in the august setting of the city theater, the Schauspielhaus (✉ Dittrichring, ☎ 0341/960–0596). Another magnet for young people is the **Moritzbastei** (✉ Universitätsstr. 9, ☎ 0341/702–590), reputedly Europe's largest student club, with bars, a disco, a café, a theater, and a cinema. Nonstudents are welcome. The *Kneipenszene* (pub scene) of Leipzig is centered around the **Drallewatsch** (a Saxon slang word for "going out"), the small streets and alleys around Grosse and Kleine Fleischergasse. One of the nicest and more upscale places to have a drink or bottle of wine is the **Weinstock** bar, pub, and restaurant (✉ Markt 7, ☎ 0341/1406–0606). It's in a Renaissance building and offers a huge selection of good wines.

Shopping

Leading off of the Markt, small streets attest to Leipzig's rich trading past. Tucked in among them are glass-roof arcades of surprising beauty and elegance, among them the wonderfully restored **Specks Hof,** the **Barthels Hof** (☞ Dining and Lodging, *above*), the **Jägerhof,** and the **Passage zum Sachsenplatz.** Invent a headache and step into the *Apotheke* (pharmacy) at Hainstrasse 9. It's spectacularly Jugendstil, with finely etched and stained glass and rich mahogany. For more glimpses into the past, check out the antiquarian bookshops of the nearby **Neumarkt Passage.**

The newly renovated **Hauptbahnhof** offers more than 150 shops, restaurants, and cafés. Thanks to the historic backdrop, it's one of the most beautiful and fun shopping experiences in eastern Germany.

SAXONY-ANHALT

Updated by
Jürgen
Scheunemann

The central state of Saxony-Anhalt is a region rich in natural attractions. In the Altmark, on the edge of the Harz Mountains, fields of grain and sugar beets stretch to the horizon. In the mountains themselves are the deep gorge of the Bode River and the stalactite-filled caves of Rubeland. The songbirds of the Harz are renowned, and though pollution has taken its toll, both the flora and fauna of the Harz National Park (which includes much of the region) are coming back. Atop the Brocken, the Harz's highest point, legend has it that witches convene on Walpurgis Night. When Germany was divided, the Brocken was a grim frontier area closed to visitors, but today large numbers of tourists come to see its Alpine flowers and the views on clear days.

Saxony-Anhalt's Letzlinger Heide (Letzling Heath), another home to rare birds and animals, is one of Germany's largest tracts of uninhabited land. The Dübener Heide (Düben Heath), south of Wittenberg, has endless woods of oaks, beeches, and evergreens that are wonderful to explore by bike or on foot. In and around Dessau are magnificent parks and gardens.

Architecturally, Saxony-Anhalt abounds in half-timber towns and Romanesque churches. Quedlinburg has both the oldest half-timber house in Germany and the tomb of Germany's first king, 10th-century Henry I. In Dessau the Bauhaus School pointed the world to modern architecture and design just before the start of World War II. Music has thrived in Saxony-Anhalt as well. Among its favorite sons are the composers Georg Philipp Telemann, of Magdeburg; Georg Friedrich Handel, of Halle; and in modern times, Kurt Weill, of Dessau. And it was in Wittenberg that Martin Luther nailed his 95 Theses to a church door.

Wittenberg

㉚ *107 km (62 mi) southwest of Berlin, 67 km (40 mi) north of Leipzig.*

Protestantism was born in the little town of Wittenberg (also called Lutherstadt-Wittenberg). In 1508 the fervent, idealistic young Martin Luther, who had become a monk only a year earlier, arrived to study and teach at the new university founded by Elector Frederick the Wise. Nine years later, enraged that the Roman Catholic Church was pardoning sins in exchange for the sale of indulgences, Luther posted his 95 Theses attacking the policy on the door of the Castle Church. Thereafter, the world became a very different place.

Martin Luther is still the center of attention in Wittenberg, and sites associated with him are marked with plaques and signs. Post-Communist Wittenberg, however, is also an increasingly sprightly home of art galleries, clothing shops, and business travelers' hotels and restaurants that take advantage of the town's historic draw. Menus offer such dishes as *Luthersuppe* (soup of tomatoes, herbs, and croutons) and *Melanchthontaler* (a plate of pasta filled with venison; the name refers to a colleague of Luther's). You can see virtually all of historic Wittenberg on a 2-km (1-mi) stretch of Collegienstrasse and Schlossstrasse that begins at the railroad tracks and ends at the Schlosskirche (Castle Church).

In a small park where Weserstrasse meets Collegienstrasse, the **Luthereiche** (Luther Oak) marks the spot where in 1517 Luther burned the papal bull excommunicating him for his criticism of the Church. The present oak was planted in the 19th century.

Within **Lutherhalle** (Luther Hall) is the Augustinian monastery where Martin Luther lived both as a teacher-monk and later, after the monastery was dissolved, as a married man. Today it is a museum dedicated to Luther and the Reformation. Enter through a garden and an elegant door with a carved stone frame; it was a gift to Luther from his wife, Katharina von Bora. In 1525 Luther broke with monasticism and married the former nun. Inside the much-restored structure is the monks' refectory, where works of Luther's contemporary, the painter Lucas Cranach the Elder, are displayed. The room that remains closest to the original is the dark, wood-paneled Lutherstube. The Luthers and their six children used it as a living room, study, and meeting place for friends and students. In it is a pulpit Luther is believed to have used. Prints, engravings, paintings, manuscripts, coins, and medals relating to the Reformation and Luther's translation of the Bible into the German vernacular are displayed throughout the house. ✉ *Collegienstr. 54,* ☎ *03491/42030.* ☞ *DM 7.* ⊙ *Apr.–Oct., daily 9–6; Nov.–Mar., daily 10–5.*

In the elegantly gabled Renaissance **Melanchthonhaus** (Melanchthon House), the humanist teacher and scholar Philipp Melanchthon corrected Luther's translation of the New Testament from Greek into German. Luther was shut up in the Wartburg in Eisenach at the time (☞ Eisenach *in* Thuringia, *below*), and as each section of his manuscript was completed it was sent to Melanchthon for approval. (Melanchthon is a Greek translation of the man's real name, Schwarzerdt, which means "black earth"; humanists routinely adopted such classical pseudonyms.) The second-floor furnishings have been painstakingly re-created after period etchings. A green tile stove in his study is thought to have been made after a Cranach design. In the tranquil back garden, a little fountain has been bubbling from a spring ever since Melanchthon's day. ✉ *Collegienstr. 60,* ☎ *03491/403–279.* ☞ *DM 5.* ⊙ *Apr.–Oct., Mon.–Sun. 9–6; Nov.–Mar., Tues.–Sun. 10–5.*

From 1514 until his death in 1546, Martin Luther preached two sermons a week in the twin-towered **Stadtkirche St. Marien** (Parish Church of St. Mary). He and Katharina von Bora were married here. The altar triptych by Lucas Cranach the Elder includes a self-portrait as well as portraits of Luther wearing the knight's disguise he adopted when hidden away at the Wartburg; Luther preaching; Luther's wife and one of his sons; Melanchthon; and Lucas Cranach the Younger. Also notable is the 1457 bronze baptismal font by Herman Vischer the Elder. On the church's southeast corner, you'll find a discomforting juxtaposition of two Jewish-related **monuments**: a 1304 mocking caricature called the Jewish Pig, erected at the time of the expulsion of the town's Jews, and, on the cobblestone pavement, a contemporary memorial to the Jews who died at Auschwitz. ✉ *Kirchpl.,* ☎ *03491/404–415.* ☞ *DM 2, including tour.* ⊙ *May–Oct., Mon.–Sat. 9–5, Sun. 11:30–5; Nov.–Apr., Mon.–Sat. 10–4, Sun. 1:30–4.*

Two statues are the centerpiece of the **Marktplatz** (market square): an 1821 statue of Luther by Johann Gottfried Schadow, designer of the Victory statue atop Berlin's Brandenburg Gate, and an 1866 statue of Melanchthon by Frederick Drake. Their backdrop is the handsome white High Renaissance **Rathaus** (town hall). Gabled Renaissance houses containing shops line part of the square. Among them, the **Cranachhaus** is believed to have been the first home in town of Lucas Cranach the Elder, the court painter, printer, mayor, pharmacist, and friend of Luther's. His son, the painter Lucas Cranach the Younger, was born here. Some of the interior has been restored to its 17th-century condition. It is now a gallery of changing art exhibits. ✉ *Markt 4,* ☎ *03491/410–912.* ☞ *DM 3.* ⊙ *Tues.–Sat. 10–5, Sun. 1–5.*

Renaissance man Lucas Cranach the Elder, probably the wealthiest man in Wittenberg in his day, lived in two different houses during his years in town. In a second **Cranachhaus,** near the Schlosskirche (Castle Church), he not only lived and painted but also operated a print shop (now being restored) and an apothecary. The courtyard, where it is thought he did much of his painting, remains much as it was in his day. ✉ *Schlossstr. 1,* ☎ *03491/420–1915.* ☞ *DM 4.* ⊙ *Tues.–Sun. 10–5.*

In 1517 the indignant Martin Luther affixed to the doors of the **Schlosskirche** (Castle Church) his 95 Theses attacking the Roman Catholic Church's policy of selling indulgences. Written in Latin, the theses might have gone unnoticed had not someone—without Luther's knowledge—translated them into German and distributed them. The incensed Holy Roman Emperor Charles V summoned Luther to appear before him in Worms. It was on the way home from his confrontation with the emperor that Luther was "captured" by his protector, Elector Frederick the Wise, and hidden from papal authorities in Eisenach for the better part of a year. The church's original wooden doors have been replaced by bronze ones that reproduce the Latin text of the theses. Inside the church, simple bronze plaques mark the burial places of Luther and Melanchthon. ⊠ *Schlosspl.,* ☎ *03491/402–585.* 🖃 *DM 2.* ◷ *May –Oct., Mon. 2–5, Tues.–Sat. 9–5, Sun. 11:30–5; Nov.–Apr., Mon. 2–4, Tues.–Sat. 9–4, Sun. 11:30–4, after service at 10.*

Dining and Lodging

$$ ✕ **Schlosskeller.** At the back of the Schlosskirche, this restaurant with historic atmosphere specializes in German dishes, such *Schlosskellerpfanne* (pork fillets with fried potatoes, tomatoes, and pepper bells). ⊠ *Schlosspl. 1,* ☎ *03491/480–805. AE, MC, V.*

$ ✕ **Luther-Schenke.** Dressed in costumes of Luther's day, waiters serve
★ the beer and the dishes they think the reformer might have eaten—roast boar and pigs' knuckles with sauerkraut—as well as such international fare as salsa, pasta, lamb, or chicken roasted on a spit. The brick-vaulted beer cellar has a laid-back ambience. ⊠ *Markt 2,* ☎ *03491/406–592. AE, DC, MC, V.*

$$–$$$ 🏨 **Best Western Stadtpalais Wittenberg.** In an old city mansion just a few steps from the Lutherhaus, this new hotel presents modern style and high-quality service. The elegant lobby and upscale rooms may suggest high prices, but the rates are more than reasonable. The best deals are the special "executive double rooms," which are 330 square ft and have many extras such as air-conditioning and an ironing set. The rooms' lack of individuality is typical of chain hotels, but their fresh and shiny look and the quality furniture make up for the blandness. ⊠ *Collegienstr. 56–57, D–06886,* ☎ *03491/4250,* FAX *03491/425–100. 78 rooms. Restaurant, bar, minibars, no-smoking rooms, sauna, steam bath, baby-sitting, dry cleaning, laundry service, meeting rooms, parking (fee). AE, DC, MC, V.*✍

$ 🏨 **Hotel Grüne Tanne.** Four hundred years ago a knight's estate stood on the land occupied today by this cozy country hotel. A hostelry since 1871, the Grüne Tanne is a starting place for walks and bicycle and horseback rides into the countryside. The outside terrace is used for summer dining. A shuttle service goes to the Wittenberg train station. ⊠ *Am Teich 1, D–06896 Wittenberg/Reinsdorf,* ☎ *03491/6290,* FAX *03491/629–250. 40 rooms, 1 apartment, 2 suites. Restaurant, sauna (fee), free parking. AE, DC, MC, V.*✍

En Route From Wittenberg take B–187 west for 13 km (8 mi), then turn onto B–107 south for 8 km (5 mi) to Wörlitz. Leopold III Friedrich Franz of Anhalt-Dessau loved gardens and sought to create a garden kingdom in his lands. He had **Wörlitz Park** laid out between 1765 and 1802, largely in the naturalistic English style. It was the first such garden created in central Europe, with meadowlands and a lake, canals and woods, rocks and grottoes. You can walk or bicycle the 42 km (26 mi) to Dessau through the park.

From Wörlitz continue another 5 km (3 mi) on B–107 to the **Oranien-baum-Park.** Leopold enlarged his garden kingdom by incorporating Oranienbaum—a 17th-century baroque palace—and adding an English-Chinese garden with a teahouse as well as a pagoda inspired by the one in England's Kew Gardens. He further developed Park Lusium on the Elbe River, which he redesigned with fountains, sculptures, and bridges, and an orangery. After visiting Oranienbaum, go west on the road that becomes B–185 in Dessau.

On B–185 9 km (5½ mi) outside Dessau you'll come to Mosigkau and its 18th-century late-baroque **Schloss Mosigkau** (Mosigkau Palace). Prince Leopold of Anhalt-Dessau commissioned the palace for his favorite daughter, Anna Wilhelmine. Never married, she lived there alone, and when she died, she left the property to an order of nuns. They immediately tore up the formal grounds to make an English-style park, and after a post–World War II attempt to restore the original baroque appearance, money and enthusiasm ran out. The palace itself, however, was always well maintained. Only a quarter of the rooms can be visited, but they include one of Germany's very few baroque picture galleries. Its stucco ceiling is a marvel of rococo decoration, a swirling composition of pastel-color motifs. ⊠ *Knobelsdorffallee 3, Dessau,* ☎ *0340/521–139.* 🎫 *Palace DM 6, palace gardens free.* ☉ *Apr.–Oct., Tues.–Sun. 10–6.*

Dessau

③① *35 km (22 mi) southwest of Wittenberg.*

The name *Dessau* is known to every student of modern architecture. In 1925–26 architect Walter Gropius set up his highly influential Bauhaus school of design here. Gropius hoped to replace the dark and inhumane tenement architecture of the turn of the century with standardized yet spacious and bright apartments. His ideas and methods were used in building 316 villas in the city's Törten section in the 1920s.

The **Bauhaus Building** is where architectural styles that would influence the appearance of such cities as New York, Chicago, and San Francisco were conceived. The architecture school is still operating, and the building can be visited. Other structures designed by Gropius and the Bauhaus architects, among them the Meisterhäuser, are open for inspection off Ebertalle and Elballee. Some of the Meisterhäuser buildings may be closed in 2000. ⊠ *Gropiusallee 38,* ☎ *0340/650–8251.* 🎫 *DM 5.* ☉ *June–Sept., Tues.–Sun. 10–6, Mon. 10–8; Oct.–May, Tues.–Sun. 10–6.*

For a contrast to the no-nonsense Bauhaus architecture, look at downtown Dessau's older buildings, including St. George's Church, built in 1712 in the Dutch baroque style.

Halle

③② *52 km (32 mi) south of Dessau.*

This 1,000-year-old city, built on the salt trade, has suffered from the shortfalls of Communist urban planning. The hastily built residential area, Halle-Neustadt, was cynically nicknamed "Hanoi." Yet the Old City has an unusual beauty, particularly its spacious central marketplace, the **Markt,** its northern side bristling with five distinctive sharp-steepled towers.

Four towers belong to the late-Gothic **Marienkirche** (St. Mary's Church). Two are connected by a vertiginous catwalk bridge. Martin Luther preached in the church; George Friedrich Handel (Händel in German), born in Halle in 1685, was baptized at its font and went on to learn to play the organ beneath its high, vaulted ceiling. The Markt's fifth tower is Halle's celebrated **Roter Turm** (Red Tower), built between 1418 and 1506 as an expression of the city's power and wealth. It houses a carillon and the local tourist office.

The **Marktschlösschen** (Market Palace), a late-Renaissance structure just off the market square, has an interesting collection of historical musical instruments, some of which could have been played by Handel and his contemporaries. ⊠ *Markt 13,* ☎ *0345/202–5977.* 🎫 *DM 2.* ☉ *Wed.–Sun. 1:30–5:30.*

Handel's birthplace, the **Händelhaus,** is now a museum devoted to the composer. The entrance hall displays glass harmonicas, curious musical instruments perfected by Benjamin Franklin in the 1760s. ⊠ *Grosse Nikolaistr. 5,* ☎ *0345/500–900.* 🎫 *DM 4, free Thurs.* ☉ *Mon.–Sat. 9:30–5:30, Thurs. 9:30–7, Sun. 9:30–5:30.*

The **Moritzburg** (Moritz Castle) was built in the late 15th century by the archbishop of Magdeburg after he had claimed the city for his archdiocese. The typical late-Gothic fortress with a dry moat and a sturdy round tower at each of its four corners was a testament to Halle's early might, which vanished with the Thirty Years' War. Prior to World War II the castle contained a leading gallery of German Expressionist paintings, which were ripped from the walls by the Nazis and condemned as "degenerate." Some of the works are back in place at the **Staatliche Galerie Moritzburg,** together with some outstanding late-19th- and early 20th-century art. You'll find Rodin's famous sculpture *The Kiss* here. ⊠ *Friedemann-Bach-Pl. 5,* ☎ *0345/212–590.* 🎫 *DM 5.* ☉ *Tues. 11– 8:30, Wed.–Sun. 10–6.*

Halle's only early Gothic church, the **Dom** (cathedral) stands about 200 yards southeast of the Moritzburg. Its nave and side aisles are of equal height, a characteristic of much Gothic church design in this part of Germany. ⊠ *Dompl. 3,* ☎ *0345/202–1379.* 🎫 *Free.* ☉ *June–Oct., Mon.–Sat. 2–4.*

The former archbishop's home, the 16th-century **Neue Residenz** (New Residence), houses the **Geiseltalmuseum** and its world-famous collection of fossils dug from brown coal deposits in the Geisel Valley near Halle. ⊠ *Domstr. 5,* ☎ *0345/552–6135.* 🎫 *Free.* ☉ *Weekdays 9–noon and 1–5; every 2nd and 4th Sun. 10–1.*

The salt trade on which Halle built its prosperity is documented in the **Technisches Halloren- und Salinemuseum** (Technical Mine Museum). The old method of evaporating brine from local springs is sometimes demonstrated. A replica salt mine shows the salt-mining process, and the exquisite silver goblet collection of the Salt Workers' Guild is on display. The museum is on the south side of the Saale River (cross the Schiefer Bridge to get there). ⊠ *Mansfelderstr. 52,* ☎ *0345/202–5034.* 🎫 *DM 3.* ☉ *Tues.–Sun. 10–5.*

Dining and Lodging

$$ ✕ **Restaurant Mönchshof.** Hearty German fare in hearty portions is served in the high-ceilinged, dark-wood surroundings. Lamb from Saxony-Anhalt's Wettin region and venison are specialties in season, but there are always fish and crisp roast pork on the menu. The wine list is extensive, with international vintages. ⊠ *Talamstr. 6,* ☎ *0345/ 202–1726. AE, MC, V.*

$$$ ✕🛏 **Hotel Restaurant zum Kleinen Sandberg.** On a quiet side street off the main pedestrian mall, where the city prison once cast its grim shadow, stands one of Halle's prettiest medieval houses, now a small, exclusive restaurant and hotel. Behind its bright brown-and-white half-timber facade is a variety of individually furnished rooms, some with their own whirlpool baths. The restaurant serves predominantly Baden specialties—marinated meats with such regional trimmings as Spätzle (homemade egg noodles)—with a wine list of Baden vintages.

⌂ *Kleiner Sandberg 5, D–06108,* ☎ *0345/202–3173,* ℻ *0345/202–5488. 9 rooms. Restaurant, minibars, free parking. AE, MC, V.*

$$–$$$ ✕🏨 **Ankerhof Hotel.** Stone walls and old wooden beams are a reminder of the tollhouse that once stood here beside the saltworks. The hotel's Alter Zollkeller (Old Customs Cellar) restaurant serves both regional and international dishes, such as *Schweinemedaillons an Metaxasauce* (roast pork medallions with Metaxa sauce—a Greek schnapps). ⌂ *Ankerstr. 2a, D–06108,* ☎ *0345/232–3200,* ℻ *0345/232–3219. 50 rooms, 5 suites. 2 restaurants, no-smoking rooms, sauna, health club, bowling, free parking. AE, DC, MC, V.* 🐾

$$$–$$$$ 🏨 **Kempinski Hotel Rotes Ross.** Behind a 265-year-old facade in the
★ city center, this friendly, well-equipped modern hotel still has a certain old-fashioned elegance in its rooms. The new wing, added in 1999, lacks the old-world atmosphere of the original main building. ⌂ *Leipziger Str. 76, D–06108,* ☎ *0345/29220,* ℻ *0345/292–2222. 75 rooms, 14 suites. Restaurant, Weinstube, in-room safes, minibars, no-smoking rooms, room service, sauna, health club, hot tub, baby-sitting, dry cleaning, laundry service, concierge, convention center, meeting rooms, parking (free). AE, DC, MC, V.* 🐾

Nightlife and the Arts

The city of Handel is of course an important music center, and Halle is famous for its opera productions, orchestral concerts, and particularly for its choirs. For **opera** schedules and ticket reservations call 0345/5110–0355; for the **State Philharmonic Orchestra** information call 0345/2213–010. The annual **Händel Festival** (☎ 0345/5009–0222) takes place in the first half of June, and two youth-choir festivals occur in May and October.

En Route To reach Quedlinburg in the Harz, you can take E–49 directly, or take a somewhat longer route via E–80 to **Eisleben** first. Martin Luther came into and out of this world here. Both the square Franconian house with the high-pitched roof that was his birthplace and the Gothic patrician house where he died are open to the public, as are, on request, the Petri-Pauli Kirche (Church of Sts. Peter and Paul), where he was baptized, and the Andreaskirche (St. Andrew's Church), where his funeral was held. From Eisleben take B–180 north to join with E–49 to Quedlinburg.

Quedlinburg

③③ *79 km (49 mi) northwest of Halle.*

This medieval Harz town has more half-timber houses than any other town in Germany: More than 1,600 of them line the narrow cobblestoned streets and squares. The town escaped World War II unscathed, and in DDR days, though not kept up, Quedlinburg was treasured, so it remains much as it was centuries ago. Today it is a UNESCO World Heritage Site.

For nearly 200 years Quedlinburg was a favorite imperial residence and site of imperial diets, beginning with the election in 919 of Henry the Fowler as Henry I, first Saxon king of Germany. It became a major trading city and a member of the Hanseatic League, equal in stature to Köln.

The Altstadt (Old Town) is full of richly decorated half-timber houses, particularly along Mühlgraben, Schuhof, the Hölle, Breitestrasse, and Schmalstrasse. Notable on the **Marktplatz** (market square) are the Renaissance **Rathaus** (town hall), with a 14th-century statue of Roland signifying the town's independence, and the baroque 1701 Haus Grünhagen. Street and hiking maps and guidebooks (almost all in German) are available at the information office at the Rathaus. ⊠ *Markt 2,* ☎ *03946/773–012.* 🎫 *Rathaus tour DM 4.* ⊙ *Tour daily 1:30.*

The oldest half-timber house in Quedlinburg, built about 1310, is now the **Ständerbau Fachwerkmuseum,** a museum of half-timber construction. ⊠ *Wordg. 3,* ☎ *03946/3828.* 🎫 *DM 4.* ⊙ *Fri.–Wed. 11–5.*

Placed behind half-timber houses so as not to affect the town's medieval feel is the sophisticated, modern **Lyonel Feininger Gallery.** When the art of American-born painter Lyonel Feininger, a Bauhaus teacher in both Weimar and Dessau, was declared "decadent" by the Hitler regime in 1938, the artist returned to America. Left behind with a friend were engravings, lithographs, etchings, and paintings. The most comprehensive Feininger print collection in the world is displayed here. ⊠ *Finkenherd 5a,* ☎ *03946/2238.* 🎫 *DM 6.* ⊙ *Apr.–Oct., Tues.–Sun. 10–6; Nov.–Mar., Tues.–Sun. 10–5.*

On top of the Schlossberg (Castle Hill), with a terrace overlooking woods and valley, perch Quedlinburg's largely Renaissance castle buildings—a church, an abbess's dwelling (Henry I's widow, Mathilde, founded a convent school here), and the building that once housed the abbey kitchens and workshops, now the **Schlossmuseum** (Castle Museum). Exhibits feature the history of the town and the castle, artifacts of the Bronze Age, and the wooden cage in which a captured 14th-century robber baron was put on public view. Restored 17th- and 18th-century rooms give an impression of castle life at that time. ⊠ *Schlossberg 1,* ☎ *03946/2730.* 🎫 *DM 5.* ⊙ *May–Sept., daily 10–5.*

The simple, graceful **Stiftskirche St. Servatius** (Collegiate Church of St. Servatius) is one of the most important and best preserved 12th-century Romanesque structures in Germany. Henry I and his wife, Mathilde, are buried in its crypt. The renowned Quedlinburg Treasure of 10th-, 11th-, and 12th-century gold and silver and bejeweled manuscripts were also kept here. Some of this treasure was stolen by an American soldier in 1945 and returned to the church in 1993. In Nazi days SS leader Heinrich Himmler made the church into a shrine dedicated to the SS, insisting that it was only appropriate since Henry I was the founder of the first German Reich. ⊠ *Schlossberg 1,* ☎ *03946/709–900.* 🎫 *DM 6.* ⊙ *May–Oct., Tues.–Sat. 10–5, Sun. noon–6; Nov.–Apr., Tues.–Sat., 10–4, Sun. noon–4.*

Dining and Lodging

$–$$$ ✕🔲 **Romantik Hotel Theophano.** This 1668 baroque half-timber merchant's house was the seat of the tanners' guild in the 18th century, a restaurant-coffeehouse in the early 20th century, and a domestic linen and store until the Communists "deprivatized" the business. Now restored with care, its elegant rooms are furnished with country antiques. The vaulted-ceiling restaurant serves such dishes as Harz trout and local wild boar. ⊠ *Markt 13–14, D–06484,* ☎ *03946/96300,* FAX *03946/963–036. 22 rooms. Restaurant, free parking. AE, MC, V.* ⊛

$–$$ ✕🔲 **Hotel Zum Bär.** There are stuffed bears in the hall and bears woven into the maroon stair carpet of this 250-year-old half-timber hostelry that has views out onto the marketplace. The French Provincial furniture is painted white and gold. Careful detail has gone into the recent interior decorating, and no two rooms are alike. The restaurant is known for its filling local dishes. ⊠ *Markt 8–9, D–06484,* ☎ *03946/7770,* FAX *03496/700–268. 50 rooms, 1 suite. Restaurant, minibars, free parking. No credit cards.*

$ ✕🔲 **Hotel Zur Goldenen Sonne.** In this recently restored baroque half-
★   timber inn, rooms are furnished in a pleasing, rustic fashion. The cozy restaurant offers such Harz fare as venison stew with plum sauce and

potato dumplings, and local smoked ham in apricot sauce. ⊠ *Steinweg 11, D–06484,* ☎ *03946/96250,* 𝔽𝔸𝕏 *03946/962–530. 27 rooms. Restaurant, minibars, no-smoking rooms, free parking. AE, MC, V.* ⊛

En Route The most scenic way to go from Quedlinburg to Braunlage is via Blankenburg, with its hilltop castle, and Wernigerode, 28 km (20 mi) away. Half-timber **Wernigerode** has a colorful twin-towered Rathaus on the marketplace, and the neo-Gothic castle above it is a starting point for walks in the Harz. Also departing from here is the steam-powered narrow-gauge **Harzquerbahn** to the heights (3,745-ft) of the Brocken. From Wernigerode take B–244 south 10 km (6 mi) to Elbingerode; then turn onto B–27 west and continue another 17 km (10 mi) along mountain roads through spruce forests to Braunlage.

Goslar

③④ *48 km (30 mi) northwest of Quedlinburg.*

Goslar, the lovely, unofficial capital of the Harz region, is one of Germany's oldest cities: Looking back on a history of more than millennium, Goslar is known for the medieval glamour expressed in the fine Romanesque architecture of the Kaiserpfalz, a medieval imperial palace of the German Empire. Thanks to the deposits of ore close to the town, Goslar also became one of the country's most wealthy hubs of trade during the Middle Ages. In this town of 46,000 today, time seems to have stood still among the hundreds of well-preserved (mostly typical northern German half-timber) houses that were built during the course of seven centuries.

Despite Goslar's rapid decline after the breakup of the medieval German empire, the city—thanks to the ore—maintained all its luxury and worldliness born of economic success. The **Rathaus** with its magnificent **Huldigungssaal** (Hall of Honor) dates to 1450 and testifies to the wealth of Goslar's merchants.

The impressive **Kaiserpfalz,** perched high above the historic downtown area, dates to the early Middle Ages. It once was the center of German imperial glory, when emperors held their regular diets here. Among the rulers who frequented Goslar were Heinrich III (AD 1039–1056) and his successor, Heinrich IV (AD 1056–1106), who was also born in Goslar. You can visit an exhibit about the German medieval kaisers who stayed here, inspect the small chapel where the heart of Heinrich III is buried (the body is in Speyer), or view the beautiful ceiling murals in the Reichssaal (Imperial Hall). ⊠ *Kaiserbleek 6,* ☎ *05321/704–358.* 🎫 *DM 4.* ☉ *Apr.–Oct., daily 9–6; Nov.–Mar., daily 10–4.*

The source of the town's riches is outside the city in the **Erzbergwerk Rammelsberg,** the world's only silver mine in continuous operation for more than 1,000 years. It was closed in 1988, but you can now inspect the many tunnels and winding plants of this old mine. ⊠ *Bergtal 19,* ☎ *05321/7500.* 🎫 *DM 15, including tour.* ☉ *Daily 10–6.*

Dining and Lodging

$$–$$$ ✕🏨 **Kaiserworth-Hotel und Restaurant.** Hidden behind the reddish-brown walls of a 500-year-old house, the seat of medieval tailors and merchants, the hotel offers small but pleasantly furnished and bright rooms. The front rooms have windows on the medieval city market. The restaurant offers standard but reliable German food. ⊠ *Markt 3, D–38640,* ☎ *05321/7090,* 𝔽𝔸𝕏 *03521/709–345. 60 rooms. Restaurant, no-smoking rooms, room service, baby-sitting, dry cleaning, laundry service, meeting rooms, parking (fee). AE, DC, MC, V.* ⊛

Braunlage

㉟ *34 km (21 mi) south of Goslar.*

One of the oldest winter-sports centers in central Germany, Braunlage gets snow from December to March and is the best spot for skiing in the Harz. In spring, summer, and fall, hiking on mountain trails is a favorite pastime, and the bald top of the Brocken is a 16-km (10-mi) walk. In the days of a divided Germany, this small resort was little more than 2 km (1 mi) from the border. Guest houses, restaurants, and ski shops are everywhere. A year-round attraction is the indoor skating rink.

Dining and Lodging

$–$$$$ ✕▥ **Romantik Hotel Zur Tanne.** Built in 1725, this is one of the old-
★ est buildings in Braunlage. Most rooms have balconies and banquette corners. The historic house connects to a modern annex, and a less expensive guest house on the outskirts of the village opens out to forest and mountains. When making a reservation, ask for a room in the new *Bachhaus* building. Diners can choose between hearty mountain dishes or lighter gourmet fare. ✉ *Herzog-Wilhelm-Str. 8, D–38700,* ☎ *05520/93120,* ℻ *05520/3992. 29 rooms, 3 suites. Restaurant, in-room safes, minibars, no-smoking rooms, room service, massage, sauna, steam bath, health club, baby-sitting, dry cleaning, laundry service, meeting room, free parking. AE, D, V.* ⊗

Outdoor Activities and Sports

SKIING

Innumerable cross-country trails (lighted at night for after-dark skiing) wend their way through the evergreen forests of Braunlage. Alpine skiers have five ski slopes and a ski jump. The jump was closed until the Wall fell—because the bottom of it was in the DDR. For Alpine skiing, a cable car rises to the top of the 3,237-ft-high Wurmberg, one of northern Germany's highest mountains. It has three ski lifts. There are also toboggan runs, horse-drawn sleigh rides, ski instruction, and equipment rentals. Contact the tourist office for more information (☞ Visitor Information *in* Saxony, Saxony-Anhalt, and Thuringia A to Z, *below*).

THURINGIA

Updated by
Jürgen
Scheunemann

The tiny state of Thuringia is one of Germany's most historic regions, with a rich cultural past still present in small villages, medieval cities, and country palaces throughout the hilly countryside. In the 14th century traders used the 168-km (104-mi) Rennsteig (fast trail) through the dark depths of the Thuringian Forest, and cities like Erfurt, Eisenach, and Gera evolved as major commercial hubs. Today the forests and the Erzgebirge Mountains are a remote paradise for hiking and fishing. The city of Weimar is one of Europe's old cultural centers, and the short-lived German democracy, the Weimar Republic, was established here in 1918. Already a prime vacation spot during Communist times, Thuringia created an economic boom for itself when it attracted investors after reunification.

Eisenach

㊱ *126 km (79 mi) south of Braunlage, 95 km (59 mi) northeast of Fulda (nearest ICE rail station).*

When you stand in Eisenach's ancient market square, it's difficult to imagine this half-timber town as an important center of the eastern German automobile industry, home of the now-shunned Wartburg. This solid, noisy staple of the East German auto trade was named after the famous castle that broods over Eisenach, atop one of the foothills of the Thuringian Forest. Today West German auto maker Opel is continuing the tradition. The GM company built one of Europe's most modern car-assembly lines on the outskirts of Eisenach.

★ Begun in 1067 (and expanded through the centuries), the mighty **Wartburg** has hosted a parade of German historical celebrities. Hermann I (1156–1217), count of Thuringia and count palatine of Saxony, was a patron of the poets Walther von der Vogelweide (1170–1230?) and Wolfram von Eschenbach (1170–1220). Legend has it that this is where Walther, the greatest lyric poet of medieval Germany, prevailed in the celebrated *Minnesängerstreit* (minnesinger contest), which features in Richard Wagner's *Tannhäuser.*

Within the castle's stout walls, Frederick the Wise (1486–1525) shielded Martin Luther from papal proscription from May 1521 until March 1522, even though he did not share the reformer's beliefs. Luther completed the first translation of the New Testament from Greek into German while in hiding, an act that paved the way for the Protestant Reformation. You can peek into the simple study in which Luther worked. Over the centuries souvenir hunters scarred its walls by scratching away the plaster and much of the wood paneling.

Frederick was also a patron of the arts. Lucas Cranach the Elder's portraits of Luther and his wife are on view in the castle, as is a very moving sculpture, the *Kneeling Angel,* by the great 15th-century artist Tilman Riemenschneider. The 13th-century great hall is breathtaking; it's here that the minstrels sang for courtly favors. Don't leave without climbing the belvedere for a panoramic view of the Harz Mountains and the Thuringian Forest. ☎ 03691/77073. ⊡ *DM 11, including guided tour.* ⊘ *Nov.–Feb., daily 9–3:30; Mar.–Oct., daily 8:30–5.*

The **Lutherhaus** in downtown Eisenach has many fascinating exhibits illustrating the life of Luther, who lived here as a student. ⊠ *Lutherpl. 8,* ☎ *03691/29830.* ⊡ *DM 5.* ⊘ *Apr.–Oct., daily 9–5; Nov.–Mar., daily 10–5.*

Johann Sebastian Bach was born in Eisenach in 1685. The **Bachhaus** has exhibits devoted to the entire lineage of the musical Bach family and includes a collection of historical musical instruments. ⊠ *Frauenplan 21,* ☎ *03691/203–714.* ⊡ *DM 5.* ⊘ *Apr.–Sept., Mon. noon–5:45, Tues.–Sun. 9–5:45; Oct.–Mar., Mon. 1–4:45, Tues.–Sun. 9–4:45.*

Composer Richard Wagner gets his due at the **Reuter-Wagner-Museum,** which has the most comprehensive exhibition on Wagner's life and work outside Bayreuth. The old **Teezimmer** (tearoom), an old concert hall with wonderfully restored French wallpaper, has reopened. Concerts are given here, and sometimes you can even listen to the Erard piano dating from the late 19th century. ⊠ *Reuterweg 2,* ☎ *03691/743–293.* ⊡ *DM 4.* ⊘ *Tues.–Sun. 10–5.*

At Johannesplatz 9, look for what is said to be the **narrowest house** in eastern Germany, built in 1890; its width is just over 6 ft, 8 inches; its height, 24½ ft; and its depth, 34 ft.

Dining and Lodging

$$–$$$ ✕⌂ **Romantik-Hotel Kaiserhof.** One of the oldest hotels in town, the
★ Kaiserhof maintains an elegant late-19th-century atmosphere. The lobby and dining room are extraordinarily beautiful and are fine examples of German Landhaus architecture. The mansion has been restored and renovated several times, so rooms are modern, spacious, and equipped with all amenities. The Turmschänke restaurant serves

local dishes. ⊠ *Wartburgallee 2, D–99817,* ☎ *03691/213–513,* FAX *03691/203–653. 64 rooms. 2 restaurants, bar, minibars, no-smoking rooms, room service, beauty salon, sauna, car rental, dry cleaning, laundry service, meeting rooms, free parking. AE, DC, MC, V.* ☜

$–$$ ✕🖼 **Hotel Glockenhof.** At the base of Wartburg Castle, this former church-run hostel has blossomed into a handsome hotel, cleverly incorporating the original half-timber city mansion into a modern extension. The excellent restaurant has been joined by a brasserie. ⊠ *Grimmelg. 4, D–99817,* ☎ *03691/2340,* FAX *03691/234–131. 38 rooms, 2 suites. Restaurant, brasserie, no-smoking rooms, room service, meeting rooms, parking (fee). AE, MC, V.* ☜

$$ 🖼 **Hotel auf der Wartburg.** In this castle hotel, where Martin Luther,
★   Johann Sebastian Bach, and Richard Wagner were guests, you'll get a splendid view over the town and the countryside. The standard of comfort is above average, and antiques and Oriental rugs mix with modern furnishings. The hotel runs a shuttle bus to the rail station and parking lot of the Wartburg. ⊠ *Wartburg, D–99817,* ☎ *03691/7970,* FAX *03691/797–100. 33 rooms, 2 apartments. Restaurant, in-room safes, minibars, no-smoking rooms, room service, dry cleaning, laundry service, meeting room, free parking. AE, DC, MC, V.* ☜

Erfurt

③⑦   *55 km (34 mi) east of Eisenach.*

The "flowers and towers" city of Erfurt emerged from World War II relatively unscathed, with most of its innumerable towers intact. Flowers? Erfurt is a center of horticultural trade and Europe's largest flower- and vegetable-seed producer. Local botanist Christian Reichart pioneered the trade in the 19th century with his seed research. The outskirts of the city are covered with greenhouses and plantations, and the annual Internationale Gartenbauaustellung, or horticultural show, takes place here from the end of March through September.

The city's highly decorative and colorful facades are easy to admire on a walking tour (though you can also take an old-fashioned horse-drawn open carriage tour of the Old Town center every weekend, leaving from the cathedral's entrance at Mettengasse between 10 and 4). Downtown Erfurt is a photographer's delight, with narrow, busy ancient streets dominated by a magnificent 14th-century Gothic cathedral, the **Mariendom.** The **Domplatz** (Cathedral Square) is bordered by houses dating from the 16th century and by the **Rathaus.** The pedestrian-zone **Anger** is also lined with restored Renaissance houses. The **Bartholomäusturm** (Bartholomew Tower), the base of a 12th-century tower, holds a 60-bell carillon.

The **Mariendom** (Erfurt Cathedral) is reached by a broad staircase from the expansive Cathedral Square. Its Romanesque origins (Romanesque foundations can still be seen in the crypt) are best preserved in the choir's glorious stained-glass windows and beautifully carved stalls. The cathedral's biggest bell, the Gloriosa, is the largest free-swinging bell in the world. Cast in 1497, it took three years to install in the tallest of the three sharply pointed towers, painstakingly lifted inch by inch with wooden wedges. No chances are taken with this 2-ton treasure; its deep boom resonates only on special occasions, such as Christmas and New Year's. ⊠ *Dompl.,* ☎ *0361/646–1265.* 🎫 *Tour DM 3.* ☉ *May–Oct., weekdays 9–11:30 and 12:30–5, Sat. 9–11:30 and 12:30–4:30, Sun. 2–4; Nov.–Apr., Mon.–Sat. 10–11:30 and 12:30–4, Sun. 2–4.*

The Gothic church of **St. Severus** has an extraordinary font, a masterpiece of intricately carved sandstone that reaches practically to the ceiling. It is linked to the cathedral by a 70-step open staircase.

Behind the predominantly neo-Gothic Rathaus, you'll find Erfurt's most outstanding attraction spanning the Gera River, the **Krämerbrücke** (Shopkeepers' Bridge). Like Florence, Erfurt has a Renaissance bridge incorporating shops and homes. Built in 1325 and restored in 1967–73, the bridge served for centuries as an important trading center. Today antiques shops fill the majority of the timber-frame houses built into the bridge, some dating from the 16th century. The area around the bridge, crisscrossed with old streets lined with picturesque and often crumbling homes, is known as **Klein Venedig** (Little Venice) simply for the recurrent flooding it endures.

The young Martin Luther spent his formative years in the **St. Augustin Kloster** (St. Augustine Monastery; ⊠ Gotthardstr.), today a seminary. Erfurt's interesting local-history museum is in a late-Renaissance house, **Zum Stockfisch.** ⊠ *Johannesstr. 169,* ☎ *0361/562–4888.* ⌑ *DM 3.* ⊙ *Tues.–Sun. 10–6.*

Dining and Lodging

$$ **Paganini im Gildehaus.** This Italian restaurant in one of the city's oldest (and most beautiful) historic mansions serves a wide variety of both basic country cooking and complex fish dishes. In summer the hotel opens its beer garden, where Thuringian specialties are served—but the focus is on Italian cooking, whose quality is far better than that of the German dishes. The chef, after all, is the Italian Mr. Pitanti. ⊠ *Fischermarkt 13–16,* ☎ *0361/6430–692. AE, DC, MC, V.*

$ ✕ **Dasdie.** Wolfgang Staub's Dasdie combines restaurant, bistro, bar, cabaret stage, and dance floor under one roof, so you can dine here (for less than DM 20), return later (or simply hang loose at the bar) for a show, and end the day with a dance. The food is hit-and-miss, but the place is always lively and prices are low. ⊠ *Marstallstr. 12,* ☎ *0361/646–4666. No credit cards. Closed Sun.–Mon.*

$$$ ✕⊡ **Radisson SAS Hotel Erfurt.** Since the SAS group gave the ugly high-rise Kosmos a face-lift and new name, the socialist-realist look of the DDR years no longer seriously intrudes on Erfurt. The hotel underwent another major renovation in 1999. The rooms have bright, modern colors and fabrics (including leather-upholstered furniture). The Classico restaurant is one of Erfurt's best. ⊠ *Juri-Gagarin-Ring 127, D–99084,* ☎ *0361/55100,* ⓕ *0361/551–0210. 314 rooms, 3 suites. Restaurant, bar, minibars, no-smoking floor, room service, beauty salon, hot tub, sauna, health club, bicycles, baby-sitting, dry cleaning, laundry service, meeting rooms, car rental, parking (fee). AE, DC, MC, V.* ✆

Weimar

㊳ *21 km (13 mi) east of Erfurt.*

Sitting prettily on the Ilm River between the Ettersberg and Vogtland hills, Weimar occupies a place in German political and cultural history completely disproportionate to its size (population 63,000). It's not even particularly old by German standards, with a civic history that started as late as 1410. By the early 19th century the city had become one of Europe's most important cultural centers, where poets Goethe and Schiller wrote, Johann Sebastian Bach played the organ for his Saxon patrons, Carl Maria von Weber composed some of his best music, and Franz Liszt was director of music, presenting the first performance of *Lohengrin.* In 1919 Walter Gropius founded his Staatliche Bauhaus here, and behind the classical pillars of the National Theater, the German National Assembly drew up the constitution of the Weimar Republic, the first German democracy. After the collapse of the ill-fated Weimar government, Hitler chose the little city as the site for the first national congress of his Nazi party. On the outskirts of Weimar the Nazis built—or forced prisoners to build for them—the infamous Buchenwald concentration camp.

Much of Weimar's greatness is owed to the widowed countess Anna Amalia, whose home, the **Wittumspalais** (Wittum Mansion), is surprisingly modest. In the late-18th century the countess went talent hunting for cultural figures to decorate the glittering court her Saxon forebears had established. Goethe was one of her finds, and he served the countess as a counselor, advising her on financial matters and town design. Schiller followed, and he and Goethe became valued visitors to the countess's home. Within this exquisite baroque house you can see the drawing room in which she held soirees, complete with the original cherrywood table at which the company sat. The east wing of the house contains a small museum that is a fascinating memorial to those cultural gatherings. ⊠ *Frauentorstr. 4,* ☎ *03643/545–377.* 💳 *DM 6.* ⊙ *Mar.–Oct., Tues.–Sun. 9–6; Nov.–Feb., Tues.–Sun. 9–4.*

A statue on **Theaterplatz,** in front of the National Theater, shows Goethe placing a paternal-like hand on the shoulder of the younger Schiller. Goethe spent 57 years in Weimar, 47 of them in a house two blocks south of Theaterplatz that has since become a shrine for millions of visitors. The **Goethe Nationalmuseum** (Goethe National Museum) consists of several houses, including the **Goethehaus,** where Goethe lived. It shows a new exhibit about life in Weimar around 1750 and contains writings that illustrate not only the great man's literary might but his interest in the sciences, particularly medicine, and his administrative skills (and frustrations) as minister of state and Weimar's exchequer. You'll see the desk at which Goethe stood to write (he liked to work standing up) and the modest bed in which he died. The rooms are dark and often cramped, but an almost palpable intellectual intensity seems to illuminate them. ⊠ *Frauenplan 1,* ☎ *03643/545–320.* 💳 *DM 8.* ⊙ *Jan.–Mar., Tues.–Sun. 9–4; Apr.–mid-May, Tues.–Sun. 9–6; mid-May–Sept., Tues.–Sun. 9–7; Oct.–Dec., Tues.–Sun. 9–6.*

The **Schillerhaus,** a sturdy, green-shuttered residence, and also part of the Goethe National Museum, is on a tree-shaded square not far from Goethe's house. He and his family spent a happy, all-too-brief three years here (Schiller died here in 1805). Schiller's study is tucked underneath the mansard roof, a cozy room dominated by his desk, where he probably completed *Wilhelm Tell.* Much of the remaining furniture and the collection of books were added later, although they all date from around Schiller's time. ⊠ *Schillerstr. 17,* ☎ *03643/545–350.* 💳 *DM 5.* ⊙ *Mar.–Oct., Wed.–Mon. 9–6; Nov.–Feb., Wed.–Mon. 9–4.*

Goethe's beloved **Gartenhaus** (Garden House), a modest country cottage where he spent many happy hours, wrote much poetry, and began his masterly classical drama *Iphigenie,* is set amid meadowlike parkland on the bank of the River Ilm. Goethe is said to have felt very close to nature here, and you can soak up the same rural atmosphere on footpaths along the peaceful little river. ⊠ *Goethepark,* ☎ *03642/545–375.* 💳 *Cottage DM 4.* ⊙ *Jan.–Mar., Tues.–Sun. 9–4; Apr.–mid-May, Tues.–Sun. 9–6; mid-May–Sept., Tues.–Sun. 9–7; Oct.–Dec., Tues.–Sun. 9–6.*

Goethe and Schiller are buried in the **Historischer Friedhof** (Historic Cemetery), a leafy cemetery where virtually every gravestone commemorates a famous citizen of Weimar. Their tombs are in the vault of the classical-style chapel. The cemetery is a short walk past Goethehaus and Wieland Platz. 💳 *Goethe-Schiller vault DM 4.* ⊙ *Wed.–Mon. 9–1 and 2–5.*

On the central town square, the **Marktplatz** (two blocks east of Theaterplatz), you'll find the home of Lucas Cranach the Elder. Cranach lived here during his last years, 1552–53. Its wide, imposing facade is richly decorated and bears the coat of arms of the Cranach family. It now houses a modern art gallery.

Weimar's 16th-century **Stadtschloss,** the city castle, is around the corner from the Marktplatz. It has a finely restored classical staircase, a festival hall, and a falcon gallery. The tower on the southwest projection dates from the Middle Ages but received its baroque overlay in circa 1730. The **Kunstsammlung** (art collection) here includes several works by Cranach the Elder and many early 20th-century pieces by such artists as Böcklin, Liebermann, and Beckmann. ⊠ *Burgpl. 4,* ☎ *03643/5460.* 🎫 *DM 6.* ☉ *Apr.–Nov., Tues.–Sun. 10–6; Dec.–Mar., Tues.–Sun. 10–4:30.*

The late-Gothic **Herderkirche** (Herder Church), on Weimar's Marktplatz, has a large winged altar started by Lucas Cranach the Elder and finished by his son in 1555.

OFF THE BEATEN PATH	**BELVEDERE PALACE –** Just 8 km (5 mi) south of Weimar, the lovely 18th-century yellow-stucco Belvedere Palace once served as a hunting and pleasure castle; today you'll find a baroque museum and an interesting collection of coaches and other historic vehicles inside. The formal gardens were in part laid out according to Goethe's concepts. ⊠ Belvederer Allee, ☎ 03643/546–162. 🎫 DM 4. ☉ Apr.–Oct., Tues.–Sun. 10–6.
	GEDENKSTÄTTE BUCHENWALD – In the Ettersberg Hills just north of Weimar is a blighted patch of land that contrasts cruelly with the verdant countryside that so inspired Goethe: Buchenwald, one of the most infamous Nazi concentration camps. Sixty-five thousand men, women, and children from 35 countries met their deaths here through forced labor, starvation, disease, and gruesome medical experiments. Each is commemorated by a small stone placed on the outlines of the barracks, which have long since disappeared from the site, and by a massive memorial tower. Besides exhibits, tours are available. To reach Buchenwald, you can take the public bus (No. 6), which leaves every 10 minutes from Goetheplatz in downtown Weimar. The one-way fare is DM 2.50. ☎ 03643/4300. 🎫 Free. ☉ May–Sept., Tues.–Sun. 9:45–3:15; Oct.–Apr., Tues.–Sun. 8:45–4:15.

Dining and Lodging

$$ ✕ **Hotel Thüringen.** The plush elegance of the Thüringen's restaurant, complete with velvet drapes and chandeliers, makes it seem expensive, but the international and regional dishes served are remarkably moderate in price. An excellent Thüringer roast beef, for instance, costs less than DM 20. ⊠ *Brennerstr. 42,* ☎ *03643/903–675. AE, DC, MC, V.*

$ ✕ **Ratskeller.** This is one of the region's most authentic city hall–cellar restaurants, its whitewashed, barrel-vaulted ceiling attesting to centuries of tradition. At the side is a cozy bar where you can enjoy a preprandial drink beneath a spectacular Art Nouveau–color skylight. The delicious *sauerbraten* (roast beef) is the highlight of the traditional Thuringian menu. If venison is in season, try it—likewise the wild duck or wild boar in red-wine sauce. ⊠ *Am Markt 10,* ☎ *03643/850–573. AE, MC, V.*

$ ✕ **Scharfe Ecke.** Thuringia's traditional *Knödel* (dumplings) are at
★ their best here—but be patient, they're made to order and take 20 minutes. The *Klösse* are salty and less dense than the Knödel and come with just about every dish, from roast pork to venison stew, and the

wait is well worth it. The ideal accompaniment to anything on the menu is one of the three locally brewed beers on tab. ⊠ *Eisfeld 2,* ☎ *03643/ 202–430. AE, DC, MC, V. Closed Mon.*

$$$$ 🖾 **Hilton Weimar.** Weimar's most modern hotel features fine, bright pear-tree wood. When making a reservation, ask for a newly renovated room on the fourth floor. The riverside Belvedere Park that Goethe helped plan is just across the road, and the Belvedere Palace is a short walk away. Frequent buses provide access to Weimar's center. ⊠ *Belvederer Allee 25, D–99425,* ☎ *03643/7220,* ℻ *03643/722–741. 294 rooms, 6 suites. 2 restaurants, café, piano bar, minibars, no-smoking floor, room service, indoor pool, beauty salon, massage, sauna, spa, exercise room, nightclub, dry cleaning, laundry service, meeting rooms, parking (fee). AE, DC, MC, V.* 🕾

$$$–$$$$ 🖾 **Kempinski Hotel Elephant.** The historic Elephant, dating from 1696,
★ is famous for its charm—even through the Communist years. Book here (well in advance), and you'll follow the choice of Goethe, Schiller, Herder, Liszt (after whom the hotel bar is named)—and Hitler—all of whom have been guests. Behind the sparkling white facade are comfortable modern rooms decorated in beige, white, and yellow in a timeless blend of Art Deco and Bauhaus styles. A sense of the past is ever present. ⊠ *Markt 19, D–99423,* ☎ *03643/8020,* ℻ *03643/802–610. 97 rooms, 5 suites. 2 restaurants, piano bar, in-room safes, minibars, no-smoking rooms, room service, dry cleaning, laundry service, meeting rooms, parking (fee). AE, DC, MC, V.* 🕾

$$ 🖾 **Amalienhof VCH Hotel.** Book far ahead to secure a room at this friendly little hotel central to Weimar's attractions. The historic and officially protected building began in 1826 as a church hostel. Double rooms are furnished with first-rate antique reproductions; public rooms have the real thing. ⊠ *Amalienstr. 2, D–99423,* ☎ *03643/5490,* ℻ *03643/549– 110. 22 rooms, 9 apartments. Free parking. AE, MC, V.* 🕾

Nightlife and the Arts

Weimar's lively after-dark scene concentrates around piano bars and nightclubs at the Hilton Weimar and Kempinski Hotel Elephant (☞ *above*).

Gera

③ *65 km (40 mi) east of Weimar.*

Once a princely residence and center of a thriving textile industry, the city has largely been rebuilt since World War II. Gera had often been compared with old Vienna, although today you have to search long and hard to discover any striking similarities between the German provincial town and the Habsburg capital. But some ornate and beautifully restored house facades hint at Gera's rich past.

Although the palace in which prince-electors once held court was destroyed in the final weeks of World War II and never rebuilt, the palace's 16th-century **orangerie** does still stand, in the former Küchengarten in the suburb of Untermhaus. It's an imposing semicircular baroque pavilion, irreverently dubbed the "roast sausage" by the people of Gera, which now houses the **Kunstsammlung**, the city's official art gallery. ⊠ *Küchengartenallee 4,* ☎ *0365/832–2147.* 🎫 *DM 4.* ☉ *Tues. 1–8, Wed.–Fri. 10–5, weekends 10–6.*

Gera's real claim to fame is artist Otto Dix (1891–1969). The residence where the satirical Expressionist painter was born is now known as the **Otto-Dix-Haus** (Otto Dix House). It has a gallery of his work and a permanent exhibition on his life. ⊠ *Mohrenpl. 4,* ☎ *03643/832–4927.*

▨ *DM 4; DM 6, including admission to Orangerie.* ☉ *Tues.–Fri. 10–5, weekends 10–6.*

Don't leave Gera without checking out the central town square, the **Marktplatz.** The Renaissance buildings surrounding it were restored with rare care. The 16th-century **Rathaus** has a vividly decorated entrance and a vaulted cellar restaurant. Note the weird angles of the lower-floor windows; they follow the incline of the staircase winding up the interior of the building's picturesque 185-ft-high tower.

Lodging

$$ ▥ **Doring Hotel Gera.** This hotel of the reliable German Doring chain has a businesslike atmosphere, and the spacious rooms have modern furnishings. Most rooms are very quiet, and for an extra DM 25, you can have a *Komfortzimmer,* which is a larger room that includes a free minibar, a free newspaper, and office equipment (two phones, fax, and data ports). The hotel is in a cul-de-sac in a nice neighborhood, and the city's sights are a 10-minute walk. ⊠ *Schülerstr. 22, D–07545,* ☎ *03651/43440,* ℻ *03651/434–4100. 278 rooms, 2 suites. Restaurant, bar, minibars, no-smoking floor, room service, pool, massage, sauna, steam room, exercise room, baby-sitting, dry cleaning, laundry service, meeting rooms, parking (fee). AE, DC, MC, V.* ▨

SAXONY, SAXONY-ANHALT, AND THURINGIA A TO Z

Arriving and Departing

By Bus
Long-distance buses service Dresden and Leipzig.

By Car
Expressways connect Berlin with Dresden (the A–13) and Leipzig (A–9). Both journeys take about two hours. The A–4 stretches east–west across the southern portion of Thuringia and Saxony.

By Plane
Berlin has the nearest international airport. **Dresden Flughafen** (☎ 0351/8810) is about 10 km (6 mi) north of Dresden. Leipzig's **Flughafen Leipzig-Halle** (☎ 0341/2240) is 12 km (8 mi) northwest of the city.

By Train
Berlin and all eastern German cities are linked (with one another and with rail hubs in western Germany) by InterCity, EuroCity (direct services to other European cities), and the high-speed InterCity Express trains. InterRegio services complete the express network.

Getting Around

By Boat
KD River Cruises of Europe has two luxury cruise ships on the Elbe River. It operates a full program of cruises of up to eight days in length from mid-April until late October that go from Hamburg as far as Prague. All the historic cities of Saxony and Thuringia are ports of call—including Dresden, Meissen, Wittenberg, and Dessau. For details of the cruises, *see* Cruise Lines *in* Smart Travel Tips A to Z.

By Bus

Bus travel is not recommended in this area. Service is infrequent and mainly connects with rail lines. Check schedules carefully at central train stations or call the service phone number of Deutsche Bahn at local railway stations.

By Car

A road-construction program is ongoing in eastern Germany, and you should expect traffic delays on any journey of more than 300 km (186 mi). The Bundesstrassen throughout Eastern Germany are narrow, tree-lined country roads, often jammed with traffic. Roads in the western part of the Harz Mountains are better and wider.

By Train

The fastest and most inexpensive way to explore the region is by train. All cities are connected by a network of trains and some—Dresden and Meissen, for example—by commuter trains. Slower D- and E-class or InterRegio trains link smaller towns. From Dresden a round-trip ticket to Chemnitz costs about DM 41 (a 1-hour, 48-minute journey); to Görlitz, DM 60 (a two-hour ride). Trains connect Leipzig and Halle or Erfurt and Eisenach within 40 minutes, and tickets cost between DM 10 and DM 16. The train ride between Erfurt and Gera (1 hour, 30 minutes) costs DM 20 one-way.

Contacts and Resources

Car Rentals

Cars can be rented at Dresden's and Leipzig's airports and train stations and through all major hotels. Be aware that you are not allowed to take rentals into Poland or the Czech Republic.

Avis (⊠ Dresden Airport, Dresden, ☎ 0351/881–4600; ⊠ Friedrichstr. 24–26, Dresden, ☎ 0351/866–800; ⊠ Torgauer Str. 231, Leipzig, ☎ 0341/259–580; ⊠ Leipzig-Halle Airport, Leipzig, ☎ 0341/224–1804; ⊠ Hauptbahnhof, Georgiring 14, Leipzig, ☎ 0341/961–1400).

Hertz (⊠ Dresden Airport, Dresden, ☎ 0351/881–4580; ⊠ Antonstr. 39, Dresden, ☎ 0351/254–0130; ⊠ Tiergartenstr. 94, Dresden, ☎ 0351/254–7030; ⊠ Leipzig-Halle Airport, Leipzig, ☎ 034204/63026; ⊠ Hauptbahnhof, Reisezentrum, Leipzig, ☎ 0341/212–5867).

InterRent-Europcar (⊠ Dresden Airport, Dresden, ☎ 0351/884–770; ⊠ Liebstädterstr. 5, Dresden, ☎ 0351/254–640; ⊠ Hauptbahnhof, Dresden, ☎ 0351/877–320; ⊠ Leipzig-Halle Airport, Leipzig, ☎ 034204/7700; ⊠ Wittenberger Str. 19, Leipzig, ☎ 0341/904–440; ⊠ Hauptbahnhof, Leipzig, ☎ 0341/141–160).

Sixt (⊠ Dresden Airport, Dresden, ☎ 0180/5252–525; ⊠ Hilton Hotel, An der Frauenkirche 5, Dresden, ☎ 0351/864–2972; ⊠ Pieschener Allee 14, Dresden, ☎ 0351/495–4105; ⊠ Leipzig-Halle Airport, Leipzig, ☎ 0180/526–2525; ⊠ Löhrstr. 2 (next to Fürstenhof Hotel), Leipzig, ☎ 0341/984–840).

Emergencies

Police and ambulance (☎ 110). **Fire** (☎ 110). For **Fire and emergency medical aid** ☎ (112).

Guided Tours

Information on travel and tours to and around eastern Germany is available from most travel agents. Most Berlin tourist offices carry brochures about travel in eastern Germany. For information about guided tours around the region, contact **Berolina Berlin-Service** (✉ Meinekestr. 3, D–10719 Berlin, ☎ 030/8856–8030) or **DER** Deutsches Reisebüro GmbH. (✉ Augsburger Str. 27, D–12309 Berlin, ☎ 030/2199–8100).

German Railways' small-gauge line penetrates deep into the Saxony countryside and the Fichtelberg Mountains. Call the Deutsche Bahn office in Dresden (☎ 0351/461–3558) for schedule and fare information.

For information on **paddle-steam tours** of the Elbe, contact the Sächsische Dampfschiffahrt GmbH (☎ 0351/496–9203). Boats depart from and stop in Dresden, Meissen, Pirna, Pillnitz, Königsstein, and Bad Schandau. The **Weisse Flotte** (White Fleet) of boats, including sidewheelers, plies the Elbe River, starting at Dresden. Besides tours in the Dresden area, boats also go upstream and into the Czech Republic. For more information contact a tour operator at Sächsische Dampfschiffahrt (✉ Hertha-Lindner-Str. 10, D–01067 Dresden, ☎ 0351/866–090).

Guided **bus tours** of Leipzig (in English) run daily at 1:30 (May–September, also on weekends at 10:30); tours leave from outside the opera house, on Goethestrasse. A **walking tour** of Leipzig (also in English) sets off from the tourist information office (✉ Sachsenpl. 1, ☎ 0341/710–4280) May–September, daily 1:30; October–April, Saturday 1:30 and Sunday 10:30. Tickets can be booked at the tourist information office.

Dresden **streetcar tours** leave from Postplatz (Tuesday–Sunday at 9, 11, and 1:30); bus tours, leaving from Dr.-Külz-Ring, run Tuesday–Thursday at 11 (☎ 0351/495–5025 for details).

Travel Agencies
American Express (✉ Burgpl. 2, D–04109 Leipzig, ☎ 0341/997–000; ✉ Hoyerswerder Str. 20, D–01099 Dresden, ☎ 0351/807–030; ✉ Leipzig-Halle Airport, D–04029 Leipzig, ☎ 0341/224–1850).

Visitor Information
Braunlage (✉ Elbingeröder Str. 17, D–3700, ☎ 5520/19433 or 5520/93070, FAX 5520/930–720, ✎). **Chemnitz** (✉ Tourist-Information (Stadthalle), Rathausstr. 1, D–09009, ☎ 0371/19433, FAX 0371/450–8725, ✎). **Dessau** (✉ Dessau-Information und Fremdenverkehrsservice, Friedrich-Naumann-Str. 12, D–06844, ☎ 0340/2041–442, FAX 0340/204–1142, ✎). **Dresden** (✉ Tourist-Information, Prager Str. 10, D–01069, ☎ 0351/491–920, FAX 0351/4919–2116,✎). **Eisenach** (✉ Eisenach-Information, Bahnhofstr. 3–5, D–99817, ☎ 03691/79230, FAX 03691/792–320, ✎). **Erfurt** (✉ Tourist-Information, Fischmarkt 27, D–99084, ☎ 0361/66400, FAX 0361/664–0290,✎). **Freiberg** (✉ Fremdenverkehrsamt Freiberg, Obermarkt 24, D–09599, ☎ 03731/273–266, FAX 03731/273–260,✎). **Gera** (✉ Gera-Information, Ernst-Toller-Str. 14, D–07545, ☎ 0365/8007–030, FAX 0365/619–304, ✎). **Görlitz** (✉ Tourist-Information, Obermarkt 29, D–02826, ☎ 03581/47570, FAX 03581/475–727,✎). **Goslar** (✉ Tourist-Information, Markt 7, D–38640, ☎ 05321/78060, FAX 05321/780–644, ✎). **Halle** (✉ Tourist-Information, Marktpl., D–06108, ☎ 0345/202–3340, FAX 0345/502–798,✎). **Leipzig** (✉ Leipzig Tourist Service e.V., Sachsenpl. 1, D–04109, ☎ 0341/7104–260, FAX 0341/710–4271). **Meissen** (✉ An der Frauenkirche 3, D–01662, ☎ 03521/41940, FAX 03521/458–240, ✎). **Quedlinburg** (✉ Tourismus-Marketing GmbH, Markt 2, D–06484, ☎ 03946/9056–208, FAX 03946/905–629,✎). **Suhl** (✉ Fremdenverkehrsamt Suhl, August-Bebel-Str. 16, D–98527, ☎ 03681/39450, FAX 03681/722–179, ✎). **Thale** (✉ Rathaustr. 1, D–06502, ☎ 03947/2597, FAX 03947/2277,✎). **Weimar** (✉ Tourist-Information Weimar, Markt 10,

D–99421, ☎ 03643/24000 or 03643/19443, ⟨FAX⟩ 03643/240–040,🐢). **Wernigerode** (✉ Nikolaipl. 1, D–38855, ☎ 03943/633035, ⟨FAX⟩ 03943/632–040,🐢). **Wittenberg** (✉ Tourist-Information, Schlosspl. 2, D–06886 Wittenberg, ☎ 03491/498–610, ⟨FAX⟩ 03491/498–611, www.wittenberg.de; **Wittenberg District Rural Information Office**, ✉ Mittelstr. 33, D–06886, ☎ 03491/402–610, ⟨FAX⟩ 03491/405–857). **Wörlitz** (✉ Neuer Wall 103, D–06786, ☎ 034905/21704, ⟨FAX⟩ 034905/20216,🐢).

17 BACKGROUND AND ESSENTIALS

Map of Germany

Chronology

Smart Travel Tips A to Z

Vocabulary

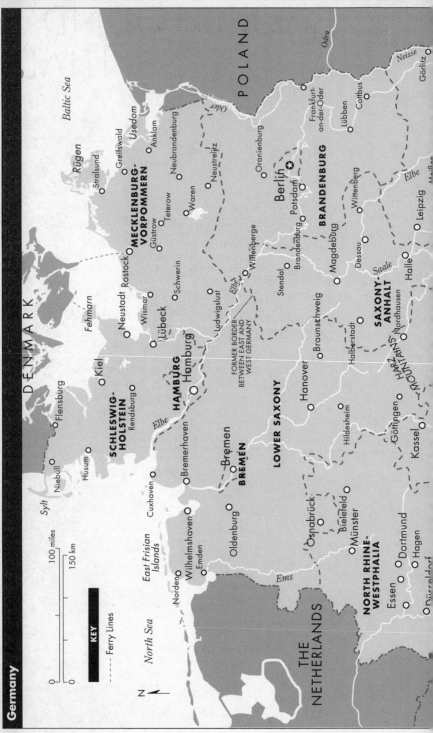

Germany

POLAND

Baltic Sea

Rügen

Usedom

DENMARK

Anklam

Stralsund

Greifswald

Neubrandenburg

MECKLENBURG-
VORPOMMERN

Neustrelitz

Waren

Oder

Görlitz

Neisse

Cottbus

Lübben

Frankfurt-
an-der-Oder

Oranienburg

Güstrow

Teterow

Rostock

Neustadt

Berlin ✪

Potsdam

BRANDENBURG

Wittenberge

Wittenberg

Elbe

Leipzig

Neustadt

Wismar

Schwerin

Ludwigslust

Brandenburg

Magdeburg

Dessau

Saale

Halle

Fehmarn

Kiel

Lübeck

HAMBURG

Hamburg

Elbe

FORMER BORDER
BETWEEN EAST AND
WEST GERMANY

Stendal

SAXONY-
ANHALT

Nordhausen

Flensburg

SCHLESWIG-
HOLSTEIN

Rendsburg

Braunschweig

Halberstadt

HARZ MOUNTAINS

Husum

Sylt

Niebüll

Elbe

Bremerhaven

Bremen

BREMEN

LOWER SAXONY

Hanover

Hildesheim

Göttingen

Kassel

East Frisian
Islands

Cuxhaven

Oldenburg

Osnabrück

Bielefeld

Münster

NORTH RHINE-
WESTPHALIA

Dortmund

Hagen

Norden

Wilhelmshaven

Emden

Ems

Essen

Düsseldorf

North Sea

THE
NETHERLANDS

100 miles

150 km

KEY

----- Ferry Lines

N

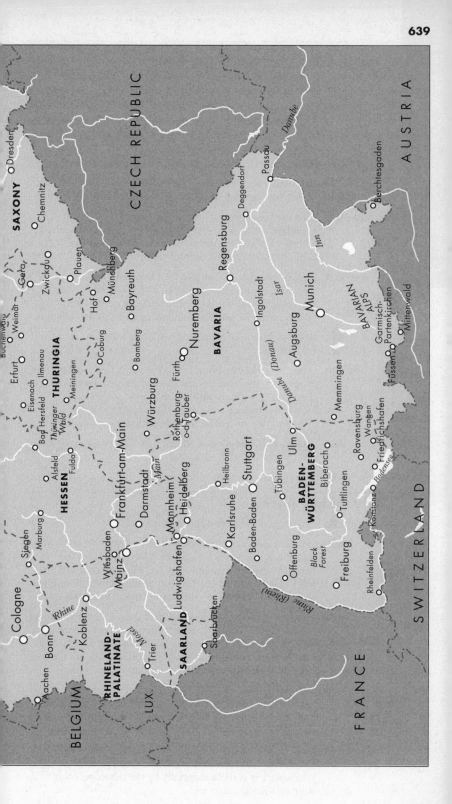

GERMANY AT A GLANCE

ca. 5000 BC Indo-Germanic tribes settle in the Rhine and Danube valleys

ca. 2000–800 BC Distinctive German Bronze Age culture emerges, with settlements ranging from coastal farms to lakeside villages

ca. 450–50 BC Salzkammergut people, whose prosperity is based on abundant salt deposits (in the area of upper Austria), trade with Greeks and Etruscans; Salzkammerguts spread as far as Belgium and have first contact with the Romans

9 BC–AD 9 Roman attempts to conquer the "Germans"—the tribes of the Cibri, the Franks, the Goths, and the Vandals—are only partly successful; the Rhine becomes the northeastern border of the Roman Empire (and remains so for 300 years)

212 Roman citizenship is granted to all free inhabitants of the Empire

ca. 400 Pressed forward by Huns from Asia, such German tribes as the Franks, the Vandals, and the Lombards migrate to Gaul (France), Spain, Italy, and North Africa, scattering the Empire's populace and eventually leading to the disintegration of central Roman authority

486 The Frankish kingdom is founded by Clovis; his court is in Paris

497 The Franks convert to Christianity

Early Middle Ages

776 Charlemagne becomes king of the Franks

800 Charlemagne is declared Holy Roman Emperor; he makes Aachen capital of his realm, which stretches from the Bay of Biscay to the Adriatic and from the Mediterranean to the Baltic. Under his enlightened patronage there is an upsurge in art and architecture—the Carolingian renaissance

843 The Treaty of Verdun divides Charlemagne's empire among his three sons: West Francia becomes France; Lotharingia becomes Lorraine (territory to be disputed by France and Germany into the 20th century); and East Francia takes on, roughly, the shape of modern Germany

911 Five powerful German dukes (of Bavaria, Lorraine, Franconia, Saxony, and Swabia) establish the first German monarchy by electing King Conrad I; Henry I (the Fowler) succeeded Conrad in 919.

962 Otto I is crowned Holy Roman Emperor by the pope; he establishes Austria—the East Mark. The Ottonian renaissance is marked especially by the development of Romanesque architecture

Middle Ages

1024–1125 The Salian dynasty is characterized by a struggle between emperors and the Church that leaves the Empire weak and disorganized; the great Romanesque cathedrals of Speyer, Trier, and Mainz are built

1138–1254 Frederick Barbarossa leads the Hohenstaufen dynasty; there is temporary recentralization of power, underpinned by strong trade and Church relations

1158 Munich, capital of Bavaria, is founded by Duke Henry the Lion; Henry is deposed by Emperor Barbarossa, and Munich is presented to the House of Wittelsbach, which rules it until 1918

1241 The Hanseatic League is founded to protect trade; Bremen, Hamburg, Köln, and Lübeck are early members. Agencies are soon established in London, Antwerp, Venice, and along the Baltic and North seas; a complex banking and finance system results

mid-1200s The Gothic style, exemplified by the grand Köln Cathedral, flourishes

1349 Black Death plague kills one-quarter of German population

Renaissance and Reformation

1456 Johannes Gutenberg (1400–68) prints first book in Europe

1471–1553 Renaissance flowers under influence of painter and engraver Albrecht Dürer (1471–1528), Dutch-born philosopher and scholar Erasmus (1466–1536), Lucas Cranach the Elder (1472–1553), who originates Protestant religious painting, portrait and historical painter Hans Holbein the Younger (1497–1543), and landscape painting pioneer Albrecht Altdorfer (1480–1538). Increasing wealth among the merchant classes leads to strong patronage of the revived arts

1517 The Protestant Reformation begins in Germany when Martin Luther (1483–1546) nails his 95 Theses to a church door in Wittenberg, contending that the Roman Church has forfeited divine authority through its corrupt sale of indulgences. Luther is outlawed, and his revolutionary doctrine splits the Church; much of north Germany embraces Protestantism

1524–30 The (Catholic) Habsburgs rise to power; their empire spreads throughout Europe (and as far as North Africa, the Americas, and the Philippines). Erasmus breaks with Luther and supports reform within the Roman Catholic church. In 1530 Charles V (a Habsburg) is crowned Holy Roman Emperor; he brutally crushes the Peasants' War, one in a series of populist uprisings in Europe

1545 The Council of Trent marks the beginning of the Counter-Reformation. Through diplomacy and coercion, most Austrians, Bavarians, and Bohemians are won back to Catholicism, but the majority of Germans remain Lutheran; persecution of religious minorities grows

Thirty Years' War

1618–48 Germany is the main theater for the Thirty Years' War. The powerful Catholic Habsburgs are defeated by Protestant forces, swelled by disgruntled Habsburg subjects and the armies of King Gustav Adolphus of Sweden. The bloody conflict ends with the Peace of Westphalia (1648); Habsburg and papal authority are severely diminished

Absolutism and Enlightenment

1689 Louis XIV of France invades the Rhineland Palatinate and sacks Heidelberg. At the end of the 17th century, Germany consolidates its role as a center of scientific thought

1708 Johann Sebastian Bach (1685–1750) becomes court organist at Weimar and launches his career; he and Georg Friederic Handel (1685–1759) fortify the great tradition of German music. Baroque and, later, rococo art and architecture flourish

1740–86 Reign of Frederick the Great of Prussia; his rule sees both the expansion of Prussia (it becomes the dominant military force in Germany) and the spread of Enlightenment thought

ca. 1790 The great age of European orchestral music is raised to new heights in the works of Joseph Haydn (1732–1809), Wolfgang Amadeus Mozart (1756–91), and Ludwig van Beethoven (1770–1827)

early 1800s Johann Wolfgang von Goethe (1749–1832) is part of the *Sturm und Drang* movement that leads to Romanticism. Painter Caspar David Friedrich (1774–1840) leads early German Romanticism. Other luminary cultural figures include writers Friedrich Schiller (1759–1805) and Heinrich von Kleist (1777–1811); the composers Robert Schumann (1810–56), Hungarian-born Franz Liszt (1811–86), Richard Wagner (1813–83), and Johannes Brahms (1833–97). In architecture, the severe lines of neoclassicism become popular

Road to Nationhood

1806 Napoléon's armies invade Prussia; it briefly becomes part of the French Empire

1807 The Prussian prime minister Baron vom und zum Stein frees the serfs, creating a new spirit of patriotism; the Prussian army is rebuilt

1813 The Prussians defeat Napoléon at Leipzig

1815 Britain and Prussia defeat Napoléon at Waterloo. At the Congress of Vienna, the German Confederation is created as a loose union of 39 independent states, reduced from more than 300 principalities. The *Bundestag* (national assembly) is established at Frankfurt. Already powerful Prussia increases its territory, gaining the Rhineland, Westphalia, and most of Saxony

1848 The "Year of the Revolutions" is marked by uprisings across the fragmented German Confederation; Prussia expands. A national parliament is elected, taking the power of the Bundestag to prepare a constitution for a united Germany

1862   Otto von Bismarck (1815–98) becomes prime minister of Prussia; he is determined to wrest German-populated provinces from Austro-Hungarian (Habsburg) control

1866   Austria-Hungary is defeated by the Prussians at Sadowa; Bismarck sets up the Northern German Confederation in 1867. A key figure in Bismarck's plans is Ludwig II of Bavaria. Ludwig—a political simpleton—lacks successors, making it easy for Prussia to seize his lands

1867   Karl Marx (1818–83) publishes *Das Kapital*

1870–71   The Franco-Prussian War: Prussia lays siege to Paris. Victorious Prussia seizes Alsace-Lorraine but eventually withdraws from all other occupied French territories

1871   The four south German states agree to join the Northern Confederation; Wilhelm I is proclaimed first kaiser of the united Empire

Modernism

1882   The Triple Alliance is forged between Germany, Austria-Hungary, and Italy. Germany's industrial revolution blossoms, enabling it to catch up with the other great powers of Europe. Germany establishes colonies in Africa and the Pacific

ca. 1885   Daimler and Benz pioneer the automobile

1890   Kaiser Wilhelm II (rules 1888–1918) dismisses Bismarck and begins a new, more aggressive course of foreign policy; he oversees the expansion of the navy

1890s   A new school of writers, including Rainer Maria Rilke (1875–1926), emerges. Rilke's *Sonnets to Orpheus* give German poetry new lyricism

1905   Albert Einstein (1879–1955) announces his theory of relativity

1906   Painter Ernst Ludwig Kirchner (1880–1938) helps organize *Die Brücke,* a group of artists who, along with *Der Blaue Reiter,* create the avant-garde art movement Expressionism

1907   Great Britain, Russia, and France form the Triple Entente, which, set against the Triple Alliance, divides Europe into two armed camps

1914–18   Austrian Archduke Franz-Ferdinand is assassinated in Sarajevo. The attempted German invasion of France sparks World War I; Italy and Russia join the Allies, and four years of pitched battle ensue. By 1918 the Central Powers are encircled and must capitulate

Weimar Republic

1918   Germany is compelled by the Versailles Treaty to give up its overseas colonies and much European territory (including Alsace-Lorraine to France) and to pay huge reparations to the Allies; Kaiser Wilhelm II repudiates the throne and goes into exile in Holland. The tough terms leave the new democracy (the Weimar Republic) shaky

1919 The Bauhaus school of art and design, the brainchild of Walter Gropius (1883–1969), is born. Thomas Mann (1875–1955) and Hermann Hesse (1877–1962) forge a new style of visionary intellectual writing

1923 Germany suffers runaway inflation. Adolf Hitler's Beer Hall Putsch, a rightist revolt, fails; leftist revolts are frequent

1925 Hitler publishes *Mein Kampf* (*My Struggle*)

1932 The Nazi party gains the majority in the *Reichstag* (parliament)

1933 Hitler becomes chancellor; the Nazi "revolution" begins

Nazi Germany

1934 President Paul von Hindenburg dies; Hitler declares himself führer (leader) of the Third Reich. Nazification of all German social institutions begins, spreading a policy that is virulently racist and anticommunist. Germany recovers industrial might and rearms

1936 Germany signs anticommunist agreements with Italy and Japan, forming the Axis; Hitler reoccupies the Rhineland

1938 The *Anschluss* (annexation): Hitler occupies Austria. Germany occupies the Sudetenland in Czechoslovakia

1939–40 In August Hitler signs a pact with the Soviet Union; in September he invades Poland; war is declared by the Allies. Over the next three years, there are Nazi invasions of Denmark, Norway, the Low Countries, France, Yugoslavia, and Greece. Alliances form between Germany and the Baltic states

1941–45 Hitler launches his anticommunist crusade against the Soviet Union, reaching Leningrad in the north and Stalingrad and the Caucasus in the south. In 1944 the Allies land in France; their combined might brings the Axis to its knees. In addition to the millions killed in the fighting, more than 6 million Jews and other victims die in Hitler's concentration camps. Germany is again in ruins. Hitler kills himself. East Berlin and what becomes East Germany are occupied by the Soviet Union

The Cold War

1945 At the Yalta Conference, France, the United States, Britain, and the Soviet Union divide Germany into four zones; each country occupies a sector of Berlin. The Potsdam Agreement expresses the determination to rebuild Germany as a democracy

1948 The Soviet Union tears up the Potsdam Agreement and attempts, by blockade, to exclude the three other Allies from their agreed zones in Berlin. Stalin is frustrated by a massive airlift of supplies to West Berlin

1949 The three Western zones are combined to form the Federal Republic of Germany; the new West German parliament elects Konrad Adenauer as chancellor (a post he held until his retirement in 1963). Soviet-held East Germany becomes the Communist German Democratic Republic (DDR)

1950s West Germany, aided by the financial impetus provided by the Marshall Plan, rebuilds its devastated cities and economy—the *Wirtschaftswunder* (economic miracle) gathers speed. The writers Heinrich Böll, Wolfgang Koeppen, and Günter Grass emerge

1957 The Treaty of Rome heralds the formation of the European Economic Community (EEC); Germany is a founding member

1961 Communists build the Berlin Wall to stem the outward tide of refugees.

1969–74 The vigorous chancellorship of Willy Brandt pursues *Ostpolitik,* improving relations with Eastern Europe, the Soviet Union, and acknowledging East Germany's sovereignty

mid-1980s The powerful German Green Party emerges as the leading environmentalist voice in Europe

Reunification

1989 Discontent in East Germany leads to a flood of refugees westward and to mass demonstrations; Communist power collapses across Eastern Europe; the Berlin Wall falls

1990 In March the first free elections in East Germany bring a center-right government to power. The Communists, faced with corruption scandals, suffer a big defeat but are represented (as Democratic Socialists) in the new, democratic parliament. The World War II victors hold talks with the two German governments, and the Soviet Union gives its support for reunification. Economic union takes place on July 1, with full political unity on October 3. In December, in the first democratic national German elections in 58 years, Chancellor Helmut Kohl's three-party coalition is reelected

1991 Nine months of emotional debate end on June 20, when parliamentary representatives vote to move the capital from Bonn—seat of the West German government since 1949—to Berlin, the capital of Germany until the end of World War II

1998 Helmut Kohl's record 16-year-long chancellorship of Germany ends with the election of Gehard Schröder. Schröder's Social Democratic Party (SPD) pursues a coalition with the Greens in order to replace the three-party coalition of the Christian Democratic Union, Christian Social Union, and Free Democratic Party

1999 The Bundestag, the German parliament, returns to the restored Reichstag in Berlin on April 19. The German federal government also leaves Bonn for Berlin, making Berlin capital of Germany again

2000 Hannover hosts Germany's first world's exposition, EXPO 2000

ESSENTIAL INFORMATION

ADDRESSES

In this book the words for street (*Strasse*) and alley (*Gasse*) are abbreviated as str. and g. within italicized service information. Brüdergasse will appear as Brüderg., for example.

AIR TRAVEL

BOOKING

When you book, **look for nonstop flights** and **remember that "direct" flights stop at least once.** Try to avoid connecting flights, which require a change of plane. Frankfurt is the most common hub for flights to Germany; flights to Berlin usually require a connecting flight, and therefore round-trip fares will be more expensive.

CARRIERS

➤ MAJOR AIRLINES: **American** (☎ 800/433–7300) to Frankfurt. **Continental** (☎ 800/525–0280) to Düsseldorf, Frankfurt. **Delta** (☎ 800/241–4141) to Berlin, Frankfurt, Munich, Stuttgart. **LTU International Airways** (☎ 800/888–0200) to Düsseldorf, Frankfurt, Munich. **Lufthansa** (☎ 800/645–3880) to Berlin, Düsseldorf, Frankfurt, Köln, Munich. **Northwest** (☎ 800/225–2525) to Berlin, Frankfurt. **TWA** (☎ 800/221–2000) to Frankfurt. **United** (☎ 800/241–6522) to Düsseldorf, Frankfurt, Munich. **US Airways** (☎ 800/428–4322) to Frankfurt, Munich.

➤ FROM THE U.K.: In the United Kingdom contact **British Airways** (☎ 0345/222–111) and **Lufthansa** (✉ 10 Old Bond St., London W1X 4EN, ☎ 020/8750–3300 or 0345/737–747).

➤ DOMESTIC AIRLINES: Contact **Deutsche BA** at its headquarters at the Munich Airport (☎ 089/9759–1500), **LTU** in Düsseldorf (☎ 0211/941–8888), or **Lufthansa** at any German airport or downtown office.

CHECK-IN & BOARDING

Assuming that not everyone with a ticket will show up, airlines routinely overbook planes. When everyone does, airlines ask for volunteers to give up their seats. In return, these volunteers usually get a certificate for a free flight and are rebooked on the next flight out. If there are not enough volunteers, the airline must choose who will be denied boarding. The first to get bumped are passengers who checked in late and those flying on discounted tickets, so **get to the gate and check in as early as possible,** especially during peak periods.

Always **bring a government-issued photo ID to the airport.** You may be asked to show it before you are allowed to check in.

CUTTING COSTS

The least expensive airfares to Germany must usually be purchased in advance and are nonrefundable. It's smart to **call a number of airlines, and when you are quoted a good price, book it on the spot**—the same fare may not be available the next day. Always **check different routings** and look into using different airports. Travel agents, especially low-fare specialists (☞ Discounts & Deals, *below*), are helpful.

Consolidators are another good source. They buy tickets for scheduled international flights at reduced rates from the airlines, then sell them at prices that beat the best fare available directly from the airlines, usually without restrictions. Sometimes you can even get your money back if you need to return the ticket. Carefully read the fine print detailing penalties for changes and cancellations, and **confirm your consolidator reservation with the airline.**

When you **fly as a courier,** you trade your checked-luggage space for a ticket deeply subsidized by a courier service. There are restrictions on when you can book and how long you can stay. Look in your yellow pages for courier company listings.

➤ CONSOLIDATORS: **Cheap Tickets** (☎ 800/377–1000). **Discount Airline Ticket Service** (☎ 800/576–1600). **Unitravel** (☎ 800/325–2222). **Up & Away Travel** (☎ 212/889–2345). **World Travel Network** (☎ 800/409–6753).

ENJOYING THE FLIGHT

For more legroom, **request an emergency-aisle seat.** Don't sit in the row in front of the emergency aisle or in front of a bulkhead, where seats may not recline. If you have dietary concerns, **ask for special meals when booking.** These can be vegetarian, low-cholesterol, or kosher, for example. On long flights try to maintain a normal routine in order to help fight jet lag. At night, **get some sleep.** By day, **eat light meals, drink water** (not alcohol), and **move around the cabin** to stretch your legs.

FLYING TIMES

Flying time to Frankfurt is 7½ hours from New York, 10 hours from Chicago, and 12 hours from Los Angeles.

HOW TO COMPLAIN

If your baggage goes astray or your flight goes awry, complain right away. Most carriers require that you **file a claim immediately.**

➤ AIRLINE COMPLAINTS: U.S. Department of Transportation **Aviation Consumer Protection Division** (✉ C-75, Room 4107, Washington, DC 20590, ☎ 202/366–2220, airconsumer@ost.dot.gov, www.dot.gov/airconsumer). **Federal Aviation Administration Consumer Hotline** (☎ 800/322–7873).

WITHIN GERMANY

Germany's internal air network is excellent, with frequent flights linking all major cities in little more than an hour. Services are operated by **Deutsche BA,** a British Airways subsidiary, **Lufthansa,** and LTU.

AIRPORTS

Frankfurt is the main hub airport in Germany. It has the convenience of its own long-distance train station.

➤ AIRPORT INFORMATION: Berlin: **Flughafen Tegel, Tempelhof, Brandenburg** (☎ 180/500–0186). Düsseldorf: **Flughafen Düsseldorf** (☎ 0211/421–2223). Frankfurt: **Flughafen Frankfurt Main** (☎ 069/6903–0511). Hamburg: **Fuhlsbüttel International Airport** (☎ 040/50750). Köln: **Flughafen Köln/Bonn** (☎ 02203/40400). Munich: **Flughafen München** (☎ 089/97500).

DUTY-FREE SHOPPING

You can purchase duty-free goods when traveling between any EU country, such as Germany, and a non-EU country. Duty-free (also called tax-free) shops at German airports are operated by the firm of Gebrüder Heinemann, which boasts that its prices (even for scotch whiskey) are "15 to 20% cheaper" than in the London duty-free shops. The big sellers, as at most duty-free shops, are perfumes and cosmetics, liquor, and tobacco products.

BOAT & FERRY TRAVEL

Eurailpasses and German Rail Passes (☞ Train Travel, *below*) are valid on all services of the KD Rhine Line and on the Mosel between Trier and Koblenz (if you use the fast hydrofoil, a supplementary fee is required). Regular rail tickets are also accepted, meaning you can **go one way by ship and return by train.** All you have to do is pay a small surcharge to KD Rhine Line and get the ticket endorsed at one of the landing-stage offices. But note that you have to buy the rail ticket first and *then* get it changed. Cruises generally operate between April and October (Cruise Travel, *below,* for specifics on the KD Rhine Line).

BUS TRAVEL

Germany has good local bus service but no proper nationwide network. A large portion of services is operated by Deutsche Touring, a subsidiary of the railroad that has offices and agents country-wide. Rail tickets are valid on its lines. Regional lines coordinate with the railroad to reach remote places.

One of the best services is the Romantic Road bus between Würzburg (with connections to and from Frankfurt and Wiesbaden) and Füssen (with connections to and from Munich, Augsburg, and Garmisch-Partenkirchen). Buses, with an attendant on board, offer one- or two-day tours in each direction in summer, leaving in the morning and arriving in the evening. Eurailpasses and German Rail Passes (☞ Train Travel, *below*) are good on this and other Deutsche Touring scenic routes.

All towns of any size have local buses, which often link up with trams (streetcars) and electric railway (S-bahn) and subway (U-bahn) services. Fares vary according to distance, but a ticket usually allows you to transfer freely between the various forms of transportation. Most cities issue 24-hour tickets at special rates.

There is direct service from London's Victoria Coach Station to some 50 German cities. Many departures are daily, some three times a week. All go via the Channel Tunnel through France, Belgium and Holland to, among other cities, Köln (14½ hours), Frankfurt (15 hours), Stuttgart/ Nürnberg (17 hours), and Munich (20 hours).

➤ INTERCITY BUSES: **Deutsche Touring** (Am Römerhof 17, D–60486 Frankfurt/Main, ☎ 069/79030).

➤ FROM THE U.K.: **Eurolines** (☎ 0990/143–219).

BUSINESS HOURS

Catholicism gives Bavaria more religious holidays than the other states of Germany. Otherwise, business hours are consistent throughout the country. Many towns' visitor information offices close by 4 during the week and might not be open on weekends.

BANKS & OFFICES

Banks are generally open weekdays from 8:30 or 9 to 3 or 4 (5 or 6 on Thursday), sometimes with a lunch break of about an hour at smaller branches. Banks at airports and main train stations open as early as 6:30 AM and close as late as 10:30 PM.

GAS STATIONS

Along the autobahn and major highways, gas stations and their small convenience shops are often open late, if not around the clock.

MUSEUMS & SIGHTS

Most museums are open from Tuesday to Sunday 10–5. Some close for an hour or more at lunch. Many stay open until 8 or 9 on Wednesday or Thursday.

SHOPS

Department stores and larger stores are generally open from 9 or 9:15 to 8 weekdays and until 4 on Saturday. Smaller shops and some department stores in smaller towns close at 6 or 6:30 on weekdays and as early as 1 on Saturday. Visit a department store in the morning or early afternoon to avoid crowds.

CAMERAS & PHOTOGRAPHY

➤ PHOTO HELP: **Kodak Information Center** (☎ 800/242–2424). *Kodak Guide to Shooting Great Travel Pictures,* available in bookstores or from Fodor's Travel Publications (☎ 800/533–6478; $16.50 plus $5.50 shipping).

EQUIPMENT PRECAUTIONS

Always **keep your film and tape out of the sun.** Carry an extra supply of batteries, and **be prepared to turn on your camera or camcorder** to prove to security personnel that the device is real. Always **ask for hand inspection of film,** which becomes clouded after repeated exposure to airport X-ray machines, and **keep videotapes away from metal detectors.** Airport personnel in Germany will not hand-inspect film, and say that their X-ray machines are not as potentially damaging as those used in the United States.

VIDEOS

The German standard for video is PAL, which is not compatible with the U.S. VHS standard.

CAR RENTAL

Rates with the major car-rental companies begin at about $45 per day and $220 per week for an economy car with a manual transmission and unlimited mileage. This does not include tax on car rentals, which is 16%. Volkswagen, Opel, and Mercedes are some standard brands of rentals; most rentals are manual, so if you want an automatic, be sure to **request one in advance.** If you're traveling with children, don't forget to **arrange for a car seat** when you reserve.

➤ MAJOR AGENCIES: **Alamo** (☎ 800/522–9696; 020/8759–6200 in the U.K.). **Avis** (☎ 800/331–1084; 800/331–1084 in Canada; 02/9353–9000 in Australia; 09/525–1982 in New Zealand; 0610 in Germany). **Budget** (☎ 800/527–0700; 0870/607–5000 in the U.K., through affiliate Europcar). **Dollar** (☎ 800/800–6000; 0124/622–0111 in the U.K., through affiliate Sixt Kenning; 02/9223–1444 in Australia). **Hertz** (☎ 800/654–3001; 800/263–0600 in Canada; 020/8897–2072 in the U.K.; 02/9669–2444 in Australia; 09/256–8690 in New Zealand; 01805/8000 in Germany). **National Car Rental** (☎ 800/227–7638; 020/8680–4800 in the U.K., where it is known as National Europe).

CUTTING COSTS

To get the best deal, **book through a travel agent who will shop around.**

Do **look into wholesalers,** companies that do not own fleets but rent in bulk from those that do and often offer better rates than traditional car-rental operations. Payment must be made before you leave home.

➤ LOCAL AGENCIES: **Sixt** (☎ 01805/252–525).

➤ WHOLESALERS: **Auto Europe** (☎ 207/842–2000 or 800/223–5555, FAX 800–235–6321, www.autoeurope.com). **DER Travel Services** (✉ 9501 W. Devon Ave., Rosemont, IL 60018, ☎ 800/782–2424, FAX 800/282–7474 for information, 800/860–9944 for brochures, www.dertravel.com). **Kemwel Holiday Autos** (☎ 800/678–0678, FAX 914/825–3160, www.kemwel.com).

INSURANCE

When driving a rented car, you are generally responsible for any damage to or loss of the vehicle. Before you rent, see what coverage your personal auto-insurance policy and credit cards already provide.

Collision policies that car-rental companies sell for European rentals usually do not include stolen-vehicle coverage. Before you buy it, check your existing policies—you may already be covered.

REQUIREMENTS & RESTRICTIONS

In Germany your own driver's license is acceptable, but an International Driver's Permit is a good idea; it's available from the American or Canadian automobile association and, in the United Kingdom, from the Automobile Association or Royal Automobile Club. These international permits are universally recognized, and having one in your wallet may save you a problem with the local authorities. In Germany you must be 21 to rent a car, and rates may be higher if you're under 25.

SURCHARGES

Before you pick up a car in one city and leave it in another, **ask about drop-off charges or one-way service fees,** which can be substantial. Note, too, that some rental agencies charge extra if you return the car before the time specified in your contract. To avoid a hefty refueling fee, **fill the tank just before you turn in the car,** but be aware that gas stations near the rental outlet may overcharge.

CAR TRAVEL

Entry formalities for motorists are few: All you need is proof of insurance, an international car-registration document, and a U.S. or Canadian driver's license (an international license is helpful but not a must). If you or your car are from an EU country, Norway, or Switzerland, all you need is your domestic license and proof of insurance. *All* foreign cars must have a country sticker.

AUTO CLUBS

There are three principal automobile clubs in Germany: **ADAC** (Allgemeiner Deutscher Automobil-Club, Am Westpark 8, D–81373 Munich), FAX 089/7676–2801. **AvD** (Automobilclub von Deutschland, Lyonerstr. 16, D–60528 Frankfurt, ☎ 069/66060), and **ACE** (Schmidener Str. 233, D–70374 Stuttgart, ☎ 0711/53030).

EMERGENCY SERVICES

ADAC and AvD (☞ Auto Clubs, *above*) operate tow trucks on all autobahns; they also have emergency telephones every 2 km (1 mi). On minor roads **go to the nearest call box and dial 01802/222–222** (if you have a mobile phone, just dial 222–222) Ask, in English, for road-service assistance. Help is free (with the exception of materials) if the work is carried out by the ADAC. If the ADAC has to use a subcontractor for the work, charges are made for time, mileage, and materials.

FROM THE U.K.

Motorists have a choice of either the Channel Tunnel or the ferry services when traveling to the Continent. Reservations are essential at peak times and always a good idea, especially when going via the Chunnel. Cars don't actually drive in the Chunnel, but instead are loaded onto trains. Cars without reservations, if they can get on at all, are charged 20% extra. It's recommended that drivers **get a green card** from their insurance companies, which extends insurance coverage to driving in Continental Europe. Extra breakdown insurance and vehicle and personal security coverage are also advisable.

GASOLINE

Gasoline (petrol) costs are between DM 1.50 and DM 2 per liter—and more expensive than in the United States. Most German cars run on lead-free fuel. Some models use diesel fuel, so if you are renting a car, **find out which fuel the car takes.** Some older vehicles cannot take unleaded fuel. German filling stations are highly competitive, and bargains are often available if you shop around, but *not* at autobahn filling stations. Self-service, or *SB-Tanken,* stations are cheapest. Pumps marked *Bleifrei* contain unleaded gas.

PARKING

In German garages you must **pay immediately on returning to retrieve your car,** not when driving out. Put the ticket you got on arrival into the machine and pay the amount displayed. Retrieve the ticket, go to your car, and upon exiting, insert the ticket in a slot to get the barrier raised.

ROAD CONDITIONS

Roads in both the western and eastern part of the country are generally excellent. *Bundesstrasse* are two-lane highways, abbreviated "B," as in B–38. Autobahns are high-speed thruways abbreviated with "A," as in A–7.

ROAD MAPS

The best-known road maps of Germany are put out by the automobile club ADAC and by Shell. They're available at gas stations and bookstores.

RULES OF THE ROAD

In Germany you **drive on the right,** and road signs give distances in kilometers. There is no speed limit on autobahns, although drivers are advised to keep below 130 kph (80 mph). Speed limits on country roads vary from 80 to 100 kph (50 to 60 mph). Alcohol limits on drivers are equivalent to two small beers or a quarter of a liter of wine (blood-alcohol level .05%). Note that **seat belts must be worn at all times by front- *and* backseat passengers.** Passing is permitted on the left side only. Headlights, not parking lights, are required during inclement weather.

SCENIC ROUTES

Germany has many specially designated tourist roads. The longest is the *Deutsche Ferienstrasse,* the German Holiday Road, which runs from the Baltic to the Alps, a distance of around 1,720 km (1,070 mi). The most famous, however, and also the oldest, is the *Romantische Strasse,* the Romantic Road (☞ Chapter 5), which runs from Würzburg to Füssen in the Alps, covering around 355 km (220 mi).

Among other notable touring routes are the *Grüne Küstenstrasse* (Green Coast Road), running along the North Sea coast from Denmark to Emden; the *Burgenstrasse* (Castle Road), running from Mannheim to Nürnberg; the *Deutsche Weinstrasse* (German Wine Road), running through the Palatinate wine country; and the *Deutsche Alpenstrasse* (German Alpine Road), running the length of the country's Alpine southern border to Bodensee. Less well-known routes are the *Märchenstrasse* (Fairytale Road ☞ Chapter 12), and the *Schwarzwälder Hochstrasse* (Black Forest High Road).

CHILDREN IN GERMANY

Almost every city in Germany has its own children's theater, and the country's puppet theaters rank among the best in the world. Many movie theaters also show films for children, normally in the morning and afternoon. Playgrounds are around virtually every corner, and there are about a half-dozen major theme parks around the country. Many tourist offices (Munich's, for example) have booklets of information for younger visitors. If you are renting a car, don't forget to **arrange for a car seat** when you reserve.

BABY-SITTING

For recommended local sitters, **check with your hotel desk.** Updated lists of well-screened baby-sitters are also available from most local tourist offices. Rates are usually between DM 20 and DM 30 per hour. Many large department stores in Germany provide baby-sitting facilities or areas where children can play while their parents shop.

FLYING

If your children are two or older, **ask about children's airfares.** As a general rule, infants under two not occupying a seat fly at greatly reduced fares or even for free. When booking, **confirm carry-on allowances** if you're traveling with infants. In general, for babies charged 10% of the adult fare you are allowed one carry-on bag and a collapsible stroller; if the flight is full, the stroller may have to be checked, or you may be limited to fewer carry-ons.

Experts agree it's a good idea to use safety seats aloft for children weighing less than 40 pounds. Airlines set their own policies: U.S. carriers usually require the child be ticketed, even if he or she is young enough to ride free, since the seats must be strapped into regular seats. Do **check your airline's policy about using safety seats during takeoff and landing.** And since safety seats are not allowed just everywhere in the plane, get your seat assignments early.

When reserving, **request children's meals or a freestanding bassinet** if you need them. But note that bulkhead seats, where you must sit to use the bassinet, may lack an overhead bin or storage space on the floor.

LODGING

Most hotels in Germany allow children under a certain age to stay in their parents' room at no extra charge, but others charge for them as extra adults; be sure to **find out the cutoff age for children's discounts.**

SIGHTS & ATTRACTIONS

Places that are especially appealing to children are indicated by a rubber duckie icon in this book's margin.

COMPUTERS ON THE ROAD

Larger German hotels now have Internet centers from which, for a fee, you can call up a Web site or send an e-mail message. There are also cybercafés in the cities, at which you can go on-line, either with their equipment or your own laptop. Buy an adapter for your laptop's phone jack. If you're plugging into a phone line, you'll need a local access number for a connection (AOL and CompuServe have numbers in Germany).

CONSUMER PROTECTION

Whenever shopping or buying travel services in Germany, **pay with a major credit card** so you can cancel payment or get reimbursed if there's a problem. If you're doing business with a particular company for the first time, **contact your local Better Business Bureau and the attorney general's offices** in your own state and the company's home state, as well. Have any complaints been filed? Finally, if you're buying a package or a tour, always **consider travel insurance** that includes default coverage (☞ Insurance, *below*).

➤ BBBs: Council of Better Business Bureaus (✉ 4200 Wilson Blvd., Suite 800, Arlington, VA 22203, ☎ 703/

276–0100, FAX 703/525–8277 www. bbb.org).

CRUISE TRAVEL

KD Rhine Line (Köln-Düsseldorfer Rheinschiffahrt) offers a program of luxury cruises along the Rhine, Main, Mosel, Neckar, Saar, Elbe, and Danube rivers. The cruises include four-day trips from Frankfurt to Trier (from DM 760), five-day journeys from Amsterdam to Basel, in Switzerland (from DM 1,460), and eight-day holidays from Regensburg to Budapest, in Hungary (from DM 2,070). Prices include all meals. The cruises are supplemented by trips of one day or less on the Rhine and Mosel. Between Easter and October there's Rhine service between Bonn and Koblenz and between Koblenz and Bingen; both trips take around five hours. The cruises, especially for the newer Elbe routes, are in great demand, so **reserve several months in advance.**

➤ CRUISE LINES: **Köln-Düsseldorfer Rheinschiffahrt** (KD Rhine Line; ⊠ Frankenwerft 1, D–50667 Köln, ☎ 0221/208–8288 for cruises, 0221/208–8813 for day trips, www.k-d.com); in the United States, **JFO CruiseService Corp.** (⊠ 2500 Westchester Ave., Purchase, NY 10577, ☎ 800/346–6525 www.rivercruises.com).

CUSTOMS & DUTIES

When shopping, **keep receipts** for all purchases. Upon reentering the country, **be ready to show customs officials what you've bought.** If you feel a duty is incorrect or object to the way your clearance was handled, note the inspector's badge number and ask to see a supervisor. If the problem isn't resolved, write to the appropriate authorities, beginning with the port director at your point of entry.

IN AUSTRALIA

Australian residents who are 18 or older may bring home $A400 worth of souvenirs and gifts (including jewelry), 250 cigarettes or 250 grams of tobacco, and 1,125 milliliters of alcohol (including wine, beer, and spirits). Residents under 18 may bring back $A200 worth of goods. Prohibited items include meat products.

Seeds, plants, and fruits need to be declared upon arrival.

➤ INFORMATION: **Australian Customs Service** (Regional Director, ⊠ Box 8, Sydney, NSW 2001, ☎ 02/9213–2000, FAX 02/9213–4000).

IN CANADA

Canadian residents who have been out of Canada for at least seven days may bring home C$500 worth of goods duty-free. If you've been away less than seven days but more than 48 hours, the duty-free allowance drops to C$200; if your trip lasts 24–48 hours, the allowance is C$50. You may not pool allowances with family members. Goods claimed under the C$500 exemption may follow you by mail; those claimed under the lesser exemptions must accompany you. Alcohol and tobacco products may be included in the seven-day and 48-hour exemptions but not in the 24-hour exemption. If you meet the age requirements of the province or territory through which you reenter Canada, you may bring in duty-free 1.14 liters (40 imperial ounces) of wine or liquor or 24 12-ounce cans or bottles of beer or ale. If you are 16 or older, you may bring in duty-free 200 cigarettes and 50 cigars. Check ahead of time with Revenue Canada or the Department of Agriculture for policies regarding meat products, seeds, plants, and fruits.

You may send an unlimited number of gifts worth up to C$60 each duty-free to Canada. Label the package UNSOLICITED GIFT—VALUE UNDER $60. Alcohol and tobacco are excluded.

➤ INFORMATION: **Revenue Canada** (⊠ 2265 St. Laurent Blvd. S, Ottawa, Ontario K1G 4K3, ☎ 613/993–0534; 800/461–9999 in Canada, FAX 613/957–8911, www.ccra-adrc.gc.ca).

IN GERMANY

Since a single, unrestricted market took effect within the European Union (EU) early in 1993, there have no longer been restrictions for persons traveling among the 15 EU countries. However, there are restrictions on what can be brought in without declaration. For example, if you have more than 800 cigarettes, 90 liters of wine, or 10 liters of alcohol, it is considered a commercial shipment and is taxed and otherwise treated as such.

For anyone entering Germany from outside the EU, the following limitations apply: (1) 200 cigarettes or 100 cigarillos or 50 cigars or 250 grams of tobacco; (2) 2 liters of still table wine; (3) 1 liter of spirits over 22% volume or 2 liters of spirits under 22% volume (fortified and sparkling wines) or 2 more liters of table wine; (4) 50 grams of perfume and 250 milliliters of toilet water; (5) other goods to the value of DM 350.

Tobacco and alcohol allowances are for visitors age 17 and over. Other items intended for personal use can be imported and exported freely. There are no restrictions on the import and export of German currency.

IN NEW ZEALAND

Homeward-bound residents 17 or older may bring back $700 worth of souvenirs and gifts. Your duty-free allowance also includes 4.5 liters of wine or beer; one 1,125-milliliter bottle of spirits; and either 200 cigarettes, 250 grams of tobacco, 50 cigars, or a combination of the three up to 250 grams. Prohibited items include meat products, seeds, plants, and fruits.

➤ INFORMATION: **New Zealand Customs** (Custom House, ✉ 50 Anzac Ave., Box 29, Auckland, New Zealand, ☎ 09/359–6655, FAX 09/359–6732).

IN THE U.K.

If you are a U.K. resident and your journey was wholly within the European Union (EU), you won't have to pass through customs when you return to the United Kingdom. If you plan to bring back large quantities of alcohol or tobacco, check EU limits beforehand.

➤ INFORMATION: **HM Customs and Excise** (✉ Dorset House, Stamford St., Bromley, Kent BR1 1XX, ☎ 020/7202–4227).

IN THE U.S.

U.S. residents who have been out of the country for at least 48 hours (and who have not used the $400 allowance or any part of it in the past 30 days) may bring home $400 worth of foreign goods duty-free.

U.S. residents 21 and older may bring back 1 liter of alcohol duty-free. In addition, regardless of your age, you are allowed 200 cigarettes and 100 non-Cuban cigars. Antiques, which the U.S. Customs Service defines as objects more than 100 years old, enter duty-free, as do original works of art done entirely by hand, including paintings, drawings, and sculptures.

You may also send packages home duty-free: up to $200 worth of goods for personal use, with a limit of one parcel per addressee per day (except alcohol or tobacco products or perfume worth more than $5); label the package PERSONAL USE and attach a list of its contents and their retail value. Do not label the package UNSOLICITED GIFT or your duty-free exemption will drop to $100. Mailed items do not affect your duty-free allowance on your return.

➤ INFORMATION: **U.S. Customs Service** (✉ 1300 Pennsylvania Ave. NW, Washington, DC 20229, www.customs.gov; inquiries ☎ 202/354–1000; complaints c/o ✉ Office of Regulations and Rulings; registration of equipment c/o ✉ Resource Management, ☎ 202/927–0540).

DINING

Almost every street of Germany has its *Gaststätte,* a sort of combination diner and pub, and every village its *Gasthof,* or inn. The emphasis in the Gaststätte and Gasthof is on *gutbürgerliche Küche,* or good home cooking—simple food at reasonable prices. People meet here in the evening for a chat, a beer, and a game of cards. Lunch rather than dinner is the main meal in Germany. The *Tageskarte,* or suggested menu, is usually less than DM 20 for soup, a main course, and a simple dessert (though this is not always offered). It's perfectly acceptable to order just a pot of coffee outside busy lunch periods. More expensive restaurants may offer a *table d'hôte* (suggested or special) daily menu, which is considerably cheaper than paying à la carte.

Regional specialties are given in the Pleasures and Pastimes sections of individual chapters. The restaurants we list are the cream of the crop in each price category. Properties indicated by an ✕⊡ are lodging establishments that also have a decent restaurant. A *Bierstube* (pub) or *Weinstube* (wine cellar) may also serve light snacks or meals.

BUDGET EATING TIPS

➤ BUTCHER SHOPS: Known as *Metzgerei*, these often serve warm snacks. The Vinzenz-Murr chain in Munich and Bavaria has particularly good-value food. Try *Warmer Leberkäs mit Kartoffelsalat*, a typical Bavarian specialty, which is a sort of baked meat loaf with sweet mustard and potato salad. In northern Germany try *Bouletten,* small hamburgers, or *Currywurst,* sausages in a piquant curry sauce.

➤ DEPARTMENT STORES: Restaurants in department stores are especially recommended for wholesome, appetizing, and inexpensive lunches. Kaufhof, Karstadt, Horton, and Hertie are names to note.

➤ FOREIGN RESTAURANTS: To save money, **consider dining in restaurants serving non-German cuisine.** Germany has a vast selection of moderately priced Turkish, Italian, Greek, Chinese, and Balkan restaurants. All offer good value. Italian restaurants are about the most popular of all specialty restaurants in Germany.

➤ PICNICS: To turn lunch into a picnic, **buy some wine or beer and some cold cuts and rolls** (called *Brötchen* in the north and *Semmel* in the south) from a supermarket or delicatessen. It's acceptable to bring fixings to a beer garden and order a beer there.

➤ STAND-UP SNACK BARS: *Imbiss* (snack) stands can be found in almost every busy shopping street, in parking lots, train stations, and near markets. They serve *Würste* (sausages), grilled, roasted, or boiled, and rolls filled with cheese, cold meat, or fish. Prices range from DM 3 to DM 6 per portion.

MEALTIMES

Gaststätte normally serve hot meals from 11:30 AM to 9 PM; many places stop serving hot meals between 2 PM and 6 PM, although you can still order cold dishes.

RATINGS

The restaurants in our listings are divided by price (representing the average cost of a three-course meal) into four categories: $$$$, $$$, $$, and $. *See* Dining or Pleasures and Pastimes *in* individual chapters for specific prices. Nearly all restaurants display their menus, with prices, outside; all prices shown will include tax and service charge. Prices for wine also include tax and service charge.

RESERVATIONS & DRESS

Reservations are always a good idea: we mention them only when they're essential or are not accepted. Book as far ahead as you can and reconfirm as soon as you arrive. We mention dress only when men are required to wear a jacket or a jacket and tie. Note, though, that even when Germans dress casual, the look is generally crisp and neat.

WINE, BEER, & SPIRITS

Chapter 10, which follows the German Wine Road, and Chapter 11, which covers the Rhine and Mosel valleys, have the most information regarding wines and wine estates.

➤ WINE INFORMATION: **German Wine Information Bureau** (245 5th Ave., #2204, New York, NY 10016, ☎ 212/896–3336 www.Germanwineusa.org).

DISABILITIES & ACCESSIBILITY

Nearly 100 German cities and towns issue special guides for visitors with disabilities, which offer information, usually in German, about how to get around destinations and suggestions for places to visit.

➤ COMPLAINTS: **Disability Rights Section** (⊠ U.S. Department of Justice, Civil Rights Division, Box 66738, Washington, DC 20035-6738, ☎ 202/514–0301 or 800/514–0301; TTY 202/514–0301 or 800/514–0301, ℻ 202/307–1198) for general complaints. **Aviation Consumer Protection Division** (☞ Air Travel, *above*) for airline-related problems. **Civil Rights Office** (⊠ U.S. Department of Transportation, Departmental Office of Civil Rights, S-30, 400

7th St. SW, Room 10215, Washington, DC 20590, ☎ 202/366–4648, FAX 202/366–9371) for problems with surface transportation.

LODGING

All the major hotel chains (Hilton, Sheraton, Marriott, Holiday Inn, Steigenberger, and Kempinski) have special facilities for guests with disabilities. Some leading privately owned hotels also cater to travelers with disabilities; local tourist offices can provide lists of these hotels and additional information.

RESERVATIONS

When discussing accessibility with an operator or reservations agent, **ask hard questions.** Are there any stairs, inside *or* out? Are there grab bars next to the toilet *and* in the shower/ tub? How wide is the doorway to the room? To the bathroom? For the most extensive facilities meeting the latest legal specifications, **opt for newer accommodations.**

TRAIN TRAVEL

The Deutsche Bahn (☞ Train Travel, *below*) provides a complete range of services and facilities for travelers with disabilities. All InterCity Express (ICE) and InterRegio trains and most EuroCity and InterCity trains have special areas for wheelchair users. Reservations for wheelchair users are free of charge. The German Red Cross and a welfare service called the Bahnhofs-Mission (Railway Station Mission) have support facilities at all major and many smaller regional stations. They organize assistance in boarding, leaving, and changing trains and also help with reservations.

Deutsche Bahn, with an English section, issues a booklet detailing its services for travelers with disabilities. For access to train platforms that are not wheelchair accessible, **call Deutsche Bahn's 24-hour hot line three working days before your trip.** For assistance from individual railroad stations **call the local number** ☎ 19419 (without the town or city prefix).

TRAVEL AGENCIES

In the United States the Americans with Disabilities Act requires that travel firms serve the needs of all travelers. Some agencies specialize in working with people with disabilities.

➤ TRAVELERS WITH MOBILITY PROBLEMS: **Access Adventures** (✉ 206 Chestnut Ridge Rd., Rochester, NY 14624, ☎ 716/889–9096, dltravel@ prodigy.net), run by a former physical-rehabilitation counselor. **CareVacations** (✉ 5–5110 50th Ave., Leduc, Alberta T9E 6V4, ☎ 780/986–6404 or 877/478–7827, FAX 780/986–8332, www.carevacations.com), for group tours and cruise vacations. **Flying Wheels Travel** (✉ 143 W. Bridge St., Box 382, Owatonna, MN 55060, ☎ 507/451–5005 or 800/535–6790, FAX 507/451–1685, thq@ll.net, www. flyingwheels.com). **Hinsdale Travel Service** (✉ 201 E. Ogden Ave., Suite 100, Hinsdale, IL 60521, ☎ 630/ 325–1335, FAX 630/325–1342, hinstrvl@interaccess.com).

➤ TRAVELERS WITH DEVELOPMENTAL DISABILITIES: **Sprout** (✉ 893 Amsterdam Ave., New York, NY 10025, ☎ 212/222–9575 or 888/222–9575, FAX 212/222–9768, sprout@interport.net, www.gosprout.org).

DISCOUNTS & DEALS

Be a smart shopper and **compare all your options** before making decisions. A plane ticket bought with a promotional coupon from travel clubs, coupon books, and direct-mail offers may not be cheaper than the least expensive fare from a discount ticket agency. And always keep in mind that what you get is just as important as what you save.

DISCOUNT RESERVATIONS

To save money, **look into discount reservations services** with toll-free numbers, which use their buying power to get a better price on hotels, airline tickets, even car rentals. When booking a room, always **call the hotel's local toll-free number** (if one is available) rather than the central reservations number—you'll often get a better price. Always ask about special packages or corporate rates.

When shopping for the best deal on hotels and car rentals, **look for guaranteed exchange rates,** which protect you against a falling dollar. With your rate locked in, you won't pay more, even if the price goes up in the local currency.

➤ AIRLINE TICKETS: ☎ 800/FLY–4–LESS. ☎ 800/FLY–ASAP.

➤ HOTEL ROOMS: **International Marketing & Travel Concepts** (☎ 800/790–4682, imtc@mindspring. com). **Steigenberger Reservation Service** (☎ 800/223–5652, www. srs-worldhotels.com). **Travel Interlink** (☎ 800/888–5898, www. travelinterlink.com).

PACKAGE DEALS

Don't confuse packages and guided tours. When you buy a package, you travel on your own, just as though you had planned the trip yourself. Fly/drive packages, which combine airfare and car rental, are often a good deal. If you **buy a rail/drive pass,** you may save on train tickets and car rentals. All Eurail- and Europass holders get a discount on Eurostar fares through the Channel Tunnel. A German Rail Pass is also good for travel aboard some KD River Steamers and some Deutsche Touring/Europabus routes.

ELECTRICITY

To use your U.S.-purchased electric-powered equipment, **bring a converter and adapter.** The electrical current in Germany is 220 volts, 50 cycles alternating current (AC); wall outlets take Continental-type plugs, with two round prongs.

If your appliances are dual-voltage, you'll need only an adapter. Don't use 110-volt outlets, marked FOR SHAVERS ONLY, for high-wattage appliances such as blow-dryers. Most laptops operate equally well on 110 and 220 volts and so require only an adapter.

EMBASSIES

➤ AUSTRALIA: ✉ Friedrichstr. 200, Berlin, ☎ 030/880–0880.

➤ CANADA: ✉ International Trade Center, Friedrichstr. 95, Berlin, ☎ 030/261–1161.

➤ NEW ZEALAND: ✉ Friedrichstr. 60, Berlin, ☎ 030/206–210.

➤ UNITED KINGDOM: ✉ Unter den Linden 32–34, Berlin, ☎ 030/201–840.

➤ UNITED STATES: ✉ Neustädtische Kirchstr. 4–5, Berlin, ☎ 030/238–5174.

EMERGENCIES

Throughout Germany call ☎ 110 for police, and ☎ 112 for an ambulance or the fire department.

ETIQUETTE & BEHAVIOR

Germans are more formal in addressing each other than Americans. Always address acquaintances as Herr (Mr.) or Frau (Mrs.) plus their last name; do not call them by their first name unless invited to do so. The German language has an informal and formal pronoun for "you": Formal is "*Sie*," informal is "*du*." Even if adults are on a first-name basis with one another, they may still keep the *Sie* form between them. A handshake is expected upon meeting someone for the first time and is often customary when simply greeting acquaintances. Germans are less formal when it comes to nudity: a sign that reads FREIKÖRPER or FKK indicates a park or beach allows nude sunbathing.

GAY & LESBIAN TRAVEL

➤ GAY- & LESBIAN-FRIENDLY TRAVEL AGENCIES: **Different Roads Travel** (✉ 8383 Wilshire Blvd., Suite 902, Beverly Hills, CA 90211, ☎ 323/651–5557 or 800/429–8747, FAX 323/651–3678, leigh@west.tzell.com). **Kennedy Travel** (✉ 314 Jericho Turnpike, Floral Park, NY 11001, ☎ 516/352–4888 or 800/237–7433, FAX 516/354–8849, main@kennedytravel.com, www.kennedytravel.com). **Now Voyager** (✉ 4406 18th St., San Francisco, CA 94114, ☎ 415/626–1169 or 800/255–6951, FAX 415/626–8626, www. nowvoyager.com). **Skylink Travel and Tour** (✉ 1006 Mendocino Ave., Santa Rosa, CA 95401, ☎ 707/546–9888 or 800/225–5759, FAX 707/546–9891, skylinktvl@aol.com, www. skylinktravel.com), serving lesbian travelers.

HOLIDAYS

The following national holidays are observed in Germany: January 1; January 6 (Epiphany—Bavaria, Saxony-Anhalt, and Baden-Württemberg only); April 13 (Good Friday); April 16 (Easter Monday); May 1

(Workers' Day); May 24 (Ascension); June 4 (Pentecost Monday); June 14 (Corpus Christi, southern Germany only); August 15 (Assumption Day—Bavaria and Saarland only); October 3 (German Unity Day); November 1 (All Saints' Day); December 24–26 (Christmas).

INSURANCE

The most useful travel insurance plan is a comprehensive policy that includes coverage for trip cancellation and interruption, default, trip delay, and medical expenses (with a waiver for preexisting conditions).

Without insurance you will lose all or most of your money if you cancel your trip, regardless of the reason. Default insurance covers you if your tour operator, airline, or cruise line goes out of business. Trip-delay covers expenses that arise because of bad weather or mechanical delays. Study the fine print when comparing policies.

If you're traveling internationally, a key component of travel insurance is coverage for medical bills incurred if you get sick on the road. Such expenses are not generally covered by Medicare or private policies. U.K. residents can buy a travel insurance policy valid for most vacations taken during the year in which it's purchased (but check preexisting-condition coverage). British and Australian citizens need extra medical coverage when traveling overseas.

Always **buy travel policies directly from the insurance company**; if you buy them from a cruise line, airline, or tour operator that goes out of business, you probably will not be covered for the agency's or operator's default, a major risk. Before making any purchase, **review your existing health and home-owner's policies** to find what they cover away from home.

➤ TRAVEL INSURERS: In the U.S.: **Access America** (✉ 6600 W. Broad St., Richmond, VA 23230, ☎ 804/285–3300 or 800/284–8300, 🖷 804/673–1583, www.previewtravel.com), **Travel Guard International** (✉ 1145 Clark St., Stevens Point, WI 54481, ☎ 715/345–0505 or 800/826–1300, 🖷 800/955–8785, www.noelgroup.

com). In Canada: **Voyager Insurance** (✉ 44 Peel Center Dr., Brampton, Ontario L6T 4M8, ☎ 905/791–8700; 800/668–4342 in Canada).

➤ INSURANCE INFORMATION: In the U.K.: **Association of British Insurers** (✉ 51–55 Gresham St., London EC2V 7HQ, ☎ 020/7600–3333, 🖷 020/7696–8999, info@abi.org.uk, www.abi.org.uk). In Australia: **Insurance Council of Australia** (☎ 03/9614–1077, 🖷 03/9614–7924).

LANGUAGE

The Germans are great linguists, and you'll find that English is spoken in most hotels, restaurants, airports, stations, museums, and other places of interest. However, English is not widely spoken in rural areas; this is especially true of the eastern part of Germany.

Unless you speak fluent German, you may find some of the regional dialects hard to follow, particularly in Bavaria. However most Germans can speak High (standard) German.

LANGUAGES FOR TRAVELERS

A phrase book and language-tape set can help get you started. Two word endings that appear frequently on vacation itineraries are -*burg*, and -*berg*. A Burg (*u* as in "burr") is a fortress; a Berg (*e* as in *ea* of "bear") is a mountain.

➤ PHRASE BOOKS & LANGUAGE-TAPE SETS: *Fodor's German for Travelers* (☎ 800/733–3000 in the U.S.; 800/668–4247 in Canada; $7 for phrasebook, $16.95 for audio set).

LODGING

The standards of German hotels are very high, down to the humblest inn. You can nearly always **expect courteous and polite service and clean and comfortable rooms.** In addition to hotels proper, the country has numerous *Gasthöfe* or *Gasthäuser*, which are country inns that serve food and also have rooms; pensions, or *Fremdenheime* (guest houses). Most hotels have restaurants, but those listed as *Garni* provide breakfast only. At the lowest end of the scale are *Fremdenzimmer,* meaning simply "rooms," normally in private houses. (Look for the sign reading ZIMMER FREI or ZU

VERMIETEN on a green background, meaning "to rent"; a red sign reading BESETZT means there are no vacancies.)

The hotels in our listings are divided by price into four categories: $$$$, $$$, $$, and $. *See* Lodging and Pleasures and Pastimes sections in individual chapters for specific prices. We always list the facilities that are available—but we don't specify whether they cost extra. **Ask about breakfast and bathing facilities** when booking. All hotels listed have a private bath unless otherwise noted. Breakfast is usually, but not always, included. Inexpensive rooms may not have a shower or tub. Larger hotels often have no-smoking rooms or even no-smoking floors, so it's always worth asking for one when you reserve. Note that double rooms often have two single beds next to one another; if a larger, single bed is important, ask. When you arrive, if you don't like the room you're offered, ask to see another.

Rates vary enormously, though not disproportionately, in comparison with other northern European countries. Room rates are by no means inflexible and depend very much on supply and demand. You can save money by inquiring about reductions: many resort hotels offer substantial ones in winter, except in the Alps, where rates often rise then. Likewise, many $$$$ and $$$ hotels in cities cut their prices on weekends and when business is quiet. If you have booked and plan to arrive late, let the hotel know. And if you have to cancel a reservation, inform the hotel as soon as possible, otherwise you may be charged the full amount for the unused room.

Tourist offices will also make bookings for a nominal fee, but they may have difficulty doing so after 4 PM in high season and on weekends, so **don't wait until too late in the day to begin looking for your accommodations.** If you do get stuck, ask someone—like a mail carrier, police officer, or waiter, for example—for directions to a house renting a Fremdenzimmer or a Gasthof.

A list of more than 7,000 lodgings is available from the Deutsche Hotel-und Gaststättenverband (DEHOGA). Regional and local tourist offices also have lists. Although there is no nationwide grading system for hotels in Germany, the DEHOGA's guide has one- to five-star ratings based on amenities offered.

➤ LODGING LISTINGS: **Deutsche Hotel-und Gaststättenverband** (DEHOGA; ✉ (An Weidendamm 1, D–10117 Berlin www.dehoga.de).

APARTMENT & VILLA RENTALS

If you want a home base that's roomy enough for a family and comes with cooking facilities, **consider a furnished rental.** These can save you money, especially if you're traveling with a group. Home-exchange directories sometimes list rentals as well as exchanges.

➤ INTERNATIONAL AGENTS: **Drawbridge to Europe** (✉ 5456 Adams Rd., Talent, OR 97540, ☎ 541/512–8927 or 888/268–1148, FAX 541/512–0978, requests@drawbridgetoeurope.com, www.drawbridgetoeurope.com). **Interhome** (✉ 1990 N.E. 163rd St., Suite 110, N. Miami Beach, FL 33162, ☎ 305/940–2299 or 800/882–6864, FAX 305/940–2911, interhomeu@aol.com, www.interhome.com). **Villas International** (✉ 950 Northgate Dr., Suite 206, San Rafael, CA 94903, ☎ 415/499–9490 or 800/221–2260, FAX 415/499–9491, villas@best.com, www.villasintl.com).

➤ CAMPING: Campsites are scattered across the length and breadth of Germany. The DCC, or German Camping Club (☞ Campsites, *below*), produces an annual listing of some 8,000 sites Europe-wide, of which some 5,500 are in Germany. It also lists a number of sites where you can rent trailers and mobile homes. Similarly, the German Automobile Association (ADAC; ☞ Car Travel, *above*) publishes a listing of campsites.

The majority of sites are open year-round, and most are crowded during high season. Prices at ordinary campsites range from around DM 20 to DM 50 for a car, tent, or trailer and two adults, though prices at fancier ones, with pools, sport facilities, and entertainment, can be considerably more. If you want to camp elsewhere, you must **get permission from the landowner beforehand; ask the police if you can't track him or her down.** Drivers of mobile homes may park for one night only on roadsides and in autobahn parking-lot areas, but may not set up camping equipment there.

➤ CAMPSITES: DCC (German Camping Club; ✉ Mandlstr. 28, D–80802 Munich, ☎ 089/380–1420).

CASTLE-HOTELS

Germany's atmospheric castle-, or *Schloss*, hotels are all privately owned and run. The simpler ones may lack some amenities, but the majority combine four-star luxury with valuable antique furnishings, four-poster beds, stone passageways, and a baronial atmosphere. Some offer full resort facilities. Nearly all are in the countryside (☞ Chapters 8 and 11, in particular, have several castle hotel reviews). Euro-Connection can provide you with a European Castle Hotels brochure listing nearly 26 castle-hotels in Germany, and advise you on castle-hotel packages, including four- to six-night tours.

➤ CONTACTS: Euro-Connection (✉ 7500 212th St. SW, Suite 103, Edmonds, WA 98026, ☎ 800/645–3876). **European Castle Hotels & Restaurants** (✉ Weinpalais, Postfach 1111, Deidesheim/Weinstr., D–67412 Germany, ☎ 6326/700–030).

FARM VACATIONS

Almost every regional tourist office has a brochure listing farms that offer bed-and-breakfasts, apartments, and entire farmhouses to rent. Staying in such a rural setting is referred to as *Urlaub auf dem Bauernhof* (vacation down on the farm).

➤ GERMAN AGRICULTURAL ASSOCIATION: **DLG Reisedienst, Agratour** (German Agricultural Association; ✉ Eschborner Landstr. 122, D–60489 Frankfurt/Main, ☎ 069/247–880, ℻ 069/2478–8110) provides an illustrated brochure listing more than 1,500 inspected and graded farms, from the Alps to the North Sea. It costs DM 14.50 in bookstores and DM 20 postpaid.

HOME EXCHANGES

If you would like to exchange your home for someone else's, **join a home-exchange organization,** which will send you its updated listings of available exchanges for a year and will include your own listing in at least one of them. It's up to you to make specific arrangements.

➤ EXCHANGE CLUBS: **HomeLink International** (✉ Box 650, Key West, FL 33041, ☎ 305/294–7766 or 800/638–3841, ℻ 305/294–1448, usa@homelink.org, www.homelink.org; $98 per year). **Intervac U.S.** (✉ Box 590504, San Francisco, CA 94159, ☎ 800/756–4663, ℻ 415/435–7440, www.intervac.com; $89 per year includes two catalogs).

HOSTELS

No matter what your age, you can **save on lodging costs by staying at hostels**—rates run DM 20–DM 25 for people under 27 and DM 25–DM 38 for those older (breakfast included). Accommodations can range from single-sex, dorm-style beds to rooms for couples and families. Germany's more than 600 *Jugendherberge* (youth hostels) are among the most efficient and up-to-date in Europe, and many are in castles. There's an age limit of 27 in Bavaria; elsewhere, there are no age restrictions, though those under 20 take preference if space is limited. In Germany you must be a member of a national hosteling association or Hostelling International (HI) in order to stay at a hostel.

Membership in any HI national hostel association allows you to stay in HI-affiliated hostels at member rates (one-year membership is about $25 for adults). Members are eligible for discounts around the world, even on rail and bus travel in some countries. For DM 14.80, the DJH Service GmbH provides a complete list of German hostels and has information on regional offices around the country. Hostels must be reserved well in advance for midsummer, especially in eastern Germany. To book a hostel, you must call the particular lodging directly.

➤ IN GERMANY: **DJH Service GmbH** (Postfach 1462, D–32704 Detmold,

☎ 05231/74010, FAX 05231/74010, www.djh.de).

➤ ORGANIZATIONS: **Hostelling International—American Youth Hostels** (✉ 733 15th St. NW, Suite 840, Washington, DC 20005, ☎ 202/783–6161, FAX 202/783–6171, www.hiayh. org). **Hostelling International—Canada** (✉ 400–205 Catherine St., Ottawa, Ontario K2P 1C3, ☎ 613/237–7884, FAX 613/237–7868, www. hostellingintl.ca). **Youth Hostel Association of England and Wales** (✉ Trevelyan House, 8 St. Stephen's Hill, St. Albans, Hertfordshire AL1 2DY, ☎ 01727/855215 or 01727/845047, FAX 01727/844126, www.yha.uk). **Australian Youth Hostel Association** (✉ 10 Mallett St., Camperdown, NSW 2050, ☎ 02/9565–1699, FAX 02/9565–1325, www.yha.com.au). **Youth Hostels Association of New Zealand** (✉ Box 436, Christchurch, New Zealand, ☎ 03/379–9970, FAX 03/365–4476, www.yha.org.nz).

HOTELS

Many major American hotel chains—Hilton, Sheraton, Holiday Inn, Radisson, Marriott—have hotels in German cities. European chains are similarly well represented.

➤ RESERVATIONS: **Tourimus Service GmbH** (✉ Yorckstr. 23, D–79110 Freiburg im Breisgau, ☎ 0761/885–810, FAX 0761/885–8129).

➤ TOLL-FREE NUMBERS: **Best Western** (☎ 800/528–1234, www.bestwestern. com). **Choice** (☎ 800/221–2222, www.hotelchoice.com). **Clarion** (☎ 800/252–7466, www.choicehotels. com). **Comfort** (☎ 800/228–5150, www.comfortinn.com).**Forte** (☎ 800/225–5843). **Four Seasons** (☎ 800/332–3442, www.fourseasons.com). **Hilton** (☎ 800/445–8667, www. hiltons.com). **Holiday Inn** (☎ 800/465–4329, www.holiday-inn.com). **Hyatt Hotels & Resorts** (☎ 800/233–1234, www.hyatt.com). **Inter-Continental** (☎ 800/327–0200). **Kempinski Hotels & Resorts** (☎ 800/426–3135; 0800/86–8588 in the U.K.; 0130/3339 in Germany). **Marriott** (☎ 800/228–9290, www.marriott. com). **Le Meridien** (☎ 800/543–4300). **Nikko Hotels International** (☎ 800/645–5687, www.nikko.com).

Quality Inn (☎ 800/228–5151, www. qualityinn.com). **Radisson** (☎ 800/333–3333, www.radisson.com). **Ramada** (☎ 800/228–2828. www. ramada.com), **Renaissance Hotels & Resorts** (☎ 800/468–3571, www. hotels.com). **Ritz-Carlton** (☎ 800/241–3333, www.ritzcarlton.com). **Sheraton** (☎ 800/325–3535, www. sheraton.com).**Sleep Inn** (☎ 800/753–3746, www.sleepinn.com). **Westin Hotels & Resorts** (☎ 800/228–3000, www.starwood.com).

ROMANTIK HOTELS

Among the most delightful places to stay—and eat—in Germany are the aptly named Romantik Hotels and Restaurants. The Romantik group has establishments throughout Europe (and even a few in the United States), with 80 in Germany. All are in atmospheric and historic buildings—a precondition of membership—and are personally run by the owners, with the emphasis on excellent food and service. Prices vary considerably but in general represent good value, particularly the special weekend and short-holiday rates. A three- or four-day stay, for example, with one main meal, is available at about DM 300–DM 400 per person. A detailed brochure listing all Romantik Hotels and Restaurants is available by mail.

➤ CONTACTS: **Romantik Hotels and Restaurants** (✉ Hörsteiner Str. 34, D–63791 Karlstein am Main, ☎ 49/6188–95020 FAX 49/6188–6007). **Euro-Connection** (✉ 7500 212th St. SW, Suite 103, Edmonds, WA 98026, ☎ 800/645–3876).

SPAS

Taking the waters in Germany, whether for curing the body or merely beautifying it, has been popular since Roman times. There are more than 300 health resorts, mostly equipped for hot mineral, mud, or brine treatments and located in pleasant country areas or historic communities (the Black Forest has many). The word *Bad* before the name of a place usually means it's a spa—offering treatments, normally at fairly high prices. Most spas in eastern Germany are not yet up to the standards of western Germany.

There are four main groups of spas and health resorts: (1) the mineral and moorland spas, where treatments are based on natural warm-water springs; (2) those by the sea on the Baltic and North Sea coasts; (3) hydropathic spas, which use an invigorating cold-water process developed during the 19th century; and (4) climatic health resorts, usually in mountainous areas, which depend on their climates and fresh air for their health-giving properties.

Using saunas, steam baths, and other hot room facilities is done "without textiles" in Germany—in other words, naked. Wearing a bathing suit is frowned upon in a sauna and sometimes even prohibited. The average cost for three weeks of treatment is from DM 3,000 to DM 5,000. This includes board and lodging, doctors' fees, treatments, and tax.

➤ CONTACTS: **Deutsche Bäderverband, the German Health Resort and Spa Association** (✉ Postfach 190 147, D–53037 Bonn, ☎ 0228/201–200) provides a complete list of spas.

MAIL

Airmail letters to the United States and Canada cost DM 3; postcards, DM 2. All letters to the United Kingdom cost DM 1.10; postcards, DM 1.

RECEIVING MAIL

You can arrange to have mail sent to you in care of any German post office; **have the envelope marked "Postlagernd."** This service is free. Or you can have mail sent to any American Express office in Germany. There's no charge to cardholders, holders of American Express traveler's checks, or anyone who has booked a vacation with American Express.

MONEY MATTERS

Western Germany has an admirably high standard of living, and eastern Germany's prices are rapidly rising. Lots of things—gas, food, hotels, and trains, to name but a few—are more expensive than in the United States, but in 2000 the strong dollar was a benefit to American tourists.

A good way to budget is to **visit lesser-known cities and towns and avoid Alpine summer and winter resorts during their high seasons.** All along the Main and Neckar rivers, for example, you will find small towns as charming as but significantly less expensive than the likes of Rothenburg and Heidelberg. Wine lovers can explore the Pfalz and Rhine Terrace area's German Wine Road (☞ Chapter 10) instead of the classic Rhine-Mosel tour. Ski enthusiasts would do well to investigate the advantages of the Harz Mountains (☞ Chapter 16) and the Bavarian Forest (☞ Chapter 3).

The five states (Brandenburg, Mecklenburg-Vorpommern, Saxony, Saxony-Anhalt, and Thuringia) of the former East Germany still have a lower standard of living than does old the former West Germany. Outside large cities, public transportation and dining are cheaper than in, say, the Black Forest or the Rhineland. Prices in leading hotels and restaurants in Dresden and Leipzig match rates in Frankfurt and Munich. As the standard of living in the new states continues to rise, so will the cost of traveling in them.

Prices throughout this guide are given for adults. Substantially reduced fees are almost always available for children, students, and senior citizens. For information on taxes, *see* Taxes, *below.*

ATMS

Twenty-four-hour ATMs (Geldautomaten) can be accessed with PLUS or Cirrus credit and banking cards. Some German banks exact DM4–DM10 fees for use of their ATMs. Your PIN number should be set for four digits; if it's longer, ask your bank about changing it for your trip. Since some ATM keypads show no letters, know the numeric equivalent of your password.

CREDIT CARDS

All major U.S. credit cards are accepted in Germany. If you get a four-digit PIN number for your card before you leave home, you can use your credit card at German ATMs.

Throughout this guide the following abbreviations are used: **AE**, American Express; **DC**, Diner's Club; **MC**, MasterCard; and **V**, Visa.

➤ REPORTING LOST CARDS: **American Express:** ☎ 01805/840–840. **Diners Club:** ☎ 05921/861–234. **Master-Card:** ☎ 0130/819–104. **Visa:** ☎ 08008/149–100.

CURRENCY

This is the last year of the Deutschmark, the currency that has sustained Germany's economic power for nearly the whole postwar period. Both D-marks and euros can be used until July 1, 2002, when the euro takes over. During the transition you may get your change in euros even if you pay in marks. Stores, restaurants, and other businesses nearly always show their prices in both the D-mark and the euro. Read all prices carefully and be sure that bills, credit card charges, and so on indicate whether the price is in the euro (EUR) or the mark (DM). There are about two marks to both the euro and the dollar. The mark is divided into 100 pfennige. There are bills of 5 (rare), 10, 20, 50, 100, 200, 500, and 1,000 marks and coins of 1, 2, 5, 10, and 50 pfennige and 1, 2, and 5 marks. At press time, the mark stood at DM 2.11 to the U.S. dollar, DM 1.42 to the Canadian dollar, DM 3.16 to the British pound sterling, DM 1.22 to the Australian dollar, and DM .95 to the New Zealand dollar.

CURRENCY EXCHANGE

For the most favorable rates, **change money through banks.** Although ATM transaction fees may be higher abroad than at home, ATM rates are excellent because they are based on wholesale rates offered only by major banks. You won't do as well at exchange booths in airports or rail and bus stations, in hotels, in restaurants, or in stores. To avoid lines at airport exchange booths, **get a bit of local currency before you leave home.**

If you are **exchanging currency from another European Union country** into German marks, do so free of charge at any branch of Germany's central bank, the **Deutsche Bundesbank** (it doesn't work the other way around,

though: You cannot get Italian lire or French francs free of charge at the Deutsche Bundesbank).

➤ EXCHANGE SERVICES: **International Currency Express** (☎ 888/278–6628 for orders, www.foreignmoney.com). **Thomas Cook Currency Services** (☎ 800/287–7362 for telephone orders and retail locations, www.us.thomascook.com).

TRAVELER'S CHECKS

Do you need traveler's checks? It depends on where you're headed. If you're going to rural areas and small towns, **go with cash**; traveler's checks are best used in cities. Lost or stolen checks can usually be replaced within 24 hours. To ensure a speedy refund, buy your own traveler's checks—don't let someone else pay for them: irregularities like this can cause delays. The person who bought the checks should make the call to request a refund.

OUTDOORS & SPORTS

Germans are very active and constantly organize themselves into sport teams and clubs, and hiking trails abound.

BIKING

There are many long-distance bicycle routes in Germany and you can rent bikes at major train stations. Rivers often have bicycle paths. Among the best are along the Danube River, which you can meet at Regensburg or Passau, and along the Weser River, which you can meet at Hannoversch-Münden. Another route, somewhat rugged, is along the Baltic Coast, mainly in the state of Mecklenburg-Vorpommern. The *Radfürerkarten,* issued by the Bielefelder Verlaganstalt, are good bike travel maps available at bookstores.

Bicycles can be rented at more than 160 train stations throughout Germany, mainly from April through October, though some are offered year-round. The cost is from DM 6 to DM 25 per day. You may have to leave cash or your passport or other identification as a deposit, depending on the arrangement with the private contractors who now handle the service. You must return the bike to the station at which you rented it. Special types, such as mountain bikes at Alpine stations, children's bikes and rickshas, are also available. Most cities also have companies that rent bikes for about DM 25 per day or DM 120 a week.

Bikes cannot be transported on Inter-City Express services, but InterCity, EuroCity, and some D-class trains and all local trains have special storage facilities, and InterRegio trains even have compartments where cyclists can travel next to their bikes. Bikes cost DM 6 on local trains. On all other trains **you must make advance reservations** and pay DM 12. Most airlines accommodate bikes as luggage, provided they are dismantled and boxed. For bike boxes, often free at bike shops, you'll pay about $5 from airlines (at least $100 for bike bags). International travelers can sometimes substitute a bike for a piece of checked luggage at no charge; otherwise, the cost is about $100. Domestic and Canadian airlines charge $25–$50.

➤ CLUBS: **Allgemeiner Deutscher Fahrrad-Club** (The German Cycle Club; Postfach 107747, D–28077 Bremen, ☎ 0421/346–290). National **Bicycle hot line** (☎ 0180/319–4194).

GOLF

The countryside along the Romantic Road is ideal golf territory, and clubs exist throughout the country.

➤ GOLF: **Deutscher Golf-Verband** (German Golf Association; ✉ Viktoriastr. 16, D–65189 Wiesbaden, ☎ 0611/990–200) has information on German golf courses.

FISHING

Anglers **must obtain a license** (DM 8–DM 12 a day) from local town halls or tourist offices.

HIKING

Hiking is popular throughout Germany. The Deutscher Alpenverein maintains more than 50 mountain huts and about 15,000 km (9,300 mi) of Alpine paths. In addition, it can provide courses in mountaineering and touring suggestions for routes in both winter and summer. Foreigners may become members. Various mountaineering schools offer week-long courses ranging from basic techniques for beginners to advanced mountaineering. Tourist offices in all Bavarian Alpine resorts have details.

➤ CONTACTS: **Deutscher Alpenverein** (✉ Von-Kahr-Str. 2–4, D–80997 Munich, ☎ 089/140–030). **Verband Deutscher Gebirgs- und Wandervereine e.V.** (✉ Wilhelmshöhe Allee 157–159, D–34121 Kassel, ☎ 0561/938–730) can provide information on routes, hiking paths, overnight accommodations, and mountain huts.

SKIING

The Black Forest maintains many cross-country ski trails, and downhill is most popular in the Bavarian Alps resorts.

PACKING

What you pack depends more on the time of year than on any particular dress code. Winters can be bitterly cold; summers are warm but with days that suddenly turn cool and rainy. In summer **take a warm jacket or heavy sweater** for the Bavarian Alps, where the nights can be chilly even after hot days.

For cities, **pack as you would for an American city:** dressy outfits for formal restaurants and nightclubs, casual clothes elsewhere. Jeans are as popular in Germany as anywhere else and are perfectly acceptable for sightseeing and informal dining. In the evening men will probably feel more comfortable wearing a jacket and tie in more expensive restaurants, although it is almost never required. Many German women are extremely fashion-conscious and wear stylish outfits to restaurants and the theater, especially in the larger cities.

To discourage purse snatchers and pickpockets, **carry a handbag with long straps** that you can sling across your body bandolier style and with a zippered compartment for money and other valuables.

For stays in budget hotels, **take your own facecloth and soap.** Many provide no soap at all or only a small bar.

In your carry-on luggage **bring an extra pair of eyeglasses or contact lenses** and **enough of any medication you take** to last the entire trip. You may also want your doctor to write a spare prescription using the drug's generic name, since brand names may vary from country to country. In luggage to be checked, **never pack prescription drugs or valuables.** To avoid customs delays, carry medications in their original packaging. And don't forget to copy down and carry addresses of offices that handle refunds of lost traveler's checks. If you are traveling with a wine opener, pocketknife or any other kind of knife, or toy weapons **pack them in check-in luggage.** These are considered potential weapons and are not permitted as carry-on items.

CHECKING LUGGAGE

How many carry-on bags you can bring with you is up to the airline. Most allow two but not always, so make sure that everything you carry aboard will fit under your seat or in the overhead bin, and get to the gate early. Note that if you have a seat at the back of the plane, you'll probably board first, while the overhead bins are still empty.

If you are flying internationally, note that baggage allowances may be determined not by piece but by weight—generally 88 pounds (40 kilograms) in first class, 66 pounds (30 kilograms) in business class, and 44 pounds (20 kilograms) in economy.

Airline liability for baggage is limited to $1,250 per person on flights within the United States. On international flights it amounts to $9.07 per pound or $20 per kilogram for checked baggage (roughly $640 per 70-pound bag) and $400 per passenger for unchecked baggage. You can buy additional coverage at check-in for about $10 per $1,000 of coverage, but it excludes a rather extensive list of items, shown on your airline ticket.

Before departure, **itemize your bags' contents** and their worth, and label the bags with your name, address, and phone number (if you use your home address, cover it so potential thieves can't see it readily). Inside each bag,

pack a copy of your itinerary. At check-in, **make sure that each bag is correctly tagged** with the destination airport's three-letter code. If your bags arrive damaged or fail to arrive at all, file a written report with the airline before leaving the airport.

PASSPORTS & VISAS

When traveling internationally, **carry your passport even if you don't need one** (it's always the best form of ID) and **make two photocopies of the data page** (one for someone at home and another for you, carried separately from your passport). If you lose your passport, promptly call the nearest embassy or consulate and the local police.

ENTERING GERMANY

U.S., Canadian, and British citizens need only a valid passport to enter Germany for stays of up to 90 days.

PASSPORT OFFICES

The best time to apply for a passport or to renew is in fall and winter. Before any trip, check your passport's expiration date and, if necessary, renew it as soon as possible.

➤ AUSTRALIAN CITIZENS: **Australian Passport Office** (☎ 131–232, www.dfat.gov.au/passports).

➤ CANADIAN CITIZENS: **Passport Office** (☎ 819/994–3500 or 800/567–6868, www.dfaitmaeci.gc.ca/passport).

➤ NEW ZEALAND CITIZENS: **New Zealand Passport Office** (☎ 04/494–0700, www.passports.govt.nz).

➤ U.K. CITIZENS: **London Passport Office** (☎ 0990/210–410) for fees and documentation requirements and to request an emergency passport.

➤ U.S. CITIZENS: **National Passport Information Center** (☎ 900/225–5674; calls are 35¢ per minute for automated service, $1.05 per minute for operator service).

REST ROOMS

If there is an attendant in the rest room, he or she will likely have a plate out "primed" with a 50-pfennig coin. This is all they expect, but a mark will be appreciated.

SENIOR-CITIZEN TRAVEL

In Germany the number of citizens over 60 is growing. The strength of this age group has won it special privileges in Germany—such as price adjustments on the railways and reduced admission to museums—and elderly visitors from abroad can also take advantage of these discounts. Contact the German National Tourist Office (☞ Visitor Information, *below*).

To qualify for age-related discounts, **mention your senior-citizen status up front** when booking hotel reservations (not when checking out). When renting a car, ask about promotional car-rental discounts, which can be cheaper than senior-citizen rates.

➤ EDUCATIONAL PROGRAMS: **Elder-hostel** (✉ 75 Federal St., 3rd floor, Boston, MA 02110, ☎ 877/426–8056, FAX 877/426–2166, www.elder-hostel.org). **Interhostel** (✉ University of New Hampshire, 6 Garrison Ave., Durham, NH 03824, ☎ 603/862–1147 or 800/733–9753, FAX 603/862–1113, www.learn.unh.edu).

STUDENTS

Most museums and modes of transportation have reduced prices for students, so have your student ID card handy. *See* Lodging, *above* for hostelling information.

➤ IDs & SERVICES: **Council Travel** (CIEE; ✉ 205 E. 42nd St., 14th floor, New York, NY 10017, ☎ 212/822–2700 or 888/268–6245, FAX 212/822–2699, info@councilexchanges.org, www.councilexchanges.org), for mail orders only (in the United States). **Travel Cuts** (✉ 187 College St., Toronto, Ontario M5T 1P7, ☎ 416/979–2406 or 800/667–2887, www.travelcuts.com), in Canada.

TAXES

VALUE-ADDED TAX

Most prices you see on items already have Germany's 16% value-added tax (VAT) included. When traveling to a non-EU country, you are entitled to a refund of the VAT you pay. Some goods, like books and antiquities, carry a 6.5% VAT as a percentage of the purchase price.

Global Refund is a VAT refund service that makes getting your money back hassle-free. The service is available Europe-wide at 130,000 affiliated stores. In participating stores, **ask for the Global Refund form** (called a Shopping Cheque). If a store is not a participating member of Global Refund, they'll probably have a form called an *Ausfuhr-Abnehmerbescheinigung,* which Global Refund can also process, for a higher fee. When you leave the European Union, you must be prepared to **show your purchases to customs officials** before they will stamp your refund form. You might not be permitted to carry these purchases in carry-on luggage, so **pack the items so that they are easily reached in your check-in luggage.** Before you check your luggage at the airport, **ask to be directed to the customs desk.** (The procedure at Frankfurt's airport is complicated and involves taking your tagged luggage one level down to the arrival area's customs desk, from where your baggage will be sent on to your flight. At Munich's airport, first go to a VAT refund counter, between the areas of B and C, as well as between C and D.) Once the form is stamped, take it to one of the more than 700 Global Refund counters—conveniently located at every major airport and border crossing—and your money will be refunded on the spot in the form of cash, check, or a refund to your credit-card account (minus a small percentage for processing). Alternatively, you can mail your validated form to Global Refund.

➤ VAT REFUNDS: **Global Refund** (✉ 707 Summer St., Stamford, CT 06901, ☎ 800/566–9828, FAX 203/674–8709, taxfree@us.globalrefund.com, www.globalrefund.com).

TELEPHONES

AREA & COUNTRY CODES

The country code for Germany is 49. When dialing a German number from abroad, drop the initial 0 from the local area code.

DIRECTORY & OPERATOR ASSISTANCE

The German telephone system is fully automatic, and it's unlikely you'll have to employ the services of an operator unless you're seeking information. If you have difficulty reaching your number, call 0180/200–1033. You can book collect calls through this number to the United States but not to other countries. For information dial 11833 for numbers within Germany and 11834 for numbers elsewhere. International operators speak English.

INTERNATIONAL CALLS

International calls can be made from just about any telephone booth in Germany. It costs only 48 pfennigs per minute to call the United States, day or night, no matter how long the call lasts. Use a phone card or make international calls from post offices. You pay the clerk the cost of the call plus a DM 2 connection fee. At a hotel, rates will be at least double the regular charge, so **never make international calls from your room.**

LOCAL CALLS

A local call from a telephone booth costs 30 pfennigs and will last for six minutes.

LONG-DISTANCE SERVICES

AT&T, MCI, and Sprint access codes make calling long distance relatively convenient, but you may find the local access number blocked in many hotel rooms. First ask the hotel operator to connect you. If the hotel operator balks, ask for an international operator, or dial the international operator yourself. One way to improve your odds of getting connected to your long-distance carrier is to travel with more than one company's calling card (a hotel may block Sprint, for example, but not MCI). If all else fails, call from a pay phone.

➤ ACCESS CODES: In Germany: **AT&T Direct** (☎ 0130–0010 or 0800/225–5288). **MCI WorldCom** (☎ 0130–0012). **Sprint** (☎ 0130–0013).

PUBLIC PHONES

Most telephone booths in Germany now are card-operated, so **buy a phone card.** You can purchase one at any German post office (also available at many exchange places). They come in denominations of DM 12 and DM 50, the latter good for DM

60 worth of calls. Most phone booths have instructions in English as well as German. Another advantage of the card: it charges only what the call cost. Coin-operated phones, which take 10-pfennig, DM 1, and DM 5 coins, don't make change.

TIME

Germany is on Central European Time, which is six hours ahead of Eastern Standard Time and nine hours ahead of Pacific Standard Time. Germans use military time (1 PM is indicated as 13) and write the date before the month, so October 3 will appear as 03.10.

TIPPING

The service charges on bills is sufficient for most tips in your hotel, though you should **tip bellhops and porters**; DM 2 per bag or service is ample. It's also customary to leave a small tip (a couple of marks per night) for the room-cleaning staff. Whether you tip the desk clerk depends on whether he or she has given you any special service.

Service charges are included in all restaurant checks (listed as *Bedienung*), as is tax (listed as *MWST*). Nonetheless, it is customary to **round up the bill to the nearest mark or to leave about 5%** (give it to the waiter or waitress as you pay the bill; don't leave it on the table, as that's considered rude). Bartenders and servers also expect a 2–5% tip.

In taxis **round up the fare a couple of marks** as a tip. Only give more if you have particularly cumbersome or heavy luggage (though you will be charged 50 pfennigs for each piece of luggage anyway).

TOURS & PACKAGES

Because everything is prearranged on a prepackaged tour or independent vacation, you'll spend less time planning—and often get it all at a good price.

BOOKING WITH AN AGENT

Travel agents are excellent resources. But it's a good idea to collect brochures from several agencies as some agents' suggestions may be influenced by relationships with tour and package firms that reward them for volume sales. If you have a special interest, **find an agent with expertise in that area**; ASTA (☞ Travel Agencies, *below*) has a database of specialists worldwide.

Make sure your travel agent knows the accommodations and other services of the place they're recommending. Ask about the hotel's location, room size, beds, and whether it has a pool, room service, or programs for children, if you care about these. Has your agent been there in person or sent others whom you can contact?

Do some homework on your own, too: local tourism boards can provide information about lesser-known and small-niche operators, some of which may sell only direct.

BUYER BEWARE

Each year consumers are stranded or lose their money when tour operators—even large ones with excellent reputations—go out of business. So **check out the operator.** Ask several travel agents about its reputation and try to **book with a company that has a consumer-protection program** (look for information in the company's brochure). In the United States members of the National Tour Association and the United States Tour Operators Association are required to set aside funds to cover your payments and travel arrangements in the event that the company defaults. It's also a good idea to choose a company that participates in the American Society of Travel Agents' Tour Operator Program (TOP); ASTA will act as mediator in any disputes between you and your tour operator.

Remember that the more your package or tour includes, the better you can predict the ultimate cost of your vacation. Make sure you know exactly what is covered and **beware of hidden costs.** Are taxes, tips, and transfers included? Entertainment and excursions? These can add up.

➤ TOUR-OPERATOR RECOMMENDATIONS: **American Society of Travel Agents** (☞ Travel Agencies, *below*). **National Tour Association** (NTA; ✉ 546 E. Main St., Lexington, KY 40508, ☎ 606/226–4444 or 800/

682–8886, www.ntaonline.com). **United States Tour Operators Association** (USTOA; ✉ 342 Madison Ave., Suite 1522, New York, NY 10173, ☎ 212/599–6599 or 800/468–7862, FAX 212/599–6744, ustoa@aol.com, www.ustoa.com).

TRAIN TRAVEL

Deutsche Bahn (DB—German Rail) is a very efficient, privatized railway. Its high-speed InterCity Express (ICE), InterCity (IC), and EuroCity (EC) trains make journeys between the centers of many cities—Munich–Frankfurt for example—faster by rail than by air. All overnight InterCity services and the slower D-class trains have sleepers with a first-class service that includes breakfast in bed. Deluxe "Hotel Trains" have been introduced with success on the Berlin–Munich and Berlin–Bonn routes. All InterCity and InterCity Express trains have restaurant cars or trolley service, and the regional InterRegio services have bright bistro cars.

With the high-speed expresses you often only have to cross to the other side of the station platform to change trains. Special train maps on platform notice boards give details of the layout of trains arriving on that track, showing the locations of first- and second-class cars and the restaurant car, as well as where they will stop along the platform. Most railroad stations have English-speaking staff handling information inquiries.

BAGGAGE SERVICE

All major train stations have luggage lockers (in three sizes). By inserting coins into a storage unit, you release the unit's key. Large lockers cost DM 4. Smaller towns' train stations may not have any storage options.

Throughout Germany you can use the Deutsche Bahn *KurierGepäck* service to deliver your baggage from a private residence or hotel to Frankfurt Airport; ask at any DB ticket counter or call 01805/236–723 to schedule a pickup. The service costs DM 28 for the first suitcase (with a valid ticket) and DM 18 for each additional piece. Delivery is guaranteed on the second weekday following pickup.

CUTTING COSTS

To save money, **look into rail passes.** But be aware that if you don't plan to cover many miles, you may come out ahead by buying individual tickets. Rail passengers with a valid round-trip air ticket can **buy a heavily discounted "Rail and Fly" ticket for DB trains** connecting with 14 German airports (Berlin's Schönefeld and Tegel airports, Bremen, Dresden, Düsseldorf, Frankfurt/Main, Hamburg, Hannover, Köln-Bonn, Leipzig/Halle, Munich, Münster/Osnabrück, Nürnberg, Stuttgart) and two airports outside Germany (Basel and Amsterdam).

If Germany is your only destination in Europe, **consider purchasing a German Railpass,** which allows 4–10 days of unlimited first- or second-class travel within a one-month period on any DB train, up to and including the ICE. A **Twin Pass** does the same for two people traveling together and is even cheaper per person. A **Youth Pass,** sold to those 12–25, is also much the same but for second class travel only. You can also **use these passes aboard KD river steamers** (☞ Cruise Travel, *above*) along certain sections of the Rhine, Main, and Moselle rivers. Prices begin at $174 for a single traveler in second class and $252 in first class. Twin Passes begin at $261 in second class and $378 in first class, and Youth Passes begin at $138. Additional days may be added to either pass.

If you're planning to visit just one region in Germany—Bavaria, for instance, or the Black Forest—consider purchasing a **FerienTicket,** which is valid for unlimited travel for one, two, or three weeks. The ticket costs just DM 40 for one week and DM 20 for each additional week (DM 60 and DM 30, respectively, for first-class travel). The ticket can be purchased at any German rail station.

Germany is one of 17 countries in which you can **use Eurailpasses,** which provide unlimited first-class rail travel in all participating countries for the duration of the pass. If you plan to rack up the miles, get a standard pass. These are available for 15 days ($554), 21 days ($718), one month ($890), two months ($1,260), and three months ($1,558). If your plans call for only limited train travel, **look into a Europass,** which costs less money than a EurailPass. Unlike with Eurailpasses, however, you get a limited number of travel days in a limited number of countries during a specified time period. For example, a two-month pass ($348) allows between 5 and 15 days of rail travel but costs $200 less than the least expensive EurailPass. Keep in mind, however, that the Europass is good only in France, Germany, Italy, Spain, and Switzerland, though it can be extended through the purchase of up to two additional zones.

In addition to standard Eurailpasses, **ask about special rail-pass plans.** Among these are the Eurail Youthpass (for those under age 26), the Eurail Saverpass (which gives a discount for two or more people traveling together), a Eurail Flexipass (which allows a certain number of travel days within a set period), the Euraildrive Pass and the Europass Drive (which combine travel by train and rental car). Eurailpasses, Europasses, and some of the German Railpasses **must be purchased before you leave** for Europe.

➤ INFORMATION AND PASSES: **DER Travel Services** (✉ 9501 W. Devon Ave., Rosemont, IL 60018, ☎ 800/782–2424, FAX 800/282–7474 for information; 800/860–9944 for brochures, www.dertravel.com). **Deutsche Bahn** (German Rail, ✉ Stephensonstr. 1, D–60326 Frankfurt am Main, ☎ 01805/996–633 for 24-hr hot line www.bahn.de/home/index.shtml). **Eurostar** (☎ 0870/518–6186 in the U.K.). **German Rail Passenger Services** (☎ 020/7307–0919 in the U.K.).Fares & Schedules

A DM 7 surcharge is added to the ticket price on all InterCity and EuroCity journeys irrespective of distance (DM 14 round-trip). The charge is DM 9 if paid on board the train. InterCity Express fares are about 20% more expensive than normal ones. Seat reservations on other trains cost DM 3.

FROM THE U.K.

There are several ways to reach Germany from London on British Rail. Travelers coming from the

United Kingdom should **take the Channel Tunnel to save time, the ferry to save money.** Fastest and most expensive is the route via the Channel Tunnel on Eurostar trains (☞ Information and Passes, *above*). They leave hourly from Waterloo and require a change of trains in Brussels. Cheapest and slowest are the 8–10 departures daily from Victoria using the Ramsgate–Ostend ferry, jetfoil, or SeaCat catamaran service.

RESERVATIONS

Many travelers assume that rail passes guarantee them seats on the trains they wish to ride. Not so. You need to **book seats ahead even if you are using a rail pass**; seat reservations are required on some European trains, particularly high-speed trains, and are a good idea during summer and on popular routes. You'll also need a reservation if you purchase sleeping accommodations.

In high season you'll frequently encounter lines at ticket offices for seat reservations. If you board the train without a reserved seat, you take the chance of not getting a seat. To avoid standing in reservations lines, **make an advance reservation by phone.** Call the ticket office (*Fahrkarten-Schalter*) of the rail station from which you plan to depart. You will probably have to make several attempts before you get through to the reservations section (*Reservierungen/Platzkarten*), but you will then be able to collect your seat ticket from a special counter without having to wait in line.

SENIOR-CITIZEN PASSES

Holders of British Rail Senior Citizens' Rail Cards can buy an "add-on" European Senior Citizens' Rail Card that permits a 30% reduction on train travel in most European countries, including Germany.

TRANSPORTATION
AROUND GERMANY

The Deutsche Bahn, Germany's privatized railway, is by far the best way to travel around the country. The basic ticket prices are not cheap, but several special offers can reduce ticket prices by as much as half. The carefully structured network of services—from the super-high-speed InterCity Express to regional InterRegio and local E-trains—ensures fast connections between cities and good access to rural areas; very few villages are more than 10 km (6 mi) or so from a railroad station.

The country's airlines—principally the national carrier, Lufthansa—are far more expensive than train travel and not always speedier. The Deutsche Bahn "Sprinter" business special, for instance, gets its passengers between Frankfurt and Munich or Berlin faster than a plane, by the time city-to-airport travel and check-in requirements are taken into account. The Frankfurt–Munich "Sprinter" stops only in Mannheim; the Frankfurt–Berlin one doesn't stop at all.

Long-distance bus services are virtually nonexistent in Germany. Those buses that do cross the country are either tourist services covering routes such as the Romantic Road or long-distance companies originating outside Germany. In rural areas local bus companies complement rail services, making even the most remote community accessible. If you're looking to save money, **take local buses,** which are generally less expensive than trains.

All major German cities have multistructure urban transportation systems, incorporating subway (U-bahn) and metropolitan suburban (S-bahn) trains, trams, and buses. Whenever possible, **take the subway.** Public transportation in cities is invariably fast, clean, and efficient. If possible, **avoid taking taxis,** which are very expensive.

TRAVEL AGENCIES

A good travel agent puts your needs first. Look for an agency that has been in business at least five years, emphasizes customer service, and has someone on staff who specializes in your destination. In addition, **make sure the agency belongs to a professional trade organization.** The American Society of Travel Agents (ASTA), with 27,000 agents in some 170 countries, is the largest and most influential in the field. Operating under the motto "Integrity in Travel," it maintains and enforces a strict code of ethics and will step in to help mediate any agent-client disputes if necessary. ASTA also maintains a Web site that includes a directory of agents. (If a travel agency is also acting as your tour operator, *see* Buyer Beware *in* Tours & Packages, *above*.)

➤ LOCAL AGENT REFERRALS: **American Society of Travel Agents** (ASTA; ☎ 800/965–2782 24-hr hot line, FAX 703/684–8319, www.astanet. com). **Association of British Travel Agents** (✉ 68–71 Newman St., London W1P 4AH, ☎ 020/7637–2444, FAX 020/7637–0713, abta.co.uk, www. abtanet.com). **Association of Canadian Travel Agents** (✉ 1729 Bank St., Suite 201, Ottawa, Ontario K1V 7Z5, ☎ 613/521–0474, FAX 613/521–0805, acta.ntl@sympatico.ca). **Australian Federation of Travel Agents** (✉ Level 3, 309 Pitt St., Sydney 2000, ☎ 02/9264–3299, FAX 02/9264–1085, www.afta.com.au). **Travel Agents' Association of New Zealand** (✉ Box 1888, Wellington 10033, ☎ 04/499–0104, FAX 04/499–0827, taanz@tiasnet. co.nz).

VISITOR INFORMATION

Local tourist offices are listed in the A to Z sections of the individual chapters. Staff at the smaller offices, especially in eastern Germany, might not speak English. Many offices keep shorter hours than normal businesses, and you can expect some to close during weekday lunch hours, and as early as 12 PM on Friday. A new centralized system allows you to reach local tourist offices through the phone number 19433 by first dialing the appropriate local area code.

➤ TOURIST INFORMATION: **U.S. Nationwide** (German National Tourist Office, ✉ 122 E. 42nd St., New York, NY 10168, ☎ 212/661–7200, FAX 212/661–7174). **Canada** (✉ 175 Bloor St. E, Suite 604, Toronto, Ontario M4W 3R8, ☎ 416/968–1570, FAX 416/968–1986). **U.K.** (✉ 18 Conduit St., London W1R ODT, ☎ 020/7317–0908, FAX 020/7495–6129). **Australia** (✉ Box A980, Sydney, NSW 1235, ☎ 9267–8148, FAX 9267–9035).

➤ U.S. GOVERNMENT ADVISORIES: **U.S. Department of State** (✉ Overseas Citizens Services Office, Room 4811 N.S., 2201 C St. NW, Washington, DC 20520, ☎ 202/647–5225 for interactive hot line, 301/946–4400 for computer bulletin board, FAX 202/647–3000 for interactive hot line); enclose a self-addressed, stamped business-size envelope.

WEB SITES

Do check out the World Wide Web when you're planning. You'll find everything from up-to-date weather forecasts to virtual tours of famous cities. Fodor's Web site, www.fodors.com, is a great place to start your on-line travels. Many German tourism-related Web sites have an English-language version. The option for English is usually indicated by an icon of the American or British flag. For more specific information on Germany, visit www. deutschland-tourismus.de/e/index. html, the German National Tourist Office's site.

WHEN TO GO

The tourist season in Germany runs from May to late October, when the weather is at its best. In addition to many tourist events, this period has hundreds of folk festivals. The winter sports season in the Bavarian Alps runs from Christmas to mid-March. Prices everywhere are generally higher during the summer, so **consider visiting out of season to save money.** Most resorts offer between-season (*Zwischensaison*) and edge-of-season (*Nebensaison*) rates, and tourist offices can provide lists of hotels that offer special low-price inclusive weekly packages (*Pauschal-angebote*). Many winter ski resorts lower rates for the period between mid-January (after local school holidays) and Easter. The disadvantages of visiting in winter are that the weather is often cold and gloomy and some attractions, especially in rural areas, are closed or have shorter hours. Ski resorts are the exception.

It's wise to **avoid cities at times of major trade fairs,** when attendees commandeer all hotel rooms and prices soar. Among the fairs to avoid are Green Week in Berlin (January), the radio-TV fair in Berlin (August and September in odd-numbered years), the boat fair in Düsseldorf (January), the computer fair in Hannover (February and March), and the auto fair in Frankfurt (September in odd-numbered years).

CLIMATE

Germany's climate is temperate, although cold spells can plunge the thermometer well below freezing, particularly in the Alps, the Harz region of Lower Saxony and Saxony-Anhalt, the Black Forest, and the higher regions of northern Franconia. Summers are usually sunny and warm, though you should **be prepared for a few cloudy and wet days,** especially in the north half of the country. The south is normally always a few degrees warmer than the north. As you get nearer to the Alps, however, the summers get shorter, often not begin-

ning until the end of May. Fall is sometimes spectacular in the south—warm and soothing. The only real exception is the strikingly variable weather in South Bavaria caused by the *Föhn,* an Alpine wind that gives rise to clear but very warm conditions. The Föhn can occur in all seasons. Sudden atmospheric pressure changes associated with the Föhn give some people headaches. Germans measure temperature in Celsius, not Fahrenheit. For example, 23.9°C is a pleasant day of 75°F; 10°C is a chilly 50°F.

➤ FORECASTS: **Weather Channel Connection** (☎ 900/932–8437), 95¢ per minute from a Touch-Tone phone.

The following are the average daily maximum and minimum temperatures for Munich.

Munich

Jan.	35F	1C	May	64F	18C	Sept.	67F	20C
	23	– 5		45	7		48	9
Feb.	38F	3C	June	70F	21C	Oct.	56F	14C
	23	– 5		51	11		40	4
Mar.	48F	9C	July	74F	23C	Nov.	44F	7C
	30	– 1		55	13		33	0
Apr.	56F	14C	Aug.	73F	23C	Dec.	36F	2C
	38	3		54	12		26	– 4

FESTIVALS AND SEASONAL EVENTS

Top seasonal events in Germany include Carnival festivities in January and February, spring festivals around Easter and Pentecost, Bayreuth's Richard Wagner Festival in August, wine festivals throughout the southern half of the country in late summer and fall, the Oktoberfest in Munich in late September and early October, the Frankfurt Book Fair in October, and December's Christmas markets.

➤ DEC.: **Christmas Markets,** outdoor festivals of light, choral and trumpet music, handcrafted gift items, and hot wine are held in just about every German city. Nürnberg's is the most famous.

➤ JAN.: **Fasching season.** The Rhineland is Germany's capital of Carnival events, including proclamations of Carnival princes, street fairs,

parades, masked balls, and more. Some of the main Carnival cities are Koblenz, Köln, Mainz, Bonn, and Düsseldorf, although there's also plenty of activity in Munich and throughout southern Germany. Festivities always run through February, finishing on Fasching Dienstag (Shrove or Fat Tuesday, or Mardi Gras).

➤ FEB.: **Frankfurt International Fair** is a major consumer-goods trade fair.

International Filmfestspiele, in Berlin, is one of Europe's leading film festivals.

International Toy Fair takes place in Nürnberg.

➤ MAR.: **ITB,** one of Europe's largest international tourism fairs, takes place in Berlin.

Strong Beer Season in Munich brings out the bands and merrymaking in all the beer halls.

➤ APR.: **Walpurgis** festivals. Towns in the Harz Mountains celebrate with spooky, Halloween-like goings on the night before May Day.

➤ MAY: **Medieval Festival.** By downing a huge tankard of wine in one gulp, the 17th-century mayor of Rothenburg-ob-der-Tauber saved the town from sacking. On Pentecost weekend his Meistertrunk is reenacted.

Religious Processions, featuring hundreds of horses, giant candles, and elaborate statues, are particularly spectacular in Catholic Eastern Bavaria during the Pentecost weekend. The best ones are at Bogen, Sankt Englmar, and Kötzting.

Wild Horse Roundup of Europe's last remaining herd takes place in late May at Dülmen, Westphalia.

➤ JUNE: **Landshut Wedding.** This elaborate event has feasting, drama, jousting, and medieval pageantry and takes place in 2001 (it happens every four years).

Kiel Week is an international sailing regatta and cultural festival in the town of Kiel in Schleswig-Holstein.

➤ JUNE–SEPT.: **Castle Illuminations,** with spectacular fireworks, are presented in Heidelberg in June, July, and September.

Pied Piper plays are performed at Hameln each Sunday at noon, from May through mid-September. The children of the town first portray the rats, then themselves as they are piped to parts unknown.

Rhine in Flames highlights the river with fireworks, Bengal lights along the bank, floodlighted castles, and a fleet of illuminated boats; it takes place around Bonn (May), Rüdesheim (July), Koblenz (August) and St. Goar (September).

The Schleswig-Holstein Music Festival takes place over six weeks in July and August. World-famous and young musicians perform in cities and towns throughout Schleswig-Holstein.

➤ JULY: **Kinderzeche** is Dinkelsbühl's medieval pageant and festival. It reenacts an incident from the Thirty Years' War, in which the children stood at the gate and pleaded with the conquerors to spare their homes.

Love Parade, a huge street party of techno-music and ravers, draws a million revelers to Berlin the second weekend in July.

➤ AUG.: **Festivals along the Main River** take place in Frankfurt in early and late August.

Kulmbach Beer Festival takes place in Franconia.

Richard Wagner Festival unfolds the Wagner operas in Bayreuth.

The Student Prince, the noted Sigmund Romberg operetta set in Heidelberg, is performed in English in the Heidelberg's castle courtyard.

➤ SEPT.: **Berlin Festival Weeks** feature classical music concerts, exhibits, and many special events.

The **International Automobile Show,** one of the world's largest, takes place at Frankfurt in mid-September of odd-numbered years.

Folk and Beer Festival at Stuttgart/Bad Cannstatt, is said to be just as big and raucous as Munich's Oktoberfest (September and October).

Oktoberfest (late September–early October) in Munich draws millions of visitors to cavernous beer tents, each with two bands, and to fairgrounds with every kind of carnival attraction imaginable.

Wine Festivals. More than a thousand of these harvest-time events take place in September and October, mainly in the valleys of the Rhine River and three of its tributaries—the Mosel, Main, and Neckar, plus the Pfalz.

Wurstmarkt, the world's biggest wine festival, is held in a field at Bad Dürkheim.

➤ OCT.: **Berlin Jazz Festival.**

Bremen Freimarkt is a centuries-old folk festival and procession in Bremen.

Frankfurt Book Fair is a famous annual literary event and a browser's paradise, sometimes with political fireworks.

➤ NOV.: **St. Martin's Festival** includes children's lantern processions, and is celebrated throughout the Rhineland and Bavaria.

WORDS AND PHRASES

English	German	Pronunciation
Basics		
Yes/no	Ja/nein	yah/nine
Please	Bitte	**bit**-uh
Thank you (very much)	Danke (vielen Dank)	**dahn**-kuh (**fee**-lun-dahnk)
Excuse me	Entschuldigen Sie	ent-**shool**-de-gen zee
I'm sorry.	Es tut mir leid.	es toot meer lite
Good day	Guten Tag	**goo**-ten tahk
Good bye	Auf Wiedersehen	auf **vee**-der-zane
Mr./Mrs.	Herr/Frau	hair/frau
Miss	Fräulein	**froy**-line
Numbers		
1	ein(s)	eint(s)
2	zwei	tsvai
3	drei	dry
4	vier	fear
5	fünf	fumph
6	sechs	zex
7	sieben	**zee**-ben
8	acht	ahkt
9	neun	noyn
10	zehn	tsane
Days of the Week		
Sunday	Sonntag	**zone**-tahk
Monday	Montag	**moan**-tahk
Tuesday	Dienstag	**deens**-tahk
Wednesday	Mittwoch	**mit**-voah
Thursday	Donnerstag	**doe**-ners-tahk
Friday	Freitag	**fry**-tahk
Saturday	Samstag/ Sonnabend	**zahm**-stakh/ **zonn**-a-bent
Useful Phrases		
Do you speak English?	Sprechen Sie Englisch?	**shprek**-hun zee **eng**-glish?
I don't speak German.	Ich spreche kein Deutsch.	ich **shprek**-uh kine doych

Vocabulary

Please speak slowly.	Bitte sprechen Sie langsam.	**bit**-uh **shprek**-en-zee **lahng**-zahm
I am American/ British	Ich bin Amerikaner(in)/ Engländer(in)	ich bin a-mer-i-**kahn**-er(in)/ **eng**-glan-der(in)
My name is . . .	Ich heiße . . .	ich **hi**-suh
Where are the restrooms?	Wo ist die Toilette?	vo ist dee twah-**let**-uh
Left/right	links/rechts	links/rechts
Open/closed	offen/geschlossen	O-fen/geh-**shloss**-en
Where is . . . the train station? the bus stop?	Wo ist . . . der Bahnhof? die Bushaltestelle?	**vo** ist **dare bahn-hof** **dee booss-hahlt-uh-**shtel-uh
the subway station? the airport? the post office? the bank? the police station? the Hospital? the telephone	die U-Bahn-Station? der Flugplatz? die Post? die Bank? die Polizeistation? das Krankenhaus? das Telefon	dee oo-bahn-**staht**-sion dare **floog**-plats dee **post** dee **banhk** dee po-lee-tsai-**staht**-sion dahs **krahnk**-en-house dahs te-le-fone
What is your . . . address? phone number? fax number?	Was ist Ihre Adresse Telefon Nummer Fax Nummer	vas ist **ear**-eh ah-**drehs**-seh tay-lay-**fon num**-mer fax **num**-mer
I'd like . . . a room the key a map a ticket	Ich hätte gerne . . . ein Zimmer den Schlüssel eine Stadtplan eine Karte	ich **het**-uh gairn . . . ein **tsim**-er den **shluh**-sul **I**-nuh **staht**-plahn **I**-nuh cart-uh
How much is it?	Wieviel kostet das?	**vee-feel cost**-et dahs?
I am ill/sick	Ich bin krank	ich bin krahnk
I need . . . a doctor the police help Stop!	Ich brauche . . . einen Arzt die Polizei Hilfe Halt!	ich **brow**-khuh **I-nen** artst dee po-li-**tsai** **hilf**-uh **hahlt**
Fire!	Feuer!	**foy**-er
Look out/Caution!	Achtung!/Vorsicht!	**ahk**-tung/for-zicht

Dining Out

A bottle of . . .	eine Flasche . . .	**I**-nuh **flash**-uh
A cup of . . .	eine Tasse . . .	**I**-nuh **tahs**-uh
A glass of . . .	ein Glas . . .	ein glahss
Ashtray	der Aschenbecher	dare **Ahsh**-en-bekh-er
Bill/check	die Rechnung	dee **rekh**-nung
Do you have . . .?	Haben Sie . . .?	**hah**-ben zee
I am a vegetarian.	Ich bin Vegetarier(in)	ich bin ve-guh-**tah**-re-er
I'd like to order . . .	Ich möchte . . . bestellen	ich **mohr**-shtuh . . . buh-**shtel**-en
Menu	die Speisekarte	dee **shpie**-zeh-car-tuh
Napkin	die Serviette	dee zair-vee-**eh**-tuh

INDEX

FODOR'S GERMANY 2001

EDITOR: Christina Knight

Editorial Contributors: Uli Ehrhardt, Phyllis Méras, Marton Radkai, Jürgen Scheunemann, Matthew Schneider, Ted Shoemaker, Kerry Brady Stewart, Robert Tilley

Editorial Production: Stacey Kulig

Maps: David Lindroth, *cartographer;* Robert Blake and Rebecca Baer, *map editors*

Design: Fabrizio La Rocca, *creative director;* Guido Caroti, *art director;* Jolie Novak, *photo editor;* Melanie Marin, *photo researcher*

Cover Design: Pentagram

Production/Manufacturing: Mike Costa

COPYRIGHT

ISBN 0–679–00568–4

ISSN 1525–5034

SPECIAL SALES

Fodor's Travel Publications are available at special discounts for bulk purchases for sales promotions or premiums. Special editions, including personalized covers, excerpts of existing guides, and corporate imprints, can be created in large quantities for special needs. For more information, contact your local bookseller or write to Special Markets, Fodor's Travel Publications, 280 Park Avenue, New York, NY 10017. Inquiries from Canada should be directed to your local Canadian bookseller or sent to Random House of Canada, Ltd., Marketing Department, 2775 Matheson Boulevard East, Mississauga, Ontario L4W 4P7. Inquiries from the United Kingdom should be sent to Fodor's Travel Publications, 20 Vauxhall Bridge Road, London SW1V 2SA, England.

PRINTED IN THE UNITED STATES OF AMERICA

10 9 8 7 6 5 4 3 2 1

IMPORTANT TIP

Although all prices, opening times, and other details in this book are based on information supplied to us at press time, changes occur all the time in the travel world, and Fodor's cannot accept responsibility for facts that become outdated or for inadvertent errors or omissions. So always confirm information when it matters, especially if you're making a detour to visit a specific place.

PHOTOGRAPHY

Owen Franken, *cover (Black Forest).*

Auf Schönburg, *30A.*

Baden-Baden Casino: *Foto-Huber, 3 bottom left.*

Baden-Baden Marketing, *29 center right.*

Berchtesgadener Landes Visitor Center, *27 top, 29 bottom right.*

Bremen Tourist Office, *2 top right, 3 bottom right, 21D.*

Jan Butchofsky-Houser, *1.*

Colombi Hotel, *30G.*

Corbis: *Jonathan Blair, 12C. Andrew Cowin/Travel Ink, 15A. Ed Eckstein, 16B. Bob Krist, 13A, 13C, 22A. Hugh Rooney/Eye Ubiquitous, 24A. Gregor Schmid, 12B. Adam Woolfitt, 9C, 12A. Michael S. Yamashita, 13B.*

FHV Rheinland-Pfalz, *17A, 29 top left.*

Owen Franken, *23B.*

Freiberg Wirtschaft und Touristik GmbH & Co., *14A.*

Kevin Galvin, *6C, 8B, 11D, 18B, 24C.*

Blaine Harrington III, *6A, 17B.*

Heidelberg Convention & Visitors Bureau, *26, 28 bottom right.*

Hotel Adlon, *30D.*

Hotel im Wasserturm, *30F.*

Dave G. Houser, *22B, 25B, 25C.*

The Image Bank: *Gary Cralle, 30C, 32. Grant V. Faint, 7D. Mahaux Photography, 16 top, 30E. Kaz Mori, 8 bottom left, 10A. Robert Müntefering, 6B. Michael Pasdzior, 19D. Andrea Pistolesi, 25A. Antonio Rosario, 24B. Harald Sund, 11B. Paul Trummer, 18A. Hans Wolf, 4–5, 18C, 23A, 23C, 30J.*

Im Schiffchen, *30I.*

Bob Krist, *14B, 19E, 20A, 21B, 21C.*

Munich City Tourist Office: *Dr. Dolling, 27 center right. Heinz Gebhardt, 7E. Stefan Moses, 2 bottom center.*

Nymphenburger Porzellanmanufaktur, *2 bottom left. Christl Reiter, 8A. Ulrike Romeis, 3 top right.*

Nördlingen Tourist Information Office, *3 top left.*

Passau Tourismus e.V., *9A, 9B.*

Photodisc, *15B.*

Residenz Heinz Winkler, *30B.*

David Sanger, *16A, 19F.*

Schlosshotel Bühlerhöhe, *2 top left, 14C, 30H.*

Staatsgalerie Stuttgart, *2 bottom right.*

Stadt Bingen am Rhein, *28 bottom left.*

Titisee-Neustadt Tourism: *Erich Spiegelhalter, 14D.*

Würzburg Congress & Tourismus Zentrale, *11C.*

ABOUT OUR WRITERS

Every vacation is important. So here at Fodor's, we've pulled out all stops in preparing *Fodor's Germany*. To help you zero in on what to see, we've gathered wonderful color photos of the key sights in every region. To show you how to put it all together, we've created great itineraries and neighborhood walks. And to direct you to the places that are truly worth your time and money, we've rallied the team of experts we're pleased to call our writers.

Uli Ehrhardt, a native German, began his long history in the travel and tourism fields as an interpreter and travel consultant within the United States. He then served for 20 years as director of the State Tourist Board Bodensee–Oberschwaben (Lake Constance–Upper Swabia). He makes his home in the city of Ulm as a tourism consultant, writer, and teacher at a state college for tourism.

Phyllis Méras, former travel editor for the *Providence Journal*, has written often about Germany, including several portions of her anecdotal guide to Europe, *Mermaids of Chenonceaux*. She also covers Germany for the magazines of US-Airways and Continental.

Marton Radkai is a native New Yorker of Bavarian/Hungarian descent. He began his professional life as an announcer at WFCR-FM Public Radio in Amherst, Massachusetts. Since 1985 he has lived in Germany, Austria, and Hungary working as a writer for radio and print media, travel photographer, translator, and editor.

Jürgen Scheunemann is a native of Hamburg and fell in love with Berlin 13 years ago when he moved there to study North American history and German literature. Since then, he has worked as a journalist and editor, and has written, published, and translated a number of books on Berlin and the United States.

Matthew Schneider found his way to Aachen from Iowa through technical means. He works as an engineer and editor for a German automotive research and development firm, helping to subsidize his travel and photography passions.

Ted Shoemaker settled in Germany more than 40 years ago when, as a U.S. Army officer, he married a German. He has been editor of three English-language magazines in Germany and a correspondent for many American publications. He lives in Frankfurt.

Kerry Brady Stewart was born in St. Louis, Missouri, and now lives in Wiesbaden, Germany. After working at the German Wine Information Bureau in New York, she moved to Germany in 1981 to coordinate the European and overseas press services of the German Wine Institute, Mainz. Today she runs Fine Line, a public relations agency specializing in wine, food, and travel. Her latest books are *The Hungry Traveler: Germany,* and *A Traveller's Wine Guide to Germany.*

Robert Tilley landed in Germany more than 25 years ago via Central Africa, South Africa, and England, intending to stay a year before settling somewhere really civilized (his German wife convinced him to stay). He runs a media company in Munich and writes and produces programs for German TV.

Don't Forget to Write

We love feedback—positive and negative—and follow up on all suggestions. So contact the Germany editor at editors@fodors.com or c/o Fodor's, 280 Park Avenue, New York, New York 10017. Have a wonderful trip!

Karen Cure

Karen Cure
Editorial Director